ENCYCLOPEDIA OF
OCCULTISM &
PARAPSYCHOLOGY

ENCYCLOPEDIA OF
OCCULTISM &
PARAPSYCHOLOGY

A Compendium of Information on the Occult Sciences,
Magic, Demonology, Superstitions, Spiritism, Mysticism,
Metaphysics, Psychical Science, and Parapsychology,
with Biographical and Bibliographical
Notes and Comprehensive Indexes

SECOND EDITION

In Three Volumes
VOLUME TWO
H-O

Edited by Leslie A. Shepard

GALE RESEARCH COMPANY ● BOOK TOWER ● DETROIT, MICHIGAN 48226

Assistant Editor:
Pamela Dear

Production:
Carol Blanchard
Cindy LaFerle

Art Director:
Arthur Chartow

BIBLIOGRAPHICAL NOTE

Based on *Encyclopedia of Occultism* by Lewis Spence, London, 1920, and *Encyclopaedia of Psychic Science* by Nandor Fodor, London [1934], substantially revised by Leslie Shepard and supplemented by new material written by him.

Library of Congress Catalog Card Number 77-92 (First Edition)

Library of Congress Cataloging in Publication Data

Main entry under title:

Encyclopedia of occultism & parapsychology.

   "A compendium of information on the occult sciences, magic, demonology, superstitions, spiritism, mysticism, metaphysics, psychical science, and parapsychology, with biographical and bibliographical notes and comprehensive indexes."
   "Based on substantially revised material from Encyclopedia of occultism by Lewis Spence, London, 1920, and Encyclopaedia of psychic science by Nandor Fodor, London [1934] with additional material edited by Leslie Shepard"--Verso CIP t.p.
   Bibliography: p.
   Includes index.
   1. Occult sciences–Dictionaries. 2. Psychical research--Dictionaries. I. Shepard, Leslie. II. Spence, Lewis, 1874-1955. An encyclopedia of occultism. III. Fodor, Nandor. Encyclopaedia of psychic science.
BF1407.E52   1983   133'.03'21   84-3990
ISBN 0-8103-0196-2

Contents

Editorial Policies

The reader is referred to the Introduction in Volume 1 for a detailed explanation of the background and overall policy of this new edition. For user convenience in consulting Volumes 2 and 3, the following editorial practices discussed in the Introduction are summarized below.

Information Extensively Updated

Each entry has been re-edited where necessary, often with substantial revision and the addition of new data, and reset in a more uniform type and style. Thousands of revisions and corrections have been made to the text.

There are hundreds of new entries or additions to existing entries relating to personalities, organizations, cults, phenomena, publications, and terms, as well as important historical data not available in the previous edition. Many birth and death dates have been added to biographical entries and some dates from the first edition have been revised in the light of recent research. Entries dealing with developments in individual countries have been brought up to date and additional entries on other countries have been added.

Bibliographical Data Expanded

Earlier limited bibliographical references have been amplified by providing author names and publication dates of cited works. In the bibliographical sections of "Recommended reading," there are many more citations of recent books as well as important out-of-print works and reprints. Where possible, paperback editions have been cited as well as hardcover, since many important books are sometimes only currently available in paperback. American publication is to be assumed after the publisher name; British or other foreign imprints are clearly identified. In the case of some unfamiliar imprints, the place of publication is given, whether American or foreign. In a few cases, the publisher's name of long out-of-print nineteenth-century works is not given where the year of publication is sufficient to trace the work in any good public or specialized library.

"See" and "See also" References

Additional cross-references have been clearly indicated within the text of individual entries by the use of bold type or the formula "See" or "See also," while significantly related entries are also indicated at the end of an entry by the formula "See also." The extensive cross-referencing in this edition is intended to assist research in new and old correlations of phenomena and overlapping areas of study.

Wherever possible, topics which are covered within more general entries are also given a brief entry in their own right which may satisfy immediate inquiry, whilst some other overlapping entries repeat information rather than involve the reader in further searches. As with most encyclopedias, the key to locating elusive material is the extensive indexing. We have continued the nine special indexes which reviewers and users have praised, and the comprehensive general index now lists further cross-references and specialized subgroupings of entries dealing with such topics as *Astrology, Parapsychology, Psychical Research, Spiritualism,* and *UFOs.*

Original Material Carefully Evaluated

Since this completely new edition is part of a progressive development from the base set, it was thought advisable to retain all the original subjects, although many new entries have been added. Although tempted to reduce some of the longer, more discursive material (particularly from Lewis Spence), the editor felt it was on balance better to retain the material in the new edition rather than eliminate facts and opinions already published. Moreover, such detailed treatment (often quotations from source works) was felt to have value for researchers. In the original edition, certain major entries included material identified as from both Lewis Spence and Nandor Fodor, in order that their complementary views could be compared. In this new edition, such different viewpoints have been integrated into an overall text after careful evaluation. Responsibility for presentation and opinion therefore lies solely with the present editor. In certain controversial areas concerned both with individuals and phenomena, the case for and against has been indicated, with sources noted for further study in depth.

Comments Are Welcome

In a work of such scope, it is difficult to avoid occasional errors of fact or omission, particularly when drawing from secondary sources. The occult field changes rapidly in modern times. Periodicals or organizations cease to exist. New names and cults become household words overnight. The publishers would greatly appreciate any corrections or additional factual information for future editions.

ENCYCLOPEDIA OF
OCCULTISM &
PARAPSYCHOLOGY

VOLUME TWO
H-O

H

Haas, George C(hristian) O(tto) (1883-)

Archbishop (Primate of Universal Spiritual Church) who took an active interest in psychical science and lectured on the subject. Born March 28, 1883, in New York, N.Y., he studied at Columbia University (M.A. 1903, Ph.D. 1909) and International University, London (D.D. 1953). In 1930 he married Rev. Beulah Thompson.

He worked as a tutor at the College of the City of New York, translator and censor U.S. Department of Justice from 1917–20, technical translator from 1921–51, founder and director of the Institute of Hyperphysical Research, director of the Institute of Life (division of IHR), from 1941 onwards priest of the Universal Spiritual Church (archbishop primate from 1956); patriarch of Holy Apostolic Church 1957 onwards. Member of the American Oriental Society, joint editor of *Journal of the American Society* from 1916–18, member of American Federation of Astrologers.

Dr. Haas was responsible for the theory of "hyperphysics" intended to reorient science, and lectured on occult and psychic science. He translated the Sanskrit treatise the *Dasarupa* in 1912, and also published *The Key to Enrichment of Life* (1949). His theory of hyperphysics is described in the article 'The New Orientation of Science' (*IS* magazine No. 23, 1960).

Habondia (or Habundia)

The queen of the witches, presiding over the **Sabbat.** She was also identified with Diana or Herodias. She was referred to as "Habonde" in the thirteenth-century poem *Le Roman de la Rose* (1. 18,624). In his work *Tableau de l'inconstance des mauvais anges* (Description of the Inconstancy of Evil Angels, 1612), the demonologist Pierre de Lancre referred to Habondia rather sweepingly as "Queen of the fairies, witches, harpies, furies; and ghosts of the wicked." (See also **Witchcraft**)

Hag of the Dribble

Welsh **banshee,** named "Gwrach y Rbibyn" who was said to carry stones across the mountains in her apron, then loosing the string, let the stones shower down, thus making a "dribble." It was believed that at twilight this hag flapped her raven wing against the window of those doomed to die, and howled "A-a-a-ui-ui-Anni."

Haggadah

The general name for the narrative or fabular portion of Rabbinical literature.

The most familiar use of the term is to the household service of *Seder* at Passover, dramatizing the Jewish exodus from Egypt led by Moses.

Haines, Frederick H(enry) (1869-1944)

Prominent British spiritualist, who was an insurance broker, author of *Chapters on Insurance History* and *The Insurance Business* which were considered classics in their field. He was converted to Spiritualism during World War I and after careful investigations, begun in a spirit of skepticism, developed powers of **clairvoyance.**

He received by **automatic writing** a large number of scripts which were published, including: *A Lamp to the Feet, Locusts and Wild Honey, The Book of Spiritual Wisdom* (1928), *A Voice from Heaven* (purporting to give the experiences of Rev. George Vale **Owen** in the After Life), *Thus Saith Celphra* (1928), *Spiritual Development, He Became Man* (an inspirational life of Christ). He also published his autobiography *Nothing But the Truth; The Confessions of a Medium* (1931).

He contributed largely to British psychic journals and was in demand as a lecturer. He founded the Watford Christian Spiritualist Fellowship and edited a monthly periodical *Spiritual Vision.*

He died February 6, 1944.

Haining, Peter (1940-)

British novelist, writer on occult subjects, anthologist of horror stories. Born April 2, 1940, in Enfield, Middlesex (England), he was educated in Buckhurst Hill. In October 1956 he married Philippa Waring. From 1957–63 he was a journalist and magazine writer; from 1963–72 editor, senior editor, editorial director of New English Library. London; from 1972 onwards editorial consultant, writer and anthologist. He is a member of the International P.E.N. Club.

His family lived for many generations in Scotland, but Haining now resides in the "witch county" of Essex, England. His researches into witchcraft and black magic resulted in a ritual curse from a group of devil worshipers in London, but this did not interfere with Haining's literary success. He claims that one of his ancestors was burned at the stake for possessing a "book of spells" and his publication *The Warlock's Book* is said to include materials based on records of this ancestor.

His other books include: (with Arthur V. Sellwood) *Devil Worship in Britain* (1964); *Four Square Holiday Guide to the Channel Islands* (1966), *Anatomy of Witchcraft* (1972), *Eurotunnel: An Illustrated History of the Channel Tunnel Projects* (1973), *The Hero* (1974), *The Witchcraft Papers* (1974), *Ghosts: An Illustrated History* (1974), *The Penny Dreadful* (1975). He edited or compiled: *The Craft of Terror: Extracts from the Rare and Infamous Gothic 'Horror' Novels* (1966), *The Evil People: Being Thirteen Strange and Terrible Accounts of*

Witchcraft, Black Magic and Voodoo (1968), *Dr. Caligari's Black Book; An Excursion into the Macabre in Thirteen Acts* (1968), *The Future Makers: A Selection of Science Fiction from Brian Aldiss* [and others] (1968), *The Midnight People: Being Eighteen Terrifying and Bizarre Tales of Vampires* (1968, American title *Vampires of Midnight,* 1970), *The Witchcraft Reader* (1969; 1970), *The Satanist* (1969; 1970), *The Unspeakable People: Being Twenty of the World's Most Horrible Horror Stories* (1969), *The Freak Show: Tales of Fantasy and Horror* (1970, American title *The Freak Show,* 1972), *The Hollywood Nightmare, Tales of Fantasy and Horror from the Film World* (1970; 1971), *A Thousand Afternoons* (1970), *The Wild Night Company: Irish Stories of Fantasy and Horror* (1970; 1971), *A Circle of Witches: An Anthology of Victorian Witchcraft Stories* (1971), *The Clans of Darkness: Scottish Stories of Fantasy and Horror* (1971), *The Ghouls* (1971), *The Necromancers: The Best of Black Magic and Witchcraft* (1971; 1972), *Gothic Tales of Terror: Classic Horror Stories from Great Britain, Europe and the United States, 1765-1840* (1972; British title *Great British Tales of Terror*), *The Magicians: Occult Stories* (1972; American title *The Magicians: The Occult in Fact and Fiction,* 1973), *The Lucifer Society: Macabre Tales by Great Modern Writers* (1972), *The Nightmare Reader* (1972; 1973), *Nightfrights: Occult Stories for All Ages* (1973), *The Dream Machines: An Illustrated History of Ballooning* (1973), *The Monster Makers* (1974), *The Hashish Club* (1974), *The Sherlock Holmes Scrapbook* (1974), *The Fantastic Pulps* (1975), *Ghost's Companion* (1975), *An Illustrated History of Witchcraft (1975),* *The Ancient Mysteries Reader* (1975), *Black Magic Omnibus* (1976), *Christopher Lee's New Chamber of Horrors* (1977), *Spring Heeled Jack* (1977), *The Second Book of Unknown Tales of Horror* (1978), *The Restless Bones* (1978), (ed.) *The Shilling Shockers* (1978), *Classic Horror Omnibus* (1979), *Third Book of Unknown Tales of Horror* (1980).

Hair

Hair has had an occult significance since ancient times. It seems to have a life of its own, since it may continue to grow after death of the body. It has been regarded as a source of strength and sexuality and has played a part in religion and magical rituals.

In various cultures, individuals dedicated to service of the priesthood have undergone ritual cutting of hair, and the tonsure of priests is said to have originated in Egypt. In Hinduism, there are hair rituals for youths, and on becoming a celibate, the head is formally shaven.

The association of hair with sexual features of the body has given it remarkable force, and distinctions between male and female hair have emphasized sexual attraction. The unisex fashions of the permissive society and rock groups have tended to create sexual confusion and neurotic behavior.

Since the hair is believed to be intimately related to the life of an individual, it has magical significance in witchcraft rituals, and many civilizations have been at pains to prevent their falling into the hands of an enemy, who might use it for black magic ill-wishing.

There is even a school of character reading from the hair, known as trichsomancy.

Extreme fright or ecstatic states have caused hair to literally "stand on end" in the goose-flesh condition of horripilation.

Recommended reading:
Berg, Charles. *The Unconscious Significance of Hair,* Allen & Unwin, London, 1951

Cooper, Wendy. *Hair; Sex Society Symbolism,* Aldus Books, London, 1971

Hajoth Hakados

According to the mystical teachings of *Kabala,* one of the spheres of angels by whose agency Jehovah's providence is spread. It was believed that these angels inhabited one of the hierarchies named "Jehovah," and that the simple essence of the divinity flowed through the *Hajoth Hakados* to the angel "Metratton" and to the ministering spirit "Reschith Hajalalim."

Hall, James A(lbert) (1934–   )

Medical student who experimented with ESP. Born February 13, 1934, he studied at University of Texas (B.A. 1955) and Southwestern Medical School, University of Texas. In 1955 he married Suzanne McKean. He is a member of the American Society for Psychical Research, an associate member of the Parapsychological Association, and a student associate of the Society for Psychical Research, London, England. He is also a student member of the American Medical Association.

In 1958 he experimented with elementary school children in Gladewater. Texas, to ascertain the effect of teacher-pupil attitudes on ESP scores, reported on in the *Journal of Parapsychology* (vol. 22, No. 4, Dec. 1958). He is also author (with H. B. Crasilneck) of 'Physiological Changes associated with Hypnosis' (*International Journal of Clinical and Experimental Hypnosis,* vol. 7, No. 1, Jan. 1959).

Hall, Manly Palmer (1901–   )

Writer and lecturer on mysticism, philosophy, psychology and comparative religion. Born March 18, 1901, in Peterborough, Ontario, Canada, he moved to the U.S. and became pastor of the Church of the People, Los Angeles, California.

He was a founder-president of the Philosophical Research Society, Inc., Los Angeles, and his other affiliations include membership of International Society for General Semantics, Pythagorean Society, Chinese Culture Society (life members), Societas Rosecrucina in Civitatibus Folderatis, Indian Association of America, American Federation of Astrologers, American Society for Psychical Research, Baconian Society, New Mexico Historical Society (life member). He was given a Distinguished Service Award by the city of Los Angeles, 1970.

His books include: *Encyclopedic Outline of Masonic, Hermetic, Qabbalistic & Rosicrucian Symbolism Philosophy* (1928), *Melchizedek and The Mystery of Fire* (1929), *Magic, A Treatise on Natural Occultism* (1929), *The Lost Keys of Masonry; The Legend of Hiram Abiff* (1929), *Man the Grand Symbol of the Mysteries* (1932), *The Story of Astrology; The Belief in the Stars as a Factor in Human Progress* (1933), *First Principles of Philosophy* (1935), *Words to the Wise; A Practical Guide to the Occult Sciences* (1936), *Twelve World Teachers; A Summary of Lives and Teachings* (1937), *Reincarnation; The Cycle of Necessity* (1939; 1971), *How to Understand Your Bible; A Philosopher's Interpretation of Obscure and Puzzling Phrases—A Study of the Bibles of the World Revealing One Spiritual Tradition* (1942), *The Philosophy of Astrology* (1943; 1970),

The Riddle of the Rosicrucians (1951), *The Secret Teachings of All Ages* (1952), *The Adepts in the Eastern Esoteric Tradition* (1952), (with Henry L. Drake) *The Basic Ideas of Man; A Program of Study Founded Upon Man's Heritage of Wisdom* (1953), *Studies in Character Analysis; Phrenology, Palmistry, Physiognomy, Graphology* (1958), *Search for Reality; Ten Lectures on Personal Growth* (1959), *Survey Course in Philosophy; Based Upon the Introduction to An Encyclopedic Outline of Symbolical Philosophy* (1960), *The Mystical and Medical Philosophy of Paracelsus* 1964), *Studies in Dream Symbolism* (1965), *Buddhism and Psychotherapy* (1967), *"Very Unusual"; The Wonderful World of Mr. K. Nakamura* (1976), *Past Lives and Present Problems* (1977).

Hall, Prescott F(arnsworth) (1868–1921)

American lawyer, author and psychic researcher. Born September 27, 1868, at Boston, Mass., he took his LL. B. in 1892 at Harvard. In 1895 he married Florence Gardiner; his second marriage in 1908 was to Lucyle Irby. Mr. Hall was in law practice in Boston from 1892–1921 and was a founder of the Immigration Restriction League, and a member of the American Society for Psychical Research.

In addition to his various writings on law, immigration and economics, he took a special interest in mediumship. His article 'Experiments with Mrs. Caton' was published in vol. 8 (1914) of the *Proceedings* of the ASPR, and he edited 'The Harrison Case' published in vol. 13 (1919) of the *Proceedings*.

Hall, Trevor H(enry) (1910–   )

Noted British author of books on parapsychological subjects. Born May 28, 1910, at Wakefield, Yorkshire, England, he was a Perrott Student in Psychical Research at Trinity College, Cambridge, England, from 1954–56. In 1937 he married Dorothy Keningley. He was chief surveyor Hudersfield Building Society from 1935–39, major in the British Army 1939–45, director of Huddersfield Building Society from 1958 onwards. He is also a city magistrate at Leeds, a director of the Legal and General Assistance Society, and a Fellow of the Royal Institution of Chartered Surveyors.

Mr. Hall is author of *The Spiritualists* (1962), (with E. J. Dingwall and K. M. Goldney), *The Haunting of Borley Rectory* (1956), (with E. J. Dingwall) *Four Modern Ghosts* (1958), *The Strange Case of Edmund Gurney* (1964), *Strange Things* (1968), *Sherlock Holmes; Ten Literary Studies* (1969), *The Late Mr. Sherlock Holmes* (1971), *Sherlock Holmes and his Creator* (1974), *The Search For Harry Price* (1977). He also contributed articles on the history of psychical research to the *International Journal of Parapsychology.*

He has special interest in conjuring and compiled *A Bibilography of Conjuring Books in English from 1580 to 1850* (1957).

Perhaps his expert knowledge of conjuring is responsible for his highly skeptical attitude towards psychic phenomena. In *The Spiritualists* he suggested that the phenomena of famous medium Florence Cook was fraudulent, and that she was having an affair with Sir William Crookes. For a discussion of this case see the important article 'William Crookes and the Physical Phenomena of Mediumship' by R. G. **Medhurst** and K.

M. **Goldney** in *Proceedings* of the SPR (vol. 54, pt. 195, March 1964).

His other books on psychical researchers are equally critical of their characters and achievements. His book on Edmund **Gurney** investigates the claimed trickery of G. A. Smith and Douglas Blackburn, whose second-sight act was investigated by Gurney, but is, on the whole, sympathetic to Gurney. Hall's book *Strange Things,* however, demolishes the character and achievements of Ada Goodrich **Freer** (known in psychical research literature as "Miss X"), and *The Search For Harry Price* effectively denigrates the character and work of famed psychical researcher Harry **Price,** just as Hall's book on Crookes and Florence Cook attempts to destroy the reputation of Crookes.

In all this Hall is a careful researcher, but his consistent attempt to demolish the reputations of famous workers in psychical research is perhaps too consistently destructive and one-sided in interpretation of claimed facts. His judgments are more those of a prosecuting counsel than magistrate and should be balanced by a careful examination of criticisms of Hall and his attitude. For example, even if one admits the various faults and weaknesses of Harry Price, it would not be just to write off all his considerable achievements as dishonest and fraudulent.

Halloween (*See* All Hallow's Eve)

Hallucination

A false perception of sensory vividness arising without the stimulus of a corresponding sense-impression. In this it differs from illusion, which is merely the misinterpretation of an actual sense-perception.

Visual and auditory hallucination are the most common, and especially the former, but hallucination of the other senses may also be experienced, although it is not so readily distinguishable. Human figures and voices most frequently form the subject of a hallucination, but in certain types other classes of objects may be seen as, for instance, the rats and insects of *delirium tremens.*

Although hallucination is often associated with various mental and physical diseases, it may nevertheless occur spontaneously while the agent shows no departure from full vigor of body and mind, and may be induced—i.e., in hypnotism—in about 90 percent of all subjects. The essential differences between sane and insane hallucinations is that in the former case the agent can, by reflection, recognize the subjective nature of the impression, even when it has every appearance of objectivity, whereas in the latter case, the patient cannot be made to understand that the vision is not real.

Until comparatively modern times hallucinatory percepts were regarded merely as intensified memory-images, but as the most intense of ordinary representations do not possess that sensory vividness which is yet a feature of the smallest sensation received from the external world, it follows that other conditions must be present besides the excitement of the brain-elements which is the correlate of representation. It is true that the seat of excitement is the same both in actual sense-perceptions and in memory images but in the former case the stimulus is peripherally originated in the sensory nerve, whereas in the latter it takes its rise in the brain itself.

Now if any neural system becomes highly excited—a state which may be brought about by emotion, ill-health, drugs, or a number of causes—it may serve to divert from their proper paths any set of impulses arising from the sense organs, and as any impulse ascending through the sensory nerves produces an effect of sensory vividness—normally, a true perception—the impulses thus diverted give to the memory-images an appearance of actuality not distinguishable from that produced by a corresponding sense-impression. In 1901, the British physician Sir Henry Head demonstrated that certain visceral disorders produced hallucinations, such as the appearance of a shrouded human figure.

In hypnosis a state of cerebral dissociation is induced, whereby any one neural system may be abnormally excited, and hallucination thus very readily engendered (see **Hypnotism**). Drugs which excite the brain also induce hallucinations (see Psychedelic **Drugs; Hallucinogens**).

The question of whether there is any relation between the hallucination and the person it represents is, and has long been, a vexed one. Countless well-authenticated stories of **apparitions** coinciding with a death or some other crisis are on record, and would seem to establish some causal connection between them. In former times apparitions were considered to be the "doubles" or "ethereal bodies" of the originals, and Spiritualists believe that they are the spirits of the dead (or in some instances, of the living) temporarily forsaking the physical organism.

But one theory among those who believe in such a causal connection between agent and hallucination (supported by the statistics collected by Professor Sidgwick and others—See **Census of Hallucinations**) is that of telepathy, or thought-transference.

That the cerebral machinery for the transmission of thought should be specially stimulated in moments of intense excitement, or at the approach of dissolution, is not to be wondered at, and thus it is sought to account for the appearance of hallucinatory images coinciding with death or other crises.

Moreover, the dress and appearance of the apparition does not necessarily correspond with the actual dress and appearance of its original. Thus a man at the point of death, in bed and wasted by disease, may appear at a distance to a friend as if in his ordinary health and wearing his ordinary garb. Nevertheless there are notable instances where some remarkable detail of dress is reproduced in the apparition.

It seems clear, however, that it is the agent's general personality which is, as a rule, conveyed to the percipient, and not, except in special cases, the actual matter of his surface-consciousness.

A similar explanation has been offered for the hallucinatory images which many people can induce by gazing in a crystal, in a pool of water or a drop of ink, and which are often declared to give information, and reproduce scenes and people of whom the agent has no knowledge. It has been suggested that those images which do not arise in the subliminal consciousness of the agent may have been telepathically received by him from other minds. (See **Crystal-Gazing**)

Collective Hallucination is a term applied to hallucinations which are shared by a number of people. There is no firm evidence, however, of the operation of any other agency than **suggestion** or telepathy.

Hallucination and Psychical Research

One of the most succinct definitions of "Hallucinations" occurs in *Phantasms of the Living* by Gurney, Myers & Podmore (2 vols., 1886): "Percepts which lack, but which can only by a distinct reflection be recognised as lacking, the objective basis which they suggest." If the sensory perception coincides with an objective occurrence or counterpart, the hallucination is called veridical, truth-telling. Such is, according to the materialistic conception, the phantasm of the dying. If the apparition is seen by several people at the same time the case is collective veridical hallucination.

In the years following the foundation of the Society for Psychical Research, London, the hallucination theory of psychic phenomena was in great vogue. If no other explanation were available the man who had a supernormal experience was told that he was hallucinated, and if several people testified to the same occurrence, that the hallucination of one was communicated to the other. However, the researcher Sir William **Crookes** stated in *Researches in the Phenomena of Spiritualism* (1870): "The supposition that there is a sort of mania or delusion which suddenly attacks a whole roomful of intelligent persons who are quite sane elsewhere, and that they all concur, to the minutest particulars, in the details of the occurrences of which they suppose themselves to be witnesses, seems to my mind more incredible than even the facts which they attest."

Such an authority as Professor Charles **Richet** deleted hallucination completely in his discussion of metapsychical phenomena (a term for paranormal). He believed that "hallucination" should be reserved to describe a morbid state when a mental image is exteriorized without any exterior reality. "It is extremely rare," he stated, "that a person who is neither ill, nor drunk, nor hypnotised should, in the walking state, have an auditory, visual or tactile illusion of things that in no way exist. The opinion of alienists that hallucination is the chief sign of mental derangement, and the infallible characteristic of insanity seems to me well grounded. With certain exceptions (for every rule there are exceptions) a normal healthy individual when fully awake does not have hallucinations. If he sees apparitions these correspond to some external reality or other. In the absence of any external reality there are no hallucinations but those of the insane and of alcoholics."

If Prof. Richet was right, the following case of Sir John Heschel does not conform to this concept. He had been watching with some anxiety the demolition of a familiar building. On the following day at evening, but in good light, he passed the spot where it had stood. "Great was my amazement to see it," he wrote, "as if still standing, projected against the dull sky. I walked on, and the perspective of the form and disposition of the parts appeared to change as they would have done if real."

From simple apparition to the theory of "local hallucination" to explain **haunting** is a very far cry. Edmund **Gurney** suggested that a person thinking of a given place which is at the time actually experienced in sense perception by some other persons, may obtain thereby to such a community of consciousness with the other persons as to be able, under some unknown circumstances, to impart into the consciousness of a second person, in the guise of hallucination, a thought existing in his own.

Of course, the testimony of registering apparatus and photography may rule out the hallucination theory provided that there is proper scientific control. It is no longer a subject of dispute that in the seance room apparently paranormal phenomena indeed occur. In haunted houses, the position is more complicated as the phenomena there do not lend themselves to experimental reproduction. Moreover one is generally not prepared for apparitions. Nevertheless, if objects are displaced the theory of hallucination becomes at once untenable. As Andrew Lang wrote on *Cock Lane and Common Sense* (1896) "Hallucinations cannot draw curtains, or open doors, or pick up books, or tuck in bedclothes or cause thumps."

The hallucinations of the mentally deranged, of the sick, drunk, or drugged do not compare with psychical experiences. They are not veridical, or telepathic, and not collective.

In the *Census of Hallucinations* (*Proceedings* of the S.P.R., 1894) the committee excluded, so far as possible, all pathological subjects. Mr. J. G. Piddington (*Proceedings,* vol. 19) in testing this census for cases that would show the same nature as hallucinations arising from visceral diseases, came to the conclusion that there was not a single case in the census report which fell into line with the visceral type.

On the other hand, hypnotic hallucinations offer ground for thought. The hypnotized subject may see apparitions if so suggested and may not see ordinary men who are in the same room. But he may hear the noises which they make, see the movement of objects which they touch and may be frightened by what appears to him to be **poltergeist** phenomena. And if the suggestion is post-hypnotic he may see a phantom shape on a signal or at the prescribed time.

The visions seen by some people on the verge of sleep were called "hypnogogic hallucinations" by F. W. H. **Myers.** The after-images on waking from sleep he named "hypnopompic hallucinations." A comprehensive study of both classes of phenomena was published by G. E. Leaning in *Proceedings* of the S.P.R., vol. 35, 1926.

The difference between hallucination and illusion is that there is an objective basis for the illusion, which is falsely interpreted. In hallucination, though more than one sense may be affected, there is no external basis for the perception. (See also **Psychical Research; Spiritualism**)

Recommended reading:

Besterman, Theodore. *Crystal-Gazing,* London, 1924; University Books, 1965

Bramwell, J. M. *Hypnotism; Its History, Practice & Theory,* London, 1903

Gurney, E., F. W. H. Myers & F. Podmore. *Phantasms of the Living,* 2 vols., Trubner, London, 1886

Huxley, Aldous. *The Doors of Perception,* London, 1954 etc.

MacKenzie, Andrew. *Apparitions & Ghosts,* Barker, London, 1971; Popular Library, N.Y., 1971

MacKenzie, Andrew. *Hauntings & Apparitions,* Heinemann, London, 1982

Myers, F. W. H. *Human Personality and Its Survival of Bodily Death,* 2 vols., Longmans Green, London & N.Y., 1903

Podmore, Frank. *Apparitions and Thought Transference,* London, 1894

Richet, Charles. *Thirty Years of Psychical Research,* W. Collins, London, 1923

Rogo, D. Scott. *Mind Beyond the Body,* Penguin, N.Y., 1973

Samuels, Mike. *Seeing With the Mind's Eye; The History, Techniques & Uses of Visualization,* Bookworks/Random, N.Y., 1973

Tyrrell, G. N. M. *Apparitions,* Duckworth, London, 1953; Society for Psychical Research, London, 1973

Hallucinogens

Drugs which induce profound changes in consciousness through interference with normal sensory perception. Typical drugs of this kind are mescaline, LSD and psilocybin.

Aldous Huxley's stimulating books *The Doors of Perception* (1954) and *Heaven & Hell* (1956) suggested that such drug experience was related to states of mysticism, but opinion is now changing to the view that drug-induced psychedelic states are qualitatively and quantitatively different from genuine mystical states. (See also **Drugs**)

Recommended reading:

Gopi Krishna. *Higher Consciousness,* Julian Press, 1974.

Lewin, L. *Phantastica, Narcotic and Stimulating Drugs,* E. P. Dutton, N.Y., 1964

Masters, R. E. L. & Jean Houston. *The Varieties of Psychedelic Experience,* Holt, Rinehart & Winston, 1966; Anthony Blond, London, 1967

Wasson, R. G. *Soma: The Divine Mushroom,* Harcourt Brace, 1971

Zaehner, R. C. *Mysticism Sacred and Profane,* London, 1957

Ham

According to Norwegian legend, Ham was a storm-fiend in the shape of an eagle with black wings, sent by Helgi to engulf Frithjof as he sailed for the island of Yarl Angantyr. The story is told in the Saga of Grettir.

Hambaruan

Among the Dayaks of Borneo the *hambaruan* or soul of a living man, was believed to be able to leave the body at will and go where it chose, however it was vulnerable to capture by evil spirits. If this should happen, the man would fall ill, and, if his soul was not speedily liberated, would die.

Hamilton, Dr. T(homas) Glen(dinning) (1873–1935)

Medical practitioner of Winnipeg, president of the Winnipeg Society for Psychical Research, a keen psychical investigator who, over a period of fifteen years, carried on systematic research in his own laboratory under scientific conditions, and often in the presence of the most distinguished people of Canada and the U.S.

He was born in Agincourt, Ontario, Canada, November 26, 1873, in a farming family. He studied at Manitoba Medical College, spent a year as house surgeon at Winnipeg General Hospital and in 1904 established a medical practice in Elmwood, Winnipeg. He served on the School Board for ten years from 1906 onwards. In late 1906 he married Lillian May Forrester. He took a great interest in community life, becoming chairman of the Winnipeg Playground Commission and in 1915 was elected Liberal Member for Elmwood to the Manitoba Legislative Assembly.

His interest in psychical phenomena dated from his days as a medical student and he took a special interest in the mediumship of Mrs. John H. Curran and "Patience Worth." His own investigations dated from 1920.

His regular circle consisted of four medical doctors, a lawyer, a civil engineer and an electrical engineer. His wife, an experienced nurse, also assisted. He secured the services of several non-professional mediums: Elizabeth M., Mary M., and Mercedes.

Through constantly attending the seances, some of the sitters also developed mediumship and fell occasionally into trance. Many of the phenomena were simultaneously photographed by a large group of cameras of which several were stereoscopic.

A unique collection of photographs of table levitations, telekinetic movements, teleplasmic structures, materialized hands, faces and full figures were obtained. The harmonious conditions of the circle enabled Dr. Hamilton to make an important contribution to the study of direct voice and psychic lights as well. A small group of famous dead individuals acted as regular controls: R. L. Stevenson, David Livingstone, W. T. Stead, Rev. C. H. Spurgeon and Camille Flammarion.

Apart from the photographs, the most valuable contribution was a critical analysis of trance which, in the hands of a competent observer, would be invaluable to researchers in eliminating imposition and fraud, whether deliberate or unintentional.

Dr. Hamilton died April 7, 1935.

Recommended reading:

Hamilton, G. *Intention and Survival; Psychical Research Studies and Bearing of Intentional Acts by Trance Personalities on the Problem of Human Survival,* Macmillan Co. of Canada, 1942, 2nd ed. Regency Press, London & New York, 1977

Hamilton, Margaret L. *Is Survival a Fact? Studies of Deep-Trance Automatic Scripts,* London, 1969

(See also articles in *Psychic Science:* 'Teleplasmic Phenomena in Winnipeg,' vol. viii, No. 3, 1929; vol. viii, No. 4, Jan. 1930, vol ix, No. 2, July 1930; 'A Lecture to the British Medical Association,' vol. ix, No. 4, Jan. 1931; 'The Mary M. Teleplasm of Oct. 27, 1929,' vol. x, No. 4, Jan. 1932).

Hammurabi, Law of

Injunction against black magic in the reign of Hammurabi, sixth king of the Amoritic or West Semitic dynasty of Babylonia, 2067–2025 B.C. (See **Semites**)

Hamon

A legendary sacred stone like gold, shaped as a ram's horn. If its possessor was in the posture of contemplation, it was believed to give the mind a representation of all divine things.

Hamon, Count Louis (1866–1936)

Famous Irish palmist and fortune-teller, who practiced and wrote under the pseudonym "**CHEIRO.**"

Hand of Glory

The hand of a dead man (preferably hanged) in which a lighted candle was placed. It was formerly believed in Ireland and Mexico to be an instrument of magic. If the candle with its gruesome candlestick was taken into a house, the sleeping inmates were believed to be prevented from waking, and the candle itself remained invisible. To be truly efficacious, however, both hand and candle had to be prepared in a special manner.

The term "hand of glory" is believed to derive from the French *main de gloire* or *mandrogore* and be related to legends of the mandrake (see **Mandragoras**). The mandrake plant was believed to grow under the gallows of a hanged man.

Belief in the efficacy of the Hand of Glory to facilitate robbery persisted as late as 1831 in Ireland (see the chapter 'The Folk-lore of the Hand' in *The Hand of Destiny* by C. J. S. Thompson, London 1932).

The belief in the Hand of Glory was the subject of 'The Nurses' Story,' one of the *Ingoldsby Legends* of Thomas Ingoldsby (Rev. Richard Barham, 1837 etc.)

Hands of Spirits

There are instances in occult history where the hand only of a spirit has become visible to the human eye.

During the reign of James I of England, a vision of this kind came to a certain clerk who was engaged in writing a will which was to disinherit a son. It took the form of a fine white hand, which appeared between the candle and the parchment, casting a shadow on the latter. It came three times, until clerk, becoming alarmed, threw down his pen and refused to finish the work.

In the book of *Daniel* in the *Bible,* it is related: "In the same hour came forth fingers of a man's hand, and wrote over against the candlestick upon the plaster of the wall of the king's palace: and the king [Belshazzar] saw the part of the hand that wrote." There are also many instances of writing being done without human hands, and in his book *Startling Facts in Modern Spiritualism* (1874), Dr. N. B. Wolfe stated that he has shaken hands with spirits, as "substantially" as one man shakes hands with another. After a certain vision, it is recorded that Daniel was touched by a hand, which set him upon his knees and upon the palms of his hands.

In his paper 'Notes of an Enquiry into the Phenomena Called Spiritual' (*Quartery Journal of Science,* Jan., 1874) Sir William **Crookes** described the appearance of a phantom hand in a seance with Kate **Fox,** then in London (see **Fox Sisters**):

"A luminous hand came down from the upper part of the room, and after hovering near me for a few seconds, took the pencil from my hand, rapidly wrote on a sheet of paper, threw the pencil down, and then rose up over our heads, gradually fading into darkness."

A similar seance took place with Kate Fox (then Mrs. H. D. Jencken) at the house of Mr. S. C. **Hall,** editor of the *Art Journal,* September 6, 1876, in the presence of nine individuals. A report in *The Spiritualist* (Oct. 13, 1876) stated:

"A luminous, small, beautifully shaped hand then descended from the side at which was sitting, that is to say, at the opposite side to Mrs. Jencken. The hand seized a pencil which was lying on the table and wrote the letters 'E.W.E.'. . ."

Phantom hands also materialized during seances with the medium D. D. **Home** in sittings with Napoleon III in 1857, as well as on many other occasions with other sitters, including Crookes. (See also **Automatic Writing**)

Recommended reading:

Medhurst, R. G. (collected). *Crookes and the Spirit World; A Collection of Writings by or concerning The Works of Sir William Crookes D.M., F.R.S., in the Field of Psychical Research,* Taplinger, N.Y./Souvenir Press, London, 1972

Moses, Rev. W. Stainton. *Direct Spirit Writing (Psychography),* London, 1878; Psychic Book Club, London, 1952

Hankey, Muriel W(inifred) Arnold
(1895–1978)

Prominent British researcher and organizer in the field of psychic science. Born May 17, 1895, in London, England, she married Herbert Anthony Hankey in 1925.

She was secretary to J. Hewat **McKenzie,** founder of the **British College of Psychic Science** and has served as principal and secretary of the College 1952-60. From 1920 onwards Mrs. Hankey investigated psychic phenomena and assisted in the training of mediums in Britain.

She cooperated with Dr. John F. **Thomas** of Detroit, Michigan, by acting as a "proxy sitter" in experiments over sixteen years. (A "proxy sitter" substitutes for the individual seeking information from a medium, in order to eliminate the possibility of telepathy between medium and sitter.)

Mrs. Hankey was author of *James Hewat McKenzie: Pioneer of Psychical Research* (1963) and also contributed to *Psychic Science, Light* and *Tomorrow.* She gave many lectures on psychic subjects.

She died in April 1978.

Hanon–Tramp

The name given by Germans to a certain kind of **nightmare.** This particular nightmare took the form of a demon which suffocated people during sleep. It was believed by the French peasantry that this was "the destruction that wasteth at noon-day," as it was supposed that people were most exposed to its attacks at that time. Its method of suffocation was to press on the breast and thus impede the action of the lungs.

Hansel, C(harles) E(dward) M(ark) (1917–)

British lecturer in psychology who has written many articles on parapsychology. Born October 12, 1917, at Bedford, England, educated at Cambridge University (M.A. 1950), married Gwenllian Evans 1953. Member of the British Psychological Society; lecturer in psychology at University of Manchester, England, from 1949 onwards.

In addition to many articles on psychology for *Nature, The Quarterly Bulletin of the British Psychological Society* and the *British Journal of Psychology,* Mr. Hansel is co-author with John Cohen of the book *Risk and Gambling* (1956). His articles on parapsychology include: 'Experiments on Telepathy' (*New Scientist,* Feb. 1959), 'Experimental

Evidence for Extrasensory Perception' *Nature,* 1959–60), 'A Critical Review of the Experiments on Mr. Basil Shackleton and Mrs. Gloria Stewart' (*Proceedings* of the SPR, May 1960), 'Experiments on Telepathy in Children: A Reply to Sir Cyril Burt' (*British Journal of Statistical Psychology,* Nov. 1960), 'A Critical Analysis of the Pearce-Pratt Experiment' and 'A Critical Analysis of the Pratt-Woodruff Experiment' (*Journal of Parapsychology,* June 1961).

In 1966 he published *ESP: A Scientific Evaluation,* a skeptical work in which he reviewed psychical research between 1880 and 1920. A new edition was published under the title *ESP and Parapsychology; A Critical Re-evaluation* (Prometheus, Buffalo, N.Y., 1980). In it he concluded: "The first forty years of psychical research produced nothing that could be regarded as scientific evidence for supernatural processes. It was in the main, a history of fraud, imposture and crass stupidity."

Hansen, F. C. C.

Danish co-author with Alfred Lehmann of the pamphlet *Veber unwilkürliches Flüstern: Eine kritische und experimentelle Untersuchung der sogenannten Gedankenübertragung,* published in the *Philosophische Studien* of W. Wundt (vol. 11, Part 4). This put forward a theory of "involuntary whispering" to account for apparent thought-transference (telepathy). The theory was discussed in *Journal* of the Society for Psychical Research (vol. 9, p. 113) and *Proceedings* (vol. 12, p. 298; vol. 14, p. 163). (See also **Telepathy**)

Hantu Penyardin

Term for a **vampire** in Malayan superstition. (See also **Malaysia**)

Hantu Pusaka

Term for a demon in Malayan superstition. (See also **Malaysia**)

Hanussen, Erik Jan (?   –1933)

Extraordinary stage clairvoyant who made a great reputation in Germany during the 1920s and 30s, combining blatant trickery with the most astounding mental phenomena. Because of the accuracy of his predictions he became known as the "Devil's Prophet." Born as Heinrich Steinschneider, he was the son of a synagogue caretaker, and left school to join a circus at an early age, becoming a knife-thrower, fire-eater and professional strong man.

He served in World War II, and when his company was cut off from water supplies demonstrated a weird talent for water-witching without apparatus. He was eventually transferred to headquarters to entertain troops. After the war, he built up a reputation as strong man at the Ronacher Circus in Vienna, and demonstrated stage clairvoyance at music halls. During one routine performance, he suddenly foretold details of the discovery of a local murderer in advance of the newspapers. At the same demonstration, he privately informed an elegant woman that she was the Baroness Prawitz, unhappily married, and that within a month she would leave her husband and become Hanussen's mistress in Berlin, although the affair would eventually break up.

Meanwhile Hanussen found himself on trial in the

Czech town of Leitmeritz, charged with extracting money under false pretences by claiming to forecast the future. With arrogant poise, Hanussen correctly told the state prosecutor the contents of his pockets, the judge the contents of his attache case, and gave other information about court officials. When the judge protested that this was just music hall telepathy, Hanussen retorted that he would give further proofs of his powers. He stated that at that moment there was a man standing on Platform Two at the Leitmeritz railway station who had just burgled the Commercial Bank, had the money in his briefcase and that the train was due in four minutes time. Police rushed to the station and found that Hanussen was right! The bank robber was arrested and Hanussen acquitted.

This case made Hanussen famous and he became a star at the Scala Theatre in Berlin during the 1920s. Here, too, the Baroness Prawitz felt under an irresistible compulsion to join him as his mistress, and was further humiliated by being obliged to dress in a revealing costume and act as his stage assistant "Jane."

In 1929, at a Scala performance, Hanussen told a banker that there was a short-circuit in his strongroom which had 360,000 Marks in the safes, and there was just over three minutes left to telephone for the fire engines. It happened just as Hanussen predicted. There was no evidence of fraud or collusion and the electrical fault in a secure strong room of a securely locked bank would have been impossibly difficult to fake. However, in spite of such sensationally accurate predictions, Hanussen also cold-bloodedly engaged an assistant to ferret out information and gossip for his regular stage performances, in order to save him from relying solely on clairvoyance.

With the rise to power of the Nazis, Hanussen obtained a favorable status as an "honorary Aryan," but over-reached himself at a seance for party members at which his medium predicted the burning of a large building as a signal for revolt. With the burning of the Reichstag, Hanussen became an embarrassment to the Nazis, and in March 1933 he was taken for a car ride and murdered by three Nazi party thugs. As it happens, he had earlier told one of his mistresses that he felt his end was near.

Although little known outside Europe, Hanussen was a celebrity in pre-war Germany and Austria, and in 1955 a German film company made a film about his life, in which this strange charlatan-clairvoyant was represented as an anti-Nazi martyr. For further details of this extraordinary character, see *Companions of the Unseen* by Paul **Tabori** (London, 1968), and Hanussen's *Meine Lebenslinie* (Berlin, 1930).

Harbinger of Light, The

The first Australian Spiritualist magazine founded by William Terry in 1870 in Melbourne, published monthly.

Harding, Douglas E. (1909–)

Modern British mystic whose teaching resembles a very practical application of Hindu Jnana Yoga and Zen Buddhist teachings.

Born at Lowestoft, Sussex, England, in a fundamental Christian atmosphere of the Plymouth Brethren sect to which his parents belonged, he studied architecture at University College, London. After breaking with the Plymouth Brethren, he was disowned by his parents and

suffered loss of religious faith until he spontaneously rediscovered the secret of mystical identity taught in various religions.

His own awakening was a matter of patient trial and error while still pursuing his profession as an architect in India and Britain, and is described in his books *On Having No Head* (1971) and *Me, The Science of the 1st Person* (1975). Harding's method is that of direct first-person experience of "headlessness," involving exercises in the location of identity and awareness. In this, Harding recalls the classic Hindu mystical question "Who Am I?" expounded by Sri **Ramana Maharshi** and other sages, but beginning at a pragmatic level of physical awareness, culminating in a kind of Western-style Zen insight. Harding lives in Suffolk, England, but spends time traveling through Europe and the U.S., lecturing and conducting experiential workshops.

Hardy, Mrs. Mary M. (c. 1875)

Boston, Massachusetts, medium through whom, in 1875, the first paraffin casts of spirit hands were obtained. She was investigated by Prof. William **Denton.**

Mrs. Hardy gave seances in public halls before many hundred spectators. On the platform there was a table, the cloth of which reached to the ground. Two vessels containing liquid paraffin and cold water were placed under the table. The lights were turned down, but spectators were able to see the medium sitting motionless. After about a quarter of an hour **raps** were heard and the paraffin mould was found floating on the water. Professor Denton made many experiments under rigid test conditions. In 1875 Mrs. Hardy visited Europe and gave many seances in England and on the Continent.

For an account of a seance in 1896 under rigid test conditions, during which moulds of spirit hands were produced, see *The Spiritualist* (1878, p. 168).

Hardy, Sir Alister Clavering (1896–)

Zoologist who was very active in the field of parapsychology. Born February 10, 1896, at Nottingham, England, educated Oundle School and Exeter College, Oxford, England (M.A., D.Sc.). In 1927 he married Sylvia Lucy Garstang. In 1920 he was a Christopher Welch Biological Research Scholar and Oxford Biological Scholar at Stazione Zoologica, Naples.

He was assistant naturalist with the Fisheries Department, Ministry of Agriculture and Fisheries, England, 1921–24; chief zoologist on the *Discovery* Expedition 1924–28; from 1928–42 professor of zoology and oceanography at University College, Hull; from 1942–45 regius professor of natural history at University of Aberdeen, Scotland; from 1946 onwards Linacre professor of zoology and comparative anatomy at Oxford University. In 1939 he was awarded the Scientific Medal of the Zoological Society, England. He is a fellow of the Royal Society, and was knighted in 1957.

In addition to his work on zoology, oceanography and marine ecology, Dr. Hardy took a keen interest in the significance of psychical research for biology, and as a member of the council of the Society for Psychical Research, London, he has sought to bring psychical and biological studies closer together. He made his views clear in his article 'Biology and Psychical Research' (*Proceedings* of the SPR vol. 50, pt. 183, 1953). His books include: *Great Waters,* London, 1967, *The Living Stream; A Restatement of Evolution Theory and its Relation to the Spirit of Man,* London, 1965.

Hare, Robert, M. D. (1781–1858)

Professor emeritus of chemistry at the University of Pennsylvania, discoverer of the oxy-hydrogen blowpipe, author of more than 150 papers on scientific subjects, writer on political and moral questions. He was born in Philadelphia January 17, 1781, and studied at the University of Philadelphia, where he filled the chair of chemistry from 1818 to 1847. As a high ranking scientist of the day, he was one of the first scientific authorities to denounce early American Spiritualism in the Press. In 1853, he wrote that he considered it "an act of duty to his fellow creatures to bring whatever influence he possessed to the attempt to stem the tide of popular madness which, in defiance of reason and science, was fast setting in favour of the gross delusion called spiritualism."

So at the age of 72, he began his investigations and devized a number of instruments which, contrary to his expectations, conclusively proved to himself that a power and intelligence, not that of those present, was in fact at work.

His first apparatus was a wooden board about four feet long, supported on a fulcrum about a foot from one end, and at the other end attached by a hook to a spring balance. A glass vessel filled with water was placed on the board near the fulcrum, a wire gauze cage attached to an independent support, and not touching the glass at any point, was placed in the water and the medium had to effect the balance by simply placing his hand into the wire cage. The medium was Henry Gordon. The balance showed variations of weight amounting to 18 lbs. This apparatus has similarities to that used later by Sir William **Crookes** to test the medium D. D. **Home**.

The other apparatus consisted of a revolving disc attached to a table in such a manner that the movements of the table actuated the pointer, which ran around the letters of the alphabet printed on the circumference of the disc and spelt out messages. The disc was so arranged that the medium could not see the letters.

Prof. Hare's book *Experimental Investigation of the Spirit Manifestation,* published in 1855, summed up the results as follows: "The evidence may be contemplated under various phases; first, those in which rappings or other noises have been made which could not be traced to any mortal agency; secondly, those in which sounds were so made as to indicate letters forming a grammatical, well-spelt sentences, affording proof that they were under the guidance of some rational being; thirdly, those in which the nature of the communication has been such as to prove that the being causing them must, agreeably to accompanying allegations, be some known acquaintance, friend, or relative of the inquiry.

"Again, cases in which movements have been made of ponderable bodies of a nature to produce intellectual communications resembling those obtained, as above-mentioned, by sounds.

"Although the apparatus by which these various proofs were attained with the greatest possible precaution and precision, modified them as to the manner, essentially all

the evidence which I have obtained tending to the conclusions above mentioned, has likewise been substantially obtained by a great number of observers. Many who never sought any spiritual communications and have not been induced to enrol themselves as Spiritualists, will nevertheless not only affirm the existence of the sounds and movements, but also admit their inscrutability."

The book, the second part of which described after-life as depicted by the communicators, passed through five editions. Reaction was quick to set in against its influence. The professors of Harvard University passed a resolution denouncing him and his "insane adherence to a gigantic humbug." He was howled down by the American Association for the Advancement of Science when in Washington in 1854 he tried to address them on the subject of Spiritualism. Finally he paid for his convictions by resigning from his chair.

A. D. Ruggles, a professional medium, who often wrote in languages unknown to him, was one of the subjects with whom Prof. Hare experimented. Later Hare himself became a medium. This is known from a letter of his to Judge **Edmonds** which contains this paragraph: "Having latterly acquired the powers of a medium in sufficient degree to interchange ideas with my spirit friends, I am no longer under the necessity of defending media from the charge of falsehood and deception. It is now my own character only that can be in question."

This simplistic acceptance of Spiritualism somewhat diminished Hare's reputation in his later years. He died in Philadelphia May 15, 1858.

In the revelations from the other world, the communications were taken at their face value. There was no careful sifting or criticism and the fact that they apparently came from spirits appears to have attested their credibility for Prof. Hare.

Hare Krishna

A sacred name of God in Hinduism, used as a mantra or prayer. "Hari" means "sin-destroyer" and Krishna was a popularly worshiped incarnation of God described in the *Bhagavad-Gita* section of the religious epic *Mahabharata.*

Sri Krishna (the "Sri" is an honorific) was born after a flight from a wicked tyrant who had ordered the slaughter of all male children in an effort to avert the divine event. However, the birth took place among the shepherds and shepherdesses on the banks of the River Jamuna in India, and a star in the heavens announced the sacred occasion. This strange foreshadowing of the Christian story is related in detail in the Hindu scripture *Srimad Bhagavatam.*

The modern **International Society for Krishna Consciousness** (ISKCON), popularly known as the "Hare Krishna movement" is a revival of the sixteenth-century Krishna cults of Bengal, and is devoted to developing "Krishna-consciousness" or divine bliss among Western people by chanting Hare Krishna mantras and assuming the dress and customs of Hindu cults. It has had a great success among young people disaffected by the generation gap, especially hippies and drug addicts. (See also Swami **Bhaktivedanta**)

Harmonial Society

Founded in Benton County, Arkansas, in 1855 by an American Methodist, the ex-reverend T. E. Spencer and his wife. It was styled "Harmony Springs" and admission to membership was subjected to the approval of the controls of the founder.

His chief doctrine was that many spirits perished with the body, some languished after death and expired shortly after. But those who followed the Spencerian system would arrive at immortality already on earth. The price of immortality was the surrender of the members' property to the founder. In the course of events, some initiates began to doubt and intended to take legal measures for the recovery of their property. The Spencers thereupon escaped but they were caught and sentenced to imprisonment.

Harodim

A degree of **Freemasonry** very popular in the North of England, and especially in the County of Durham, and probably founded in Gateshead in 1681. It was brought under the Grand Lodge in 1735. They were the custodians of the Ritual of All Masonry, or the Old York Ritual. There were nine lodges in all. A London version of this society was the Harodim-Rosy-Cross, of Jacobite origin, probably carried to London by the Earl of Derwentwater.

In 1787 a Grand Chapter of the Ancient and Venerable Order of Harodim was founded by William Preston, author of *Illustrations of Masonry* (London, 1775).

Harris, Mrs. Susannah (c. 1920)

American direct voice medium (later Mrs. Harris Kay), pastor of a Spiritualist Church in Columbus, Ohio, controlled by a child "Harmony." The last years of her life were spent in England.

After accusations of fraud, Dr. Abraham Wallace applied the water test, filling the medium's mouth with water which changed color according to the length of time it was affected by saliva, Dr. Wallace claimed to have established the independence of the medium's voices.

In 1913 and 1914 the journal *Light* contained many testimonies in favor of Mrs. Harris' mediumship. In 1919 at the Steinway Hall, while blindfolded, she executed a painting in oils upside down and nearly completed another in over two hours.

However, in 1920 the Norwegian Society for Psychical Research published a very unfavorable report on twenty-five sittings held in Christiania. Proof was adduced that the German voice of "Rittmeister Hermann" was an accomplished fraud to which "Harmony" was an accomplice (*Light,* May 1, 1920).

Mrs. Harris had been accused of fraud at seances in Holland in 1914 (see K. H. Jong, 'The Trumpet Medium Mrs. Harris,' *Journal* of the Society for Psychical Research, vol. 16, 1914).

For a favorable view of her phenomena, see James Coates, *Is Spiritualism Based on Facts or Fancy* (1920).

Harris, Rev. Thomas Lake (1823–1906)

Mystic, poet, medium, fascinating orator and religious reformer. He was born at Fenny Stratford, England, May 15, 1823, and brought to America as a child. He became a Universalist Minister at the age of 20 and was one of the little band of enthusiasts who gathered around Andrew Jackson **Davis** after the publication of *The Principles of Nature, Her Divine Relations and a Voice to Mankind* in 1847.

In the same year Harris formally withdrew from the Universalist Church and went on a lecture tour to spread the knowledge of the New Revelation. On his return he broke off relations with Davis. His ideas were stern and rigid and he was shocked to find that the Poughkeepsie Seer's views on marriage were rather lax. Davis had association with a married woman whose husband was still living and he taught that if married partners discovered that they were no longer adapted to one another they ought to separate and seek truer affinities.

Although they became reconciled after Davis married the lady in question, they never again worked together. Harris became pastor of the First Independent Christian Society of New York. In 1851 he joined the Apostolic Movement of Auburn of which J. D. Scott, a Baptist preacher, was the head (see **Apostolic Circle**). Scott, a trance speaker, fancied that he was the chosen vessel of St. John. The imagination of Harris was fired by messages, coming through Mrs. Benedict, the official medium of the movement, stating that St. Paul was expected to communicate and that he might be the fortunate mouthpiece. He went to Auburn and in joint editorship with Scott published a new periodical *Disclosures from the Interior and Superior Care of Mortals.* The **Mountain Cove** community was founded soon afterwards. The faithful band of settlers yielded themselves and all their possessions to J. D. Scott, the "perfect medium." Harris did not join the community. When, however, dissension arose and a break was threatening, Scott went to New York and induced him to come to the rescue. As Harris prevailed upon several men of property to follow them the crisis was averted. There were now two "perfect mediums" and Harris, as the representative of St. Paul, assumed directing influence. His autocratic rule did not last long. A revolt broke out and he left for New York to preach Spiritualism at Dodworth Hall, then the headquarters of the movement.

During November and December 1853, in a state of trance or inspiration he dictated his first great poetic composition: *An Epic of the Starry Heavens.* According to Arthur A. Cuthbert's biography *The Life and World Work of Thomas Lake Harris* (Glasgow, 1908), the poem was ingerminated in Harris' subconscious self three years and nine months previous to its dictation and its six thousand lines were delivered in twenty-one sittings from November 24 to December 8, 1853 in twenty-six hours and sixteen minutes. Cuthbert also recorded that Harris was, from his earliest childhood, a very remarkable poetical improvisatore. In proof of this he quoted the letter of a lady from Richard M'Cully's *The Brotherhood of the New Life* (1893) which stated: "When in Utica he would come to my sitting room of an evening, and sitting down in a rather high chair, he would compose poetry by the mile; and it was really poetry—exquisite thoughts exquisitely worded."

The Epic of the Starry Heavens was followed by *The Lyric of the Morning Land* and *The Lyric of the Golden Age* similarly dictated in a state of trance. Of the former, a poem of five thousand words and of great beauty, he claimed entire ignorance in his conscious state. He spoke and sang it during parts of fourteen days in about thirty hours. It was finished by August 4, 1854.

The *Lyric of the Golden Age* is superior in poetical composition to the first two and reflects the highest ideas of Byron, Shelley, Coleridge and others. Harris actually claimed them, and also Dante, as his inspirers.

In view of such impressive evidence of supernormal powers manifesting through him, Harris aspired to be the leader of the Spiritualist movement. When he met with repudiation his attitude underwent a singular change. He professed himself to be the champion of Christianity versus Spiritualistic Pantheism and published his *Song of Satan* in which the communicating spirits, with the exception of those who visited Harris' Sacred Family, were declared to be demons in the worst sense of the word. Yet apparently he himself was not quite immune from the influence of these demons. In his life work *Arcana of Christianity* (1857) he complained of obsession in writing: "It was resolved upon by Evil Spirits that my physical existence should be destroyed, the demon, by name Joseph Balsamo, planned a subtle scheme to bring to bear upon the enfeebled physical system the magic of the Infernal World."

In his esoteric system, **fairies** occupied a large place. There is a long disquisition in the *Arcana* under the title "The Divine Origin of the Fay." He claimed constant intercourse with fairyland and poured forth a number of infantile communications in which the "Little Brothers" playfully called him "Little Yabbit." The mouthpiece of his movement, *The Herald of Light* (1857–1861), was called "a journal of the Lord's New Church" and was almost entirely written by Harris.

In 1859 he announced to his congregation in New York that the spirits had entrusted him with a mission to go to England and preach there. He arrived in May 1859 and, in inspirational addresses of striking eloquence, preached his mystic Christianity both in London and various provincial centers. In his very first sermon he presented "in bold relief the danger of Spiritualists giving themselves up to production of physical phenomena, and allowing their minds to be held captive by the teachings of the low forms of Spiritualism." The *Morning Advertiser* considered the sermon "an extraordinary and triumphant exposure of Spiritualism."

In his *History of the Supernatural* (1863) William Howitt paid great tribute to his eloquence: "His extempore sermons" he wrote, "were the only realisation of my conceptions of eloquence; at once full, unforced, outgushing, unstinted and absorbing. They were triumphant embodiments of sublime poetry, and a stern unsparing, yet loving and burning theology. Never since the days of Fox were the disguises of modern society so unflinchingly rent away, and the awful distance betwixt real Christianity and its present counterfeit made so startlingly apparent. That the preacher was also the prophet was most clearly proclaimed, by his sudden hastening home, declaring that it was revealed to him that the nethermost hells were let loose in America. This was before the public breach betwixt North and South had taken place. But it soon followed, only too deeply to demonstrate the truths of the spiritual intimation."

Laurence Oliphant, a brilliant writer and politician and Lady Oliphant, his mother, the widow of an ex-chief justice of Ceylon, came under Harris' influence during his stay in England. Oliphant was a man of varied career. He held various diplomatic missions, was private secretary to Lord Elgin during his Vice-Royalty of India, secretary of

legation in Japan, special correspondent of *The Times* in Crimæa and M.P. for the Stirling Burghs in 1865. During his two years of parliamentary life he observed unbroken silence. This was in obedience to Harris' influence.

In 1867 the prophet decided to impose a still more severe probation. Oliphant disappeared from London and was not seen until 1870. He was summoned to America to work as a manual laborer in the theo-socialistic community "The Use," which T. L. Harris founded in 1861 in a small hill farm near Wassaic in the State of New York. The Holy Ghost, named "Divine Breath," was expected to descend in seven stages upon the members of this community. It appears, however, from Cuthbert's biography that Harris and subsequently his wife were about the only ones who attained to the seventh stage. The practice of "open breathing," a form of respiration to bring the Divine Breath into the body sounds very much like a form of *pranayama* or yoga breathing (see **Kundalini**).

In 1863, "The Use" moved to Amenia, about four miles distant from Wassaic, where a mill was purchased and The First National Bank of Amenia was founded under Harris' presidency.

This was soon given up for a settlement in Brockton, on the shore of Lake Erie, which was bought largely with Lady Oliphant's money.

Laurence Oliphant was ordered to report in Brockton and the first task he was set to was to clean a stable. According to Frank Podmore, the stable must have been of Augean dimensions as he was engaged in it for many days in absolute loneliness, sleeping in a loft which was only furnished with a mattress and empty orange boxes. He had no one to speak to. His meals were brought to him by a silent messenger. He was but rarely allowed to meet his mother to whom he was very much attached.

After a period of probation, Harris allowed him to go out into the world. During the Franco-Prussian war Oliphant acted as correspondent for *The Times* but always held himself in readiness to return if Harris summoned him. He met his future wife in 1872. Harris withheld his consent to the marriage and only agreed when the lady placed all her property in his hands.

After the marriage had taken place, the couple were summoned to Brockton. The lady was set down to housework and Oliphant was quickly dispatched to New York to labor for the community as director of a cable company. For years, husband and wife were kept apart. For a period of three years Oliphant was not even allowed to see her. During this time, Mrs. Oliphant was sent out of the community penniless and alone to earn her living.

In 1880, Harris permitted their reunion in Europe. This was after his community migrated to Santa Rosa, California. The grape and wine culture which they began in Amenia was developed to a profitable industry in the new settlement. The teetotallers' abuse was ingeniously answered. It was stated that the curse which attends intemperance was in this case occultly met with and counteracted. Another reason for scandal was the relationship of Harris with a lady whom he afterwards married.

In the meantime Oliphant's mother was reported dying. Laurence came to bid her farewell. When she died, the spell in which Oliphant was held by Harris was broken. He charged Harris with fraud and, with the help of friends, recovered a considerable part of the fortune entrusted to him.

Nevertheless until the end of his days in December 1888 Oliphant persisted in the belief that Harris had genuine psychic powers. It is a fact that his hold on his followers was very strong. He was implicitly believed when in 1891 he announced that he had discovered the **elixir of life** and renewed his youth thereby. Consequently, when he died March 23, 1906, his disciples refused to believe in his death and only acknowledged the fact three months later.

Recommended reading:

Noyes, John Humphrey. *History of American Socialisms*, Lippincott, 1970; reissued as *Strange Cults & Utopias of 19th-Century America*, Dover Publications, 1966

Schneider, Herbert Wallace. *A Prophet and a Pilgrim, Being the Incredible History of Thomas Lake Harris and Laurence Oliphant; Their Sexual Mysticisms and Utopian Communities*, Columbia University Press, N.Y., 1942

Hart, Hornell (Norris) (1888-1967)

American professor of sociology and parapsychologist. Born August 2, 1888, at St. Paul, Minnesota, he studied at Oberlin College, Ohio (B.A. 1910), University of Wisconsin (M.A. in sociology 1914), State University of Iowa (Ph.D. child welfare and sociology 1921). In 1915 he married Ella Brockhausen.

He was a faculty member of Bryn Mawr College, Pennsylvania 1924-30, professor of social economy 1930-33. From 1933-38 he was professor of social ethics at Hartford Theological Seminary, Hartford, Connecticut; 1938-57 professor of sociology at Duke University, Durham, N.C.; 1957-60 John Hay Whitney Foundation professor of sociology at Centre College of Kentucky, Danville, Kentucky; from 1960 onwards head of sociology department, Florida Southern College.

He was winner of the Edward L. Bernays Award for Best Action-Related Study on the Social Effects of Atomic Energy, 1948. He is a charter member of the Parapsychological Association and member of American Society for Psychical Research, Society for Psychical Research, London, American Sociological Society, Southern Sociological Society. He published several books and a number of articles on sociology.

In the field of Parapsychology, he took special interest in apparitions and the evidence for survival. His articles in *Proceedings* of the Society for Psychical Research, London, included: 'Visions and Apparitions Collectively and Reciprocally Received' (May 1933), 'Six Theories About Apparitions' (May 1956), and in *Journal of the ASPR:* 'The Psychic Fifth Dimension' (1953), 'ESP Projection: Spontaneous Cases and the Experimental Method' (1954), 'Psychical Research and the Methods of Science' (1957). He discussed the question **Out-of-the-Body** traveling or "Astral Projection" in his article "Man Outside His Body?' (*Tomorrow*, Winter 1954). His books included: *The Science of Social Relations* (1927), *The Technique of Social Progress* (1931), *Personality and the Family* (1935, 1941), *Living Religion* (1937), *Newspapers and the News* (1937), *Skeptic's Quest* (1938), *Chart for Happiness* (1940), *New Gateways to Creative Living* (1941), *Can World Government be Predicted by Mathematics?* (1944), *Social Science and the Atomic Crisis* (1949), *The "Great Debate" on American Foreign Policy* (1951), *McCarthy versus the State Department*

(1951, 1952), *Your Share of God* (1958), *The Enigma of Survival; The Case For and Against an After-Life* (1959), *A Laboratory Manual for Introductory Sociology* (1961, 1964). He contributed articles to: *American Journal of Sociology, Social Forces, Philosophy of Science, New Republic, Forum, New York Times, Christian Century, International Journal of Religious Education, Proceedings* of the Society for Psychical Research.

He died February 1967.

Hartlaub, Gustav Friedrich (1884-1963)

German museum director and professor of art who studied the relationship of occultism and magic to art.

Born March 12, 1884, at Bremen, Germany, he obtained his Ph.D. from Heidelberg, 1863. He married Félice Meyer (died 1930); his second marriage in 1914 was to Erika Schellenberg. He was director of the Municipal Art Museum, Mannheim, Germany, from 1921 until dismissed by the Nazis in 1933.

From 1946 onwards he was professor, history of art, at Heidelberg University. His books included *Magic of the Mirror* (1950), *The Inexplicable: Study of the Magic World View* (1951), *The Philosopher's Stone: Character and Image of Alchemy* (1959). He died April 30, 1963.

Hartmann, Dr. Edward von (1842-1906)

German philosopher, author of *The Philosophy of the Unconscious*, the ground work of modern psychoanalysis, and of Phenomenology. Born February 23, 1842, in Berlin, he was originally educated for an army career, but later turned to philosophy and was awarded D. Phil. by the University of Rostock in 1867.

One of the first investigators of Spiritualism in Germany, he desired to give a definite place to both physical and mental phenomena in his philosophy and in his book *Spiritualism*, (translated into English by C. C. Massey, 1885) put forward the following hypothesis: "A nervous force producing outside the limits of the human body mechanical and plastic effects. Duplicate hallucinations of this same nervous force and producing also physical and plastic effects. A latent, somnambulistic consciousness, capable (the subject being in his normal state) of reading in the intellectual background of another man, his present and his past, and being able to divine the future." It was in reply to this book that A. N. **Aksakoff** wrote his *Animismus und Spiritismus* (1890).

Dr. von Hartmann died at Grosslichterfelde June 5, 1906.

Hartmann, Franz (1838-1912)

Noted Theosophist and writer on occultism. Born November 22, 1838, in Bavaria, Germany, he claimed descent on his mother's side from the old Irish kings of Ulster, Ireland.

He became a physician and emigrated to America in 1865, traveling as a doctor to various cities and also visiting Indian tribes and studying their religious beliefs. He became interested in Spiritualism, and also corresponded with leading Theosophists.

He was invited to the Theosophical Society headquarters at Adyar, India, where he lived during the furor of Madame **Blavatsky's** alleged miracle working. When Richard **Hodgson** of the Society for Psychical Research, London, published his devastating exposure of trickery and fraudulent phenomena by Madam Blavatsky, Dr. Hartmann accompanied her to Europe and then returned to his home town in Bavaria. Here he encountered a sect of secret Rosicrucians, from whom he acquired many mystical insights.

He was President of the Theosophical Society in Germany, but eventually resigned in order to found independent societies. During his later years, he spent much time in the Untersberg Mountains near Salzburg, Austria, where he believed he encountered gnomes, water nymphs and other nature spirits. He died at Kempten, Bavaria, August 7, 1912. His books on occult subjects included: *Magic, Black and White* (1885, reissued University Books, N.Y., 1970), *An Adventure Among the Rosicrucians* (1897), *Life and Doctrines of Paracelsus* (1891), *Occult Science in Medicine* (1893).

Hasidim

Devotees of a mystical phase of Judaism. The term means "pious ones." They are first referred to in the pre-Maccabean age. They again occur in the first centuries of the Christian era, sometimes supposed to be the descendants of the earlier sect. The later *Hasidim* were saints and workers of miracles, gifted with esoteric wisdom and the prophetic faculty.

Early in the eighteenth century there arose yet another group of the same name, having for its aim the revival of spirituality in the Jewish religion. A founder of this movement was the **Baal Shem Tor** ("Master of the Good Name") (c. 1700-1760). Representatives of this mystical movement are still to be found in Europe, the U.S. and Israel.

The characteristic formation of groups surrounding a noted *zaddik* or holy leader is reminiscent of the Hindu tradition of similar groups of devotees around a noted holy man.

Recommended reading:

Buber, Martin. *The Origin and Meaning of Hasidism,* Horizon Press, N.Y., 1960

Buber, Martin. *Tales of the Hasidim; Early Masters,* Schocken Books, 1947

Buber, Martin. *Tales of the Hasidim; Later Masters,* Schocken Books, 1948

Hasted, John B(arrett) (1921–   )

British physicist who has also conducted important researches in parapsychology. He commenced his professional training as a chemist, then worked in the field of physics at the Clarendon Laboratory, Oxford, England, during World War II. He was responsible for important developments in the microwave region of the electromagnetic spectrum in communications, and was reader in physics at the University College of London. His published works include: *Physics of Atomic Collisions* (1964; 1972), *Aqueous Diaelectrics* (1973). Dr. Hasted is Professor of Experimental Physics and Head of the Physics Department of Birkbeck College, University of London.

In the field of parapsychology, he conducted careful experiments with the psychic Uri **Geller** on Psychokinetic phenomena. These experiments, together with colleagues David Bohm, Edward W. Bastin and Brendan O'Regan took place between February and September 1974 at Birkbeck College, and were designed to investigate Gel-

ler's ability to bend metal, deform crystals and activate a Geiger counter without contact. Witnesses at some of the sessions included authors Arthur Koestler and Arthur C. Clarke. The results, which were largely successful, were reported in the paper 'Experiments on Psychokinetic Phenomena' by Hasted, Bohm, Bastin & O'Regan in *The Geller Papers* by Charles Panati (1976).

Dr. Hasted's involvement with paranormal metal bending dates back to 1974, when Uri Geller visited Britain. Hasted was one of a group of scientists who met Geller and was impressed with his talents. Subsequently Hasted conducted experiments with many children who claimed to be able to reproduce the Geller effect.

Because there have been frequent criticisms that metal bending experiments are not properly controlled and that children, in particular, are given to blatant frauds, Dr. Hasted took care to experiment under conditions in which touching the targets was ruled out and observers closely watched the experiments, some of which were videotaped. Since critics of metal-bending phenomena like James **Randi** allege imperfect experimental control, it is only fair to say that Dr. Hasted is aware of the possibility of fraud and has taken advice on methods from noted conjurers.

Dr. Hasted has also devoted special attention to what happens to metal during paranormal bending. The targets are connected with a strain gauge sensor to register the strength of the deformation. He suggests that children may have special aptitude in paranormal bending in the same way that they are often centers of disturbance in **Poltergeist** phenomena. In contrast to Prof. John **Taylor,** who now discounts the possibility of an electromagnetic phenomenon being involved, he believes that there is evidence of an electromagnet field in paranormal metal bending. (See also **Movement; Psychokinesis**)

Recommended reading:

Hasted, John. *The Metal-benders,* Routledge & Kegan Paul, London, 1981

Taylor, John. *Superminds,* Viking Penguin/Macmillan, London, 1975

Taylor, John. *Science and the Supernatural,* Temple Smith, London, 1980

Hastings, Arthur Claude (1935–   )

Assistant professor of speech and drama who has investigated paranormal phenomena. Born May 23, 1935, at Neosho, Missouri, he studied at Tulane University (B.A. 1957) and Northwestern University (M.A. 1958). He is a member of the Parapsychological Association, Speech Association of America, Western Speech Association. From 1960 onward he was assistant professor at the Department of Speech and Drama, University of Nevada.

He investigated poltergeist phenomena in Gutenberg, Iowa, for the Parapsychology Laboratory at Duke University, Durham, N.C. His articles include: 'Poltergeist Phenomena and Expectancy Set' (*Northwestern Tri-Quarterly,* vol. 3, No. 3, spring 1961), 'Expectancy Set and "Poltergeist" Phenomena' (*ETC* magazine, vol. 18, No. 3, Oct. 1961).

Hastraun

A small mystical sect of Judaism, whose members were to be found in some parts of Palestine and Babylon. They practiced some sort of communism, and were known also as "fearers of sin."

Hatha Yoga

The ancient Hindu science of physical exercise. This system differs essentially from Western gymnastics in featuring static postures *(asanas)* instead of active movements and in being related to spiritual development.

The Sanskrit syllable *Ha* indicates the sun and *tha* the moon. The "yoga" or union of the sun and moon is through *Pranayama* the subtle vitality of breath and essence of food. Pranayama is induced by actual practice of the asanas and also by special breathing exercises and cleansing techniques.

Good physical health is regarded as an important step towards spiritual development rather than an end in itself. Thus, the traditional Hatha Yoga treatises insist upon *yama* and *niyama* (moral observances and ethical restraints) as an essential preliminary to yoga practice. These include: non-violence, not stealing, truthfulness, abstinence from sexual impropriety and greed, observance of purity, austerity, religious study, and faith in God. Without such observance, Hatha Yoga becomes merely a gymnastic achievement.

Of the theoretical 8,400,000 asanas, 84 are said to be the best, and 32 the most useful for good health. Most of these are named after living creatures, e.g., cow, peacock, locust, cobra, lion, etc. An asana is considered to be mastered when the yogi can maintain the position without strain for three hours. Asanas clearly develop flexibility in associated muscle groups throughout the body, and also affect the tone of veins and arteries, particularly through the inverted positions such as the yoga headstand. Many asanas develop maximum flexibility of the spine through a series of backward and forward bending positions at different points of gravity. Asanas are also claimed to improve the function of the ductless glands through persistent gentle pressure.

The mastery of basic asanas and associated cleansing techniques prepares the yogi for meditation positions, and the practice of mental concentration, detachment and meditation itself. When associated with special breathing techniques, the subtle current of the body *(prana)* flows through nerve channels, culminating in the arousal of a latent energy called **Kundalini,** located at the base of the spine. The task of the yogi is to induce this current to flow up the spine to a subtle center in the head, resulting in mystical or transcendental experience.

Evidence for the reality of this mystical awakening, described by the great Hindu sages of the past, can be found in the lives of living yogis, notably Pandit **Gopi Krishna** and Swami **Muktananda.** (See also **Prana; Kundalini; Yoga**)

Recommended reading:

Bernard, Theos. *Hatha Yoga,* London, 1950; paperback Weiser, N.Y., 1970

Dvivedi, M. N. (transl.) *The Yoga-Sutras of Patanjali,* Theosophical Publishing House, 1890, etc.

Gopi Krishna. *The Awakening of Kundalini,* Dutton paperback, 1975

Gopi Krishna. *The Secret of Yoga,* Harper & Row, 1972

Iyangar, Yogi S. (transl.) *Hatha-Yoga-Pradipika of Svat-*

marama Svamin. Theosophical Publishing House, India, 1893, etc.

Iyengar, B. K. S. *Light on Yoga,* London, 1965 [describes over 200 asanas]

Majumdar, S. M. *Introduction to Yoga Principles & Practices,* University Books, 1964

Vishnudevananda, Swami. *The Complete Illustrated Book of Yoga,* Bell Publishing Co., 1960, Pocket Books, 1971.

Hauffe, Frau Frederica (1801–1829)

The "Seeress of Prevorst," so known from the book of that title (*Die Seherin von Prevorst,* 1829 etc.) by Dr. Justinus **Kerner,** a physician, poet, and philosopher of Weinsberg. She was born in the village of Prevorst near Löwenstein (Württemburg), Germany, in 1801 and married in 1819 and from that time on until her death ten years later, she was bedridden, subject to various ailments. She had convulsive fits, her body became rigid like a corpse and in this state she was possessed by spirits. She saw clairvoyantly, made predictions and exhibited a wide range of curious psychic phenomena.

At one time she spoke for three days in verse only. Occasionally she saw her own **double** clad in white, seated on a chair, whilst she was lying in bed.

She could draw with tremendous speed perfect geometrical designs in the dark, used with great skill the **divining rod,** exhibited disturbances of a **poltergeist** character and communicated extraordinary revelations from the spirit world. The spirits of the dead were said to be in constant attendance on her both by night and day and in confirmation of this were occasionally seen by others. Dr. Kerner himself observed once in her bedroom a grey pillar of cloud as though with a head. Another curious phenomenon recorded by Dr. Kerner was seeing with the **stomach** (see also **Eyeless Sight**).

Troubled souls came to Frau Hauffe for help and disclosed secrets of their doings on earth which made them restless. They made various noises, rapped, threw things about, pulled off the boots of Frau Hauffe with violence in Dr. Kerner's presence, extinguished the nightlight and made the candle glow.

The teachings of Frau Hauffe in a trance state mainly consisted of the triune doctrine of body, soul and spirit. The soul is clothed by an ethereal body (Nervengeist) which carries on the vital processes when the body is in trance and the soul wanders about. After death it withdraws with the soul but later decays and leaves the soul free.

The unique part of the spiritual revelations of the Seeress of Prevorst consisted of the description of systems of circles, Sun-circles and Life-Circles, corresponding to spiritual conditions and the passage of time. They were illustrated by amazing diagrams. The interpretation was furnished partly by ciphers, partly by words of a primeval language written in primitive ideographs.

On the basis of these revelations, a mystic circle was founded which claimed that the teachings disclose analogies with the philosophical ideas of Pythagoras, Plato and others. They issued a journal of their own, *Blaetter aus Prevorst,* of which twelve volumes were published from 1832–39.

The "Universal language" which the Seeress of Prevorst described compares, as in the case of Dr. John **Dee,** with Hebrew. A philologist also discovered in it a resemblance to Coptic and Arabic. It was said to be the language of the inner life.

The written characters, preserved by Dr. Kerner, were always connected with numbers. Some of them are as complicated as an Egyptian hieroglyph. Frau Hauffe said that the words with numbers had a much deeper significance than without. In this respect the language had affinity with Hebrew **gematria,** a forerunner of **Numerology.**

The names of things in this language expressed the properties and qualities of the things. Frau Hauffe spoke it quite fluently and in time the listeners vaguely understood her. Dr. Kerner quoted a few words of the language in his book which, in an abbreviated form, was translated into English by Mrs. Catharine Crowe as *The Seeress of Prevorst* (London, 1845).

In 1823, Frau Hauffe was delivered of a child, which was also seized with spasms and convulsions and died within a few months.

In January 1829, Frau Hauffe in trance state announced that she had only four months left before her death, but in spite of severe illness she was still living in May. She stated "it is hard to know the moment of one's death," and continued to see visions of specters and a coffin. Three days before her death she stated that she could not endure another three days. She died August 5, 1829.

Haunted Houses

About 1919, a number of British newspapers contained, throughout several consecutive weeks, an advertisement offering for sale "an ancient Gothic Mansion, known as Beckington Castle, ten miles from Bath and two from Frome". After expatiating on the noble scenery around Beckington and the rare architectural beauty of the house itself, the writer of this advertisement proceeded to say that the place was the more desirable because it was reported to be haunted!

No doubt there are people who long for a house containing a genuine ghost, and it was sometimes said that the rich tradesman, anxious to turn himself into a squire used to look for a haunted manor, while humorists declared that ghosts were on sale at department stores and that the demand for them among American millionaires was stupendous. Such a story formed the plot of René Clair's movie comedy *The Ghost Goes West* (1936), script by Robert Sherwood.

And, if the purchaser of Beckington Castle had to pay an additionally high price because the place rejoiced in a veritable ghost, in reality anything of this sort used to make a house almost unsaleable. At Lossiemouth, on the east coast of Scotland, a fine old mansion stood untenanted for years, and was eventually sold for a merely nominal sum. The reason was simply that according to popular tradition, the building was paraded nightly by a female figure draped in white, her throat bearing an ugly scar, and her hands tied behind her back with chains. Nor was it merely concerning old country mansions that stories of this nature were current. Even in many densely-populated towns there were houses reputed to be haunted, which were quite unsaleable.

Since World War II, the acute housing shortage in

Britain has made house buyers less finicky or agents less forthcoming about ghosts.

It would seem that royal palaces, closely watched and guarded as they invariably have been, are not altogether destitute of such inhabitants. Legend contends that Windsor Castle is frequently visited by the ghost of Sir George Villiers, and it is said, moreover, that in the reign of Charles I, this ghost appeared to one of the king's gentlemen-in-waiting and informed him that the Duke Buckingham would shortly fall by the hand of an assassin—a prophecy which was duly fulfilled soon after, as all readers of *Les Trois Mousquetaires* will doubtless remember, the incident figuring in that immortal story.

Then at Hackwood House, near Basingstoke Hampshire, there is a room in which no one dares to sleep, all dreading "the grey woman" supposed to appear there nightly, while Wyecoller Hall, near Colne, boasts a specter horseman who visits the place once a year, and rides at full speed through the garden.

Very different is the legend attached to Dilston, in Tyneside, where a bygone Lady Windermere is said to appear from time to time and indulge in loud lamentations for her unfortunate husband who was executed for his share in the Jacobite rising of 1715. Dilston Hall is now an educational establishment, but permission can be obtained to visit the castle ruins.

At Salmesbury Hall, Blackburn, there is a ghost of yet another kind, neighborhood tradition affirming that a ghostly weird lady and her knight promenade the grounds of the Hall, indulging the while in silken dalliance. At the present time, the Hall houses an exhibition center and may be visited by tourists.

It need hardly be said that ghosts bulk largely in the spiritual lore of nearly every British county, but there are more gruesome apparitions and among these is the ghost of Amy Robsart, which haunts the manor of Cumnor, in Oxfordshire. For it must be borne in mind that Amy was a real woman, and not a mere creation of novelist Sir Walter Scott.

She was married in 1550 to the Earl of Leicester and her tragic death is commonly laid to his charge, but a tradition exists to the effect that Queen Elizabeth was really the responsible person, and recalling an authentic portrait of Amy, which depicts her as a woman of charm and of no ordinary beauty, it is easy to believe that the ill-favored queen hated her and took strong measures to get her out of the way.

Numerous rectories rejoice in the ghost of a clergyman murdered by his parishioners, and there are several haunted monasteries and convents, while at Holy Trinity Church at York a phantom nun was said to appear occasionally on winter evenings and walk about muttering paternosters. The story concerning her is that, on one occasion, during the Civil War, a band of soldiers intended to loot the church. On approaching it with this intention they were confronted by an abbess, who bade them beware of the divine wrath they would surely incur if they committed such an act of sacrilege. They laughed at her piety, never thinking that she would offer any resistance and they tried to march *en masse* into the building, but hardly had they commenced the assault when their opponent snatched a sword from one of them and stood bravely on the defensive. A fierce battle ensued, the abbess proving herself a veritable amazon, and slaying a host of her foes, yet she lost her life ultimately, and her ghost was supposed to frequent the church she sought to defend.

There are few parts of England so rich in romance as Sherwood Forest in Nottinghamshire, once the scene of Robin Hood's exploits. One place in this region which claims a number of ghosts is Newstead Abbey, the seat of Lord Byron's ancestors. A part of the garden there is popularly known as "the devil's wood," a name which points to the place having been infested once by minions of the foul fiend, while one of the rooms in the house was haunted by a certain "Sir John Byron, the little, of the grey beard," who presumably ended his days in some uncanny fashion. His portrait hung over the hall in the dining room, and a young lady staying at Newstead about the middle of last century insisted that once she had entered this room to find the portrait gone, and its subject seated by the fireside reading a black-letter folio volume!

The poet Byron himself cherished very fondly all the ghostly traditions which clung round his home and it is recorded that, on his learning that there were stone coffins underneath the house, he immediately had one of them dug up and then opened. He used some of its gruesome contents to "decorate" his own library, while he had the coffin itself placed in the great hall through which thereafter the servants were afraid to pass by night. He also utilized the supernatural lore of Newstead in one of his poems, and from this we learn that a specter friar used to parade the mansion whenever some important event was wont to befall its owners:

> "When an heir is born he is heard to mourn,
>   And when aught is to befall
> That ancient line, in the pale moonshine
>   He walks from hall to hall.
> His form you may trace, but not his face,
>   'Tis shadowed by his cowl;
> But his eyes may be seen from the folds between,
>   And they seem of a parted soul.
> Say nought to him as he walks the hall,
>   And he'll say nought to you:
> He sweeps along in his dusky pall,
>   As o'er the grass the dew.
> Then, gramercy! for the black friar;
>   Heaven sain him, fair or foul,
> And whatsoe'er may be his prayer,
>   Let ours be for his soul."

There are many stories of hauntings at that grim ancient fortress the Tower of London, but visitors must remember that those were usually reported at night time, when the gates were closed to tourists.

Passing from England to Ireland, we find many traditions of haunted houses. For instance, at Dunseverick in Antrim dwells the soul of a bygone chief so wicked in his lifetime that even hell's gates were closed to him. Other haunted houses in Ireland, now open to visitors, include castle Matrix in Limerick, castle Malahide in County Dublin and Springhill Manor in County Londonderry.

In Scotland there are also numerous haunted buildings, notably Holyrood Palace and the castles of Hermitage and Glamis. It is the ghost of the murdered Rizzio which

frequents Holyrood, yet it should be added that the vision is seldom seen nowadays and maybe the fates, aware that the Italian minstrel was shamefully treated, have at length accorded his soul a resting-place more cosy than the dismal Edinburgh Palace.

But the ghost of Hermitage, on the contrary, is still considerably addicted to exercise and in truth his story marks him as having been a man of rare activity and ambition. Lord Soulis was his name and, possibly hearing of the exploits of Dr. Faustus, (see **Faust**) he vowed that he too would invoke the devil, who generously made his appearance.

"Vast power will be yours on earth," said the devil to Soulis "if you will but barter your soul therefor," so his lordship signed the requisite compact with his life's blood and thenceforth his days were given over to the enjoyment of every conceivable pleasure.

Soon, however, he felt that his end was near, and calling some of his vassals around him he told them of the awful fate awaiting him after death. They were thunderstruck, but soon after Soulis was gone it occurred to them that, if they could destroy his mortal remains completely, they might save his soul from the clutches of Beelzebub. So having sheathed the corpse in lead they flung it into a burning fiery furnace, and (so the story goes) manifestly this cremation saved his lordship from the nether regions, for had he gone there his soul would not have been active still at Hermitage.

The ghost story associated with Glamis Castle, the family seat of the Earl of Strathmore, is quite different from the rank and file of supernatural tales and bears a more naked semblance of veracity than pertains to any of these. It is a matter of tradition that there is a secret chamber at Glamis, a chamber which enshrines a mystery known only to a few members of the Strathmore family, and three or four generations ago a lady, staying as a visitor at Glamis, vowed she would solve the riddle.

Her first difficulty was to locate the actual room, but one afternoon, when all the rest of the household were going out, she feigned a headache and thus contrived to be left completely alone. Her next move was to go from room to room, putting a handkerchief in the window of each, and having done this she went outside and walked round the castle to see whether any room had evaded her search.

Very soon she observed a window which had no handkerchief in it, so she hastened indoors again, thinking that her quest was about to be rewarded. But try as she might she could not find the missing room, and while she was searching the other guests returned to the house, along with them being the then Lord Strathmore.

He was fiercely incensed on learning what was going on and that night shrieks were heard in a long corridor in the castle. The guests ran out of their rooms to find out what was wrong, and in the dim light they perceived a curious creature with an inhuman head, wrestling with an aged man-servant who eventually contrived to carry the monster away. There the story ends, but as remarked before, it bears a semblance of truth, the probability being that some scion of the Glamis castle family was mad or hideously deformed, and was accordingly incarcerated in a room to which access was difficult and secret.

Another explanation was offered by the nineteenth-century writer the Rev. F. G. Lee, who claimed that strange, weird and unearthly sounds were regularly heard in the Castle. The then head of the family unlocked the haunted room, then swooned away in the arms of his companions. What had he seen? The story goes that there had been a feud between the Ogilvie and Lindsay clans, and that one day a party of fleeing Ogilvies demanded sanctuary in the Castle. The lord of the day could not refuse, but feared to offend the Lindsays. He thereupon led the Ogilvies to a remote room and locked them in—forever. What the later head of the family saw was the skeletons of the starved Ogilvies, who still had the bones of their arms clenched in their teeth, having been driven in desperation to eat their own flesh.

Be that as it may, there are traditions of other ghosts at Glamis, including a White Lady, a tall thin man known as "Jack the Runner" and a small black servant. Glamis is Scotland's oldest inhabited castle and has many dark and gloomy legends. As a stately home, it is accessible to visitors at the present time.

The reputation of "The Most Haunted House in England" was bestowed upon Borley Rectory in Suffolk by psychical researcher Harry Price in his book *'The Most Haunted House in England'; Ten Years' Investigation of Borley Rectory* (London, 1940). Price rented the Rectory for a year and advertised for observers. Over a period of fourteen months, 2,000 paranormal phenomena were reported: voices, footsteps, ringing of bells, locking and unlocking of doors, messages on walls, transportation of objects, crashes, breaking of windows, starting of fires, lights in a window, the apparitions of a nun and a ghost coach with a headless coachman. Price died in 1948, two years after publication of another book *The End of Borley Rectory*, following demolition of the Rectory. Seven years later, psychical investigators E. J. Dingwall, Kathleen M. Goldney and Trevor H. Hall published another book *The Haunting of Borley* (1956) alleging that Price deliberately faked phenomena and distorted the Borley story. Trevor H. Hall later followed this work by *The Search for Harry Price* (1978) in which he attempted methodically to demolish Price's reputation not only as a psychical researcher but also as an individual. It has to be said that the case against Price has been grossly overstated. Like many other people, he had certain faults but these should not detract from his pioneer achievements as a psychical researcher. So far as Borley Rectory is concerned, the claimed hauntings stretch way back in time, long before the appearance of Price on the scene.

Visiting Haunted Houses

British ghosts are exceptionally well documented by recent books. *Haunted Britain* by Antony Hippisley-Coxe (1975) lists the haunts of varied ghosts of the British countryside, including grey ladies, headless horesmen, phantom hounds, healing wells and witches. The pretty village of Pluckley in Kent has no fewer than twelve phantoms, including a White Lady, a Red Lady, a poltergeist, a monk, the Mistress of Rose Court, a schoolmaster who hanged himself, a miller, a watercress woman who was burnt to death, a highwayman impaled to a tree by a sword, a screaming man who died in a clay pit, and a coach and horses in the main street. Mr. Coxe also conducted a weekend ghost safari in conjunction with Grand Metropolitan Hotels and Boswell and Johnson

Travel of New York. A coach trip took tourists to supernatural sites in the West Country frequented by ghosts, witches and poltergeists. (In the U.S., similar **Ghost Tours** were organized by Richard T. Crowe in Chicago, Illinois).

Jack Hallam, former picture editor of the British *Sunday Times* newspaper, published *The Ghost Tour; A Guidebook to Haunted Houses Within Easy Reach of London* (1967), and *The Ghost Who's Who* (1977) which lists some five hundred frequently reported apparitions in England and Wales, ranging from a Bronze Age ghost through kings and queens to a man in a bowler hat haunting a runway at London Airport. Hallam claims that Britain is the most haunted country in the world, with 25,000 phantoms in England and Wales as well as thousands more in Scotland and Ireland. He states that the most haunted English village is Bramshott in Hampshire, with 300 living residents and 17 ghosts.

Another useful guide to ghost-ridden Britain is *Ghosts Over Britain* by Peter Moss (Elm Tree Books, U.K., 1977). Peter **Underwood** of the British **Ghost Club** has published *Hauntings* (1977), as well as *Gazetteer of British Ghosts* (1975) and *Gazetteer of Scottish & Irish Ghosts* (1975). Irish ghosts are also documented in *Haunted Ireland: Her Romantic & Mysterious Ghosts* by John J. Dunne (Appletree Press, Belfast, 1977), which lists 52 traditional Irish phantoms.

Of course, hauntings are not confined to the stately homes of the British Isles. In America there have also been celebrated haunted houses, including the Audubon House of Key West, Florida, San Antonio's Brooks House, Fort Sam Houston's Service Club, the Dakota Apartments in New York City (which inspired the setting of *Rosemary's Baby*) and the Governor's Mansion in Delaware, right up to modern times with the claimed phenomena of the **Amityville Horror.** Some of the most famous earlier hauntings such as the Great Amherst Mystery are more accurately classified as cases of Poltergeist, and are discussed under that heading. (See also **Apparitions; FOG Newsletter; Ghost Club; Ghost Tours; Haunting; Poltergeist**)

Recommended reading:

Alexander, Marc. *Haunted Houses You May Visit,* Sphere Books paperback, London, 1982

Anson, Jay. *The Amityville Horror,* Bantam paperback, N.Y./Pan Books paperback, London, 1978

Bennett, E. T. *Apparitions & Haunted Houses; A Survey of Evidence,* Faber & Faber, London, 1939; Gryphon Books, Ann Arbor, 1971

Dunne, John J. *Haunted Ireland; Her Romantic & Mysterious Ghosts,* Appletree Press, Belfast, 1977

Flammarion, Camille. *Haunted Houses,* T. Fisher Unwin, London, 1924; Tower Books, Detroit, 1971

Hallam, Jack. *The Ghost Tour; A Guidebook to Haunted Houses Within Easy Reach of London,* Wolfe Publishing paperback, London, 1967

Harper, Charles G. *Haunted Houses; Tales of the Supernatural, With Some Account of Hereditary Curses and Family Legends,* Palmer, London, 1924; Tower Books, Detroit, 1974

Hippisley-Coxe, A. D. *Haunted Britain; A Guide to Supernatural Sites Frequented by Ghosts, Witches, Poltergeists & Other Mysterious Beings,* Hutchinson, London/McGraw Hill, N.Y., 1973; Pan paperback, London, 1975

Holzer, Hans. *Hans Holzer's Haunted Houses; A Pictorial Register of the World's Most Interesting Ghost Houses,* Crown, N.Y., 1971

Price, Harry. *'The Most Haunted House in England'; Ten Years' Investigation of Borley Rectory,* Longmans, London, 1940

Price, Harry. *The End of Borley Rectory,* George G. Harrap, London, 1946

Smith, Susy. *Ghosts Around the House,* World Publishing Co., N.Y., 1970; Pocket Books paperback, 1971

Tabori, Paul & Peter Underwood. *The Ghosts of Borley; Annals of the Haunted Rectory,* David & Charles, Newton Abbot, U.K., 1973

Underwood, Peter. *Gazetteer of British Ghosts,* Souvenir Press, London, 1971; Walker & Co., N.Y., 1975

Underwood, Peter. *Gazetteer of Scottish & Irish Ghosts,* Souvenir Press, London, 1973; Walker & Co., N.Y., 1975

Haunting

Disturbances of a paranormal character, attributed to the spirits of the dead. Tradition established two main factors in haunting: an old house or other locale and restlessness of a spirit. The first represents an unbroken link with the past, the second is believed to be caused by remorse over an evil life or by the shock of violent death.

The manifestations vary greatly. In most cases, strange noises are heard alone (auditory effects), in some others objects are displaced, lights are seen (visual effects), a chilliness is felt in the atmosphere, not infrequently unbearable stench pervades the room, an evil influence imparts feelings of unspeakable horror (sensory effects), and phantoms, both human and animal, appear in various degrees of solidity. The more noise they make the less solid they are.

The phenomena of haunting are often classed as objective and subjective. This classification is rather arbitrary as it does not take count of auditive hyperaesthesia. Sounds below the ordinary limit of audition may be heard objectively although nobody else is aware of a beginning disturbance. The phantoms themselves are often harmless and aimless, sometimes malevolent. "Since the days of ancient Egypt, ghosts have learned, and have forgotten nothing," stated Andrew **Lang,** noted folklorist and writer on psychical manifestations. The usual type display no intelligence, appear irregularly and act like a sleep-walker or a mechanical recording.

Cap. A. W. Monckton, F.R.G.S., in his *Some Experiences of a New Guinea Resident Magistrate* (1927) told the story of ghostly footsteps at Samarai, in the house where he was staying. In brilliant illumination he could see the depression at the spots from which the sound of the footsteps came.

Perhaps the most ancient case of haunting is attributed to the spirit of the traitorous general Pausanias (second century A.D.) who was immured in the Temple of Athene of Sparta to die of starvation. Terrifying noises were heard in the temple until a necromancer finally laid the ghost.

John H. Ingram, in *The Haunted Homes and Family Traditions of Great Britain* (1890) published many accounts of haunting. According to him there are at least 150 haunted houses in Britain. To quote one account, he recorded, on the source of an article in *Notes and Queries,* 1860, that Edmund Lenthal Swifte, who was appointed

Keeper of the Crown Jewels in the Tower of London in 1814, experienced various unaccountable disturbances and that one night one of the sentries saw a huge phantom bear issue from underneath the Jewel Room door. The bear dissolved into the air after the sentry thrust at it with his bayonet. The sentry died of fright next day.

Haunted "B. House"

The story of the book *The Alleged Haunting of B. House* (1899, 1900) was investigated on the spot by Sir Oliver Lodge, F. W. H. Myers, Col. L. M. Taylor, the Marquis of Bute and Miss X. (Goodrich-Freer). "B. House" is Ballechin House, Perthshire, Scotland. Miss Goodrich-Freer, who was in charge of the investigation, spent about three months there. In her diary she stated: "I was startled by a loud clanging sound which seemed to resound through the house. The mental image it brought to my mind was of a long mental bar, such as I have seen near iron foundries, being struck at intervals with a wooden mallet. The noise was distinctly across the house. It sounded so loud, though distant, that the idea that any inmate of the house should hear it seemed ludicrous."

Several phantoms were seen, most often a nun whom the investigators named "Ishbel" and a lay woman dressed in grey who was called "Margaret." The nun was sketched by a member of the party. She often appeared to be talking with the lay woman who seemed to upbraid or reprove her. The attempt to catch their words was unsuccessful. The phantoms were seen by the dogs who were terrified.

The clanging sounds sometimes continued for a long time and were succeeded by other sounds. "It might have been made by a very lively kitten, jumping and pouncing, or even by a very large bird; there was a fluttering noise too. It was close, exactly opposite the bed. We heard noises of pattering in Room No. 8 and Scamp [the dog] got up and sat apparently watching something invisible to us, turning his head slowly as if following the movements of some person or thing across the room from West to East. During the night Miss Moore had heard footsteps crossing the room, as of an old or invalid man shuffling in slippers." Attempts to produce the same noises naturally were unsuccessful.

The phantoms apparently desired to be noticed. Miss X., absorbed in writing, was gently, then firmly and more decidedly pushed to make her look up. Nothing was visible, but the dog was gazing intently from the hearth-rug at the place where the phantoms might have been expected.

Once the phantom of a living man was seen, the Rev. Father H., who was supposedly sleeping at the time. Twice the vision of a wooden crucifix presented itself, preceded by an acute chill on the part of someone present. Phantom dogs were heard pattering and bounding in play, one was seen. Miss Goodrich-Freer and Miss Moore felt more than once being pushed as if by a dog and on one occasion two forepaws of a large black dog were seen resting on the edge of a table. The melancholy and depressing character of the phenomena later changed to a horrible and evil influence. Gradually the manifestations died down and finally ceased altogether.

Animal Ghosts

The family history of the owners of this haunted house appears to bear out the theory that the animals seen in haunted houses have also lived there. Major S., who was commonly believed to be one of the haunting spirits was convinced in his lifetime that the spirit of the dead can enter the body of animals, and intended to possess, after his death, the body of a favorite black spaniel from among his many dogs. The family was so distressed by the idea that they had all his dogs shot after his burial. Curiously enough, among the dog apparitions at B. House several witnesses saw a black spaniel.

The writer Elliott **O'Donnell** believed that there are as many animal phantasms as human, the most frequent being the cat, as cats meet more often with a sudden and violent end in the house in which they live than any other animal. Investigating a haunted house he generally used to take a dog with him as a dog seldom fails to give early "notice—either by whining, or growling, or crouching shivering of one's feet, or springing on one's lap and trying to bury its head in one's coat—of the proximity of a ghost." O'Donnell stated that belief in spectral dogs was common all over the British Isles.

Haunted Hampton Court

Miss Goodrich-Freer claimed to have seen ghost manifestations in Hampton Court, the famous London palace built for Cardinal Wolsey but taken over by Henry VIII: "In the darkness before me," she wrote, "there began to glow a soft light. I watched it increase in brightness and in extent. It seemed to radiate from a central point, which gradually took form, and became a tall, slight woman, moving slowly across the floor." She asked the phantom whether she could help her. "She then raised her hands, which were long and white, and held them before her as she sank upon her knees and slowly buried the face in her palms, in the attitude of prayer—when, quite suddenly, the light went out, and I was alone in the darkness."

Miss Goodrich-Freer nevertheless did not believe that the visitor in this case was a departed spirit. She conjectured that it was a telepathic impression of the dreams of the dead "just as the figure which, it may be, sits at my dining-table, is not the friend whose visit a few hours later it announces but only a representation of him, having no objective existence apart from the truth of the information it conveys—a thought which is personal to the brain which thinks it."

A Haunted Chateau

At the Chateau T. in Normandy, near Caen, knocking phenomena were recorded in a diary (see *Annales des Sciences Psychique,* 1892–93) as follows: "One o'clock. Twelve blows followed by a long drumming, then thirty rapid single knocks. One would have thought that the house was shaken; we were rocked in our beds on every storey . . . then a long rush of feet; the whole lasting only five minutes. A minute later the whole house was shaken again from top to bottom; ten tremendous blows on the door of the green room. Twelve cries outside, three bellowings followed by furious outcries. Very loud drumming in the vestibule, rhythmical up to fifty knocks. 1.30 a.m. The house shaken twenty times; strokes so quick that they could not be counted. Walls and furniture alike quivered; nine heavy blows on the door of the green room, a drumming accompanied by heavy blows. At this moment bellowings like those of a bull were heard, followed by wild non-human cries in the corridor. We rang up all

the servants and when all were up we again heard two bellowings and one cry."

The Laying of Uneasy Spirits

There are many cases of hauntings by uneasy spirits which required certain acts to take place before the manifestation ceased.

A highly curious mixture of haunting, poltergeist and obsession phenomena is found in the old case of The Maid of Orlach, told in Dr. Justinus Kerner's *Geschichten Besessener neurer Zeit* (1834). The disturbances began in the cowhouse. The cows were found tied up in unusual ways and places. Sometimes their tails were so finely plaited together as if done by a lace weaver.

Strange cats and birds came and went and invisible hands boxed Magdalene's ears while milking and struck her cap off with violence. Mysterious fires broke out from time to time in the cottage and a contest between a black and white spirit ensued.

There was a white spirit, a benign influence, a nun born at Orlach in 1412, guilty of many crimes. She tried to give protection against the increasing violence of a black spirit and asked for the house to be pulled down. The black spirit threw Magdalene into a cataleptic state and obsessed her. The persecution suddenly stopped when the house was demolished. Under an ancient piece of masonry a mass of human bones, among them the remains of several infants, was discovered. The girl never saw ghosts thereafter.

According to Emma Hardinge's *Modern American Spiritualism* (1869; 1970) the **Hydesville** phenomena developed to formal haunting after the discovery of the rapping intelligence. "The furniture was frequently moved about; the girls were often clasped by hard, cold hands; doors were opened and shut with much violence; their beds were so shaken that they were compelled to "camp out" as they termed it, on the ground; their bed-clothes were dragged off from them, and the very floor and house made to rock as in an earthquake. Night after night they would be appalled by hearing a sound like a death struggle, the gurgling of the throat, a sudden rush as of falling blood, the dragging as if of a helpless body across the room, and down the cellar stairs; the digging of a grave, nailing of boards, and the filling in of a new-made grave. These sounds have been subsequently produced by request."

Proceedings of the Society for Psychical Research (vol. 11, p. 547) contains one of the most curious and well-authenticated cases in which a haunting spirit established communication with a living and was laid after its wishes were carried out. The percipient was Mrs. Claughton, time 1893, place 6 Blake Street, a house reputed to have been haunted by the spirit of its former owner, Mrs. Blackburn. Mrs. Claughton was awakened in the night by a female apparition which was also perceived by her elder child. The apparition bid her "follow me," led her to the drawing room, said "to-morrow" and disappeared. Next night the apparition returned, made a statement to Mrs. Claughton and asked her to do certain things. To prove to her the reality of her experience, the apparition gave the date of her marriage which, on subsequent inquiry, was found to be correct. During this period, a second phantom appeared who stated himself to be George Howard, buried in Meresby churchyard and gave the date of his marriage and death. He asked Mrs. Claughton to go to Meresby (she had never heard of the place before), verify the dates and wait at Richard Hart's grave in the aisle of the church after midnight. He also said that her railway ticket would not be taken, that Joseph Wright, a dark man to whom she should describe him, would help her and that she would lodge with a woman who would tell her that she had a child (drowned) buried in the same churchyard. The rest of the story would be told to her at the churchyard. A third phantom also appeared. He was in great trouble standing with his hands on his face, behind Mrs. Blackburn. Thereafter the three phantoms disappeared. Mrs. Claughton found that such a place as Meresby exists, went there and found lodgings with Joseph Wright who turned out to be the parish clerk. The woman who lost a child was Mrs. Wright. She spoke to Joseph Wright about George Howard, and he took her to his and Richard Hart's graves and locked her in after midnight. Richard Hart appeared and made a communication which Mrs. Claughton did not feel at liberty to disclose. She carried out the desires of the dead in full and received no communications from them thereafter.

Dr. Kerner's book *The Seeress of Prevorst* (1845) contains an account of a poor family in Weinsberg that was disturbed by a ghost. Kerner brought the woman of the house to see Frau Hauffe. The ghost attached itself to the Frau Hauffe and told her that he previously lived in the house which he haunted about 1700 under the name Belon, died at the age of 79 and could not rest because he had defrauded two orphans. After a search in the records it was found that the information tallied with a Burgomaster of the town who died in 1740 at the age of 79 and had been guardian of orphans.

Premonitory Haunting

Premonitory haunting, foretelling death or another catastrophe, is in a class by itself. The White Lady of the Royal Palace in Berlin and of the Castle of Schönbrunn, the White Lady of Avenel (in Sir Walter Scott's book *The Monastery*), the Dark Lady of Norfolk and the Grey Lady of Windsor, are all said to be heralds of death. The White Lady of the Royal Palace of Berlin is supposed to be the ghost of the Countess Agnes of Orlemunde who murdered her two children. She appeared in 1589, eight days before the death of the Prince Elector John George, in 1619, twenty-three days before the death of Sigismund, and also in 1688. In 1850 her appearance preceded the attempt on the life of Count Frederick William. The White Lady of Schönbrunn was seen in 1867 before the tragic death of Emperor Maximilian of Mexico in 1889, prior to the Meyerling drama and before the news arrived that John Orth, the ex-Archduke, was lost at sea.

The forms of premonitory haunting show great variety, from death lights and phantom funeral processions to symbolic sounds, stopping of clocks, the apparition of banshees and ominous animals. Deathbed visions are in a different class as there is no periodicity in their occurrence.

Augustus Hare, in his book *The Story of My Life* (3 vols., 1896) tells of the visit of Sir David Brewster to the Stirling family at Kippenross, in Scotland. Brewster was so terrified by strange noises heard in the night that he fled to his daughter's room. Next day Miss Brewster saw at the head of the stairs a tall woman leaning against the banisters.

She asked her to send her her maid. She nodded three times and, pointing to a door in the hall, descended the stairs. When Miss Brewster spoke of the matter to Miss Stirling she became deeply agitated. Major Wedderburn and his wife were sleeping in the room pointed to. The tradition said that whoever was pointed out by the ghost died within the year. Strangely enough, before the year was out both the Major and his wife were killed in the Sepoy rebellion in India.

The Vanishing Bread and Other Weird Phenomena

The British Spiritualist publication *Light,* Oct. 24, 1903, reprinted from the *Daily Express* newspaper an account of the mystery of the vanishing bread of Raikes Farm, Beverley, Yorkshire. The Websters, a family of seven children, apparently lived in a haunted farmstead. Strange noises, footsteps and mysterious choir singing was heard in the night but the thing which mostly disturbed the family was that the bread, from the first week of March, 1903, crumbled away during the night. It had the appearance as if gnawed by rats or mice.

All sorts of precautions were taken but nothing could arrest the dwindling of the loaves. They were set in a closed pan, with a rat-trap set inside, another on top of the lid, the floor was sprinkled with flour, two lengths of cotton were stretched across the room and the doors were locked.

In the morning, everything was found intact but one of the loaves had entirely disappeared, the other had dwindled to half of its original size. For nearly three months the Websters kept the mystery to themselves. The situation became desperate. Mrs. Webster had seen the end of a loaf waste to nothingness on the kitchen table within an hour.

So the services of ex-police-constable Berridge, of Bishop Burton were requested and he was put in sole charge of the dairy for several days.

But Berridge frankly confessed that he was baffled. He came with two loaves of bread to the farm, and locked them in the dairy with his own special lock. The next day they appeared to be all right but a day after, cutting them open, he found the loaves quite hollow. He suspected faulty baking but the cavity gradually grew wider and wider, and the second loaf began to dwindle before his eyes.

He secreted pieces of bread in other places about the house, but in every instance they wasted away to nothing. Ten leading chemists of Beverley and Hull visited the farm and analyzed the bread. Microscopic examination did not reveal the presence of any microbe or fungus, and the bread had been pronounced absolutely pure.

When Mrs. Webster resorted to baking cakes for the household, she was relieved to find that although they lay side by side with the blighted bread they showed no sign of harmful contact. But when the last crumb of bread disappeared, the mysterious destroyer of the loaf attacked the cakes as well. The decay of the loaf was immediately arrested if it was removed from the precincts of the farmhouse. This proved that the blight was local and possibly, a bizarre form of haunting.

The gruesome traits of the traditional haunting ghost are well reflected in the story which the Earl of Bective told British psychical researcher Harry **Price.** As reported in the journal *Psychic Research* (June 1930), the Earl, stayed with some friends at a Scottish castle and wished to explore a certain wing which had been closed for generations. In the state ballroom, he saw to his amazement "the trunk of a man near the door by which he had just entered and which he had closed after him. No head, arms or legs were visible, and the trunk was dressed in red velvet, with slashings of white across the breast and a good deal of lace. The period was perhaps Elizabethan and the trunk was undoubtedly that of a man.

"The apparition gradually became less distinct and finally vanished, apparently through the closed door. Lord Bective then hurried to the other end of the room with the intention of ascertaining whether the phantom had passed into the next apartment.

"And now comes the most extraordinary part of the story. Although he had a few minutes previously passed through the doorway (the door swinging very easily and with a simple latch), he now found that something was on the other side of the door which prevented his opening it. He could still raise the latch and the door would give a fraction of an inch, with a pronounced resilience, exactly as if someone were on the far side attempting to bar his entry into the room. After two or three good pushes he gave an extra powerful one and the door flew open and he was alone."

The story of the haunted vaults at Barbados sounds like fiction, yet Commander R. T. Gould, R.N., assured us in his book *Oddities: A Book of Unexplained Facts* (1928) that it is a true tale. Time after time, heavy leaden coffins were found standing on end and tossed about as if by the hand of a giant. Lord Combermere, Governor of Barbados, decided to test the matter. The six coffins of the haunted vault were placed in order, a stone weighing five tons was cemented into the doorway and Lord Combermere and others placed their seals on the vault. On April 18, 1820, eight months afterwards, the vault was opened. The sand on the floor bore no mark, yet the six coffins were found thrown all over the vault.

A recurring spectral light, subsequently named the Fire of St. Bernardo, was seen in Italy in Quargnento by Signor Sirembo during the early months of 1895, and afterwards by Prof. Garzino, the Civil Engineer Capello and others. At about half past eight in the evening, a luminous mass, sometimes of a diameter of 24–28 inches, appeared and moved by leaps from the little church of St. Bernardo to the cemetery and about midnight returned to the church. The event took place at all seasons, but it was not seen by everybody. At the church the members of the Guasta family are buried. The case was described in Prof. C. **Lombroso**'s book *After Death-What?* (1909).

In all these cases the locality was very definite. In some others, the space-bound condition has to be conceived in a larger sense.

The medium Mme. **d'Esperance,** as a young girl, was greatly frightened on the Mediterranean in 1867 seeing a "strange ship, her sails gleaming rosy red in the light of the setting sun, looming full over the bows of the Sardinian on which she was sailing. One man on her deck was leaning with folded arms against the bulwarks watching the on-coming of our vessel." The strange ship passed through their own. Mme. d'Esperance saw the vessel in the wake of her boat, with sails fully set; she saw each rope

of the rigging, men moving about on the deck, the pennant flying at the mast-head.

To Prof. Charles **Richet,** the idea that nonhuman intelligences might be behind the phenomena of haunting was greatly appealing. However, almost nothing which would amount to evidence is available of such haunting. The German "Berg Geister," the spirits of mountains and mines or the "little people" (fairies) would be in this class. In *Nineteenth Century Miracles* (1883), Emma H. Britten related that Mr. Kalozdy, a Hungarian author on mineralogy and teacher in the Hungarian School of Mines, collected many narratives of knockings in Hungarian and Bohemian mines. He and his pupils often heard these knockings. The miners took them for signals of the Kobolds (underground goblins) not to work in the direction against which they were warned. The materialized appearance of these Kobolds was seen by Mme. Kalozdy, herself an authoress, in the hut of a peasant, Michael Engelbrecht. Lights of the size of a cheese plate suddenly emerged; surrounding each one was the dim outline of a small human figure, black and grotesque. They flitted about in a wavering dance and then vanished one by one. This visit was announced to Michael by knockings in the mine.

A more prosaic explanation of underground knockings is that they could be caused by seismic disturbances.

Speculations of the Early Psychical Researchers

Such instances, complemented with poltergeist disturbances and other famous cases (see **Bealing Bells; Drummer of Tedworth; Epworth Phenomena;** Rev. Eliakim **Phelps; Poltergeist; Willington Mill**) give a comprehensive idea of the complexity of haunting. What has psychical research made out of it? Early investigation pointed to a disproval of the general belief that some great crime or catastrophe is always to be sought as the ground work of haunting.

There is a chapter on "Local Apparitions" in the *Report on the Census of Hallucinations* published by the Society for Psychical Research, England, in 1894, which concluded: "The cases we have given, in addition to others of the same kind to be found in previous numbers of the Proceedings, constitute, we think, a strong body of evidence, showing that apparitions are seen in certain places independently by several percipients, under circumstances which make it difficult to suppose that the phenomena are merely subjective, or that they can be explained by telepathy without considerable straining of our general conception of it. It appears, however, that there is in most cases very little ground for attributing the phenomena to the agency of dead persons, but as we have said, in the great majority of cases they are unrecognised; and in these cases, if they really represent any actual person, there is often no more reason to suppose the person dead than living."

Miss Goodrich-Freer's comment is worth quoting: "The public seems to have been singularly reticent in confiding stories of hauntings to the S.P.R. or the officials of the Society have been as singularly reticent in confiding their information to its members. The interest of the subject of haunted houses was acknowledged by the early appointment of a committee of inquiry which was, to say the least, unfortunate as to its results. At the end of a few months they discarded a subject of which the literature and well-attested records are especially abundant, and which required years of patient research. They found only twenty-eight cases which they considered really worth inquiry and these rested upon no better evidence than an average of one person and a half to each." (*Essays in Psychical Research* by "Miss X," 1899)

Andrew **Lang** objected mainly on the ground that the committee "neglected to add a seer to their number." This he considered a wanton mistake. He added that ghosts do not have benefit nights, they are not always on view and even where they have been there are breaks of years without any manifestations.

Mrs. Henry **Sidgwick,** who drew up the report, was the first to make a serious attempt to face the difficulties of the problem of haunting. In a paper in 1885 she offered four hypotheses for consideration:

1. The apparition is something belonging to the external world that, like ordinary matter, it occupies and moves through space, and would be in the room whether the percipient were there to see it or not.

2. The apparition has no real relation to the external world but is an hallucination caused in some way by some communication, without the intervention of the senses, between the disembodied spirit and the percipient, its form depending on the mind of either the spirit or of the percipient, or of both. This hypothesis does not account for the apparent dependence of the haunting on the locality.

3. The first appearance in haunted houses is a purely subjective hallucination, and subsequent similar appearances, both to the original percipient and to others, are the result of the first appearance, unconscious expectancy causing them in the case of the original percipient in the case of others. This hypothesis assumes that a tendency to a particular hallucination is very infectious.

4. There is something in the actual building itself which produces in the brain that effect which, in its turn, becomes the cause of hallucination.

Personally, she did not find any of these hypotheses satisfactory and stated: "I can only say that having made every effort—as my paper will, I hope, have shown—to exercise a reasonable scepticism, I yet do not feel equal to the degree of unbelief in human testimony necessary to avoid accepting, at least provisionally, the conclusion that there are in a certain sense, haunted houses, i.e., that there are houses in which similar quasi-human apparitions have occurred at different times to different inhabitants, under circumstances which exclude the hypothesis of suggestion or expectation."

Frank **Podmore** believed that the story of a haunting was begun by some subjective hallucination on the part of a living person, which lingered on in the atmosphere and was telepathically transmitted to the next occupant of the room or house in question. Miss Goodrich-Freer, in her *Essays in Psychical Research,* aptly remarked that on this theory the story of her vision in Hampton Court Palace ought to be transmitted to future occupants of her room whether she really saw or only imagined what she saw, or mistook what she saw, or even if she told lies as to what she saw.

F. W. H. **Myers** defined the ghost as a manifestation of persistent personal energy. He made many interesting suggestions. One was that haunting may be the result of

past mental actions which may persist in some perceptible manner, without fresh reinforcement, just as the result of our bodily actions persist. The perception may be retro-cognition owing to some curious relation of supernormal phenomena in haunted houses to time. In another suggestion he attributed the phenomena to the dreams of the dead, which are somehow being made objective and visible to the living. In his *Human Personality and its Survival of Bodily Death* (2 vols., 1903 etc.) he went much further and offered for consideration his theory of "psychorrhagic diathesis" as applied to a spirit. He defined it as "a special idiosyncrasy which tends to make the phantasm of a person easily perceptible; the breaking loose of a psychical element, definable mainly by its power of producing a phantasm, perceptible by one or more persons in some portion of space."

The theory is a bolder exposition of what Edmund **Gurney** suggested: that spectral pictures, like the recurring figure of an old woman on the bed where she was murdered, may be veridical after-images impressed we know not how on what we cannot guess by that person's physical organism and perceptible at times to those endowed with some cognate form of sensitiveness. The image is veridical because it contains information as regards the former inhabitant of the haunted place.

Why are Spirits Earthbound?

The same suggestion was contained in E. **Bozzano's** "psychical infestation" theory. Bozzano made a special study of haunting and compiled statistics which indicated that out of 532 cases of haunting, 374 were caused by ordinary ghosts and 158 by the poltergeist type. Psychometric impressions are frequently referred to as another possibility of explanation. (See **Psychometry**). As Longfellow wrote: "All houses wherein men have lived and died are haunted houses, through the open doors the harmless phantoms on their errands glide, with feet that make no sound upon the floors."

To explain how psychometric impressions may become intensified, the theory may be combined with the emotional energy of the dreams or the remorse of the dead. Remorse is said to make a spirit earthbound. The same conditions may be brought about by a variety of reasons.

Plato quoted Socrates in *Phaedo:* "And in this case [impure life] the soul which survives the body must be wrapped up in a helpless and earthy covering, which makes it heavy and visible, and drags it down to the visible region, away from the invisible region of spirit world, Hades—which it fears. And thus these wandering souls haunt, as we call it, the tombs and monuments of the dead, where such phantoms are sometimes seen. These are apparitions of souls which departed from the body in a state of impurity, and still partake of corruption and the visible world, and therefore are liable to be still seen. And these are not the souls of good men, but of bad, who are thus obliged to wander about suffering punishment for their former manner of life which was evil."

The poet W. B. Yeats was less censorious in suggesting: "We carry to Anima Mundi our memory, and that memory is for a time our external world; and all passionate moments recur again and again, for passion desires its own recurrence more than any event." (*Per Amica Silentia Lunae,* 1918).

It is interesting to quote, at this juncture, Sylvan J.

Muldoon. In the book *The Projection of the Astral Body* (written in collaboration with Hereward **Carrington,** 1929 etc.) he stated: "the most upright earthly being is just as apt to become the victim of an earthbound condition as the most wicked." It is not the moral but the psychic conditions which make a spirit earthbound. "How often do we hear of the murderer haunting a place? No, it is always the victim—the innocent party, who figures in haunted house phenomena." This is not always true, however, as there have been many accounts of hauntings by murderers.

Spirits may be earthbound for four reasons: desire, habit, dreams and insanity. Revenge may be just as potent a factor in making a spirit earthbound as love. Often the haunter appears to be dreaming, yet occasionally he can be drawn into conversation. According to Muldoon, it is the "crypto-conscious" mind which does the talking, while the conscious mind is engaged in the dream.

The crypto-conscious mind of Muldoon is a department of the unconscious which has a will of it own. Violent death is, however, the most frequent cause of haunting. It results in a stress on the mind which influences the crypto-conscious mind to re-enact the last scene on earth. As an analogy Muldoon pointed to the "very common occurrence during the World War to see soldiers, while dreaming, jump from their beds and re-enact terrors which they had met with and which had left a deep stress in their subconscious minds."

Prof. C. **Lombroso** investigated many cases of haunting and always found a certain purpose: inflicting punishment for the reoccupation of the house, revenging the honor of the family, moral or religious warning. The disturbances appear specially powerful if the victims of the tragedy, enacted perhaps centuries before, died a violent death in the flower of their life. Lombroso called the haunted houses "necrophanic houses."

Vexed by the problem how the haunting spirits obtain matter for their materializations in uninhabited houses where no human organism is available, he asked explanation from the **control** during a seance and twice received the answer that the haunters derive the material of their incarnations from the animals and plants of the deserted house. Nevertheless, human organisms, if available, may be drawn upon by the haunters.

Miss R. C. Morton, in her record of a haunted house (*Proceedings* of the Society for Psychical Research, vol. 8, p. 311) stated: "I was conscious of a feeling of loss, as if I had lost power to the figure. Most of the other percipients speak of a feeling of cold wind, but I myself had not experienced this." The ghosts which Miss Morton saw sometimes appeared so solid that they were mistaken for the living. A dog mistook the phantom for a living man and fled in abject terror after discovering his mistake. However solid the phantoms are, material objects do not apparently impede their progress.

Successful experiments were conducted in haunted houses by crystal gazers to locate the source of the trouble. The picture of the haunter was often disclosed when no materialization took place. Dr. J. Grasset recorded a case in *Proceedings* of the S.P.R., (vol. 18, p. 464) in which a girl saw the haunting spirit in a glass of water.

Experience shows that of decent burial of the remains of the victims of foul deeds, division of ill-gotten treasure, **exorcism,** prayer, mass, often lays the ghost. This suggests that the haunters are conscious of causing the disturbance, that the physical effects are not simple repercussions of the spirit's tormented mental state. But, as Andrew Lang remarked, "the ghost can make signs, but not the right signs." They suffer from what he calls "spectral aphasia," imperfect expression on the physical plane. He believed that lights in haunted houses are partial failures of ghosts to appear in form. The possibility of causing physical effects often disappears if the haunted house is rebuilt, or if the furniture is taken out. The psychical researcher Col. Taylor once cured a haunted house by ordering the inhabitants to burn an old, moth-eaten bed which he discovered in the attic. Whether the bed was a focal point of evil or not, the manifestations soon ceased.

Ancient laws made special dispositions in the case of haunting. In *Cock Lane and Common Sense* (1894) Andrew Lang gave a summary of old cases carried to court. Law suits over haunting were started in 1915 at Altavilla (Italy), in 1907 at Naples and in 1907 at Egham, England, in the latter case by the author Stephen Philips. In November 1930, the question came up before the Berlin courts in Germany whether one had the right to keep his family ghosts on the premises. An eleven-year-old girl, Lucie Regulski, was pursued by poltergeist disturbances that purported to emanate from her dead uncle. As the house acquired the reputation of being haunted, the owner applied for an order of eviction. The court decided in favor of the tenant, stating that Herr Regulski could harbor as many ghosts as he pleased and that they did not lessen the value of the house.

Present Position

Cases of haunting are still reported in modern times and old-fashioned apparitions are said to appear occasionally in their traditional locales. However, in spite of the development of scientific apparatus superior to that of the past, such as tape recorders, temperature measurement devices, infra-red photography, etc., investigation of haunting is still difficult. Ghosts do not appear to order, and many individuals do not report their experiences for fear of ridicule. On the other hand, the tendency of mass media to sensationalize claims of haunting raises doubts about cases that are reported or which become publicized in bestselling paperbacks (e.g. The **Amityville Horror**).

There seems to be a strong subjective aspect to apparitions and most informants speak of reactions which suggest energy being drawn from themselves to assist the manifestations in haunting. In this sense those who perceive apparitions appear to function like mediums in seances and such subjective factors do not register on cameras and tape recorders.

Moreover spontaneous cases and anecdotal reports are difficult to evaluate by modern parapsychologists.

Much more frequent than traditional style hauntings are the reports of poltergeist phenomena, which appear to be impersonal as distinct from the personalities of apparitions. Poltergeist phenomena is more accessible to psychical investigation with cameras and tape recorders.

Although there are many well authenticated cases of haunting over a long period of time, there is still no evidence to show how apparitions are produced and why they persist. An intriguing aspect of apparitions is the question of those of living individuals, of which there are many reliable reports (see *Phantasms of the Living* by E. Gurney, F. W. H. Myers & F. Podmore, 2 vols., 1886). It should be mentioned that hypnotists have shown that apparently real apparitions may be evoked in subjects by suggestion and one subject was able to produce such images at will (see *The Story of Ruth* by M. Schatzman, London, 1980). The term "hallucination" (without popular misconceptions of lunacy) still seems a useful scientific description of apparitions until there is decisive evidence of how haunting takes place.

In 1970, a team of sociologists at Birmingham University, England, investigated religious beliefs and behavior in one Shropshire town and found that 15 percent of the 8,000 inhabitants accepted the existence of ghosts, while ten percent claimed to have seen or felt a ghost. Another survey by the **Institute of Psychophysical Research** in Oxford, England, collated 1,500 first-hand accounts of encounters with ghosts reported by individuals in all walks of life. This report was edited by Celia **Green** and Charles McGreery under the title *Apparitions* (1977) and emphasized that the majority of ghost sightings are in the familiar surroundings of people's homes rather than eerie old sites. (See also **Apparitions; FOG Newsletter; Ghost Club; Ghost Seers; Ghost Tours; Haunted Houses; Poltergeist**)

Recommended reading:

Anson, Jay. *The Amityville Horror,* Bantam paperback, N.Y./Pan Books paperback, London, 1978

Automobile Association of Great Britain. *Haunts & Hauntings,* Publications Division of the Association, Basingstoke, U.K., 1974

Bell, Charles Bailey. *The Bell Witch, A Mysterious Spirit,* Lark Bindery, Nashville, Tennessee, 1934 (reissued as *A Mysterious Spirit* with *Bell Witch of Tennessee* by Harriet Parks Miller, C. Elder, Nashville, 1973)

Bord, Janet. *Ghosts,* David & Charles, Newton Abbot, U.K., 1974

Bozzano, Ernesto. *Dei Fenomeni d'Infestazione,* Rome, 1919

Cox, Katharine. *Haunted Royalties,* W. Rider, London, 1916

Crowe, Catherine. *The Night Side of Nature; or Ghosts & Ghost Seers,* 2 vols., London, 1848 etc.

Dingwall, Eric J. *Ghosts & Spirits in the Ancient World,* Kegan Paul, London, 1930

Flammarion, Camille. *Haunted Houses,* T. Fisher Unwin, London, 1924; Tower Books, Detroit, 1971

Green, Celia & Charles McGreery. *Apparitions,* Hamish Hamilton, London/State Mutual Book, N.Y., 1977

Green, Andrew M. *Ghost Hunting; a Practical Guide,* Garnstone Press, London, 1973

Gauld, Alan & A. D. Cornell. *Poltergeists,* Routledge & Kegan Paul, London, 1979

Gurney, E., F. W. H Myers & Frank Podmore. *Phantasms of the Living,* 2 vols., London, 1886 (abridged edition University Books, N.Y., 1962)

Haining, Peter. *Ghosts: The Illustrated History,* Sidgwick & Jackson, London, 1974; Macmillan, N.Y., 1975

Harper, Charles G. *Haunted Houses,* Cecil Palmer, London, 1927

Harris, Joh. *Inferences from Haunted Houses & Haunted Men,* London, 1901

Hubbell, Walter. *The Great Amherst Mystery,* New York, 1888

Ingram, John H. *Haunted Houses & Family Traditions of Great Britain,* 2 series, London, 1884 etc.

Ingram, M. V. *An Authenticated History of the Famous Bell Witch,* W. P. Titus, Clarksville, Tennessee, 1894

Lombroso, Cesare. *After Death—What?* T. Fisher Unwin, London, 1909

Mackenzie, Andrew. *Apparitions & Ghosts,* Barber, London/Popular Library, N.Y., 1971

Mackenzie, Andrew. *Hauntings & Apparitions,* Heinemann, London, 1982

Middleton, Jessie A. *The White Ghost Book,* Cassell, London, 1918

Moore, Edward. *Bealings Bells,* Woodbridge, U.K., 1841

O'Donnell, Elliot. *Haunted Places in England,* Sands & Co., London, 1919

O'Donnell, Elliot. *The Banshee,* Sands & Co., London, 1920

O'Donnell, Elliot. *Family Ghosts & Ghostly Phenomena,* Philip Allan, London, 1933

Podmore, Frank. *Apparitions and Thought-Transference,* Walter Scott Publishing Co., London, 1894 etc.

Prince, Walter F. *The Psychic in the House,* Boston Society for Psychical Research, Boston, Mass., 1926

Roll, W. G. *The Poltergeist,* Scarecrow Press, 1976

Schatzman, Morton. *The Story of Ruth,* Duckworth, London, 1980

Smith, Susy. *Haunted Houses for the Million,* Bell Publishing Co., 1967

Smith, Susy. *Prominent American Ghosts,* World Publishing Co., 1967

Stead, William T. *Real Ghost Stories,* London, 1891 etc.; University Books, N.Y., 1970 (under new title: *Borderland; A Casebook of True Supernatural Stories*)

Thompson, C. J. S. *The Mystery & Lore of Apparitions,* Shaylor, London, 1930; Gale Research Co., 1975

Tweeddale, Violet C. *Ghosts I Have Seen,* Herbert Jenkins, London, 1919

Tyrrell, G. N. M. *Apparitions,* revised ed. Gerald Duckworth, London, 1953; Society for Psychical Research, London, 1973

Walter, W. Grey. *The Neurophysiological Aspects of Hallucinations and Illusory Experience,* Society for Psychical Research, London, 1963

Wright, Dudley. *The Epworth Phenomena,* London, 1917

X, Miss (Miss Goodrich-Freer, with John, Marquess of Bute). *The Alleged Haunting of B—House,* London, 1899

Zingaropoli, F. *Case Infestate degli Spiriti,* Naples, 1907

Haxby, W. (c. 1878)

English physical medium of the nineteenth century, a postal employee of whom Dr. Alfred Russel **Wallace** wrote in *My Life* (1902): "He was a small man, and sat in a small drawing-room on the first floor separated by curtains from a larger one, where the visitors sat in a subdued light. After a few minutes, from between the curtains would appear a tall and stately East Indian figure in white robes, a rich waistband, sandals, and large turban, snowy white, and disposed with elegance. Sometimes this figure would walk round the room outside the circle, would lift up a large and very heavy musical box which he would wind up and then swing around his head with one hand.

"He would often come to each of us in succession, bow and allow us to feel his hands and examine his robes. We asked him to stand against the door-post and marked his height, and on one occasion Mr. Hensleigh Wedgwood brought with him a shoe-maker's measuring rule and at our request, Abdullah, as he gave his name, took off a sandal, placed his foot on a chair and allowed it to be accurately measured with the sliding rule. After the seance Mr. Haxby removed his boot and had his foot measured by the same rule, when that of the figure was found to be full one inch and a quarter the longer, while in height it was about half a foot taller. A minute or two after Abdullah had retired into the small room, Haxby was found in a trance in his chair, while no trace of the white-robed stranger was to be seen. The door and window of the back room were securely fastened and often secured with gummed paper which was found intact."

It was recorded in the contemporary Spiritualist press that Haxby materialized dogs which ran about the room. However, Prof. Charles Richet in *Thirty Years of Psychical Research* (1923) stated: "Haxby cheated impudently."

For a critical report on Haxby's phenomena, see 'Alleged Mediumship of W. Haxby' (*Proceedings* of the Society for Psychical Research, vol. 4, p. 60).

Hayden, Mrs. Maria B. (c. 1852)

Influential American medium of Boston, wife of W. R. Hayden, editor of the *Star Spangled Banner*. Mrs. Hayden was the first American medium after the beginnings of modern Spiritualism in America to visit England and thus had a great influence on the development of the spiritualist movement.

She arrived in October 1852, in the company of a man named Stone, who professed to be a lecturer on "electrobiology," the art of inducing hypnotism by gazing at metallic discs.

Mrs. Hayden was an educated woman and possessed a limited type of mediumship consisting mainly of raps which, however, furnished information beyond the knowledge of the sitters. In the British press she was treated as an American adventuress. The magazine *Household Words* was the first to ridicule her. *Blackwood's Magazine, The National Miscellany* and other papers followed in the same line and many disclosures were published claiming that the medium could not give correct answers unless she saw the alphabet.

However, the first man who confessed to have been puzzled and unable to account for the phenomena was Robert **Chambers.** He described his visit to Mrs. Hayden in an unsigned article in *Chambers' Journal* on May 21, 1853, and admitted to having witnessed correct information when the alphabet was behind the medium's back. *The Critic* was the next to call attention to the inadequacy of the theory put forward by the skeptics. Dr. Ashburner, one of the Royal Physicians, came forward for the defence and so did Sir Charles Isham. Other people of importance admitted that the phenomena were worthy of serious investigation although they were unwilling to commit themselves.

Mrs. Hayden's most important conquest was the conversion of Professor Augustus **de Morgan,** the famous

mathematician and philosopher to Spiritualism. The book by Mrs. de Morgan *From Matter to Spirit* (1863, first edition anonymous), the preface of which was written by Prof. de Morgan, gave a detailed account of Mrs. Hayden's seances. Additional notes were published in Mrs. Morgan's *Memoir of Augustus de Morgan* (1882).

The veteran socialist Robert Owen, at the time in his 83rd year, also had several sittings. The result was that he boldly embraced Spiritualism and proclaimed in the *Rational Quarterly Review* a formal profession of his new faith. The publication of the first English periodical on Spiritualism dates from Mrs. Hayden's visit. The publisher was W. R. Hayden, who joined his wife in England; the title: *The Spirit World*. The first and last number appeared in May 1853.

After a year's stay in England Mrs. Hayden returned to America, graduated as a doctor of medicine and practiced for fifteen years with such remarkable healing powers that Dr. James Rhodes **Buchanan,** the famous pioneer in **psychometry,** declared her to be "one of the most skillful and successful physicians I have ever known." She was offered a medical professorship in an American College.

It is interesting to note that the great medium D. D. **Home** gave one of his first public seances at the house of Mr. and Mrs. Hayden in March 1851. It is possible that Mrs. Hayden's mediumship dated from that visit.

Haynes, Renee (Oriana) (1906-   )

British novelist, historian, and writer on psychical research. Born July 23, 1906, in London, England, she was educated at private schools and an open-air establishment run by Theosophists before going on to St. Hugh's College, Oxford (B.A. honors 1927, M.A.), studying law and history. In 1929 she married writer Jerrard Tickell (died 1966), and had three children. From 1928-30 she worked for the publishers Geoffrey Bles, Ltd., London, and from 1941-67 with the British Council, London, becoming director of book reviews.

She joined the **Society for Psychical Research,** London, in the 1940s, becoming editor of the Society's *Journal* and *Proceedings* from 1970 to 1981, and is a vice-president of the Society. In addition to her novels and other writings, she contributed to *Cassell's Encyclopedia of Literature and Twentieth Century Catholicism, Times Literary Supplement, Catholic Herald, International Journal of Parapsychology* and other publications. In her writings on psychical research she has shown that serious study of this subject need not preclude a sense of humor.

Her publications include: *Neapolitan Ice* (1928, 1929), *Immortal John* (1932), *The Holy Hunger* (1935), *Pan, Caesar and God: Who Spake by the Prophets* (1938), *Hilaire Belloc* (1953), (transl.) *Psychical Phenomena* by Reginald Omez (1958), *The Hidden Springs: An Enquiry into Extra-Sensory Perception* (1961, 1973), *Philosopher King: The Humanist Pope Benedict XIV* (1970), (author of postscript) *Roots of Coincidence* by Arthur Koestler (1970, 1972), (author of foreword) *The Guidebook for the Study of Psychical Research* (1972), (contributed) *Book of Ghosts and Hauntings* by Aidan Chambers (1973), *The Seeing Eye, The Seeing I* (1976), *The Society for Psychical Research: A History 1882-1982* (1982).

Hazel Tree

The Hazel was dedicated to the god Thor and was esteemed a plant of great virtue for the cure of fevers.

Hazel branches were a favorite for use as a divining rod. If the rod was cut on St. John's Day or Good Friday it was believed to be certain as a successful instrument of divination. A hazel rod was also a badge of authority, and it was probably this notion which caused it to be made use of by schoolmasters. Among ancient Romans, a hazel rod was also a symbol of authority.

Head of Baphomet

An interesting discovery was made public in 1818 dealing with the history of secret societies. There was found, among the antiquities of the Imperial Museum of Vienna, some of those idols named heads of Baphomet, which the **Templars** were said to have venerated. These heads represented the divinity of the Gnostics, named *Mêtê* or Wisdom. For a long time there was preserved at Marseilles one of these gilded heads, seized in a retreat of the Templars when the latter were pursued by the law. (See also **Baphomet**)

Healing, Psychic

A popular early theory of psychic healing was that it was effected by a sudden and profound nervous change. The conception of the therapeutic power of such a change we owe to Anton **Mesmer** (1733–1815). He brought it about by a combination of passes, unconscious suggestion and supposed metallotherapy, the "baquet." The baquet involved an oak tub filled with water and iron filings, with flasks of "magnetized water." Patients were connected to this baquet by holding rods or cords which supposedly conveyed the "magnetism." The atmosphere was enhanced by music.

Mesmer contended that a nervous effluence was passing into the patients.

There are many sensitives even now who claim curative power by such a fluid which they perceive. But the discovery of magnetic action was put forward long before Mesmer as the basis of the sympathetic system of medicine.

The magnet itself was an illustration of the interaction of living bodies. Every substance was supposed to radiate a force. This force was guided by the in-dwelling spirit of the body from which it proceeded. A dissevered portion of a body retained something of the virtue of the body. This led to the deduction that instead of the wound, the weapon which caused it should be anointed, as the wound cannot heal whilst a portion of the vital spirit remains in disastrous union with the weapon and exerts an antipathetic influence upon its fellow spirit in the body.

The sway of Mesmerism was long and powerful. It yielded place to hypnotism when James **Braid** proved that **somnambulism** can be induced without passes by mere suggestion, moreover that the patients can bring it about by themselves by staring at bright objects.

This discovery threw the nervous effluence theory overboard, although its possibility as a coordinating factor was by no means ruled out. Indeed, "**animal magnetism**" was often rediscovered. A. A. Liébeault (1823–1901), by treating children under four and curing some under three, claimed that magnetic healing was not due to suggestion. Similar successes were registered later by psychologist Julien **Ochorowitz** (1850–1917) on children under two. Liebeault even came to the conclusion that a living being can, merely by his presence, exercise a salutary influence on another living being quite independently of suggestion.

However that may be, the mysterious power which after Braid was ascribed to suggestion did not bring us to any closer understanding of the curative process. It is more than likely that the ordinary hypnotizer has no curative power at all, and that his command simply starts a train of self-suggestion from the conscious mind, which otherwise would not have penetrated sufficiently deeply to bring about a nervous change.

It is even legitimate to suppose that in the form of the stimulus given to our imagination the same power may be at work in charms, **amulets,** fetishes and incantations. Sergeant E. W. **Cox** may have hit upon the truth when he wrote: "The use of the passes is to direct the attention of the patient to the part of the body then being operated upon. The effect of directing the attention of the mind to any part of the frame is to increase the flow of nerve force [or vital force] to that part."

The healer himself may have no knowledge of the process. The supposition that when he lays his hand on the diseased part of the body a magnetic current passes through may not be correct at all, even if the patients often experience a feeling of warmth as of an electric shock. The healer's influence appears to be rather a directive one for our own powers which he turns into a more efficient channel. If the hypnotizer is more successful than the average psychic healer, an explanation may be found in the trance state into which the patient is thrown, giving him direct access to the subconscious self to which, to use the words of F. W. H. **Myers**, "a successsful appeal is being made through suggestion."

"Beneath the threshold of waking consciousness," (he wrote in *Proceedings* of the Society for Psychical Research, vol. 14), "there lies, not merely an unconscious complex of organic processes but an intelligent vital control. To incorporate that profound control with our waking will is the great evolutionary end which hypnotism, by its group of empirical artifices, is beginning to help us to attain." This vital control he believed to be the result of some influx from the unseen world; the efficacy of suggestion was dependent on the quantity of new energy which could be imbided from the spiritual world by directing subliminal attention to a corporeal function.

The problem of psychic healing, however, is much more complex than it appears. It bristles with interesting and stubborn facts which refuse to be fitted into convenient pigeon-holes. Suggestion is surely ruled out when healers cure animals. The process of healing seems interwoven with psychical manifestations, the success of healing often serving as evidence of the paranormal, and the paranormal serving as evidence of extraneous intervention. Medical **clairvoyance, psychometry** and direct and indirect action by spirits are concepts which demand consideration.

The somnambules of the early magnetizers diagnosed their own diseases. This was known later as "**autoscopy.**" It is now a rare phenomenon. As an intermediate instance between autoscopy and clairvoyant diagnosis for others the curious case in Baron Carl du Prel's *Experimental-Psychologie* (1890) is worth mention. To a hypnotic subject it was suggested that, in his dream, he would find a certain cure for his ailments. The dream was very vivid, a voice giving medical advice was heard, and on following the instructions thus imparted the patient's health considerably improved.

To the eyes of medical clairvoyants, the human body appears to be transparent. They see and describe in lay terms the seat and appearance of the disease. Some have a more restricted power and diagnose from the changes in the **aura** of the patient, the color being allegedly affected by illness.

Psychometrists do not require the presence of the patient at all. A lock of hair may be sufficient to put the medium on the right track. Sometimes an index, i.e., the mere mention of the name, will suffice. The medium, however, sometimes suffers sympathetically. Temporarily he often assumes the bodily conditions of the afflicted man and vividly experiences his ailments.

The therapeutic services of psychical research are now often acknowledged by psychoanalysts and physicians. **Crystal-gazing** and **automatic-writing** help to explore the subconscious mind. Long forgotten memories may be recalled and events of importance may be traced to their source and enable the psychoanalyst to form conclusions without hypnotic experiments. The **divining rod** (the diviner holding bacterial cultures in his hand) has also been discovered as a means of successful diagnosis, and the use of the pendulum in place of the rod has developed in the art of **Radiesthesia.**

Often diagnosis and cure take place through alleged spirit influence, advice or direct action.

Dr. Josiah A. Gridley of Southampton, Mass., confessed in his *Astounding Facts from the Spirit World* (1854) to have been constantly impressed (long before the advent of Spiritualism) with the disease and treatment to be followed of the patient before he went to see him. He attributed the remarkable success of his practice to his communion with the spirit world.

In England, the first spiritual healer, a lecturer on mesmerism named Hardinge, became convinced through spirit communications that epilepsy was due to demonic **possession** and undertook to cure such cases by spirit instruction. J. D. Dixon, a homeopathic doctor, was the next English healer who, being converted to Spiritualism in 1857, treated his patients with prescriptions obtained by raps. Daniel Offord, a nine-year-old English boy, wrote prescriptions in Latin, a language which he did not know. He predicted the 1853 cholera epidemic two months in advance and prescribed a daily dose of half a teaspoonful of carbon as an antidote.

The spirits who assist mediums mostly claim to have been physicians on earth who have attained to a higher knowledge in the Beyond. **Jacob** the Zouave, actually saw the spirits ministering to his patients. Mrs. J. H. **Conant** attributed Jacob's curative powers to the knowledge of "Dr. John Dix Fisher" in spirit; similarly "Dr. Lascelles" who worked through C. A. Simpson in "**The Seekers**" group in London, and "Dr. **Beale**" who worked through the medium Miss Rose claimed to have followed the medical profession on earth. The strange cure of Mme X. (*Proceedings* of the Society of Psychical Research, vol. 9) was effected by a spirit doctor and the Indian controls like "Old John" who healed, in the case of Dr. Kenney, were said to have been medicine men in their tribes.

The methods of Indian controls are sometimes extraor-

dinary. Thus the medium Mrs. Gladys Osborne **Leonard** described in *My Life in Two Worlds* (1931): "Mrs. Massey's chair was a wooden rocking one. Suddenly her chair began to rock backwards and forwards gently at first, then gathering speed, till it rocked at a tremendous rate. Then, to our horror, the chair turned a complete somersault. So did Mrs. Massey. She fell right on her head, and lay where she fell. I rushed to her, and before I realised what was happening North Star had taken control of me. A lump, the size of an egg, had come up on Mrs. Massey's head. North Star placed my hands upon it; in a few moments it had gone. North Star then left her head alone and proceeded to make passes over her body, particularly over the heart. He gave loud grunts of satisfaction, and seemed extremely well pleased with something. After about half an hour's hard work he stopped controlling me, and Mrs. Massey then disclosed the fact that she had felt very ill for some days past, and she felt better now then she had done for months."

Further on Mrs. Leonard stated: "When North Star controlled me for healing, he always appeared to appeal to someone far higher than himself before commencing his treatment. He never spoke, but he used to hold his hands upward and outward as if he expected something to be put, or poured into them. His attitude was so obviously one of prayer, or supplication, though he was usually in a standing position."

The most sensational modern development of psychic healing is **Psychic Surgery**, which takes two forms. First, in which the medium mimes operations, allegedly guided by the spirit of a dead doctor; secondly in which psychic healers appear to perform real operations, either with bare hands or with primitive instruments, wounds healing instantaneously. The latter type of psychic surgery, practiced widely in the Philippines and Brazil, remain's highly controversial, with conflicting evidence of genuineness and fraud.

Ernesto **Bozzano** recorded this instance of distant diagnosis: "In October, 1928, M. Paolo Rossi sat in London in a direct voice seance with a private medium. Cristo d'Angelo, speaking in Italian communicated with him, saying that Marquis Centurione Scotto's deceased son, by advice of Dr. Barnett (one of Valiantine's spirit guides) wished to give a message of supreme importance concerning the health of someone dear to the Marquis' son. He therefore begged M. Rossi to take his wife to Millesimo during the first fortnight of November in order to sit in a private sitting, at which no persons were to be present except the Marquis Centurione Scotto and his wife, M. and Mme. Rossi and Ernesto Bozzano. Even Marquis Centurione Scotto was to be kept in ignorance of what transpired at the sitting (in order that he should not be alarmed) and so Cristo d'Angelo decided to put him into trance. We five assembled on November 12 at Millesimo according to Cristo d'Angelo's instructions, and almost immediately, as had been predicted in London, but contrary to his usual practice, Marquis Centurione Scotto fell into trance. Cristo d'Angelo at once communicated, at the request—he informed us—of Marquis Centurione Scotto's deceased son. He spoke for half an hour, giving a masterly diagnosis of a disease of the blood, called leukemia. He told us the cause of the disease and prescribed a cure, after which he ordered the sitting to be closed. The diagnosis was absolutely correct and the cure prescribed rapidly brought back health to a person in precarious condition the reason of whose ill health had been a mystery."

The most well-known psychic healer was Edgar **Cayce** (1877–1945) who diagnosed and prescribed for thousands of ailments in a state of self-induced trance.

Cases of healing at a distance are also on record. When the healer's magnetism is said to be transferred into water, paper or cloth one may argue for suggestion as an explanation; there are, however, more difficult instances. According to a letter from E. W. Capron, quoted in Mrs. Underhill's *The Missing Link* (1885) on the occasion of Capron's first visit to the **Fox sisters** in Rochester, he mentioned casually that his wife was affected with a severe and troublesome cough. Leah Fox in trance suddenly declared: "I am going to cure Rebecca of the cough." She then gave an accurate description of Rebecca and pronounced her cured. Returning home, Capron found her extremely well and the trouble never returned. Absent healing, through prayer groups, is now a regular activity of healing centers.

Cases are recorded in which an apparition at the bedside of a sick person effected a cure by laying on of hands or by giving instructions. Materialized spirit hands made passes over the head, throat, chest and back of the Rev. Stainton **Moses** to relieve his bronchitis. Whilst it may have been the faith of Stainton Moses in the powers of his guides which effected the cure, this does not, however, explain how the healing took place.

"The faith which was healing power," said the neurologist J. M. Charcot (1825–1893), "seems to me to be the greatest of medicines, for it may succeed where all other remedies have failed. But why should faith, which works on the soul, be considered more miraculous than a drug, which acts on the body? Has anyone yet understood how a drug can cure?"

St. Bernard, the Abbot of Clairvaux (1090–1153), Valentine **Greatrakes** (1662), **Jacob** the Zouave (1828–1913), Dr. J. R. **Newton** (1810–1883), the Earl of **Sandwich** (1839–1916), author of *My Experiences in Spiritual Healing* (London, 1915) and such modern healers as the late Henry **Edwards** (1893–1976) to mention a few names only, put many astonishing cures on record which seem to be authentic.

The mind-cures of **Christian Science** must also be considered. These are wrought by the belief that neither matter nor evil exists and the sick will invariably recover if they believe that they are spirits superior to physical trouble or pain. There is little essential difference between mind-cure and faith-cure (the removal of pain by faith in God's power and by prayer) and for examples one may go back to the ancient days when sleeping in the temple, after having invoked the help of God, often brought about healing at the shrines of Aesculapius, Isis and Seraphis.

Thus, although the subject of spiritual healing or **Healing by Faith** is considered in a separate article, the psychic and religious aspects are clearly related. Twenty-two archbishops and bishops of Languedoc wrote to Clement XI: "We are witnesses that before the tomb of Father John Francis Regis, the blind see, the lame walk, the deaf hear, the dumb speak."

Astonishing instances of healing are recorded in Carré

de Montgeron's book *La Verité des Miracles opérés par l'intercession de M. de Paris* (Cologne, 1745–47), dedicated to the King of France. Miracles took place at the tomb of the Abbé Paris, the Jansenist, in 1731 and the three or four years following. The cure of Mlle. Coirin was without precedent. Cancer had completely destroyed her left breast, the case was utterly hopeless. A visit to the tomb not only cured her, but restored the breast and nipple without any trace of a scar. She was examined in Paris by the royal physician, M. Gaulard, who declared the restoration of the nipple an actual creation. Other physicians deposed before notaries that the cure was perfect. Other amazing cures followed.

The cemetery of St. Médard became so famous for this occurrence that the ire of the Jesuits was aroused and soon afterwards, according to Voltaire, it was inscribed on the churchyard wall:

De par le Roi—défense à Dieu
De faire miracle en ce lieu.

Voltaire said that God obeyed. This, however, is contradicted by cures which kept on occurring for a space of twenty-five years.

Miraculous cures were effected at Treves in Germany by touching a relic known as the **Holy Coat** in 1891. Holywell in Wales was called the Welsh Lourdes for similar occurrences. **Lourdes** itself has become an established site for miracles in healing. (See also **Christian Science; Convulsionnaires of St. Médard;** Psychic **Dentistry;** Harry **Edwards; Healing by Faith; Healing by Touch;** Kathryn **Kuhlman; Lourdes**)

Recommended reading:

Carter Mary Ellen & W. McGarey. *Edgar Cayce on Healing,* Warner paperback, 1972

Dooley, Anne. *Every Wall a Door,* Abelard-Schuman, London, 1973; Dutton, N.Y., 1974

Edwards, Harry. *A Guide to the Understanding & Practice of Spiritual Healing,* Spiritual Healing Sanctuary, Surrey, England, 1974

Edwards, Harry. *Thirty Years a Spiritual Healer,* Spiritual Healing Sanctuary, 1968

Flammonde, Paris. *The Mystic Healers,* Stein & Day, 1975

Guirdham, Arthur. *Obsession; Psychic Forces and Evil in the Causation of Disease,* Neville Spearman, London, 1972

Hammond, Sally. *We Are All Healers,* Random House, 1974

Hutton, Bernard. *Healing Hands,* W. H. Allen, London, 1966

James, R. L. L. *The Church and Bodily Healing,* C. W. Daniel, Essex, England, 1929

Kiev, Ari. *Magic, Faith and Healing,* Macmillan, 1964

Macmillan, W. J. *The Reluctant Healer,* Victor Gollancz, London, 1952

Montgomery, Ruth. *Born to Heal,* Popular Library paperback, 1973

Nolen, William. *Healing,* Fawcett paperback, 1974

Rose, Louis. *Faith Healing,* Victor Gollancz, London, 1952

Sherman, Harold. *Wonder Healers of the Philippines,* DeVorss & Co., 1966; Psychic Press, London, 1967

Tenhaeff, W. H. C. *Paranormal Healing Powers,* Olten, 1957

Valentine, Tom. *Psychic Surgery,* Henry Regnery Co., 1974

Healing by Faith

Faith healing by itinerant Deliverance evangelists has been a regular feature of the American religious scene since the nineteenth century. There is no clear single strand of descent in the tangled spread of dozens of different church movements and star preachers, but in general, faith healing can be considered a branch of the Pentecostal churches. (See also **Pentecostalism**) Tradition, of course, assigns the healing faculty to that liberated by Jesus Christ and spread through his disciples.

In the 1870s, G. O. Barnes, formerly a Presbyterian minister, joined forces with evangelist D. L. Moody and also encountered Holiness preachers. In 1876, Barnes traveled through Kentucky, saving souls and healing the sick by laying on hands in the name of the Lord. By 1882, Barnes had joined forces with another famous faith healer, A. B. Simpson, founder of a large Holiness group.

Another influential evangelist healer was John Alexander Dowie, who came to America from Australia in 1888. During the 1890s, Dowie preached a kind of **Christian Science,** declaring that physicians and medication were instruments of the Devil and divine healing was available to those with religious faith. He leased three hotels in Chicago, turning them into faith cure centers.

In 1895, following numerous deaths, the city authorities charged him with manslaughter and practicing medicine without license, but the higher courts upheld Dowie. In 1899, he founded the Christian Catholic Church of Zion, and two years later declared himself a reincarnation of Elijah, preparing the world for the second coming of Christ. In 1906, he was forced to curtail all activities, after numerous scandals, bankruptcy, and even physical illness. His own daughter had died after her nightdress had caught fire and Dowie had banished physicians who wanted to treat her burns. Dowie himself died in 1907.

Dowie's healing evangelism was a forerunner of a number of Pentecostal and Holiness movements. In 1898, Charles F. Parham opened his Bethel Healing Home in Topeka, Kansas, and two years later the Bethel Bible School. It was here that the Pentecostal phenomenon of "speaking in tongues" became conspicuous. In his revival campaigns, Parham practiced healing through laying on of hands, and hundreds of cures were claimed. Parham's campaigns influenced the Negro Holiness preacher William J. Seymour, who carried a healing mission to California, where he established a church at Azusa Street, Los Angeles.

One of the most colorful healing evangelists of the 1920s was Aimee Semple McPherson (1890–1944), whose Church of the Foursquare Gospel had some affinity to the doctrines of A. B. Simpson. Although MacPherson's following was initially small, a revival campaign in San Diego became immensely successful through claims of miraculous healing under her ministry, and her followers eventually provided funds for a huge Angelus Temple in Los Angeles. A charismatic figure, McPherson had a flair for publicity, and was one of the early evangelists to establish a strong following on radio. She had purchased a radio station in Los Angeles, and her services were broadcast to thousands of followers in the U.S. In 1926, she was supposed to have been kidnapped for a month, but critics have stated that this story covered a "love-nest" scandal. Some doubt also surrounds the claimed miraculous cures under her ministry.

During the depression, healing evangelism suffered something of a decline, although there were still many missions and itinerant preachers. There was a great upsurge in evangelism after World War II with the ministry of William Marrion Branham, an independent Baptist preacher who attracted huge crowds with his healing during the 1940s. There were rumors that he had even raised a man from the dead. Amongst those influenced by Branham's gospel campaigns were Oral Roberts, O. L. Jaggers, Gayle Jackson, T. L. Osborn and Gordon Lindsay, all of whom developed their own ministries. In spite of a great expansion of such evangelism during the 1950s, there was again some decline by 1960, largely through opposition from the major Pentecostal churches, as well as newspaper exposures of frauds and fanatics.

Marjoe Gortner, the golden boy of healing evangelism, who was a charismatic figure as a teenage preacher, appeared in a documentary film (*Marjoe,* 1972) in which he frankly exposed all the tricks of the trade, and disillusioned thousands of would-be followers, as well as throwing doubt on other evangelists.

During the 1970s, the days of the traveling tents seemed numbered, as increasingly sophisticated audiences expected comfortable seats and air conditioning. Healing itself became a risky enterprise, since evangelists faced accusations of fraud or even lawsuits if they appeared to succeed, and failing congregations if they could not cure. In 1970, it cost $2,000 just to buy a tent and start out on the gospel circuit. Renting church auditoriums, advertising, radio spots and other expenses involved a considerable investment. Some evangelists were obliged to take part-time jobs to support themselves and accumulate the necessary capital for a campaign.

Nonetheless, many new names emerged—Oral Roberts, Rex Humbard, Don Stewart, A. A. Allen, Kathryn Kuhlman, Roxanne Brandt, Leroy Jenkins, W. V. Grant, Paul Wells and many others. Increasingly the high cost of organizing evangelist campaigns demanded more attention to modern business techniques, and in an age of television, the millions of living room sets constituted a larger and more responsive audience than the tent and stage. Some evangelists moved successfully into the awesome finances of weekly television services, in which the regular miracle of soliciting subscriptions for saving souls and maintaining an expensive full-time ministry tended to displace the earlier miracles of faith healing. Many successful evangelists like the famous Billy Graham ignored healing and concentrated on the gospel message. Today, what has been called "The Electronic Church" has a vast financial investment in regular television programs, in which evangelical missions must be organized as efficiently as large business corporations, with scores of full-time employees.

However, many evangelists still conduct public healing, and some, like the late Kathryn Kuhlman (1910?–1976) built up a great reputation for miracle cures. One remarkable evangelist healer is Willard **Fuller,** who specializes in dental healing. An eyewitness reported: "He prays for people and God fills their teeth. I have actually seen fillings appear in teeth that had cavities; some gold, some silver, some white enamel-like substances, and some are completely restored to their original condition."

Skeptics maintain that all faith healing is either fraud or "spontaneous remission." It cannot be as simple as that. Undoubtedly there have been some frauds, some deliberate, some little more than attempts to "prime the pump" by enhancing the atmosphere of faith in which genuine miracles flourish, much as some genuine psychics have cheated when real phenomena were scarce. Some of the claimed cures may indeed have been spontaneous remission (whatever that is, since there is as yet no wholly convincing explanation of its rationale), and certainly some cures were not permanent, the individual relapsing after the excitement of the healing meeting was over. But the great number of claimed cures of a great variety of illnesses and physical disabilities cannot all be explained away, particularly to the individuals that have benefited by the healing.

It is a common experience that large groups of people can generate emotional and psychic force, even higher states of consciousness. There seems little reason to doubt that, under the right circumstances, faith healers may be able to direct such energy, together with the subject's own energies, into paranormal healing. All healing, in the final analysis, rests upon the unknown vital force in the individual that causes cells to be renewed, wounds healed, or broken bones united. It is not beyond belief that such processes can be speeded up in the healing process. To the grateful sufferer cured by faith healing, of course, it is simply a welcome miracle that cannot be explained away by terms like "spontaneous remission."

However, faith healing may tell us less about religion than the dynamics of group psychic energies, since paranormal healing has been claimed as a feature of both Eastern and Western religions. Moreover the concept of a benevolent divinity that bestows sickness and disability without justification but permits a cure in a few random cases, constitutes something of a theological paradox, perhaps best expressed in the Judeo-Christian story of Job.

The field of faith healing presents a fascinating challenge for parapsychologists. The supercharging of emotional energies in mass religious groups through music and oratory cannot be studied in the clinical atmosphere of the laboratory, and demands a sympathetic and flexible technique. More study is needed to correlate religious healing with the secular healing of gifted operators like Harry **Edwards** and Ted **Fricker.**

The case against faith healing is ably presented by Louis Rose, a consulting psychiatrist, in his book *Faith Healing* (1968). Rose stated that not even a single case of miraculous healing has yet been verified to his satisfaction, although this sweeping statement somewhat avoids the issue of the satisfaction of the individual cured at a healing mission. (See also **Christian Science;** Psychic **Dentistry; Healing By Touch;** Psychic **Healing;** Kathryn **Kuhlman**)

Recommended reading:

Allen, A. A. *Bound to Lose, Bound to Win*, Doubleday, 1970

Edwards, Harry. *The Power of Spiritual Healing*, Herbert Jenkins, London, 1963, etc.

Hart, Ralph. *Doctors Pronounced Me Dead in Dallas*, Ralph Hart, Detroit, n.d.

Lindsay, Gordon. *William Branham, A Man Sent From God*, Voice of Healing Publ. Co., 1950

Roberts, Oral. *My Twenty Years of a Miracle Ministry*, Tulsa, 1967

Rose, Louis. *Faith Healing*, Victor Gollancz, London, 1968; Penguin paperback, 1970

Simpson, Eve. *The Faith Healer: Deliverance Evangelism in North America*, Concordia, 1977; Pyramid paperback, 1977

Spraggett, Allen. *Kathryn Kuhlman; the Woman Who Believes in Miracles*, Thomas Y. Crowell Co., 1970; Signet paperback, 1971

Stegall, C. & C. C. Harwood. *The Modern Tongues and Healing Movement*, Western Bible Institute, n.d.

Tenhaeff, W. H. C. *Paranormal Healing Powers*, Olten, 1957

Healing by Touch

In England, Scotland and also in France, the idea that a touch of the royal hand was a sure remedy for scrofula was long prevalent, and consequently this complaint acquired the now familiar name of "king's evil."

In France, so far as can be ascertained, this interesting practice dates from the reign of Louis IX, and in England from that of Edward III, who is recorded to have performed a considerable number of cures. He used to wash the affected part of the sufferer, but gradually the use of actual ablutions was discontinued, and most subsequent kings contented themselves with mere touching, while at the same time prayers were offered up on behalf of the patient.

Eventually the religious ceremony used on such occasions grew more elaborate, while during the reign of Henry VII a special "king's evil" petition was drawn up by a body of divines for insertion in the Service Book and it prevailed for a surprisingly long time thereafter, being found in some editions printed as late as the beginning of the eighteenth century.

The idea that kings ruled by divine right emanated mainly from Scotland, and so it is natural to assume that the early inhabitants of that land regarded their sovereigns as capable of miracles. There is little or no evidence, nevertheless, that the Stuarts, prior to the Union of the Crowns, practiced touching for king's evil, but scarcely was Charles I on the British throne before he began to demonstrate his powers, and scrofulous persons flocked from far and near accordingly.

Indeed, they came in such numbers that early in the fifth year of his reign, Charles found it essential to specify certain times for their reception at court, and the proclamation which he issued on the subject may be read in the *Historical Collections* of John Rushworth, sometimes secretary to Oliver Cromwell.

Here it is stated that, in the future, those who wish to benefit from the king's thaumaturgic gift will be welcomed at Michaelmas or Easter, although it is clear that his Majesty saw fit to make exceptions to this rule for, during his visit to Edinburgh in 1633, he ministered to numerous unfortunates in the month of June. It was at Holyrood that he received them, the palace being transformed temporarily into a forerunner of **Lourdes** and Sir James Balfour, the Historian, who was knighted at this time, and created Lyon King-at-Arms, affirmed in an unpublished manuscript still extant in the Advocates Library, Edinburgh, that Charles successfully "heallit 100 persons of the cruelles or kingis eivell, yong and olde."

In the proclamation cited above, king spoke at length of the many cures wrought by his "royal predecessors." Now this, of course, may allude purely to the Plantagenets or Tudors, but it is equally possible that these references indicate touching for scrofula on the part of the early Stuarts, and be that as it may, Charles I was not the only member of that dynasty who essayed the act.

John Evelyn, in his *Diary,* wrote repeatedly of Charles the Second's activities in this relation, while Samuel Pepys referred to the same thing, and in one passage he stated that the sight failed to interest him in the least, for he had seen it often before. Clearly, then, quite a host of the monarch's subjects were "heallit" by the royal touch, nor did the practice end with the ousting of the Stuarts in 1689. The lexicographer Dr. Samuel Johnson had been taken to London from Litchfield when a boy by his father to be touched "for the evil" by Queen Anne in 1712. The Chevalier de St. George essayed it on several occasions, and his son Prince Charles, when in Scotland in 1745, made at least one attempt, though whether with success or not is unrecorded.

At a late period, coins which had been touched by the king were believed to ward off evil or scrofula. These were known as "royal touch-pieces" and specimens of several were preserved in the British Museum, London.

In early history when laws of nature were but partially known and understood by man, it was most natural that these inexplicable powers should be directly ascribed to a divine influence. Healing of the sick was supposed to proceed alone from God, or through the priest and saints His servants. Faith was therefore necessary to the cure, and the magical powers were therefore transferred by words, prayers, and ceremonies, and the science was transmitted among the mysteries. Healing by touch, by laying on of hands and by the breath, belonged to this secret influence, also the use of talismans and amulets, which were composed of organic as well as inorganic substances (minerals, stones, and plants), the wearing of rings, of images of saints, and other symbolical objects, lastly, healing the sick by words and prayers.

As regards the resemblance which this science bears to **animal magnetism,** it is certain that not only were the ancients acquainted with an artificial method of treating disease but also with somnambulism itself. Amongst others, Agrippa von Nettesheim spoke of this plainly when he stated, in his *De Occulta Philosophia* (1531): "There is a science, known but to very few, of illuminating and instructing the mind, so that at one step it is raised from the darkness of ignorance to the light of wisdom. This is produced principally by a species of artificial sleep, in which a man forgets the present, and, as it were, perceives the future through the divine inspiration. Unbelieving wicked persons can also be deprived of this power by secret means."

The healing of the sick by the touch and the laying on of hands among primitive peoples, in India, Egypt and especially among the Jews. In Egypt sculptures have been found where one hand of the operator is placed on the stomach and the other on the back. Even the Chinese, according to the accounts of early missionaries such as Athanasius Kircher, *China . . . Illustrata* (1667), healed sickness by the laying on of hands. In the Old Testament we find numerous examples, such as the following:

When Moses found his end approaching, he prayed for a worthy successor, and there occurs the following passage (*Numbers,* xxvii, 18, 20): "And the Lord said unto Moses, Take thee Joshua, the son of Nun, a man in whom is the spirit, and lay thine hand upon him." . . . . "And thou shalt put some of thine honour upon him, that all the congregation of the children of Israel may be obedient."

Another instance is to be found in the healing of the seemingly dead child by Elisha, who stretched himself three times upon the child, and called upon the Lord. The manner in which Elisha raised the dead son of the Shunamite woman was still more remarkable. He caused Gehazi to proceed before him to lay his staff upon the face of the child. As this was of no avail, Elisha went up into the room, and laid himself upon the child, etc., and his hands upon the child's hands, so that the child's body became warm again. After that the child opened his eyes.

Elisha's powers even survived his death: "And Elisha died, and they buried him, and the bands of the Moabites invaded the land in the coming of the year. And it came to pass, as they were buying a man that, behold, they spied a band of men; and they cast the man into the sepulchre of Elisha, and when the man let down, and touched the bones of Elisha, he revived and stood upon his feet." (*2 Kings,* xiii, 20, 21).

Naaman the leper, when he stood before Elisha's house with his horses and chariots, and had been told to wash seven times in the Jordan said, "Behold I thought, he will surely come out to me, and stand, and call upon the name of the Lord his God, and strike his hand over the place, and recover the leper." (*2 Kings,* v. 4).

The New Testament is particularly rich in examples of the efficacy of laying on of the hands. "Neglect not the gift that is in thee, which was given thee by prophecy, with the laying on of the hands of the presbytery." (*1 Timothy,* iv, 14), was the principal maxim of the Apostles, for the practical use of their powers for the good of their brethren in Christ. In *Mark* (xvi, 18) it is stated: "They shall lay hands on the sick and they shall recover."

St. Paul was remarkable for his powers: "And it came to pass that the father of Publius lay sick of a fever and of a bloody flux; to whom Paul entered in, and prayed and laid his hands on him and healed him." (*Acts,* xxviii, 8).

"And Ananias went his way, and entered into the house, and putting his hands on him, said, Brother Saul, the Lord, even Jesus that appeared unto thee in the way as thou camest, hath sent me that thou mayest receive thy sight and be filled with the Holy Ghost. And immediately there fell from his eyes as it had been scales, and he received sight." (*Acts,* ix, 17, 18).

The gospel of Mark also states: "And they brought young children to him, that he might touch them, and his disciples rebuked those who brought them. But Jesus said, 'Suffer the little children to come unto me, for of such is the kingdom of heaven.' And he took them up in his arms, put his hands upon them, and blessed them." "And they bring unto him one that was deaf and had an impediment in his speech, and they besought him to put his hand upon him. And he took him aside from the multitude, and put his fingers into his ears, and he spit and touched his tongue and, looking up to heaven, he sighed, and said unto him, 'Ephphatha'—that is, Be opened. And straightway his ears were opened, and the string of his tongue was loosed, and he spake plain." (*Mark,* vii, 33).

Other passages may be met with in *Matth.* ix, 18; *Mark* v, 23; vi, 5; viii, 22; x, 13; xvi, 18; *Luke* v, 13; xviii, 15; *John* ix, *17; Acts* ix, 17. In the histories of the saints, innumerable examples are recorded, and the command "In my name shall they cast out devils; they shall speak with new tongues; they shall take up serpents, and if they drink any deadly thing it shall not hurt them; they shall lay their hands on the sick and they shall recover," applies to all true followers of Christ. Those, however who are wanting in the power of the spirit and in faith cannot perform these acts like the saints, on whom they cast doubts because they cannot imitate them. In modern times, this text has been interpreted as an actual injunction to take up serpents or drink poison, as in the **snake-handling** sects in the U.S.

The saints are said to have accomplished everything through absolute faith in Christ, and were therefore able to perform miracles. St. Patrick, the Irish apostle, healed the blind by laying on his hands. St. Bernard is said to have restored eleven blind persons to sight, and eighteen lame persons to the use of their limbs, in one day at Constance. At Cologne he healed twelve lame individuals, caused three dumb persons to speak, ten who were deaf to hear, and, when he himself was ill, St. Lawrence and St. Benedict appeared to him, and cured him by touching the affected part. Even his plates and dishes are said to have cured sickness after his death.

The miracles of saints Margaret, Katherine, Elizabeth, Hildegarde, and especially the miraculous cures of the two holy martyrs Cosmas and Damianus, belong to this class. Among others, they were said to have freed the Emperor Justinian from an incurable sickness. St. Odilia embraced a leper who was shunned by all men in her arms, warmed him, and restored him to health.

Remarkable above all others are those cases where persons who were at the point of death have recovered by holy baptism or extreme unction. The Emperor Constantine is one of the most singular examples. Pyrrhus, king of Epirus, was reputed to have the power of assuaging colic and affections of the spleen by laying the patients on their backs and passing his great toe over them. (Plutarch, *Vita Pyrrhi:* "Digitum maximum pedis divinitatem habuisse adeo quod igne non potuit comburi.") The Emperor Vespasian cured nervous affections, lameness, and blindness, solely by the laying on of his hands (Suelin, *Vita Vespas*). According to Coelius Spartianus, Hadrian cured those afflicted with dropsy by touching them with the points of his fingers, and recovered himself from a violent fever by similar treatment. King Olaf healed Egill on the spot by merely laying his hands upon him and singing proverbs according to the *Edda.*

The kings of England and France cured diseases of the throat by touch. It is said that the pious Edward the Confessor, and in France Philip the First, were the first who possessed this power. The French formula used on such occasions was: "Le roi te touche, allez at guerissez,"

so that the word was connected with the act of touching. In England the disease was therefore called "King's Evil." In France this power was retained until the time of the Revolution, and it is said that at the coronation the exact manner of touching, and the formula "Le roi te touche, dieu te guerisse" were imparted to the monarch. In the reign of Louis XIII, the Duke d'Epernon is said to have exclaimed, when Richelieu was made generalissimo against the Spaniards, "What! has the king nothing left but the power of healing wens?"

Among German princes this curative power was ascribed to the Counts of Hapsburg, and it was also believed that they were able to cure stammering by a kiss. Pliny stated: "There are men whose whole bodies possess medicinal properties, as the Marsi, the Psyli, and others, who cure the bite of serpents merely by the touch." This he remarked especially of the Island of Cyprus, and later travelers confirmed these cures by the touch. In later times, the Salmadores and Ensalmadores of Spain became very celebrated, who healed almost all diseases by prayer, laying on of hands and by breathing.

In Ireland, Valentine **Greatrakes** cured "king's evil" and other diseases by touch. In the seventeenth century, the gardener Levret and the notorious Streeper performed cures in London by stroking with the hand. In similar manner, cures were performed by Michael Medina, and the Child of Salamanca; also Marcellus Empiricus (Sprengel, *Gesch. der Med.* Part 2). Richter, an innkeeper at Royen, in Silicia cured, in the years 1817–18, many thousands of sick persons in the open fields, by touching them with his hands. Under the Popes, laying on of hands was called Chirothesy. Diepenbroek wrote two treatises on it, and, according to Lampe, four-and-thirty Chirothetists were declared to be holy. Franz Anton **Mesmer** and his assistants also employed manipulations for healing purposes. (See also **Christian Science;** Psychic **Dentistry; Willard Fuller; Healing by Faith;** Psychic **Healing;** Kathryn **Kuhlman**)

Recommended reading:

Greatrakes, Valentine. *A Brief Account of Mr. Valentine Greatrake's [sic], and divers of the strange cures by him lately performed . . .,* London, 1666

Hocart, A. M. *Kingship,* Humphrey Milford, London, 1927

Rose, Louis. *Faith Healing,* Victor Gollancz, London, 1968

Thompson, C. J. S. *Magic and Healing,* Rider & Co., London & New York, 1947; Gale Research Co., 1973

Healing Center for the Whole Person

A project of a religious corporation which meets at **International Cooperation Council** World Headquarters, Northridge, California. The Healing Center is directed by various types of professional people who specialize in healing, and seeks to transcend traditional disciplines, incorporating all valid methods of healing the whole person "in the spirit of the emerging new age."

The Center grew out of a conference on "Healing the Whole Person" held in Los Angeles, California, in May 1974. The I.C.C. encourages development of area councils and member groups. Address: International Cooperation Council, World Headquarters, 17819 Roscoe Boulevard,

Northridge, California 91324. (See also **Academy of Parapsychology and Medicine**)

Heard, Gerald (Henry Fitz Gerald Heard) (1889–1971)

British author and lecturer, with special interests in parapsychology. Born October 6, 1889, in London, England, he studied at Cambridge University (B.A. hons. history, postgraduate work in philosophy and philosophy of religion, 1908–13). He gave lectures for Oxford University Board of Extramural Studies from 1926–29; science commentator for British Broadcasting Corporation and lecturer for British Ethical Society, 1930–34. He lectured on historical anthropology at Duke University, Durham, N.C., in 1937. He was a council member of the Society for Psychical Research, London, from 1932–42, and studied on a Bollingen Trust grant 1945–47.

He lectured on history, philosophy, religion, theology and morals at colleges and universities in the U.S. He contributed articles on parapsychological topics to *Tomorrow* magazine.

Amongst his many books, *Is Another World Watching?* (1951) was an early discussion of the flying saucer or UFO phenomenon. His other books included: *The Social Substance of Religion* (1930), *Pain, Sex and Time* (1939), *Is God in History?* (1950), *The Human Venture* (1955), *Training for a Life of Growth* (1959).

In his later years, Mr. Heard resided in California. He died August 14, 1971.

Heart

The belief in the heart as a psychic structure is a very ancient one, stemming from the characteristic responses of that organ to emotional crises. However, mystical writers have indicated that there is a subtle or spiritual heart center which is slightly to the right of one's body as distinct from the physical heart on the left.

In the Bible *(Ecclesiastes)* it is said that the heart of the wise is at the right side, the heart of the foolish at the left. If this is not simply a symbolic statement, it may coincide with the ancient Hindu yoga concept of the *anahata chakra* or subtle heart center, which yogis have experienced as slightly to the right in the body. (See also **Chakras; Kundalini**)

Heat and Light (Journal)

American Spiritualist journal published during 1851. (See also **Spiritualism**)

Heavenly Man, The

A concept of Jewish mysticism or Kabala. According to the *Zohar,* the first of the Sephiroth or divine emanations. Before the creation God was without form, above and beyond all attributes. But when He had created the Heavenly Man, he used him as a Chariot in which to descend. And desiring to make Himself known by His attributes, "He let Himself be styled as the God of pardon, the God of Justice, the God Omnipotent, the God of Hosts and He Who Is (Jahveh)." The Heavenly Man is to be distinguished from the "earthly man." The creation of the earthly man was, indeed, the work of the Heavenly Man—that is, of the first emanation from God, the

Supreme Manifestation, the Divine activity. (See also **Kabala**)

Hecate

A Greek goddess, daughter of Zeus and Demeter, but of uncertain origin. She appears to have been originally one of the Titans who ruled the heaven, earth and sea and could bestow gifts on mortals at pleasure. Later she was confused with other goddesses until she became at length a mystic goddess having all the magic powers of nature at command. Magicians and witches sought her aid and sacrifices of dogs, honey and female black lambs were offered to her where three ways met or at crossroads or graveyards. Festivals were celebrated to her annually at Ægina. In appearance she was frightful, and serpents hung hissing around her shoulders.

As a dark goddess of ghosts and moonlight, her propitiation was an early form of **black magic** and **witchcraft.**

Hefferlin, Gladys

With her husband in Livingston, Montana, publicist for the story of a mysterious underground world culminating in an Antarctic kingdom called Rainbow City, supposed to have been constructed 2½ million years ago of plastic material.

It is warmed by hot springs and has eluded discovery by polar explorers because it is surrounded by ice walls ten thousand feet high.

As distinct from the evil **Dero** of the "Shaver Mystery," Rainbow City and its subterranean world is ruled by "The Ancient Three," originally from the planet Mars, who take a benevolent interest in world politics and use their occult influence on behalf of the good guys. The story is told in *Rainbow City & The Inner Earth Story* by "Michael X" (Saucerian Press paperback, Clarksburg, Va., c. 1971). (See also **Agharta; Hollow Earth; Shaver Mystery**)

Hefley, Report, The

Psychic newspaper edited by Carl D. Hefley, reporting and discussing a wide range of paranormal topics for popular readership. Published by U.S. Research, Inc. Address: The Hefley Report, P.O. Box 7242, Burbank, California 91510. (See also **Hefley's Secret Journal**)

Hefley's Secret Journal

Publication edited by Carl D. Hefley, supplementing his newspaper The **Hefley Report** by in-depth stories and research on paranormal topics. Address: P.O. Box 7242, Burbank, California 91510.

Heim, Roger (1900–   )

Botanist specializing in Cryptogamy, who has contributed to knowledge of the hallucinogenic properties of mushrooms. Born February 12, 1900, at Paris, France, he studied at the University of Paris (D.Sc. 1931) and Uppsala University, Sweden (Hon. Ph.D.). Dr. Heim was appointed director of the French National Museum of Natural History, and also director of the laboratory for the study of mycology and tropical phytopathology at the Ecole Pratique des Hautes Etudes.

His interest in parapsychology was stimulated by his studies of mushrooms and their hallucinogenic properties and he has written scholarly articles on the sacred mushroom rites of Mexican Indians. He was coauthor with R. B. **Wasson** of *Les champignons hallucinogens du Mexique* (1958). (See also Psychedelic **Drugs; Hallucinogens; Mushrooms**)

Heindel, Max (1865–1919)

Pseudonym of Carl Louis van Grasshoff, born in Germany, who emigrated to America in 1895. He became a Theosophist in 1903 and lectured widely.

While visiting Europe in 1907, he claimed that he encountered a mysterious Rosicrucian who took him to a Rose Cross temple on the border of Germany and Bohemia. Here he was initiated into the order. The following year he publicized the secret wisdom in his book *The Rosicrucian Cosmo-Conception* (1908 etc.).

However, much of his writing appears to be based on the lectures of Rudolf **Steiner,** who may have been his real Rosicrucian mentor. After publication of his book, Heindel founded various Fellowship Centers and a temple of his Rosicrucian Fellowship at Mount Ecclesia, Oceanside, San Diego, California. In addition to his Rosicrucian activities, including further books on the subject, Heindel was also interested in astrology and wrote *The Message of the Stars* (1919) and *Simplified Scientific Astrology* (1928). His wife Augusta Foss Heindel was also an editor, lecturer and writer on Rosicrucian subjects. She died in 1938. The Mount Ecclesia temple was the subject of a half a century lawsuit by various factions, resolved only by the deaths of the principals. (See also **AMORC; Rosicrucians;** H. Spencer **Lewis**)

Hekalot

According to the Jewish mysticism of the Kabalistic work the *Zohar,* the seven halls of the world of *Yetsirah,* the divine halls into which the seekers for the Chariot *(Merkabah)* strive to enter. Here dwell the angels, presided over by *Metatron;* likewise the souls of men not specially noted for their piety. (The souls of the pious dwell in the world of *Beriah.*) (See also **Kabala**)

Hel (or Hela)

In Teutonic mythology, the goddess of death, one of the offspring of Loki and the giantess Angurbodi. The gods became alarmed at her and the other monsters which were coming to life in Jotunheim, so it was deemed advisable by All-father that they should be brought before him. Hel was cast into Niflheim, the realm beneath the roots of the world tree Yggdrasil, reserved for all those who die of sickness or old age. Hel governs this world, which is composed of nine regions, into which she distributes those who come to her, and in which she inhabits a strongly-protected abode.

Niflheim is said to be "a dark abode far from the sun", its gates open to the "cutting north," "its walls are formed of wreathed snakes and their venom is ever falling like rain," and it is surrounded by dark and poisonous streams. "Nidhog, the great dragon, who dwells beneath the central root of Yggdrasil, torments and gnaws the dead."

It is said that one-half of Hel's body is livid, and the other half flesh-colored. Hunger is her table, Starvation, her knife, Delay, her man, Slowness, her maid, Precipice, her threshold, Care, her bed, and Burning Anguish forms the hangings of her apartments.

Heliotrope

A plant which follows the sun with its flowers and leaves, popularly known as "turnsole," it was believed to render its possessor invisible if rubbed over with the juice of this herb, which was also reputed to stop bleeding and avert danger from poison.

Hell

The derivation of this word is believed to be from the Teutonic root *helan* to cover, designating a subterranean or hidden place. It is sometimes used in the form of *Hel* as a "place of the dead" alone, by no means a place of punishment. "Hel" or "Hela" is also the name of the Teutonic goddess who was guardian of the dead.

This conception has a more or less clear train of evolution behind it. The Christian idea of a place of punishment was directly colored by the Jewish conception of *Sheol,* which in turn took shape from Babylonian sources. When exactly the idea began to form itself as a place of punishment is not clear, as among the ancient Semites, Egyptians and Greeks, we find the under-world regarded as a place of the dead alone.

Thus in Egypt we find "Amenti" distinctly a place of the dead, in which the tasks of life are for the most part duplicated. This is the case also among primitive people, who merely regard the land of the dead as an extension of human existence, in which people lead a more or less shadowy life. The primitive does not generally believe in punishment after death and conceives that any breach of moral rule is summarily dealt with in this life. It is usually when a higher moral code emerges from totemic or similar rule that the idea of a place of punishment has been invented by priest-craft.

However, this is not always the case. In Greece, Rome and Scandinavia, Hades was merely looked upon as a place of the dead, where, like shadowy ghosts, people flitted to and fro, gibbering and squeaking as phantoms were supposed to do.

According to the Greeks, Hades was only some twelve feet under the surface of the ground, so that Orpheus would have had no very long journey from the subterranean spheres to reach earth once more. Hell was generally regarded as a sovereignty, a place definitely ruled in an ordinary manner by a monarch set there for the purpose by the celestial powers.

Thus the Greek Hades ruled the Sad Sphere of the Dead, Osiris was lord and governor of the Egyptian Amenti, while in Central America there were twin rulers in the Kiche Hades, Xibalba, whose names were given as Hun-came and Vukub-came. These latter were actively malignant, unlike the Mictlan of the Mexican, whose empire was for the generality of the people. These could only exist there for the space of four years, after which they finally became entirely extinct.

The Mexicans represented Mictlan as a huge monster with open mouth ready to devour his victims, and this was also paralleled in the Babylonian Tiawith. It seems then that at a certain stage in all mythologies, the concept of a place of the dead was confounded with the idea of a place of punishment.

The Greeks generally bewailed the sad end of humanity which was condemned forever to dwell in semi-darkness after death. The possibility of the existence of a place of reward never seemed to appeal to them. To the vivid Greek mind, life was all in all and it was left to the finer and altogether more upright Semitic conscience to evolve in the near East the conception of a place of punishment. Thus Sheol, from being regarded as a place of the dead became the home of fire, into which the wicked and unjust were thrust for their sins.

This was certainly foreshadowed by Babylonian and Egyptian ideals, for we find the Egyptian unable to pass the test of justification simply rejected. From the idea of rejection would soon spring the idea of active punishment. The Semitic conception of Hell was probably reinforced on the introduction of Christianity into Europe, and colored by the concept of the places of the dead belonging to the other mythologies of Europe. Thus the Scandinavian idea, which was also that of Saxon forefathers, undoubtedly colored the English conception of the place of punishment.

"Hela," or "Death," in the prose *Edda,* is one of the offspring of Loki and the giantess Angurbodi; their other two being the wolf Fenrir and the Midgard serpent. The gods were not long ignorant that these monsters continued to be bred up in Jötunheim, and having had recourse to divination, became aware of all the evils they would have to suffer from them; their being sprung from such a mother was a bad presage, and from such a sire one still worse. All-father therefore deemed it advisable to send one of the gods to bring them to him. When they came, he threw the serpent into that deep ocean by which the earth is engirdled.

But the monster had grown to such an enormous size that, holding his tail in his mouth he encircled the whole earth. "Hela" he cast into Niflheim, and gave her power over nine worlds (regions), into which she distributed those sent to her, that is to say, all who die through sickness or old age. Here she possessed a habitation protected by exceedingly high walls and strongly-barred gates. Her hall was called Elvidner; Hunger is her table; Starvation, her knife; Delay, her man; Slowness, her maid; Precipice, her threshold; Care, her bed; and Burning Anguish forms the hangings of her apartments. The one-half of her body is livid, the other half the color of human flesh.

A description of Niflheim itself, the abode of Loki and his evil progeny, is given in the *Voluspa.* It is "a dark abode far from the sun"; it gates are open to "the cutting north"; "its walls are formed of wreathed snakes, and their venom is ever falling like rain." It is surrounded by the dark and poisonous streams "Elivagar." Nidhog, the great dragon, who dwells beneath the central root of Yggdrasil, torments and gnaws the dead.

The probabilities are that the ideas concerning the Celtic other-world had little to do in forming the British conception of Hell. The Brythonic "Annwyl" was certainly a subterranean locality, but it was by no means a place of punishment, being merely a microcosm of the world above, where folk hunted, ate and drank, as in early Britain. Nor was the Irish other-world much different and after crossing the waters of oblivion the possessed person found himself in a sphere in many ways resembling the earth-life.

In southern Europe again the idea of Hell appears to have been strongly colored by both classical and Jewish conceptions. The best picture of the medieval conception of the place of punishment is undoubtedly the *Inferno* of Dante, who in most things followed the teaching of contemporary schoolmen in describing it. Acknowledging Virgil as his master, he followed him in many descriptions of Tartarus, but we find the Semitic idea cropping up here and there, as in the beginning of one of the cantos, where what looks suspiciously like a Hebrew incantation is set down.

The *dramatis personae* are classical, thus we have Pluto and many of the breed of Tartarus. In later medieval times the ingenuity of the monkish mind came to the rescue and concept which in some instances appear to be perfectly original sprang up.

For instance, Hell obtained an annexe, Purgatory. Its inhabitants took on a form which may distinctively be alluded to as European, in contradistinction to the more satyr-like shape of the earlier hierarchy of Hades. It featured grizzly forms of bird-like shape, with exaggerated beaks and claws, and the animal forms and faces of later medieval gargoyles give a good idea of what the denizens of Hades seemed like in the eyes of the superstition of the sixteenth and seventeenth centuries.

It was only a modifed version of these ideas which came down to later generations, and one may suspect that such superstitions were not altogether disbelieved by our fathers.

This is not the place to embark upon a theological discussion as to whether the Hell of the Christians exists, or does not exist, but it may be interesting to remark that a great controversy has raged ever since the time of Origen as to the question whether or not the punishments of Hell are eternal. Those who denied that this was so were called Universalists and believed in the final redemption of all.

Enough has been said to show that most Eastern mythological systems possess a Hades which does not differ in any fundamental respect from that of most barbarian races, except that it is perhaps rather more specialized and involved. Many later writers, such as **Swedenborg, Boehme, Blake** and others (not to forget Milton), have given us vivid pictures of the hierarchy and general condition of Hell. For the most part these are based on the patristic writings. In the Middle Ages endless controversy took place as to the nature and offices of the various inhabitants of the place of punishment (see **Demonology**), and the descriptions of later visionaries are practically mere repetitions of the conclusions then arrived at.

The locality of Hell has also been a question of endless speculation. Some believed it to be resident in the sun, giving as their reason for this the fact the Greek name of the luminary, *Helios,* but such childish etymologies appear to have been in disfavor with most writers on the subject, and the grand popular idea that Hell is subterranean has had no real rival.

Recommended reading:

Fox, Samuel J. *Hell in Jewish Literature,* Whitehall Co., Wheeling, Ill., 1969

Kohler, Kaufmann. *Heaven & Hell in Comparative Literature,* Folcroft, Pa., 1923

Lehner, Ernest & J. Lehner. *Picture Book of Devils, Demons & Witchcraft,* Dover paperback, 1972

MacCullough, John A. *The Harrowing of Hell: A Comparative Study of an Early Christian Doctrine,* T. & T. Clark, London, 1930; AMS Press, c. 1981

Mew, James. *Traditional Aspects of Hell,* Swan, Sonnenschein, London, 1903; Gale Research Co., 1971

Swedenborg, Emanuel. *Heaven & Hell,* Swedenborg Foundation, New York & London, reprint of work originally published 1758

Walker, Daniel P. *Decline of Hell; Seventeenth Century Discussions of Eternal Torment,* Routledge, London/University of Chicago Press, 1964

Hell-Fire Club

An eighteenth-century British Satanist society of rich men, politicians and eccentrics, based at Medmenham Abbey in Buckinghamshire and later in caves at High Wycombe. The founder was the notorious profligate Sir Francis Dashwood (1708–1781), member of parliament, appointed chancellor of the exchequer in 1762. His ignorance and incapacity for this latter post resulted in his resignation a few months later.

As a young man, Dashwood had plunged into a life of pleasure and dissipation. When only seventeen, he became a member of one of the earlier Hell-Fire clubs which conducted secret orgies in a cellar. There were rumors that during Dashwood's subsequent European travels, he was initiated into a diabolic cult in Venice and brought back to England various magical grimoires and manuals.

About 1745, Dashwood founded the brotherhood known as "The Knights of St. Francis of Wycombe" or "The Franciscans of Medmenham," more popularly known as "the Hell-Fire Club." From 1750 onwards, Dashwood rented the old Cistercian abbey of Medmenham on the river Thames, near Marlow, originally founded in 1201. Dashwood made costly renovations to the premises, which he furnished with an altar in the chapel, candlesticks and pornographic pictures. The entrance to the abbey bore the inscription "Fay ce que voudras" (Do What Thou Wilt) derived from the Abbey of Thelema in Rabelais' *Gargantua.* The same motto was adopted by occult Aleister **Crowley** for his own Abbey of Thelema nearly two centuries later.

Although it has been claimed that Dashwood's "Franciscans" (derived from his own forename) were largely rakes of the period seeking drunken sex orgies, there was an inner circle or "Superior Order" of twelve members who held obscene parodies of Catholic ritual in the chapel as an elementary form of Satanism. As Grand-Master, Dashwood used a communion cup to pour libations to pagan gods, and even administered the sacrament to a baboon in a contemptuous mockery of sacred ritual. Members of this Superior Order included Lord Sandwich, the libertine Paul Whitehead, the debauchee George Selwyn and Thomas Potter (son of the Archbishop of Canterbury). A fictionalized account of the "Franciscans" was published in Charles Johnston's novel *Crysal* (1760).

The brotherhood flourished at Medmenham for no less than twelve years, until it was exposed by John Wilkes, who had joined in 1762 but was later expelled, probably through political quarrels. At one of the Satanic rituals, Wilkes secretly brought an ape with horns tied in its head, dressed in a long black cloak. The creature was released at the height of the ceremony and sprang upon the Satanists, who screamed with fear at the devil they thought they had raised by their mockery. Wilkes and the politician Charles Churchill exposed the brotherhood in an issue of the *North Briton* newspaper, and a satirical print appeared entitled "The Saint of the Convent." In the face of public exposure, the Medmenham chapel was hastily stripped and its contents taken away to West Wycombe, where Dashwood attempted to revive his ceremonies. He built a church on Wycombe Hill, where he and his companions drank heavily and blasphemed the Psalms. In the caves underneath the hill, they attempted to revive the orgies and rituals of Medmenham, but some of Dashwood's friends had passed away, others tired of their folly.

After resigning from the post of chancellor of the exchequer, Dashwood retired from the ministry, and in 1763 became the fifteenth Baron Le Despencer, premier baron of England. In 1763 he became lord-lieutenant of Buckinghamshire. He died at West Wycombe after a prolonged illness on December 11, 1781, and was buried in the mausoleum he had built there.

Other Hell-Fire Clubs existed in eighteenth-century England at Oxford and Cambridge, as well as in Scotland (Edinburgh) and Ireland (Dublin). The contemporary influences which brought about such societies were an increasing religious skepticism, the growth of free-thought, romantic Gothic literature with mad monks and devils, and male chauvinism in an atmosphere of class privilege and debauchery.

Hellawes

A medieval sorceress, Lady of the Castle Nigramous. She attempted to win the love of Lancelot, but being unable to do so, she perished. Her story is told in Sir Thomas Mallory's *Morte d'Arthur* first published 1485.

Hellenbach, Baron Lazarus De Paczolay (1827–1887)

Hungarian philosopher of whose numerous important works *Birth and Death* and *The Philosophy of Sound Common Sense* closely concern psychical research. In the first, which was translated into English in 1886, he put forward the original idea that no change of world occurs at the moment of birth and death, and that the only change is in the method of perception. In the second, published in 1876, he told the story of his psychical investigations.

It was in 1857 that he met with the first convincing mediumistic experience at Countess D.'s castle in Croatia. Thereafter, for six years, he engaged the services of two ladies as mediums. Through one of them he communicated with the philosopher Schopenhauer.

In 1870 he made the acquaintance of Baroness Adelma Vay, whose powers as seeress opened up new fields of research for him.

In 1875 he witnessed strong physical manifestations with Lottie **Fowler.** Following these he invited many well known mediums to Vienna. Henry **Slade** came in 1878. The result of the sittings was published in a pamphlet: *Mr. Slade's residence in Vienna; an open letter to my friend.* In

February 1880, Karl Hansen, the famous hypnotist came to Vienna. To the controversy which arose in the Press, Baron Hellenbach contributed another pamphlet: *Is Hansen a Swindler? A Study of Animal Magnetism.*

In the same year he stood up with similar vigor for the medium William **Eglinton** who sat for him under strictest test conditions, immediately after the Munich exposure which Baron Hellenbach considered to have been based on ignorance.

The medium Harry **Bastian** paid him two visits of which he gave an account in a leaflet: *The Latest Communications from the "Intelligible" World.* In 1884 Bastian came for the third time. The sitters were Crown Prince Rudolph and Archduke John. The Archduke seized the "materialized spirit." It was found to be the medium. Of this exposure, the Archduke published a pamphlet: *A Glimpse into Spiritism.* Baron Hellenbach countered with another: *The Logic of Facts,* in which he essayed to clear the medium. In the same year Baron Hellenbach invited to Vienna Frau Valeska Topfer of Leipzig, Weber Scraps of Mulsen and Margit Morgenstern of Budapest.

In 1885, after a second visit from Eglinton, Baron Hellenbach gave up his residence in Vienna and returned to his second home in Croatia. Here he was engaged on another book. Of this, however, only a series of essays was published in the periodical *The Sphynx,* under the title: *Ether as a Solution of the Mystic Problem.*

Hellström, Eva Backström (1898–　)

Founder and secretary of the Swedish Psychical research organization in 1947 (Sällskapet för Parapsykologisk Forskning). Born September 26, 1898, at Stockholm, Sweden. Educated at Djursholm College, Sweden. In 1918 she married Professor Bo Hellström.

Mrs. Hellström became a member of the Society for Psychical Research, London, and a charter member of the Parapsychological Association. Her interests included mediumship, psychokinesis and psychometry, and she studied the work of various Swedish, Dutch and Danish mediums. She was herself a clairvoyant and manifested faculties of precognition. See her articles 'Precognition of Girls Dancing' (*Journal* of the Society for Psychical Research, vol. 41, p. 252-54; vol. 44, p. 411) and 'Collection of Spontaneous Cases (*Journal* of S.P.R. vol. 43, p. 164-65).

Helvetius, John Friedrich (1625–1709)

A physician of the Hague, Holland, who in 1667 published a work concerning a strange adventure of his life in which he claimed to have taken part in a veritable act of metallic transmutation by alchemical processes. The book was translated into English and published in London in 1670, under the title *The Golden Cult Which the World Adores and Desires: In which is handled the most Rare and Incomparable Wonder of Nature, in Transmuting Metals.* As it is one of the few exact descriptions of such an experiment, it is given in full, as follows:

"On the 27th December, 1666, in the afternoon, a stranger, in a plain, rustic dress, came to my house at the Hague. His manner of address was honest, grave authoritative; his stature was low, with a long face and hair black, his chin smooth. He seemed like a native of the north of Scotland, and I guessed he was about forty-four years old. After saluting me he requested me most respectfully to pardon his rude intrusion, but that his love of the pyrotechnic art made him visit me. Having read some of my small treatises, particularly that against the sympathetic powder of Sir Kenelm Digby (see **Powder of Sympathy**) and observed therein my doubt of the Hermetic mystery, it caused him to request this interview. He asked me if I still thought there was no medicine in Nature which could cure all diseases, unless the principal parts, as the lungs, liver, etc. were perished, or the time of death were come. To which I replied I never met with an adept, or saw such a medicine, though I read of much of it and often wished for it. Then I asked if he was a physician. He said he was a founder of brass, yet from his youth learned many rare things in chemistry, particularly of a friend—the manner to extract out of metals many medicinal arcana by the use of fire.

"After discoursing of experiments in metals, he asked me, would I know the philosophers' stone if I saw it? I answered, I would not, though I read much of it in Paracelsus, Helmont, Basil, and others, yet I dare not say I could know the philosophers' matter. In the interim he drew from his breast pocket a neat ivory box, and out of it took three ponderous lumps of the stone, each about the size of a small walnut. They were transparent and of a pale brimstone colour, whereto some scales of the crucible adhered when this most noble substance was melted. The value of it I since calculated was twenty tons weight of gold. When I had greedily examined and handled the stone almost a quarter of an hour, and heard from the owner many rare secrets of its admirable effects in human and metallic bodies, also its other wonderful properties, I returned him this treasure of treasures, truly with a most sorrowful mind, like those who conquer themselves, yet, as was just, very thankfully and humbly. I further desired to know why the colour was yellow, and not red, ruby colour, or purple, as the philosophers write. He answered that was nothing, for the matter was mature and ripe enough.

"Then I humbly requested him to bestow a little piece of the medicine on me, in perpetual memory of him, though but the size of a coriander or hemp seed. He presently answered, 'Oh no, this is not lawful, though thou wouldst give me as many ducats in gold as would fill this room, not for the value of the metal, but for some particular consequences. Nay, if it were possible,' said he, 'that fire could be burnt by fire, I would rather at this instant cast all this substance into the fiercest flames.' He then demanded if I had a more private chamber, as this was seen from the public street.

"I presently conducted him into the best furnished room backward, not doubting but he would bestow part thereof or some great treasure on me. He entered without wiping his shoes, although they were full of snow and dirt. He asked me for a little piece of gold, and, pulling off his cloak, opened his vest, under which he had five pieces of gold. They were hanging to a green silk ribbon, and were of the size of breakfast plates. This gold so far excelled mine that there was no comparison for flexibility and colour. The inscriptions engraven upon them he granted me to write out; they were pious thanks-givings to God, dated 20th August, 1666, with the characters of the Sun, Mercury, the Moon, and the signs of Leo and Libra.

"I was in great admiration, and desired to know where and how he obtained them. He answered, 'A foreigner, who dwelt some days in my house, said he was a lover of this science, and came to reveal it to me. He taught me various arts—first, of ordinary stones and chrystals, to make rubies, chrysolites, sapphires, etc., much more valuable than those of the mine; and how in a quarter of an hour to make oxide of iron, one dose of which would infallibly cure the pestilential dysentery, or bloody flux; also how to make a metallic liquor to cure all kinds of dropsies, most certainly and in four days; as also a limpid, clear water, sweeter than honey, to which in two hours of itself, in hot sand, it would extract the tincture of garnets, corals, glasses, and such like.' He said more, which I Helvetius did not observe, my mind being occupied to understand how a noble juice could be drawn out of minerals to transmute metals. He told me his said master caused him to bring a glass of rain-water, and to put some silver leaf into it, which was dissolved therein within a quarter of an hour, like ice when heated. 'Presently he drank to me the half, and I pledged him the other half, which had not so much taste as sweet milk, but whereby, methought, I became very light-headed. I thereupon asked if this were a philosophical drink, and wherefore we drank this potion; but he replied, I ought not to be so curious.' By the said masters directions, a piece of a leaden pipe being melted, he took a little sulphureous powder out of his pocket, put a little of it on the point of a knife into the melted lead, and after a great blast of the bellows, in a short time he poured it on the red stones of the kitchen chimney. It proved most excellent pure gold, which the stranger said brought him into such trembling amazement that he could hardly speak; but his master encouraged him saying, 'Cut for thyself the sixteenth part of this as a memorial and give the rest away among the poor,' which the stranger did, distributing this alms, as he affirmed if my memory fail not, at the Church of Sparenda. 'At last,' said he, 'the generous foreigner taught me thoroughly this divine art.'

"As soon as his relation was finished, I asked my visitor to show me the effect of transmutation and so confirm my faith; but he declined it for that time in such a discreet manner that I was satisfied, he promising to come again in three weeks, to show me some curious arts in the fire, provided it were then lawful without prohibition. At the three weeks end he came, and invited me abroad for an hour or too. In our walk we discoursed of Nature's secrets, but he was very silent on the subject of the great elixir, gravely asserted that it was only to magnify the sweet fame and mercy of the most glorious God; that few men endeavoured to serve Him, and this he expressed as a pastor or minister of a church; but I recalled his attention, entreating him to show me the metallic mystery, desiring also that he would eat, drink, and lodge at my house, which I pressed, but he was of so fixed a determination that all my endeavours were frustrated. I could not forbear to tell him that I had a laboratory ready for an experiment, and that a promised favour was a kind of debt. 'Yes, true,' said he, 'but I promised to teach thee at my return, with this proviso, if it were not forbidden.'

"When I perceived that all this was in vain, I earnestly requested a small crumb of his powder, sufficient to transmute a few grains of lead to gold, and at last, out of his philosophical commiseration, he gave me as much as a turnip seed in size, saying, "Receive this small parcel of the greatest treasure of the world, which truly few kings or princes have ever seen or known.' 'But,' I said, 'this perhaps will not transmute four grains of lead,' whereupon he bid me deliver it back to him, which, in hopes of a greater parcel, I did, but he, cutting half off with his nail, flung it into the fire, and gave me the rest wrapped neatly up in blue paper, saying, 'It is yet sufficient for thee.' I answered him, indeed with a most dejected countenance, 'Sir, what means this? The other being too little, you give me now less.'

"He told me to put into the crucible half an ounce of lead, for there ought to be no more lead put in than the medicine can transmute. I gave him great thanks for my diminished treasure, concentrated truly in the superlative degree, and put it charily up into my little box, saying I meant to try it the next day, nor would I reveal it to any. 'Not so, not so,' said he, 'for we ought to divulge all things to the children of art which may tend alone to the honour of God, that so they may live in the theosophical truth.' I now made a confession to him, that while the mass of his medicine was in my hands, I endeavoured to scrape away a little of it with my nail, and could not forbear; but scratched off so very little, that, it being picked from my nail, wrapped in a paper, and projected on melted lead, I found no transmutation, but almost the whole mass sublimed, while the remainder was a glassy earth.

"At this unexpected account he immediately said, 'You are more dexterous to commit theft than to apply the medicine, for if you had only wrapped up the stolen prey in yellow wax, to preserve it from the fumes of the lead, it would have sunk to the bottom, and transmuted it to gold; but having cast it into the fumes, the violence of the vapour, partly by its sympathetic alliance, carried the medicine quite away.' I brought him the crucible, and he perceived a most beautiful saffron-like tincture sticking to the sides. He promised to come next morning at nine o'clock, to show me that this tincture would transmute the lead into gold. Having taken his leave, I impatiently awaited his return, but the next day he came not, nor ever since. He sent an excuse at half-past nine that morning, and promised to come at three in the afternoon, but I never heard of him since.

"I soon began to doubt the whole matter. Late that night my wife, who was a most curious student and inquirer after the art, came soliciting me to make an experiment of the little grain of the stone, to be assured of the truth. 'Unless this be done,' said she, 'I shall have no rest or sleep this night.' She being so earnest, I commanded a fire to be made, saying to myself, 'I fear, I fear indeed, this man hath deluded me.' My wife wrapped the said matter in wax, and I cut half an ounce of lead, and put it into a crucible in the fire. Being melted, my wife put in the medicine, made into a small pill with the wax, which presently made a hissing noise, and in a quarter of an hour the mass of lead was totally transmuted into the best and finest gold, which amazed us exceedingly. We could not sufficiently gaze upon this admirable and miraculous work of nature, for the melted lead, after projection, showed on the fire the rarest and most beautiful colours imaginable, settling in green, and when poured forth into an ingot, it had the lively fresh colour of blood.

When cold it shined as the purest and most splendid gold. Truly all those who were standing about me were exceedingly startled, and I ran with this aurified lead, being yet hot, to the goldsmith, who wondered at the fineness, and after a short trial by the test, said it was the most excellent gold in the world.

"The next day a rumour of this prodigy went about the Hague and spread abroad, so that many illustrious and learned persons gave me their friendly visits for its sake. Amongst the rest, the general Assay-master, examiner of coins of this province of Holland, Mr. Porelius, who with others earnestly besought me to pass some part of the gold through all their customary trials, which I did, to gratify my own curiosity. We went to Mr. Brectel, a silversmith, who first mixed four parts of silver with one part of the gold, then he filled it, put *aquafortis* to it, dissolved the silver, and let the gold precipitate to the bottom; the solution being poured off and the calx of gold washed with water, then reduced and melted, it appeared excellent gold, and instead of a loss in weight, we found the gold was increased, and had transmuted a scruple of the silver into gold by its abounding tincture.

"Doubting whether the silver was now sufficiently separated from the gold, we mingled it with seven parts of antimony, which we melted and poured out into a cone, and blew off the regulus on a test, where we missed eight grains of our gold; but after we blew away the red of the antimony, or superfluous *scoria,* we found nine grains of gold for our eight grains missing, yet it was pale and silverlike but recovered its full colour afterwards, so that in the best proof of fire we lost nothing at all of this gold, but gained, as aforesaid. These tests I repeated four times and found it still alike, and the silver remaining out of the *aquafortis* was of the very best flexible silver that could be, so that in the total the said medicine or elixir had transmuted six drams and two scruples of the lead and silver into most pure gold."

Helvetius died at the Hague August 29, 1709. (See also **Alchemy; Philosopher's Stone**)

Henslow, Prof. George (1834–1925)

A clergyman of the Church of England, a noted scholar and medallist of Christ College, Cambridge, Vice-President of the British Association for the Advancement of Science in 1919, a celebrated authority on botany on which he wrote sixteen learned works, and a convinced Spiritualist. In his researches he was closely associated with Archdeacon **Colley** and took much interest in **psychic photography.** He was the author of *Proofs of the Truth of Spiritualism* (1919), *The Religion of the Spirit World* (1920), and part author (with D. J. D'Aute Hooper) of *Spirit Psychometry* (1914).

He died December 20, 1925, at the age of 92.

Hereburge

Frankish title for a witch. (See **France**)

Hermes Trismegistus

"The thrice greatest Hermes," the name given by the Greeks to the Egyptian god Thoth or Tehuti, the god of wisdom, learning and literature. Thoth was alluded to in later Egyptian writings as "twice very great" and even as "five times very great" in some demotic or popular scripts (c. third century B.C.).

To him was attributed as "scribe of the gods" the authorship of all sacred books which were thus called "Hermetic" by the Greeks. These, according to Clemens Alexandrinus, were forty-two in number and were subdivided into six portions, of which the first dealt with priestly education, the second with temple ritual and the third with geographical matter. The fourth division treated of astrology, the fifth of hymns in honor of the gods and a textbook for the guidance of Kings, while the sixth was medical.

It is unlikely that these books were all the work of one individual, and it is more probable that they represent the accumulated wisdom of Egypt, attributed in the course of ages to the great god of wisdom.

As "scribe of the gods," Thoth was also the author of all strictly sacred writing. Hence by a convenient fiction the name of Hermes was placed at the head of an extensive cycle of mystic literature produced in post-Christian times. Most of this Hermetic or Trismegistic literature has perished, but all that remains of it has been gathered and translated into English. It includes the *Poimandres,* the *Perfect Sermon,* or the *Asclepius,* excerpts by Stobacus, and fragments from the Church Fathers and from the philosophers, Zosimus and Fulgentius.

Hitherto these writings were neglected by theologians, who dismissed them as the offspring of third-century Neo-Platonism. According to the generally accepted view, they were eclectic compilations, combining Neo-Platonic philosophy, Philonic Judaism and Kabalistic theosophy in an attempt to supply a philosophic substitute for Christianity. The many Christian elements to be found in these mystic scriptures were ascribed to plagiarism.

By an examination of early mystery writings and traditions it has been shown with some degree of certainty that the main source of the Trismegistic Tractates is the wisdom of Egypt, and that they "go back in an unbroken tradition of type and form and context to the earliest Ptolemaic times."

The *Poimandres,* on which all later Trismegistic literature is based, must, at least in its original form, be placed not later than the first century. The charge of plagiarism from Christian writings, therefore, falls to the ground. If it can be shown that the *Poimandres* belongs to the first century, we have in it a valuable document in determining the environment and development of Christian origins.

G. R. S. Mead, author of *Thrice Greatest Hermes* (1906) stated in a illuminating passage:—

"The more one studies the best of these mystical sermons, casting aside all prejudices, and trying to feel and think with the writers, the more one is conscious of approaching the threshold of what may well be believed to have been the true adytum of the best in the mystery traditions of antiquity. Innumerable are the hints of the greatnesses and immensities lying beyond that threshold—among other precious things the vision of the key to Egypt's wisdom, the interpretation of apocalypsis by the light of the sun-clear epopteia of the intelligible cosmos."

Recommended reading:

Hermes Trismegistus (ed. J. D. Chambers). *Theological & Philosophical Works,* 2 vols., London, 1882

Mead, G. R. S. *Thrice-Greatest Hermes*, London, 1906; University Books, 1964

Bell, H. Idris. *Cults and Creeds in Graeco-Roman Egypt*, Liverpool University Press, England, 1957

Hermetic Society (Dublin)

Founded in 1898 by mystical poet "AE" (George W. **Russell**) in Dublin, Ireland, after leaving the Theosophical Society. The Hermetic Society placed great emphasis on meditation. It was not connected with the **Hermetic Society, London**.

Hermetic Society (London)

Founded by Anna **Kingsford** and Edward **Maitland** in London, England, in 1884, connected with the Theosophical Society of Madame **Blavatsky**. Occultists S. L. MacGregor **Mathers** and W. Wynn **Westcott** lectured to the Hermetic Society, London. Soon afterwards they launched the famous Hermetic Society of the **Golden Dawn**. (See also **Alchemy**)

Hermetica

The body of secret mystical wisdom which honored Hermes Trismegistos ("Thrice-Greatest Hermes") between the 3rd century B.C. and first century A.D., identifying the Greek god Hermes with the Egyptian god Thoth.

This wisdom literature involved two levels of writing: a popular Hermetic teaching of astrology, magic and alchemy, and a later higher religious philosophy. The Hermes-Thoth literature had a profound effect on the development of Western magic. Hermetic works include *Poimandres* (Shepherd of Men), *Asclepius* and *The Secret Discourse on the Mountain*. (See also **Hermes Trismegistus**)

Recommended reading:

Atwood, M. A. *A Suggestive Inquiry into the Hermetic Mystery*, Belfast, Ireland 1918

Hermes Trismegistus (ed. J. D. Chambers). *Theological & Philosophical Works*, 2 vols., London, 1882

Hermes Trismegistus (transl. Dr. Everard). *The Divine Pymander*, Theosophical Publishing Society, 1894

Scott, W. *Hermetica*, Oxford University Press, England, 1924–36

Hernandez Montis, Vicente (1925–　　)

Associate professor of physics, University of Seville, who has published papers on parapsychology. Born April 23, 1925, at Seville, Spain, he studied at the University of Seville and the University of Madrid. He is a member of Colegio Official de Doctores y Licenciados en Letras y Ciencias, Seville, and the Parapsychological Association. He has studied ESP in relation to the hypnotic state, and also dowsing or water-witching.

Herne, Frank (c. 1870)

Famous nineteenth-century English medium. His first seances were given in January, 1869. He gave clairvoyant descriptions of spirits and of the sitter's aura. Physical manifestations soon developed. In 1870 at the house of Dr. Dixon he was said to have manifested **elongation of the human body**. Miss Florence **Cook** held her first sittings with Herne.

In 1871 Herne joined partnership with Charles **Williams**. Their seances at 61 Lamb's Conduit Street, Lon-

don, were very impressive. Voices, psychic lights, independent music, **apports** and **levitations** were often witnessed. Mrs. Guppy's famous **transportation** occurred in one of these joint sittings. In 1875 Mr. St. George Stock made an attempt to expose Herne as fraudulent but did not succeed and two years later in *The Spiritualist* apologized for the part he played.

However, much suspicion surrounds the mediumship of Herne and Williams. The latter, who worked closely with Herne was caught cheating in seances in Paris in 1874 and in Amsterdam in 1879.

For a critical account of Herne's phenomena, see the article 'Alleged Mediumship of F. Herne' (*Proceedings* of Society for Psychical Research, vol. 7, p. 272) and *Journal* of the S.P.R., vol. 10, p. 105. See also references to the phenomena of Mrs. P. Bassett (Herne's wife) in *Proceedings* of S.P.R., vol. 54, p. 49, 59, 71.

Hesse, Hermann (1877–1962)

Famous German novelist (later acquired Swiss nationality) whose books on mystical themes have been influential in the contemporary spiritual and occult revival amongst young people. His novel *Siddharta* (1922, translated 1954) dealt with the relationship between father and son, and the quest for self-discovery through a journey to India. Both themes have great significance in modern times. His novel *Das Glasperlenspiel* (1943, translated as *Magister Ludi*, 1950) resolves world disorder through a religious game played by rulers.

Hex (or Hexerai)

General term for witchcraft spells amongst the Pennsylvania Dutch and German settlers of America. A standard textbook of hex spells and folk remedies is *The Long Lost Friend or Pow-Wows* by John George Hohman of Berks County, Pennsylvania, first published in 1820.

Versions of this book still circulate. It includes pagan, Christian and gypsy spells such as: "Against Mishaps and Dangers in the House," "Treating a Sick Cow," "To Stop Bleeding at Any Time," "To Charm Enemies, Robbers and Murderers." Many Pennsylvania barns are still decorated with "hex signs" to drive away evil spirits.

Hexenhaus

A prison for witches built in Bambert, Germany, in 1627 during the rule of the "Witch-Bishop" Prince Gottfried Johann George II Fuchs von Dornheim. It contained two chapels, a torture chamber and cells to accommodate twenty-six witches.

Heyd

A Norwegian sea-witch or storm-fiend in the shape of a white bear, alluded to in the *Frithjof Saga*. With the other storm-fiend Ham, she was sent by Helgi to engulf Frithjof as he sailed for the island of Yarl Angantyr.

Heydon, John (1629–c. 1668)

English astrologer and attorney. He was born in London, September 10, 1629, and educated at Tardebigg in Worcestershire. Because of the outbreak of the Civil War, he did not go on to university, but joined the King's army.

He is said to have been successful as a soldier, and to have won to the captaincy of a troop of horse under

Prince Rupert, but on the ultimate triumph of the Round-head party, the young man found it advisable to leave England, and for some years lived in various countries on the Continent, notably Spain and Turkey. Indeed, if his contemporaneous biographers are to be trusted, he penetrated so far afield as Zante, the island in the Levant whose praise has been sung so beautifully by Edgar Allan Poe, but by 1652 Heydon was back in England. In 1655 he studied law and was established in the Temple.

However, law was not his only study, for soon he was deep in that craft of **astrology** with which his name was destined to become associated, and on one occasion, having prophesied that Cromwell would shortly die by hanging, he was immediately imprisoned. According to Thomas Carte in his life of the great Marquis of Ormonde, Heydon was imprisoned for two years.

In 1656, Heydon married the widow of Nicholas Culpeper, who, after fighting for the Parliament in the Civil War, had devoted a wealth of energy to compiling elaborate treatises on astrology and pharmacopia, arts which went hand in hand in the seventeenth century. It would seem that a daughter was born of their union, for among the astrologer's writings is a volume entitled *Advice to a Daughter* (1658). Whether Heydon continued living in the Temple after his marriage is not recorded, nor does it seem that he even attended greatly to legal business. It is likely, on the contrary, that astrology occupied all his time, while it appears that his first imprisonment was not the only one he suffered. He became intimate with many of the great scientists of the Restoration, but quarrelled with a number of them, and although he always maintained that he was not actually affiliated with the Rosicrucians, it is a fact that he explained their theories publicly. In 1667 he was imprisoned for "Treasonable practices in sowing sedition in the navy, and engaging persons in a conspiracy to seize The Tower [of London]."

Heydon was considered something of a charlatan in his own time, and he undoubtedly rehashed the writings of others on mystical subjects.

Nevertheless Heydon must be credited with considerable assiduity, and his Rosicrucian books alone are numerous, the best of them being probably *The New Method of Rosie-Crucian Physick* (1658), *The Rosie-Crucian Infallible Axiomater* (1660), *The Wise Man's Crown,* or *The Glory of the Rosie-Cross* (1664), and *The Rosie-Cross Uncovered* (1662). In addition to those, he was author of *Theomagia or The Temple of Wisdom* (1664), and *The Prophetic Trumpeter, sounding an Allarum to England* (1655), the latter being dedicated to Henry Cromwell, while according to Wood's *Athenæ Oxonicsis,* Heydon was likewise the compiler of *A Rosiecrucian Theological Dictionary.*

Yet another book from his pen was *Idea of the Law,* and at the end of this there are advertisements of several works of his, probably pamphlets, none of which is known to exist nowadays, but whose titles are worth recording here. One is called *The Familiar Spirit,* another *The Way to Converse with Angels,* while the others are *A New Method of Astrology, Of Scandalous Nativities,* and *Cabballa, or the Art by which Moses and Elijah did so many Miracles.*

It is quite possible, of course, that these pamphlets were advertised while yet in course of preparation, and that the author was prevented from bringing them to a finish, but

their titles are significant, showing how far *Heydon* waded into the sea of mysticism.

Heym, Gerard (died c. 1974)

Scholar, bibliophile and student of the occult during the 1930's in Britain. Although Heym was a close associate of S. L. MacGregor **Mathers** and other members of the **Golden Dawn** secret order, he does not appear to have been a member himself. Although he was reported to have signed a copy of Aleister **Crowley's** journal **The Equinox** as: "Gerard Heym 10° = 1°. Supreme Magus of the R + C, G. D. Paris, 1931," this may well have been a private joke, implying that Heym had achieved the status of a Secret Chief.

Heym had a special interest in alchemy, and was a founder-member of the Society for the Study of Alchemy and Early Chemistry, founded c. 1937 in Britain "for the scientific and historical study of the branches of learning named in its title." Heym contributed to the Society's journal *Ambix.* Heym's remarkable personal collection of books on the subject was dispersed some years before his death.

Heyn, F(rans) A(driaan) (1910–   )

Dutch professor of nuclear physics who studied telepathy. Born November 2, 1910, at Delft, Netherlands, he studied science at the University of Delft. From 1947 onwards he was professor, nuclear physics, electrical engineering, University of Delft. He became a charter member of the Parapsychological Association. In 1937 he married Y. C. Steentjes.

He was co-author with Dr. S. **Mulckhuyse** of *Vorderingen en Problemen van de Parapsychologie* (Progress and Problems in Parapsychology, 1950).

Heywood, Rosalind (Hedley) (1895–1980)

Prominent British researcher in the field of psychical science. Born February 2, 1895, at Gibralter, she was educated at London University. In 1921 she married Col. Frank Heywood. Mrs. Heywood became a member of the Women's Voluntary Services, and served on the board of governors of the English-Speaking Union. She joined the Society for Psychical Research, London, 1938 and served on the council soon afterwards. She has translated various plays from the French of Gabriel Marcel, and lectured and broadcast on parapsychology.

She experimented together with Whateley **Carington** on ESP, and was also a subject for physicians studying the effects of mescaline. She wrote a significant book on ESP: *The Sixth Sense* (1959; American edition titled *Beyond the Reach of Sense* (1974).

She contributed a number of articles to the *Journal* of the Society for Psychical Research, including: 'Pseudo-Communicator' (vols. 34, 36), 'Visit to Brook House' (vol. 35), 'Experience in Village Shop' (vol. 38), 'Something Told Me to Go to Victoria' (vol. 38), 'Apparition of Dog and Mistress' (vol. 39), 'Case of Auditory Hallucination' (vol. 40), 'Luminous Apparition' (vol. 40), 'Report of Sitting with Medium' (vol. 40), 'Tangle for Unravelling (Palm Sunday Case)' (vol. 40), 'Collective Hallucinations of Non-Existent Buildings' (vols. 41, 42), 'Labyrinth of Associations' (vol. 42), 'Precognition by Rhys-Williams' (vol. 42), 'Telepathic Dream' (vol. 43), 'Margins of the

Mind (TV Programme)' (vol. 44), 'Telepathic Impression of Illness' (vol. 44).

In her book *ESP: A Personal Memoir* (1964) she gave a lucid explanation of the possibilities and implications of ESP based on her own experience.

She died June 27, 1980, in England.

Hickling, Alan Micklem (1936–   )

British aeronautical engineer who has experimented in the field of ESP. Born February 22, 1936, at London, England, he studied at Cambridge University (B.A. hons. in mechanical sciences 1958) and served as a pilot in the Royal Navy from 1959 onwards. He is a graduate member of the Royal Aeronautical Society and the Institute of Mechanical Engineers, and a charter member of the Parapsychological Association. He has experimented with ESP in an endeavor to establish conditions which might be conducive to successful scoring.

Hieroglyphs

This term, normally applied to ancient Egyptian picture writing, is also used for the symbolic illustrations in astrological almanacs and for symbols produced by **automatic** and **direct writing** through mediumship.

Direct writing, i.e., messages produced without contact between mediums and writing materials, although sometimes produced at seances, has also occurred during outbreaks of **poltergeist** phenomena, when the poltergeist has distributed messages through the house.

Thus, in the disturbance in the house of Dr. **Phelps,** Stratford, in 1850–51, hieroglyphs were found on the walls and ceilings, while turnips covered with them were seen to grow from the pattern of the carpet. On this occasion, the matter was investigated by Andrew Jackson **Davis,** who claimed to recognize the hieroglyphs as spiritual symbols, which he was inspired to interpret as friendly messages from high spiritual powers.

Higgins, Godfrey (1772–1833)

British archaeologist, humanist, social reformer and author. He became convinced that there was an ancient universal religion from which later creeds developed, and devoted twenty years to a search for a secret tradition.

The result of his researches was his great work *Anacalypsis, An Attempt to draw aside the Veil of the Saitic Isis; or An Inquiry into the Origin of Languages, Nations and Religions,* first published posthumously in 2 vols., London, 1833–36 (a new edition was issued by University Books Inc., New York, 1965). It is a work of tremendous scope, more than 1,250 pages in length, and supplied material and inspiration for the Theosophical writings of Madame **Blavatsky,** who even echoed the title in her own book *Isis Unveiled* (1877).

Hill, J(ohn) Arthur (1872–1951)

An important British psychical researcher and author. Born December 4, 1872, at Halifax, England, he was educated at Thornton Grammar School, Bradford. He worked as a business manager until 1898, when he suffered a heart ailment and became an invalid. He then spent his time studying the literature of psychical research and also sat with various mediums.

Later he assisted the work of Sir Oliver **Lodge,** noted

British Spiritualist. Hill was a member of the Society for Psychical Research, London, and served on the council between 1927 and 1935.

His books included: *Religion and Modern Psychology* (1911), *New Evidences in Psychical Research* (1911), *Spiritualism and Psychical Research* (1912), *Psychical Investigations* (1917), *Spiritualism, its History, Phenomena and Doctrine* (1918), *Man Is a Spirit* (1918), *Emerson and His Philosophy* (1919), *Psychical Miscellanea* (1919), *From Agnosticism to Belief* (1924), *Psychical Science and Religious Belief* (1928). He also published a number of articles on psychical research and Spiritualism in various journals. He died March 22, 1951.

Hillman, James (1926–   )

Analytical psychologist who is concerned with the relationship of parapsychology to depth psychology. Born April 12, 1926, at Altantic City, New Jersey, he studied at Trinity College, Dublin, Irish Republic (M.A. 1953) and University of Zurich (Ph.D. summa cum laude 1958). In 1952 he married Catharina Kempe. From 1959 onwards was an analytical psychologist and director of studies at the C. G. Jung Institute, Zurich. He is a member of the Swiss Society for Analytical Psychology, and founding associate editor of *Envoy: An Irish Review of Literature and Art* (1949–51). He is author of *Emotion: A Comprehensive Phenomenology of Theories and their Meanings for Therapy* (published U.K. 1960, U.S. 1961).

During a visit to India, he met **Gopi Krishna,** a retired civil servant from Srinagar who had attained a condition of higher consciousness through arousing the legendary **Kundalini** energy of Hindu mysticism. Hillman was favorably impressed with Gopi Krishna and wrote a psychological commentary for his book *Kundalini; the evolutionary energy in man,* first published New Delhi, 1967, reissued London, 1970, Shambala, California, 1970). This commentary interpreted the experiences of Gopi Krishna in relation to Jungian psychology.

Hills, Christopher

Contemporary **New Age** teacher, director of **University of the Trees.** Born in England, he left home at an early age and attended a naval school, serving in World War II. By the age of 30, he had become a businessman in the West Indies with an international organization of ten companies, but after 1957 became concerned with psychic and spiritual life after his son was miraculously healed through prayer. Hills retired from his business practice and spent two years in India, studying yoga and Hindu philosophy.

In 1960, he became honorary director of research at the Indian Institute of Philosophy, Psychology and Psychical Research, and was elected president of a World Conference on Scientific Yoga attended by eight hundred yogis and fifty Western scientists. In 1962, he formed the Commission for Research into the Creative Faculties of Man, bringing together the work of scientists, psychical researchers, philosophers, holy men, educationalists and politicians.

One aspect of this project was the formation in 1965 with Professor Hiroshi Nakamura, of the International Union of Leading Microbiologists, advising on production of edible algae as a means of solving world food problems by photosynthesis of solar energy.

During 1966, he founded **Centre House** community in England, a free fellowship for those interested in spiritual development, serving a social and educational program aimed at a "conscious evolution towards a society based on love and peace." Training is given in yoga, meditation, awareness, sensitivity development and related subjects. In 1973, Hills founded the **University of the Trees** in Boulder Creek, California, with a comprehensive program of New Age teachings, and granting degrees in consciousness research. The university has also formed a **Research Institute for Supersensonic Healing Energies** for practical research into subtle energy therapeutics.

Hills has written a number of books, published by University of the Trees Press, including: *Nuclear Evolution: A Guide to Cosmic Enlightenment* (1968), *Christ Yoga of Peace; Proposal for a World Peace Center* (1970; new ed. titled *Universal Government by Nature's Laws,* 1978), *Supersensonics: the Science of Radiational Physics* (1975), *Supersensic Instruments of Knowing* (1976), *Rays from the Capstone* (1976), *Nuclear Evolution; Discovery of the Rainbow Body* (1977), *For the One I Love* (3 vols., 1978), *Rise of the Phoenix* (1979).

HIM

Acronym for Human Individual Metamorphosis, a flying saucer cult founded in the Amercan West by two individuals calling themselves **Bo and Peep,** claiming they will lead their followers to literal ascension to heaven in a spacecraft.

Himalayan International Institute of Yoga Science and Philosophy

Organization which grew out of the work of Dr. E. E. and Alyne M. Green in their Voluntary Controls Research Project at Menninger Foundation in 1965.

This concerned experiments with Autogenic Training, involving the use of **Biofeedback** instrumentation. During their later researches, they met Swami Rama from the Himalayas, India, an expert on yoga techniques, who cooperated on psychophysiological programs at the Menninger Foundation.

As a result of this work, the present Institute was formed, with programs of psychosomatic self-regulation and awareness. Address: 907 Camp McDonald Road, Prospect Heights, Illinois 60070.

Himalayan News

Monthly newspaper with articles on yoga, Eastern philosophy and Psi faculty; includes information on the activities of the **Himalayan International Institute of Yoga Science and Philosophy.** Address: 1505 Greenwood Road, Glenview, Illinois 60025.

Hindu Spiritual Magazine, The

Founded in Calcutta, India, March 1906, by Babu Shishir Kumar Ghose (1840–1911), a Bengalee scholar; edited by him as a thoroughly outspoken Spiritualist journal until his decease. It ceased publication in July 1916.

Hippomancy

A method of **divination** practiced by the ancient Celts, who kept certain white horses in consecrated groves. These were made to walk immediately after the sacred car and auguries were drawn from their movements.

The ancient Germans kept similar steeds in their temples. If on leaving these on the outbreak of hostilities, they crossed the threshold with the left forefoot first, the presage was regarded as an evil one, and the war was abandoned.

Hmana Zena

Slavonic name for a witch in Dalmatia. The term means "common woman." (See **Slavs**)

Hmin Nat

A Burmese evil spirit. (See **Burma**)

Hobgoblin (or **Robin Goodfellow** or **Puck**)

An English domestic fairy or brownie of nocturnal habits. His disposition was a merry one and he was believed to be one of the courtiers, probably the jester, at the court of Oberon.

In *Discovery of Witchcraft* (1584 etc.) Reginald Scot stated: "Your grandames maids were wont to set a bowl of milk for him for his pains in grinding of malt and mustard, and sweeping the house at midnight. This white bread, and bread and milk, was his standard fee."

He is perhaps best known in Britain by his appellation of Puck, and his qualities and attributes are represented under this name in Shakespeare's *Midsummer Night's Dream.*

In some folklore traditions he is malicious rather than mischievous, and in medieval times was associated with the devil. By some he was believed to be a demon who led men astray during the night. Sometimes he was represented as clothed in a suit of leather close to his body, and sometimes he wore green. He was usually considered to be full of tricks and mischief. (See also **Fairies**)

Hockley, Frederick (1809–1885)

British occultist who was a member of the **Societas Rosicruciana in Anglia.** Hockley collected some important occult texts, including a Rosicrucian manuscript of Dr. Sigismond Bacstrom, who had been initiated into an occult society in Mauritius in 1794. This text had a great influence on British occultism.

Hockley had some gift of **crystal gazing,** and was a close friend of Kenneth R. H. **Mackenzie** and other British occultists of his period. He had been a pupil of Francis Barrett, author of *The Magus* (1801). Hockley died November 10, 1885. (See also **Rosicrucians**)

Hocus Pocus

Words of pseudo-magical import. According to Sharon Turner in *The History of the Anglo-Saxons* (4 vols., 1799–1805), they were believed to be derived from "Ochus Bochus," a magician and demon of the north. It is more probable, however, that they are a corruption of the Latin words "hoc est corpus," and an imitation of the act of transubstantiation practiced by priests of the Church of Rome.

The term has been used from the seventeenth century

onwards to indicate the tricks of conjuring magicians. A conjurer of the period used to introduce his tricks with the sham Latin formula "Hocus pocus, tontus talontus, rade celeriter jubeo." (See also **Conjuring; Magicians**)

Hod

The name assigned in the Jewish mysticism of **Kabala** to the number eight and meaning "Eternity"—that is, Eternity of the conquests achieved by mind over matter, active over passive, life over death.

Hodgson, Dr. Richard (1855–1905)

One of the leading members of the **Society for Psychical Research,** London, in its early years, the keenest, most critical investigator, a man of brilliant intellect and scholarly education. He was born September 24, 1855, in Melbourne, Australia. His interest in psychical research began in Australia.

At Cambridge, where he continued legal studies after his arrival in England in 1878, he took an active part in the undergraduate Ghost Society for the investigation of psychical phenomena. His name appears in the first published list of the members of the S.P.R. in 1882–83 and in 1885 he was a council member. His legal training and personal attainments made him specially qualified for the detection of fraud.

His exposure of Mme. Blavatsky was his first brilliant achievement. It was in November 1884 that, as a member of the S.P.R. committee he was sent to India to investigate the phenomena of Theosophy.

His report alleging fraud by Mme. **Blavatsky** created an immense sensation.

Next, in conjunction with Mr. S. J. **Davey,** he undertook important experiments into the possibilities of malobservation and lapse of memory in connection with seance phenomena. His paper on the subject is his most original work.

As to physical phenomena he was extremely skeptical. He believed that "nearly all professional mediums form a gang of vulgar tricksters, who are more or less in league with one another." All his early investigations ended with a negative result.

He was convinced that Eusapia **Palladino** whose sittings he attended at Cambridge in 1895, was an impostor, although investigations by other psychical researchers indicated that she produced genuine phenomena when properly controlled, but cheated on other occasions.

The change in Hodgson's general attitude towards the phenomenal side of Spiritualism was brought about very slowly and after desperate resistance by his unparalleled opportunities of investigation of the mediumship of Mrs. **Piper** for a period of fifteen years. He was sent to America in 1887 to act as secretary to the **American Society for Psychical Research** in Boston. He continued in this capacity until his sudden death of heart failure while playing a game of handball at the Boat Club in Boston on December 20, 1905.

The papers which he contributed to the *Proceedings* of the Society for Psychical Research are masterpieces of psychical studies. His life work, the systematic study of the Piper mediumship, cannot be overestimated in importance.

The attention of the S.P.R. was drawn to Mrs. Piper by Professor William **James.** Between him and Hodgson a lifelong friendship developed. Each admired the qualities of the other. Hodgson, being extremely skeptical, had Mrs. Piper watched by detectives to learn whether she attempted to collect information by normal means. He took every precaution to prevent such acquisition of knowledge and finally became convinced not only of the genuineness of her mediumship, but also of spirit return.

His first report on the Piper phenomena was published in 1892 in *Proceedings* of the S.P.R. (vol. 8). In it no definite conclusions were announced. Yet, at this time Hodgson had obtained conclusive evidence of genuineness. But it was of a private character and as he did not include the incident in question in his report he did not consider it fair to point out its import.

As told by Hereward **Carrington** in *The Story of Psychic Science* (1930), Hodgson, when still a young man in Australia, had fallen in love with a girl and wished to marry her. Her parents objected on religious grounds. Hodgson left for England and never married. One day, in a sitting with Mrs. Piper, the girl suddenly communicated, informing Dr. Hodgson that she had died shortly before. This incident, the truth of which was verified, made a deep impression on his mind. In his second report, published in *Proceedings* of the S.P.R. (vol. 13, 1897), his tone was definite in stating: "At the present time I cannot profess to have any doubt that the chief communicators to whom I have referred in the foregoing pages are veritably the personages that they claim to be, that they have survived the change we call death, and that they have directly communicated with us whom we call living, through Mrs. Piper's entranced organism."

After ten years spent in these investigations he returned to England for one year and became editor of the S.P.R. *Journal* and *Proceedings*. Then he went back to America and resumed his Piper studies. He intended to publish a third report but he did not live to do it.

His personal experiences changed his whole outlook upon life. He lived in one room in Boston, dependent on an inadequate salary. Nevertheless, in order to devote all his time to psychical research, he refused remunerative offers from colleges and universities. In his latter years he lived an austere life and could hardly wait until he died.

It appears from the revelations of Carrington that, like so many other famous investigators in the past, Hodgson also developed mediumship at the end. In the last years of his life he allowed no one to enter his room at 15 Charles Street. In the evenings when alone there, he received direct communications from "Imperator," "Rector" and the other controls of Mrs. Piper. These communications were of a very convincing nature but he told very few people of their reception. The room was closed to everyone so as not to disturb the "magnetic atmosphere."

In an interesting critical remark on Dr. Hodgson's life, James Robertson said that Dr. Hodgson traveled all over America in search of psychic phenomena, yet he missed meeting the greatest marvels of spirit action: Andrew Jackson **Davis** and Hudson **Tuttle.**

After Dr. Hodgson's death communications under his control were received in England by the psychic "Mrs. **Holland.**" They contained a cipher, similar entries to which were found in Dr. Hodgson's notebook but it could not be solved. Not even by the dramatic and very lifelike

Hodgson control of Mrs. Piper was the key ever given. There he first communicated eight days after his death and delivered many messages bearing the stamp of his surviving self as a source.

However, many test questions were left unanswered. "If we could suppose," wrote Frank **Podmore**, "that sometimes the real Hodgson communicated through the medium's hand, and that sometimes, more often, when he was inaccessible, the medium's secondary personality played the part as best it could, these difficulties would, no doubt, be lessened."

Many evidential messages bearing on the continued identity of Dr. Hodgson were received by Prof. James **Hyslop.** One of the first came through a friend who asked Dr. Hodgson, the communicator, if he would get in touch with him through another "light." The reply was: "No, I will not, except through the young light. She is all right."

Later in the sitting, one of the other controls remarked that Prof. Hyslop would know what the reference meant. It referred to a young, nonprofessional medium whose powers were a subject of discussion between the living Dr. Hodgson and Prof. Hyslop. It appears that the surviving Dr. Hodgson investigated her case from the other side, as the young lady's control about the time of the incident remarked that he had seen Dr. Hodgson. The news of his death was carefully kept from the medium at the time.

The detailed records of these seances from the time of Hodgson's death until January 1, 1908, were handed over to Prof. William James for examination. In his report (*Proceedings* of the Society for Psychical Research, vol. 23, pp. 120–21) he said: "I myself feel as if an external will to communicate were probably there; that is, I find myself doubting that Mrs. Piper's dream-life, even equipped with telepathic powers, accounts for all the results found. But if asked whether the will to communicate be Hodgson's or some mere spirit-counterfeit of Hodgson, I remain uncertain and await more facts—facts which may not point clearly to a conclusion for fifty or a hundred years."

In England the Hodgson messages were studied by Mrs. **Sidgwick**, J. G. **Piddington** and Sir Oliver **Lodge** during Mrs. Piper's visit to England. They did not find their authenticity proved.

Hoene-Wronski, Joseph Maria (1776–1853)

Polish mathematician and inventor who developed a philosophy of Messianism, deriving from **Kabalism** and Gnosticism. He claimed to have discovered the secret of the Absolute, which he revealed for 150,000 francs to Pierre Arson, a businessman who agreed to publish Hoene-Wronski's Messianic works.

When Arson backed out of the deal, Hoene-Wronski declared him to be the Beast of the Apocalypse, and published a pamphlet against him with the immortal title: *Yes or No—that is to say, have you or have you not, yes or no, purchased from me for 150,000 francs my discovery of the Absolute?* Not surprisingly, Hoene-Wronski lost his court battle to obtain return of the money, but the unfortunate Arson had already expended some 40,000 francs on the works of Hoene-Wronski.

About 1850, Hoene-Wronski became an occult teacher of Alphonse Louis Constant, who later wrote many books on the occult under the pseudonym Éliphas **Lévi.**

Hoffer, Abram (1917–   )

Psychiatrist who studied the effect of psychedelic drugs on human consciousness. Born November 11, 1917, at Saskatchewan, Canada, he studied at the University of Saskatchewan (B.S. 1938, M.S. 1940), University of Minnesota (Ph.D. 1944) and University of Toronto (M.D. 1945). He worked as director of psychiatric research, Psychiatric Services Branch, Department of Public Health, Saskatchewan. In 1942 he married Rose Beatrice Miller. His memberships include the American Association for the Advancement of Science, American Psychiatric Association, Canadian Psychiatric Association, Saskatchewan Psychiatric Association.

With Dr. Humphrey **Osmond**, Dr. Hoffer was co-author of *Chemical Concepts of Psychiatry* (1960). In 1959 Dr. Hoffer spoke at the Conference on Parapsychology and Psychedelics in New York.

His books include *How to Live with Schizophrenia* (1978), (with H. Osmond) *Hallucinogens* (1967), (with Morton Walker) *Orthomolecular Nutrition* (1978), *Nutrients to Age Without Senility* (1980). He also contributed to *Clinical & Other Uses of the Hoffer-Osmond Diagnostic Test* (1975). (See also Psychedelic **Drugs; Hallucinogens; Mushrooms**)

Hohenlohe, Prince (1794–1849)

Full name: Alexander Leopold Franz Emmerick, Prince of Hohenlohe-Waldenburg-Schillings-Furst, priest and claimed miracle healer. He was born at Kupferzell, near Waldenburg, August 17, 1794; ordained as a Catholic priest in 1815. He went to Rome, where he entered the Society of the Fathers of the Sacred Heart.

He gained a great reputation as a miraculous healer at Bamberg and Munich and attracted large crowds. Eventually the authorities intervened to prevent his healing work. He traveled to Vienna and Hungary, becoming titular Bishop of Sardica in 1844. He died at Vöslau, near Vienna, November 17, 1849.

For an account of his healing, see: F. N. Baur *A Short and Faithful Description of the Remarkable Occurrences and . . . Conduct of . . . Prince Alexander of Hohenlohe* (1822), J. Doyle, *Miracles Said to Have Been Wrought by the Prince Hohenlohe* (1823). The Prince's own writings were collected by S. Brunner: *Aus dem Nachlasse des Furstein Aloysius von Hohenlohe* (1851).

Hohenwarter, Peter (1894–   )

Theologian who conducted important researches into mediumistic phenomena. Born May 18, 1894, at Obervellach, Austria, he studied at Graz University, Austria (Theol.D., 1924). He was a professor of mathematics, physics and philosophy at Klagenfurt but was removed by the Nazis in 1938. Dr. Hohenwarter became vice-president of the International Society of Catholic Parapsychologists and a member of the Austrian Society for Psychical Research.

He organized a great many sittings with the Viennese medium Maria **Silbert** and the Danish medium Einer **Nielsen,** whose phenomena he endorsed in lectures. His articles include: 'Our Experiments with Maria Silbert' (*Schweizer Rundschau,* Feb. 1954), 'Hauntings at Schwarzach in the Voralberg Region' (*Neue Wissenschaft,* July 1954), 'Should We Study Parapsychology?' (*Der Seelsorger,* March 1958), 'The Experiments of Astro-

Physicist Dr. Alois Gatterer, S. J. with Maria Silbert' (*Vergorgene Welt,* Nos. 2 & 3, 1957), 'Germany's Leading Parapsychologist: The 100th Anniversary of Schrenck-Notzing's Birth' (*Vergorgene Welt,* Nos. 3-5, 1959).

Holistic

A **New Age** term implying wholeness or an integrated approach to life which includes a culture complex of such things as whole grain foods, environmental concern, alternative energy, unorthodox healing, experimental communes, meditation, spiritual growth and higher consciousness. (See also **Findhorn; Lindisfarne;** William Irwin **Thompson**)

HOLLAND

For general early occultism amongst Germany peoples, see entry on **Teutons.**

Spiritualism

Since the introduction of Spiritualism into Holland in 1857–58, no small part of its history has been enacted in that country, notwithstanding popular belief that the temperament of the Dutch people would seem to be unsuited to mediumship. In fact Holland later produced some interesting psychics and notable psychical researchers.

The first Dutch Spiritualist of whom we have record is J. N. T. Marthese who, after studying psychic phenomena in foreign countries, finally returned to his native Holland, bringing with him the American medium D. D. **Home.** The latter held seances at the Hague before several learned societies, and by command of Queen Sophia, a seance was given in her presence. The medium himself, in an account of the performance, stated that the royal lady was obliged to sit seven seances on consecutive evenings, before any results were obtained. These results, however, were apparently satisfactory, for the Queen was thereafter a staunch supporter of the movement.

During Home's visit, Spiritualism gained a considerable following in Holland and the practice of giving small private seances became fairly widespread. Spirit voices were heard at these gatherings, the touch of spirit hands was felt, and musical instruments were played upon by invisible performers.

Particularly were these seances appreciated which were held at the house of Mr. J. D. van Herwerden, in the Hague, and which were attended by many enthusiastic students of Spiritualist phenomena. His medium was, as a rule, a Javanese boy of his household, about fourteen years old, and very ignorant.

The manifestations ranged from spirit rapping and **table turning** in the earlier seances to **direct voice, direct writing, levitation** and **materializations** in those of a later date. The seances were described in van Herwerden's book *Ervaringen en Mededeeling op een nog Geheimzinnig Gebied* and took place between 1858–62. One of the principal spirits purported to be a monk, Paurellus, who had been assassinated some three hundred years previously in that city. Afterwards Mr. van Herwerden was induced by his friends to publish his diary, under the title of *Experiences and Communications on a still Mysterious Territory.*

For a time, Spiritualist seances were only conducted in family circles, and were of a quite private nature. But as the attention of the intellectuals became more and more

directed to the new science, societies were formed to promote research, and to throw light upon that which was obscure and perplexing.

The first of these was the society called the "Oromase," or Ormuzd, which was founded by Major J. Revius, a friend of Marthese, in 1859, and which included among its members many people of high repute. They met at the Hague, and the records of their transactions were carefully preserved. Major Revius was president and continued to act in that capacity till 1871, the year of his death. The society's secretary, A. J. Rita, was also a prominent worker in the cause.

The "Oromase" library contained a fine collection of works on Spiritualism, mesmerism, and kindred subjects, and included American, French, German and English books. Another society, the "Veritas," was founded in Amsterdam in 1869. The studies of this latter association were conducted in a somewhat less searching and scientific spirit than those of the "Oromase." Its mediums specialized in trance utterances and written communications from the spirits, and its members inclined to a belief in reincarnation, which was at variance with the opinions of the older society.

Rotterdam had, for a time, a society with similar objects known as the "Research after Truth," but it soon came to an end, although its members continued to devote themselves privately to the investigation of spirit phenomena.

Other equally short-lived societies were formed in Haarlem and other towns. In all of these, however, there was a shortage of mediums able to produce form materializations, and to supply this want a number of foreign mediums hastened to Holland. Hitherto the comparatively private nature of the seances, and the high standing of those who took part in them, had prevented the periodicals from making any but the most cautious comments on the seances.

But the advent of professional mediums on the scene swept away the barrier and let loose a flood of journalistic ridicule and criticism. This in turn provoked the supporters of Spiritualism to retort, and soon a lively battle was in progress between the Spiritualists and the skeptics. The consequence was, that "the cause" was promoted as much by the articles which derided it as by those which were in favor of it.

Such mediums as Mrs. Margaret Fox Kane (see **Fox Sisters**), the **Davenport** brothers, A. **Rita,** D. D. **Home,** Florence **Cook** and Henry **Slade,** came over to Holland. Writers arose who were prepared to devote their abilities to the defence of Spiritualism. Such a one was Madame Elise van Calcar, who not only wrote a novel expounding Spiritualist principles, but also conducted a monthly journal *On the Boundaries of Two Worlds,* and held a sort of Spiritualist salon, where enthusiasts could meet and discuss their favorite subject.

Dr. H. de Grood, Dr. J. Van Velzen, Dr. Van der Loef, Herr Schimmel, were among other prominent Dutch authors who wrote in defence of the same opinions. The writings of Professors **Varley, Crookes,** and **Wallace** were translated into the Dutch language, and lecturers helped to spread the belief in communication with the Other World.

A mesmerist, Signor Donata, carried on the practice of

"Animal Magnetism" in Holland, and endeavored to identify the "magnetic force" emanating from the operator with the substance of which disembodied spirits were believed to be composed. Many exposures were made of unscrupulous mediums, and these, naturally, cast discredit upon the entire movement. But on the whole the mediums, professional or otherwise, were well received. Such phases of psychic phenomena as haunted houses and **poltergeist** were also common, but were so similar to these manifestations in other countries that they require no separate discussion.

Psychical Research & Parapsychology

Some of the pioneers of psychical research in Holland were: Frederik van Eeden (1860–1932), Dr. K. H. E. de Jong (1872–1960), Dr. P. A. Dietz (1878–1953) and Florentin J. L. Jansen (1881–   ).

Dr. Van Eeden was an author and physician who sat with the English medium Mrs. R. Thompson and was also acquainted with F. W. H. Myers. Van Eeden contributed 'A Study of Dreams' to *Proceedings* of the Society for Psychical Research (vol. 26, p. 431) in which he used the term "lucid dream" to indicate those conditions in which the dreamer is aware that he is dreaming. This condition of walking consciousness in the dream state has been emphasized by the British writer "Oliver **Fox**" as a frequent preliminary to **astral projection.**

Dr. de Jong was a classical student whose doctoral thesis dealt with the Mysteries of Isis. In 1940 he was a lecturer in parapsychology at the University of Leiden, and was responsible for a number of books and articles dealing with psi faculty.

Dr. Dietz had attempted to organize a student social for psychical research when studying biology at the University of Groningen. Although this was short-lived, Dr. Dietz went on to investigate parapsychological card tests, using himself as subject. After qualifying as a medical doctor in 1924, he became a neurologist in the Hague. A few years later, he was a co-founder with W. H. C. **Tenhaeff** of the periodical **Tijdschrift voor Parapsychologie** and contributed many articles to it. In his book *Wereldzicht der Parapsychologie* (Parapsychological View of the Universe) he coined the term "paragnosy" for psychical phenomena and "parergy" for physical phenomena. He became a lecturer in parapsychology at the University of Leyden in 1931 and had a reputation as an excellent speaker.

Dr. Florentin Jansen seems to have established a parapsychological laboratory as early as 1907, while still a medical student. He founded the quarterly periodical *Driemaandelijkse verslagen van het Psychophysisch Laboratorium te Amsterdam*. He took a special interest in experiments with the **Sthenometer** of Dr. **Joire** and conducted a number of experiments to verify the **Od** of Baron von **Reichenbach.** In 1912 he emigrated to Buenos Aires, where he worked as a physician.

Other pioneers included Marcellus Emants (1848–1932), a novelist who experimented with the famous medium Eusapia **Palladino**; engineer Felix Ortt (1866–1959), who published articles on parapsychology and published a book on "Philosophy of Occultism & Spiritualism"; Captain H. N. de Fremery published a manual of Spiritualism and also contributed to *Tijdschrift voor Parapsychologie.*

In 1920, a Dutch Society for Psychical Research was founded in Amsterdam through the enterprise of Prof. G. Heymans (1857–1930) of Groningen University. Although the Society began well, it was soon criticized for an unsympathetic atmosphere for mediums, but in 1927 it received a new impetus from the psychologist W. H. C. Tenhaeff and the founding of the periodical *Tidschrift voor Parapsychologie*. Some notable investigations over the years included a study of **dowsing** (water-witching), physics and parapsychology, and precognitive elements in dreams.

The Society was suppressed during World War II and the German occupation, the library removed to Germany and destroyed. After the war, the Society was reconstructed and soon numbered a thousand members, including G. Zorab, who contributed important papers. Some of the work in this modern period included observations on the noted psychic Gerard Croiset, an attempt to replicate the Whately **Carington** tests with Zener cards (F. A. Heyn & J. J. Mulckhuyse, 1950), investigation of "objective clairvoyance" (A. Mak, 1953).

Meanwhile the Parapsychology Institute of the State University of Utrecht was founded in 1933 by Dr. W. H. C. Tenhaeff; it later became known as the **Parapsychological Division of the Psychological Laboratory, Utrecht.**

In 1953, the First International Conference of Parapsychological Studies, sponsored by the **Parapsychology Foundation,** New York, was held in Utrecht.

In 1959, the Amsterdam Foundation for Parapsychological Research was established and commenced an investigation of the influence of psychedelics on ESP. Another investigation was a widely conducted inquiry into the occurrence of spontaneous phenomena.

By 1967, there was growing interest in parapsychology amongst students of five major universities, and various societies were set up. These were later grouped in the Study Center for Experimental Parapsychology.

The Federation of Parapsychological Circles of the Netherlands includes the following organizations:

Amsterdamse Parapsychologische Studiekring, Jan van Goyenkade 4, Amsterdam.

Haarlemse Parapsychologische Studiekring, Jacob van Lennplaan 11, Haarlem.

Haagse Parapsychologische Studiekring, Norte Potan, The Hague.

Rottendamse Parapsychologische Studiekring, Nachtegaallaan 15, Rotterdam 13.

"Holland, Mrs." (1868–1948)

Pseudonym of Alice Kipling **Fleming,** who took part in famous "cross correspondence" tests of the Society for Psychical Research, London, and produced significant **automatic writing** scripts.

Holleran, Eugene M(artin) (1922–   )

Professor of chemistry who has investigated psychokinesis. Born June 25, 1922, at Kingston, Pennsylvania, he studied at Scranton University (B.S., 1943) and Catholic University, Washington, D.C. (Ph.D. in chemistry, 1949). In 1947 he married Margaret Walter. From 1950 onwards he was professor of chemistry at St. John's University, Jamaica, New York. He is a member of the American Chemical Society and the Parapsychological Association.

From 1960–61 he worked under a Parapsychology Foundation grant on tests to establish psychokinetic ability.

Hollis, Mrs. Mary J. (Mrs. Hollis-Billing) (1837–   ?)

American **direct voice** and **materialization** medium, of the nineteenth century, controlled by spirit guides "James Nolan" and "Skiwaukee" (an Indian). She visited England in 1874 and 1880, was one of the earliest slate writers (see **Slate-writing**), the script frequently being said to be produced by a materialized hand in full view.

She was born April 24, 1837, in Jeffersonville, Indiana in a wealthy family. She became an exemplary member of the Episcopal church until she began to see and talk with spirits. After that she ceased to be a fashionable worshiper and dedicated her life to service of the spirit world.

During the years 1871–73, Dr. N. B. Wolfe of Chicago made exhaustive investigations into her phenomena. The account is incorporated in his *Startling Facts in Modern Spiritualism* (1873). According to Wolfe, Mrs. Hollis' direct voice mediumship was well developed. As many as thirty-forty spirits were said to have come in one single sitting. They only spoke in the dark. They could sing with the sitters. Sometimes the sitters were given the Freemasonry challenge.

Movements of objects were very frequent. Sometimes the medium was levitated to the ceiling and left a pencil mark there. One of her manifesting spirits was fond of making dolls and rosettes from the material provided for this purpose. The process of sewing was done accurately in the dark.

Mrs. Hollis produced materialized forms from a cabinet without going into trance. The appearance of phantom hands was very quick. As a test the medium's right hand was blackened with cork. The spirit hand was clean. The faces were often flat. The sitters looked at them through opera glasses. On one occasion six heads materialized simultaneously. Famous people were claimed to have manifested at the seances of Mrs. Hollis, including Napoleon and the Empress Josephine wearing a jewelled crown and strings of pearls.

Hollow Earth

Many occult speculations revolve around heterodox cosmologies in which the earth is not simply a solid sphere in a universe of other celestial bodies. Today there are still followers of Wilbur Glen Voliva (died 1942) who kept alive the Flat Earth theories of John Alexander Dowie.

The Hollow Earth heresy is equally durable, and takes two basic forms. The first turns the world inside out and claims that we live on the inside of a sphere or oval, with sun, moon and planets in the center. The second is that we live on the *outside* of a hollow sphere with a mysterious inner kingdom known only to a few initiates or intrepid travelers.

An early Hollow Earth theory was proposed by the English astronomer Edmund Halley in 1692, who suggested that the earth was a shell 500 miles thick, with two inner shells and a solid inner sphere, all capable of sustaining life. In 1721, Cotton **Mather** (prominent in the Salem Witchcraft mania) put forward a similar view.

In 1818, John Cleves Symmes, a retired Captain of U.S. Infantry, spent the last years of his life trying to prove that the earth consisted of five concentric spheres, with holes several thousand miles in diameter at the poles. His theories were explained in detail in the book *Symmes' Theory of Concentric Spheres* (1826) by James McBridge, and *The Symmes' Theory of Concentric Spheres* (1878) by Americus Symmes, son of the Captain. In 1820, a writer with the probably pseudonymous name "Captain Seaborn" published in fictional narrative of a hollow earth under the title *Symzonia*. Captain Seaborn finds his steamship drawn by strong currents to a south pole opening, where he finds an inner world of happy Utopiates. Edgar Allan Poe's *Narrative of Arthur Gordon Pym* developed a similar theme.

A later development of the Symmes theories was propounded with Messianic zeal by Cyrus Reed Teed (1839–1908), who spent thirty-eight years lecturing and writing on the hollow earth theme. He had a laboratory in Utica for the study of alchemy, and claimed that in 1869 he had a vision of a beautiful woman who revealed to him the secret of the hollow earth. This discovery was given to the world in a pamphlet titled *The Illumination of Koresh; Marvelous Experience of the Great Alchemist at Utica, N.Y.* In 1870 he published *The Cellular Cosmogony* under the pseudonym "Koresh" and after many years of enthusiastic lecturing established a College of Life in Chicago, Illinois, in 1886. This was the beginning of a commune called Koreshan Unity. By the 1890s this blossomed into the town of Estero, near Fort Meyers, Florida, under the name The New Jerusalem.

Long after Teed's death and the decline of his Koreshan communities in the U.S., his ideas influenced eccentric Nazis in Germany during the Hitler period, and remnants of the "Hohlweltlehre" or Hollow Earth Teaching still have some following. A secondary offshoot of the Koresh revelations was that the name itself was later exploited by two famous occult swindlers, Mr. and Mrs. Frank Jackson, operating under the names "Mr. and Mrs. Theodore **Horos**." The name "Horos" had also been taken from the publicity of Cyrus Reed Teed. Mrs. Jackson aka Mrs. Diss Debar aka Angel Anna aka Editha Gilbert Montez appears to have been born as Editha Salomon. As well as representing herself as a founder of "Koreshan Unity," she also stole the rituals of the Hermetic Order of **Golden Dawn**.

Another Hollow Earth theorist was Marshall B. Gardner, an Illinois maintenance engineer who worked for a corset manufacturer. His book *Journey to the Earth's Interior* (1906) might have been influenced by Jules Verne's story *Journey to the Center of the Earth* (1864). It rejected the theory of several concentric spheres and claimed as a positive fact that there was only one hollow earth and that we lived on the outside of it. It was 800 miles thick and the interior had its own sun, and there were openings at the poles each 1,400 miles wide, through which the mammoths of Siberia and the Eskimos people had come. An enlarged edition of Gardner's book was published in 1920, with many impressive illustrations showing the everlasting summerland of the interior.

Six years after the second edition of Gardner's book, Admiral Richard E. Byrd flew over the north pole and three years later over the south pole. The Admiral found no holes in the poles. Incredibly enough, however, his statements about his explorations have since been quoted out of context to make it seem as if he actually endorsed the hollow earth myth. **Flying saucers** are supposed to emerge from the polar openings. This version of the hollow earth story is revived by Raymond Bernard's book *The Hollow Earth* (Dell, 1969).

A persistent variant of the hollow earth cosmology is the legend of secret subterranean kingdoms under the ground, modern versions of older folklore about fairies and gnomes (see **Agharta; Shaver Mystery; Subterranean Cities**).

Holly

This name is probably a corruption of the word "holy" as this plant has been used from time immemorial as a protection against evil influence. It was hung round, or planted near houses, as a protection against lightning.

Its common use at Christmas is apparently the survival of an ancient Roman custom, occurring during the festival to Saturn, to which god the holly was dedicated. While the Romans were holding this feast, which occurred about the time of the winter solstice, they decked the outsides of their houses with holly; at the same time the Christians were quietly celebrating the birth of Christ, and to avoid detection, they outwardly followed the custom of their heathen neighbors, and decked their houses with holly also. In this way the holly came to be connected with our Christmas customs. This plant was also regarded as a symbol of the resurrection.

The use of mistletoe along with holly is probably due to the notion that in winter the **fairies** took shelter under its leaves, and that they protected all who sheltered the plant. The origin of kissing under the mistletoe is considered to have come from Saxon ancestors of the British, who regarded this plant as dedicated to Freya, the goddess of love.

Holmes, Mr. and Mrs. Nelson (c. 1874)

Materialization mediums of Philadelphia who claimed "Katie King" and "John King" as their **controls.** The claim was supported by Dr. Henry Child, another medium, who published particulars of their earth-life as privately communicated to him in his study.

The Holmes had a good reputation and in 1873 they came to England. Here they were charged with dishonorable attempts to raise money. The account of their powers of mediumship varied. Dr. and Mrs. Speer and the latter's brother recognized in a sitting a spirit face as that of a departed relative, and the Rev. Stainton **Moses,** in giving an account in *The Spiritualist,* stated that the light was good and the face was only a few feet away from the sitters. After their return to America, General Lippitt publicly endorsed their mediumship in *The Galaxy* in December 1874. They found another powerful advocate in Robert Dale **Owen.**

"I have seen Katie," he wrote, "on seven or eight different occasions, suspended, in full form, about two feet from the ground for ten or fifteen seconds. It was within the cabinet, but in full view; and she moved her arms and feet gently, as a swimmer upright in the water might. I have seen her, on five different evenings, disappear and reappear before my eyes, and not more than eight or nine feet distant. On one occasion, when I had given her a calla lily, she gradually vanished, holding it in her hand; and the lily remained visible after the hand which held it

was gone; the flower, however, finally disappearing also. When she reappeared the lily came back also, at first a bright spot only, which gradually expanded into a flower."

On November 2, 1874, Owen yet wrote, "I stake whatever reputation I may have acquired, after eighteen years' study of spiritualism, as a dispassionate observer upon the genuine character of these phenomena."

Nevertheless, on December 6, 1874, he declared in *The Banner of Light:* "Circumstantial evidence, which I have just obtained, induces me to withdraw the assurances which I have heretofore given of my confidence in the geniune character of certain manifestations presented last summer, in my presence, through Mrs. and Mr. Nelson Holmes." A similar notice was published by Henry T. Child.

The reason for the sudden change was the revelation that Eliza White, the landlady of the Holmeses, claimed that she had impersonated Katie King by slipping in through a false panel of the cabinet. A demonstration of the impersonation was given to Robert Dale Owen and Dr. Child. The newspapers made a great sensation of the exposure. The Holmeses appeared to have been ruined.

Then Col. Henry **Olcott** came to the rescue. He investigated and soon discovered very serious discrepancies in Eliza White's story. Affidavits were handed to him proving the bad moral reputation and lying character of this woman. Mr. Allen, Justice of Peace of New Jersey, testified to having heard Eliza White singing in the neighboring room while "Katie King" appeared before them. General Lippitt told of a thorough investigation of the cabinet, once with a professional magician who was perfectly satisfied that there was no chance of any trick.

Letters were produced by the Holmeses which spoke against the probability of any conspiracy between them and Eliza White. On the contrary they proved that Eliza White tried to blackmail them much earlier by alluding to promises made to her if she were to confess that she impersonated "Katie King."

The final proof was obtained in the following form: At the time of the mock seance before Dr. Child and Robert Dale Owen the Holmeses had a real seance with twenty people at which the spirits appeared just the same. On the basis of all these facts and also making allowance for the dubious part which Dr. Child appeared to have played in the affair, Col. Olcott concluded that the conflicting nature of the evidence justified them in giving a chance to the Holmeses testing them again without reference to the past.

This he did. He netted a cabinet to make it proof against surreptitious entry and put Mrs. Holmes into a bag tied around her neck. The experiments were repeated in his own room. He became satisfied that Mrs. Holmes was a genuine and powerful medium for materializations. General Lippitt shared his conclusions.

For a full account of Col. Olcott's investigations and conclusions, see his book *People from the Other World* (1875; 1972).

Holms, A(rchibald) Campbell (1861–1954)

Scottish expert on shipbuilding, who also studied Spiritualism and psychic science. In addition to his classic work *Practical Shipbuilding* (first published 1904), he also compiled one of the most valuable and comprehensive encyclopedias of psychical phenomena ever published: *The Facts of Psychic Science* (1925; reissued University Books, 1969). Although not a critical study, it analyzed and classified every major phenomenon of psychic science, with detailed indexes.

Holon

Newsletter issued by the **Holonomics Group,** devoted to "the unified and impartial study of the pattern of law and purpose of the universe as a whole." Address: The Holonomics Group, c/o Alan Mayne, 63A Muswell Avenue, London, N10 2EH, England.

Holonomics

Term coined by the **Holonomics Group** to denote "the unified and impartial study of the pattern of law and purpose of the universe as a whole," deriving from the ancient Greek words "holon" (whole) and "nomos" (law). It is "a new approach to fundamental knowledge, adopting a holistic mode of thinking and action, and aiming to coordinate and integrate the approaches of science, philosophy, religion, personal experience, ethics and the arts, and to have direct applications to the human situation."

Holonomics Group, The

Founded in November 1977 to help promote a unified approach to science, parascience, philosophy, religion, the arts, human development and human affairs, and to provide a forum for the discussion of ideas relevant to this theme. The Group issues a newsletter *Holon,* presenting concepts and principles of Holonomics, as well as notices of relevant societies, meetings, reports and projects. The Group is also compiling a register of interests and personal statements of members to assist them to contact each other on related interests and experiences, and to stimulate the exchange of ideas. A communication network is being set up as a framework through which members and other interested individuals can arrange informal discussions and meetings. The Group also aims to provide an environment for the encouragement of relevant interdisciplinary researchers. Address: The Holonomics Group, c/o Alan Mayne, 63A Muswell Avenue, London, N10 2EH, England. (See also **Institute of Parascience;** Alan James **Mayne**)

Holt, Henry (1840–1926)

American publisher who encouraged the publication of books on psychic phenomena. Born January 3, 1840, at Baltimore, Maryland, he studied at Yale University (B.S., 1862), Columbia University Law School (LL.B. 1864), University of Vermont (hon. LL.D. 1901). In 1863 he married Mary Florence West (died 1879), his second marriage in 1886 was to Florence Tabor. He was a Fellow of the American Association for the Advancement of Science, a trustee and council member of the American Society for Psychical Research, and a founding member of Yale Club, New York. He was also a member of Sons of the American Revolution, Authors Club and Century Club.

In 1866 Holt became a partner in the publishing company of George P. Putnam, later founding his own company Henry Holt & Co. His interest in psychic

phenomena led him to promote research and to publish books on the subject, including his own work *On The Cosmic Relations* (2 vols., 1914). A revised edition was issued after World War I with additional matter on immortality under the title *The Cosmic Relations and Immortality* (1918). His other books include: *Calmire* (1892), *Man and Nature* (1892), *Man and Man* (1905) and a book of reminiscences *Garrulities of an Octogenarian Editor* (1923). He died February 13, 1926.

The company continued in existence, and in 1941 published the important one-volume edition of *The Books of Charles Fort,* dealing with bizarre, inexplicable and mysterious phenomena (see also Charles **Fort**).

Holy Coat of Treves

Sacred relic believed to be the seamless robe worn by Jesus Christ at the time of crucifixion. It is located in the cathedral at Treves, on the River Moselle in the Rhineland of Germany. The coat has been venerated by many thousands of pilgrims. For a discussion of its history and claimed authenticity, see *The Holy Coat of Treves* by Richard F. Clark, S.J., London, 1892.

For details of an even more highly regarded relic, see **Turin Shroud.**

Holzer, Hans W. (1920–)

Researcher and writer on paranormal topics. Born January 26, 1920 at Vienna, Austria, he studied at Vienna University, and Columbia University. From 1945 onwards he became a freelance writer, playwright and composer and was a drama critic of *London Weekly Sporting Review* from 1949-60. He has also acted as a television consultant.

He is a member of the American Society for Psychical Research, the Society for Psychical Research, London, the British College for Psychic Science, Authors Guild, Dramatists Guild, and is research director of the New York Committee for the Investigation of Paranormal Occurrences.

He has written over 300 newspaper and magazine articles on various subjects, including many on psychic phenomena. He contributed the chapter 'The Rockland County Ghost' to the book *Beyond the Five Senses* (1957). His books include: *Beyond Medicine; the facts about unorthodox and psychic healing* (1973), *The Habsburg Curse* (1973), *The Power of Hypnosis* (1973), *The Alchemist; The Secret Magical Life of Rudolf von Hapsburg* (1974), *The Directory of the Occult* (1974), *Haunted Hollywood* (1974), *Patterns of Destiny* (1974), *The Truth About ESP; what it is, how it works and how you develop it* (1974), *The Great British Ghost Hunt* (1975), *Handbook of Parapsychology* (1975), (ed.) *Heather: Confessions of a Witch, as told to Hans Holzer* (1975), *The Prophets Speak* (1975), *Psychic Investigator* (1975), *Psychic Detective No. 1* (1976), *White House Ghosts* (1976; original title *Ghosts,* 1971), *Elvis Presley Speaks* (1978), *Occult Power* (1978), *Possessed* (1978), *The Powers of the New Age* (1978), *Some of My Best Friends Are Ghosts* (1978), *Word Play* (1978), *Dreams; Gateway to the Unconscious* (1979), *Hidden Meanings in Dreams* (1979), *Houses of Morror* (1979), *In Search of Ghosts* (1979), *Pagans & Witches* (1979), *Psychic Healing* (1979), *Signs of Love & Glory* (1979), *Star Ghosts* (1979), *Super Seduction* (1979), *There is an Afterlife; A Scientific Evaluation* (1979), *Wicca: The Way of the Witches* (1979), *The Clairvoy-*

ant (1980), *Demonic Possession* (1980), *Inside Witchcraft* (1980), *More Than One Life* (1980), *Westghosts; The Psychic World of California* (1980, original title *Ghosts of the Golden West*), *The Amityville Curse* (1981), *The Entry* (1981).

Home, Daniel Dunglas (1833–1886)

The greatest physical medium in the history of Spiritualism. There was a certain mystery about his parentage. According to his own footnote in *Incidents in My Life* (1863), his father was a natural son of Alexander, the tenth Earl of Home. Through his mother, he was descended from a Highland family in which the traditional gift of **second sight** had been preserved. He was born March 20, 1833, in Scotland.

He was a sensitive, delicate child of a highly nervous temperament and of such weak health that he was not expected to live. Adopted by Mrs. McNeill Cook, a childless aunt, he passed his infancy at Portobello, Scotland, and was taken to America at the age of 9, growing up in Greeneville, Conn., and Troy, N.Y. It was noticed that he had keen powers of observation and a prodigious memory. He saw his first vision at the age of 13. His schoolfellow, Edwin, died in Greeneville and appeared to him in a bright cloud at night in Troy, thus keeping a childish promise with which they had bound themselves that he who should die first should appear to the other. The second vision came four years later. It announced the death of his mother to the hour.

From that time onwards his thoughts turned more and more to the life beyond. One night he heard loud, unaccountable blows. Next morning a volley of **raps.** His aunt, remembering the **Hydesville** rappings that were then two years old (see **Fox Sisters**), believed him to be possessed of the devil and called in turn for a Congregationalist, a Baptist and a Wesleyan minister for exorcism. This being unsuccessful she turned him out of doors.

Thenceforth, although he never asked or received direct payment, Home appears to have been living on the hospitality of friends attracted by his curious gift.

The intelligence behind the raps was soon discovered. The first scientist to investigate the phenomenon and the communications thus received was Prof. George Bush, a distinguished theologian and Oriental scholar of New York. The celebrated American poet, Bryant and Prof. Wells of the University of Harvard, testified in a written statement to the reality of the phenomena. Prof. Robert **Hare** and Prof. James **Mapes,** both famous chemists, and Judge **Edmonds** of the United States Supreme Court, owed much of their conversion to Spiritualism to the young man of frail health whose fame now began to spread.

The first **levitation** of Home occurred in the South Manchester house of Ward Cheney, an eminent American manufacturer. Strains of music were heard when no instrument was near.

Nobody understood at that time the part which the physical organism plays in the production of the phenomena. The claims made on Home were very heavy, the drain of nervous energy excessive. His intended medical studies had to be broken off owing to illness and a trip to Europe being advised, Home went to England, landing in April 1855.

He first stayed at Cox's Hotel in Jermyn Street, London, and was later the guest of Mr. J. S. Rymer, an Ealing solicitor. While in America his name was spelt "Hume," he was known now as Home, which is the correct spelling for the Scottish family. According to Mme. Home's biography the name was always Home but it was pronounced *Hoom,* which is nearer to the correct pronunciation for the Scottish family.

The conversion of many of the later leaders of the Spiritualist movement in England was due to Home's phenomena. No sooner had they attracted public attention when Home found himself in the midst of a Press warfare. Among the first who asked Home to attend a seance was Lord Brougham. He came with Sir David **Brewster.** Home was proud of the deep impression he produced upon these two distinguished men and wrote about it to a friend in America. The letter was published in America and found its way to the London Press, whereupon Sir David Brewster at once disclaimed all belief in Spiritualism and set down the phenomena to imposture.

As this, however, contradicted his statements in private; these statements also found their way into the Press and have, to a considerable degree, discredited his attitude, the more so as Lord Brougham preserved silence and Sir David Brewster did not even attempt to refer to his testimony.

More harm was done to Home's reputation by Robert **Browning**'s poem, *Mr. Sludge, the Medium,* which was generally taken to refer to Home, as Browning, together with his wife, who accepted Spiritualism, attended seances with Home. The poem was a malignant attack, since Browning had never claimed in public to have caught Home at trickery and in private admitted that imposture was out of the question. The reason for this vicious attack may have been jealousy of his wife's enthusiasm for Home's phenomena.

Other famous men of the day, such as Bulwer **Lytton** and William **Thackeray,** never spoke of their experiences in public. Thackeray was very incredulous. He made Home's acquaintance in America when he lectured there. Both there and in London he availed himself of every opportunity of control. He admitted to have found a genuine mystery and warmly endorsed Robert Bell's anonymous article "Stranger than Fiction" published in the *Cornhill Magazine* which he then edited.

The account of Robert Bell of a seance with Home started with a quotation of Dr. Treviranus to Coleridge: "I have seen what I would not have believed on your testimony, and what I cannot therefore, expect you to believe upon mine." Thackeray was bitterly attacked for the publication of the article and it was said that the *Cornhill Magazine* lost considerably in circulation as a consequence.

In the early autumn of 1855, Home went to Florence to visit Mr. and Mrs. **Trollope.** His name and fame soon spread there, too. False rumors arose among the peasants that he was a necromancer, who administered the sacraments of the Church to toads in order to raise the dead by spells and incantations.

This may explain the attempt which was made against his life on December 5, 1855. A man lay in wait for him late at night and struck him three times with a dagger. Home had a narrow escape. The would-be murderer was never arrested, but Home was warned the following month by Signor Landucci, Minister of the Interior to the Grand Duke of Tuscany, of his sinister reputation among the populace.

About this time he was told by the spirits that his power would leave him for a year. In this state of seclusion from supernormal contact, Catholic influences found an easy inroad into his religious ideas. He became a convert to Catholicism and decided to enter a monastery. He was received by Pius IX and treated with favor. Home, however, changed his mind and left Italy for Paris, where, exactly to a day from the announced suspension, his powers returned. The news reached the French Court and Napoleon III summoned him to the Tuilleries.

The story of the seance with Napoleon was not made public. The curiosity of the Press was aroused, as the first seance was followed by many others. There is an account, however, in Home's autobiography, *Incidents in My Life,* according to which Napoleon followed every manifestation with keen and skeptical attention and satisfied himself by the closest scrutiny that neither deception nor delusion was possible. His and the Empress' unspoken thoughts were replied to and the Empress was touched by a materialized hand in which, from a defect in one of the fingers, she recognized that of her late father.

The second seance was still more forceful. The room was shaken, heavy tables were lifted and then held down immoveably to the floor by an alteration of their weight. At the third seance a phantom hand appeared above the table, lifted a pencil and wrote the single word "Napoleon" in the autograph of Napoleon I. As Prince Murat related later to Home, the Duke de Morny told the Emperor that he felt it a duty to contradict the report that the Emperor believed in Spiritualism. The Emperor replied "Quite right, but you may add when you speak on the subject again that there is a difference between believing a thing and having proof of it, and that I am certain of what I have seen."

When, soon after these seances, Home left Paris for America, rumors were rife that his departure was compulsory. The truth was that the Empress had offered to take Home's sister under her protection and educate her at her expense and Home simply went to America to bring her over. On his return he was speedily summoned to Fontainebleau, where the King of Bavaria was another interested party for a seance. Home was in great power at the time and so much sought after that the Union Club, where the fashionable sophisticates congregated, offered him 50,000 francs for a single seance. Home refused. A book, privately printed in France, recorded the strange experiences which high society had at this time with Home's mediumship.

Earlier, in Italy, Home was introduced to the King of Naples. The German Emperor and the Queen of Holland soon joined the ranks of the curious who were besieging Home with requests for seances. While enjoying the benevolence of crowned heads and the highest members of the aristocracy Home had to wage a desperate struggle against the scandalmongers. Fantastic stories began to circulate as soon as he left Paris and while he was regaining his shattered health in Italy it was even rumored that he was in the prison of Mazas. Henri Delange, the author, on receiving a letter from the unsuspecting

Home from Rome, was instrumental in laying the calumny in *Le Nord.*

In Rome, in the Spring of 1858, Home was introduced to Count Koucheleff-Besborodka and his wife. Not many days after he became engaged to Mlle. Alexandrina de Kroll, the Count's sister-in-law. The wedding took place in St. Petersburg. It was a great society affair. Count Alexis Tolstoy, the poet, and Count Bobrinsky, one of the Chamberlains of the Emperor, acted as groomsmen, Alexandre Dumas, the guest of Count Koucheleff-Besborodka, was one of the witnesses.

Dumas was disappointed when Emperor Alexander II sent a request to Home to present himself at Peterhoff but then consoled himself with the grandiose remark: "There are many crowned heads in Europe but there is only one Alexandre Dumas."

Many of Dumas' fantastic stories about spirits entering into inanimate objects derived their source from Home's mediumship. In Russia, as well as in many other countries, queer rumors circulated as regards Home's mysterious powers. It was said that he had a great number of cats to sleep with him, and by this means his body became so charged with electricity that he could produce raps at pleasure! In Paris the favorite story was that he carried a trained monkey in his pocket to twitch dresses and shake hands during the seances! From chloroforming and magnetizing the sitters, to the magic lantern, and secret police to obtain information for the sittings, every sort of wild explanation was attempted while none of them could match the inspired inanity of an old woman in America: "Lor, sirs, it's easy enough, he only rubs himself all over with a gold pencil first."

From the marriage a son was born to Home. Shortly after Home returned to England. Friends tried to bring about a meeting between him and Michael **Faraday,** the famous scientist, the proponent of the involuntary muscular action theory to explain table movement, whose stubborn attitude to face certain facts was strongly criticized by A. R. Wallace and Professor De Morgan.

As the *Morning Star* reported, Faraday was not satisfied with demanding an open and complete examination, but wished Home to acknowledge that the phenomena, however produced, were ridiculous and contemptible. Thereafter, the idea of giving him a sitting was abandoned.

More satisfaction was derived by Home from his experiences with Dr. Ashburner, one of the Royal physicians and Dr. John **Elliotson,** F.R.S., sometime president of the Royal Medical and Chirurgical Society of London, a character-study of whom, as "Dr. Goodenough," was drawn by Thackeray in *Pendennis* and to whom the work was dedicated. When Dr. Ashburner became a believer in Spiritualism, Dr. Elliotson, who was one of the hardest materialists, became estranged from him and publicly attacked him for his folly. A few years later, however, in Dieppe, Home and Elliotson met. The result was a seance, a strict investigation and the complete conversion of Dr. Elliotson. On his return to London he hastened to seek reconciliation with Dr. Ashburner and publicly declared that he was satisfied of the reality of the phenomena and that they were tending to revolutionize his thoughts and feelings on almost every subject.

Another headstrong dogmatist whose belief was radically changed through Home's phenomena was Robert

Chambers, co-author, with Leitch Ritchie, of the anonymous *Vestiges of the Natural History of Creation* (1844) which startled the public by its outspoken skepticism. Chambers attended the seance of which Robert Bell wrote in the *Cornhill Magazine.* But he was too afraid of his reputation to make a public statement, although he received startling evidences of continued personal identity from his deceased father and daughter. Nevertheless, he undertook to write anonymously the preface to Home's autobiography in 1862. Eight years later, during the Lyon-Home trial, he abandoned his attitude of reserve and gave an affidavit in Home's favor.

For a time during the years of 1859–60, Home gave frequent joint seances with the American medium, J. R. M. **Squire,** one of the editors of the Boston *Banner of Light.* Squire was introduced to London society under Home's auspices and later in the year he was presented at Court.

Home's wife died in July 1862. Six months later, his book *Incidents in My Life* was published. It attracted widespread notice in the Press. The *Morning Herald* remarked: "We must note also the strangeness of the fact that Mr. Home has never been detected, if indeed he is an impostor."

The book sold very well. A second edition was published in a very few months. This, however, did not relieve the pecuniary difficulties Home began to feel. Relatives disputed his right of inheritance to the fortune of his wife and looking about for a means of livelihood he decided to develop his keen artistic perceptions. He hoped to become a sculptor and went to Rome to study.

The Papal Government, however, did not forgive the breaking of his promise to enter a monastery. In January 1864, he was summoned before the chief of the Roman police and ordered, on the ground of "sorcery," to quit Rome within three days. Home claimed the protection of the English Consul and the order of expulsion was suspended on his promising that, during his stay in Rome, he would have no seance and would avoid, as much as possible, all conversations upon Spiritualism.

As, however, the manifestations were beyond his control, he was soon ordered to quit the Papal territory. He left for Naples, where he was received by Prince Humbert, and returned in April to London to demand diplomatic representations on the subject of his expulsion. There was a debate in the House of Commons, but no representation was resolved upon.

Soon after, Home made another trip to America and there became filled with hope that he might achieve success as a reader. He had undoubted talents as a stage reciter. His public rendering of Henry Howard Brownell's poems was very well received, and on returning to Europe he started on this new career with a lecture on Spiritualism in London.

His health, however, would not stand the strain. Friends came to the rescue with the post of residential secretary at the foundation of the **Spiritual Athenaeum,** a kind of headquarters for London Spiritualists.

Then came the disastrous proposition of Mrs. Jane Lyon, a wealthy widow, that she adopt Home, with the intention of securing his financial stability. Mrs. Lyon took a fancy to Home and proposed to adopt him if he added her name to his own, in which case she was prepared to settle a handsome fortune upon him. Home assented and changed his name to Home-Lyon.

Mrs. Lyon transferred £60,000 to Home's account and drew up a will in his favor. Later she repented her action and sued him for the recovery of her money on the basis that she was influenced by spirit communications coming through Home from her late husband. Home, when on the point of leaving for Germany, was arrested. He was liberated the following day on depositing in the Court of Chancery the deeds of gift relating to the £60,000.

In spite of weighty testimony against Mrs. Lyon's credibility, the court put the onus of proof on the defendant and refused to accept it, denouncing the belief in Spiritualism as "mischievous nonsense, well calculated on the one hand to delude the vain, the weak, the foolish, and the superstitious, and on the other to assist the projects of the needy and of the adventurer."

Although in the judgment Vice-Chancellor Gifford branded the plaintiff's "misstatements so perversely untrue that they have embarrassed the Court to a great degree," Home did not appeal, as public sentiment and the Press were against him when the judgment was delivered in May 1868.

While the suit was in progress, an attempt was made against his life. He parried the blow of the assassin's stiletto with his hand which was pierced. The fantastic and quite untrue stories that were then and later on circulated are best illustrated by a reminiscence in the *New York World* on the report of his death, that Mrs. Lyon had a false left hand and Home actually made her believe that by mediumistic power he could create life in the artificial limb.

Of the years 1867–69, we have important records of Home's phenomena in Lord Adare's *Experiences with D. D. Home in Spiritualism* (1870). The book was printed for private circulation and contains the account of eighty seances.

In 1869 an important event took place. The **London Dialectical Society** appointed a committee for the investigation of spiritualistic phenomena. The committee before which Home appeared had some of the most skeptical members of the society on its list, among others Charles **Bradlaugh** and Dr. Edmunds. Four seances were held, but owing to Home's illness the manifestations did not extend beyond slight raps and movements of the table. The committee reported that nothing material had occurred, but added that "during the inquiry Mr. Home afforded every facility for examination."

The most important phase in the history of D. D. Home's mediumship began when Sir William **Crookes** entered the arena. His investigations commenced in May 1871, and were highly acclaimed by the press. His verdict as regards the occurrence of paranormal phenomena was decidedly in the affirmative.

Previous to this investigation, other important events had taken place in the life of D. D. Home. He gained the lawsuit for his deceased wife's fortune, became engaged to an aristocratic lady of wealth and gave several seances in the Winter Palace in St. Petersburg. During a lecture on Spiritualism he referred to some particulars of a seance held in the presence of a distinguished professor of the University of St. Petersburg. At the end of the lecture Prof. Boutlerof rose from his place and announced that he was the investigator to whom Home had referred. This dramatic scene was followed by an investigation of a committee of five from the University. The result was negative, as Home's powers were then, owing to recurring illness, at an ebb.

In 1872, Home published the second series of his *Incidents in My Life,* including the principal affidavits in the Lyon law suit, and in 1873 he brought out his *Lights and Shadows of Spiritualism.* His opinions on fraudulent mediumship and his protest against holding seances in the dark were bitterly resented by other mediums. They said, with some justification, that he had little experience of the powers of others.

Mrs. Jencken, the former Miss Kate Fox (see **Fox Sisters**), was the only medium with whom he was friendly. On a few occasions he sat jointly with William Stainton **Moses.** After the first such sitting on December 22, 1872, Moses wrote in his notebook: "Mr. D. D. Home is a striking-looking man. His head is a good one. He shaves his face with the exception of a moustache, and his hair is bushy and curly. He gives me the impression of an honest, good person whose intellect is not of high order. I had some talk with him, and the impression that I have formed of his intellectual ability is not high. He resolutely refuses to believe in anything that he has not seen for himself. For instance, he refuses to believe in the passage of matter through matter, and when pressed concludes the argument by saying 'I have never seen it.' He has seen the ring test, but oddly enough, does not see how it bears on the question. He accepts the theory of the return in rare instances of the departed, but believes with me that most of the manifestations proceed from a low order of spirits who hover near the earth sphere. He does not believe in Mrs. Guppy's passage through matter, nor in her honesty. He thinks that regular manifestations are not possible. Consequently he disbelieves in public mediums generally. He said he was thankful to know that his mantle had fallen on me, and urged me to prosecute the inquiry and defend the faith. He is a thoroughly good, honest, weak and very vain man, with little intellect, and no ability to argue, or defend his faith."

Whether it was owing to failing health, or the influence of his aristocratic wife, Home slowly broke with nearly all of his friends and spent most of his time on the Continent. In 1876, his death was falsely reported in the French press. In declining health he lived for ten more years and died on June 21, 1886. His grave is at St. Germain, Paris, and his tombstone is inscribed "To another discerning of Spirits." In the Canongate of Edinburgh there is a fountain erected to his memory. It is not known who erected it nor why it was placed opposite the Canongate Parish Church.

Excepting **apports** and **direct voice,** Home demonstrated every known physical phenomenon of Spiritualism. In an undeveloped state he even possessed a latent faculty of direct voice. Faint whisperings were sometimes heard in his seances, but of single words only. He was mostly in a normal state during the phenomena but went into trance during the fire test, **elongations,** and occasionally during **levitations.**

In the spirit teachings delivered through Home's mouth by his control we find manifest absurdities. The control, criticizing the slight knowledge of scientists says that the sun is covered with a beautiful vegetation and full of organic life. When Lord Adare asks: "Is not the sun hot?" he answers "No, the sun is cold; the heat is produced and transmitted to the earth by the rays of light passing through various atmospheres."

Lord Adare, then Earl of Dunraven, gave Home the following character in the 1925 edition of *Experiences in Spiritualism with D. D. Home:* "He had the defects of an emotional character, with vanity highly developed (perhaps wisely to enable him to hold his own against the ridicule and obloquy that was then poured out upon spiritualism and everyone connected with it). He was liable to fits of great depression and to nervous crisis difficult at first to understand; but he was withal of a simple, kindly, humorous, lovable disposition that appealed to me. He never took money for seances, failed as often as not. He was proud of his gift but not happy in it. He could not control it and it placed him sometimes in very unpleasant positions. I think he would have been pleased to have been relieved of it, but I believe he was subject to these manifestations as long as he lived."

Sir William Crookes summed up his opinion as follows: "During the whole of my knowledge of D. D. Home, extending for several years, I never once saw the slightest occurrence that would make me suspicious that he was attempting to play tricks. He was scrupulously sensitive on this point, and never felt hurt at anyone taking precautions against deception. To those who knew him Home was one of the most lovable of men and his perfect genuineness and uprightness were beyond suspicion."

Frank **Podmore,** a most skeptical psychical researcher, said of Home in his *Modern Spiritualism* (2 vols., 1902): "A remarkable testimony to Home's ability whether as medium or simply as conjurer, is the position which he succeeded in maintaining in society at this time [1861] and indeed throughout his later life, and the respectful treatment accorded to him by many leading organs of the Press. No money was ever taken by him as the price of a sitting; and he seemed to have had the entree to some of the most aristocratic circles in Europe. He was welcomed in the houses of our own and of foreign nobility, was a frequent guest at the Tuilleries, and had been received by the King of Prussia and the Czar. So strong, indeed, was his position that he was able to compel an ample apology from a gentleman who had publicly expressed doubts of his mediumistic performance (Capt. Noble in the *Sussex Advertiser* of March 23, 1864) and to publish a violent and spiteful attack upon Browning on the occasion of the publication of Sludge (*Spiritual Magazine,* 1864, p. 315). His expulsion from Rome in 1864 on the charge of sorcery gave to Home for the time an international importance."

He further stated: "Home was never publicly exposed as an impostor; there is no evidence of any weight that he was even privately detected in trickery."

Between the publication of his *Modern Spiritualism* in 1902 and *The Newer Spiritualism* in 1910, Podmore nevertheless succeeded in unearthing a single piece of so-called "evidence" of imposture in a letter from Mr. Merrifield, dated August 1855, and printed in the *Journal* of the Society for Psychical Research (1903), in which the writer claims to have noticed that the medium's body or shoulder sank or rose in concordance with the movements of a spirit hand and to have seen afterwards "the whole connection between the medium's shoulder and arm and the spirit hand dressed out on the end of his own." This slender and highly speculative statement was sufficient for Podmore to proceed to talk of Home as a practiced conjurer who dictated his own conditions in the experiments and produced his feats by trickery. The only admission Podmore made was this final conclusion: "We don't quite see how some of the things were done and we leave the subject with an almost painful sense of bewilderment."

Long after Home's death, various writers have speculated how Home's feats might have been achieved by trickery, and from this have gone on to impute that there must have been trickery. It cannot be emphasized too strongly that Home was never detected in trickery, which would have been inconsistent with his character and outlook, nor is there any sound ground for suspicion in this matter.

Attempts have also been made to discredit Home's unfortunate association with Mrs. Lyon, and to suggest that Home tried to take advantage of a wealthy widow. But the evidence is clear that Home was pressurized by a foolish and unstable woman. Her claim that Home used undue influence "from the spirit world" is worthless in view of the fact that when Mrs. Lyon reneged on her commitment to Home, she had actually transferred allegiance to Miss Nicholls, another medium. A significant point is the claim that Mrs. Lyon had wanted him to be "something nearer than an adopted son" and her change of heart stemmed from Home repulsing her advances.

So far as Browning's extraordinarily spiteful attack in "Mr. Sludge the Medium" is concerned, the veteran psychical researcher E. J. Dingwall made the interesting suggestion in his book *Some Human Oddities* (1947) that Home might have given the impression of latent homosexual tendencies, which might have incensed Browning.

It has often been said of D. D. Home after his death that his phenomena remains a great enigma. What people mean by that is that since it is impossible to prove that it was fraudulent it must be considered as unsolved mystery! A much more sensible and fair-minded conclusion is that it was genuine. As with much Spiritualist phenomena, "spirit messages" were often inaccurate or inconclusive, sometimes astonishingly accurate. But the paranormal phenomena of levitation, elongation, spirit hands, raps, table movements, etc., whatever their psychical origin, are the most credible and sensational of their kind and the experiments of Sir William Crookes with Home must be considered *prima facie* evidence for a genuineness of Home's strange powers.

Recommended reading:

Adare, Viscount. *Experiences in Spiritualism with D. D. Home,* privately printed, 1870 (reissued by Society for Psychical Research, 1924)

Alexander, Patrick P. *Spiritualism; A Narrative with a Discussion,* Edinburgh, Scotland, 1871

Browning, Elizabeth Barrett. (ed. L. Huxley) *Letters to her Sister,* 1846-1859, J. Murray, London, 1929; Dutton, N.Y., 1930

Burton, Jean. *Heyday of a Wizard; Daniel Home the Medium,* George G. Harrap, London, 1948

Chevalier, J. C. *Experiences in Spiritualism or the Adjuration of Spirits, by a late member of Mr. Home's Spiritual Athaeneum,* London, 1867

Cox, Edward W. *Spiritualism Answered by Science,* London, 1871

Crookes, William. *Research in the Phenomena of Spiritualism,* J. Burns, London, 1874; London & Manchester, 1926

Dingwall, E. J. *Some Human Oddities,* Home & Van Thal, London, 1947, University Books, 1962

Jenkins, Elizabeth. *The Shadow and the Light; A Defence of Daniel Dunglas Home, the Medium,* Hamish Hamilton, London, 1982

Gordon, Mrs. M. M. *The Home Life of Sir David Brewster,* Edinburgh, Scotland, 1869, 1870

Home, D. D. *Incidents in My Life,* Longman, Green, London, 1863; University Books, 1972

Medhurst, R. G. (coll.). *Crookes and the Spirit World,* Souvenir Press, London/Taplinger, N.Y., 1972

Molloy, J. Fitzgerald. *The Romance of Royalty,* London, 1904

Porter, Katherine H. *Through a Glass Darkly; Spiritualism in the Browning Circle,* University of Kansas Press, 1958

Rymer, J. Snaith. *Spirit Manifestations* (a lecture), London, 1857

Wilkinson, J. J. Garth. *Evenings with Mr. Home and the Spirits,* London, 1855

Homunculus

An artificial man supposed to have been made by the alchemists, and especially by **Paracelsus.** To manufacture one, he stated that the needful spagyric substances should be taken and shut up in a glass phial, and afterwards be placed to digest in horse-dung for the space of forty days. At the end of this time, there will be something which will begin to move and live in the bottle. This sometimes is a man, but a man who has no body and is transparent.

Nevertheless he exists, and nothing remains but to bring him up—which is not more difficult to do than to make him. It may be acomplished by daily feeding him (over a period of forty weeks, and without extricating him from his dung-hill) with the arcanum of human blood. At the end of this time there should be a veritable living child, having every member as well-proportioned as any infant born of a woman. He will only be much smaller than an ordinary child, and his physical education will require more care and attention.

The term "spagyric" was probably originated by Paracelsus and implied a alchemical process using male semen. (See also **Frankenstein; Golem**)

Honorton, Charles (1946-   )

Parapsychologist; senior research associate at the Division of Parapsychology & Psychophysics, Department of Psychiatry, Maimonides Medical Center, Brooklyn, New York. Born at Deer River, Minnesota, he studied at University of Minnesota, where he was research coordinator for the Minnesota Society for Psychic Research 1965-66. In 1966 he became Research Fellow at the Institute for Parapsychology, FRNM, and joined the research staff at Division of Parapsychology, Maimonides Medical Center in 1967. He has served on the council of the Parapsychological Association, holding office as Secretary, Vice-President and President (1975). He is a member of the Board of Trustees of the American Society for Psychical Research.

His special interests concern the psycho-physiological correlates of psi processes, altered states of consciousness and development of techniques of psi augmentation.

His published papers include: (in *Journal of Parapsychology*) 'Separation of High- and Low-Scoring ESP Subjects Through Hypnotic Preparation' (vol. 28, 1964), 'A Further Separation of High- and Low-Scoring ESP Subjects Through Hypnotic Preparation' (vol. 30, 1966), 'Creativity and Precognition Scoring Level' (vol. 31, 1967); (in *Journal* of American Society for Psychical Research), 'A Combination of Techniques for the Separation of High- and Low-Scoring ESP Subjects: Experiments with Hypnotic and Waking-Imagination Instructions' (vol. 63, 1969), (with J. P. Stump) 'A Preliminary Study of Hypnotically-Induced Clairvoyant Dreams' (vol. 63, 1969), (with S. Krippner) 'Hypnosis and ESP Performance: A Review of the Experimental Literature' (vol. 63, 1969), 'Relationship Between EEG Alpha Activity and ESP in Card-Guessing Performance' (vol. 63, 1969), 'Effects of Feedback on Discrimination Between Correct and Incorrect ESP Responses' (vol. 64, 1970), 'Effects of Feedback on Discrimination Between Correct and Incorrect ESP Responses: A Replication Study' (vol. 65, 1971), (with R. Davidson & P. Bindler) 'Feedback Augmented EEG Alpha, Shifts in Subjective State, and ESP Card-Guessing Performance' (vol. 65, 1971), (with M. Carbone) 'A Preliminary Study of Feedback Augumented EEG Alpha Activity and ESP Card-Guessing Performance' (vol. 65, 1971), 'Significant Factors in Hypnotically-Induced Clairvoyant Dreams' (vol. 66, 1972), (with W. Barsdale) 'PK Performance with Waking Suggestions for Muscle Tension Versus Relaxation' (vol. 66, 1972), 'Reported Frequency of Dream Recall and ESP' (vol. 66, 1972), (with S. Drucker & H. Hermon) 'Shifts in Subject State and ESP Under Conditions of Partial Sensory Deprivation: A Preliminary Study' (vol. 67, 1973), (with S. Harper), 'Psi-Mediated Imagery and Ideation in an Experimental Procedure for Regulating Perceptual Input' (vol. 68, 1974), 'State of Awareness Factors in Psi Activation' (vol. 68, 1974), (with L. Tierney & D. Torres) 'The Role of Mental Imagery in Psi-Mediation' (vol. 68, 1974), (with M. Ramsey & C. Cabibbo) 'Experimenter Effects in Extrasensory Perception' (vol. 69, 1975); (in *Psychophysiology*) (with R. Davidon & P. Bindler) 'Shifts in Subjective States Associated with Feedback-augmented EEG Alpha' (1972, abstract); 'Signal Increasing in ESP' (*Osteopathic Physician*, vol. 41, April 1974). The following papers were published in books: (with S. Krippner) 'Hypnosis and ESP Performance: A Review of the Experimental Literature,' and 'State of Awareness Factors in Psi Activation' (in *Surveys in Parapsychology* by Rhea A. White, 1976), 'Has Science Developed the Competence to Confront Claims of the Paranormal?' (in *Research in Parapsychology 1975*, ed. J. D. Morris, W. G. Roll & R. L. Morris, 1976), 'ESP and Altered States of Consciousness' (in *New Directions in Parapsychology*, ed. J. Beloff, 1975).

Hoodoo Sea

One of many terms for an area of the Western Atlantic between Bermuda and Florida where ships and planes are said to have vanished without trace. (See **Bermuda Triangle**)

Hooper Dr. T. d'Aute (c. 1910)

Extraordinary British medium of the early twentieth century. Although a busy physician in Birmingham, England, he was also credited (in Prof. G. Henslow's *The Proofs of the Truths of Spiritualism* 1919), with a wide range of psychic phenomena, physical and mental.

Hooper's Indian **control**, "Segaske" (Rising Sun), produced scents and **apports;** an Indian fakir demonstrated the fire test, made articles appear and vanish in daylight and spoke in Hindustani; a deceased Chicago preacher, calling himself "Ajax," and many other more or less frequent spirit visitors produced **direct voice** manifestations and **psychic photography.**

In another book published anonymously (*Spirit Psychometry and Trance Communications by Unseen Agencies through a Welsh Woman and Dr. T. d'Aute Hooper*, London, 1914) Prof. Henslow recorded important investigations in **psychometry.**

Hope, William (1863–1933)

Famous spirit photographer, a carpenter of Crewe, England, whose psychic power was discovered accidentally about 1905. He and a friend photographed each other on a Saturday afternoon. The plate which Hope exposed showed an extra figure, a transparent woman, behind whom the brick wall was visible. It was the sister of Hope's comrade, dead for many years.

With the help of Mr. Buxton, the organist at the Spiritualist Hall at Crewe, a circle of six friends was formed to sit for **spirit photography.**

For fear of being accused by devout Catholics of being in league with the devil, the circle destroyed all the original negatives until Archdeacon **Colley** came on the scene. He tested Hope's powers, endorsed them and gave him his first stand camera which Hope refused to give up long after it had become old fashioned, its box battered and its leg broken. The first controversy about Hope and his psychic photographs arose in 1908 in connection with Archdeacon Colley's first sitting. He recognized his mother in the psychic extra. Hope thought it was more like a picture he had copied two years earlier. Mrs. Spencer, of Nantwich, indeed, recognized her grandmother in it, after Hope took it to her. Hope informed Archdeacon Colley of his mistake. Colley said it was madness to think that a man did not know his own mother and advertised in the Leamington paper asking all who remembered his mother to meet him at the rectory. Eighteen persons selected the photograph from several others and testified in writing that the picture was a portrait of the late Mrs. Colley who had never been photographed.

The second case of public controversy arose in 1922 and was, on the surface, damning for Hope. In a report published in the *Journal* of the Society for Psychical Research he was accused of imposture by Harry **Price**. The accusations were later published in a sixpenny pamphlet.

The basis of the revelation was that Price, in a sitting at the British College of Psychic Science, caught Hope in the act of substituting the dark slide, holding the exposed plates, by another; further, that he (Hope) handed him two negatives (one of which contained a psychic extra) that did not bear the secret mark which the Imperial Dry Plate Company specially impressed on the packet of films by X-rays and which were different in color and thickness from the original plates.

Subsequent investigation proved that the counter-accusation raised by Spiritualists of an organized conspiracy against Hope deserved examination. The wrapper of the packet was found, and it bore marks of tampering. Moreover, one of the original marked plates was returned anonymously and undeveloped to the Society for Psychical Research a week after the experiment and three weeks before the revelation. On being developed it showed an image. As the packet of marked plates was lying about for four weeks in the office of S.P.R. it was open to tampering and substitution, it being also likely, in the view of the Hope-apologists, that the abstractor sent back the missing plate out of pure mischief.

Immediately after the revelation, Hope offered new sittings and declared his willingness to submit himself to stringent tests. The offer was refused. Harry Price, however, signed a statement to the effect that the test of February 24, 1922, "does not rule out the possibility that Hope has other than normal means." Indeed, no less authority than Sir William **Crookes** bears out the true mediumship of William Hope in an authorized interview published in the *Christian Commonwealth* on December 4, 1918. On his own marked plates, under his own conditions, Crookes obtained a likeness of his wife different from any he possessed.

On the other hand, Sir Oliver Lodge was emphatic in stating concerning a test of his own with a sealed packet sent to Hope: "I have not the slightest doubt that the envelope including the plates had been opened." Again Sir William **Barrett** claimed to have received with Hope "indubitable evidence of supernormal photography" (*Proceedings* of the S.P.R., vol. 34, 1924).

After the Harry Price exposure, Allerton F. Cushman, of Washington, also bore witness to having obtained psychic extras on his own plates, similarly marked by the Imperial Dry Plate Company, and also on plates purchased previous to the sitting by Dr. Hereward **Carrington.**

The great number of signed testimonies, with a detailed account of the precautions taken, speaks in an impressive manner for the genuine powers of Hope. The charges of fraud advanced by Mr. Fred Barlow and Major W. Rampling Rose (*Proceedings* of the S.P.R., vol. 41, 1933) were largely built on surmise and suspicion, not on facts. Barlow, in 1923, associated himself with Sir Arthur Conan Doyle in the publication of *The Case for Spirit Photography* (1923) a book written in answer to the Hope exposure. At that time he could not "get away from the fact that many of these photographic effects are produced by discarnate intelligences." Two years previously in *Budget No. 58* of the **Society for the Study of Supernormal** Pictures, dated January 20, 1921, Barlow said: "I have got results with Mr. Hope here in my own home under conditions where fraud was absolutely impossible. I have loaded my dark slides in Birmingham and taken them to Crewe with my own camera and apparatus, have carried out the whole of

the operation myself (even to the taking of the photograph) and have secured supernormal results."

In answer to these quotations by Hope apologists Mr. Barlow replied: "A further ten years of careful continuous experimenting has enabled me to say quite definitely that I was mistaken. During the whole of this period no single instance has occurred, in my experience, that would in any way suggest that Hope has genuine gifts." (*Light*, April 14, 1933).

Hope never commercialized his gift. He charged 4s/6d. (about 50 cents) for a dozen prints. This was calculated on the basis of his hourly earnings as a carpenter. He was very devout, almost fanatical and relied blindly on the advice of his spirit guides.

"During all his career as a medium," wrote David **Gow** in *Light*, March 17, 1933, "he had become so accustomed to accusation and abuse that he had grown case-hardened. His attitude seemed to be that, knowing himself to be honest, it did not matter how many people thought otherwise. I found, too, that in his almost cynical indifference, he was given to playing tricks on skeptical inquirers by pretending to cheat and then boasting that he had scored over his enemies in that way. . . . Mr. Hope, in my view, was a genuine medium, but of a type of mentality which might easily lead to the opposite conclusion on the part of an unsympathetic observer."

According to Harry Price, the *Scientific American* inquiry into psychic matters in 1922 was based largely on Price's exposure of Hope.

During his lifetime, Hope obtained more than 2,500 claimed spirit photographs. He died March 7, 1933. (See also **Psychic Photography; Spirit Photography; Thoughtforms**)

Hope Diamond

Famous precious stone with a reputation of bringing disaster to its owners. It is one of the largest colored diamonds known, being a 44.4 carat vivid blue. It is believed to have been cut from an even larger stone of over 67 carats. The name derived from Mr. Henry Thomas Hope, a former owner who bought it for £18,000.

Fact and legend are inextricably tangled in the story of this unlucky diamond. The known history begins in the seventeenth century with the explorer Jean Baptiste Tavernier (1605–1689), who is reputed to have acquired the stone from the Indian mines of Killur, Golconda, circa 1642. He sold the stone to Louis XIV in 1668, and subsequently lost all his money through the speculations of his son.

The diamond was worn by Madame de Montespan at a court ball, and she fell from favor soon afterwards. From this time onwards, the diamond had a sinister reputation. It was worn by Marie Antoinette, who had misfortune in connection with diamonds when the celebrated affair of the Diamond Necklace preceded the French Revolution.

The Princesse de Lamballe, who was lent the diamond, was executed on the guillotine and her head was paraded on a pike under the windows of the prison in which Louis XVI and his family were imprisoned.

The diamond disappeared for thirty years, reappearing in the possession of a Dutch lapidary named Fals. As in the case of Tavernier, a son brought Fals misfortune. He stole the diamond and left his father to die in poverty. The son entrusted the diamond to a Frenchman named Beaulieu who committed suicide after selling it to a London Dealer Danile Eliason, who died under mysterious circumstances. It was then that the diamond was acquired by Henry Thomas Hope, and it remained in the Hope family for seventy years.

Lord Francis Hope, last of the line, married an actress but divorced her and lost all his money. The diamond disappeared for a time, but was later acquired by an American who went bankrupt, a Russian who was stabbed, and a French dealer who committed suicide. A Greek merchant sold it to Abdul Hamid II, sultan of Turkey, who lost his throne. In 1908 the diamond was bought by Habib Bey for £80,000 but auctioned the following year at only a fifth of the price. The diamond traveled to America through a New York jeweller, who was said to have arranged a sale to a man who returned to America on the ill-fated *Titanic.* The next owner was the millionaire McLean. His wife Evalyn published a book *Father Struck It Rich* (1938), in which she described the misfortunes that befell the family, in spite of having the diamond blessed by a priest.

In November 1958, the Hope Diamond was acquired by the Smithsonian Institution, Washington, D.C.

Hopedale Community

Founded by the Rev. Adin **Ballou** (1828–1886) in 1842 near Milford, Massachusetts. From 1850 on, this religio-socialistic community was the scene of various spirit manifestations and made good propaganda service in the spreading of Spiritualism in America. The Rev. Adin Ballou proclaimed his new faith in *Modern Spirit Manifestations,* published in 1852, the year in which he received the first communications from his deceased son.

Hopkins, Matthew (died 1647)

The infamous English "witchfinder" who, with his equally evil accomplices persecuted, imprisoned, tortured or killed hundreds of unfortunate individuals.

William Godwin commented, "Nothing can place the credulity of the English nation on the subject of witchcraft in a more striking point of view, than the history of Matthew Hopkins, who, in a pamphlet published in 1647 in his own vindication, assumes to himself the surname of the Witchfinder. He fell by accident, in his native country of Suffolk, into contact with one or two reputed witches, and, being a man of an observing turn and an ingenious invention, struck out for himself a trade, which brought him such moderate returns as sufficed to maintain him, and at the same time gratified his ambition by making him a terror to many, and the object of admiration and gratitude to more, who felt themselves indebted to him for ridding them of secret and intestine enemies, against whom, as long as they proceeded in ways that left no footsteps behind, they felt they had no possibility of guarding themselves."

After two or three successful experiments, Hopkins engaged in a regular tour of the counties of Norfolk, Suffolk, Essex and Huntingdonshire. One of his confederates was a man named John Stern. They visited every town in their route that invited them, and secured to them the renumeration of twenty shillings and their expenses, leaving what was more than this to the spontaneous gratitude of those who should deem themselves indebted to the exertions of Hopkins and his gang.

By this expedient they secured to themselves a favorable reception and a set of credulous persons who would listen to their dictates as so many oracles. They were able to play the game into one another's hands, and were sufficiently strong to overawe all timid and irresolute opposition. In every town to which they came, they inquired for reputed witches, and having taken them into custody, were secured for the most part of a certain number of zealous abettors, and took care that they should have a clear stage for their experiments.

They overawed their helpless victims with a certain air of authority, as if they had received a commission from heaven for the discovery of misdeeds. They assailed the poor creatures with a multitude of questions constructed in the most artful manner. They stripped them naked, in search for the "devil's marks" in different parts of their bodies, which they ascertained by running pins to the head into those parts, that, if they were genuine marks, would prove themselves such by their insensibility.

They swam their victims in rivers and ponds, it being accepted as an undoubted fact that, if the persons accused were true witches, the water (which was the symbol of admission into the Christian Church) would not receive them. If the persons examined continued obstinate, they seated them in constrained and uneasy attitudes, occasionally binding them with cords, and compelling them to remain so without food or sleep for twenty-four hours. They walked them up and down the room, two taking them under each arm, till they dropped down with fatigue. They carefully swept the room in which the experiment was made so that they might keep away spiders and flies, which were supposed to be devils or their imps in disguise.

The most plentiful inquisition of Hopkins and his confederates was in the years 1644, 1645, and 1646. At length there were so many persons committed to prison upon suspicion of witchcraft that the government was compelled to take in hand the affair. The rural magistrates before whom Hopkins and his confederates brought their victims were obliged, willingly or unwillingly, to commit them for trial.

A commission was granted to the Earl of Warwick and others to hold a session of jail-delivery against them for Essex at Chelmsford. Lord Warwick was at this time the most popular nobleman in England. He was appointed by the Parliament lord high admiral during the civil war. He was much courted by the independent clergy, was shrewd, penetrating and active, and exhibited a singular mixture of pious demeanor with a vein of facetiousness and jocularity. With him was sent Dr. Calamy, the most eminent divine of the period of the Commonwealth, to see (according to Richard Baxter) that no fraud was committed or wrong done to the parties accused.

It may well be doubted, however, whether the presence of this clergyman did not operate unfavorably to the persons suspected. He preached before the judges. It may readily be believed, considering the temper of the times, that he insisted much upon the horrible nature of the sin of witchcraft, which could expect no pardon, either in the world or the world to come.

He sat on the bench with the judges and participated in their deliberations. In the result of this inquisition, sixteen persons were hanged at Yarmouth in Norfolk, fifteen at Chelmsford, and sixty at various places in the county of Suffolk. Bulstrode Whitelocke in his *Memorials of English Affairs,* under the date of 1649, spoke of many witches being apprehended about Newcastle, upon the information of a person whom he calls "the Witch-finder," who, as his experiments were nearly the same, though he is not named, we may reasonably suppose to be Hopkins, and in the following year about Boston in Lincolnshire. In 1652 and 1653 the same author spoke of women in Scotland who were put to incredible torture to extort from them a confession of what their adversaries imputed to them.

The fate of Hopkins was such as might be expected in similar cases. The multitude are at first impressed with horror at the monstrous charges that are advanced. They are seized, as by contagion, with terror at the mischiefs which seem to impend over them and from which no innocence and no precaution appear to afford them sufficient protection. They hasten, as with an unanimous effort, to avenge themselves upon these apparently malignant enemies, whom God and man alike combine to expel from society.

But, after a time, they begin to reflect and to apprehend that they have acted with too much precipitation, that they have been led on with uncertain appearances. They see one victim led to the gallows after another, without stint or limitation. They see one dying with the most solemn asseverations of innocence and another confessing apparently she knows not what, put into her mouth by her relentless persecutors. They see these victims old, crazy and impotent, harrassed beyond endurance by the ingenious cruelties that are practiced against him. They were first urged on by implacable hostility and fury, to be satisfied with nothing but blood. But humanity and remorse also have their turn. Dissatisfied with themselves, they are glad to point their resentment against another.

The man that at first they hailed as a public benefactor, they presently come to regard with jealous eyes, and begin to consider as a cunning imposter, dealing in cool blood with the lives of his fellow creatures for personal gain, and, still more horrible, for the lure of a perishable and short-lived fame.

The multitude, it is said, after a few seasons, rose upon Hopkins and resolved to subject him to one of his own criteria. They dragged him to a pond and threw him into the water for a witch. It seems he floated on the surface, as a witch ought to do. They then pursued him with hootings and revilings, and drove him for ever into that obscurity and ignominy which he had amply merited.

Whether this story be true or not, Hopkins retired to Manningtree, Essex, in 1646 and died of tuberculosis within a year. (See also **Witchcraft**)

Horbehutet

The ancient Egyptian winged disk, symbol of a solar deity who accompanied the sun-god Ra on his daily journey across Egypt, for the purpose of warding off evil from him. His symbol was placed over the gates and doors of temples to protect them from malign influences.

Hörbiger, Hans (1860–1931)

German engineer who developed an eccentric cosmology of "Cosmic Ice." Hörbiger's theories were taken up by Nazi occultists and sponsored by Heinrich Himmler.

According to Hörbiger, space is filled with cosmic ice, a basic material from which stellar systems are generated when a large block of cosmic ice collides with a hot star. Stellar systems are governed by a law of spiral motion and propelled towards a central sun and smaller planets, eventually being captured by larger ones, becoming moons. Earth is supposed to have had several previous moons which were drawn to it. These earlier moons caused geological upheavels when they spiralled to our earth, and myths and legends are said to preserve race memories of such cataclysms. When a former moon circled the earth with ever-increasing rapidity during such a capture, its appearance generated legends of the Judaeo-Christian Devil, as well as dragons and other monsters.

Hörbiger's complex theories included occult concepts of Platonic World Soul. With Phillipp Fauth, he published *Glazialcosmogonie* in 1912. It provoked enraged opposition from German astronomers, but Nazi sympathizers associated it with ideas of lost **Atlantis** and a master Aryan race. A Hörbiger cult called WEL (Welt Eis Lehre) sprang up with millions of supporters. Hörbiger himself was intolerant of all opposition to his theories, and once wrote to rocket expert Willy Ley: ". . . either you believe in me and learn, or you must be treated as an enemy."

After the death of Hörbiger, Hans Schindler Bellamy, a British mythologist, continued the propaganda for WEL in his book *Moons, Myths and Man* (1936) and in further books on the subject. During the height of the Nazi rule in Europe, the teachings of Hörbiger and Bellamy were combined with paranoid propaganda and anti-Semitism.

Horos, Theodore (c. 1866–   ?) & Laura (1849–c. 1906)

A notorious man-and-wife team of occult swindlers who were sentenced for fraud in Britain December 20, 1901.

Mrs. Horos aka Ellora aka Madame Helena aka Swami Viva Ananda aka Mrs. Diss Debar aka Angel Anna aka Claudia D'Arvie aka Editha Gilbert Montez aka Blanche Solomons appears to have been born in Harrodsburg, Kentucky, February 9, 1849, daughter of "Professor John C. F. R. Salomon."

In 1870 under the name Editha Gilbert Montez, she collected money by representing herself as the daughter of famous adventuress Lola Montez. In the 1880s she became a fradulent Spiritualist medium, in partnership with "General" Joseph H. Diss Debar. In 1888 she was sentenced to six months imprisonment for fraud. In 1898 she married Frank Dutton Jackson in New Orleans, and the couple engaged in a fake mediumship partnership in Bucktown, Jefferson Parish, and after complaints were arrested and served a short prison sentence. At that time there were rumors of unsavory sexual practices in their "Order of the Crystal Star."

The Jacksons reappeared in Europe in 1899 under the name "Mr. & Mrs. Horos," and in Paris became acquainted with S. L. Macgregor **Mathers,** from whom they stole rituals of the Hermetic Order of the **Golden Dawn.** At that time they variously represented themselves as being principals of "Koreshan Unity" and the "Theocratic Unity." They removed to South Africa in 1890, where they opened a "College of Occult Science" in Cape Town. Mrs. Horos lectured and gave clairvoyant readings under the names "Madame Helena" and "Swami Viva Ananda," assisted by Mr. Theodore Horos. The Swami issued certificates of occult proficiency to students, based on the stolen teachings of the Golden Dawn. In October 1900 they set up headquarters in Britain. Their "College of Life and Occult Sciences" was established in London, teaching mental and magnetic therapeutics, psychology, clairvoyance, mediumship, materialization, thaumaturgic power and Divine Healing. Under this cover they operated an esoteric order using the Golden Dawn rituals, with secret mysteries of their own in which gullible young women were raped as well as swindled. Theodore and Laura Horos were arrested for fraud in September 1901. Jackson was sentenced to fifteen years imprisonment and his wife seven years.

For a detailed study of this famous couple, see E. J. Dingwall, *Some Human Oddities* (London, 1947; University Books, 1962).

Horoscope

Astrological journal published since 1935 by Dell Publishing Co., Inc., 1 Dag Hammarskjold Plaza, 245 East 47 Street, New York, N.Y. 10017.

Horoscope Guide

Monthly popular-type magazine featuring a year's forecast for each sign of the month. Address: J.B.H. Publishing Company, 350 Madison Avenue, Cresskill, New Jersey 07626.

Horse Shoes

Horse shoes were nailed on the thresholds in the Middle Ages to keep out witches.

The magical significance of the horse shoe is probably of more ancient origin, being related to the two-horn shape which was believed to repel the **evil eye** in more ancient civilizations. This shape may have derived from a belief in animal horns as a symbol of good fortune, and the shape of the crescent moon.

Iron as a metal is also traditionally believed to repel witches, fairies and evil spirits and the horse shoe combined both the shape and the metal which would ensure good fortune and avert evil.

For protection, the horse shoe charm was placed outside buildings with the prongs pointing upwards, so that the luck would not "run out," but in many buildings the horse shoe was used indoors with the prongs pointing down, so that good luck would be diffused inside the house.

Horse-Whispering

A secret method by which certain persons are supposed to be able to acquire power over refractory horses. As is well known to students of gypsy lore, gypsies are reputed to be in possession of some secret by which they are enabled to render vicious horses entirely tame.

Opinions are divided as to whether this secret consists in the application of a certain odor or balm to the horse's muzzle, or whispering into its ear a spell or incantation. It has been claimed, that the gypsy horse-charmer applies aniseed to the nose of the animal. But besides the gypsies, horse-whispering has been in vogue amongst many other peoples. The antiquary William Camden in his recital of Irish superstitions stated, "It is by no means allowable to praise a horse or any other animal unless you say 'God save him.' If any mischance befalls a horse in three days after, they find out the person who commended him, that he may whisper the Lord's Prayer in his right ear."

It was said by Con Sullivan, a famous Irish horse-whisperer of the eighteenth century, that it was out of the power of the professors of the art to explain the source of their influence, the same thing being affirmed by those who practiced it in South America, where a couple of men would tame half a dozen wild horses in three days. The same art was widely practiced in Hungary and Bohemia, and it was from a Bohemian gypsy that a family in the county of Cork claimed to hold a secret by which the wildest or most vicious horse could be tamed. For generations this secret was regularly transmitted as a parting legacy at the time of death from the father to the eldest son.

Throughout the North of Scotland there are disseminated members of a secret society for the breaking in of refractory horses, which is believed to be called the Horseman's Society, and which purports to be able to trace its origin away back into the dark ages. Only those who gain their livelihood by the care and management of horses are admitted and the more affluent and better educated are jealously excluded.

Many farmers entertain a prejudice against the members of the society, but they are forced to admit that they are always very capable in the management of their teams and can perform services which would otherwise require the calling in of a veterinary surgeon. They are usually skilled in the knowledge of herbs and simples, and a great deal of the marvelous is imputed to them.

In fact it is stated that they hold their meetings at night in the clear moonlight, going through various equestrian performances with horses borrowed for the occasion from their masters' stables.

There is further said to be an inner circle in the society, where the black art and all the spells and charms of **witchcraft** are the objects of study, and the members of which can smite the horses and cattle with mysterious sickness, and even cast a glamor over human beings. Indeed one local writer stated that the inner circle of the Horsemen employed hypnotic influence both on men and animals, as it is said certain North-American Indians, and some of the jungle tribes of Hindustan, do.

The famous Con Sullivan has already been alluded to, and his achievements were really wonderful. On one occasion his services were requisitioned by Colonel Westenra (afterwards Earl of Rosmore) who possessed a racehorse called "Rainbow," of the most savage description, which would attack any jockey courageous enough to mount him by seizing him by the leg with his teeth, and dragging him from the saddle.

A friend of the Colonel's told him that he knew a person who could cure Rainbow, and a wager of £1,000 was laid on the matter. Con Sullivan, who was known throughout the countryside as "The Whisperer," was sent for and after being shut up alone with the animal for a quarter of an hour, he gave the signal for the admission of those who had been waiting on the result.

When they entered, they found the horse extended on his back, playing like a kitten with Sullivan, who was quietly sitting by him, but both horse and operator appeared exhausted, and the latter had to be revived with brandy. The horse was perfectly tame and gentle from that day.

Another savage steed named "King Pippin" took an entire night to cure, but in the morning he was seen following Sullivan like a dog, lying down at the word of command, and permitting any person to put his hand into his mouth. Shortly afterwards he won a race at the Curragh. Sullivan was described by one who knew him well as an ignorant rustic of the lower class, but there can be no question as to his extraordinary powers.

The statement of Sullivan that the successful whisperer is not acquainted with the secret of his own power may well be true. "The reason," stated Elihu Rich (in E. Smedley's *The Occult Sciences*, 1855) "is obvious. A force proceeding immediately from the will or the instinctive life would be impaired by reflection in the understanding and broken up or at least diminished by one half. The violent trembling of the animal under this operation is like the creaking and shivering of the tables before they begin to 'tip,' and indicates a moral or nervous force acting physically, by projection perhaps from the spirit of the operator. None of these cases are, after all, more wonderful than the movement of our own limbs and bodies by mental force, for how does it move them with such ease? And may not the same power that places its strong but invisible little fingers on every point of our muscular frames, stretch its myriad arms a little further into the sphere around us, and operate by the same laws, and with as much ease, on the stalwart frame of a horse, or even a clothes horse?"

Horseman's Word

A persistent theme in British folklore is the magic word or phrase which can tame an unruly horse. Gypsies were reputed to have this secret, and it was also known to members of a mysterious group of individuals known as the Brotherhood of the Horseman's Word.

In other parts of Britain, horse-handlers with the secret were sometimes known as "Whisperers." It has been suggested that the secret was in substances which had an attractive smell for the horse, and that the whispering was simply a blowing in the ear of the animal. (See also **Horse-Whispering**)

Houdini, Harry (1874–1926)

Born Ehrich Weiss, he later changed his name to "Houdini" and became the most sensational escapologist of modern history. He was born March 24, 1874, in Budapest, Hungary, and brought to Appleton, Wisconsin, as a child although he later claimed to have been born on April 6, 1874. His mother had always celebrated this date, possibly to give the child the security of American citizenship. Weiss began his professional life as a trapeze performer. He went on to become the foremost conjuring magician and escapologist.

Weiss derived the name "Houdini" from Jean Eugene Robert Houdin (1805–1871), a famous French illusionist who took pride in exposing "fake" performers of religious marvels. Houdini was similarly very proud of his amazing feats and spent many years exposing so-called Spiritualist frauds. Although he undoubtedly unmasked some tricksters, his enthusiasm became almost a mania. He was a member of the committee appointed by the *Scientific American* to investigate the mediumship phenomena of "Margery" (Mrs. M. **Crandon**) in 1924. In his anxiety to prove fraud, Houdini himself was guilty of fraudulently tampering with the experiments.

Ironically enough, Sir Arthur Conan **Doyle,** famous creator of Sherlock Holmes and an enthusiastic Spiritualist, claimed that some of Houdini's own incredible feats must be due to psychic or supernatural powers. This infuriated Houdini, and at one time caused a break in his long-standing friendship with Doyle.

Houdini's uneasy feud with Spiritualism persisted after his death, when various mediums claimed to convey messages from him lamenting his arrogant denunciation of Spiritualism. But one message was quite different.

Amongst the challenges which Houdini constantly issued to mediums was one which could operate only after his death. He stated that if spirit survival was possible, he would communicate with his wife Bess in a secret two-word code message known to no one else. A reward of $10,000 was offered for successfully communicating this code message.

Three years after Houdini's death, the medium Arthur **Ford** gave Bess Houdini a two-word message "Rosabelle believe" in the special code used by the Houdinis in an early mind-reading act. "Rosabelle" had been a pet name used by Houdini for his wife. Mrs. Houdini signed a statement that Ford was correct. This was witnessed by a U.P. reporter and an associate editor of the *Scientific American,* but forty-eight hours later the New York *Graphic* stated that the story was untrue, that a reporter had perpetrated a hoax, possibly with the connivance of Ford and Mrs. Houdini. The original scoop story evaporated in a confusion of charges, counter-charges and denials, and Mrs. Houdini did not refer to the matter again in public. But the evidence favors the original claim that Arthur Ford really did break the Houdini code by a mediumistic message from the beyond. (See also **Magicians**)

Houdini's books included: *The Right Way to Do Wrong* (1906), *The Unmasking of Robert Houdin* (1908), *A Magician Among the Spirits* (1924). A book about his exploits *The Secrets of Houdini* by magician J. C. Cannell (London, 1931) was reissued by Gale Research Co., 1976.

Houghton, Michael (died c. 1956)

British poet and occultist, associate of Aleister **Crowley.** Under the pseudonym "Michael Juste," Houghton published some volumes of poetry, including *Escape, and other verse* (Leeds, 1924), *Shoot—and be Damned* (London, 1935), *Many Brightnesses, and other verse* (London, 1954). He also published *The White Brother* (London, 1927), described as an occult biography.

Houghton was proprietor of the famous **Atlantis Book Shop** in London, specializing in occultism, and also edited the journal *Occult Observer* (1949–50) with contributions from leading occultists of the period.

Houghton, Miss Georgina (died 1887)

Nineteenth-century English private medium, author of *Evenings at Home in Spiritual Seance* (1882) and of *Chronicles of the Photographs of Spiritual Beings and Phenomena invisible to the Material Eye* (1882). She never sat for research, knew nothing of test conditions and her mediumship, which developed after a visit to Mrs. Mary **Marshall,** appears to have consisted of **automatic drawing,** other acts of automatism, as house haunting under spirit guidance, minor telekinetic phenomena, unconfirmed cases of **levitation** or rather floating above the ground while apparently walking like anyone else, **apports** and vision of colored **auras** about the heads of others.

She claimed a band of seventy archangels as her guardian spirits and implicitly believed and obeyed every subconscious impulse, even to the extent of leaving it to the spirit to choose the wallpapers and carpets in her house.

The spirit photographs in her book *Chronicles of the Photographs of Spiritual Beings* were taken at the studio of Frederick **Hudson,** the first English spirit photographer, who was exposed as a fraud. The pictures themselves, which include spirit forms of Joan of Arc, the wife of Manoah (mother of Samson) and St. John the Evangelist are for the most part, obvious fakes, but have a certain nineteenth-century period charm. (See also **Psychic Photography; Spirit Photography**)

House of Wisdom

The *tarik* or "path" of the *House of Wisdom* was founded by Moslem mystics at Cairo in the ninth century, and had seven initiatory degrees. The original founder appears to have been Abdallah, a Persian, who, believing in the Gnostic doctrine of the Aeons or Sephiroths, applied the system to the successors of Mohammed, stating that Ismael was the founder of his *tarik* and one of his descendants as the seventh Imaum.

Abdallah established an active system of propaganda and sent missionaries far and wide. He was succeeded in his office as chief of the society by his son and grandson. After the institution had been in existence for some time it was transferred to Cairo, and assemblies were held twice a week, when all the members appeared clothed in white. They were gradually advanced through the seven degrees of which the *tarik* consisted, and over which a *Dai-al-doat* or "Missionary of missionaries" presided. A later chief, Hakem-bi-emir-Illah, increased the degrees to nine, and in 1004 erected a stately home for the society, which he elaborately furnished with mathematical instruments.

As the institution did not meet with the approval of the authorities, it was destroyed in 1123 by the then Grand Vizier, but meetings continued elsewhere. The officers of the society were:—*Sheik, Dai-el-keber,* or Deputy, *Dai,* or Master, *Refik,* or Fellow, *Fedavie,* or Agent, *Lassik,* or Aspirant, *Muemini,* or Believer. The teaching was to the effect that there had been seven holy Imaums, that God had sent seven Lawgivers, who had each seven helpers, who in turn had each twelve apostles. (See also **Assassins**)

Houston, Jean

Professor of psychology, formerly an actress and N.Y.C. Drama Critics award-winning playwright. She has taught at Columbia University and the New York School of Social Research. With her husband Robert E. L. **Masters** she collaborated on the book *The Varieties of Psychedelic Experience* (1966). Together the couple organized the **Foundation for Mind Research** in New York in 1964, to conduct experiments in the borderland between mental and psychical experiences.

Other books by Masters & Johnson include: *Mind Games; The Guide to Inner Space* (1972), *Listening to the Body* (1978).

Howe, Ellic (1910–   )

British authority on printing history, who has also written on occult subjects. Born September 20, 1910, in London, England; educated Hertford College, Oxford, 1929–31. In 1947 he married Elsa Antweiler. He was a director of printing companies from 1947–62, served with the British Army 1939–41 and was seconded to the Foreign Office 1941–45. He is a member of the Worshipful Company of Stationers, London (liveryman), and was president of the Double Crown Club 1967–68.

In addition to his comprehensive studies of the history of British printing, he has published: *Urania's Children: The Strange World of the Astrologers* (London, 1967; U.S. title *Astrology: a recent history including the untold story of its role in World War II,* Walker, 1968), *The Magicians of the Golden Dawn* (London, 1972). The latter work is a comprehensive study of the history and membership of this famous secret order. (See also **Golden Dawn**)

Howitt, William (1792–1879)

Author, pioneer British Spiritualist was born December 18, 1792, at Heanor, Derbyshire, son of a Quaker. The boy published his first poem at the age of 13. He studied chemistry and natural philosophy of Tamworth and read widely. He married Mary Botham in 1821 and they co-authored a number of works. Howitt traveled through England and Germany, extending his knowledge of foreign languages.

In 1852 he went to Australia, and it was there that he first heard of the outbreak of American Spiritualism, while digging for gold in the Australian bush. Into his novel, *Tallengetta or the Squatters' Home* which he conceived there, he weaved many incidents entirely of Spiritualist and supernatural character. Before the novel was published, in 1857, two and a half years after his return to England, he had some interesting experiences.

His wife attended a seance in April 1856 in the home of Mrs. de Morgan (see Augustus **de Morgan**) and within a month mediumship developed in the Howitt family. It started with **automatic writing and drawing,** and continued with **clairvoyance** and spirit vision. There may have been some inherited tendency, as William Howitt's mother was a seeress and he himself was a sleepwalker in early youth.

The phenomena started with his son and daughter. In January 1858, he himself gained the power to write and draw automatically. It suddenly commenced after a visit to Mr. and Mrs. Wilkinson. Mrs. Wilkinson was a good drawing medium.

The first public debut of William Howitt as a champion of Spiritualism occurred with a lively exchange of letters in *The Critic* regarding a haunted house and ghosts in general. Charles **Dickens** desired to visit some well-known haunted houses and asked for information. Howitt told him of **Willington Mill** which he had visited and of a house at Cheshunt, near London, of which he had heard. This house was mentioned in Mrs. Catharine Crowe's *Night Side of Nature* (2 vols., 1848 etc.). The account was furnished, anonymously, by Robert **Chambers.** But the house was partly pulled down and Dickens could not find it. As a consequence its existence and that of ghosts in general were questioned.

When William Wilkinson's *Spiritual Magazine* was started in 1860, Howitt became a regular contributor and in the thirteen years of its existence wrote more than a hundred articles on the supernatural in the life of men and nations, on the religious and philosophical aspects of the manifestations and of personal experiences. His most important work was a book of two volumes, *The History of the Supernatural in all ages and nations and in all churches, Christian and Pagan, demonstrating a Universal Faith,* published in 1863. His other writings included: *Popular History of Priestcraft in all Ages and Nations* (1833), *Homes and Haunts of the Most Eminent British Poets* (1847), (ed.) *Howitt's Journal of Literature and Popular Progress* (3 vols., 1847-49) and a translation of J. Ennemoser, *The History of the Supernatural* (2 vols., 1854; reissued University Books, 1970).

Howitt died in Rome March 3, 1879. His biography was written by his daughter, Mrs. Howitt-Watts, and published under the title: *Pioneers of the Spiritual Reform* (1883).

Howling of Dogs

It was a common superstition in Europe and Asia that the howling of dogs at night presaged death to someone in the vicinity.

Huaca

Peruvian oracle. (See **Divination**)

Hubbard, L(afayette) Ron(ald) (1911–   )

Brilliant science-fiction writer who developed the cults of **Dianetics** and **Scientology.** To his millions of followers, "Ron" has become a legendary figure and many biographical accounts of his life are as fictional as his own stories.

The basic facts appear to be as follows. He was born in Tilden, Nebraska, March 13, 1911. In the early 1930s he enrolled in the Engineering School of the George Washington University, Washington, D.C., but does not appear to have graduated. During World War II he served in the U.S. Navy with the rank of lieutenant. He also worked briefly in naval intelligence. He was married three times. His first wife was Margaret Louise Grubb, by whom he had two children. Hubbard traveled widely and spent much time away from home. Eventually he was divorced and some time after 1947 married Sarah Northrup by whom he had a daughter. This marriage was also unsuccessful and his second wife sued for divorce in May 1951. In the same year Hubbard married Mary Sue Whipp, by whom he had four children.

As a writer, Hubbard had a prodigious output and wrote at amazing speed. In the 1930s he turned out Westerns for pulp magazines under the pseudonym "Winchester Remington Colt." His early science-fiction pulp stories were under the pseudonyms "Kurt von Rachen" and "René Lafayette." He wrote for Columbia Pictures in Hollywood in 1935.

The first draft of his scheme of Dianetics was published in *Astounding Science Fiction* (May 1950) with the announcement of his book *Dianetics: the Modern Science of Mental Health* (Hermitage). Both the article and the book created a sensation and launched a vast new industry of do-it-yourself psychotherapy, culminating in the more occult development of Scientology, now organized as a new religion.

According to some writers, Hubbard was at one time associated with occultism through his friendship with Cal. Tech. rocket propulsion chemist Jack Parsons. Parsons became head of the California Lodge of Aleister **Crowley's** O.T.O. and in 1946 is said to have performed a magical ritual with Hubbard. This was to secure an incarnation of the goddess Babalon by occult influences on an unborn human embryo. However, the affair ended in some confusion, and Hubbard's version is that he was courageously exposing a black magic group.

In recent years, Hubbard's empire of Scientology has been riven by internal disputes and defections, and externally by civil actions on the part of former members who allege harassment or swindling; by IRS tax-court claims, and by judgment against leading officials of the Scientology organization for theft and conspiracy against the government, in Watergate style of operations. In January 1983, Hubbard's third wife Mary Sue was sentenced to four years in prison by a federal judge in Washington. There are power struggles within Scientology.

In this confused scene, Hubbard himself has remained a recluse as legendary as Howard Hughes and many people believe that he may even be dead.

For critical views of Hubbard and his development of Dianetics and Scientology, see *Fads & Fallacies in the Name of Science* by Martin Gardner (Dover, 1957) and *Cults of Unreason* by Dr. Christopher Evans (Farrar, Straus & Giroux, 1973; Dell paperback, 1975). The article 'Scientology, Anatomy of a Frightening Cult' by Eugene H. Methvin (*Reader's Digest*, May 1980) and a followup article Sept. 1981, 'Mystery of the Vanished Ruler' (*Time* magazine, Jan. 31, 1983). For an official Scientology view see their own literature available from The Church of Scientology, Los Angeles, California, and branches throughout the world, and an interview with Hubbard first published in *Freedom!*, Hollywood (May-June 1975), since included in *Biography News* (Gale Research, July/August 1975).

Huby, Pamela M(argaret) Clark (1922–   )

British university lecturer in philosophy who experimented in parapsychology. Born April 21, 1922, at London, England, she studied at Oxford University (B.A. 1944, M.A. 1947). In 1956 she married Dr. Ronald Huby. From 1945-47 Mrs. Huby was a research student at Oxford University, and from 1947-49 lecturer in philosophy at St. Anne's Society, Oxford; from 1949 onwards lecturer in philosophy at Liverpool University. She is a member of Mind Association, Hellenic Society, Classical Association, Parapsychological Association, Society for Psychical Research, London.

She conducted experiments in group telepathy and clairvoyance (some in collaboration with Dr. C. W. M. **Wilson**). Her papers in *Journal* of the Society for Psychical Research include: 'Effects of Centrally Acting Drugs on ESP Ability' (vol. 41, p. 60-67), 'Case of Xenoglossy' (vol. 44, p. 48-49), 'New Evidence About "Rose Morton"' (vol. 45, p. 391-92).

Hudson, Frederick A. (c. 1872)

The first British exponent of **spirit photography**. In March 1872, Mr. and Mrs **Guppy**, who made several unsuccessful experiments to obtain psychic photographs in their own home, went on an impulse to Hudson's studio which was nearby. A white patch, resembling the outline of a draped figure, was obtained behind Mr. Guppy's portrait. The experiment was repeated with increasing success.

After report of these pictures spread, the accusation of imposture soon arose but, according to Dr. Alfred Russel **Wallace,** even those who were most emphatic about fraud believed that a large number of genuine pictures were taken.

William **Howitt** obtained the likeness of two deceased sons, of the very existence of one of whom even the friend who accompanied him was ignorant. Dr. Thompson, of Clifton, obtained the extra of a lady whom his uncle in Scotland identified as the likeness of Dr. Thompson's mother. She died in childbirth and no picture of her remained. Dr. Alfred Russel **Wallace** obtained two different portraits of his mother, unlike any photograph taken during her life, representing two different periods in the life of the deceased.

The editor of the *British Journal of Photography* investigated, using his own collodion and new plates. He found abnormal appearances on the pictures. Nevertheless, it appears to be a fact that, from time to time, Hudson was caught cheating. Once he was exposed by the Rev. Stainton **Moses** for whom he produced many spirit photographs that agreed with his clairvoyant visions. To play the part of the ghost, Hudson occasionally dressed up or made double exposure. The duplication of the pattern of the carpet and other parts of the background showing through the legs of the sitter and of the ghost was ingeniously explained by refraction, the spirits being quoted as saying that the spirit aura differs in density and refracting power from the ordinary terrestrial atmosphere. Such explanations, coupled with the belief that Hudson produced many genuine spirit photographs, helped to reestablish his shaken credit.

However, according to psychical researcher Harry **Price**, in his book *Confessions of a Ghost-Hunter* (1936, reprinted Causeway Books, 1974), Hudson used an ingenious camera manufactured by Howell, a famous London maker of conjuring apparatus. This camera was of the old square wooden type and contained a light metal frame which in its normal position rested on the bottom of the smaller of two telescopic portions of which the camera was constructed. This frame held a waxed paper positive of the desired ghostly "extra." When the dark-slide was pushed into the camera, it actuated a lever raising the frame to a vertical position in contact with the photographic plate. When the picture was taken, the "extra" image was also printed on the plate. When the plate was drawn out of the camera, the frame automatically fell back to its hidden position.

Fifty-four "spirit photographs" taken in this way are reproduced in the book *Chronicles of Spirit Photography* by Georgina **Houghton** (1882). (See also **Psychic Photography; Spirit Photography**)

Hudson, Thomson Jay (1834–1903)

American author and lecturer who attained prominence by an ingenious anti-Spiritualist theory expounded in his books. He was born February 22, 1834, in Windham, Ohio. He attended public schools in Windham and later studied law. He was admitted to the bar at Cleveland, Ohio, in 1857 and practiced for a time in Michigan, before entering upon a journalistic career, culminating in editorship of the Detroit *Evening News*.

In 1880, he left journalism to enter the U.S. Patent Office, becoming principal examiner. In 1893, he resigned and devoted himself, to the study of experimental psychology and was awarded an honorary LL.D. by St. Johns College, Annapolis, in 1896.

The essence of his special theory of psychic phenomena was that man has within him two distinct minds: the objective, with which he carries on his practical daily life, and the subjective, which is dormant but is infallible as a record, registering every single impression of life. The objective mind is capable of both inductive and deductive reasoning, the subjective mind of deductive only.

The change of death is survival in another state of consciousness with which, however, communication is impossible. Any attempt is simply playing the fool with the subjective mind which presents reflections of the experimenter's complete life record and lures him on to believe that he is communicating with his departed friends.

The Law of Psychic Phenomena (1893) in which this theory was expounded, became very popular and made a deep impression. It was followed by *Scientific Demonstration of the Future Life* (1896), *Divine Pedigree of Man* (1900), *Law of Mental Medicine* (1903), and *Evolution of the Soul and other Essays* (1904).

Hudson died in Detroit, Michigan, May 26, 1903. Admiral Usborne Moore wrote in *Glimpses of the Next State* (1911) that through Mrs. Georgie, a young dramatist of Rochester, who wrote automatically in mirror writing, he received manifestations of Hudson's spirit. Evidential details of his life, unknown to both of them, were given and he communicated through different mediums in Detroit and Chicago, carrying as a test messages of the Admiral from one medium to another and describing his doings to them.

Huebner, Louise

Designated as "The Official Witch of Los Angeles, California" July 21, 1968. Mrs. Huebner is the wife of a Hollywood set designer and has three children. An attractive dark-haired, dark-eyed beauty, she has practiced witchcraft for a number of years and claims a six generation witch pedigree on her grandmother's side. She has given astrological and psychic readings in Los Angeles supermarkets and was featured in radio and television programs, as well as contributing regular newspaper columns on occult topics.

Her title as an official witch started as a promotional gimmick for the Folk Day at Hollywood Bowl in 1968 by Los Angeles supervisor Eugene Debs, and the County government attempted to withdraw the designation after Mrs. Huebner's use of the title to promote her own writings on witchcraft. However, she threatened to withdraw her spell for sexual vitality for the area, and after press conferences which made front-page news, the County capitulated. It seems possible that Mrs. Huebner's spells for sexual vitality may draw some of their power from her own seductive personality.

She has published *Power Through Witchcraft* (1969) and *Never Strike a Happy Medium* (1971) and has also issued a long-play record titled *Seduction Through Witchcraft.* (See also **Witchcraft**)

Huet, Pierre-Daniel (1630–1721)

A celebrated French bishop of Avrenches, who collected some early reports of vampires.

He was born February 8, 1630, at Caen, educated at a Jesuit school and by a Protestant pastor. He became a great classical scholar. In addition to editing Origen's *Commentary on St. Matthew,* he studied mathematics, astronomy, anatomy, ocular research, and chemistry as well as learning Syriac and Arabic. With Ann Lefèvre, he edited 60 volumes of Latin classics.

He took holy orders in 1676 and became bishop of Soissons in 1685, later bishop of Avránches. He died February 26, 1721. In his *Memoirs* (transl., 2 vols., 1810) there are many interesting passages relating to the vampires by the Greek Archipelago. "Many strange things," he stated, "are told of the broucolagnes, or vampires of the Archipelago. It is said in that country that if one leads a wicked life, and dies in sin, he will appear again after death as he was wont in his lifetime, and that such a person will cause great affright among the living." Huet believed that the bodies of such people were abandoned to the power of the devil, who retained the soul within them for the vexation of mankind.

Father Richard, a Jesuit, employed on a mission in these islands, provided Huet with details of many cases of vampirism. In the Island of St. Erini, the Thera of the ancients, occurred one of the greatest chapters in the history of vampirism. He stated that these people were tormented by vampires, that they were constantly disinterring corpses for the purpose of burning them. Huet stated that this evidence is worthy of credence as emanating from a witness of unimpeachable honesty, who had ocular demonstrations of what he wrote about. He further said that the inhabitants of these islands after the death of a person cut off his feet, hands, nose, and ears, and they called this act *acroteriazein.* They hung all these round the elbow of the dead.

It is noteworthy that the bishop appeared to think that the modern Greeks might have inherited the practice of burning bodies from their fathers in classical times, and that they imagined that unless the corpse was given to the flames, all could not be well with the soul of the deceased. (See also **Vampire**)

Hughes, Irene (Finger)

Well-known modern psychic. Born in a Tennessee log cabin near Mississippi, she combined Cherokee Indian and Scots-Irish ancestry. Her psychic abilities were manifest even in childhood. Later she worked in a hospital in New Orleans and married William Hughes in 1945. After war service in Pearl Harbor and the South Pacific, Mr. Hughes moved to Chicago, Illinois, with his wife. They had four children. Mrs. Hughes used her psychic abilities to sponsor the trip to Chicago by correctly forecasting horse race winners.

After 1961, after various secretarial posts, Mrs. Hughes had a major operation and subsequently became aware of a Japanese "spirit guide." In later years, Mrs. Hughes became established as a professional psychic, lecturing and contributing syndicated newspaper columns, as well as giving private consultations. She also edited a medical publication *The International Journal of Neuropsychiatry.*

In 1963 she founded the **Golden Path** in Chicago, an organization devoted to teaching students to develop their psychic talents. In 1967 she visited the **Psychical Research Foundation** in Durham, N.C., where her psychic abilities were tested by parapsychologist W. B. **Roll.** Mrs. Hughes has hosted a television show on Chicago's WSNS and has been interviewed on other television programs. She had a correct premonition of the assassination of Robert Kennedy, and has filed other predictions with the **Central Premonitions Registry.** She believes that the present age will be one of expansion of man's consciousness. She has published *ESPecially Irene; A Guide to Psychic Awareness* (1972). For an account of her psychic abilites in action, see *Irene Hughes on Psychic Safari* by Brad Steiger, Warner Paperback Library, 1972.

Hugo, Victor (1802–1885)

The great French novelist, was keenly interested in the **spiritism** movement. He wrote: "To avoid phenomena, to make them bankrupt of the attention to which they have a right, is to make bankrupt truth itself."

He left an unpublished manuscript on Spiritism in the possession of Paul Meurice, who died in 1905. It appears from this and from Claudius Grillet's *Victor Hugo spirite* (Paris, 1929) that he met with his first experiences in **table turning** at the house of Mme. de Girardin during his exile in the island of Jersey in September 1853. He had at first refused to attend but was greatly moved when the table spelt out the name of his lost daughter, Leopoldine. Soon regular communications were established.

At the table were seated the exiles and their visitors, especially General Le Flo, Count Paul Teleki, Charles Hugo, Vacquerie and Mme. Hugo. Victor Hugo himself was never at the table, sometimes not even in the room. Many fabulous and symbolical personages came through: "The Lion of Androcles," "the Ass of Balaam," the Dove of Noah." They were very intellectual. "The Shadow of the Tomb" expressed itself in verses in the style and language of Victor Hugo, with all the grandiloquence of romantic poetry.

Sometimes verses in the same style were signed by Aeschylus. Shakespeare challenged Victor Hugo to a poetic competition. André Chenier, the guillotined poet, finished the fragmentary poem which was interrupted by his execution.

Charles Hugo was the principal medium in all these experiments, of which interesting descriptions are given in Henry Malo's *Life of Delphine Gray* [Mme. de Girardin]

(1925). The full records were published two years earlier: *Chez Victor Hugo. Les Tables Tournantes de Jersey. Procés-verbeaux des seances présentés et commentés par Gustave Simon.*

In 1892, the spirit of Victor Hugo, or a secondary **personality** assuming the name, appeared as the control of Mlle. Hélène **Smith,** the medium, famous for her pseudo-Martian communication. He was in exclusive control for five months. After a struggle lasting for a year he was ousted by another control, "Leopold," the *soi-disant* spirit of **Cagliostro.**

Human Dimensions Institute

Educational organization pioneering research on the "whole" person—physical, emotional, mental and spiritual. The Institute operates through scientific research, publications, lectures, seminars, experience groups and continuing courses at Rosary Hill, Buffalo, and surrounding colleges and institutions. Seminars are also held at Swen-i-o, the new HDI Retreat Center at Canandiagua, New York. International authorities have discussed such areas as parapsychology, consciousness-expansion, nutrition, unorthodox healing, holistic philosophy and spiritual experience. Address: 4380 Main Street, Buffalo, N.Y. 14226.

Human Dimensions Institute-West

Research center and forum concerned with scientific and metaphysical disciplines. Advisors include: Stanley **Krippner,** Ph.D., Charles Muses, Ph.D., Elizabeth Rauscher, Ph.D., David Spangler and Fred Wolfe, Ph.D. The center supplements the **Human Dimensions Institute** at Buffalo, New York, and provides classes, lectures and workshops. Address: P.O. Box 5037 or 10773 Highway 150, Ojai, California 93023.

Human Dimensions Magazine

Quarterly publication of **Human Dimensions Institute;** includes significant articles and professional papers on new frontiers of human experience. Address: 4620 W. Lake Road, Canandaigua, N.Y. 14424.

Human Nature (Journal)

London monthly journal, founded by British Spiritualist James **Burns** in 1867, which was published for ten years. It was a major forum for non-Christian or "Progressive Spiritualism."

Humpfner, Winfried G(oswin) (1889–1962)

German priest who was actively interested in parapsychological studies. Born August 4, 1889, at Aidhausen, Bavaria, Germany, he studied at the University of Würsburg (D. Theol. 1930). He entered the Augustinian Order in 1909 and was ordained as a priest in 1914. He studied in Rome and became general archivist and sub-secretary general 1931, assistant general from 1936–47.

He was a life member of the Society for Psychical Research, London, associate member of the American Society for Psychical Research, Società Italiana di Parapscicologia, Association Italiana Scientifica de Metapsichica, and member of the Internationale Gesellschaft Katholischer Parapsychologen. He wrote the book *L'Interpretazione di Fenomeni Metapsichici, ovvero L'Anima in Metapsichica, in Psicologia, ecc. (The Interpretation of Metapsychical*

Phenomena, or The Soul in Metapsychics, Psychology, etc., 1951). He died November 3, 1962.

Humphreys, Mrs. (W.) Desmond (?   –1938)

Popular British novelist and Spiritualist who wrote under the pseudonym "Rita." She was a daughter of John Gilbert Gollan of Inverness-shire, Scotland. She was educated in Sydney, Australia, where she went with her parents during childhood, later returning to England. She was married twice; her second husband being W. Desmond Humphreys of Ballin, Co. Cork, Ireland.

She commenced literary work at an early age and during her lifetime published more than sixty popular novels, as well as *Recollections of a Literary Life* (1936). She was a convinced Spiritualist and in her book *The Truth of Spiritualism* (1918) she stated that her interest began in early girlhood, "when, owing to my father's interest in the subject, we used to try for communications sitting at a table with joined hands in dim light, and received messages by means of the alphabet and raps . . . and my father used to keep a written record of communications."

She died January 1, 1938.

Huna

The secret knowledge of Hawaiian priest sorcerers known as "Kahunas" or keepers of the secret. This knowledge includes healing, weather control and mastery of fire-walking on red hot lava without injury. An important aspect of their miracles is the concept of *mana,* a vitalistic force which has close parellels with the Odic force of von **Reichenbach,** the **Animal Magnetism** of nineteenth-century Europe, and **Orgone** energy of **Wilhelm Reich,** as well as the **Kundalini** of Hindu tradition.

According to Max Freedom **Long** who studied Huna magic in Hawaii, the Kahunas recognize three entities of *aka* bodies of the human being: a low, middle and higher self. The low self generates *mana* through food and other vital processes and is concerned with the physical body and the emotions. The middle self is a reasoning entity, whilst the higher self transcends memory and reason. Mr. Long devised a technique of establishing partnership between the three selves which he believed embodied the secret of the Hawaiian Kahunas, and later established the **Huna Research Associates,** succeeded by the Order of **Huna International,** an organization for research and teaching in Huna magic.

Huna International, The Order of

A non-sectarian spiritual order dedicated to the teaching, application and research into laws governing man and the universe, with special reference to the Huna magic of Polynesian sorcerer priests known as "Kahunas" or keepers of the secret. These laws were first publicly discussed by Max Freedom **Long** in various books, notably *Recovering the Ancient Magic* (London, 1936) and *The Secret Science Behind Miracles* (California, 1948 etc.)

Huna International was founded in 1973 by Dr. Sage King and includes amongst its objectives the training of kahunas, and the establishment of a center of knowledge for individuals to learn Huna techniques. Their address is: 1535 6th St., #202, Santa Monica, California 90401.

Huna Research Associates

Established by Max Freedom **Long** circa 1949 for research and experiment in the field of **Huna** magic, the secret knowledge of Polynesian sorcerer priests. The work of HRA is now continued on a world scale by the Order of **Huna International.** HRA issues a newsletter for members, *Huna Vista Research Bulletin.* Address: 126 Camellia Drive, Cape Girardeau, Missouri 63701.

Huna Vista Research Bulletin

Quarterly publication of **Huna Research Associates,** reporting on experiments and research in **Huna,** the occult system of Hawaiian priest sorcerers, as elucidated by Max Freedom **Long.** Huna phenomena included healing, weather control and fire walking. HRA also issues a newsletter for members. Address: 126 Camellia Drive, Cape Girardeau, Missouri 63701.

Huns

The people who invaded the East Roman empire c. 372–453 A.D., and who were particularly ruthless in their war campaigns under the leadership of Attila. Ancient historians credited the Huns with a monstrous origin. They were often called "children of the devil," because it was said that they were born of a union between demons and hideous witches, the latter cast out of their own county by Philimer, king of the Goths, and his army. The old writers state that the Huns were of horrible deformity, and could not be mistaken for anything but the children of demons.

The German historian C. Besoldus (1577–1638) claimed that their name of Huns came from a Celtic or barbaric word signifying "great magicians." Many stories are told of their magic prowess, and of their raising specters to assist them in battle.

Hunt, H(arry) Ernest (died 1946)

British Spiritualist, lecturer and author. A tutor at St. Paul's School, London, England, he resigned in order to devote his attention to the study of practical psychology. His publications included: *Manual of Hypnotism* (1915), *Self Training* (1919), *Hidden Self and Its Mental Processes* (1921), *Spirit and Music* (1922), *Nerve Control* (1923), *A Book of Auto-Suggestion* (1923), *Why We Survive* (1928), *Spiritualism For the Enquirer* (1931). He died January 6, 1946.

Hurkos, Peter (1911–)

Prominent modern psychic born May 21, 1911, as Peter Van Der Hurk in Dordrecht, Holland. He worked as a merchant seaman before becoming a member of the Dutch underground movement in occupied Holland during World War II.

As a result of a fall from a ladder in 1941 he discovered a psychic faculty. However, he was arrested and imprisoned in Buchenwald, Germany, until the camp was liberated by U.S. and Canadian troops. Afterwards his psychic abilities were too distracting for him to follow a normal occupation, and he began to appear on stage and television shows, demonstrating feats of ESP.

He was brought to the U.S. in 1956 by Dr. Andrija **Puharich,** who tested his abilities for two and a half years. These tests are discussed in Puharich's book *Beyond Telepathy* (Doubleday, 1962).

The psychic abilities of Hurkos in tracing missing persons and objects, and discovering criminals, have been much publicized, but he has often been inaccurate or misleading. When he was brought in to assist the police in tracing the Boston Strangler, his psychic descriptions had no relevance to Albert DeSalvo who confessed to the crimes. However, Hurkos has cooperated with police departments throughout Europe and the U.S. His story is told in his autobiography *Psychic: the Story of Peter Hurkos* (Bobbs-Merrill, 1961) and *The Psychic World of Peter Hurkos* by Norma Lee Browning (Doubleday, 1970). For a skeptical account, see the chapter 'Peter Hurkos—Psychic Sleuth' in Milbourne Christopher's *Mediums, Mystics & The Occult* (Thomas Y. Crowell, 1975), and 'The Mystery Men From Holland, I: Peter Hurkos' Dutch Cases' by Piet Hein Hoebens (*Zetetic Scholar*, No. 8, July 1981).

Husk, Cecil (1847–1920)

British professional singer, member of the Carl Rosa Opera Company, who owing to failing eyesight, abandoned his vocation and, having been strongly psychic from early childhood, changed it for professional mediumship.

His **materialization** seances began about 1875 and were well known for the strength and varied nature of the phenomena. "John King" was claimed as his chief control with five subordinates: "Uncle," "Christopher," "Ebenezer," "Tom Hall" and "Joey" (the latter apparently the same control as manifesting through medium William **Eglinton**). Their voices, according to Florence Marryat, were heard as soon as the medium entered the cabinet. They prepared the manifestations for "John King."

One of his favorite phenomena was the demonstration of the passage of **matter** passing through matter. The threading of chairs or iron rings on the medium's arms while the sitters held his hands was a frequently observed manifestation.

An often mentioned experiment was done by Dr. George Wyld, of Edinburgh. In his book, *Theosophy, or Spiritual Dynamics and the Divine and Miraculous Man* (1884), he described in detail how he carried about himself a specially made iron ring of 5–6 inches diameter for four years in the hope that eventually it would be placed on his arm or on the medium's while he held his hand. The iron ring was of oval shape. Its size did not allow its passage over the hand.

Dr. Wyld's wish was satisfied by Cecil Husk in 1884. While Dr. Wyld held the left hand of the medium, the ring was taken from his right, the medium cried out in pain and when the light was turned on, it was found on Husk's left wrist. An hour later it fell on the floor.

Encouraged by this success, Dr. Wyld had a still smaller ring made. This was also put on Husk's wrist whilst his hand was held by a friend. The ring was identified by microscopic markings. The Society for Psychical Research examined the ring and undertook to force it off if the medium permitted himself to be chloroformed. When he refused they brought the verdict: "We cannot infer that it is impossible that the ring should have come into the position in which we found it by known natural means." This verdict was based on experiments carried on with the hands of three other men, by etherizing them and compressing their hands with metallic tape.

The ring could not be passed over. Still the investigators concluded that they might have been successful in the case of Husk. He, by the way, wore the ring to his dying day.

In 1890, through Cecil Husk's mediumship, Stanley **de Brath** made his first acquaintance with psychic phenomena. In the following year at a public seance with about twenty sitters Cecil Husk was exposed. In the light of an electric tie-pin he was seen leaning over the table and illuminating his face with a phosphorized slate. The "spirit drapery" which enveloped his head did not disappear. The apology of Spiritualists ,that a case of **transfiguration** was taking place and that the drapery was aported instead of being materialized is provoking to common sense. "When, he was waked up from his trance in that sudden way," wrote Florence **Marryat,** "he was paralysed with terror, and ran about like a mad creature." He was very ill for some time afterwards and was unable to sit for months except with friends.

In an article in the July 1906 issue of the *Annals of Psychic Science,* Henry A. Fotherby described an interesting materialization seance with Husk in which the phantasms appeared to develop from a sort of phosphorescent vapor in the air, dotted all over with countless numbers of minute points of bright light, like little glow lamps. They were rendered visible by luminous slates which rose by themselves from the table and cast a weird bluish light on the phantom faces.

Gambier Bolton published some unusual experiences with Cecil Husk in his book *Psychic Force* (1904). In his own house, in the presence of fourteen investigators, the medium, while tightly held, was levitated in his chair on to the top of the table.

Important experiences were described by Admiral Usborne Moore in *Glimpses of the Next State* (1911). He was introduced to the subject by Cecil Husk. In the first seance in 1904, a zither rose from the table and soared above the circle. Its movements could be watched by the phosphorescent spots on its underside. After two or three swirls it dashed on to the floor and apparently went through, for faint music could be heard from underneath.

In the light of illuminated cards, Admiral Moore witnessed the materialization of about fifteen spirits. The faces were about two-thirds of life size. "John King" always spoke in a stentorian voice. This was not exceptional. When a sitter asked the control "Uncle": "Are you using the medium's throat?" the answer came in a bellowing voice close to him: "Do you think that this is the medium's throat? If so, he must have a long neck."

The voices spoke in many languages. The singing, tenor, bass and all the shades between, went on in astonishing volume just the same even when Husk had a cold. Admiral Moore sat over forty times with Husk and had only once suspected fraud. On that occasion, conditions were bad and he was by no means sure that his doubts were reasonable.

Hutin, Serge Roger Jean (1929-   )

French author who wrote extensively on occult subjects. Born April 2, 1929 at Paris, France, he studied at the Sorbonne. His memberships include: Institut Métapsychique International, Paris, Association Francaise d'Etudes Métapsychiques, Paris, Jacob Boehme Society, New York, Swedenborg Institut, Basel, the Rosicrucian Order. He has written a number of articles on parapsychological topics, especially retrocognition and reincarnation, including the following, all published in *Revue Métapsychique:* Swedenborg et le mond invisible' (March–April 1953), 'A propos du "Cas de Trianon" ' (July–August 1953), 'Du Nouveau sur le cas de Trianon' (November–December 1953), and the following in *Revue Spirite:* 'Peut-on prouver La Pluralité des existences?' (July–August 1959), 'A propos des "Fantômes de Trianon"' (May–June 1960).

His books include: *L'Alchimi* (Alchemy), *Les Sociétés secrétes, La Philosophie anglaise et américaine,* and *Les Gnostiques* (in the series Que Sais-Je? 1951–58), (with M. Caron) *Les Alchimistes* (1959), *Les Francs-Macons* (The Freemasons, 1960) *Les Disciples anglais de Jacob Boehme* (1959), *Histoire mondiale des sociétés secrétes* (World History of Secret Societies, 1959), *Les Civilisations inconnues* (Unknown Civilizations, 1961) *Histoire des Rose-Croix* (History of the Rosicrucians, 1962), *Voyages vers Ailleurs* (Travels to Elsewhere, 1962).

Huxley, Aldous (Leonard) (1894–1963)

Eminent British novelist whose book *The Doors of Perception* (1954) triggered modern controversies on the relationship between drug experience and mysticism. Born in Godalming, Surrey, England, July 27, 1894, Huxley was a grandson of a famous biologist. He was educated at Eton and at Balliol College, Oxford. He suffered from defective vision, and about 1935 began special eye training exercises according to the system of W. H. Bates. These involved special visualization techniques. Huxley found a remarkable improvement in vision, and has described his experiences in his book *The Art of Seeing* (1942).

He went on to write intellectually brilliant novels, short stories and essays, mostly critical and sometimes cynical in their view of modern society. His better known works are: *Crome Yellow* (1921), *Antic Hay* (1923), *Point Counter Point* (1928), *Brave New World* (1932), *Eyelessin Gaza* (1936), *Ape and Essence* (1949).

In 1919, he married Maria Nys from Belgium, and they had one son. Through Huxley's friendship with novelist D. H. Lawrence, he began to be interested in mystical perception, and towards the end of his life, this interest deepened and mellowed in his later writings. After a period of living in southern France, the Huxleys eventually settled in Los Angeles, California. After Huxley's wife Maria died in 1955, he married Laura Archera a year later. Huxley himself died November 22, 1963.

His developing interest in occult themes is indicated by his book *The Devils of Loudon* (1952), *The Doors of Perception* (1954), and *Heaven and Hell* (1956). The latter two works are only short essays, but they had a profound influence in generating discussion on possible connections between drug experience and mysticism. Huxley had met occultist Aleister **Crowley** in Berlin in 1930 and through him was familiar with the effects of mescaline, but it was not until summer 1953 that Huxley took the four-tenths of a gramme of mescaline that resulted in *The Doors of Perception* and *Heaven and Hell.*

Huxley's dazzling intellectual discussions of consciousness-expanding drugs were widely drawn upon by such apostles of the psychedelic revolution as Timothy **Leary** and Richard **Alpert,** but Huxley himself was not in favor of undiscriminating drug-taking. According to his brother, the famous biologist Sir Julian Huxley, he realized "that LSD would not bring liberation and understanding to everyone, and in his last book, 'Island', he points out its potential danger . . . though his warnings were not heeded."

Hwyl

A special characteristic of traditional Welsh revivalist preaching, indicating a surge of intense emotional and spiritual fervor released by chanting. "Hwyl" is also Welsh for the sails of a ship, and a possible derivation is that as a breeze ("awel") fills the sails and transports the vessel, so a strong current of emotion lifts the spiritual awareness of the preacher and his congregation.

Traditional Welsh revivalism is comparable with the fervor of Kentucky backwoods preaching. The congregation catch the spirit of the preacher and ejaculate deeply felt responses of *Bendigedig!* (Praise the Lord!) or *Diolch byth!* (Amen!). The *Hwyl* is sometimes induced by a chanting of the attributes of God in a rhythmic sequence.

Hydesville

A little hamlet in New York State, in the township of Arcadia thirty miles east of Rochester, the birthplace of nineteenth-century Spiritualism in 1848. Here in the house of John D. Fox, his wife Margaret and two daughters, mysterious rappings first took place on March 31, 1848. The raps responded intelligently to questions. Various neighbors were called in, and one of them, Mr. Duesler, displayed great ingenuity in reciting letters of the alphabet and eliciting responses by raps at meaningful letters. This was a forerunner of the technique of "spirit communication" in the development of Spiritualism.

In 1927 from December 4–7, an International Hydesville Memorial and Spiritualist Congress was held at Rochester, N.Y., and it was resolved to erect a twenty-five feet high shaft to commemorate the advent of Spiritualism at Hydesville.

In 1915, the old Fox house was purchased by B. F. Bartlett of Cambridge, Pennsylvania, who had it dismantled and removed to the Lily Dale Spiritualist camp in western New York. In 1955 the building was totally destroyed by fire. (See also **Fox Sisters; Rochester Rappings**)

Hydromancy

Divination by water, said by Natalis Comes (died 1582) to have been the invention of Nereus ancient god of the sea, but the term covers various methods of divination, ranging from forms of **crystal gazing** (using a large or small pool of water) to what is now known as **Radiesthesia,** using as a pendulum a wedding ring on the thread, held over a glass of water (see **Pendulums**).

The writer M.A. Delrio (1561–1608) described one example of hydromancy (cited by Iamblichus) to which the Emperor Andronicus Comnenus had recourse; not in person, for regard for his character forbade this humiliation.

This worthy applied to Sethos, a diviner, who from his youth upward had been addicted to magic, and on that account had been deprived of sight by the Emperor Manuel. The question proposed by hydromancy was, who was to be the successor of Andronicus, a doubt which grievously perplexed the superstitious tyrant and left him in hesitation as to the fittest victim whom his suspicious vengeance might first sacrifice.

The spirit when summoned, showed upon the water the letters "S.I." and upon being asked at what time the person so designated should succeed, he replied, before the Feast of the exaltation of the Cross. His prediction was verified, for, within the time named, Isaac Angelus had thrown Andronicus to be torn in pieces by the infuriated populace of Constantinople. It should be remembered here that the devil spells, as he repeats the Lord's Prayer, not in the natural order, but backwards. "S.I.," when inverted, would fairly enough represent Isaac, according to all laws of magic.

The same story was related with great spirit by Nicetas (died 1216). The arts with which the tempter cheats the ear of his votary are vividly displayed, and there is one very picturesque touch, when the spirit was asked respecting time, a point which surprisingly escaped Delrio, who evidently borrowed from this source, although he refered to Iamblichus.

However, Delrio cited several kinds of hydromancy. In one, a ring was suspended by a thread in a vessel of water, and this being shaken, a judgment was formed according to the strokes of the ring against the sides of the vessel.

In a second method, three pebbles were thrown into standing water and observations were drawn from the circles which they formed. A third method depended upon the agitations of the sea, whence the learned Jesuit deduced a custom prevalent among the Oriental Christians of annually baptizing that element; at the same time taking especial care to show that the betrothment of the Adriatic by the Doge of Venice had a widely different origin.

A fourth divination was taken from the color of water and certain figures appearing in it, which Varro said afforded numerous prognostics of the event of the Mithridatic War. But this branch was of sufficient importance to deserve a separate name, and accordingly there arose a method of divination by fountains, these being the waters most frequently consulted. Among the most celebrated fountains for this purpose were those of Palicorus in Sicily, which invariably destroyed the criminal who ventured to adjure them falsely in testimony of his innocence. A full account of their usage and virtue is given by the Roman philosopher Macrobius (c. 345–423 A.D.)

Pausanias (2nd century A.D.) described a fountain near Epidaurus, dedicated to Ino, into which on her festival, certain loaves were wont to be thrown. It was a favorable omen to the applicant if these offerings were retained; on the other hand, most unlucky if they were washed up again. So, also, Tiberius cast golden dice into the fountain of Apomus, near Padua, where they long remained as a proof of the imperial monster's good fortune in making the highest throw.

Several other instances of divining springs were collected by the antiquary J. J. Boissard (1528–1602) and Delrio ascribed to them the origin of the custom of the ancient Germans, who threw their newborn children into the Rhine, with a conviction that if they were spurious they would sink, if legitimate they would swim. This custom also sounds like a precursor of the seventeenth-century custom of "swimming witches," perhaps related to the Anglo-Saxon law of King Athelstan of trial by water.

In a fifth method of hydromancy, certain mysterious words were pronounced over a cup full of water, and observations were made upon its spontaneous ebullition. In a sixth method, a drop of oil was let fall on water in a glass vessel, and this furnished a kind of mirror upon which many wonderful objects were said to become visible. This, stated Delrio, is the *Modus Fessanus.*

Clemens Alexandrinus is cited for a seventh kind of hydromancy in which the women of Germany watched the sources, whirls, and courses of rivers, with a view to prophetic interpretation; the same fact was mentioned by J. L. Vives in his *Commentary upon St. Augustine.* In modern Italy, continued the learned Jesuit, diviners were still to be found who wrote the names of any three persons suspected of theft upon a like number of little balls, which they threw into the water and some went to so profane an extent as to abuse even holy water for this most unsanctified purpose. Boissard, as cited above, explained more fully than Delrio two of these methods of hydromancy: that by the ring suspended in a vessel of water, and the method by its spontaneous ebullition. A very similar account was given by Johan **Weyer.**

In a fragment of M. T. Varro's book, *de Cultu Deorum,* the practice of hydromancy is attributed to Numa. Upon this statement, St. Augustine had commented in the passage to which we have already referred, and he mentioned that the practice of hydromancy was attributed by Varro to the Persians, and afterwards to the philosopher Pythagoras. Strabo, in like manner, ascribed the practice to the Persians.

Hydromancy is, in principal, the same thing as divination by the crystal or mirror, and in ancient times a natural basin of rock kept constantly full by a running stream, was a favorite medium. The double meaning of the word "reflection" ought to be considered here, and how when gazing down into clear water the mind is disposed to self-retirement and to contemplation, deeply tinctured with melancholy. Rocky pools and gloomy lakes figure in many stories of witchcraft—the Craic-pol-nain in the Highland woods of Laynchork; the Devil's Glen in the county of Wicklow, Ireland; the Swedish Blockula; the witch mountains of Italy; and the Bibiagora, between Hungary and Poland. Similar resorts in the glens of Germany were marked, as Tacitus mentions, by salt springs.

It was really only another form of divination by the gloomy water pool that attracted so much public attention at that time when E. W. Lane, in his work *An Account of the Manners & Customs of the Modern Egyptians* (1836), testified to its success as practiced in Egypt and Hindostan. That author, having resolved to witness the performance of this species of sorcery, the magician commenced his operations by writing forms of invocation to his familiar spirits on six slips of paper. A chafing dish with some live charcoal in it was then procured and a boy summoned who had not yet reached the age of puberty. Lane inquired who were the persons that could see in the fluid mirror, and was told that they were a boy not arrived at puberty, a virgin, a black female slave, or a pregnant woman.

To prevent any collusion between the sorcerer and the boy, Lane sent his servant to take the first boy he met. When all was prepared, the sorcerer threw some incense and one of the strips of paper into the chafing dish; he then took hold of the boy's right hand and drew a square with some mystical marks on the palm. In the center of the square he poured a little ink, which formed the magic mirror, and desired the boy to look steadily into it without raising his head. In this mirror the boy declared that he saw, successively, a man sweeping, seven men with flags, an army pitching its tents, and the various officers of state attending on the Sultan. The rest is told by Lane himself.

"The sorcerer now addressed himself to me, and asked me if I wished the boy to see any person who was absent or dead. I named Lord Nelson, of whom the boy had evidently never heard, for it was with much difficulty that he pronounced the name after several trials. The magician desired the boy to say to the Sultan: 'My master salutes thee and desires thee to bring Lord Nelson; bring him before my eyes that I may see him speedily.' The boy then said so, and almost immediately added, 'A messenger has gone and brought back a man dressed in a black (or rather, dark blue) suit of European clothes; the man has lost his left arm.' He then paused for a moment or two, and looking more intently and more closely into the ink, said 'No, he has not lost his left arm, but it is placed on his breast.'

"This correction made his description more striking than it had been without it; since Lord Nelson generally had his empty sleeve attached to the breast of his coat; but it was the right arm that he had lost. Without saying that I suspected the boy had made a mistake, I asked the magician whether the objects appeared in the ink as if actually before the eyes, or as if in a glass, which makes the right appear left. He answered that they appeared as in a mirror. This rendered the boy's description faultless.

"Though completely puzzled, I was somewhat disappointed with his performances, for they fell short of what he had accomplished in many instances in the presence of certain of my friends and countrymen. On one of these occasions, an Englishman present ridiculed the performance, and said that nothing would satisfy him but a correct description of the appearance of his own father, of whom he was sure no one of the company had any knowledge.

"The boy, accordingly, having called by name for the person alluded to, described a man in a Frank dress, with his hand placed on his head, wearing spectacles, and with one foot on the ground and the other raised behind him, as if he were stepping down from a seat. The description was exactly true in every respect; the peculiar position of the hand was occasioned by an almost constant headache, and that of the foot or leg by a stiff knee, caused by a fall from a horse in hunting.

"On another occasion Shakespeare was described with the most minute exactness, both as to person and dress, and I might add several other cases in which the same magician has excited astonishment in the sober minds of several Englishmen of my acquaintance."

Lane's account may be compared with a similar one given by Mr. Kinglake, the author of *Eöthen.*

Encyclopedia of Occultism and Parapsychology, 2nd Ed.

It may be worth adding, that in another case of hydromancy known to Elihu Rich, part author of *The Occult Sciences* (1855), the boy could see better without the medium than with it—although he could also see reflected images in a vessel of water. This fact may be admitted to prove that such images are reflected to the eye of the seer from his own mind and brain: how the brain becomes thus enchanted or the eye disposed for vision, is another question. Certainly it is no proof that the recollected image in the mind of the inquirer is transferred to the seer, as proofs can be shown to the contrary. (See also **Crystal Gazing; Divination**)

Hyena

A fabled many-colored stone, taken from the eye of the animal so called. Put under the tongue, it was said to enable its possessor to foretell future events. It was also supposed to cure gout and quartan ague.

Hyle

The primordial matter of the universe, also the name given by Gnostics to one of the three degrees in the progress of spirits. (See also **Gnosticism**)

Hynek, J(oseph) Allen (1910-   )

Prominent astrophysicist and author, authority on UFOs or flying saucers, founder-director of the **Center for UFO Studies,** Evanston, Illinois. Born May 1, 1910, in Chicago, Illinois, he studied at University of Chicago (B.S. 1931; Ph.D. astrophysics 1935). In 1942 he married Miriam Curtis. He became assistant at Yerkes Observatory, Chicago, in 1934, instructor in physics and astronomy at Ohio State University from 1935-41, assistant professor 1941-46, associate professor 1946-50, professor of astronomy 1950-56, chief of section dealing with upper atmosphere studies and satellite tracking and associate director of Smithsonian Astrophysics Observatory 1956-60, director of Dearborn Observatory, Northwestern University, Evanston, Illinois, from 1961 onwards, chairman of department of astronomy from 1960 onwards, director Lindheimer Astronomical Research Center 1965.

He was in charge of UFO investigations on "Project Bluebook," the U.S. Air Force official investigation of UFO sightings. He is a Fellow of the Royal Astronomical Society, member of American Astronomical Society, International Astronomical Union. Prof. Hynek founded the Center for UFO Studies in conjunction with other professional scientists. CUFOS serves as a clearinghouse for UFO data from all over the world and encourages systematic research on UFOs. Hynek was technical consultant on the Spielberg movie **Close Encounters of the Third Kind.** His books include: *Astrophysics: a topical symposium commemorating the fiftieth anniversary of the Yerkes Observatory and a century of progress in astrophysics* (1951), (with G. F. Schilling) *Observational Information on Artificial Earth Satellites* (1958), *Challenge of the Universe* (1962; 1965); (with Necia H. Apfel) *Astronomy One* (1972), *The UFO Experience; a scientific inquiry* (1972), (with Jacques Vallee) *The Edge of Reality; a progress report on Unidentified Flying Objects* (1975), *The Hynek UFO Report* (1977), (with Necia H. Apfel) *Architecture of the Universe* (1979).

Hyperaesthesia

An actual or apparent exaltation of the perceptive faculties, or superacuity of the normal senses, characteristic of the hypnotic state. It has been noticed frequently with hysterics. They may feel a piece of wire on their hands as heavy as a bar of iron.

The smallest suggestion, whether given by word, look, gesture, or even breathing or unconscious movement, is instantly seized upon and interpreted by the entranced subject, who for this reason is often termed "sensitive."

The phenomenon of hyperaesthesia, observed but wrongly interpreted by the early magnetists and mesmerists, was largely responsible for the so-called **clairvoyance, thought-reading, community of sensation,** and other kindred phenomena. In its phenomenal appearance, hyperaesthesia is often difficult to distinguish from **telepathy** or clairvoyance. Theoretically, the dividing line is that hyperaesthesia is a peripheral perception. Telepathy, or clairvoyance is a central perception which does not reach us through the end organs. In practice, it is difficult to decide whether the perception takes place through the end organs or not.

The realization of suggestion and hyperaesthesia was the great achievement of Bertrand and Braid, which brought hypnotism into the domain of scientific fact. The significance of hyperaesthesia in connection with every form of psychic phenomena can hardly be over estimated. Nor is it met with only in the trance state. It enters into the normal existence to an extent that is but imperfectly understood. Dreams, for instance, frequently reproduce impressions which have been recorded in some obscure stratum of consciousness, while much that we call intuition is made up of inferences subconsciously drawn from indications too subtle to reach the normal consciousness.

Hyperaesthesia has been defined as "an actual or *apparent* exaltation of the perceptive faculties." The reason for this is that modern scientists declare that it is not known whether the senses are actually sharpened or not. Most probably the hyperaesthetic perception is merely a normal perception which by reason of the state of cerebral dissociation operates in a free field. Very slight sense-impressions may be recorded in the brain during normal consciousness, but such is the inhibiting effect of the excitement occasioned by other similar impressions, that they do not reach full consciousness.

Prof. Gilbert **Murray** conducted telepathic experiments by placing himself in a different room from the sensitive and having a sentence spoken to him in a very low voice. The sensitive in the other room reproduced the sentence.

The British Society for Psychical Research considered this a case of telepathy. Prof. **Richet** considered it exceptional auditory hyperaesthesia. Similarly, the sudden movements which save people from falling masonry in the street may be due to a subconscious hearing of an almost inaudible sound as a consequence of which an urgent impulse is sent up to the motor centers.

Emile **Boirac** recorded interesting cases of tactile and visual hyperaesthesia. His subject read with his fingertips in complete darkness. Being bandaged, his back turned to Boirac, but holding his elbow he could also read if Boirac passed his own fingertips along the lines of a newspaper. It did not make the least difference if Boirac closed his eyes. (See also **Eyeless Sight**)

Another subject could tell the time from a watch wrapped up in a handkerchief. Mme. M., before the Medical Society of Tamboff, could tell the colors of thirty flasks wrapped in paper and placed under a thick cloth.

A further complication in the way of explanation is that Mme. Tamboff could taste by the sense of touch. James **Braid** found the olfactory sense so acute in some hypnotic patients, that by the smell of a glove they could unhesitatingly and unerringly detect its owner in a large company. It is very questionable whether auditory hyperaesthesia could explain the astounding phonic imitations he observed such as patients repeating accurately what was spoken in any language, or singing correctly in any language which they had never heard before.

For example, Braid stated: "A patient of mine who, when awake, knew not the grammar even of her own language, and who had very little knowledge of music, was enabled to follow Mlle. Jenny Lind correctly in songs in different languages, giving both words and music so correctly and simultaneously with Jenny Lind, that two parties in the room could not for some time imagine that there were two voices, so perfectly did they accord, both in musical tone and vocal pronunciation of Swiss, German and Italian songs."

Hypnagogic State

A condition between waking and sleeping, characterized by illusions of vision or sound. These appear to have been first noted by J. G. F. Baillarger (1809–1890) in France and W. Griesinger (1817–1868) in Germany about 1845.

They were studied by the scholar and antiquary Alfred L. F. Maury, who gave them the name "illusions hypnagogiques." They are distinguished from "hypnopompic visions" which appear at the moment when sleep recedes and which momentarily persist into waking life. Both illusions are related to the faculty of dreaming. Some hypnagogic visions are often the precursor to **Out-of-the-Body** experiences. (See also **Astral Projection**)

Hypnotism

A peculiar state of cerebral dissociation distinguished by certain marked symptoms, the most prominent and invariable of which is a highly-increased suggestibility in the subject.

The hypnotic state may be induced in a very large percentage of normal individuals, or may occur spontaneously. It is recognized as having an affinity with normal sleep, and likewise with a variety of abnormal conditions, among which may be mentioned somnambulism, ecstasy, and the trances of Hindu fakirs and primitive Shamans. In fact, in one form or another hypnosis has been known in practically all countries and all times.

Hypnotism is no longer classed with the occult sciences. It has gained, though only within comparatively recent years, a definite scientific status, and no mean place in legitimate medicine. Nevertheless its history is inextricably interwoven with occultism, and even today much hypnotic phenomena is classed as "Spiritualist," so that a consideration of hypnotism is very necessary to a proper understanding of much of the occult science of our own and former times.

The Early Magnetists

As far back as the 16th century, hypnotic phenomena were observed and studied by men of science, who attributed them to "magnetism," an effluence supposedly radiating from every object in the universe, in a greater or lesser degree, and through which all objects might exercise a mutual influence one on another.

From this doctrine was constructed the "sympathetic" system of medicine, by means of which the "magnetic effluence" of the planets, of the actual magnet, or of the physician, was brought to bear upon the patient. **Paracelsus** is generally supposed to be the originator of the sympathetic system, as he was its most powerful exponent. Of the magnet he stated:

"The magnet has long lain before all eyes, and no one has ever thought whether it was of any further use, or whether it possessed any other property, than that of attracting iron. The sordid doctors throw it in my face that I will not follow the ancients; but in what should I follow them? All that they have said of the magnet amounts to nothing. Lay that which I have said of it in the balance, and judge. Had I blindly followed others, and had I not myself made experiments, I should in like manner know nothing more than what every peasant sees—that it attracts iron. But a wise man must enquire for himself, and it is thus that I have discovered that the magnet, besides this obvious and to every man visible power, that of attracting iron, possesses another and concealed power." That power, he believed, was of healing the sick.

And there is no doubt that cures were actually effected by Paracelsus with the aid of the magnet, especially in cases of epilepsy and nervous affections. Yet the word "magnet" is most frequently used by Paracelsus and his followers in a figurative sense, to denote the *magnes microcosmi,* man himself, who was supposed to be a reproduction in miniature of the earth, having, like it, his poles and magnetic properties. From the stars and planets, he taught, came a very subtle effluence which affected man's mind or intellect, while earthly substances radiated a grosser emanation which affected his body. The human mummy especially was a "magnet" well suited for remedial purposes, since it draws to itself the diseases and poisonous properties of other substances. The most effective mummy was that of a criminal who had been hanged, and it was applied in the following manner.

"If a person suffer from disease," stated Paracelsus, "either local or general, experiment with the following remedy. Take a magnet impregnated with mummy, and combined with rich earth. In this earth sow some seeds that have a likeness to, or homogeneity with, the disease; then let this earth, well sifted and mixed with mummy, be laid in an earthen vessel, and let the seeds committed to it be watered daily with a lotion in which the diseased limb or body has been washed. Thus will the disease be transplanted from the human body to the seeds which are in the earth. Having done this, transplant the seeds from the earthen vessel to the ground, and wait till they begin to flourish into herbs. As they increase, the disease will diminish, and when they have reached their mature growth, will altogether disappear."

The quaint but not altogether illogical idea of "weapon-salve"—anointing the weapon instead of the wound—was also used by Paracelsus, his theory being that part of the vital spirits clung to the weapon and exercised an ill effect on the vital spirits in the wound, which would not heal until the ointment had first been applied to the weapon. This also was an outcome of the magnetic theory.

Towards the end of the 16th century, Paracelsus was worthily succeeded by J. B. **van Helmont,** a scientist of distinction and an energetic protagonist of magnetism. "Material nature," he wrote, "draws her forms through constant magnetism from above, and implores for them the favour of heaven; and as heaven, in like manner, draws something invisible from below, there is established a free and mutual intercourse, and the whole is contained in an individual."

Van Helmont believed also in the power of the will to direct the subtle fluid. There was, he held, in all created things, a magic or celestial power through which they were allied to heaven. This power or strength is greatest in the soul of man, resides in a lesser degree in his body, and to some extent is present in the lower animals, plants, and inorganic matter.

It is by reason of his superior endowment in this respect that man is enabled to rule the other creatures, and to make use of inanimate objects for his own purposes. The power is strongest when one is asleep, for then the body is quiescent, and the soul most active and dominant, and for this reason dreams and prophetic visions are more common in sleep. "The spirit," he stated, "is everywhere diffused, and the spirit is the medium of magnetism; not the spirits of heaven and of hell, but the spirit of man, which is concealed in him as the fire is concealed in the flint. The human will makes itself master of a portion of its spirit of life, which becomes a connecting property between the corporeal and the incorporeal, and diffuses itself like the light."

To this ethereal spirit he ascribed the visions seen by "the inner man" in ecstasy, and also those of the "outer man" and the lower animals. In proof of the mutual influence of living creatures he asserted that men may kill animals merely by staring hard at them for a quarter of an hour.

That Van Helmont was not ignorant of the power of imagination is evident from many of his writings. A common needle, he declared, may by means of certain manipulations and the will-power and imaginations of the operator, be made to possess magnetic properties. Herbs may become very powerful through the imagination of him who gathers them. And again: "I have hitherto avoided revealing the great secret, that the strength lies concealed in man, merely through the suggestion and power of the imagination to work outwardly, and to impress this strength on others, which then continues of itself, and operates on the remotest objects. Through this secret alone will all receive its true illumination—all that has hitherto been brought together laboriously of the ideal being out of the spirit—all that has been said of the magnetism of all things—of the strength of the human soul—of the magic of man, and of his dominion over the physical world."

Van Helmont also gave special importance to the stomach as the chief seat of the soul, and recounted an experience of his own in which, on touching some aconite

with his tongue, he found all his senses transferred to his stomach. In after years this was to be a favorite accomplishment of somnambules and cataleptic subjects (see Seeing with the **Stomach**).

A distinguished English magnetist was Robert **Fludd,** who wrote in the first part of the 17th century. Fludd was an exponent of the microcosmic theory, and a believer in the magnetic effluence from man. According to Fludd, not only were these emanations able to cure bodily diseases, but they also affected the moral sentiments, for if radiations from two individuals were, on meeting, flung back or distorted, negative magnetism, or antipathy resulted, whereas if the radiations from each person passed freely into those from the other, the result was positive magnetism, or sympathy. Examples of positive and negative magnetism were also to be found among the lower animals and among plants. Another magnetist of distinction was the Scottish physician, William Maxwell, author of *De Medicina Magnetica* (1679), who is said to have anticipated much of Mesmer's doctrine. He declared that those who are familiar with the operation of the universal spirit can, through its agency, cure all diseases, at no matter what distance. He also suggested that the practice of magnetism, though very valuable in the hand of a well-disposed physician, is not without its dangers, and is liable to many abuses.

The Healers Valentine Greatrakes and J. J. Gassner

While the theoretical branch of magnetism was thus receiving attention at the hands of the alchemical philosophers, the practical side was by no means neglected. There were, in the seventeenth and eighteenth centuries, a number of "divine healers," whose magic cures were without doubt the result of hypnotic suggestion.

Of these perhaps the best known and most successful were Valentine **Greatrakes,** an Irishman, and a Swabian priest named John Joseph **Gassner.** Greatrakes was born in 1628, and on reaching manhood served for some time in the Irish army, thereafter settling down on his estate in Waterford.

In 1662 he had a dream in which it was revealed to him that he possessed the gift of curing the king's evil (scrofula). The dream was repeated several times before he paid heed to it, but at length he made the experiment, his own wife being the first to be healed by him.

Many people who came to him from the surrounding country were cured when he laid his hands upon them. Later the impression came upon him strongly that he could cure other diseases besides the king's evil.

News of his wonderful powers spread far and wide and patients came in hundreds to seek his aid. Despite the fact that the bishop of the diocese forbade the exercise of these apparently magical powers, Greatrakes continued to heal the afflicted people who sought him. In 1666 he proceeded to London, and though not invariably successful, he seems to have performed there a surprising number of cures, which were testified to by Robert Boyle, Sir William Smith, Andrew Marvell, and many other eminent people.

Greatrakes himself described them in a work entitled *A brief account of Mr. V. Greatrak's* [sic], *and divers of the strange cures by him . . . performed, written by himself* (London, 1666). His method of healing was to stroke the affected part with his hand, thus (it was claimed) driving the disease into the limbs and so finally out of the body. Sometimes the treatment acted as though by magic, but if immediate relief was not obtained, the rubbing was continued and very few cases were dismissed as incurable. Even epidemic diseases were healed by a touch.

It was said that during the treatment the patient's fingers and toes remained insensible to external stimuli, and frequently he or she showed every symptom of such a "magnetic crisis" as was afterwards to become a special feature of mesmeric treatment.

Personally Greatrakes was a simple and pious gentleman, persuaded that his marvelous powers were a divinely-bestowed gift, and most anxious to make the best use of them.

The other healer mentioned earlier, J. J. Gassner, belongs to a somewhat later period—about the middle of the eighteenth century. J. J. Gassner (1727–79) was a priest of Bludenz in Vorarlberg, where his many cures gained for him a wide celebrity. All diseases, according to him, were caused by evil spirits possessing the patient, and his mode of healing thus consisted of exorcizing the demons.

Gassner too was a man of kindly disposition and piety, and made reference to the Scriptures in his healing operations.

The ceremony of **exorcism** was a rather impressive one. Gassner sat at a table, the patient and spectators in front of him. A blue red-flowered cloak hung from his shoulders. The rest of his clothing was "clean, simple, and modest." On his left was a window, on his right, the crucifix. His fine personality, deep learning, and noble character inspired the faith of the patient and his friends and doubtless played no small part in his curative feats. Sometimes he made use of "magnetic" manipulations, stroking or rubbing the affected part, and driving the disease, after the manner of Greatrakes, into the limbs of the patient. The formula of exorcism he generally pronounced in Latin, with which language the demons showed a perfect familiarity.

Not only could Gassner control sickness by these means, but the passions also were amenable to his treatment: "Now anger is apparent, now patience, now joy, now sorrow, now hate, now love, now confusion, now reason,— each carried to the highest pitch. Now this one is blind, now he sees, and again is deprived of sight, etc."

These curious results suggest the "phreno-magnetism" of later years, where equally sudden changes of mood were produced by touching with the fingertips those parts of the subject's head which **phrenology** associated with the various emotions to be called forth.

Emanuel Swedenborg

Hitherto it will be seen that the rational and supernatural explanations of magnetism had run parallel with one another, the former most in favor with the philosophers, the latter with the general public. It was reserved for Emanuel **Swedenborg** (1688–1772), the Swedish philosopher and Spiritualist, to unite the doctrine of magnetism with that of Spiritualism—i.e., the belief in the action in the external world of the discarnate spirits of deceased human beings. That Swedenborg accepted some of the theories of the older magnetists is evident from his mystical writings, from which the following passage has been extracted:

"In order to comprehend the origin and progress of this influence [i.e., God's influence over man], we must first know that that which proceeds from the Lord is the divine sphere which surrounds us, and fills the spiritual and natural world. All that proceeds from an object, and surrounds and clothes it, is called its sphere.

"As all that is spiritual knows neither time nor space, it therefore follows that the general sphere or the divine one has extended itself from the first moment of creation to the last. This divine emanation, which passed over from the spiritual to the natural, penetrates actively and rapidly through the whole created world, to the last grade of it, where it is yet to be found, and produces and maintains all that is animal, vegetable, and mineral. Man is continually surrounded by a sphere of his favourite propensities; these unite themselves to the natural sphere of his body, so that together they form one. The natural sphere surrounds every body of nature, and all the objects of the three kingdoms. Thus it allies itself to the spiritual world. This is the foundation of sympathy and antipathy, of union and separation, according to which there are amongst spirits presence and absence.

"The angel said to me that the sphere surrounded man more lightly on the back than on the breast, where it was thicker and stronger. This sphere of influence peculiar to man operates also in general and in particular around him by means of the will, the understanding, and the practice.

"The sphere proceeding from God, which surrounds man and constitutes his strength, while it thereby operates on his neighbour and on the whole creation, is a sphere of peace, and innocence; for the Lord is peace and innocence. Then only is man consequently able to make his influence effectual on his fellow man, when peace and innocence rule in his heart, and he himself is in union with heaven. This spiritual union is connected with the natural by a benevolent man through the touch and the laying on of hands; by which the influence of the inner man is quickened, prepared, and imparted. The body communicates with others which are about it through the body, and the spiritual influence diffuses itself chiefly through the hands, because these are the most outward or *ultimum* of man; and through him, as in the whole of nature, the first is contained in the last, as the cause in the effect. The whole soul and the whole body are contained in the hands as a medium of influence."

Mesmerism or Animal Magnetism

In the latter half of the eighteenth century, a new era was inaugurated in connection with the doctrine of a "magnetic fluid." The fresh impetus which the doctrine of magnetism received at that period was due in a very large measure to the works of Franz Anton **Mesmer,** a physician from whose name the word "**Mesmerism**" was taken.

Mesmer was born at Wiel, near Lake Constance in 1733, and studied medicine at the University of Vienna, taking his doctor's degree in 1766. In the same year he published his first work, *De Planetarum Influxu* ("De l'influence des Planettes sur le corps humain"). Although he claimed to have thereby discovered the existence of a "universal fluid," to which he gave the name of *magnétisme animal,* there is no doubt that his doctrine was in many respects identical with that of the older magnetists mentioned above.

The idea of the universal fluid was suggested to him in the first place by his observation of the stars, which led him to believe the celestial bodies exercised a mutual influence on each other and on the earth. This he identified with magnetism, and it was but a step (and a step which had already been taken by the early magnetists) to extend this influence to the human body and all other objects, and to apply it to the science of medicine.

In 1776, Mesmer met with Gassner, the Swabian priest whose miraculous cures have already been considered and, setting aside the supernatural explanation offered by the healer himself, Mesmer declared that the cures and severe crises which followed on his manipulations were attributable to nothing but magnetism.

Nevertheless this encounter gave a new trend to his ideas. Hitherto he himself had employed an actual magnet in order to cure the sick, but seeing that Gassner dispensed with that aid, he was led to consider whether the power might not reside in a still greater degree in the human body. Mesmer's first cure was performed on an epileptic patient by means of magnets, but the honor of it was disputed by a Jesuit Fr. Hell (a professor of astronomy at the University of Vienna), who had supplied the magnetic plates, and who claimed to have discovered the principles on which the physician worked.

Thereafter for a few years Mesmer practiced in various European cities, and strove to obtain recognition for his theories, but without success. In 1778, however, he went to Paris, and there attained an immediate and triumphant success in the fashionable world, although the learned bodies still refused to have anything to say to him.

Aristocratic patients flocked in hundreds to Mesmer's consulting rooms, which were hung with mirrors, it being one of the physician's theories that mirrors augmented the magnetic fluid. He himself wore, it was said, a shirt of leather lined with silk, to prevent the escape of the fluid, while magnets were hung about his person to increase his natural supply of magnetism. The patients were seated round a *baquet* or magnetic tub, of which the following description was given by Seifert, one of Mesmer's biographers:

"This receptacle was a large pan, tub, or pool of water, filled with various magnetic substances, such as water, sand, stone, glass bottles (filled with magnetic water), etc. It was a focus within which the magnetism was concentrated, and out of which proceeded a number of conductors. These being bent pointed iron wands, one end was retained in the *baquet,* whilst the other was connected with the patient and applied to the seat of the disease. This arrangement might be made use of by any number of persons seated round the *baquet,* and thus a fountain, or any receptacle in a garden, as in a room, would answer for the purpose desired." For the establishment of a school of *Animal Magnetism* Mesmer was offered 20,000 livres by the French government, with an annual sum of 10,000 livres for its upkeep; but this he refused. Later, however, the sum of 340,000 livres was subscribed by prospective pupils, and handed over to him. One of Mesmer's earliest and most distinguished disciples was M. D'Eslon, a prominent physician, who laid the doctrines of animal magnetism before the Faculty of Medicine in 1780. Consideration of Mesmer's theories was, however, indignantly refused, and D'Eslon warned to rid himself of such

dangerous doctrine. Another disciple of Mesmer who attained to distinction in magnetic practice was the Marquis de Puységur, who was the first to observe and describe the state of induced somnambulism now as well known as the hypnotic trance. It has been suggested, and seems not improbable, that Mesmer himself knew something of the induced trance, but believing it to be a state full of danger, steadfastly set his face against it. However that may be, Puységur's ideas on the subject began to supersede those of Mesmer, and he gathered about him a distinguished body of adherents, among whom was numbered the celebrated Lavater. Indeed, his recognition of the fact that the symptoms attending the "magnetic sleep" were resultant from it, was a step of no small importance in the history of mesmerism. In 1784 a commission was appointed by the French government to enquire into the magnetic phenomena. For some reason or another its members chose to investigate the experiments of D'Eslon, rather than those of Mesmer himself. The commissioners, including among their number Benjamin Franklin, Lavoisier, and Bailly, observed the peculiar crises attending the treatment, and the *rapport* between patient and physician, but decided that imagination could produce all the effects, and that there was no evidence whatever for a magnetic fluid. The report, edited by M. Bailly, gives the following description of the crisis.

"The sick persons, arranged in great numbers, and in several rows around the *baquet* (bath), received the magnetism by means of the iron rods, which conveyed it to them from the *baquet* by the cords wound round their bodies, by the thumb which connected them with their neighbours, and by the sounds of a pianoforte, or an agreeable voice, diffusing magnetism in the air.

"The patients were also directly magnetised by means of the finger and wand of the magnetiser, moved slowly before their faces, above or behind their heads, or on the diseased parts.

"The magnetiser acts also by fixing his eyes on the subjects; by the application of his hands on the region of the solar plexus; an application which sometimes continues for hours.

"Meanwhile the patients present a very varied picture.

"Some are calm, tranquil, and experience no effect. Others cough and spit, feel pains, heat, or perspiration. Others, again, are convulsed.

"As soon as one begins to be convulsed, it is remarkable that others are immediately affected.

"The commissioners have observed some of these convulsions last more than three hours. They are often accompanied with expectorations of a violent character, often streaked with blood. The convulsions are marked with involuntary motions of the throat, limbs, and sometimes the whole body; by dimness of the eyes, shrieks, sobs, laughter, and the wildest hysteria. These states are often followed by languor and depression. The smallest noise appears to aggravate the symptoms, and often to occasion shudderings and terrible cries. It was noticeable that a sudden change in the air or time of the music had a great influence on the patients, and soothed or accelerated the convulsions, stimulating them to ecstasy, or moving them to floods of tears.

"Nothing is more astonishing than the spectacle of these convulsions.

"One who has not seen them can form no idea of them. The spectator is as much astonished at the profound repose of one portion of the patients as at the agitation of the rest.

"Some of the patients may be seen rushing towards each other with open arms, and manifesting every symptom of attachment and affection.

"All are under the power of the magnetizer; it matters not what state of drowsiness they may be in, the sound of his voice, a look, a motion of his hands, spasmodically affects them."

Although Mesmer, Puységur, and their followers continued to practice magnetic treatment, the report of the royal commission had the effect of quenching public interest in the subject, although from time to time a spasmodic interest in it was shown by scientists. M. de Jussieu, at about the time the commission presented its report, suggested that it would have done well to inquire into the reality of the alleged cures, and to endeavor to find a satisfactory explanation for the phenomena they had witnessed, while to remedy the deficiency he himself formulated a theory of "animal heat," an organic emanation which might be directed by the human will. Like Mesmer and the others, he believed in action at a distance (see also **Absent Healing**).

Mesmeric practitioners formed themselves into "Societies of Harmony" until the political situation in France rendered their existence impossible. Early in the nineteenth century Pététin and Deleuze published works on Animal Magnetism. But a new era was inaugurated with the publication in 1823 of Alexandre Bertrand's *Traité du Somnambulisme,* followed three years later by a treatise *Du Magnétisme Animal en France.*

From Animal Magnetism to Phreno-Magnetism and Hypnotism

Bertrand was a young physician of Paris, and to him belongs the honor of having discovered the important part played by suggestion in the phenomena of the induced trance. He had observed the connection between the magnetic sleep, epidemic ecstasy, and spontaneous sleep-walking, and declared that all the cures and strange symptoms which had formerly been attributed to "animal magnetism," "animal electricity," and the like, resulted from the suggestions of the operator acting on the imagination of a patient whose suggestibility was greatly increased.

It is probable that had he lived longer (he died in 1831, at the age of thirty-six), Bertrand would have gained a definite scientific standing for the facts of the induced trance, but as it was, the practitioners of animal magnetism still held to the theory of a "fluid" or force radiating from magnetizer to subject, while those who were unable to accept such a doctrine, ignored the matter altogether, or treated it as vulgar fraud and charlatanry.

Nevertheless Bertrand's works and experiments revived the flagging interest of the public to such an extent that in 1831 a second French commission was appointed by the Royal Academy of Medicine. The report of this commission was not forthcoming until more than five years had elapsed, but when it was finally published, it contained a definite testimony to the genuineness of the magnetic phenomena, and especially of the somnambulic state, and

declared that the commission was satisfied of the therapeutic value of "animal magnetism."

The report was certainly not of great scientific worth. The name of Bertrand was not even mentioned therein, nor his theory considered. On the other hand, a good deal of space was given to the more supernatural phenomena, clairvoyance, action at a distance, and the prediction by somnambulic patients of crises in their maladies. This is the more excusable, however, since these ideas were almost universally associated with somnambulism.

Community of sensation was held to be a feature of the trance state, as was also the transference of the senses to the stomach (see Seeing with the **Stomach**), while thought-transference was suggested by some of these earlier investigators, notably by J. P. F. Deleuze, who suggested that thoughts were conveyed from the brain of the operator to that of the subject through the medium of the subtle "magnetic fluid."

Meanwhile the Spiritualist theory was becoming more and more frequently advanced to explain the "magnetic" phenomena, including both the legitimate trance phenomena and the multitude of supernormal phenomena which was supposed to follow the somnambulic state. This will doubtless account in part for the extraordinary animosity which the medical profession showed towards animal magnetism as a therapeutic agency. Its anesthetic properties they ridiculed as fraud or imagination, notwithstanding that serious operations, even of the amputation of limbs, could be performed while the patient was in the magnetic sleep.

Thus Dr. John **Elliotson** was forced to resign his professorship at the University College Hospital; Dr. James **Esdaile,** a surgeon who practiced at a government hospital at Calcutta, had to contend with much ignorance and stupid conservatism in his professional brethren. Similar contemptuous treatment was dealt out to other medical men who were really pioneers of hypnotism, against whom nothing could be urged but their defense of mesmerism.

In 1841 James **Braid**, a British surgeon, arrived independently at the conclusions which Bertrand had reached some eighteen years earlier. Once more the theory of abnormal suggestibility was offered to explain the various phenomena of the so-called "magnetic" sleep, and once more it was utterly ignored, alike by the world of science and by the public.

Braid's explanation was essentially that which is offered now. He placed the new science, which he called "hypnotism," on a level with other natural sciences, above the mass of medieval magic and superstition in which he had found it. Yet even Braid did not seem to have entirely separated the chaff from the grain, for he countenanced the practice of phreno-**mesmerism,** a combination of mesmerism and **phrenology** wherein the entranced patient whose head was touched by the operator's fingers, exhibited every sign of the emotion or quality associated with the phrenological organ touched.

Braid asserted that a subject, entirely ignorant of the position of the phrenological organs, passed rapidly and accurately from one emotion to another, according to the portion of the scalp in contact with the hypnotist's fingers. His physiological explanation is a somewhat inadequate one, and we can only suppose that he was not fully appreciative of his own theory of suggestion.

In 1843 two periodicals dealing with "magnetism" appeared: the *Zoist,* edited by Dr. John Elliotson and a colleague, and the *Phreno-Magnet,* edited by Spencer T. Hall. The first, adopting a scientific tone, treated the subject mainly from a therapeutic point of view, while the latter was of a more popular character. Many of the adherents of both papers, and notably Elliotson himself, afterwards became Spiritualists.

In 1845 an additional impetus was given to animal magnetism by the publication in that year of Baron von **Reichenbach**'s researches. Reichenbach claimed to have discovered a new force, which he called "odyle," "od" or "odylic force", and which could be seen in the form of flames by "sensitives," i.e., sensitive individuals or psychics. Reichenbach meticulously classified the indications of such sensitivity as a more acute form of normal human faculty.

In the human being these emanations might be seen to radiate from the fingertips, while they were also visible in animals and inanimate things. Different colors issued from the different poles of the magnet. Reichenbach experimented by putting his sensitives in a dark room with various objects—crystals, precious stones, magnets, minerals, plants, animals—when they could unerringly distinguish each object by the color and size of the flame visible to their clairvoyant eye.

These emanations appeared so invariable and so permanent that an artist might paint them and, indeed, this was frequently done. Feelings of temperature, of heat or cold, were also experienced in connection with the "odylic force."

Baron von Reichenbach's experiments were spread over a number of years, and were made with every appearance of scientific care and precision, so that their effect on the mesmerists of the time was very considerable. But notwithstanding the mass of dubious and occult phenomena which was associated with hypnotism at that time, there is no doubt that the induced trance, with its therapeutic and anesthetic value, would soon have come into its own had not two other circumstances occurred to thrust it into the background. The first was the application of chloroform and ether to the purposes for which hypnotism had hitherto been used, a substitution which pleased the medical faculty greatly, and relieved its members from the necessity of studying hypnotism. The second circumstance was the introduction of the movement known as modern **Spiritualism,** which so emphasized the occult side of the trance phenomena as to obscure for nearly half a century the true significance of induced somnambulism.

Later Views of Hypnotism

But if the great body of medical and public opinion ignored the facts of hypnotism during the period following Braid's discovery, the subject did not fail to receive some attention from the more enlightened scientists of Europe, and from time to time investigators took upon themselves the task of inquiring into the phenomena.

This was especially the case in France, where the study of mesmerism or hypnotism was most firmly entrenched and where it met with least opposition. In 1858 Dr. Azam of Bordeaux investigated hypnotism from Braid's point of view, aided by a number of members of the Faculty of Paris. An account of his researches was published in 1860, but cast no new light on the matter. Later the same set of facts was examined by E. Mesnet, M. Duval, and others. In 1875, the noted psychical researcher Professor Charles **Richet** also studied the science of artificial somnambulism.

It was, however, from the Bernheim and the Nancy school that the generally accepted modern view of hypnotism is taken. H. Bernheim was himself a disciple of Liébeault, who, working on independent lines, had reached the same conclusion as Bertrand and Braid and once more formulated the doctrine of suggestion. Bernheim's work *De la Suggestion,* published in 1884, embodied the theories of A. A. Liébeault and the result of Bernheim's own researches therein.

According to this view, hypnotism is a purely psychological process, and is induced by mental influences. The "passes" of Mesmer and the magnetic philosophers, the elaborate preparations of the *baquet,* the strokings of Valentine Greatrakes, and all the multitudinous ceremonies with which the animal magnetists used to produce the artificial sleep, were only of service in inducing a state of expectation in the patient, or in providing a soothing and monotonous, or violent, sensory stimulus.

And so also with the modern methods of inducing hypnosis—the fixation of the eyes, the contact of the operator's hand, the sound of his voice, are only effective through the medium of the subject's mentality. Other investigators who played a large part in popularizing hypnotism were Professor J. M. Charcot, of the Salpêtrière, Paris, a distinguished pathologist, and R. Heidenhain, professor of physiology at Breslau. The former taught that the hypnotic condition was essentially a morbid one, and allied to hysteria, a theory which, becoming widely circulated, exercised a somewhat detrimental effect on the practice of hypnotism for therapeutic purposes, until it was at length proved erroneous. As a result, prejudice lingered against the use of the induced hypnotic trance in medicine until relatively modern times. Heidenhain laid stress on the physical operations to induce somnambulism, believing that thereby a peculiar state of the nervous system was brought about wherein the control of the higher nerve centers was temporarily removed, so that the suggestion of the operator was free to express itself automatically through the physical organism of the patient. The physiological theory also is somewhat misleading, nevertheless its exponents did good work in bringing the undoubted facts of hypnosis into prominence.

Besides these theories there was another to be met with chiefly in its native France—the old doctrine of a magnetic fluid. But it rapidly died out.

Among the symptoms which may safely, and without reference to the supernatural, be regarded as attendant on hypnotism are the *rapport* between subject and operator, implicit obedience on the part of the former to the smallest suggestion (whether given verbally or by look, gesture, or any unconscious action) anesthesia, positive and negative hallucinations, the fulfilment of post-hypnotic promises, control of organic processes and of muscles not ordinarily under voluntary control.

Other phenomena which have been allied from time to time with magnetism, mesmerism, or hypnotism and for which there is not the same scientific basis, are clairvoyance, telekinesis, transference of the senses from the ordinary sense organs to some other parts of the body (usually the finger tips or the pit of the stomach), community of sensation, and the ability to commune with the dead.

The majority of these, like the remarkable phenomena of phreno-magnetism, can be directly traced to the effect of suggestion on the imagination of the patient. Ignorant as were the protagonists of mesmerism with regard to the great suggestibility of the magnetized subject, it is hardly surprising that they saw new and supernormal faculties and agencies at work during the trance state.

To the same ignorance of the possibilities of suggestion and hyperesthesia may be referred the common belief that the hypnotizer can influence his subject by the power of his will alone, and secure obedience to commands which are only mentally expressed. At the same time it must be borne in mind that if belief in telepathy be accepted, there is a possibility that the operation of thought transference might be more freely carried out during hypnosis, and it is notable, in this respect, that the most fruitful of the telepathic experiments conducted by psychical researchers and others have been made with hypnotized percipients (see **Telepathy**).

An Extraordinary Experiment

One of the most bizarre and dangerous experiments in hypnotic telepathy is related in M. Larelig's biography of the celebrated Belgium painter Antoine Joseph Wiertz (1806–1865) and also in the introductory and biographical note affixed to the *Catalogue Raisonné du Musée Wiertz*, by Dr. S. Watteau (1865). Wiertz was the hypnotic subject and a friend, a doctor, was the hypnotizer. Wiertz had long been haunted by a desire to know whether thought persisted in a head severed from the trunk. His wish was the reason for the following experiment being undertaken, this being facilitated through his friendship with the prison doctor in Brussels, and another outside practitioner. The latter had been for many years a hypnotic operator and had more than once put Wiertz into the hypnotic state, regarding him as an excellent subject.

About this time a trial for murder in the Place Saint-Géry had been causing a great sensation in Belgium and the painter had been following the proceedings closely. The trial ended in the condemnation of the accused. A plan was arranged and Wiertz, with the consent of the prison doctor, obtained permission to hide with his friend, Dr. D., under the guillotine, close to where the head of the condemned would roll into the basket. In order to carry out more efficiently the scheme he had determined upon, the painter desired his hypnotizer to put him through a regular course of hypnotic suggestion, and when in the sleep state to command him to identify himself with various people and tell him to read their thoughts and penetrate into their psychical and mental states.

The following is a resumé given in *Le Progrès Spirite*: "On the day of execution, ten minutes before the arrival of the condemned man, Wiertz, accompanied by his friend the physician with two witnesses, ensconced themselves underneath the guillotine, where they were entirely hidden from sight. The painter was then put to sleep, and told to identify himself with the criminal. He was to follow

his thoughts and feel any sensations, which he was to express aloud. He was also 'suggested' to take special note of mental conditions during decapitation, so that when the head fell in the basket he could penetrate the brain and give an account of its last thoughts.

"Wiertz became entranced almost immediately, and the four friends soon understood by the sounds overhead that the executioner was conducting the condemned to the scaffold, and in another minute the guillotine would have done its work. The hypnotized Wiertz manifested extreme distress and begged to be demagnetized, as his sense of oppression was insupportable. It was too late, however—the knife fell.

" 'What do you feel? What do you see?' asks the doctor. Wiertz writhes convulsively and replies, 'Lightning! A thunderbolt falls! It thinks; it sees!' 'Who thinks and sees?' 'The head. It suffers horribly. It thinks and feels but does not understand what has happened. It seeks its body and feels that the body must join it. It still waits for the supreme blow for death, but death does not come.'

"As Wiertz spoke, the witnesses saw the head which had fallen into the basket and lay looking at them horribly; its arteries still palpitating. It was only after some moments of suffering that apparently the guillotined head at last became aware that is was separated from its body.

"Wiertz became calmer and seemed exhausted, while the doctor resumed his questions. The painter answered: 'I fly through space like a top spinning through fire. But am I dead? Is all over? If only they would let me join my body again! Have pity! give it back to me and I can live again. I remember all. There are the judges in red robes. I hear the sentence. Oh! my wretched wife and children. I am abandoned. If only you would put my body to me, I should be with you once more. You refuse? All the same I love you, my poor babies. Miserable wretch that I am I have covered you with blood. When will this finish!—or is not a murderer condemned to eternal punishment?'

"As Wiertz spoke these words, the witnesses thought they detected the eyes of the decapitated head open wide with a look of unmistakable suffering and of beseeching.

"The painter continued his lamentations: 'No, such suffering cannot endure for ever; God is merciful. All that belongs to earth is fading away. I see in the distance a little light glittering like a diamond. I feel a calm stealing over me. What a good sleep I shall have! What joy!' These were the last words the painter spoke. He was still entranced, but no longer replied to the questions put by the doctor. They then approached the head and Dr. D. touched the forehead, the temples, and teeth and found they were cold. The head was dead."

In the Wiertz Gallery in Brussels are to be found three pictures of a guillotined head, presumably the outcome of this gruesome experiment.

Theory of Hypnotic Action

Among numerous explanations of the physiological conditions accompanying the hypnotic state there is one, the theory of cerebral dissociation, which was generally accepted by science, and which may be briefly outlined as follows.

The brain is composed of innumerable groups of nerve cells, all more or less closely connected with each other by means of nervous links or paths of variable resistance.

Excitement of any of these groups, whether by means of impressions received through the sense organs or by the communicated activity of other groups, will, if sufficiently intense, occasion the rise into consciousness of an idea. In the normal waking state, the resistance of the nervous association-paths is fairly low, so that the activity is easily communicated from one neural group to another. Thus the main idea which reaches the upper stratum of consciousness is attended by a stream of other, subconscious ideas, which has the effect of checking the primary idea and preventing its complete dominance.

Now the abnormal dominance of one particular system of ideas—that suggested by the operator—together with the complete suppression of all rival systems, is the principal fact to be explained in hypnosis. To some extent the physiological process conditioning hypnosis suggests an analogy with normal sleep. When one composes oneself to sleep there is a lowering of cerebral excitement and a proportionate increase in the resistance of the neural links, and this is apparently what happens during hypnosis, the essential passivity of the subject raising the resistance of the association-paths.

But in normal sleep, unless some exciting cause be present, all the neural dispositions are at rest, whereas in the latter case such a complete suspension of cerebral activities is not permitted, since the operator, by means of voice, gestures, and manipulations of the patient's limbs, keeps alive that set of impressions relating to himself. One neural disposition is thus isolated, so that any idea suggested by the operator is free to work itself out in action, without being submitted to the checks of the sub-activity of other ideas.

The alienation is less or more complete according as the degree of hypnotism is light or heavy, but a comparatively slight raising of resistance in the neural links suffices to secure the dominance of ideas suggested by the hypnotizer.

Hyperesthesia, mentioned so frequently in connection with the hypnotic state, really belongs to the doubtful class, since it has not yet been decided whether or not an actual sharpening or refining of the senses takes place. Alternatively it may be suggested that the accurate perception of very faint sense-impressions, which seems to furnish evidence for hyperesthesia, merely recalls the fact that the excitement conveyed through the sensory nerve operates with extraordinary force, being freed from the restriction of sub-excitement in adjacent neural groups and systems.

In putting forward this viewpoint it must be conceded that in normal life, very feeble sensory stimuli must act on nerve and brain just as they do in hypnosis, save that in the former case they are so stifled amid a multitude of similar impressions that they fail to reach consciousness. In any case the occasional abnormal sensitiveness of the subject to very slight sensory stimuli is a fact of hypnotism as well authenticated as anesthesia itself, and the term "hyperesthesia," if not entirely justified, may for want of a better, be practically applied to the observed phenomenon.

The hypnotic state is not necessarily induced by a second person. "Spontaneous" hypnotism and "autohypnotization" are well known. Certain Indian fakirs and the shamans of primitive races can produce in themselves a state closely approximating to hypnosis, by a prolonged fixation of the eyes, and by other means. The mediumistic trance is also, as will be shown hereafter, a case in point.

Hypnotism and Spiritualism

Spiritualism was a legacy bequeathed by the magnetic philosophers of medieval times, and through them, from the still older astrologers and magi. It has been shown that at a very early date, phenomena of a distinctly hypnotic character were ascribed to the workings of spiritual agencies, whether angelic or demonic, by a certain percentage of the observers. Thus Greatrakes and Gassner believed themselves to have been gifted with a divine power to heal diseases.

Cases of ecstasy, catalepsy and other trance states were given a spiritual significance, i.e., demons, angels, elementals, and so on, were supposed to speak through the lips of the possessed. Witchcraft, in which the force of hypnotic suggestion seems to have operated in a very large degree, was thought to result from the witches' traffic with the devil and his legions. Even in some cases the souls of deceased men and women were identified with these intelligences, although not generally until the time of Swedenborg. Although the movement known as "Modern Spiritualism" is usually dated from 1848, the year of the "**Rochester Rappings**," the real growth of Spiritualism was much more gradual, and its roots passed through animal magnetism.

Emanuel Swendenborg, whose affinities with the magnetists have already been referred to, exercised a remarkable influence on the Spiritualist thought of America and Europe, and was in a sense the founder of that faith. Automatic phenomena were even then a feature of the magnetic trance, and clairvoyance, community of sensation, and telepathy were believed in generally, and regarded by many as evidences of spiritual communication.

In Germany, Professor Jung-Stilling (see J. J. **Jung**), Dr. C. Römer, Dr. Werner, and the poet and physician Justinus **Kerner,** were among those who held opinions on these lines, the latter pursuing his investigations with a somnambule who became famous as the "Seerers of Prevorst"—Frau Frederica **Hauffe.**

Frau Hauffe could see and converse with the spirits of the deceased, and gave evidence of prophetic vision and clairvoyance. Physical phenomena were witnessed in her presence, knockings, rattling of chains, movement of objects without contact, and, in short, such manifestations as were characteristic of **poltergeist.** She was, moreover, the originator of a "primeval" language, which she declared was that spoken by the patriarchs.

Thus Frau Hauffe, although only a somnambule or magnetic patient, possessed all the qualities of a successful Spiritualist medium.

In England also there were many circumstances of a supernatural character associated with mesmerism. Dr. Elliotson, one of the best-known of English magnetists, became in time converted to a Spiritualist theory, as offering an explanation of the clairvoyance and similar phenomena which he thought to have observed in his patients.

France, the headquarters of the rationalist school of magnetism, had indeed a good deal less to show of Spiritualist opinion. Nonetheless even in that country the latter doctrine made its appearance at intervals prior to 1848. J. P. F. Deleuze, a good scientist and an earnest protagonist of magnetism, who published his *Histoire Critique du Magnétisme Animal* in 1813, was said to have embraced the doctrines of Spiritualism before he died.

Dr. G. P. Billot was another believer in spirit communication, and one who succeeded in obtaining physical phenomena in the presence of his somnambules. It was, however, Alphonse Cahagnet, a man of humble origin, who began to study induced somnambulism about the year 1845, and who thereafter experimented with somnambules, and who became one of the first French Spiritualists of distinction. So good was the evidence for spirit communication furnished by Cahagnet and his subjects that it remains among the most impressive which the annals of the movement produced.

In America, the Rev. Laroy **Sunderland,** Andrew Jackson **Davis,** and others who became pillars of Spiritualism were first attracted to it through the study of magnetism. Elsewhere we find hypnotism and Spiritualism identified with each other until in 1848 a definite split occurs, and the two go their separate ways.

Even so, however, the separation is not quite complete. In the first place, the mediumistic trance is obviously a variant of spontaneous or self-induced hypnotism, while in the second, many of the most striking phenomena of the seance room have been matched time and again in the records of animal magnetism.

For instance, the diagnosis of disease and prescription of remedies dictated by the control to the "healing medium" have their prototype in the cures of Valentine Greatrakes, or of Mesmer and his disciples. Automatic phenomena—speaking in "**tongues**" and so forth—early formed a characteristic feature of the induced trance and kindred states.

Even the physical phenomena, **movement** without contact, **apports, rappings,** were witnessed in connection with magnetism long before the movement known as modern Spiritualism was so much as thought of. In some instances, though not in all, it is possible to trace the operation of hypnotic suggestion in the automatic phenomena, just as we can perceive the result of fraud in much of the physical manifestations. The question whether, after the factors of hypnotism and fraud have been removed, a section of the phenomena remains inexplicable say by the hypothesis of communication with the spirit world is one which has been in the past, and is today, answered in the affirmative by many individuals of the highest distinction in their various walks of life, and one which we would do well to treat with due circumspection. This, however, is reserved for consideration elsewhere, the scope of the present article being to show how closely Spiritualism and hypnotism have been connected in their historical development and phenomena.

Hypnotism and Psychical Phenomena

The three classical states of hypnotism were thus described by psychical researcher Dr. Paul **Joire:**

1. Lethargy, the state of complete relaxation with variable amount of anesthesia, with neuro-muscular excitation as its fundamental characteristic. In this state the subject has the eyes closed and is generally only slightly open to suggestion.

2. Catalepsy, the eyes are open, the subject is as though petrified in the position which he occupies. Anesthesia is complete, and there is no sign of intelligence. Immobility is characteristic of this state.

3. Somnambulism. The condition of the eyes varies, the subject appears to sleep. Simple contact, or stroking along any limb is sufficient to render that limb rigid. Suggestibility is the main characteristic of this state. The somnambulistic state presents three degrees:

(i) Waking somnambulism, slight passivity with diminution of the will and augmentation of suggestibility.

(ii) The second personality begins to take the place of the normal one. Torpor of consciousness and memory. Sensibility decreases.

(iii) Complete anesthesia. Disappearance of consciousness and memory. Inclination to peculiar muscular rigidity.

It is very likely that the depth of hypnotic sleep may infinitely vary. Distinct trains of memory may correspond to each stage, presenting alternating personalities of a shallow type.

The means to induce the hypnotic state differ. In many cases simple suggestion will do, even from a distance; in others passes and the close proximity of the hypnotizer will be necessary. Some subjects feel the old "mesmerizer" influence, some do not.

The implicit obedience to suggestion has great therapeutical and psychological significance. Bad habits may be improved, phobias, manias, criminal propensities, diseases cured, inhibitions removed, pain banished, the ordinary working of defective senses restored, the ordinary senses vivified, an increased intelligence and ability in professional pursuits result and new senses of perception developed.

Subconscious calculation discloses flashes of mathematical genius and the rapport once established, the possibility is open for the development of supernormal faculties. The subject may see clairvoyantly, give psychometric descriptions, see into the future, read the past, make spiritual excursions to distant places, hear and see events occurring there and give correct medical diagnoses. Dr. Eugène **Osty** believed that the number of hypnotizable subjects was getting less and less and in support of his contention, referred in the *Revue Metapsychique* (November-December, 1930) to the similar experiences of Dr. Berillon, Prof. **Richet** and M. Emile Magnin. However, modern hypnotists have shown that there is no shortage of subjects and that a high percentage of ordinary individuals are susceptible to hypnosis.

The exact nature of the hypnotic trance is still unknown. Its relation to the mediumistic trance is of absorbing interest. The first essential difference is that the mediumistic trance is voluntary and self-induced, although hypnotism, for the purpose of relieving the medium from the attendant physiological suffering, is sometimes employed to bring it about. Dr. J. **Ochorowicz** saved Mlle. **Tomczyk** much exhaustion by hypnotizing her. Mme. **Bisson** similarly facilitated the materialization phenomena of **Eva C.** Kathleen **Goligher** was hypnotized by Dr. W. S. **Crawford,** the **Didier Brothers** were always accompanied by a magnetizer and the mediumship of Andrew Jackson **Davis** was initiated by hypnotic clairvoyance.

Generally, if the hypnotized subject is a medium, he or

she exhibits faculties of a far more transcendental character than ordinary subjects. Ordinary faculties of clairvoyance may progress to traveling clairvoyance and it is very likely that many of the wonderful phenomena of early mesmerizers was due to the fact that their subjects, unknown to them, were mediums.

The hypnotized subject has great powers of personation. But he does not claim, unless so suggested, communication with the dead. In the mediumistic trance such suggestion does not work. Those whose appearance is yearned for often do not communicate at all, many strangers come and go and all the controls exhibit a distinct personality far surpassing in variety the imitative efforts of any hypnotized subject. If they were subjective creations of the medium's mind they would not exhibit those special peculiarities by which the sitters establish their identity with their departed friends. The hypnotic self does not normally exhibit such cunning as the personation of hundreds of individuals and the acquisition of facts deeply buried in the subconscious or totally unknown to the sitters, although there is evidence that the subconscious mind may sometimes invent plausible personalities, just like the waking consciousness of a novelist.

The hypnotic personality has an uncanny sense of time. Spirit controls, on the other hand, are very vague and uncertain on this point. Their messages are not exactly located in time, and are sometimes borne out by past or near future happenings.

Professor William **James** made many attempts to see whether Mrs. **Piper**'s medium-trance had any community of nature with ordinary hypnotic trance. The first two attempts to hypnotize her failed but after the fifth attempt she had become a pretty good hypnotic subject "as far as muscular phenomena and automatic imitations of speech and gesture go; but I could not affect her consciousness, or otherwise get her beyond this point. Her condition in this semi-hypnosis is very different from her medium-trance. The latter is characterized by great muscular unrest, even her ears moving vigorously in a way impossible to her in her waking state, but in hypnosis her muscular relaxation and weakness are extreme. She often makes several efforts to speak before her voice becomes audible; and to get a strong contraction of the hand, for example, express manipulation and suggestion must be practised. Her pupils contract in the medium-trance. Suggestions to the control that he should make her recollect after the medium-trance what she had been saying were accepted, but had no result. In the hypnotic trance such a suggestion will often make the patient remember all that has happened."

From time to time hypnotism has been used in an attempt to validate theories of **Reincarnation.** A hypnotized subject is made to recall experiences which progressively regress to birth and then (allegedly) to memories of former births. An early experimenter in this technique was Col. Albert **Rochas** in France. Two of his subjects were Marie Mayo and Juliette. In modern times, the hypnotist Morey **Bernstein** created a sensation with his book *The Search for Bridey Murphy* (Doubleday, 1956) based on his experiences with the subject "Ruth Simmons" (Mrs. Virginia Tighe), who was alleged to recover memories of a previous life as an Irish girl named Bridey Murphy.

Another modern experimenter is Denys Kelsey, who hypnotized his wife novelist Joan **Grant.** Their book *Many Lifetimes* (1969) presents Joan Grant's claimed memories of former lives.

The British hypnotherapist Arnall **Bloxham** conducted many experiments with hypnotic regression and many of these have been recorded on magnetic tape and in 1970 were the subject of a British television documentary. (See also **Animal Magnetism; Autosuggestion; Mesmerism; Reincarnation; Spiritualism; Trance**)

Recommended reading:

Ambrose, G. & G. Newbold. *A Handbook of Medical Hypnosis,* 4th ed., Macmillan, 1980

Bernheim, H. *Hypnosis & Suggestion in Psychotherapy; A Treatise on the Nature and Uses of Hypnotism,* London, 1888; University Books, 1964

Braid, James. *Braid on Hypnotism; the Beginnings of Modern Hypnosis,* Julian Press, 1960 (reissue of *Neurypnology,* 1843)

Brown, Slater. The Heyday of Spiritualism, Hawthorn Books, 1970

Cahagnet, L. Alphone. *The Celestial Telegraph,* London, 1850

Deleuze, J. P. F. *Practical Instructions in Animal Magnetism,* New York, 1879

Edmunds, Simeon. *Hypnotism & Psychic Phenomena,* Wilshire paperback, n.d.

Erskine, Alex. *A Hypnotist's Casebook,* Rider & Co., London, 1932

Esdaile, James. *Hypnosis in Medicine and Surgery,* Institute for Research in Hypnosis Publication Press, N.Y., 1957 (reissue of *Mesmerism in India,* 1850)

Fahnestock, William B. *Statuvolism, or Artificial Somnambulism,* Chicago, 1871

Frankau, Gilbert (ed.). *Mesmerism by Doctor Mesmer (1779); Being the first translation of Mesmer's historic* Mémoire sur la découverte du Magnétisme Animal *to appear in English,* Macdonald, London, 1948

Goldsmith, Margaret. *Franz Anton Mesmer; The History of an Idea,* Arthur Barker, London, 1934

Gregory, William. *Animal Magnetism or Mesmerism and its Phenomena,* London, 1884 etc.

Grossi, Ralph. *Reliving Reincarnation Through Hypnosis,* Exposition Press, Smithtown, N.Y., 1975

Hull, C. L. *Hypnosis and Suggestibility; An Experimental Approach,* Century Psychology Service, N.Y., 1933

Milne, J. Bramwell. *Hypnotism; Its History, Practice, and Theory,* London, 1903

Moll, Albert. *Hypnotism; Including a Study of the Chief Points of Psycho-Therapeutics and Occultism,* Walter Scott Publishing Co., London, 1889 etc.

Ochorowicz, J. *De la Suggestion Mentale,* Paris, 1887

Podmore, Frank. *Mesmerism and Christian Science,* Methuen, London, 1909

Reichenbach, Karl von (transl. William Gregory). *Researches on Magnetism, Electricity, Heat, Light, Crystallization, and Chemical Attraction in their relations to the Vital Force,* London, 1850; University Books, N.Y., 1974

Reichenbach, Karl von. (transl. William Gregory). *Letters on Od and Magnetism,* Hutchinson, London, 1928 (reissued under title *The Odic Force: Letters on Od & Magnetism,* University Books, 1968)

Rutter, J. O. N. *Human Electricity; The Means of Its*

Development, Parker, London, 1854

Smith, Susy. *ESP and Hypnosis,* Macmillan, 1973

Tinterow, Maurice M. *Foundations of Hypnosis; From Mesmer to Freud,* Chas. C. Thomas, Springfield, Ill., 1970

Toksvig, Signe. *Emmanuel Swedenborg, Scientist and Mystic,* Yale University Press, 1948

Wambach, Helen. *Reliving Past Lives; The Evidence Under Hypnosis,* Harper & Row, 1978

Hypocephalus

A disk of bronze or painted linen found under the heads of Græco-Roman mummies in Egypt. It was inscribed with magical formulae and divine figures, and its object was probably to secure warmth for the corpse. There is frequently depicted upon such amulets a scene showing cynocephalus apes adoring the solar disk seated in his boat.

Hyslop, George Hall (1892–1965)

American physician and neuropsychiatrist who was a prominent figure in the field of psychic research. Born December 20, 1892, at New York, N.Y., he studied at University of Indiana (B.A. 1913, M.A. Psychology 1914) and Cornell University Medical College (M.D. 1919). In 1916 he married Esther McNaull. He had a distinguished medical and psychiatric career, and was President of the New York Neurological Society 1955–56, fellow of the American Medical Association, New York Academy of Medicine, Chairman of the section on Neurology and Psychiatry, New York Academy of Medicine 1941–42, founding fellow of American Academy of Compensation Medicine 1948. He was a member of the Society for Psychical Research, London, and the Parapsychological Association.

He was also a member of the American Society for Psychical Research from 1913 onwards and served as President for twenty-one years.

His articles in the *ASPR Journal* included: 'Certain Problems of Psychic Research' (August 1930), 'Report of the Questionnaire Committee' (November 1930), 'The Biological Approach to Psychic Phenomena' (April 1942), 'An Instance of Apparent Spontaneous Telepathy' (April 1948). Dr. Hyslop was the son of pioneer psychic researcher James Hervey **Hyslop** and contributed an appreciation of his father's work to the *ASPR Journal:* 'James H. Hyslop: His Contribution to Psychical Research' (October 1950).

Hyslop, James Hervey (1854–1920)

Professor of Logic and Ethics from 1889–1902 at Columbia University, New York, one of the most distinguished American psychical researchers.

He was born August 18, 1854 at Xenia, Ohio. He was educated at Wooster College, Ohio (B.A., 1877), University of Leipzig, 1882–84 (Ph.D., 1877); Johns Hopkins University (L.L.D., 1902). He was one of the first Ameri-can psychologists to connect psychology with psychic phenomena.

In 1888, in a skeptical frame of mind, he was brought for the first time in touch with the supernormal through the psychic Mrs. **Piper.** Messages from his father and relatives poured through. They reminded him of facts known and unknown to him. He was intensely puzzled. Out of 205 incidents mentioned in the record of his sixteenth sitting, he was able to verify no fewer than 152. The personality of the communicators was so strong and impressive that after twelve sittings he had no hesitation in declaring: "I have been talking with my father, my brother, my uncles. Whatever supernormal powers we may be pleased to attribute to Mrs. Piper's secondary personalities, it would be difficult to make me believe that these secondary personalities could have thus completely reconstituted the mental personality of my dead relatives. To admit this would involve me in too many improbabilities. I prefer to believe that I have been talking to my dead relatives in person; it is simpler."

When Dr. Richard **Hodgson** died in 1905, he took his place as chief investigator of Mrs. Piper and devoted the following year to the organization of a new **American Society for Psychical Research**. The work was successful and he became the active spirit of the new society, the first *Journal* of which was published in January 1907. For the first two years he was assisted by Dr. Hereward **Carrington,** later by Dr. W. F. **Prince.**

Hyslop was a prolific writer and a great American propagandist of survival. In his *Life After Death* (1918) he forcefully stated: "I regard the existence of discarnate spirits as scientifically proved and I no longer refer to the skeptic as having any right to speak on the subject. Any man who does not accept the existence of discarnate spirits and the proof of it is either ignorant or a moral coward. I give him short shrift, and do not propose any longer to argue with him on the supposition that he knows anything about the subject."

Hyslop contributed many ingenious theories to psychical literature. He made a deep study of multiple **personality** and of **obsession,** and came to the conclusion that in many cases it was due to spirit **possession.** In his will, he founded an institute for the treatment of obsession through the instrumentality of mediums. He died June 17, 1920, in upper Montclair, New Jersey. The evidence of his own spirit return is discussed by his secretary, Gertrude O. Tubby, in her book *James Hyslop X.—His Book* (1929). For an appreciation of Hyslop's work, see the article 'James H. Hyslop: His Contribution to Psychical Research' by his son George Hall Hyslop in the *ASPR Journal* (October, 1950).

J. H. Hyslop's own publications included: *Science and a Future Life,* (1906), *Borderland of Psychical Research* (1906), *Enigmas of Psychical Research* (1906), *Psychical Research and the Resurrection* (1908), *Psychical Research and Survival,* (1913), *Life After Death* (1918), *Contact with the Other World* (1919).

I

I Am Movement

Cult founded in 1930 by Guy W. **Ballard** (1878-1939) with his wife Edna. Writing under the pseudonym "Godfré Ray King," Ballard published his first book *Unveiled Mysteries* (1934) after allegedly encountering a godlike figure named as "The Master Saint-Germain" in the wood near Mount Shasta in northern California. Ballard's claimed divine power named as "The Mighty I Am Presence" was immediately available to him through the Ascended Masters of the past.

Ballard's cult teachings were an offshoot of Theosophical concepts, together with a new mythology of underground adepts, lost civilizations, flying boats and strange lights. Great emphasis was placed on the importance of colors as an occult influence, and Ballard wore pastel suits, colored shoes, and preached in a setting of electric violet drapes.

After the death of Ballard, the cult was continued by Edna Ballard until her death in 1971, and subsequently by the Saint-Germain Foundation. The "I Am" movement is still based at Mount Shasta and holds an annual pageant on the life of Christ, firmly established as a tourist attraction. Much of the aura of mystery and romantic occult legend surrounding Mount Shasta stems from the cult's publicity. (See also Guy W. **Ballard**)

I Ching (Yi King or Y-Kim)

The ancient Chinese *Book of Changes,* attributed to the Emperor Fo-Hi in 3468 B.C. It expounds a classical Chinese philosophy based on the dual cosmic principles of Yin and Yang and claims to elucidate the implications of any given moment by a technique involving interpretation of sixty-four hexagrams, each composed of two groups of three lines. These lines are each either divided or undivided.

The implications of any given moment are traditionally ascertained by a process of selecting sticks or yarrow stalks, which indicate the appropriate hexagram and the interpretation associated with it.

A bundle of fifty sticks is used. These should be kept wrapped in clean silk or cloth. When consulting the I Ching, it is traditional to face south and incorporate the divination procedure in a ritual. Prostrations are made, then incense lighted, and the sticks passed through the fumes. The question to be answered should be unambiguous, usually related to the favorable or unfavorable anguries of a given project. One of the fifty sticks is taken out and put on one side. The remaining forty-nine are bunched together then quickly divided into two heaps by the right hand. The enquirer then takes one stick from the

right-hand pile and places it between the last two fingers of the left hand. He now pushes away four sticks at a time from the left-hand pile until only one, two, three or four remain. This remainder is placed between the next two fingers of the left hand. Next, four sticks at a time are pushed away from the right-hand pile until only one, two, three or four remain. The left hand should now contain either five or nine sticks, thus: $1 + 1 + 3$; $1 + 2 + 2$; $1 + 3 + 1$; or $1 + 4 + 4$. These sticks are now laid in the *second* heap. The process is then repeated with the remaining sticks from the first heap, which are pushed together with the right hand and then divided as previously. This will yield a total of either four or eight sticks, thus: $1 + 1 + 2$; $1 + 2 + 1$; $1 + 3 + 4$; or $1 + 4 + 3$. These four or eight sticks are then placed on the first pile, but kept slightly apart from those already there.

The process is now repeated with sticks remaining on the first heap, resulting in either four or eight, as in the second phase. After these three counts, the second heap will now contain $(5 \text{ or } 9) + (4 \text{ or } 8) + (4 \text{ or } 8)$. These three figures indicate the bottom line of the appropriate hexagram, i.e., unbroken or broken, and whether moving or not.

Now the forty-nine sticks are again bunched together and the whole process repeated to discover the second line from the bottom of the hexagram, and so on until the six lines have been found. A table of interpretations of the upper and lower trigrams can now be consulted.

A quicker system of divining the appropriate hexagrams involves the tossing of six coins. More recently a set of I Ching playing cards has been marketed in the U.S. permitting an even more rapid divination.

There are several translations of the I Ching currently available, and it is advisable to study more than one, because the interpretations of the ancient Chinese concepts and symbols sometimes varies.

For parallels between the I Ching and Western occultism, see entry under **Y-KIM,** Book of.

Recommended reading:

Baynes, C. F. & R. Wilhelm (transl.). *The I Ching or Book of Changes,* Princeton, 1967

Blofeld, John (transl.). *I Ching: The Book of Changes,* E. P. Dutton, 1968

Legge, James (transl.). *I Ching; Book of Changes,* Causeway Books, 1973

Legge, James (transl., edited Ch'u Chai & Winberg Chai). *I Ching: Book of Changes,* University Books, 1964

Liu, Da. *I Ching Coin Prediction,* Harper & Row, 1975

Reifler, Sam. *I Ching: A New Interpretation for Modern Times,* Bantam, 1974

Schoenholtz, Larry. *New Directions in the I Ching; The Yellow River Legacy,* University Books, 1975

Iao (or I-ha-ho)

A mystic name said by Clement of Alexandria (c. 150-c. 213 A.D.) to have been worn on their persons by the initiates of the Mysteries of Serapis. It was said to embody the symbols of the two generative principles.

Serapis was an Egyptian divinity who, with Isis, supplanted Osiris and Apis and acquired their attributes. As a healing divinity, Serapis was a rival of Aesculapius in Rome and in vogue in the Greek cult of Asklepios at Pergamon and Alexandria.

ICELAND

Icelandic interest in psychical research goes back many years with the founding of Salarrannsoknafelag Island, the Society for Psychical Research of Iceland in Reykjavik in 1918. The founder was Prof. Einar Hjöleifsson Kvaran (1859–1938), a well-known writer who edited *Morgunn,* a Spiritualist magazine. A prominent member was Prof. Haraldur **Nielsson** (died 1928) of the University of Reykjavik, who spent five years investigating the phenomena of the medium Indride **Indridason.**

A contemporary researcher is Thorstein Thorsteinsson, at University of Iceland, Rekjavik.

Ichthyomancy

Divination by the inspection of the entrails of fish. (See also **Divination**)

Identity

The identity of spirit communicators is a comparatively modern problem. In olden times every spirit voice was considered the voice of God or of the devil. The prophets communed with God. Mediums commune with spirits. God could not be asked to prove his identity, but the spirits have to. John the Apostle said: "Beloved, believe not every spirit, but try the spirits whether they be of God; because many false prophets are gone out into the world."

It has been generally admitted that in the seances of Mrs. **Piper** far better evidence of identity has been adduced over and again than any ordinary telephone conversation with someone living could provide. However, the argument of the opponents of the spirit hypothesis is basically that "in the latter case we know that an intelligent operator is present, we do not have to prove that. But in the former case we have to prove the very existence of the intelligent operator; hence the standard of evidence must be far higher."

What kind of evidence can stand the supreme test? A. N. **Aksakof,** the well-known Russian Spiritualist, said in despair: "Absolute proof of spirit identity is impossible to obtain; we must be content with relative proof." The critical spirit of Prof. Charles **Richet** echoed the same opinion: "Subjective metapsychics will always be radically incapable of proving survival."

According to Sir Oliver **Lodge,** the question of identity in spirit communication could be established (1) by gradually accumulated internal evidence, based on pertinacious and careful record; (2) by **cross correspondences** or the reception of unintelligible parts of one consistent and coherent message, through different mediums; (3) by

information or criteria especially characteristic of the supposed communicating intelligence, and if possible, in some sense new to the world.

Ingenious efforts to furnish proof have been variously made in sealed letter tests, **book tests,** newspaper tests and cross references. The human element of the problem is well illustrated by an amusing experiment of Sir Oliver Lodge as told by H. Dennis **Bradley** in his book *The Wisdom of the Gods* (1925). Lodge has twelve children, who sat around him at the table. "Now, let's play a game," he said. "You will pretend that I am dead, and you cross-examine me as to whether I am your father or not. Ask me all the questions that you think would prove it." For an hour they asked him about things in his past life and theirs and he couldn't remember one of the things they could remember. So, at the end, he said: "That proves it's not me. I'm not your father."

The communicator in a Spiritualist seance is mostly in the background. He acts like a prompter in the theater. The automatic script or trance speech delivered through the medium seldom represents his own hand or his own voice. The medium's organism acts like a freshly painted sieve, it tints whatever it lets through. Besides, communication is an art itself and has its own inherent difficulties (see **Communication**). **Direct voice** seances, **materialization** in good light, life-like personation of the departed or the **transfiguration** of the medium which afford more dramatic evidence with less opportunity for self-deception are comparatively rare.

With ancient names or historic personalities, the problem of establishing the identity of the communicator is almost hopeless. Impersonation is of frequent occurrence. The entity "Imperator" said in a script of the Rev. Stainton **Moses**: "There is much insanity among lower spirits. The assumption of great names, when it is not the work of conscious deceivers, is the product of insanity. The spirit imagines itself to be some great one, fancies how he would act, and so projects his imaginings on the sphere of the medium's consciousness."

If the information claimed as proofs of identity as regards famous personages is verifiable, it cannot be proved that such facts were inaccessible to the medium's subconsciousness or to his powers of **clairvoyance.** It should also be borne in mind that "Rector," another **control** of Stainton Moses, had the power of reading books. This opens up a storehouse of pertinent information for so-called deceiving spirits.

Theoretically, therefore, the difficulties of proof of spirit identity are almost insurmountable. Practically, the human element, the complexity of life, often provides very strong assumptions in favor of identity.

One of the earliest cases of convincing identity proof was registered by the Rev. J. B. Ferguson in his book *Spirit Communion* (1854). O. F. Parker died on August 5, 1854, at St. Louis. On the following day at Maryville, Kentucky, Mrs. Ferguson was controlled by his spirit. Part of the communication was: "My books I ordered to be sold to defray my funeral expenses, but it was not done. I am afraid, too, that there will be some flaw picked in my life policy, and if so I wish you to order my books to be sold to pay my debts, and if they fail, do not fail then from any delicacy of feeling to write to my mother, and she will have all properly settled. The policy is now in the hands of Mr. Hitchcock." The Rev. Ferguson affirmed that until the communication, the only account they had of his cousin's decease was a short telegram. As every detail was found correct, he considered the evidence of identity overwhelming.

C. H. Foster was visited in 1874 in San Francisco by the Hon. Charles E. de Long, a perfect stranger to him. He said he had a message for "Ida" and asked the visitor if this name meant anything to him. It was the name of his wife. Foster asked him to bring her and when she came, he wrote automatically the following message: "To my daughter, Ida. Ten years ago I entrusted a large sum to Thomas Madden to invest for me in certain lands. After my death he failed to account for the investment to my executors. The money was invested and 1,250 acres of land were bought, and one half of this land now belongs to you. I paid Madden on account of my share of the purchase 650 dollars. He must be made to make a settlement. Your father, Vineyard."

This story proved to be true. Madden admitted the commission and made restitution.

A very often-quoted case in Spiritualist literature is that of the steam-roller suicide. The notes of the Rev. Stainton Moses are as follows: "February 20, 1874. Dr. and Mrs. Speer and I dined with Mrs. Gregory, to meet the Baron du Potet, the celebrated magnetist and spiritualist. Mr. Percival was of the party. During dinner I was conscious of a strange influence in the room and mentioned the fact. The Baron had previously magnetised me very strongly, and had rendered me more than usually clairvoyant. He also recognised a spirit in the room, but thought it was the spirit of a living person. After dinner, when we got upstairs, I felt an uncontrollable inclination to write, and I asked the Baron to lay his hand upon my arm. It began to move very soon and I fell into a deep trance. As far as I can gather from the witnesses, the hand then wrote out 'I killed myself to-day.' This was preceded by a very rude drawing, and then 'Under steam-roller, Baker Street, medium passed,' (i.e., W. S. M.) was written. At the same time I spoke in the trance and rose and apparently motioned something away, saying 'Blood' several times. This was repeated and the spirit asked for prayer. Mrs. G. said a few words of prayer, and I came out of the trance at last, feeling very unwell. On the following day Dr. Speer and I walked down Baker Street and asked the policeman on duty if any accident had occurred there. He told us that a man had been killed by the steam-roller at 9 a.m. and that he himself had helped to carry the body to Marylebone Workhouse."

The only flaw in this case is that the *Pall Mall Gazette* published a short account of the suicide the same evening and this might conceivably have been subconsciously seen by the medium. The name was not known, nor was it disclosed in Moses' experience.

Dr. Isaac **Funk,** the New York editor, handed a letter to Mrs. Piper containing the word "mother." Mrs. Piper gave the Christian name of Mr. Funk's mother, told him that she was walking on only one leg and asked: "Don't you remember that needle?" She had hurt herself by thrusting a needle into her foot. Mrs. Piper also described a grandson, Chester, of whom Funk knew nothing. Upon inquiry, however, he found out that a grandson of this name died twenty years previously.

Dr. Joseph Vezzano established the identity of a materialized form in a seance given by Eusapia **Palladino** and described it in *Annals of Psychic Science* (Vol. 6, p. 164, September, 1907) as follows: "In spite of the dimness of the light I could distinctly see Mme. Palladino and my fellow sitters. Suddenly I perceived that behind me was a form, fairly tall, which was leaning its head on my left shoulder and sobbing violently, so that those present could hear the sobs. It kissed me repeatedly. I clearly perceived the outline of the face, which touched my own, and I felt the very fine and abundant hair in contact with my left cheek, so that I could be quite sure that it was a woman."

"The table then began to move, and typtology gave the name of a close family connection who was known to none present except myself. She had died some time before and on account of incompatability of temperament there had been serious disagreements with her. I was so far from expecting this typtological response that I at first thought this was a case of coincidence of name, but while I was mentally forming this reflection I felt a mouth, with warm breath, touch my left ear and whisper in a low voice in Genoese dialect, a succession of sentences, the murmur of which was audible to the sitters. These sentences were broken by bursts of weeping and their gist was repeatedly to implore pardon for injuries done to me, with a fullness of detail connected with family affairs which could only be known to the person in question.

"The phenomenon seemed so real that I felt compelled to reply to the excuses offered me with expressions of affection and to ask pardon in my turn if any resentment of the wrongs referred to had been excessive. But I had scarcely uttered the first syllables when two hands, with exquisite delicacy, applied themselves to my lips and prevented my continuing. The form then said to me: 'Thank you,' embraced me, kissed me, and disappeared."

According to Prof. T. Flournoy, this case was nothing else than the objectification of the emotional complex existing within the subconscious mind of M. Vezzano. There is food for thought, even for those who incline to differ, in his following remark: "The invasion or subjugation of the organism of the medium by a psychic complex belonging to a strange individual is not more easy to explain if that individuality be a spirit of the dead than if it is or belongs to one of the sitters in flesh and blood. And in this equally difficult question there is no reason to attribute to the discarnate or to the spirit world phenomena which can as readily be explained by the phenomena of our empirical world."

The Pearl Tie-Pin Case of Sir William **Barrett** has been often quoted. Through the medium Hester Dowden (Mrs. Travers Smith), the daughter of Prof. Edward Dowden, Mrs. C. obtained a message spelt out on the **ouija board:** "Tell mother to give my pearl tie-pin to the girl I was going to marry." The message allegedly came from a cousin of Mrs. C., an officer who was killed a month previously. The name and address of the girl was also given. The letter written to the address was returned and the whole message was thought fictitious. Six months later, however, it was discovered that the officer had been engaged to the very lady. The War Office sent back his effects and it was found that he put the lady's name in his will as his next-of-kin. A pearl tie-pin was also found in his effects."

Ernesto **Bozzano** recorded that in a sitting held on July 23, 1928, with the Marquise Centurione **Scotto** in **Millesimo Castle,** a voice addressed him as follows: "O Ernesto Bozzano, O my dear, my dear, I sought you in London, I sought you in Genoa, at last I find you." He immediately recognized the voice, a strong southern accent as that of the medium Eusapia Palladino. "This, her first manifestation, was a great revelation to me from the point of view of personal identification of the communicating spirit; because, without the faintest shadow of doubt, I recognised the person who was speaking to me the moment she pronounced my name. In life she had her own particular way of enunciating my surname, for she pronounced the two z's in an inimitable manner. Not only so, for when she spoke to me in life, she never called me simply by my surname, but invariably added my Christian name, though she never used the word 'Mr.' These small but most important idiosyncrasies of language are really what constitute the best demonstration of the real presence of the agency which affirms that it is actually present. I must add that she spoke with the identical timbre of voice which she had in life and with the very marked accent of her Italianized Neapolitan dialect."

Many visions of deceased soldiers were recorded by clairvoyants during world war. Mrs. E. A. Cannock, of London, described at a Spiritualist meeting a novel and convincing method employed by the fallen soldiers to make their identity known. In her vision, they advanced in single file up the aisle, led by a young lieutenant. Each man bore on his chest a large placard with his name and the place where he lived inscribed. Mrs. Cannock read the names and the place. The audience identified them one after the other. After recognition the spirit form faded and made way for the next one.

There has been no shortage of evidence of communication from servicemen who died in World War II. One of the most distinguished champions of such communication was Air Chief Marshal Lord **Dowding,** who was head of Fighter Command in the Battle of Britain. He obtained convincing evidence of spirit communication from servicemen at sittings with such famous mediums as Estelle **Roberts,** and has discussed Spiritualist evidence for survival in his books *Many Mansions* (1943) and *Lychgate* (1945).

Of course, evidence of identity in spirit communication can never be wholly scientific, depending as it does on the meaning which spirit messages have for the sitter. But thousands of people from all walks of life have been convinced of survival through the impressive clairaudient and clairvoyant messages through such remarkable British mediums as Doris **Stokes,** who has traveled to a number of countries giving impressive public and private demonstrations, as recorded in her books *Voices in My Ear* (1980) and *More Voices in My Ear* (1981).

Ideoplasm

Another term for **ectoplasm,** a subtle substance claimed to issue from the body of a **materialization** medium in a vaporous or solid form, taking on the appearance of phantom forms or limbs. "Ideoplasm" stems from the investigations of such French psychical researchers as Dr.

Gustave **Geley,** and conveys the additional idea that the substance may be molded by the operators into any shape to express ideas of the medium or of the sitters.

Ifrits

Hideous specters probably of Arabian origin, now genii of Persian and Indian mythology. They assume diverse forms, and frequent ruins, woods and wild desolate places, for the purpose of preying upon human beings and other living things. They are sometimes confounded with the Jinns or **Divs** of Persia.

Ignath, Mrs. Lujza Linczegh (1891– ?)

Hungarian clairvoyant, healing and **apport** medium, controlled by "Nona," a pure spirit who claimed to have never been incarnated and came, like "Sally" in the famous Beauchamps case, without **trance** in the manner of an alternating personality.

Mrs. Ignath's curious psychic powers were first described in an Hungarian pamphlet by William Tordai, of Budapest. In vol. 5 of the *Tidskrift for Psykisk Forskning* (the journal of the Norwegian Society for Psychical Research), Mrs. Lujza Lamaes-Haughseth, a high school teacher and experimental psychologist, published a long report of her observations with the medium in Budapest. As a consequence the Norwegian S. P. R., headed by Prof. Jaeger and Prof. Wereide, of the University of Oslo, sent an invitation to Mrs. Ignath. She accepted.

According to a report in the *Tidens Tegn* (Nov. 20, 1931), the medium produced **direct writing** in the presence of 100 people on places selected by the audience. In an experimental sitting for the S.P.R. conducted by Dr. Jorgen Bull, a distinguished chemist of Oslo, direct writing was produced on wax tablets in a specially prepared and closed box.

In religious ecstatic condition, stigmatic wounds were observed on the medium's head. On such occasions "Nona" delivered impressive lectures on the subject of religion.

The most curious phenomena of Mrs. Ignath's were the miniature heads which she materialized in drinking glasses filled with water. "Nona" asserts that the heads, the size of a walnut, were "plastic thoughts." Having been shown the photograph of Mrs. Haughseth's husband, "Nona" materialized his likeness. Flashlight photographs of these forms were published in vol. 6 of the *Psykisk Forskning.*

In *Proceedings* of the Society for Psychical Research, England (vol. 38, p. 466–671), Theodore Besterman described some psychometric experiments with Mrs. Ignath in Budapest. On November 18, 1928, he left a sealed vial with Mrs. Haughseth for testing. His conclusion of the reading was that "the experiment is very instructive from a negative point of view."

Ignis Fatuus

A wavering luminous appearance frequently observed in meadows and marshy places, around which many popular superstitions cluster. Its folk-names, Will o' the Wisp and Jack o' Lantern, suggest a country fellow bearing a lantern or straw torch (wisp).

Formerly these lights were supposed to haunt desolate bogs and moorlands for the purpose of misleading travellers and drawing them to their death. Another superstition says that they are the spirits of those who have been drowned in the bogs, and yet another, that they are the souls of unbaptized infants.

Science refers these *ignes fatui* to gaseous exhalations from the moist ground, or more rarely, to night-flying insects.

Ike, Rev.

Real name Dr. Frederick Eikenerkoetter, born c. 1935, a highly successful American revivalist preacher whose message is that with mental power all things are possible, and that life should be enjoyed here and now.

His multimillion dollar United Evangelical Association, financed by voluntary contributions, is witness to the efficiency of his gospel of success. It grew from a simple healing mission in Boston and spread to New York, and is now housed in a large building in Harlem that used to be a movie theater.

The Rev. Ike preaches his own colorful version of the power of positive thinking. He believes that God is within every individual and that kneeling down to pray only "puts you in a position to get a kick in the behind." He says that "lack of money is the root of all evil" and that his "Rolls-Royces and Mercedes don't run on Glory Hallelujah." His Blessing Plan rests upon "right thinking" and "right giving." By pledging regular money to his organization as a "giving person" one is supposed to receive in full measure. The Rev. Ike states "You can be anything you want to be, do anything you want to do, and have anything you want to have."

His own career seems to have proved that there is some truth in this. (See also **Healing by Faith**)

Illuminati

The term used first of all in the 15th century by enthusiasts in the occult arts signifying those who claimed to possess "light" directly communicated from a higher source, or due to a larger measure of human wisdom.

We first find the name in Spain about the end of the 15th century. Its origin was probably a late Gnostic one hailing from Italy, all sorts of people, many of them charlatans, claimed to belong to the brotherhood. In Spain, such persons as laid claim to the title had to face the rigor of the Inquisition, and this is perhaps one reason that numbers of them were found in France as refugees in the early seventeenth century.

Here and there, small bodies of those called Illuminati, sometimes known as **Rosicrucians**, rose into publicity for a short period. But it is with Adam Weishaupt, Professor of Law at Ingolstadt, that the movement first became identified with republicanism. He founded the order of the Illuminati in Bavaria in 1776. It soon secured a strong hold throughout Germany, but its founder's object was merely to convert his followers into blind instruments of his supreme will.

He modeled his organization on that of the Jesuits, adopted their system of organization, and the maxim that the end justified the means. He induced mysticism into the workings of the brotherhood, so that an air of mystery might prevade all its doings, adopted many of the classes and grades of Freemasonry, and held out hopes of the communication of deep occult secrets in the higher ranks.

Only a few of the members knew Weishaupt personally, and thus, although the society had many branches in all parts of Germany, to these people alone was he visible, and he began to be regarded by those who had not seen him almost as a god.

He took care to enlist in his ranks as many young men of wealth and position as possible, and within four or five years the power of Illuminism became extraordinary in its proportions, its members even had a hand in the affairs of the state, and not a few of the German princes found it to their interest to having dealings with the fraternity.

Weishaupt's idea was to blend philanthropy and mysticism. He was only 28 when he founded the sect in 1776, but he did not make much progress until a certain Baron von Knigge joined him in 1780. A gifted person of strong imagination, he had been admitted master of most of the secret societies of his day, among them Freemasonry. He was also an expert occultist and the supernatural had strong attractions for him. These two rapidly spread the gospel of the Revolution throughout Germany. But they grew fearful that, if the authorities discovered the existence of such a society as theirs, they would take steps to suppress it. With this in view they conceived the idea of grafting it on to Freemasonry, which they considered would protect it, and offer it means of spreading more widely and rapidly.

The Freemasons were not long in discovering the true nature of those who had just joined their organization. A chief council was held with the view of thoroughly examining into the nature of the beliefs held by them and a conference of masons was held in 1782 at which Knigge and Weishaupt attended and endeavored to capture the whole organization of Freemasonry, but a misunderstanding grew up between the leaders of illuminism. Knigge withdrew from the society, and two years later those who had reached its highest grade and had discovered that mysticism was not its true object, denounced it to the Bavarian Government as a political society of a dangerous character. It was suppressed in 1786. Weishaupt fled, but the damage had been done, for the fire kindled by *Illuminism* was soon to burst forth in the French Revolution.

The title "Illuminati" was later given to the French Martinists, followers of the French mystic Louis Claude de **St. Martin** (1743–1803), known as "le philosophe inconno."

Famous members of the Order of Illuminati include **Cagliostro** and Franz Anton **Mesmer.** Cagliostro was initiated in 1781 at Frankfurt where the Illuminati used the name of the Grand Masters of the Templars, and was said to have received money and instructions from Weishaupt to influence French masonry. Cagliostro later became associated with the Martinist Order which had been founded in 1754. The Illuminati are believed to have maintained a complex network of secret orders of their time.

The Order of Illuminati was revived in recent times, notably by Leopold Engel in 1880 at Dresden, Germany. Notable names connected with this revival include Rudolph **Steiner** and Franz **Hartmann.** The revival was taken over in 1895 by Dr. Karl Kellner, who named it "Order Templi Orientis" (**O.T.O.**) and after Kellner's death in 1905, the German occultist Theodor **Reuss,** with Franz Hartmann, continued on the inner council.

Recommended reading:

Barruel, Augustin. *Memoirs Illustrating the History of Jacobinism,* 4 vols., London, 1797

Gould, R. F. *History of Freemasonry,* revised ed., 5 vols., Caxton Publishing Co., London, 1931 etc.

Waite, Arthur E. *A New Encyclopaedia of Freemasonry,* 2 vols., Rider & Co., London; David McKay Co., 1921; 2 vols. in 1, University Books/Weathervane Books, 1970

Illusion

Sensory perception originated by an actual sensory stimulus to which wrong interpretation is attached. (See also **Hallucination**)

Imhotep

Ancient Egyptian deity, son of Ptah and Nut, to whom great powers of **exorcism** were attributed. He was often appealed to in cases of demonic **possession.**

Immortality

Psychical research is concerned primarily with survival as a matter of inference from intelligently observed and interpreted psychic phenomena. It does not attempt to answer the question whether survival means continued existence through eternity or for a limited period.

With few exceptions, psychical researchers have been concerned with the question of authenticity of claimed phenomena, and the enigma of whether there is really evidence for survival of personality after death.

The issue of whether there is continued existence of a personality or a soul, which is gradually perfected either in an afterlife or in a series of reincarnations, properly belongs to religion.

Many religions have proclaimed the immortality of the soul, although in modern times the precise stages of afterlife evolution have been somewhat vague in Christian eschatology. On the other hand, Eastern religions have been much more detailed, and in Hinduism these stages are carefully described, although they vary with different schools which have variant claims on the relationship between the human soul and God. In advaita **Vedanta,** the individual soul is perfected by infinite reincarnations to reassert its true reality as a group soul, then as the infinite Divine itself; in vishadvaita Vedanta, however, there remains some distinction between Divinity and the perfected human souls. In general, however, Vedanta does not view immortality in terms of an achievement of individual souls in a period of time, but rather the reassertion of an infinite Divine reality when the illusions of ego, body, mind, time, space and causality have disappeared. This postulates the Divine infinity as the eternal reality which is veiled by illusions of individual consciousness and the world of matter.

Since Spiritualism is a religion, with its roots in traditional Christianity, the question of immortality and perfectibility of the soul is an important doctrine, although there is no universal agreement on the question of reincarnation.

Some of the pioneers of psychical research in the nineteenth century were, of course, religious men or enlightened psychologists open to unprejudiced examina-

tion of religious beliefs in relation to survival and psychical research. For this reason, the earlier period of psychical research deserved a closer rescrutiny in a more materialistic age when parapsychology is so often a clinical affair of laboratory evidence and assessment rather than a matter of claimed phenomena which have an important bearing on the meaning and purpose of life. (See also **Reincarnation**)

Recommended reading:

Augustine, St. *Immortality of the Soul* (*Fathers of the Church* series, vol. 4), Catholic University of America Press, Washington, D.C., c. 1973.

Bernard, Theos. *Philosophical Foundations of India,* Rider & Co., London & N.Y., n.d.

Carrington, Hereward. *Death; The Causes & Phenomena with Special Reference to Immortality,* London, 1911, Arno Press, N.Y., 1977.

Charles, R. H. *A Critical History of the Doctrine of a Future Life in Israel, in Judaism and in Christianity,* London, 1899

Ducasse, C. J. *Critical Examination of the Belief in a Life After Death,* Charles C. Thomas, Springfield, Ill., 1974.

Fournier, D'Albe. *New Light on Immortality,* London, 1908

Hyslop, James H. *Psychical Research & the Nature of Life After Death,* American Institute for Psychological Research, Albuquerque, New Mexico, 1980

James, William. *The Will to Believe* & *Human Immortality,* (two books), Dover Books paperback, n.d.

Lombroso, Cesare. *After Death—What?,* T. Fisher Unwin, London/Small, Mayard & Co., 1909

Myers, Frederick W. *Human Personality & Its Survival of Bodily Death,* 2 vols., London, 1903 etc., Arno Press, N.Y. 1975

Steiner, Rudolf. *Reincarnation & Immortality,* Harper & Row paperback, 1980

Immortality (Magazine)

Spiritualist monthly "for Progressive thinking people," founded in 1919, official organ of the General Assembly of Spiritualists, New York. It was still in existence in the 1930s.

Immortality and Survival (Magazine)

British monthly, incorporated, after a short existence, into *Survival* Magazine. No longer published.

"Imperator"

The famous spirit **control** of the Rev. W. Stainton **Moses,** commanding a band of spirits engaged in a missionary effort to uplift the human race by teachings through automatic writing.

He first announced his presence on September 19, 1872, and signed as "Imperator." Yielding to the pressure of Stainton Moses, he revealed, on July 6, 1873, in *Book IV,* that he was the prophet Malachias, and charged the medium not to speak of his identity (except to those intimately associated with him) without his express permission.

He was seen clairvoyantly by Stainton Moses and his appearance was described in *Book VI.* His communications were not written by himself, but by "Rector." The signature was: "Imperator S. D. (Servus Dei)" or "I.S.D.," preceded by a Latin cross, later by a crown.

In 1881 a story was circulated from Theosophical sources that "Imperator" was a living man, a Theosophical "Brother," and that his dealings with Stainton Moses had been perfectly known to Madame **Blavatsky.** "Imperator," on Stainton Moses' query, branded the whole story as false. Of Mme. Blavatsky, who once hinted that "Imperator" was connected with the "Lodge," he said: "She does not know or speak with us, though she has the power of ascertaining facts concerning us." He claimed to have directed the whole course of the life of Stainton Moses, preparing him for the role of a messenger.

Complaining of the latter's incredulity regarding his personal identity, he summed up the case on January 18, 1874, as follows: "We are real in power over you; real in the production of objective manifestations; real in the tests and proofs of knowledge which we adduce. We are truthful and accurate in all things. We are the preachers of a Divine Gospel. It is for you to accept the individual responsibility from which none may relieve you, or deciding whether, being such as we are, we are deceivers in matters of vital and eternal import. Such a conclusion, in the face of all evidence and fair inference, is one which none could accept save a perverted and unhinged mind; least of all one who knows us as you do now."

"Imperator" and his band took over the control of Mrs. **Piper** in 1897. Doubts were raised by Sir Oliver **Lodge** and Professor William **James** as to their identity with the "Imperator" group of Stainton Moses. These entities could not give the names which they had given to Stainton Moses. The Myers and Hodgson control endorsed them. "I conjecture, however," wrote Sir Oliver Lodge, "that whatever relationship may exist between these personages and the corresponding ones of Stainton Moses, there is little or no identity." (*Proceedings* of the Society for Psychical Research, vol. 23., p. 235).

Mrs. **Sidgwick,** in *Proceedings* of the S.P.R., vol. 27, also rejected their claims for identity. Hyslop slightly inclined to admit it. He argued (*Journal* of the American Society for Psychical Research, vol. 16, p. 69) that "Malachi" means "Messengers" and that this was the very function which "Imperator" assumed in English through Mrs. Piper and Mrs. Chenoweth, as well as Stainton Moses.

A. W. Trethewy, who made a deep study of the scripts of Stainton Moses in a paper in *Proceedings* of the S.P.R., vol. 25, stated: "that the internal evidence points to the two groups not having been identical. There are, it is true, slight resemblances, but they are either so vague as to be well within the sphere of coincidence where two good bands of controls are concerned, or they are of a nature to suggest an origin from the mind of Mrs. Piper or her sitter. On the other hand, the ignorance and the errors of her controls concerning the earth-lives of the guides of Stainton Moses whose names they bore, and concerning important features of his mediumship, are altogether inconsistent with their claim to identity."

Dr. Richard **Hodgson,** in the last years of his life, received direct communications from the "Imperator" group in his room. In giving a character sketch of Dr. Hodgson, Dr. Hereward Carrington stated in *The Story of Psychic Science* (1930): "He possessed a keen sense of humour, and was always buoyant and cheerful, but would become serious when the name of Imperator was mentioned. It is now realised, perhaps, that this Personality—

together with Rector and the other members of the group—played a large part in many people's lives, and that numerous old Piper Sitters (as they were called) prayed to Imperator for comfort and guidance—as one might pray to any favourite Saint."

At a later date, communications by Imperator were received through Mrs. Minnie M. **Soule** (Mrs. Chenoweth). Gwendolyn Kelley Hack, in *Modern Psychic Mysteries at Millesimo Castle* (1929) also claimed the control of "Imperator" in her own automatic scripts.

For an account of the "Imperator" scripts, see the book *Spirit Teachings* by "M. A. (Oxon.)" (Rev. W. Stainton Moses) (1898; 1949 etc.).

Incommunicable Axiom, The

According to occultist Éliphas Lévi in his book, *Transcendental Magic* (1896 etc.), it was believed that all magical science was embodied in knowledge of this secret. The Axiom is to be found enclosed in the four letters of the Tetragram arranged in a certain way; in the words "Azoth" and "Inri" written Kabalistically; and in the monogram of Christ embroidered in the labarum. He who succeeded in elucidating it became humanly omnipotent from the magical standpoint.

This is a Western occultist interpretation of Jewish mysticism and Eastern teachings about the creative power of the Ineffable Name of God. (See also **AUM; Divine Name; Kabala; Mantra; Shemhamphorash**)

Incorporeal Personal Agency (IPA)

Rather cumbersome term used by parapsychologist J. B. Rhine to indicate survival of bodily death; i.e., aspects of personality surviving without a body.

Incubus

A demon spirit which has intercourse with mortal women. The concept may have arisen from the idea of the commerce of gods with women which was rife in pagan times. The female demon having intercourse with men is the **succubus.** These demons associated with an individual witch or sorcerer are known as **familiars.**

Belief in incubi and succubi goes back to ancient times but was incorporated into Christian belief from medieval times onwards and such churchmen as Thomas Aquinas (1225-74) discussed these demons.

The *Description of Scotlande* of Hector Boethius as translated in the first volume of Holinshed's Chronicles (1577) has three or four notable examples, which obtain confirmation from the pen of Jerome Cardan. One of these is quoted below in the quaint language which Holinshed had given it:

"In the year 1480 it chanced as a Scottish ship departed out of the Forth towards Flanders, there arose a wonderful great tempest of wind and weather, so outragious, that the maister of the ship, with other the mariners, woondered not a little what the matter ment, to see such weather at that time of the yeare, for it was about the middest of summer. At length, when the furious pirrie and rage of winds still increased, in such wise that all those within the ship looked for present death, there was a woman underneath the hatches called unto them above, and willed them to throw her into the sea, that all the residue, by God's grace, might yet be saved; and thereupon told them how she had been haunted a long time with a spirit dailie coming unto hir in man's likenesse. In the ship there chanced also to be priest, who by the maister's appointment going down to this woman, and finding her like a most wretched and desperate person, lamenting hir great misfortune and miserable estate, used such wholesome admonition and comfortable advertisements, willing her to repent and hope for mercy at the hands of God, that, at length, she seeming right penitent for her grievous offences committed, and fetching sundrie sighs even from the bottome of her heart, being witnesse, as should appeare, of the same, there issued forth of the pumpe of the ship, a foule and evil-favoured blacke cloud with a mighty terrible noise, flame, smoke, and stinke, which presently fell into the sea. And suddenlie thereupon the tempest ceassed, and the ship passing in great quiet the residue of her journey, arrived in saftie at the place whither she was bound." (*Chronicles,* vol. 5, p. 146, 1808 ed.)

In another case related by the same author, the Incubus did not depart so quietly. In the chamber of a young gentlewoman, of excellent beauty, and daughter of a nobleman in the country of Mar, was found at an unseasonable hour, "a foule monstrous thing, verie horrible to behold," for the love of which "Deformed" nevertheless, the lady had refused sundry wealthy marriages. A priest who was in the company began to repeat St. John's Gospel, and ere he had proceeded far "suddenlie the wicked spirit, making a verie sore and terrible roaring noise, flue his waies, taking the roofe of the chamber awaie with him, the hangings and coverings of the bed being also burnt therewith."

Other writers on the incubus include Erastus, in his Tract *de Lamiis,* Jakob **Sprenger** and Heinrich **Kramer** in **Malleus Maleficarum** (1486), which contains a report of a nun who slept with an incubus in the form of a bishop, H. Zanchius in de Operibus Del, (1597, xvi, 4); G. Dandini in *Aristotelis Tres de Anima* (1610), J. G. Godellman in *Tractatus de Magis* (1591), and M. A. Del Rio in *Disquisitionum Magicarum* (1599) and F.-M. Guazzo in *Compendium Maleficarum* (1608) are just a few writers who have discussed the subject.

Jean Bodin, author of *Démonomaie* (1580) cited the case of Joan Hervilleria, who at twelve years of age was solemnly betrothed to Beelzebub by her mother, who was afterwards burnt alive for compassing this clandestine marriage.

The bridegroom was very respectably attired, and the marriage formulary was simple. The mother pronounced the following words to the bridegroom: "Ecce filiam meam quam spospondi tibi," and then turning to the bride, "Ecce amicum tuum qui beabit te."

It appears, however, that Joan was not satisfied with her spiritual husband alone, but became a bigamist by intermarrying with real flesh and blood.

Besides this lady, we read of Margaret Bremont, who, in company with her mother, Joan Robert, Joan Guillemin, Mary, wife of Simon Agnus, and Wilhelma, spouse of one Grassus, were in the habit of attending diabolic assignations. These unhappy wretches were burnt alive by Adrian Ferreus, General Vicar of the Inquisition.

Magdalena Crucia of Cordova, an abbess, was more fortunate. In 1545 she became suspected by her nuns of magic, an accusation very convenient when a superior

was at all troublesome. She encountered them with great wisdom by anticipating their charge, and going beforehand to the Pope, Paul III, she confessed a thirty years' intimate acquaintance with the devil, and obtained pardon.

For an authoritative study of beliefs in incubi and succubi, see *Demoniality* by Fr. Sinistrari, tranl. by Isidore Liseux (Paris 1879) or another English translation by the Rev. Montague Summers (1927). For a portrait of "The Incubus" see *The Magus* by Francis Barrett (1801; reprinted University Books, 1967). (See also **Demonology; Succubus; Witchcraft**)

Independent Drawing & Painting (*See* **Direct Drawing & Painting**)

Independent Voice (*See* **Direct Voice**)

Independent Writing (*See* **Direct Writing**)

INDIA

Many occult beliefs and practices stem from the complex religious and mystical concepts of Indian people.

It might be said that the mysticism of the Hindus was a reaction against the austere religion and practical ceremonial of the sacred scriptures *Vedas.* If its trend were summarized it might justly be said that it partakes strongly of detachment, in a pantheistic identifying of subject and object, worshiper and worship, aimed at ultimate absorption in the Infinite, inculcating transcendent from the material world through the most minute self-examination, the cessation of physical powers, and belief in the spiritual guidance of the **guru** or mystical adept.

For the Indian theosophist there is only one Absolute Being, the One Reality. However, in popular Hinduism, the pantheistic doctrine of *Ekam advitiyam* "the One without Second" posits a countless pantheon of gods, great and small, and a rich demonology, but these should be understood ultimately as merely illusions of the soul and not realities. Upon the soul's coming to fuller knowledge, its illusions are totally dispelled, but to the ordinary man and woman the impersonality of the Absolute being is they require a symbolic deity to bridge the gulf between the impersonal Absolute and the very material self, hence the numerous gods of Hinduism which are regarded by the initiated merely as manifestations of the Supreme Spirit.

Even the everyday forms of temple idols in this way possess higher meaning. As Sir Alfred Lyall stated: "It [Brahminism] treats all the worships as outward visible signs of the same spiritual truth, and is ready to show how each particular image or rite is the symbol of some aspect of universal divinity. The Hindus, like the pagans of antiquity, adore natural objects and forces,—a mountain, a river, or an animal. The Brahmin holds all nature to be the vesture or cloak of indwelling divine energy which inspires everything that produces all or passes man's understanding."

A life time of asceticism has from the remotest times been regarded in India as a true preparation for communion with the deity. Asceticism has been extremely prevalent especially in connection with the cult of the god

Siva, who is in great measure regarded as the prototype of this class.

The Yogis (disciples of the Yogi philosophy), practice mental abstraction, and are popularly supposed to attain to superhuman powers. In some cases their extreme ascetic practices have resulted in madness or mental vacancy and many claimed supernatural powers have turned out to be jugglery and conjuring. However, there are charlatans in all religions, and the authentic prerequisites of the training of a yogi preclude such imposture and indeed warn against the vanity of displaying supernatural powers.

The Parama-Hamsas, that is "supreme swans," are believed to have achieved communion with the world-soul through spiritual disciplines and **meditation.** They are said to be equally indifferent to pleasure or pain, insensible to heat or cold, and incapable of satiety or want.

The Sannyasis are those who renounce the world and live as wandering monks or residents in an ashram or spiritual retreat. The *Dandis,* or staff-bearers, are worshippers of Siva in his form of Bhairava the Terrible.

J. C. Oman in *Mystics, Ascetics and Sects of India* (1903) says of these Sadhus or holy men: "Sadhuism whether perpetuating the peculiar idea of the efficacy of asceticism for the acquisition of far-reaching powers over natural phenomena or bearing its testimony to the belief of the indispensableness of detachment from the world as a preparation for the ineffable joy of ecstatic communion with the Divine Being, has undoubtedly tended to keep before men's eyes as the highest ideal, a life of purity and restraint and contempt of the world of human affairs. It has also necessarily maintained amongst the laity a sense of the rights and claims of the poor upon the charity of the more opulent members of the community. Further, Sadhuism by the multiplicity of the independent sects which have arisen in India has engendered and favoured a spirit of tolerance which cannot escape the notice of the most superficial observer."

One of the most esoteric branches of Hinduism is the Shakta cult. The Shaktas are worshipers of the Shakti or female principle as a creative and reproductive agency. Each of the principal gods possesses his own Shakti, through which his creative acts are performed, so that the Shakta worshippers are drawn from all sects. But it is principally in connection with the cult of Siva that Shakta worship is practiced.

It is divided into two distinct groups. The original self-existent gods were supposed to divide themselves into male and female energies, the male half occupying the right-hand and the female the left-hand side. From this conception we have the two groups of "right-hand" observers and "left-hand" observers. The left-hand path of Tantra involves decadent sexual activities. In the *Tantras* or mystical writings, Siva answers questions asked by his spouse Parvati regarding the mysteries of Shakta occultism.

In the genuine mystical form of *Tantra,* sexual energy in the yogi is manifested in a pure form as **Kundalini,** a psycho-physiological force which is directed to **chakras** or mystical centers in the body, culminating in a chakra in the head, which bestows higher consciousness and spiritual enlightenment. In modern times, the reality of *Kundalini* experience has been affirmed in the writings of Pandit **Gopi Krishna.**

Brahmanism

Brahmanism is a system originated by the Brahmans, the sacerdotal caste of the Hindus, at a comparatively early date. It is the mystical religion of India *par excellence,* and represents the older beliefs of its peoples. It states that the numerous individual existences of animate nature are but so many manifestations of the one eternal spirit towards which they tend as their final goal of supreme bliss.

The object of life is to prevent oneself sinking lower in the scale, and by degrees to raise oneself in it, or if possible to attain the ultimate goal immediately from such state of existence as one happens to be in.

The socio-religious Code of *Manu* concludes "He who in his own soul perceives the supreme soul in all beings and acquires equanimity towards them all attains the highest state of bliss." Mortification of animal instincts, absolute purity and perfection of spirit, were the moral ideals of the Brahman class. But it was necessary to pass through a succession of four orders or states of existence before any hope of union with the deity could be held out. These were: that of *brahmacharin,* or student of religious matters; *grihastha,* or householder; *Varnaprastha* or hermit; and *sannyasin* or *bhikshu,* religious mendicant.

Practically every man of the higher castes practiced at least the first two of these stages, while the priestly class took the entire course. Later, however, this was by no means the rule, as the scope of study was intensely exacting, often lasting as long as forty-eight years, and the neophyte had to support himself by begging from door to door.

He was usually guided by a spiritual preceptor and after several years of his tuition was usually married, as it was considered absolutely essential that he should leave a son behind him to offer food to his spirit and to those of his ancestors. He was then said to have become a "House-holder" and was required to keep up perpetually the fire brought into his house upon his marriage day.

Upon his growing older, the time for him arrived to enter the third stage of life, since having fulfilled his *dharma* (social and religious obligations) he now became aware of the transitory nature of the material life and found it necessary to become preoccupied with more eternal spiritual truth. He therefore cut himself off from family ties except (if she wished) his wife who might accompany him, and went into retirement in a lonely place, carrying with him his sacred fire, and the instruments necessary for his daily sacrifices. Scantily clothed, the anchorite lived entirely on food growing wild in the forest—roots, herbs, wild grain, and so forth. The acceptance of gifts was not permitted him unless absolutely necessary, and his time was spent in studying the metaphysical portions of the *Vedas* under the guidance of a *guru,* in making offerings, and in practicing austerities with the object of producing entire indifference to worldly desires.

In this way he fitted himself for the final and most exalted order, that of religious mendicant or *bhikshu.* This consisted solely of meditation. He took up his abode at the foot of a tree in entire solitude and only once a day at the end of his labors might he go near the dwellings of men to beg a little food. In this way he waited for death, neither desiring extinction nor existence, until at length it reached him, and he was absorbed in the eternal Brahma.

The purest doctrines of Brahmanism are to be found in the Vedanta philosophic system, which recognizes the *Vedas* or collection of ancient Sanskrit hymns, as the revealed source of religious belief through the visions of the ancient *Rishis* or seers. The *Upanishads* are later versions of the *Vedas* and another popular scripture is the *Bhagavad-Gita.*

It has been already mentioned that the Hindu regarded the entire gamut of animated nature as being traversed by the one soul, which journeyed up and down the scale as its actions in its previous existence were good or evil. To the Hindu the vital element in all animate beings appears essentially similar, and this led directly to the Brahmanical theory of transmigration, which has taken such a powerful hold upon the Hindu mind.

Demonology

A large and intricate demonology has clustered around Hindu mythology. The gods are at constant war with demons. Vishnu slays more than one demon, but Durga appears to have been a great enemy of the demon race. The Asuras, probably a very ancient and aboriginal pantheon of deities, later became demons in the popular imagination, and the Rakshasas may have been cloud-demons. They were described as cannibals, could take many forms, and were constantly menacing the gods. They haunted cemeteries, disturbed sacrifices, animated the dead, harried and afflicted mankind in all sorts of ways. In fact they were almost an exact parallel with the **vampires** of Slavonic countries; and this greatly assisted the conjecture that the Slavonic vampires were originally cloud-spirits.

We find the gods constantly harassed by demons, and on the whole may be justified in concluding that just as the Tuatha-de-danaan harassed the later deities of Ireland, so did these aboriginal gods lead an existence of constant warfare with the divine beings of the pantheon of the immigrant Aryans.

Popular Witchcraft & Sorcery

The popular witchcraft and sorcery of India greatly resembles that of Europe. The Dravidian or aboriginal races of India have always been strong believers in **witchcraft,** and it is possible that this is an example of the mythic influence of a conquered people. They are, however, extremely reticent regarding any knowledge they possess of it.

It seems possible that the extraordinarily high demands made upon the popular religious sense by Brahmanism crushed the superstitions of the lower cultus of a very early period, and confined the practice of minor sorcery to the castes of Dravidian or aboriginal stock. Witchcraft seems most prevalent among the more isolated and least advanced races, like the Kols, Bhils, and Santals. The nomadic peoples were also strong believers in sorcery, one of the most dreaded forms of which is the *Jigar Khor,* or liver-eater, of whom Abul Fazl (1551–1602) stated: "One of this class can steal away the liver of another by looks and incantations. Other accounts say that by looking at a person he deprives him of his senses, and then steals from him something resembling the seed of a pomegranate, which he hides in the calf of his leg; after being swelled by

the fire, he distributes it among his fellows to be eaten, which ceremony concludes the life of the fascinated person. A *Jigar Khor* is able to communicate his art to another by teaching him incantations, and by making him eat a bit of the liver cake. These *Jigar Khors* are mostly women. It is said they can bring intelligence from a long distance in a short space of time, and if they are thrown into a river with a stone tied to them, they nevertheless will not sink. In order to deprive any one of this wicked power, they brand his temples and every joint of his body, cram his eyes with salt, suspend him for forty days in a subterranean chamber, and repeat over him certain incantations."

The witch does not, however, devour the man's liver for two and a half days, and even if she has eaten it, and is put under the hands of an exorcizer, she can be forced to substitute a liver of some animal in the body of the man whom she victimized. There are also folk tales of witches taking out the entrails of people, sucking them, and then replacing them.

All this undoubtedly illustrates, as in ancient France and Germany, and probably also in the Slavonic countries, the original combination of witch and vampire, how, in fact, the two were believed identical. In India the arch-witch *Ralaratri,* or "black night" has the joined eyebrows of the Slavonic **werwolf** or vampire, large cheeks, widely-parted lips, projecting teeth, and is a veritable vampire. But she also possesses the powers of ordinary witchcraft— **second-sight,** the making of philtres, the control of tempests, the **evil eye,** and so forth.

Witches also took animal forms, especially those of tigers, and stories of trials are related at which people gave evidence that they had tracked certain tigers to their lairs, which upon entering they had found tenanted by a notorious witch or wizard. For such witch-tigers the usual remedy was to knock out their teeth to prevent their doing any more mischief.

Strangely enough, the Indian witch, like her European prototype, was very often accompanied by a cat. The cat, said the jungle people, is aunt to the tiger, and taught him everything but how to climb a tree. Zalim Sinh, the famous regent of Kota, believed that cats were associated with witches, and imagining himself enchanted ordered that every cat should be expelled from his province.

As in Europe, witches were known by certain marks. They were believed to learn the secrets of their craft by eating offal of all kinds. The popular belief concerning them was that they were often very handsome and neat, and invariably applied a clear line of red lead to the parting of their hair. They were popularly accused of exhuming dead children and bringing them to life to serve occult purposes of their own. They could not die so long as they were witches and until (as in Italy) they could pass on their knowledge of witchcraft to someone else.

They recited charms backwards, repeating two letters and a half from a verse in the *Koran.* If a certain charm was repeated "forwards," the person employing it would become invisible to his neighbor, but if he repeated it backwards, he would assume whatever shape he chose.

A witch could acquire power over her victim by getting possession of a lock of hair, the paring of nails, or some other part of his body, such as a tooth. For this reason Indian people were extremely careful about the disposal of such, burying them in the earth in a place covered with grass, or in the neighborhood of water, which witches universally disliked. Some people even flung the cuttings of their hair into running water.

Like the witches of Europe, they too made images of persons out of wax, dough, or similar substances, and tortured them with the idea that the pain would be felt by the person whom they desired to injure.

In India the witches' **familiar** was known as *Bir* or the "hero," who aided her to inflict injury upon human beings. The power of the witch was greatest on the 14th, 15th and 29th of each month, and in particular on the Feast of Lamps *(Diwali)* and the Festival of Durga.

Witches were often severely punished amongst the isolated hill-folk and diabolical ingenuity was shown in torturing them. To nullify their evil influence, they were beaten with rods of the castor-oil plant and usually died in the process. They were often forced to drink filthy water used by curriers in the process of their work, or their noses were cut off, or they were put to death. It has also been said that their teeth were often knocked out, their heads shaved and offal thrown at them. In the case of women, their heads were shaved and their hair was attached to a tree in some public place. They were also branded, had a ploughshare tied to their legs or were made to drink the water of a tannery.

During the Mutiny, when British authority was relaxed, the most atrocious horrors were inflicted upon witches and sorcerers by the Dravidian people. Pounded *chilli* peppers were placed in their eyes to see if they would bring tears, and the wretched beings were suspended from a tree head downwards, being swung violently from side to side. They were then forced to drink the blood of a goat, and to exorcize the evil spirits that they had caused to enter the bodies of certain sick persons. The mutilations and cruelties practiced on them were sickening, but one of the favorite ways of counteracting the spells of a witch was to draw blood from her, and the local priest would often prick the tongue of the witch with a needle and place the resulting blood on some rice and compel her to eat it.

In Bombay state, the aboriginal Tharus were supposed to possess special powers of witchcraft, so that the "Land of Tharus" is a synonym for witch-land. In Gorakhpur, witches were also very numerous and the half-gypsy *Banjaras,* or grain-carriers, were notorious believers in witchcraft. In his interesting *Popular Religion and Folk-lore of Northern India* (2 vols., 1896) W. Crooke, who had exceptional opportunities for the study of the Indian character, and who did much to elucidate dark places of Indian popular mythology, stated regarding the various types of Indian witches:

"At the present day [c. 1895] the half-deified witch most dreaded in the Eastern Districts of the North-western Provinces is Lona, or Nona, a *Chamarin* or woman of the currier caste. Her legend is in this wise. The great physician Dhanwantara, who corresponds to Luqman Hakim of the Muhammadans, was once on his way to cure King Parikshit, and was deceived and bitten by the snake king Takshaka. He therefore desired his sons to roast him and eat his flesh, and thus succeed to his magical powers. The snake king dissuaded them from eating the unholy meal, and they let the cauldron containing it float down the Ganges. A currier woman, named Lona, found it and ate

the contents, and thus succeeded to the mystic powers of Dhanwantara. She became skilful in cures, particularly of snake-bite. Finally she was discovered to be a witch by the extraordinary rapidity with which she could plant out rice seedlings. One day the people watched her, and saw that when she believed herself unobserved she stripped herself naked, and taking the bundle of the plants in her hands threw them into the air, reciting certain spells. When the seedlings forthwith arranged themselves in their proper places, the spectators called out in astonishment, and finding herself discovered, Nona rushed along over the country, and the channel which she made in her course is the Loni river to this day. So a saint in Broach formed a new course for a river by dragging his clothes behind him. . . .

"Another terrible witch, whose legend is told at Mathura, is Putana, the daughter of Bali, king of the lower world. She found the infant Krishna asleep, and began to suckle him with her devil's milk. The first drop would have poisoned a mortal child, but Krishna drew her breast with such strength that he drained her life-blood, and the fiend, terrifying the whole land of Braj with her cries of agony, fell lifeless on the ground. European witches suck the blood of children; here the divine Krishna turns the tables on the witch.

"The Palwar Rajputs of Oudh have a witch ancestress. Soon after the birth of her son she was engaged in baking cakes. Her infant began to cry, and she was obliged to perform a double duty. At this juncture her husband arrived just in time to see his demon wife assume gigantic and supernatural proportions, so as to allow both the baking and nursing to go on at the same time. But finding her secret discovered, the witch disappeared, leaving her son as a legacy to her astonished husband. Here, though the story is incomplete, we have almost certainly, as in the case of Nona Chamarin, one of the Melusina type of legend, where the supernatural wife leaves her husband and children, because he violated some taboo, by which he is forbidden to see her in a state of nudity, or the like.

"The history of witchcraft in India, as in Europe, is one of the saddest pages in the annals of the people. Nowadays, the power of British law has almost entirely suppressed the horrible outrages which, under the native administration were habitually practised. But particularly in the more remote and uncivilized parts of the country this superstition still exists in the minds of the people and occasional indications of it, which appear in our criminal records, are quite sufficient to show that any relaxation of the activity of our magistrates and police would undoubtedly lead to its revival in some of its more shocking forms."

The aborigines of India lived in great fear of ghosts and invisible spirits, and a considerable portion of their time was given up to averting the evil influences of these. Protectives of every description littered their houses, and the approaches to them, and they wore numerous amulets for the purpose of averting evil influences. Regarding these, W. Crooke stated:

"Some of the Indian ghosts, like the *Ifrit* of the Arabian Nights, can grow to the length of ten *yojanas* or eighty miles. In one of the Bengal tales a ghost is identified because she can stretch out her hands several yards for a vessel. Some ghosts possess the very dangerous power of entering human corpses, like the Vetala, and swelling to an enormous size. The Kharwars of Mirzapur have a wild legend which tells how long ago an unmarried girl of the tribe died, and was being cremated. While the relations were collecting wood for the pyre, a ghost entered the corpse, but the friends managed to expel him. Since then great care is taken not to leave the bodies of women unwatched. So, in the Panjab, when a great person is cremated the bones and ashes are carefully watched till the fourth day, to prevent a magician interfering with them. If he has a chance, he can restore the deceased to life, and ever after retain him under his influence. This is the origin of the custom in Great Britain of waking the dead, a practice which 'most probably originated from a silly superstition as to the danger of a corpse being carried off by some of the agents of the invisible world, or exposed to the ominous liberties of brute animals.' But in India it is considered the best course, if the corpse cannot be immediately disposed of, to measure it carefully, and then no malignant *Bhut* can occupy it.

"Most of the ghosts whom we have been as yet considering are malignant. There are, however, others which are friendly. Such are the German Elves, the Robin Goodfellow, Puck, Brownie and the Cauld Lad of Hilton of England, the Glashan of the Isle of Man, the Phouka or Leprehaun of Ireland. Such, in one of his many forms, is the *Brahmadaitya,* or ghost of a Brahman who has died unmarried. In Bengal he is believed to be more neat and less mischievous than other ghosts; the Bhuts carry him in a palanquin, he wears wooden sandals, and lives in a Banyan tree."

Eastern & Western Occultism

It is interesting to note that much of Western magical ritual and belief is a decadent descend from Hindu religion and folklore, sometimes by way of Arabic influence. Alchemy itself was a study from Arabic sources. The ritual magical diagrams of the Western occultist derive from the **yantra** or mystical diagram inscribed on metal and other materials by Hindu priests as religious symbols to invoke divine favor. The magical spells of Western magicians resemble the **mantra** or sacred religious prayers of power in Hinduism. The sex magic of Western occultists like Aleister **Crowley** is a decadent version of Indian **tantra.** In the same way, the pop Hinduism of American and European cults, as well as much vaunted meditation techniques is again a packaging of traditional Hindu practice but without the intense spiritual and ethical disciplines meant to accompany them.

Psychical Research & Parapsychology

The scientific study of psychical phenomena in India really belongs to the period following independence. A small beginning took place in 1951 at the Department of Philosophy and Psychology of Benares Hindu University under Prof. B. L. Atreya, when parapsychology was included as a postgraduate subject, but it did not make much progress. But various other Indian scholars such as Prof. C. T. K. Chari and Prof. S. Parthasarthy of Madras, and Prof. & Mrs. Akolkar of Poona became keenly interested in psychical phenomena. Prof. Chari took a special interest in scientific and statistical approaches and published papers in the *Journal* of the American Society for Psychical Research.

Another pioneer was Dr. K. Ramakrishna Rao, Professor and Head of the Department of Psychology and Parapsychology at Andhra University who worked for several years at Duke University, North Carolina, and then established the Department at Andhra University and collaborated with Dr. B. K. Kanthamani. Dr. Rao subsequently became president of the Parapsychological Association for 1965 and 1978, and was later director of the Institute for Parapsychology, Durham, North Carolina.

In North India, Dr. Sampurananand first became interested in parapsychology when Education Minister, and later initiated study of the paranormal at the University of Lucknow in conjunction with Prof. Kali Prasad, head of the Department of Philosophy and Psychology. When Dr. Sampurananand was appointed Governor of Rajasthan, he helped to establish a department of parapsychology at the Rajasthan University at Jaipur, although this was subsequently closed. Since then, however, there has been interest in the subject for postgraduate degree in Lucknow and Agra Universities.

In 1962–63, the Bureau of Psychology in Allahabad took up a research project in parapsychology, studying ESP in schoolchildren. The results were published in the *International Journal of Parapsychology* (Autumn 1968).

In 1964, Dr. Jamuna Prasad, president of the Indian Institute of Parapsychology, Allahabad, assisted Prof. Ian Stevenson who visited India to investigate reported cases of reincarnation at first hand. A group of researchers took part in this project, which involved a Specific Trait Questionnaire designed to assess the possible impressions of past experiences carried over to another incarnation. With the formal establishment of the Indian Institute of Parapsychology, another valuable project was undertaken with a grant from the Parapsychology Foundation: "Paranormal Powers Manifested During Yogic Training."

In December 1966, Dr. Karan Singh, Minister of Health and Family Planning inaugurated "Project Consciousness" at the National Institute of Mental Health and Neuro Sciences, Bangalore. This important project was largely concerned with modern interest in the ancient Hindu concepts of *Kundalini* as a psycho-physiological force in the human being related to sexual energy, and in a sublimated form, to levels of higher consciousness. This stemmed from the work of Pandit Gopi Krishna, who revived interest in the subject through his books describing his own experiences in arousing *Kundalini.*

Indian publications concerned with parapsychology include: *Darshan International* (quarterly journal of philosophy, psychology, psychical research, religion and mysticism), *Psychics International* quarterly journal of psychic and yoga research), *Parapsychology* (Indian Journal of Parapsychological Research, Dept. of Parapsychology, Rajasthan University, Jaipur), although the latter journal was discontinued with the closure of the Department of Parapsychology at Rajasthan University. On a more general mystical basis, the journal *Kundalini* (formerly *Kundalini & Spiritual India*) is devoted to the study of consciousness evolution arising from the work of Pandit Gopi Krishna. In this connection, a Central Institute for Kundalini Research has now been established at Srinagar, Kashmir. (See also **Indian Rope Trick; Kundalini; Reincarnation; Vedanta; Yoga**)

Recommended reading:

Abbott, John. *The Keys of Power; A Study of Indian Ritual and Belief,* London, 1932; University Books, 1974

Atreya, B. L. *An Introduction to Parapsychology,* International Standard Publications, Banaras, India, 1957

Bernard, Theos. *Philosophical Foundations of India,* Rider & Co., London & New York, 1945 etc.

Crooke, William. *The Popular Religion & Folk-Lore of Northern India,* Government Press, Allahabad, India, 1894; new edition 2 vols., A. Constable & Co., London, 1896

Garrison, Omar. *Tantra—The Yoga of Sex,* Causeway Books, N.Y., 1973 etc.

Gervis, Pearce. *Naked They Pray,* Cassell & Co., London, 1956

Gopi Krishna, Pandit. *Kundalini; The Evolutionary Energy in Man,* Stuart & Watkins, London, Shambhala, Boulder, Colorado, 1967 etc.

Gopi Krishna, Pandit. *The Biological Basis of Religion & Genius,* Harper & Row, 1971

Oman, J. Campbell. *Cults, Customs & Superstitions of India,* T. Fisher Unwin, London, 1908

Oman, J. Campbell. *The Mystics, Ascetics & Saints of India,* T. Fisher Unwin, London, 1903

Sanyal, J. M. (transl.) *The Srimad Bhagavatam,* 2 vols., Munshiram Manocharlal, New Delhi, India, 1973

Indian Journal of Parapsychology

Published by University of Rajasthan, Department of Parapsychology, Jaipur, India.

Indian Rope Trick

A legendary illusion said to have been witnessed by a number of travelers in India and other Oriental countries.

In its most characteristic form, the demonstration starts with the magician throwing a rope high into the air. The rope stays vertical, and a boy assistant of the magician climbs up it and disappears from sight. The magician calls to the boy in apparent anger, demanding his return, then puts a sharp knife in his teeth and also climbs the rope and disappears high in the air. Presently there is the sound of fierce quarrel then the dismembered limbs of the boy, followed by his bleeding trunk and head are thrown down to the ground. The magician comes down the rope, kicks the limbs, throws a cloth over them or puts them in a basket, and in a moment the boy reappears whole, none the worse for the experience.

Travelers tales over the last century often include the detail that a photographer took a picture which proved blank on developing the negative, or alternatively showed only the magician sitting on the ground without a rope, suggesting that the whole exhibition was a collective hallucination induced by the magician.

An early account of the illusion is that of the great Moslem traveler Ibn Batuta (1304–1378) who claimed to witness it in Hang-chow, China. Two centuries later, a wandering juggler demonstrated a version of the trick in Germany. Pu Sing Ling, a seventeenth-century Chinese author, wrote that he saw the trick at Delhi, India, in 1630, but using a 75 foot chain instead of a rope. Edward Melton, a British sailor, saw the trick performed at Batavia by Chinese conjurers about 1670. Since then there have been many reports and rumors of the trick by British travelers and residents in India until modern

times. A correspondence on the subject in the British newspaper the *Daily Mail* (commencing January 8, 1919) drew several first-hand accounts of versions of the trick, and even a photograph.

It seems possible that like so many other apparently supernatural demonstrations, there may be two versions—one a rare but genuinely occult occurrence, the other a clever conjuring illusion.

The conjuring trick relies upon a specially prepared rope, sometimes made of bamboo sections with a central wire which can stiffen the rope when manipulated by the conjurer.

Another version of the trick was demonstrated in India by the American illusionist John **Keel,** who used carefully suspended wires invisible to the spectators, over which a rope was thrown and secured by a hook. Keel claimed that he learned this trick from an Indian holy man who was no longer interested in false illusions.

According to traditional Hindu yoga teachings, **levitation** and other supernormal powers are possible at a certain stage of yogic development. The material world itself is regarded as *Maya* or illusion, an inferior reality which may be transcended by advanced yogis. The great Hindu religious teacher Shankaracharya (born 8th century A.D.) actually cited the classic form of the Indian Rope Trick in his commentary on the scripture *Mandukya Upanishad,* using this as an example of the illusory nature of empirical reality.

He pointed out that although the spectators appeared to witness the marvels of the trick, in reality the magician was simply seated on the ground veiled by his own magic. This would suggest that Shankaracharya had seen the trick performed, and that he knew it to be achieved by the ability of the magician to transcend empirical reality and communicate an illusory demonstration to the spectators. In modern terms, this would validate the possibility of a collective hallucination, achieved by the supernormal powers of the magician.

Recommended reading:

Keel, John A. *Jadoo,* London, 1958 [contains an account of the author's performance of the Indian Rope Trick]

Gould, Rupert T. *More Oddities and Enigmas* (original title *The Stargazer Talks*), University Books, 1973 [includes a chapter on the Indian Rope Trick]

Indra Devi (1899-   )

Pioneer teacher, writer and lecturer on Yoga. Born May 12, 1899, in Riga, Russia, as Eugenie Petersen, part Russian, part Swedish, she was educated in St. Petersburg (now Leningrad). Her first marriage was to a diplomat, now deceased; second marriage to Sigfrid Knauer, a medical doctor, March 14, 1953. She was fascinated by Oriental philosophy and mysticism and lived in India for twelve years and in Shanghai, China, for seven years.

While in India, she actively supported the movement for Indian freedom, and was a friend of Mahatma Gandhi, Rabindranath Tagore and Pandit Nehru. She suffered from a supposed "incurable" heart disease for some years, but was cured miraculously by yoga healing. As a result, she studied yoga under Swami **Kuvalanayananda,** a noted Hatha Yogi, and took the name "Indra Devi."

She started a school of yoga in Shanghai, which she maintained throughout the Japanese occupation.

She returned to India, where she was the first Western woman to teach yoga, but in 1947 went to the U.S. where she started a yoga school in Los Angeles. She also traveled widely, lecturing on yoga. During her lecture tours she visited the U.S.S.R. and lectured on yoga to a group which included members of the Praesidium. She established and directed an International Yoga Center in Tecate, Baja, California.

She speaks twelve languages, and in addition to many articles on yoga has also published the following books: *Yoga—the Technique of Health and Happiness* (Kitabistan, India, 1948), *Forever Young, Forever Healthy* (1953, 1976), *Yoga for Americans* (1959, 1971), *Renew Your Life Through Yoga* (1953). Her books are frequently reprinted, and some of them have been translated into eight languages.

Indridason, Indride (died 1912)

Powerful Icelandic medium (discovered by the novelist Einar H. Kuaran) who was the subject of systematic experiments between the years 1904–1909 by the Psychic Experimental Society of Reykjavik, which was established for the purpose of studying this mediumship, the first which Iceland had known.

Indridason, who was under exclusive contract to the Society, began with **automatic writing** and **trance** speaking. After that **telekinesis, levitation, materialization** and **direct voice** developed. He also had healing powers. The phenomena was so strong that direct voice was heard and levitations took place in the presence of sixty-seventy sitters.

Indridason's chief **control** claimed to be a brother of his grandfather, a University Professor of Copenhagen. The power of the medium was at its height in 1909. During the summer he contracted typhoid fever and later consumption, dying in a sanatorium in August 1912.

The experimental society disbanded after his death. Haraldur Nielsson, Professor of Theology at the University of Reykjavik, was the chief exponent of the genuineness of Indridason's power (*Light,* Oct.–Nov. 1919). The *Journal* of the American Society for Psychical Research (1924, p. 239) published a long critical analysis of the phenomena by Professor Gudmundur Hanneson of the University of Reykjavik. He concluded: "The phenomena are unquestionable realities."

Inedia

Technical term for the claimed ability to survive without taking nourishment. This ability has been reported of various saints throughout history, and in modern times of the Bavarian peasant woman Therese **Neumann,** who is said to have existed for many years without food, taking only a little water.

Infernal Court

Johan **Weyer** (1515–1588) and other demonologists learned in the lore of the infernal regions, have discovered therein princes and high dignitaries, ministers, ambassadors, and officers of state, whose names and occupations are listed as precisely as any earthly census. Satan is no longer the sovereign of Hades, but is, so to speak, leader of the opposition, the true leader being Beelzebub.

According to Weyer, the demons number 7,405,926, commanded by 72 princes. Howard, an anonymous author of *Le Cabinet du Roy de France* (1581) amends these figures to 7,409,127 demons and evoked 79 princes.

Although demons are specifically named in many inspired catalogues and involved by sorcerers from their **grimoires,** there is no real agreement on names and numbers, and in all these fantastic works it is not difficult to see that they represent a distorted reflection of social organization of the world of their time.

Influence

In mediumistic terminology influence is equivalent to spirits. The British medium Mrs. **Piper** applied it to objects which, by virtues of association of ideas, or "magnetism" of the late owner, helped her to establish communication with the deceased. The presence of such objects, she declared, helped her to clear the ideas of the communicators. (See also **Psychometry**)

INFO

Journal of the International Fortean Organization, continuing the researches of the late Charles **Fort** into inexplicable events, prodigies, mysteries, etc. Address: INFO, P.O. Box 367, Arlington, Virginia 22210. (See also **Doubt; Fortean Times**)

Information Services for Psi Education

A clearinghouse for information on sources and resources in parapsychology. It has been formed to provide facts on individuals, organizations, and research findings for the benefit of librarians and educators. Address: P.O. Box 221, New York, N.Y. 10001.

Informazioni de Parapsicologia

Semi-annual publication in Italian language, reporting research in parapsychology; includes news and book reviews. Published by: Centro Italiano di Parapsicologia, Via Belvedere 87, 81027 Naples, Italy.

Ingeborg, Mrs. (c. 1930)

Daughter of Judge Ludwig Dahl of Fredrikstad, Norway, whose trance mediumship, with impressive evidence for spirit return, was discussed in Judge Dahl's *We Are Here* (1931). An interesting account of personal experiences was given in *Psychic Science* (April 1931) by Prof. Thorstein Wereide, Professor at the University of Oslo.

Inglis, Brian (1916–)

Irish author and journalist, an authority on alternative medicine and paranormal topics. Born July 31, 1916, in Dublin, Ireland, he was educated at Shrewsbury and Magdalene College, Oxford, Dublin University (Ph.D.). He served in the R.A.F. during World War II, afterwards becoming a journalist and author. He was editor of *The Spectator* 1959–62. His original outlook and mistrust of scientific dogma led him to join the Society for Psychical Research in the early 1960s and make his own investigation into paranormal subjects. He was a founding member of the **K.I.B. Foundation,** with Arthur **Koestler,** formed to encourage and promote research in fields at present outside scientific orthodoxies, such as parapsychology and alternative medicine. (After the death of Arthur Koestler, the organization was renamed "The Koestler Foundation").

Publications by Inglis include: *The Freedom of the Press in Ireland* (1954), *The Story of Ireland* (1956), *Revolution in Medicine* (1958), *West Briton* (1962), *Fringe Medicine* (1964), *Private Conscience, Public Morality* (1964), *Drugs, Doctors, and Disease* (1965), *A History of Medicine* (1965), *Abdication* (1966), *Poverty and the Industrial Revolution* (1971), *Roger Casement* (1973), *The Forbidden Game; A Social History of Drugs* (1975), *The Opium War* (1976), *Natural and Supernatural; A History of the Paranormal from Earliest Times to 1914* (1977), *The Book of the Back* (1978). He was also a consultant to the serial publication *The Unexplained* (1982 etc.).

Initiation

The process of entry into a secret society, an occult group, or a mystical stage of religion. The idea of initiation was inherited by the Egyptians and Assyrians from older neoblithic peoples, who possessed secret organizations or "mysteries" analogous to those of the Medwiwin of the North American Indians or those of the Australian Blackfellows.

Initiation was a stage in the various grades of the Egyptian priesthood and the "mysteries" of Eleusis and Bacchus. These processes probably consisted of tests of courage and fidelity (as with the ordeals of primitive peoples) and included such acts as sustaining a severe buffeting, the drinking of blood, real and imaginary, and so forth.

In the *Popol Vuh*, the saga of the Kiche Indians of Guatemala, there is a description of the initiation tests of two hero-gods on entrance to the native Hades. Indeed, many of the religious mysteries typified the descent of man into Hell, and his return to earth, based on the corn-mother legend of the resurrection of the wheat plant.

Initiation into the higher branches of mysticism, magic and Theosophy is, of course, largely symbolical, and is to be taken as implying a preparation for the higher life and the regeneration of the soul. Typical of such rites are the ceremonies for initiation and advancement of Freemasons. (See also **Freemasonry; Mysteries**)

Inner Forum Newsletter

Monthly publication featuring development in Parapsychology; includes sections on Yoga, astrology, pyramids and related subjects. Address: Inner Forum, Inc., P.O. Box 1611, Boise, Idaho 83701.

Inner-Space Interpreters

Publishers of three valuable guides to periodicals, recordings and services in the fields of psi phenomena and New Age spiritual awareness: *Guide to Psi Periodicals* (Newspapers, Magazines, Newsletters), *California Directory of Psi Services* (Organizations, individuals, shops, services), *Guide to Psi Tape Recordings*. All three guides are edited by Elizabeth M. Werner. Address: P.O. Box 1133, Magnolia Park Station, Burbank, California 91507.

Inner Voice

An auditory sensation covered, whether subjective or objective, by the term **Clairaudience**. However, clairaudience is conceived of as a purely mental phenomenon, whereas the following unusual testimony of the medium T. Herbert Noyes, B.A., before the **London Dialectical Society** in the nineteenth century suggests interesting physiological aspects: "I know that I should excite the derision of the sceptics if I were to say that I have conversed with spirits after a fashion which was asserted to be that in which spirits communicate with each other—by an 'inner voice,' which I could only compare to the sensation which would be caused by a telegraphic apparatus being hooked on to one of the nerve-ganglia—a distinctly audible click accompanying every syllable of the communication, which one could not say one heard, but of which one was made conscious by a new sense, and which was clearly distinguishable from thoughts originated in one's own mind." (See also **Clairaudience; Clairvoyance**)

Insight (Magazine)

Quarterly magazine of occultism with a wide range of coverage, published by Deric Robert James, 25 Calmore Close, Stourvale Meadows, Bournemouth, Dorset, England.

Insights (Journal)

Monthly publication of the Jersey Society of Parapsychology, reporting on the Society's activities and experiments in Psi phenomena. Address: P.O. Box 2071, Morristown, New Jersey 07960.

Inspiration

A psychic state in which one becomes susceptible to creative spiritual influence or, to a varying degree, unwittingly lends oneself as an instrument for through-flowing ideas.

The philosopher Schiller wondered where his thoughts came from; they frequently flowed through him "independent of the action of his own mind." The composer Mozart stated: "When all goes well with me, when I am in a carriage, or walking, or when I cannot sleep at night, the thoughts come streaming in upon me most fluently; whence or how is more than I can tell." Beethoven stated: "Inspiration is for me that mysterious state in which the entire world seems to form a vast harmony, when every sentiment, every thought re-echoes within me, when all the forces of nature become instruments for me, when my whole body shivers and my hair stands on end." Lord Beaconsfield, British statesman and novelist, admitted: "I often feel that there is only a step from intense mental concentration to madness. I should hardly be able to describe what I feel at the moment when my sensations are so strangely acute and intense. Every object seems to be animated. I feel that my senses are wild and extravagant. I am no longer sure of my own existence and often look back to see my name written there and thus be assured of my existence."

The two satellites of Mars were discovered in 1877 by Professor A. Hall. One hundred and seventy-five years earlier, Jonathan Swift wrote in *Gulliver's Travels* of the astronomers of Laputa: "They have discovered two small stars, or satellites, which revolve round Mars. The inner one is three diameters distant from the centre of the planet, the outer one five diameters; the first makes its revolution in ten hours, the second in twenty hours and a half." These figures, taken at the time as a proof of Swift's ignorance of astronomy, show a striking agreement with the findings of Prof. Hall.

W. M. Thackeray wrote in one of his "Roundabout Papers" (*Cornhill Magazine,* August 1862): "I have been surprised at the observations made by some of my characters. It seems as if an occult power was moving the pen. The personage does or says something and I ask: 'How did he come to think of that?' "

The writing of Lafcadio Hearn (1850–1904) was done in "periods of hysterical trance." He saw things that were not, and heard things that were not (Nina H. Kennard, *Lafcadio Hearn, his Life and Work,* 1912).

Of the inception of the chapter "The Death of Uncle Tom" in *Uncle Tom's Cabin,* the biography of Harriet Beecher Stowe states: "It seemed to her as though what she wrote was blown through her mind as with the rushing of a mighty wind."

Bogdan Hasdeu, the great Roumanian writer, became a convinced Spiritualist following messages which he automatically obtained from his deceased daughter. His father was a distinguished linguist and had in mind a standard dictionary of the Roumanian language. He himself was a historian. When half through his *History of the Roumanian People,* he suddenly plunged into the compilation of a vast dictionary. He felt that he was forced to do so. It is difficult to explain this case by ordinary psychological processes, as in a seance, which he was attending, the medium (who could not speak Russian) passed into trance and wrote messages from his father in Russian urging him to complete the work.

The popular novelist and playwright Edgar Wallace wrote in the London *Daily Express* (June 4, 1928): "Are we wildly absurd in supposing that human thought has an indestructible substance, and that men leave behind them, when their bodies are dead, a wealth of mind that finds employment in a new host? I personally do not think we are. I am perfectly satisfied in my mind that I have received an immense amount of help from the so-called "dead." I have succeeded far beyond the point my natural talents justified. And so have you—and you. I believe that my mind is furnished with oddments of intellectual equipment that have been acquired I know not how."

Sitting with W. T. **Stead** and Miss **Goodrich-Freer,** the medium, David Anderson went into trance and gave the name of the hero, and some incidents of his life, of a story which Miss Goodrich-Freer had written but never published. The spirits asserted that the story had been impressed on her mind from the spirit side. A similar occurrence is recorded in H. Travers Smith's *Voices from the Void* (1919).

Hannen **Swaffer** interviewed a number of distinguished artists and writers on the method by which their work was produced. The majority of the statements, recorded in Swaffer's book *Adventures with Inspiration* (1929) attributed the creative afflatus to a supernormal source.

According to ancient Hindu mysticism, there is a psycho-physiological mechanism in human beings by which a condition of higher consciousness may be brought about by meditation or yoga practice, and in modern times there is some evidence that this condition has occurred spontaneously in inventors and men of genuis (see **Kundalini**). (See also **Inspirational Speakers**)

Inspirational Speakers

Trance mediums who deliver impromptu platform addresses on various subjects, often chosen by the audience, the contents of which greatly surpass their normal intellectual power and knowledge.

The history of Spiritualism is rich in inspirational mediums. The most famous names are: Mrs. **Richmond** (first known as Miss Cora Scott, later, as Mrs. Hatch and Mrs. Tappan), Mrs. Emma Hardinge **Britten,** Thomas Lake **Harris,** Thomas Gale Forster, Nettie Colburn (Mrs. **Maynard**) and in Britain, W. J. **Colville,** J. J. **Morse,** Mrs. Meuring **Morris,** Estelle **Roberts** and Winifred **Moyes.**

The first American inspirational speaker who visited England shortly after the arrival of Mrs. Hayden, was Miss Emma Frances Jay (later Mrs. Emma Jay Bullene). Among early American inspirational speakers the following names are mentioned in Emma Hardinge's *Modern American Spiritualism* (1869): Miss Sprague, Mrs. Charlotte Tuttle, Mrs. Hattie Huntley, Mrs. Frances Hyzer and Mrs. M. S. Townsend.

Mrs. Maynard (Nettie Colburn) has a special claim to fame since her trance speaking influenced Abraham **Lincoln** in the issue of the anti-slavery proclamation. (See also **Inspiration**)

Institut für Grenzgebiete der Psychologie (Institute for Border Areas of Psychology)

Important institute for parapsychology founded in 1966 by Prof. Hans **Bender** in conjunction with Freiburg University, West Germany. The University considers parapsychology an integral part of psychology, and Freiburg students take courses in parapsychology at the Institute. Since 1957, the Institute has published the journal *Zeitschrift für Parapsychologie und Grenzgebiete der Psychologie,* in which many articles contain summaries in English language.

Institut Général Psychologique

Founded in Paris in 1904 for the pursuance of psychical research, first president Professor Duclaux (Pasteur's successor in L'Institut Pasteur), second, M. d'Arsonval, (member of the Academy), third, Professor Borda.

Owing to the intervention of Czar Nicholas, the French government authorized a lottery on behalf of the Institut which produced 800,000 francs. The depreciation of the franc, however, wiped out most of this capital, and the Institut, the most memorable investigation of which was conducted between 1905–08 with Eusapia **Palladino,** ceased to be active. For some time past it occupied itself more with normal than supernormal psychology. The moving spirit of the Institut was M. Serge Yourievitch, Secretary to the Russian Embassy in Paris and the secretarial duties were attended to by M. J. Courtier.

Institut Métapsychique International

Founded by Jean Meyer at 89 Avenue Niel, Paris, France, in 1918, recognized as an institute of public utility. The first director was Dr. Gustave **Geley;** the first committee: Prof. **Richet,** Prof. Santoliquido, Count de Gramont of the Institut of France, Medical Inspector General Dr. Calmette, Camille **Flammarion,** Ex-Minister of State Jules Roche and Dr. Treissier, of the Hospital of

Lyons; later members: Sir Oliver **Lodge,** Ernesto **Bozzano** and Prof. Leclainche, member of the Institut and Inspector General of Sanitary Services; official organ: *La Revue Métapsychique.* Later, Dr. Eugene **Osty** became director and Prof. Richet president.

An important phase of the work of the Institut was to invite public men of eminence in science and in literature to witness the investigations. Invitations to a hundred men of science were extended by Dr. Geley to the seances with "Eva C." The Institut installed an infra-red ray installation with which it was possible to take one thousand fully exposed pictures per second. The apparatus cost about $2,500, but owing to the noise which it produced and for other technical reasons it could not be turned to much practical use.

The most important experiments when Dr. Osty took office were conducted with Rudi **Schneider,** the medium having produced an invisible and non-photographable substance which, however, intercepted the passage of an infra-red ray, emitted from an apparatus outside his reach. The interception was automatically registered on a revolving cylinder.

In modern times, the Institut has been headed by Dr. Jean Berry, and is now situated at 1 Place Wagram, Paris 17. The *Revue Métapsychique* is still published.

Institute for Parapsychology

A division of the **Foundation for Research on the Nature of Man,** housing the Duke University collection on parapsychology, comprising over 10,000 accounts of spontaneous PSI experiences. The director is Dr. K. Ramakrishna **Rao.** The Institute conducts research and serves as an international forum. It holds meetings attended by researchers from other parapsychology centers, and many of their papers and reports are published in the **Journal of Parapsychology.** Address: Box 6847, College Station, Durham, North Carolina 27708.

Institute for the Development of the Harmonious Human Being

A Sufi form of **Fourth Way** teachings (related to the work of G. I. **Gurdjieff**). The Institute encourages a search for God which transcends human concepting, and by assimilation with God the discovery of truth and happiness. The Institute holds workshops on conscious birth, sex and death, and teaches meditation techniques. Address: P.O. Box 370, Nevada City, California 95959. (See also **Sufism**)

Institute for the Study of American Religion

Educational research organization formed to further the study of the numerous small religious bodies and psychic/occult organizations in American culture during the nineteenth and twentieth centuries.

The director is Dr. J. Gordon **Melton,** lecturer and author of various books, including: *A Reader's Guide to the Church's Ministry of Healing* (1972), *Directory of Religious Bodies in the United States* (1977), *Encyclopedia of American Religions* (1978).

The center derived from a large collection of research materials originally located at Garrett Theological Seminary in 1969. The Institute's present holdings cover some 20,000 volumes, in addition to research files, magazines

and ephemeral literature. Amongst special collections is the Elmer T. Clark Memorial of volumes donated by Dr. Clark, author of the classic work *The Small Sects in America* (Abingdon, 1949). The Institute's library of books is available to the public for serious research, and the Institute also offers information services and lectures. Address: Box 1311, Evanston, Illinois 60201.

Institute Magazine

A journal of **Fourth Way** teachings, stemming from the philosophy of G. I. **Gurdjieff** as taught by J. G. **Bennett.** Address: Coombe Springs Press, Daglingworth Manor, Daglingworth, Gloucestershire, GL7 7AH, England.

Institute of Noetic Sciences

Founded in 1973 by former astronaut Edgar D. **Mitchell** to encourage and conduct basic research and education programs on mind-body relationships, for the purpose of gaining new understanding of human consciousness. The term "noetic" is defined as "pertaining to, or originating in intellectual or rational activity." Institute programs include research in parapsychology, healing, personal awareness and control of interior states. Address: 575 Middlefield Road, Palo Alto, California 94301.

Institute of Parascience

Founded in 1971 in Devon, England, to investigate scientific aspects of parapsychology. The first president was Alan J. **Mayne.** Beginning with a mimeographed publication *Parascience,* the Institute has since held symposia on experimental Psi research and started to publish *Parascience Proceedings* and *Parascience Newsletter* (1975). Subjects covered include Psychical research and the theory of Resonance; Notes on the Macromechanics of Psychokinesis; Evaluations of Field-Theoretical Approaches to Psi; Experimental and experiential methods in Psi research; Problems of Precognition; Mediumship and the Survival Question. The Institute is located at: Spryton, Lifton, Devon, U.K.

Institute of Psychophysical Research

Founded at Oxford, England, by members of the **Society for Psychical Research,** London, at Oxford University, to research psychophysiological aspects of Psi phenomena. It is an independent group and the director is Celia E. **Green,** who authored the book *Out-of-the-body Experiences,* published 1968 as Vol. II of *Proceedings of the Institute of Psychophysical Research.* The address of the Institute is: 118 Banbury Road, Oxford, OX2 6JU England.

Insufflation

According to occultist Éliphas **Lévi,** in his book *Transcendal Magic,* (1896 etc.), insufflation "is one of the most important practices of occult medicine, because it is a perfect sign of the transmission of life. To inspire, as a fact, means to breath upon some person or thing, and we know already, by the one doctrine of Hermes, that the virtue of things has created words, and that there is an exact proportion between ideas and speech, which is the first form and verbal realisation of ideas. The breath attracts or repels, according, as it is warm or cold. The warm breathing corresponds to positive electricity, and the cold breathing to negative electricity.

"Electrical and nervous animals fear the cold breathing, and the experiment may be made upon a cat, whose familiarities are important. By fixedly regarding a lion or tiger and blowing in their face, they would be so stupefied as to be forced to retreat before us.

"Warm and prolonged insufflation restores the circulation of the blood, cures rheumatic and gouty pains, re-establishes the balance of the humours, and dispels lassitude. When the operator is sympathetic and good, it acts as a universal sedative.

"Cold insufflation soothes pains occasioned by congestions and fluidic accumulations. The two breathings must, therefore, be used alternately, observing the polarity of the human organism, and acting in a contrary manner upon the poles, which must be treated successfully to an opposite magnetism. Thus, to cure an inflamed eye, the one which is not affected must be subjected to a warm and gentle insufflation, cold insufflation being practised upon the suffering member at the same distance and in the same proportion.

"Magnetic passes have a similar effect to insufflations, and are a real breathing by transpiration and radiation of the interior air, which is phosphorescent with vital light; slow passes constitute a warm breathing which fortifies and raises the spirits; swift passes are a cold breathing of dispersive nature, neutralising tendencies to congestion. The warm insufflation should be performed transversely, or from below upward, the cold insufflation is more effective when directed downward from above."

Integral Yoga Institute

Founded in 1966 by Swami **Satchidananda,** disciple of the late Swami **Sivananda** of Rishikesh, India. Integral Yoga combines various yoga methods such as Hatha Yoga (physical development), Karma Yoga (selfless service), Bhakti Yoga (devotion), Japa Yoga (mantra repetition), Jnana Yoga (knowledge) and Raja Yoga (meditation and mind control), thus harmonizing the personality and enhancing spiritual awareness.

There are now a number of I.Y.I branches in the U.S., covering Los Angeles, San Diego and San Francisco, California; Denver, Colorado; Washington, D.C.; Danbury and New Britain, Connecticut; St. Louis, Missouri; Garfield, New Jersey; New York, N.Y.; Dallas and San Antonio, Texas. These institutes offer instruction for beginners and advanced students, community service and drug rehabilitation programs, yoga instruction in schools and prisons. Record albums and cassette tapes are available, as well as spiritual publications. For information: Satchidananda Ashram—Yogaville, Route 1, P.O. Box 172, Buckingham, Virginia 23921.

Inter Cosmic Spiritual Association

Founded by Dr. Rammurti S. Mishra, endocrinologist, neuro-surgeon and psychiatrist, who has also published authoritative works on Hatha Yoga and yoga philosophy. ICSA is responsible for Dr. Mishra's lectures and study groups throughout the world, operating through **Ananda Ashram,** Rt 3, P.O. Box 141, Monroe, N.Y. 10950.

International Academy for Continuous Education

Founded in 1971 by mathematician philosopher **J. G. Bennett** to propagate the work of G. I. **Gurdjieff.** It aims "to achieve, in a short space of time, the effective transmission of a whole corpus of practical techniques for self-development and self-liberation, so that people could learn effectively to direct their own inner work and to adapt to the rapid changes in the inner and outer life of man." The organization is based in Sherborne House, a Victorian mansion in the Cotswold countryside of Britain. Candidates for admission must be eighteen years or over, and undergo preliminary tests. Students study psychology, art, history, cosmology and linguistics, and practice spiritual and psychological exercises which make a considerable demand at all levels, mental, physical and emotional.

Since the death of J. G. Bennett, the Academy expects that there may be considerable changes, largely necessitated by the creative evolution of the inner and outer work. Address: Sherborne House, Sherborne, Gloucestershire, GL54 3DZ, England. (See also **Claymont Society for Continuous Education;** The **Dicker; Gurdjieff Foundation of California**)

International Association for Psychotronic Research

Publishers of reports, bulletins, newsletters and a Journal concerned with **Psychotronics**—defined as the mutual interactions of consciousness, energy and matter; embracing such subjects as Dowsing, Radiesthesia, Radionics, Bio-electric fields, Aura phenomena, etc. Address: 43 Eglinton Avenue, Suite 803, Toronto, Ontario M4P 1A2, Canada.

International Association for Religion and Parapsychology

Founded in Tokyo, Japan, in 1972 by Dr. Hiroshi Motoyama. The Association aids and supports efforts of individuals to clarify truths of mind, matter and religious experience, and to verify the reality of paranormal phenomena. The Association holds yoga classes, seminars and retreats, maintains an **acupuncture** clinic and laboratories for parapsychology experiments. The IARP issues a periodic Journal and Newsletter, and publishes books and monographs. Address: 4-11-7 Inokashira, Mitaka-shi, Tokyo 181, Japan.

International Association for Religion and Parapsychology Newsletter

Quarterly publication from Japan in English language, reporting on researches connected with Psi and religious realization. Address: 4-11-7 Inokashira, Mitaka-shi, Tokyo 181, Japan.

International Congress of Psychical Research

Periodical gathering of psychical researchers from all over the world from 1921 onwards. The first Congress was held in Copenhagen, the second in 1923 in Warsaw, the third in 1927 in Paris, and the fourth in 1930 in Athens.

World War II interrupted such international congresses, but in 1953 the first International Conference on

Parapsychological Studies was held at Utrecht University, Holland, sponsored by the **Parapsychology Foundation.**

International Cooperation Council

An international coordinating body composed of educational, scientific, cultural and religious organizations which in their own ways "foster the emergence of a new universal person and a civilization based on unity in diversity among all peoples." Originally formed to propagate the ideals and activities of several such organizations during International Cooperation Year, it was voted into being in 1965 by the General Assembly of the United Nations. The I.C.C. seeks to publicize the aims and ideas of humanitarian groups which bring together the methods and discoveries of modern science and the deeper insights of religion, philosophy and the arts. Much of this synthesis is concerned with developing areas of awareness in human consciousness and unorthodox healing techniques.

As a World Headquarters, the I.C.C. has developed area councils in various parts of the U.S. and abroad. Activities include International Cooperation Festivals, Action Projects, the New Age Institute and the Worldview Exploration Seminar. The festivals are held annually each January in or near Los Angeles, when cooperating organizations participate through displays, dialog sessions and interest groups, and leading specialists explain new developments in their fields. Action Projects bring about the convergence of new consciousness organizations to exchange information and work together on education, healing and media.

The New Age Institute arose as a result of a new age education conference held in 1974 in Los Angeles, directed towards public and private education. The Worldview Exploration Seminar, formed in spring 1969, grew out of the Fifth Annual International Cooperation Festival, and is composed primarily of professional individuals from the fields of science, religion, art, education and philosophy. It meets monthly on the campus of the California State College at Los Angeles to explore "the meaning of the new universal person and the world civilization." Papers presented during seminars are published by I.C.C. World Headquarters. Other publications include *Spectrum,* a monthly semiannual magazine of art, poetry and other materials of intergroup work, *Directory of Organizations* (published 1974, with 1975 Supplement). Address of I.C.C.: World Headquarters, 17819 Roscoe Boulevard, Northridge, California 91324.

International Flat Earth Society

Successor to the Universal Zetetic Society of America and Great Britain, dedicated to the view that "so called modern astronomy is false; that no proof has been brought forth to show the earth as a spinning ball." (The term "Zetetic" refers to an ancient Greek school of skeptical inquiry, and has also been used as the title of the **Zetetic,** journal of the Committee for the Scientific Investigation of Claims of the Paranormal; this has no connection with the International Flat Earth Society). Address: P.O. Box 2533, Lancaster, California 93534.

International General Assembly of Spiritualists

Founded in 1936 to charter Spiritualist churches and promote spiritual healing. It holds classes and training sessions in the art of spiritual healing. Address: 1809 Bayview Boulevard, Norfolk, Virginia 23505.

International Ghost Registry

Formed in California to preserve and investigate records of hauntings and ghostly phenomena throughout the world. The major objectives include preserving firsthand records of ghost sightings which might otherwise be lost, cataloging and recording ghost lore from individual geographical regions, encouraging careful evaluation and documentation of ghostly phenomena, providing a central file for the use of researchers and writers in parapsychology. The Registry is administered by the International Society for the Investigation of Ghosts. Address: International Ghost Registry, P.O. Box 5011, Salinas, California 93901.

International Institute for Psychic Investigation

British organization formed in January 1939 as an amalgamation between the **British College of Psychic Science** and the **International Institute for Psychical Research.** It continued publication of the journal *Psychic Science* and maintained the reference library of the College, transferred to the Institute's premises at Walton House, Walton Street, London, S.W.3. The Institute ceased in 1947, after its library and records were dispersed or destroyed in bombing. However, its objectives were largely continued by a separate organization, the **College of Psychic Science,** London, formed in 1955 from the **London Spiritualist Alliance,** originally founded in 1884.

International Institute for Psychical Research

British organization for psychical research founded in 1934 by Mrs. Dawson Scott, pupil and associate of pioneer psychical researcher J. Hewat **McKenzie,** J. Arthur **Findlay,** and Shaw **Desmond.** The Institute had as its aim investigation of psychic phenomena by the objective methods of laboratory research. Prof. Fraser Harris was appointed Research Officer, followed by Dr. Nandor **Fodor,** who held this position until summer 1938.

The I.I.P.R. premises were in Harrington Road, London, S.W., later removing to Walton House, Walton Street, London, S.W.3. The Institute emphasized the need for experimental work and secured photographic and recording apparatus to investigate and record voice and physical phenomena. The Council consisted of both Spiritualists and non-Spiritualists, ensuring a balanced approach to the investigation of paranormal phenomena. The Institute published papers on their experiments, including the following: *Bulletin I. Historic Poltergeists* by Hereward Carrington; *The Saragossa Ghost* by Nandor Fodor; *Bulletin II. The Lajos Pap Experiments* by Nandor Fodor; *Bulletin III. Enquiry into the Cloud-Chamber Method of Studying the "Intra-Atomic Quantity"* by G. J. Hopper.

As from January 1939, the Institute was amalgamated with the British College of Psychic Science under the name of The International Institute for Psychic Investigation. The B.C.P.S. transferred many of its workers and its excellent reference library to the I.I.P.R. at the Walton House premises. Publication of the College's valuable journal *Psychic Science* continued under the auspices of the Institute. However, with the outbreak of war, the organization had a difficult time, and eventually ceased in 1947.

The library and records were dispersed or destroyed by bombing.

However, its place was to a large extent filled by the **College of Psychic Science** in London, formed in 1955 from the long-established **London Spiritualist Alliance,** originally founded in 1884. The College of Psychic Science had very similar objectives to the B.C.P.S. and I.I.P.R. and at one time or another leading Spiritualists or psychical researchers connected with the earlier organizations also took part in its activities. The College also maintained an excellent loan and reference library at its premises in 16 Queensberry Place, South Kensington, London, S.W.7., and arranges for experimental investigations and consultations with mediums, currently continued under a new name of **The College of Psychic Studies.**

International Journal of Parapsychology

Former scholarly journal which appeared quarterly from vol. 1 (Summer 1959) through vol. 10 (Winter 1968), published by **Parapsychology Foundation** (228 East 71st Street, New York, N.Y. 10021) "as a forum for scholarly inquiry, linking parapsychology with psychology, physics, biochemistry, pharmacology, anthropology, ethnology and other scientific disciplines." Resumes of main articles were given in French, German, Italian and Spanish. The purpose of the *International Journal of Parapsychology* has now been taken over by the bimonthly *Parapsychology Review,* published by the Parapsychology Foundation. Back issues of the *Journal* are available from University Microfilms, Ann Arbor, Michigan 48106.

International Parascience Institute

Originally founded in 1971 as Institute of Parascience in Devon, England, to investigate scientific aspects of parapsychology. The first president was Alan J. **Mayne.**

Beginning with a mimeographed publication *Parascience,* the Institute has since held symposia on experimental Psi research and published *Parascience Proceedings* and *Parascience Newsletter.* Subjects covered included Psychical research and the theory of Resonance; Notes on the Macromechanics of Psychokinesis; Evaluations of Field-Theoretical Approaches to Psi; Experimental and experiential methods in Psi research; Problems of Precognition; Mediumship and the Survival Question.

Address: Cryndir, Nantmel, Llandrindod Wells, Powys LD1 6EH, Wales, U.K.

International Plant Consciousness Research Newsletter

Monthly publication reporting meetings and seminars on matters relating to plant consciousness. The directors include pioneer researcher Cleve **Baxter** and Mrs. Charles Musés. Address: 5210 East 25th Street, Long Beach, California 90815. (See also **Plants, Psychic Aspects**)

International Psychic Gazette

Monthly magazine founded in 1912 as the official organ of the International Club for Psychical Research. Publication ceased after a few months.

International Psychic Register

First issue of a directory of practitioners of the psychic arts in the U.S., Canada and Great Britain. Includes classified list of healers, psychics, teachers and parapsychologists, with addresses and telephone numbers. Published by Ornion Press, Box 1816, Erie, Pa. 16507.

International Society for Krishna Consciousness (ISKCON)

A modern Hindu religious cult for Western youth, founded by Swami Prabhupada **Bhaktivedanta** in New York in the 1960s. It is derived from the sixteenth-century Bengal cults of devotion to Shri Krishna, a popular incarnation of the god Vishnu, and Western devotees are initiated with Hindu names and costumes.

They may be seen chanting the praises of Shri Krishna on the streets of large cities in many countries of the world. Devotees live in communities with temples and images of Shri Krishna in traditional Hindu style.

It is claimed that incessant chanting of mantras or sacred prayers praising Shri Krishna will develop spiritual consciousness.

The movement has gained great popularity with former drug addicts and hippies, who have ceased to be anti-social dropouts by becoming spiritual drop-outs in a family commune atmosphere. It should be said, however, that traditional Hinduism does not favor widespread renunciation of everyday *dharma* or duties and responsibilities of individuals.

In December 1976, the Society incurred unfavorable comment through its practice of dressing up fund collectors as Santa Claus, in rivalry with the accepted traditional Santas collecting for charities on the streets of large cities. Santa Claus does not figure in Hindu religious mythology, and cannot be said to enhance Krishna Consciousness. These episodes appear uncharacteristic of the aims and ideals of the Society.

The movement has continued to grow and before the passing of its founder in 1977, it had become a worldwide confederation of more than one hundred ashrams, schools, temples, institutes and farm communities. In 1968, an experimental Vedic community named New Vrindaban was established in the hills of West Virginia, and similar communities have been formed elsewhere. Educational school centers have been founded in the U.S. and abroad and several large cultural centers in India. The center at Sridhama Mayapura in West Bengal is the site for an ambitious spiritual city.

The Bhaktivedanta Book Trust has published a large number of authoritative books on Indian religion and philosophy edited by Swami Bhaktivedanta, including classic Hindu scriptures.

Address for inquiries regarding ISKCON: ISKCON-Berkeley, 2334 Stuart Street, Berkeley, California 94705.

International Society for the Investigation of Ghosts

An organization which maintains an **International Ghost Registry** to preserve and investigate records of hauntings and related phenomena throughout the world. The Society publishes a bi-monthly newsletter *FOG,* which includes ghost accounts sent by members, articles and book reviews. Members of the Society have access to the International Ghost Registry. Address: International Society for the Investigation of Ghosts, International Ghost Registry, P.O. Box 5011, Salinas, California 93901.

International Spiritualist Congress

First was held at Liege in 1923, the second congress at Paris in 1925, the third in London in 1928, and the fourth at the Hague in 1931. The Paris Congress expressed the philosophy and fundamental principles of Spiritualism in the following propositions: 1. The existence of God as the Intelligent and Supreme Cause of all things. 2. The affirmation that Man is a spirit related, during terrestrial life, to a perishable body by an intermediate body (the etheric or perispirit), which is indestructible in nature. 3. The immortality of the spirit and its continuous evolution towards perfection through progressive stages of life. 4. Universal and personal responsibility, both individual and collective, between all beings. Later congresses have reaffirmed these principles.

International Spiritualists Federation, The (Fédération Spirite Internationale)

Founded c. 1923 with headquarters at Maison des Spirites, 8 Rue Copernic, Paris (XVIe), original presidents Sir Arthur Conan Doyle and Ernest W. Oaten (editor of *Two Worlds* journal). It had many affiliated associations in England, France, Germany, Spain, Holland, Belgium, Switzerland, U.S.A., Cuba, Costa Rica, Mexico and South Africa. The first International Spiritist Congress was held at Liège, Belgium, in 1923, the second in 1925 at the headquarters in Paris, the third in London, England, in 1928, the fourth at La Haye in 1931, the fifth at Barcelona in 1934. As with many international organizations, its work was suspended by World War II.

International UFO Reporter

Monthly journal published by **Center for UFO Studies,** 1609 Sherman Avenue, Room 207, Evanston, Illinois 60201. It is edited by J. Allen **Hynek,** who was in charge of UFO investigations on "Project Bluebook," the U.S. Air Force official investigation of UFO sightings, and technical consultant on the Steven Spielberg movie **Close Encounters of the Third Kind.** A special feature of *International UFO Reporter* is the monthly statistical account of UFO or related sightings reported to the CUFOS hotline.

International Yoga Guide

Monthly magazine of the International Yoga Society; includes extracts from Hindu scripture, yoga exercises, news of Society activities. Address: 6111 S.W. 74th Avenue, Miami, Florida 33143.

Interplanetary Space Travel Research Association

Non-profit society founded in 1957 to promote public interest in space activities (including UFOs and extraterrestrials) and science fiction. Membership is free. The first issue of *Space Digest* (1977) is available from ISTRA through: Robert Morison (editor), 30 Grosvenor Road, London, E. 11, England.

Intuition

Human faculty by which individuals are aware of facts not accessible to normal sensory or mental processes. Some apparent intuition may be due to unconscious sensory or mental perception or deduction. Other intuitive awareness suggests paranormal faculty.

Intuitional World

Theosophical term for the Buddhic Plane or the fourth world, from which come intuitions. (See also **Intuition; Solar System; Theosophy**)

IRELAND

Pagan and Christian Beliefs

For information regarding ancient Ireland, see **Celts.**

Although nominally Christianized, there is little doubt that the early medieval Irish retained many relics of their former condition of paganism, especially those which possessed a magical tendency. This is made clear by the writings of the Welsh historian Giraldus Cambrensis (c. 1147–1220), the first account we have of Irish manners and customs after the invasion of the country by the Anglo-Normans. His description, for example, of the Purgatory of St. Patrick in Lough Derg, Co. Donegal, suggests that the demonology of the Catholic Church had already fused with the animism of earlier Irish tradition. He stated:

"There is a lake in Ulster containing an island divided into two parts. In one of these stands a church of especial sanctity, and it is most agreeable and delightful, as well as beyond measure glorious for the visitations of angels and the multitude of the saints who visibly frequent it. The other part, being covered with rugged crags, is reported to be the resort of devils only, and to be almost always the theatre on which crowds of evil spirits visibly perform their rites. This part of the island contains nine pits, and should any one perchance venture to spend the night in one of them (which has been done, we know, at times, by some rash men), he is immediately seized by the malignant spirits, who so severely torture him during the whole night, inflicting on him such unutterable sufferings by fire and water, and other torments of various kinds, that when morning comes scarcely any spark of life is found left in his wretched body. It is said that any one who has once submitted to these torments as a penance imposed upon him, will not afterwards undergo the pains of hell, unless he commit some sin of a deeper dye.

"This place is called by the natives the Purgatory of St. Patrick. For he, having to argue with a heathen race concerning the torments of hell, reserved for the reprobate, and the real nature and eternal duration of the future life, in order to impress on the rude minds of the unbelievers a mysterious faith in doctrines so new, so strange, so opposed to their prejudices, procured by the efficacy of his prayers an exemplification of both states even on earth, as a salutary lesson to the stubborn minds of the people."

Human Animals

The ancient Irish believed in the possibility of the transformation of human beings into animals, and Giraldus in another narrative of facts purporting to have come under his personal notice shows that this belief had lost none of its significance with the Irish of the latter half of the twelfth century. The case is also interesting as being one of the first recorded examples of **lycanthropy** in the British Isles:

"About three years before the arrival of Earl John in Ireland, it chanced that a priest, who was journeying from Ulster towards Meath, was benighted in a certain wood on the borders of Meath. While, in company with only a young lad, he was watching by a fire which he had kindled under the branches of a spreading tree, lo! a wolf came up to them, and immediately addressed them to this effect: 'Rest secure, and be not afraid, for there is no reason you should fear, where no fear is!' The travellers being struck with astonishment and alarm, the wolf added some orthodox words referring to God. The priest then implored him, and adjured him by Almighty God and faith in the Trinity, not to hurt them, but to inform them what creature it was in the shape of a beast uttered human words. The wolf, after giving catholic replies to all questions, added at last: 'There are two of us, a man and a woman, natives of Ossory, who, through the curse of Natalis, saint and abbot, are compelled every seven years to put off the human form, and depart from the dwellings of men. Quitting entirely the human form, we assume that of wolves. At the end of the seven years, if they chance to survive, two others being substituted in their places, they return to their country and their former shape. And now, she who is my partner in this visitation lies dangerously sick not far from hence, and, as she is at the point of death, I beseech you, inspired by divine charity, to give her the consolations of your priestly office.'

"At this wood the priest followed the wolf trembling, as he led the way to a tree at no great distance, in the hollow of which he beheld a she-wolf, who under that shape was pouring forth human sighs and groans. On seeing the priest, having saluted him with human courtesy, she gave thanks to God, who in this extremity had vouchsafed to visit her with such consolation. She then received from the priest all the rites of the church duly performed, as far as the last communion. This also she importunately demanded, earnestly supplicating him to complete his good offices by giving her the viaticum. The priest stoutly asserting that he was not provided with it, the he-wolf, who had withdrawn to a short distance, came back and pointed out a small missal-book, containing some consecrated wafers, which the priest carried on his journey, suspended from his neck, under his garment, after the fashion of the country. He then intreated him not to deny them the gift of God, and the aid destined for them by Divine Providence; and, to remove all doubt, using his claw for a hand, he tore off the skin of the she-wolf, from the head down to the navel, folding it back. Thus she immediately presented the form of an old woman. The priest, seeing this, and compelled by his fear more than his reason, gave the communion; the recipient having earnestly implored it, and devoutly partaking of it. Immediately afterwards the he-wolf rolled back the skin and fitted it to its original form.

"These rites having been duly, rather than rightly performed, the he-wolf gave them his company during the whole night at their little fire, behaving more like a man than a beast. When morning came, he led them out of the wood, and, leaving the priest to pursue his journey pointed out to him the direct road for a long distance. At his departure, he also gave him many thanks for the benefit he had conferred, promising him still greater returns of gratitude, if the Lord should call him back from his present exile, two parts of which he had already completed.

"It chanced, about two years afterwards, that I was passing through Meath, at the time when the bishop of that land had convoked a synod, having also invited the assistance of the neighbouring bishops and abbots, in order to have their joint counsels on what was to be done in the affair which had come to his knowledge by the priest's confession. The bishop, hearing that I was passing through those parts, sent me a message by two of his clerks, requesting me, if possible, to be personally present when a matter of so much importance was under consideration; but if I could not attend he begged me at least to signify my opinion in writing. The clerks detailed to me all the circumstances, which indeed I had heard before from other persons; and, as I was prevented by urgent business from being present at the synod, I made up for my absence by giving them the benefit of my advice in a letter. The bishop and synod, yielding to it, ordered the priest to appear before the pope with letters from them, setting forth what had occurred, with the priest's concession, to which instrument the bishops and abbots who were present at the synod affixed their seals.

"In our own time we have seen persons who, by magical arts, turned any substance about them into fat pigs, as they appeared (but they were always red), and sold them in the markets. However, they disappeared as soon as they crossed any water, returning to their real nature; and with whatever care they were kept, their assumed form did not last beyond three days. It has also been a frequent complaint, from old times as well as in the present, that certain hags in Wales, as well as in Ireland and Scotland changed themselves into the shape of hares, that, sucking teats under this counterfeit form, they might stealthily rob other people's milk."

Witchcraft in Ireland

In Anglo-Norman times, sorcery was widely practiced but notices are scarce. It is only by fugitive passages in the works of English writers who constantly comment on the superstitious nature and practices of the Irish that we glean any information concerning the occult history of the country. The great scandal of the Lady Alice **Kyteler** shook the entire Anglo-Norman colony during several successive years in the first half of the fourteenth century. The party of the Bishop of Ossory, the relentless opponent of the Lady Alice, boasted that by her prosecution they had rid Ireland of a nest of sorcerers, but there is reason to believe that Ireland could have furnished numerous similar instances of black magic had the actors in them been of similar rank to the ill-fated lady—that is of sufficient importance in the eyes of chroniclers.

In this connection a work on *Irish Witchcraft and Demonology* by Mr. St. John D. Seymour (1913) is of striking interest. The author appears to take it for granted that witchcraft in Ireland is purely an alien system, imported into the island by the Anglo-Normans and Scottish immigrants to the north. This undoubtedly is the case so far as the districts of the Pale and of Ulster are concerned, but surely it cannot be applied to the Celtic districts of Ireland.

Regarding these Mr. Seymour is silent, but it will occur to many readers that the analogy of Celtic Scotland, which abounded in witches and witch-customs, is powerful evidence that a system similar to that in vogue in the Highlands obtained in the aboriginal districts of Ireland. Early Irish works contain numerous references to sorcery, and practices are chronicled in them which bear a close resemblance to those of the shamans and medicine men of savage tribes all over the world. Animal transformation, one of the most common feats of the witch, is alluded to frequently in the ancient Irish cycles, and there are few heroes in Hibernian legend who do not have a fair stock of working magic at their finger-ends. Wonder-working druids abound too.

Mr. Seymour claims that "In Celtic Ireland dealings with the unseen were not regarded with such abhorrence, and indeed had the sanction of custom and antiquity." He also states that "the Celtic element had its own superstitious beliefs, but these never developed in this direction" i.e., Witchcraft). This is very difficult to believe. The lack of records of such a system is no criterion that it never existed, and it is possible that a thorough examination of the subject would prove that a veritable system of witchcraft obtained in Celtic Ireland as elsewhere, although it may not have been of "Celtic" origin.

Be that as it may, Mr. Seymour's book is most interesting as dealing with those Anglo-Norman and Scottish portions of Ireland where the belief in witchcraft followed the lines of those in vogue in the mother-countries of the immigrant populations. He sketches the famous Kyteler case, touches on the circumstances connected with the Earl of Desmond and notes the case of the Irish prophetess who insisted upon warning the ill-fated James I of Scotland on the night of his assassination at Perth.

It is not stated by the ancient chronicler quoted by Mr. Seymour, from what part of Ireland the witch in question emanated—for a witch she undoubtedly was as she possessed a **familiar** spirit "Huthart" whom she alleged had made her cognisant of the coming catastrophe. Mr. Seymour does not seem to be aware of the history of this spirit. He is the Teutonic *Hudekin* or *Hildekin,* the wearer of the hood, sometimes also alluded to as *Heckdekin,* well known throughout Germany and Flanders as a species of house-spirit or brownie. Trithemius alludes to him as a "spirit known to the Saxons who attached himself to the Bishop of Hildesheim" and he is cited here and there in occult history. From this circumstance it might with justice be inferred that the witch in question came from some part of Ireland which had been settled by Teutonic immigrants, and more probably from Ulster, but the data is insufficient to permit us to conclude this definitely.

From the most scanty materials, Mr. Seymour has compiled a book of outstanding interest. He passes in review the witchcraft trials of the sixteenth century, the burning of Adam Dubh, of the Leinster trial of O'Toole and College Green in 1327 for heresy, and the passing of the statute against witchcraft in Ireland in 1586.

The prevalence of witchcraft in Ireland during the sixteenth century is proved by him to have been very great indeed, but a number of the authorities he cites, as to the existence of sorcerers in the Green Isle, almost certainly refer to the more Celtic portions of it, for example Rich and Stanihurst.

He has an excellent note upon the enchantments of the Earl of Desmond who demonstrated to his young and beautiful wife the possibilities of animal transformation by changing himself into a bird, a hag, a vulture, and a gigantic serpent.

Human relations with the Devil are dwelt upon at length by Mr. Seymour in a racy chapter, and we are told how the Devil was cheated by a doctor of divinity and raised on occasion by certain sorcerers.

Florence Newton, the witch of Youghal claims an entire chapter to herself, and worthily, for her case is one of the most absorbing in the history of witchcraft. At any rate, whatever her occult powers, she splendidly succeeded in setting a whole community by the ears.

Ghostly doings and **apparitions,** fairy possession, and dealings with the **fairies** are also included in the volume, and Mr. Seymour has not confined himself to Ireland, but has followed one of his countrywomen to America, where he shows how she gave congenial employment to the fanatic Cotton **Mather.**

Witchcraft notices of the seventeenth century in Antrim and Island Magee comprise the eighth chapter, and the ninth and last bring down the affairs of sorcery in Ireland from the year 1807 to the early twentieth century. The last notice is that of a trial for murder in 1911, when a wretched woman was tried for killing another (an old-age pensioner) in a fit of insanity. A witness deposed that he met the accused on the road on the morning of the crime holding a statue or figure in her hand and repeating three times, "I have the old witch killed. I got power from the Blessed Virgin to kill her." It appears that the witch quoted in question threatened to plague the murderess with rats and mice. A single rodent had evidently penetrated to her abode and was followed by the bright vision of a lady who told the accused that she was in danger, and further informed her that if she received the senior citizen's pension-book without taking off her clothes and cleaning them and putting out her bed and cleaning up the house, she would "receive dirt for ever and rats and mice." This is not an isolated case, and shows how hard such superstitions die in the more remote portions of civilized countries.

Modern Occultism

During the late nineteenth and early twentieth century, Celtic mysticism and legends of ghosts and fairies received a new infusion from Hindu mysticism through the Dublin lodge of the **Theosophical Society** and the writings of poets W. B. **Yeats** and "AE" (George W. **Russell**). Through the Society, Russell was profoundly influenced by the great Hindu scripture *Bhagavad-Gita* which teaches that mysticism should be interfused with one's everyday social responsibilities. Russell wrote mystical poems, and painted pictures of nature spirits but gave himself unstintingly to the hard work of establishing Irish cooperatives.

W. B. Yeats became a noted member of the **Golden Dawn** occult society and its teachings had a primary influence on the symbolism of his poems and on his own mystical vision. He too was greatly impressed by Hindu mystical teachings, and collaborated with Shree **Purohit Swami** in translation of Hindu religious works.

After the death of Yeats and Russell, occultism did not make much headway in Irish life and literature and the occult and witchcraft boom of the 1950s and 60s was largely ignored, but in recent years, Mr. & Mrs. Stewart Farrar, both "white witches," have taken up residence in the Republic of Ireland. Stewart Farrar is the author of a number of books on witchcraft as a nature religion, including *What Witches Do; The Modern Coven Revealed* (1971).

There is also The **Fellowship of Isis** at Huntingdon Castle, Clonegal, Enniscorthy, devoted to the deity in the form of the Goddess and publishing material concerning matriarchal religion and mysticism.

Irish author Desmond **Leslie** was coauthor with George **Adamski** of the influential book *Flying Saucers Have Landed* (1953) which played a dominant part in publicizing the subject. The book was translated into sixteen languages.

Psychical Research & Parapsychology

Although Ireland is traditionally a land of ghosts, fairies, banshees and haunted castles, there has been little systematic attempt to conduct psychical research in the Republic, although there has been some interest in dowsing (water-divining). However, there is a **Society for Psychical & Spiritual Studies** in Dublin which holds lecture meetings and issues an occasional Newsletter. There is a Belfast Psychical Society at Gateway House, 57 Dublin Road, Belfast, Northern Ireland. There is also the Belfast Spiritualist Alliance and Church of Psychic Science in Belfast. (See also **Banshee; Fairies**)

Recommended reading:

AE (George W. Russell). *The Candle of Vision,* Macmillan, London, 1918; University Books, 1965

Curtin, Jeremiah. *Tales of the Fairies and of the Ghost World, Collected from Oral Tradition in Southwest Munster,* D. Nutt, London, 1895; Talbot Press paperback, Dublin, Eire, 1974

Dunne, John J. *Haunted Ireland; Her Romantic & Mysterious Ghosts,* Appletree Press, Belfast, N. Ireland, 1977

Farrar, Stewart. *What Witches Do; The Modern Coven Revealed,* Coward, McCann & Geoghegan, 1971

Giraldus Cambrensis (transl. R. C. Hoare). *The Historical Works of Giraldus Cambrensis, Containing The Topography of Ireland, and The History of the Conquest of Ireland,* Bohn's Antiquarian Library, London, 1847

Gregory, Lady. *Visions and Beliefs in the West of Ireland,* 2 vols., Putnam, 1920

Harper, George Mills. *Yeats's Golden Dawn,* Macmillan, London, 1974

O'Donnell, Elliot. *The Banshee,* Sands & Co., London, 1920

McAnally, D. R., Jr. *Irish Wonders; The Ghosts, Giants, Pookas, Demons, Leprechawns, Banshees, Fairies, Witches, Widows, Old Maids and Other Marvels of the Emerald Isle,* Houghton Mifflin, 1888; Grand River Books, Detroit, 1971

Seymour, St. John D. *Irish Witchcraft & Demonology,* London/Dublin, 1913; EP Publishing, Wakefield, U.K., 1972; Causeway Books, 1973

Seymour, St. John D. & Harry L. Neligan. *True Irish Ghost Stories,* Oxford University Press, London, 1915; Causeway Books, 1974

White, Carolyn. *A History of Irish Fairies,* Mercier Press paperback, Cork, Eire, 1976

Yeats, W. B. (ed.) *Fairy & Folk Tales of the Irish Peasantry,* Walter Scott Publishing Co., London, 1888; Grosset & Dunlap paperback, 1957

Iremonger, Lucille (d'Oyen)

British novelist, journalist and broadcaster who has taken over parapsychological topics. She studied at Oxford University (M.A. hons.), and married Thomas L. Iremonger, M.P., in 1939. She was awarded the Society of Women Journalists' Lady Britain trophy for the best book of the year in 1948 for *It's A Bigger Life* and also the Lady Violet Astor trophy for the best article of the year, and the Silver Musgrave Medal (Jamaica) for her contributions to literature relating to the West Indies, 1962.

In addition to her novels, her books on various themes include: *West Indian Folk Tales: Anansi Stories* (retold for English children) (1956) and *The Ghosts of Versailles: Miss Moberly and Miss Jourdain and Their Adventure—A Critical Study* (1957).

Iridis (Newsletter)

Monthly newsletter of the California Society for Psychical Study, Inc. Address: P.O. Box 844, Berkeley, California 94709.

Irish Diviner

Quarterly journal of the Irish Society of Diviners, dealing with various mysterious forces in life as well as **Dowsing.** No longer published.

Iron

The occult virtues of iron are thus described by **Pliny** (in the translation by Philemon Holland, 1601): "As touching the use of Yron and steele in Physicke, it serveth otherwise than for to launce, cut, and dismember withal; for take the knife or dagger, an make an ymaginerie circle two or three times round with the point thereof upon a young child or an elder bodie, and then goe round withall about the partie as often, it is a singular preservative against all poysons, sorceries, or enchantments. Also to take any yron naile out of the coffin or sepulchre wherein man or woman lieth buried, and to sticke the same fast to the lintle or side post of a dore, leading either to the house or bed-chamber where any dooth lie who is haunted with Spirits in the night, he or she shall be delivered and secured from such phanasticall illusions. Moreover, it is said, that if one be lightly pricked with the point of sword or dagger, which hath been the death of a man, it is an excellent remedy against the pains of sides or breast, which come with sudden prickes or stitches."

In certain parts of Scotland and Ireland, there is a belief in the potency of iron for warding off the attacks of fairies. An iron poker, laid across a cradle, will, it is believed, keep the fairies away until the child is baptized. The Rev. John G. Campbell in his *Superstitions of the*

Highlands and Islands of Scotland (1900) related how when a child, he and another boy were believed to be protected from a fairy which had been seen at a certain spot by one possessing a knife, and the other a nail. This was at Appin in Argyllshire.

Many other countries have folklore beliefs about iron as a religious taboo or a charm against witchcraft and the supernatural. Iron tools were prohibited in Greek and Hebrew temples in ancient times. In Korea, the body of the king was never to be touched by iron. Roman priests were forbidden to shave with an iron blade. In India and China, evil spirits are warded off by iron.

Irving, Rev. Edward (1792–1834)

Famous Scottish preacher whose Catholic Apostolic Church in London was the scene of extraordinary psychic manifestations in 1831. The "Irvingites" were seized with the gift of speaking in **tongues,** they prophesied and effected cures. The manifestations continued for about two years. They were described by Robert Baxter, a member of the Church, in a pamphlet: "*A Narrative of Facts Characterising the Supernatural Manifestations in the Members of Mr. Irving's Congregation, and Other Individuals in England and Scotland, and formerly in the Writer Himself* (London, 1833).

The story of Irving's life is told by Washington Wilks in *Edward Irving: An Ecclesiastical and Literary Biography* (London, 1854).

Isaac of Holland (c. 15th century)

Very little is known about the life of this alchemist, but he is commonly supposed to have lived and worked early in the fifteenth century, the principal reason for assigning his career to that period being that in his writings he refers to Geber, Dastin, Morien and **Arnaldus de Villanova,** but not to more modern authorities, while again, he appears to have been acquainted with various chemical processes discovered towards the close of the fourteenth century, and hence it may reasonably be deduced that he did not live anterior to that time.

According to tradition, Isaac worked with his son, whose name is not recorded and the pair are usually regarded as having been the first men to exploit chemistry in the Netherlands. They are said to have been particularly skillful in the manufacture of enamels and artificial gems, and it is noteworthy that no less distinguished an alchemist than **Paracelsus** attached value to the Dutchmen's researches while these are also mentioned with honor by the seventeenth-century English scientist, Robert Boyle.

Isaac compiled two scientific treatises, one entitled *Opera Mineralia Joannis Isaaci Hollandi, sive de Lapide Philosophico* (1600) and the other *De Triplici Ordine Elixiris et Lapidis Theoria* (1608) and both were published at the beginning of the seventeenth century. The more important of the two is the last named, wherein the author sets forth his ideas on the exalting of base metals into *Sol* and *Luna,* and shows by the aid of illustrations exactly what kind of vessels should be used for this purpose. (See also **Alchemy**)

Isian News

Quarterly publication of the Fellowship of Isis, an Irish-based religious organization founded in 1976 to revive worship and communion with the feminine principle in deity in the form of the Goddess, and to promote knowledge of the world's matriarchal religions. Address: Huntingdon Castle, Clonegal, Enniscorthy, Eire.

ISKCON

Initialism for **International Society for Krishna Consciousness.**

ISRAEL

Ever since the Balfour Declaration of November 2, 1917, there was a great influx of Jewish immigrants into Palestine, and this was intensified with the establishment of the State of Israel on May 14, 1948. Refugees from persecutions and the aftermath of two world wars brought the rich folklore of Europe into the new homeland. Stories of the Hasidim, the miracle-working mystical rabbis and their followers, exist side by side with legends of the Angel of Death, or the **Golem** created by Rabbi Loew of Prague. As in the United States, mystical groups in Israel have kept alive the study of **Kabala.**

However, beyond the legends of miracles and occult phenomena which really have a basically mystical purpose, speculation on the after-life is alien to the general trend of Judaism and there has been little basis for studies of Spiritualism and psychical research.

In recent years, however, there has been a growing interest in parapsychology in Israel, given added topical interest by the furious controversies over the phenomena of Uri **Geller,** who encountered great opposition from scientists and psychologists who were convinced that he was fraudulent.

Enlightened scientific interest in parapsychology in Israel owes much to Prof. H. S. Bergman, who was a great friend of the famous psychic Eileen **Garrett,** founder of the **Parapsychology Foundation** in the U.S. With the cooperation of Prof. Bergman, Prof. F. S. Rothschild, Prof. Peri, Dr. Jacobson and Dr. H. C. Berendt, the Israel Parapsychology Society was formed. In 1965, Eileen Garrett visited the group in Jerusalem for the opening of the Parapsychology Foundation Library. Dr. H. C. Berendt published the first Hebrew language book on Parapsychology (*Parapsychology—The World Beyond,* Jerusalem, 1966).

In 1968, the Israel Society for Parapsychology was founded in Tel Aviv, under the chairmanship of Mrs. Margot Klausner. The Society has organized lectures and courses on a wide range of subjects, such as clairvoyance, telepathy, reincarnation, dowsing, spiritual healing, meditation, astrology. It also publishes a journal *Mysterious Worlds,* and maintains a library of over 1,200 volumes.

ITALY

For information regarding Ancient Italy, see **Rome, Medieval Legends of Magic.**

Strangely enough, magic and sorcery in medieval Italy seem to have centered around many great personalities of the church, and even several popes have been included by the historians of occult science in the ranks of Italian sorcerers and alchemists.

There appears to have been some sort of folk tradition that the popes had been given over to the practice of magic ever since the tenth century, and it was alleged that Silvester II confessed to this charge on his death bed. Éliphus **Lévi** stated that Honorius III, who preached the Crusades, was an abominable necromancer, and author of a **grimoire** or book by which spirits were evoked, the use of which was reserved exclusively to the priesthood (see **Grimoire of Honorius**).

Bartholomew Platina (1421–1481), quoting from Martinus Polonus, stated that Silvester, who was a proficient mathematician and versed in the **Kabala**, on one occasion evoked Satan himself and obtained his assistance to gain the pontifical crown. Furthermore he stipulated as the price of selling his soul to the Devil that he should not die except at Jerusalem, to which place he inwardly determined he would never betake himself.

He duly became Pope, but on one occasion whilst celebrating mass in a certain church at Rome, he felt extremely ill, and suddenly remembered that he was officiating in a chapel dedicated to the Holy Cross of Jerusalem. He had a bed set up in the chapel, to which he summoned the cardinals and confessed that he had held communication with the powers of evil. He further arranged that when dead his body should be placed upon a car of green wood and should be drawn by two horses, one black and other white, that they should be started on their course, but neither led nor driven, and that where they halted there his remains should be entombed. The conveyance stopped in front of the Lateran, and at this juncture most terrible noises proceeded from it, which led the bystanders to suppose that the soul of Silvester had been seized upon by Satan in virtue of their agreement.

There is no doubt whatsoever that such ridiculous legends concerning papal necromancers are absolute inventions and can be traced through Platina and Polonus to Galfridus and the chronicler Gervase of Tilbury, whom Gabriel Naudé termed "the greatest forger of fables, and the most notorious liar that ever took pen in hand!"

On a par with such myths is that of Pope Joan, who for several years was supposed to have sat on the papal throne although a woman, and who was supposed to be one of the blackest sorceresses of all time. Many magic books were attributed to Pope Joan. Lévi has an interesting passage in his *History of Magic* (1913 etc.) in which he stated that certain engravings in a Life of this female pope, purporting to represent her, are nothing else than ancient tarots representing Isis crowned with a tiara. "It is well-known," he stated, "that the hieroglyphic figure on the second **tarot** card is still called 'The Female Pope,' being a woman wearing a tiara, on which are the points of the crescent moon, or the horns of Isis." It is much more possible that the author of the grimoire in question was Honorius II, the anti-pope, or perhaps another Honorius described as the son of Euclid and master of the Thebans.

But all Italian necromancers and magicians were by no means churchmen—indeed, medieval Italy was hardly a place for the magically inclined, so stringent were the laws of the church against the Black Art. **Astrology,** however, flourished to some extent, and its practitioners do not appear to have been unduly persecuted. A Florentine astrologer, named Basil, who flourished at the beginning of the fifteenth century, obtained some repute for successful predictions, and was said to have foretold to Cosmo de Medici that he would attain exalted dignity, as the same planets had been in ascendency at the hour of his birth, as in that of the Emperor Charles V.

Many remarkable predictions were made by Antiochus Tibertus of Romagna, who was for some time counselor to Pandolpho de Maletesta, Prince of Rimini. He foretold to his friend Guido de Bogni, the celebrated soldier, that he was unjustly suspected by his best friend, and would forfeit his life through suspicion. Of himself he predicted that he would die on the scaffold, and of the Prince of Rimini, his patron, that he would die a beggar in the hospital for the poor at Bologna. It is stated that the prophecies came true in every detail.

Although the recorded notices of sorcery in medieval times are few in Italian history, there is reason to suspect that although magic was not outwardly practiced, it lurked hidden in bypaths and out-of-the-way places. We have an excellent portrait of the medieval Italian magician in those popular myths regarding Virgil the Enchanter.

The Legend of Virgil

The fame of Virgil the Poet had waxed so great in ancient Italy that in due course of time his name was synonymous with fame itself. From that it was a short step to the attribution of supernatural power, and Virgil the Roman poet became in the popular mind the medieval Enchanter. His myth is symptomatic of magic in medieval Italy as a whole and is therefore described here at some length.

When the popular myth of Virgil the Enchanter first grew into repute is uncertain, but probably the earliest conception arose about the beginning of the tenth century and each succeeding generation embroidered upon it some fantastic impossibility. Soon, in the South of Italy (for the necromancer's fame was of southern origin) there floated dim, mysterious legends of the enchantments which he had wrought.

Thus he fashioned a brazen fly and planted it on the gate of fair Parthenope to free the city from the inroads of the insects of Beelzebub. On a Neapolitan hill he built a statue of brass and placed in its mouth a trumpet. Lo! when the north wind blew there came from that trumpet so terrible a roar that it drove back into the sea the noxious blasts of Vulcan's forges, which, even to this day, seethe and hiss near the city of Puossola. At one of the gates of Naples, Virgil raised two statues of stone and gifted them respectively with the power of blighting or blessing the strangers who passed by one or the other of them on entering the city. He constructed three public baths for the removal of every disease afflicting the human frame, but the physicians, in a wholesome dread of losing their patients and their fees, caused them to be destroyed.

Other wonders which he was supposed to have wrought, which in time assumed a connected form, were woven into a life of the enchanter, first printed in French about 1490–1520. A still fuller history appeared in English as "The Life of Virgilius," about 1508, printed by Hans Doesborcke at Antwerp. It set forth with tolerable clearness the popular type of the medieval magician, and is drawn upon in the following biographical sketch.

"Virgil was the son of a wealthy senator of Rome, wealthy and powerful enough to carry on war with the Roman Emperor. As his birth was heralded by extraordinary portents, it is no marvel that even in childhood he showed himself endowed with extraordinary mental powers, and his father having the sagacity to discern in him an embryo necromancer sent him, while still very young, to study at the University of Toledo, where the 'art of magick' was taught with extraordinary success.

"There he studied diligently, for he was of great understanding, and speedily acquired a profound insight into the great Shemaia of the Chaldean lore. But this insight was due not so much to nocturnal vigils over abstruse books, as to the help he received from a very valuable **familiar.** And this was the curious fashion in which he was introduced to the said familiar:

" 'Upon a tyme the scholers at Tolenten hadde lycence to goo to playe and sporte them in the fyldes after the usuance of the olde tyme; and there was also Virgilius therby also walkynge among the hylles all about. It fortuned he spyed a great hole in the syde of a great hyll, wherein he went to depe that he culde not see no more lyght, and than he went a lytell ferther therein, and then he sawe soon lyght agayne, and than wente he fourth streyghte. And within a lytell wyle after he harde a voice that called, "Virgilius, Virgilius," and he loked aboute, and he colde nat see nobodye. Than Virgilius spake, and asked, "Who calleth me?" Than harde he the voyce agayne, but he sawe nobodye. Than sayd he, "Virgilius, see ye not that lytell bourde lyinge byside you there, marked with that worde?" Than answered Virgilius, "I see that borde well enough." The voyce said, "Doo away that bourde, and lette me out theratte."

" 'Then answered Virgilius to the voyce that was under the lytell bourde, and sayd, "Who art thou that talkest me so?" Than answered the devyll, "I am a devyll conjured out of the body of a certeyne man, and banysshed here tyll the daye of jugement, without that I be delyvered by the handes of men. Thus, Virgilius, I pray thee delyver me out of this payn, and I shall show unto thee many bokes of nygromancy, and how thou shalt cum by it lytly, and shalte knowe the practyse therein, that no man in the science of nygromancy shall (sur)pass thee; and, moreover, I shall showe and informe thee so that thou shalt have all thy desyre, whereby methinke it is a great gyfte for so lytell a donyge, for ye may also thus all your poor frendys helpen, and make ryghte your ennemyes unmighty."

" 'Thorough that great promise was Virgilius tempted. He badde the fynd showe the bokes to hym, that he myght have and occupy them at his wyll. And so the fynd showed hym, and then Virgilius pulled open a bourde, and there was a lytell hole, and thereat wrange the devyll out lyke a yeel, and cam and stode before Virgilius lyke a bigge man.

" 'Thereof Virgilius was astonied, and merveyled greately thereof, that so great a man myght com out at so lytell a hole!

" 'Then sayd Virgilius, "Shulde ye well passe into the hole that ye cam out of?" "Yes, I shall well," sayd the devyll. "I holde the beste pledge that I have, ye shall not do it." "Well," sayd the devyll, "thereto I consente." And then the devyll wrange hymself into the lytell hole agen, and as he was therein, Virgilius kyvered the hole agen with the bourde close, and so was the devyll begyled, and myght not there come out agen, but there abydeth shutte styll therein. Than called the devyll dredefully (drearily) to Virgilius, and sayd, "What have ye done?" Virgilius answered, "Abyde there styll to your day apoynted.' And fro thensforth abydeth he there." '

The story goes on that Virgil's father died soon after this event and his estates being seized by his former colleagues, his widow sunk into extreme poverty. Virgil accordingly gathered together the wealth he had amassed by the exercise of his magical skill, and set out for Rome, to replace his mother in a position proper to her rank. At Toledo he had been regarded as a famous student; at Rome he was a despised scholar, and when he besought the Emperor to execute justice and restore to him his estate, that potentate, ignorant of the magician's power, simply replied, "Methinketh that the land is well divided to them that have it, for they may help you in their need; what needeth you for to care for the disheriting of one school-master Bid him take heed, and look to his schools, for he hath no right to any land here about the city of Rome."

Four years passed, and only such replies as this were vouchsafed to Virgil's frequent appeals for justice. Growing at length weary of the delay, he resolved to exercise his wondrous powers in his own behalf. When the harvest-time came, he accordingly shrouded the whole of his rightful inheritance with a vapor so dense that the new proprietors were unable to approach it, and under its cover his men gathered in the entire crop with perfect security. This done, the mist disappeared.

Then a great indignation possessed the souls of his enemies, and they assembled their swordsmen, and marched against him to take off his head. Such was their power that the Emperor fled out of Rome in fear, "for they were twelve senators that had all the world under them, and if Virgilius had had right, he had been one of the twelve, but they had disinherited him and his mother." When they drew near, Virgil once more baffled their designs by encircling his patrimony with a rampart of cloud and shadow.

The Emperor, with surprising inconsistency, now joined forces with the senators against Virgil, whose magical powers he probably feared far more than the rude force of the senatorial magnates, and made war against him. But who can prevail against the arts of necromancy? Emperor and senators were duly beaten, and from that moment Virgil, with marvelous generosity, became the faithful friend and powerful supporter of his sovereign.

It may not generally be known that Virgil, besides being the savior of Rome, was supposed to be the founder of Naples. This feat had its origin, like so many other great actions, in the power of love.

Virgil's imagination had been fired by the reports that reached him of the surpassing loveliness of the Sultan's daughter. Now the Sultan lived at Babylon (that is, at Cairo, the "Babylon" of medieval romancers) and the distance might have daunted a less ardent lover and less potent magician. But Virgil's necromantic skill was equal to magically raising a bridge in the air (where other glowing spirits have often raised fair castles) and passing over it, he found his way into the Sultan's palace and into the Princess's chamber. Speedily overcoming her natural modesty, Virgil bore her back with him to his Italian bower. There, he enjoyed his fill of love and pleasure, then restored the princess to her bed in her father's palace. Meanwhile, her absence had been noted, but she was soon discovered on her return, and the Sultan hastening to her chamber, interrogated her respecting her disappearance. He found that she knew not who it was that had carried her off, nor whither she had been carried.

When Virgil abducted and restored the lady on the following night, she took back with her, by her father's instructions, some of the fruit plucked from the enchanter's garden, and from its quality the Sultan guessed that she had been carried to a southern land "on the side of France." These nocturnal journeys being several times repeated and the Sultan's curiosity growing ungovernable, he persuaded his daughter to give her lover a sleeping draught. The deceived magician was then captured in the Babylonian palace and flung into prison, and it was decreed that both he and his mistress should be punished for their love by death at the stake.

Necromancers, however, are not so easily outwitted. As soon as Virgil was apprized of the fate intended for him, he made, by force of his spells, the Sultan and all his lords believe that the mighty Nilus, great river of Babylon, was overflowing in the midst of them, and that they swam and lay and sprang like geese, and so they took up Virgil and the princess, tore them from their prison, and placed them upon the aerial bridge. And when they were thus out of danger, Virgil delivered the Sultan and all the lords from the river, and lo, when they recovered their wits they beheld the enchanter bearing the beautiful princess across the Mediterranean, and they marveled much, and felt that they could not hope to prevail against such supernatural power.

And in this manner Virgil conveyed the Sultan's daughter over the sea to Rome. And he was highly enamoured of her beauty. "Then he thought in his mind how he might marry her [apparently forgetting that he was already married] and thought in his mind to found in the midst of the sea a fair town with great lands belonging to it; and so he did by his cunning, and called it Naples, and the foundation of it was of eggs. And in that town of Naples he made a tower with four corners and on the top he set an apple upon an iron yard, and no man could pull away that apple without he brake it; and through that iron set he a bottle, and on that bottle set he an egg, and he hanged the apple by the stalk upon a chain, and so hangeth it still. And when the egg stirreth, so should the town of Naples quake, and when the egg brake, then should the town sink. When he had made an end, he let call it Naples."

After accomplishing so much for his Babylonian beauty, Virgil did not marry her, but endowing her with the town of Naples and its lands, gave her in marriage to a certain grandee of Spain. Having thus disposed of her and her children, the enchanter returned to Rome, collected all his treasures, and removed them to the city he had founded, where he resided for some years, and established a school which speedily became of illustrious renown. Here he lost his wife, by whom he had had no issue, built baths and bridges, and wrought the most extraordinary miracles. So passed an uncounted number of years, and Virgil at length abandoned Naples for ever, and retired to Rome.

"Outside the walls of the Imperial City, he built a goodly town, that had but one gate, and was so fenced round with water as to bar any one from approaching it. And the entry of its one gate was made with twenty-four iron flails, and on each side was there twelve men smiting with the flails, never ceasing, the one after the other, and no man might come in without the flails stood still, but he was slain. And these flails were made with such a gin [contrivance] that Virgilius stopped them when he list to enter in thereat, but no man else could find the way. And in this castle put Virgilius part of his treasure privily and, when this was done, he imagined in his mind by what means he might make himself young again, because he thought to live longer many years, to do many wonders and marvelous things. And upon a time went Virgilius to the Emperor, and asked him of licence [of absence] by the space of three weeks. But the Emperor in no wise would grant it unto him for he would have Virgilius at all times by him."

Italian Witchcraft

In his *Aradia, or the Gospel of the Witches of Italy* (1899) folklorist Charles Godfrey **Leland** gave a valuable account of the life and practice of the Italian *strega* or witch as described by a Florentine hereditary witch named Maddalena. He stated:

"In most cases she comes of a family in which her calling or art has been practised for many generations. I have no doubt that there are instances in which the ancestry remounts to medieval, Roman, or it may be Etruscan times. The result has naturally been the accumulation in such families of much tradition. But in Northern Italy, as its literature indicates, though there has been some slight gathering of fairy tales and popular superstitions by scholars, there has never existed the least interest as regarded the strange lore of the witches, nor any suspicion that it embraced an incredible quantity of old Roman minor myths and legends, such as Ovid has recorded, but of which much escaped him and all other Latin writers. . . . Even yet there are old people in the Romagna of the North who know the Etruscan names of the Twelve Gods, and invocations to Bacchus, Jupiter, and Venus, Mercury, and the Lares or ancestral spirits, and in the cities are women who prepare strange amulets, over which they mutter spells, all known in the old Roman time and who can astonish even the learned by their legends of Latin gods, mingled with lore which may be found in Cato or Theocritus. With one of these I became intimately acquainted in 1886, and have ever since employed her specially to collect among her sisters of the hidden spell in many places all the traditions of the olden times known to them. It is true that I have drawn from other sources but this woman by long practice has perfectly learned what few understand, or just what I want, and how to extract it from those of her kind.

"Among other strange relics, she succeeded, after many years, in obtaining the following 'Gospel,' which I have in her handwriting. A full account of its nature with many details will be found in an Appendix. I do not know definitely whether my informant derived a part of these traditions from written sources or oral narration, but believe it was chiefly the latter. . . .

"For brief explanation I may say that witchcraft is known to its votaries as *la vecchia religione,* or the old religion, of which Diana is the Goddess, her daughter *Aradia* (or Herodias) the female Messiah, and that this little work sets forth how the latter was born, came down to earth, established witches and witchcraft, and then returned to heaven. With it are given the ceremonies and invocations or incantations to be addressed to Diana and Aradia, the exorcism of Cain, and the spells of the holy-stone, rue, and verbena, constituting, as the text declares, the regular church service, so to speak, which is to be chanted or pronounced at the witch meetings. There are also included the very curious incantations or benedic-tions of the honey, meal, and salt, or cakes of the witch-supper, which is curiously classical, and evidently a relic of the Roman Mysteries."

Briefly the ritual of the Italian witches as reported by Leland was: At the Sabbath they take meal and salt, honey and water, and say a conjuration over these, one to the meal, one to the salt, one to Cain, one to Diana, the moon goddess. They then sit down naked to supper, men and women, and after the feast is over they dance, sing and make love in the darkness, quite in the manner of the medieval Sabbath of the sorcerers. Many charms are given connected with stones, especially if these have holes in them and are found by accident. A lemon stuck full of pins we are told is a good omen. Love spells fill a large space in the little work, which for the rest recounts several myths of Diana and Endymion in corrupted form.

Leland's interesting book was clearly the inspiration for the British witchcraft revival of Gerald B. **Gardner** in the 1950s and served as a model for the so-called *Book of Shadows* which modern witches claim as a traditional descent in their covens.

Spiritualism

An early indication of the rise and spread of Spiritual-ism in Italy was continued in an article published in *Civitta Catholica,* the well-known Roman organ, entitled "Modern Necromancy." The conclusions of the article were:

"1st. Some of the phenomena may be attributed to imposture, hallucinations, and exaggerations in the re-ports of those who describe it, but there is a foundation of reality in the general sum of the reports which cannot have originated in pure invention or be wholly discredited without ignoring the value of universal testimony.

"2nd. The bulk of the theories offered in explanation of the proven facts, only cover a certain percentage of those facts, but utterly fail to account for the balance.

"3rd. Allowing for all that can be filtered away on mere human hypotheses, there are still a large class of phenom-ena appealing to every sense which cannot be accounted for by any known natural laws, and which seem to manifest the action of intelligent beings."

The famous medium D. D. **Home** visited the principal cities of Italy in 1852 and had been so active in his propaganda that numerous circles were formed after his departure. Violent journalistic controversies arose out of the foundation of these societies, with the result that public interest was so aroused that it could only be satisfied with the publication of a paper on the subject. It was titled *Il amore del Vero,* issued from Geneva and edited by Dr. Pietro Suth and Signor B. E. Manieri. In this journal accounts of the spiritual movements in the various countries of Europe, and America were published al-though the Church and press leveled anathemas against the journal.

In the spring of 1863, a society was founded at Palermo named Il Societa Spiritual di Palermo, which had for president Signor J. V. Paleolozo, and such members as Paolo Morelle, professor of Latin and Philosophy.

It was about the autumn of 1864 that lectures were first given on Spiritualist subjects in Italy. They were started in Leghorn and Messina, and although of a very mixed character and often partaking largely of the lecturer's peculiar idiosyncrasies on religious subjects, they served to draw attention to the upheaval of thought going on in all directions, in connection with the revelations from the Spirit world. It could not be expected that a movement so startling and unprecedented as that which opened up direct communication between the natural and the Spirit world could gain ground in public acceptance without arousing latent elements of enthusiasm, fanaticism, and bigotry, which prevailed in the Italian as in every other community.

In the year 1870, over a hundred different societies were formed, with varying success, in different parts of Italy. Two of the most prominent flourishing at that date were conducted at Naples, and according to the French journal *Revue Spirite,* represented the two opposing schools which have prevailed in Continental Spiritualism, namely, the "Reincarnationists" or "Spiritists" and the "Immortalists," or those known in America and England merely as "Spiritualists." (For information on **Spiritism,** see also **France;** Allan **Kardec**)

About 1868, an immense impulse was communicated to the cause of Spiritualism (at least in the higher strata of Italian Society) by the visit of Mr. and Mrs. **Guppy** to Naples, where they took up their residence for two or three years. Mrs. Guppy (née Miss **Nichol**) of London, was renowned throughout Europe for her marvelous powers as a physical force medium and as Mr. Guppy's wealth and social standing enabled him to place his gifted wife's services at the command of the distinguished visitors who crowded his salons, it soon became a matter of notoriety that the highest individuals in the land, includ-ing King Victor Emmanuel and many of his nearest friends and counselors, had yielded conviction to the truth of the astounding phenomena exhibited through Mrs. Guppy's mediumship.

About the year 1863 Spiritualism began to enjoy the advantage of fair and honorable representation in the columns of a new paper named the *Annali dello Spiritismo* (Annals of Spiritualism). This journal was published in Turin by Signor Niceforo Filalete with liberality, energy, and talent.

The columns of the *Annali* recorded that a Venetian Society of Spiritualists named "Atea" elected General Giuseppe Garibaldi their honorary president, and received the following reply by telegraph from the distinguished hero, the liberator of Italy: "I gratefully accept the presidency of the Society Atea. Caprera, 23rd September."

The same issue of the *Annali* contained a verbatim report of a "grand discourse, given at Florence, by a distinguished literary gentleman, Signor Sebastiano Fenzi, in which the listeners were considerably astonished by a rehearsal of the many illustrious names of those who openly avowed their faith in Spiritualism."

The years 1863-64 appear to have been rich in Spiritualist efforts. Besides a large number of minor associations, (the existence of which was recorded from time to time in the early numbers of the *Annali* and *Revue Spirite*), one society which continued for a long time to exert a marked influence in promoting the study of occult forces and phenomena, was formed about this time in Florence, under the title of the Magnetic Society of Florence. The members of this association were all persons remarkable for literary and scientific attainments or of high influential position in society.

About this time, Mr. Seymour Kirkup, well known to the early initiators of Spiritualism, resided in Florence and contributed many records of spiritual phenomena to the *London Spiritual Magazine.* Nearly ten years after the establishment of the Magnetic Society of Florence, Baron Guitern de Bozzi, an eminent occultist, founded the Pneumatological Psychological Academy of Florence, but it was discontinued after his death.

Psychical Research and Parapsychology

In Italy, the divisions between Spiritualism and psychical research have tended to be blurred. Many eminent psychical researchers were sympathetic to Spiritualism if not actually endorsing its beliefs.

One of the most famous investigators was the psychiatrist and criminologist Prof. Cesare **Lombroso** (1836-1909) who accepted the evidence for survival after death. Prof. Marco Tullio **Falcomer,** who conducted experiments with the famous medium Florence **Cook,** was a Spiritualism, as was also Prof. Enrico **Morselli** (1852-1929) who had investigated the phenomena of Eusapia **Palladino.**

Amongst other Italian psychical researchers were Dr. Giovanni Batista Ermacora (1869-98), Dr. Enrico Imoda (who investigated the phenomena of Linda **Gazzera**), Prof. P. B. Bianchi, Prof. Angelo **Brofferio** (who became a Spiritualist), Dr. Ercole Chiaia, Prof. Philippe **Bottazzi,** Augusto Tamburini and Dr. Rocco Santoliquido (1854-1930, who played a part in the founding of the **Institut Métapsychique** in Paris). Later researchers were Prof. Ernesto Bozzano (1862-1943), Prof. Giovanni Pioli of Milan, Prof. Lidio Cipriani of the University of

Naples), Dr. William McKenzie of Genoa, Count Cesar Baudi **De Vesme** (1862-1938), Prof. Ferdinando Cazzamalli of Como, Prof. Fabio Vitali, Prof. G. C. Trabacchi and Prof. Sante de Sanctis.

In 1901, The Società di Studi Psichici (Society of Psychic Studies) was founded in Milan. It was responsible for investigations of the mediums Augustus **Politi,** Eusapia **Palladino** and Lucia **Sordi.**

In 1937, The Società Italiana di Metapsichica (Italian Society of Metapsychics) was founded in Rome, in memory of Prof. Charles Richet, the noted psychical researcher. In 1946, one group from the Society headed by Prof. Cazzamalli formed the Association di Metapsichica, in Milan; at a later date the name was changed to Società Italiana di Parapsicologia, replacing the older term "metapsychics" by "parapsychology." It is currently headed by Dr. Emilio **Servadio,** at Via de Montecatini 7, 00186 Rome.

Another active organization is the Centro Studi Parapsicologici (Center for Parapsychological Studies) established in Bologna in 1948, directed by Dr. Piero **Cassoli.** Other organizations include the Facoltà di Scienze Psichiche e Psicologiche (Faculty of Psychic and Psychological Sciences) of Academia Tiberina, established in 1960 (address: Via del Vantaggio 22, Rome) the Centro Italiano di Studi Metapsichici (Italian Center of Metapsychic Studies) founded in Pavia in 1968, which has conducted studies in psychic healing (address: Via Calascione 5/A, Naples); Centro Studi Parapsicologici de Bologna, Via Tamagno 2, Bologna.

Amongst periodicals, the oldest is *Luce e Ombre* (Light & Shadow) founded in 1900 in Rome, edited from January 1932 from Milan under the title *Ricerca Psichica.* The journal *Uomini e Idee* (Men & Ideas) was published in Naples in 1959; in 1965 it was replaced by *Informazioni di Parapsicologia* (Parapsychology News) as a publication of the Centro Italiano di Parapsicologia.

Iubdan

In Ultonian romance (the Ossianic stories of Ireland), the King of the Wee Folk. One day he boasted of the might of his strong man Glower, who could hew down a thistle at one blow. His bard Eisirt retorted that beyond the sea there existed a race of giants, any one of whom could annihilate a whole battalion of the Wee Folk.

Challenged to prove his words, Eisirt brought Creda, King Fergus' dwarf and bard. He then dared Iubdan to go to Fergus' palace and taste the king's porridge.

Iubdan and Bebo, his queen, arrived at the palace at midnight, but in trying to get at the porridge so as to taste and be away before daybreak, Iubdan fell in. He was found in the pot next morning by the scullions, and he and Bebo were taken before Fergus, who after a while released them in exchange for a pair of water shoes, which a man wearing could go over or under water as freely as on land.

Ivan III (1440-1505)

Ivan, son of Vasily Vasilievich, Grand Duke of Moscow, became Grand Duke of Muscovy in the fifteenth century. According to legend, when he was at the point of death, he fell into terrible swoons, during which his soul made laborious journeys. In the first he was tormented for having kept innocent prisoners in his dungeons; in the second, he was tortured still more for having ground the people under heavy tasks; during the third voyage he died, but his body disappeared mysteriously before he could be buried, and it was thought that the devil had taken him.

Ivunches

Chilian familiars. (See United States of **America**)

Iynx

A Chaldean symbol of universal being, the name of which signifies "power of transmission." It was repro-duced as a living sphere or winged globe, and said to be projected forth by divine Mind on the plane of reality, to be followed by three others called "paternal" and "ineffable," and latterly by hosts of Iynxs of a subordinate character, described as "free intelligences." The Iynx was described by occultist Éliphas **Lévi** as "corresponding to the Hebrew Yod or to that unique letter from which all other letters were formed," and thus related to the Jewish mysticism of the *Sepher Yetsirah* or Book of Creation (See **Kabala**). For reference to Chaldean concepts, see the complex Gnostic emanations discussed by G. R. S. **Mead** in his version of *The Chaldean Oracles* (2 vols., London, 1908).

J

Jachin and Boaz

The names of two symbolical pillars of King Solomon's Kabalistic temple, which were believed to explain all mysteries. One was black and the other white, representing the powers of good and evil. It was said that they symbolized the need of "two" in the world. Human progression requires two feet, the worlds gravitate by means of two forces, generation needs two sexes. The addition of a third pillar would seem to indicate the equilibrium of opposing forces. (See also **Kabala**)

Jachowski, Jan (1891–   )

Polish publisher who experimented with the **divining rod** and **pendulum,** and also studied in the field of astrology. Born December 13, 1891, at Jaktorowo, Chodziez Poznanskie, Poland, he married Zenona Nowicka in 1954. Mr. Jachowski was an editor, Publications Services, University of Poznan, and winner in 1936 of the Silver Wreath of the Polish Academy of Literature.

Jacinth

A gem stone, a variety of zircon, which was believed to preserve the wearer from plague and from lightning to strengthen the heart and bring wealth, honor, prudence, and wisdom. It was recommended by **Albertus Magnus** as a soporific on account of its coldness, and was ordered by Psellus in cases of coughs, ruptures, and melancholy, to be drunk in vinegar. Marbodæus described the wonderful properties of three species of the jacinth. Pliny and Leonardus also spoke highly of it.

Jacks, L(awrence) P(earsall) (1860–1955)

British author and professor of philosophy who investigated physical phenomena, and was President of the Society for Psychical Research, London (1917–18), vice-president 1909–55. Born October 9, 1860, at Nottingham, England, he was educated at University School, Nottingham, London University (M.A. 1886), Manchester College, Göttingen, and Harvard. In 1889 he married Olive Cecilie Brooke (died 1945). He was professor of Philosophy at Manchester College, Oxford, in 1903, and principal from 1915–31.

Dr. Jacks was particularly concerned with the relationship of psychical research to philosophy. He also sat with a number of mediums, including Mrs. Osborne **Leonard,** one of the great British trance mediums.

His articles included: 'Dramatic Dreams, an Unexplored Field for Psychical Research' (*Journal* of the S.P.R., vol. 17, 1915), 'Presidential Address: The Theory of Survival in the Light of Its Context' (*Proceedings* of the

S.P.R., vol. 29, 1918). His books included: *All Men Are Ghosts* (1913), *My Neighbour the Universe* (1928), *The Inner Sentinel* (1930), *My American Friends* (1933), *Elemental Religion* (1934), *The Confessions of an Octogenarian* (1942), *Near the Brink* (1955). He died February 17, 1955.

Jacob, Auguste Henri ("Jacob the Zouave") (1828–1913)

Famous French spiritual healer, whose curative and clairvoyant powers became known in 1867 while he was still attached to his French regiment. Born March 6, 1828, he volunteered to serve in the 7th Hussars (the Zouaves). He became interested in Spiritualism and his healing probably began while serving in the Crimea and Algeria, but his fame spread when stationed in central France. He was soon discharged from the army, since the crowds that assembled daily around his tent made army discipline impossible. After removing to Versailles, he came to Paris to effect his cures and at a house in the Rue de la Roquette he was besieged by crowds of crippled and diseased individuals.

He commenced a career of healing mediumship, claiming that he saw spirits ministering to the patients who called upon him and prescribed healing. He not only refused to charge for his healing, but also declined to accept freewill offerings, even when it was requested that they be devoted to healing the poor. However, his father became a self-constituted manager, standing at the door selling Jacob's photograph for one franc to all who would buy.

Jacob's method of healing often resembled that of modern evangelists—a forceful command to be well. In other cases he simply stared at the patient. Many spectacular cures were reported. He was not uniformly successful, and in some cases, he simply dismissed the sufferer with the remark "I can do nothing for your disease."

In his later years, he recommended natural health treatment and condemned the use of alcohol. He ascribed his own healing powers to "the spirits of white magnetism" (see **Animal Magnetism**). He published several books, including: *Les Pensées du Zouave Jacob* (Paris, 1868), *L'Hygiène naturelle, out l'art de consevèr sa santé et de se guérir soi-même* (Paris, 1868), *Poisons et contre-Poisons dévoilés* (Paris, 1874). For a brief account of his healing, see *Nineteenth Century Miracles* by Emma Hardinge Britten (1884, pp. 66-69). (See also **Healing by Faith**)

Jacob, Mr. ("Jacob of Simla") (c. 1850–1921)

A reputed wonder-worker of India during the late nineteenth and early twentieth centuries. A rich diamond merchant, he had a reputation for generosity and also for working miracles. He was immortalized in literature as the original of the novel *Mr. Isaacs* (1882) by F. Marion Crawford. In the novel, Isaacs was a disciple of a Brahmin initiate Ram Lal, whose mystical powers included appearing and disappearing at will. Jacob was also the model for "Lurgan Sahib," the mysterious secret agent with hypnotic powers in Rudyard Kipling's great novel *Kim* (1901). Lurgan, too, is a dealer in precious stones and describes himself as a "Healer of Pearls." He boasts: "There is no one but me can doctor a sick pearl and reblue turquoises. I grant you opals—any fool can cure an opal—but for a sick pearl there is only me. Suppose I were to die! Then there would be no one."

F. Marion Crawford had met Mr. Jacob in a hotel in Simla, India. Jacob invited him to his room, where Crawford was astounded by an Aladdin's cave of wealth and beauty: ". . . it appeared as if the walls and the ceiling were lined with gold and precious stones. . . . Every available space, nook and cranny was filled with gold and jeweled ornaments, shining weapons or uncouth but resplendent idols. . . . The floor was covered with a rich, soft pile, and low divans were heaped with cushions of deep-tinted silk and gold . . . superbly illuminated Arabic manuscripts. . . . At last I turned, and from contemplating the magnificence and inanimate wealth, I was riveted by the majestic face and expression of the beautiful living creature, who by a turn of his want, or, to speak prosaically, by an invitation to smoke, had lifted me out of the humdrum into a land peopled with all the effulgent fantasy and the priceless realities of the magic East."

After publication of Crawford's novel, wild rumors spread about the magical powers of Mr. Jacob, aided by his spirit guide "Ram Lal" who was said to have died one hundred and fifty years earlier. An article by a European occultist calling himself "Tautriadelta," "a pupil of Lord Lytton," in *Borderland* (April 1896) recounted miracles performed by Jacob, such as growing bunches of ripe black grapes on a walking stick, thrusting a sword into a man's body without injury, and walking on water. Some time later, interviewed by a member of the Society for Psychical Research, Jacob was quoted as saying that the growing of buds and blossoms on a walking stick was a trick with a prepared stick, and that pushing a sword into the body was only a matter of skill and knowledge, but that the walking on water was achieved by being supported in the air by his spirit guide, who also acted as a kind of astral "postman," delivering messages over vast distances when needed.

This last phenomenon is of particular interest in view of the fact that Jacob met the famous wonder worker Madame **Blavatsky,** who later acquired fame for the magical precipation of "**Mahatma Letters**" over a distance. Could she have possibly had the idea from stories about Mr. Jacob? Jacob himself regarded Madame Blavatsky as no more than "a clever conjurer."

The early life of Jacob was as romantic as his later reputation. He was born a Turkish or Armenian Jew near Constantinople and sold into slavery at the age of ten. He was bought by a rich and intelligent pasha who saw that the boy had great abilities and instead of giving him menial tasks educated him in Eastern life, literature, philosophy and occultism. On the death of his patron,

Jacob made a pilgrimage to Mecca, then took passage to Bombay, landing without money or friends. Through his knowledge of Arabic, he soon obtained a position as scribe to a nobleman at the Nizam's court in Hyderabad. Here he started dealing in precious stones, later moving to Delhi, then to Simla, where he became one of the most famous jewelers of the time. Maharajahs from all over India engaged his services and he became a rich man, furnishing his house in Oriental splendor with priceless and lavish possessions. Here he received Indian princes, Viceroys, Governors and distinguished members of the civil and military services. Lord Lytton, then viceroy, visited him and remained for several days.

In spite of his lavish surroundings, Jacob lived a simple vegetarian life, occasionally entertaining guests with occult marvels which became the gossip of Simla.

The story of his eventual downfall was equally remarkable. He had incurred the displeasure of a prime minister at Hyderabad through giving information about the brutal execution of a Hindu by the minister's brother. Knowing that the Imperial Diamond was being sold in England, Jacob offered to buy it for the Nizam of Hyderabad, who agreed to pay him forty-six lakhs of rupees (over $600,000). Jacob knew that he could buy for half that sum and saw the chance of a good bargain. The Nizam paid him twenty lakhs of rupees on account. After the diamond arrived in India and was paid for by Jacob, the prime minister urged the Government of India to prevent the sale, knowing that there was an official embargo on princes spending such large sums. The sale was vetoed, and Jacob was left with the diamond and less than half the sum promised by the Nizam. Next, the prime minister urged the Nizam to sue Jacob for return of the money already paid. The trial lasted fifty-seven days and after returning the Nizam's deposit and paying legal costs, Jacob was ruined. In desperation he offered the diamond to the Nizam at any price from one rupee upwards and the Nizam agreed to pay seventeen lakhs of rupees. But Jacob never received any money after handing over the diamond, and was penniless. He retired to Bombay, living in penury, later becoming blind.

Many years later, Dr. Nandor **Fodor** discovered that Jacob's downfall stemmed from a hoax perpetrated by Colonel Angelo, staff officer to General Nicolson in India. Angelo concocted a letter allegedly from a Persian ascetic, reproving Jacob for his attachment to material pleasures and promising him great spiritual development. Other letters followed, and Jacob was convinced that they were from a real "Ram Lal." The correspondence lasted for some years and culminated in a direction for Jacob to journey to a cave nine miles from Simla in the mountains, where he would find a treasure of diamonds which must be used for holy ends. Jacob was to make the journey alone on foot at night, otherwise the treasure would vanish. Angelo knew that Jacob would be afraid to make the journey alone and had him watched, finding that he took his servant with him. Next day Jacob returned with a handful of small diamonds, claiming that he had traveled alone and found the cave and the treasure! Angelo sent him an angry letter from "Ram Lal," cursing him for deception and promising vengeance, ruin and desolation. It should have been a good joke on Jacob, but he was deeply superstitious and from that day onward everything went wrong with him. For a full account of this strange story, see the chapter 'The Healer of Pearls' in Nandor Fodor's book *The Haunted Mind* (1959; 1963).

What is not clear from Fodor's account is whether Jacob did actually perform any occult marvels as well as conjuring tricks. For other accounts of the strange story of Jacob of Simla, see 'The Story of Mr. Isaacs' Life' by Frederick W. Heath (*Occult Review,* October 1912) and '"Mr. Issacs" of Simla' by Edmund Russell (*Occult Review,* March 1917).

Jacobi, Jolande Szekacs (Mrs. Andrew Jacobi) (1890–   )

Psychologist, psychotherapist and author who has written on parapsychology in the context of Jungian psychology. Born March 25, 1890, at Budapest, Hungary, she studied at the University of Vienna (PhD. psychology, 1938). She trained as a psychotherapist with C. G. **Jung** from 1938–43. In 1909 she married Andrew Jacobi.

Mrs. Jacobi was a lecturer for the Institute for Applied Psychology, University of Zürich, C. G. Jung Institute from 1947 on. She has written a number of articles on depth psychology, Jungian psychology and parapsychology, and lectured on such topics throughout Europe. Her books include: *Die Psychologie von C. G. Jung* (1940; U.S. ed. 1943), *Paracelsus* (1951), *Komplex, Archetypus, Symbol in der Psychologie von C. G. Jung* (1957; U.S. ed. 1959), *Case Studies in Counselling & Psychotherapy* (1959), (ed. & contrib.) *Man and His Symbols* (1964), *The Way of Individuation* (1967), *Frauenprobleme—Eheprobleme* (1968), *Vom Bilderreich der Seele* (1969). She also contributed a chapter on 'Dream of the Oracle' in the volume honoring Dr. Jung's eightieth birthday.

Jacob's Ladder

According to the Kabalistic view, Jacob's Ladder, which was disclosed to him in a vision, was a metaphorical representation of the powers of **alchemy,** operating through visible nature.

The "Ladder" was a "Rainbow," or prismatic staircase, set up between heaven and earth. Jacob's dream implied a history of the whole hermetic creation. There were said to be only two original colors, red and blue, representing "spirit" and "matter," for orange is red mixing with the yellow light of the sun, yellow is the radiance of the sun itself, green is blue and yellow, indigo is blue tinctured with red, and violet is produced by the mingling of red and blue. The sun is alchemic gold, and the moon is alchemic silver. In the operation of these two potent spirits or mystic rulers of the world, it was supposed astrologically that all mundane things were produced.

Jade

A term covering minerals of varying color and chemical composition, credited with occult properties.

Jade may be jadeite, nephrite or chloromelanite, with a range of colors—black, brown, red, lavender, blue, green, yellow or white. The mineral is found mainly in New Zealand, Mexico, Central America and China. In prehistoric times, jade was used for utensils and weapons, but in Mexico, Egypt and China it was employed in burial rites. In China, Burma and India, jade has been used for amulets.

Jade is chiefly associated with China, where it has been carved into ornaments for thousands of years. The blue variety of jade was traditionally associated with the heavens, and Chinese emperors are supposed to have made contact with Heaven through a disk of white jade. There was a Chinese superstition that rubbing a piece of jade in the hand would give good fortune to any decision or business venture. The Chinese word for jade is *yü,* indicating beauty, nobility and purity. Because of its *yang* qualities, jade is believed to prolong life. It is taken medicinally in water or wine, and believed to protect against heat and cold, hunger and thirst. Powdered jade is taken to strengthen the heart, lungs and voice. It is also considered an indicator of health and fortune, becoming dull and lusterless in ill health or misfortune. In Burma, Tibet and India, jade is considered a cure for heart trouble and a means of deflecting lightning. It has the property of bringing rain, mist or snow when thrown into water. In Scotland, it has been used as a touchstone to cure illness.

The carving of jade into beautiful ornaments reached its peak in China, where even a small carving involved skilled and patient work over several months. In modern times, there is a large jade market in Hong Kong.

Jadian

A wer-tiger or human animal in Malayan superstition (see **Malays**).

Jadoo

A Hindu term for magic or wonder working, usually applied to traveling conjurers or *jadoo-wallahs.* The term was popularized in the U.S. by writer-magician John A. **Keel** in his book *Jadoo* (1957; London, 1958). Keel traveled through India where his skill as an amateur magician earned him the confidence of Indian conjurers, who disclosed their own tricks, including a version of the famous **Indian Rope Trick.**

Although most of present-day *jadoo* is skillful conjuring, this does not preclude the possibility of genuine paranormal versions of the same wonders. For example, the traditional Indian Rope Trick may well exist in different versions, genuine or illusory.

Jaffé, Aniela (1903–   )

Jungian psychologist who has written on parapsychology. Born February 20, 1903, in Berlin, Germany, she was secretary at the C. G. Jung Institute, Zurich, from 1947–55 and personal secretary to Dr. C. G. **Jung** from 1955 to 1961.

In addition to her various important papers on psychology, she has also written widely on parapsychology, particularly connections between psi phenomena and the unconscious, and the psychological interpretation of paranormal phenomena. Her article 'The Psychic World of C. G. Jung' was published in *Tomorrow* magazine, Spring 1961. Her books include: *Apparitions and Precognition; a study from the point of view of C. G. Jung's analytical psychology* (1963), *From the life and work of C. G. Jung* (1971 rev. ed. 1979), *The Myth of Meaning* (1971). She also recorded and edited the reminiscences of C. G. Jung, published as *Memories, Dreams, Reflections* (1963).

Jahagirdar, Keshav Tatacharya (1914–)

Indian professor of philosophy and psychology who has studied parapsychological phenomena. Born April 16, 1914, at Agarkhed, Mysore, India, he studied at Allahabad University, Uttar Pradesh (M.A. 1941) and was awarded a research scholarship in the Philosophy Department, Allahabad University 1941–44. He was professor of philosophy at Nagpur University from 1944–46, professor, head of departments of Psychology and Philosophy M.T.B. College, Surat, Bombay 1946–54, professor, head of departments of Psychology and Philosophy, D. & H. National College, Bombay from 1954 onwards.

He became a charter member and general secretary of the Society for Psychical Research, Bombay, from 1956 onwards, and member of the managing committee of Bombay Psychological Association, co-editor and contributor to *Manav* magazine 1956–58. Prof. Jahagirdar has studied mediumship, psychokinesis and clairvoyance. His research papers include (with Edwin C. May) 'From Where Does the Kum-Kum Come? A Materialization Attempt' (*Research in Parapsychology 1975* ed. J. D. Morris, W. G. Roll & R. L. Morris, 1976). ("Kum-kum" is a red powder used in sacred Hindu religious rituals.)

Jahoda, Gustav (1920–)

Lecturer in social psychology who has written on parapsychological topics. Born October 11, 1920, at Vienna, Austria, he studied at London University, England (B.Sc. 1945, M.Sc. 1948, Ph.D. 1952). In 1950 he married Jean C. Buchanan. From 1948–49 he was an Oxford University extramural delegate, 1949–52 lecturer at University of Manchester, 1952–56 faculty member of the University College of Ghana (Gold Coast), 1956 onwards senior lecturer in social psychology at Glasgow University, Scotland.

He is a member of the British Sociological Association and associate of the British Psychological Society. In addition to his various papers on psychological, anthropological and sociological subjects, Dr. Jahoda has written on the supernatural beliefs of West Africans. His article 'Emotional Stress, Mental Illness and Social Change' (*International Journal of Social Psychiatry*) describes West African healers, and 'Aspects of Westernization' (*British Journal of Sociology*) analyses West African belief in the paranormal. His books include *White Man; A Study of the Attitudes of Africans to Europeans Before Independence* (1961), *The Psychology of Superstition* (1974).

James, T. P. (c. 1874)

The **automatic writing** medium of Brattleboro, Vermont, who published a completion of the novel *The Mystery of Edwin Drood* by Charles Dickens, allegedly from the spirit of Dickens (see Charles **Dickens**).

James, William (1842–1910)

Professor of Psychology at Harvard University, one of the founders of the American Society for Psychical Research, president of the Society for Psychical Research (in Britain) in 1894–95, vice-president from 1809–1910. His name and prestige, his open espousal of the cause of psychical research was a great benefit to this nascent science.

James was born in New York, N.Y., January 11, 1842,

and obtained his M.D. in 1869 from Harvard Medical School but was a semi-invalid until 1872, when he was appointed instructor in physiology at Harvard College. He went on to study psychology and in 1891 published his famous work *The Principles of Psychology.* In 1897, he became professor of philosophy at Harvard and lectured at universities in the U.S. and Britain. He developed the doctrine of pragmatism and one of his most important philosophical books was *The Varieties of Religious Experience* (1902), which has always been a very influential work in the attempt to reconcile science and religion.

The first case which decided William James to believe in metapsychical phenomena was reported in *Proceedings* of the American S.P.R., Vol. 1, part 2, pp. 221–31. It is the case of a drowned girl whose body was seen by Mrs. Titus, of Lebanon, New Hampshire, in her dream head downwards under the timber work of a bridge at Enfield. Divers had searched for the body in vain, but following Mrs. Titus' vision it was found.

The discovery of Mrs. **Piper's** mediumship for the Society for Psychical Research was due to Prof. James. Mrs. Gibbins, his mother-in-law, led by curiosity, paid a visit to Mrs. Piper in 1885. She returned with a perplexing story. Prof. James took a rationalist view, seeking to explain by simple considerations the marvelous character of the facts. A few days later, with his wife, he went to get a direct personal impression. Their names were not announced and they were careful not to make any reference to their relative who had preceded them.

"My impression," wrote Prof. James, "after this first visit was that Mrs. P. was either possessed of supernormal powers or knew the members of my wife's family by sight and had by some lucky coincidence become acquainted with such a multitude of their domestic circumstances as to produce the startling impression which she did. My later knowledge of her sittings and personal acquaintance with her has led me to absolutely reject the latter explanation, and to believe that she has supernormal powers."

For eighteen months after his first experiments, Prof. James was virtually in charge of all arrangements for Mrs. Piper's seances. When, owing to other duties, he dropped his inquiries for a period of two years, he wrote to the S.P.R. and induced them to engage Mrs. Piper for experiments. "The result," he wrote of his personal investigations, "is to make me feel as absolutely certain as I am of any personal fact in the world that she knows things in her trances which she cannot possibly have heard in her waking state." He admitted that a strong presumption in favor of survival exists when the following message, obtained while Miss Robbins had a sitting with Mrs. Piper, was submitted to him: "There is a person named Child, who has suddenly come and sends his love to William and to his own wife who is living. He says L . . ." Neither Miss Robbins nor Mrs. Piper knew Child who was an intimate friend of William James and whose Christian name begins with L.

In the autumn of 1899 Mrs. Piper paid Prof. James a visit at his country house in New Hampshire. There he learned to know her personally better than ever before. "It was in great measure," wrote Alta L. Piper in her biography of Mrs. Piper, "due to his sympathetic encouragement and understanding of the many difficulties, with which she found herself confronted in the early days of her career, that my mother was able to adhere unfalteringly to the onerous course which she had set herself to follow."

In an often quoted lecture in 1890 Prof. James declared: "To upset the conclusion that all crows are black, there is no need to seek demonstration that no crow is black; it is sufficient to produce one white crow; a single one is sufficient." He proclaimed Mrs. Piper as his "one white crow." Since then, this concept of the single "white crow" has become a cliché in psychical research.

Prof. James published several papers in the *Proceedings* of the S.P.R., an important essay on psychical research in his book *The Will to Believe* (1902; 1956) and a valuable contribution for the reconciliation of science with religion in his *Varieties of Religious Experience* (1902).

In a lecture at Oxford in 1909, he announced his firm conviction that "most of the phenomena of psychical research are rooted in reality."

Shortly before his death he stated in the *American Magazine* the principal effect upon his opinion of twenty-five years of psychical research. He held the spiritistic hypothesis unproven and inclined "to picture the situation as an interaction between slumbering faculties in the automatist's mind and a cosmic environment of other consciousness of some sort which is able to work upon them."

Prof. James was honored by Hon. LL.D. degrees at Princeton, Edinburgh, and Harvard. He died at Chocorua, New Hampshire, August 26, 1910.

His alleged return after death is discussed in a long chapter in James **Hyslop**'s *Contact with the Other World* (1919).

James IV of Scotland

It was almost inevitable that the romantic nature of James IV of Scotland should have encouraged the study of alchemy and the occult sciences. William Dunbar in his *Remonstrance,* referred to the patronage which James bestowed upon alchemists and charlatans, and in the Treasurer's accounts there are numerous payments for the "Quinta Essentia," including wages to the persons employed, utensils of various kinds and so forth. In a letter to one Master James Inglis, James stated:

"*James,* etc. . . . to dear Master James Inglis greeting. We graciously accept your kindness, by which in a letter brought to us you signify that you have beside you certain books learned in the philosophy of the true Alchemy, and that although most worthy men have sought them from you, you have nevertheless with difficulty kept them for our use, because you had heard of our enthusiasm for the art. We give you thanks; . . . and we have sent our familiar, Master James Merchenistoun, to you, that he may see to the transfer hither of those books which you wish us to have; whom receive in good faith in our name. Farewell. From our Palace at Edinburgh."

From the Treasurer's Accounts.

27 Sept.—Item, for a pan in Stirling for the quinta
    essencia, and "potingary" there.   vi. *s.*
29 Sept.—For aqua vitae for the quinta essencia. . .
18 Oct.—Gallons aqua vitae for quinta essencia.   iii.
    l. iiij. *s.*
10 Nov.—For four cauldrons to quinta essencia   xlv. *s.*
24 Dec.—V cakes glass for quinta essentia.   xxv. *s.*

31 Dec.—Paid to William Foular apothecary (*potingair* for potingary to the King and Queen, distillation of waters, aqua vitae, and potingary books in English, from the 17 day of December, 1506.

(See also **Scotland**)

Janet, Pierre (Marie Félix) (1859–1947)

French psychologist and neurologist, noted for his researches on hysteria and neuroses. Born May 30, 1859, in Paris, he studied at the École Normale and the École de Medecine, Paris. He became a lecturer on philosophy at the lycées of Chateauroux and The Hague, at the College Rollin, and the lycées Louis-le-Grand and Condorcet.

From 1889–98 he was director of the psychological laboratory of the Saltpêtrière in Paris. He also lectured on psychology at the Sorbonne, and became professor of psychology at the Collège de France in 1902. He published many important works on psychology and hysteria. Together with Prof. J. M. **Charcot,** his work includes the serious medical and scientific study of the phenomena of **hypnotism** in place of the earlier occult connotations of **Mesmerism.**

JAPAN

Magical concepts are to be found amongst the Japanese, in their traditional religious beliefs and rites, in their conception of Nature. According to such beliefs, all forms and objects animate or inanimate possess, equally with man, a soul with good or evil tendencies and these entities, either of their own volition or by evocation, come into close touch with man either to his advantage or detriment. Much of Japanese folklore and tradition is permeated with a belief in the supernatural.

Shinto Religion and Ancestor-Worship

The predominant feature of the Japanese religion Shintoism is the worship of ancestors, allied to that of Nature. There are twelve main sects of Shintoism all with ancestor-worship as their cardinal principle.

The belief was that the disembodied spirits acquired the powers of deities and possessed supernatural attributes. They become potential for good or evil and exercised their potentialities in the same mundane sphere upon which their interests and affections centered during life.

They thus become guardian divinities and as such the object of ceremonies in their honor is to show gratitude for their services whilst upon earth and to solicit a continuance of these services beyond the grave.

On this point, Lafcadio Hearn wrote: "An intimate sense of relation between the visible and invisible worlds is the special religious characteristic of Japan among all civilized countries. To Japanese thought the dead are not less real than the living. They take part in the daily life of the people—sharing the humblest sorrows and the humblest joys. They attend the family repasts, watch over the well-being of the household, assist and rejoice in the prosperity of their descendants. They are present at the public pageants, at all the sacred festivals of Shinto, at the military games, and at all the entertainments especially provided for them. And they are universally thought of as finding pleasure in the offerings made to them or the honors conferred upon them."

Every morning, before the family shrine to be found in Japanese homes, flowers are set and food-emblems placed as offerings of pious affection, while ancient prayers are repeated, for on the shrine, beside the symbols of the Sun-goddess and the tutelary god of the family, are put the memorial tablets containing names, ages and dates of death of members of the household. There are stories of the souls of ancestors taking material form and remaining visible through centuries.

In the month of July three days are set apart for the celebration of the Festival of the Dead. At this time it is thought that the disembodied souls return from the dismal region of the Shades to gaze for a while upon the beauty of their country and to visit their people. On the first morning, new mats are placed upon all altars and on the household shrine, while in the homes, tiny meals are prepared in readiness for the ghostly guests. The streets at night are brilliant with many torches. In front of the houses gaily-colored lanterns are lit in welcome. Those who have recently lost some relative go to the cemeteries to pray and burn incense and leave offerings of water and flowers set in bamboo vases.

On the third day, the souls of those who are undergoing penance are fed, also those who have no friends among the living to care for them. The evening of this day is the time of the ghosts' departure, and for this thousands of little boats are fashioned and laden with food-offerings and tender messages of farewell. When the night falls, tiny lanterns are lit and hung at the miniature prows and the ghosts are supposed to step aboard. Then the craft are set free upon river, lake and sea, the water gleaming with glow of thousands of lights. On this day no sailor dreamt of putting out to sea—for this one night belonged to the dead. It was believed that if a ship failed to come to port before the sailing of the ghost-fleet the dead arose from the deep and the sailors could hear their mournful whispering, while the white breakers were dead hands clutching the shores, vainly trying to return.

In the Shinto pantheon, deities represent almost everything in heaven and earth, from the mountain of Fijiyama to the household kitchen, from Wisdom to Scarecrows, from Calligraphy to Poverty, Laughter to Smallpox. When babes were a week old they were taken to the temple and placed under the protection of some god chosen by the parents, but in later years the child might choose his patron god for himself beside the tutelary one.

In remote parts of Japan may still be found traces of an older form of Shinto in which phallic symbols had their place as representing life-giving power and therefore used as a magical exorcism of evil influences, especially that of disease. In this connection appears a dwarf-god who is said to have first taught mankind the art of magic and medicine.

In Shinto there are no idols, their place being taken by *shintia*, god-bodies, concrete objects in which the divine spirit was supposed to dwell, such as the mirror, jewel and sword of the Sun-goddess, worshipped at the famous Ise shrine. Pilgrims from all parts of Japan made their way to this shrine, acquiring merit and purification thereby.

These pilgrims received from the priests objects of talismanic properties called *harai*, these also serving as evidence of having been at the holy place. In former days they were recognized as passports.

The term *harai* signifies to "drive out" or "sweep away," and had reference to the purification of the individual from his sins. These objects were in the form of small envelopes or paper boxes, each containing shavings of the wands used by the Ise priests at the half-yearly festivals held to purify the nation in general from the consequences of the sins of the preceding six months. The list included witchcraft, also wounding and homicide, these latter being regarded more as uncleanness than as a moral stigma. On the pilgrims returning home, the *harai* were placed upon the "god's-shelf."

On certain festival days the ancient ordeals were practiced. These were three in number: the *Kugadachi*, in which priests, wrought to ecstatic frenzy by participation in a rhythmic dance, poured upon their bodies boiling water without receiving harm from the process; the *Hiwatari* consisting of walking barefoot over a bed of live coals, priests and people alike participating, and *Tsurugi-watari*, the climbing of a ladder of sword-blades. These were regarded as tests of purity of character, this being thought to confer an immunity from hurt in these ordeals. The attendant rites consisted of exorcism of evil spirits by the waving of wands and magical finger-knots, and invocation of the gods who were then believed to be actually present.

Possession by Divinities

In connection with some of the Shinto sects, occult rites were practiced to bring about possession of a selected person by the actual spirits of the gods. Priests and laymen alike developed and practiced this art, undergoing a period of purification by means of various austerities. Prophecy, divination and the cure of disease were the objects of these rites. The ceremony took place in a temple or ordinary house where the "gods' shelf" made the shrine. In the rites *gohei*, the Shinto symbols of consecration were used, the pendant form for purification and exorcism of evil influences, and an upright *gohei* affixed to a wand signifying the *shintai*, or god-body, is the central object.

The medium, called *nak aza*, took his seat in the midst. Next to him in importance was the functionary, the *maeza* who presided over the ceremony. It was he who built the magical pyre in a brass bowl and burnt in the flames strips of paper inscribed with characters, effigies of disease and trouble. There was a clapping of hands to call the attention of the gods and chants were intoned, accompanied by the shaking of metal-ringed crosiers and the tinkle of pilgrim bells.

After the fire was burnt out, the bowl was removed and sheets of paper placed in symbolic form, upon which was then put the upright gohei wand. There was further chanting, the medium closed his eyes and clasped his hands into which the *maeza* now thrust the wand. All then awaited the advent of the god which was indicated by the violent shaking of the wand and convulsive throes on the part of the medium, who was now considered to have become the god. The *maeza* reverently prostrated himself before the entranced *nakaza,* and asked the name of the god who had deigned to come. This done and answered, he next offered his petitions, to which the god replied. The ceremony concluded by a prayer and the medium was awakened by beating upon his back and the massaging of his limbs out of their cataleptic contraction. These possession-rites were also conducted by the pilgrims who ascended the mountain of Ontaké.

Buddhist Sects

Buddhism shared with Shinto the devotions of Japan, enjoining meditation as a means of attaining to supernatural knowledge and occult power. It was said that to those who in truth and constancy put into force the doctrines of Buddha the following ten powers would be granted. (1) They know the thoughts of others. (2) Their sight, piercing as that of the celestials, beholds without mist all that happens in the earth. (3) They know the past and present. (4) They perceive the uninterrupted succession of the ages of the world. (5) Their hearing is so fine that they perceive and can interpret all the harmonies of the three worlds and the ten divisions of the universe. (6) They are not subject to bodily conditions and can assume any appearance at will. (7) They distinguish the shadowing of lucky or unlucky words, whether they are near or far away. (8) They possess the knowledge of all forms, and knowing that form is void, they can assume every sort of form; and knowing that vacancy is form, they can annihilate and render nought all forms. (9) They possess a knowledge of all laws. (10) They possess the perfect science of contemplation.

It was said that methods were thus known by which it was possible to so radically change the psychological condition of the individual that he would be enabled to recognize the character of the opposition between subjective and objective. These two extremes were reconciled in a higher condition of consciousness, a higher form of life, a more profound and complete activity which concerns the inmost depths of the self. Such beliefs reflected Hindu **yoga** philosophy, probably imported into Japan from India by Buddhist influence during the twelfth and fourteenth centuries A.D. Early Buddhist influence in Japan from the sixth century onwards was from China.

Zen Buddhism in Japan belongs to the later period of the twelfth century. Zen monasteries were instituted, to which anyone so inclined could retire for temporary meditation and for the development of these special faculties, which are mainly produced by entering upon a calm mental state, not exactly passive, but in which the attention was not devoted to any one thing, but evenly distributed in all directions, producing a sort of void and detachment. The spirit thus obtained entire repose and a satisfaction of the thirst for the ideal. This mystical retirement was sought by statesmen and generals, by scientific, professional and businessmen, and it is said that the force which accumulated within them by practicing the Zen was of effective service even in practical life.

Customs and Occult Lore

Many of the customs of the Japanese have a magical significance. At the Festival of the New Year, extending over three days, it is considered of the first importance to insure good luck and happiness for the coming year by means of many traditional observances. Houses are thoroughly cleansed materially and spiritually, this last is getting rid of the evil spirits by throwing out beans and peas from the open slides of the houses. The gateways are decorated with straw ropes made to represent the lucky Chinese numbers of three, five and seven. Mirror cakes, associated with the sun-goddess, are eaten, also lobsters, longevity being symbolized by their bent and ancient appearance, the pine-tree branches used for decoration at this time also signifying long life.

Divination was performed by various methods: by **divining-rods,** by the reading of lines and cracks in the shoulder-blade of a deer, and by the classical form taken from the Confucian **I Ching** or *Book of Changes,* this involving the use of eight trigrams and sixty-four diagrams. One method of "raising spirits" used by the Japanese, especially by girls who had lost their lovers by death was to put into a paper lantern a hundred rushlights and repeat an incantation of a hundred lines. One of these rushlights was taken out at the end of each line and the would-be ghost-seer then went out in the dark with one light still burning and blew it out when the ghost ought to appear.

Charms used to be popular, fashioned of all substances and in all forms, such as strips of paper bearing magical inscriptions to avert evil, fragments of temples, carven ricegrains representing the gods of Luck, *sutras* (sacred texts) to frighten the demons, copies of Buddha's footprint, and paper tickets bearing the name of a god were often affixed outside the doors of houses to combat the god of Poverty.

Nature and her manifestations are the result of indwelling soul-life and the Japanese mind, imbued with this belief peopled nature with multiform shapes. There were dragons with lairs in ocean and river which yet could fly abroad in the air, while from their panting breath came the clouds of rain and tempests of lightning. In the mountains and forests were bird-like gnomes who often beset wayfaring men and women and stole away their wits. There were also mountain men, huge hairy monkeys, who helped the woodcutters in return for food, and mountain-women, ogres with bodies grown over with long white hair, who flitted like evil moths in search of human flesh.

Then legend also told of the *Senrim,* hermits of the mountains, who knew all the secrets of magic, wizards who were attended by wise toads and flying tortoises, who could conjure magical animals out of gourds, who could project their souls into space.

Supernatural powers were also ascribed to animals. The fox was believed to possess such gifts to an almost limitless extent, for he had miraculous vision and hearing, could read the inmost thoughts of man, could transform himself and assume any shape at will. He loved to delude mankind and work destruction thereby to this end often taking the form of a beautiful and seductive woman whose embrace meant madness and death. To the agency of this animal was attributed demoniacal possession, this occurring mostly among ignorant and superstitious women of the lower classes.

The cat was not regarded with any kindly feeling by the Japanese, this being ascribed to the fact that this animal, together with the serpent, were the only creatures who did not weep at Buddha's death. This animal also had the power of bewitchment and possessed **vampire** proclivities. Among sailors, however, the cat was held in high estimation, for it was thought to possess the power of warding off the evil spirits which haunt the sea.

The images of animals were thought to be also endowed with life. There are tales of bronze horses and deer, of huge carven dragons and stone tortoises wandering abroad at night, terrorizing the people and only laid to rest by summary decapitation. Butterflies were thought to be the wandering souls of the living who might be dreaming or sunk in reverie; white butterflies were the souls of the dead. Fireflies kept afar evil spirits, and an ointment compounded of their delicate bodies defied any poison.

Trees occupied a foremost place in the tradition and legends of Japan. The people regarded them with great affection, and there are stories of men who, seeing a tree they loved withering and dying, committed *hara-kiri* before it, praying to the gods that their life so given might pass into the tree and give it renewed vigor. The willow is one of the most eerie of trees, the willow-spirit often becoming a beautiful maiden and wedding a human lover. The pine tree brought good fortune, especially in the matter of happy marriages. It was also a token of longevity. Tree spirits could sometimes be inimical to man and it is recorded of one that to stay its disturbing wanderings it was necessary to cut it down, when from the stump flowed a stream of blood.

The element of Fire figured largely in the Japanese world of marvels. It was worshiped in connection with the rites of the Sun-goddess and even the kitchen-furnace became the object of a sort of cult. There is the lamp of Buddha, while messages from Hades came to this world in the shape of fire-wheels, Phantom-fires flickered about and flames burnt in the cemeteries; there were demon-lights, fox-flames and dragon-torches. From the eyes and mouths of certain birds such as the blue heron, fire darted forth in white flames. Globes of fire, enshrining human faces and forms, sometimes hung like fruit in the branches of the trees.

The dolls of Japanese children were believed to be endowed with life, deriving a soul from the love expended upon them by their human possessors. Some of these dolls were credited with supernatural powers, they could confer maternity upon a childless woman, and they could bring misfortune upon any who ill-treated them. When old and faded these dolls were dedicated to Kojin the many-armed who dwelt in the *enokie* tree, and they were reverently laid upon his shrine, bodies which once held a tiny soul.

New Religions in Japan

Many ancient beliefs and superstitions changed in Japan following World War II, and although Shinto and Buddhist religions still predominate, an astonishing number of new sects have arisen, some combining original Shinto and Buddhist beliefs with elements of Christianity. The defeat of Japan in the war was a crushing blow to national morale and weakened belief in traditional religions. Again, the post-war period of high technology and industrialization also created receptivity to new directions in the religious life. There was a need for updating and streamlining religious belief and practice.

In modern times, over 170 new religions have been registered officially, two-thirds of them developments of Shinto or Buddhism, but also many heterodox sects with a following of over 3½ million people.

Among the new sects is a group known as *Omoto* (Teaching of the Great Origin), which originally began in 1892 as a Messianic sect, founded by a farmer woman named Deguchi Nao. The sect was developed by Deguchi Onisaburo and featured the healing of diseases by mystical power. By 1934, the sect had links with Chinese groups and the *Baha'i* religion, with some 2½ million followers. In 1935, the Japanese government imprisoned the founders and leading followers and their headquarters were dynamited. After World War II, the sect was revived under the name of *Aizen-en* (Garden of Divine Love). Onisaburo died in 1948, but the movement continued to flourish and also gave rise to various splinter sects.

Amongst unrelated new religions is *Tensho Kotai Jingu Kyo,* more generally known as *Odoru Shukyo* (The Dancing Religion) deriving from the founder Kitamura Sayo, a farmer's wife regarded by followers as divinely inspired. She is addressed as "Goddess" and her son as "Young God." She is believed to have prophetic insight and power to heal diseases.

Psychical Research & Parapsychology

Although little has been published in Western countries about Japan in relation to paranormal phenomena, Japanese interest in the subject goes back to the last century. As already mentioned, shamanistic techniques and mediumistic faculty were characteristic of some Japanese religions, and from the middle of the nineteenth century onwards, such phenomena began to be studied objectively. One early investigator was Atsutane Hirat (1776–1843) who was a pioneer in drawing attention to reported cases of reincarnation and poltergeist. Chikaatsu Honda (1823–1889) studied the techniques of *Chinkon,* a method of meditation involving revelation through divine possession, becoming mediumistic himself. His techniques were developed by Onisaburo Deguchi (1871-1948), a leading figure in the *Omoto* sect. The *Chinkon Kishin* technique involved spirit communication, and Wasaburo Asano, then a member of *Omoto*, perceived that this had much in common with European Spiritualism. He subsequently became independent of *Omoto* and promoted the study of Spiritualism.

A pioneer of psychical research was Dr. Enryo Inoue (1858–1919) who founded the Research Society for Supernormal Phenomena at the University of Tokyo in 1888. Another early investigator was Prof. Oguma of Meiji University, who had studied abnormal psychology, hypnosis and dreams and who began to make Western psychical research known in Japan. Dr. Oguma published books on psychical science.

Another pioneer was Prof. Tomokichi **Fukurai** (1869–1952) of the University of Tokyo, whose experiments on clairvoyance and psychic photography (which he called "Thoughtography") commenced in 1910. An English translation of his book *Clairvoyance & Thoughtography* (1913) was published in 1921. His experiments in Thoughtography were a remarkable anticipation of the phenomena of Ted Serios in modern times, investigated by Dr. Jule Eisenbud. Unfortunately the experiments of Dr. Fukurai caused dissension at Tokyo University, and he was obliged to resign. He went to the Buddhist university of Kohyassan where he became president of a Psychical Institute of Japan. He also published a second book *Spirit and Mysterious World* (1932), in which he attempted to reconcile psychical phenomena with Buddhism.

In 1923, the Japanese Society for Psychic Science was founded at Tokyo, under the presidency of W. Asano. Progress in psychical research was slow, however. After the war, Dr. J. B. **Rhine**'s book *The Reach of the Mind* (1947) was translated into Japanese and stimulated investigation of ESP. Meanwhile Dr. Fukurai, who had removed to Sendai in Honshu, organized a research group of psychologists and engineers for the study of parapsychology. The Fukurai Institute of Psychology was founded after his death in 1952. Another organization about this period was the Institute for Religious Psychology, founded by Dr. Hiroshi Motoyama.

After a visit to Japan by Dr. Pratt of Duke University Parapsychology Laboratory in 1963, a Japanese Society for Parapsychology was founded through the initiative of Dr. Soji Otani, who visited Duke University and studied their techniques. In 1967, the Society held a conference of parapsychologists in Tokyo, when Prof. Oguma lectured on the history of parapsychology in Japan. Parapsychology has since become a recognized area for research at various Japanese universities.

The showing of a program featuring psychic Uri **Geller** on Japanese television stimulated interest in the phenomena of **psychokinesis.** In 1977, experiments were reported with a 17-year-old boy Masuaki Kiyota, who claimed unusual faculties in **metal-bending** and in Thoughtography (now investigated as "Nengraphy"). Some of these experiments were filmed by an American unit and incorporated in the 90-minute program "Exploring the Unknown" shown by NBC October 30, 1977.

Recently advised addresses for Japanese organizations concerned with parapsychological investigations are as follows:

International Association for Religion & Parapsychology, 4-11-7 Inokashira, Mitaka, Tokyo 181

Japan Nengraphy Association, Awiji-cho 2-25, Kannda, Chioda, Tokyo

Japan Association for Psychotronic Research, c/o 284-6 Anagawa-cho. Chiba-shi

Japan Society for Parapsychology, 26-14 Chun 4, Nakano, Tokyo 164

Recommended reading:

Anesaki, Masaharu. *History of Japanese Religion,* Kegan Paul, London, 1930

Davis, F. Hadland. *Myths and Legends of Japan,* Harrp & Co., 1912

Deguchi, Onisaburo. *Memoirs,* Kameoka, Japan, 1957

Fukurai, T. *Clairvoyance & Thoughtography,* Rider & Co., London, Arno Press, N.Y., 1975

Hearn, Lafcadio. *Kokoro; Hints & Echoes of Japanese Inner Life,* Houghton Mifflin, 1906

Lowell, Percival. *Occult Japan,* Houghton Mifflin, 1895

Offner, C. B. & H. van Straelen. *Modern Japanese Religions,* E. J. Brill, Leyden, Netherlands, 1963

Thomsen, Harry. *The New Religions of Japan,* Charles E. Tuttle Co., 1963

Uphoff, Walter & Mary Jo. *Mind Over Matter: Implications of Masuaki Kiyota's PK Feats with Metal and Film,* New Frontiers Center, Oregon, Wisconsin/Colin Smythe, U.K., 1980

Jaquin, Noel (1894–1974)

One of the best known British experts in **palmistry,** who attempted to establish a scientific rationale for study of what has so often been regarded as a superstition. He was able to diagnose disease from markings on the hand, and also worked with police authorities in studying palmistry indications with criminals. His books included: *Scientific Palmistry* (1925), *The Hand and Disease* (1926), *Hand-reading Made Easy* (1928), *The Hand of Man* (1933), *Man's Revealing Hand* (1934), *The Signature of Time* (1940), *Its in Your Hands: The Secrets of the Human Hand* (1941), *The Human Hand* (1956, 1959), *The Theory of Metaphysical Influence; a Study of Human Attunements, Perception, Intelligence & Motivation* (1958).

Jarman, Archibald Seymour (1909–   )

Writer on parapsychological subjects. Born June 23, 1909, at Richmond, Surrey, England, he married Helene Mariana Klenk in 1937. He has worked as an estate administrator, and was associate editor of *Tomorrow* magazine from 1962 onwards. His articles in *Tomorrow* include 'Unsolved Animal Mysteries' (Spring 1960), 'Physical Phenomena: Fraud or Frontier?' (Autumn 1960). He has also written articles for British journals dealing with parapsychology including the *Journal* of the Society for Psychical Research. His article 'High Jinks on a Low Level' (originally from *Tomorrow* magazine), published in *Spiritualism; A Critical Survey* by Simeon Edwards (1966), is an amusing description of three seances attended by the writer and illustrates the crude frauds of bogus mediums.

Jarricot, Jean (1877–1962)

French physician and experimenter in the field of radiesthesia. Born July 14, 1877, at Saint Genis Lavel, Rhone, France; died November 13, 1962. Dr. Jarricot's article 'A quel cadre de references rattacher les faits de parapsychologie?' (In what terms of reference should we consider parapsychology?) was published in *La Tour Saint Jacques* (May 1958). His books included: *Pendule at Médecine* (Pendulum and Medicine, 1949), *Radiesthesie* (Radiesthesia, 1958).

Jasper

A variety of quartz, to which many medicinal values were attributed in ancient times. It was believed to prevent fever and dropsy, strengthen the brain, and promote eloquence. It was said to be a preservative against defluxions (discharge of catarrhal mucous), prevent the nightmares and epilepsy, and was often met with in the east as a counter-charm. Bishop Marbodæus mentioned seventeen species of this stone, but noted that "like the emerald" it was most noted for its magical virtues. As late as 1609, it was still believed that jasper worn about the neck would strengthen the stomach.

Jean

According to Lewis *Spence* (in *Encyclopedia of Occultism,* 1920), Jean was a French magician, votary of **Apollonius of Tyana.** He went from town to town, wearing an iron collar, and making his living by the performance of deeds of charletanry. At Lyons he attained some measure of fame by his miraculous cures, and was admitted to the presence of the sovereign, to whom he presented a magnificent enchanted sword. In battle, this weapon became surrounded by nine score drawn knives. Jean also gave this prince a shield containing a magic mirror which would divulge the greatest secrets. The arms vanished, or were stolen.

(Unfortunately, Spence did not state the period or the ruler involved, but this is probably a medieval legend of France.)

Jean d'Arras (c. 1387)

A French writer of the fourteenth century, who compiled for his patron John, Duke of Berry, The *Chronique de la princesse* in 1387 from popular stories of Mélusine.

Mélusine was a fairy doomed to change into the form of a serpent every Saturday unless she found a husband who would never see her on Saturdays. She married Raymond of Poitiers of the house of Lusignan. He was rich and powerful and Mélusine was able to be instrumental in the building of the castle of Lusignan and other family fortresses.

One Saturday, her husband was overcome by curiosity and spied on her, whereupon she cried out and flew away in serpent form. Since then, the cry of Mélusine was said to herald death in the family of Lusignan (see also **Banshee**).

The book of Jean d'Arras was first printed in Geneva in 1478 and frequently reprinted.

Jean de Meung (or Mehun) (1250?–1305?)

French poet who owes his celebrity to his continuation of the *Roman de la Rose* of Guillaume de Saint-Amour rather than to his rhyming treatise upon **alchemy.** He was born Jean Clopinel (or Chopinel) at Meun-sur-Loire, and flourished through the reigns of Louis X, Philip the Long, Charles IV and Philip de Valois.

He appears to have possessed a light and railing wit and a keen appreciation of a jest, and it may well be doubted whether he was altogether sincere in his praises of alchemy.

Having composed a quatrain on woman, which stigmatized her in the strongest terms, the ladies of Charles IV's court resolved to revenge their affronted honor. Surrounding him in the royal antechanber they desired the courtiers present to strip him preparatory to their inflicting a sound flogging. Jean begged to be heard before he was condemned and punished, and having obtained an interval of grace set forth, with fluent eloquence, that he was certainly the author of the calumnious verses, but that they were not intended to disparage all womankind. He referred only to the vicious and debased, and not to such models of purity as he saw around him. Nevertheless, if any lady present felt that the verses really applied to her, he was her very humble servant, and would submit to a well-deserved chastisement!

Like most of the medieval poets, Jean de Meung was a bitter enemy of the priesthood, and he contrived with great ingenuity a posthumous satire upon their inordinate greed. He bequeathed in his will, as a gift to the Cordeliers, a chest of immense weight. Since his fame as an alchemist was widespread, the brotherhood accepted the legacy in the belief that the chest contained the golden results of his quest of the **Philosopher's Stone.** But when they opened it, their dismayed eyes rested only on a pile of *slates,* covered with the most unintelligible hieroglyphics and kabalistic characters. The perpetrator of this practical joke was hardly, it seems, a very sincere believer in the wonders of alchemy.

Jean de Meung's book on alchemy was published as *Le Miroir d'alchymie* (1557) and in German as *Der Spiegel der Alchimie* (1771), but some critics believe it is spurious. Also doubtfully attributed to de Meung are the poetical treatises, *Les Remonstrances de Nature à l'Alchimiste errant* and *La Reponse de l'Alchimiste à Nature.*

Jeanne D'Arc, St. (1412–1431)

Joan was born Jeanette with the surname Arc or Romée in the village of Domrémy, near Vaucouleurs, on the border of Champagne and Lorraine, on January 6, 1412. In documents of her time, she is known as Jeanne.

She was taught to spin and sew, but not to read or write, these accomplishments being unusual and unnecessary to people in her station of life. Her parents were devout, and she was brought up piously. Her nature was gentle, modest, and religious but with no physical weakness or morbidity. On the contrary, she was exceptionally strong, as her later history shows.

At or about the age of thirteen, she began to experience what modern psychology calls "auditory hallucinations." In other words, she heard "voices" (usually accompanied by a bright light) when no visible person was present. This, of course, is a common symptom of impending mental disorder, but no insanity developed in Jeanne d'Arc. She was naturally startled at first, but continuation of the experience led to familiarity and trust. The voices gave good counsel of a very commonplace kind, as, for instance, that she "must be a good girl and go often to church."

Soon, however, she began to have visions. She saw St. Michael, St. Catharine, and St. Margaret and was given instructions as to her mission. She eventually made her way to the Dauphin, put herself at the head of 6,000 men, and advanced to the relief of Orleans, which was surrounded by the victorious English. After a fortnight of hard fighting, the siege was raised and the enemy driven off. The tide of war turned, and in three months the Dauphin was crowned king at Rheims as Charles the Seventh.

At this point, Jeanne felt that her mission was accomplished. But her wish to return to her family was overruled by king and archbishop, and she took part in the further fighting against the allied English and Burgundian forces, showing great bravery and tactical skill. But in November 1430, in a desperate sally from Compiégne (which was besieged by the Duke of Burgundy), she fell into the enemy's hands, was sold to the English and thrown into a dungeon at their headquarters in Rouen.

After a year's imprisonment, she was brought to trial before the Bishop of Beauvais, in an ecclesiastical court. The charges were heresy and sorcery. Learned doctors of the Church, subtle lawyers, did their best to entangle the simple girl in their dialectical toils, but she showed a remarkable power of keeping to her affirmations and of avoiding heretical statements. "God has always been my Lord in all that I have done," she said.

But the trial was only a sham, for her fate was already decided. She was condemned to the stake. To the end, she solemnly affirmed the reality of her "voices," and the truth of her depositions. Her last word, as the smoke and flame rolled round her, was "Jesus." Said an English soldier, awestruck by the manner of her passing: "We are lost; we have burned a Saint." The idea was corroborated in popular opinion by events which followed, for speedy death (as if by Heaven's anger) overtook her judges and accusers. Inspired by her example and claims, and helped by dissension and weakening on the side of the enemy, the French took heart once more, and the English were all but swept out of the country.

Jeanne's family was rewarded by ennoblement, under the name of De Lys. Twenty-five years after her death, the Pope acceded to a petition that the *procés* by which she was condemned should be reexamined. The result was that the judgment was reversed, and her innocence established and proclaimed.

The life of the Maid supplies a problem which orthodox science cannot solve. She was a simple peasant girl, with no ambitious hankering after a career. She rebelled pathetically against her mission. "I had far rather rest and spin by my mother's side, for this is no work of my choosing, but I must go and do it, for my Lord wills it."

She cannot be dismissed on the "simple idiot" theory of Voltaire, for her genius in war and her aptitude in repartee undoubtedly prove exceptional mental powers, unschooled though she was in normal education. She cannot be dismissed as a mere hysteric, for her health and strength were superb.

It is on record that a man of science said to an Abbé: "Come to the Salpêtrière Hospital [the refuge for elderly, poor and insane patients in Paris] and I will show you twenty Jeannes d'Arc." To which the Abbé responded: "Has one of them given us back Alsace and Lorraine?" The retort was certainly neat. Still, although the Salpêtrière hysterics have not won back Alsace and Lorraine, it is nevertheless true that many great movements have sprung from fraud or hallucination. Jeanne delivered France, and her importance in history is great, but it is arguable that her mission and her actions might have been the outcome of merely subjective hallucinations, induced by the brooding of her specially religious and patriotic mind on the woes of her country. The army, being ignorant and superstitious, would readily believe in the supernatural nature of her mission, and great energy and valor would result—for a man fights well when he feels that Providence is on his side.

This is the most usual kind of theory in explanation of the facts. But it is not fully satisfactory. How was it ordinary that this simple untutored peasant girl could persuade not only the soldiers, but also the Dauphin of France and the Court, of her Divine appointment? How came she to be given the command of an army? Surely a post of such responsibility and power would not be given to an ignorant girl of eighteen, on the mere strength of her own claim to inspiration. It seems, at least, very improbable.

Now it so happens (although the materialistic school of historians conveniently ignore or belittle it) that there is strong evidence in support of the idea that Jeanne gave the Dauphin some proof of the possession of supernormal faculties. In fact, the evidence is so strong that Mr. Andrew Lang called it "unimpeachable," and Lang did not usually err on the side of credulity in such matters.

Among other curious things, Jeanne seems to have repeated to Charles the words of a prayer which he had made *mentally,* and she also made some kind of clairvoyant discovery of a sword hidden behind the altar of Fierbois church. Schiller's magnificent dramatic poem, "Die Jungfrau von Orleans," although unhistorical in some details, is positive on these points concerning clairvoyance and mind-reading.

Certain other aspects of the story of Jeanne d'Arc should be mentioned, even although these run counter to popular belief. First of all, there is some evidence that Jeanne was connected with fairies, which were also part of witchcraft beliefs. Not far from Domrémy was a tree called "the Fairies' Tree" (*Arbor Fatalium,* or *des Faés*) beside a spring said to cure fevers. The wife of the local mayor stated that he had heard it said that "Jeanne received her mission at the tree of the fairy-ladies" and that St. Katharine and St. Margaret came and spoke to her at the spring beside the fairies' tree. During Jeanne's trial, the fourth article of accusation was that Jeanne was not instructed in her youth in the belief and primitive faith, but was imbued by certain old women in the use of witchcraft, divination, and other superstitious works or magic arts, and that Jeanne herself had said she heard from her godmother and other people of visions and apparitions of fairies.

Moreover, Pierronne, a follower of Jeanne d'Arc, was burnt at the stake as a witch. She stated on oath that God appeared to her in human form and spoke to her as a friend, that he was clothed in a scarlet cap and a long white robe.

It has been suggested that the "Voices" heard by Jeanne may have been those of human beings rather than Christian saints, and Jeanne herself stated "Those of my party know well that the Voice had been sent to me from God, they have seen and known this Voice. My king and many others have also heard and seen the Voices which came to me . . . I saw him [St. Michael] with my bodily eyes as well as I see you." It should also be noted that Jeanne's references to "the King of Heaven" in the original Latin and French were translated with a Christian bias as "Our Lord," and "my Lord" as "Our Saviour." The scholar Margaret A. Murray in her book *The Witch-Cult in Western Europe* (1921) also suggested if Jeanne was a member of a Dianic [witch] cult, the wearing of male clothing may have been for Jeanne an outward sign of that faith, hence the importance attached to it.

In another book, *The God of the Witches* (1931 etc.), Dr. Margaret Murray examined the tradition that Jeanne was not actually burnt at the stake, but survived for a number of years afterwards. The *Chronique de Metz* states: "Then she was sent to the city of Rouen in Normandy, and there was placed on a scaffold and burned in a fire, so it was said, but since then was found to be the contrary." Some of the evidence for this view had been cited earlier by Andrew Lang in his essay 'The False Jeanne d'Arc' in his book *The Valet's Tragedy and Other Studies* (1903).

The period between the trial at Rouen and the Trial of Rehabilitation in 1452–1456 is crucial. Five years after the Rouen trial (i.e. in 1436), the herald-at-arms and Jeanne's brother Jean du Lys announced officially in Orleans that Jeanne was still alive. The city accounts record that on Sunday, August 6, Jean du Lys, brother of "Jehane la Pucelle" [Jeanne the Maid] was in Orleans with letters from his sister to the king. In July 1439, Jeanne's brothers were in Orleans together with their sister Jeanne now married to the Sieur des Armoises (or Harmoises), and the city council presented Jeanne des Armoises with 210 livres parisis "for the good that she did to the said town during the siege of 1429." Accounts are also recorded of the wine merchant and draper who supplied Jeanne with wine and clothing. Her own mother was in Orleans at the time. Moreover the masses which had been celebrated in Orleans for the repose of Jeanne's soul were discontinued after the visit.

It is not conclusive that this Jeanne was an imposter (as Andrew Lang believed), and it seems unlikely that many people in Orleans, including Jeanne's own brothers, could have been deceived, or would have lent themselves to imposture. The riddle of conflicting evidence of burning at the stake or substantiated appearances years later has never been satisfactorily resolved. Many such questions remain unresolved, in spite of various books, mainly by French writers, dealing with the questions at issue. Dr. Margaret Murray researched the subject in great detail and devoted a chapter to it in her book *The God of the Witches.* Earlier French books on the subject include *La Survivance et le Mariage de Jeanne D'Arc* by Grillot de Givry (Paris, n.d.) and *La Legende Detruite; indications pour essayer de suivre l'histoire de Jeanne d'Arc* by Paraf-Javal (Paris, 1929). More recently, another French writer, Pierre de Sermoise, published *Jeanne d'Arc et la Mandragore* (Paris, 1983) has revived the claim that the veiled woman burnt at the stake in the market-place was a prisoner condemned to death as a witch, substituting for France's national heroine.

More speculative is the conclusion of American biologist Robert Greenblatt (reported in 1983) that Jeanne was really a man. It was claimed, however, that two midwives who had examined Jeanne to establish her virginity were astonished to find that she had not reached puberty.

Jehovah's Witnesses

A popular Christian cult, also embracing the Watch Tower Bible and Tract Society, People's Pulpit Association, International Bible Students Association. Although the title "Jehovah's Witnesses" was officially adopted in 1931, the movement stems from the evangelism of "Pastor" C. T. Russell (1870–1916), and for many years followers have been known as "Russellites." After the death of Russell, the new leader was "Judge" Joseph Rutherford (1916–1942).

The basic concept of the movement, arising from interpretation of Biblical prophecy, is that within the present generation the divine forces of King Jesus will defeat and annihilate Satan, and those "witnesses" who have already accepted the creed of the movement will have everlasting life. A popular phrase often used in the literature is "Millions now living will never die." It is also claimed that the second coming took place discreetly in 1914, unnoticed except to the eye of faith.

In spite of a complex religious teaching on the Trinity, sin and hell, the movement has a strong simplistic following, and members have shown courage in refusing to take up arms for any cause. Since the death of Joseph Rutherford, the movement was led by Nathan H. Knorr.

Jensen, Wiers (1866–1925)

Norwegian dramatist who was active in the field of psychical research. Born November 25, 1866, at Bergen, Norway, he was educated at the University of Oslo. In 1894 he married Rigmor Nicolowna Danielsen. In addition to his work as a playwright and an instructor at theaters in Bergen and Oslo, Mr. Jensen was editor of the journal *Norsk Tidsskrift for Psykisk Forksning,* dealing with psychical research, from 1922 to 1925. His play "Anne Pedersdotter" is about a mediumistic woman believed to be a witch.

Mr. Jensen made a special study of the phenomenon of the "**vardøgr**" or psychic **double** known in Norway and Scotland. His experiences and those of other individuals are described by Dr. Thorstein **Wereide** in the article 'Norway's Human Doubles' (*Tomorrow,* vol. 3, No. 2, Winter 1955). After the death of Mr. Jensen, communications apparently from him were received through the automatic writing of the medium Ingeborg Koeber.

Jephson, Ina (died 1961)

British artist and expert in child guidance, who was a member of the council of the Society for Psychical Research, London. Miss Jephson devoted special attention to researches designed to set up repeatable experiments dealing with clairvoyance. Her articles in the *Proceedings* of the S.P.R. included: 'Evidence for Clairvoyance in Card-Guessing' (pt. 109, vol. 38, December 1928), 'Report on a Series of Experiments in Clairvoyance' (with S. G. **Soal** and Theodore **Besterman** (pt. 118, vol. 39, April 1931), 'A Behaviourist Experiment in Clairvoyance' (pt. 128, vol. 41, Jan. 1933). She also contributed a number of useful comments in both *Proceedings* and *Journal* of the S.P.R. as well as book reviews.

Jersey Devil

Strange creature on the borderline between fact and legend, reported from southern New Jersey for over two centuries.

The Jersey Devil appears to have a kangaroo body, bat's wings, pig's feet, dog's head, face of a horse and a forked tail. The creature is said to be anything from eighteen inches to twenty feet in size and impervious to gunshot.

It terrorized inhabitants of the Delaware Valley in 1909 when people stayed home even in daylight and factories and theaters closed. In another famous scare in 1951, the Jersey Devil is supposed to have attacked and mutilated poultry, cats and dogs. The creature has been reported as appearing in thirty different towns, leaving footprints, and there are numerous eyewitness accounts.

Recommended reading:
McCloy, J. F. & Ray Miller, Jr. *The Jersey Devil,* Middle Atlantic Press, Pa., 1976

Jesodoth

According to Jewish mysticism, the angel through which Elohim, the source of knowledge, understanding and wisdom, was imparted to the earth. (See also **Kabala**)

Jesus Freaks

A general term for Christian revivalist cults amongst young people in the 1970s, also known as the "Jesus Revolution." It began in the U.S. and spread to Britain and elsewhere, representing a reaction against orthodox theology and the negative aspects of hippie life.

Typical of the Jesus Freaks movement is the **Children of God** characterized by intense fervor and a communal life-style. It seems that much of the the energy of the Jesus Revolution is a pop style revivalism, fed by the same attitudes of trendy radicalism formerly expressed in political nonconformity but now channelized into religious oversimplifications. Moreover some evangelical cults undoubtedly develop into antisocial fanaticisms. However, it also cannot be denied that the Jesus Revolution contains much sincerity and a desire for valid belief. (See also **Communes; Cults**)

Jet

A substance which is a variety of lignite as anthracite. Its occult virtues were thus described by Pliny (in the translation of Philemon Holland, 1601): "In burning, the perfume thereof chaseth away serpents, and bringeth women again that lie in a traunce by the suffocation or rising of the mother; the said smoke discovereth the falling sicknesse and bewraieth whether a young damsel be a maiden or no; the same being boiled in wine helpeth the toothache, and tempered with wax cureth the swelling glandules named the king's evil. They say that the magicians use this jeat stone much in their sorceries, which they practice by the means of red hot axes, which they call axinomancia, for they affirm that being cast thereupon it will burne and consume, if that ewe desire and wish shall happen accordingly." Jet was known in Prussia as black amber. (See also **Electrum; Gagates**)

Jettatura

The Italian name for the power of the "evil eye." In order to guard against it magicians said that horns must be worn on the body or the phallic gesture of horns be made with the fingers.

Jinn

(Singular *Jinnee*, plural *Jineeyeh*). Arabian spirits, perhaps animistic, but more probably strictly mythological like the Persian *divs*. The jinns were said to have been created out of fire and occupied the earth for several thousand years before Adam. They were perverse and would not reform, although prophets were sent to reclaim them; they were eventually driven from the earth, and took refuge in the outlying islands of the sea.

One of the number named Azazeel (afterwards called Iblees) had been carried off as a prisoner by the angels. He grew up amongst them, and became their chief, but having refused, when commanded, to prostrate himself before Adam, he was degraded to the condition of a sheytân, and become the father of the sheytâns, or devils.

The jinns are not immortal and destined ultimately to die. They eat and drink and propagate their species, live in communities and are ruled over by princes. They can make themselves visible or invisible, and assume the forms of various animals, such as serpents, cats and dogs. There are good jinns and bad jinns. They frequent baths, wells, latrines, ovens, ruined houses, rivers, crossroads and marketplaces. Finally, like the demons of Jewish traditions, they ascend to heaven and learn the future by eavesdropping. But with all their power and knowledge, they are liable to be reduced to obedience by means of **talismans** or occult arts, and become obsequious servants until the spell is broken.

It is far from clear or certain that the jinn of the east was derived from the mythology or philosophy of the west, and the practice of translating the Arabic word jinn by the Latin term "genius" arose more from an apparent resemblance in the names than from any identity in the nature and functions of those imaginary beings. This similarity of name, however, must have been purely accidental, for the Arabs knew little or nothing of the Latin language, and not a single term derived immediately from it. Therefore "dæmon" and not "genius" was the word which they would have used if they had borrowed this part of their creed from the west. "Jinn" appears, moreover, to be a genuine Arabic word, derived from a root signifying "to veil" or "conceal"; it therefore means properly "that which is veiled and cannot be seen."

"In one sense," stated Frús-àbàdí (*Câmús*, vol. 3, p. 611), "the word Jinn signifies any spiritual being concealed from all our senses, and, for that reason, the converse of a material being. Taken in this extensive sense, the word *Jinn* comprehends devils as well as angels, but there are some properties common to both angels and *Jinn*; some peculiar to each. Every angel is a *Jinn*, but every *Jinn* is not an angel. In another sense, this term is applied peculiarly to a particular kind of spiritual being; for such beings are of three kinds; the good, which are angels; the bad, devils; and the intermediate, comprehending both good and bad, who form the class of *Jinn*."

Thus Arabs acknowledged good and bad genii, in that respect agreeing with the Greeks, but differing from the Persians. The genii so long familiarized to European readers by the Arabian Nights, were not the same beings, mentioned by the Arabian lexicographer, but the *Divs* and *Dévatàs* of Indian romance, dressed up in a foreign attire, to please the taste of readers in Persia and Arabia.

The principal differences, therefore, between the genii of the west and the jinns of the east, seem to have been as follows: the genii were deities of an inferior rank, the constant companions and guardians of men, capable of giving useful or prophetic impulses, acting as a species of mediators and messengers between the gods and men. Some were supposed to be friendly, others hostile, and many believed one of each kind to be attached, from his birth, to every mortal. The former was called "Agathodæmon," the latter "Cacodæmon"; and one of the latter who appeared to Cassius was represented as a man of vast stature and of a black hue, whence, no doubt, that color was given, in latter times, to the devil. The good genius prompted men to good, the evil to bad actions. That of each individual was as a shadow of himself. Often he was represented as a serpent. His age also varied. He was generally crowned with a chaplet of plane leaves. In coins of Trajan and Hadrian the genius placed a *patera* with his right hand on an altar, and held a sort of scourge in his left. His sacrifices were wholly bloodless, consisting of wine and flowers, and the person who performed the oblation was the first to taste the cup. He was adored with prostrations, particularly on the birthday, which was placed under his especial care.

The Roman men swore by their Genius, the women by their Juno. The genius of the reigning Prince was an oath of extraordinary solemnity. There were local as well as individual genii, concerning whom many particulars may be found in *De Idolatria liber* of Dionysius Vossius (editions 1633, 1641).

The jinns, on the contrary, who seem to be the lineal descendants of the *Dévatés* and *Rakshasas* of the Hindu mythology, were never worshiped by the Arabs, nor considered as anything more than the agents of the Deity. Since the establishment of Mohammedanism, indeed, they have been described as invisible spirits, and their feats and deformities which figure in romance are as little implicitly believed by Asiatics as the tales of King Arthur's Round Table are by Westerners. Their existence as superhuman beings was maintained by the Moslem doctors, but that had little connection with their character and functions as delineated by poets.

Jinnistan

An imaginary country which, according to a popular belief among the ancient Persians, was the residence of the **jinn** who had submitted to King Solomon.

Jobson, Mary (c. 1840)

Nineteenth-century psychic of Bishop Weatmouth, England. Her strange case was recorded in a little book by Dr. Reid Clanny, *A Faithful Record of the Miraculous Case of Mary Jobson* (1841).

At the age of 13, in November 1839, Mary was taken ill and had convulsions for eleven weeks. The first time she was seized her mother heard three loud knocks in the sick room. The knocks repeated themselves, the noise of violent scratching was heard and the door opened and shut with violence four or five times.

While in a helpless and apparently hopeless condition, the girl heard voices and occasionally made accurate predictions. In May 1840, she foretold an attempt on the life of Queen Victoria. The voices claimed to come from the Virgin Mary, from apostles and martyrs. Dr. R. B. Embleton once heard the voice begin: "I am the Lord thy God which brought thee out of the land of Egypt."

Dr. Drury, Dr. Beattie and many other witnesses testified to a series of occult phenomena. Water appeared from nowhere and was sprinkled in the room, an astronomical design in green, yellow and orange colors appeared on the ceiling and music was constantly heard. This latter phenomena was confirmed by her governess, Elizabeth Guantlett, and by Dr. Drury. He stated: "On listening I distinctly heard most exquisite music which continued during the time I might count a hundred. This she told me she often heard." The girl alternately became blind, deaf and dumb. After eight months of unaccountable illness she was mysteriously cured.

Jogand-Pagès, Gabriel (1854–c. 1906)

Nineteenth-century French journalist, who, under the name of "Léo Taxil" perpetrated an extraordinary and prolonged hoax in which he claimed to have exposed a Satanist activity within **Freemasonry.** The motives of Jogand are not entirely clear even today, but it seems that his hoax was also designed to embarrass the Roman Catholic Church.

In 1892, a book entitled *Le Diable du XIXe Siecle* was published in Paris, attributed to "**Dr. Bataille.**" For a time, the book was thought to be the work of Dr. Charles Hacks, who contributed a preface entitled 'Revelations of an Occultist.' Dr. Hacks was a real, although shadowy figure. It was not until five years later that the hoax was revealed by Jogand himself.

The groundwork for the hoax began as early as 1885 when "Léo Taxil," who edited an anti-clerical newspaper, began to publish exposés of Freemasonry, claiming that there were lodges that practiced rites deriving from Manichaean heresy. With the publication of "Dr. Bataille's" book, Jogand had invented a sinister High Priestess of Satanic Freemasons. She was "Diana Vaughan," said to be a descendent of the seventeenth-century alchemist Thomas Vaughan. She had been chosen as a high priestess of Lucifer to overthrow Christianity and win over the world for Satanism. Diana was supposed to head a feminine cult of Freemasonry named Palladism. Periodicals claiming to emanate from the Palladium were published by Jogand.

His next audacious stroke was to announce that Diana Vaughan had been converted from Satanism to the true Roman Catholic faith! Her *Memories d'une Ex-Palladist* (1895–97) attracted enormous interest and enthusiasm. They were read by Pope Leo XIII, together with a short devotional work supposedly composed by Diana, and His Holiness responded with a Papal benediction. By now, it seemed that Jogand himself had repented of his former Freethinking, and created a saintly impression. He was received in private audience by the Pope, who had expressed approval of his anti-Masonic writings, and an anti-Masonic congress was summoned in 1887 at Trent, famous for its sixteenth-century Council.

By now, there was great pressure for Diana Vaughan herself to be produced from the unnamed convent where Jogand claimed she was residing. It was announced that she would appear on Easter Monday 1897 and give a press conference in Paris.

Instead, Jogand himself appeared, and calmly announced that he had invented the whole conspiracy! He claimed that he himself had written Diana Vaughan's confessions, but asserted that "Diana" actually existed. She was his secretary, he said, and it had appealed to her sense of humor to be involved.

After this astounding denoument, Jogand calmly left the hall by a side door, and enjoyed a coffee and cognac in a nearby cafe, while something like a riot erupted in the lecture hall and the police were called in.

The whole affair was so extraordinary and deceived so many people, including exalted ecclesiastics, that much confusion still remains about Jogand's motives. Clearly he was a great liar, and even some details of his brazen confession are suspect. In general, he seems to have developed the hoax to discredit both the Freemasons and the Catholic Church, but there also seem elements of personal neurosis. Jogand came from a deeply religious family, but rebelled against his father's authority. As a young man, Jogand early came into contact with Freemasonry and revolutionary circles, for which he was punished by being sent to a special school.

He developed an aversion to authority and became a freethinker, later earning his living as a journalist concerned with freethinking publications.

Many questions remain unanswered about his great hoax as "Leo Taxil." The book by "Dr. Bataille" is a substantial work, and some of its revelations appear to be an imaginative embroidering of known facts. It is undoubtedly true that there were some Rosicrucian elements in certain Masonic temples, and some of Taxil's inventions are not unlike the claims made against the **Templars.** Undoubtedly other individuals were concerned in the hoax, including Dr. Hacks and someone willing to pose as "Diana Vaughan" for photographs, and for correspondence which was unlikely to have been written by Jogand. Perhaps he was aware of **devil-worship** actually in existence in nineteenth-century Paris, as described in the writings of J.K. Huysman and Jules Bois. At all events, his final confessions of an immense fraud against the Catholic Church created a unique scandal, with repercussions in anti-Masonry for a long time afterwards. (See also **Devil worship;** Diana **Vaughan**)

Recommended reading:

Bataille, Dr. *Le Diable au XIXe Siècle,* Paris, 1892

Bataille, Dr. *Memoire à l'Adresse des Members du Congrès de Trent,* 1897

Lea, H. C. *Léo Taxil, Diana Vaughan et l'Eglise romaine,* Paris, 1901

Vaughan, Diana. *Mémoires d'une Ex-Palladiste, parfaite Initiée, Indépendante,* Paris (1895–97)

Waite, A. E. *Devil Worship in France,* London, 1896

Johannine Daist Communion

Group deriving from the life and teachings of American mystic Da Free **John** (born Franklin Albert Jones, known for some years as "Bubba Free John").

The Johannine Daist Communion comprises various sections. The Laughing Man Institute is the public education division, also serving beginning students of what is described as "the Way of Radical Understanding or Divine Ignorance."

The Free Communion Church comprises maturing practitioners engaged in practices relevant to "the Way of Divine Communion" or, at a higher level, of "the Way of Faith or the Way of Insight."

The Advaitayana Buddhist Order consists of mature practitioners who practice the first or the second stage of "the Perfect Practice," i.e., "Be Consciousness" or who, in the second stage are engaged in "the contemplation of Consciousness."

The Crazy Wisdom Fellowship consists of free renunciates who have "Realized the seventh stage of life or Enlightenment."

These various organizations stem from the entry of Da Free John into the "hermitage phase" of his work. Publications include numerous books by Da Free John issued by the Dawn Horse Press.

The address of the Johannine Daist Community and

the Dawn Horse Press is: P.O. Box 3680, Clearlake, California 95422.

Johannites

A mystical sect of prerevolutionary Russia, founded on tenets of Father John of Kronstadt. They published a periodical and pursued their propaganda by means of itinerant pamphlet sellers. They were said to abduct Jewish children and because of this rumor they sometimes came under police supervision. On various occasions they unsuccessfully forecast the date of the Last Judgment. They declared in Father John's lifetime that all the powers of heaven had descended into Kronstadt and were personified in the entourage of Father John.

They exhorted all believers to make confession to Father John, who alone could rescue sinners from the depths of hell. The orthodox clergy would not know the Lord, but Father John would gather together in Kronstadt 144,000 of the blessed, and then "leave the earth." Another affirmation of theirs was that all children who were newborn were "little devils," who must be "stamped out" immediately after birth.

The Johannites urged people to sell all their possessions and send the proceeds to Father John, or entrust them to the keeping of the pamphlet sellers. It seems, however, that Father John was unaware of the abuse of his name, and on one occasion, in reply to a telegram from Bishop Nikander, of Perm, he strongly repudiated any connection with certain Johannite propagandists in the Perm Government.

Another well-known sect of Johannites in seventeenth-century Holland was a less rigid branch of the Mennonites. They were first known as Anabaptists, but this name became distasteful in view of the excesses of the Anabaptists under such fanatics as John of Leyden, and in 1537 the priest Menno Simonis gave his name to the movement. The Johannite branch was also known as "Waterlanders," from the name of the Waterland district in North Holland where they lived. Other Mennonite sects emigrated to America.

John, Bubba Free (*See* **John, Da Free**)

John, Da Free (1939–   )

Name assumed by Franklin Albert Jones, contemporary American mystic, spiritual head of the **Johannine Daist Communion** concerned with spiritual enlightenment.

Jones was born November 3, 1939. According to his own account, he was aware of a sense of joy and light illuminating his head and heart as a baby. As he grew up, he became specially attracted to speculations about the nature of consciousness and reality, although these were often overshadowed by thirty years of ordinary life, including a period at Columbia University studying philosophy, and graduate study in English at Stanford University, California, where he was incidentally involved as a volunteer in drug experiments with mescaline, LSD and psilocybin. On several occasions he claimed to have experienced the arousal of energy at the base of the spine, clearly a manifestation of the traditional mystical Hindu force known as **Kundalini.**

He was drawn to Eastern spiritual concepts and studied

the lives and teachings of such individuals as Sri **Ramana Maharshi,** Sri **Ramakrishna,** and Sri **Aurobindo** and **J. Krishnamurti.** He moved to New York, where he had a vision that he would find a teacher at an oriental art store. This proved to be "Rudi," a disciple of Swami **Muktananda,** and he taught Jones a system of Kundalini Yoga which resulted in further experiences of higher consciousness. At the request of Rudi, Jones spent a year studying at a Lutheran seminary in Philadelphia. He also spent several months in a Scientology group, but found that this did not enhance his experiences and left. He paid visits to India, where he had personal contact with Swami Muktananda who bestowed the name "Dhyananda" (roughly "bliss of meditation") upon him and gave him a letter confirming his ability to initiate others in meditation.

The relationship of Jones to Swami Muktananda as explained in Jones' autobiography *The Knee of Listening* in 1972 is currently revised in a new edition prepared eleven years later. Muktananda's letter is retranslated to indicate that the Swami confirmed that Jones had attained "the highest human condition" or "yogic liberation" and was not simply a promising student of meditation who had not yet attained the highest experience. At the time, Jones certainly felt that he was not wholly in agreement with the traditional pattern of spiritual seeking, guru-pupil relationship and spiritual realization as exemplified by Swami Muktananda and others.

After his return to the U.S. in August 1969, Jones spent several months investigating problems of spiritual consciousness. A supportive figure at this period was his wife Nina, whom he had met in Scientology in 1968 who, together with Patricia Morley became early devotees. In 1970, the three went to India to the Muktananda Ashram where Jones had further spiritual experiences and visions but seemed distant from Swami Muktananda. The trio did not stay there, but moved on in a pilgrimage that took them to Israel, Greece, Italy, France, England and Spain, visiting religious sites, eventually returning to the U.S. and settling in Los Angeles.

Jones established his own ashram community as the Dawn Horse Communion, based on the traditional Hindu concept of imparting Kundalini experience and spiritual awareness, but later emphasized the paradoxical philosophy that seeking for spiritual enlightenment could actually be an obstacle to discovering it. In his ashram life he was then known as "Bubba Free John" ("Bubba" being a childhood name). He has dramatized the necessity for freedom from dependence either on the guru, a teaching or a particular ashram sanctuary, by moving around to different addresses. He distinguished four stages of development: the way of Divine Communion, the way of Relational Enquiry, the way of Re-cognition (a rediscovery of reality) and the way of Radical Intuition.

More recently he has dropped the prefix "Bubba" and is now known as Da Free John, the name "Da" presenting itself to him in a vision. He no longer teaches Kundalini Yoga in any form, but rather emphasizes transmission of awareness between himself and devotees, at the same time publishing a number of books relating to his concepts of radical transcendentalism. A considerable organization has grown up around him under the present name of the Johannine Daist Communion, with the Laughing Man Institute division, the Free Communion Church, the Advaitayana Buddhist Order and the Crazy Wisdom Fellowship. Publications are issued by the Dawn Horse Press, P.O. Box 3680, Clearlake, California 95422. The books of Da Free John include: *The Knee of Listening* (1972 etc.), *The Method of the Siddhas* (1973), *The Heart of the Ribhu Gita as Taught by Sri Ramana Maharshi* (1973), *The Spiritual Instructions of Saint Seraphim of Sarov* (1973), *No Remedy: An Introduction to the Life & Practices of the Spiritual Community of Bubba Free John* (1975), *Conscious Exercise & the Transcendental Sun* (1975), *Love of the Two-Armed Form* (1978), *The Yoga of Consideration & The Way That I Teach* (1978), *The Enlightenment of the Whole Body* (1978), *The Eating Gorilla Comes in Peace; the Transcendental Principle of Life Applied to Diet & the Regenerative Discipline of True Health* (1979), *Garbage and the Goddess* (1980), *Scientific Proof of the Existence of God Will Soon Be Announced by the White House* (1980), *The Lion Sutra; On the Sacred Ordeal of Keeping Attention in the Sacrifice* (1981), *The Bodily Location of Happiness* (1982), *Nirvanasara* (1982), *Crazy Da Must Sing, Inclined to His Weaker Side* (1982).

The paradoxes of individual and universal consciousness, spiritual striving versus actual realization, intellectualism versus experience, empirical versus higher reality have been exhaustively dealt with in traditional Hindu Vedanta and Yoga philosophy, in particular the traps of the guru-chela relationship as both liberation or enslavement. Da Free John has read widely and has been greatly impressed by such sages as Sri Ramana Maharshi, with whom he claimed affinity of experience. Many of the concepts presented in his books read like a restatement of other writers, and ideas of the evolutionary nature of the psycho-physiological mechanism of human beings will be familiar to readers of the books of Pandit Gopi Krishna dealing with Kundalini. Da Free John is a colorful writer and his style varies from a highly complex intellectual presentation to a Zen-like humorous demolition of the conventions of ideas and intellectualism. This ambivalence can be confusing for the neophyte, producing a kind of semantic fog, whilst for Da Free John himself, there is a certain irony that his earlier misgivings about the conventional concepts of "spiritual life," "seeking," "pathways" and guru-chela relationship, should result in a community where he himself is venerated as "the Master" and "My Lord" with offerings of fruit and flowers from adoring devotees, just like the conventional Eastern guru. In his book *The Knee of Listening* he had stated ". . . I sorely needed to get out of the spiritual game."

There can be no doubt, however, of his sincerity and the reality of his Kundalini experiences culminating in higher consciousness. As such experiences became more widely known and widespread in occurrence, it will be necessary to exercise great discrimination in evaluating such phenomena and their meaning, in particular assessing grades of transcendence and their applicability to empirical reality and individual consciousness. Much confusion may be avoided by reading various writers on the subject of Kundalini Yoga and spiritual realization, both Eastern and Western. The books of Pandit **Gopi Krishna** may provide a valuable starting point.

"John King"

Claimed spirit entity manifesting at many Spiritualist seances. (See **"King, John"**)

John of Nottingham

Famous occult magician of fourteenth-century England. (See **England**)

John XXII, Pope (1249-1334)

Jacques Duèse, subsequently Pope John XXII, was born at Cahors in France. His parents were in affluent circumstances, and it has even been suggested that they belonged to the *noblesse.* Jacques was educated first at a Dominican priory in his native village, and afterwards at Montpellier, while subsequently he proceeded to Paris, where he studied both law and medicine.

Leaving the Sorbonne, he was still at a loss to know what profession to follow, but, chancing to become intimate with Bishop Louis (a son of Charles II, King of Naples) the young man decided to enter the church, being doubtless prompted to this step by the conviction that his new friend's influence would help him forward in the clerical career.

Nor was the future pontiff disappointed herein, for in the year 1300, at the instance of the Neapolitan sovereign, he was elevated to the episcopal see of Fréjus, while in 1308 he was appointed Chancellor of Naples. He soon showed himself a man of no mean ability in ecclesiastical affairs, and in 1310 Pope Clement V saw fit to summon him to Avignon, being anxious to consult him on the question of the legality of suppressing the **Templars** and also whether to condemn the memory of Boniface VIII. Jacques was in favor of suppressing the Templars but rejected condemnation of Boniface. In 1312 Jacques was made Bishop of Porto, and four years later was elected to the pontifical crown and scepter.

Thenceforth he lived always at Avignon, but his life was by no means a quiet or untroubled one. Early in his reign the throne of Germany became vacant. Louis of Bavaria and Frederick of Austria both contended for it and Jacques gave great offense by supporting the claims of the latter, while at a later date he raised a storm by preaching a somewhat heterodox sermon, its purport being that the souls of those who have died in a state of grace go straight into Abraham's bosom and do not enjoy the beatific vision of the Lord till after the Resurrection and the Last Judgment. This doctrine was hotly opposed by many clerics, notably Thomas of England, who had the courage to preach against it openly at Avignon, and so great was the disfavor which John incurred that, in fact, for several years after his death he was widely regarded as Anti-Christ.

Jacques has frequently been credited with avarice, and it is true that he made stupendous efforts to raise money, imposing numerous taxes unheard of before his régime. Indeed, he manifested considerable ingenuity in this relation, and so the tradition that he dabbled in hermetic philosophy (**alchemy**) may be founded on fact. It must be conceded, on the one hand, that in the course of his reign he issued a stringent bull against alchemists, but then, this was directed rather against the charlatans of the craft than against those who were seeking the **philosopher's stone** with real earnestness, and with the aid of scientific knowledge.

It seems possible that Jacques sent forth this mandate largely with a view to blinding those who had charged him with essaying the practice at issue himself. Be that as it may, it is probable that he believed in magic and was interested in science. His credulity as regards the former is indicated by his bringing a charge of sorcery against Géraud, Bishop of Cahors, while his scientific predilections are evinced by the fact that he kept up a laboratory in the palace at Avignon, and spent much time therein.

Doubtless some of this time was given to physiological and pathological studies, for various works of a medical nature are ascribed to Jacques, in particular a collection of prescriptions, a treatise on diseases of the eye, and another on the formation of the fetus. But it may well be that the prelate's activities in his laboratory were also bestowed in some measure on alchemistic researches, and this theory is buttressed by his having been a friend of **Arnaldus de Villanova.** More significantly, among the writings attributed to Jacques is the alchemical work *L'Art Transmutatoire,* published at Lyons in 1557. Moreover, the pontiff left behind him on his death a vast sum of money and a mass of priceless jewels, and it was commonly asserted among the alchemists of the day that these and also two hundred huge ingots had all been manufactured by the deceased. The story of the unbounded wealth amassed in this way gradually blossomed and bore fruit, and one of Jacques' medieval biographers credited him with having concocted a quantity of gold equivalent to a million dollars.

Johnson, Alice (186?-1940)

Prominent figure in British psychical research in the early period. Miss Johnson was organizing secretary of the **Society for Psychical Research,** London, from 1903-16, research officer from 1908-16, and editor of the Society's *Proceedings* from 1899-1916. Born in Cambridge, England, she was educated at Newham College, Cambridge University (Bathurst student 1882); from 1884-90 was a demonstrator in animal morphology at the Balfour Laboratory.

She became interested in psychical research through her association with Mrs. Henry **Sidgwick** and became her personal secretary. Miss Johnson participated in the first sittings in England with the American medium Mrs. Leonore **Piper** in 1889, and assisted in the SPR Census of Hallucinations between 1889-94.

In 1901 she collaborated with Richard **Hodgson** on the preparation of the Frederic **Myers** book *Human Personality and Its Survival of Bodily Death,* published after Myers' death.

Miss Johnson also reported on the "SPR" group of mediums investigated in connection with automatic phenomena (writing and trance messages). Her articles in the SPR *Proceedings* included: 'Report of Some Recent Sittings for Physical Phenomena in America' (1908-09), 'On the Automatic Writing of Mrs. Holland' (1908-09), 'The Education of the Sitter' (1908-09), 'Supplementary Notes on Mrs. Holland's Scripts' (1910), 'Second Report on Mrs. Holland's Scripts' (1910), 'Third Report on Mrs. Holland's Scripts' (1910), 'Mrs. Henry Sidgwick's Work in Psychical Research' (1936-37). She died January 13, 1940.

Johnson, Douglas

Modern British medium who has investigated haunted houses in the U.S. and appeared on television programs.

He was born in London, England before World War I. His powers were evident at an early age. He has given many clairvoyant sittings at the **College of Psychic Studies,** London, but also spent time in the U.S., where he has worked with Dr. W. J. **Roll,** Mrs. Eileen **Garrett,** Dr. Thelma Moss, Dr. Stanley Krippner and other parapsychologists.

Johnson, Mrs. Roberts (c. 1927)

Direct voice medium of Stockton-on-Tees, England. Her powers developed after a sitting with Mrs. Thomas **Everitt.** Her principal **control** claimed to be David **Duguid,** the famous trance painting medium of Glasgow.

A sitter at a seance held March 5, 1918, reported in *Light* as follows: "I have never had two sittings alike with Mrs. Johnson. They are marked each time by some different characteristic. On this occasion, before each new speaker used the trumpet, I saw a faintly-luminous figure moving about. Then, again, all the voices were louder than is usual in ordinary conversation, so much so, that Mrs. Johnson on more than one occasion asked the male speakers to moderate their tone; otherwise neighbours and pedestrians outside might be attracted by the unusual noise. Most of our spirit visitors remained throughout the sitting, and verbally called our attention to the fact. This was the best direct-voice sitting which, so far, it has been my good fortune to attend."

Sir Arthur Conan Doyle remarked on her remarkable power with direct-voice phenomena but commented on the non-religious atmosphere of her sittings with humorous spirit communicators.

Johnson, Raynor C(arey) (1901–)

Master of Queen's College, University of Melbourne, Australia, author, and writer on parapsychology. Born April 5, 1901, at Leeds, England, he studied at Bradford Grammar School, Balliol College, Oxford, University of London (B.A., M.A., D.Sc.). He was also awarded an Hon. D.Sc. by University of Melbourne. In 1925 he married Mary Robina Buchanan.

He has been successively lecturer in physics, Queen's University of Belfast, lecturer in physics, King's College, University of London, Master of Queen's College, University of Melbourne 1934 onwards. He has been a member of the Society for Psychical Research, London. In addition to his books on physics, Dr. Johnson has also written works dealing with aspects of parapsychology: *The Imprisoned Splendour* (1953; 1971), *Psychical Research* (1955), *Nurslings of Immortality* (1957), *Watcher on the Hills* (1959), *The Spiritual Path* (1971).

Joire, Dr. Paul (1856– ?)

Professor at the Psycho-physiological Institute of Paris, France, President of the Societé Universelle d'Etudes Psychiques, distinguished French psychical researcher, whose studies in hypnotism and in the obscure region of exteriorized sensibility were especially noteworthy.

His book *Psychical and Supernormal Phenomena* (1916) was an important contribution to psychical literature. Other books published by Dr. Joire but not translated into English included: *Précis historique et pratique de Neuro-Hypnologie* (1892), *Traité de Graphologie scientifique* (1906), *Traité de l'Hypnotisme expérimental et thérapeutique* (1908).

He invented a device named the **Sthenometer** to demonstrate the existence of a force which seemed to emanate from the nervous system which was capable of acting at a distance and causing movement of objects without contact. (See also **Exteriorization of Sensitivity**)

Jones, Charles Stansfeld (1886–1950)

British occultist and author who lived in Canada and assumed the magical name of "Frater Achad." Jones was an accountant in Vancouver when he became a disciple of occultist Aleister **Crowley,** who considered him his "magical son," as prophesied in Crowley's *The Book of the Law.* Crowley believed that Jones had discovered a Kabalistic key to *The Book of the Law.* As a disciple, Jones progressed to the grade of Master of the Temple in Crowley's secret order A.·.A.·. There is a record of his achievement in Liber CLXV, partially published in Crowley's journal **The Equinox** (vol. III, p. 127).

In attempting a magickal rebirth as "Babe of the Abyss," Jones had a nervous breakdown. He returned briefly to England and joined the Roman Catholic Church, hoping to convert other Catholics to Crowley's Law of Thelema, but upon returning to Vancouver wandered around the city wearing only a raincoat, which he threw off in public, crying that he had renounced all the veils of illusion.

After his recovery, Jones became hostile to Crowley who had expelled him from his Order. In spite of his eccentricities, Jones wrote some remarkable books on occultism, including *Q.B.L. or the Bride's Reception* (1923) and *The Anatomy of the Body of God* (1925). The latter work (published Chicago, Collegium ad Spiritum Sanctum), attempts a three-dimensional projection of the Kabalistic "Tree of Life." (See also **Kabala**)

Jones, Franklin Albert (1939–)

Former name of contemporary American mystic and spiritual teacher later known as "Bubba Free John, head of the **Dawn Horse Communion,** now known as Da Free John,** head of the **Johannine Daist Communion.**

Jones, Marc Edmund (1888–)

Well-known writer on occult and astrological subjects. Born in St. Louis, Missouri, October 1, 1888, he was educated privately. From 1911–18 he was a pioneer motion picture writer, author of nearly 200 original screen plays. He was ordained a minister of the United Presbyterian Church and also founded the **Sabian Assembly** (concerned with the Solar Mysteries).

He was founder of the Photoplay Authors' League (later renamed Screen Writers' Guild of the Authors' League of America). He was a member of The Writers' Club, New York, the Writers (Hollywood), Playwrights Club (New York). From 1922 onwards, he was a freelance writer and lecturer on metaphysical subjects. He was founder editor of the *Message,* to which he contributed regularly from 1926 onwards. He was an active proponent of **New Thought,** and was responsible for two weekly students' lessons of 1,200 words each prior to 1927, later conducting 36 correspondence courses averaging 40,000 words each.

His books included: *The New Genesis* (1915), *Key Truths of Occult Philosophy* (1948), *The Ritual of Living* (1930, later expanded as *The Sabian Manual,* 1957), *How to Learn Astrology* (1941; 1969), *The Guide to Horoscope Interpretation* (1941), *Problem Solving By Horary Astrology* (1943; 1971), *Astrology, How and Why It Works* (1945; 1969), *Gandhi Lives* (1948), *George Sylvester Morris* (1948), *Sabian Symbols in Astrology* (1935), *Essentials of Astrological Analysis* (1960), *Scope of Astrological Prediction* (1969), *The Sabian Book* (1973), *Mundane Perspectives in Astrology* (1974), *The Marc Edmund Jones 500* (consists of 500 horoscope sessions presented to students of the Sabian Assembly) (1977).

Jones, Rev. Jim (1931–1978)

Charismatic leader of the **Peoples Temple** cult of San Francisco, Los Angeles and Guyana, which made headline news with the horrific murders of Congressmen Leo J. Ryan, newsmen Gregory Robinson, Robert Brown and Don Harris, followed by mass suicide of the Guyana cult and its founder in a death ritual of over 900 men, women and children.

James Warren Jones, popularly known as Jim Jones, was born in Lynn, Indiana, in 1931. He became involved with evangelism while still in his teens, and gave a sermon at the age of 14. At school, he planned to study for a medical career, but soon after his marriage to Marceline Baldwin in 1949, he became a Christian pastor. He founded the Community Union Church, and in 1956 the Peoples Temple, later affiliated with the Disciples of Christ mission.

Jones was much impressed by the career of the black evangelist **Father Divine** (died 1965) who had a reputation for miracle working. Jones organized sensational "faith healing" services at which individuals were supposed to be cured of heart conditions, rheumatoid arthritis, calcified joints, cancer and many other ailments. Former associates have stated that these miracles were deliberate fakes, and they were eventually discontinued. In building up a career as a charismatic leader, Jones also carefully contrived a front of social welfare and sponsorship of liberal causes, eventually enlisting the support of many politicians. Although Jones used evangelical Christianity to develop his powerful following, he was privately obsessed by the goal of achieving social change through his own somewhat naive brand of Marxist philosophy.

By 1971 he had attracted thousands of followers and opened a successful Peoples Temple in San Francisco and later in Los Angeles. From 1973 onwards he established an agricultural commune in Guyana, planned as a socialist utopia. In 1977 he moved to his Jonestown commune together with large numbers of his San Francisco congregation.

Soon there were rumors of bizarre activities of the cult and its founder, with stories of armed guards, brutal punishments, rehearsals for mass suicide as a "loyalty" ordeal, and mysterious deaths. After persistent complaints that cult members were prevented from leaving Jonestown, Congressman Leo J. Ryan led an on-the-spot investigation with pressmen and a newsreel team.

On November 18, 1978, the party was attacked by cult members before boarding their plane at the airstrip near Jonestown. Ryan was killed, together with press photographer Gregory Robinson, NBC cameraman Robert Brown, NBC news correspondent Don Harris, and cult members trying to leave Jonestown. In late afternoon the same day,

the Peoples Temple cult of Guyana ended in an incredible mass suicide of over 900 men, women and children. The method of self-destruction was a cyanide laced Kool-Aid drink, although there were a few cases of cultists killed by shooting or other violent means. Some escaped into the jungle. Jim Jones died with his congregation, but his son Stephen missed the mass suicide because he was playing in a basketball game in Georgetown at the time. In a press interview he later declared that there had been "a growing paranoia in the group."

After the incredible tragedy of Jonestown, journalists and psychologists have attempted to explain the enigma of the Rev. Jim Jones and his cult. The dominant factors appear to have been Jones's intensely disturbed personality, in which a genuine desire for social justice and a simplistic view of life was associated with egocentricity and sex hangups. In the supercharged emotional atmosphere of Jones's cult, his followers became increasingly identified with their leader's paranoia. Former associates of Jones have testified to his ambiguous sexual drives. Wayne Pietila, a former bodyguard, stated that Jones "had a voracious appetite for both men and women." Fannie Mobley, a church member until 1976, stated that Jones "would talk for hours about sex, about how good he was and how women should think he was making love to them, not their husbands . . ." and that "He told everybody not to have sex until they got to the Promised Land [Guyana]."

The mixture of disordered sexual drives, desire to shine as a messiah and alternating megalomania and guilt feelings is characteristic of many cult leaders, and is often associated with real or fake paranormal phenomena. The danger of such unstable personalities gaining power over their followers is intensified by present day mass media susceptibility and the desire for simplistic instant solutions to social, personal and mystical problems. (See also **Communes; Cults**)

Jonson, Mr & Mrs. J. B. (c. 1923)

Celebrated American mediums of Toledo, who later moved to Altadena, California. Jonson was a painter and paper-hanger who, jointly with his wife, sat for **materialization** and **direct voice** phenomena. Homer Taylor Yaryan, chief of the secret police under the Grant government, watched the mediums carefully for years and assured Admiral Usborne Moore that they were genuine. The Admiral himself in his book *Glimpses of the Next State* (1911) reached the same conclusion. He saw 15–16 phantoms in circumstances which apparently excluded confederacy emerge from the cabinet in a single sitting. Some of them dematerialized into the floor and it was possible to follow their heads with the eye until the shoulders were level with the carpet; some came too far out in the light, doubled up and collapsed, some dissipated after falling over on one side.

Each phantom had a distinctive movement of the limbs and carriage by which, in successive seances, they were identified. They were mostly etherealizations, the faces and heads were alone tangible. The Admiral put his arms around the waist of a phantom relative and found nothing.

A white-robed figure, with a bright silver band on her forehead and bracelets and jewels on her arm, gave her name as "Cleopatra, Queen of Egypt," another form as "Josephine." Apparently "Cleopatra" made a hit with Jonson's Indian control, "Grayfeather," for he declared: "I like that squaw, she is a very nice squaw."

In 1923 the Jonsons were visited in California by Sir Arthur Conan **Doyle,** who was greatly impressed by their materialization phenomena, which he believed genuine. He described the seance in his book *Our Second American Adventure* (1923).

The Jonsons, however, did not live up to the favorable reputation which the experiments of Yaryan and Admiral Moore established for them and in view of the experiences of J. Hewat **McKenzie** in Toledo in 1917, those who accused them of fraud apparently had grounds to rely on. "I proved on this visit," wrote McKenzie in *Psychic Science* (April 1927) "that the daughter of the Jonsons' masqueraded as a spirit, and would appear from the back room to dance as a materialised form in highly illuminated garments, the illumination for these being produced in an adjoining room with the help of magnesium wire used on clothing impregnated with phosphorescent paint. The smoke from the magnesium wire was seen by me in clouds in the room where she danced, and my sense of smell also recognized the well-known odour. Here we have a striking instance of what the abuse of spirit intercourse may lead to."

For the favorable evidence of Homer T. Yaryan, see his narrative 'An Investigator's Experience of Materialization Phenomena' in *Psychic Science* (October 1926), which includes remarkable photographs of claimed materializations.

Jonsson, Olaf

Famous Swedish-born psychic who took part in telepathic experiments with Apollo astronaut Edgar **Mitchell** during Mitchell's flight to the moon. Jonsson trained as an engineer in Sweden, qualifying in 1941. He worked with various companies and in 1946 was appointed a design engineer at the Monarch Motorcycle factory in Varberg. At this time, his psychic gifts (which had been evident in childhood) became more widely manifested and he became known as the "psychic engineer" through his demonstrations of **clairvoyance, telepathy** and **psychokinesis.** He was tested by parapsychologists in Sweden and Denmark. From 1949 onwards, he visited South America, Canada, China, Japan and Australia, studying paranormal phenomena at first hand amongst primitive peoples.

In 1953, Dr. J. B. **Rhine** of Duke University invited Jonsson to come to the U.S., where he was tested by parapsychologists in such areas as telepathy, clairvoyance, precognition, psychometry and psychokinesis. His notably successful card-guessing led to him being chosen to participate in the Apollo 14 tests of ESP with Edgar Mitchell during the three days before and after the moon landing. The tests were described in detail by Mitchell in *Journal of Parapsychology* (June 1971). The results indicated scoring significantly above chance expectation. However, for a skeptical view of claimed success, see the chapter 'ESP in Outer Space' in *Mediums, Mystics & The Occult* by Milbourne Christopher (1975).

Amongst other psychic achievements, Jonsson is said to have elucidated thirteen murder cases after visiting the scenes of the crimes, and located three missing women. He

was also supposed to have predicted accurately the time and place of death of Nasser and De Gaulle.

Recommended reading:

Steiger, Brad. *The Psychic Feats of Olaf Jonsson,* Popular Library paperback, 1971

Jordan, Pacual (1902–   )

Physicist, who was concerned with the relationship of physics, psychology and parapsychology. Born October 18, 1902, at Hanover, Germany, he studied at Göttingen University (Ph.D. 1924). He was professor of theoretical physics at University of Rostock from 1929–44, and professor of theoretical physics at the University of Hamburg. He won the Max Planck Medal for his work in physics in 1942. He was a member of the International Conference on Philosophy and Parapsychology, St. Paul de Vence, France, 1954.

He conducted joint research with Dr. Niels Bohr and Dr. Werner Heisenberg in quantum mechanics. He published *Verdrängung und Komplementarität* (Repression and Complementarity, 1951), and lectured on 'New Trends in Physics and their Relation to Parapsychology' at the International Conference on Philosophy and Parapsychology, France, 1954. This lecture was published in *Parapsychology Foundation Newsletter* (July-August 1955). Dr. Jordan also contributed on the subject of 'Quantum Field Theory' to the *Journal* of the Society for Psychical Research.

Journal du Magnetisme et du Psychisme Experimental

Monthly publication founded by Baron **Du Potet** in 1845, and edited by Henri **Durville,** as the official organ of the Société Psychiques Internationale. It continued publication until 1861.

Journal of Automatic Writing

Published by Spiritual Press, Box 464, Don Mills, Ontario M3C 2T3 Canada.

Journal of Borderland Research

Bi-monthly publication of **Borderland Sciences Research Foundation,** concerned with such subjects as psychical research, psychic surgery, radionics, radiesthesia and related occult topics. Address: P.O. Box 548, Vista, California 92083.

Journal of Holistic Health

Annual publication dealing with **New Age** teachings of a comprehensive and integrated approach to life, combining diet, environmental concern, personal responsibility and spiritual growth. Contributors have included Pir Vilayat Inayat Khan, Dr. Olga **Worrall,** Ruth Carter **Stapleton** and Dr. Jonas Salk. Address: Mandala Holistic Health, P.O. Box 1233, Del Mar, California 92014.

Journal of Humanistic Psychology

Quarterly professional journal of the Association for Humanistic Psychology, concerned largely with aspects of consciousness expansion from a psychological viewpoint, presenting research, theory and discussion on various aspects of consciousness, health and growth. Address: 325 9th Street, San Francisco, California 94103.

Journal of Instrumented UFO Research

Published at irregular intervals, specializing in detection of UFOs by sophisticated equipment. Edited by Ray Stanford, Box 5310, Austin, Texas 78763.

Journal of Man

Dr. J. R. **Buchanan**'s journal of research in **psychometry.** Founded in 1853 in Cincinnati, it succeeded S. B. Brittan's Spiritualist monthly *The Shekinah.*

Journal of Occult Studies

Quarterly publication of the Occult Studies Foundation, in cooperation with the University of Rhode Island, as "an interdisciplinary approach to Paranormal Phenomena." Commencing in May 1977, it published several issues until 1980, when it changed its name to *MetaScience Quarterly* and the foundation name to MetaScience Foundation. The change of name reflects reservations about the contemporary connotations of the word "occult," since the MetaScience Foundation intends to maintain a high standard of scientific information in the field of parapsychology and related subjects. Address: MetaScience Quarterly, Box 32, Kingston, Rhode Island 02881.

Journal of Orgonomy

Bi-annual journal representing an authoritative view of the life, work and writings of the late Dr. Wilhelm **Reich.** The Journal is published by a group of accredited Reichian physicians, and includes previously unpublished writings of Dr. Reich as well as contemporary views and research on **Orgone** energy and associated topics. Address: P.O. Box 565, Ansonia Station, New York, N.Y. 10023.

Journal of Our Time

Canadian journal concerned with **Fourth Way** teachings deriving from the philosophy of **Gurdjieff.** Address: Box 484, Adelaide Street P.O., Toronto, Canada M5C 2K4.

Journal of Parapsychology

Quarterly journal published from 1937 onwards, edited by Louisa E. **Rhine** and Dorothy H. **Pope.** It is a scholarly publication "devoted primarily to the original publication of experimental results and other research findings in extrasensory perception and psychokinesis. In addition, articles presenting reviews of literature relevant to parapsychology, criticisms of published work, theoretical and philosophical discussions, and new methods of mathematical analysis" are included in its scope. Published by Parapsychology Press, Box 6847, College Station, Durham, North Carolina 27708.

Journal of Research in Psi Phenomena

Published by Kingston Association for Research in Parasciences, P.O. Box 141, Kingston, Ontario, K7L 4V6, Canada.

Journal of the American Society for Psychical Research

This publication ran from 1906 until 1928, when vol. 22 was continued under the title *Psychic Research.* From January 1932, however, the original title was resumed.

The *Journal* and also *Proceedings* of the A.S.P.R., however, are now published from 5 West 73rd Street, New York, N.Y. 10023.

Journal of the American Society for Psychosomatic Dentistry and Medicine

Quarterly professional journal relating parapsychological phenomena, hypnosis, acupuncture and similar subjects to medicine and the welfare of patients. Address: 2802 Mermaid Avenue, Brooklyn, N.Y., 11224.

Journal of the Society for Psychical Research

Published from 1884 onwards. Vols. 1–34 (1884–1948) were restricted to members of the Society, but issues from September 1949 onwards were available for purchase by the public. The Journal is now published quarterly by the Society at 1 Adam & Eve Mews, Kensington, London, W8 6UQ, England. A Combined Index to the *Journal* and the Society's *Proceedings* is also published.

Journal of Transpersonal Psychology

Semi-annual journal with authoritative contributions concerned with a psychological approach to dreams, meditation, psychic experiences, biofeedback and consciousness expanding techniques. Address: P.O. Box 4437, Stanford, California 94305.

Journal of Vampirism

Published by the **Vampire Studies Society.** Address: Martin V. Riccardo, 7809 South LaPorte Avenue, Burbank, Illinois 60459.

Journal UFO

Canadian publication reporting on UFO activities and related mysteries, now incorporating *Canadian UFO Report* (formerly published from British Columbia). Address: UP Investigations Research Inc., Box 455, Streetsville, Mississauga, Ontario, Canada L5M 2B9.

Joy, Sir George Andrew (1896–1974)

Official of the British Colonial and Foreign Office, also active in the field of psychical research. Born February 20, 1896, at London, England, he served in the British Army and was successively assistant commissioner, New Hebrides Condominium, resident commissioner and deputy commissioner for Western Pacific, consult for the Hoorn and Wallace Islands, resident adviser to the Quaiti and Kathiri Sultans, Hadhramaut States of Arabia, civil secretary to the Government of Adam, Commissioner for Civil Defense, governor and commander-in-chief St. Helena.

He was awarded many distinctions, notably Companion of the Order of St. Michael and St. George, 1945, Knight Commander of the British Empire, 1949, British War Medal, Victory Medal, Silver Jubilee Medal, 1935, Coronation Medal, 1937, Coronation Medal, 1953, Defense Medal. He was Secretary of the **Society for Psychical Research,** London, from 1958 and a member of the SPR Council, later vice-president.

Judah Ha-Levi (1085–1140)

Celebrated Jewish theologian and mystic. He seems to have had some conception of **elementary spirits,** for of the angels he said that "some are created for the time being, out of the subtle elements of matter."

Judd, Pearl (1908–   ?)

Direct voice medium of Dunedin, New Zealand, who held seances in a well-lighted room, or in daylight, with remarkable manifestations, as described in Clive Chapman's book *The Blue Room* (1927).

In *Psychic Research* (November 1930) psychical researcher Harry **Price** quoted the testimony of Dr. W. P. Gowland, professor of anatomy and neurologist at the Medical School, Dunedin, given personally on the occasion of the professor's visit to London. He witnessed the **levitation** of heavy tables, the playing of a specified tune on an ordinary piano when three people were sitting on the closed and locked lid, heard invisible instruments and many voices.

An entity named "Sahnaei," who first manifested in 1923 and stated he lived hundreds of years ago and was an Arab, appeared to be in charge of the band of communicators: "Captain Trevor," "Ronald," "George Thurston," "Charlie," "Grace," "Oliver," "Jack," "Vilma," etc. Miss Judd's uncle, Clive Chapman, was also a medium and was also present at the most impressive seances. These were held in a blue room, hence the title of Chapman's book.

Pearl Judd retired some years after publication of the book. Chapman died August 10, 1967, at the age of 84.

Judge, William Q(uan) (1851–1896)

Prominent American Theosophist and one of the founders of the **Theosophical Society** of Madame **Blavatsky** and Col. H. S. **Olcott.** Born in Ireland, he studied occult literature and emigrated to the U.S. where he became a lawyer. Judge founded many branches of the Theosophical Society in America. After the death of Madame Blavatsky, he was involved in the case of the **Mahatma Letters,** in which communications allegedly from the Master **Koot Hoomi,** a mysterious adept, appeared to favor his taking charge of the Society, as opposed to the presidency of Annie **Besant.**

At the convention of the American section of the Theosophical Society, it was decided to secede from the parent Society. Judge was elected president of the Theosophical Society in America for life.

Amongst his various writings, Judge produced his own edition of the *Yoga Sutras of Patanjali,* study notes on the *Bhagavad-Gita,* and a book *The Ocean of Theosophy* (1893).

Julia's Bureau

A public institution founded by W. T. **Stead** in 1909 in London for free communication with the Beyond. Visitors were allowed to have three sittings with three different mediums to check the communication. Shorthand records were kept. For distant inquirers, psychometric readings were given.

Robert **King,** Alfred Vout **Peters,** Mrs. Wesley Adams, J. J. Vango, and, during her visit to London, Mrs. Etta **Wriedt,** were employed as mediums. In its three years' existence about 1,300 sittings were given and the running of the bureau cost Stead about £1,500 a year.

The idea for the establishment of the bureau was suggested to Stead in his own automatic scripts by the spirit of Julia A. Ames, an American journalist, who was his constant communicator. In 1914 the work of Julia's Bureau was taken up by a new organization: The W. T. Stead **Borderland Library,** founded by Estelle W. Stead on the lines of other Spiritualist societies.

The Stead Bureau closed in 1936.

Jung, Carl Gustav (1875–1961)

Swiss psychologist who made various occult ideas a valid study within the framework of psychology. Born July 26, 1875, at Kesswil Thurgau, Switzerland, he studied medicine at the University of Basel, Switzerland, 1895–1900 and took his M.D. in 1902, University of Zurich. While still a student he read various works on occultism and attended Spiritualist seances. In 1903 he married Emma Rauschenbach (died 1961); they had four daughters and one son.

Jung became a physician and assisted Eugene Bleuler at the Burghölzli Mental Hospital in Zurich. Between 1907 and 1913 Jung became a disciple of Freud, but eventually went his own way as a result of what he regarded as Freud's over-emphasis on sexual theories and opposition to occult ideas. In fact, much of Jung's life was influenced by paranormal phenomena, some of which even took place in the presence of Freud.

Jung's break with Freudian theory was marked by a paper on 'Symbols of the Libido' in 1913. Jung's analytical psychology emphasized the importance of symbols in the spiritual journey of the individual psyche through life, and proposed a collective unconscious as well as a personal unconscious. Jung distinguished archetypal symbols which had a universal application in human experience, as well as symbols appearing in waking or dreaming life with special significance for the individual.

Much of Jung's scheme of psychology reinstated earlier religious and particularly Eastern teachings within a context of modern Western scholarship in the field of psychology. One of Jung's theories which has special application in such borderline studies as astrology is that of **Synchronicity,** an a-casual connecting principle between events, as distinct from conventional cause-and-effect.

During the 1930s in Germany, some of Jung's concepts of a collective unconscious were identified with Nazi concepts of a racial unconscious. This resulted in later accusations that Jung was a supporter of the Nazis. This did less than justice to the broader scope of Jung's thought and work.

Jung was a professor of psychology at the Federal Polytechnical University, Zurich, from 1933–41, professor of medical psychology at the University of Basel 1943–44 and consultant and lecturer at the C. G. Jung Institute 1948–61. He was awarded an honorary LL.D. by Clark, Fordham and Calcutta Universities, Hon. D. Litt. Benares and Geneva Universities, H.D.Sc. Harvard, Oxford, Allahabad Universities; honorary fellow Royal Society of Medicine, London, honorary member of the Royal Medico-Psychological Association; co-founder of the International Psychoanalytic Society.

His most significant works include: *The Theory of Psychoanalysis* (1916), *Psychological Types* (1923), *Modern Man in Search of a Soul* (1933), *Psychology and Religion* (1938), *Psychology and Alchemy* (1953), *The Interpretation of Nature and the Psyche* (1955), *Archetypes and the Collective Unconscious* (1959). His many writings have been issued in *Collected Works* (Pantheon, New York/Routledge, London, 1953).

Jung's breadth of thought and perception covered every major area of human experience. He even published a book on *Flying Saucers; a modern myth of things seen in the skies* (1959). His occult experiences are indicated in his book *VII Sermones ad Mortuoso*, published anonymously, which dramatizes Jung's journey into the unconscious. Some of his reminiscences are recorded in *Memories, Dreams, Reflections* (Pantheon, 1963).

Jung, Johann Heinrich (1740–1817)

German author, physician, best known by his assumed name of Heinrich Stilling. He was Professor of Political Economy at the University of Marburg, a contemporary of Mesmer and founder of a German spiritual school of cosmology.

His book *Theory of Pneumatology* (1834) contained a great number of authentic narratives of **apparitions** and similar phenomena. In *Theorie der Geisterkunde* (1827) he expounded the doctrine of a psychic body, based on the luminiferous ether.

He put forward the following propositions: **Animal Magnetism** undeniably proves that we have an inward man, a soul, which is constituted of the divine spark, the immortal spirit, possessing reason and will, and of a luminous body which is inseparable from it. Light, electric, magnetic, galvanic matter and ether appear to be all one and the same body under different modifications. This light-substance or ether is the element which connects body and soul, and the spiritual and material world together. When the inward man, the human soul, forsakes the outward sphere, where the senses operate and merely continue the vital functions, the body falls into an entranced state, or a profound sleep, during which the soul acts more freely, powerfully and actively. All its faculties are elevated.

The more the soul is divested of the body, the more extensive, free and powerful is its inward sphere of operation. It has, therefore, no need whatever of the body in order to live and exist. The latter is rather a hindrance to it. The soul does not require the organs of sense in order to be able to see, hear, smell, taste and feel in a much more perfect state. The boundless ether that fills the space of our solar system is the element of spirits in which they live and move. The atmosphere that surrounds our earth, down to its center, and particularly the night, is the abode of fallen angels, and of such human souls as die in an unconverted state.

Jung-Stilling discouraged communications with the spirit world as sinful and dangerous. He considered trance as a diseased condition. He believed implicitly in the efficacy of prayer and had psychic powers himself. More than ten weeks before the event, he predicted the tragic fate of Lavater who was shot by a soldier in Zurich in 1799.

Jürgenson, Friedrich

Russian-born Swedish painter and film producer who first dicovered the paranormal voice phenomenon which has since come to be known as "Raudive Voices" or the "Electronic Voice Phenomenon."

In July 1959, Jürgenson recorded the song of a Swedish finch on his tape recorder and on playback heard what appeared to be a human voice. He thought there must be some fault in the apparatus, but subsequent recordings contained a message which seemed to be recognizably from his dead mother. Jürgenson mentioned his experiences in a book which made a deep impression on the Latvian psychologist Dr. Konstantin **Raudive.**

The two men met and conducted further research into paranormal voices on tape recordings, collaborating with other scientists, for a period between 1964–69. The collaborators included Professor Hans **Bender** of the University of Freiburg and Dr. Friedebert Karger of the Max Planck Institute in Munich. After 1969, Mr. Jürgenson and Dr. Raudive had some differences of opinion and conducted their further researches on independent lines. Dr. Raudive's researches were very extensive, and included the collection and study of over 100,000 recordings. Following publication of his book on the subject, translated into English as *Breakthrough; An Amazing Experiment in Electronic Communication with the Dead* (Colin Smythe, Gerrards Cross, U.K./Taplinger, New York, 1971), the phenomenon became generally known and discussed as "Raudive Voices," although more recently the term Electronic Voice Phenomenon is preferred by parapsychologists.

Essentially this phenomenon consists of paranormal voice communications (apparently from dead individuals) which are apparent on recordings made on a standard tape recorder, sometimes enhanced by a simple diode circuit. The voices are also apparent on the "white noise" of certain radio bands.

In view of traditional opposition to Spiritualist phenomena from the Catholic church in the past, it is significant that the work of Mr. Jürgenson on paranormal voice recordings has been known to the Holy See since 1960, and according to Mr. Jürgenson the suggestion that these recordings are voices from the dead has been sympathetically considered. In 1969, Archbishop Dr. Bruno B. Heim presented Mr. Jürgenson to Pope Paul VI for investiture as Commander of the Order of St. Gregory. It must be stressed, however, that this honor was in respect of Mr. Jürgenson's work as a filmmaker.

In view of the initial discovery of the paranormal voice phenomenon through tape recordings of bird song, some confusion has been caused subsequently by the announcement that Dr. Raudive recently investigated mediumistic messages conveyed by a budgerigar. Such "Bird Voices" may be related to the electronic voice phenomenon discovered by Mr. Jürgenson, but are basically of a different nature. They are discussed in more detail in the entry under **Raudive Voices.**

Juste, Michael

Pseudonym of poet and occultist Michael **Houghton,** associate of Aleister **Crowley.**

Jyotir Maya Nanda, Swami (1931–   )

Disciple of the late Swami **Sivananda** of Rishikesh, India, now president of **Yoga Research Foundation,** Inc. of Miami, Florida.

Born February 3, 1931, in Dumari Buzurg, District Saran, Bihar, India, he became a renunciate at the age of

22 on February 3, 1953, and was religious professor at the Sivananda Ashram in Rishikesh for nine years, lecturing on Yoga and Vedanta, also editing the journal *Yoga Vedanta.*

In 1962, at the invitation of Swami Lalitananda (formerly Miss Leonora Rego), also a disciple of Swami Sivananda, he came to Puerto Rico to head the Hindu religious center Sanatan Dharma Mandir. In 1969, he moved with Swami Lalitananda to Miami as head of the International Yoga Society, now reformed as Yoga Research Foundation. The Foundation has issued a number of publications on yoga and Hindu philosophy, as well as tape recordings and study courses. Address: 6111 S.W. 74th Avenue, Miami, Florida 33143.

K

Ka

The human **double** of ancient Egyptians belief. It was usually depicted as a sort of bird-like duplicate of the deceased. The Egyptogist Gaston Maspero defined it as "a kind of second copy of the body in matter less dense than the corporeal, a coloured though real projection of the individual, an exact reproduction of him in every part."

The Ka lived in the tomb and the purpose of mummification and burial provisions was to prolong its life. If no attention was paid to it, the Ka was thought to come out of the tomb and haunt the relatives guilty of neglect. The Ka was not confused with the soul, called *Ba* or *Bai*. This left the material body and the double at the moment of death. (See also **Astral Projection; Ba; Double; Egypt; Out-of-the-Body**)

Kabala (Cabbala, Kabbala)

A Hebrew and Jewish system of theosophy. The word signifies "doctrines received from tradition." In ancient Hebrew literature the name was used to denote the entire body of religious writings, the Pentateuch excepted. It was only in the early Middle Ages that the system of theosophy known as Kabalism was designated by that name.

A major source which went to the making of the *Kabala* was the *Sepher Yesirah* or Book of Creation, a combination of medieval mysticism and science. The date of origin of this work has been a matter of great argument, but it is perhaps safest to say that it seems to be earlier than the ninth century A.D. The *Bahir* or "brilliance" is first quoted by Nahmanides (1194-c. 1293) and is usually attributed to his teacher, Ezra. It owed much to the *Sepher Yesirah*, and to a great extent foreshadowed the *Zohar*, which is a commentary on the *Pentateuch*, including eleven dissertations on that book, the most important of which are the *Book of Secrets*, the *Secret of Secrets*, the *Mysteries of the Pentateuch*, and the *Hidden Interpretation*.

The *Zohar* was attributed to the authorship of Simon ben Yohai in the second century, and it was alleged that he drew his sources from traditional dialogues between God and Adam in Paradise. It was also stated that it was discovered in a cavern in Galilee where it had been hidden for one thousand years. It seems more likely, however, that it was written in the thirteenth century, since the capture of Jerusalem by the Crusaders is alluded to. It is also believed that Moses de Leon, who died in 35, and who circulated and sold the *Zohar*, was himself its author. At the same time there is no doubt that it enshrined a large number of very ancient and important Hebrew traditions.

The matter contained in the *Kabala* deals with the nature of God, the *sephiroth* or divine emanations, of angels and of man. God, known in the *Kabala* as *En Soph*, fills and contains the universe. As he is boundless, mind cannot conceive him, so in a certain mystical sense God is non-existent or pre-existent.

The doctrine of the *sephiroth* is undoubtedly the most important to be met with in the pages of the *Kabala*. To justify existence, the Deity had to become active and creative, and this was achieved through the medium of the ten sephiroth or intelligences which emanated from God like rays proceeding from a luminary. The first *sephiroth* or emanation was the wish to become manifest, and this contained nine other intelligences or *sephiroth*, which again emanated one from the other—the second from the first, the third from the second, and so forth. These were known as the "Crown," "Wisdom," "Intelligence," "Love," "Justice," "Beauty," "Firmness," "Splendor," "Foundation" and "Kingdom." From the junction of pairs of *sephiroth*, other emanations were formed; thus from Wisdom and Intelligence proceeded Love or Mercy and from Mercy and Justice, Beauty. The *sephiroth* were also symbolic of primordial man and the heavenly man, of which earthly man was the shadow. They formed three triads, which respectively represented intellectual, moral, and physical qualities: the first, Wisdom, Intelligence and Crown; the second Love, Justice and Beauty; the third Firmness, Splendor and Foundation. The whole was circled or bound by Kingdom, the ninth *sephiroth*. Each of these triads symbolized a portion of the human frame; the first the head, the second the arms, the third the legs. It must be understood that although those *sephiroth* were emanations from God they remained a portion, and simply represented different aspects of the One Being.

Kabalistic cosmology posits four different worlds, each of which forms a sephiric system of a decade of emanations, which were verified in the following manner: the world of emanations or the heavenly man, a direct emanation from the *En Soph*. From it is produced the world of creation, or the *Briatic* world of pure nature, but yet not so spiritual as the first. The angel Metatron inhabits it and constitutes the world of pure spirit. He governs the visible world and guides the revolutions of the planets. From this is formed the world of formation or the *Yetziratic* world, still less refined, which is the abode of angels. Finally from these emanates the world of action or matter, the dwelling of evil spirits, which contains ten hells, each becoming lower until the depths of diabolical degradation is reached. The prince of this region is Samael, the evil spirit, the serpent of Genesis, otherwise "the Beast."

But the universe was incomplete without the creation of man, the heavenly Adam, that is the tenth *sephiroth,* created the earthly Adam, each member of whose body corresponds to a part of the visible universe. The human form is said to be shaped after the four letters which constitute the Jewish tetragrammaton, the letters JHVH. The souls of the whole human race preexist in the world of emanations, and are all destined to inhabit human bodies. Like the *sephiroth* from which it emanates, every soul has ten potencies, consisting of a trinity of triads—spirit, soul, cruder soul or *neptesh.* Each soul, before its entrance into the world, consists of male and female united into one being, but when it descends to this earth, the two parts are separated and animate different bodies.

The destiny of the soul upon earth is to develop the perfect germs implanted in it, which must ultimately return to *En Soph.* If it does not succeed in acquiring the experience for which it has been sent to earth, it must re-inhabit the body three times till it becomes duly purified. When all the souls in the world of the *sephiroth* shall have passed through this period of probation and returned to the bosom of *En Soph,* the jubilee will commence. Even Satan will be restored to his angelic nature, and existence will be a Sabbath without end. The *Kabala* states that these esoteric doctrines are contained in the Hebrew scriptures, but cannot be perceived by the uninitiated; they are, however, plainly revealed to persons of spiritual mind.

Considering the *Kabala* as occult literature, it is stated that the philosophical doctrines developed in its pages are found to have been perpetuated by the secret method of oral tradition from the first ages of humanity. "The Kabbalah," stated Dr. Christian D. Ginsburg, in his book of that title (1863), "was first taught by God Himself to a select company of angels, who formed a theosophic school in Paradise. After the Fall the angels most graciously communicated this heavenly doctrine to the disobedient child of earth, to furnish the protoplasts with the means of returning to their pristine nobility and felicity. From Adam it passed over to Noah, and then to Abraham, the friend of God, who emigrated with it to Egypt, where the patriarch allowed a portion of this mysterious doctrine to ooze out. It was in this way that the Egyptians obtained some knowledge of it, and the other Eastern nations could introduce it into their philosophical systems. Moses, who was learned in all the wisdom of Egypt, was first initiated into the Kabbalah in the land of his birth, but became most proficient in it during his wanderings in the wilderness, when he not only devoted to it the leisure hours of the whole forty years, but received lessons in it from one of the angels. By the aid of this mysterious science the lawgiver was enabled to solve the difficulties which arose during his management of the Israelites, in spite of the pilgrimages, wars, and frequent miseries of the nation. He covertly laid down the principles of this secret doctrine in the first four books of the Pentateuch, but withheld them from Deuteronomy. Moses also initiated the seventy Elders into the secrets of this doctrine, and they again transmitted them from hand to hand. Of all who formed the unbroken line of tradition, David and Solomon were the most deeply initiated into the Kabbalah. No one, however, dared to write it down till Schimeon ben Jochai, who lived at the time of the destruction of the second.

After his death, his son, Rabbi Eleazar, and his secretary, Rabbi Abba, as well as his disciples, collated Rabbi Simon Ben Jochai's treatises, and out of these composed the celebrated work called Z H R, *Zohar,* Splendor which is the grand storehouse of Kabbalism."

This history of Kabalistic origins, however, has been shown to be almost wholly fabulous, and no evidence worthy of the name can be adduced in its support. The mysticism of the *Mishna* and the *Talmud* must be carefully distinguished from that of the Kabalistic writings, as they are undoubtedly of very considerable antiquity. But the *Kabala* has certain claims upon the modern student of mysticism.

Its philosophical value is not depreciated by its relatively modern origin, and it is regarded by many as an absolute guide to knowledge in all the most profound problems of existence. Its thesis is extensive and profound, but examination unfortunately shows it to be a series of dogmatic hypotheses, a body of positive doctrine based on a central assumption which is incapable of proof.

This tradition, stated occultist Éliphas **Lévi,** wholly reposes on the single dogma of magic, that the Visible is for us a proportional measure of the Invisible. In fact, it proceeds by analogy from the known to the unknown. At the same time, it is a most remarkable and stimulating effort of the human mind.

Medieval magic was deeply indebted to Kabalistic combinations of the divine names for the terms of its rituals, and from it it derived the belief in a resident virtue in sacred names and numbers. Certain definite rules were employed to discover the sublime source of power resident in the Jewish scriptures. Thus the words of several verses in the scriptures which were regarded as containing an occult sense, were placed over each other, and the letters formed into new words by reading them vertically, or the words of the text were arranged in squares in such a manner as to be read vertically or otherwise.

Words were joined together and re-divided, and the initial and final letters of certain words were formed into separate words. Again, every letter of the word was reduced to its numerical value, and the word explained by another of the same quantity. Every letter of a word too was taken to be an initial of an abbreviation of it. The twenty-two letters of the alphabet were divided into two halves, one half placed above the other, and the two letters which thus became associated were interchanged. Thus *a* became *l, b, m,* and so on. This cipher alphabet was called *albm* from the first interchanged pairs. The commutation of the twenty-two letters was effected by the last letter of the alphabet taking the place of the first, the last but one the place of the second and so forth. This cipher was called *atbah.* These permutations and combinations are much older than the *Kabala,* and obtained amongst Jewish mystics from time immemorial.

It should be pointed out that the *Kabala* was often condemned among the Jews themselves. Jewish orthodoxy has always been suspicious of it, and as the mystical writer A. E. Waite aptly stated: "The best lesson we can learn from it is the necessity of scrupulously separating the experimental knowledge of the mystics from their bizarre fields of speculation."

Kabalism has recently seen a revival, but many Jewish scholars rightly resent such studies being appropriated by non-Jewish occultists, as has often occurred over the centuries.

However, it is of great interest that the mysticism of the *Sepher Yesirah,* with its relationship of letters to parts of the body and to the macrocosm, as well as the diagramatic representation of mystical evolution, has something in common with Hindu mysticism. (See also **Gematria; Yantra; Yoga**)

Recommended reading:

Abelson, Joshua. *Jewish Mysticism: An Introduction to Kabbalah,* Sepher-Hermon Press, New York (paperback), 1981

Achad, Frater. *The Anatomy of the Body of God; Being the Supreme Revelation of Cosmic Consciousness,* Collegium ad Spiritum Sanctum, Chicago, 1925; Weiser, New York, 1969

Bension, Ariel. *The Zohar in Moslem & Christian Spain,* Sepher-Hermon Press, New York, 1932

Berg, Phillip S. *Kabbalah for the Laymen,* Research Center of Kabbalah, New York, n.d.

Franck, Adolphe. *The Kabbalah,* University Books, 1967; Citadel paperback, 1979

Gaster, Moses. *The Origin of the Kabbalah,* Gordon Press, N.Y., 1976

Halevi, Z'ev Ben Shimon. *An Introduction to the Cabala—Tree of Life,* Weiser, 1972

Kalisch, Isidor (transl.). *Sepher Yezirah,* New York, 1877; Rosicrucian Press, California, 1950; Symbols & Signs, N.Hollywood, California, n.d.

Lévi, Éliphas. *The Book of Splendors,* Weiser, 1973

Luzzatto, Moses. *General Principles of the Kabbalah,* Research Center of Kabbalah, 1970

Meltzer, David (ed.). *The Secret Garden; An Anthology of the Kabbalah,* Seabury Press, New York, 1976

Pick, Bernhard. *The Cabala,* Open Court Publishing Co., Illinois 1903

Scholem, Gershom (ed.). *Zohar—The Book of Splendor; Basic Readings from the Kabbalah,* Schocken paperback, 1963

Scholem, Gershom. *On the Kabbalah & Its Symbolism,* Schocken, 1960

Sperling, Harry & Maurice Simon (transl.). *The Zohar,* 5 vols., Rebecca Bennet Publishing, New York, n.d.

Waite, Arthur E. *The Holy Kabbalah,* University Books, 1960; Citadel paperback, 1976

Kabbalist, The

Quarterly journal of the International Order of Kabbalists, devoted to study of Hebrew mysticism and related subjects. Address: 25 Circle Gardens, Merton Park, London, SW 19 3JX, England. (See also **Kabala**)

Kabir (1450?–1518?)

One of the most celebrated mystics of fifteenth to sixteenth century India, who practiced yoga and attempted to reconcile Hindus and Moslems. After his death he was claimed by both religions. Kabir's inspirational hymns are very moving, and are still popular in present-day India. Kabir was a contemporary of Guru Nanak who founded the Sikh religion.

Recommended reading:

Kabir (transl. Rabinadrath Tagor). *One Hundred Poems of Kabir,* London, 1915

Kay, Frank E. *Kabir and his Followers.* London, 1931

Westcott, G. H. *Kabir and the Kabir Path,* 1907

Kaboutermannekens

According to the folklore of Flemish peasants, these were little spirits which played tricks on the women of the country, particularly on those who worked in the dairy. In this respect they are similar to the **fairies** of other folklore beliefs.

Kaempffert, Waldemar B(ernhard) (1877–1956)

Editor and writer associated with pioneer physical researchers. Born New York, N.Y., September 23, 1877, he studied at the City College of New York (B.S. 1897) and New York University (LL.B. 1903). He married Carolyn Lydia Yeaton (died 1933).

Kaempffert was a friend of James H. **Hyslop** and Walter Franklin **Prince,** and believed that psychical research could help human beings to know more about themselves from the viewpoints of physical, psychological and philosophical knowledge.

As science editor of *The New York Times* from 1927–28 and 1931–56, Kaempffert's favorable reports on the work of Dr. J. B. **Rhine** and other parapsychologists helped to spread public awareness of research in parapsychology and its implications. His books include: *Science Today and Tomorrow* (1939), *Invention and Society* (1930), *Explorations in Science* (1953).

Kaf

According to Arabian tradition, a great mountain that stretches to the horizon on every side. The earth is in the middle of this mountain, like a finger in the middle of a ring. Its foundation is the stone *Sakhrat,* the least fragment of which is capable of working untold marvels. This stone is said to cause earthquakes. It is made of a single emerald.

The mountain, which is frequently referred to in Eastern tales, is said to be the habitation of genii. To reach it one must pass through dark wildernesses, and it is essential that the traveler be guided by a supernatural being.

Kagyu Droden Kunchab

A center founded by the Venerable Kalu Rinpoche, concerned with the teaching and practice of Mahayana and Vajrayana Buddhism. The practice taught includes mantra, visualization, form and formless meditations. The Rinpoche's representative in San Francisco is the Lama Lodru. Address: 1892 Fell Street, San Francisco, California 94117.

Kahn, Ludwig (c. 1925)

German clairvoyant, whose faculty of "lucidity" in reading sealed messages created a sensation in Paris in 1925. He demonstrated his powers to Prof. Schottelius in Fribourg. In 1925 and 1926 he appeared in Paris before the Institut Métapsychique. In the presence of a distinguished gathering of scientists he read the contents of eleven mixed paper pellets.

When his residence permit in France was expiring he went with a letter of introduction from Prof. Charles **Richet,** to M. Maurain, commissioner of police. Richet wrote that his stay in France was very desirable from the scientific point of view. Maurain said that he would extend the permit if Kahn proved his lucidity to him. Kahn successfully convinced him of his powers and was duly given the permit.

The literature concerning Kahn was summarized by E. J. Dingwall in *Journal* of the Society for Psychical Research (vol. 23, 1926, p. 94-95).

Kahn, S. David (1929-   )

Psychiatrist who has written on experimental parapsychology. Born February 15, 1929, in New York, N.Y., he studied at Harvard University (B.A. 1950, M.D. 1954). In 1958 he married Caroline Phelps. Dr. Kahn was appointed senior psychiatrist at Montefiore Hospital, New York, in 1960. He is a member of the American Psychiatric Association, the Parapsychology Association, and a trustee of the American Society for Psychical Research.

His articles include: 'A Mechanical Scoring Technique for Testing GESP' [General Extrasensory Perception] (*Journal of Parapsychology* vol. 13, No. 3, 1949), 'Studies in Extrasensory Perception: Experiments Utilizing an Electronic Scoring Device' (*ASPR Proceedings,* vol. 25, October 1952), 'Extrasensory Perception and Friendly Interpersonal Relations' (symposium *Explorations in Altruistic Love and Behavior,* edited by Pitirim A. **Sorokin,** 1950), 'The Enigma of Psi: A Challenge for Scientific Method' (*ASPR Journal,* July 1962).

Kai

The seneschal of King **Arthur,** known in the French romances as Messire Queux, or Maitre Queux or Kuex. He is prominent in the *Morte d' Arthur.*

In the tale of Kilhwuh and Olwen in the *Mabinogion,* he is identified with a personage whose "breath lasted nine nights and days under water" and who "could exist nine nights and nine days without sleep." A wound from his sword could not be cured; he could make himself as tall as the highest tree, and so great was the heat of his nature that, during rain, whatever he carried remained dry.

Originally a deity, a rain-and-thunder god, he had apparently degenerated, through a series of mythological processes, into a mere folk hero.

Kaiser, A. W. (c. 1933)

American **direct voice** medium of Detroit, Michigan. "Blackfoot" and "Leota," both Indians, and "Dr. Jenkins," were his chief controls. The medium did not go into trance.

Kaivalyadhama S.M.Y.M. Samhiti

Center for the medical and scientific study of **Hatha Yoga,** established since 1935 by Swami **Kuvalayananda.** The center has been officially recognized as a research institute by the Government of Bombay and by Bombay State. It publishes **Yoga-Mimamsa** Journal. Address: Yoga-Mimamsa Office, Lonavla (C.R.), India.

Kalé, Shrikrishna Vasudeo (1924-   )

Psychologist actively concerned with parapsychology. Born April 10, 1924, in Poona, India, he studied at University of Bombay (B.A. 1944, M.A. 1947), Columbia University, New York (M.A. 1950, Ph.D. 1953). In 1954 he married Premala Prabhavati Joshi.

Dr. Kalé has been reader in psychology at University of Bombay from 1959 on, and is an associate of the American Psychological Association, secretary of Shikshana Prasaraka Mandali, member of Society for the Psychology of Social Issues, National Productivity Council, All India Philosophy Congress, Indian Psychological Association.

He has written a number of papers on psychology and was president of the Psychology Section at a symposium on parapsychology at the All-India Philosophical Congress held at Ahmedabad in 1958. His article 'Parapsychology and Science' was published in the *Indian Journal of Parapsychology* (vol. 1, No. 2, 1959), and he has also written the article 'Parapsychology and Science' published in the *Indian Journal of Parapsychology,* vol. 2, No. 1, 1961. His publications include: *Learning and Retention of English-Russian Vocabulary under Different Conditions of Motion Picture Presentation* (1953).

Kale Thaungto

A town of wizards in Lower Burma. (See **Burma**)

Kali Yuga

The "Iron Age" of Hindu mythology. There are said to be four ages of the world: Krita Yuga (Golden Age of truth) lasting 4,800 years of the gods; Treta Yuga (Silver Age), 3,600 years of the gods; Dwapara Yuga, 2,400 years of the gods; Kali Yuga (Iron or Evil Age), 1,200 years of the gods.

Since a year of the gods equals 360 years of men, the extent of Kali Yuga is said to be 432,000 years and would have commenced 540 B.C. In Kali Yuga, righteousness has been diminished by three quarters, and the age is one of devolution, culminating in the destruction of the world prior to new creation and another Krita Yuga in an endless cycle of time.

Kammerdiener, Franklin Leslie, Jr. (1932-   )

Director of the Parapsychology Laboratory at Wayland Baptist College, Plainview, Texas. Born September 1, 1932, at Oklahoma City, Oklahoma, he studied at Oklahoma Baptist University (B.S. 1954), Southwestern Baptist Theological Seminary, Fort Worth, Texas (B.D. 1957, M.Th. 1959), Stephen F. Austin State College, Macogdoches, Texas (M.A. 1960). In 1952 he married Margaret Marie Wilburn. From 1960 on, Mr. Kammerdiener has been Instructor in psychology at Wayland as well as director of Parapsychology Laboratory. He has been responsible for evaluation of experiments in telepathy involving the use of objects in various shapes.

Kane, Dr. Elisha Kent (1820–1857)

Arctic explorer husband of Margaret Fox, one of the pioneers of American Spiritualism (See **Fox Sisters**). After the death of Kane, his relatives refused to accept the marriage (said to have been a simple Quaker ceremony) or Margaret's claim to Kane's estate.

With the publication of his letters in *The Love-Life of Dr. Kane; containing the correspondence . . .* (1866), a lively controversy arose about the meaning of his accusations against Margaret for "living in deceit and hypocrisy." He did not believe in spirits, but on the other hand there is nothing in his letters to show that he actually discovered fraud. On the contrary, in a letter to Kate he says: "Take my advice and never talk of the spirits either to friends or strangers. You know that with my intimacy with Maggie after a whole month's trial I could make nothing of them. Therefore they are a great mystery." In another letter he had written: "I can't bear the thought of your sitting in the dark, squeezing other peoples hands. I touch no hand but yours; press no lips but yours; think of no thoughts that I would not share with you; and do no deeds that I would conceal from you."

Kant, Immanuel (1724-1804)

The great German philosopher anticipated the modern pictographic conception of apparitions when analyzing the experiences of Swedenborg in his *Dreams of a Spirit Seer.* He wrote: "Departed souls and pure spirits . . . can still act upon the soul of man . . . For the ideas they excite in the soul clothe themselves according to the law of fantasy in allied imagery and create outside the seer the apparition of the objects to which they are appropriate." He did not distinguish between veridical and objective apparitions and after some perfunctory speculation laid the subject aside.

Kapila (c. 6th century B.C.)

Celebrated Hindu sage, founder of the *Sankya* school of philosophy. He is believed by some Hindus to be the god Vishnu in the fifth of his twenty-four incarnations.

The *Sankya* system seeks to explain the creation of the phenomenal universe and the part played by Spirit and Matter (*Purusha* and *Prakriti*), and attempts to harmonize rational analysis and the religious authority of the *Vedas.* It is the oldest of the Hindu philosophical systems and regarded as the cornerstone of Hindu philosophy. The Yoga system popularized in the *Yoga Sutras* of Patanjali is based on the *Sankya* system. (See also **Vedanta; Yoga**)

Kappers, Jan (1914-)

Dutch physician who has been active in the field of parapsychology. Born July 30, 1914, at Rotterdam, Netherlands, he studied at the University of Leiden (M.S. 1938). In 1940 he married Alida Johanna Frederika Hulscher. From 1938-40 he was a medical officer with the Netherlands Army, and has been in private practice in Amsterdam from 1941 on. From 1959 on he was research officer of Amsterdam Foundation for Parapsychological Research, board member of the Dutch Society for Psychical Research from 1958 on, a board member of the Foundation for the Investigation of Paranormal Healing from 1955 on, President of the Parapsychological Circle, Amsterdam. In 1959, Dr. Kappers set up the Amsterdam Foundation for Parapsychological Research in order to facilitate funding.

Dr. Kappers was concerned with Arie **Mak**, F. v.d. Berg and A. H. de Jong in investigating clairvoyance with apparatus devised by Mr. Mak. A report on this project was published in *Tijdschrift voor Parapsychologie* (1957). Dr. Kappers also undertook a statistical evaluation of astrological findings, an inquiry into spontaneous paranormal phenomena in Amsterdam, and a study of paranormal events among subjects using hallucinogens. He edited the

bimonthly journal *Spiegel der Parpsychologie* and contributed a number of articles. His article 'The Investigation of Spontaneous Cases' was published in *Tijdschrift voor Parapsychologie,* 1954. He contributed to the special issue of *International Journal of Neuropsychiatry* on 'ESP Status in 1966' (Sept.-Oct., 1966).

Karagulla, Shafica

Medical doctor and psychiatrist who has taken a special interest in psychic perception. Born in Turkey in a Christian family, she was educated at the American School for Girls in Beirut, Lebanon, the American Junior College for Women, Beirut, and the American University of Beirut (M.D. and surgery degree, 1940).

She went on to specialize in psychiatry in Scotland, where she took her residency at the Royal Edinburgh Hospital for Mental and Nervous Disorders. She was awarded the Walter Smith Kay Research Fellowship in Psychiatry and the Lawrence McLaren Bequest by the University of Edinburgh. During this period she reported unfavorably on the effect of the then fashionable electric shock therapy. In 1948 she was awarded the D.P.M. by the Royal College of Physicians of Edinburgh, one of the highest medical qualifications in Britain.

In 1952, she visited the neurosurgeon Dr. Wilder Penfield at McGill University, Montreal, to discuss the investigation of hallucinations by electrode probes, after which she was associated as consultant psychiatrist with the work of Dr. Penfield on temporal lobe epilepsy and the study of hallucinations by electrical stimulation of the brain.

In 1956, whe came to the U.S. as a practicing physician, where she joined the faculty of the State University of New York as assistant professor in psychiatry. She also became an American citizen.

After reading the book *Edgar Cayce: Mystery Man of Miracles* (1961) by Joseph Millard, she became interested in psychic research, and sought for other individuals with similar abilities to those of Cayce so that she could study them. She spent several years researching what she called "higher sense perception" and published her findings in the book *Breakthrough to Creativity* (1967). Her book has had a powerful impact in universities, colleges of philosophy, psychology and other areas. With her associate Viola P. Neal, Ph.D., she has been teaching the study of Higher Sense Perception at the University College of Los Angeles, California. She has also taken a special interest in the psychic ability of Dora **Van Gelder.**

Kardec, Allan (1804-1869)

The father of French **Spiritism** as distinct from spiritualism. His real name was Hypolyte Leon Denizard Rivail. The pseudonym originated in mediumistic communications. Both "Allan" and "Kardec" were said to have been his names in previous incarnations.

The story of his first investigations into spirit manifestations is somewhat obscure. *Le Livre des Esprits* (The Spirits' Book), which expounded a new theory of human life and destiny, was published in 1856. According to an article by Alexander **Aksakof** in *The Spiritualist* in 1875, the book was based on trance communications received through Mlle. Celina Bequet, a professional somnambulist who, for family reasons, took the name of Celina Japhet and, controlled by her grandfather, M. Hahnemann and Franz **Mesmer,** gave under this name medical advice. Her mesmerist, M. Roustan, believed in the plurality of existences. This may or may not have had an influence. The fact is that in her automatic scripts the spirits communicated the doctrine of **reincarnation.**

In 1856 Rivail was introduced to the circle by Victorien **Sardou.** Rivail was entrusted with the scripts, correlated the material by a number of questions and published it without mentioning the name of the medium. It is difficult to say how far Aksakof's information covers the truth. He obtained it in the course of a personal interview with Celina Japhet in Paris. It was she who revealed that the name "Allan" was borne in a previous incarnation by Rivail. "Kardec" was revealed by Rose, another medium by whose help Rivail formed a circle of his own.

In 1857, *Le Livre des Esprits* was issued in a revised form and later went into more than twenty editions. It has since become the recognized textbook of Spiritistic philosophy in France. This philosophy is distinct from Spiritualism as it is built on the main tenet that spiritual progress is effected by a series of compulsory reincarnations. Allan Kardec became so dogmatic on this point that he always disparaged physical mediumship in which the objective phenomena did not bear out his doctrine and encouraged **automatic writing** where the danger of contradiction was less, owing to the psychological influence of preconceived ideas. As a consequence, experimental psychic research was retarded for many years in France.

Several French physical mediums were never mentioned in *La Revue Spirite,* the monthly magazine which Allan Kardec founded. Nor did the Society of Psychologic Studies, of which he was the president, devote attention to them. Camile **Brédif,** a very good physical medium, only acquired celebrity in St. Petersbourg and Allan Kardec even ignored the important mediumship of D. D. **Home** after the medium declared himself against reincarnation.

In 1864, Kardec published *Le Livre des Mediums.* In this book the formerly unpublished portion of the Japhet scripts were said to have been liberally used. His next books were: *The Gospel as Explained by Spirits* (1864), *Heaven and Hell* (1865), *Genesis* (1867), *Experimental Spiritism and Spiritualist Philosophy.*

In England, Miss Anna **Blackwell** was the most prominent exponent of the philosophy of Allan Kardec. She translated his books into English. In 1881 a three-volume work was published in London on the esoteric aspect of the Gospels under the title *The Four Gospels.* This book, with the publication of which Miss Blackwell was associated, was described as a further development of Allan Kardec's religious philosophy. (See also **France; Spiritism; Spiritualism**)

Karma

A doctrine common to Hinduism, Buddhism and Theosophy, although Theosophists have not adopted it wholly as it is taught in the two religions mentioned.

The word *karma* itself means "action," but implies action and reaction. All actions have consequences, some immediately, some delayed, others in future incarnations. Thus we bear responsibility for all our actions and cannot escape the consequences, although bad actions may be expiated by good actions.

Action is not homogeneous, but on the contrary contains three elements: the thought which conceives it, the will which finds the means of accomplishment, and the union of thought and will which brings the action to pass. It is plain, therefore, that thought is very potent for good or evil, for as the thought is, so will the action be.

The miser, thinking of avarice, is avaricious, the libertine, thinking of vice, is vicious, and on the contrary, those of virtuous thoughts show virtue in their actions. Arising naturally from such teaching is the attention devoted to thought-power. Taking the analogy of the physical body which may be developed by regimen and training, based on natural scientific laws, Theosophists teach that character may, in a similar way, be scientifically built up. Physical weakness can be eradicated and an opposite state of affairs brought about by special exercise of the weak part, and by a similar method, weakness of character may be converted into strength.

Every vice is considered to evidence the lack of a corresponding virtue, avarice for instance showing the absence of generosity. Instead, however, of allowing matters to rest at this, under the plea (arising from ignorance) that the individual was naturally avaricious, Theosophists teach that constant thought directed to generosity will in time change the individual's nature in this respect. This result cannot, of course, be brought about immediately, and the length of time necessary depends on at least two factors, the strength of thought and the strength of the vice, for the latter may be the sum of the indulgence of many ages and hence correspondingly difficult to eradicate.

The doctrine of *karma* must, therefore, be considered not in its relation to one life only, but in the light of the Theosophical teaching of reincarnation. Reincarnation is carried on under the law of *karma* as well as of evolution. The new-born person bears within the seeds of former lives. His or her character is the same as it was. It is as the individual made it in past existences and accordingly as he or she made it, so does it continue unless the individual himself change it as he or she had the power to do. Each succeeding existence finds that character more definite in one direction or another and if it be evil, the effort to change it becomes increasingly difficult, indeed a complete change may not be possible until many existences of effort have passed.

In such cases as these, the promptings of evil may be too strong to be resisted, yet the individual who has an intelligent knowledge of the workings of *karma,* though he or she must eventually yield, does so only after the most desperate struggle of which his or her nature is capable, and thus, instead of yielding weakly and increasing the power of the evil, has helped to destroy its potency. Only in the most rare cases can he free himself with a single effort. (See also **Evolution; Reincarnation; Theosophy; Yoga**)

Kat, Willem (1902–   )

Dutch psychiatrist and neurologist who has been active in the field of parapsychology. Born June 13, 1902, at Medemblick, Netherlands, he studied at the University of Amsterdam. In 1929 he married Wilhelmina Enjelina Lorje. Dr. Kat spent many years on the teaching staff of the biochemical laboratory at Amsterdam University, where he became head.

He has investigated unorthodox healing. As a member of the Dutch Society for Psychical Research and the Netherlands Committee for the Study of Unorthodox Healing and its Social Consequences, he has contributed articles on parapsychology to *Tijdschrift voor Parapsychologie.*

Katean Secret Society

A secret society of the Moluccas or Spice Islands of the Malay archipelago. Anyone who wished to become a member was introduced into the Katean house through an aperture in the form of a crocodile's jaws or a cassowary's beak. After remaining there for a few days, he was secretly removed to a remote spot. At the end of two months he was permitted to return to his relatives hitherto unaware of his whereabouts, as a member of the Katean Society.

Kathari (*See* Cathari)

"Katie King"

Claimed spirit entity manifesting at many Spiritualist seances, daughter of "John King." (See "**King, Katie**")

Katika Lima

Malay system of Astrology. (See **Malays**)

Katika Tujo

Malay system of Astrology. (See **Malays**)

Kauks

Fabulous bird, said to be hatched from a cock's egg. (See **Cock**)

Keel, John A(lva) (1930–   )

Writer on magic, mysteries and **UFOs**; conjuring magician. Born in Hornell, New York State, March 25, 1930, son of Harry Eli Kiehle, musician.

From an early age he was interested in magic tricks and idolized the great **Houdini.** After the divorce of his parents he lived with grandparents until the age of ten, then returned to his mother and stepfather, working on their farm near Perry, New York State. At Perry High School he edited a mimeographed one-sheet journal called *The Jester.* At the age of 14, he edited a column in the local weekly the *Perry Herald,* using the name John A. Keel, studying at Perry Public Library and planning to be a professional writer.

In 1947 he left home, hitchhiking to New York, where he earned a meager living as a writer in Greenwich Village for four years, before being drafted in the Korean War. Later, while quartered in Western Germany, he contributed to *American Forces Network* and was responsible for a Halloween broadcast from Frankenstein Castle, which started a monster scare on the lines of the famous Orson Welles Martian program.

Several years later he produced another Halloween forces broadcast from the Great Pyramid of Giza in Egypt. Attracted by the mystery of the East, he resigned from the American Forces Network and at the age of 24 started a series of adventurous world travels, hoping to write his way round the world as a journalist.

His travels in search of mysteries took him from Egypt to India and Tibet, searching out mystics, fakirs, lamas and magicians. In India, he discovered the secrets of snake-charming, being buried alive, walking on water, the basket trick and the **Indian Rope Trick,** as well as other feats of **Jadoo** or conjuring illusion.

However, he also admitted that there were mysteries which were not tricks. In Darjeeling he met Sherpa Tensing Norgay, hero of the Everest expeditions, who talked about the *Yeti* or Abominable Snowman (see **Monsters**). Keel went on to Sikkim, where he saw what he believed to be the *Yeti* footprints and heard the creature's strange cry. All these adventures are recounted in his entertaining book *Jadoo* (1957; London, 1958). In recent years he has also written extensively on UFOs. His books include: *UFOs: Operation Trojan Horse* (1970), *The Mothman Prophecies* (1975), *The Eighth Tower* (1975), *Our Haunted Planet* (1977), *Why UFOs* (1978).

Keeler, Pierre L.O.A. (c. 1886)

American slate-writing medium who sat for physical phenomena before the **Seybert Commission** in 1885. The committee did not find the phenomena unexplainable by normal means and came to no definite conclusion except that "we can dismiss the theory of a spiritual origin of the hand behind Mr. Keeler's screen."

Dr. Alfred Russel **Wallace** described in his book *My Life* (2 vols., 1905) some remarkable sittings with the suspected medium in 1886 in the company of Prof. Elliott Coues, General Lippitt and Mr. D. Lyman. In good light Wallace examined the enclosed space, the curtain, the floor, the walls.

After various telekinetic demonstrations, a hand appeared above the curtain, the fingers moving excitedly. "This was the signal for a pencil and a pad of notepaper, then rapid writing was heard, a slip of paper was torn off and thrown over the curtain, sometimes two or three in rapid succession, in the direction of certain sitters. The director of the seance picked them up, read the name signed, and asked if anyone knew it, and when claimed it was handed to him. In this way a dozen or more of the chance visitors received messages which were always intelligible to me and often strikingly appropriate. . . . On my second visit a very sceptical friend went with us and seeing the writing pad on the piano marked several of the sheets with his initials. The medium was very angry and said that it would spoil the seance. However, he was calmed by his friends. When it came to the writing the pad was given to me, over the top of the curtain, to hold. I held it just above the medium's shoulder, when a hand and pencil came through the curtain and wrote on the pad as I held it."

At a third seance, "most wonderful physical manifestations occurred. A stick was pushed through the curtain. Two watches were handed to me through the curtain, and were claimed by the two persons who sat by the medium. The small tambourine, about ten inches in diameter, was pushed through the curtain and fell on the floor. These objects came through different parts of the curtain, but left no holes as could be seen at the time, and was proved by a close examination afterwards. More marvellous still (if that be possible) a waistcoat was handed to me over the curtain, which proved to be the medium's, though his coat was left on and his hands had been held by his companion all the time; also about a score of people looking on all the time in a well-lighted room. These things seem impossible, but they are nevertheless facts.''

In his later career, Keeler concentrated solely on slate-writing which he combined with **pellet reading.** A. B. Richmond in his book *What I Saw at Cassadaga Lake,* (1888) described a sitting in which he received an answer to a pellet inside a pair of locked slates the key of which was in his pocket.

Admiral Moore, in his book *Glimpses of the Next State,* wrote of a successful seance in which on five slates 474 words were written and two pictures drawn in a period not exceeding ten minutes. The letters signed by names on the pellets were very commonplace. They contained no proof of identity. Still, the Admiral believed that the sitting was a most striking exhibition of spirit power as there was full light and the slates were held above the table with no cloth or covering of any sort over them. He knew the reports of past slate-writing through William **Eglinton,** S. T. **Davey** and others. He thought that no explanation he had read would meet Keeler's case.

Hereward **Carrington,** during his investigations in the Lily Dale Camp in August 1907, came to a different conclusion. He admitted that Keeler's slate writings were the most puzzling phenomena of their kind he ever witnessed, but, as pointed out in his report (*Proceedings,* A.S.P.R., Vol. II) there was sufficient evidence of palpable fraud. In the *Journal,* A.S.P.R. (July, 1908) an instance was mentioned in which Keeler was accidentally seen writing on a slate held in his lap under the table.

Carrington also stated that Dr. Richard **Hodgson,** Mr. Henry Ridgely Evans, Mr. David P. **Abbot,** and others united in thinking that Keeler was a clever trickster, yet he did not wish to be dogmatic on the point since he was unable to explain many stories told to him by apparently good observers and only reported that his own sittings, both the slate writing and **direct voice,** were certainly fraudulent. He was inclined to agree that the case needed careful re-investigation.

In retrospect, it is difficult to doubt that Keeler's phenomena, as with so many other exponents of slate-writing, must have been fraudulent.

Keeler, William M. (c. 1887)

American spirit photographer brother of Pierre L. O. A. **Keeler,** also mentioned in the report of the **Seybert Commission.** No formal investigation took place as his terms ($300 for three sittings) and his conditions were considered unacceptable.

Keeler was exposed by Dr. Walter F. **Prince** (see 'Supplementary Report on the Keeler-Lee Photographs' in *Proceedings* of the American Society for Psychical Research, vol. XII, 1919). (See also **Spirit Photography**)

Keely, John (Ernst) Worrell (1837–1898)

Founder of the Keely Motor Company, formed to promote his inventions powered by energy claimed to be derived from "vibratory etheric force" or cosmic energy. Born in Philadelphia September 3, 1837, son of a musician, Keely worked as a carpenter before developing his famous inventions. The Keely Motor Company was incorporated April 29, 1874, out of the Keely Motor Association. The company expended $60,000 on experimental work on Keely's first engine called "The Multiplicator." The company attracted investment which was spent by Keely on his researches, but he had no practical motor to show for the money.

In 1881, the managers threatened Keely with imprisonment if he would not disclose his secret. He did in fact spend a brief period in jail, but was befriended by Mrs. Clara Sophia Bloomfield Moore, a Theosophist, who provided further funds for Keely's experiments and defended him from criticism. She wrote a stirring defense of his work: *Keely and his Discoveries* (London, 1893; reprinted University Books, New York, 1972).

In addition to the famous Motor, Keely also demonstrated other devices, including a "Compound Disintegrator," "Musical Ball," "Globe Engine," "Pneumatic Rocket Gun" and a model airship, all powered by the same mysterious etheric force. He wrote a number of articles purporting to explain this force, but they were shrouded in such resounding pseudo-technical jargon that they only deepened the mystery. He spoke of "Vibro-Molecular, Vibro-Atomic, and Sympathetic Vibro-Etheric Forces as applied to induce Mechanical Rotation by Negative Sympathetic Attraction."

However, there was no doubt about the startling demonstrations of force given in his laboratory at Philadelphia, and many scientists, professors and businessmen were greatly impressed.

After Keely's death November 18, 1898, startling evidence of fraud was uncovered, and it has since been assumed that all his inventions were fraudulent. The real motive force seems to have been compressed air, concealed in cylinders in a secret basement and conveyed to the apparatus by thin hollow wires.

None the less, many individuals even today believe that any fraud may have been merely because of the intense pressure to show practical results, and that there may have been some genuine basis to Keely's life work. However, there is no evidence that Keely ever discovered a more powerful force than the inspired jargon of his theoretical expositions.

For details of another mysterious motor, see entry under John Murray **Spear.** (See also **Orgone**)

Keely Motor

An invention of John E. Worrell **Keely** (1837–1898), who claimed that it was powered by "vibratory etheric force" or cosmic energy. The motor was developed from what was called a "Hydro-Pneumatic-Pulsating-Vacuo-Engine."

The Keely Motor Association was formed in 1873 with headquarters in New York, while Keely experimented in Philadelphia. It developed into the Keely Motor Company.

Although Keely gave startling test demonstrations of motor force, together with other inventions using a similar mysterious energy, and convinced many reputable individuals and investors of the reality of his discoveries, there was evidence of fraud after his death. As a result of these disclosures, the Keely Motor Company dissolved. (See also John E. Worrell **Keely; Orgone;** John Murray **Spear**)

Keevan of the Curling Locks

In Irish mythology, the lover of Cleena, a Danaan maiden, who went off to hunt in the woods, leaving her to be abducted by the fairies. (See also **Danaans**)

Keil, H(erbert) H(ans) J(urgen) (1930–   )

Lecturer in psychology and active parapsychologist. Born May 30, 1930 at Freiberg, Germany, he studied at University of Tasmania, Hobart, Australia (B.A. 1957, Dip. Ed. 1959, B.A. hons. 1960). In 1955 he married Gloria Ruth Whitburn.

He has worked at the University of Tasmania and the University of Hamburg, Germany; from 1960–61 was a teaching fellow, psychology, University of Tasmania, 1961–62 research fellow, Parapsychology Laboratory, Duke University, 1962 onwards lecturer in psychology, University of Tasmania. He is an associate member of the Parapsychological Association. His parapsychology investigations include study of psychokinesis with improved controls and automated experimental paraphernalia. He has published articles in the *Australian Journal of Psychology* and the *Medical Journal of Australia.*

Keingala

The weatherwise mare of Asmund in the Icelandic saga of Grettir the Strong, c. eleventh century. Her master believed in her weather prophecies, and, in setting his second son, Grettir, to look after the horses, told him to be guided by Keingala, who would always return to the stable before a storm.

As she persisted in remaining on the cold hillside, grazing on the scanty grass until the lad was nearly frozen with cold, Grettir determined to make her return home regardless of the weather. One morning, before turning out the horses, he tore off a long strip of her skin from wither to flank. This had the effect of making the mare soon seek her stable. The same thing occurring the next day, no storm impending, Asmund himself let out the horses, when he discovered what had been done.

Kelpie, The

A water spirit of Scotland, which was believed to haunt streams and torrents. Kelpies appear to have been of a mischievous nature and were often accused of stopping the water-wheels of mills, and of swelling streams. The Kelpie was occasionally used as a name of terror to frighten unruly children, and it was believed that he devoured women.

The Kelpie was also said to tempt travelers to mount him, then plunge them into deep water and drown them. An Irish version of the Kelpie was the *Eac Visge.* (See also **Phouka**)

Kenawell, William Wooding (1920–   )

Assistant professor of history at Stroudsburg State College, East Stroudsburg, Pennsylvania; has also written on parapsychology. Born November 19, 1920, at Reedsville, Pennsylvania, he studied at Franklin and Marshall College, Lancaster, Pa. (B.A. 1953), Lehigh University,

Bethlehem, Pa. (M.A. 1955). In 1944 he married Doris Belle Drenning.

From 1954–55 he was research assistant at Department of History, York Junior College, York, Pa., teaching assistant 1955–56; from 1956–61 librarian at Lehigh University. As a grantee of the Parapsychology Foundation he engaged in a study of the life of Frederick Bligh **Bond,** a British archaeologist who used automatic writing in connection with excavations at Glastonbury Abbey, England. This study was published as *The Quest at Glastonbury; A Biographical Study of Frederick Bligh Bond,* (Helix Press, 1965).

Kephalonomancy

A method of divination which was practiced by interpreting various signs on the baked head of an ass. It was familiar to the Germans and the Lombards substituted for it the head of a goat. The ancient diviners placed lighted carbon on an ass's head, and pronounced the names of those who were suspected of any crime. If a crackling coincided with the utterance of a name, that name was taken as being the guilty person.

Kephu

A vampire of the Karen tribes of Burma. (See also **Vampire**)

Kepler, Johann (1571–1630)

Famous German mathematician, astronomer and astrologer. He was born December 27, 1571, at Weil in Würtemburg and educated at a monastic school at Maulbrunn and afterwards at the University of Tübingen, where he studied philosophy, mathematics, theology and astronomy. In 1593, he became professor of mathematics and morals at Gratz in Styria, where he also continued his astrological studies. He had an unhappy home life, and was somewhat persecuted for his doctrines.

In 1626 were printed the famous Rodolphine tables, which he had prepared with the astronomer Tycho de Brahe. Kepler died November 15, 1630 at Ratisbon.

Some of Kepler's writings were influenced by occult and mystical concepts. In his work *De Harmonice Mundi* (1619), he expounded a system of celestial harmonies. His book *Somnium* (1634) was an early speculation on life on the moon. For a discussion of the concept of archetypes in the work of Kepler, see 'The Influence of Archetypal Ideas on the Scientific Theories of Kepler' in the book *The Interpretation of Nature and the Psyche* by C. G. Jung & W. Pauli (1955).

The laws of the courses of the planets, deduced by Kepler from observations made by Tycho, and known as *The Three Laws of Kepler,* became the foundation of Newton's discoveries, as well as the whole modern theory of the planets. His services in the cause of astronomy have placed him high amongst the distinguished men of science, and in 1808 a monument was erected to his memory at Ratisbon. His most important work is his *Astronomia nova, seu Physica Coelestis tradita Commentariis de Motibus Stellae Martis* (1609) which is still regarded as a classic by astronomers.

Kerheb

The priestly caste of ancient Egyptian scribes (see **Egypt**).

Kerner, Justinus (Andreas) (Christian) (1786–1862)

Noted German poet and physician, born September 18, 1786, at Ludwigsburg, Württemberg. He studied medicine at Tübingen and practiced as a physician at Wildbad. In addition to books of poetry, he was author of a remarkable record of supernormal phenomena and experiments in **Animal Magnetism** therapeutics: *Die Seherin von Prevorst, Eröffnungen über das innere Leben des Menschen und über das Hereinragen einer Geisterwelt in die Unsere*. It is the story of Frau Frederica **Hauffe**, "the Seeress of Prevorst," who arrived in Weinsberg in November 1826, and became Kerner's patient.

Frau Hauffe was the picture of death, exhibited many frightful symptoms and fell into trance every evening at seven o'clock. For a while, Dr. Kerner ignored her somnambulic condition and seriously declared that he was not going to take any notice of what she said in her sleep. He commenced to treat her by homeopathic remedies.

The medicine produced the reverse effect to the one expected and she was fast approaching death. In trance she prescribed a gentle course of animal magnetism, with which Dr. Kerner at first desired to have nothing to do. Finally he became convinced of the extraordinary character of the case and began to study it in an earnest spirit.

His book, published in 1829, passed through three enlarged editions in 1832, 1838 and 1846. In a translation by Catherine Crowe it was published in English in 1845 under the title *The Seeress of Prevorst; or Openings-up into the Inner Life of Man, and Mergings of a Spirit World into the World of Matter*.

In Germany the book had made a great sensation. Among those who inquired into the case of the Seeress of Prevorst were Kant, Schubert, Eschenmayer, Görres, Werner and David Strauss. On the revelations of the Seeress a school of philosophy was built and, to have an organ of its own, Dr. Kerner established in 1831 a periodical, *Blätter aus Prevorst; Originalien und Lesefrüchte für Freunde des innern Lebens* (Leaves from Prevorst; or, Original Literary Fruits for Lovers of the Inner Life). Its chief contributors were Prof. Eschenmayer, Frederik von Mayer of Frankfort, Gotthelf, Heinrich von Schubert, Guido Görres and Franz von Baader. Twelve volumes were published until 1839 when the periodical was superseded by *Magikon; Archive für Beobachtungen aus dem Gebiete der Geisterkunde und des magnetischen und magischen Lebens* (Magikon, or Archives for Observations concerning the Realms of the Spirit World and of Magnetic Life). It ran until 1853. Kerner died February 21, 1862.

Kerner's reputation was very high. King Ludwig of Bavaria in 1848 and the King of Württemberg in 1858 bestowed pensions upon him, while King Frederick William IV of Prussia expressed his admiration in 1848 by sending him the gold medal of art and science. King Ludwig made him the first knight of the newly instituted Maximilian Order of Science and Art.

Besides the *Seeress of Prevost*, Kerner was author of the following volumes: *The History of Two Somnambulists; together with certain other Notable Things from the Realms of Magical Cure and Psychology* (1826); *History of Modern Cases of Possession, together with Observations made in the Realm of Kako-demoniac, Magnetic Appearances* (1834); *Letter to the Superior Medical Counsellor Schelling concerning the Appearance of Possession, Demoniacal, Magnetic Suffering and its Cure through Magnetic Treatment, as known to the Ancients* (1836); *An appearance from the Night Realms of Nature; proved Legally by a Series of Witnesses, and communicated to Searchers into Nature for their careful consideration* (1836); *Somnambulic Tables; or, the History and Explanation of that Phenomenon* (1853); *Anton Mesmer, the Discoverer of Animal Magnetism, with Recollections of Him, etc.* (1856).

For biographies of Kerner, see Aime Reinhard, *Justinus Kerner und das Kernerhaus zu Weinsberg* (Tübingen, 1862); A. M. Howitt-Watts, *The Pioneers of Spiritual Reformation* (London, 1883).

Kether

The Kabalistic name for the number one, and meaning "Reason" (the Crown), the equilibrating power. Also a Hebrew occult name for one of the three essentials of God—Reason. (See also **Kabala**)

Kettner, Frederick (died 1957)

Founder of the Biosophical Institute and **Biosophy,** a system of spiritual self-education and self-improvement intended to create a world-fellowship of peace-loving men and women who have overcome religious, national, racial and social prejudices, to work creatively for the growth of democracy and world peace.

Dr. Kettner was inspired by the writings of the philosopher Spinoza, and became a leading authority on his teachings. Dr. Kettner created the Institute for the Advancement of Cultural and Spiritual Values in cooperation with leading educators and thinkers in the U.S., and in 1935 inaugurated a movement for a Secretary of Peace in every government. He toured the U.S. and lectured on his ideals.

In 1936, the Secretary of Peace idea was partially endorsed by the Inter-American Peace Conference in Buenos Aires, where Dr. Kettner founded the Instituto Biosofico Argentino. He also founded the Biosophical Institute, which continues his teachings. Dr. Kettner's work with the Bisophical Institute was warmly endorsed by Prof. Albert Einstein, who wrote "Your group is the embodiment of that spirit which Spinoza served so passionately."

"Key of Solomon the King" (Clavicula Salomonis)

A **grimoire** or magical treatise of medieval origin, of which a number of manuscripts are extant. It is supposed to be the work of King **Solomon,** but is manifestly of later origin, and was probably written in the fourteenth or fifteenth century. It was published under the title *Clavicula Salomonis* c. 1456.

It is permeated with late Jewish ideas, and its chief intention appears to be the finding of treasure and the making of such experiments as have for their object the interference with the freewill of others. The power of the **Divine Name** is much in evidence, but the work appears to combine both Black and White Magic.

The *Lemegeton*, or Lesser Key of Solomon, is much more

noteworthy. Its earliest examples date from the seventeenth century, and it invokes the hierarchies of the abyss by legions and millions. It is divided into four parts, which control the offices of all spirits at the will of the operator. The first part, *Göetia,* contains forms of conjuration for seventy-two demons with an account of their powers and offices. The second part, *Theurgia Göetia,* deals with the spirits of the cardinal points, who are of mixed nature. The third book is called the *Pauline Art,* the significance of which name is unaccountable. It deals with the angels of the hours of the day and night, and of the signs of the Zodiac. The fourth part is entitled *Almadel,* which enumerates four other choirs of spirits. The usual homilies regarding purity of life are insisted upon, as is the circumstance that none of the conjurations shall be applied to the injury of another.

For fuller discussion of this grimoire and its contents, see: Idries Shah, *The Secret Love of Magic* (1957); Arthur E. Waite, *The Book of Ceremonial Magic* (1961). The work was originally translated into English by S. L. MacGregor **Mathers** (a member of the **Golden Dawn** society) in 1909, reissued by Routledge & Kegan Paul, London, in 1972.

Keyhoe, Donald Edwards (1897–   )

Prominent figure in **flying saucer** controversies. He was a graduate of the U.S. Naval Academy and became a Marine aircraft and balloon pilot during World War II, with the rank of Major. He began writing about Unidentified Flying Objects in 1950 with his article 'Flying Saucers Are Real' (*True* magazine, Jan. 1950), which caused a sensation with its claim that the U.S. Air Force was covering up evidence for the reality of flying saucers.

He contributed numerous magazine articles on the subject of flying saucers, and appeared on hundreds of radio and television programs. His books on UFOs included: *The Flying Saucers Are Real* (1950), *Flying Saucers From Outer Space* (1953), *The Flying Saucer Conspiracy* (1955), *Flying Saucers: Top Secret* (1960), *Aliens From Space* (1973).

In 1956, Keyhoe founded NICAP (**National Investigations Committee on Aerial Phenomena**), with prominent military men and politicians on the board of governors, including Senator Barry Goldwater. NICAP was beset with financial problems over the years, and after a stormy meeting in 1969, Keyhoe retired as director, although remaining on the board. (See also **UFO**)

Khaib

The ancient Egyptian name for the shadow, which at death was supposed to quit the body to continue a separate existence of its own. It was represented under the form of a sunshade. (See also **Egypt**)

Khérumian, Raphaël (1903–   )

Painter and writer on parapsychological topics. Born at Baku, Azerbaidzhan. He was a member of the board of directors of the Institut Métapsychique International, Paris, France, with special interest in the physiological mechanisms of telepathy and certain moral implications of parapsychology.

His articles in the *Revue Métapsychique* included: 'Introduction à l'étude de la connaissance parapsychologique' (Introduction to the Study of Parapsychology Knowledge, Nos. 1, 2, 3, 1948), 'Essai d'interprétation des expériences de Soal et Goldney' (Interpretative Essay on the Experiments of Soal and Goldney, No. 8, 1949), 'Les propriétés groupales des organismes et la parapsychologie' (The Group Properties of Organisms and Parapsychology, No. 10, 1950), 'Procédés mécaniques pour faciliter les transmissions télépathiques (Mechanical Procedures to Facilitate Telepathic Messages, No. 26, 1953), 'Remarques sur les déformations des dessins télépathiques' (Remarks on the Distortions of Telepathic Drawings, in collaboration with René **Warcollier,** No. 27, 1954), 'Physiologie et parapsychologie' (Physiology and Parapsychology, 1955), 'A propos de l'hypothèse cryptesthésique' (Regarding the Cryptesthestic Hypothesis, vol. 1, No. 2, 1955), 'Réflexions sur l'état actuel et les perspectives de la parapsychologie' (Remarks on the Present Status and the Future of Parapsychology, vol. 2, Nos. 8, 9, 1958–59). He also published *Léonard de Vinci et les mystères* (Paris, 1952).

Khu

The ancient Egyptian name for one of the immortal parts of man, probably the spirit. The word means "clear" or "luminous" and was symbolized by a flame of fire.

Khunrath, Heinrich (1560–1605)

German alchemist and hierophant of the physical side of the *Magnum Opus.* He was certainly aware of the greater issues of Hermetic theorems and may be regarded as a follower of **Paracelsus.**

He was born in Saxony in 1560. At the age of 28 he graduated in medicine at the University of Basle. He practiced in Hamburg and thereafter in Dresden. He died in poverty and obscurity in Leipzig in 1605 at the age of forty-five.

The most remarkable of his works, some of which are still in manuscript, is the *Anphitheatrum Sapientiæ Æternæ solius veræ, Christiano Kabbalisticum divino magicum, &c.* It is an unfinished work and appeared in 1602, although an earlier edition of 1598 has been suggested. An edition of 1609 contains a preface and conclusion by his friend Erasmus Wohlfahrt. It is a mystical and magical treatise. The seven steps leading to the goal of universal knowledge are described in a commentary on the Wisdom of Solomon. The work has been described as being the voice of ancient chaos, and its folding plates are particularly curious. Khunrath believed in the transmutation of stones and metals and in the **Elixir of Life.** The physician and chemist Conrad Khunrath (c. 1594) may have been a brother of Heinrich Khunrath. (See also **Alchemy**)

Kian

In Irish mythology, father of Lugh (father of the Ulster warrior hero Cuchulain). After his magical cow with her wonderful supply of milk had been stolen by Balor, (King of the Fomorians), he revenged himself by making Balor's daughter, Ethlinn, the mother of three sons. Of these, two were drowned by Balor, and the third, Lugh, escaped by falling into a bay and was wafted back to his father, Kian.

Some years later, while fighting in Ulster, Kian fell in with the three sons of Turenn whose house was at enmity with him. To escape their notice, he turned himself into a pig, but they recognized him and he was wounded by one of them. He begged to be restored to his human shape before dying. This being granted, he rejoiced in having outwitted his enemies, as they would now have to pay the blood-fine for a man instead of a pig. The brothers, determined that there should be no blood-stained weapon to publish the deed, stoned Kian and buried his body.

K.I.B. Foundation

British organization founded in 1980 to encourage and promote research in fields at present outside the scientific orthodoxies, such as parapsychology and alternative medicine. The trustees were Arthur **Koestler,** Brian **Inglis,** Tony Bloomfield, Michael Fullerlove and Sir William Wood, and the Foundation's title derives from initials of the first three names. After the death of Arthur Koestler in 1983, the Foundation was renamed "The Koestler Foundation."

The Foundation acts as a clearing house for information about research in various parts of the world and acts as a bridge between sponsors and research projects. Selection of projects is by an advisory group which includes individuals of distinction in relevant fields of science and medicine. Projects already undertaken include publication of significant books, such as *A Glossary of Terms Used in Parapsychology* compiled by Michael A. Thalbourne (1982) on behalf of the Society for Psychical Research. Address: 23 Harley House, Marylebone Road, London, NW1 5HE, England.

Kidd, James (1879–c. 1949)

American copper miner and prospector, whose disappearance in 1949 led to the discovery of his will bequeathing nearly a quarter of a million dollars towards "research or some scientific proof of a soul of the human body which leaves at death . . . ." As a result, there ensued what newspapers called "The Ghost Trial of the Century," in which no less than 134 scientific researchers, organizations and institutions filed a claim on the Kidd estate.

Kidd was something of a mystery man, a quiet well-mannered unobtrusive loner who lived in Phoenix, Arizona, and worked in the copper mines or prospected in the mountains. He vanished after undertaking a prospecting trip in the area of Superstition Mountain, claimed as the locale of the almost legendary Lost Dutchman gold mine.

Kidd had set out November 9, 1949, and his disappearance was not noticed until some weeks later. Routine inquiries ascertained that he was born July 18, 1879 in Ogdensburg, New York, had lived in Reno, Nevada, and Los Angeles, California. He had worked for the Miami Copper Company, Arizona, lived simply and had few acquaintances.

By 1954, Kidd was officially registered as a missing person but no proof of death was established. It was not until 1957 that the contents of Kidd's unclaimed safe deposit box together with stock certificates, were delivered to the Estate Tax Commissioner's office in Arizona. In January 1964, official examination of Kidd's papers disclosed assets totalling $174,065.69 and a will written at Phoenix, Arizona, reading:

> "this is my first and only will and is dated the second of January, 1946. I have no heirs and have not been married in my life and after all my funeral expenses have been paid and #100. one hundred dollars to

some preacher of the gospel to say fare well at my grave sell all my property which is all in cash and stocks with E. F. Hutton Co. Phoenix some in safety deposit box, and have this balance money to go in a research or some scientific proof of a soul of the human body which leaves at death I think in time their can be a Photograph of soul leaving the human at death, James Kidd."

Even before the will was validated, the first claim to the estate came from the University of Life Church Inc., Arizona, as an organization conducting research on scientific proof of the existence of a human soul. Meanwhile two Canadians, claiming to be blood brothers of Kidd, contested the will. By now, widespread press coverage had resulted in claims to the estate from a number of individuals and organizations, including the **Parapsychology Foundation,** the **Psychical Research Foundation** and the Neurological Sciences Foundation of the University of Arizona College of Medicine.

On May 6, 1965, the Court of Maricopa County, Arizona, declared the will fully acceptable for probate. More petitions flooded into the Court, some of them merely facetious and invalid, others from reputable organizations like the **American Society for Psychical Research.** The hearings were presided over by Judge Robert L. Myers of the Supreme Court of Maricopa County, and occupied ninety days and some 800,000 words of testimony. Eventually a decision of October 20, 1967, awarded the Kidd funds to the Barrow Neurological Institute, Phoenix, Arizona.

For a detailed study of this remarkable story, see *The Great Soul Trial* by John G. Fuller, Macmillan, 1969, which includes Fuller's own discussions with parapsychologists and psychics on the issues raised by the trial.

Kilner, Walter J(ohn) (1847–1920)

British physician who first studied the phenomenon of the human **aura** and its changed appearances in sickness or health.

Born May 23, 1847, at Bury St. Edmunds, Suffolk, England, he was educated at Bury St. Edmunds Grammar School and St. John's College, Cambridge University, and was a medical student at St. Thomas's Hospital, London. He took his B.A. in 1870, M.R.C.S. and L.S.A. in 1871 and M.B. in 1872. In June 1879, he was appointed in charge of electro-therapy at St. Thomas's Hospital. In 1883, he became a member of the Royal College of Physicians, then opened a private practice as a physician at Ladbroke Grove, London.

He took a scientific interest in the aura, a kind of radiating luminous cloud surrounding individuals, usually perceived only by clairvoyants. He was familiar with the work of Baron von **Reichenbach,** who had claimed to perceive auras round the poles of magnets and human hands.

In 1908, Kilner believed that the human aura might be made visible if viewed through a suitable filter. He experimented with dicyanin, a coaltar derivative and after careful study reported his findings in his book *The Human Atmosphere* (London, 1911). This book was the first to study the human aura as a scientific fact instead of a somewhat questionable psychic phenomenon. The revised edition of Kilner's book was published in 1920, and some medical men endorsed his findings, although they were very unconventional for his time. Kilner, however, died June 23, 1920.

The revised edition of his book was reprinted under the title *The Human Aura* by University Books, New York, 1965.

After Kilner's death, his findings were endorsed by the experimenter Oscar Bagnall, in his book *The Origin and Properties of the Human Aura* (London, 1937; revised edition University Books, N.Y., 1970). In recent years, a special photographic technique has been devised by which it is claimed that the aura can be reproduced. (See also **Aura; Kirlian Aura; Od, Odie Force, Odyle; Reichenbach**)

Kimmell, Susan C(randall) (Mrs. Leslie Frederic Kimmell) (1894–   )

Public relations director who collaborated with Steward Edward **White** on preparations of books on parapsychological topics: *Anchors to Windward* (1945), *The Stars Are Still There* (1946), *With Folded Wings* (1947), *The Job of Living* (1948). Born January 1, 1894 at Chicago, Illinois, she studied at University of Minnesota (B.A. 1917). In 1924 she married Leslie Frederic Kimmell. From 1953-62, she was director of public relations, American Institute of Family Relations, Los Angeles, California.

King, Bruce (1897–1976)

A modern tycoon of **astrology,** using the pseudonym "Zolar." Born in Chicago, Illinois, he became an actor, salesman and stockbroker, eventually part-owner of a radio station in Los Angeles. The station had an astrologer named Kobar as general manager, and King was impressed with his financial success.

In the same week that Kobar left the station to go to Hollywood, another astrologer demonstrated a dime-in-the-slot horoscope machine to King, and the two men went into partnership in the Astrolograph Company, putting the machines in movie theaters.

King later conceived the idea of making horoscopes for chain stores and established a highly successful business. It was then that he took the pseudonym "Zolar," derived from the word "Zodiac" with echoes of "Kobar." He later merchandised something like 100 million horoscopes, and published bestselling books on astrology and occultism, notably *The Encyclopedia of Ancient and Forbidden Knowledge* (Nash, 1970). He died January 16, 1976.

King, Francis (Xavier) (1904–   )

Contemporary British author who has also written or edited a number of important studies on occultism, including: *Ritual Magic in England: 1887 to the present day* (London, 1970; U.S. title *The Rites of Modern Occult Magic,* Macmillan, 1971), *Astral Projection, Ritual Magic and Alchemy* (London, 1971), *Sexuality, Magic and Perversion,* (London, 1971); *Magic; The Western Tradition* (London & N.Y., 1975), *Wisdom From Afar* (N.Y., 1975), *Satan and Swastika; The Occult and the Nazi Party* (London, 1976), (with Stephen Skinner) *Techniques of High Magic* (London, 1980), (with Isabel Sutherland) *The Rebirth of Magic* (London, 1982). He has also contributed to such reference books as *Encyclopedia of Mythology* and the *Encyclopedia of the Unexplained.*

King, George (c. 1919–   )

British cultist, founder of the **Aetherius Society,** later resident in California. King was a British cabdriver, son of a woman who ran a healing sanctuary. King studied occultism and practiced hatha **yoga** for many years. He frequently went into trance states in which he received or delivered inspirational messages. In 1954 a mysterious voice told him "Prepare yourself, you are to become the voice of Interplanetary Parliament." Subsequently King gave trance addresses claimed to be from various Masters, including "Aetherius" from Venus, and a Chinese rejoicing in the name "Goo-ling."

The Aetherius Society was founded in London in 1956, with tape-recorded trance communications from the Master Aetherius, organizing military-sounding operations to rescue the world from dramatic spiritual perils.

Such missions included charging holy mountains by means of "Cosmic Batteries" of prayer, "Operation Sunbeam," "Operation Karmalight" and "Operation Bluewater" as well as "Special Power Transmissions." These hazardous operations involved cult members in pilgrimages, prayers and direction of currents of spiritual force from the Cosmic Brotherhood.

News bulletins delivered through the mediumship of George King often commenced with messages from such entities as "Mars, Sector 6." The dark astral forces are always defeated, but like the evil villains of Superman comics, they always plan further mischief.

In 1959, George King brought his Society to the U.S. and resided in a large house in Hollywood, L.A. It contains a chapel, a bookstore, offices, conference rooms, and an air conditioned trance room in which King delivers his interplanetary messages. In recent years, the Aetherius Society has extended its range of interests to include spiritual healing, psychometry, Mantra Yoga, Yoga breathing, chromotherapy, Personal Magnetism, Kinesiology, and Pendulum Dowsing. Meanwhile the Society now lists King's qualifications as "Sir George King, Kt.C., G.C.J., D.Sc., Ph.D., D.D., Hu. Sa.D."

King, Godfré Ray

Pseudonym of Guy W. **Ballard** (1878–1939), leader of the "I AM" cult at Mount Shasta, northern California. Ballard was born in Kansas and worked as a mining engineer before studying Theosophical literature and later launching his own successful cult with his wife Edna, a professional medium. Under the name Godfré Ray King, Ballard wrote *Unveiled Mysteries* (The Saint-Germain Press, 1934), in which he reported meeting a godlike figure described as "the Master Saint-Germain" who imparted the "Mighty I Am" Presence, which became the basis of Ballard's cult.

The publishers printed the sweeping claim: "Each copy of this book carries with it the mighty Presence of the ascended Host, their radiation and sustaining power. The Masters have become a blazing outpouring of Light into which no discordant thought or feeling can enter."

Ballard also used the pseudonyms Lotus Ray King and B. B. Ballard Bryan. After Ballard's death in 1939, discordant feelings entered into the cult, when the new leaders were put on trial on a charge of obtaining money under false pretenses. However, the movement rallied again, even after the death of Edna Ballard in 1971, and still exists in Mount Shasta.

"King, John"

One of the most romantic and frequently claimed spirit entities, manifesting at many spiritualist seances of different mediums over many decades. He claimed to have been Henry Owen Morgan, the buccaneer, who was knighted by Charles II and appointed Governor of Jamaica.

He first manifested with the **Davenport Brothers** in 1850, and was first seen in the flash of a pistol fired by Ira Davenport in the dark. He remained as spirit manager with the Davenports throughout their career and in **typtology** and **direct voice** gave them sound advice in difficult positions.

His ostensible activity was multifarious. While faithfully serving the Davenport Brothers he took charge of the performances in the loghouse of Jonathan **Koons** in the wilds of Ohio. Here he assumed an august mien. As the head of a band of 160 spirits he claimed descent from a race of men known by the generic title "Adam," and having as leaders "the most ancient angels." They signed their communications as "King No. 1," "No. 2," etc., and sometimes: "Servant and Scholar of God." In his last incarnation King had strayed from the path of virtue and become a redoubtable pirate. He communicated in direct voice through a trumpet, his own invention, and through direct scripts. The tone of these writings was sanctimonious and upbraiding, i.e.: "We know that our work will be rejected by many, and condemned as the production of their King Devil, whom they profess to repudiate, but do so constantly serve by crucifying truth and rejecting all that is contrary to their own narrow pride and vain imaginings."

The *Telegraph Papers* of 1856 published a psychometric reading of the writing of John King by Mrs. Kellog and Miss Jay of New York to whom the paper was handed in a sealed envelope. Mrs. Kellog became entranced and said: "A person of great might and power appears before me—a power unknown. I cannot compare him to anyone on earth. He wields a mighty weapon. I can neither describe nor explain the influence that emanates from him. I can only compare it to one of whom we read in the Bible. It seems like unto one who 'rules the world.' It does not seem to have been done by any human being. It does not seem to me that a mortal could have been employed even as the instrument for this writing. This is beyond human effort." Miss Jay had given a similar reading: "It must be a power so far exalted in the scale of development as to grasp the great laws that govern all material combinations. He does not seem to be of the earth, but to belong to another race of beings, whose spiritual growth has continued for ages."

In the early years of British Spiritualism, it was the aspiration of many mediums to secure the influence of "John King." Mrs. Mary **Marshall** was the first, Mrs. **Guppy,** Miss Georgina **Houghton,** Mrs. A. H. Firman, Charles **Williams,** William **Eglinton** and Cecil **Husk** followed, whilst in America he was claimed by Mr. & Mrs. Nelson **Holmes** and Mme. **Blavatsky** in her early career as a Spiritualist. V. S. Solovyoff, in his book *A Modern Priestess of Isis* (1895), even suggested that Blavat-

sky's Mahatma Koot Hoomi was "John King" transformed by the addition of an Eastern garb.

On March 20, 1873, in a daylight seance of Charles Williams, "John King" manifested so successfully that a sketch was made of him by an artist. A week later he appeared again in solid and material form. He was usually seen in the light of a peculiar lamp which he carried and which illuminated his face and sometimes the room. In Paris, on May 14, 1874, a young man tried to seize him. "John King" eluded his grasp and left a piece of drapery behind. The medium was found entranced. On being searched, no paraphernalia for a make-up was discovered.

In times, "John King" took charge of the physical phenomena of Mrs. Etta **Wriedt** in London. He greeted the sitters of Williams' and Cecil Husk's circle by their names. W. T. **Stead** once found a mislaid manuscript through communication in automatic writing from "John King." More recently "Feda," the control of Mrs. Osborne **Leonard,** informed H. Dennis **Bradley** during a seance of his own that "John King" often helped with the voices and that the volume of his own voice was enormous.

Of all the public activities of "John King," his association with Eusapia **Palladino** was the most memorable. Scientists all over the world made his acquaintance and found him ever anxious to produce good and convincing phenomena. He said in many messages that Eusapia Palladino was his reincarnated daughter but he seldom spoke, if so only in Italian and through the entranced medium.

A curious story of his appearance in strong light was told by Chevalier Francesco Graus, an Italian engineer, in a letter to Vincent Cavalli, the letter being published in *Luce e Ombra* in April 1907. At the time of the narrative, Eusapia worried herself ill over the theft of her jewels. She was so affected by the reproaches of the police inspector that she fainted. The table began to move and rapped out: "Save my daughter, she is mad." "A minute later," wrote Graus, "in full light, a phenomenon occurred which I shall never forget. On my left, in the space separating me from Mme. Palladino, appeared the form of an old man, tall, rather thin, with an abundant beard who, without speaking, laid the full palm of his right hand on my head, which he squeezed between his fingers as if to draw from it some vital fluid, and when he saw fit he raised his hand and spread over Eusapia's head the fluid he had withdrawn from my brain. He repeated this operation three times in succession, then the figure dissolved. Mme. Palladino immediately returned to her normal state. I remained for three consecutive days in such a condition of cerebral prostration, on account of the fluid that had been drawn from me, that I could not carry on the smallest intellectual work."

The identity of "John King" with Henry Owen Morgan, the pirate, has never been satisfactorily established. Sir Arthur Conan **Doyle** had in his possession a contemporary picture of the buccaneer king but it bore no resemblance to the tall, swarthy man with a noble head and full black beard, who presented himself in materialized form. But Doyle stated that a daughter of a recent governor of Jamaica was confronted in a seance in London with "John King," who said to her: "You have brought back from Jamaica something which was mine." She asked: "What was it?" He answered: "My will." It was a fact. Her father had brought back this document.

To Admiral Usborne Moore, in a sitting with Cecil Husk on March 28, 1905, "John King" said that he had been hunting up old records and found that he succeeded Lynch as Governor of Jamaica. There was a Richard Morgan who came before him as Governor and the names were sometimes confused. He believed that he was governor three separate times, not consecutively, but he would make further inquiries.

A correspondent to *Light* (June 29, 1912) looked up the official handbook of the island and found that Morgan succeeded Sir Thomas Lynch in 1673, Lord Vaughan in 1677 and the Earl of Carlisle in 1680. The other Morgan to whom he referred was Colonel Edward (not Richard) Morgan and he was Deputy Governor in 1664.

Through Mrs. Wriedt in **Julia's Bureau** in London, "John King" gave many particulars in regard to his earth life in Jamaica and made beautiful bugle calls through the trumpet, saying that was how he used to call his men together, in the old buccaneering days, one most terrific blast illustrating his signal to fight.

In February 1930, "John King" manifested in Dr. Glen **Hamilton**'s circle in Winnipeg, Canada, and carried on a dialogue with "Walter" who controlled another medium, feigning that they were abroad the pirateship amongst a crew of ruffians. This play-acting had a psychological purpose—the recovery of past memories and the imagining of a sailing ship which was afterwards objectively built out of **ectoplasm.**

The continued manifestation of "John King" with different mediums over a period of some eighty years raises a number of interesting questions. If the manifestations are genuine, why should a relatively unimportant individual continue to dominate seance phenomena? Why should such a personality continue to exist virtually unchanged for nearly a century? Is there so little progress in the spirit world? Or does the interest of mediums in a well defined personality bring about conscious or unconscious fraud? Or is this perhaps a fictitious personality like the experimental "ghost" created by members of the Toronto Society for Psychical Research? (see **Philip**") (see also "Katie **King**").

"King, Katie"

The famous spirit **control** of Miss Florence **Cook.** "Katie" claimed to be the daughter of the equally famous spirit entity "John **King,**" but of her identity even less proof is available than of her father's.

She began to manifest in the Cook house when Florence was a girl of 15. She was seen almost daily, the first time in April, 1872, showing a death-like face between the seance curtains. Later her materializations became more perfect, but it was only after a year of experimental work that she could walk out of the cabinet and show herself in full figure to the sitters.

She became a nearly permanent inhabitant of the Cook household, walked about the house, appeared at unexpected moments, and went to bed with the medium, much to her annoyance. When Florence married, complications arose. According to Florence **Marryat**, Capt. Corner used

to feel at first as if he had married two women, and was not quite sure which of the two was his wife.

According to all accounts "Katie" was a beautiful girl. In his famous investigations of psychic phenomena, Sir William **Crookes** had forty flashlight photographs of "Katie." In most of them she noticeably resembled Miss Cook, but Crookes had no doubt of her independent identity. "Photography was inadequate," he wrote, "to depict the perfect beauty of Katie's face, as words are powerless to describe her charm of manner. Photography may, indeed, give a map of her countenance; but how can it reproduce the brilliant purity of her complexion, or the ever varying expression of her most mobile features, now overshadowed with sadness when relating some of the bitter experiences of her past life, now smiling with all the innocence of happy girlhood when she had collected my children round her, and was amusing them by recounting anecdotes of her adventures in India?"

Her original name was claimed to have been Annie Owen Morgan. She was about twelve years old when Charles I was beheaded. She married, had two children and committed many crimes, murdering men with her own hands. She died quite young, at the age of 22 or 23. Her attachment to Florence Cook served the purpose of convincing the world of the truth of Spiritualism. This work was given her on the other side as a service to expiate her earthly sins. On her farewell appearance, after three years of constant manifestations, she declared that her years of suffering were now over, she would ascend to a higher sphere from where she could only correspond with her medium through **automatic writing** at long intervals, although Florence would be able to see her clairvoyantly.

In her early manifestations in the seances of the **Davenport Brothers,** "Katie King" was apparently far less spiritual than at the time of the Crookes records. Robert Cooper, describing a **direct voice** consultation of the spirits by the Davenports, wrote: "The next minute a shrill female voice was heard immediately in front of us. It was like that of a person of the lower walks of life and talked away, like many persons do, for the mere sake of talking. It was intimated that it was 'Kate' who was speaking. There was a great attempt on her part at being witty, but according to my ideas on such matters, most of what was said would come under the category of small— very small—wit." In another passage he wrote: "Unlike John, Kate will talk any length of time, as long in fact as she can find anything to talk about, even if it be the most frivolous nonsense; but I must do her the justice to say that she talks sensibly enough at times, and I have heard great wisdom in her utterances, and satisfactory answers given to profound philosophical questions."

The "Katie" who assisted "John King" in the seances of Frank **Herne** and Charles **Williams** was apparently not identifiable with "Katie King," as the former, after the materialization of a negro hand, was described as a descendant of a black. Her voice was like a whisper but perfectly distinct. The transportation of Mrs. **Guppy** to the room of Williams was put down to her achievement.

A rather dubious "Katie King" manifested through the mediumship of Mr. and Mrs. Nelson **Holmes** of Philadelphia. Dr. Henry T. Child and Robert Dale Owen stated that they had seen her materialize on May 12, 1874.

Robert Dale Owen believed that she was identical with the control of Miss Cook, though her features differed from those in the photograph of the London Katie. The nose was straight, not aquiline and the expression was more intellectual. Sir William Crookes, who had seen a photograph of the Philadelphia "Katie," had no hesitation in declaring her as a fraud. To justify her appearance in America the Philadelphia "Katie King" declared: "Some of my English friends misinterpreted my parting words. I took final leave not of your earth, but of dear Florrie Cook, because my continuance with her would have injured her health." A rather limp explanation which was further disproved by the circumstance that Florence Cook, under the control of another spirit "Marie," continued her materialization seances without injury to her health.

On November 2, 1874, Owen reaffirmed his belief in the genuineness of the "Katie King" phenomena but only a month later withdrew his assurances in the face of convincing evidence that he had been the victim of fraud. Dr. Child made a similar statement. (For further details, see entry on Mr. & Mrs. Nelson **Holmes.**)

In October 1930, "Katie King" unexpectedly manifested in the circle of Dr. Glen **Hamilton** in Winnipeg, Canada. Photographs were taken. According to Dr. Glen Hamilton: "Obviously it is wholly impossible to say whether or not this Mary M.-Mercedes-Katie King is the same being as the entity appearing in the experiments of Crookes and others. We have the word of the controls in this case that it is so and we have seen how, so far, these controls have repeatedly established the fact that they know whereof they speak. . . . While there are, I may say, some points of similarity to be traced between Katie as photographed by Crookes and Katie as photographed in the Winnipeg experiments, both faces for instance being rather long in formation, the eyes in both being large and luminous, the angle of the jaw in both being rather pronounced, the later Katie is so much younger in appearance, her beauty so much more apparent that it is evident that we cannot use the earlier record of her presence in any way as conclusive proof that there is any connection between the two."

Since then, "Katie King" reportedly materialized in Rome in July 1974 with the medium Fulvio Rendhell (see *Spirits and Spirit Worlds* by Roy Stemman, 1975). (See also John **King; Materialization; Spiritualism**)

King, Robert (1869– ?)

British professional clairvoyant and lecturer in occult science. He sat for Sir William **Crookes**, with whom he was acquainted, worked with A. P. **Sinnett**, with whom he served on the *Daily Mail* committee for the investigation of **psychic photography** in 1908, and was the chief psychic of **Julia's Bureau** from 1909–1913.

He toured Europe as a lecturer. His particular psychic faculty was diagnosing mental emotions in relation to physical disease. He equipped himself to this profession by a three years' course in biology, physiology and chemistry. He was not a trance medium and reflected spirit messages in a perfectly still but fully conscious state.

"King Robert of Sicily"

English romance of the fourteenth century, author unknown. It tells how King Robert of Sicily was beguiled by pride into sneering at a priest who read mass. To punish him, an angel was sent down by God, and he, assuming Robert's shape, transformed the King into the likeness of his own fool, sent out to lie with the dogs. He was at length allowed to resume his proper shape after a long and ignominious penance. The theme is an ancient one, with parallels in early Buddhist and Hindu tales. It was revived in modern times by the poet H. W. Longfellow in one of his *Tales of a Wayside Inn.* For a discussion of the theme in earlier literature, see *Curiosities of Olden Times* by S. Baring-Gould (1895).

King's Evil

For centuries, the kings of England and France were credited with the ability to cure scrofula by touching the sufferer with the fingers, a healing ritual known as "touching for the king's evil."

Many thousands of subjects regularly assembled for this royal touch, and some English kings were credited with hundreds of cures. The custom seems to have arisen during the reign of Edward the Confessor, as a result of a young woman's dream. It was discontinued in England during the Hanoverian period, when it was considered "papist" or Roman Catholic. (See also **Healing by Touch**)

Kingsford, Anna Bonus (1846–1888)

Founder of Esoteric Christianity, embracing some of the teachings of the Gnostics, Sufis and proponents of spiritual alchemy.

She was born Anna Bonus at Stratford, Essex, England, September 16, 1846. Even as a child, Anna Bonus displayed unusual psychic gifts and claimed kinship with fairies, who were said to have visited her during sleep. She told fortunes at school and seems to have been something of a seeress.

After her marriage in 1867 to the Rev. Algernon G. Kingsford, an Anglican clergyman, she edited a ladies' journal and conducted a feminist campaign with special emphasis on womanly attributes. She considered masculinity in women degrading. In 1870, she became a Roman Catholic, and ten years later took her medical degree in Paris, France.

About this time she discovered in Edward Maitland a "twin soul" for mystical mission, although their platonic association resulted in some mischievous gossip. In fact, the Maitland and Kingsford families were related by marriage.

In 1884 Kingsford and Maitland founded the **Hermetic Society** in Britain, for the study of mystical Christianity, with a strong emphasis on vegetarianism and anti-vivisection. It was Anna Kingsford who introduced the occultist S. L. Macgregor **Mathers** to Madame **Blavatsky.** Mathers sympathized with the campaign against vivisection, although his occult interests were wider than the **Theosophical Society** and he eventually became a leading figure in the Hermetic Order of the **Golden Dawn.** Anna Kingsford was a passionate advocate of animal rights and believed that her furious indignation against the cruel vivisection experiments of Prof. Claude Bernard caused his death at a distance. Her own death was on February 22, 1888.

Kingsford and Maitland were innovators in the field of mystical Christianity, but their Society was largely ineffectual, and much of their inspiration was eventually subsumed in the all-inclusive conspectus of Theosophy.

Recommended reading:

Kingsford, A. & E. Maitland. *The Perfect Way: or, the Finding of Christ,* London, 1886 (originally published anonymously 1882)

Maitland, Edward. *Anna Kingsford; Her Life, Letters, Diary,* London, 1896

Kinocetus

A fabled precious stone, said to be effective for casting out devils.

Kirby, Bernard C(romwell) (1907–   )

Professor of sociology who has conducted investigations in parapsychology. Born October 9, 1907 at Indianapolis, Indiana, he studied at Denison University, Granville, Ohio (B.A. 1929), University of Washington (M.A. 1950, Ph.D. 1953). In 1930 he married Pauline Robion.

From 1931–33 he was Probation officer, Juvenile Court of Cook County, Chicago, Illinois; 1940–42 field representative, Idaho Department of Public Assistance; 1942–44 administrator, Walla Walla (Wash.) County Welfare Department; 1946–48 instructor, Farragut (Idaho) College and Technical Institute; 1950–53 instructor, University of Washington; 1953–54 parole officer, State of Washington; 1954 on, assistant professor, associate professor, professor, Department of Sociology and Anthropology, San Diego State College, California.

His memberships have included American Sociological Association, Pacific Sociological Society, Society for the Study of Social Problems, American Correctional Association, National Association of Social Workers. Dr. Kirby investigated the linkage question in clairvoyance and conducted experiments in telepathy. He read a paper before the Parapsychological Association in September 1959 on 'The "Linkage" Effect in ESP.' His thesis at University of Washington *A Parole Prediction Study Using The Discriminant Function* was published by University Microfilms, Ann Arbor (1953).

Kirlian Aura

Although the human **aura** has long been considered a psychic phenomenon, visible only to gifted sensitives, some scientists have always maintained that the aura is an objective reality, and that such a radiation around human beings varies in different states of health. In the nineteenth century Karl von **Reichenbach** spent many years in experiments to validate the aura, although he was ridiculed by other scientists of the day. In Britain, the physician Walter J. **Kilner** (1847–1920) who knew of Reichenbach's experiments, devised a method of making the aura visible through spectacle screens or goggles impregnated with the chemical dicyanin. His work was developed further by other experimenters, notably Oscar Bagnall.

In 1958, Semyon Davidovich and his wife Valentina Khrisanova Kirlian, two Soviet scientists, described a photographic technique of converting the non-electrical properties of an object into electrical properties recorded on photographic film (electrophotography). They spent some thirteen years in painstaking researches. Eventually their work was endorsed by Soviet authorities and a new laboratory provided for them in Krasnodar in the Kuban

region of South Russia. Their technique of photographing what has become generally known as the "Kirlian Aura" has become internationally famous.

The method is a modern development of a technique known as early as the 1890s but not formerly applied to the human aura. In 1898, a Russian engineer and electrical researcher named Yakov Narkevich-Todko had demonstrated "electrographic photos" by using high voltage spark discharges. The modern development by the Kirlians was influenced by study of **Acupuncture,** after Viktor Adamenko, a Soviet physicist, demonstrated the "tobiscope," a device to detect the acupuncture points of the human body. Various Kirlian photography devices are now marketed in the U.S. and Europe to record biological fields around human beings, animals and even plants. A recent compact Kirlian device marketed in Europe is known as a Verograph.

Recommended reading:

Kilner, Walter J. *The Human Atmosphere,* London, 1911 (reissued as *The Human Aura,* University Books, 1965)

Bagnall, Oscar. *The Origin and Properties of the Human Aura,* London, 1937 (revised edition University Books, 1970)

Krippner, Stanley & Daniel Rubin. *Galaxies of Life; the Human Aura in Acupuncture and Kirlian Photography,* Gordon & Breach, 1973 (reissued as: *The Kirlian Aura: Photographing the Galaxies of Life,* Anchor, 1974)

Kischuph

In the **Kabala,** the higher magical influence. It was divided into two branches, an elementary and a spiritual, and included exorcism. Sometimes Kischuph exhibited a striking resemblance to the witchcraft of medieval times. Sorcerers were said to change themselves into animals, and go long distances in a very short time. They might also induce pain and disease and death in men and animals. Still further allied to witches were the "women who make a contract with the Schedim, and meet them at certain times, dance with them, and visit these spirits who appear to them in the shape of goats. In many countries such women are killed." This form of Kischuph is true sorcery; the other form, material Kischuph, is rather evil sympathy, consisting of disturbing influences on the natural elements produced by exciting false "rapports" in various substances.

Kiss, Bewitchment by

Florence Newton, a notorious Irish witch of the seventeenth century, was on several occasions accused of having bewitched people by means of a kiss. The first was a servant-maid who had refused alms to her. About a week later the witch kissed her violently, from which time the servant suffered from fits and was transported from place to place, now being carried mysteriously to the top of the house, now being placed between two feather beds, and so on.

The witch was also said to have caused the death of one David Jones, who stood sentinel over her in prison, by kissing his hand, and by the same means brought about the death of the children of three aldermen of Youghall, County Cork. Florence Newton was tried at Cork Assizes in 1661. For details of the accusations, see *Irish Witchcraft and Demonology* by St. John Seymour (1913, reprinted Causeway Books, 1973).

Kitson, Alfred (1855–1934)

British pioneer of teaching Spiritualism to children through the **Lyceum** system first founded in America by Andrew Jackson **Davis,** c. 1863. Kitson, son of a Yorkshire coal miner, was a veteran of the Spiritualist movement at a time when it was violently opposed in Britain.

In 1876, he organized evening classes for children on the Lyceum system as a wing of the newly formed Spiritualist Society in Yorkshire. Kitson campaigned vigorously for the Lyceum movement, and became known as the "Father of British Lyceums." He collaborated with Harry A. Kersey on the *English Lyceum Manual,* first published 1887. Kersey and Kitson were also largely instrumental in bringing into existence the Spiritualists' Lyceum Union in 1890. The Union started a monthly *Spiritualists' Lyceum Magazine* in January 1890, published at Oldham; when this ceased publication in November 1890 it was replaced by the **Lyceum Banner,** edited by J. J. **Morse** from Liverpool until 1902, when Kitson became editor. In 1894, the Union changed its name to the British Spiritualists' Lyceum Union.

The Lyceum movement prospered for many years, but Kitson resigned from secretaryship of the Union in 1919, owing to ill health.

Kiyota, Masuaki (1962–   )

Remarkable young Japanese psychic, who appears to have extraordinary talents in metal-bending and nengraphy (paranormal photography). Kiyota rivals famed psychics Uri **Geller** and Matthew **Manning** in his unusual demonstrations. Kiyota has been elaborately tested and filmed during the production of his phenomena. In addition to a Nippon Television program, he was also featured in the American program "Exploring the Unknown" (narrated by Burt Lancaster) presented on NBC Television October 30, 1977. He was the subject of a detailed investigation by Walter and Mary Jo **Uphoff,** who visited him in Japan, and he is the subject of their book *Mind Over Matter; Implications of Masuaki Kiyota's PK Feats with Metal and Film,* published by New Frontiers Center, Oregon, Wisconsin, 1980 (British edition published Colin Smythe Ltd., U.K.). (See also **Japan)**

Klinckowstroem, Graf Carl von (1884–1970)

German research scientist who has written on water divining and other parapsychological subjects. Born August 26, 1884 at Potsdam, Germany, he studied at University of Munich (physics, philosophy, psychology, history). In 1942 he married Charlotte Anders.

He was a corresponding member of the Society of Psychical Research, London, from 1928 on and an honorary member of Deutscher Erfinder-Verband, Nuremberg. He published books on science, notably *Geschichte der Technik* (History of Technology, 1959; 1960). His books on parapsychology included: *Bibliographie Der Wünschelrute* (Bibliography of the Divining Rod, 1911), *Yogi-Künste* (Yogic Arts, 1922), *Der Physikalische Mediumismus* (Physical Mediumship, with Dr. W. von Gulat-Wellenburg and Dr. Hans Rosenbusch, 1925), *Handbuch der Wunschelrute* (Handbook of the Divining Rod, with Rudolph von Maltzahn, 1931), *Die Zauberkunst* (The Art of Magic, 1954).

Klinschor (or Klingsor)

According to Arthurian romance, he was Lord of the Magic Castle wherein were kept Arthur's mother and other queens. He was nephew to Virgilius of Naples and was overcome by Sir Gawain. He was alluded to in the *Parsival* of Wolfram von Eschenbach. (See also King **Arthur;** Holy **Grail)**

Kloppenburg, Bonaventura (1919–   )

Professor of theology and Franciscan priest, who studied **Spiritism** in Brazil. Born November 2, 1919 at Molbergen (Oldenburg), Germany, he studied at Antonianum University, Rome (D.Th.).

His books include: *De Relatione inter Peccatum et Mortem* (The Relationship between Sin and Death, 1951), *Nossas Superstiçoes* (Our Superstitions, 1959), *O Espiritismo no Brasil* (Spiritism in Brazil, 1960), *O Reencarnacionismo no Brasil* (Reincarnationism in Brazil, 1961), *A Maçonario no Brasil* (Masonry in Brazil, 4th ed. 1961), *The Priest; Living Instrument & Minister of Christ the Eternal Priest* (1974), *The People's Church* (1978), *Pastoral Practice and the Paranormal* (1979). He also published pamphlets on the Theosophical Societies, and the Rosicrucian Society in Brazil.

Kluski, Franek (1874–   ?)

Pseudonym of a distinguished Polish professional poet and writer whose remarkable physical powers co-existed with intellectual psychic gifts. As a child of five or six he had presentiments, visions of distant events and saw phantoms. He thought them natural and talked with them familiarly.

In 1919 his psychic gifts were discovered when he attended a seance of Jan Guzyk. It annoyed him at first, but curiosity prevailed and he consented to experiments. Various phases of physical phenomena developed, culminating in materialization, during which, like Mme. **d'Esperance,** he retained consciousness.

For scientific research he placed himself readily at the disposition of the Polish Society for Psychic Research and the **Institut Métapsychique** of Paris, where his first sittings took place in 1920 in the presence of Prof. Charles **Richet,** Count de Grammont and Gustav **Geley.** The paraffin casts of materialized limbs made in these seances are amongst the best objective evidences of supernormal power ever produced. Another curious feature of his materialization seances was the appearance of animal forms, which included squirrels, dogs, cats, a lion and a buzzard. One of the most disturbing manifestations was a large primitive creature like a huge ape or a hairy man. The face was hairy and the creature had long strong arms and behaved roughly to the sitters, trying to lick their hands and faces. This materialization, which Geley named the "Pithecanthropus," exuded a strong odor like "a wet dog." Geley considered Kluski as a universal medium, a king among his contemporaries. He found his clairvoyance which was manifest in his **automatic writing** scripts almost terrifying.

The best account of Kluski's mediumship is the book (in Polish) by Col. Norbert Ocholowicz, *Wspomnienia Z, Seansow Z (Medium Frankiem Kluskim)* (Warsaw, 1926). See also Geley's book *Clairvoyance and Materialisation* (London, 1927).

Kneale, Martha Hurst (Mrs. William Calvert Kneale) (1909–)

University fellow and tutor who has written on psychical research. Born at Skipton, Yorkshire, England, she studied at Somerville College, Oxford University (B.A. 1933) and was a Graham Kenan fellow, University of North Carolina from 1933–34, graduate fellow Bryn Mawr College, Pennsylvania 1934–36; Oxford University (M.A. 1936). In 1938 she married William Calvert Kneale. Mrs. Kneale was a tutor at Lady Margaret Hall, Oxford University, and a member of the Aristotelian Society, the Mind Association, and the Society for Psychical Research, London.

She reviewed books on psychical research for *Philosophy* journal and wrote articles for the *Encyclopaedia Britannica.* With W. C. Kneale she was co-author of *The Development of Logic* (1962). Her papers on parapsychology include 'Is Psychical Research Relevant to Philosophy?' (*Proceedings, Aristotelian Society,* supplementary volume 24, 1950), 'Time and Psychical Research' (*Proceedings* of Four Conferences of Parapsychological Studies, 1957).

Knock

Irish village in County Mayo which was the scene of spiritual manifestations of the type associated with **Lourdes.** On the evening of August 21, 1879, shortly before dusk, three strange figures were observed by one or two parishioners of the village. The figures were standing motionless by the gable of the Catholic church. At first, this occasioned no surprise, as the parishioners assumed that the figures were statues ordered by the parish priest, but as the evening advanced, the figures appeared to be surrounded by a strange light, and presently a small crowd of villagers assembled to observe the apparitions. The main figure was a woman clothed in white, wearing a golden crown. On each side of her was a man, one wearing a bishop's mitre, the other elderly and bearded.

As it was raining at the time, the crowd eventually dispersed. Some villagers went home to dry their clothes, others to assist an elderly woman who had collapsed on her way to church. The priest's housekeeper went to tell the priest about the apparitions, but it seems that he was not impressed, and did not go to the church to see for himself. Later that night, the apparitions disappeared.

The apparitions had been witnessed by nearly thirty people, and a few weeks later the Archbishop of Tuam set up a commission to investigate the phenomenon and interview the witnesses. Fifteen villagers were interviewed, ranging from a boy of six to an old woman of seventy-five. Their evidence was given in a frank down-to-earth manner that carried absolute conviction, and their accounts were never changed throughout their lives.

A Marian shrine was constructed at Knock, with the permission of the Catholic Church for pilgrimages. In addition to the original Knock Shrine at the apparition church, there is now a large new Church of Our Lady, and, as at Lourdes, there are mass services for healing the sick. The shrine achieved worldwide recognition when Pope John Paul II visited Knock in September 1979. In the 1980s, an ambitious project commenced to build an airport at Knock.

Recommended reading:
Rynne, Catherine. *Knock 1879–1979,* Veritas, Eire, 1979

Knockers

Underground sprites of Cornish folklore, England, inhabited tin mines. They resemble the friendly type of German **kobolds,** but are basically friendly, since they knock to indicate places underground where there is a rich ore. (See also **Elementary Spirits**)

Knodt, William Charles (1936–)

Administrative employee, Illinois Bell Telephone Company. He conducted experiments in psychokinesis (influencing casting of dice), and correlation between physical pain and ESP in hospital patients.

Knorr von Rosenroth, Christian (1636–1689)

German alchemist and mystic who edited Kabalistic works under the title *Kabbala Denudata* (1677, 1684). This work included three fragments from the book *Zohar* with extensive commentaries, as well as treatises by Isaac Luria, founder of a Kabalistic sect in the sixteenth century and the *Treatise on the Soul* by Moses Cordovero. Rosenroth translated these Hebrew works into Latin, and thus made them available to non-Jewish readers. An English translation of *Kabbala Denudata* was published by S. L. MacGregor **Mathers** in 1887. (See also **Kabala**)

Knowles, Elsie A(nna) G(race) (1908–)

Statistician who wrote and experimented in the field of parapsychology. Born July 14, 1908 at Berlin, Germany, she studied at the University of Jena (Ph.D. education, 1932). From 1935–37 she was a demonstrator in mathematics, University of Southampton, England; 1937–38 assistant lecturer in mathematics, Royal Holloway College (University of London), England; 1938–42 lecturer in mathematics, South-West Essex Technical College, and from 1942–45 at Brighton Technical College, Sussex; 1945–50 statistical mathematician, electronics, fiber industries; 1950–54 lecturer in applied statistics, Department of Engineering Production, University of Birmingham, England; 1954 on, manager of Statistics Department, Ferodo Ltd. Associate, Institute of Physics, London; fellow, Royal Statistical Society; charter member, Parapsychological Association.

Dr. Knowles reported on experiments in Psi dexterity, and her articles for the *Journal of Parapsychology* include: 'Report on an Experiment Concerning the Influence of Mind Over Matter' (vol. 13, No. 3, September 1949), 'Report on the Susceptibility of Manually Operated Random Selector to Psi Dexterity' (vol. 16, No. 1, March 1952).

Knowles, Frederick W(ilfred) (1911–)

Physician and surgeon who has written on psychic healing. Born June 7, 1911 at Berlin, Germany, he studied at Royal College of Surgeons, England (Member 1950), Royal College of Physicians (Licentiate 1950). In 1954 he married Lindsay Ellen June Le Lievre. Dr. Knowles was a life member of the Society for Psychical Research, London, and a charter member of the Parapsychological Association. His medical practice took him to

Canada, India, New Guinea, Australia and New Zealand as well as England.

His studies on psychic healing include Indian yoga techniques, hypnosis and phenomena formerly known as mesmerism. In addition to his medical and anatomical papers, he has published the following articles in the *Journal* of the American Society for Psychical Research: 'Some Investigations into Psychic Healing' (vol. 48, No. 1, January 1954), 'Psychic Healing in Organic Disease' (vol. 50, No. 3, July 1956), 'Rat Experiments and Mesmerism' (vol. 53, No. 2, April 1959). He contributed to the special issue of *Corrective Psychiatry and Journal of Special Therapy* titled 'ESP Today' (vol. 12, No. 2, March 1966).

Kobolds

The sprites or **fairies** of German folklore. They are of two kinds. The first is a household sprite, rather like the English brownie, helping with the housework if properly fed and treated, but mischievous, playing pranks on people. They are often given names, like "Chimmeken," "Heinze" or "Walther."

The second type are underground spirits who haunt caves and mines and are often evil and malicious. The metallurgist Georg Landmann described these spirits in his book *De Animatibus subterraneis* (1657). (See also **Elementary Spirits; Fairies; Knockers**)

Koch, Walter A(lbert) (1895–   )

Teacher and astrologer, who wrote books and articles on parapsychology topics. Born September 18, 1895, at Esslingen/Neckar, Württenberg, Germany, he studied at the University of Tübingen (Ph.D. 1920). In 1947 he married Ingeborg Egenolf, also a teacher. He was scientific adviser to the Association of German Astrologers, and leader of the investigation circle of the Cosmobiosophical Association, Hamburg. He served in the German Army during World War I, but was arrested for resistance to the Nazis in 1941, spending three years in prisons (including the concentration camp at Dachau).

His books included *Astrologische Farbenlehre* (Astrological Science of Colors, 1930), *Psychologische Farbenlehre* (Psychological Science of Colors, 1931), *Die Seele der Edelsteine* (The Psyche of Precious Stones, 1934), *Deine Farbe-Dein Charakter* (Your Color—Your Character, 1953), *Prophetie und Astrologische Prognose* (Prophecy and Astrological Prediction, 1954), *Dr. Korsch und Die Astrologie* (Dr. Korsch and Astrology, 1956), *Innenmensch und Aussenmensch* (Man: Introversion and Extraversion, 1956), *Häusertabellen* (Astrologies tables, 1962), *Regiomontanus und das Häusersystem des Geburtosortes* (Regiomontanus and the System of Houses of Birthplaces, 1960). He also contributed articles on psychokinesis, card divination and prophecy to various journals, include *Neue Wissenschaft* and *Mensch und Schicksal.*

Koestler, Arthur (1905–1983)

World-famous novelist, writer on political, scientific and philosophical themes, who was also interested in parapsychology. Born in Budapest, Hungary, September 5, 1905, he was the only son of a Hungarian father and an Austrian mother. He described his early life as "lonely, precocious and neurotic, admired for my brains and detested for my character by teachers and schoolfellows alike." He attended the Polytechnic High School in Vienna and studied engineering, then science and psychology at the University of Vienna.

As a young man, he became a Zionist, but when working as a journalist he joined the Communist party. He was a reporter in Spain during the Civil War, where he was imprisoned as a Communist and only released after the intervention of the British government. He was in Paris during World War II, where he was arrested and sent to a concentration camp. His prison experiences became the basis of his brilliant but depressing book *Darkness at Noon* (1940). In this book, as in his contribution to the later symposium *The God That Failed; Six Studies in Communism* (1949), he expressed rejection of Communism and other totalitarian regimes, which he saw as corrupted by inhuman and cynical power politics. In 1941, he joined the British Army and after the war became a British citizen. By 1955, he had ceased to be actively involved in political campaigning.

In addition to his novels, he published a series of brilliant questing works concerned with human faculty and destiny in relation to scientific findings. Although it was not widely recognized that he had a longstanding interest in parapsychology, his book *The Roots of Coincidence* (1972) touched on the question of scientific validation of psychic gifts and stated that extrasensory perception might be "the highest manifestation of the integrative potential of living matter," whilst in *The Challenge of Chance,* published a year later, he reviewed possible connections between parapsychology and quantum physics. However, he maintained a characteristic skepticism, as expressed in a television interview: "I am still skeptical. I've got a split mind about it. I know from personal experience, from intuition, whatever you call it, that these phenomena exist. At the same time, my rational or scientific mind rejects them. And I'm quite happy with that split of the mind."

He participated in three annual international conferences of the **Parapsychology Foundation.** At the 1972 Amsterdam conference on "Parapsychology and the Sciences," he contributed a paper on 'The Perversity of Physics,' in which he stated: "I do believe that there is a positive, not only a negative rapprochement between those two black sheep: parapsychology and quantum physics. But let us not try to rush things. The great new synthesis in the history of science occurred when each component, which ultimately went into synthesis, was already there and they only needed to be together. I do not think that the time is ripe, but I think there is this affinity between parapsychology and modern physics which is more intuitive than logical, more potential than actual . . . a kind of 'gestalt' affinity."

In the 1974 conference at Geneva, he again discussed parapsychology in relation to quantum physics and stated: "So there is now a radical wing in parapsychology, a sort of Trotskyite wing, of which I am a member, with Alister Hardy and others, who are trying really radically to break away from causality, not only paying lip service to the rejection of causality, or confining this rejection of causality and determinism to the micro-level, but who really wonder whether a completely new approach, indicated in holism, Jung's synchronicity, and so on, might not be theoretically more promising."

Koestler was also a founder member of the **K.I.B. Foundation,** a British organization fostering research into unorthodox and paranormal phenomena.

Koestler published some thirty-five books, including: *Darkness at Noon* (1943), *The Yogi and the Commissar* (1945), *Thieves in the Night* (1946), *Promise and Fulfilment; Palestine 1917–1949* (1949), *The Age of Longing* (1951), *The Lotus and the Robot* (1961), *Suicide of a National; An Enquiry into the State of Britain Today* (1963), *The Act of Creation* (1964), *The Ghost in the Machine* (1967), *Drinkers of Infinity* (1968), (ed., with J. R. Smythies) *Beyond Reductionism—New Perspectives in the Life Sciences* (1969), *The Case of the Midwife Toad* (1971), *The Roots of Coincidence* (1972), (with Sir Alister Hardy & Robert Harvie) *The Challenge of Chance* (1973), *Janus: A Summing Up* (1978).

Koestler died at his London home March 3, 1983 in a joint suicide with his third wife Cynthia. Koestler, aged 77, had been suffering from leukemia and advanced Parkinson's Disease. In his will, he included a bequest to a British university for the study of paranormal faculties such as metal-bending, telepathy and healing.

Koestler was generally recognized as one of the most stimulating intellects of the twentieth century. In 1968, at the University of Copenhagen, he was awarded the Sooning Prize for his political and philosophical writings, a distinction earlier awarded to Bertrand Russell and Winston Churchill. Koestler was also honored by such awards as Commander of the British Empire and Companion of the Royal Society of Literature. In 1976, Roy Webberly edited the volume *Astride the Two Cultures: Arthur Koestler at 70,* containing essays by Koestler's contemporaries. For other biographical background, see: *Arthur Koestler* by John Atkins (1956), *Arthur Koestler, Das Literarische Werk* by Peter Alfred Huber (Zürich, 1962), *Arthur Koestler, Cahiers de l'Herne* (1975).

Koestler Foundation

Current name of the former **K.I.B. Foundation.** (See also Arthur **Koestler**)

Koilon

The name given to the ether by Annie **Besant** and Charles W. **Leadbeater** in their book on *Occult Chemistry* (1919). (See also **Ether; Theosophy**)

Kommasso

Burmese evil spirits inhabiting trees. (See **Burma**)

Koons, Jonathan (c. 1855)

Early American Spiritualist medium, a well-to-do farmer in Millfield Township, Athens County, a wild district of Ohio. He became interested in Spiritualism in 1852 and was told at a seance that he was "the most powerful medium on earth" and that all his eight children, from the seven-month-old baby, upwards, had psychic gifts.

Acting on spirit instructions, he built a "Spirit Room," a single room log-house, sixteen feet by twelve, for the use of the spirits and equipped it with every conceivable noise-making apparatus. This log-house soon became famous and people flocked from great distances to see a great variety of curious phenomena. The eldest boy,

Nahum, a youth of 18 and the head of the family, sat at the "spirit table," the audience in benches beyond.

When the lights were put out a fearful din ensued which was sometimes heard a mile away. Surprising feats of strength were also manifested, yet none present was struck or injured by the flying objects or target shooting pistol bullets. The sitters were touched by materialized hands which, in the light of phosphorized paper, were seen carrying objects around. Spirit faces were also seen and through a trumpet, which sailed about in the air, voices called out the names of the guests even if they concealed their identity, deceased relatives and friends spoke to them and gave proof of survival.

The circle was attended by a host of ministering spirits, said to number 165. They claimed to belong to a race of men known under the generic title "Adam" (red clay), antedating the theological Adam by thousands of years. They represented their leaders as the most ancient angels. One of these ancient angels, who instructed the circle, was called "Oress." Generally they signed themselves in the written communications as "King" No. 1, No. 2, and No. 3, and sometimes "Servant and Scholar of God." Foremost among them was the "John **King**" who claimed to have been Henry Morgan the pirate.

Two or three miles distant, there was another lonely farmhouse, belonging to John Tippie where another "spirit room" was laid out on the same plan. The manifestations in the Tippie family were identical with those in the Koon log-house. Both had a "spirit machine" which consisted of a complex arrangement of zinc and copper for the alleged purpose of collecting and focalizing the magnetic aura used in the demonstrations. The Tippies had ten children, all mediums.

Dr. J. Everett of Athens County, Ohio, who investigated the Koons' phenomena, published the messages of the spirits under the title *Communications from Angels* (1853) and also printed a number of affidavits testifying to the occurrences in the spirit house, with a chart of the spheres drawn by Nahum Koons in trance.

Charles Partridge wrote of his visit in the American *Spiritual Telegraph* of 1855: "The spirit rooms will hold from 20-30 persons each. After the circle is formed and the lights extinguished, a tremendous blow is struck by the drum-stick, when immediately the bass and tenor drums are beaten with preternatural power, like calling the roll on a muster field, making a thousand echoes. The rapid and tremendous blows on these drums are really frightful to many persons; it is continued for five minutes or more and when ended, 'King' usually takes up the trumpet, salutes us with 'Good evening, friends' and asks what particular manifestations are desired. After the introductory piece on the instruments, the spirits sang to us. They first requested us to remain perfectly silent; then we heard human voices singing, apparently in the distance, so as to be scarcely distinguishable; the sounds gradually increased, each part relatively, until it appeared as if a full choir of voices were singing in our room most exquisitely. I think I never heard such perfect harmony. Spirit hands and arms were formed in our presence several times, and by aid of a solution of phosphorus, prepared at their request by Mr. Koons, they were seen as distinctly as in a light room."

The Koons family did not fare well at the hands of their

neighbors. Their house was attacked by mobs, fire was set to their crops and barns, their children were beaten. Finally they left the countryside and began missionary wanderings, lasting for many years. Their mediumship was given free to the public and they did a great propaganda service to the cause of early American Spiritualism.

The phenomenon noisy "spirit room" of Koons bears a striking resemblance to the **shaman** performances of primitive peoples, where the medicine man enters an enclosed area and manifests noisy "spirit" communications (see **Eskimos**).

Koot Hoomi Lal Singh (or **Kut Humi**)

One of the **adepts** or **Masters** who inspired the founders of the **Theosophical Society.** Madame **Blavatsky** claimed that such Masters were high spiritual beings dwelling in Tibet who exerted supernatural influence over the welfare of mankind. Messages allegedly from Koot Hoomi were signed "K. H" and appeared mysteriously in the vicinity of Madame Blavatsky.

Koot Hoomi was also claimed as the inspiration of Alice **Bailey,** a former Theosophist who founded her own Arcane School.

During the power struggles for leadership of the Theosophical Society after the death of Madame Blavatsky, messages allegedly from Koot Hoomi were cited to enhance the claims of William Q. **Judge.** More recently Koot Hoomi was claimed as the inspiration of Robert and Earlyne Chaney in setting up the Astara Foundation in 1951. (See also **Mahatma Letters**)

Kooy, J(ohannes) M(arie) J(oseph) (1902–   )

Lecturer in mathematics and physics, who made special studies of problems of space travel and precognition in dreams. Born July 13, 1902 at Rotterdam, Netherlands, he studied at the Technical University of Delft and the University of Leyden (Ph.D, physics and mathematics). In 1937 he married Cornelia M. van der Heyden. From 1927–32 he was an engineer with De Nederlandsche Staalindustrie, Rotterdam; 1936–39 chief scientific adviser in the Aeronautical Department of the Technical University, Delft; from 1939 on, lecturer, theoretical physics, mechanics and mathematics, Royal Military Academy, Breda; 1960 on, lecturer, space-flight mechanics, Technical University of Delft. He was a charter associate member of the Parapsychological Association; academician, International Academy of Astronautics.

With J. W. H. Uytenbogaart Dr. Kooy was co-author of *Ballistics of the Future* (1946). He contributed papers on space travel to International Astronautical Congresses, and wrote articles for *De Ingenieur, Astronautica Acta, Journal of the British Society.*

He published many articles on parapsychology in *Tijdschrift voor Parapsychologie,* including 'Introspectief Onderzoek naar Het Dunne-Effect' (Introspective Investigation of the Dunne-Effect, vol. 6, No. 3, March 1934), 'Paragnosie en Kansrekening' (Extrasensory Perception and the Calculus of Probability, vol. 7, No. 3, March 1935), 'Tijd, Ruimte en Paragnosie' (Time, Space and Extrasensory Perception, vol. 15, Nos. 3, 4, May-July 1947). Other papers included: 'Tijd, Ruimte en Bewustzijn' (Time, Space and Consciousness, *Thersofia,* vol. 52, Nos. 9-10, vol. 53, No. 102), 'Space, Time, Consciousness

and the Universe (lecture at International Conference of Parapsychological Studies, Utrecht, 1953, 'Space, Time and Consciousness' (*Journal of Parapsychology,* vol. 21, No. 4, December 1957), 'Reply to Dr. Chari' (*Journal of Parapsychology,* vol. 22, No. 1, March 1958).

Koresh

Name assumed by Cyrus Reed Teed (1839–1908), proponent of a hollow earth theory. He founded the Koreshan Unity cult, which later constructed a settlement in Estero, Florida, in the hope that it would become the capital of the world. (See **Hollow Earth**)

Koreshan Unity

Cult founded by Cyrus Reed Teed (1839–1908) under the name "Koresh." (See **Hollow Earth**)

Koschei the Deathless

A demon of Russian folklore. This horrid monster is described as having a death's head and fleshless skeleton, "through which is seen the black blood flowing and the yellow heart beating." He is armed with an iron club, with which he knocks down all who come in his path. In spite of his ugliness, he is said to be a great admirer of young girls and women. He is avaricious, hates old and young alike, and particularly those who are fortunate. His dwelling is amongst the mountains of the Koskels and the Caucasus, where his treasure is concealed. For references to Koschei, see *Russian Folk-Tales* by W. R. S. Ralston (1873).

Kosh

A wicked forest fiend of the Bangala of the Southern Congo. (See also **Africa**)

Kosmon Unity

Semi-annual publication of the Confraternity of Faithists, concerned with the teachings of the "New Bible" **OAHSPE.** This was an automatic script received on a typewriter by J. B. **Newbrough** and published in 1882. The address for *Kosmon Unity* is: Kosmon Press, BM/KCKP, London, WCIV 6XX, England, or in the U.S.: Kosmon Service Center, P.O. Box 664, Salt Lake City, Utah 84110.

Kosmos

Quarterly publication of the International Society for Astrological Research, Inc.; includes a cumulative digest of astrological activities and research. The Society also publishes a Newsletter. Address: 70 Melrose Place, Montclair, New Jersey 07042.

Kostka, Jean

Pseudonym of Jules Stanislas Doinel (died 1903). A late Gnostic and initiate of the 33rd degree, who, converted to the Christian standpoint, he claimed to reveal his diabolic adventures in the pages of *La Verité* under the title of "Lucifer démasqué" (Lucifer Unmasked). He told of diabolic happenings in the private chapel of a lady "Madame X." who figured frequently in his pages, and who was thought to be the late Countess of Caithness, of visions of Jansen, and the classical deities.

It seems probable from the evidence that "Jean

Kostka" never came into personal contact with a Satanic or Luciferian cultus, and that his diabolic experiences were merely those of the intellectual Satanist. Doinel's revelations came in the same period as the impudent fake Satanist writings of "Léo Taxil" (Gabriel **Jogand-Pagès**) and seem to partake of the same contemporary anti-Masonic and anti-Semitic conspiracies.

Krafft, Karl Ernest (1900–1945)

Swiss astrologer of German descent who was employed by the Nazis for propaganda work during World War II. He participated in tests by the German parapsychologist Prof. Hans **Bender** in 1937 upon moving to Germany.

Krafft had formerly conducted an ambitious statistical investigation of cosmic influences on individuals and developed his own system of "Typocosmy." His book *Traité d'Astro-Biologie* was printed in Brussels, 1939.

Krafft was introduced to the German Propaganda Ministry by C. Loog, another astrologer, who had worked on interpretations of the famous **Nostradamus** prophecies. Krafft's pro-German edition of *Nostradamus* was used for psychological warfare, and Krafft himself became highly regarded after a successful prediction of the Munich attempt on Hitler's life November 9, 1939. In fact, this prophecy was so remarkable that Krafft was at first interrogated by the Gestapo, who thought he might have had a hand in the plot.

After the 1941 flight of Rudolf Hess to Britain, many astrologers and occultists in Germany were arrested, including Krafft, who was imprisoned for a year. After his release he again worked for the German Propaganda Ministry, interpreting horoscopes of leaders of the Allies in a manner favorable to Germany. However, he was arrested again in 1943 and sent to Oranienburg concentration camp. He died January 8, 1945 on the way to Buchenwald camp.

Recommended reading:

Howe, Ellic. *Astrology & Psychological Warfare during World War II,* Rider, 1972

Kral, Josef (1887–   )

Publisher, editor and writer on parapsychology. Born August 15, 1887 at Munich, Germany. In 1910 he married Anna Jaeger. He was awarded the Distinguished Service Cross of the German Federal Republic. He published an autobiography *Auftrag des Gewissens: Documente Katholischen Widerstandes gegen das N. S. Regime* (Command of Conscience: Documents of Catholic Resistance to the Nazi Regime, 1958).

He was general secretary of the International Society of Catholic Parapsychologists, and publisher of the journal *Vergorgene Welt* (Hidden World) founded by him with Abbé Alois **Wiesinger** in 1951, dealing with occult and parapsychological subjects. His other works included: *Die Irrelehre vom Zufall und Schicksal im Lichte der Wissenschaften und des Glaubens* (The Heresy of Coincidence and Fate in the Light of Science and Faith, 1953), *Der Neue Gottesbeweis: Parapsychologie, Mystik, Unsterblichkeit* (New Proof of God: Parapsychology, Mysticism, Immortality, 1956), *Das Heisse Eisen: Das Aussersinnliche als Wissenschaft und Glaube* (The Hot Iron: The Paranormal as Science and Faith, 1962).

Kramer, Heinrich (c. 1430–1505)

Dominican inquisitor who played a leading part in the great witchcraft persecutions as co-author with Jakob **Sprenger** of the infamous *Malleus Maleficarum,* the authoritative sourcebook for inquisitors, judges and magistrates.

Born at Schlettstadt, in Lower Alsace, near Strasburg, Kramer entered the Dominican Order, where he progressed so rapidly that he was appointed Prior of the Dominican House in Schlettstadt while still a young man. He became Preacher-General and Master of Sacred Theology, P.G. and S.T.M. (two Dominican Order distinctions), and around 1474 was appointed Inquisitor for the districts of Tyrol, Salzburg, Bohemia and Moravia. He received praise from Rome and from the Archbishop of Salzburg, becoming Spiritual Director of the Dominican church in Salzburg.

In 1484, Pope Innocent VIII was responsible for the famous Bull *Summis desiderantes affectibus* of December 9, which deplored the power of the witch organization and delegated Kramer and Jakob Sprenger as inquisitors throughout Northern Germany, especially in Mainz, Cologne, Treves, Salzburg and Bremen. By 1485, Kramer had written a treatise on witchcraft circulated in manuscript; this was later incorporated in the *Malleus Maleficarum,* first published circa 1486. This became the foremost manual for inquisitors, judges and magistrates in the great witchcraft persecutions, and went into many editions, some in French, Italian and English, as well as German.

Kramer resided for a period at the priory of Santi Giovanni e Paolo (X. Zanipolo), returning to Germany in 1497, where he lived at the convent of Rohr, near Regensburg. On January 31, 1500, he was appointed Nuncio and Inquisitor of Bohemia and Moravia by Alexander VI, and empowered to proceed against the Waldenses and Picards as well as witches. He died in Bohemia in 1505. (See also **Malleus Maleficarum**)

"Krata Repoa"

Title of a book published in Berlin in 1782, which claimed to be an "Initiation into the ancient Mysteries of the Priests of Egypt." The authors were C. F. Köppen (1734–c. 1797) and J. W. B. von Hymmen (1725–1786). Köppen was a German official and a founder of the Order of **African Architects.**

The term *Krata Repoa,* said to be of Egyptian origin, possessed no real affinity to that language. The work was of a Masonic ritual nature, divided into seven grades. That of Postophoris (a word used by Apuleius to signify a priest of Isis) corresponds to the apprentice or keeper of the sacred threshold. Secondly comes the degree of Neokaros, in which are to be found many ordeals and temptations. The third degree is the State of Death—of degree of judgment and of the passage of the Soul. The candidate was restored to light in the following degree, that of the Battle of the Shadows. In the fifth grade, a drama of Vengeance was enacted, and the sixth is that of the astronomer before the gate of the gods. In the final grade, the whole scheme of initiation was expounded.

It was believed that these degrees corresponded to the actual procedure of a secret society, and it may be that in some measure they did, as one of their authors was a prominent member of the **African Architects,** but although there would seem to be elements of real tradition in the work, most of it is probably mere invention. For a detailed discussion of the ritual, see *A New Encyclopaedia of Freemasonry* by Arthur E. Wait (1921; 1951).

Kraus, Joseph

Famous European performer of stage telepathy and clairvoyance during the 1930s, known under the stage name of Frederick **Marion** (1892–   ?). He appears to have possessed genuine paranormal powers.

Kreskin

Contemporary mentalist magician who performs amazing feats apparently through telepathy and suggestion. Real name George Kresge, Jr., he worked for eight years as consultant to a psychologist.

He disclaims supernatural powers, but appears to use some degree of ESP in such feats as influencing a member of his audience to select a name (previously placed by Kreskin in an envelope) from a pile of telephone directories. His own interpretation of telepathy is "just a heightening of the senses," and he suggests that "ESP" should read "PSE"—phenomena scientifically explainable.

Recommended reading:

Kreskin. *Amazing World of Kreskin,* Random, 1973; Avon paperback 1974

Krippner, Stanley Curtis (1932–   )

Psychologist and writer on parapsychology. Born October 4, 1932 at Edgerton, Wisconsin, he studied at University of Wisconsin (B.S. 1954), Northwestern University (M.A. 1957, Ph.D. 1961). From 1954–56 he was a speech therapist at Warren, Illinois, and at Richmond, Virginia, public schools from 1956–59.

From 1957–60 he was assistant director at Northwestern University Psychoeducational Clinic, teaching assistant at Northwestern University School of Education; 1959–60 head counselor, Elder Hall, Northwestern University; 1960 graduate assistant, University of Hawaii Department of Psychology; 1961 on, director, child Study Center, Kent State University, Kent, Ohio. Memberships include: Parapsychological Association, Council for Exceptional Children, American Association for the Advancement of Science, American Psychological Association, American Speech and Hearing Association, American Personnel and Guidance Association, National Council on Psychological Aspects of Disability, National Association for Gifted Children, National Vocational Guidance Association, International Society for General Semantics. He has written various articles on vocational development, exceptional children and reading disability.

An internationally known humanistic psychologist, Dr. Krippner has explored dreams, altered states of consciousness and paranormal phenomena for many years. His interest in such things began as a teenager on a Wisconsin farm: "When I was about 14 years of age, I had a very dramatic sense of my uncle's death at the very time that my parents received a phone call announcing his death. The effect of that was quite electrifying. Also I was an avid science fiction reader and an amateur magician, and all of these interests coalesced."

Such interests were reinforced by contacts with parapsychologist J. B. **Rhine** and Gardner **Murphy** during his undergraduate and graduate college years.

In 1964, Dr. Krippner left his position at Kent State University to become director of the **Dream Laboratory** at Maimonides Medical Center in Brooklyn, New York. With Dr. Montague **Ullman** and, later, Charles **Honorton,** Krippner spent ten years in a systematic exploration of dreams, including ESP in dreams and other altered states of consciousness. This work is described in the book *Dream Telepathy* (1973, 1974) by Montague Ullman, Stanley Krippner & Alan Vaughan.

In 1973, Dr. Krippner was the first parapsychologist to become vice-president for the western hemisphere of the International Psychotronic Research Association. He chaired sessions of the Psychotronic Congress in Czechoslovakia in 1973 and Monte Carlo in 1975, and became editor of the international journal *Psychoenergetic Systems.*

His investigations in parapsychology have taken him to many countries, including Mexico, Brazil, Columbia, Puerto Rico, the Philippines, India, Czechoslovakia, U.S.S.R., described in his book *Song of the Siren; A Parapsychological Odyssey* (1975). In 1974, he became visiting professor at California State College, Sonoma. He served as president of the Association for Humanistic Psychology from 1974–75, and was a faculty member of the Institute since 1973, working extensively with graduate students in this experimental graduate program. Originally serving as program planning coordinator at Saybrook, he became faculty chairman. In 1973, he became president of the **Parapsychological Association.**

He has written extensively on parapsychology, contributing to various symposia. He has also published: (with Daniel Rubin) *Galaxies of Life; The Human Aura in Acupuncture & Kirlian Photography* (1973; reissued in paperback as *The Kirlian Aura; The Galaxies of Life,* 1974), (with D. Rubin) *The Energies of Consciousness; Exploration in Acupuncture, Auras & Kirlian Photography* (1975), (ed.) *Advances in Parapsychological Research, vol. 1: Psychokinesis* (1977) & *Advances in Parapsychological Research, vol. 2: Extrasensory Perception* (1978), *Psychoenergetic Systems; The Interaction of Consciousness, Energy & Matter* (1979), *Human Possibilities; Mind Exploration in the USSR & Eastern Europe* (1980), (with Sidney Cohen) *LSD Into the Eighties* (1981). He has served on the editorial boards of: *Gifted Child Quarterly, Journal of Humanistic Psychology, Journal of Transpersonal Psychology, Journal of the American Society of Psychosomatic Dentistry & Medicine.*

Krishna Venta

Pseudonym of Francis Heindswater Pencovic aka Ben Covic. He started the **Foundation of the World Cult** in California in 1949, and was dynamited by dissident disciples in 1958. Pencovic had a criminal record in several states.

Krishnamurti, Jiddu (1895–   )

Philosopher and spiritual guide who might be described as a commonsense mystic. Born at Madanapelle, South India, he was educated privately. While still a child, he was "discovered" by C. W. **Leadbeater** in 1909 and confirmed later by Mrs. Annie **Besant** of the **Theosophical Society** who announced that he would be a forthcoming World Leader.

He traveled the world with Mrs. Besant and gave inspiring talks, but in 1929 publicly announced that he did not accept the Messianic role which had been thrust upon him. However, be continued to give informal discussions on spiritual topics and founded the Krishnamurti Foundation at Ojai, California.

Many of his discussions were published in book form. He did not normally lecture in the accepted pattern of speaker and audience, but rather encouraged questions and discussion to which he would respond with deep insights, stimulating individuals to assess their experiences in a more profound way than verbalization. His philosophical position stems from his background of Hinduism but goes beyond sectarian categories. He has traveled widely and inspired audiences all over the world. He has also made some shrewd no-nonsense comments on the more phoney aspects of mass media cults popularizing Eastern religions. His books include: *The First and Last Freedom* (1954), *Commentaries on Living* (1st series 1956, 2nd series 1958, 3rd series 1960); *Life Ahead* (1963), *Think on These Things* (1964), *Freedom from the Known* (1969), *The Only Revolution* (1970), *The Urgency of Change* (1971), *The Impossible Question* (1973); *Beyond Violence* (1973), *Flight of the Eagle* (1972), *The Awakening of Intelligence* (1973). Other books about Krishnamurti include: *Candles in the Sun* by Lady Emily Lutyens (1957), *To Be Young* by Mary Lutyens (1959), *Krishnamurti, The Awakening Years* by Mary Lutyens (1975).

Kristensen, H(arald) Kromann (1903–)

Danish engineer, chairman of the Danish Society for Psychical Research in 1963. Born March 5, 1903 at Charlottenlund, Denmark, he studied at the Polytechnic University of Denmark (M.S., electrical engineering, 1927). He married Ingeborg Mortensen. From 1928 on he was a staff member of the City of Copenhagen Lighting Department. He has published many technical papers on engineering.

Krohn, Sven I(lmari) (1903–)

Professor of philosophy and writer on parapsychology. Born May 9, 1903 at Helsinki, Finland, he studied at the University of Helsinki (M.A. 1929), University of Turku, Finland (Ph.D. 1949). In 1930 he married Ruth Grônroos. He has been a school teacher, lecturer in theoretical philosophy and professor of philosophy, from 1960 on, head of the Philosophical Institution, University of Turku.

From 1934–40 he was president of the Society for Psychical Research, Finland; Finnish representative, International Congress for Psychical Research, Oslo, in 1935; founder and president of the Society for Parapsychological Studies in Finland; member of the Philosophical Society of Finland, president, Society for Philosophy and Phenomenological Research in Finland.

In addition to his books and paper on philosophical subjects, he was co-author with Ake Tollet of the book *Jälleenlöydetty sielu: Keskusteluja parapsykologiasta* (Soul Rediscovered: Dialogues concerning Parapsychology, 1936). He published a number of articles on parapsychology for various journals in Finland and elsewhere.

Krstaca

Dalmatian name for a witch. (See **Slavs**)

Kübler-Ross, Elisabeth

Contemporary physician who has become a world authority on the subject of death, dying and after-death states. Born in Switzerland, she worked as a country doctor before moving to the U.S.

During World War II, she spent weekends at the Kantonspital (Cantonai hospital) in Zürich, where she volunteered to assist escaped refugees. After the war, she visited Majdanek concentration camp, where the horrors of the death chambers stimulated a desire to help people facing death and to understand the human impulses of love and destruction. She extended her medical background by becoming a practicing psychiatrist. Her formal work with dying patients commenced in 1965, when she was a faculty member at the University of Chicago, Illinois. She also conducted researches on basic questions concerning life after death when at the Manhattan State Hospital, New York.

Her studies of death and dying have involved accounts by patients who reported **Out-of-the-Body** experiences. Her researches tend to show that while dying can be painful, death itself is a peaceful condition.

In 1978, Dr. Ross helped to found Shanti Nilaya (Final Home of Peace), a healing and growth center in Escondido, California. This was an extension of her well-known "Life-Death and Transition" workshops conducted in various parts of the U.S. and Canada, involving physicians, nurses, social workers, lay people and terminally ill patients. Shanti Nilaya is located in San Diego County and offers courses with short and long-term therapeutic sessions.

Dr. Ross is author of *On Death and Dying* (New York, 1970), *Questions & Answers on Death & Dying* (1974), *The Final Stage of Growth* (1975), (with M. Warshaw) *To Live Until We Say Good-Bye* (1978), *Coping With Death & Dying* (1980), *Living With Death & Dying* (1981), and has edited *Death: The Final Stage of Growth* (New Jersey, 1975), and recorded a series of five cassette tapes on *Coping With Death and Dying* (Ross Medical Associates, Flossmoor, Illinois). In May 1977, Dr. Ross was included in the *Ladies' Home Journal* "Women of the Year" awards.

Kuda Bux (1905–)

Kashmiri stage magician, who has demonstrated claimed feats of "eyeless sight" and fire-walking. Born at Akhnur, Kashmir, on October 15, 1905, he came to London in 1935. He first practiced fire-walking at the age of 14, and subsequently devoted himself to public performances of stage magic. He normally performed fire-walking only at an annual religious festival and claimed that his immunity from burns was due to his "faith," conferred by a "higher power" in India. He also claimed to be able to convey his immunity to another person and take him over the fire walk without burns.

During 1935, Kuda Bux cooperated with psychical researcher Harry **Price** in two fire walk tests under control conditions on September 9 and September 17, 1935. Scientific observers carefully monitored all aspects of the fire walk. Kuda Bux's feet were examined and no chemical or other preparation was discovered. The temperature of the feet was taken before and after the walk, and found to be slightly lower after than before. The feet were not blistered or injured in any way. The skin was soft and not calloused, moreover the feet were washed and dried before the walk. The surface temperature of the fire trench on the second day was 430°C. The trench was 25 feet long by

6 feet wide but with a 36 inch wide platform of earth in the center, in effect being two trenches, each 11 feet long, 6 feet wide and 9 inches deep place end to end. Kuda Bux walked the trench deliberately and steadily in 4.5 seconds; the estimated time of contact of each foot with the burning embers was half a second. The tests were photographed and a cinematographic record taken. A volunteer European, Digby Moynagh, attempted the walk on both days but suffered some blistering of the feet. A full report of the tests appeared in *Bulletin II* of the University of London Council for Psychical Investigation, 1936.

After these tests, the resulting publicity made Kuda Bux well known and he performed in British variety theaters with his impressive act of "eyeless sight." Managements and fire departments would not permit fire trenches to be built on stage for demonstrations of fire walking.

In 1938, Kuda Bux came to the U.S. to demonstrate his fire walk for a Robert Ripley "Believe It or Not" radio program, and later became a member of the Society of American Magicians. He demonstrated his eyeless vision act widely and in 1945 rode a bicycle through the heavy traffic of Times Square in New York while blindfolded. Magicians claim that such performances are a trick, in spite of the performer being heavily blindfolded by balls of dough being placed over the eyes, secured with yards of bandages. The skeptical view is that the dough and bandages are shifted sufficiently by the performer to enable him to squint underneath them. However, Kuda Bux claimed that his performance was due to feats of mental concentration, establishing a link between his mind and outside objects, even although he admitted to practicing conjuring tricks in his acts. (See also **Conjuring; Eyeless Sight; Fire-Ordeal; Magicians;** Rosa **Kuleshova;** Jules **Romains;** Seeing with the **Stomach; Transposition of the Senses**)

Kuhlman, Kathryn (1910?–1976)

One of the most well-known spiritual healers in modern America. Born in Concordia, Missouri, she had a religious experience at the age of 13 and felt a strong call to the ministry. She dropped out of school and started preaching from the age of 15 on. She became an itinerant evangelist, traveling through the midwest states.

Her first healing took place while she preached in Franklin, Pennsylvania, in 1946. A woman stood up and gave testimony that she had been cured of a tumor. From 1947 on, Miss Kuhlman held regular services in the Carnegie Auditorium at Pittsburgh, where a number of cases of miraculous healing were reported during her ministry. She held services at the Carnegie Auditorium for twenty years before transferring to the First Presbyterian Church in downtown Pittsburgh.

During her services, she would speak with simplicity and emotional sincerity and presently become transformed by what she called "the Holy Spirit." Members of the congregation reported a feeling of power building up, with a healing effect. At this point Miss Kuhlman would become clairvoyantly aware of various diseases and symptoms of ill health which she would locate and "rebuke" from her place on the stage: "To my right in the first balcony, somebody is being healed of diabetes . . . a growth has disappeared. It's a man up there in the top balcony . . .". She spoke rapidly in a kind of transported trance-like condition. She often introduced medical doctors into her programs, and they confirmed the reality of her miraculous cures. A sincere and dedicated individual, Miss Kuhlman appeared regularly on television and radio programs. She died in Tulsa, Oklahoma, February 20, 1976, following open-heart surgery.

Recommended reading:

Kuhlman, Kathryn. *I Believe in Miracles,* Prentice-Hall 1962

Spraggett, Allen. *Kathryn Kuhlman: the Woman Who Believes in Miracles,* Thomas Y. Crowell Co., 1970; Signet paperback, 1971

Kulagina, Nina

Contemporary Russian psychic who demonstrates the ability to move objects at a distance (**Psychokinesis**). Nina Kulagina, a Leningrad housewife, has been tested under laboratory conditions by noted researchers, including physiologist L. L. Vasiliev, Dr. Genady A. Sergeiev of the Uktomskii Physiological Institute, Leningrad, Dr. Zdenek Rejdak, Czech psychical researcher, B. Blazek, a psychologist and Dr. J. S. Zvierev.

Mrs. Kulagina causes a compass needle to spin by holding her hand a few inches above it; she also moves matchboxes at a distance. Mrs. Kulagina was filmed demonstrating her ability to move small objects such as a pen or cigarettes without contact. A report of experiments with Mrs. Kulagina was published by Z. Rejdak in the article 'Nina Kulagina's Mind Over Matter' (*Psychic* magazine, June 1971). (See also **Movement; U.S.S.R.**)

Kuleshova, Rosa (died 1978)

Remarkable contemporary Russian psychic who demonstrated the ability to "read" ordinary printed words with the fingers of her right hand when normal vision was completely excluded. She could also determine color tones on paper and objects by touch. Experiments with Kuleshova were reported in 1963 by the Soviet scientist I. M. Gol'dberg in an article 'On Whether Tactile Sensitivity Can Be Improved by Exercise' (*Soviet Psychology & Psychiatry,* vol. II, No. 1).

Kuleshova had been a relatively unimportant individual in her home town of Nizhniy Tagil in the Urals, but after news of her remarkable abilities spread through the scientific world in the U.S.S.R., she was invited to Moscow to undergo experiments at the Biophysics Institute of the Soviet Academy of Sciences in Moscow. Here Kuleshova demonstrated her abilities to scientists, and it seems likely that the attention and excitement of being famous went to her head. She found it difficult to adjust to ordinary life back in Tagil, and insisted on returning to Moscow for further experiments. She made wild claims which she often failed to fulfill, and was even caught cheating. After this led to skepticism about "skin vision," further scientific tests were undertaken with precautions against fraud, and these validated Kuleshova's basic achievements.

In 1964, *Life* reporter Bob Brigham saw Kuleshova in Moscow and stated that she was able to read the small print on his business card accurately *with her elbow* under conditions when normal vision was entirely excluded. Soon other Soviet subjects were discovered to have the ability of eyeless sight, and new programs of scientific investigation were undertaken. Recently the faculty of "skin vision" has been renamed "bio-introscopy" in the Soviet Union.

Rosa Kuleshova died in 1978 from a brain tumor. Reports of her successful demonstrations of eyeless sight in the editorial offices of the Moscow journal *Technika Molo-geji* shortly before her death were reported in *The International Journal of Paraphysics* (vol. 13, Nos. 3 & 4). For details of Kuleshova's life and the Soviet experiments with other individuals demonstrating eyeless vision, see: *Psi: Psychic Discoveries Behind the Iron Curtain* by Sheila Ostrander & Lynn Schroeder (1970; Bantam paperback, 1971). (See also **Dermo-Optical Perception; Eyeless Sight;** Jules **Romains;** Seeing with the **Stomach; Transposition of the Senses; U.S.S.R.**)

Kumbha Mela

Important Hindu religious festival, held every twelve years at the appropriate planetary conjunction; an *Ardh-Kumbha* (half-Kumbha) is held midway between the major *Kumbha* festivals. *Kumbha* is equivalent to the sign of Aquarius, and the festival is calculated at the conjunction of Jupiter, Aquarius, Aries and the sun.

The festival takes place at either Hardwar, Allahabad, Ujjain or Nasik. In 1977, the festival was at Allahabad, a specially holy place where the sacred river Ganges merges with the Jamuna and the Saraswati.

Ritual bathing by pilgrims is a special feature of the festival, which originated in ancient times as an occasion for spiritual instruction from great sages and yogis. Some two million pilgrims attend the festival to visit wandering holy men and yogis from all over India. The festival is divided into different camps relating to individual Hindu sects and subsects.

In modern times, the Indian government provides sanitary facilities and a system of barricades to prevent accidents caused by vast crowd movements. *Kumbha Mela* is one of the most colorful mass festivals of India, a kind of non-generation gap super-Woodstock of the spiritual life.

Kundalini

According to ancient Hindu religious teachings and yoga science, a latent force in the human organism, responsible for sexual activity and (in a sublimated form) higher consciousness. In Hindu mythology, Kundalini is personified as a goddess, sometimes with the aspect of Durga (a creator) and sometimes Kali (the destroyer) or Bhujangi (the serpent). Kundalini is often described as a serpent that sleeps at the base of the spine, and when aroused darts upwards, bringing enlightenment or pain. The traditional Hindu yoga texts state that Kundalini may be aroused by a combination of **hatha yoga** *asanas, pranayama* (breathing exercises), meditation and spiritual practices. It seems clear, however, that when Kundalini is incorrectly aroused, this can result in physical disability or even death.

The *Panchastavi* is an esoteric Hindu scripture in which Kundalini is addressed as the Mother of all beings, and the arousal of Kundalini for mystical enlightenment is described in ecstatic terms:

"Flawless, exceedingly sweet and beautiful, soul-enchanting, fluent speech manifests in all ways in those [devotees] blessed with genius who keep Thee, O Shakti [power] of Shiva, the destroyer of Kamadeva [god of love] constantly in mind, as shining with the stainless luster of the moon in the head . . ." (III-12)

"O Goddess, rising from the cavity of Muladhara [chakra or center at the base of the spine], piercing the six lotuses [chakras] like a flash of lightning, and then flowing from the moon into the immovable sky-like center [in the head] as a stream of Supreme nectar, Thou then returnest [to Thy abode]." (IV-6)

These descriptions, in context, indicate that Kundalini is the creative force expressed in procreation, which is also responsible for mystical enlightenment when sublimated by rising up the spine through chakras or psychic centers to the highest center in the head.

There are foreshadowings of the Biblical story of the Garden of Eden in this poetic myth of the serpent and the tree with the fruit of knowledge or of sexual force, and there are similar myths in many ancient religions, suggesting a lost secret of the relationship between sex and mysticism. Esoteric cults in many countries have guarded this secret, and there are evidences of meditation systems in ancient Egypt, China and Tibet which under one name or another taught the arousal of the serpent-like force for higher consciousness instead of procreation. Many other religions have emphasized a relationship between sex and mysticism by enjoining celibacy for priests and monks. A third aspect of Kundalini is its claimed connection with certain psychic powers, known to yogis as *siddhis*.

In modern times, the ancient concept of Kundalini has been revived by Pandit **Gopi Krishna** of Srinagar, India, who has aroused this legendary force and experienced a continuing state of higher consciousness. He has described his experience in *Kundalini; The Evolutionary Energy in Man* (1970) and a number of other books. Amongst other modern Hindus who claim to have aroused Kundalini is Swami **Muktananda,** who is said to have the power to communicate this arousal by touch, a technique traditionally known in India as *shaktipat.*

The controversial psychoanalyst Dr. Wilhelm **Reich,** originally a pupil of Freud, developed a theory of "**Orgone** Energy" expressed in different segments of the human body, closely paralleling the course of Kundalini through the *chakras* or psychic centers. Reich also associated this energy with sexual activity. However, he was strongly opposed to Yoga, which he mistakenly considered merely a system of fixed physical positions with rigid musculature. In fact, hatha yoga exercises progressively improve the tone of groups of associated muscles and enhance flexibility.

Identification of Kundalini and the *chakras* with nervous energy and the main plexi of the human body was made by Dr. B. D. Basu of the Indian Medical Service in a prize essay on 'The Hindu System of Medicine' (*Guy's Hospital Gazette,* London, 1889) and this theory was enlarged by Dr. Vasant G. Rele in his book *The Mysterious Kundalini* (1927).

It is now clear that there is a biological basis for the mystical anatomy relating to Kundalini, and it is to be expected that the recent scientific interest in the nerve currents of **Acupuncture** may be correlated with the pathways of Kundalini.

Pandit Gopi Krishna believes that Kundalini is an

evolutionary force which will play an increasingly important part in the development of the human race and its goals, indicating new directions for both science and religion. His books have already attracted the serious attention of such eminent thinkers as Prof. Carl von Weizsäcker of the Max Planck Institute for the Life Sciences, Germany.

Following upon the writings of Pandit Gopi Krishna, Dr. Karan Singh, Union Minister of Health in India, announced in 1974 an ambitious Kundalini Research project to be sponsored by the All-India Institute of Medical Science, to research "Kundalini concept and its relevance to the development of higher nervous functions." Meanwhile sympathizers with the work of Pandit Gopi Krishna have founded the Central Institute for Kundalini Research at Srinagar, Kashmir, India, and there is also a Kundalini Research Foundation located at 10 East 39 Street, New York, N.Y. 10016. (See also **Breathing; Chakras; Emanations; Hatha Yoga; Orgone; Siddhis; Yoga**)

Recommended reading:

Avalon, Arthur (Sir John Woodroffe). *The Serpent Power,* Madras, 1922

Gopi Krishna. *Kundalini; the evolutionary energy in man,* Shambala, 1970

Gopi Krishna. *The Biological Basis of Religion and Genius,* Harper & Row, 1972

Gopi Krishna. *The Awakening of Kundalini,* F. P. Dutton & Co., 1975

Rele, Vasant G. *The Mysterious Kundalini,* Taraporevala, Bombay, 1927

Narayananda, Swami. *The Primal Power in Man or the Kundalini Shakti,* N. K. Prasad, Rishikesh, 1950

Vyasdev, Brahmachari Swami. *Science of Soul (Atma Vijnana),* Yoga Niketan Trust, Gangotri, 1964

Kundalini Quarterly

Quarterly publication of the Kundalini Research Institute, California, concerned with the relationship of **Kundalini** energy and yoga techniques to the emotional, physical and spiritual life of human beings. Address: P.O. Box 1020, Claremont, California 91711.

Kuppuswami, B(angalore) (1907–   )

Professor of psychology, active in the field of parapsychology. Born February 29, 1907 at Bangalore, Mysore, India, he studied at University of Mysore (B.A. 1927, M.A. 1929, D.Litt. 1944). In 1932 he married Peddada Kameswaramma. From 1929–49 he was a lecturer in psychology at University of Mysore; 1949–52 professor of psychology at Presidency College, Madras; 1952 on, professor of psychology at University of Mysore.

In 1945 he was president of the Psychology section, Indian Science Congress; member of educational board, *Journal of General Psychology* (U.S.); 1952, secretary of Education and Employment Section. U.S.A. Educational Reforms Committee of Mysore; 1954, chairman of Elementary Education Committee, Andhra State; 1956, director of Mysore State Seminar on the Welfare of Scheduled Castes and Tribes; 1956, editor of *Psychological Studies* (Mysore); chairman of Section on Social Change, International Conference on Human Relations, Netherlands (1956); president of Psychology Section, All India

Philosophical Conference (1956); president of Regional Conference of Psychology, Mysore (1956); leader of general education team assigned to the U.S. (1958); president of the Parapsychology Conference, Indian Science Congress (1960).

In addition to his work in the fields of psychology, sociology and education, Dr. Kuppuswamy studied the effect of education and variation in distance on Psi ability.

Kusche, Lawrence David (1940–   )

Author of an important critical work on the **Bermuda Triangle** mystery. His carefully researched book *The Bermuda Triangle Mystery—Solved* (1975) examined popular theories of time warps, black holes, UFOs etc. and opted for a rational view that there is no single overall mysterious explanation, but rather a mystery built up from inaccurate research, exaggeration, omission of important facts and repetition of misleading rumors.

Kusche has had considerable experience as a flight instructor and also as research librarian. In commenting on his approach to such matters as the Bermuda Triangle question, he has stated: "I might be called a skeptic. It's not that I disbelieve anything and everything, but I *especially* question much of the present day written and televised information that passes for 'fact.' Much of it is nothing more than a half-fact attempt to earn as much money as possible with as little regard for truth as possible."

Kuvalayananda, Swami (1883–1966)

Famous Indian pioneer of the scientific study of Yoga. Born as Jagannath Ganesh Gune on August 30, 1883, at Dabhoi, Baroda, his mother tongue was Marathi but his publications on Yoga are in English. He was a noted scholar, educationalist and national freedom fighter. He organized the Khandesh Education Society in 1916 and was principal of the Society's college from 1921–23. He was chairman of the Physical Education Committee appointed by the Kher Ministry of Bombay in 1937, chairman of the Bombay Board of Physical Education, member of the Central Advisory Board of Physical Education.

His guru was Paramhamsa Shree Madhavadasji Maharaj at Malsar, on the banks of the river Narmada in Gujarat State, who trained him in Yoga.

In 1932 he established a Yogic Health Center at Santa Cruz, Bombay; new premises were secured in 1935 and the Center renamed Ishwardas Chunilal Yoga Health Centre, Kaivalyadhama. Later a spiritual center was added at Kanakesvara Hill in the Kolaba District of Bombay. An additional center named the Kaivalyadhama Saurashtra Mandal was established in Rajkot in 1943.

By the end of 1943, it was decided to divide the main organization into two wings: Kaivalyadhama Ashrama with emphasis on spiritual development, and Kaivalyadhama Sreeman Madhava Yoga Mandira Samiti at Lonavla, Poona, specializing in the medical and scientific investigation of Yoga. The latter wing was officially recognized as a research institute by the Government of Bombay and by Bombay State.

From 1935 onwards, the Kaivalyadhama S.M.Y.M. Samhiti has published *Yoga-Mimamsa* Journal, edited by

Swami Kuvalayananda, with both popular and scientific sections devoted to the serious study of Yoga. Swami Kuvalayananda is also the author of two books: *Asanas* (a manual of Hatha Yoga exercises) and *Pranayama* (yoga breathing exercises), both published by Yoga-Mimamsa Office, Lonavla (C.R.), India, reprinted 1966 by Popular Prakashan, Bombay. (See also **Hatha Yoga; Yoga**)

Kyphi

Among the ancient Egyptians, an aromatic substance, with soothing and healing properties, prepared from sixteen materials according to the prescription of the sacred books. (See also **Egypt**)

Kyteler, Dame Alice (c. 1324)

Fourteenth-century witch of Kilkenny, Ireland, of a good Anglo-Norman family. She was indicted by Bishop de Ledrede, but being well connected and wealthy was able to defy the Bishop, who thereupon excommunicated her. Lady Alice then imprisoned the Bishop, who responded by indicting the whole community.

However, the Lord Justice, who supported Lady Alice, obliged the Bishop to lift his ban. The Bishop eventually succeeded in instituting a case against Lady Alice and others accused with her of sorcery, but she fled to England. Her maid Petronilla de Meath was arrested and flogged, after which she confessed to various orgies involving Lady Alice. Petronilla was excommunicated and burned as a witch at Kilkenny November 3, 1324, but Lady Alice spent the rest of her life peacefully in England.

The case is significant as the first witchcraft trial in Ireland. A full account was printed as vol. 24 in the series of the Camden Society, England, under the title: *A Contemporary Narrative of the Proceedings against Dame Alice Kyteler, prosecuted for Sorcery in 1324,* edited by Thomas Wright, 1843.

L

Labadie, Jean (1610-1674)

A French fanatic of the seventeenth century, born in 1610 at Bourg, on the Dordogne. He declared himself a second John the Baptist, sent to announce the second coming of the Messiah.

He even went so far as to claim some measure of divinity for himself. But to his ambition as a votary he joined a taste for more worldly pleasures, which he indulged under the mask of religion. He left the Jesuit College in Bordeaux in 1639 and became canon of Amiens. He became the favorite confessor of upper-class ladies, but was obliged to leave Amiens after a number of scandals. He was also in trouble in Toulouse and eventually discredited with the Church.

In 1650, he joined the Calvinists and became pastor at Montauban but was banished after charges of sedition. He was similarly obliged to move from Geneva and moved to Middleburg in Zealand with a band of followers. He was opposed by the Lutherans and eventually expelled with his band. He died February 16, 1674 at Erfurt. A sect of Labadists persisted for a few years at Wiewart, North Holland, professing austerity of manners similar to early Quakers. The Labadists emphasized community of property within the church and continuance of prophecy.

Among the works of Labadie (which were condemned) was *Le Veritable Exorcisme, au l'unique moyen de chasser le diable du monde chrétien.*

Laboratoire d'études des relations entre rythmes cosmiques et psychophysiologiques

Established by psychologist Michel **Gauquelin** and his wife Françoise for the study of cosmic influences in relation to the psychology of personality. Over twenty publications have been issued. Address: 8 Rue Amyot, Paris 75005, France.

Laburum

A Kabalistic sign, embodied in the Great Magical Monogram which is the seventh and most important pentacle of the **Enchiridion** ascribed to Pope Leo III, a collection of sixteenth-century prayers and charms.

Lacteus

A fabled precious stone said by ancient writers to be efficacious when applied to rheumatic eyes.

Lady of Lawers

Name given to a woman, one of the Breadalbane family, of Scotland, who was married to Campbell of Lawers. This gentlewoman was believed to be gifted with prophetic powers, and her prophecies were said to be written in a book shaped like a barrel and kept in the charter room of Taymouth Castle and named "The Red Book of Balloch."

These all had reference to the house and lands of Breadalbane. One of these stated that when the red cairn on Ben Lawers fell, the church would split. In the same year that the cairn, built by the sappers and miners on Ben Lawers, fell, the Disruption in the Church of Scotland took place.

Ladybug (or Ladybird)

Popular name of the colorful red-spotted beetle of the coccinellidae group of the Coleoptera order. It is the subject of many folklore superstitions. It brings children, warns of danger, forecasts length of life by the number of its spots, or warns of death. In British and European folklore, the lady-bird was captured by a maid and bidden to fly "north, south, or east, or west" in the direction in which her lover lived. Whichever way the insect flew, there dwelt her future husband.

A well known children's rhyme is: "Ladybird, ladybird, fly away home, your house is on fire, And your children all roam."

Lafleche, Pierre (1892–)

French poet and government official who studied telepathy and ESP, also collaborated with René **Warcollier.** Born February 6, 1892 in Paris, France, he studied at Collège de Juilly (Seine-et-Marne), Bachelier ès lettres 1909; University of Paris (licencié en droit 1918). In 1918 he married Johanne Kristiansen. He served in the French army in World War I and was awarded Croix de Guerre and chevalier, Legion of Honor.

He took up a position with the French Ministry of Public Works in 1920, retiring in 1952. He published three volumes of poetry. He wrote on parapsychology in various journals: *Psychica, Revue Métapsychique, Lotus Bleu* and *Tomorrow.*

Laidlaw, Robert W(ordsworth) (1901–)

Physician and psychiatrist who took an active part in parapsychology. Born February 26, 1901 at Englewood, New Jersey, he studied at Princeton University (B.A. 1924), College of Physicians and Surgeons, Columbia University (M.D. 1931). He married twice, his second wife being Beatrice Snedeker. He was chief, Psychiatric Service, Roosevelt Hospital, New York, N.Y. from 1949 on; consultant in psychiatry, Union Theological Seminary, New York, 1949 on; president, American Association of Marriage Counselors, Inc., 1950-52; member of

New York State Board of Social Welfare from 1958. He is a Fellow of the American Psychiatric Association, New York Academy of Medicine, and member of American Medical Association, Medical Societies of the State of New York and County of New York, Association for Research in Nervous and Mental Disease, New York Society for Clinical Psychiatry; trustee of the American Society for Psychical Research; and author of a number of papers on marriage counseling and clinical psychiatry.

His interest in parapsychology led him to study mediumship, and the effect of chemical substances on the human mind. He presented a paper on 'Psychedelics: A New Road to the Understanding of Mediumistic Phenomena?' at the Conference on Parapsychology and Psychedelics held in New York 1958. He also wrote on hypnosis and hypnoanalysis in *Tomorrow* Magazine (Autumn 1958). He also studied the effect on the mind of LSD 25, and clinical aspects of spiritual healing.

Lam

A mystical word in Hindu yoga practice, associated with the Muladhara **chakra** or subtle energy center situated at the base of the human spine near the anus.

Each chakra has its characteristic shapes, colors, symbolic figures and mantras (mystical sounds formed by combinations of letters. "Lam" is a *bija* or seed mantra, i.e., a special form of natural power which can be liberated by meditation. (See also **Chakras; Kundalini; Mantra; Yoga**)

Lamb, Dr. John (died 1628)

Dr. Lamb was a noted astrologer and reputed sorcerer in the time of Charles the First. Richard Baxter, in his *Certainty of the World of Spirits* (1691) recorded the following apocryphal account of the miraculous performance of Lamb.

Meeting two of his acquaintances in the street, and they having intimated a desire to witness some examples of his skill, he invited them home with him. He then conducted them into an inner room, where presently, to their great surprise, they saw a tree spring up in the middle of the apartment. They had scarcely ceased wondering at this phenomenon, when in a moment there appeared three diminutive men, with little axes in their hands for the purpose of cutting down this tree. The tree was felled; and the doctor dismissed his guests, fully satisfied of the solidity of his pretensions.

That very night, however, a tremendous hurricane arose, causing the house of one of the guests to rock from side to side, with every appearance that the building would come down, and bury him and his wife in the ruins. The wife in great terror asked "Were you not at Dr. Lamb's to-day?" The husband confessed it was true. "And did you not bring something away from his house?" The husband owned that, when the little men felled the tree, he had picked up some of the chips, and put them in his pocket. Nothing now remained to be done but to produce the chips, and get rid of them as fast as they could. This ceremony performed, the whirlwind immediately ceased, and the remainder of the night passed quietly.

Originally a medical doctor, Lamb became known for practicing "other mysteries, as telling of fortunes, helping of divers to lost goods, shewing to young people the faces of their husbands or wives that should be in a crystal glass." It is possible that popular resentment against Lamb was due less to the success of his magical practices than his position as a favorite of the Duke of Buckingham. It was generally believed that Lamb used magic charms to corrupt women to serve the pleasure of the Duke.

Dr. Lamb at length acquired such an odious reputation for infernal practices that the populace rose upon him and tore him to pieces in the streets. Nor did the effects of his ill-fame terminate here. Thirteen years after, a woman, who had been his servant maid, was apprehended on a charge of witchcraft, was tried, and in expiation of her crime was executed at Tyburn.

A broadside ballad by Martin Parker titled "The Tragedy of Doctor Lambe, the great suposed conjurer, who was wounded to death by saylers and other lads, on Friday the 14 of June, 1628. And dyed in the Poultry Counter, neere cheap-side, on the Saturday morning following" was sold and sung in the streets. In fact, the dates of June 14 and 15 are mistakes, as Lamb was mobbed on June 13 and died the following day.

Lambert, G(uy) W(illiam) (1889–   )

British government official who took an active interest in psychical research. Born in London, England, December 1, 1889, he studied at St. John's College, Oxford University (B.A. hons. 1912). In 1917 he married Nadine F. W. Noble. He was a member of the British Civil Service from 1913–51; Assistant Undersecretary of State for War from 1938–51. He was awarded Chevalier, Legion of Honor 1920, Silver Jubilee Medal 1935, Coronation Medal 1937, Companion of the Bath, 1942.

Mr. Lambert was a member of the Council of the Society for Psychical Research, London, from 1925 on, president 1955-58, honorary secretary from 1958 on. He has studied spontaneous phenomena involving ESP, haunting and poltergeists. He contributed various articles to publications of the SPR, including: 'The Dieppe Raid Case' (*Journal,* vol. 35, May-June 1952), 'Antoine Richard's Garden' (*Journal,* vol. 37, July-October 1953, March-April 1954, vol. 41 June 1962), 'Poltergeists: A Psychical Theory' (*Journal,* vol. 38, June 1955).

Lambert, R(ichard) S(tanton) (1894–   )

Broadcasting official and author, who explored the field of parapsychology and published books and articles on the subject. Born August 25, 1894 at Kingston-on-Thames, England, he studied at Oxford University (M.A. 1921). In 1918 he married Kate Elinor Klein; his second marriage in 1944 was to Joyce Morgan.

He was sub-editor of *The Economist,* London, from 1914–15, tutorial class tutor at University of Sheffield 1919–23, staff tutor of tutorial classes at University of London 1923-28, editor of *The Listener* (published by the British Broadcasting Corporation) 1928-39, Supervisor of School Broadcasts, Canadian Broadcasting Corporation 1943 on, Counselor for radio, UNESCO 1947. He was winner of the Governor General of Canada Medal for Juvenile Literature in 1949.

Mr. Lambert wrote over thirty books dealing with biography, children's adventure, travel, art, crime, radio, films, propaganda and various school textbooks. In the field of parapsychology he investigated poltergeist phenomena with Harry **Price** and was joint author with Price of *The Haunting of Cashen's Gap* (1936). The publicity accorded to this celebrated case nearly cost Lambert his career as editor of the B.B.C. journal *The Listener* when one of the governors of the B.B.C. concluded that an interest in the supernatural was a reflection on Lambert's competence. As a result of his actions, Lambert was obliged to bring a court case for defamation. The story of this case is told by Lambert in his biographical work *Ariel and All His Quality* (1940). Lambert's book *Exploring the Supernatural* (1954) also deals with parapsychology. (See also **Cashen's Gap**)

Lamia

In ancient Greek folklore, a shape-shifting monster that sucked blood and ate flesh, similar to stories of the succubus and vampire. In Greek myth, Lamia was the daughter of Belus and Libya, loved by Zeus and punished by Hera. Because Hera took Lamia's children away, Lamia took her revenge on the children of men and women, since she has no power over gods. According to folk beliefs, Lamia might be in the form of a beautiful woman, a snake with a woman's head, or a monster with deformed lower limbs and the power to take out her eyes. (See also **Striges**)

Lamps, Magic

Stories of magic lamps are of great antiquity. According to G. Panciroli (1523–1599), the sepulchre of Tullia, daughter of the Roman statesman Cicero (106–43 B.C.), was found to have a lamp which had burnt for over 1,550 years. St. Augustine described a lamp placed by the seashore which was not extinguished by wind or rain. Mgr. Guerin, chamberlain of Pope Leo XIII, told of a lamp in St. Denis's Church before the shrine of St. Genevieve, which contained oil that was always consumed but never diminished in quantity.

Another legend concerned Rabbi Jachiel of Paris, who was regarded by the Jews as one of their saints, and by the Parisians as a sorcerer. During the night when everyone was asleep, he was believed to work by the light of a magic lamp which cast through his chamber a glow like that of day itself. He never replenished this lamp with oil, nor otherwise attended to it, and folks began to hint that he had acquired it through diabolic agencies. If anyone chanced to knock at his door during the night they noticed that the lamp threw out sparks of light of various colors, but if they continued to rap the lamp failed and the Rabbi turning from his work touched a large nail in the middle of his table which connected magically with the knocker on the street-door, giving to the person who rapped upon it something of the nature of an electric shock (see **France**).

One of the most familiar stories is that of Aladdin and his Wonderful Lamp from the *Arabian Nights Entertainment* or *Book of a Thousand and One Nights*. Here the lamp is a magic wish-fulfilling talisman. Although versions of the stories in the *Arabian Nights* are of some antiquity, some of the tales, like that of Aladdin, are from late Egyptian sources.

Another well-known legend is that of the tomb of Christian Rosenkreutz, founder of the Order of the Rosy Cross or Rosicrucians. According to the Rosicrucian manifesto *Fama Fraternitatis* (first printed 1614), translated together with the manifesto *Confessio Fraternitatis* (1615) by "Eugenius Philalethes" (pseudonym used by alchemist Thomas Vaughan) in London, 1652. According to the *Fama*, Christian Rosenkreutz was buried in a wonderful tomb. When it was opened many years after the death of Rosenkreutz, a secret vault was discovered with an ever-burning lamp, together with magical mirrors, sacred books, bells, more ever-burning lamps and "artificial songs." The latter items sound intriguingly like precursors of the phonograph record! For an attempt to separate history from legend and symbolism in this story, see *The Brotherhood of the Rosy Cross* by Arthur E. Waite (1924; reprinted University Books, 1961).

Many stories of ever-burning lamps may have stemmed from phosphorescent phenomena, or from spontaneous combustion caused by the sudden influx of air into a gaseous vault.

Lancashire Witches

A famous episode of ignorance, superstition and persecution in Lancashire, England, involving a mass trial of twenty alleged witches. Not far from Manchester lies Pendelbury Forest, a gloomy although romantic and picturesque spot. At the beginning of the seventeenth century, it was supposed to be inhabited by witches and held in such terror by law-abiding folks that they scarcely dared to approach it. They imagined it to be the scene of all sorts of frightful orgies and diabolical rites. So that when Roger Nowel, a country magistrate, hit upon the plan of routing the witches out of their den, and thus ridding the district of their malevolent influence, he fancied he would be performing a public-spirited and laudable service.

He promptly began by seizing Elizabeth Demdike and Ann Chattox, two women of eighty years of age, one of them blind and the other threatened with blindness, both of them living in squalor and abject poverty. Demdike's daughter, Elizabeth Device, and her grandchildren, James and Alison Device, were included in the accusation, and Ann Redferne, daughter of Chattox, was apprehended with her mother.

Others were seized in quick succession—Jane Bulcock and her son John, Alice Nutter, Catherine Hewitt, and Isabel Roby. All of them were induced to make a more or less detailed confession of their communication with the Devil. It is not known how these confessions were obtained, but considering the age and condition of the women, no real value can be attached to their claimed admissions. When these had been extorted from them, they were sent to prison in Lancaster Castle, some fifty miles away, to await trial for their misdeeds.

They had not lain in prison very long when the authorities were informed that about twenty witches had assembled on Good Friday at Malkin's Tower, the home of Elizabeth Device, in order to compass the death of one Covel, to blow up the castle in which their companions were confined and rescue the prisoners, and also to kill a man called Lister by means of diabolical agency.

In the summer assizes of 1612, the prisoners were tried for witchcraft and were all found guilty. The woman Demdike had died in prison, and thus escaped a more ignominious death at the gallows. The principal witnesses who appeared against Elizabeth Device were her grandchildren, James and Jannet Device. Directly the latter entered the witness-box, her grandmother set up a terrible yelling punctuated by bitter execrations. The child, who was only nine years of age, begged that the prisoner might be removed as she could not otherwise proceed with her evidence. Her request was granted, and she and her brother swore that the Devil had visited their grandmother in the shape of a black dog, and asked what were her wishes. She had intimated that she desired the death of one John Robinson, whereupon the fiend told her to make a clay image of Robinson and gradually crumble it to pieces, saying that as she did so the man's life would decay and finally perish. On such evidence, ten persons were hanged, including the aged Ann Chattox.

It is shocking to reflect that, at a period when literature and learning were at their height, such cruelty could be tolerated, not only by the vulgar and uneducated, but by the learned judges who pronounced the sentence. The women were old and ignorant and probably weak-minded. No doubt they began in time to invest themselves with those powers, which their neighbors credited to them, and to believe themselves fit objects for the awe and terror of the people. It is even possible that they may have seen some sort of visions or hallucinations which they persuaded themselves were evil spirits attending on them. Thus their own superstition and ignorance may have hastened their downfall.

The story of the Lancashire witches became the subject of Thomas Shadwell's play of that name in 1681, and a novel by W. H. Ainsworth in 1848. Twenty-two years after the events of 1612, a similar outrage in the same area of Lancashire was narrowly avoided, by the shrewdness of the judge who tried the case. A certain misguided man, by name Edmund Robinson, thought to profit by the general belief in witchcraft. To this end he taught his young son, a boy of eleven, to say that one day he encountered in the fields two dogs, with which he tried to catch a hare. But the animals would not obey his bidding, and at length he tied them to a post and whipped them, when they immediately turned into a witch and her imp.

This monstrous story gained such credence that when Robinson declared that his son possessed a sort of **second-sight,** which enabled him to distinguish a witch at a glance, no-one thought of denying his statement. Accordingly, he took the boy to the neighboring churches, set him on a bench, and bade him point out the witches. No less than seventeen persons were thus accused and might have been hanged had not the judge's suspicions been aroused by the story, for the jury did not hesitate to convict them.

However, the doubts of the worthy judge gained a respite for the prisoners, some of whom were sent to London for examination by the King's physician and by King Charles I himself. The boy's story was investigated and found to be merely a tissue of lies, as, indeed, the child himself confessed it to be. For details, see *An History of The Original Parish of Whalley* by Thomas D. Whitaker, London, 1818 etc. (See also **Witchcraft**)

Lancaster, John B(usfield) (1891–)

Engineering technician who experimented in the field of parapsychology. Born January 19, 1891 at Philadelphia, Pennsylvania, he studied structural design and building at the Drexel Institute, Philadelphia, 1914-18. In 1917 he married Annetta Persing. He was a draftsman, power plant engineer, and chief draftsman at the Philadelphia Gas Works 1911-55.

Mr. Lancaster developed games for testing telepathy and psychokinesis, presented to the Parapsychology Laboratory, Duke University, Durham, North Carolina. During 1959, he conducted long-distance experiments in telepathy with students of Cambridge and Oxford Universities in England, and Wayland College, Plainview, Texas. His article 'A GESP Experiment with a Dual (Color-Symbol) Target' was published in *Journal of Parapsychology,* December 1959.

Lancelin, Charles (c. 1927)

French physician and occultist who was an early experimenter in the field of **astral projection** (see also **out-of-the-body** travel). He published a number of important books in the active period of French interest in occultism which preceded World War II. These included: *Histoire mythique de Shatan; de la légende au dogme* (1903), *Comment on meurt, comment on nait* (1912), *La fraude dans la production des phénomènes mediumiques* (1912), *Méthode de dédoublement personnel* (1913), *L'âme humaine; etudes expérimentales de psycho-physiologie* (1921), *La vie posthume* (1922), *La sorcellerie des campagnes* (1923), *L'occultisme et la Science* (1926), *L'occultisme et la vie* (1928), *L'humanité posthume et le monde angélique* (n.d.), *Qu'est-ce l'âme?* (n.d.), *La réincarnation* (n.d.)

Landau, Lucian (1912–)

Industrial consultant who experimented and lectured in the field of parapsychology. Born April 13, 1912 in Warsaw, Poland, he came to Britain as a business executive and consultant in rubber, plastics and electronics industries. He invented various devices and processes used in Britain, France and Italy and was author of a study on latex published by the British Rubber Development Board in 1954.

He also experimented with dowsing, clairvoyance and psychic photography, and lectured on such subjects to the Medical Society for the Study of Radiesthesia, Cambridge University Society for the Study of Parapsychology, and the College of Psychic Science, London. He published various articles in *Light* journal, including a report on the Delawarr Camera (vol. lxxvii, No.3430, March 1957) (see also **Black Box**). His paper on 'Radionics: General Considerations' was published in the *Journal of the British Society of Dowsers* (Sept. 1958).

Lang, Andrew (1844-1912)

Philosopher, poet, scholar, author of significant books on anthropology, folklore, mythology, psychology, ghost lore, history, biography, and fairy tales.

He was born at Selkirk Scotland, March 31, 1844. He was educated at Selkirk Grammar School and Edinburgh Academy, matriculating at St. Andrews University. He continued his studies at Glasgow University and Oxford University (Balliol and Merton Colleges). In 1875 he married Leonora Blanche Alleyne. He abandoned his fellowship at Merton College to become a journalist and author in London.

He joined the Society for Psychical Research in 1906 but his interest in psychical phenomena was of longer standing. He studied them rather from the historic and anthropologic, than from the experimental viewpoint. He contributed some valuable personal evidence on crystal gazing. His earliest paper was read before the S.P.R. on the **Cock Lane Ghost** in 1894. Subsequently, he frequently contributed to the society's *Proceedings* and *Journal.* In *Journal* vol. 7 he wrote on Queen Mary's Diamonds, in *Proceedings* vol. 11 on the Voices of Joan of Arc. The telepathy *à trois* (involving three individuals) was his conception in a paper on the mediumship of Mrs. Leonora **Piper.** His book *Custom and Myth,* published in 1884, contained a chapter on the **divining rod,** which he regarded as a mischievous instrument of superstition. However, the investigations of Prof. W. **Barrett** convinced him that it was "a fact, and a very serviceable fact."

Lang wrote several articles on psychical research for the *Encyclopaedia Britannica* in 1902. His books *The Making of Religion* (1898), *Magic and Religion* (1901), *Cock Lane and Common Sense* (1894), *The Book of Dreams and Ghosts* (1897) are valuable for students of psychical research. *The Mind of France* (1908) was the first attempt to consider Joan of Arc in the light of psychical phenomena. In 1911 he became President of the Society for Psychical Research. According to the Rev. M. A. Bayfield's appreciation in *Proceedings* (vol. 26) it is fair to infer from his later writings that he found the exclusion of an external agency from some phenomena increasingly difficult.

Lang's books and writings over an astonishing wide field of literature demonstrated a remarkable originality and scholarship. He was the first scholar to correlate properly the mythology of ancient society with the folklore and psychical phenomena of modern civilization. His rainbow-colored series of fairy tale books for children, commencing with *The Blue Fairy Book* in 1889 is still popular today. His valuable study *The Book of Dreams and Ghosts* was reissued by Causeway Books in 1974.

Lang was honored by St. Andrews and Oxford Universities and he was elected an honorary fellow of Merton College in 1890. The freedom of his native town of Selkirk was conferred on him in 1889. He died July 20, 1912.

Lanz Von Liebenfels, Jörg (1874-1954)

Austrian astrologer, part of the occult underground preceding the Nazi movement. His **Order of New Templars** only admitted members who satisfied his racist concepts of Nordic purity. He also founded the Ariosophical Movement, another occult and anti-Semitic organization.

Born in Vienna July 19, 1874 as Adolf Lanz, he claimed to be the son of Baron Johannes Lancz de Liebenfels. He circulated an incorrect birth date to mislead other astrologers. He became a novice at a Cistercian monastery but was expelled for improper behavior. Soon afterwards he founded his Order of New Templars, which claimed divine support for Hitler's race theories and the supremacy of a master race. Lanz advocated special breeding colonies or stud farms for the master race, as well as elimination of lesser breeds.

The Order used the swastika symbol before it was officially adopted by the Nazi party, and Hitler met Lanz as early as 1909, when he collected some issues of Lanz's journal *Ostara.* Lanz prophecied the success of Hitler as a world figure, but failed to find favor with the Nazis after the invasion of Austria in 1938.

His ideas were certainly used by the Nazis, but Hitler may have been reluctant to admit their origin. Lanz died April 22, 1954. He was the subject of a book by W. Daim, *Der Mann, der Hitler die Ideen gab* (The man who gave Hitler the ideas) published 1958.

Lapis Exilis

A fabulous precious stone which was believed to cause the phoenix to renew her youth. *Lapis Exilis,* according to Wolfram von Eschenbach, was synonymous with the Holy **Grail.** (See also **Lapis Judaicus**)

Lapis Judaicus

A fabulous precious stone also identified with the Holy **Grail** and the talismanic stone of inexhaustible feeding power. It was sometimes called "Theolithos," and may have been another name for the **Lapis Exilis.** It has also been known as the Phoenix stone. Another legend which clung to it was that it had fallen from the crown of Lucifer as he was banished from heaven, and remained in the keeping of the angels of the air.

LAPLAND

The Laplanders acquired a reputation for magical practice which was almost proverbial throughout Europe, and certainly so among the peoples of the Scandinavian Peninsula. Indeed the Finns used to credit them with extraordinary power in sorcery and divination. Many Scandinavian scions of nobility were in ancient times sent to Lapland to obtain a magical reputation, and Eric the son of Harold Haarfager found Gunhild, daughter of Asur Tote, living among the Lapps in A.D. 922 for that purpose. English literature abounds with reference to Lapland witches. But Sorcery in Lapland was a preserve of the male shamans or magicians. Like the Celtic witches, the Lapps were addicted to the selling of wind or tempests in knotted ropes.

In his book *The History of Lapland* (1674), Joannes W. Scheffer described Lapp magic as follows: "The melancholic constitution of the Laplanders, renders them subject to frightful apparitions and dreams, which they look upon as infallible presages made to them by the Genius of what is to befall them. Thus they are frequently seen lying upon the ground asleep, some singing with a full voice, others howling and making a hideous noise not unlike wolves.

"Their superstitions may be imputed partly to their living in solitudes, forests, and among the wild beasts, partly to their solitary way of dwelling separately from the society of others, except who belong to their own families sometimes several leagues distance. Hereafter it may be added, that their daily exercise is hunting, it being observed that this kind of life is apt to draw people into various superstitions, and at last to a correspondence with spirits. For those who lead a solitary life being frequently destitute of human aid, have ofttimes recourse to forbidden means, in hopes to find that aid and help among the spirits, which they cannot find among men; and what encourages them in it is impunity, these things being committed by them, without as much as the fear of any witnesses; which moved Mr. Rheen to allege, among sundry reasons which he gives for the continuance of the impious superstitions of the Laplanders, this for one: because they live among inaccessible mountains, and at a great distance from the conversation of other men. Another reason is the good opinion they constantly entertain of their ancestors, whom they cannot imagine to have been so stupid as not to understand what God they ought to worship, wherefore they judge they should be wanting in their reverence due to them, if, by receding from their institutions, they should reprove them of impiety and ignorance.

"The parents are the masters, who instruct their own sons in the magical art. 'Those,' says Tornaeus, 'who have attained to this magical art by instructions receive it either from their parents, or from somebody else, and that by degrees which they put in practice as often as an opportunity offers. Thus they accomplish themselves in this art, especially if their genius leads them to it. For they don't look upon every one as a fit scholar; nay, some are accounted quite incapable of it, notwithstanding they have been sufficiently instructed, as I have been informed by very credible people.' And Joh. Tornaeus confirms it by these words: 'As the Laplanders are naturally of different inclinations, so are they not equally capable of attaining to this art.' And in another passage, they bequeath the demons as part of their inheritance, which is the reason that one family excels the other in this magical art. From whence it is evident, that certain whole families have their own demons, not only differing from the familiar spirits of others, but also quite contrary and opposite to them. Besides this, not only whole families, but also particular persons, have sometimes one, sometimes more spirits belonging to them, to secure them against the designs of other demons, or else to hurt others.

"Olaus Petri Niurenius speaks to this effect, when he says—'They are attended by a certain number of spirits, some by three, others by two, or at least by one. The last is intended for their security, the other to hurt others. The first commands all the rest. Some of those they acquire with a great deal of pains and prayers, some without much trouble, being their attendants from their infancy.' Joh. Tornaeus gives us a very large account of it. 'There are some,' says he, 'who naturally are magicians; an abominable thing indeed. For those who the devil knows will prove very serviceable to him in this art, he seizes on in their very infancy with certain distemper, when they are haunted with apparitions and visions, by which they are, in proportion of their age, instructed in the rudiments of this art. Those who are a second time taken with this distemper, have more apparitions coming before them than in the first, by which they receive much more insight into it than before. But if they are seized a third time with this disease, which then proves very dangerous, and often not without the hazard of their lives, then it is they see all the apparitions the devil is able to contrive, to accomplish them in the magical art. Those are arrived to such a degree of perfection, that without the help of the drum (see infra), they can foretell things to come a great while before; and are so strongly possessed by the devil, that they foresee things even against their will. Thus, not long

ago, a certain Laplander, who is still alive, did voluntarily deliver his drum to me, which I had often desired of him before; notwithstanding all this, he told me in a very melancholy posture, that though he had put away his drum, nor intended to have any other hereafter, yet he could foresee everything without it, as he had done before. As an instance of it, he told me truly all the particular accidents that had happened to me in my journey into Lapland, making at the same time heavy complaints, that he did not know what use to make of his eyes, those things being presented to his sight much against his will.'

"Lundius observes, that some of the Laplanders are seized upon by a demon, when they are arrived to a middle age, in the following manner: 'Whilst they are busie in the woods, the spirit appears to them, where they discourse concerning the conditions, upon which the demon offers them his assistance, which done, he teaches them a certain song, which they are obliged to keep in constant remembrance. They must return the next day to the same place, where the same spirit appears to them again, and repeats the former song, in case he takes a fancy to the person; if not, he does not appear at all. These spirits make their appearances under different shapes, some like fishes, some like birds, others like a serpent or dragon, others in the shape of a pigmee, about a yard high; being attended by three, four, or five other pigmees of the same bigness, sometimes by more, but never exceeding nine.'

"No sooner are they seized by the Genius, but they appear in the most surprising posture, like madmen, before bereaved of the use of reason. This continues for six months; during which time they don't suffer any of their kindred to come near them, not so much as their own wives and children. They spend most of this time in the woods and other solitary places, being very melancholy and thoughtful scarce taking any food, which makes them extremely weak. If you ask their children, where and how their parents sustain themselves, they will tell you, that they receive their sustenance from their Genii.

"The same author gives us a remarkable instance of this kind in a young Laplander called Olaus, being then a scholar in the school of Liksala, of about eighteen years of age. This young fellow fell mad on a sudden, making most dreadful postures and outcries, that he was in hell, and his spirit tormented beyond what could be expressed. If he took a book in hand, so soon as he met with the name of Jesus, he threw the book upon the ground in great fury, which after some time being passed over, they used to ask him whether he had seen any vision during this ecstacy? He answered that abundance of things had appeared to him, and that a mad dog being tied to his foot, followed him wherever he stirred. In his lucid intervals he would tell them, that the first beginning of it happened to him one day, as he was going out of the door of his dwelling, when a great flame passed before his eyes and touching his ears, a certain person appeared to him all naked. The next day he was seized with a most terrible headache, so that he made most lamentable outcries, and broke everything that came under his hands. This unfortunate person's face was as black as coal, and he used to say, that the devil most commonly appeared to him in the habit of a minister, in a long cloak; during his fits he would say that he was surrounded by nine or ten fellows of a low stature, who did use him very barbarously, though at the same time the standers-by did not perceive the least thing like it. He would often climb to the top of the highest fir trees, with as much swiftness as a squirrel, and leap down again to the ground, without receiving the least hurt. He always loved solitude, flying the conversation of other men. He would run as swift as a horse, it being impossible for anybody to overtake him. He used to talk amongst the woods to himself no otherwise than if several persons had been in his company.

"I am apt to believe, that those spirits were not altogether unknown to the ancients, and that they are the same which were called by Tertullian *Paredri,* and are mentioned by Monsieur [Herride] Valois, in his *Ecclesiastical History of Eusebius.*

"Whenever a Laplander has occasion for his familiar spirit, he calls to him, and makes him come by only singing the song he taught him at their first interview; by which means he has him at his service as often as he pleases. And because they know them obsequious and serviceable, they call them *Sveie,* which signifies as much in their tongue, as the companions of their labour, or their helpmates. Lundius has made another observation, very well worth taking notice of, viz.:—That those spirits or demons never appear to the women, or enter into their service, of which I don't pretend to allege the true cause, unless one might say, that perhaps they do it out of pride, or a natural aversion they have to the female sex, subject to so many infirmities."

For the purposes of augury or divination, the Lapps employed a magic drum, which, indeed, was in use among several Arctic peoples. Writing in 1827, De Capell Brooke stated that the ceremonies connected with this instrument had almost quite disappeared at that date. The encroachments of Lutheranism had been long threatening the existence of the native shamanism. In 1671 the Lapp drum was formally banned by Swedish law, and several magicians were apprehended and their instruments burnt. But before that date the religion which the drum represented was in full vigor.

The Lapps called their drum *Kannus* (Regnard, 1681), also *Kaunus, Kabdas, Kabdes Gabdas,* and *Keure* (Von Duben, 1873), its Scandinavian designations being *trolltrumma,* or *Rune-bomme,* "magic or runic drum," otherwise *Spa-trumma,* "fortune-telling drum." J. A. Friis has shown that the *sampo* of the Finnish national epic poem *Kalevala* is the same instrument. According to G. W. von Düben, the best pictures and explanations of the drum are to be found in *Lappisk Mythologi* (Christiania, 1871) by J. A. Friis (pp. 30–47) but there are good descriptions in G. W. von Düben's own work (*Om Lappland och Lapparne,* Stockholm, 1873), as also in the books of Scheffer, Leem, Jessen, and others.

The appearance of the Lapp drum was thus described by Jean François Regnard in 1681: "This instrument is made of a single piece of wood, hollowed in its thickest part in an oval form, the under part of which is convex, in which they make two apertures long enough to suffer the fingers to pass through, for the purpose of holding it more firmly. The upper part is covered with the skin of the reindeer, on which they paint in red a number of figures, and from whence several brass rings are seen hanging, and some pieces of the bone of the reindeer."

A wooden hammer, or, as among the Samoyeds (1614), a hare's foot was used as a drum-stick in the course of the incantation. An *arpa* or divining-rod was placed on a definite spot showing from its position after sounding the drum what magic inference might be drawn. By means of the drum, the priest could be placed in sympathy with the spirit world, and was thus enabled to divine the future, to ascertain synchronous events occurring at remote distances, to forecast the measure of success attending the day's hunting, to heal the sick, or to inflict people with disease and cause death. Although long obsolete in Lapland, these rites survived for a long time among the Samoyeds and other races of Arctic Asia and America. It is interesting to note how exactly the procedure among the Vaigatz Samoyeds in 1556 (*Pinkerton's Voyages,* London, 1808, I, 63) tallied with that of the Sakhalin Ainos in 1883 (J. M. Dixon in *Transactions of the Asiatic Society of Japan,* Yokohama, 1883, 47). The same practices can be traced eastward through Arctic America, and the drum was used in the same fashion by the Eskimo shaman priests in Greenland (Hinrich Johannes Rink's *Tales and Traditions of the Eskimos,* 1875, pp. 60–61). The shape of the drum varied a little according to locality. The form of the Eskimo drum was that of a tambourine.

"Their most valuable instrument of enchantment," stated J. J. Tornæus, "is this sorcerer's kettle-drum, which they call Kannas or Quobdas. They cut it in one entire piece out of a thick tree stem, the fibres of which run upwards in the same direction as the course of the sun. The drum is covered with the skin of an animal; and in the bottom holes are cut by which it may be held. Upon the skins are many figures painted, often Christ and the Apostles, with the heathen gods, Thor, Noorjunkar, and others jumbled together; the picture of the sun, shapes of animals, lands and waters, cities and roads, in short, all kinds of drawings according to their various uses. Upon the drum there is placed an indicator, which they call *Arpa,* which consists of a bundle of metallic rings. The drumstick is, generally, a reindeer's horn.

"This drum they preserve with the most vigilant care, and guard it especially from the touch of a woman. When they will make known what is taking place at a distance,—as to how the chase shall succeed, how business will answer, what result a sickness will have, what is necessary for the cure of it, and the like, they kneel down, and the sorcerer beats the drum; at first with light strokes, but as he proceeds, with ever louder stronger ones, round the index, either till this has moved in a direction or to a figure which he regards as the answer which he has sought, or till he himself falls into ecstasy, when he generally lays the kettle-drum on his head.

"Then he sings with a loud voice a song which they call *Jogke,* and the men and women who stand round sing songs, which they call *Daura,* in which the name of the place whence they desire information frequently occurs. The sorcerer lies in the ecstatic state for some time— frequently for many hours, apparently dead, with rigid features; sometimes with perspiration bursting out upon him. In the meantime the bystanders continue their incantations, which have for their object that the sleeper shall not lose any part of his vision from memory; at the same time they guard him carefully that nothing living may touch him—not even a fly. When he again awakes to consciousness, he relates his vision, answers the questions put to him, and gives unmistakable evidence of having seen distant and unknown things."

The inquiry of the oracle does not always take place so solemnly and completely. In everyday matters as regards the chase, etc., the Lapp consults his drum without falling into the somnambulic crisis. On the other hand, a more highly developed state of prophetic vision may take place without this instrument, as has already been stated. Claudi relates, that at Bergen, in Norway, the clerk of a German merchant demanded of a Norwegian Finn-Laplander what his master was doing in Germany. The Finn promised to give him the intelligence. He began then to cry out like a drunken man, and to run round in a circle, till he fell, as one dead, to the earth. After a while he woke again, and gave the answer, which time showed to be correct.

Finally, that many Lapp shamans, while wholly awake, free from convulsions and a state of unconsciousness, were able to become clairvoyant, seems placed beyond all doubt by the account of Tornæus. "The use which they make of their power of clairvoyance, and their magic arts, is, for the most part, good and innocent; that of curing sick men and animals; inquiring into far-off and future things, which in the confined sphere of their existence is important to them. There are instances however, in which the magic art is turned to the injury of others."

In addition to the works quoted, see also E. J. Jessen-Schardebøl, *Afhandling om de Norske Finners og Lappers Hedenske Religion* (1765), N. H. Sioborg, *Tympanum Schamanico-lapponicum* (1808); Émile Petitot, *Les Grands Esquimaux* (1887), John Abercromby, *The Pre- and Proto-historic Finns* (2 vols., 1898).

Larcher, Hubert (1921–   )

French physician and authority on industrial medicine active in the field of parapsychology. Born June 26, 1921 in Paris, France, he studied at the University of Grenoble (Licencié, philosophy, 1943) and University of Paris (M.D. 1951; diploma in industrial hygiene and industrial medicine, 1955). In 1949 he married Edda Ritzhaupt. From 1961 onwards was professor of hygiene and safety, Ecole Normale Sociale, Paris. He became a council member of the Institut Métapsychique International.

In addition to his work on industrial medicine, he has taken a special interest in paranormal psychophysiology, pathogenesis and paranormal cures. He has studied the relationship between parapsychology, psychic research and mysticism, and investigated physiological aspects of metamorphosis and survival, as well as such parapsychological phenomena as levitation and psychokinesis.

He published numerous articles on parapsychology, including: 'Prodiges sanguins après la mort' (Wonders of the Blood after Death, *Revue Métapsychique,* Sept.-Oct. 1953; Nov.-Dec. 1953), 'Trois cas extraordinaires d'oncorruption de la chair' (Three Remarkable Cases of Lack of Decay of Flesh, *Revue Métapsychique,* March-April 1954), 'Towards a Science of Healing' (*Proceedings* of Four Conferences on Parapsychological studies, 1957), 'Perspectives parapsychochimiques: La Drogue' (Parapsychochemical Outlook: Narcotics, *La Tour St. Jacques,* No. 1, 1960). He is also author of *Le sang peut-il vaincre la mort?* and edited *Aux frontières de la science* (1957).

Lascaris (c. 18th century)

Mysterious alchemist who was almost legendary. It is impossible to determine the proper name or date at which this person was born, or to say, exactly, whence he came and where he chiefly lived. He was commonly supposed to have been active about the beginning of the eighteenth century, while Germany is said to have been the principal scene of his activities, but everything recorded concerning him reads like a romance, and suggests the Middle Ages.

According to popular belief he assured people that he was of Oriental origin, sometimes he maintained that his native land was the Ionian Isles, and that he was a scion of the Greek royal house of Lascaris, while on other occasions he declared that he was an archimandrite of a convent in the Island of Mytilene. His object in coming to Europe was supposed to be to solicit alms for the ransom of Christian prisoners in the East, but in view of his claimed alchemical achievements, this seems paradoxical. However, this was his story when, about 1700, he commenced wandering in Germany. While staying in Berlin, he happened to fall ill and sent for medical aid. This appeared shortly in the shape of Johann Friedrich Bötticher, a young apothecary, who chanced to be deeply interested in alchemy. A friendship sprang up between physician and patient and when Lascaris left the Prussian capital he gave Bötticher a packet of transmuting powder, at the same time instructing him how to use it successfully, yet refraining from telling him how to manufacture the powder itself.

Bötticher set to work speedily, concocted considerable quantities of gold and silver, grew rich, and was raised to the peerage, while simultaneously he began to find his society, and more especially his services as a scientist, courted by kings and nobles. The title of Baron was conferred on him. Meanwhile, however, his supply of the precious powder had run short, and being unable to make more, he found his reputation waning rapidly. Worse still, he had spent his newly-acquired wealth and now found himself reduced to penury. He was placed under house arrest, and when he attempted to escape he was removed to prison. During his detention he was allowed to experiment with chemistry and discovered a process for the manufacture of red porcelain, and by the sale of this he eventually restored his fallen fortunes.

We presume naturally that it was gratitude to his physician which had inspired the alchemist to give Bötticher the powder, but why did Lascaris make an analogous present to someone else at a later date? The recipient on this occasion was Schmolz de Dierbach, a lieutenant-colonel in the Polish Army. He, like the German apothecary, succeeded in making a quantity of gold, although no more is known about him after this transmutation. A certain Baron de Creux was likewise favored by Lascaris, the Baron's experiments proving just as successful as those of the others.

Nor were these the only people on whom this alchemist bestowed his indulgence, for one Domenico Manuel, the son of a Neapolitan mason, was likewise given a packet of transmutatory powder, and armed with this, he wandered through Spain, Belgium, and Austria, performing alchemical operations before princes and noblemen, and reaping wealth accordingly.

Pride was the inevitable result of this, and although

there is no reason to suppose that any patent of nobility was ever conferred on Domenico, he was soon styling himself Comte Gautano, then Comte di Ruggiero, while in one town he maintained that he was a Prussian major-general. Elsewhere he declared that he was field-marshal of the Bavarian forces. Going to Berlin in the course of his perambulations, he offered to make gold in the presence of the king but unfortunately his operation proved utterly futile, and he was hanged as a charlatan in consequence.

That was in 1709, and in the same year, according to tradition, Lascaris himself performed some successful transmutations before a German politician named Liebknech, a citizen of Wurtembourg. Nothing further was heard of the mysterious alchemist, however, so it may be assumed that he died soon after these events. His was indeed a curious career, his generosity having scarcely a parallel in the whole history of hermetic philosophy. (See also **Alchemy**)

Laszlo, Laszlo (1898-1936)

One of the most famous fake mediums of Hungary during the 1920s. Born in Budapest, September 23, 1898, he was the son of a locksmith. He left school at the age of 13 and was apprenticed to an electrician. He was harshly treated, and ran away on several occasions, but was returned by the police. After three and a half years apprenticeship, he beat up his master before finally leaving him.

Laszlo earned a living as an electrician until 1915, when he joined a Polish Legion of the Austro-German campaign against Russia. He was in the front line for nearly a year, but deserted after being wounded. He was court-martialed, then escaped, later serving in a Hungarian unit on the Italian front in 1916. He deserted again when his sweetheart became a prostitute, and, since ordinary employment was barred to him, joined a gang of burglars. He gave much of his ill-gotten gains to his sweetheart to keep her off the streets, but when he found that she was still living as a prostitute and even keeping pimps, he began to drink heavily and attempted suicide. He was arrested and imprisoned until October 1918, when the revolution in Hungary decreed a general amnesty.

After that, he again took to a life of crime, and while escaping from police, took refuge in southeast Hungary, became involved with an anti-Communist plot, was arrested and sentenced to be shot. Freed by anti-Communists, he fought against Romanians until captured and taken to the death camp of Jassy, where he was beaten and starved for three months before escaping.

He returned to Budapest, hoping that his criminal record had been lost in archives burnings, and (according to his own account) took a succession of jobs as actor, film extra, variety artist, playwright, painter, and electrical technician. The performance of a music hall hypnotist led him to become interested in Spiritualism and occultism.

With his picaresque background and emotional instability, it was a fatal mixture. Influenced by Laszlo's seances, several young men committed suicide as a journey to the "Great Beyond." In 1920, Laszlo fell off a tram, and during two weeks in a hospital met a girl with whom he fell deeply in love. After recovery, he telephoned her demanding that they become engaged, and when she refused him, shot himself in the telephone booth. Again in the hospital, he fell in love with another girl, with whom he later formed a suicide pact. In a somewhat confused scene with a gun, the girl died, while Laszlo was only wounded. He was arrested for homicide.

Astonishingly enough, the police agreed to hold a Spiritualist seance at their headquarters with Laszlo as medium, during the course of which Laszlo claimed that he was the victim of an evil entity from the thirteenth century, desiring to use psychic force to destroy victims. Laszlo was released, but later claimed that the seance was a deliberate fake on his part to fool the authorities.

He now turned journalist on a Budapest newspaper, and published articles about occultism and Spiritualism, and through them was introduced to William Torday, president of the Hungarian Metapsychical Society. Torday and his colleagues believed that Laszlo had brilliant occult talents, and persuaded him to sign an exclusive contract with them for seances. Laszlo duly produced fake spirit heads and hands, and built up a reputation as a great medium.

After reading a classic work on **materialization** by famous psychical researcher Baron **Schrenck-Notzing,** Laszlo deliberately contrived to fake such effects in order to deceive the Baron. The materials used by Laszlo for fake **ectoplasm** were gauze and cottonwool soaked in goose-fat. These props were hidden in the furniture in the seance room, and when this became impossible through strict controls, Laszlo was impudently adroit in slipping his props into the pockets of his investigators when searched, and picking their pockets during the seance! It is by no means certain that Schrenck-Notzing was actually deceived, but certainly many prominent psychical researchers were.

Laszlo was tricked into exposure of his frauds by Eugene Schenck, a music-hall hypnotist and stage clairvoyant. Anticipating publicity for his tricks, Laszlo himself admitted fraud at a public lecture, when he revelled in his clever frauds. In the subsequent disillusionment, Torday was discredited as a psychical researcher and sixty-seven of the seventy members of the Hungarian Metapsychical Society resigned. According to Laszlo, he was then visited by two young men who were members of a Spiritualist circle. They said they had received a spirit message that Laszlo should retract his confessions of fraud or be killed. Laszlo accordingly drew up a public statement that his materialization phenomena were genuine, and undertook not to combat Spiritualism in any way. However, it is possible that this melodramatic episode was yet another instance of Laszlo's fertile fantasy. For a time, it was believed that Laszlo might have been part genuine, part fraud.

Laszlo resumed his everyday work as an electrician, and in due course became a criminal again. After ten years, he was arrested for burglary and house-breaking. Before the hearing could be completed, he died of a lung hemorrhage in 1936.

For further details of this extraordinary fake medium and his fraudulent career, see *Companions of the Unseen* by Paul Tabori (London, 1968) and *My Occult Diary* by Cornelius Tabori (London, 1951). See also *Proceedings* of the Society for Psychical Research, London (vol. xxiv, pp. 329–32; xxvi, p. 339) and the Society's *Journal* (vol. xxi, p.

280). The story of Laszlo also makes interesting comparison with that of the famous British fake medium William **Roy,** who was equally neurotic and shameless. (See also **Fraud**)

Latihan

A spiritual exercise which is a basic feature of the **subud** movement (the term is Indonesian). The object of the latihan is worship of God. In a state of submission, contact is said to be made with the divine life force, resulting in a process of regeneration.

In principle, the latihan can be practiced individually but usually a number of individuals gather together for this purpose. The preliminary stages of the latihan are characterized by marked physical reactions. Urges to cry, weep, dance or speak in tongues are followed but may be stopped if need be. No particular stress is laid on the manifestations as such, but they are said to result in a release of tension that culminates in a state of inner quietude, in which communion with God takes place. All this is believed to have a strong resemblance to what is supposed to have occurred at the original Pentecostal scene. In contrast to other spiritual movements and sects involving Pentecostal phenomena, there are no anticipatory stimulating speeches, music, ceremonies or rituals, the ecstatic state emerging spontaneously.

The cathartic quality of the latihan is said to manifest in a gradual integration of the entire being. In conjunction with the latihan, the problems of members are "tested," answers being received in a state of inner receptivity.

The characteristic physical features of the latihan make interesting comparison with the spiritual exercise of earlier cults such as the Shakers. The backwoods revivalists of Kentucky and Tennessee in the early nineteenth century often excited "the jerks," similar to the physical convulsions of the early Methodists in Britain, who sometimes jumped and danced until they became insensible. In Hindu **yoga** practice, the onset of **Kundalini,** or divine force is also accompanied by jerking and twitching in the body.

Launoy, Jean de (1603-1678)

A celebrated doctor of the Sorbonne, canonist and historian, born in Valdesie, Normandy, France. He studied at the University of Paris and after being ordained as a priest was admitted as a doctor of divinity at Navarre.

He resisted the claims of the court of Rome and specialized in exposing legendary religious fables and demolishing dubious claims for saints. He undoubted thinned the ranks of sainthood by his keen scrutiny. One commentator remarked: "He suspected the whole martyrology, and examined all the saints as they do the nobility of France."

In spite of his shrewd judgments, he was known as a kind-hearted and benevolent man. He published many learned volumes.

Laurel

A tree which Lucius (c. 126–173 A.D.) Apuleius classed among the plants which preserved men from the influence of evil spirits. It was also believed to give protection from lightning.

The laurel was regarded as sacred to Apollo and associated with purifying, since Apollo was the great purifier. It was a symbol of immortality as an evergreen and its intoxicating properties were associated with prophetic and poetic inspiration. The Pythian priestess at Delphi used to chew laurel leaves to enhance oracular powers (see **Greece**).

The laurel also symbolizes victory and peace. The victors in the Pythian games were crowned with laurel. Roman generals sent news of their victories in messages wrapped in laurel leaves, delivered to the Senate.

"Laurin" (or "Der Kleine Rosengarten")

A Tyrolese romance of the late thirteenth century, attached to the saga-cycle of Dietrich of Bern. Laurin, a dwarf, possesses a magic rose-garden into which no one may enter without the loss of a hand or a foot. Dietrich and his follower Witege enter the garden, and the latter rides through the rose bushes. Laurin, the dwarf, appears, on horseback and dismounts Witege. He is challenged by Dietrich and, assuming his cloak of invisibility, wounds him.

Dietrich now persuades him to a wrestling match and wrenches off the dwarf's belt which gives him superhuman strength. Thus he overthrows Laurin.

Laurin then invites Dietrich and his followers to his mountain home, prepares them a banquet, makes them tipsy, and throws them all into a dungeon. They are released by Künhild, a mortal woman, who restores their weapons. They take Laurin prisoner and carry him to Bern where he becomes a Christian convert and receives Künhild in marriage. For further details see *Epics and Romances of the Middle Ages* by M. W. MacDowall (London, 1883).

La Vey, Anton Szandor (1930–   )

High priest of the First Church of Satan in San Francisco, California, some time lion tamer, calliope player as well as occultist and Satanist. Born April 11, 1930 in Chicago, Illinois, of Alsatian-French-German-Romanian-Russian ancestry. From the age of seven onwards, he studied books on occultism and the supernatural, including *Dracula, Frankenstein* and pulp horror magazines. At high school he detested his schoolmates and lived in a world of literary black magic. He read the books of Aleister **Crowley,** whom he was later to eclipse as a sensational occultist. He also studied music, and at the age of sixteen was second oboist in the San Francisco Ballet Orchestra.

Through an uncle who had supplied alcohol to the Al Capone gang during Prohibition, young La Vey was introduced to the sleazy world of Las Vegas mobsters, and found their self-serving life-style appealing. He dropped out of high school and hung around pool halls with hustlers, pimps and gamblers. Here he was impressed by a friend who had worked in a circus, and in spring 1947 La Vey joined the Clyde Beatty circus as roustabout and cage boy.

In due course he was promoted to being a trainer of lions and tigers, and developed the magical willpower that was to dominate his later activities. In his own words: "That's when you really learn power and magic, even how to play God: when you're lying in the sawdust with a lion breathing in your face." He went on to become a celebrated circus calliope player, hypnotist, palmist, phrenologist and magician. In 1948 he became friendly with Marilyn Monroe, and as musical accompanist orchestrated her bumps and grinds at burlesque theaters in Los Angeles.

During the Korean War he avoided being drafted by enrolling as a college student, and his course in criminology led to a position as assistant criminologist and photographer with the San Francisco Police Department in 1951.

His first wife Carole was divorced in 1960, and La Vey married Diane, a seventeen-year old usherette who assisted his Friday night occult seminars in San Francisco. One of these was on cannibalism, illustrated practically by serving a well cooked meal of human flesh with fried bananas and yams (the flesh was obtained from a cadaver in a San Francisco hospital). La Vey's workshops on the black arts became known as "The Magic Circle."

One of the members was Kenneth **Anger,** underground movie-maker, who produced *Inauguration of the Pleasure Dome,* based on rituals of an American Aleister Crowley cult. La Vey played Satan in Anger's film *Invocation of My Demon Brother.*

With his black scarlet-lined cape, his weird activities and strange pets (tarantula, leopard and lion), La Vey attracted great publicity, and in due course he decided to formalize his life-style by founding a new cult.

On Walpurgis Night (April 30) 1966, he shaved his head and announced the First Church of Satan. This was a new religion celebrating carnal indulgence and self-satisfaction in place of self-denial, vengeance instead of tolerance, Satan in place of the Christian God. The principles of this trendy diabolism, deriving from the neo-hedonism of the affluent society, are set forth in La Vey's book *The Satanic Bible* (1969). After only a few years, La Vey's new cult claimed over a million followers. One famous convert was movie actress Jayne Mansfield, who died in a tragic auto crash with her lover, on whom La Vey is supposed to have laid a curse. La Vey's daughters Karla (by his first marriage) and Zeena Galatea have grown up in the Church of Satan.

La Vey played the Devil to world audiences when film director Roman Polanski selected him for the diabolic role in the movie version of Ira Levin's sensational book *Rosemary's Baby.* La Vey was also able to advise on authentic Satanic details of the movie.

The publicity accorded to La Vey and his cult was a signal for an explosion of sordid criminal black magic all over the world, and the association of Hollywood film stars with Satanism culminated in the horrifying murders of the Charles **Manson** gang. Such lower levels of black magic were publicly deplored by La Vey, who affected an elitist Satanism.

However, it would be a mistake to classify La Vey simply as a circus showman of sexy diabolism for showbiz personalities, even if the publicity pranks and sensationalist rituals inevitably become as tedious and boring as the bourgeois Christianity which they mock. La Vey undoubtedly has charisma, power and a keen intellect, and his Satanist philosophy has penetrated many influential areas of human activity. His socio-political concepts of Superman Satanism invite comparison with the theories

of Adolf Hitler, whose doctrine of a Master Race grew from a background of black magic cults. (See also **Rosemary's Baby**)

Recommended reading:

La Vey, Anton Szandor. *The Satanic Bible,* Avon, 1969

La Vey, Anton Szandor. *The Satanic Rituals,* Avon, 1972

Lyons, Arthur. *The Second Coming: Satanism in America,* Dodd, 1970; Award Books, 1970

Wolfe, Burton H. *The Devil's Avenger. A biography of Anton Szandor La Vey,* Pyramid, 1974

Lavritch, Sophie Bentkowski (1905–   )

Editor and writer on parapsychological subjects. Born May 8, 1905 in St. Petersburg, Russia, she studied at the University of Paris Law School (Licenciée en droit, 1926). In 1949 she married Jean Lavritch. She was editorial director of the journal *Initiation et Science,* and from 1945-46 was welfare officer at United Nations Relief and Rehabilitation Administration.

She described her experimental studies in clairvoyance in the article 'La Voyance, ses limites et ses erreurs' (Clairvoyance, its limits and errors, *Initiation et Science,* No. 49). She wrote under the names Sophie Bentkowski, Sonia Bentkowski-Lavritch and Sophie de Trabeck.

Law, William (1686–1761)

English mystic and theologian. William Law was born at King's Cliffe, Northamptonshire. His father followed the humble calling of a grocer, but it is manifest that he was in tolerably affluent circumstances nevertheless, and ambitious besides, for in 1705 William was sent to Cambridge University. Entering Emmanuel College, he became a fellow in 1711, but on the accession of George I, felt himself unable to subscribe the oath of allegiance, the inevitable consequence being that he forfeited his fellowship.

In 1727 he went to Putney, having acquired there the post of tutor to the father of Edward Gibbon, the historian of the Roman Empire. He acted in his capacity for ten years, winning universal esteem for his piety and theological erudition.

In 1737, on the death of his employer, Law retired to his native village of King's Cliffe, and it would seem that thenceforth he was chiefly supported by some of his devotees, notably Miss Hester Gibbon, sister of his guardian pupil, and a widow named Mrs. Hutcheson. These two ladies had a united income of fully £3000 a year, so Law must have been comfortable indeed, yet wealth and luxury did not tend to corrupt his piety, and it is recorded that he was wont to get up every morning at five, and spend several hours before breakfast in prayer and meditations. At a early stage in his career he had begun publishing theses on mysticism, and on religion in general. Now, being blessed with abundance of leisure, and having acquired fresh inspiration from reading the works of Jakob **Boehme,** of which he was an enthusiastic admirer, he produced year after year a considerable mass of writing. Thus his life passed away placidly, and he died in 1761.

Law's works amount in all to some twenty volumes. He first published in 1717, with an examination of certain tenets lately promulgated from the pulpit by the Bishop of Bangor, and this was followed soon afterwards by a number of analogous writings, while in 1726 he employed his pen to attack the theater, bringing out a book entitled *The Absolute Unlawfulness of the Stage Entertainment fully Demonstrated.* In the same year he issued *A Practical Treatise upon Christian Perfection,* and this was followed shortly by *A Serious Call to a Devout and Holy Life, adapted to the State and Condition of all Orders of Christians.*

This last is the best-known of his works, but others which are well regarded are *The Grounds and Reason of Christian Regeneration* (1739), *The Spirit of Prayer* (1749), *The Way to Divine Knowledge* (1752), *The Spirit of Love* (1752), and *Of Justification by Faith and Works* (1760).

Most of his books, but especially the *Serious Call,* have been reprinted again and again, while in 1762 a collected edition of *Law's* works was published. In 1893 there appeared a kind of anthology, made up of extracts from the writer, chosen by Dr. Alexander Whyte. In his preface the editor spoke of Law's "golden books," while he added that "In sheer intellectual strength Law is fully abreast of the very foremost of his illustrious contemporaries, while in that fertilising touch which is the true test of genius, Law stands simply alone."

Numerous other encomiums no less enthusiastic than this have been offered to the insight of this mystic, and it is noteworthy that he has engaged the interest of many great writers. Sir Leslie Stephen, for example, cited him in his *English Thought in the Eighteenth Century* (1876) and again in his *Studies of a Biographer* (2 vols., 1899, 1902) while the mystic figures also in the brilliant pages of W. E. H. Lecky's *History of England in the Eighteenth Century* (1878). In Edward Gibbon's *Autobiography* (1896) he was hailed as "a worthy and pious man, who believed all that he professed, and practised all that he enjoined."

Lawton, George (1900–1957)

Psychologist, gerontologist and lecturer, who wrote on Spiritualism. Born June 22, 1900 in New York, N.Y., he studied at Columbia University (B.A. 1922, M.A. 1926, Ph.D. 1936). He was in private practice as a psychologist from 1936 onwards and also acted as a consultant on problems of retirement for various industrial and governmental agencies.

He was author of *Straight to the Heart* (1957). *Aging Successfully* (1946), *The Drama of Life After Death* (1932). The latter book deals with the psychological motivations involved in Spiritualism. Dr. Lawton died October 9, 1957.

Laya Yoga

That practice of the yogi by which he listens to sounds which can be heard within his own body when the ears are closed. These sounds are termed "Nada," and are of various kinds, ranging from the roar of the ocean to the humming of bees. (See also **Nada; Vibrations; Yoga**)

Lazare, Denys (c. 622 A.D.)

A prince of Serbia said to have lived in the year of the Hegira (flight of Mohammed from Mecca), i.e. in 622 A.D. He was author of a work entitled *Dreams,* published over a century later in 1686. He himself claimed to have had nocturnal visions.

Leadbeater, C(harles) W(ebster) (1847–1934)

British clergyman, occultist and author who played a prominent part in the **Theosophical Society.** Born February 17, 1847, he became a curate in the Church of England in Hampshire. In 1884 he went to Adyar, headquarters of the Theosophical Society at Madras, India and devoted himself to the cause of Theosophy.

He traveled in Ceylon with Col. H. S. **Olcott,** one of the founders of Theosophy, and publicly professed himself a Buddhist. He returned to England in 1890 and became a tutor.

After the death of Madame **Blavatsky** in 1891, Leadbeater had a considerable influence over Mrs. Annie **Besant,** with whom he worked closely, and through his psychic ability acquired the reputation of a seer. However, he lacked profound spiritual insight, and his psychic gifts were of a confused character.

Moreover he appears to have been a confirmed homosexual. In 1906, several mothers in the U.S. brought charges against Leadbeater for immoral practices with their sons. Mrs. Besant found it impossible to accept these charges. The mothers thereupon appealed to Col. Olcott, then in London, and a judicial committee of the Society summoned Leadbeater to appear before them. In the face of clear evidence, Leadbeater was obliged to resign from the Society. However, after the death of Col. Olcott, the Leadbeater scandal took a bizarre turn with an Open Letter from Dr. Weller van Hook, General Secretary of the American Section, who vigorously defended Leadbeater's sex theories on the upbringing of young boys, and even claimed that this defense was dictated to him by a Theosophical Master or Mahatma.

In July 1908 the British Convention of the Society carried a resolution to the President and General Council requesting that Leadbeater and his practices be repudiated. Astonishingly enough the Council did not agree, and "saw no reason why Mr. Leadbeater should not be restored to membership." Thereupon some 700 members of the Society (including the scholar G. R. S. **Mead**) resigned forthwith. Leadbeater rejoined the Society and exerted a powerful influence over the Indian section, emphasizing clairvoyant teachings and an exalted lineage of reincarnation. He also entered the Liberal Catholic Church, founded by Theosophist James Ingall Wedgewood.

In 1908, Leadbeater and Mrs. Besant adopted a young Brahmin boy called Jiddu **Krishnamurti,** who they claimed was to be a future World Teacher or Messiah. The Order of The Star in the East was formed to propagate his mission. Unfortunately in 1929 Krishnamurti publicly renounced his Messianic role and dissolved the Order, repudiating Theosophy. Curiously enough he later became a noted spiritual lecturer of remarkable insight and sincerity, and taught all over the world.

Meanwhile Leadbeater removed to Australia, where he became Bishop of the Liberal Catholic Church. He died in 1934. His many publications included: *Man Visible and Invisible* (1902), *Outline of Theosophy* (1902), *The Astral Plane* (1905), *The Science of the Sacraments* (1911), *A Textbook of Theosophy* (1912), *The Hidden Side of Things* (2 vols., 1913), (with Annie Besant) *Man: Whence, How and Whither* (1913).

Leaf, Horace (c. 1886–1971)

Well known British lecturer and author in the cause of Spiritualism and psychical research. He also had psychic faculties as a clairvoyant, psychometrist and healer. He was a Fellow of the Royal Geographical Society.

During the course of his extensive traveling, he met most of the important mediums in the U.S. and Canada and did not hesitate to condemn frauds. He lectured on mediumship and Spiritualism at Johns Hopkins University, Dartmouth College, Swarthmore College and at Oxford and Cambridge Universities. He contributed regular articles to such Spiritualist journals as *Light.*

He was well known to the pioneer Spiritualist James Hewat **McKenzie**, who he met at the beginning of the twentieth century when Leaf was a member of a debating society in North London, discussing philosophical, political, social and religious topics. Soon after McKenzie established the British College of Psychic Science in London, Leaf became a staff lecturer on psychology and the development of mediumship. His publications included: *What Is This Spiritualism?* (1918), *Under the Southern Cross* (1923), *Psychology and Development of Mediumship* (1923), *Ahmed's Daughter* (1933), *What Mediumship Is* (1938), *Death Cannot Kill* (1959).

Leaf, Walter (1852-1927)

Classical scholar, banker and pioneer of psychical research in Britain. Born November 28, 1852 in London, England, he was educated at Harrow School, and Trinity College, Cambridge (B.A. 1874, M.A. 1877). In 1894 he married Charlotte Mary Symonds.

He was president of the Institute of Bankers from 1919-21, president of the International Chambers of Commerce 1924-26, member of London County Council 1901-04. He was awarded D. Litt, Oxford in 1904, was president of the Hellenic Society 1914-19, president of the Classical Association 1921, and honorary fellow of Trinity College Cambridge.

A versatile and talented individual, Leaf was a fine linguist, musician, political economist and Greek scholar. He was an active member of the Society for Psychical Research, London, and served on the council from 1889-1902. He took part in the SPR sittings with the medium Mrs. Leonore **Piper** in 1889-90. He contributed to the *Journal* of the SPR and the Society's *Proceedings.* He died March 8, 1927.

Leanan Sidhe

Gaelic words meaning "fairy sweetheart" who may be of either sex. According to one tradition, mortals are advised to have nothing to do with such beings, as no good ever comes of the connection. So long as the fairy lover is pleased with his or her mortal, all goes well, but when offended, life may be the forfeit.

However, in Ireland the fairy mistress has sometimes been considered the spirit of life, inspiring poets and singers but making their lives short through their all-consuming burning vision.

Another tradition regards the *leanan sidhe* of a man as more like a **vampire** or **succubus.**

Leary, Timothy (1920–   )

With Dr. Richard **Alpert,** Dr. Leary became a controversial figure in the psychedelic revolution of the 1960s.

Born October 22, 1920 in Springfield, Mass., he was a student at Holy Cross College, 1938-39; U.S. Military Academy 1940-41; University of Alabama (A.B. 1943); Washington State University 1946; University of California at Berkeley (Ph.D. in Psychology, 1930). He married Rosemary Woodruff August 17, 1965, two children.

From 1950-55 he was assistant professor at University of California at Berkeley, from 1955-58 director of psychological research, Kaiser Foundation, Oakland, from 1959-63 lecturer at Harvard University; first guide of the League of Spiritual Discovery from 1964 onwards.

Leary and Albert were both dismissed from Harvard for their experiments with psilocybin. They subsequently obtained financial backing for widespread experiments and publicity for the use of such drugs as LSD in producing altered state of consciousness, and launched the psychedelic revolution which in less than a decade had a traumatic impact on a whole generation.

In propagating the belief that mystical experience could be obtained from a drug, Leary and Alpert were rehashing the suggestions in Aldous **Huxley's** book *The Doors of Perception* (1954), which cited the sacramental use of peyote by certain North American Indians. However, the motivations and cultural values of such small closely-knit groups had nothing in common with the confused hedonism of the affluent society. The psychedelic revolution may have popularized the idea of mystical experience in a materialistic society, but at the cost of widespread decadence, hard-line narcotic addition, crime and violence.

In 1967, Alpert went to India in search of traditional mysticism and suffered a change of life-style, studying with a guru in the Himalayas and returning to the U.S. as "Baba Ram Dass." He abandoned the use of psychedelic drugs and has since propagated traditional Hindu mysticism. Leary, however, continued to advocate the psychedelic revolution, and in 1969 was an appellant in the U.S. Supreme Court decision which invalidated the federal marijuana law test case. After various brushes with the law on drug charges, Leary was sentenced to ten years imprisonment by a federal judge in Houston January 21, 1970 and another ten years in Santa Ana, California March 22, 1970, both charges involving marijuana offences. He was interred at the California Men's Colony West, San Luis Obispo, but escaped in September 1970, and was later reported to have associated with the Weatherman underground group, the Black Panthers and other radicals. Escaping to Lebanon, he became a counter-culture hero, with a gospel of "Turn On, Tune In, Drop Out," later taking refuge in Switzerland. He was subsequently rearrested in the U.S. and confined to Folsom Prison, California.

His publications include: *Social Dimensions of Personality* (1950), *Interpersonal Diagnosis of Personality* (1950), *Multilevel Assessment of Personality* (1951), *The Psychedelic Experience* (1964), (with G. Weil) *The Psychedelic Reader* (1965), *Psychedelic Prayers* (1965), *High Priest* (1968), *The Politics of Ecstasy* (1968), *The Psychology of Pleasure* (1969), *Jail Notes* (1970), *Confessions of a Hope Fiend* (1973), *Neurologic* (1973),

Terra II (1973), *Seven Up* (1973). (See also Psychedelic **Drugs; Hallucinogens; Mushrooms**)

Le Brun, Charles (1619-1690)

A celebrated French painter, born in Paris February 24, 1619. When only fifteen years old, he received commissions from Cardinal Richelieu, and his paintings were also praised by Poussin. Le Brun was later one of the founders of the Academy of Painting and Sculpture (1648) and The Academy of France at Rome (1666). He also became director of the Gobelins, a famous school for the manufacture of tapestries and royal furniture.

His remarkable treatise on physiognomy (*Traité sur la physionomie humaine comparée avec celle des aminaux*) was written at a time when the subject was considered one of the occult sciences. In this book Le Brun executed remarkable drawings of human and animal faces compared, a theme later developed with reference to the emotions by Charles Darwin in his book *The Expression of the Emotions in Man and Animals* (1872 etc.). Le Brun died February 22, 1690.

Lebrun, Pierre (1661-1729)

French Theologian, born at Brignolles. He published a book on the **divining-rod**, *Lettres qui décovrent l'illusion des philosophes sur la Baguette et qui détruisent leurs systèmes* (1693), and an interesting work on occult curiosities and popular beliefs, *Histoire critique des pratiques superstitieuses qui ont séduit les peuples et embarrassé les savants* (1702).

Lecour, Paul (1871-1954)

French government official and writer on psychical research. Born April 5, 1871 at Blois, France, he was a tax collector and head of department of the French Ministry of Public Works from 1896-1934. In 1926 he organized the Society for Atlantean Studies at the Sorbonne, which issued the journal *Atlantis* from 1927 onwards.

His books on religion and mysticism included: *Hellénisme et Christianisme* (Hellenism and Christianity), *Le Septième sens* (The Seventh Sense), *Saint Paul et les Mystères chrétiens* (St. Paul and the Christian Mysteries) and *Ma Vie mystique* (concerned with his own experiences). He was present at sittings with the famous physical medium **Eva C** (Marthe Beraud) and his own photographs of her ectoplasm phenomena were reproduced in *Annales des Sciences Psychique* (1919, No. 1). He died February 5, 1954.

Lecron, Leslie (1892-)

Psychologist and expert on hypnotism, who wrote on parapsychological topics. Born October 27, 1892 at Minneapolis, Minnesota, he studied at University of Colorado (B.A. 1916). In 1956 he married Ethelyn Lancaster.

In addition to his private practice his memberships included the Society for Clinical and Experimental Hypnosis, the Academy of Psychosomatic Medicine, and an honorary member and consultant of the Los Angeles Society for Psychic Research. He was joint author with Jean Bordeaux of *Hypnotism Today* (1947) and edited *Experimental Hypnosis* (1952). He wrote articles for *Tomorrow* magazine, including 'The Paranormal in Hypnosis' (Spring 1955).

Lee Penny

Famous Scottish **amulet** in the possession of Sir Simon Locard on Lockhart of Lee, circa 1330. The stirring story of this relic suggested the title of Sir Walter Scott's novel *The Talisman*, and in his introduction to the book he related the incident which led to the acquisition of the Lee Penny.

After the death of Robert the Bruce, King of Scotland in 1329, his friend Lord James of Douglas set out to take the dead king's heart to the Holy Land, to make the pilgrimage which the king was not able to undertake in his lifetime. On the way east, Douglas and his band of knights visited Spain and became involved in a battle with the Saracens. Douglas died on the battlefield but the king's heart in a silver casket was rescued by Sir Simon Locard of Lee, who brought it back to Scotland for burial (Scott, however, believed it was taken on to the Holy Land). Sir Simon Locard was made prisoner in battle by a wealthy Emir. His aged mother ransomed the Emir, and in the course of counting out the money, a pebble inserted in a coin fell out of the lady's purse. She was in such a hurry to retrieve it that the Scottish knight realized it must be valuable to her, and insisted on this amulet being added to the ransom. The lady reluctantly agreed, and also explained to Sir Simon Locard what its virtues were. Apparently it was a medical talisman which drove away fever and stopped bleeding. The stone was a dull heart-shaped pebble of dark red color, semi-transparent, set in a piece of silver said to be an Edward IV groat.

The Lockhart family tradition credits the Lee Penny with the ability to cure all diseases in cattle and the bite of a mad dog. The stone should be dipped in water three times and swirled around, and the water given to the man or beast to be cured. The amulet has been used frequently in the past, according to tradition. In 1629 the Lee Penny was used in the curing of sick oxen, but as a result a young woman was burnt at the stake for witchcraft. There are records of an accusation of witchcraft against Sir Thomas Lockhart during the Reformation, but the Church Synod at Glasgow merely reproved Sir Thomas and advised him to cease using the Penny as a charm. During the reign of Charles I, the citizens of Newcastle requested the use of the Penny to cure a cattle plague. Sir James Lockhart required from the Corporation a bond for £6,000. The Penny was used, the plague abated, and the Corporation offered to purchase the amulet with the money. The offer was refused and the Lee Penny returned to Scotland. During the eighteenth century it was housed in a gold casket presented to the head of the family by the Empress Maria Theresa of Austria. Many cures are recorded, extending into the middle of the nineteenth century.

In modern times the Penny has passed into the possession of Simon Macdonald Lockhart of Lee, living at Dolphinton, Scotland.

Leek, Sybil (1923-1983)

Astrologer, "white witch," author, one of the most popular figures of the modern occult revival. Born in the Midlands, England, she left school at sixteen, had a television play broadcast at 17, and traveled through France, taking part-time jobs. Back in England she continued writing for television and also managed three antique shops before specializing in the occult.

Her early experiences are described with lively humor in her book *A Shop in the High Street* (David McKay, 1964).

After moving to the U.S., Mrs. Leek acquired a great reputation as a witch and astrologer.

She died in Melbourne, Florida, in 1983. She wrote over sixty books, most of which acquired great popularity. Her books included: *Diary of a Witch* (1968); *Sybil Leek Book of Fortune Telling* (1969); *Tree that Conquered the World* (1969), *Numerology* (1969), *How to Be Your Own Astrologer* (1970), *Guide to Telepathy* (1971), *Phrenology* (1971), *Complete Art of Witchcraft* (1971), *Pictorial Encyclopedia of Astrology* (1971), *Astrological Guide to Financial Success* (1971), *Astrological Guide to the Presidential Candidates* (1972), *ESP: The Magic Within You* (1972), *The Zodiac of Love* (1974), *Reincarnation; The Second Chance* (1974) (with Rosamond V. Kaufman) *Astrological Guide to Love & Sex* (1975), *The Night Voyagers* (1976), *Sybil Leek's Book of The Curious & The Occult* (1976), *Moon Signs* (1977).

Lees, Robert James (died c. 1931)

British clairvoyant, a pensioner of the Privy Purse, who was often received at Buckingham Palace by Queen Victoria and whose supernormal powers in the famous Jack-the-Ripper case—as revealed by the *Daily Express* on March 9, 1931, shortly after the seer's death—rendered the greatest service to the English police.

According to this revelation, Lees had unaccountable premonitions of the crime which the Ripper was going to commit. In a vision he saw the victim and the place. When his descriptions, communicated to the police, agreed with later findings and the visions kept on recurring, the police asked him to track down the murderer. Much in the same way as a bloodhound pursues a criminal, Lees, followed by an inspector and detectives, set out, in a state of trance, to find the trail and at four o'clock in the morning halted at the gates of a West End mansion where a prominent physician was living and, pointing to an upper chamber where a faint light gleamed, declared: "There is the murderer."

According to this story, the physician confessed that he was liable to fits of obsession in which he committed acts of fiendish cruelty. Evidence connecting him with victims of the Ripper, was found in his rooms and on the findings of a medical committee, he was confined to an insane asylum. However, it has to be said that there are several conflicting claims to the identity of Jack the Ripper and no definitive version. For a review of the main suspects, see *The Complete Jack the Ripper* by Donald Rumbelow (London, 1975). (See also Mabel **Collins**)

The spirit controls of Lees often diagnosed disease and also effected remarkable instantaneous cures.

Lees published several books which he claimed were inspired psychically, including: *Through the Mists* (1898), *The Heretic* (1901), *The Life Elysian* (1905), *The Car of Phoebus; An Astral Bridegroom* (1909). The posthumous manuscript titled *The Gate of Heaven* was claimed to be the autobiography of a soul in paradise. For Lees' own account of these books see 'My Books: How They Were Written' (*Occult Review*, December 1931).

Lefebure, Francis (1916–   )

Physician, experimenter and writer on parapsychological subjects. Born September 17, 1916 in Paris, France, he studied at Paris Medical School, University of Paris (M.D.). He married Thérèse Delecourt. He was a physician in the French Army from 1939–44, school physician 1944–59, subsequently director of "cervoscopy" (his own technique of brain exploration) at Dynam Institut, Paris. He is a member of the Assn. Francais d'Etudes Métapsychiques, Paris.

Dr. Lefebure has experimented successfully with projecting his "psychic double" at a distance to individuals who had no prior knowledge of the attempt. This conscious projection of a "double" is related to **Out-of-the-Body** traveling. Dr Lefebure's publications include: *Expériences Initiatiques* (3 vols., 1954, 1956, 1959), *Les Homologies, ou La Lumière secrète de l'Asie devant la Science modernes* (Homologies, or the Secret Light of Asia in relation to Modern Science). He has also contributed articles on clairvoyance and occultism to the magazine *Initiation et Science*.

Leg Cake

The name given in the Highlands of Scotland to a cake presented to a herdsman when he came with the news that a mare had foaled, or to a dairy-maid when she brought word that a cow had calved.

Lehman, Alfred

Danish co-author with F.C.C. **Hansen** of a pamphlet proposing a theory of "involuntary" whispering to account for apparent thought-transference (telepathy). (See also **Telepathy**)

Leippya

Burmese term for human soul. (See **Burma**)

Leland, Charles Godfrey (1824–1903)

Versatile American writer and folklorist who researched traditional witchcraft lore. Born in Philadelphia August 15, 1824, he graduated at Princeton and also studied at Heidelberg and Munich. He resided in Europe for a number of years. He became well known for his humorous dialect verse *The Breitmann Ballads* (1871) and for his researches in gypsy lore and language. He first discovered and elucidated Shelta, the secret language of the tinkers (see **Shelta Thari**). He died in Florence, Italy, March 20, 1903.

His many valuable books included: *The English Gypsies and their Language* (1872; Gale Research 1968), *The Gypsies* (1882), *Gypsy Sorcery and Fortune-Telling* (1891; University Books 1963; Dover 1971), (in collaboration with Albert Barrére) *A Dictionary of Slang, Jargon and Cant* (1889; Gale Research 1967).

From 1886 onwards, Leland was friendly with Maddalena, a Florentine fortune-teller and hereditary witch from Tuscany, who communicated to him the traditional witchcraft lore which he published in *Aradia: or the Gospel of the Witches* (1899; Weiser 1974). The book played a prominent part in the modern revival of witchcraft and has been widely adapted by many so-called "hereditary witches" as the *Book of Shadows* and similar witch manuals.

Leland was a genial giant of a man, fascinated by anything occult or mysterious. For biographical information, see his *Memoirs* (1893; Gale Research 1968) and *Charles Godfrey Leland* by Elizabeth R. Pennell (his niece), 1906.

Le Loyer, Pierre (1550-1634)

Sieur de la Brosse, royal councilor and demonographer, was born at Huillé in Anjou, France. He became a magistrate at Angers. He was the author of a work entitled *Discours et histoires des spectres, visions et apparitions des esprits, anges, demons et âmes se montrant aux hommes* (Discourse and Histories about Specters, Visions and Apparitions of Spirits, Angels, Demons and Souls that appeared visibly to Men). It was published at Paris in 1605 in one quarto volume.

The work is divided into eight books dealing with the marvelous visions and prodigies of several centuries, and the most celebrated authors sacred as well as profane, who have dealt with occult subjects, the cause of **apparitions,** the nature of good and evil spirits, of demons, of ecstasy, of the essence, nature and origin of souls, of magicians and sorcerers, of the manner of their communication, of evil spirits, and of imposters.

The first book deals with specters, apparitions and spirits; the second with the physics of Le Loyer's time, the illusions to which the senses are prone, wonders, the elixirs and metamorphoses, of sorceries and of philters; the third book establishes the degrees, grades and honors of spirits, gives a resumé of the history of Philinnion and of Polycrites, and recounts diverse adventures with specters and demons; the fourth book gives many examples of spectral appearances, of the speech of persons possessed of demons, of the countries and dwelling-places of these specters and demons, of marvelous portents, and so forth; the fifth treats of the science of the soul, of its origin, nature, its state after death, and of haunting ghosts; the sixth division is entirely taken up with the apparition of souls, and shows how the happy do not return to earth, but only those whose souls are burning in purgatory; in the seventh book the case of the Witch of Endor and the evocation of the soul of Samuel are dealt with, as is evocation in general and the methods practiced by wizards and sorcerers in this science; the last book gives some account of exorcism, fumigations, prayers, and other methods of casting out devils, and the usual means employed by exorcists to destroy these. The work as a whole is exceedingly curious if disputatious and a little dull in parts, and throws considerable light upon the occult science of the times.

It is interesting to note, however, that in spite of Le Loyer's credulities, he was skeptical regarding **alchemy,** of which he wrote: "As to transmutation, I wonder how it can be reasonably defended. Metals can be aduterated, but not changed . . . Blowing [the bellows], they may exhaust their purses, they multiply all into nothing. Yes, I do not believe, and may the philosophers excuse me if they wish, that the alchemists can change any metal into gold."

Lemuria

A Pacific Ocean equivalent of the lost continent of **Atlantis.** During the nineteenth century, zoologist P. L. Sclater drew attention to the similarities between animal and plant life in land masses separated by thousands of miles of ocean, and suggested that there might have been a land-bridge from the Malay Archipelago to the south coast of Asia and Madagascar during the Eocene Age, thus explaining the wide distribution of the lemur, a mammalian primate. A number of reputable scientists supported the hypothesis of "Lemuria," including T. H. Huxley, Alfred Russel Wallace and Ernst Haeckel.

Less scientific was the endorsement of occultist Madame **Blavatsky,** who declared that a lost continent under the Pacific Ocean was formerly inhabited by the third of five root-races of mankind. These Lemurians were four-armed hermaphroditic giants.

Equally fantastic were the speculations of Col. James **Churchward** (1852–1936) who wrote several books about a Lemurian continent called "Mu." He claimed his knowledge came from a Hindu priest who had shown him clay tablets which had been hidden in a cave in India. These tablets were inscribed with hieroglyphics in a lost language called "Naacal." According to Churchward, the priest helped him to decipher these inscriptions, which told the story of Mu as a kind of primeval Garden of Eden. The colonel supplemented his palaeographical researches by occult means in trance visits to former incarnations. Equally unverified are the translations from the clay tablets, which remain as elusive as the golden plates of the Mormons.

Another occult investigator of Lemuria and Atlantis was W. Scott-Elliot, a Theosophist who used astral clairvoyance for his writings. Lemuria and Atlantis were also endorsed by anthroposophist Rudolf **Steiner** in his book *Atlantis and Lemuria* (1913).

Recommended reading:

Churchward, James. *Children of Mu,* Washburn, 1931; Paperback Library 1968

Churchward, James. *Cosmic Forces of Mu,* Washburn 1934; Wehman 1967

Churchward, James. *The Lost Continent of Mu,* Washburn, 1926; Paperback Library 1968

Churchward, James. *The Sacred Symbols of Mu,* Washburn, 1933; Paperback Library 1968

De Camp, L. Sprague. *Lost Continents: The Atlantis Theme in History, Science & Literature,* Dover, 1954; Ballantine, 1970

Scott-Elliot, W. *The Story of Atlantis and the Lost Lemuria,* Theosophical Publishing House, 1893; 1962; 1972

Spence, Lewis. *The Problem of Lemuria,* London, 1932; McKay, 1933

Le Normand, Marie-Anne Adélaide (1772–1843)

Famous French clairvoyant and fortune teller, known as "The Sybil of the Faubourg Saint Germain." She was born at Alençon and became one of the most celebrated occultists and diviners of her day, but it might be said that her art was much more the product of sound judgment than of any supernatural gift.

She predicted their futures to Danton, Marat, Robespierre, and St. Just, but we hear no more of her under the Directory. When Josephine Beauharnais came into prominence as the intended wife of Napoleon, Mlle. Le Normand was received at all those houses and salons where the future empress had any influence. Josephine was extremely credulous, and used to read her own fortunes to herself on the cards, but when she found that Mlle. Le Normand was an adept at this art, she often had her in attendance to assist her in it. Even Napoleon himself, who was not without his own superstitions, had his horoscope read by her.

Mlle. Le Normand soon set up her own salon in Paris, where she read people's fortunes by means of the cards. It is not certain whether these cards were of the nature of Tarot cards, but it is more than likely that Mlle. Le Normand used various methods. She occasionally divined the fortunes of others through playing the games of piquet, sept, and other well known card games. There is anecdotal evidence that she told fortunes with ordinary playing cards, but there is also a tradition that she used a specially designed pack. She did not hide her methods from others, but the Parisian society of her day appears to have thought that her power of divination lay not only in the cards she manipulated but in her personality or occult insight.

After the fall of the Emperor she was in great demand amongst the Russian, German and English officers in Paris, and even the Emperor Alexander and other potentates consulted her. Shortly after this she went to Brussels, where she read the fortune of the Prince of Orange, but as she tried to cheat the Customs officials she soon found herself the occupant of a Belgian prison.

By the year 1830, she had become quite forgotten and when the newspapers announced her death on June 25, 1843, a great many people failed to remember her name. There is very little doubt that she had a great reputation for the accuracy of her predictions and was clearly more than a mere charlatan. Opinions are divided on her powers, but there is no denying her successful reputation amongst all classes, from revolutionary heroes to emperors and royalty.

What is said to be an authentic reproduction of the "Mlle. Le Normand Fortune Telling Cards" has long been reprinted in Europe and elsewhere and is currently marketed by U.S. Games Systems, Inc., New York, N.Y.

Leo, Alan

Pseudonym of British astrologer William Frederick Allen (1860–1917). He was born in London August 7, 1860. His mother was a member of the Plymouth Brethren sect; his father abandoned her and the child. Young Allen was apprenticed as a draper, chemist and grocer in turn, but did not serve out his time. At the age of 16 he was destitute in Liverpool, but within only a few years was a prosperous employer, then just as suddenly ruined by a dishonest manager.

He became a salesman for a manufacturer of sewing machines, and eventually learned about Astrology from an old herbalist, who treated him for an illness. He also became friendly with the astrologer "Sepharial" (Walter Gorn **Old**).

Allen joined the **Theosophical Society** in 1890 and became a successful mail-order astrologer. In 1895 he married Bessie Phillips, a professional palmist and phrenologist.

Allen became proprietor of *Modern Astrology* journal, and under the name "Alan Leo" compiled a number of popular books on astrology, which are still highly regarded today, including: *The Horoscope and How to Read It* (1902), *How to Judge a Nativity* (2 vols., 1904), *Astrology for All* (2 vols., 1904). His Modern Astrology Publishing Co.

was the first large-scale venture of its kind, and had branches in Paris and New York.

In 1914 Allen was prosecuted for fortune-telling and again in 1917. He was acquitted in the first case and fined in the second. At that date, prosecution of Spiritualist mediums and other seers was not infrequent (see **Fortune Telling Act**). He died August 30, 1917 at Cornwall, England. His wife, who also published several books under the name "Bessie Leo," edited his biography: *The Life and Works of Alan Leo* (1919).

Leonard, Mrs. Gladys Osborne (1882–1968)

Celebrated trance medium. Dr. Hereward **Carrington** designated her as "the British Mrs. Piper." She was generally regarded as one of the greatest trance mediums. Even as a child, she saw visions.

"In whatever direction I happened to be looking," she wrote in *My Life in Two Worlds* (London, 1931), "the physical view of the wall, door, ceiling, or whatever it was, would disappear, and in its place would gradually come valleys, gentle slopes, lovely trees and banks covered with flowers, of every shape and hue. The scene seemed to extend for many miles, and I was conscious that I could see much farther than was possible with the ordinary physical scenery around me."

When she was a professional singer, she acquired experimental acquaintance with the phenomena of Spiritualism through **table-turning** experiences. She sat with two girl friends in her dressing room. After twenty-six futile attempts, a communicator appeared who called herself "Feda" and said that she was the wife of an ancestor of Mrs. Leonard who married her, a very young Indian girl, and that she died at the age of thirteen about 1800.

From her first appearance, "Feda" remained a faithful attendant of Mrs. Leonard and was always the first to come through when she passed into trance. During her first manifestations through the table communications, her form and that of other spirit friends were quite distinctly seen in the subdued light on the white walls "like clearly-cut shadows, which showed up perfectly against the light background." However, significant physical phenomena such as **ectoplasm** or **materialization** did not develop. Mrs. Leonard sometimes heard voices objectively, slight **touches** and little manifestations when alone, being always aware of "suspended" or blank feeling whenever this happened.

Generally, however, her acquaintance with physical phenomena came about through sittings with other mediums who had power in this direction. The first time she herself heard the voice of "Feda" was in a direct voice sitting in the house of H. Dennis **Bradley.** It appears that even part of her own power, necessary for the trance control, was contributed by her husband, as "Feda" was very clamorous against a separation which came about through her husband's professional engagements. "Feda" said that she could not use the power well enough during his absence.

Occasionally, for medical purposes, "Feda" gave place to "North Star," another Indian, who was never able to speak through Mrs. Leonard, but used her "hands and arms in an extraordinary way, making passes over the patient, and certainly he cured several people of different maladies."

In March 1914, "Feda" gave instructions that Mrs. Leonard must begin work as a professional medium as soon as possible. At the same time the medium was deluged with messages ending with the words: "Something big and terrible is going to happen to the world. Feda must help many people through you."

During the winter of 1914, Mr. Hewat **McKenzie,** the founder of the **British College of Psychic Science,** had some satisfactory sittings with Mrs. Leonard. On his recommendation, Lady Lodge and Sir Oliver **Lodge** came, after their son Raymond was killed in World War I in the autumn of 1915. The first evidence of Raymond's survival was obtained through Mrs. Leonard. Through the attendant publicity, Mrs. Leonard became a celebrity. Sir Oliver Lodge secured a sitting with her each week for several years.

In 1916, two sitters, Miss Radcliffe Hall and (Una) Lady Troubridge, approached Mrs. Leonard after the death of their friend "A.V.B." Although the sitters and subject were unknown to Mrs. Leonard, "Feda" gave remarkably detailed information on the subject and the house where the ladies had lived. The sitters not only approached Mrs. Leonard anonymously, but also employed a private detective to make sure whether Mrs. Leonard had obtained the information in a mundane way. No subterfuge was discovered. See 'On a series of sittings with Mrs. Osborne Leonard' by Radcliffe Hall & (Una) Lady Troubridge in *Proceedings* of the S.P.R., vol. 30, pp. 339–547.

In 1918, for a period of three months, she was exclusively engaged by the Society for Psychical Research. Out of seventy-three sittings, all but three were anonymous. The report of Mrs. W. H. Salter stated that the sitters generally agreed that good evidence of surviving personality had been obtained and the complete trustworthiness of the medium could not be questioned. (See contributions by Mrs. W. H. Salter to *Proceedings* of the S.P.R., [vol. 32, pp. 1–143; vol. 36, pp. 187–332; vol. 39, pp. 306–332])

The Rev. C. Drayton **Thomas** carried on experiments with Mrs. Leonard for years. Important book and newspaper tests were evolved. The story is told in his books *Some New Evidence for Human Survival* (1922) and *Life Beyond Death with Evidence* (1928). The deceased father of the Rev. Drayton Thomas acquired the ability to come through without "Feda," who usually acted as interpreter for others, and he spoke directly from Mrs. Leonard's mouth. Evidential messages came on numerous occasions in the following kind of form: "In to-morrow's *Times,* on page 8, column 5, about six inches from the bottom, you will find a name which will recall intimate associations of your youth between the ages of 16–18." The *Times* appears to have been "invaded" systematically for information by this communicator who also disclosed personal traits in referring to his favorite books, indicating passages on certain pages in answer to questions put by his son.

In her autobiography, Mrs. Leonard narrated many interesting **out-of-the-body** experiences. She stated that she often met people in the spirit world and brought back memories of such meetings into the waking state. These spiritual excursions often received striking confirmation through other means. Mrs. Leonard also cooperated with

parapsychologist W. W. Carington in tests to establish whether "Feda" was a secondary personality or a genuine communicator. (See *Telepathy* by W. W. Carington, London, 1945 etc.) For a useful guide to the early mediumship of Mrs. Leonard, see 'Books and Reports on Leonard Mediumship' in *Psychic Science* (vol. 16, No. 4, January 1938).

Mrs. Leonard had abandoned her career as a professional singer after her mediumistic gifts developed. After nearly fifty years of mediumship, she died March 10, 1968.

Recommended reading:

Broad, C. D. *Lectures on Psychical Research,* Humanities, New York, 1962

Leonard, Gladys Osborne. *My Life In Two Worlds,* Cassell, London, 1931

Lodge, Sir Oliver J. *Raymond or Life and Death,* Metheun, London/George H. Doran, New York, 1916

Salter, W. H. *Trance Mediumship; An Introductory Study of Mrs. Piper & Mrs. Leonard,* Society for Psychical Research, London, 1962 (pamphlet)

Smith, Susy. *The Mediumship of Mrs. Leonard,* University Books, 1964

Thomas, C. Drayton. *Some New Evidence For Human Survival,* Collins, London, 1922

Thomas, John F. *Beyond Normal Cognition; An Evaluative and Methodological Study of the Mental Content of Certain Trance Phenomena,* Boston Society for Psychical Research, 1937; University Microfilms, Ann Arbor, Michigan

Leroy, Olivier-Gilbert (1884–   )

Author of books on the lives of the saints, and on parapsychology. Born October 9, 1884 at Tours, France, he studied at the Law School, University of Paris (LL.D. 1925), and the Sorbonne (docteur ès lettres, 1931). From 1941–50 he was a Director of Education in Madagascar.

As a student of hagiography, he wrote on saints and mysticism. His books included: *La Raison primitive* (Primitive Reason, 1926), *La Lévitation* (1928; translated into English same year), *Le Chevalier Thomas Browne* (1931), *Les Hommes-Salamandres* (The Salamander Men, 1931), *Sainte Jeanne d'Arc, Les Voix* (The Voices of St. Joan of Arc, 1956). He also contributed various articles to *Revue d'Ascétique et de Mystique,* including: 'Examen des témoignages sur la lévitation extatique chez Sainte Thérèse de Jésus' (Study of the Testimony on Ecstatic Levitation of Saint Theresa, No. 131, 1937), 'Apparitions de Sainte Thérèse de Jésus' (Apparitions of Saint Theresa of Jesus, No. 134, 1958), La Pénétration des consciences chez Sainte Thérèse de Jésus' (The Penetration of Consciousness in Saint Theresa of Jesus, No. 136, 1958).

Lescoriere, Marie (c. 16th century)

A witch of the sixteenth century, arrested at the age of ninety years. On being examined she declared that she was no longer a witch, that she prayed daily, and that she had not visited the **Sabbat** for forty years. Questioned on the subject of the Sabbat, she confessed that she had seen the devil, and that he had visited her in the shape of a dog or a cat. On one occasion, she said, she had killed a neighbor by praying to the devil.

LeShan, Lawrence (L.) (1920–)

American author and parapsychologist. Born September 8, 1920 in New York, N.Y., he was educated at College of William and Mary (B.A. 1942), University of Nebraska (M.S. 1943), University of Chicago (Ph.D. 1954). He was an instructor (later assistant professor), psychology, 1948–51; associate psychologist, Worthington Associates, Inc., 1950–51; research associate, Foundation for Human Research, 1952-54; chief of department of psychology, Institute of Applied Biography, New York, 1954–64; research associate, Ayer Foundation, Inc., New York, 1954–70; research psychologist, Union Theological Seminary Program in Psychiatry and Religion, 1943–46. He served in the U.S. Army 1943-46, 1950-52, with rank of second lieutenant. He is a member of the American Psychological Association, Federation of American Scientists, American Psychical Research Society.

Originally a skeptic in his attitude to paranormal phenomena, he devoted some 500 hours to testing the famous psychic Eileen **Garrett,** and was particularly impressed by her powers in the field of **psychometry.** He also made a special study of psychic **healing,** and from 1970 onwards held training seminars in New York for psychologists and students. In his book *The Medium, the Mystic & the Physicist* (1974), he proposed a theory of different types of reality: Sensory Reality (that of everyday experience), Clairvoyant Reality (in which the time structure is modified and the identities of "you" and "I" become part of a total "One" in the cosmos), and a Transpsychic Reality (in which there is total identification with the "All").

His other books include: (with Bowers, Jackson & Knight) *Counselling the Dying* (1964); *Psychosomatic Aspects of Neoplastic Disease* (1964), *How to Meditate: A Guide to Self-Discovery* (1973), *Alternative Realities* (1976), *You Can Fight For Your Life; Emotional Factors in the Causation of Cancer* (1977). He has also contributed some fifty articles to psychology and psychiatry journals, and published short stories.

Leslie, Desmond (Peter Arthur) (1921–)

Irish novelist, film scriptwriter, musician, coauthor of a key book on **flying** saucers. Born in London, he was the youngest son of novelist Sir Shane Leslie. Desmond Leslie was educated at Ampleforth, England, and Trinity College, Dublin. From 1940–44 he served in the Royal Air Force. In addition to his novels and scripts, he has composed electronic music for films and television.

His books include: *Careless Lives* (1945), *Pardon My Return* (1946), *Angels Weep* (1949), *Hold Back the Night* (1956), *The Amazing Mr. Lutterworth* (1959), (with P. Moore) *How Britain Won the Space Race* (1973), *The Jesus File* (1974).

His most famous book written with George Adamski was *Flying Saucers Have Landed* (1953) which created a sensation and launched a trend. It passed through many editions and was translated into sixteen different languages.

Leventhal, Herbert (1941–)

Author of scholarly studies on occultism. Born October 9, 1941 in Brooklyn, N.Y., he was educated at Brooklyn College of the City University of New York (B.A. 1962;

Ph.D. 1973). From 1970-74 he was part-time instructor at Brooklyn College of the City University of New York; from 1974–75 visiting assistant professor of history. From 1974 onwards he was assistant editor of *Papers of Robert Morris;* 1971–74 research associate. Program for Loyalist Studies and Publications. In 1976 he was a member of Tom Paine Independent Democrats; member of executive board of Kings County Democratic Coalition. He is also a member of the American Historical Association, Organization of American Historians, American Association for Eighteenth Century Studies, American Studies Association, Historians Film Committee. He has contributed to *Proceedings of the American Antiquarian Society.*

In 1976 his doctoral dissertation was *In the Shadow of the Enlightenment; Occultism and Renaissance Science in Eighteenth-Century America* (published New York University Press). This was prompted by his researches on political thought in eighteenth-century American culture, when he identified relics of occultism and Renaissance science which played an important part in the outlook of their time.

Lévi, Éliphas (1810–1875)

Pseudonym of Alphonse Louis Constant, a French occultist of the nineteenth century, who has been called "the last of the magi." He was born in Paris, the son of a shoemaker, and through the good offices of the parish priest was educated for the church at St. Sulpice. In due course he became a deacon, taking a vow of celibacy. Shortly after this he was expelled from St. Sulpice for teaching doctrines contrary to those of the Church.

How he lived during the ensuing years is not known, but about 1839 under the influence of a political and socialistic prophet named Ganneau, he wrote a pamphlet entitled *The Gospel of Liberty,* for which he received six-months imprisonment. In Paris, notwithstanding his vow of celibacy, he married a beautiful girl of sixteen, who afterwards had the marriage annulled. It was probably not until Madame Constant had left him that he studied the occult sciences. At all events his writings previous to this show little trace of occult influence.

In 1850, he had contributed a "Dictionary of Christian Literature," to a series of theological encyclopedias published by Abbé Migne. About a year or so later he was giving lessons on occultism to pupils. According to a paragraph by M. Chauliac: "The Abbé Constant, for a second time repudiating his name, assumed the title of the Magus Éliphas Lévi, giving consultations in great number to credulous clients, who paid as much as twenty-five francs a time for a prediction from Lucifer." There is no evidence that Lévi was actually ordained as a priest, but the title "Abbé" was normally given to those wearing a clerical style of costume. It is clear that Lévi affected a quasi-clerical garb in his capacity of a Magus or master of magic.

In 1853, he traveled to London and made the acquaintance of Lord **Lytton,** whom he assisted in various magical evocations and theories, which were later fictionalized in Lytton's occult stories, such as *Zanoni, A Strange Story,* and *The Haunted and the Haunters.*

Lévi's own works on occultism had a great influence. They included *Dogme de la Haute Magie* (1854), *Rituel de la Haute Magie* (1856), *Histoire de la Magie* (1860), *La Clef des Grands Mystères* (1861), *Fables et Symboles* (1862), *La Science des Esprits* (1865). Two of Lévi's major works were translated into English by the British scholar of occultism Arthur Edward **Waite:** *Transcendental Magic* (1896), *The History of Magic* (1913). Waite also translated *The Mysteries of Magic; A Digest of the Writings of Éliphas Lévi* (1886; reprinted University Books, 1974). In spite of some shortcomings, these books have played a prominent part in the occult revival. Waite's critical notes add considerable value.

Lévi's knowledge of the occult sciences was often more imaginative than circumstantial, and in perusing his works the reader requires to be on guard against the adoption of hasty generalizations and hypotheses.

Lévi died in April 1875. There is an interesting firsthand account of Lévi during his lifetime by Kenneth R. H. **Mackenzie,** who visited the magus in Paris in 1861. (See *Occult Review,* December 1921)

Levitation

The rising of physical objects, tables, pianos, etc., or of human beings into the air, contrary to the laws of gravitation and without any visible agency. More often the term is used in a restricted sense and refers to the levitation of the human body. As such, the phenomenon was known from ancient times. Instances of **transportation,** which is levitation in its highest form, are recorded both in the Old and New Testament, while in the walking of Jesus on the water, a feat duplicated by many of the saints, we find a plain illustration.

The power was claimed by wizards of many primitive tribes, by mystics in the East, and it has been repeatedly claimed, in less sensational degrees, by many modern Spiritualist mediums. These furnished the first evidence to science that the miracles of rising in the air recorded in the life of saints, ecstatics, witches and victims of demoniac possession might rest on a solid basis of fact.

Levitating Saints

J. J. von Görres, in his monumental work *Die Christliche Mystik* (5 vols., 1836–42) spoke of seventy-two levitated saints, but Olivier Leroy (in *Levitation,* 1928) stated that out of 14,000 at least two hundred had experienced the phenomenon.

St. Dunstan (918–988), St. Dominic (1170–1221), St. Francis of Assisi (1186–1226), Thomas Aquinas (1226–1274), St. Edmund, Archbishop of Canterbury (+1242), Blessed James of Illyria (+1485), Savonarola (1452–1498), St. Ignatius Loyola (1491–1556), St. Philip Neri (1515–1595), St. Peter of Alcantara (1499–1562), St. Joseph of Copertino (1603–1663) and St. Alphonsius Liguori (1696–1787)—to mention a few out of a multitude—were variously reportedly seen raised a foot, a palm, a hand's breath, a cubit and more in the air. Olivier Leroy found the average elevation twenty inches. But in some cases, exceptional height was recorded.

St. Joseph of Copertino who, in the *Acta Sanctorum,* is credited with seventy separate flights, once flew up into a tree and perched on a branch which quivered no more than if he had been a bird. According to von Görres, St. Peter of Alcantara was, on one occasion, carried up in the air to a great height, far above the trees, when with his arms crossed on his chest he continued to soar while hundreds of little birds gathered around him, making a most agreeable concert with their songs.

St. Dunstan, archbishop of Canterbury, was observed to rise from the ground shortly before his death in 988. St. Bernard Ptolomei, St. Philip Benitas, St. Albert of Sicily, and St. Dominic, founder of the Dominican order, were all seen to be levitated while engaged in their devotions. An ecstatic nun "rose from the ground with so much impetuosity, that five or six of the sisters could hardly hold her down." It is related by his biographers that Savonarola, shortly before he perished at the stake, remained suspended at a considerable height above the floor of his dungeon, absorbed in prayer.

Levitation Before the Altar

The scene of the elevation of saints and ecstatics was most often the altar in the church, and the state which seemed to condition it was deep religious meditation or "rapture." St. Joseph of Copertino experienced fifteen levitations in front of images of the Holy Virgin; his raptures in saying Mass were of frequent occurrence and "his ecstasies and ascensions were witnessed not only by the people and the members of his order, but Pope Urban VIII saw him one day in this state and was intensely astonished. Joseph, bethinking himself that he was in the presence of the Vicar of Christ, fell into an ecstasy and was raised above the ground."

According to an official report, the original of which is in the Bibliotheque National of Paris, Françoise Fontaine, a young servant of Louviers, exorcized in 1591, was three times raised before the altar and the third time was carried through the air head downwards.

Anne Catherine Emmerich (1774–1824), the stigmatic visionary, was quoted by Fr. K. A. Schmöger:

"When I was doing my work as vestry-nun, I was often lifted up suddenly into the air, and I climbed up and stood on the higher parts of the church, such as windows, sculptured ornaments, jutting stones; I would clean and arrange everything in places where it was humanly impossible. I felt myself lifted and supported in the air, and I was not afraid in the least, for I had been accustomed from a child to being assisted by my guardian angel."

Of Abbé Claude Dhière (1757–1820), Director of the Grand Séminaire of Grenoble, his biographer Mlle. de Franclieu noted that: "when he experienced ecstasies during his Mass, it was usually at the Memento of the living and the dead, and the students who used to serve his Mass declare that, when enraptured, his feet did not touch the floor."

The *Frankfurter Zeitung* published the following paragraph on September 8, 1861: "We read in the *Gegenwart* of Vienna that a Catholic Priest was preaching before his congregation last Sunday in the Church of St. Mary, at Vienna, on the subject of the constant protection of angels over the faithful committed to their charge, and this in words of great exaltation, and with an unction and eloquence which touched profoundly the hearts of numbers of the congregation. Soon after the commencement of the sermon, a girl of about 20 years of age, showed all signs of ecstasy, and soon, her arms crossed upon her bosom, and with her eyes fixed on the preacher, she was seen by the whole congregation to be raised gradually from the floor into the air, and there to rest at an elevation of more than a foot until the end of the sermon. We are assured that the same phenomenon had happened several days previously at the moment of her receiving the communion."

The French psychical investigator Col. **Rochas** received a personal testimony from Abbé Petit that once, to his great terror, he was levitated in the church.

In religious chronicles, one even meets with the antithesis of the phenomenon of levitation—excessive gravitation. G. Neubrigensis recorded the case of Raynerus, the wicked minister, who so overweighted a ship with his iniquity that in the midst of the stream it was unable to stir. As soon as he was put out of the ship they could easily sail away.

However legendary the account may appear, there is an analogy in the case of hysterics who often claim such an increase of weight that they are unable to stir. That the feeling may not be purely imaginary is indicated by the case of the medium, Alberto Fontana who, after a levitation, remained as if nailed to the floor and nobody was able to move him.

Levitation in Witchcraft

In the tenth century, it was popularly believed that women who followed the pagan goddess Diana flew in the air to their rituals, but the church considered this a heretical delusion. However, during the great **witchcraft** manias of the sixteenth and seventeenth centuries, confessions or accusations of **transvection** (flying through the air) were accepted as describing a reality. It was believed that witches smeared themselves with a special ointment which gave them the power of flight, usually mounted on a broomstick, a shovel, a distaff or even an animal.

The church considered that the transvection of witches was a fact, but a diabolical parody of the transports of saints. It now seems possible that some of the claimed transvection of witches may have been **out-of-the-body** experiences, and other apparent transvection may have been hallucination, perhaps induced by the special ointment. However, since the transvection of saints was well attested by many witnesses, it seems possible that there may have been some genuine cases of levitation of witches. The idea that this was the result of demonic agency persisted.

From Witchcraft to Spiritualism

In ancient rituals, levitation was mentioned as a sign of **possession.** Charges of witchcraft or bewitchment usually followed the manifestation. Henry Jones, a twelve-year-old English boy of Shepton-Mallet was believed to be bewitched in 1657, as he was carried by invisible means from one room to another, and sometimes was wholly lifted up, so that his body hung in the air, with only the flat of his hands placed against the ceiling. One afternoon in the garden of Richard Isles, he was raised up and transported over the garden wall for about thirty yards.

Patrick Sandilands, a younger son of Lord Torpichen, was similarly believed to be the victim of witchcraft in 1720 at Caldor in Scotland. His tendency to rise entranced into the air was so great that his sisters had to watch him, and sometimes only could keep him down by hanging to his skirts.

Mary London, a hysterical servant girl who was tried in 1661 at Cork, Ireland, for witchcraft, was frequently transported by an invisible power to the top of the house.

The phenomenon was frequently witnessed in **poltergeist** cases. The **Drummer of Tedworth** would lift all the children up in their beds. Nancy Wesley, during the disturbances at the Epworth Vicarage in 1716, was several times successfully lifted up with the bed on which she was sitting to a considerable height. Four of her sisters were present, among them Hetty whom the disturbances chiefly followed (see **Epworth Phenomena**).

Harry Phelps, the twelve-year-old son of the Rev. Eliakim **Phelps** around whom the Stratford, Connecticut disturbances centered in 1850, was often lifted from the floor, and was once put into a water cistern, at another time suspended from a tree.

In the age of **animal magnetism,** Dr. G. **Billot** reported that his somnambules sometimes rose into the air. The Seeress of Prevorst (see Frau Frederica **Hauffe**), if put into a bath during her trance, floated on the top of the water like a cork. If Dr. Justinus **Kerner** placed his fingers against her own, he could act like a magnet and lift her from the ground.

Louis J. J. Charpignon, in his book *Physiologie, médecine et métaphysique du magnétisme* (1848), stated that Bourguignon, a mesmerist of Rouen, could lift several of his subjects from the ground by placing his hand over the epigastrium. Other experimenters have recorded with the same experience.

The levitation of Spiritualist mediums represents a simple continuity of an age-old phenomenon. When modern Spiritualism was introduced with the **Rochester rappings,** the phenomenon soon appeared. It was recorded for the first time with Henry C. Gordon in February 1851. A year later, in Dr. Gray's house in New York, he was carried through the air to a distance of sixty feet.

If we accept Dr. R. T. Hallock's account before the New York Conference of June 18, 1852, there was an instance of Gordon's levitation in daylight in a crowded assembly room. According to Dr. Hallock, while he was delivering a lecture, Gordon, who sat at some distance from but in front of him, rose into the air, swayed from side to side, his feet grazing the top seats, and sank to the ground when the attention of the entire congregation became riveted on him. It was afterwards declared by the spirits that they intended to carry him over the heads of the sitters to the rostrum but that the audience had broken the necessary conditions of passivity.

The Levitations of D. D. Home

The next medium to exhibit the phenomenon was D. D. **Home.** His first levitation occurred on August 8, 1852, in Ward Cheney's house at Manchester, Connecticut. The report of the *Hartford Times* stated: "Suddenly and without any expectation on the part of the company, Mr. Home was taken up in the air. I had hold of his hand at the time, and I felt his feet—they were lifted a foot from the floor. He palpitated from head to foot with the contending emotions of joy and fear which choked his utterance. Again and again he was taken from the floor, and the third time he was carried to the ceiling of the apartment with which his hands and feet came in gentle contact. I felt the distance from the soles of his boots to the floor, and it was nearly three feet. Others touched his feet to satisfy themselves."

With no other medium was levitation so often and so reliably attested as with Home. In Britain, Sir William **Crookes** narrated his own experiences as follows: "On one occasion I witnessed a chair, with a lady sitting on it, rise several inches from the ground. On another occasion, to avoid the suspicion of this being in some way performed by herself, the lady knelt on the chair in such a manner that its four feet were visible to us. It then rose about three inches, remained suspended for about ten seconds and then slowly descended.

"At another time two children, on separate occasions, rose from the floor with their chairs, in full daylight under (to me) most satisfactory conditions; for I was kneeling and keeping close watch upon the feet of the chair, observing distinctly that no one touched them.

"The most striking instances of levitation which I have witnessed have been with Mr. Home. On three separate occasions I have seen him raised completely from the floor of the room. Once sitting in an easychair, and once standing up. On each occasion I had full opportunity of watching the occurrence as it was taking place."

"There are at least a hundred instances of Mr. Home's rising from the ground, in the presence of as many separate persons; and I have heard from the lips of three witnesses to the most striking occurrence of this kind—the Earl of Dunraven, Lord Lindsay and Captain C. Wynne—their own most minute accounts of what took place. To reject the recorded evidence on this subject is to reject all human testimony whatever; for no fact in sacred or profane history is supported by a stronger array of proofs."

In the *Journal* of the Society for Psychical Research (vol. 6, part 15, 1889), Crookes further stated: "On several occasions Home and the chair on which he was sitting at the table rose off the ground. This was generally done very deliberately, and Home sometimes tucked up his feet on the seat of the chair and held up his hands in full view of all of us. On such an occasion I have got down and seen and felt that all four legs were off the ground at the same time, Home's feet being on the chair. Less frequently the levitating power was extended to those sitting next to him. Once my wife was thus raised off the ground in her chair."

The striking occurrence to which Crookes referred in the first quotation was the most famous case in the history of levitation. It was witnessed on December 13, 1868, at Ashley House, Victoria Street, London, in the presence of Lord Adare, the Master of Lindsay and Charles Wynne, Lord Adare's cousin. Home floated out of a third storey window and came in through the window of another room. As a veritable literature of controversy grew up around this incident, it is well to quote Lord Adare himself: "He [Home] then said to us, 'Do not be afraid, and on no account leave your places' and he went out into the passage. Lindsay suddenly said 'Oh, good heavens! I know what he is going to do; it is too fearful.'

"Adare: 'What is it?'

"Lindsay: 'I cannot tell you, it is too horrible! Adah [the spirit of a deceased American actress] says that I must tell you; he is going out of the window in the other room, and coming in at this window.' We heard Home go into the next room, heard the window thrown up, and presently Home appeared standing upright outside our window; he opened the window and walked in quite coolly. 'Ah,' he said, 'you were good this time'—referring to our having sat still and not wished to prevent him. He sat down and laughed.

"Charlie: 'What are you laughing at?'

"Home: 'We [the spirits; Home always was spoken of in third person when in trance] are thinking that if a policeman had been passing and had looked up and had seen a man turning round and round along the wall in the air he would have been much astonished. Adare, shut the window in the next room.' I got up, shut the window, and in coming back remarked that the window was not raised a foot, and that I could not think how he managed to squeeze through. He arose and said, 'Come and see.' I went with him; he told me to open the window as it was before. I did so; he told me to stand a little distance off; he then went through the open space, head first, quite rapidly, his body being nearly horizontal and apparently rigid. He came in again, feet foremost, and we returned to the other room. It was so dark I could not see clearly how he was supported outside. He did not appear to grasp, or rest upon, the balustrade, but rather to be swung out and in. Outside each window is a small balcony or ledge, 19 inches deep, bounded by stone balustrades, 18 inches high; the balustrades of the two windows are 7 feet 4 inches apart, measuring from the nearest points. A string-course, 4 inches wide, runs between the windows at the level of the bottom of the balustrade; and another 3 inches wide at the level of the top. Between the window at which Home went out, and that at which he came in, the wall receded 6 inches. The rooms are on the third floor. I asked Lindsay how Adah had spoken to him on the three occasions. He could scarcely explain; but said it did not sound like an audible human voice; but rather as if the tones were whispered or impressed inside his ear. When Home awoke he was much agitated; he said he felt as if he had gone through some fearful peril, and that he had a most horrible desire to throw himself out of the window; he remained in a very nervous condition for a short time, then gradually became quiet." (Viscount Adare; *Experiences in Spiritualism with D. D. Home,* privately printed, London, 1870).

The Master of Lindsay gave an account of the incident before the Committee of the **Dialectical Society** in London in 1869 and wrote out an account in 1871. Before the Dialectical Society he stated: "I saw the levitation in Victoria Street, when Home floated out of the window; he first went into a trance and walked about uneasily; then he went into the hall; while he was away, I heard a voice whisper in my ear 'He will go out of one window and in at another.' I was alarmed and shocked at the idea of so dangerous an experiment. I told the company what I had heard, and we then waited for Home's return. Shortly after he entered the room, I heard the window go up, but I could not see it, for I sat with my back to it. I, however, saw his shadow on the opposite wall; he went out of the window in a horizontal position, and I saw him outside the other (that in the next room) floating in the air. It was eighty-five feet from the ground. There was no balcony along the window, merely a string course an inch and a half wide; each window had a small plant stand, but there was no connection between them."

In his account of 1871, there was a further addition to the story: "The moon was shining full into the room. My back was to the light; and I saw the shadow on the well of the window sill, and Home's feet about six inches above it. He remained in this position for a few seconds, then raised the window and glided into the room feet foremost, and sat down."

Frank **Podmore,** the author of *Modern Spiritualism* (2 vols., 1906), who discredited the phenomenon of levitation stated that he looked up a Nautical Almanack of 1868 and found that the moon was new and could not have lit the room, however faintly. But in Lord Adare's almost contemporary account there is no mention of the moon. He only stated that "the light from the window was sufficient to enable us to distinguish each other." As the moon is not mentioned in the Master of Lindsay's account before the Dialectical Committee either, Podmore's criticism is probably based on a misstatement of facts.

Another line of attack was chosen by Dr. W. B. Carpenter, Vice-President of the Royal Society. In the *Contemporary Review* of January 1876, he wrote: "A whole party of believers will affirm that they saw Mr. Home float out of the window and in at another, whilst a single honest sceptic declares that Mr. Home was sitting in his chair all the time." The "single honest sceptic" could be no other than Captain Wynne, the third witness of the occurrence. However, when he narrated to Sir William Crookes, S. C. Hall and others what he saw, he was actually in accord with Lord Adare and the Master of Lindsay. When Carpenter's assertion found echo in an American book, W. A. Hammond's *Spiritualism and Allied Causes and Conditions of Nervous Derangement* (1876), Capt. Wynne being explicitly mentioned as the honest skeptic, D. D. Home challenged his testimony. Wynne, answering him explicitly declared: "The fact of your having gone out of the window and in at the other I can swear to."

A different basis of suspicion was raised by Podmore in a letter which H. D. Jencken sent to *Human Nature.* According to this, a few days before the much-discussed miracle of levitation Home had opened the same window in the presence of two of his later witnesses, stepped on the ledge outside, and to the great alarm of the Master of Lindsay, remained standing there, looking down at the street some eighty feet below. Podmore believed that this was a rehearsal and "What, no doubt, happened was that Home, having noisily opened the window in the next room, slipped back under cover of darkness into the seance room, got behind the curtains, opened the curtains, opened the window, and stepped on the window ledge."

Joseph McCabe in his *Spiritualism; A Popular History from 1847* (1920), also attacked the case on the grounds of visibility and held it likely that it was only the shadow of Home which was seen. Andrew Lang took the stand that people in a room can see even in a fog a man coming in by the window, and going out again, head first, with body rigid.

A curious entry in the diary of the famous escapologist **Houdini** (May 6, 1920) should also be mentioned: "I offered to do," it stated "the D. D. Home levitation stunt at the same place that Home did it in 1868, and G. shirked and messed it up." According to the authors of *Houdini and Conan Doyle,* "he had evidently made a careful examination of the premises, with his customary thoroughness, and had decided that it would be possible to duplicate the performance, with suitable assistance. The assistant was apparently to have been G.; but the latter for some reason or other became frightened at the prospect, and backed out of the bargain."

It is hardly necessary to stress that the possibility of Home having an accomplice is a most unreasonable one in the light of the circumstances of this celebrated levitation.

Subjective Sensations of Levitation

As Home was not always in trance when levitation occurred, he could give an account of his sensations. He wrote in his autobiography *Incidents in My Life* (1863): "During these elevations or levitations I usually experience in my body no particular sensation other than what I could only describe as an electrical fulness about the feet. I feel no hands supporting me, and since the first time have never felt fear, though if I had fallen from the ceiling of some rooms in which I have been raised, I could not have escaped serious injury. At times, when I reach the ceiling, my feet are brought on a level with my face, and I am, as it were, in a reclining position. I have frequently been kept so suspended four or five minutes."

It is interesting to compare this account with that of the Rev. Stainton **Moses** of August 1872: "I was carried up. I made a mark on the wall opposite to my chest. I was lowered very gently until I found myself in my chair again. My sensation was that of being lighter than the air. No pressure on any part of the body, no unconsciousness or entrancement. From the position of the mark on the wall it is clear that my head must have been close to the ceiling. The ascent of which I was perfectly conscious, was very gradual and steady, not unlike that of being in a lift, but without any perceptible sensation of motion other than that of feeling lighter than the atmosphere." His only discomfort was a slight difficulty in breathing accompanied by a sensation of fulness in the chest.

For a fuller account of subjective sensations, we have to go back to St. Teresa of Avila, the famous reformer of the Carmelite Order. Explaining the difference between union and rapture, the saint wrote:

"Rapture, for the most part, is irresistible. It comes, in general, as a shock, quick and sharp, before you can collect your thoughts or help yourself in any way, and you see and feel it as a cloud or a strong eagle rising upwards and carrying you away on its wings. . . . Occasionally I was able, by great efforts, to make a slight resistance; but afterwards I was worn out, like a person who had been contending with a strong giant; at other times it was impossible to resist at all: my soul was carried away, and almost always my head with it—and now and then the whole body as well, so that it was lifted up from the ground. . . . It seemed to me, when I tried to make some resistance, as if a great force beneath my feet lifted me up, I know of nothing with which to compare it; . . . for it is a great struggle, and of little use, whenever our Lord so wills it. There is no power against this power. . . . When the rapture was over, my body seemed frequently to be buoyant, as if all weight had departed from it; so much so that now and then I scarcely knew that my feet touched the ground."

Home stated "I am generally lifted up perpendicularly, my arms frequently become rigid, and are drawn above my head, as if I were grasping the unseen power which slowly raises me from the floor."

Crookes saw him, in one instance, levitate in a sitting posture. On April 21, 1872, he recorded: "He was sitting almost horizontally, his shoulders resting on his chair. He asked Mrs. Walter Crookes to remove the chair from under him, as it was not supporting him. He was then seen to be sitting in the air, supported by nothing visible."

This account compares in an interesting manner with the deposition of the surgeon Francesco Pierpaoli about the last illness of St. Joseph of Copertino. The saint was sitting on a chair with his leg laid on the surgeon's knee. The surgeon began to cauterize it when he noticed that Father Joseph was "rapt out of his senses." "I noticed," he said, "that he was raised about a palm over the said chair, in the same position as before the rapture. I tried to lower his leg down, but I could not; it remained stretched out. . . . He had been a quarter of an hour in this situation when Father Silvestro Evangelista of the monastery of Osimo came up. He observed the phenomenon for some time, and commanded Joseph under obedience to come to himself, and called him by name. Joseph then smiled and recovered his senses."

A similar levitation in sitting posture was put on record by Col. Rochas (*Recueil de documents relatifs à la lévitation du corps humain,* 1897) of the stigmatist from Ardeche, Victoire Claire of Coux, who died in 1883. Mme. D., an eye witness, said: "I saw her with great amazement remain with her eyes fixed but lively, and gradually raised above the chair whereon she was sitting. She stretched forth her arms, leaned her body forward, and remained thus suspended, her right leg bent up, the other touching the earth but by a toe. I saw Victoire in this position, impossible for anyone to keep up normally, every time she was in an ecstatic trance . . . more than a thousand times."

D. D. Home was often levitated in good light. Lord Lindsay categorically stated before the Dialectical Society: "I once saw Home in full light standing in the air seventeen inches from the ground."

Strength of Levitating Power

Such clear contemporary testimony makes Home's levitations vie in importance with any hagiologic account of levitating saints. Olivier Leroy, with ecclesiastic bias, attributes mediumistic levitations to diabolic agency but it is difficult to see more a quantitative difference of levitating power between floating saints, demoniacs and mediums.

According to von Görres, it is impossible to cause the levitants to descend. Thus the Blessed Gilles, while one day reading a passage relative to ecstasy, was lifted up above the table. When found in this state by some of the brethren he was seized and pulled at with all their strength, but they could not get him down.

When Curé Peller wanted to give the Sacrament to Francoise Fontaine, the girl "kneeling down had been almost alarmingly carried away, without being able to take the Sacrament, opening her mouth, rolling her eyes in her head in such a horrible way that it had been necessary, with the help of five or six persons, to pull her down by her dress as she was raised into the air, and they had thrown her down on the floor."

According to Dom La Taste, Mlle. Thevenet, the Jansenist convulsionaire "was sometimes raised seven or eight feet high up to the ceiling, and then could carry two persons pulling her down with all their might, three feet above the ground."

Joseph **Glanvill** quoted the testimony of Valentine **Greatrakes,** the famous healer, as given at Lady Con-

way's castle in 1665 in the case of a butler who rose from the ground and notwithstanding that Greatrakes and another man caught hold of him and held him with all their strength, he was forcibly taken up, and for a considerable time floated about in the air just over their heads.

Domic de Jesus-Marie was raised up to the ceiling of his cell and remained there without earthly support for a day and night. A skeptic who seized the floating body by the feet, was on another occasion, borne on high. Frightened, he let go and fell to the earth.

In the days of the Salem witchcraft persecutions (see **America**), the tormentors of Margaret Rule once "pulled her up to the ceiling of the chamber, and held her there before a numerous company of spectators who found it as much as they could do to pull her down again."

In modern experience, the power which effects levitation is often short-circuited as soon as the chain of hands is broken, the gaze of the sitters is too intense, the light is switched on, or the levitated body is touched.

The following occurrence was reported as taking place in the house of Mrs. Guppy-Volckman (see Mrs. Samuel **Guppy** II) in the presence of Mrs. Mary **Hardy,** the American medium:

"Mrs Volckman did not wish to take part in the experiments, so she retired to the back drawing-room with the Baroness Adelma Vay and other visitors, and left Mrs. Hardy with the rest of the guests in the front drawing-room. Suddenly, however, Mrs. Volckman was levitated and carried in sight of us all into the middle of the ring. As she felt herself rising in the air she called out: "Don't let go hands, for Heaven's sake." We were just standing in a ring, and I had hold of the hand of Prince Albert of Solme. As Mrs. Volckman came sailing over our heads, her feet caught his neck and mine, and in our anxiety to do as she told us we gripped tight hold of each other and were thrown forward on our knees by the force with which she was carried past us into the centre of the ring. The influence that levitated her, moreover, placed her on a chair with such a bump that it broke the two front legs off."

The levitations of the medium A. **Zuccarini** were photographed. The flash of magnesium light caused the medium to fall back into the cabinet, but he was not hurt. One of the photographs showed the medium with his feet about 20–24 inches above the table. According to Prof. Murani, the duration of the levitation was about 12–14 seconds.

M. Macnab, an engineer, wrote in 1888 in Gaborieau's *Lotus Rouge* of the levitation of M. C., a sculptor: "Another time, having accidentally lighted up while he was levitated on the music-stool, he fell heavily from a height of from fifty to sixty centimetres, so heavily that the foot of the stool was broken." Mr. Macnab devised an ingenious means of control. He spread on the ground a square of very thin material, placed a chair in the middle and had M.C. sit on it. The sitters then held a corner of the material and, when the medium was levitated, could lift it up and test the height of the chair on which the medium was sitting in the air."

D. D. Home often asked the sitters not to look at him at the moment he was being carried up. Robert Bell touched his feet when he passed over him in the air. It "was withdrawn with a palpable shudder," he wrote, "it sprang from touch as a bird would." In another instance, however, James Wason, a Liverpool solicitor, testified: "Laying hold and keeping hold of his hand I moved along with him five or six paces as he floated above me in the air, and I only let go his hand when I stumbled against a stool." Apparently the conditions greatly depend upon the available power. Sir William Crookes observed instances in which it was ample to impart levitation to others.

The psychical investigator Gambier Bolton had a similar experience in a seance with the medium Cecil **Husk.** "At one of our experimental meetings," he reported in his book *Psychic Force* (1904), "one of the observers (a man weighing quite 12 stones) was suddenly raised from the floor, with the chair in which he was sitting; and releasing the hands of those who were holding his hands, he was levitated in his chair, greatly to his surprise, until his feet were just above the heads of the other experimenters present. He remained stationary in the air for a few seconds and then slowly descended to the floor again. Fourteen observers were present."

Lord Lindsay has seen D. D. Home floating with an armchair in his hand: "I felt something like velvet touch my cheek, and on looking up, was surprised to find that he had carried with him an armchair which he held out in his hand and then floated round the room, pushing the pictures out of their places as he passed along the walls. They were far beyond the reach of persons on the ground."

The medium William **Eglinton** was levitated in the presence of the Emperor and Empress of Russia, the Grand Duke of Oldenburg and the Grand Duke Vladimir. "My neighbours," he wrote, "had to stand on their chairs to follow me. I continued to rise till my feet touched two shoulders on which I leaned. They were those of the Czar."

Simultaneous Levitations

At a levitation of William Eglinton in Calcutta, India, in 1882, the stage magician Harry Kellar, while holding firmly the left hand of the medium, was pulled after him: "his own body appeared for the time being to have been rendered nonsusceptible to gravity."

In his book *What Am I?* (2 vols., 1873), Sergeant E. W. Cox described a violent outburst of power: "Mr. Williams, although held firmly by myself on one side and an F.R.S. on the other, was instantaneously lifted from his chair and placed in a sitting posture on the table. Mr. Herne was in like manner thrown flat upon his back upon the table, while his hands were held by two others of the party. While thus lying he was suddenly raised from the table, as if he had been flung by a giant, and thrown over the heads of the sitters to the corner of the room. The height to which he was actually thrown may be judged by this, that he knocked down a picture that was hung upon the wall, at a height of eight feet."

Dr. Nicholas Santangeno of Venosa wrote in a letter to psychical researcher Dr. Paul **Joire:** "When the medium Ruggieri commenced to rise I held him firmly by the hand, but seeing myself drawn with such force as almost to lose my footing I held on to his arms, and thus I was raised in the air with my companion, who was on the other side of the Medium. We were all three raised in the air to a height of at least three yards above the floor, since I distinctly touched with my feet the hanging lamp which

was suspended from the centre of the ceiling." Before this, "the three mediums, Cecrehini, Ruggieri and Boella were also raised into space until they almost touched the ceiling." On another occasion, Dr. Santangelo and M. Gorli, holding the hands of the medium, Alberto Fontana, were suddenly lifted on the table, Gorli standing, Santangelo kneeling. Later the medium, who was seated in his chair, was suddenly thrown full length under the table with such force that M. Gorli was dragged with him and Dr. Santangelo was thrown down.

Such cases of simultaneous levitation are rare. A very early account was cited in Col. Henry Yule's *The Book of Ser Marco Polo* (1871). The story told by Ibn Batuta, the Moor who lived in the fourteenth century, concerned seven Indian jugglers who rose in the air in a sitting posture. As, however, Ibn Batuta confessed to a loss of consciousness it is possible that the experience was the result of hypnotic suggestion.

Another yet earlier account from the second century A.D. is found in Philostratus' *Life of Apollonius of Tyana* has still less evidential value. Damis, a disciple of Apollonius, stated that he had seen Brahmins suspended in the air at the height of two cubits, and walk there without visible support.

The evidential value of records improves as we progress in time. St. Joseph of Copertino was seen to rise in the air with a lamb on his shoulder. Once he grasped the confessor of the convent by the hand, snatched him off the floor and began whirling round with him in mid-air. Another time he seized an insane nobleman who was brought to him to be healed by the hair of the head, uttered his usual shout and soared up with the patient who finally came down cured.

St. Teresa of Avila and St. John of the Cross, while engaged in a conversation about the Trinity, were seen lifted up simultaneously.

In the mediumistic age, the first record is of the **Davenport Brothers.** The three children, Ira, William and Elizabeth were seen, at an early age, floating high up in the air at the same time.

A joint levitation of Frank **Herne** and Mrs. **Guppy** was described in an attested record in Catherine **Berry's** *Experiences in Spiritualism* (1876) as follows: "After this, Mr. Herne was floated in the air, his voice being heard near the ceiling, while his feet were felt by several persons in the room, Mrs. Guppy who sat next to him being struck on the head by his boots as he sank into the chair. In a few minutes he recommenced ascending, and as Mrs. Guppy on this occasion determined, if possible, to prevent it, she held his arm, but the only result was that she ascended with him, and both floated together with the chairs on which they sat. Rather unfortunately, at this moment the door was unexpectedly opened, and Mr. Herne fell to the ground, injuring his shoulder, Mrs. Guppy alighting with considerable noise on the table where, on the production of light, she was found comfortably seated though considerably alarmed."

On occasions, the American medium Charles **Foster** also registered great anxiety. According to Dr. John Ashburner, author of *Notes and Studies on the Philosophy of Animal Magnetism and Spiritualism* (1867): "He grasped my right hand, and beseeched me not to quit my hold of him; for he said there was no knowing where the spirits might convey him. I held his hand, and he was floated in the air towards the ceiling. At one time Mrs. W. C. felt a substance at her head, and putting up her hands, discovered a pair of boots above her head."

The following case is an interesting contrast. About 1858, strong physical phenomena were recorded in the Poston Circle in America. The seven-year-old son of Charles Cathcart, an ex-Congressman of Indiana, was often levitated and tossed about in the air. The spirit control "John **King**" was credited with the manifestation. The little boy shouted with delight and cried: "Go it, old King. I am not a bit afraid; take me again." For details of the Poston Circle see *Modern American Spiritualism* by Emma Hardinge (1869; 1970).

Another "baby story" was told by Florence **Marryat** of "Dewdrop," the child control of Bessie **Williams,** who grew very impatient when the medium's fifteen-month-old baby interrupted her chats with crying. She usually went up to quiet him, relinquishing the control of the medium for a few minutes and re-assuming it after. One day, her attempt at pacifying the baby failed for she returned saying: "It is no good, I have had to bring him down. He is on the mat outside the door." The baby, who was on the top storey and could not yet walk, was found there, wailing, in his night shirt.

Cases in which mediums have been levitated to the top of the table while sitting in a chair and holding the hands of the sitters are very numerous. Professor Charles **Richet** classified them as semi-levitations, including as such the loss of weight of the medium also. Many physical mediums have at one time or other performed this feat.

A curious testimony of the medium Henry **Slade** was given by Dr. Kettredge, a schoolmate, in *Light* (1909), according to which Slade was once levitated when sound asleep and was carried from one bed to another in a recumbent position.

The Levitations of Eusapia Palladino and Other Mediums

The levitations of Eusapia **Palladino** were among the best observed cases. Prof. C. **Lombroso,** Dr. E. **Chiaia,** Dr. J. **Ochorowitz,** Col. **Rochas,** Prof. Porro, Prof. E. **Morselli** and Dr. de Albertis testified to the facts. Dr. Chiaia reported a case in which "we found the medium stretched out, her head and a small portion of her back supported on the top of the table, and the remainder of the body extended horizontally, straight as a bar, and without any support to the lower part, whilst her dress was adhering to her legs as if her clothing was fastened or stitched around her. One evening I saw the medium stretched out rigid in the most complete cataleptic state, holding herself in a horizontal position, with only her head resting on the edge of the table for five minutes, with the gas lighted and in the presence of Prof. de Cinties, Dr. Capuano, the well-known writer, and Mr. Frederic Verdinois and other persons."

In Prof. Lombroso's *After Death—What?* (1909) there is an account of Eusapia's levitation by a semi-materialized phantom: "On the evening of the 28th September, while her hands were being held by MM. Richet and Lombroso, she complained of hands which were grasping her under the arms; then, while in trance, with the changed voice characteristic of this state, she said: 'Now I lift my medium up on the table.' After two or three seconds the

chair, with Eusapia in it, was not violently dashed, but lifted without hitting anything, on the top of the table and M. Richet and I are sure that we did not even assist the levitation by our force. After some talking in the trance state the medium announced her descent and (M. Finzi having been substituted for me) was deposited on the floor with the same security and precision, while Mme. Richet and Finzi followed the movements of her hands and body without at all assisting them, and kept asking each other questions about the position of the hands. Moreover during the descent, both gentlemen repeatedly felt a hand touch them on the head."

At a later date, there are records by Dr. Schwab on the levitation of Maria **Vollhardt** and by Baron **Schrenck-Notzing** on Willy Schneider (see **Schneider Bros.**). Willy, to quote from René Sudre's *Introduction à la Metapsychique Humaine* (1926), "rose horizontally and seemed to rest on an invisible cloud. He ascended to the ceiling and remained five minutes suspended there, moving his legs about rhythmically. The descent was as sudden as the uplighting. The supervision had been perfect. Geley in his last journey to Vienna, also witnessed a levitation of Willy at Dr. Holub's and he told me he felt absolutely sure of the genuineness of the phenomenon."

Carlo **Mirabelli,** the South American medium, was fastened to an armchair in the presence of several members of the **Academia de Estudo Psychicos "Cesare Lombroso."** After that he rose from the ground and remained two minutes suspended twelve feet over the floor. The witnesses passed under the levitated body. At Santos, in the street, he was lifted up from a motor car for about three minutes.

Length of Time, Height, Luminosity

The period of mediumistic levitation seldom exceeds a few minutes. The fakir Covindassamy of whom Louis Jacolliot wrote in *Occult Science in India* (1919) established a fairly good duration. "At the moment when he left me for lunch . . . the fakir stopped in the doorway opening from the terrace into the back-stairs, and folding his arms, he was lifted—or so it seemed to me—gradually without visible support, about one foot above the ground. I could determine the exact height, thanks to a landing mark upon which I fixed my eyes during the short time the phenomenon lasted. Behind the fakir hung a silk curtain with red, golden and white stripes of equal breadth, and I noticed that the fakir's feet were as high as the sixth stripe. When I saw the rising begin, I took my watch out. From the time when the magician began to be lifted until he came down to earth again, about ten minutes elapsed. He remained about five minutes suspended without motion." In this case, however, we have only Jacolliot's unsupported statements.

Ten minutes is far behind the achievements of the saints. St. Joseph of Copertino was testified to have once remained suspended in the air at the height of the trees in the garden for more than two hours. And accounts of his levitations were confirmed by reliable witnesses.

The record of height attained belongs to a fakir who, according to Count Perovsky-Petrovo Solovovo in *Proceedings* of the Society for Psychical Research (vol. 38, p. 276) was levitated, in the presence of a crowd, about twice the height of a five-storey building.

The levitation of saints is often accompanied by luminous phenomena. The light which surrounds their body is said to be dazzling, sometimes lighting up the room (see also **Aura**). In mediumistic cases, the **luminous phenomena** are of a separate order. But they may also accompany levitation. We read in Home's *Incidents in My Life* (1863): "Just before this took place [levitation] we saw his whole face and chest covered with the same silvery light which we had observed on our host's [Mr. S. C. Hall's] face."

With some of the saints, intense corporeal heat was also noticed during their elevation. The difference between the ecstatic and ordinary trance state may eventually shed light on such epiphenomena.

Modern Accounts of Levitation

The best and most impressive cases of claimed levitation date back to the nineteenth century and are therefore not amenable to validation by modern scientific method. But it must be admitted that the phenomena of D. D. Home as investigated by Sir William Crookes and others must stand as highly evidential.

During the 1930s, various mediums apparently demonstrated levitations. In 1938, the British newspaper *Daily Mirror* (June 13) published an impressive photograph of the medium Colin Evans apparently levitating. However, such photographic evidence is far from conclusive, as Mrs. A. P. Goldney, Mrs. H. Richard and others have shown in their article on 'Photographs of Jumping Model Imitating Levitation' in *Proceedings* of the Society for Psychical Research (vol. 45, part 158, pp. 196-98).

In his book *The Haunted Mind* (1959), Dr. Nandor **Fodor** devoted a chapter to 'Phenomena of Levitation' and described his own investigation of the claimed levitation of the medium Harry Brown. A photograph of the medium apparently levitated in trance showed his coat-line dead straight and the buttons without blurring. Had the medium jumped from his chair, one would have expected the coat to have flapped and the buttons to blur.

In modern times, accounts of mediumistic levitation are rare. In the **Enfield Poltergeist** case in 1977, one of the children involved claimed to have floated about a room and there is a photograph of her apparently levitated during an investigation.

A case of levitation associated with demonic possession was reported in Rome. The British newspaper *Sunday People* (May 15, 1977) described how the nun "Sister Rosa" in a Rome convent was the center of poltergeist type disturbances in which objects around her in a room would rise up and fly around, and the nun herself was levitated on several occasions. The Sisters of the convent stated to a reporter that Sister Rosa had once floated through the ceiling, and was found standing on the floor above. The Mother Superior of the convent consulted Padre Candido, a leading exorcist in Rome, but the phenomena persisted. Sister Rosa was sent to no less than five different exorcists in other parts of Italy, but after returning was again surrounded by diabolic disturbances. These included persecution of the nun by inanimate objects, such as cactus thorns which became embedded in her head and could not be removed until washed with holy water. An iron bar is said to have broken loose from a door and moved through walls to materialize in the nun's cell and commenced beating her while she slept. Kitchen knives were reported as flying from a table and trying to stab the nun in the chest. On other occasions, the nun is said to have spoken obscenities, using a gutteral "animal-like" voice, and had to be restrained by five nuns from attacking the cross and the altar.

A few years ago, a documentary film "Journey into the Beyond" (Burbank International Pictures) featured a spectacular scene of the apparent levitation of an African witch-doctor. It was filmed in a small village somewhere between Dahomey and Togo. Witch-doctor Togo Owaku is shown meditating on the shores of a lake, then at dusk walking in front of a large palm tree and drawing a circle in the sand with his staff. A fire is built, and as darkness falls drummers build up an impressive rhythm. Inside the circle, Owaku spreads out his arms and begins to float upwards to a height of about three feet. The scene is shown by two cameras, one in front and the other in the rear, and the ascent occupies about ten seconds. The film was directed by Frank Martin Lang, now known as "Rolf Olsen." He was interviewed two years ago by Alan Vaughan, one of the editors of *New Realities* magazine, and it seemed that the film team believed this to be a genuine case of levitation. However, some doubts remain, since the witch-doctor himself picked the site and the incident took place in darkness illuminated by the light of the fires.

A surprising recent development is the teaching course in levitation offered by an academy organized by **Maharishi Mahesh Yogi** in Lucerne, Switzerland. This novel development of Transcendental Meditation was reported by various British newspapers between May and July 1977. The London *Evening News* (May 16) stated that twelve individuals had just graduated from the first six-month course in levitation. One of them, Mrs. Albertine Haupt stated: "I suddenly found myself six feet above the floor and thought 'Heavens, I've done it.'" Although the floor was covered with foam rubber, she landed precipitately, and other students, equally successful in levitating, sustained bruises. Mrs. Haupt stated: "It is just a matter of learning to control the power." The *Daily Mirror* (July 14, 1977) stated that reporter Michael Hellicar interviewed the Maharishi but was refused a demonstration of levitation. His followers refused to permit photographs being taken and stated, "We will not turn this into a circus." However, they produced their own picture taken two days earlier showing disciples apparently levitating, and this was reproduced in the *Daily Mirror* report. In the London *Evening News* (May 18, 1977), professional magician David Berglas offered to pay £2,000 to any levitator who could hover six inches or more above the ground in a public demonstration, and up to £10,000 if as many as five of the Maharishi disciples demonstrated the ability together. To date, the challenge has not been accepted. In spite of the apparent incongruity of associating meditation with such paranormal feats as levitation, it seems unlikely that Maharishi Mahesh Yogi would permit any deception, and there is a strong tradition in India that certain yoga practices might result in the ability to levitate, as well as other *siddhis* or psychic powers. However, yogis are enjoined to avoid pride in such feats, which might hinder spiritual emancipation.

Theories of Levitation

How is levitation achieved? We know little of the power which accomplishes it. What might be considered as the first attempt at explanation is little more than legendary—the possession of a word of mystical power. This appears in an ancient Jewish anti-gospel *(Toledoth Jeshu: Life of Jesus)*, composed about the sixth century A.D. which G. R. S. **Mead** quoted in his book *Did Jesus Live 100 Years B.C.?:*

"And there was in the sanctuary a foundation stone— and this is its interpretation: God founded it and this is the stone on which Jacob poured oil—and on it were written the letters of the Shem [Shem Hamephoresch, the ineffable name, of which only the consonants Y.H.V.H. are given to indicate the pronunciation as known to the initiated] and whosoever learned it, could do whatsoever he would. But as the wise feared that the disciples of Israel might learn them and therewith destroy the world, they took measures that no one should do so."

"Brazen dogs were bound to two iron pillars at the entrance of the place of burnt offerings, and whosoever entered in and learned these letters—as soon as he went forth again, the dogs bayed at him; if he then looked at them the letters vanished from his memory."

"This Jeschu came, learned them, wrote them on parchment, cut into his hip and laid the parchment with the letters therein—so that the cutting of the flesh did not hurt him—then he restored the skin to its place. When he went forth the brazen dogs bayed at him, and the letters vanished from his memory. He went home, cut open his flesh with his knife, took out the writing, learned the letters . . ."

Queen Helene, being greatly troubled by the miracles of Jesus, sent for the wise men of Israel. They decided to use against Jesus his own medicine and taught Juda Ischariota the secret of learning the letters of the Shem. In the presence of Queen Helene and the wise men Jesus (says the chronicle) "raised his hands like unto the wings of an eagle and flew, and the people were amazed because of him: How is he able to fly twixt heaven and earth?"

"Then spake the wise men of Israel to Juda Ischariota: Do thou also utter the letters and ascend after him. Forthwith he did so, flew in the air, and the people marvelled: How can they fly like eagles?"

"Ischariota acted cleverly, flew in the air, but neither could overpower the other, so as to make him fall by means of the Shem, because the Shem was equally with both of them."

The belief expressed in Robert Kirk's *Secret Commonwealth of Elves, Fauns & Fairies* (written 1691, published 1815 etc.) that levitation is accomplished by fairies explains as little as crediting spirits with the feat or ascribing it to Taoist charms which, when swallowed, have the effect of carrying people to any place they think of. But curiously enough the legend of the word of power persists alongside with the fairy agency. Writing of the **transportation** of Lord Duffus, John Aubrey stated in his *Miscellanies* (1696 etc.) that the fairies cry "Horse and Hattock" and whenever a man is moved to repeat the cry he will be caught up.

As the scientific age was drawing near, "electric," "magnetic," "mesmeric" and "odic" forces were speculated upon. They are now antiquated notions.

From a theological viewpoint, J. J. von Görres groped in a promising direction, but explained nothing, in stating that the source of levitation is in the human organism and is produced by a pathological process or a mystic disposi-

tion of the soul. The pathological process which he applies to somnambules is a "kind of interior tempest aroused by the mechanical forces of the organism being suddenly upset." The mystical disposition is a condition for the reception of the Holy Ghost and levitation is then due to this special gift setting the natural mechanism of the body in motion.

This is a halfway house between naturalistic and supernatural theories. It is more satisfactory than the Catholic view which ascribed the levitation of the saints to a divine marvel and that of "demoniacs" and mediums to diabolic trickery. While the first claim is unacceptable to science, the second is too much in agreement with the extreme Spiritualistic idea that spirits have the power to act on matter direct.

Anti-Gravity Phenomena

Scientific interest in anti-gravity phenomena goes back many years. Variations of the gravitational field of the earth were noted as early as 1672 by Jean Richer, and the first practical gravity meter was invented in 1833 by Sir John Herschel.

The repulsion effect of aluminum to electromagnetism is well known, and in 1914 the French inventor M. Bachelet demonstrated a working model of his Levitated Railway system. A Bachelet Levitated Railway Syndicate was formed to promote a full-scale layout, but the development was abandoned on the outbreak of World War I.

For some years, scientists in various countries have conducted secret researches in "electro-gravitics," the science of anti-gravity effects and some devices have been constructed in which levitation of disk-like forms has been achieved in laboratory tests. Little has so far been published on such work. It is tempting to suppose that some **UFO** reports may concern such levitated devices. The Gravity Research Foundation, New Boston, New Hampshire, founded by Roger W. Babson, investigates various aspects of scientific inquiry into gravity and its anomalies.

The Cantilever Theory of Levitation

Some investigators have attempted to explain human levitation on the same basis as movement of objects by **psychic force** (**telekinesis** or **psychokinesis**). (See **Movement**)

Between 1917 and 1920, Dr. W. J. Crawford of Belfast, Ireland, investigated the phenomena of the **Goligher Circle.** He studied alteration in weight of the medium Kathleen Goligher during levitation of a table, and claimed that the levitation was effected by "psychic rods" of ectoplasm emanating from the medium, which found leverage in the medium's body, acting as cantilevers. He obtained flashlight photographs of these psychic structures.

The parapsychologist René **Sudre** believed that Dr. Crawford's cantilever theory accounted for the movement of distant objects by the extrusion of elastic and resisting pseudopods from the body of the medium and thus sufficiently explained levitation. "From a theoretical point of view," he wrote, "the levitation of a person is as easy to understand as that of an object. The teleplastic levers have naturally their fulcrum on the floor. Their shape is not definite; it may be that of a simple stay, of a cloudy cushion, or even a complete human materialization. The force of gravity is not eluded, but simply opposed by a contrary upward power. The spent amount of energy is not above that required for the production of a fair phenomenon of telekinesis."

It should be kept in mind, however, that the sphere of action of pseudopods was limited to about 7 feet, that the extreme mobility of the levitated body had to be accounted for and that the cantilever structure was very sensitive to light. Therefore this hardly lends itself as a mechanism for daylight levitation as in the case of the medium D. D. Home, or saints and stigmatics.

Possibly there are differing mechanisms of levitation amongst different individuals and as distinct from the movement of objects by psychic force.

The Effect of Will-Power

The possibility of the effect of will-power on levitation was suggested by Capt. J. Alleyne Bartlett in a lecture before the **London Spiritualist Alliance** on May 3, 1931. He often had the feeling that he could lighten his weight at will. Getting on to the scale of a weighing machine he willed that his weight should be reduced and the scale indicated, in fact, a loss of several pounds. To make such observations unobjectionable, the possible pressure of cantilever structures on the floor around the weighing machine ought to be made a matter of control.

The loss of weight in the levitated body may be an appearance due to the effect of a force which lifts or, if internally applied, makes the body bouyant. The best evidence as to the alleged extraordinary lightness of the bodies of saints and ecstatics is furnished in a case quoted by Col. Rochas of an ecstatic who lived in a convent near Grenoble. Three eye witnesses: a parish priest, a university professor and a student of the polytechnic school stated that "her body would sometimes become stiff and so light that it was possible to lift her up like a feather by holding her by the elbow."

According to some hypnotists, the phenomenon could be accomplished by simple hypnotic suggestion.

The question of possible paranormal changes of weight was recently the subject of experiments by parapsychologists John B. **Hasted,** David Robertson and Ernesto Spinelli. Their paper 'Recording of Sudden Paranormal Changes of Body Weight' was published in *Research in Parapsychology 1982* edited by W. G. Roll, John Beloff & Rhea A. White (Scarecrow Press, 1983).

Special Breathing Techniques

Breathing exercises which form an important part in Eastern psychic development are said to have a curious effect on the weight of the human body. According to Hindu **yoga** teachings, they generate a force which partially counteracts gravitation. They say that he who awakens the Anahata **Chakra** (a psychic and spiritual center situated in the region of the heart) "can walk in the air."

The psychical researcher Camille **Flammarion** believed that by breathing even the ordinary sitters of a circle release a motor energy comparable to that which they release when repeatedly moving their arms. Dr. Hereward **Carrington**'s experiments with the "lifting game" (see **Breathing**) seemed to show that, for some mysterious reason, rhythmical breathing may considerably reduce the weight of the human body.

At the third International Psychical Congress in Paris in 1927 Baron **Schrenck-Notzing** described the case of a young man who claimed that by breathing exercises he had levitated his own body twenty-seven times.

There is a description in Alexandra **David-Neel**'s *With Mystics and Magicians in Tibet* (1931 etc.) of a practice which especially enabled its adepts to take extraordinary long tramps with amazing rapidity. It is called *lung-gom* and it combines mental concentration with various breathing gymnastics. Meeting a *lung-gom-pa* in the Chang thang of Northern Tibet she noticed:

"The man did not run. He seemed to lift himself from the ground, proceeding by leaps. It looked as if he had been endowed with the elasticity of a ball and rebounded each time his feet touched the ground. His steps had the regularity of a pendulum." The fact that Mme. David-Neel, a highly respected witness, actually observed a *lung-gom-pa* is of very special interest.

The breathing exercises of the *lung-gom-pa* had to be practiced for three years and three months during strict seclusion in complete darkness. It was claimed that the body of those who trained themselves for years became exceedingly light; nearly without weight: "These men, they say, are able to sit on an ear of barley without bending its stalk or to stand on the top of a heap of grain without displacing any of it. In fact the aim is levitation."

Some initiates asserted that "as a result of long years of practice, after he has travelled over a certain distance, the feet of the *lung-gom-pa* no longer touch the ground and that he glides on the air with an extreme celerity."

Some *lung-gom-pas* wore iron chains around their body for "they are always in danger of floating in the air."

Mme. David-Neel discovered that during their walk the *lung-gom-pas* were in a state of trance. They concentrated on the cadenced mental recitation of a mystic formula with which, during the walk, the in and out breathing must be in rhythm, the steps keeping time with the breath and the syllables of the formula. The walker must neither speak, nor look from side to side. He must keep his eyes fixed on a single distant object and never allow his attention to be attracted by anything else.

The use of a mystical formula or **mantra** as an adjunct to levitation recalls the legends of sacred words in the Judeo-Christian tradition.

The Elevation of Famous Dancers

The expression that the *lung-gom-pas* are able to sit on an ear of barley without bending its stalk finds a suggestive parallel in the history of famous dancers. It was said of Maria Taglioni that "she seemed to be able to walk on a cornfield without bending the ears." While such unusual lightness may be purely illusory there is little doubt that the *élévation* of some famous dancers demonstrated the rudimentaries of levitation.

Vestris père, the "Dioux de la Dance," said of his famous son, Augustus Vestris: "Il resterait toujours en l'air, s'il ne craignait d'humilier ces camarades." (He would always remain in the air but feared to humiliate his comrades.)

Cyril W. Beaumont wrote of Vaslav Nijinski that "in the execution of leaps he displayed a rare quality which contemporaries observed in the dancing of both Vestris and Taglioni—the ability to remain in the air at the highest point of *élévation* before descending."

The technique of remaining in the air appears to be this: Before taking the leap, the dancer takes a deep breath and keeps on drawing in during the leap. He holds his breath while up and tightens his thigh muscles so that his trunk should rest on his thighs.

Curiously enough the capacity of the lungs appears to have less to do with the feat than the development of thigh muscles. Diaghilev noticed of Nijinski: "His *élévation* is nearly three feet . . . Nature has endowed him with tendons of steel and tensile muscles so strong that they resemble those of the great cats. A real lion of the dance, he could cross the diagonal of the stage in two bounds."

Nikolai Legat, who was leader of the class of perfection at the Imperial Theatre School of Warsaw, disclosed in *Der Tanz* (Berlin, February, 1933) the following observations: "As an example of phenomenally high, beautiful and elastic *élévation* I hold the memory of N. P. Damaschoff, the dancer of the great Imperial Theatre of Moscow . . . I have never seen such an *élévation* in my life. The impression was that Damaschoff, after the high jump, remained for a longer time in the air. Rather smaller than of middle stature he possessed extraordinary leg muscles with respectable thighs and impressive calves. Tightening his leg muscles, especially those of the thighs in the air, he made all his moderate jumps fairly high. During the leap he held his breath, i.e., he breathed in shortly before the spring and breathed out as soon as he was down again."

It is for future research to elucidate the relationship between muscular tension in the thighs, deep breathing and suspension in the air.

The question of levitation remains a fascinating one. The evidence for levitation of Christian saints is strong, even if anecdotal. Particular interest is attached to the subjective aspect, as expressed in the writings of St. Teresa of Avila and other saints.

There seems good ground for believing that levitation has sometimes been characteristic of possession and poltergeist cases, possibly involving similar psycho-physical mechanics, but the evidence is less reliable. Abnormal morbid mental states may involve uncontrolled muscular feats such as leaps in the air that could be mistaken for levitation. Moreover the spectator moods of horror or loathing could impede clear observation. It is not clear whether movement of objects without contact (psychokinesis) is related to the same mechanisms as levitation of human beings. On the face of things, it seems unlikely since the subjective human aspects of levitation are distinct from the objective application of some kind of psychic force to inanimate objects.

The Hindu yoga teachings on *pranayama* breathing techniques offer an explicit and promising line of inquiry. The concept of **prana** as the dynamic force in the human body, connected with the latent power of **Kundalini,** deserves closer experimental investigation. In this connection, the expensive special TM-Siddhi courses of the **Transcendental Meditation** movement (*siddhi* is a yoga term for special accomplishment) are clearly a packaging of the standard Hindu yoga teachings of Patanjali and others. There seems no good reason to doubt that some of the TM meditators may have achieved degrees of levitation, accelerated by the suggestible aura of success.

It seems possible that suggestion may be one secondary factor in achieving levitation, in much the same way that Jules **Romains** claimed that it assisted the development of the special faculty of "**eyeless sight.**"

In some cases, out-of-the-body phenomena may have been confused with levitation, particularly from the point of view of the subjective sensations of floating in the air.

The evidence for the reality of the claimed levitations,of some psychic mediums, in particular D. D. Home, is impressive. It is possible that special aspects of breathing may play some part, as with the elevation of some dancers, but combined with states of exaltation.

The connection between levitation and transportation phenomena (movement of individuals over distances) remains obscure. (See also **Breathing; Kundalini; Movement; Out-of-the-Body; Possession; Prana; Psychic Force; Psychokinesis; Transportation; Yoga**)

Recommended reading:

Crawford, W. J. *The Reality of Psychic Phenomena,* John M. Watkins, London, E.P., Dutton, New York, 1916

Crawford, W. J. *Experiments in Psychic Science,* John M. Watkins, London, E. P. Dutton, New York, 1919

Crawford, W. J. *The Psychic Structures in the Goligher Circle,* John M. Watkins, London, E. P. Dutton, New York, 1921

Dingwall, E. J. *Some Human Oddities,* Home & Van Thal, London, 1947; University Books, New York, 1962, contains extensive chapter on the levitations of Joseph of Copertino

Dunraven, Earl of. *Experiences in Spiritualism With D. D. Home,* Society for Psychical Research, London, printed Robert Maclehose, Glasgow (formerly printed for private circulation by Viscount Adare, London, 1869); reprinted under author Adare, Viscount, Arno Press, New York, 1976

Feilding, Everard. *Sittings With Eusapia Palladino & Other Studies,* University Books, 1963

Fodor, Handor. *The Haunted Mind; A Psychoanalyst Looks at the Supernatural,* Helix Press, New York, 1959

Kuvalayananda, Swami. *Pranayama,* Bombay, India, 1931 etc. (frequently reprinted)

Leroy, Olivier. *Levitation,* Burns, Oates, London, 1928

Patanjali (transl. M. N. Dvivedi). *The Yoga-Sutras of Patanjali,* Theosophical Publishing House, Madras, India, 1890 etc.

Prasad, Rama. *The Science of Breath and the Philosophy of the Tattvas . . . Nature's Finer Forces,* Theosophical Publishing Society, London, India, New York, 1897

Richards, Steve. *Levitation; What It Is, How It Works, How to Do It,* Aquarian Press, Northamptonshire, U.K., 1980

Underhill, Evelyn. *Mysticism; A Study in the Nature & Development of Man's Spiritual Consciousness,* E. P. Dutton, 1911 etc. (frequently reprinted)

Von Görres, J. J. *Die Christliche Mystik,* 5 vols., Regensburg & Landshut, 1836–42

Leviticon

A gospel adopted by revivalist French Templars of the nineteenth century, and alleged by them to have been discovered in the Temple at Paris, along with other objects. It was supposed to have been composed in the fifteenth century by a Greek monk, Nicephorus, who sought to combine Moslem tenets with Christianity.

Levy, Walter J., Jr.

Director of the **Institute for Parapsychology,** Durham, North Carolina in 1974. Dr. Levy was accused of manipulation in one of his studies concerned with rodent precognition. In the summer of 1974, Dr. J. B. Rhine stated that Levy had been discovered deliberately falsifying experimental results. Details were reported in 'Comments on the Levy Affair' by James Davis of the Institute for Parapsychology, published in *Research in Parapsychology 1974* (Scarecrow Press, 1975).

This exposure naturally threw doubt on Levy's other studies, and research was undertaken by other parapsychologists attempting independent replication of the Levy researches. The results, on the whole, were ambiguous (see *Research in Parapsychology 1975,* Scarecrow Press, 1976). As far back as 1972, parapsychologist Helmut **Schmidt** had done an independent replication of the Levy research with a lack of positive results.

The prompt exposure of the alleged manipulation reflects credit on Levy's fellow parapsychologists, anxious to maintain the integrity of their scientific researches. Levy's papers included the following: (with James Davis) 'A Potential Animal Model for Parapsychological Interaction Between Organisms' (*Research in Parapsychology 1973,* Scarecrow Press, 1974), (with Brian Artley, Al Mayor & Carol Williams) 'The Use of an Activity Wheel Based Testing Cage in Small Rodent Precognition Work' (*Research in Parapsychology 1973*), 'Possible PK by Rats to Receive Pleasurable Brain Stimulation' (*Research in Parapsychology 1973*). Levy had developed some special techniques of parapsychological research.

Lewis, H(arvey) Spencer (1883–1939)

Founder of AMORC (Ancient and Mystic Order Rosae Crucis), a modern revival Rosicrucian order, with extensive headquarters at San Jose, California.

Born in Frenchtown, New Jersey, November 25, 1883, Lewis was of Welsh ancestry. He was educated in New York State and raised as a Methodist. He became a journalist, sat on a committee investigating Spiritualism in New York and was eventually elected president of the New York Institute for Psychical Research. He was closely associated with Elbert Hubbard and Ella Wheeler Wilcox. In 1903 he was president of the Publishers' Syndicate in New York and edited several scientific and research magazines. Lewis married Martha Morphier.

In 1925 he founded the AMORC in Florida, claiming a special charter from the French Order of the Rose Croix. Soon afterwards the organization moved to present headquarters at San Jose. Lewis applied his special talents as an advertising man to forming a worldwide fraternal organization teaching philosophical and mystical practices to develop the latent faculties of man, and selling literature by mail order.

The large headquarters includes an Egyptological museum, a temple, an auditorium and modern computerized offices.

During his lifetime Lewis was named Imperator or Chief Executive of AMORC. After his death in 1939, his son Ralph Maxwell Lewis succeeded him as Imperator.

Lewis, Matthew Gregory (1775–1818)

English author commonly known as "Monk" Lewis, born in London July 9, 1775. His father was Matthew Lewis, deputy secretary of war, and proprietor of several valuable estates in Jamaica; his mother was Anna Maria Sewell, a lady of cultured tastes, devoted to music and

various other arts. The future author showed precocity during childhood and on reaching boyhood he was sent to Westminster School, but while he was there an ugly cloud rose to dim his horizon when his parents quarrelled and agreed to separate.

Matthew managed to remain friendly with both his father and mother, and in 1791 he visited Paris, while about the same time he made his literary efforts, an attempt at a novel and a force. In 1792 he went to Weimar in Germany where he made the acquaintance of **Goethe,** and also learnt German thoroughly. Two years later he was appointed attaché to the British Embassy at the Hague, and while staying there he wrote his famous sensational story, *Ambrosio; or the Monk,* completed in ten weeks and published in 1795. It earned him his now familiar nickname of "Monk" Lewis.

In 1796, he entered Parliament as member for Hindon, in Wiltshire, and during the next few years he necessarily resided chiefly in London, or near it, becoming friendly the while with most of the notable people of the day.

Meantime his interest in the occult had been developing, and in 1798 his play *Castle Spectre* was staged at Drury Lane; ghosts and the like played a prominent part in this production, which won great popularity among a public increasingly interested in Gothic romances. In 1788, he published his *Tales of Terror,* and in 1801 a volume entitled *Tales of Wonder,* this being virtually an anthology of popular occult verses, some of which were supplied by novelist Sir Walter Scott.

In 1812 Lewis father died, and the author accordingly found himself a very rich man. His conscience was troubled, nevertheless, by the fact that his wealth was derived from slave labor, and so in 1815, he sailed to Jamaica, intent on making arrangements for the generous treatment of the negroes on his estates. Returning to England in 1816, he went soon afterwards to Geneva, where he met Byron and Shelley, while in 1818 he paid a last visit to the West Indies, and died at sea May 14, 1818, while returning home.

The books of Lewis are memorable chiefly for the sensational way in which he exploited the rapidly developing public taste for Gothic romance inaugurated by Horace Walpole's *The Castle of Otranto* (1764). Mrs. Ann Radcliffe's *The Mysteries of Udolpho* appeared in April 1794, and Lewis was greatly impressed by it before publishing his own *Ambrosio; or The Monk* only a few months later. For a concise study of Lewis against the Gothic literary background of his time, see Chapter 5 of *The Gothic Quest* by Montague Summers (1968 etc.). (See also English Occult **Fiction**)

Ley Hunter, The (Journal)

Bi-monthly British publication concerned with **Leys** (ancient straight tracks formed by alignment of burial mounds, beacon hills, earthworks and other sites) and associated theories of occult earth energies and UFOs. Formerly published in Hartlepool, England, the journal is now issued bi-monthly from: P.O. Box 152, London, N10 1EP, England.

Leys

(Pronounced "lays"). A term now used to indicate ancient straight tracks formed by the alignment of burial mounds, beacon hills, earthworks, moats and church sites in Britain. The term had long been thought by philologists to indicate a pasture or enclosed field, but this meaning was challenged by Alfred Watkins (born 1855) in his book *The Old Straight Track,* first published London, 1925. Watkins pointed out the world "ley" in its various place-name forms "lay," "lee," "lea" or "leigh" must have predated the enclosure of fields or pastures.

Watkins was an original thinker, an early photographer, inventor of a pinhole camera and the Watkins exposure meter. In 1922 he published his book *Early British Trackways,* based on a lecture to the Woolhope Club of Hereford, England.

Three years later he published *The Old Straight Track,* in which he detailed his investigations which tended to show a vast network of straight tracks in Britain, aligned with either the sun or a star path. He also claimed evidence that such sighted straight tracks existed in other parts of the world. The purpose of such tracks remains a mystery, but in modern times they have been connected with occult beliefs and ancient lines of earth power. Such lines of force have been reported in primitive magical systems such as the *mana* of the Polynesian Islands. It has also been suggested that certain line marks of ground sites indicate gigantic zodiacs (*see* **Glastonbury Zodiac**).

A British journal *The Ley Hunter* is devoted to the study of leys, ancient wisdom, sacred sites, cosmic energy, UFOs and related subjects. Issued bi-monthly from P.O. Box 152, London, N10 1EP, England.

Lhermitte, Jacques Jean (1877–1959)

French physician and writer, who also published works on parapsychology. Born January 20, 1877 at Mont Saint Pere, Aisne, France, he was a Professor of medicine at Paris Medical School from 1923–47, honorary professor from 1947–59, staff physician at l'Hospice Paul Brouse from 1919–45.

He was a member of the French National Academy of Medicine, doctor honors causa University of Zurich, commander French Legion of Honor. In 1907 he married Lucie Mégret, who died 1916; in 1918 he married Marcelle Berthe Duflocq.

In addition to his many books on medical subjects, he also published: *Psychopathologie de la Vision* (1942), *Les Reves* (Dreams, 1942), *Le Cerveau et La Pensée* (The Brain and Thought, 1951), *Les Hallucinations* (1951), *Mystiques et Faux Mystiques* (Mystics and False Mystics, 1952), *Vrais et Faux Possédés* (True and False Possession, 1956, also published in English translation, Hawthorn Books), *Le Probléme des Miracles* (1956). He died January 24, 1959.

Lia Fail

The Stone of Destiny in medieval Irish romance. It was said that when the feet of rightful kings rested upon it, the stone would roar for joy.

According to tradition, this became the famous Stone of Scone, on which Scottish kings were formerly crowned at Scone, near Perth, removed from Scotland by Edward I in 1296 and brought to Westminster Abbey, London, where it was housed under the Chair of St. Edward. It was stolen by Scottish Nationalists on Christmas Eve, 1950, as a protest, but recovered and restored to Westminster Abbey in February 1952. Also known as the Tanist Stone, or Jacob's Stone. (See also **Danaans**)

"Libellus Merlini"

(Little Book of Merlin). A Latin tract on the subject of the prophecies of **Merlin** written by Geoffrey of Monmouth about 1135.

Geoffrey prefaced his account of the prophecies with one concerning the deeds of a supernatural youth named Ambrosius whom he deliberately confounded with Merlin. Vortigern, King of the Britons, asks Ambrose Merlin the meaning of a vision in which appear two dragons red and white in combat. Merlin replies that the Red Dragon signifies the British race which would be conquered by the Saxon, represented by the White Dragon. A long prophetic rhapsody follows, relating chiefly to the Saxon wars, and with this the work, as given in the Seventh Book of Geoffrey's *Historia Regum Britanniae,* concludes.

It was, however, known in Iceland before 1218 in a form independent of the *Historia.* (H. C. Leach, *Modern Philology,* viii, pp. 607 et seq.). This tract must not be confounded with the *Vita Merlini* (1145 or 1148) generally attributed to Geoffrey.

Liberal Catholic Church

Founded by James Ingall Wedgewood in London, England in 1916. Wedgewood was a Theosophist who had earlier been an Anglican priest, and the new Church was developed in order to provide sacred ritual in line with Theosophical concepts of Masters, angels, auras and colors.

A powerful leader of this ecclesiastical dimension of Theosophy was C. W. **Leadbeater,** who went to Australia as Bishop of the Liberal Catholic Church after the scandals in the Theosophical Society over his alleged homosexual activities.

There are at present three Liberal Catholic denominations in the U.S. with some 1,500 members, and related churches in Canada, Britain and Holland, with a total world membership of about 10,000. The rituals are said to invoke powerful psychic forces. A standard guide to ceremonial is C. W. Leadbeater's *The Science of the Sacraments* (Theosophical Publishing House, 1929). (See also Jiddu **Krishnamurti; Theosophical Society**)

Licking (a Charm)

The following was believed to be a remedy for enchantment: to lick the child's forehead first upward, then across, and lastly up again; and then to spit behind its back.

It was said that if on licking a child's forehead with the tongue a salt taste was perceived, this was an infallible proof of **fascination.**

Lien Hypnotique, Le

French-language publication concerned with hypnosis and related subjects. Address: L'Union Magnetique de Tersac, C.P. 482, Quebec, 8 P.Q., Canada G1K 6W8. (See also **Hypnotism**)

Life Waves

According to Theosophists life waves are three in number. It is necessary to remember that the Deity (the **Logos**) is said to have three aspects analagous to the Christian Trinity. These aspects are first that of Will, second, that of Wisdom, and third, that of Activity, and each has its definite scope in the creation of a universe.

When the Logos sets about the great work of creation it sends the first life wave through the aspect of Activity into the multitude of bubbles in the ether, and thereby forms the various kinds of matter. The universe having been thus far prepared, the second life wave is sent through the aspect of Wisdom, which, bringing with it *life* as we usually understand that term and penetrating matter from above, gradually descends to the grosser forms and again ascends to the finer forms. In its descent, this life wave makes for an ever-increasing heterogeneity, but in its ascent the process is reversed and it makes for an ever-increasing homogeneity.

The work of creation is now far enough advanced to permit of the creation of humanity, for matter has now been infused with the capacity of form and provided with life, and the Logos, therefore, through the aspect of Will, bears forth the Divine Spark, the Monad, and, along with the form and the life, ensouls man. (See also **Ether; Evolution; Logos; Monad; Solar System; Theosophy**)

Light

Light is believed to have a destructive effect upon physical phenomena. The reasons are not fully known, but analogies help to make it admissible. Light waves are the very rapid vibrations (the visible light waves are from 3900 A.U. to 7700 A.U. ie., the wave lengths range from 0.00000077 to 0.00000039 meters). Broadcasting practice demonstrates that the fast vibrations tend to nullify the slower vibrations on which radio is based. When the days are long and the sunlight intense, radio reception drops down. With the oncoming of night it improves again. With short waves which vibrate faster, reception is better.

It is claimed that psychic vibrations are in the same position. The slowest light vibration is red and its destructive effect is correspondingly less. Filtering of daylight by glasses of various colors makes little difference. Cold light, devoid of actinic rays is the least injurious. "I have had many opportunities," wrote Sir William **Crookes,** "of testing the action of light of different sources and colours, such as sunlight, diffused daylight, moonlight, gas, lamp and candle light, electric light from a vacuum tube, homogeneous yellow light, etc. The interfering rays appear to be those at the extreme end of the spectrum." He found moonlight ideal.

Sulphide of zinc or calcium screens have been also tried. They have the disadvantage that their illumination is poor, unless they are extremely large and the intensity of their phosphorescence rapidly diminishes. Dr. Gustave **Geley** experimented with biological light. It did not affect the phenomena. However, the cultures of photogenic microbes are very unstable. In Brazil, luminous insects were tried with success.

We know that light has marked physical, chemical and electrical properties, that many of the lower forms of life are destroyed by ultra-violet rays, that vegetable growth takes place mainly at night, that the function of chlorophyl seems to be the protection of delicate tissues against light, that life itself begins in darkness. The objection, therefore, that genuine mediums should be able to produce their manifestations in good light does not appear to be quite reasonable. Some of the powerful mediums were actually able to produce extraordinary phenomena in

good light. D. D. **Home** seldom sat in darkness. Eusapia **Palladino** once levitated a table in blazing sunshine. The French psychical researcher Dr. J. **Maxwell** was probably right in stating that the action of light is not such as to constitute an insurmountable obstacle to the production of telekinetic movements.

Whenever the phenomena are intense in obscurity, we ought to be able to obtain weaker phenomena of the same kind in light, yet Maxwell himself pointed out that the table appears to play the role of condenser for the accumulated nervous energy. May it not be that light acts as certain rays of cathodic origin which discharge the electricized condensers placed in their vicinity?

In *Psychic Research* (January 1930) a curious accident was recorded which may bear out Maxwell's speculation. According to a communication by Mr. Irving Gaertner of St. Louis, Missouri, in a sitting with Eveling Burnside and Myrtle Larsen in Camp Chesterfield, Indiana, a ray of light, owing to the turning of a switch outside, penetrated through a crack between the lower edge of the door and the floor into the seance room.

"Agonized groans were heard (presumably from the entranced medium, Mrs. Larsen) and one of the two trumpets which had been levitated for the voice immediately fell at the feet of Mr. Nelson. At the same moment, Mrs. Nelson received an electric shock which formed a blister on one of her fingers, resembling one which would be produced by a burning of the skin. All the sitters testified to having felt the electric shock both in the region of the solar plexus, the back and the forehead."

Mrs. Larsen was discovered prostrate on the floor. Her heart did not beat and the body was rigid. It took considerable effort to restore her to consciousness. Mrs. Burnside, the other medium, suffered from the shock for several days after the sitting. Frederick Bligh **Bond,** editor of *Psychic Research,* offered a speculation different from Maxwell's idea for the understanding of the electric shock. He asked: "Is it the light, *qua* light, which in this case causes the violent disturbance of conditions, or is it light as an avenue of conductivity, linking the psychic circuit to the current on the wires of the lamp in the hall?"

The dangers of the shock from the slightest unexpected light ray are indicated in an interesting manner in J. Hewat **McKenzie's** report on the mediumship of Miss Ada **Besinnet** in *Psychic Science* (April 1922). The smallest red spark burning was sufficient to prevent the medium from going into trance. "Upon another occasion, when drawing the electric plug from the wall socket, behind a piece of furniture, and about 8 feet from the medium, the small spark, about 1/16 inch long, which usually accompanies the withdrawal of a plug of this kind when the power is on, was sufficient to create such a psychic shock that the medium immediately fell forward on the table in a cataleptic state."

That psychic structures may objectively exist beyond the range of our optical capacity was demonstrated by quartz lens photography. The quartz lens transmits ultra-violet rays, i.e., it makes visible on the photographic plate, things of which our eyes are not cognisant. Mrs. J. H. McKenzie and Major Mowbray conducted important experiments in this field with the mediums J. Lynn and Lewis. The quartz lens not only disclosed fluorescing lights, vibrating, spinning substances, and psychic rods, but also the dematerialization of the medium's hand when added force had to be borrowed.

Similar results were achieved by Dr. Daniel Frost Comstock in seances with the medium Margery (Mina Stinson **Crandon**) in Boston. Several of his exposed plates showed curious, indefinable white patches, one of which was fairly recognizable as a human face, although it could not be identified. The most important advance in this field of research was registered at the **Institut Métapsychique** in Paris with the mediumship of Rudi **Schneider** in 1931.

Of course, skeptics claim that the alleged destructive effect of light on psychic phenomena and the health of the medium is merely a cover for fraud in the darkness of the seance room. In a number of cases this has certainly been true.

Meanwhile recent developments in fast infra-red photography and heat sensory apparatus have now provided the technical means for psychical researchers to make film or video records in darkness. Unfortunately such technical advances come at a period when there is a shortage of great physical mediums of the caliber of D. D. Home or Eusapia Palladino. Hopefully it may one day be possible to make records which give incontrovertible evidence of the reality or otherwise of **ectoplasm.** (See also **Ectoplasm; Materialization**)

Light (Journal)

The oldest British Spiritualist weekly, official organ of the **London Spiritualist Alliance,** founded in 1881 by Dawson Rogers and the Rev. Stainton **Moses.** Successive editors were E. W. **Wallis** and David **Gow.**

It is now published quarterly as the journal of the **College of Psychic Studies,** London, 16 Queensberry Place, South Kensington, London SW7 2EB England.

Lignites

According to ancient belief, this was a beautiful stone like glass. If hung about a child, it preserved him or her from witchcraft, and if bound on the forehead it stopped bleeding of the nose, restored the loss of senses, and helped to foretell future events.

It is not clear what stone is indicated and it seems unlikely to have been the lignite which is a brown or black variety of coal.

Lilith

According to Johan **Weyer** and other demonologists, Lilith was the prince or princess who presided over the demons known as succubi (see **Succubus**). The demons under Lilith bore the same name as their chief, and sought to destroy newborn infants. For this reason the Jews wrote on the four corners of a birth-chamber a formula to drive Lilith away.

The name Lilith means "night monster" and is referred to in *Isaiah* 34, 14. Lilith is also mentioned in the *Midrash* as a demon of the night. According to ancient Jewish legend, Lilith had the shape of a seductive woman, but seduced men and killed the children she bore them.

It was said that God created Lilith as the first wife of Adam, but that the couple quarreled because Lilith was an archetypal feminist and insisted on equality. When Adam refused, she pronounced the Shem (ineffable Name

of God) and fled. Three angels were sent to bring her back, but she refused, declaring that she was created in order to have power over young children. Eventually she agreed to spare infants in homes which carried an amulet bearing the names of the three children.

Meanwhile Eve was created as a more docile mate for Adam, while Lilith continued to roam the world with a band of 480 demons, seeking vengeance on mankind.

Lilith was also the name of one of the three female demons of ancient Assyria.

Lilly, William (1602–1681)

One of the most famous early English astrologers. Born April 30, 1602, at Diseworth, Leicestershire, he was the son of a yeoman farmer, although a rival astrologer John Heydon later insisted that his father was "a laborer or ditcher." In 1613, Lilly began his education at the grammar school of Ashby-de-la-Zouch, studying Latin, Greek and Hebrew. In 1620, he traveled to London and obtained employment as a servant, helping with his master's accounts. He also nursed his master's first wife, who died of cancer in 1624. The following year, his master remarried, but died in 1627. Lilly accepted an offer of marriage from the widow and was well provided for, being made a freeman of the Salter's Company and spending time in angling or listening to Puritan sermons.

Lilly became interested in **astrology** in 1632, reading many books on the subject and contacting leading astrologers of the day. Soon after the death of his wife in 1633, Lilly studied the famous **Ars Notoria** grimoire, and took part in an occult ceremony with hazel rods to locate treasure said to be buried in the cloisters of Westminster Abbey (see **Divining-Rod**). In the event, only a coffin was found.

In 1634, Lilly married a second time. He taught astrology to pupils and began to write astrological books. His first almanac *Merlinus Anglicus Junior, the English Merlin Revived, or a Mathematicall Prediction upon the Affairs of the English Commonwealth, and of All or Most Kingdoms of Christendom, this present year 1644* was published June 12, 1644. This was followed by other books of predictions. Although ostensibly a parliamentarian, Lilly was several times in trouble with the authorities for apparently helping the royalist cause.

Some of his prophecies also got him into difficulties, notably the engravings in his *Monarchy and No Monarchy* (1651) which illustrated the Great Plague and the Fire of London. In 1666, Lilly was called before the committee set up to investigate the cause of the great fire, predicted in the hieroglyphics of his book five years earlier. In the trial of conspirators charged with having set the fire, it was stated that the date of September 3, 1666 was selected because Lilly had designated it a "lucky day" (the fire actually started September 2).

A few years later, Lilly studied medicine, and through his friend the antiquary Elias Ashmole was granted a license to practice. From 1670 onwards he became celebrated as a physician as well as an astrologer. He published fifteen major works on astrology as well as thirty-six almanacs and was consulted by famous individuals of the time. He died June 9, 1681. His posthumous autobiography *The History of Lilly's Life and Times* was published in 1715.

Lily Dale (Spiritualist Assembly)

One of the oldest central headquarters (formerly called "Camp Meetings") of American Spiritualism. It was established in 1880 as the Cassadaga Free Lake Association situated in beautiful countryside in the Chautauqua hills, scarcely two hours drive from the city of Buffalo. In 1906 it was renamed Lily Dale. It comprised eighty acres with hundreds of cottages, meeting places, a hotel, post office and a library.

For many years it became a focal point for world famous lecturers and mediums demonstrating every variety of phenomena. Not surprisingly it also attracted many fraudulent mediums from time to time.

In 1916, the old Hydesville house, which was the center of the Fox family knockings which founded American Spiritualism, was removed to Lily Dale, but was unfortunately burned to the ground in 1955. It was recreated in 1968 as a tourist attraction on the Hydesville site.

For a general view of Spiritualist centers in their heyday, see 'The Spiritualistic Camp-Meetings in the United States' by Lilian Whiting in *The Annals of Psychical Science* (January, 1907).

Limachie

According to ancient belief, this resembled a chip of a man's nail and was squeezed out of the head of a slug, which had to be done the instant it was seen. It was said to be a good **amulet** to preserve from fever.

Lincoln, Abraham (1809–1865)

President Lincoln, the emancipator, was influenced in his decision to free the slaves by Spiritualist experiences. Immediately after his election to the presidency, an article was published in the Cleveland *Plaindealer* which, on the statements of the medium J. B. **Conklin**, identified him as a sympathizer with Spiritualism. Conklin recognized in him the unknown individual who was a frequent guest at his seances in New York, asked mental questions and departed unnoticed, as he came.

When the article was shown to Lincoln he said, instead of contradicting it: "The only falsehood in the statement is that the half of it has not been told. This article does not begin to tell the wonderful things I have witnessed."

In a letter to Horace Greely in August 1862, Lincoln stated: "My paramount object is to save the union, and not either to save or destroy slavery." The anti-slavery proclamation was dated September 1862, and was issued in January 1863. The change in Lincoln's attitude was mainly brought about by the influence of Senator Thomas Richmond, by his experiences through the mediums J. B. Conklin, Mrs. Cranston Laurie, Mrs. Miller, Nettie Colburn and by Dr. Farnsworth's predictions.

Senator Richmond was one of the leading business men of Chicago. He had a controlling interest in the grain and shipping industry of that city. While chairman of the committee on banks and corporations he became a personal friend of Lincoln. In his book, *God Dealing with Slavery* (1870) he reproduced the letters which, under psychic influence, he sent to the President.

Col. S. P. Kase testified in the *Spiritual Scientist* that "for four succeeding Sundays Mr. Conklin, the test medium, was a guest at the presidential mansion. The result of these interviews was the President's proposition to his cabinet to issue the proclamation." Col. Kase also narrated President Lincoln's visit, in the company of his wife, in Mrs. Laurie's house. Mrs. Laurie was a well known medium. The Colonel's daughter, Mrs. Miller, produced strong physical phenomena.

Nettie Colburn (see Mrs. **Maynard**) was another guest. She later became famous as an inspirational speaker, but then she was scarcely out of her teens. She passed into trance, approached the President with closed eyes, and addressed him for a full hour and a half. The sum total of her address was: "This civil war will never cease. The shout of victory will never ring through the North, till you issue a proclamation that shall set free the enslaved millions of your unhappy country." It is significant enough that from the intermediate time between the drawing up of the proclamation in September and its issue in January, the Union army had in diverse places twenty-six battles and every one of them was a success upon the Union side. In the same seance President Lincoln witnessed powerful physical manifestations. The piano on which the medium was playing rose four inches from the floor in spite of the efforts of Col. Kase, Judge Wattles and the two soldiers who accompanied the President to weigh it down.

In 1891, Nettie Colburn (then Mrs. Maynard) published a book, *Was Abraham Lincoln a Spiritualist?* (frequently reprinted since 1956 by Psychic Book Club, London) In this she described her very first meeting with President Lincoln. In 1862 in Washington, Mrs. Lincoln had a sitting with her and was so much impressed that she asked her to come and see the President.

According to Mrs. Maynard's account in her book, she delivered a trance address in which the President "was charged with the utmost solemnity and force of manner not to abate the terms of its [Emancipation Proclamation] issue and not to delay its enforcement as a law beyond the opening of the year; and he was assured that it was to be the crowning event of his administration and his life; and that while he was being counselled by strong parties to defer the enforcement of it, hoping to supplant it by other measures and to delay action, he must in no wise heed such counsel, but stand firm to his convictions and fearlessly perform the work and fulfill the mission for which he had been raised by an overruling Providence. Those present declared that they lost sight of the timid girl in the majesty of the utterance, the strength and force of the language, and the importance of that which was conveyed, and seemed to realise that some strong masculine spirit force was giving speech to almost divine commands. I shall never forget the scene around me when I regained consciousness. I was standing in front of Mr. Lincoln, and he was sitting back in his chair, with his arms folded upon his breast, looking intently at me. I stepped back, naturally confused at the situation—not remembering at once where I was; and glancing around the group where perfect silence reigned. It took me a moment to remember my whereabouts. A gentleman present then said in a low tone: 'Mr. President, did you notice anything peculiar in the method of address?' Mr. Lincoln raised himself, as if shaking off his spell. He glanced quickly at the full-length portrait of Daniel Webster that hung above the piano, and replied: 'Yes, and it is very singular, very!' with a marked emphasis."

On Mr. Some's inquiry whether there had been any pressure brought to bear upon him to defer the enforcement of the Proclamation, the President admitted, "It is taking all my nerve and strength to withstand such a pressure."

For information on Lincoln's association with Spiritualists, see *Nineteenth Century Miracles* by Emma Hardinge Britten, London & Manchester, 1883 (pp. 484–87).

Recommended reading:

Fleckles, Elliott V. *Willie Speaks Out; The Psychic World of Abraham Lincoln.* Llewellyn Publications, St. Paul, Minn., 1974

Maynard, Nettie Colburn. *Was Abraham Lincoln A Spiritualist?* R. C. Hartrampft, Philadelphia, 1891; Psychic Book Club, 1956

Shirley, Ralph. *Short Life of Abraham Lincoln,* London, 1919

Lindisfarne

Educational community in Southampton, New York, founded in 1973 by William Irwin **Thompson,** author of *Passages About Earth: An Exploration of the New Planetary Culture* (1974). Lindisfarne takes its name from the English monastery founded by St. Aidan on Holy Island in Northumberland in 635 A.D.

The island is now owned by Robin Henderson who keeps racing pigeons, and the monastery is a ruin, but Thompson was impressed by the symbolic associations of the place, which he described in *Passages About Earth.* He regarded Lindisfarne as typifying a historic clash between esoteric Christianity and ecclesiastical Christianity, between religious experience and religious authority.

A visit to **Findhorn** community in Scotland helped to develop Thompson's concept of a new "planetary culture" involving a synthesis of science, art and spiritual awareness. He founded the Lindisfarne Association as an educational community "in which people of all ages could work and study together in new forms of growth and transformation." Spiritual self-discipline is regarded as a basis for artistic and cultural learning, and Lindisfarne offers seminars in science and the humanities for students rooted in daily meditational practice. All this has much in common with contemporary outlooks loosely labelled **New Age.** Address: Fish Cove Road, Southampton, Long Island, New York, N.Y. 11968.

Lindsay, The Master of (1847–1913)

Later the Earl of Crawford and Balcarres. A famous figure in the early history of English Spiritualism owing to his association with Viscount Adare in testimony to the phenomena of the medium D. D. **Home.** He appeared before the committee of the **London Dialectical Society** in 1869 and testified to Home's mysterious powers. His account of Home's most famous levitation and floating out of the third-storey window of Lord Adare's house led to sharp controversy in later literature, but the evidence vindicated the reality of Home's phenomena. (See also **Levitation**)

Link, The

An international association of Spiritualist home circles, founded by N. Zerdin in 1931 for the interchange of psychic information obtained in the home circles, publishing a privately circulated monthly, *The Link.*

Mr. I. S. Beverley, president of the Link Association and treasurer of the Great Metropolitan Spiritualist Association, died January 9, 1947. He had also edited *The Link* journal.

Linton, Charles (c. 1855)

One of the most remarkable American writing mediums of early Spiritualism. Originally a blacksmith with limited education he became, at the age of 22, a clerk in a store in Philadelphia and bookkeeper afterwards.

Soon after he developed **automatic writing,** under the alleged **control** of Daniel Webster. Governor Talmadge and the actor Fenno claimed to have received, through his hand, communications from Shakespeare.

In 1853, Linton began his great work. In the space of only four months, he produced a remarkable book, a religious rhapsody which was published in 1855 under the title *The Healing of the Nations,* with a preface by Governor Talmadge who often witnessed the writing. The book consists of more than 100,000 words; it came very fluently and in a different handwriting from the medium's who was quite conscious during its production. It was one of the most remarkable inspirational books of the period, although its aphorisms would now seem rather trite. (See also **Automatic Writing and Speaking**)

Lippares (or Liparia)

According to ancient belief, he who has this stone "needs no other invention to catch wild beasts." On the other hand, no animal can be attacked by dogs or huntsman if it look upon it. It is not clear whether this was a known or a fabled precious stone.

List, Guido von (1848–1919)

Austrian occultist, author, journalist and playwright whose racist theories preceded National Socialism in Germany. He grew up obsessed by pagan folklore of gods and demons, and after publication of his first books a small group of admirers founded a Guido von List Society, which issued further books of a pseudo-mystical nature.

List developed a theory of a mysterious ancient race called the "Armanen," whose symbol was the swastika, and founded a secret occult lodge of the Armanen. After a press scandal in which it was revealed that he practiced medievel black magic with blood rituals and sexual perversion, he fled from Vienna. Many of his associates, like **Lanz von Liebenfels,** were rabid anti-Semites, part of the occult underground that nourished perverted Nazi beliefs. List died in Berlin in May 1919.

Litanies of the Sabbat

According to one account, on Wednesdays and Saturdays it was the custom to sing at the witches' Sabbat the following Litanies:

"Lucifer, Beelzebub, Leviathan, have pity on us.

"Baal, prince of the seraphim; Baalberith, prince of the cherubim; Astaroth, prince of the thrones; Rosier, prince of denominations; Carreau, prince of the powers; Belial, prince of the vertues; Perrier, prince of the principalities; Oliver, prince of the arch angels; Junier, prince of the angels; Sarcueil, Fume-bouche, Pierre-le-Feu, Carniveau, Terrier, Contellier, Candelier, Behemoth, Oilette, Belphegor, Sabathan, Garandier, Dolers, Pierre-Fort, Axaphat, Prisier, Kakos, Lucesme, pray for us."

It is interesting to note that Satan was evoked in these litanies only in company with a crowd of other demons.

However accounts of different Sabbats vary and many litanies appear to have been merely anti-Christian parodies. This particular litany sounds more like an evocation of demons for a magical ritual than a celebration of witches at a Sabbat. (See also **Lucifer; Sabbat; Witchcraft**)

Lithomancy

A species of divination performed by stones, but in what manner it is difficult to ascertain. Thomas Gale, in a "Note upon Iamblichus," confessed that he did not clearly understand the nature of it; whether it referred to certain motions observable in idols, or to an insight into futurity obtained by demons [familiars] enclosed in particular stones. That these supernatural beings might be so commanded is clear from a passage of Nicephorus.

The old rabbis attributed *Leviticus* xxvi, 1 to Lithomancy, but the prohibition of stones there given is most probably directed against idolatry in general. J. C. Boulenger has a short chapter on Lithomancy. He showed from Tzetzes that Helenus ascertained the fall of Troy by the employment of a magnet, and that if a magnet be washed in spring water, and interrogated, a voice like that of a sucking child will reply.

The pseudo-Orpheus related at length this legend of Helenus. "To him," he stated, "Apollo gave the true and vocal sideritis, which others call the animated ophites, a stone possessing fatal qualities, rough, hard, black, and heavy, graven everywhere with veins like wrinkles. For one and twenty days Helenus abstained from the nuptial couch, from the bath, and from animal food. Then, washing this intelligent stone in a living fountain, he cherished it as a babe in soft clothing; and having propitiated it as a god, he at length gave it breath by his hymn of mighty virtue. Having lighted lamps in his own purified house, he fondled the divine stone in his hands, bearing it about as a mother bears her infant; and you, if ye wish to hear the voice of the gods, in like manner provoke a similar miracle, for when ye have sedulously wiped and dandled the stone in your arms, on a sudden it will utter the cry of a new-born child seeking milk from the breast of its nurse. Beware, however, of fear, for if you drop the stone upon the ground, you will rouse the anger of the immortals. Ask boldly of things future, and it will reply. Place it near your eyes when it has been washed, look steadily at it, and you will perceive it divinely breathing. Thus it was that Helenus, confiding in this fearful stone, learned that his country would be overthrown by the Atridæ."

Photius, in his abstract of the life of Isodorus by Damascius, a credulous physician of the age of Justinian, wrote of an oracular stone, the *bætulum,* to which Lithomancy was attributed. A physician named Eusebius used to carry one of these wonder-working stones about with him.

One night, it seems, actuated by an unaccountable impulse, he wandered out from the city Emesa to the summit of a mountain dignified by a temple of Minerva. There, as he sat down fatigued by his walk, he saw a globe of fire falling from the sky and a lion standing by it. The lion disappeared, the fire was extinguished, and Eusebius ran and picked up a *bætulum.* He asked it to what god it appertained, and it readily answered, to Gennæus, a deity worshiped by the Heliopolitæ, under the form of a lion in the temple of Jupiter. During this night, Eusebius said he traveled not less than 210 stadia (more than 26 miles).

He never became perfectly master of the *bætulum,* but was obliged very humbly to solicit its responses. It was of a handsome, globular shape, white, a palm in diameter, though sometimes it appeared more, sometimes less; occasionally, also, it was of purple color. Characters were to be read on it, impressed in the color called "tingaribinus." Its answer seemed as if proceeding from a shrill pipe, and Eusebius himself interpreted the sounds.

Damascius believed its animating spirit to be divine; Isodorus, on the other hand, thought it demoniacal, that is, not belonging to evil or material demons, nor yet to those which are quite pure and immaterial.

It was with one of these stones, according to Hesychius, that Rhea fed Saturnus, when he fancied that he was devouring Jupiter, its name being derived from the skin in which it was wrapped, and such the commentator supposed to have been the *Lapides divi,* or *vivi,* which the insane monster Heliogabalus wished to carry off from the temple of Diana, built by Orestes at Laodicea (ÆL. Lampid, *Heliogab,* 7). In *Geographia Sacræ* (ii, z, 1646), Samuel Bochart traced the name and the reverence paid to the bætylia, to the stone which Jacob anointed at Bethel. Many of these bætylia, Photius assured us from Damascius, were to be found on Mount Libanus.

Little World (Society)

The name given to a secret society which was said to have conspired in England, during the eighteenth century to reestablish the Stuart dynasty. Various strange stories are told of this society, for instance, that the devil presided over their assemblies in person. The members were believed to be Freemasons.

Lively Stones World Healing Fellowship, Inc., The

Organization to support the healing mission of Willard **Fuller,** famous for his psychic **dentistry.** The Fellowship is supported by voluntary offerings. Address: P.O. Box 23908, Jacksonville, Florida 32217.

Livingston, Mrs. Marjorie (c. 1935)

British inspirational writer, psychic lecturer, authoress of some remarkable books received clairaudiently. Her first work, *The New Nuctemeron* (1930) was claimed to have been inspired by **Apollonius of Tyana** and claimed to expound some remnants of his teachings, the originals were lost during the burning of the Alexandrian Library.

This book was followed by *The Harmony of the Spheres* (1931), *The Elements of Heaven* (1932) and *The Outline of Existence* (1933), all containing new and illuminative information on after-death conditions and the scheme of life in the universe.

Llewellyn Publications

Founded as Llewellyn Publishing Co. in Los Angeles, California, by Welsh astrologer Llewellyn **George** (1876–1954). The company was purchased by Minnesota businessman Carl L. **Weschke** (also a well-known astrologer and occultist) and is now situated in St. Paul, Minnesota, under the name Llewellyn Publications. It is one of the largest publishing and wholesaling organizations of occult books in the U.S.

During the witchcraft boom of the 1960s, Llewellyn was one of the first to publish a version of the witchcraft manual **Book of Shadows;** other popular publications include the magazines *Gnostica, Astrology Now* and *Aquarian Age Preview,* as well as the annual *Moon Sign Book* (first edited by founder Llewellyn George in 1905) and many other occult titles, casette tapes and correspondence courses.

A large retail bookstore Gnostica was opened in Minneapolis January 15, 1970, housed in a 12,000 square foot former mortuary. Through *Gnostica Aquarian Booksales,* the company maintains a large mail order operation. Gnostica sponsors an annual Aquarian Age Festival, which includes lectures, readings and consultations. Carl L. Weschke also presents daily horoscope readings for Twin Cities radio audiences and has discussed occult topics on television programs.

Loathly Damsel, The

Kundrie (or Kundry), the "Grail Messenger." One would imagine that the holder of such an office would be saint-like, but Cretien de Troyes described her as "a damsel more hideous than could be pictured outside hell." Wolfram referred to her in his work as "Kundrie la Sorciére." Kundry in Wagner's music-drama "Parsifal" represents sin. (See also Holy **Grail**)

Lobb, John (1840–1921)

Prominent British businessman and public figure who became active in the cause of **Spiritualism.** Born August 7, 1840 in Middlesex, he became a lay preacher in the Methodist ministry as well as editor of successful journals. In 1876 he raised a fund for the Rev. Josiah Henson (original of Mrs. Stowe's *Uncle Tom's Cabin*), lecturing and preaching on the subject. He also edited the story of Henson's life, which sold over 30,000 copies in six weeks, later being translated into twelve languages. Lobb and Henson were honored with a command to meet the Queen at Windsor Castle on March 5, 1877.

Lobb became a well-known public figure in London life, member of the London School Board, Guardian of the City of London Union, the Metropolitan Asylums Board, serving on the Central Markets committees and becoming a Councilman of the City of London. He was a governor of St. Bride's Foundation, Fellow of the Royal Historical Society and of the Royal Geographical Society.

During his busy public life, he exposed many scandals and abuses in the field of education, the police force and other areas of social and public life. From 1903 onwards he became active in the cause of Spiritualism and campaigned vigorously by lectures and publications. He traveled all over Britain and claimed to have addressed some 40,000 individuals. He lectured on the survival of personality after death and the evidence of **spirit photog-**raphy and **materialization** phenomena. His books included: *'Uncle Tom's Story of His Life* (1877), *Talks with the Dead* (1906).

Loch Ness Investigation Bureau

Founded in 1962 to obtain scientific evidence of the existence of the Loch Ness monster, a marine animal or animals believed by some to inhabit Loch Ness and other lakes in Scotland, Ireland, Canada, Siberia and the Scandinavian countries. Formerly titled Loch Ness Phenomena Investigation Bureau. Address: % David James, M.B.E., D.S.C., M.P., House of Commons, London, SW1A 0AA, England. (See also **Loch Ness Monster; Monsters**)

Loch Ness Monster

A persistently reported monster or colony of monsters in the vast area of Loch Ness, Scotland. The loch is some 24 miles long and about a mile wide, with a depth from 433 to 754 feet. A monster was reported here in ancient Gaelic legends as well as in a biography of St. Columba circa 565 A.D. The modern history dates from 1933 onwards, when the monster received a good deal of publicity.

Convincing films and photographs of a monster in the loch have been made in the last few decades, and new evidence of a large unknown creature in Loch Ness made the front page of the *New York Times* (April 8, 1976), featuring records of an underwater camera using a sonar echo technique June 20, 1975. A scientific report by Mr. Martin Klein and Dr. Harold E. Edgerton appeared in *Technology Review* (March-April 1976).

Two impressive photographs of the head and neck of the monster were taken by monster-hunter and conjurer Tony "Doc" Shiels on May 21, 1977 near Castle Urquhart at Loch Ness, Scotland. One of these photographs was reproduced in both *Cornish Life* and London *Daily Mirror* for June 9, 1977 and both photographs were reproduced and discussed in *Fortean Times* (No. 22, Summer 1977).

Interest in the Loch Ness and similar monsters was stimulated by reports and photographs of the decomposing body of a sea creature caught by Japanese fishermen April 25, 1977 off the coast of New Zealand. The accumulated evidence for the reality of the Loch Ness phenomenon is now substantial and persuasive.

As the observations on a monster in the loch extend over many centuries, it seems reasonable to suppose that there might be a continuing colony of creatures rather than a single monster.

Known in Britain affectionately as "Nessie," the creature was recently given the monstrous name of *Nessiteras rhombopteryx* by Sir Peter Scott and Robert Rines (see 'Naming the Loch Ness Monster,' *Nature,* December 11, 1976) in an attempt to secure official protection as a rare species qualifying for conservation.

In 1961, the Loch Ness Phenomena Investigation Bureau was founded at 23 Ashley Place, London S.W.1. England.

The Loch Ness monster is not unique, since similar creatures have been reported in lakes in a number of different countries. (See also **Crytozoology; Loch Ness Investigation Bureau; Monsters**)

Recommended reading:

Costello, Peter. *In Search of Lake Monsters,* London, 1974

Dinsdale, Tim. *The Story of the Loch Ness Monster,* London, 1973

Gould, Rupert T. *The Loch Ness Monster,* London, 1934; University Books, 1969

Heuvelmans, Bernard. *In the Wake of the Sea Serpents,* London, 1968

Holiday, F. W. *The Dragon and the Disc,* London, 1973

Oudemans, A. C. *The Loch Ness Animal,* Leyden, 1934

Witchell, Nicholas. *The Loch Ness Story,* London, 1974

Lodestone (or Loadstone)

A magnetic stone of magnetite (oxide of iron) showing polarity when suspended. It was believed to possess magical properties of various kinds. If one was ill, it should be held in the hands and shaken well. It was said to cure wounds, snakebites, weak eyes, headaches and restore hearing.

The possessor of the lodestone was supposed to be able to walk through reptiles in safety, even when they were accompanied by "black death." Orpheus stated that "with this stone you can hear the voices of the gods and learn many wonderful things," that it had the property of unfolding the future; and if held close to the eyes it would inspire with a divine spirit.

Lodge, Sir Oliver (Joseph) (1851-1940)

World famous British physicist, a fearless champion of after-death **survival,** who missed no opportunity to affirm his belief in public that death is not the end, that there are higher beings in the scale of existence and that intercommunication between this world and the next is possible. Sir Oliver Lodge was one of the first great thinkers to bring the transcendental world into close relationship with the physical one. He was convinced that life is the supreme, enduring thing in the universe, that it fills the vast interstellar spaces and that the matter of which the physical world is composed of is a particular condensation of ether for the purpose of isolating life into conscious, individual form.

He was born June 12, 1851 at Penkhull Staffordshire, England, and studied at Newport Grammar School and University College, London (B.S., 1875, D.Sc. 1877). He was professor of physics at University College 1877 and at University College, Liverpool 1881-90; principal of Birmingham University 1900-19. In 1877, he married Mary F. Marshall (died 1929). He was elected Fellow of the Royal Society 1887, awarded the Albert Medal of the Royal Society of Arts for his pioneer work in wireless telegraphy. He was president of the British Association in 1913.

His great reputation as a physicist was established by his researches in electricity, thermo-electricity and his experiments in wireless (radio) and theories of matter and ether. He developed the spark plug which bears his name. He was knighted in 1902.

His first experiences in psychical research dated from 1883-84, when he was invited by Mr. Malcolm Guthrie to join his investigations in **thought-transference** in Liverpool. Next he undertook similar experiments himself in 1892 in Carinthia at Portschach am See where he spent the summer. They were reported in *Proceedings* of the Society for Psychical Research (vol. 7, part 20, 1892).

In physical research his most notable observations were made with the medium Eusapia **Palladino.** In Prof. **Richet's** house on the Ile Roubaud he attended four seances and in his report for the *Journal* of the S.P.R., (November 1894) he accepted the reality of Palladino's phenomena as follows: "However the facts are to be explained the possibility of the facts I am constrained to admit; there is no further room in my mind for doubt. Any person without invincible prejudice who had had the same experience would come to the same broad conclusion, viz., that things hitherto held impossible do actually occur. If one such fact is clearly established, the conceivability of others may be more readily granted, and I concentrated my attention mainly on what seemed to me the most simple and definite thing, viz., the movement of an untouched object in sufficient light for no doubt of its motion to exist. This I have now witnessed several times; the fact of movement being vouched for by both sight and hearing, sometimes also by touch, and the objectivity of the movement being demonstrated by the sounds heard by an outside observer, and by permanent alteration in the position of the objects. The result of my experience is to convince me that certain phenomena usually considered abnormal do belong to the order of nature, and as a corollary from this, that these phenomena ought to be investigated and recorded by persons and societies interested in natural knowledge."

When Eusapia Palladino was exposed in fraud in the following year at Cambridge, Sir Oliver Lodge, who attended two of the sittings there, had no hesitation in maintaining his former opinion, declaring that he failed to see any resemblance between the Cambridge phenomena and those observed on the Ile Roubaud.

In the field of mental phenomena, Mrs. Leonore **Piper** was his chief source of enlightenment. His first investigations with Mrs. Piper took place in 1889 when the medium was tested in England by the Society for Psychical Research. He received many evidential messages which soon convinced him that the dead still live. His first report was published in 1890. Nineteen years later, in discussing the evidence for the return through the mediumship of Mrs. Piper of F. W. H. Myers, Edmund Gurney and many others, he referred to his first experiences in the following words: "The old series of sittings with Mrs. Piper convinced me of survival for reasons which I should find it hard to formulate in any strict fashion, but that was their distinct effect. They also made me suspect—or more than suspect—that surviving intelligences were in some cases consciously communicating—yes, in some few cases consciously; though more usually the messages came, in all probability, from an unconscious stratum, being received by the medium in an inspirational manner analogous to psychometry. The hypothesis of surviving intelligence and personality—not only surviving but anxious and able with difficulty to communicate—is the simplest and most straightforward and the only one that fits all the facts." (from *The Survival of Man,* 1909)

It was a year earlier in 1908, that for the first time he came into the open with the statement that he believed he had held genuine converse with old friends and that at last the boundary wall between the two worlds was wearing thin in places. Five years later, speaking from the Presidential Chair to the British Association in September 1913, he boldly declared that his own investigations had convinced him that "memory and affection are not limited to that association with matter by which alone they can manifest themselves here and now, and that personality persists beyond bodily death."

The widest publicity to his belief in survival was given by his famous book, *Raymond, or Life and Death* (1916). The story of the return of his son, who died in action in World War I, is one of the best-attested cases of spirit identity. It begins with the celebrated "Faunus" message, delivered through Mrs. Piper on August 8, 1915. It purported to come from the spirit of Dr. Richard **Hodgson** and began abruptly as follows: "Now, Lodge, while we are not here as of old, i.e., not quite, we are here enough to give and take messages. Myers says you take the part of the poet, and he will act as Faunus. Faunus. Myers. Protect: he will U.D. (understand). What have you to say Lodge? Good work as Verrall, she will also U.D. Arthur says so."

The message reached Sir Oliver Lodge in early September 1915. On September 17, the War Office notified him that Raymond was killed in action on September 14. Before this blow fell, Sir Oliver Lodge wrote to Mrs. A. W. **Verrall,** a well-known classical scholar and asked her: "Does the poet and Faunus mean anything to you? Did one protect the other?" She replied at once that "the reference is to Horace's account of his narrow escape from death, from a falling tree, which he ascribes to the intervention of Faunus." The Rev. M. A. Bayfield attached to the incident the following interpretation: "Horace does not, in any reference to his escape, say clearly whether the tree struck him, but I have always thought it did. He says Faunus lightened the blow; he does not say 'turned it aside.' As bearing on your terrible loss, the meaning seems to be that the blow would fall, but would not crush; it would be 'lightened' by the assurance, conveyed afresh to you by a special message from the still living Myers, that your boy still lives."

On September 25, Lady Lodge had a sitting with the medium Mrs. Gladys Osborne **Leonard.** Raymond communicated and sent this message: "Tell Father I have met some friends of his." On asking for names, Myers was mentioned. Another medium, Alfred Vout **Peters,** two days later spoke about a photograph of a group of officers with Raymond among them. Various other messages came from different mediums, also **cross-correspondence** on the Faunus message.

On November 25, Mrs. Cheves, a complete stranger, wrote a letter saying that she had a photograph of the officers of the South Lancashire Regiment of which Raymond Lodge was a second lieutenant and offered to send it. On December 3, Mrs. Leonard, in a seance, gave a complete description of the photograph. Raymond was described as sitting on the ground, an officer placing his hand on his shoulder. On December 7, the photograph had arrived and corresponded with the description in every detail.

Many other messages, bearing the authentic stamp of Raymond's identity, were obtained. The most curious was one about "Mr. Jackson." "Feda," Mrs. Leonard's **control,** said that Raymond mixed it up with a bird and a pedestal. The truth of the matter was that Jackson was a

peacock which, after its death, was stuffed and put on a pedestal.

Sir Oliver Lodge displayed the whole mass of evidential communications in his book *Raymond,* without cutting out a reference to cigars and whisky and soda in the after-life. Owing to this, the book was ridiculed by many, although there is nothing intrinsically absurd in the idea that dead spirits continue to furnish the after-life with familiar associations of everyday physical life. It was also said that Sir Oliver Lodge was led into Spiritualism by his bereavement. This is, however, repudiated in the book itself. "My conclusion," the author wrote, "has been gradually forming itself for years, though, undoubtedly, it is based on experience of the same sort of thing. But this event has strengthened and liberated my testimony. It can now be associated with a private experience of my own, instead of with the private experience of others."

The book *Raymond* was followed by other important publications on psychical research in which Sir Oliver Lodge elaborated his previous conclusions.

Before the Modern Churchmen's Conference in September 1931, in Oxford, Sir Oliver Lodge declared: "If I find myself an opportunity of communicating I shall try to establish my identity by detailing a perfectly preposterous and absurdly childish peculiarity which I have already taken the trouble to record with some care in a sealed document deposited in the custody of the English S.P.R. I hope to remember the details of this document and relate them in no unmistakable fashion. The value of the communication will not consist in the substance of what is communicated, but in the fact that I have never mentioned it to a living soul, and no one has any idea what it contains. People of sense will not take its absurd triviality as anything but helpful in contributing to the proof of the survival of personal identity."

He reiterated this viewpoint two years later in his book *My Philosophy* and stated with simple directness and assurance: "Basing my conclusions on experience I am absolutely convinced not only of survival but of demonstrated survival, demonstrated by occasional interaction with matter in such a way as to produce physical results." Sir Oliver Lodge died August 22, 1940 at Amersham, Wiltshire, England.

The post-mortal identity test of survival involved the depositing of a set of envelopes with the Society for Psychical Research and the London Spiritualist Alliance, with instructions for consecutive opening of the envelopes. These instructions were somewhat complex and owing to the war years following his death could not be applied. Therefore the test has not so far led to the evidence of survival hoped for (see *Journal* of the S.P.R., vol. 38, pp. 121–134). (See also **Spiritualism**)

Recommended reading:

Books by Sir Oliver Lodge included: *Man and the Universe* (1908), *Survival of Man* (1909), *Reason and Belief* (1910), *Life and Matter* (1912), *Modern Problems* (1912), *Science and Religion* (1914), *The War and After* (1915), *Raymond, or Life and Death* (1917), *Christopher* (1918), *Raymond Revised* (1922), *The Making of Man* (1924), *Ether and Reality* (1925), *Relativity* (1926), *Evolution and Creation* (1926), *Science and Human Progress* (1927), *Modern Scientific Ideas* (1927), *The Natural History of a Savant* (trans. from Charles Richet) (1927), *Why I Believe in Personal Immortality*

(1928), *Phantom Walls* (1929), *Beyond Physics* (1930), *The Reality of a Spiritual World* (1930), *Conviction of Survival* (1930), *Past Years* (1932), *My Philosophy* (1933)

Loehr, Franklin (Davison) (1912–   )

Clergyman and parapsychologist. Born November 19, 1912, at Oskaloosa, Iowa, he studied at Monmouth College, Illinois (B.A.) and Theological Seminary, Chicago, Illinois (B.D., Presbyterian). He was a pastor in various churches and a chaplain in the U.S. Army Air Force. In 1958 he married Grace Wittenberger.

From 1952 onwards he was director of research, Religious Research Foundation, Los Angeles, California. He is a member of the Central Ministerial Association of Los Angeles, Los Angeles Association of Congregational-Christian Churches and Ministers, Southern California Academy of Sciences.

The Rev. Mr. Loehr conducted research on the power of prayer, mediumship and paraphysics. His wife, Grace Wittenberger, is a medium, and her "life readings" have been investigated under the auspices of the Religious Research Foundation. These readings are concerned with claimed former incarnations of individuals, throwing light on their present-day personality.

Mr. Loehr's book *The Power of Prayer on Plants* (1959) describes a three-year laboratory study. Mr. Loehr has also lectured at the Second British Conference on Science and Religion (1959) and contributed articles to *Parade* and *Fortnight* magazines, as well as reporting in *Religious Research* (Journal of the Religious Research Foundation).

Logan, Daniel (1936–   )

Modern American psychic. Born as Daniel Olaschinez April 24, 1936 in Flushing, N.Y., he changed his name when he planned to be an actor. However, he achieved fame as a professional psychic as well as a writer and lecturer on psychic subjects.

His first public appearance as a psychic was on David Susskind's television show, later appearing in an hour-long television special. He successfully forecast the prolonging of the Vietnam war into the 1970s, the race riots of 1967, and named the Academy Award winners for 1966, 1967 and 1968 weeks in advance.

His insights are verbal rather than visual and he sometimes makes predictions before he is aware of what he is saying. His publications include: *Do You Have ESP?* (1970), *Your Eastern Star* (1972), *America Bewitched; the Rise of Black Magic and Spiritism* (1973), *Vibrations* (1976), and two off-Broadway musical revues. He has also published an autobiography *The Reluctant Prophet* (Doubleday, 1968).

Logos

"Fohat" is the term very commonly used in **Theosophy** to designate the Deity. Along with the great religions, Theosophy has as the beginning of its scheme a Deity who is altogether beyond human knowledge or conception, whether in the ordinary or the clairvoyant states. But when the Deity manifests to man through his works of creation, He is known as the Logos.

Essentially He is infinite, but when He encloses a "ring-pass-not" within which to build a cosmos, He has set limits to Himself, and what we can know of Him is contained in these limits.

He appears in a triple aspect like the Christian Trinity but this is, of course, merely an appearance, and in reality He is a unity. This triple aspect shows Him as Will, Wisdom and Activity, and from each of these came forth one of the creative life waves which formed the universe. From the third, came the wave which created matter, from the second, the wave which aggregated diffuse matter into form, and from the first, the wave which brought with it the **Monad,** that scintillation of Himself which took possession of formed matter, to start thereby the evolutionary process. (See also **Evolution; Life Waves; Monad; Sphere; Theosophy**)

Loka

In Hindu religion, a term for a world or division of the universe. For general purposes, there are three *lokas:* heaven, earth and hell, but different philosophical schools have enumerated seven or even eight *lokas.* The seven lokas are: *Bhur-loka* (earth), *Bhuvar-loka* (space between earth and the sun, inhabited by semi-divine beings), *Swar-loka* (region between the sun and polar star, the heaven of the god Indra), *Mahar-loka* (the abode of great sages and saints), *Jana-loka* (abode of the sons of the god Brahma), *Tapar-loka* (abode of other deities), *Satya-loka* or *Brahma-loka* (abode of Brahma, where souls are released from the necessity of rebirth).

In Buddhism, there are three world or world systems named *lokas.* These are: *kamaloka* (world of desire), *rupaloka* (world of matter or form), *arupaloka* (world without form). These terms are used by the Theosophical Society. (See also **Lokaloka**)

Loka (Journal)

Annual publication of Naropa Institute, concerned with Buddhism and its meditation techniques. Address: Vajradhatu Books, 78 Fifth Avenue, New York, N.Y. 10011.

Lokaloka

A fabulous region of Hindu mythology—"world and no world." It was said to be a chain of mountains at the edge of the seven seas, dividing the visible world from the regions of darkness. (See also **Loka**)

Lombroso, Cesare (1836–1909)

Famous Italian psychiatrist, criminal anthropologist and psychical investigator, who became convinced of **survival** and in communication with the dead.

Born November 18, 1836 at Verona, he studied at Padua, Vienna and Paris. In 1862, he became professor of psychiatry at Pavia. He was later director of the lunatic asylum at Pesaro, then professor of forensic medicine and psychiatry at Turin, where he later had the chair of criminal anthropology.

In 1872, he discovered that the disease known as *pellagra* in Italy was due to a poison in diseased maize eaten by the peasants. He had established a great reputation for his researches on madness and genius before turning his attention to psychical research.

In July 1888, he wrote an article in the *Fanfulla della Domenica* on the "Influence of Civilization and Opportunity of Genius," which he concluded: "Who knows whether I and my friends who laugh at spiritism are not in error, since, just like hypnotised persons, thanks to the dislike of novelties which lurks in all of us, we are unable to perceive that we are in error, and just like many lunatics, being in the dark as regards the truth, we laugh at those who are not in the same condition."

After reading this article, Cavaliere Ercole **Chiaia** of Naples addressed an open letter to Prof. Lombroso and invited him to sittings with the medium Eusapia **Palladino** in Naples. In March 1891, Lombroso accepted the invitation and in company with Professors Tamburini, Bianchi and Violi and Drs. Ascenzi, Prenta, Limoncelli, Gigli and Ciolfi, witnessed the phenomena of an extraordinary medium. In a letter to Dr. Ciolfi, the reporter of the sittings, Lombroso openly declared: "I am ashamed and grieved at having opposed with so much tenacity the possibility of the so-called spiritistic facts; I say the facts because I am still opposed to the theory. But the facts exist, and I boast of being a slave to facts."

This admission caused a great sensation in Italy. As a direct consequence, a memorable series of sittings was held in October 1892, at Milan, in Dr. Finzi's house with the same medium. The reality of the facts was completely confirmed. Lombroso pursued his researches with assiduity. He carried out important experiments in thought-transmission, and from 1896, in a special section in the *Archivio di Psichiatria,* wrote many articles on the phenomena of mediumship. His investigation of a haunted house in Turin is of special interest (see **Poltergeist**).

In 1900, Lombroso wrote to Prof. M. T. **Falcomer:** "I am like a little pebble on the beach. As yet I am uncovered; but I feel that each tide draws me a little closer to the sea."

In 1901 and 1902, Lombroso participated at further sittings with Eusapia Palladino in Genoa and in 1907 in Turin. He progressively came nearer to the spirit hypothesis and finally ended in openly accepting it. Against the clamour of his friends and their protest that he would ruin an honorable reputation, he published his findings in a memorable book entitled *After Death—What?* (1909).

The book is richly illustrated and presents a very lucid and sincere account of the phenomena of mediumship. Lombroso's chief credit was his fearless confession to the truth of his strange observations at a period when, despite the courage of Sir William **Crookes,** Dr. Alfred Russel **Wallace** and Prof. J. C. F. **Zöllner,** the physical phenomena of Spiritualism were held in utter disdain. Following Lombroso's open declaration, a group of scientists resolved to put aside prejudice and investigate in a serious frame of mind.

Some of Lombroso's other books translated into English include: *The Man of Genius* (1891), *The Female Offender* (1895), *Criminal Anthropology* (1895), *Crime; Its Causes & Remedies* (1911), *Criminal Man* (1911). He died suddenly at Turin on October 19, 1909.

London Dialectical Society

An important nineteenth-century British investigation of the phenomena of Spiritualism. The London Dialectical Society established in 1867 was a highly regarded association of professional individuals. A resolution was carried January 26, 1869 "to investigate the phenomena

alleged to be Spiritual Manifestations, and to report thereon." A committee was appointed on which thirty-three members acted: H. G. Atkinson, G. Wheatley Bennett, J. S. Bergheim, Charles Bradlaugh, G. Fenton Cameron, George Cary, E. W. Cox, Rev. C. Maurice Davies, D. H. Dyte, Mrs. D. H. Dyte, James Edmunds, Mrs. James Edmunds, James Gannon, Grattan Geary, William B. Gower, Robert Hannah, Jenner Gale Hillier, Mrs. J. G. Hillier, Henry Jeffery, H. D. Jencken, Albert Kisch, J. H. Levy, Joseph Maurice, Isaac L. Meyers, B. M. Moss, Robert Quelch, Thomas Reed, G. Russel Roberts, W. H. Sweepstone, William Volckman, Alfred Russel Wallace, Josiah Webber and Horace S. Yeomans.

The cooperation of Prof. Huxley and George Henry Lewes was invited but both refused, Huxley stating "supposing the phenomena to be genuine, they do not interest me."

The report with evidence was presented to the Council of the London Dialectical Society on July 20, 1870. It was accepted but since it appeared to favor Spiritualist phenomena it was not published by the Society. However, the Committee felt that it was in the public interest to be published and it was accordingly privately printed in 1871.

The principal work was done in six sub-committees. The general Committee, in fifteen meetings, received oral evidence of personal spiritual (i.e., psychic) experience from thirty-three written statements from thirty-one persons and stated that the report of the sub-committees "substantially corroborate each other, and would appear to establish the following propositions:

"1. That sounds of a very varied character, apparently proceeding from articles of furniture, the floor and wall of the room—the vibrations accompanying which sound are often distinctly perceptible to the touch—occur without being produced by muscular action or mechanical contrivance.

"2. That movements of heavy bodies take place without mechanical contrivance of any kind or adequate exertion of muscular force by the persons present, and frequently without contact or connection with any person.

"3. That these sounds and movements often occur at the times and in the manner asked for by persons present, and by means of a simple code of signals, answer questions and spell out coherent communications.

"4. That the answers and communications thus obtained are, for the most part, of a commonplace character; but the facts are sometimes correctly given which are only known to one of the persons present.

"5. That the circumstances under which the phenomena occur are variable, the most prominent fact being that the presence of certain persons seems necessary to their occurrence and that of others generally adverse; but this difference does not appear to depend upon any belief or disbelief concerning the phenomena.

"6. That, nevertheless, the occurrence of the phenomena is not insured by the presence or absence of such persons respectively."

The evidence was summarized in the report as follows:

"1. Thirteen witnesses state that they have seen heavy bodies—in some instances men—rise slowly in the air and remain there for some time without visible or tangible support.

"2. Fourteen witnesses testify to having seen hands or figures, not appertaining to any human being, but life-like in appearance and mobility, which they have sometimes touched or even grasped, and which they are therefore convinced were not the result of imposture or illusion.

"3. Five witnesses state that they have been touched, by some invisible agency, on various parts of the body, and often where requested, when the hands of all present were visible.

"4. Thirteen witnesses declare that they have heard musical pieces well played upon instruments not manipulated by an ascertainable agency.

"5. Five witnesses state that they have seen red-hot coals applied to the hands or heads of several persons without producing pain or scorching; and three witnesses state that they have had the same experiment made upon themselves with the like immunity.

"6. Eight witnesses state that they have received precise information through rappings, writings, and in other ways, the accuracy of which was unknown at the time to themselves or to any persons present, and which, on subsequent inquiry was found to be correct.

"7. One witness declares that he has received a precise and detailed statement which, nevertheless, proved to be entirely erroneous.

"8. Three witnesses state that they have been present when drawings, both in pencil and colours, were produced in so short a time, and under such conditions as to render human agency impossible.

"9. Six witnesses declare that they have received information of future events and that in some cases the hour and minute of their occurrence have been accurately foretold, days and even weeks before.

"In addition to the above evidence has been given of trance speaking, of healing, of automatic writing, of the introduction of flowers and fruits into closed rooms, of voices in the air, of visions in crystals and glasses, and of the elongation of the human body.

"In presenting their report your Committee, taking into consideration the high character and great intelligence of many of the witnesses to the more extraordinary facts, the extent to which their testimony is supported by the reports of the sub-committees, and the absence of any proof of imposture or delusion as regards a large portion of the phenomena; and further, having regard to the exceptional character of the phenomena, the large number of persons in every grade of society and over the whole civilised world who are more or less influenced by a belief in their super-natural origin, and to the fact that no philosophical explanation of them has yet been arrived at, deem it incumbent upon them to state their conviction that the subject is worthy of more serious attention and careful investigation than it has hitherto received."

Of the sub-committees, two reported failure to obtain phenomena, one investigated with the medium D. D. **Home** with very feeble results, three witnessed strong physical manifestations without contact and intelligence behind the operations. Dissenting opinion to the report was registered by Dr. James Edmunds, the Chairman of the General Committee and by three other members: Henry Jeffrey, Grattan Geary and H. G. Atkinson.

According to a statement of Dr. Alfred Russel **Wallace** in *On Miracles and Modern Spiritualism* (1875), of the thirty-three acting members of the committee, only eight were, at the commencement, believers in the phenomena, while not more than four accepted the spiritual theory. During the course of the inquiry at least twelve of the complete skeptics became convinced of the reality of many of the physical phenomena through attending the experimental sub-committees, and almost wholly by means of the mediumship of members of the committee. At least three of the previous skeptics later became thorough Spiritualists. The degree of conviction was approximately proportionate to the amount of time and care bestowed on the investigation.

Among those who gave evidence or read papers before the committee were: Dr. Alfred Russel **Wallace,** Mrs. Emma Hardinge (**Britten**), H. D. Jencken, Benjamin Coleman (later a member of the **British National Association of Spiritualists**), Cromwell F. **Varley,** D. D. **Home** and the Master of **Lindsay.** Correspondence was received from Lord **Lytton,** Robert **Chambers,** Dr. Garth Wilkinson, William **Howitt,** Camille **Flammarion** and others.

For the opposition, very little evidence was brought in. Lord Lytton believed in material influences of whose nature we are ignorant, Dr. Carpenter in unconscious cerebration, Dr. Kidd in the Devil.

The reception of the report in the Press was largely hostile. According to *The Times,* it was "nothing more than a farrago of impotent conclusions, garnished by a mass of the most monstrous rubbish it has ever been our misfortune to sit in judgment upon."

The *Morning Post* considered it entirely worthless. The *Saturday Review* was disappointed that it did not discredit a little further "one of the most unequivocally degrading superstitions that has ever found currency among reasonable beings." The *Standard* took a more open-minded view. The *Daily News* stated that "it may be regarded as an important contribution to a subject which someday or other, by the very number of its followers will demand more extended investigation." The *Spectator* agreed with the conclusion of the report that the phenomena justified further cautious investigation.

Although the report only embraced the phenomenal aspect of Spiritualism and left the question of survival outside its pale, it had a far-reaching influence in turning the attention of qualified investigators to the subject. Even the arch skeptic, Frank **Podmore,** admitted so much in his book *Modern Spiritualism* (2 vols., 1902): "The work done by the Dialectical Society was, no doubt, of value, since it has brought together and preserved for us a large number of records of personal experience by representative Spiritualists. For those who wish to ascertain what Spiritualists believed at this time, and what phenomena were alleged to occur, the book may be of service. But, except in the Minority Report by Dr. Edmunds, there is no trace of any critical handling of the materials, and the conclusions of the committee can carry little weight."

Originally published by Longmans, Green, Reader & Dyer, London, 1871, the *Report* was reissued in a cheap edition, by J. Burns, London, 1873. It was recently reprinted by Arno Press, New York, 1976.

London Spiritualist Alliance

Organized from the **British National Association of Spiritualists** in 1884, incorporated under the Companies

Act in 1896. The first president was the Rev. Stainton **Moses.** Many other famous names were associated with the Alliance over the years. In the 1930s, Sir Arthur Conan **Doyle** was president.

The Alliance accepted and investigated psychic phenomena, not as a new religion, but the basis of all religions. Its aims were: "To seek, collect, and obtain information respecting, and generally to investigate the phenomena commonly known as psychical or as spiritualistic, including hypnotism, somnambulism, thought-transference, second-sight, and all matters of a kindred nature. To aid students and enquirers in their researches." Visitors from abroad were welcomed. The library was one of the finest of its kind. Consultations with psychic mediums were arranged. The Alliance published the important newspaper *Light.*

In 1955, the Alliance was renamed the "**College of Psychic Science**" (not to be confused with the **British College of Psychic Science,** which flourished from 1920–47).

In 1970, the C.P.S. was renamed the "College of Psychic Studies." In its present form, the College continues valuable work in the study of psychic and spiritual exploration after a century of existence. It arranges lectures, study groups and conferences and arranges consultations with reputable psychics. It continues to maintain a large and comprehensive library and to publish *Light,* now a quarterly journal. Address: 16 Queensberry Place, London, SW7 2EB England.

Long, Max Freedom (1890–   )

Pioneer researcher into the mystery of **Huna** magic, the secret techniques of Kahunas or Polynesian priest sorcerers. Mr. Long spent time in Hawaii from around 1918 onwards, where he discussed Huna magic with Dr. William Tufts Brigham, then curator of the Bishop Museum in Honolulu. Dr. Brigham had studied the miraculous feats of the Kahunas, including paranormal healing, weather control and fire-walking over red-hot lava.

After the death of Dr. Brigham, Long continued to study kahuna magic, but was unable to discover the secret before leaving Hawaii in 1921. Three years later it occurred to him that the secret might be indicated by the terms used for various aspects of Huna in the Polynesian language. After prolonged study, he believed he had discovered the secret, which he made the subject of experiment with his associates and discussed in his various books. He established **Huna Research Association,** an organization for further research, the aims of which are now continued by the Order of **Huna International.** Long believed that his concept of Huna magic was a key to understanding of occult and mystical systems in other countries.

Recommended reading:

Long, Max Freedom. *Recovering the Ancient Magic,* London, 1936

Long, Max Freedom. *The Secret Science Behind Miracles,* Kosmon Press, 1948; Huna Research Publications, 1954.

Long, Max Freedom. *The Secret Science at Work,* Huna Research Publications, 1953

Long, Max Freedom. *Growing Into Light,* Huna Research Publications, 1955

Lopato, David (1911–   )

South African accountant, medium and spiritual healer. Born October 13, 1911, he studied at University of Witwatersrand, Johannesburg, South Africa. From 1934 onwards he has been in practice as a chartered accountant and auditor. He was also chairman of the Society for Psychic Advancement, Johannesburg from 1945–60 and president from 1961 onwards.

He worked as a healing medium in conjunction with physicians, treating patients who had failed to respond to orthodox treatment. He also lectured on parapsychology.

Lopukhin, I. V. (1756–1816)

Russian lawyer and politician with special interests in mysticism and Freemasonry, who published anonymously a work titled *Characteristics of the Interior Church.* This tract was first published in Russian in 1798. It was translated into English in 1912, from a French edition by D. H. S. Nicholson and occultist Arthur E. **Waite.** Lopukhin's teaching was similar to that of Karl von **Eckhartshausen.** It is a kind of Christian transcendentalism and resembles the higher literature of the **Grail.**

Loquifer, Battle of

A tale incorporated in the Charlemagne saga, supposed to have been written about the twelfth century. Its hero is Renouart, the giant brother-in-law of William of Orange, and the events take place on the sea. Renouart and his barons are on the shore at Porpaillart, when a Saracen fleet is seen. He is persuaded to enter one of the ships, which immediately set sail, and he is told by Isembert, a hideous monster, that the Saracens mean to flay him alive.

Renouart, armed only with a huge bar of wood, kills this creature, and makes the Saracens let him go, while they return to their own country. It is arranged that Renouart will fight one Loquifer, a fairy giant and leader of the Saracens, and on the issue of this combat the war will depend.

They meet on an island near Porpaillart. Loquifer is in possession of a magical balm, which heals all his wounds immediately, and is concealed in his club, but Renouart, who is assisted by angels, at length succeeds in depriving Loquifer of his club, so that his strength departs. Renouart slays him, and the devil carries off his soul.

The romance goes on to tell of a duel between William of Orange and Desrame, Renouart's father, in which the latter is slain. Renouart is comforted by fairies, who bear him to Avalon where he has many adventures. He is finally wrecked, but is rescued by mermaids, and awakes to find himself on the sands at Porpaillart, from which spot he had been taken to **Avalon.**

Lord, Jenny (c. 1854)

Nineteenth-century American physical medium of Maine, New England. She later became Mrs. J. L. Webb. She produced remarkable musical phenomena, either by herself or with her sister Annie, who was also mediumistic.

In her book *Modern American Spiritualism* (1870), Emma Hardinge (Britten) stated: "These young ladies, both very slight, fragile persons, suffering under the most pitiable conditions of ill-health, and in their normal state unable to play upon any instrument, became mediums for various phases of 'the power' requiring the most astounding physical force in execution, in addition to which, spirits, in their presence and in darkened rooms, would play upon a double bass violon cello, guitar, drums, accordion, tambourine, bells, and various small instruments, with the most astonishing skill and power. Sometimes the instruments would be played on singly, at others all together, and not infrequently the strange concert would conclude by placing the young medium, seated in her invalid chair, silently and in a single instant in the center of the table, piling up all the instruments around her, and then calling for a light to exhibit their ponderous feats of strength and noiseless agility to the eyes of the astonished circle. The sisters rarely sat together, and though it would be impossible to conceive of any persons more incapable of giving off *physical power* than these two fragile and afflicted girls, yet their manifestations with one alone acting as medium, have surpassed, in feats of vast strength and musical achievements, any that are recorded in the annals of Spiritualism."

In his book *The Scientific Basis of Spiritualism* (1882), Epes Sargent described similar amazing seances with Jenny Lord, and introduced the Scottish writer Robert **Chambers** to her phenomena on a visit to America. Sargent expressed absolute conviction of the genuineness of the phenomena of Jenny Lord.

Lord, Mrs. Maud E. (1852–1924)

(Mrs. Maud Lord-Drake). American **direct voice** medium. She was born March 15, 1852 in Marion County, West Virginia, with a double veil or **caul** over her face. Her father was a Baptist deacon, her mother a Methodist.

She appeared before the **Seybert Commission** in 1885. Nothing more than hoarse whispers were heard and these were never simultaneous with the speech of the medium. Touches were felt here and there. The committee did not find the phenomena convincing. However, Sir Arthur Conan **Doyle** believed that the members of the commission were prejudiced against Spiritualist phenomena.

Usually Mrs. Maud Lord sat in the middle of her circle and clapped her hands in the darkness to prove that she did not change position while the voices spoke from different parts of the room. Her favorite **control** was an Indian child, "Snowdrop." She manifested remarkable phenomena for sixty-five years, including full-form **materializations** in daylight, independent music from a levitated guitar, independent voices and singing, **clairvoyance, clairaudience** and **psychometry.** She was invited to Buckingham Palace, England, where she gave two readings to Queen Victoria. Her autobiography: *Psychic Light: The Continuity of Law and Life* (1904), published under her married name, gives a good impression of her mediumistic work.

Lords of the Flame (or Children of the Fire Mist)

According to Theosophists, there were adepts sent from the planet Venus to aid terrestrial evolution. It is necessary to explain that, in the evolution of the **Solar System,** Venus was said to be considerably in advance of the Earth, but by the efforts of these adepts directed towards intellectual development, the inhabitants of the earth now became really further advanced than to be expected in ordinary course of events. These adepts are not permanent inhabitants of the Earth, and, while a few yet remain, most of them have returned whence they came, the time of crisis at which they assisted having now passed. (See also **Evolution; Chains; Theosophy**)

Lost Word of Kabalism (in Freemasonry)

Also known as the Lost Word in Masonry. A word relating to some mystic plan, which, although it is held to have disappeared, will at some time be restored, and will then make the whole system plain. It is not really lost, only withheld for a season. In the same way the **Grail** was not lost, but withdrawn to its own place and the search for it occupied the noblest figures in chivalry. It represented the Key to the enigma of Creation, or, in terms of Christianity, the Kingdom of Heaven.

In his *New Encyclopedia of Freemasonry* (1921), occultist and mystic Arthur E. **Waite** associated the Lost Word with the virtues of faith, hope and charity, stating: "The quest of the Lost Word is followed in one of the High Degrees within a spiritual area which is delineated by these Pillars [Wisdom, Strength and Beauty], and that which is hidden within them, leading to the term of quest, is symbolical of these virtues, connoting their inward and sacramental sense."

Lou (1898–1968)

Name assumed by a Dutch fisherman Louwrens van Voorthuizen (or Voorthuyzen), who claimed to experience the annihilation of his human self and the taking over by a divine self, as a kind of Christian avatar.

Born in 1898 at Anna Paulowna, N.H., Netherlands, Lou did not begin to preach in public until 1950, when he commenced his testimony with the words: "I preach Jesus Christ bodily, his resuscitated body, with his new name, which is Lou. Those who accept this shall experience it and those who have experienced, shall be as Jesus Christ was on earth. Brothers and sisters of Jesus, sons and daughters of God."

A mimeographed magazine was published in English by the Lou-group from 1963 onwards in Amsterdam, Holland.

In his later years, Lou declared himself to be God and Creator of the universe, and as such, immortal. However, he died in 1968. His death created a crisis amongst his followers, and the sect has now dispersed.

Loudun, Nuns of

In the year 1633, the convent of Ursulines established at Loudun in France was the scene of an outbreak of diabolical possession. The numerous nuns who inhabited the convent showed signs of diabolic possession, spoke with **tongues,** and behaved in the most extraordinary and hysterical manner. The affair grew in volume until practically all the nuns belonging to the institution were in the same condition of temporary insanity.

The Mother Superior of the convent, Jeanne de Belfiel, appears to have been of hysterical temperament, and she was not long in infecting the other inmates of the institution. She, with a sister named Claire and five other nuns, were the first to be obsessed by the so-called evil spirits. The outbreak spread to the neighboring town and so scandalous did the whole affair become that Cardinal

Richelieu appointed a commission to examine into it. The devils were subjected to the process of **exorcism,** which, however, proved to be fruitless in this instance, and the attacks of the nuns continued. But on a more imposing ceremony being held, they took themselves off, but only for a little while, returning again with greater violence than ever.

Suspicion, fixed upon the person of Urbain **Grandier,** confessor of the convent, as the head and source of the whole affair. He was arrested and accused of giving over the nuns to the possession of the Devil by means of the practice of sorcery.

The truth seems to have been that the neighboring clergy were madly jealous of Grandier because he had obtained two benefices in their diocese, of which he was not a native, and they had made up their minds to compass his destruction at the first possible moment. Despite his protests of innocence, the unfortunate priest was haled before a council of judges of the neighboring presidencies, who found upon his body the various marks which were said to be the undoubted signs of a sorcerer, and the inquest also brought to light the fact that Grandier had none too good a reputation.

However, the sources regarding this are undoubtedly tainted by religious prejudice. It was said that on his papers being seized, much matter subversive of religious practice was found amongst them. The authorities failed, however, to find that pact with Satan for which they had looked, although afterwards several versions of it were published by more or less credulous persons and sold as broadsheets.

The unfortunate man was condemned to be burnt at the stake, a sentence which was duly carried out in 1634. Prior to his execution, Grandier had been so severely tortured that the marrow of his bones oozed through his broken limbs, but he had persistently maintained his innocence.

After his death the possession of the hysterical sisters did not cease. The demons became more obstreperous than ever and flippantly answered to their names of Asmodeus, Leviathan, and Behemoth, and so forth. A very holy Brother called Surin was delegated to put an end to the affair. Frail and unhealthy, he possessed, however, an indomitable spirit, and after much wrestling in prayer succeeded in finally exorcising the demons.

The whole affair is set forth in the *Historie des Diables de Loudun,* published in 1839, which gave a detailed account of one of the most extraordinary obsessions of the time. For a good account in English, see *The Devils of Loudun* by novelist Aldous Huxley (London, 1952). A somewhat sensational movie, based loosely on this book, was produced in 1971 under the title "The Devils," directed by Ken Russell. (See also **Exorcism;** Louis **Gaufridi;** Urbain **Grandier;** Nuns of **Louviers; Obsession and Possession**)

Lourdes

French watering resort, famous for miracle cures, attributed to the Virgin Mary who, in 1858, appeared in a grotto to the peasant girl Bernadette Soubirous (1844-1879), canonized as St. Bernadette in 1933. The following inscription on a marble tablet records the apparition:

Dates of the Eighteen apparitions

and words of the Blessed Virgin
in the year of grace 1858.
In the hollow of the rock where her statue is now seen the Blessed Virgin appeared to Bernadette Soubirous Eighteen times.
the 11*th and the* 14*th of February;*
Each day, with two exceptions, from February 18*th till*
March 25*th, April* 7*th, July* 16*th.*
The Blessed Virgin said to the child on February 18*th,*
"Will you do me the favour of coming here daily for a fortnight?
I do not promise to make you happy
In this world, but in the next;
I want many people to come.
The Virgin said to her during the fortnight:
" You will pray for sinners; you will kiss the earth for sinners.
Penitence! penitence! penitence!
Go, and tell the priests to cause a chapel to be built;
I want people to come thither in procession.
Go and drink of the fountain and wash yourself in it
Go and eat of the grass which is there."
On March 25*th The Virgin said:*
" I Am the Immaculate Conception."

The apparition was seen by Bernadette alone. There was no coinciding objective event which would make it veridical. There was, however, a later incident of a supernormal character in the life of Bernadette for which evidence is available in the testimony of Dr. Dozous, to whose advocacy the credence bestowed on Bernadette and the fame of Lourdes is mainly due. It was quoted in Dr. Boisserie's book *Lourdes,* which gives a summary of the miraculous cures, published in the *Annales des Lourdes* from 1868 until 1891. While praying in ecstasy, the girl held her interlaced fingers over the flame of a lighted taper. The point of the flame came out between the fingers without causing her any harm.

In the story of the apparition, there was no promise of miraculous cures. Bernadette was an invalid child subject to fits, and nobody would have paid attention to her visions but for the grotto in the rocks to which she was conducted by the white angel, and the water of which made her feel lighter and stronger.

A quarryman of the name of Bourriette was the first to conceive the idea that the water of the spring in the grotto uncovered by Bernadette's bare hands, might benefit his eyes, which had been injured by an explosion. He was healed and the rumor soon spread that the Virgin Mary was effecting miraculous cures.

In *Proceedings* of the Society for Psychical Research (vol. 9, part 24, 1893) a long analysis was published of these miracles by A. T. Myers, M.D., and F. W. H. Myers under the title 'Mind-Cure, Faith-Cure, and the Miracles of Lourdes.' The conclusions were: "Many forms of psycho-therapeutics produce, by obscure but natural agencies, for which at present we have no better terms than suggestion and self-suggestion, effects to which no definite limit can yet be assigned. Thus far Lourdes offers the best list of cures; but this superiority is not more than can be explained by the greater number of patients treated there than elsewhere, and their greater confidence in the treatment. There is no real evidence, either that the apparition of the Virgin was itself more than a subjective hallucination, or that it has any more than a merely subjective connection with the cures."

The Catholic Church was also cautious in assessing

claimed cures at Lourdes, and a Medical Bureau was established, reorganized in 1947. Strict criteria are established for claimed cures. In the first place, the sick are expected to bring with them a diagnosis from their own doctors and are given an examination upon arrival in Lourdes. If a cure is claimed, the patient must return to Lourdes a year later for examination and if the cure appears permanent and inexplicable by normal explanations, the case is then put to a higher medical tribunal in Paris. Even then, it is submitted to members of an ecclesiastical tribunal before being pronounced miraculous, or, in some cases, a genuine cure but still non-miraculous.

Approximately three million pilgrims visit Lourdes each year, and some 6,000 cures have been considered genuine but not miraculous. About sixty cures are considered in the miraculous category and of these, some appear quite remarkable.

Lourdes is now one of the most famous pilgrim sites and the whole area is well organized for great annual pilgrimages. In 1876, a huge basilica was constructed above the rock, and in the case where Bernadette had her vision a marble state of the Virgin was placed. The grotto is festooned with crutches from disabled pilgrims who did not need assistance after their visit. Not all pilgrims visit the shrine expecting a cure. Thousands come on pilgrimage as an act of piety, and the grotto has a remarkable atmosphere of faith and grace. (See also **Apparitions; Fatima; Garabandhal; Healing by Faith;** Psychic **Healing**)

Recommended reading:

Estrade, J. B. *The Appearances of the Blessed Virgin Mary at the Grotto of Lourdes; Personal Souvenirs of an Eyewitness,* Art & Book Co., London, 1912

Neame, Alan. *The Happening at Lourdes,* Hodder & Stoughton, London, 1968

Trochu, Francis. *Saint Bernadette Soubirous, 1844–1879,* Longmans, London, 1957

West, Donald J. *Eleven Lourdes Miracles,* Garrett/Helix, New York, 1957

Louviers, Nuns of

The third case of demonic possession reported in seventeenth century France. The first was that involving Father Louis **Gaufridi** and Sister Madeleine de la Palud de Demandolx at Aix-en-Provence in 1611, the second the great scandal of Father Urbain **Grandier** and the nuns of **Loudun** in 1633.

The case of the Nuns of the Franciscan Tertiaries at Louviers concerned Sister Madeleine Bavent and Father Thomas Boullé and was documented by Madeleine's Bavent's own written confession, which included her earlier life story. Born in Rouen in 1620, she was apprenticed to a dressmaker. At the age of 18 she was seduced by a Franciscan Father who had also been intimate with other girls. Madeleine decided to enter the convent at Louviers. Here she found that the first chaplain, Father Pierre David, had strange heretical ideas, believing that an illuminated individual (such as himself) could not sin, and that he should worship God naked like Adam.

During three years as a novice under Father David, Madeleine was obliged to be received by him naked, although he did not have intercourse with her. Father

David was succeeded as chaplain by Father Mathurin Picard in 1628 and his assistant Father Thomas Boullé.

According to Madeleine, she became pregnant by Father Picard, who also made revolting love charms from altar wafers to secure favors from other nuns. Both priests conducted a Black Mass at midnight sabbats with Madeleine and other nuns, involving disgusting practices, as a result of which Madeleine was visited by the devil in the shape of a huge black cat.

Between 1628 and 1642, such orgies involved other nuns, who exhibited frenzied symptoms of hysterical possession by specific devils. When the scandal became public, the nuns confessed but blamed Madeleine Bavent. Exorcisms were performed, and the Bishop of Evreux investigated the convent for witchcraft. Madeleine was charged with sorcery, witchcraft and making a pact with the Devil. She confessed and was expelled from the order, being punished with perpetual imprisonment in an underground dungeon with only bread and water three days of the week. She died soon afterwards in 1647. Father Picard had died in 1642, but his corpse was exhumed and excommunicated. Father Thomas Boullé was imprisoned for three years, tortured, then burned alive in 1647. The remaining nuns of Louviers were sent away to other convents. (See also **Exorcism;** Louis **Gaufridi;** Nuns of **Loudon; Possession**)

Lovecraft, H(oward) P(hillips) (1890–1937)

Celebrated American writer of supernatural fiction. Born August 20, 1890 in Providence, Rhode Island. Both his parents suffered from insanity, and Lovecraft himself grew up as a lonely neurasthenic with a love of eighteenth-century English literature. He was also strongly influenced by the fantasy fiction of Edgar Allan Poe. He began writing stories at the age of five, and as a young man became something of an eccentric recluse. At the age of sixteen, he contributed a series of articles on astronomy to the Providence *Tribune.* A shy, imaginative and delicate individual, he was much influenced in his own stories by such fantasy authors as Algernon Blackwood, Lord Dunsany, Arthur Machen and Walter de la Mare. His own somewhat Augustan prose style and highly individual preoccupation with fantasy and horror themes remained too specialized for conventional literary outlets, and much of his work was for little magazines like *Vagrant* and *Home Brew,* or pulps like *Weird Tales, Amazing Stories* and *Astounding Stories.*

In 1924, he married Sonia Greene of New York City, also a writer, but the marriage only lasted a couple of years and he was later divorced, returning to Providence where he wrote late into the night at his stories. His most impressive creation was the **Cthulhu Mythos,** involving a group of stories about entities from other time and space. Another Lovecraft invention was the **Necronomicon;** the Book of Dead Names compiled by the "mad Arab Abdul Alhazred," a **Grimoire** or text-book of black magic for the purpose of evoking demons.

In spite of his considerable literary output, Lovecraft made very little money out of his fiction, which he supplemented by editing and ghost-writing. He died from cancer March 15, 1937.

After his death, his friend and biographer August Derleth revived and reissued his stories through Arkham

House Press, "Arkham" being a fictional city in Lovecraft's stories. It has been suggested that some of the fantasy inventions of Lovecraft may have had some real existence in some other plane of reality, contacted through his subconscious mind.

Lovecraft's main works include: *The Shadow Over Innsmouth* (1936), *The Notes & Commonplace Book Employed by the Late H. P. Lovecraft* (1938), *The Outsider & Others* (1939), *Beyond the Wall of Sleep* (1943), *The Weird Shadow Over Innsmouth & Other Stories of the Supernatural* (1944), *Marginalia* (1944), *The Best Supernatural Stories of H. P. Lovecraft* (1945), *The Dunwich Horror* (1945), *Something About Cats & Other Pieces* (1949), *Haunter of the Dark & Other Tales* (1951), *The Case of Charles Dexter Ward* (1952).

Since his death, there has been extensive interest in Lovecraft and his writings, amounting almost to a Lovecraft Mythos. Biographical studies include: *H.P.L.: A Memoir* by August Derleth (Ben Abramson, 1945), *Howard Phillips Lovecraft: Dreamer on the Night Side* by Frank Belknap Long (Arkham House, 1975), *Lovecraft: a Biography* by L. Sprague de Camp (Doubleday, 1975). (See also English Occult **Fiction**)

Lubin

The fish whose gall was used by Tobias to restore his father's sight. It was said to be very powerful against ophthalmia, and its heart potent in driving away demons. (See the book of **Tobit** in Apocrypha)

Luce E Ombra (Journal)

(Light and Shade), the principal Italian Spiritualist monthly, founded in 1900, edited by Prof. Angelo Marzorati until his death in the autumn of 1931. The title was changed from January 1932 to *La Ricerca Psichica* (Psychic Review), with a transfer of editorial offices from Rome to Milan.

Lucidity

A faculty by which paranormal knowledge may be obtained. It is a collective term for the phenomena of **clairvoyance, clairaudience, psychometry, premonitions,** etc. It was first used by experimenters describing the condition of sensitives in relation to the phenomena of **Animal Magnetism** and **Mesmerism** but was later used by French psychical researchers.

Lucifer

Literally "light-bringer," a name applied to the conception of the devil, who has often been likened to a fallen star or angel. The Miltonic conception of Lucifer as a force potent for good or evil, one who might have done good greatly, intensely proud and powerful exceedingly, is one which is inconsistent with enlightenment. He represents simply the absence of good, a negative not a positive entity.

According to the ideas of the old magicians, he was said to preside over the east (possibly an identification with the rising sun). He was invoked on Mondays in a circle in the center of which was his name. As the price of his compliance in appearing to the magician, he asked only a mouse. Other superstitions state that Lucifer commands Europeans and Asiatics. He sometimes appears in the shape of a beautiful child. When he is angry his face is flushed, but there is nothing monstrous about him. He is, according to some students of **demonology,** the grand justiciary of Hades. He is the first to be invoked by witches in the **Litanies of the Sabbat.** (See also **Demonology; Devil-Worship; Witchcraft**)

Lugh

In medieval Irish romance, son of Kian and father of Cuchulain. He was brought up by his uncle Goban, the Smith, and by Duach, King of Fairyland. It was prophesied of Lugh that he should eventually overcome his father's old enemy **Balor,** his own grandfather. So instead of killing the three murderers of his father Kian, he put them on oath to obtain certain wonders, including the magical spear of the King of Persia and the pig-skin of the King of Greece, which, if laid on a patient, would heal him of his wound or cure him of his sickness.

Thus equipped, Lugh entered the Battle of Moytura against the Fomorians, and by hurling a stone which pierced through the eye to the brain of Balor, fulfilled the Druidic prophecy.

Lugh was the Irish Sun god; his final conquest of the Fomorians and their leader symbolizes the victory of light and intellect over darkness. Balor was god of darkness, and brute force as embodied in the Fomorians. By his title of Ildanach, or "All Craftsman," Lugh is comparable to the Greek Apollo. He was widely worshipped by Continental Celts.

Lully, Raymond (or Ramon Lull)
(c. 1232–1315)

The life of this alchemist was a curious and eventful one, and all its various chapters show him to be a man of titanic physical and mental energy, quite incapable of doing anything in dilettante fashion, but instead throwing himself heart and soul into every quest which chanced to appeal to him. Raymond's father was a Spanish knight, who, having won the approval of John I, King of Arragon, was granted an estate in Majorca, and it was in that island of the Balearic group that the future alchemist was born, probably in the year 1232, but the date is uncertain. Thanks to the royal favor which his father enjoyed, Raymond was appointed Seneschal of the Isles while he was still a mere youth, but hardly had he acquired this position before, much to the chagrin of his parents, he began to show a strong predilection for debauchery.

He paid amorous addresses to women of all sorts, while at length, becoming enamoured of a married lady named Eleonora de Castello, he began to follow her wherever she went, making no attempt to conceal his illicit passion. On one occasion, indeed, he actually sought the lady while she was attending mass. And so loud was the outcry against this bold, if not sacrilegious act, that Eleonora found it essential to write in peremptory style to her *cavaliere servente*, bidding him desist from his present course. The letter failed to cool the youth's ardor, but when it transpired that the lady was smitten with the deadly complaint of cancer, her admirer's frame of mind began to alter speedily. Sobered by the frustration of his hopes, he vowed that henceforth he would live differently, consecrating his days to the service of God.

So Raymond took holy orders, but, as was natural in the case of a man of such active and impetuous temperament, he felt small inclination for monastic life. His aim was to carry the Gospel far afield, converting the followers of Mahomet, and with this in view he began to study Arabic. Having mastered that tongue he proceeded to Rome, eager to enlist the Pope's sympathy in his project.

Raymond failed in the latter particular, yet nothing daunted he embarked on his own account at Genoa about the year 1291, and having reached Tunis he commenced his crusade. His ardor resulted in his being fiercely persecuted and ultimately banished, so he returned for a while to Europe, visiting Paris, Naples and Pisa, and exhorting all good Christians to aid his beloved enterprise.

In 1308 he went to Africa, and at Algiers he made a host of converts, yet was once more forced to fly for his life before the angry Moslems. He traveled to Tunis, thinking to escape thence to Italy, but his former activities in the town were remembered and consequently he was seized and thrown into prison. Here he languished for a long time, never failing to seize every opportunity which presented itself of preaching the gospel, but at last some Genoese merchants contrived to procure his release, and so he sailed back to Italy.

Proceeding to Rome, he made further and strenuous efforts towards obtaining the Pope's support for a well-equipped foreign mission, but Raymond's importunity proved abortive, and after resting for a brief space at his native Majorca, the heroic zealot took his life in his hands and returned to Tunis. Here he even proclaimed his presence publicly, but scarcely had he begun preaching when he reaped the inevitable harvest, and after being savagely attacked he was left lying on the seashore, his assailants imagining him dead. He was still breathing, however, when some Genoese found him, and carrying him to a ship they set sail for Majorca. But the missionary did not rally, and he died while in sight of his home on June 30, 1315.

Raymond's proselytizing ardor had made his name familiar throughout Europe, and while many people regarded him as a heretic because he had undertaken a mission without the Pope's sanction, there were others who admired him so much that they sought to make him a saint. In fact, he was canonized as a martyr, and a mausoleum erected to him.

He also attained some notoriety as an alchemist, and was reported to have made a large sum of gold for the English king, and while there is really no proof that he ever visited Britain, the remaining part of the story holds a certain significance. For it is said that Lully made the money on the strict understanding that it should be utilized for equipping a large and powerful band of missionaries, and the likelihood is that he thought to employ his alchemical skill on behalf of his beloved object, and approached some European sovereign with this in view, thus giving rise to the tradition about his dealings with the English monarch.

Be that as it may, Raymond's voluminous writings certainly include a number of alchemistic works, notably *Alchimia Magic Naturalis, De Aquis Super Accurtationes, De Secretis Medicina Magna* and *De Conservatione Vitæ.* It is interesting to find that several of these won considerable popularity and were repeatedly reprinted, while as late as 1673, two volumes of *Opera Alchima* purporting to be written by him were issued at London. Five years before

this, a biography by De Vernon had been published at Paris, while at a later date a German historian of chemistry named Gruelin referred to Lully as a scientist of exceptional skill, and mentioned him as the first man to distil rosemary oil.

A modern biography *Raymond Lully, Illuminated Doctor, Alchemist & Christian Mystic* by Arthur E. Waite was published in London 1922, reprinted London, 1939. An American issue by David McKay appeared in 1940.

Lumieres dan la Nuit

French-language publication concerned with Unidentified Flying Objects, published annually. Address: R. Veillith (ed.), "Les Pins," 43400 Le Chambon-sur-Lignon, France.

Luminous Bodies

Dead bodies were frequently supposed to glow in the dark with a sort of phosphorescent light. Possibly the belief arose from the idea that the soul was like a fire dwelling in the body.

Luminous Phenomena

A frequent occurrence in physical mediumship. On rare occasions, they have been witnessed in apparent independence of mediumistic conditions. The chronicles of religious revivals are full of instances of transcendental lights.

Of the great Irish revival in 1859 and of the Welsh Revival in 1904 there are various accounts. Mr. Jones of Peckham, editor of the *Spiritual Magazine* (1877, vol. 18), quoted a leading official belonging to the Corporation of London: "Having heard that fire had descended on several of the great Irish assemblies during the Revivals, I, when in Ireland, made inquiry and conversed with those who had witnessed it. During the open-air meetings, when some 600–1,000 people were present, a kind of cloud of fire approached in the air, hovered and dipped over the people, rose and floated on some distance, again hovered on that which was found afterwards to be another revival meeting, and so it continued. The light was very bright and was seen by all, producing awe."

Of the Welsh Revival an interesting account was published by Beriah G. Evans in the *Daily News* (February 9, 1905). The lights he saw appeared for the first time on the night when Mrs. Jones commenced her public mission at Egryn. The first light "resembled a brilliant star emitting sparklets. All saw this. The next two were as clearly subjective, being seen only by Mrs. Jones and me, though the five of us walked abreast. Three bars of clear white light crossed the road in front, from right to left, climbing up the stone wall to the left. A blood-red light, about a foot from the ground in the middle of the roadway at the head of the village street was the next manifestation." The *Daily Mirror* correspondent confirmed the account of Evans. He saw the subjective, at another time the objective light. A third confirmation was published in the July 1905 *Review of Reviews,* by the Rev. Llewellyn Morgan.

These lights seem to have been the result of an outpouring of combined psychic forces which religious ecstasy generates. It is a well-known fact that religious enthusiasm and ecstasy in general is often accompanied by luminous phenomena. Christ was the light of the world. The saints and martyrs spoke of an interior illumination. St. Ignatius Loyola was seen surrounded by a brilliant light while he prayed, his body shone with light when he was levitated and St. Columba was said to have been continually enveloped in a dazzling, golden light.

William James quoted many interesting instances in *Varieties of Religious Experience* (1902 etc.). The cosmic consciousness of Maurice **Bucke** (author of *Cosmic Consciousness,* 1901) was heralded by an influx of dazzling light. The body of the medium Mrs. Leonore **Piper** was described by the communicators as an empty shell filled with light. "A medium," said "Phinuit," spirit control of the Rev. Stainton **Moses,** is for us a lighthouse, while you, non-mediums are as though you did not exist. But every little while we see you as if you were in dark apartments lighted by a kind of little windows which are the mediums."

This light or flame, according to communications obtained by Mrs. Hester Travers-Smith (See Hester **Dowden**), appears to be pale "a clear white fire" which seems to grow more vivid as the medium gets into better touch with the spirit world.

Spectral lights may also have a psychic origin. The Fire of St. Bernardo was studied in 1895 in Quargnento by Prof. Garzino. It was a mass of light which wandered every night from the church to the cemetery and returned after midnight. A similar light was observed at Berbenno di Valtellina. The light passed through trees without burning them. The phenomenon does not appear amenable to known chemical laws. The main difficulty which such lights present is the absence of human organism to which their origin could be traced. But such an absence is also noted in uninhabited haunted houses where the human link is strongly emphasized.

Leaving the deeper mystery aside, a general survey of the cases that will follow justifies the comparatively simple conclusion that psychic lights are the result of a chemical operation on the human body and disclose a close analogy to the organic lights observable in nature. The ways and means of this operation are at present unknown to our physiology but appear to be an easy process to the intelligences that continually claim to stand behind the phenomena.

The Psychic Lights of D. D. Home and Stainton Moses

"Under the strictest test conditions," wrote Sir William **Crookes** in *Researches in the Phenomena of Spiritualism* (1874), "I have seen a solid luminous body, the size and nearly the shape of a turkey's egg float noiselessly about the room, at one time higher than anyone present could reach on tiptoe, and then gently descending to the floor. It was visible for more than ten minutes, and before it faded away it struck the table three times with a sound like that of a hard solid body. During this time the medium was lying back, apparently insensible, in an easy chair."

"I have seen luminous points of light darting about and settling on the heads of different persons; I have had questions answered by the flashing of a bright light a desired number of times in front of my face. I have had an alphabetic communication given me by luminous flashes occurring before me in the air, whilst my hand was moving about amongst them. In the light, I have seen a luminous cloud hover over a heliotrope on a side table, break a sprig off and carry the sprig to a lady."

Viscount Adare wrote in *Experiments in Spiritualism with D. D. Home* (privately printed, 1870): "We all then observed a light, resembling a little star, near the chimney piece, moving to and fro; it then disappeared. Mr. Home said: Ask them in the name of the Father, the Son and the Holy Ghost, if this is the work of God. I repeated the words very earnestly; the light shone out, making three little flashes, each one about a foot higher above the floor than the preceding."

The color of the lights was sometimes blue, yellow or rose. They did not light up their surroundings. Special effort was necessary to produce an effect of illumination. When Ada Menken's spirit tried to make her form visible "the surface of the wall to Home's right became illuminated three or four times; the light apparently radiating from a bright spot in the centre. Across the portion of the wall thus illuminated we repeatedly saw a dark shadow pass."

Adare had seen the extended hand of Home become quite luminous. On another occasion his clothes commenced to shine. Once the top of his head glowed with light as if a halo surrounded it. The tongues or jets of flame described by the Master of Lindsay and Capt. Charles Wynne as issuing from Home's head probably refer to this experience. The Master of Lindsay and many other witnesses often saw luminous crosses in and out of doors in Home's presence. They were variously globular, columnar, or star-shaped.

Reading a paper before the **London Dialectical Society,** the Master of Lindsay said: "I saw on my knee a flame of fire about nine inches high. I passed my hand through it, but it burnt on, above and below. Home turned in his bed and I looked at him, and saw that his eyes were glowing with light. It had a most disagreeable appearance. The flame which had been flitting about me now left me, and crossed the room about four feet from the ground, and reached the curtains of Home's bed. These proved no obstruction; for the light went right through them, settled on his head and then went out."

A letter to the London Dialectical Society narrated a further experience of his as follows: "At Mr. Jencken's house I saw a crystal ball, placed on Mr. Home's head, emit flashes of coloured light, following the order of the spectrum. The crystal was spherical, so that it could not have given prismatic colours. After this it changed and we all saw a view of the sea, as if we were looking down at it from the top of a high cliff. It seemed to be the evening as the sun was setting like a globe of fire, lighting up a broad path over the little waves. The moon was faintly visible in the south, and as the sun set, her power increased. We saw also a few stars; and suddenly the whole thing vanished, like shutting the slide of a magic lantern; and the crystal was dead. This whole appearance lasted about ten minutes."

Many similar observations were recorded in the mediumship of the Rev. Stainton Moses. Dr. Stanhope Templeman Speer observed that the light could be renewed when it grew dim, by making passes over it with the hand. The light had a nucleus and an envelope of drapery. It seemed to be more easily and fully developed if he rubbed his hands together or on his coat. The drapery passed over the back of his hand several times. It was perfectly tangible. These large globes of light could knock distinct blows on the table. A hand was more or less distinctly generated in their nucleus.

These globular lights ceased after a time. The drain on the vital strength of Stainton Moses was too great. They were supplanted by a round disc of light which had a dark side, generally turned towards the medium, while the light side gave answers to questions by flashes. On rarer occasions the light was a tall column, about half an inch or rather more in width, and six or seven feet high. The light was of bright golden hue and did not illuminate objects in the neighbourhood. For a minute a cross developed at its top, and rays seemed to dart from it.

Around the head of Stainton Moses was a halo, perceptible by natural vision and another cluster of light of an oblong shape at the foot of the tall column. It moved up and the big, luminous cross gradually travelled near the wall until it had passed over an arc of 90 degrees. Solid objects afforded no obstacles to one's view of the lights. If they appeared under a mahogany table they could be seen from above just as well as if the top of the table had been composed of glass. Sometimes as many as thirty lights were seen flashing about like comets in the room. The big lights were usually more stationary than the smaller ones, which darted swiftly about the room.

Accidents in Light Production

The chemical operation for the production of these lights miscarried on April 14, 1874: "Suddenly there arose from below me, apparently under the table, or near the floor, right under my nose, a cloud of luminous smoke, just like phosphorus. It fumed up in great clouds, until I seemed to be on fire, and rushed from the room in a panic. I was very frightened and could not tell what was happening. I rushed to the door and opened it, and so to the front door. My hands seemed to be ablaze and I left their impress on the door and handles. It blazed for a while after I had touched it, but soon went out, and no smell or trace remained. I have seen my own hands covered with a lambent flame; but nothing like this I ever saw. There seemed to be no end of the smoke. It smelt phosphoric, but the smell evaporated as soon as I got out of the room into the air. I was fairly frightened, and was reminded of what I had read about a manifestation given to Mr. Peebles similar to the burning bush. I have omitted to say that the lights were preceded by very sharp detonations on my chair, so that we could watch for their coming by hearing the noises. They shot up very rapidly from the floor."

Next day, "Imperator" (his spirit control) said that the phosphoric smoke was caused by an abortive attempt on the part of "Chom" (another spirit) to make a light. There were, he said, ducts leading from our bodies to the dark space beneath the table, and into this space these ducts conveyed the substance extracted for the purpose of making the light. The phosphoric substance was enclosed in an envelope which was materialized. It was the collapse of this envelope that caused the escape of the phosphoric smoke and the smell. This substance was the vital principle, and was drawn from the spine and nerve centers principally, and from all the sitters, except those who were of no use or were deterrent.

Another miscarriage of psychic light was described by W. H. Harrison of a seance of the mediums Frank **Herne** and Charles **Williams** as follows: "The name of the spirit was then written rapidly in large phosphorescent letters in the air near Mr. Williams. In the same rapid manner the spirits next began writing 'God Bless—' when there was a snap, like an electrical discharge, and a flash of light which lit up the whole room." At the end of the sitting a slight smell of phosphorus was perceptible. However, a more mundane explanation of this phenomenon could be that it was caused by the sudden striking of a match, since suspicion of fraud is attached to the seances of Herne and Williams.

The strong smell of ozone which Dr. Gustave **Geley** recorded in later years during luminous phenomena may be a quite different phenomenon.

The following description is from the Livermore records of seances with Kate Fox (see **Fox Sisters**): "A spherical ovoid of light rises from the floor as high as our foreheads and places itself on the table in front of us. At my request the light immediately became so bright as to light up that part of the room. We saw perfectly the form of a woman holding the light in her outstretched hand."

Dr. Nichols, in whose house William **Eglinton** gave a series of sittings in Malvern, wrote of: "masses of light of a globular form, flattened globes, shining all through the mass, which was enveloped in folds of gauzy drapery. 'Joey' [a spirit control] brushed the folds aside with his finger to show us the shining substance. It was as if a gem—a turquoise or a pearl—three inches across, had become incandescent, full of light, so as to illuminate about a yard round. This light also we saw come and go. 'Joey' allowed his larger light to go almost dark, and then revived it to its former brilliancy. I need hardly say that all the chemists of Europe could not, under these conditions, produce such phenomena, if indeed they could under any."

The spirit entity "John King" often brought a spirit lamp when he materialized. Once in a seance with Williams, the lamp was placed in the hands of Alfred Smedley. He stated in his book *Some Reminiscences* (1900): "To my great surprise it was like a lump of solid, warm flesh, exactly similar to my own." Others observed that the lamp was often covered with lace-like drapery. This is not a surprising fact, as the appearance of psychic lights often heralds materializations. A disc of light may transform itself into a face, a star into a human eye. To the touch, the light is sometimes hard, sometimes sticky.

Later Observations

In a seance with Franek **Kluski** on May 15, 1921, Dr. Geley recorded: "A moment later, magnificent luminous phenomena; a hand moved slowly about before the sitters. It held in the palm, by a particular bending of the fingers, a body resembling a piece of luminous ice. The whole hand appeared luminous and transparent. One could see the flesh colour. It was admirable."

In another seance on April 12, 1922, "A large luminous trail like a nebulous comet, and about half a metre long, formed behind Kluski about a metre above his head and seemingly about the same distance behind him. This nebula was constituted of tiny bright grains broadcast, among which there were some specially bright points. This nebula oscillated quickly from right to left and left to right, and rose and fell. It lasted about a minute, disappeared and reappeared several times. After the sitting I found that the medium, who had been naked for an hour, was very warm. He was perspiring on the back and armpits; he was much exhausted."

With the same medium, Prof. Pawlowski recorded the appearance of a completely luminous figure of an old man. It made the impression of a light column. It illuminated all of the sitters and even the more distant objects in the room. His hands and the region of the heart were much more strongly luminous than the rest of the body.

Admiral Usborne Moore stated that he had seen tongues of spirit light issue from the body of the medium Ada **Bessinet.** They were about one third of an inch broad at one end and tapered away for a length of about one and a half inches to nothing.

In a seance with the medium Indride **Indridason,** Prof. Haraldur **Nielsson** counted one evening more than sixty tongues of light of different colors. "I could not help thinking of the manifestations described in the second chapter of the Acts of the Apostles," he wrote in *Light* (Oct. 25, 1919), "especially as a very strong wind arose before the lights appeared. Later on the whole wall behind the medium became a glow of light."

An unusual type of psychic light was shown by the medium Pasquale **Erto** ("the human rainbow") in seances at the Metapsychical Institute of Paris, on the genuineness of which serious doubt was thrown afterwards. Flashes like electric sparks proceeded from the lower part of Erto's body, lighting up the floor and sometimes the walls of the room; luminous white rays up to 8 meters in length, luminous spheres from the size of a walnut to an orange in white, reddish or bluish color, zig-zag flashes and rocket-like lights. They were cold lights, devoid of actinic rays.

Before each seance, Erto was completely stripped and medically examined in all cavities—mouth, ears, rectum and even urethra. Erto demanded absolute darkness and did not permit hand control. Dr. Geley found out that the phenomena could be produced by the use of ferro-cerium, and that the medium seemed to have used this trick.

Erto's phenomena were not entirely unique. Frau Maria **Silbert** occasionally produced somewhat similar psychic flashes. But her mediumistic reputation was far above that of Erto.

In the Boston seances of the medium "Margery" (see M. S. **Crandon**) a glowing light was located on Margery's left shoulder. On touch, no luminosity was rubbed off and it continued to be seen through a black sock though with decreased frequency and brilliance. On examination the medium's left shoulder strap was found to be luminous. There was a less distinct brightness on her chest and luminous patches on her right shoulder which soon faded out. The luminous shoulder strap being brought into the seance room, a sudden growth of its intensity was noticed. During a minute examination a whisper in the voice of "Walter" (the spirit control) said "goodnight." At approximately the same time, the light of the shoulder strap faded out and was not seen thereafter, except for one minute luminous point which seemed more persistent than the rest. At another time, Dr. Hereward **Carrington,** holding the left hand of Margery, noticed at the end of the sitting that his hand was faintly luminous.

Prof. Charles **Richet** attempted to imitate psychic lights by a neon tube six feet long and one inch in diameter. By rubbing, he induced a frictional electric charge which made a brilliant glow in the neon at the point of the tube

where the hand had the contact. It looked like a realistic psychic phenomenon in the dark.

Prof. Dubois collected a number of examples to prove in exceptional, yet normal conditions, that the human organism is capable of creating light. A woman suffering from cancer of the breast, under treatment in an English hospital, showed luminosity of the sore, sufficiently strong to be recognized at several paces distant, and bright enough to enable watch hands to be read at night a few inches away. The discharge from it was also very luminous. Bilious, nervous, red-haired, and more often alcoholic subjects have sometimes shown phosphorescent wounds.

Dr. Geley concluded that organic light and ectoplasmic light are rigorously analogous. They have the same properties. They are cold light, giving off neither calorific nor chemical radiations. Both are nearly inactinic and have considerable powers of penetration into opaque bodies. They impress photographic plates through cardboard, wood and even metal. Geley believed it likely that analysis of ectoplasmic secretion would reveal the two constituents—luciferin and luciferase—discovered in the normal luminous secretion by Professor Dubois.

Dr. Julien **Ochorowicz,** in his researches into the radiography of etheric hands, found it a curious and significant fact that when an etheric hand radiates light it does not, and apparently cannot, materialize at the same time. By the act of materializing, it loses its luminosity. This may be true. There are, however, experiences on record which caution against generalization.

Morever the incidence of known fraud, as well as the ease with which lumious phenomena can be produced chemically, must make for caution in assessing the genuineness of claimed phenomena. At the same time, certain accounts appear reliable.

It may be that a study of phosphorescent and electrical phenomena in nature, such as displayed by insects and certain fishes, may indicate possible mechanisms in psychic phenomena.

Lusus Naturae

A general term for freaks or sports of nature, sometimes applied to the area of collecting stones and minerals which appear to contain pictures on their surfaces when cut and polished. Such pictures may appear as landscapes or even portraits, arising from the principle of duplication of shapes in nature, rather as if nature draws doodles and tests out forms. The resemblance of certain roots, notably mandrake (see **Mandragoras**), to human shape is a well-known example of this strange principle.

Lutin, The

The Lutin of Normandy in many respects resembled Robin Goodfellow, the mischievous sprite also identified with Puck. Like Robin, he had many names, and also the power of assuming many forms, but the Lutin's pranks were usually of a more serious nature than those of the tricky spirit of Merrie England. Many a man ascribed his ruin to the malice of the Lutin, although it must be confessed that in these cases neighbors were uncharitable enough to say, that the Lutin had less to do with it than habits of Want-of-Thrift and Self-Indulgence.

Thus, on market days, when a farmer lingered late over

his ale, whether in driving a close bargain or in enjoying the society of a boon companion, he declared the Lutin was sure to play him some spiteful trick on his way home. His horse would stumble and he would be thrown. He would lose his purse or else his way. If the farmer persisted in these habits the tricks of the Lutin would become more serious. The sheep pens would be unfastened, the cowhouse and stable doors left open, and the flocks and cattle be found moving among the standing corn and unmown hay, while every servant on the farm would swear to his own innocence, and unhesitatingly lay the blame on the Lutin.

Similar tricks were played on the fishermen by the Nain Rouge—another name for the Lutin. He opened the meshes of the nets and set the fish free. He removed the floats and let the nets sink to the bottom, or let the nets float away on the retiring tide. True, if closely questioned, the fishermen would confess that on these occasions, the night was dark and stormy, the cottage warm and the grog plentiful, and that instead of drawing their nets at the proper time, they had delayed until morning.

Again, the Lutin might appear like a black nag, ready bridled and saddled, quietly feeding by the wayside, but woe to the luckless wight who mounted him! Unless he did so for some charitable or holy purpose, he was borne with the speed of the wind to his destination. In this form the Lutin played his wildest pranks and was called Le Cheval Bayard. (See also **Fairies; Kaboutermannekens**)

Lutoslawski, Wincenty (1863–1954)

Polish occultist and mystic. Born in Warsaw, he studied chemistry and philosophy before developing his own synthesis of psychic phenomena, sex and mysticism. He corresponded with psychologist William **James,** and with psychical researcher Prof. Charles **Richet.**

In 1902 he proposed the term "metapsychic" for studies in psychical science, independently adopted by Richet for his own investigations. Lutoslawski also founded a short-lived political party named the Philaretes.

Amongst his books, the following have been translated into English: *The World of Souls* (1924), *Pre-existence and Reincarnation* (1928), *The Knowledge of Reality* (1930).

Lycanthropy

The transformation of a human being into an animal. The belief is an ancient one. The term derives from the Greek words *lukos* a wolf, and *anthropos* a man, but it is employed regarding a transformation into any animal shape. It is chiefly in those countries where wolves are numerous that we find such tales concerning them. But in India and some parts of Asia, the tiger takes the place of the wolf. In Russia and elsewhere it is the bear and in Africa the leopard.

It is usually savage animals regarding which these beliefs are prevalent, but even harmless ones sometimes figure in them. There is considerable confusion as to whether such transformations were voluntary or involuntary, temporary or permanent. The human being transformed into the animal may be the physical individual or, on the other hand may be only a double, that is, the human spirit may enter the animal and the body remain unchanged. Magicians and witches were credited with the power of transforming themselves into wolves and other animal shapes, and it was asserted that if the animal were wounded then the marks of the wound would be discovered upon the wizard's body.

The belief was current amongst many primitive tribes that every individual possessed an animal form which could be entered at death, or at will. This was effected either by magic or natural agency.

As mentioned, the wolf was a common form of animal transformation in Europe. In ancient Greece, the belief was associated with the dog, which took the place of the wolf. Other similar beliefs have been found in India and Java and in the former country we find the **wer-wolf** in a kind of **vampire** form.

Magical Transformation

The seventeenth-century writer Louis Guyon related the history of an enchanter who used to change himself into different beasts.

"Certain people," said he, "persuaded Ferdinand, first Emperor of that name, to command the presence of a Polish enchanter and magician in the town of Nuremberg to learn the result of a difference he had with the Turks, concerning the kingdom of Hungary; and not only did the magician make use of divination, but performed various other marvels, so that the king did not wish to see him, but the courtiers introduced him into his chamber. There he did many wonderful things, among others, he transformed himself into a horse, anointing himself with some grease, then he took the shape of an ox, and thirdly that of a lion, all in less than an hour. The emperor was so terrified by these transformations that he commanded that the magician should be immediately dismissed, and declined to hear the future from the lips of such a rascal.

"It need no longer be doubted," added this writer, that Lucius Apuleius Plato was a sorcerer, and that he "was transformed into an ass, forasmuch as he was charged with it before the proconsul of Africa, in the time of the Emperor Antonine I, in the year 150 A.D., as Apollonius of Tyana, long before, in the year 60, was charged before Domitian with the same crime. And more than three years after, the rumour persisted to the time of St. Augustine, who was an African, who has written and confirmed it; as also in his time the father of one Prestantius was transformed into a horse, as the said Prestantius declared. Augustine's father having died, in a short time the son had wasted the greater part of his inheritance in the pursuit of the magic arts, and in order to flee poverty he sought to marry a rich widow named Pudentille, for such a long time that at length she consented. Soon after her only son and heir, the child of her former marriage, died. These things came about in a manner which led people to think that he had by means of magic entrapped Pudentille, who had been wooed in vain by several illustrious people, in order to obtain the wealth of her son. It was also said that the profound knowledge he possessed—for he was able to solve difficult questions which left other men bewildered—was obtained from a demon or familiar spirit he possessed. Further, certain people said they had seen him do many marvellous things, such as making himself invisible, transforming himself into a horse or into a bird, piercing his body with a sword without wounding himself, and similar performances. He was at last accused by one Sicilius Œmilianus, the censor, before

Claudius Maximus, proconsul of Africa, who was said to be a Christian; but nothing was found against him.

"Now, that he had been transformed into an ass, St. Augustine regards as indubitable, he having read it in certain true and trustworthy authors, and being besides of the same country; and this transformation happened to him in Thessaly before he was versed in magic, through the spell of a sorceress, who sold him, and who recovered him to his former shape after he had served in the capacity of an ass for some years, having the same powers and habits of eating and braying as other asses, but with a mind still sane and reasonable as he himself attested. And at last to show forth his case, and to lend probability to the rumour, he wrote a book entitled *The Golden Ass,* a mélange of fables and dialogues, to expose the vices of the men of his time, which he had heard of, or seen, during his transformation, with many of the labours and troubles he had suffered while in the shape of an ass.

"However that may be, St. Augustine in the book of the *City of God,* book XVIII, chapters XVII and XVIII, relates that in his time there were in the Alps certain sorceresses who gave a particular kind of cheese to the passers by, who, on partaking of it, were immediately changed into asses or other beasts of burden, and were made to carry heavy weights to certain places. When their task was over, they were permitted to regain their human shape.

"The bishop of Tyre, historian, writes that in his time, probably about 1220, some Englishmen were sent by their king to the aid of the Christians who were fighting in the Holy Land, and that on their arrival in a haven of the island of Cyprus a sorceress transformed a young English soldier into an ass. He, wishing to return to his companions in the ship, was chased away with blows from a stick, whereupon he returned to the sorceress who made use of him, until someone noticed that the ass kneeled in a church and did various other things which only a reasoning being could do. The sorceress who followed him was taken on suspicion before the authorities, was obliged to give him his human form three years after his transformation, and was forthwith executed.

"We read that Ammonius, a peripatetic philosopher, about the time of Lucius Septimius Severus, in the year 196 A.D., had present at his lessons an ass whom he taught. I should think that this ass had been at one time a man, and that he quite understood what Ammonius taught, for these transformed persons retain their reason unimpaired, as St. Augustine and other writers have assured us.

"Fulgose writes, book VIII, chapter II, that in the time of Pope Leon, who lived about the year 930, there were in Germany two sorceresses who used thus to change their guests into beasts, and on one occasion she changed a young mountebank into an ass, who, preserving his human understanding, gave a great deal of amusement to the passers-by. A neighbour of the sorceresses bought the ass at a good price, but was warned by them that he must not take the beast to a river, or he would lose it. Now the ass escaped one day and running to a near-by lake plunged into the water, when he returned to his own shape. Apuleius says that he regained his human form by eating roses.

"There are still to be seen in Egypt asses which are led into the market-place to perform various feats of agility and tricks, understanding all the commands they receive, and executing them: such as to point out the most beautiful woman of the company, and many other things that one would hardly believe; and Belon, a physician, relates in his observations that he has seen them, and others also, who have been there, and who have affirmed the same to me."

Augustine Calmet, author of *The Phantom World* (2 vols., 1850) stated: "One day there was brought to St. Macarius, the Egyptian, an honest woman who had been transformed into a mare by the wicked art of a magician. Her husband and all who beheld her believed that she had really been changed into a mare. This woman remained for three days without taking any food, whether suitable for a horse or for a human being. She was brought to the priests of the place, who could suggest no remedy. So they led her to the cell of St. Macarius, to whom God had revealed that she was about to come. His disciples wished to send her away, thinking her a mare, and they warned the saint of her approach, and the reason for her journey. He said to them: 'It is you who are the animals, who think you see that which is not; this woman is not changed, but your eyes are bewitched.' As he spoke he scattered holy water on the head of the woman, and all those present saw her in her true shape. He had something given her to eat and sent her away safe and sound with her husband."

Modern Beliefs in Transformation

Belief in transformation of human beings into predatory animals persisted into relatively modern times in Africa, India, Java, Malaya and other countries. In Africa there were tiger men and even a leopard society of wizards. It seems very likely, however, that many apparent cases of transformation were effected by wearing the skin of an animal when hunting victims. In some cases there may have been a perverse desire for blood-drinking or cannibalism, as in the celebrated sixteenth-century case of the French lycanthrope Gilles **Garnier.**

In July 1919, the *Journal* of the Society for Psychical Research published a summary of Richard Bagot's article, *The Hyaenas of Pirra* (*Cornhill Magazine*, October 1918), in which some experiences reported by Lieutenant F. personally and an experience of the late Capt. Shott, D.S.O., dealt with the killing of Nigerians when in the form of supposed hyenas. The main facts which deeply impressed the officers were as follows:

"Raiding hyenas were wounded by gun-traps, and tracked in each case to a point where the hyena traces ceased and were succeeded by human footprints, which made for the native town. At each shooting a man mysteriously dies in the town, all access being refused to the body. In Lieut. F.'s experiences the death wail was raised in the town almost immediately after the shot; but Capt. Shott does not mention this. In Capt. Shott's experience the beast was an enormous brute, readily trackable, which after being hard hit made off through the guinea-corn. It was promptly tracked, and a spot was come upon where 'they found the jaw of the beast lying near a large pool of blood.' Soon after the tracks reached a path leading to the native town. The natives next day came to Capt. Shott—and this is the curious part of the affair—and told him, without any regrets, that he had shot the Nefada—a lesser head-man—who was then lying dead with his jaw shot away. The natives gave their reasons as having seen and spoken to the Nefada, as he was, by his own admission, going into the bush. They heard the gun and saw him return with his head all muffled up and walking like a very sick man. On going next morning to see what was the matter . . . they found him as stated . . ."

Mr. Bagot, a member of the S.P.R., added in response to further questions:

"In the article in question I merely reproduced verbatim the reports and letters sent to the said official . . . by British officers well known to him, and said that the authenticity and good faith of the writers can be vouched for entirely. I have evidence of precisely similar occurrences that have come under the notice of Italian officers in Eritrea and Somaliland; and in all cases it would seem that a gravel patch thrown up by the small black ants is necessary to the process of metamorphosis. I drew the attention of Sir James G. Frazer (author of *The Golden Bough*) to this coincidence and asked him if he had come across in his researches anything which might explain the connection between gravel thrown up by the ants and the power of projection into animal forms; but he informed me that, so far as he could recollect, he had not done so. Italian officials and big game hunters assure me that it is considered most dangerous (by natives in Somaliland, Abyssinia, etc.) to sleep on ground thrown up by ants; the belief being that anyone who does so is liable to be possessed or obsessed by some wild animal, and that this obsession once having taken place, the victim is never afterwards able entirely to free himself from it and is compelled periodically to assume the form and habits of some beast or reptile."

Psychical Aspects

Psychical research does not normally admit such phenomena as lycanthropy within its scope. It is well to remark, however, that there are two possible points of contact. The first is the projection of the **double** (or **astral body**), provided it will be proved that the double may assume any desired shape.

Col. **Rochas** asserted that the double of his hypnotic subject, on being so suggested, assumed the shape of her mother. If it were proved that the shape of animals could be assumed, we would have to consider lycanthropy as a psychic possibility. But the animal, in that case, would not be more than a phantom, and we would have to prove that this phantom can be hurt and transfer, by repercussion, the wound to the projector.

The second possibility brings us nearer to this aspect of the problem. Dr. Paul **Joire** succeeded in transferring the exteriorized sensitivity of his subject to a figure made of putty. If the hand of the putty figure was scratched by a needle, a corresponding red mark appeared on the somnambule's hand.

The question which suggests itself is this: would it not be possible to transfer sensitivity to a living being, to an animal? In that case it would be natural to expect a repercussion from the animal to the human body. Experiments along this line may precipitate a number of absorbingly interesting problems on researchers.

What would be the effect of such transference of sensitivity on the animal? Could the animal will be dominated by such influence? Would there be a reaction from the animal consciousness on the human one? What dangers would attend such experiments? A third line of approach is indicated by animal materializations which, however, psychical research finds restricted to the dark seance room and of very rare occurrence. (See also **Double; Exteriorization of Sensitivity; Vampire; Wer-wolf**)

Recommended reading:

Baring-Gould, Sabine. *The Book of Were-Wolves*, London, 1865; Causeway Books, New York, 1973

Hamel, Frank. *Human Animals*, London, 1915; University Books, 1969

Kaigh, Frederick. *Witchcraft & Magic of Africa*, Richard Lesley & Co., London, 1947

Maclean, Charles. *The Wolf Children*, Hill & Wang, 1977

Summers, Montague. *The Werewolf*, London, 1933; University Books, 1966

Woodward, Ian. *The Werewolf Delusion*, Paddington Press, London & New York, 1979

Lyceum Banner, The

Spiritualist publication, founded in 1890 as the official monthly organ of the **British Spiritualists Lyceum Union.** It was published by J. J. **Morse** in Liverpool until 1902, when the paper was passed to the Lyceum Union under the editorship of Frank **Kitson.** Publication continued through the 1930s.

Lynn, Thomas (c. 1928)

A coal miner medium in the North of England, the subject of remarkable experiments by Hewat **McKenzie** and Major C. Mowbray in photographing the arrival and ectoplasmic mechanism of **apports.** Lynn's mediumship developed around 1913 in his home circle, but he did not exercise physical mediumship before 1926. Extrusions of **ectoplasm,** small coils or rods of varying shapes, were seen to issue from the region of his solar plexus, to perform minor physical feats and leave, after their disappearance, red marks like punctures behind on the medium's skin.

Apports of small, insignificant objects were the most impressive phenomena. In earlier seances, held in the dark, it was said that small bottles arrived containing wax in various shapes, molded images, etc. In the experimental seances held in light by the investigators of the **British College of Psychic Science,** no such bottles had been aported.

The first series of these experimental sittings took place in July 1928. Two cameras were used, one whole-plate ordinary lens, and a half-plate with quartz lens. The medium was put in a bag, his hands were tied to his knees with tapes.

The flashlight photographs showed luminous connections between the medium's body and the apports. The sittings were continued in September 1928, and were repeated at the College in March 1929. By then, Lynn abandoned his former occupation and became a professional medium. The curious photographs secured in these seances throw an interesting light on the problem of apports.

For a detailed report on the Lynn phenomena, including photographs, see *Psychic Science* (vol. 8, No. 2, July 1929, pp. 129–37).

Lyttelton, Edith (Mrs. Alfred Lyttelton)
(187?–1948)

Author, playwright, psychic, past president of the Society for Psychical Research, London. A daughter of Arthur Balfour, she was educated privately. In 1892 she married the Hon. Alfred Lyttelton. She was a member of the Joint Council of Vic-Wells and National Theatre and a governor of Stratford Memorial Theatre. During World War I she served on War Refugees Committee, and from 1917–19 was deputy director of the Women's Branch, Ministry of Agriculture. She was British Substitute Delegate to the League of Nations Assembly at Geneva between 1923 and 1931; appointed Dame Commander of the Order of the British Empire 1917; Dame Grand Cross 1929.

In 1902 she joined the Society for Psychical Research, and from 1928 onwards was a member of the council. In 1913, soon after her husband's death, she experimented with automatic writing, and received predictions of the outbreak of World War I. Her scripts also predicted the sinking of the liner "Lusitania" in 1915, and other predictions referred to World War II. Her books include: *The Faculty of Communion* (1925?), *Florence Upton, Painter* (1926), *Our Superconscious Mind* (1931), *Some Cases of Prediction* (1937). Her Presidential Address to the SPR was published in the Society's *Proceedings* (vol. 41, part 132, 1933). She died September 2, 1948.

Lytton, Bulwer (1801–1872)

According to his baptismal certificate, the full name of this once famous author was Edward George Earle Lytton Bulwer-Lytton and in signing some of his early writings he used all these names with occasional variations in their order, an act which was regarded by many people as springing from pride and pompousness, and which elicited the withering satire of Thackeray in *Punch.*

Lytton was born in London, February 13, 1801. His father was a Norfolk squire, Bulwer of Heydon Hall; his mother was Elizabeth Barbara Lytton, a lady who claimed kinship with Cadwaladr Vendigaid, the semi-mythical hero who led the Strathclyde Welsh against the Angles in the seventh century. As a child the future novelist was delicate, but he learned to read at a surprisingly early age, and began to write verses before he was ten years old. Going first to a small private school at Fulham, he soon passed on to another one at Rottingdean, and here he continued to manifest literary tastes, Byron and Scott being his chief idols at this time. He was so talented that his relations decided it would be a mistake to send him to a public school. Accordingly he was placed with a tutor at Ealing, under whose care he progressed rapidly with his studies. Thereafter he proceeded to Cambridge, where he took his degree easily, and won many academic laurels, while on leaving the University he traveled for a while in Scotland and France, and then bought a commission in the army. He sold it soon afterwards, however, while in 1827 he was married, and now he began to devote himself seriously to writing.

His first publications of note were the novels *Falkland, Pelham* and *Eugene Aram.* These won an instant success, and placed considerable wealth in the author's hands, the result being that in 1831 he entered Parliament as liberal member for St. Ives, Huntingdonshire. During the next ten years he was an active politician yet still found time to produce a host of stories, such as *The Last Days of Pompei, Ernest Maltravers, Zanoni* and *The Last of the Barons.* These were followed shortly by *The Caxtons,* and simultaneously Lytton achieved some fame as a dramatist, perhaps his best play being *The Lady of Lyons.*

In 1851 he was instrumental in founding a scheme for pensioning authors. In 1862, he increased his reputation greatly by his occult novel entitled *A Strange Story,* and four years later his services to literature and politics were rewarded by a peerage. He now began to work at yet another story, *Kenelm Chillingly,* but his health was beginning to fail, and he died May 23, 1872 at Torquay.

The works cited above constitute but a fragment of Lytton's voluminous achievement. Besides further novels too numerous to mention, he issued several volumes of verses notably *Ismael* and *The New Union,* while he did translations from German, Spanish and Italian. He produced a history of Athens, he contributed to endless periodicals, and was at one time editor of *The New Monthly Magazine.*

But although so busy throughout the whole of his career, and while winning great fame Lytton's life was not really a happy one, various causes conducing to make it otherwise. Long before meeting his wife, he fell in love with a young girl who died prematurely, and this loss seems to have left an indelible sorrow while his marriage was anything but a successful one, the pair being divorced comparatively soon after their union.

Even as a child, Lytton had evinced a predilection for mysticism, while he had surprised his mother once by asking her whether she was "not sometimes overcome by the sense of her own identity" (almost exactly the same question was put to his nurse in boyhood by another mystic, William Bell Scott). Lytton sedulously developed his leaning towards the occult, and it is frequently manifest in his literary output. It transpires, for example, in his poem *The Tale of a Dreamer,* and again in *Kenelm Chillingly,* while in *A Strange Story* he tried to give a scientific coloring to old-fashioned magic. However, Sir Leslie Stephen shrewdly commented that Lytton's "attempts at the mysterious too often remind us of spirit-rapping rather than excite the thrill of supernatural awe."

He was a keen student of psychic phenomena. The great medium D. D. **Home** was his guest at Knebworth in 1855. Home's phenomena greatly aroused Lytton's curiosity. He never spoke about his experiences in public but his identity was at once detected in an account in Home's autobiography (*Incidents in My Life,* 1863) which reads: "Whilst I was at Ealing, a distinguished novelist, accompanied by his son, attended a seance, at which some very remarkable manifestations occurred that were chiefly directed to him. The rappings on the table suddenly became unusually firm and loud. He asked: 'What spirit is present?' The alphabet was called over, and the response was: 'I am the spirit who influenced you to write Z (Zanoni).' 'Indeed,' said he, 'I wish you would give me some tangible proof of your presence.' 'What proof? Will you take my hand.' 'Yes.' And putting his hand beneath the surface of the table it was immediately seized by a powerful grasp, which made him start to his feet in evident trepidation, exhibiting a momentary suspicion that a trick had been played upon him. Seeing, however, that all the persons around him were sitting with their hands quietly reposing on the table, he recovered his composure, and offering an apology for the uncontrollable excitement caused by such an unexpected demonstration, he resumed his seat."

"Immediately after this," wrote Home, "another message was spelt out: 'We wish you to believe in the . . .' On inquiring after the finishing word a small cardboard cross which was lying on a table at the end of the room was given into his hand."

When the Press asked Lord Lytton for a statement, he refused to give any. His wariness to commit himself before the public was well demonstrated by his letter to the secretary of the **London Dialectical Society,** February 1869: "So far as my experience goes, the phenomena, when freed from impostures with which their exhibition abounds, and examined rationally, are traceable to material influences of the nature of which we are ignorant.

"They require certain physical organisations or temperaments to produce them, and vary according to these organisations and temperaments."

Lord Lytton sought out many mediums after his experiences with Home and often detected imposture. His friendship with Home extended over a period of ten years and when he commenced the wildest of his romances, *A Strange Story,* he intended first to portray Home in its pages, but abandoned this intention for the fantastic conception of Margrave. The joyousness of Home's character, however, is still reflected in the mental make-up of Margrave.

Lytton also became acquainted with the French occultist Éliphas Lévi, whom he assisted in magical evocations, and Lévi was clearly a model for the character of the magus in *The Haunted and The Haunters.*

M

M. A., Oxon.

Pseudonym of the Rev. William Stainton **Moses,** prominent British Spiritualist, author of *Spirit Teachings* (1833) and other books.

Maa-Kheru

According to Egyptologist G. Maspero, the Egyptian name of the true intonation with which the dead must recite those magic incantations which would give them power in Amenti, the Egyptian Hades. (See also **Egypt**)

McConnell, R. A. (1914–   )

Associate research professor actively concerned with parapsychology, who was president of the Parapsychological Association in 1958. Born in Pennsylvania, he studied at Carnegie Institute of Technology (B.S. physics, 1935), University of Pittsburgh (Ph.D. physics, 1947). He worked as a physicist with Gulf Research & Development Co., and with a U.S. Naval aircraft factory between 1937 and 1941 and subsequently went to Massachusetts Institute of Technology Radiation Laboratory where he was a group leader from 1944–46. From 1947–53 he was assistant professor of physics, 1953–59 assistant research professor of biophysics, 1959 onwards associate research professor of biophysics, at University of Pittsburgh. He is a member of the American Physical Society, Biophysical Society, Institute of Radio Engineers, Parapsychological Association.

Dr. McConnell was a founding member of the **Parapsychological Association,** president 1957–58, 1977–78. From 1964 onwards he was resident professor of physics at University of Pittsburgh.

In addition to his articles in technical journals, Dr. McConnell has written widely on parapsychology. With Dr. Gertrude **Schmeidler** he was co-author of the book *ESP and Personality Patterns* (1958). He contributed chapters to a Ciba Foundation symposium on *Extrasensory Perception* (1956) and a symposium edited by Eileen J. Garrett, *Does Man Survive Death?* He also published *ESP Curriculum Guide* (Simon & Schuster, 1971), prepared for secondary-school and college teachers of psychology, biology and general science who may wish to teach extrasensory perception and related subjects. His many articles on parapsychology include: 'ESP, Fact or Fancy?' (*Scientific Monthly,* vol. 69, 1949), 'Why Throw Dice?' (*Journal of Parapsychology,* vol. 16, 1952), 'Wishing With Dice' (co-author, *Journal of Experimental Psychology,* vol. 50, 1955) 'Psi Phenomena and Methodology' (*American Scientist,* vol. 45, 1957); (*Journal of Parapsychology*): 'Modern Experiments in Telepathy' (vol. 18, 1954, 'Price in "Sci-

ence" ' (vol. 19, 1955), 'Scaled Measurement in Psi Research' (vol. 22, 1958), 'Continuous Variable Trials' (vol. 22, 1958); (*Journal of Psychology*): 'Nature of the Discontinuity in Schmeidler's ESP-Rorschach Data' (vol. 52, 1961), 'Fantasy Testing for ESP in a Fourth and Fifth Grade Class' (co-author, vol. 52, 1961), (with J. Forwald) 'Psychokinetic Placement: I. A Re-examination of the Forwald-Durham Experiment' (*Journal of Parapsychology 1973,* Scarecrow Press, 1974), 'Parapsychology and the Occult' (*Journal* of the American Society for Psychical Research, vol. 67, 1973).

In addition to his work in the field of parapsychology, Dr. McConnell has also specialized in radar moving target indication, theory of the iconoscope and ultrasonic microwaves.

McDonnell Laboratory for Psychic Research

Psychic research laboratory at Washington University, St. Louis, Missouri, funded by a grant from James S. McDonnell, chairman of the McDonnell Foundation. The director of the laboratory is Dr. Peter R. Philips, who has worked on high energy physics and psychical research.

McDougall, William (1871–1938)

Professor of Psychology at Harvard University, author of *Body and Mind* and *Social Psychology,* president of the **Society for Psychical Research** 1920–21 and of the **American Society for Psychical Research** 1921, member of the Scientific American Committee for the investigation of the mediumship of "Margery" (Mina S. **Crandon**), a keen but reserved investigator who took great care not to commit himself as to the genuine occurrence of the supernormal and agencies of an extra-terrene origin.

Born June 22, 1871 in Lancashire, England, he was educated at Owens College, Manchester, St. Thomas Hospital, London, Cambridge, Oxford and Göttingen Universities. He was a fellow of St. John's College, Cambridge, 1898 (hon. fellow 1938), reader, University College, London, reader in mental philosophy and fellow, Corpus Christi College, Oxford, before becoming a professor at Harvard. In 1900 he married Anne Amelia Hickmore.

Professor McDougall was one of the leading psychologists of his time, and his later interest in psychical research was a dominant influence in the development of modern parapsychology. When head of the Psychology Department at Duke University from 1927–38, he encouraged J. B. **Rhine** in founding the **Parapsychology Laboratory,** from which modern research in laboratory controlled experiments developed. Prof. McDougall published a number of articles on psychical subjects, including: 'The

Case of Sally Beauchamp' (*Proceedings* of the Society for Psychical Research, London, vols. 19-20, 1905-07), 'The Need for Psychical Research' (*Harvard Graduate Magazine*, reprinted *ASPR Journal*, vol. 17, 1923), 'Further Observations on the "Margery" Case' (*ASPR Journal*, vol. 19, 1925), 'The Margery Mediumship' (*Psyche*, vol. 26, 1926). He contributed the important article on Hypnotism to the eleventh edition of the *Encyclopaedia Britannica* (1910), as well as articles on Hallucination, Suggestion and Trance (11th-14th editions). His books include: *Pagan Tribes of Borneo* (1911), *Psychology* (1912), *Group Mind* (1920), *Is America Safe for Democracy?* (1926), *Janus* (1927), *Character and Conduct of Life* (1927); *Modern Materialism and Emergent Evolution* (1929), *World Chaos—The Responsibility of Science* (1931), *Energies of Men* (1933). He died November 28, 1938.

Machen, Arthur (Llewellyn) (1863–1947)

British novelist, born March 3, 1863 at Carleon-on-Usk, Wales, who became one of the leading authors of occult fiction, although undeservedly neglected during his lifetime. He was a close friend of Arthur Edward **Waite,** one of Britain's greatest authorities on occult literature.

One of Machen's short stories brought a legend to real life. This was "The Bowmen," first published in the newspaper *The Evening News,* London, September 29, 1914. In the story, British troops hopelessly outnumbered in the French trenches of World War I, are miraculously rescued by phantom English archers from Agincourt, led by St. George.

A few months after publication, a number of eyewitness accounts of 'The Angels of Mons' began to appear, and Machen was taxed with elaborating a true story. This strange example of nature imitating art is detailed by Machen in his introduction to *The Bowmen and other legends of the War* (London, 1915). His other books include: *The Great God Pan* (1894), *The House of Souls* (1906), *The Hill of Dreams* (1907), *The Great Return* (1915), *The Terror* (1917). In addition to his powerful stories on occult themes, he also published a number of volumes of essays and translations. For biographical and bibliographical details, see: *Arthur Machen; a short account of his life and work* by Aidan Reynolds & William Charlton (London, 1963). He died December 15, 1947 at Beaconsfield, Buckinghamshire. (See also English Occult **Fiction**)

M'Indoe, John B. (c. 1936)

A prominent Scottish Spiritualist, past president of the **Spiritualists National Union** in Britain, trustee and advisory committee member of Edinburgh Psychic College and Library. He was a great authority on the subject of **spirit photography,** and also reported on the controversial mediumship of Mrs. Helen **Duncan.**

Macionica

Slavonic name for a witch. (See **Slavs**)

McKenzie, James Hewat (1870–1929)

Founder of the **British College of Psychic Science.** He was born in Edinburgh, Scotland, November 11, 1869.

He began the study of psychic facts in 1900, led to this by dissatisfaction with the failure of science or theology to throw any light on human destiny. Years of private study

and investigation followed, and in 1915 he gave a series of various lectures in London, Edinburgh and Glasgow.

In 1916, he published *Spirit Intercourse, Its Theory and Practice* and a pamphlet *If a Soldier Die,* which had a wide circulation. In 1917, he toured the U.S. as far as Chicago in search of mediums and again in 1920, spending a good deal of time in California on the latter visit.

In 1920, the British College of Psychic Science was established, and for this venture Mr. McKenzie found the entire initial cost. In 1922, *Psychic Science,* the College quarterly journal, was started on its career. In the same year he and Mrs. Barbara McKenzie, who was associated closely in all his investigations, visited Germany, Austria and Poland and had sittings with many of the best Continental psychics.

In Warsaw, they sat with the materializing medium Franek **Kluski,** and secured plaster casts of materialized hands, which they brought to London, the only ones in England. They also brought Frau Maria **Silbert,** of Graz, Austria, to the College for valuable experimental work, and also a **poltergeist** medium, of whom valuable first-hand reports were made.

Mr. McKenzie had a deep interest in physical mediumship in all its aspects and a profound knowledge of the conditions necessary for good results. On many occasions he was asked to investigate cases of haunting and of disturbances and was able to clear up annoying conditions.

He also made an intensive study of trance mediumship with Mrs. Osborne **Leonard** and Mrs. Eileen **Garrett,** and himself helped to develop the psychic talents of several trance mediums. A strong courageous personality, convinced that only through psychic facts is there any proved knowledge of **survival,** he affirmed this continuously by his writings and lectures for the years in which he acted as honorary president of the College, the first substantial organization in London to become a center for psychic demonstration and instruction.

Mrs. McKenzie, who brought a fine intellect and understanding to the study of psychic phenomena, was honorary secretary of the College until 1929, and then became honorary president for one year, being succeeded by Mrs. Champion **de Crespigny.**

Mr. McKenzie died August 29, 1929 in London. For biographical information, see the book *J. Hewat McKenzie, Pioneer of Psychical Research* by Muriel Hankey (Aquarian Press, U.K., 1963).

Mackenzie, Kenneth R. H. (1833–1886)

Prominent British occultist who was a Honorary Magus of the **Societas Rosicruciana in Anglia** and a member of the Hermetic Society of the **Golden Dawn.** From 1858–59 he edited four numbers of *Biological Review,* devoted to Spiritualism, homeopathy and electro-dentistry.

He was author of the *Royal Masonic Cyclopaedia* (1877), and as early as 1879 planned a work called *The Game of Tarot, Archaeologically and Symbolically Considered* which was announced but not published. In 1861 Mackenzie visited the famous French occultist Éliphas Lévi (Alphonse Louis Constant) in Paris, and recorded vivid personal recollections of the man and his outlook, published in *Rosicrucian,* Journal of the Soc. Ros. in Anglia.

Mackenzie died July 3, 1886. (See also **Rosicrucians**)

Mackenzie, William (1877–)

British biologist and writer, living in Italy, who played a prominent part in the scientific study of parapsychology. Born March 25, 1877 at Genoa, Italy, he studied at University of Turin (Ph.D. 1900). In 1902 he married Marie Bühler. In 1905 he founded the first Marine Biological Laboratory at the University of Genoa, and from 1912–13 conducted research in Germany on the phenomenon of "thinking animals." During World War I he was a volunteer in the Italian Army; from 1939–45 he lectured on biological philosophy at the University of Geneva, and was consultant on foreign scientific literature to publishers in Florence from 1960 onwards.

He was president of the Second International Congress of Psychical Research, Warsaw, 1923, president of the Italian Society for Parapsychology 1951–54, honorary president from 1954 onwards. He was president of the Third National Congress of Parapsychology, University of Rome, 1956, honorary member of the Institut Métapsychique, Paris, and Institut Francais de Florence.

He edited *Parapsicologia* (quarterly journal of parapsychology) from 1955–56. Dr. Mackenzie made a special study of psychobiology (parapsychology in living organisms) and has also investigated psychic animals and mathematical mediumship. He published many articles on parapsychology in *Psiche, Archives de Psycholgie, Proceedings of the Italian Society for the Advancement of Science, Quaderni di Psichiatria, Journal of the American Society for Psychical Research, Revue Métapsychique, Uomini e Idee.* His books include: *Alle Fonti della Vita* (At the Sources of Life, 1912; 1916), *Nuove Rivelazioni della Psiche Animale* (New Revelations of Animal Psyche, 1914), *Significato Bio-Filosofico della Guerra* (The Meaning of War from the Viewpoint of Biological Philosophy, 1915), *Metapsichica Moderna* (Modern Psychical Research, 1923).

Mackey, Albert Gallatin (1807–1881)

American authority on **Freemasonry,** editor of numerous books on the subject, including *Encyclopedia of Freemasonry* (1874). He was a disciple of Albert Pike (1809–1891), one of the leaders of Masonry in Charleston, U.S.A. falsely charged by "Miss Diana Vaughan," and others with the practice of Satanism and sorcery. The whole campaign proved to be an audacious conspiracy on the part of journalist Gabriel **Jogand-Pagès** to discredit and embarrass both the Catholic Church and Freemasonry. One of the earliest writers to throw doubt on the revelations of "Diana Vaughan" (as expressed in the writings of "Dr. Bataille") was British occultist and mystic Arthur E. **Waite** in his book *Devil-Worship in France* (1896). (See also Dr. **Bataille; Devil Worship;** Gabriel **Jogand-Pagès;** Diana **Vaughan**)

McMahan, Elizabeth Anne (1924–)

Assistant professor of zoology, also active in the field of parapsychology. Born May 5, 1924 at Mocksville, North Carolina, she studied at Duke University (M.A. 1948), University of Hawaii (Ph.D. 1960). From 1943–48 she was a research assistant, from 1948–54 research fellow at the Parapsychology Laboratory, Duke University, Durham, N.C.; graduate teaching assistant, Zoology Department, Duke University from 1954–56; graduate teaching assistant, entomology from 1956–59, research assistant, entomology from 1959–60, Department of Zoology and Entomology, University of Honolulu; fellow, University of Chicago 1960–61; assistant professor of zoology, University of North Carolina 1961 onwards.

She is a charter member of the Parapsychological Association, member of American Association for the Advancement of Science, Entomological Society of America. In addition to her many articles on entomology, she published a number of papers on parapsychology, based on her own investigations in telepathy, psychokinesis and precognition.

Her contributions to the *Journal of Parapsychology* include: 'PK Experiments With Two-Sided Objects' (vol. 9, 1945), 'An Experiment in Pure Telepathy' (vol. 10, 1946), 'A Second Zagreb-Durham ESP Experiment' (with J. B. **Rhine,** vol. 11, 1947), 'A Review of the Evidence for Dowsing' (vol. 11, 1947), 'Extrasensory Perception of Cards in an Unknown Location' (vol. 12, 1948), 'Report of Further Marchesi Experiments' (with E. K. Bates, vol. 18, 1954).

MacRobert, Russell Galbraith (1890–)

Psychiatrist, neurologist, who took a special interest in parapsychology. Born June 4, 1890 at London, Ontario, Canada, he studied at University of Western Ontario (M.D. 1912) and University of Toronto (M.D. 1916). In 1936 he married Fannie G. Perkinson. From 1922–41 he was associate neuropsychiatrist, Lenox Hill Hospital, New York, 1941–46 captain, Medical Corps, USNR; 1946–55 attending physician at Lenox Hill Hospital, 1955 onwards consulting neuropsychiatrist; instructor in clinical neurology New York University, Bellevue Hospital Medical Center, New York. His memberships include: American Medical Association, American Academy of Neurology, American Board of Psychiatry and Neurology, Academy of Religion and Mental Health, American Society for Psychical Research. He is a fellow of the American Psychiatric Association, the American Society of Clinical Hypnosis.

In addition to his many published articles on medical, psychiatric and neurological subjects, he took great interest in clairvoyance and mediumship and was author of the survey 'Current Attitudes of American Neuropsychiatrists towards Parapsychology' (*Journal of Parapsychology,* Nov. 1948). In the *Journal of Insurance Medicine* he wrote on 'Psychiatry and Intuition' (vol. 4, No. 3, 1949) and 'Hallucinations of the Sane' (vol. 5, No. 3, 1950). His articles in *Tomorrow* magazine included: 'Science Studies Intuition' (May 1950), 'When is Healing "Psychic"?' (Spring 1955), 'Where is Bridey Murphy?' (Spring 1956). He contributed the chapter 'Something Better Than Reincarnation' to the book *Reincarnation* (1956) and preface to R. DeWitt **Miller**'s book *You Do Take It With You* (1956).

Macrocosm, The

The whole universe (Greek *Macros,* long, *Kosmos,* the world) symbolized by a six-pointed star, formed of two triangles, and the sacred symbol of Solomon's seal. It represents the infinite and the absolute—that is, the most simple and complete abridgment of the science of all things. **Paracelsus** stated that every magical figure and Kabalistic sign of the pantacles which compel spirits may be reduced to two—the Macrocosm and the **Microcosm** (world in miniature). (See also **Magical Diagrams; Microcosm**)

Macroprosopus, The

One of the four magical elements in the **Kabala,** and probably representing one of the four simple elements—air, water, earth, or fire. Macroprosopus means "creator of the great world."

Macumba

General term for the magical practices of spiritists in Brazil. These include spirit **possession** and both white and black magic. For detailed study see A. J. Langguth, *Macumba* (Harper & Row, 1975). (See also **Spiritism**)

Madre Natura

An old and powerful secret society of Italy, who worshiped and idealized nature. It seems to have been founded by members of the ancient Italian priesthood. It had a tradition that one of the Popes as Cardinal de Medici became a member of the fraternity, and there appears to be some documentary evidence for this claim. The Society accepted the allegorical interpretation which the Neo-Platonists had placed upon the pagan creeds during the first ages of Christianity.

Maeterlinck, Maurice (1862–1949)

Famous Belgian writer and poet, to whom the Nobel Prize of literature was awarded in 1911, a profound thinker in whom the mystic sense and the spirit of inquiry was fortunately blended.

He was born in Ghent August 29, 1862 and educated at the Collège Sainte-Barbe and the University of Ghent. For a time, he lived in Paris, where he became associated with the symbolist school of French poetry. His first publication was *Serres Chaudes,* a volume of poems in 1889. His play *La Princesse Maleine* in the following year was praised by novelist Octave Mirbeau. Although Maeterlinck had already qualified for a legal profession, he decided to follow a literary life.

From the very beginning of his great literary career, he was attracted by the problems of the inner life. His early plays were dominated by the grim specter of death as the destroyer of life. In his later works his interest in psychical phenomena developed and the fearful mystery gave place to wondrous fascination.

The Unknown Guest, Our Eternity and *The Wrack of the Storm* disclosed a familiarity with all the prevailing ideas on psychical subjects and he showed no doubt whatever as to the genuineness of phenomena. "The question of fraud and imposture are naturally the first that suggest themselves," he wrote, "when we begin the study of these phenomena. But the slightest acquaintance with the life, habits and proceedings of the three or four leading mediums is enough to remove even the faintest shadow of suspicion. Of all the explanations conceivable, the one which attributes everything to imposture and trickery is unquestionably the most extraordinary and the least probable . . . From the moment that one enters upon this study, all suspicions are dispelled without leaving a trace behind them; and we are soon convinced that the key to the riddle is not to be found in imposture . . . Less than

fifty years ago most of the hypnotic phenomena which are now scientifically classified were likewise looked upon as fraudulent. It seems that man is loth to admit that there lie within him many more things than he imagined."

He considered survival proved, but was uncertain as to the possibility of communication with the dead. Between the telepathic and spirit hypotheses he could not make a choice in favor of the latter. He admitted that "the survival of the spirit is no more improbable than the prodigious faculties which we are obliged to attribute to the medium if we deny them to the dead; but the existence of the medium, contrary to that of the spirit, is unquestionable, and therefore it is for the spirit, or for those who make use of its name, first to prove that it exists."

He added that in his view there were five imaginable solutions of the great problem: the religious solution, annihilation, survival with our consciousness of today, survival without any sort of consciousness and survival with a modified consciousness. The religious solution he ruled out definitely because it occupied "a citadel without doors or windows into which human reason does not penetrate." Annihilation he considered unthinkable and impossible. "We are the prisoners of an infinity without outlet, wherein nothing perishes, wherein everything is dispersed but nothing lost." Survival without consciousness of today is inconceivable as the change of death and the casting aside of the body must bring about an enlarged understanding and an expansion of the intellectual horizon. Survival without any consciousness amounted to the same thing as annihilation.

The only solution which appealed to him was survival with a modified consciousness. He argued: since we have been able to acquire our present consciousness why should it be impossible for us to acquire another in which our present consciousness is a mere speck, a negligible quantity: "Let us accustom ourselves to regard death as a form of life which we do not as yet understand; let us learn to look upon it with the same eye that looks upon birth; and soon our minds will be accompanied at the steps of the tomb with the same glad expectation that greets a birth."

Maeterlinck died May 6, 1949. Two of his books dealing with the paranormal were reissued by University Books, Inc. as follows: *The Great Secret* (1969), *The Unknown Guest* (1975).

Magi

Priests of ancient Persia, and cultivators of the wisdom of Zoroaster (or Zarathustra) (possibly 1500 B.C.) They were instituted by Cyrus when he founded the new Persian empire, and are supposed to have been of the Median race. The German scholar K. W. F. von Schlegel stated in his *Lectures on the Philosophy of History* (2 vols., 1829): "they were not so much a hereditary sacerdotal caste as an order or association, divided into various and successive ranks and grades, such as existed in the mysteries—the grade of apprenticeship—that of mastership—that of perfect mastership." In short, they were a theosophical college; and either its professors were indifferently "magi," or magicians, and "wise men" or they were distinguished into two classes by those names.

Their name, pronounced "Mogh" by later Persians, and "Magh" by the ancients, signified "Wise," and such was the interpretation of it given by the Greek and Roman writers. Stobæus expressly called the science of the magi, the "service of the gods," so Plato. According to Joseph Ennemoser in his book *The History of Magic* (1847), "Magiusiah, Madschusie," signified the office and knowledge of the priest, who was called "Mag, Magius, Magiusi," and afterwards magi and "Magician." The philosopher J. J. Brucker maintained that the primitive meaning of the word was "fire worshiper," "worship of the light," an erroneous opinion. In modern Persian, the word is "Mog," and "Mogbed" signifies high priest. The high priest of the Parsees at Surat is called "Mobed." Others derive the word from "Megh," "Meh-ab" signifying something which is great and noble, and Zoroaster's disciples were called "Meghestom."

A. J. E. B. Salverte, author of *Des Sciences Occulte* (1829), stated that these Mobeds were named in the Pehivi dialect "Magoi." They were divided into three classes: Those who abstained from all animal food; those who never ate of the flesh of any tame animals; and those who made no scruple to eat any kind of meat. A belief in the transmigration of the soul was the foundation of this abstinence.

They professed the science of **divination,** and for that purpose met together and consulted in their temples. They professed to make truth the great object of their study, for that alone, they said, can make man like God "whose body resembles light, as his soul or spirit resembles truth."

They condemned all images, and those who said that the gods were male and female; they had neither temples nor altars, but worshiped the sky, as a representative of the Deity, on the tops of mountains; they also sacrificed to the sun, moon, earth, fire, water, and winds, said Herodotus, meaning, no doubt that they adored the heavenly bodies and the elements. This was probably before the time of Zoroaster, when the religion of Persia seems to have resembled that of ancient India. Their hymns in praise of the Most High exceeded (according to Dio Chrysostom) the sublimity of anything in Homer or Hesiod. They exposed their dead bodies to wild beasts.

Schlegel maintained that it was an open question "whether the old Persian doctrine and wisdom or tradition of light did not undergo material alterations in the hands of its Median restorer, Zoroaster, or whether this doctrine was preserved in all its purity by the order of the magi." He then remarked that on them devolved the important trust of the monarch's education, which must necessarily have given them great weight and influence in the state. They were in high credit at the "Persian gates" (the Oriental name given to the capital of the empire, and the abode of the prince) and they took the most active part in all the factions that encompassed the throne, or that were formed in the vicinity of the court.

In Greece, and even in Egypt, the sacerdotal fraternities and associations of initiated, formed by the mysteries, had in general but an indirect, although not unimportant influence on affairs of state, but in the Persian monarchy they acquired a complete political ascendency.

Religion, philosophy, and the sciences were all in their hands, they were the universal physicians who healed the sick in body and in spirit, and, in strict consistency with that character, ministered to the state, which is only the individual in a larger sense. The three grades of the magi

alluded to were called the "disciples," the "professed," and the "masters." They were originally from Bactria, where they governed a little state by laws of their own choice, and by their incorporation in the Persian empire, they greatly promoted the consolidation of the conquests of Cyrus. Their decline dates from the reign of Darius Hystaspes, about 500 B.C., by whom they were fiercely persecuted. This produced an emigration which extended to Cappadocia on the one hand, and to India on the other, but they were still of so much consideration at a later period as to provoke the jealousy of Alexander the Great.

"Magia Posthuma" (of F. de Schertz)

A short treatise on Vampirism published at Olmutz in 1706, and written by Ferdinand de Schertz. Reviewing it, Augustin **Calmet** stated in his *Dissertation sur les apparitions des anges . . . et sur les revenaus et vampires* (1746 etc.):

"The author relates a story of a woman that died in a certain village, after having received all the sacraments, and was buried with the usual ceremonies, in the churchyard. About four days after her death, the inhabitants of the village were affrighted with an uncommon noise and outcry, and saw a spectre, sometimes in the shape of a dog, and sometimes in that of a man, which appeared to great multitudes of people, and put them to excessive pain by squeezing their throats, and pressing their breasts, almost to suffocation. There were several whose bodies he bruised all over, and reduced them to the utmost weakness, so that they grew pale, lean, and disfigured. His fury was sometimes so great as not to spare the very beasts, for cows were frequently found beaten to the earth, half dead; at other times with their tails tied to one another, and their hideous lowings sufficiently expressed the pain they felt. Horses were often found almost wearied to death, foaming with sweat, and out of breath, as if they had been running a long and tiresome race; and these calamities continued for several months."

The author of the treatise examined the subject in the capacity of a lawyer and discussed both the matter of fact and the points of law arising from it. He was clearly of the opinion that if the suspected person was really the author of these noises, disturbances, and acts of cruelty, the law would justify the burning of the body, as is practiced in the case of other specters which come again and molest the living.

He related also several stories of apparitions of this sort and listed the mischiefs done by them. One, among others, was of a herdsman of the village of Blow near the town of Kadam in Bohemia, who appeared for a considerable time and called upon several persons, who all died within eight days. At last, the inhabitants of Blow dug up the herdsman's body and fixed it in the ground, with a stake driven through it. The man, even in this condition, laughed at the people that were employed about him, and told them they were very obliging to furnish him with a stick to defend himself from the dogs.

The same night, he extricated himself from the stake, frightened several persons by appearing to them, and occasioned the death of many more than he had hitherto done. He was then delivered into the hands of the hangman, who put him into a cart in order to burn him outside the town. As they went along, the carcass shrieked in the most hideous manner, and threw its arms and legs about as if it had been alive, and upon being again run through with a stake, it gave a loud cry, and a great quantity of fresh, florid blood issued from the wound. At last the body was burnt to ashes, and this execution put a final stop to the specter's appearing and infesting the village.

The same method was practiced in other places where these apparitions were seen, and upon taking them out of the ground, their bodies seemed fresh and florid, their limbs pliant and flexible, without any worms or putrefaction, but not without a great stench.

The author quoted several other writers, who attested what he related concerning these specters, which, he stated, still appeared in the mountains of Silesia and Moravia. They were seen, it seems, both by day and night, and the things which formerly belonged to them were observed to stir and change their place without any person being seen to touch them. And the only remedy in these cases, he claimed, was to cut off the head and burn the body of the persons supposed to appear. (See also **Dracula;** Pierre-Daniel **Huet; Vampire**)

Magic

General term for "magic art," believed to derive from Greek *magein,* the science and religion of the priests of Zoroaster (see **Magi**), or, according to philologist Skeat, from Greek *megas* ("great") thus signifying the great science.

Early History

The earliest traces of magical practice are found in the European caves of the middle Paleolithic Age. These belong to the last interglacial period of the Pleistocene period, which has been named the Aurignacian, after the cave-dwellers of Aurignac, whose skeletons, artifacts and drawings link them with the Bushmen of South Africa.

In the cave of Gargas, near Bagnères de Luchon, occur, in addition to spirited and realistic drawings of animals, numerous imprints of human hands in various stages of mutilation. Some hands had been first smeared with a sticky substance and then pressed on the rock, others had been held in position to be dusted round with red ocher, or black pigment. Most of the imprinted hands have mutilated fingers; in some cases the first and second joints of one or more fingers are wanting; in others the stumps only of all fingers remain.

A close study of the hand imprints makes it evident that they are not to be regarded as those of lepers. There can be little doubt that the joints were removed for a specific purpose, and on this point there is general agreement among anthropologists.

A clue to the mystery is provided by the magical custom among the Bushmen of similarly removing finger joints. G. W. Stow, in his book *The Native Races of South Africa* (1905) referred to this strange form of sacrifice. He once came into contact with a number of Bushmen who "had all lost the first joint of the little finger" which had been removed with a "stone knife" for the purpose of ensuring a safe journey to the spirit world. Another writer told of an old Bushman woman whose little fingers of both hands had been mutilated, three joints in all having been removed. She explained that each joint had been sacrificed to express her sorrow as each one of three daughters died. No doubt, however, there was a deeper meaning in the custom than she cared to confess.

In his *Report on the Northwestern Tribes of the Dominion of Canada* (1889), Franz Boas gave evidence of the custom among these peoples. When frequent deaths resulted from disease, the Canadian Indians used to sacrifice the joints of their little fingers in order (they explained) "to cut off the deaths." Among the Indian Madigas (Telugu pariahs), the **evil eye** was averted by sacrificers who dipped their hands in the blood of goats or sheep and impressed them on either side of a house door. This custom was also known to Brahmans. Impressions of hands were also occasionally seen on the walls of Indian Mohammedan mosques. As among the northwest Canadian tribes, the hand ceremony was most frequently practiced in India when epidemics took a heavy toll of lives. The Bushmen also removed finger joints when stricken with sickness. In Australia, where during initiation ceremonies the young aborigine men had teeth knocked out and bodies scarred, the women of some tribes mutilated the little fingers of daughters in order to influence their future careers.

Apparently the finger chopping customs of Paleolithic times had a magical significance. On some of the paintings in the Aurignacian caves appear symbols which suggest the slaying with spears and cutting up of animals. Enigmatical signs are another feature. Of special interest are the figures of animal-headed demons, some with hands upraised in the Egyptian attitude of adoration, and others apparently dancing like the animal-headed dancing gods of the Bushmen.

In the Marsonlas Paleolithic cave, there are semi-human faces of angry demons with staring eyes and monstrous noses. In the Spanish Cave at Cogul, several figures of women wearing half-length skirts and shoulder shawls, are represented dancing round a nude male. So closely do these females resemble such as usually appear in Bushmen paintings that they might well, but for their location, be credited to this interesting people. Religious dances among the Bushman tribes are associated with marriage, birth and burial ceremonies; they are also performed to exorcise demons in cases of sickness. "Dances are to us what prayers are to you," an elderly Bushman once informed a European.

Whether the cave drawings and wood, bone and ivory carvings of the Magdalenian, or late Paleolithic period at the close of the last ice epoch, are of magical significance is a problem on which there is no general agreement. It is significant to find, however, that several carved ornaments bearing animal figures or enigmatical signs are perforated as if worn as charms. On a piece of horn found at Lorthet, Hautes Pyrénées, are beautiful incised drawings of reindeer and salmon, above which appear mystical symbols. An ape-like demon carved on bone was found at Mas d'Azil. On a reindeer horn from Laugerie Basse, a prostrate man with a tail is creeping up on all fours towards a grazing bison. These are some of the instances which lend color to the view that late Paleolithic art had its origin in magical beliefs and practices—that hunters carved on the handles of weapons and implements, or scratched on cave walls, the images of the animals they desired to capture—sometimes with the secured co-operation of demons, and sometimes with the aid of magical spells.

Coming to historic times, we know that the ancient Egyptians possessed a highly-developed magical system (see **Egypt**), as did the Babylonians (see **Semites**) and other pristine civilizations. Indeed, from these the medieval European system of magic is believed to have evolved. **Greece** and **Rome** also possessed distinct national systems, which in some measure were branches of their religions, and thus, like the Egyptian and Babylonian, were preserves of the priesthood.

Magic in early Europe was, of course, merely an appendage of the various religious systems which obtained throughout that continent, and it was these systems which later generated into **witchcraft.** But upon the foundation of Christianity, the church soon began to regard the practice of magic as foreign to the spirit of its religion. Thus the Thirty-sixth Canon of the Ecumenical Council held at Laodicea in 364 A.D. forbad clerks and priests to become magicians, enchanters, mathematicians or astrologers. It ordered, moreover, that the Church should expel from its bosom those who employed ligatures or phylacteries, because, it said, phylacteries are the prisons of the soul. The Fourth Canon of the Council of Oxia, A.D. 525, prohibited the consultation of sorcerers, augurs, diviners, and divinations made with wood or bread, while the Sixtieth Canon of the Council of Constantinople A.D. 692, excommunicated for a period of six years diviners and those who had recourse to them. The prohibition was repeated by the Council of Rome in 721. The Forty-second Canon of the Council of Tours in 613 was to the effect that the priests should teach to the people the inefficacy of magical practices to restore the health of men or animals, and later Councils practically endorsed the church's earlier views.

Medieval Magic

It does not appear that what may be called "medieval magic" took final and definite shape until about the twelfth century. Modeled upon the systems in vogue among the Byzantines and Moors of Spain, which were evolved from the Alexandrian system (see **Neoplatonism**), what might be called the "oriental" type of magic gained footing in Europe, and quite superseded the earlier and semi-barbarian systems in use among the various countries of that continent, most of which, as has been said, were the relics of older pagan practice and ritual. To these relics clung the witch and the wizard and the professors of lesser magic, whereas among the disciples of the imported system we find the magician (black and white), the necromancer and the sorcerer.

The manner in which the theosophy and the magic of the East was imported was probably two-fold. First, there is evidence that it was imported into Europe by persons returning from the Crusades; secondly, we know that in matters of wisdom, Byzantium fell heir to Alexandria, and that from Constantinople magic was disseminated throughout Europe, along with other sciences.

It is not necessary to detail here the history of witchcraft and lesser sorcery, as that is already covered in the article **witchcraft.** It is sufficient to confine ourselves strictly to the history of the higher branches of magic. But it is relevant to remark that Europe appears to have obtained its pneumotology largely from the Orient through Christianity, from Jewish and early Semitic sources, and it is an

open question how far eastern demonology colored that of the Catholic Church.

Medieval magic of the higher type has practically no landmarks save a series of great names. Its tenets experienced but little alteration during six centuries. From the eighth to the thirteenth century, there does not appear to have been much persecution of the professors of magic, but after that period the opinions of the church underwent a radical change, and the life of the magus was fraught with considerable danger. However, it is pretty clear that he was not victimized in the same manner as his lesser brethren, the sorcerers and wizards, although we find Paracelsus consistently baited by the medical profession of his day. **Agrippa** was also constantly persecuted, and even mystics like Jakob **Boehme** were imprisoned and ill-used.

It is difficult at this distance of time to estimate the enormous vogue that magic experienced, whether for good or evil during the Middle Ages. Although severely punished if discovered, or if its professors became sufficiently notorious to court persecution, the power it seems to have conferred upon them was eagerly sought by scores of people—the majority of whom were quite unfitted for its practice and clumsily betrayed themselves into the hands of the authorities. In the article **Black Magic,** there is an outline of the history of that lesser magic known as sorcery or "black magic," and the persecutions which overtook those who practiced it.

As already mentioned, the history of higher magic in Europe is a matter of great names, and these are somewhat few. They do not include alchemists, who are strictly speaking not magicians, as their application of arcane laws was particular and not universal, but this is not to say that some alchemists were not also magicians (see also **Alchemy**). The two great names which stand out in the history of European magic are those of Paracelsus and Agrippa, who formulated the science of medieval magic in its broad outlines. They were also the greatest practical magicians of the Middle Ages, as apart from pure mystics, alchemists and others, and their thaumaturgic and necromantic experiences were probably never surpassed. With them, medieval magic comes to a close and the further history of the science in Europe will be found outlined in the division below entitled "Modern Magic."

Scientific Theories Regarding the Nature of Magic

General agreement as to the proper definition of magic is lacking, as it depends upon the view taken of religious belief. According to Sir James George Frazer, author of *The Golden Bough* (1890), magic and religion are one and the same thing, or are so closely allied as to be almost identical. This may be true of peoples in a primitive condition of society, but can scarcely apply to magic and religion as fully fledged, as for example in medieval times, however fundamental may be their original unity.

The objective theory of magic would regard it as entirely distinct from religion, possessed of certain well-marked attributes, and traceable to mental processes differing from those from which the religious idea springs. Here and there, the two have become fused by the superimposition of religious upon magical practice.

The objective idea of magic, in short, rests on the belief that it is based on magical laws which are supposed to operate with the regularity of those of natural science. The subjective view, on the other hand, is that many practices seemingly magical are in reality religious, and that no rite can be called magical which is not so designated by its celebrant or agent.

It has also been said that religion consists of an appeal to the gods, whereas magic is the attempt to force their compliance. Henri Hubert and Marcel Mauss (*Greatness and Decline of the Celts,* 1934) believed that magic is essentially traditional. Holding that the primitive mind is markedly unoriginal, they satisfied themselves that magic is therefore an art which did not exhibit any frequent changes amongst primitive folk, and was fixed by its laws. Religion, they claimed, was official and organized, magic prohibited and secret. Magical power appeared to them to be determined by the contiguity, similarity and contrast of the object of the act, and the object to be effected.

Sir J. G. Frazer believed all magic to be based on the law of sympathy—that is, the assumption that things act on one another at a distance because of their being secretly linked together by invisible bonds. He divided sympathetic magic into homeopathic magic and contagious magic. The first is imitative or mimetic, and may be practiced by itself, but the latter usually necessitates the application of the imitative principle. Well-known instances of mimetic magic are the forming of wax figures in the likeness of an enemy, which are destroyed in the hope that he will perish. This belief persisted in European **witchcraft** into relatively modern times. Contagious magic may be instanced by the savage anointing the weapon which caused a wound instead of the wound itself, in the belief that the blood on the weapon continues to feel with the blood on the body.

L. Marillier divided magic into three classes: the magic of the word or act; the magic of the human being independent of rite or formula, and the magic which demands a human being of special powers and the use of ritual. A. Lehmann believed magic to be a practice of superstition, and founded in illusion.

The fault of all such theories is that they strive after too great an exactness, and that they do not allow sufficiently for the feeling of wonder and awe which is native to the human mind. Indeed they designate this "strained attention." We may grant that the attention of savages to a magical rite is "strained," so strained in some cases that it terrifies them into insanity, and it would seem therefore as if the limits of "attention" were overpassed, and as if it shaded into something very much deeper. Moreover it is just possible that in the future it may be granted that so-called sympathetic magic does not partake of the nature of magic at all, but has greater affinities (owing to its strictly natural and non-supernatural character) with pseudoscience.

Magic is recognized by many primitive peoples as a force rather than an art—something which impinges upon the thought of man from outside. It would appear that many tribes believed in what would seem to be a great reservoir of magical power, the exact nature of which they are not prepared to specify.

Thus amongst certain American-Indian tribes we find a force called *Orenda* or spirit-force. Amongst the ancient Peruvians, everything sacred was *huaca* and possessed of magical power. In Melanesia, we find a force spoken of called *mana,* transmissible and contagious, which may be seen in the form of flames or even heard. The Malays used the word *kramat* to signify the same thing, and the Malagasy the term *hasma.* Some of the tribes around Lake Tanganyika believed in such a force, which they called *ngai,* and Australian tribes had similar terms, such as *churinga* and *boolya.* In Mexico there was a strange creed named *nagualism,* which partook of the same conception—everything *nagual* was magical or possessed an inherent spiritual force of its own.

Theories of the Origin of Magic

Many theories have been advanced regarding the origin of magic—some authorities believing that it commenced with the idea of personal superiority, others through animistic beliefs (see **Animism**), and still others through such ideas as that physical pains for which the savage could not account, were supposed to be inflicted by invisible weapons. This last theory is, of course, in itself, merely animistic.

It does not seem, however, that writers on the subject have given sufficient attention to the great influence exerted on the mind of man by odd or peculiar occurrences. Whilst it would be unreasonable to advance the hypothesis that magic entirely originated from such a source, it may have been a powerful factor in the growth of magical belief. To which, too, animism and taboo contributed their quota. The cult of the dead and their worship might also have become fused with magical practice, and a complete demonology would thus speedily arise.

The Dynamics of Magic

Magical practice is governed by well-marked laws, limited in number. It possesses many classes of practitioner, as, for example, the diviner or augur, whose duties are entirely different from those of the witch-doctor (see **Divination**). Chief among these laws, as has been already hinted, is that of sympathy, which, as has been said, must inevitably be subdivided into the laws of similarity, contiguity and antipathy.

The law of similarity and homeopathy is again divisible into two sections: (1) the assumption that like produces like—an illustration of which is the destruction of a model in the form of an enemy, and (2) the idea that like cures like—for instance, that the stone called the bloodstone can staunch the flow of bleeding.

The law dealing with antipathy rests on the assumption that the application of a certain object or drug expels its contrary.

There remains contiguity, which is based on the concept that whatever has once formed part of an object continues to form part of it. Thus, if a magician can obtain a portion of a person's hair, he can work harm upon that person through the invisible bonds which are supposed to extend between the individual and the hair in the sorcerer's possession. It is commonly believed that if the animal **familiar** of a witch be wounded, that the wound will react in a sympathetic manner on the witch herself (see **Wer-wolf**). This is called "repercussion."

Another widespread belief is that if the magician procures the name of a person he can gain magical dominion over that person. This, of course, arose from the idea that the name of an individual was identical with himself. The doctrine of the "Incommunicable Name," the hidden name of the god or magician, is well instanced by many legends in Egyptian history, the deity usually taking extraordinary care to keep his name secret, in order that no one might gain power over him (see **Egypt**). The spell or incantation is connected with this concept, and with these, in a lesser degree, may be associated magical gesture, which is usually introduced for the purpose of accentuating the spoken word.

Gesture is often symbolic or sympathetic, it is sometimes the reversal of a religious rite, such as marching against the sun, which is known as walking "widdershins." The method of pronouncing rites is, too, one of great importance. Archaic or foreign expressions are usually found in spells ancient and modern, and the tone in which the incantation is spoken, no less than its exactness, is also important. To secure exactness, rhythm was often employed, which had the effect of aiding memory.

The Magician

In early society, the magician, which term includes the shaman, medicine-man, piagé, and witch-doctor, may hold his position by hereditary right; by an accident of birth, as being the seventh son of a seventh son; to revelation from the gods; or through mere mastery of ritual. In primitive life, we find the shaman a good deal of a medium, for instead of summoning the powers of the air at his bidding, as did the magicians of medieval days, he found it necessary to throw himself into a state of trance and seek them in their own sphere. The magician is also often regarded as possessed by an animal or supernatural being. The duties of the priest and magician are often combined in primitive society, but it cannot be too strongly asserted that where a religion has been superseded, the priests of the old cult are, for those who have taken their places, nothing but magicians.

Medieval Definition of Magic

The definitions of magic by the great magicians of medieval and modern times naturally differ greatly from those of anthropologists. For example, Éliphas **Levi** stated in his *History of Magic* (1913): "Magic combines in a single science that which is most certain in philosophy with that which is eternal and infallible in religion. It reconciles perfectly and incontestably those two terms so opposed on the first view—faith and reason, science and belief, authority and liberty. It furnishes the human mind with an instrument of philosophical and religious certainty, as exact as mathematics, and even accounting for the infallibility of mathematics themselves. . . . There is an incontestable truth, and there is an infallible method of knowing that truth; while those who attain this knowledge and adopt it as a rule of life, can endow their life with a sovereign power, which can make them masters of all inferior things, of wandering spirits, or in other words, arbiters and kings of the world."

Paracelsus stated: "The magical is a great hidden wisdom, and reason is a great open folly. No armour shields against magic for it strikes at the inward spirit of life. Of this we may rest assured, that through full and powerful imagination only can we bring the spirit of any man into an image. No conjuration, no rites are needful; circle-making and the scattering of incense are mere humbug and jugglery. The human spirit is so great a thing that no man can express it; eternal and unchangeable as God Himself is the mind of man; and could we rightly comprehend the mind of man, nothing would be impossible to us upon the earth. Through faith the

imagination is invigorated and completed, for it really happens that every doubt mars its perfection. Faith must strengthen imagination, for faith establishes the will. Because man did not perfectly believe and imagine, the result is that arts are uncertain when they might be wholly certain."

Agrippa also regarded magic as the true road to communion with God, thus linking it with mysticism.

Later Magic

With the death of Agrippa in 1535, the old school of magicians may be said to have ended. But the traditions of magic were handed on to others who were equally capable of preserving them, or revived by modern sensationalists.

We must carefully discriminate at this juncture between those practitioners of magic whose minds were illuminated by a high mystical ideal, and persons of doubtful occult position, like the Comte de **Saint Germain** and others. At the beginning of the seventeenth century, there were many great alchemists in practice, who were also devoted to the researches of transcendental magic, which they carefully and successfully concealed under the veil of hermetic experiment. These included Michael **Maier,** Robert **Fludd,** Cosmopolite, Jean **D'Espagnet,** Samuel Norton (see Thomas **Norton**), Baron de **Beausoleil,** and J. **Van Helmont;** another illustrious name is also that of Eirenaeus **Philalethes** (see also **Alchemy**).

The eighteenth century was rich in occult personalities, as for example the alchemist **Lascaris,** Martinez **de Pasqually,** and Louis de **Saint Martin,** who founded the Martinist school, which was continued by "Papus" (Gerard **Encausse**). After this magic merged for the moment into **Mesmerism,** and many of the secret magical societies which abounded in Europe about this period practiced **Animal Magnetism** experiments as well as **astrology, Kabalism** and **ceremonial magic.** Indeed Mesmerism powerfully influenced mystic life in the time of its chief protagonist, and the mesmerists of the first era are in direct line with the Martinist and the mystical magicians of the late eighteenth century. Indeed mysticism and magnetism are one and the same thing, in the persons of some of these occultists (see **Secret Tradition**) the most celebrated of which were Cazotte, Ganneau, Comte, Wronski, Du Potet, Hennequin, Comte d'Ourches, and Baron de Guldenstubbé, and last of the initiates known to us, Éliphas Lévi.

Modern Revivals of Magic

During the 1890s, there was a revival of interest in ritual magic in Europe amongst both intellectuals and sensationalists. This "occult underground" permeated much of the intellectual life and progressive movements in Europe, in contrast to the more popular preoccupation with Spiritualism and Table-turning. At the sensational level, this interest was characterized by Devil Worship cults, and later by hoaxes of claimed devil worship aimed at discrediting the Catholic Church and Freemasonry (see Gabriel **Jogand-Pagès**). For an excellent survey of nineteenth-century irrationalism, see *The Flight from Reason* (vol. 1 of *The Age of the Irrational*) by James Webb (1971).

On a more dignified level was the founding of the famous Hermetic Order of the Golden Dawn, which numbered amongst its members such individuals as Annie Horniman (sponsor of the Abbey Theatre, Dublin), Florence Farr (mistress of George Bernard Shaw), Israel Regardie, S. L. MacGregor Mathers, Arthur Machen, Arthur Edward Waite and poet W. B. Yeats. Another famous G. D. member was the magician Aleister Crowley, who left the order to found his own organization A.˙.A.˙.. Crowley's book *Magick in Theory and Practice* (1929 etc.) is an interesting analysis of the methods of Magic, although marred by some egocentricity and revelations stemming from psychedelic drugs.

A more sinister aspect of magical belief and practice is the claim that Adolf Hitler was strongly influenced by occultism in the formation of Nazi politics. This aspect of magic is explored in *The Spear of Destiny* by Trevor Ravenscroft (1973) and *Satan and Swastika; The Occult and the Nazi Party* by Francis King (1976).

During the 1930s, there was another popular outbreak of public interest in the occult in Britain and Europe, and a number of significant books on Magic were published. Their influence was limited only by the relatively smaller influence of mass media at that time, and the conservatism of intellectual life. Exceptional individuals like Aleister **Crowley** flourished in the 1920s and 30s, but were deplored by polite society, who regarded such occultists as scandalous misfits.

A second wave of popular occultism flared up again in the 1950s in Britain and the U.S., fueled largely by reprints of key books published during the 1930s (see Felix **Morrow**). This modern interest in Magic, however, had little in common with the outlook and ideals of medieval magicians and followers of the hermetic art, stemming largely from the trendiness of post-war affluence and the desire for sensationalist indulgence. At the seediest level, the occult explosion led to Witchcraft, Satanism and Black Magic cults. Not surprisingly, much of modern occultism has been influenced by drug taking.

During this period, one long kept secret of occultism became generally discussed—that of the important factor of sexual energy in dynamizing the processes of Magic. Although this factor was well known to the occultists of ancient India under the study of Tantra, it was openly discussed in modern times through the practices and writings of Aleister Crowley.

Although the present-day occult revival has generated many neurotic and exhibitionist magicians, whose magical feats have been greatly overrated, certain talented individuals with some special psychic gifts may well have achieved paranormal feats. There are still two opinions amongst occultists as to how such feats are achieved. First, that it is the achievement of desired effects in the physical world by the exercise of the operator's will-power, assisted by rituals. Secondly, that the desired effects are achieved by means of spirits, evoked by rituals.

There is some anecdotal evidence that old-fashioned magic does achieve minor miracles, mainly in the field of relatively small personal gains in influencing events such as success in love, business or acquiring power over others, or in causing harm to one's enemies. However, the subject is riddled with fraudulent claims and self-deception. In a modern world, science and technology have triumphed as the highest magic, achieving amazing results which the ancient magicians would have considered incredible.

Conjuring Tricks and Stage Magic

Nowadays the term "magic" normally denotes the performance of conjuring, legerdemain or illusion, although it is interesting to note that even the term "conjuring" was originally used to indicate the evocation of spirits.

It should not be supposed, however, that conjuring tricks are only a modern kind of "magic." There is evidence that tricks have been used by priests thousands of years ago to create an illusion of magical miracles. For a brief survey of the conjuring of antiquity see the fascinating and authoritative book *The Illustrated History of Magic* by Milbourne **Christopher** (1975).

The astonishing and skillful illusions of modern stage magicians show that special caution is necessary in evaluating many apparently paranormal feats of magic, and stage magicians have also performed valuable service in exposing fraudulent "psychic" feats, notable in such areas as **slate-writing.** Because of this, there is a tendency for stage magicians to be occupationally skeptical of all claimed paranormal feats. (See also **Abraham the Jew; Black Magic; Ceremonial Magic; Egypt; Magic Darts; Magical Diagrams; Magical Instruments; Magical Numbers; Magical Union of Cologne; Magical Vestments; Magicians; Medieval Magic**)

Recommended reading:

Agrippa, Henry Cornelius. *The Philosophy of Natural Magic,* London, 1651; University Books, 1974

Barrett, Francis. *The Magus; A Complete System of Occult Philosophy,* London, 1801; University Books, 1967

Bonewits, Philip E. I. *Real Magic,* Coward, McCann & Geoghegan, 1971; Berkley Medallion paperback, 1971

Christopher, Milbourne. *The Illustrated History of Magic,* Thos. Crowell, 1973/Robert Hale, London, 1975 [deals with conjuring and stage magic]

Christopher, Milbourne. *Panorama of Magic,* Dover, New York, 1962 [deals with conjuring and stage magic]

Christian, Paul. *The History & Practice of Magic,* 2 vols., Forge Press, London, 1952

Crow, W B. *A History of Magic, Witchcraft & Occultism,* Aquarian Press, U.K., 1968; Abacus paperback, U.K., 1972

(Crowley, Aleister) The Master Therion. *Magick in Theory and Practice,* Paris, 1929; Castle Books, New York, n.d.; Routledge & Kegan Paul, London, 1973; Samuel Weiser, 1974

Ennemoser, Joseph. *The History of Magic,* 2 vols., London, 1854; University Books, 1970

Freedland, Nat. *The Occult Explosion,* Putnam/Michael Joseph, London, 1972

Grant, Kenneth. *The Magical Revival,* Frederick Muller, London, 1972; Samuel Weiser, 1973

King, Francis. *Ritual Magic in England (1887 to the Present Day),* Neville Spearman, London, 1970; Macmillan, New York, 1971

King, Francis. *Sexuality, Magic & Perversion,* Neville Spearman, London, 1971; Citadel Press, 1972

Lévi, Éliphas. *Transcendental Magic,* London, 1896; revised edition Rider & Co., 1923 etc.

Lévi, Éliphas. *The History of Magic,* Rider & Co., London, 1913; David McKay, 1914.

Lévi, Éliphas. (edited A. E. Waite) *The Mysteries of*

Magic; A Digest of the Éliphas Lévi, London, 1886, 1897; University Books, 1974

Seligmann, Kurt. *The History of Magic,* Pantheon Books, New York, 1948 etc. (also titled *Magic, Supernaturalism & Religion*)

Shah, Sayed Idries. *Oriental Magic,* Rider & Co., London, 1956

Shah, Sayed Idries. *The Secret Lore of Magic; The Books of the Sorcerers,* Frederick Muller, London, 1957

Summers, Montague. *Witchcraft & Black Magic,* Rider & Co., London, 1946; Causeway, 1974

Thompson, C. J. S. *The Mysteries and Secrets of Magic,* London, 1927; Causeway, 1973

Waite, Arthur Edward. *The Book of Ceremonial Magic,* London, 1911; University Books, 1961

Webb, James. *The Flight From Reason* (Volume 1 of *The Age of the Irrational*), Macdonald, London, 1971; (American title *The Occult Underground,* Open Court, Illinois, 1974)

Webb, James. *The Occult Establishment,* Open Court, Illinois, 1975

Magic Circle, The

British organization of professional and amateur conjuring magicians. It was founded in July 1905 at the famous Pinoli's restaurant in Wardour Street, London (long since vanished), and was originally intended to honor a young professional magician Martin Charpender who had just died. Some members preferred an impersonal name to "The Martin Charpender Club," but when it was pointed out that the initials "M. C." might also stand for "Magic Circle" the latter name was agreed.

In its early period, the Magic Circle convened at St. George's Hall in Portland Place, where the famous stage magicians Maskelyne and Devant performed their feats. In 1910 the Magic Circle moved to Anderton's Hotel, Fleet Street, where it held meetings and monthly concerts (named "seances"). Individual magicians showed off their latest tricks. There were many changes of address over the years, and in the 1970s the Magic Circle was established in Chenies Mews, London, W.C.1.

In addition to providing a club for professional and amateur magicians, the Circle also gave many charity shows. Members have included doctors of medicine, philosophy and divinity as well as engineers and plumbers and a taxi-driver.

Magic Darts

The Laplanders, at one time said to be great magicians, were supposed to launch lead darts, about a finger-length, against their absent enemies, believing that with such magic darts they were sending grevious pains and maladies. (See also **Magic**)

Magical Diagrams

These were geometrical designs, representing the mysteries of deity and creation, therefore supposed to be of special virtue in rites of evocation and conjuration.

The chief of these were the Triangle, the Double Triangle, forming a six-pointed star and known as the Sign or Seal of Solomon; the Tetragram, a four-pointed star formed by the interlacement of two pillars, and the Pentagram, a five-pointed star.

These signs were traced on paper or parchment, or engraved on metals and glass and consecrated to their various uses by special rites.

The Triangle was based on the idea of trinity as found in all things, in deity, time and creation. The triangle was generally traced on the ground with the magic sword or rod, as in circles of evocation where the triangle was drawn within it and, according to the position of the magician at its point or base, so the spirits were "conjured" (summoned up) from heaven or hell.

The Double Triangle, the Sign of Solomon, symbolic of the Macrocosm, was formed by the interlacement of two triangles, thus its points constituted the perfect number six. The magicians wore it, bound on their brows and breasts during the ceremonies and it was engraved on the silver reservoir of the magic lamp.

The Tetragram was symbolic of the four elements and used in the conjuration of the **elementary spirits**—sylphs of the air, undines of the water, the fire salamanders and gnomes of the earth. In **alchemy** it represented the magical elements, salt, sulphur, mercury and azoth; in mystic philosophy the ideas Spirit, Matter, Motion and Rest; in hieroglyphs the man, eagle, lion and bull.

The Pentagram, the sign of the Microcosm, was held to be the most powerful means of conjuration in any rite. It might represent evil as well as good, for while with one point in the ascendant it was the sign of Christ, with two points in the ascendant it was the sign of Satan. By the use of the pentagram in these positions, the powers of light or darkness were evoked. The pentagram was said to be the star which led the Magi to the manger where the infant Christ was laid.

The preparation and consecration of this sign for use in magical rites was prescribed with great detail. It might be composed of seven metals, the ideal form for its expression, or traced in pure gold upon white marble never before used for any purpose. It might also be drawn with vermilion upon lambskin without a blemish prepared under the auspices of the Sun. The sign was next consecrated with the four elements, breathed on five times, dried by the smoke of five perfumes (incense, myrrh, aloes, sulfur and camphor). The names of five genii were breathed above it, and then the sign was placed successively at the north, south, east and west and center of the astronomical cross, pronouncing the letters of the sacred tetragram and various Kabalistic names (see **Kabala**).

It was believed to be of great efficacy in terrifying phantoms if engraved upon glass, and the magicians traced it on their doorsteps to prevent evil spirits from entering and the good from departing.

This symbol was used by many secret and occult societies, by the **Rosicrucians**, the **Illuminati**, down to the **Freemasonry** of modern times. Modern occultists translate the meaning of the pentagram as symbolic of the human soul and its relation to God.

The symbol is placed with one point in the ascendant. That point represents the Great Spirit, God. A line drawn from there to the left-hand angle at base is the descent of spirit into matter in its lowest form, whence it ascends to right-hand angle typifying matter in its highest form, the brain of man. From here, a line is drawn, across the figure to left angle representing man's development in intellect, while progress in material civilization, the point of danger from which all nations have fallen into moral corruption, is signified by the descent of the line to right angle at base. But the soul of man being derived from God cannot remain at this point, but must struggle upward, as is symbolized by the line reaching again to the apex, God, whence it issued.

It seems likely that the magical diagrams of Western magicians have descended from the comparable magical designs of Hindu religion known as **Yantra.** (See also **Ceremonial Magic; Magic; Magical Instruments & Accessories; Magical Vestments & Appurtenances**)

Recommended reading:

Barrett, Francis. *The Magus; A Complete System of Occult Philosophy,* London, 1801; University Books, 1967

Thompson, C. J. S. *The Mysteries and Secrets of Magic,* London, 1927; Causeway, 1974

Waite, Arthur Edward. *The Book of Ceremonial Magic,* London, 1911; University Books, 1961

Woodroffe, Sir John. *Sakti and Sakta,* Ganesh & Co., Madras, India, 1918 etc.

Magical Instruments and Accessories

In magical rites these were considered of the utmost importance. Indispensable to the efficacy of the ceremonies were the altar, the chalice, the tripod, the censer; the lamp, rod, sword, and magic fork or trident; the sacred fire and consecrated oils; the incense and the candles.

The altar might be of wood or stone, but if of the latter, then of stone that had never been worked or hewn or even touched by the hammer.

The chalice might be of different metals, symbolic of the object of the rites. Where the purpose was evil, a black chalice was used, as in the black masses of sorcerers and witches. In some talismans, the chalice was engraved as a symbol of the moon.

The tripod and its triangular stand were also made in symbolic metals.

The censer might be of bronze, but preferably of silver.

In the construction of the lamp, gold, silver, brass and iron must be used; iron for the pedestal, brass for the mirror, silver for the reservoir and at the apex a golden triangle. Various symbols were traced upon it, including an androgynous figure about the pedestal, a serpent devouring its own tail, and the Sign of Solomon.

The rod must be specially fashioned of certain woods and then consecrated to its magical uses. A perfectly straight branch of almond or hazel was to be chosen. This was cut before the tree blossomed, and cut with a golden sickle in the early dawn. Throughout its length must be run a long needle of magnetized iron; at one end there had to be affixed a triangular prism, to the other, one of black resin, and rings of copper and zinc bound about it. At the new moon, it must be consecrated by a magician who already possessed a consecrated rod.

The secret of the construction and consecration of magical rods was jealously guarded by all magicians and the rod itself was displayed as little as possible, being usually concealed in the flowing sleeve of the magician's robe.

The sword must be wrought of unalloyed steel, with copper handle in the form of a crucifix. Mystical signs were engraved on guard and blade and its consecration took place on a Sunday in full rays of the sun, when the

sword was thrust into a sacred fire of cypress and laurel, then moistened with the blood of a snake, polished, and next, together with branches of vervain, swathed in silk. The sword was generally used in the service of **Black Magic.**

The magic fork or trident used in **necromancy** was also fashioned of hazel or almond, cut from the tree at one blow with an unused knife, from whose blade must be fashioned the three prongs. Witches and sorceresses were usually depicted using the trident in their infernal rites.

The fire was lit with charcoal on which were cast branches of trees, symbolic of the end desired. In Black Magic, these generally consisted of cypress, alderwood, broken crucifixes and desecrated hosts.

The oil for anointing was compounded of myrrh, cinnamon, galingale and purest oil of Olive. Unguents were used by sorcerers and witches, who smeared their brows, breasts, and wrists with a mixture composed of human fat and blood of corpses, combined with aconite, belladonna and poisonous fungi, thinking thereby to make themselves invisible.

Incense might be of any odoriferous woods and herbs, such as cedar, rose, citron, aloes, cinnamon, sandal, reduced to a fine powder, together with incense and storax. In Black Magic, alum, sulfur and assafoetida were used as incense.

The candles, belonging solely to practices of Black Magic were molded from human fat and set in candlesticks of ebony carved in the form of a crescent.

Bowls also were used in these ceremonies, fashioned of different metals, their shape symbolic of the heavens. In necromantic rites, skulls of criminals were used, generally to hold the blood of some victim or sacrifice. (See also **Ceremonial Magic; Magic; Magical Diagrams; Magical Vestments & Appurtenances**)

Recommended reading:

Barrett, Francis. *The Magus; A System of Occult Philosophy,* London, 1801; University Books, 1967

Knight, Gareth. *The Practice of Ritual Magic,* Weiser paperback n.d.

Lévi, Éliphas. *Transcendental Magic,* Rider & Co., London, 1923 etc.

Waite, Arthur Eward. *The Book of Ceremonial Magic,* Rider & Co., London, 1911; University Books, 1973

Magical Numbers

Certain numbers and their combinations were traditionally held to be of magical power, by virtue of their representation of divine and creative mysteries.

The doctrines of Pythagoras (see **Greece**) furnished the basis for much of this belief. According to his theory numbers contained the elements of all things, of the natural and spiritual worlds and of the sciences. The real numerals of the universe were the primaries one to ten and in their combination the reason of all else might be found. To the Pythagoreans, One represented unity, therefore God; Two was duality, the Devil; Four was sacred and holy, the number on which they swore their most solemn oaths; Five was their symbol of marriage. They also attributed certain numbers to the gods, planets and elements; one represented the Sun, two the Moon; while five was fire, six the earth, eight the air, and twelve water.

Cornelius **Agrippa** in his work *Occult Philosophy* first published in Latin 1531–33, discoursed upon numbers as those characters by whose proportion all things were formed. He enumerated the virtues of numerals as displayed in nature, instancing the herb cinquefoil, which by the power of the number five exorcises devils, allays fever and forms an antidote to poisons. Also the virtue of seven, as in the power of the seventh son to cure king's evil.

One was the origin and common measure of all things. It is indivisible, not to be multiplied. In the universe there is one God; one supreme intelligence in the intellectual world, man; in the sidereal world, one Sun; one potent instrument and agency in the elementary world, the **philosopher's stone;** one chief member in the human world, the heart; and one sovereign prince in the nether world, Lucifer.

Two was the number of marriage, charity and social communion. It was also regarded sometimes as an unclean number; beasts of the field went into the Ark by twos.

Three had a mysterious value as shown in Time's trinity—Past, Present and Future; in that of Space—length, breadth and thickness; in the three heavenly virtues—faith, hope and charity; in the three worlds of man—brain (the intellectual), heart (the celestial), and body (elemental).

Four signifies solidity and foundation. There are four seasons, four elements, four cardinal points, four evangelists.

Five, as it divides ten, the sum of all numbers, is also the number of justice. There are five senses; the **Stigmata,** the wounds of Christ were five; the name of the Deity, the Pentagram, is composed of five letters; it also is a protection against beasts of prey.

Six is the sign of creation, because the world was completed in six days. It is the perfect number, because it alone by addition of its half, its third and its sixth reforms itself. It also represents servitude by reason of the Divine injunction "Six days shalt thou labour."

Seven is a miraculous number, consisting of one, unity, and six, sign of perfection. It represents life because it contains body, consisting of four elements, spirit, flesh, bone and humor (ancient concept of bodily fluids affecting the mind); and soul, made up of three elements, passion, desire and reason. The seventh day was that on which God rested from his work of creation.

Eight represents justice and fullness. Divided, its halves are equal; twice divided, it is still even. In the Beatitude, eight is the number of those mentioned—peace-makers, they who strive after righteousness, the meek, the persecuted, the pure, the merciful, the poor in spirit, and they that mourn.

Nine is the number of the muses and of the moving spheres.

Ten is completeness because one cannot count beyond it except by combinations formed with other numbers. In the ancient mysteries, ten days of initiation were prescribed. In ten is found evident signs of a Divine principle.

Eleven is the number of the commandments, while Twelve is the number of signs in the Zodiac, of the apostles, of the tribes of Israel, of the gates of Jerusalem.

This theory of numbers Agrippa applied to the casting of horoscopes. Divination by numbers was one of the favorite methods employed in the Middle Ages.

In magical rites, numbers played a great part. The instruments, vestments and ornaments must be duplicated. The power of the number three is found in the magic triangle: in the three prongs of the trident and fork, and in the three-fold repetition of names in conjurations. Seven was also of great influence, the seven days of the week each representing the period most suitable for certain evocations and these corresponded to the seven magical works: 1) works of light and riches; 2) works of divination and mystery; 3) works of skill, science and eloquence; 4) works of wrath and chastisement; 5) works of love; 6) works of ambition and intrigue; 7) works of malediction and death. (See also **Kabala; Numerology**)

Recommended reading:

Agrippa, Henry Cornelius. *The Philosophy of Natural Magic,* London, 1651; University Books, 1974

Bosman, Leonard. *The Meaning and Philosophy of Numbers,* Rider & Co., London, 1932

Butler, Christopher. *Number Symbolism,* Routledge, Kegan Paul, U.K., 1970

Redgrove, H. Stanley. *A Mathematical Theory of Spirit,* Rider & Co., London, 1912

Waite, Arthur Edward. *The Holy Kabbalah,* Williams & Norgate, London, 1929; University Books, 1960

Westcott, W. Wynn. *Numbers: Their Occult Power & Mystic Virtues,* Theosophical Publishing Society, London, 1890 etc.

Magical Union of Cologne

A society stated in a manuscript of the **Rosicrucians** (under the pseudonym "Omnis Moriar") at Cologne, Germany, to have been founded in that city in the year 1115. In the *Rosenkreutzer in seiner blosse* (1786) of F. G. E. Weise it was stated that the initiates wore a triangle as symbolizing power, wisdom and love. The more exalted orders among them were called Magos, and these held the greater mysteries of the fraternity.

Magical Vestments and Appurtenances

These were prescribed needful adjuncts to magical rites. Their color, name, form and substance, symbolic of certain powers and elements, added, it was supposed, greater efficacy to the evocations.

Abraham the Jew, a magician of the Middle Ages, prescribed a tunic of white linen, with upper robe of scarlet and girdle of white silk. A crown or fillet of silk and gold was to be worn on the head and the perfumes cast on the fire might be incense, aloes, storax, cedar, citron or rose.

According to other authorities on the subject, it was advisable to vary color of robe and employ certain jewels and other accessories according to the symbolism of the end desired. Éliphas **Lévi,** a magician of the nineteenth century, gave a detailed description of ritual, from which the following details are taken.

If the rites were those of White Magic and performed on a Sunday, then the vestment should be of purple, the tiara, bracelets and ring of gold, the latter set with chrysolith or ruby. Laurel, heliotrope and sunflowers are the symbolic flowers, while other details include a carpet of lionskins and fans of sparrow-hawk feathers. The appropriate perfumes were incense, saffron, cinnamon and red sandal.

If, however, the ceremonial took place on a Monday, the Day of the Moon, then the robe must be of white embroidered with silver and the tiara of yellow silk emblazoned with silver characters, while the wreaths were to be woven of moonwort and yellow ranunculi. The jewels appropriate to the occasion were pearls, crystals and selenite; the perfumes, camphor, amber, aloes, white sandalwood and seed of cucumber.

In evocations concerning transcendent knowledge, green was the color chosen for the vestment, or it might be green shot with various colors. The chief ornament was a necklace of pearls and hollow glass beads enclosing mercury. Agate was the symbolic jewel; narcissus, lily, herb mercury, fumitory, and marjoram the flowers; whilst the perfumes must be benzoin, mace and storax.

For operations connected with religious and political matters, the magician must don a robe of scarlet and bind on his brow a brass tablet inscribed with various characters. His ring must be studded with an emerald or sapphire, and he must burn for incense, balm, ambergris, grain of paradise and saffron. For garlands and wreaths, oak, poplar, fig and pomegranate leaves should be entwined.

If the ceremonial dealt with amatory affairs, the vestment must be of sky blue, the ornaments of copper, and the crown of violets. The magic ring must be set with a turquoise, while the tiara and clasps were wrought of lapis-lazuli and beryl. Roses, myrtle and olive were the symbolic flowers, and fans must be made of swan feathers.

If vengeance was desired on anyone, then robes must be worn whose color was that of blood, flame or rust, belted with steel, with bracelets and ring of the same metal. The tiara must be bound with gold and the wreaths woven of absinthe and rue.

To bring misfortune and death on a person, the vestment must be black and the neck encircled with lead. The ring must be set with an onyx and the garlands twined of cypress, ash and hellebore; whilst the perfumes to be used were sulfur, scammony, alum and assafœtida.

For purposes of **Black Magic,** a seamless and sleeveless robe of black was donned, while on the head was worn a leaden cap inscribed with the signs of the Moon, Venus and Saturn. The wreaths were of vervain and cypress; and the perfumes burned were aloes, camphor and storax. (See also **Ceremonial Magic; Magic; Magical Diagrams; Magical Instruments & Accessories**)

Recommended reading:

Knight, Gareth. *The Practice of Ritual Magic,* Weiser paperback, n.d.

Lévi, Éliphas. *Transcendental Magic,* Rider & Co., London, 1923 etc.

Waite, Arthur Edward. *The Book of Ceremonial Magic,* Rider & Co., London, 1911; University Books, 1973

Magicians (Illusionists)

Nowadays the term "magician" is used to denote professional illusionists. Such magicians and mediums have been in opposing camps since the earliest days of modern Spiritualism. The first important challenge of a magician to Spiritualism was issued in 1853 by J. H. Anderson of New York. He offered a thousand dollars to any "poverty-stricken medium" who would come to his hall and attempt to produce **raps** there. The **Fox Sisters** accepted immediately and, accompanied by Judge J. W. **Edmonds** and Dr. Grey, went to the hall. But Anderson backed out and, amid the hisses of the audience, refused them admission to the stage.

Some of the most famous magicians acknowledged having witnessed genuine phenomena.

The clairvoyant powers of Alexis **Didier** stupefied the famous conjurer Robert Houdin. His signed declaration was published by Dr. Edwin Lee in his book *Animal Magnetism* (1866) as follows: "I cannot help stating that the facts above related are scrupulously exact and the more I reflect upon them the more impossible do I find it to class them among the tricks which are the objects of my art."

In a letter to M. de Mirville who introduced him to Alexis Didier, Houdin wrote: "I, therefore, came away from this seance as astonished as anyone can be, and fully convinced that it would be quite impossible for anyone to produce such surprising effects by mere skill."

The stage magician Leon Bosco used to laugh immoderately at the belief that the phenomena of the famous medium D. D. **Home** could be thought imitable by the resources of his art. Canti similarly declared to Prince Napoleon "that he could in no way account for the phenomena he saw on the principles of his profession." He also published a letter expressing the same opinion. (See *Outlines of Investigation Into Spiritualism* by T. Barkas, 1862) Robert Houdin also stated: "I have come away from that seance as astounded as I could be, and persuaded that it is perfectly impossible by chance or adroitness to produce such marvellous effects." (*Experimental Psychologie* by Carl DuPrel, Leipzig, 1891)

The stage magician Hamilton (Pierre Etienne Chocat), successor of Robert Houdin, in a letter to the **Davenport Brothers,** published in the *Gazette des Etrangers,* September 27, 1865, declared: "Yesterday I had the pleasure of being present at the seance you gave, and came away from it convinced that jealousy alone was the cause of the outcry raised against you. The phenomena produced surpassed my expectations; and your experiments were full of interest for me. I consider it my duty to add that those phenomena are inexplicable, and the more so by such persons as have thought themselves able to guess your supposed secret, and who are, in fact, far indeed from having discovered the truth."

This letter was accompanied by a similar statement from M. Rhys, a manufacturer of conjuring implements who examined the cabinet and instruments of the Davenports and declared that the insinuations cast about them were false and malevolent and, the cabinet being completely isolated, all participation in the manifestations by strangers was absolutely impossible.

Prof. Jacobs wrote on April 10, 1881 to the editor of *Licht, Mehr Licht* about the phenomena which occurred through the Davenport Brothers in Paris: "As a prestidigitator of repute and a sincere spiritualist, I affirm that the medianimic facts, demonstrated by the two brothers were absolutely true, and belonged to the spiritualistic order of things in every respect. Messrs. Robin and Robert Houdin, when attempting to imitate these said facts, never presented to the public anything beyond an infantile and almost grotesque parody of the said phenomena, and it would be only ignorant and obstinate persons who could regard the question seriously as set forth by these gentlemen."

However, one should add that in modern times the Davenports are considered to be illusionists rather than mediums.

Samuel Bellachini, Court Conjurer at Berlin, stated in an authenticated statement given to the medium Henry **Slade:** "I must, for the sake of truth, hereby certify that the phenomenal occurrences with Mr. Slade have been thoroughly examined by me with the minutest observation and investigation of his surroundings, including the table, and that I have not in the smallest degree found anything produced by means of prestidigitative manifestations, or by mechanical apparatus; and that any explanation of the experiments which took place under the circumstances and conditions then obtaining by any reference to prestidigitation is absolutely impossible. It must rest with such men of science as Crookes and Wallace in London, Perty in Berne, Butleroff in St. Petersburg to search for the explanation of this phenomenal power, and to prove its reality."

The great illusionist Harry Kellar witnessed, in January 1882 in Calcutta a levitation of the medium William **Eglinton.** He wrote (*Proceedings* of the Society for Psychical Research, vol. 9, p. 359): "A circle having been formed, I was placed on Mr. Eglinton's left and seized his left hand firmly in my right. Immediately on the extinction of the lights I felt him rise slowly in the air and as I retained firm hold of his hand, I was pulled to my feet, and subsequently compelled to jump on a chair and then on the table, in order to retain my hold of him. That his body did ascend into the air on that occasion with an apparently utter disregard to the law of gravity, there can be no doubt. What most excited my wonder was the fact, for I may speak of it as a fact without qualification, that Mr. Eglinton rose from my side, and, by the hold he had on my right hand, pulled me up after him, my own body appeared for the time being to have been rendered non-susceptible to gravity."

However, the case of S. J. Davey is especially noteworthy. He was a magician who attended some **slate-writing** seances of Eglinton and was impressed. He made a deep study of the problem and, in agreement with Dr. Richard **Hodgson,** presented himself as a medium and produced all the characteristic phenomena of the seance room to the entire satisfaction of his sitters. An account of his demonstration is published in *Proceedings* of the Society for Psychical Research, vol. 4. His revelation that he did everything by trickery was disbelieved. Even Alfred Russel **Wallace** suggested that Davey was also a good physical medium and could get phenomena supernormally as he exhibited all the characteristic physiological symptoms of trance convulsions as other mediums.

Largely as a consequence of the acute controversy which slate-writing aroused, the Society for Psychical Research asked the conjurer Professor Hoffman (Angelo J. Lewis) to report upon Eglinton's performance in his professional capacity. He concluded in his report, published in August, 1886: "If conjuring were the only explanation of the slate-writing phenomena, I should

certainly have expected that their secret would long since have become public property."

The two most tenacious magician opponents of Spiritualism, J. N. Maskelyne and Harry **Houdini,** focused public attention on themselves for many years. They both led crusades against mediums. Maskelyne started by claiming to have unmasked the Davenport Brothers. He admitted that in their effect upon the public mind no alleged manifestations of mediums could be compared with their exhibitions. "Certain it is, England was completely taken aback for a time by the wonders presented by these jugglers." Maskelyne, however, was not too successful in dispelling this wonderment. Dr. George Sexton, the former editor of the *Spiritual Magazine,* publicly explained the tricks of Maskelyne and said: "The two bear about as much resemblance to each other as the productions of the poet Close to the sublime and glorious dramas of the immortal bard of Avon." (*Spirit Mediums and Conjurers,* London, 1873.) (John Close was a notoriously bad poet of the nineteenth century who achieved a brief notoriety by bombarding the nobility and gentry with his verses.)

Maskelyne nevertheless did not absolutely disbelieve in the supernatural. In a letter to the *Daily Telegraph* in 1881 he wrote: "It may surprise some of your readers to learn that I am a believer in apparitions. Several similar occurrences to those described by many of your correspondents have taken place in my own family, and in the families of near friends and relations."

In the *Pall Mall Gazette,* April 20, 1885, he acknowledged the phenomenon of **table-turning** as genuine. He declared that Faraday's explanation was insufficient and some psychic or nerve force was responsible for the result. At the same time he asserted that he could imitate any Spiritualistic phenomenon, provided his own apparatus, which in many cases exceeded a ton in weight, was at his disposal.

This very point is the one which marks the main difference between the performances of a stage magician and a medium. The former is always master of ceremonies, whereas the latter has to submit himself to the conditions imposed upon him. It is very likely that mediums could discover many of the sleight-of-hand tricks if they were admitted to the stage. The magicians always have a privileged position. They can watch the performance very closely. In the investigations of the **London Dialectical Society** in 1869, the committee invited the services of the two best prestidigitators of London when their sessions were in progress.

Many later psychical researchers were amateur conjurers (notably Hereward **Carrington,** Harry **Price,** W. W. **Baggally**) who were well acquainted with the tricks of the trade. If the seance room phenomena were simply due to trickery it would be reasonable to expect that many mediums, after an exposure, should turn professional magicians. No such incidents are on record, except perhaps the case of Colchester, an American medium, who was compelled, by the verdict of a jury, to take out a license as a juggler. But Colchester was exposed years before by the Spiritualists themselves (see *Spiritual Magazine,* 1861). In one instance quoted in du Prel's *Experimental Psychologie,* a medium named Thorn advertised his seances as "anti-Spiritualistic." But when he met Spiritualists he admitted that the sole purpose of the advertisement was to draw the public.

A conjurer's performance may in fact afford presumptive evidence that the phenomena as produced by the medium are genuine. Admiral Usborne Moore (author of *Glimpses of the Next State,* 1911) saw a conjurer reproduce the phenomena of the **Bangs Sisters** on the stage. The effect was crude at first, afterwards very satisfactory. But the point, as he remarked, was that the conjurer's conditions were as different to the conditions of the seances of the Bangs Sisters as a locomotive boiler is different from a teapot. His efforts finally convinced him that he had witnessed genuine spirit manifestations with the Bangs Sisters.

After the Rev. F. W. **Monck** was accused of fraud in 1876, Archdeacon **Colley** offered a thousand pounds to J. N. Maskelyne if he could duplicate Monck's materialization performance. Maskelyne accepted the challenge. His performance was declared unsatisfactory. He sued for the money and lost heavily in prestige when Archdeacon Colley won. When, later, Sir Hiram Maxim, the great inventor, challenged Maskelyne to produce some psychic effect he had seen in America under the same conditions, he refused. The challenge and its result were described by the inventor in a pamphlet: *Maxim versus Maskelyne* (1910).

The descendants of J. N. Maskelyne followed in his footsteps. Capt. Clive Maskelyne issued a challenge in February 1925, when the visit of the medium "Margery" (Mrs. **Crandon**) to England was reported, that he could produce any of the phenomena she had produced in America. The author H. Dennis **Bradley,** in an interview to the *Daily Sketch,* promised a hundred guineas to Capt. Maskelyne if he could duplicate the **Valiantine** phenomena. Capt. Maskelyne at first accepted, but withdrew when he heard what was expected from him.

In 1930, psychical researcher Harry **Price** offered a thousand pounds to any conjurer who could repeat Rudi **Schneider's** phenomena under the same conditions. Nobdy came forward, but a skit, under the title "Olga," was produced in imitation of Rudi Schneider's phenomena at the Coliseum Theatre ("Olga" was the claimed spirit **control** of Schneider). Harry Price publicly challenged Noel Maskelyne from the stage of that theater on December 10, 1929, to simulate by trickery one single phenomenon of Rudi Schneider under the identical conditions as imposed by the **National Laboratory of Psychic Research.** He offered Maskelyne £250 if he could show the trick. Maskelyne refused.

Earlier than this occurrence, Will Goldston, one of the greatest professional magicians in Europe, the author of forty works on legerdemain, founder and ex-president of the Magicians' Club of London, declared in the *Sunday Graphic* (December 2, 1929) concerning the same phenomena: "I am convinced that what I saw at the seance was not trickery. No group of my fellow-magicians could have produced those effects under such conditions."

Goldston told the story of his conversion to spiritualism in *Secrets of Famous Illusionists* (London, 1933). Two of his great fellow magicians—Ottokar Fischer, of Vienna, and Harry Rigoletto—accepted psychic phenomena.

In the *Sunday Dispatch* (August 1931), Will Goldston testified to Miss Hazel **Ridley's** **direct voice** phenomena as follows: "Miss Ridley sat at a table in our midst, and

without the use of trumpets or any of the usual paraphernalia spoke in three different voices. No ventriloquist could possibly produce the effect this girl produced, and I say that after a long experience of ventriloquists. First there was a powerful, clear, man's voice, ringing through the room in tones one would have thought no woman's throat could have produced. The next voice, a very quiet one, like that of a child of six or seven years of age, added to my surprise. The third guide also spoke in a woman's or a child's voice, but quite unlike the normal voice of the medium. The seance lasted an hour and three quarters." A year later, he also spoke up in favor of Mrs. Helen **Duncan** and declared that he was not aware of any system of trickery which could achieve the astounding results which he witnessed. However, there is alternative testimony from others that Mrs. Duncan was fraudulent on some occasions.

During the Harry Price-Maskelyne controversy, Goldston also stated that Mr. J. N. Maskelyne and Mr. Nevil Maskelyne, grandfather and father respectively of Noel, were secret believers in Spiritualism. He added that Houdini's exposures were simply part of a great publicity stunt and that he, too, was secretly a believer. On this latter point Harry Price remarked in his book *Rudi Schneider* (1930) that he had a letter from Houdini in which he stated that a spirit extra of Prof. James Hyslop, which he had seen, was a genuine one.

But it is a far cry from the inclination to believe in the supernormal to the possession of such powers and Houdini was the first to ridicule the statement of J. Hewat **Mackenzie** in *Spirit Intercourse* (1916) that it was by psychic means that he freed himself from handcuffs and that his feat of escaping from a small iron tank filled with water was performed by the dematerialization of his body within one and a half minutes and its reintegration after passing through the tank.

Nevertheless, the belief was not so easily given up, although clearly mistaken. It was sustained by A. Campbell Holms in *Facts of Psychic Science* (1925) and Sir Arthur Conan Doyle devoted about sixty pages in *The Edge of the Unknown* (1930) to the claim that Houdini was really a medium masquerading as a conjurer! Whatever the true nature of Houdini's inner belief, his demonstrations during the *Scientific American* investigation of the mediumship of "Margery" did not greatly redound to his prestige (see **Crandon**). The exposures which he advertised throughout the United States were not at all supported by substantial proofs. Privately he made some admissions.

On January 5, 1925, he wrote to Harry Price: "Another strange thing happened: with the aid of the spirit slates I produced a photograph of Mrs. Crandon's brother, Walter, who was killed, and of all the miracles in the world, I ran across the photograph of the boy as he was crushed between the engine and the tender of the train, and which was taken one minute before he died . . . I doubt very much if there are any duplicates about." (*Light,* August 12, 1932).

Houdini was a very clever magician, but according to Conan Doyle, his narrow-mindedness was sufficiently indicated by the fact that he died disbelieving that the phenomena of **hypnotism** were genuine. In *Houdini and Conan Doyle* by Bernard M. L. Ernst and Hereward

Carrington, many interesting letters were published on Houdini's strange adventures in psychic realms.

After his death there was a long controversy in the American press about the code word which he left behind to prove his identity if messages be claimed to originate from him. Will Goldston, in *Sensational Tales of Mystery Men,* quoted a letter from Mrs. Houdini with this admission: "I have gotten the message that I have been waiting for from my beloved, how, if not by spiritual aid, I do not know." The medium was Arthur **Ford.** The story of the messages, Mrs. Houdini's statements, and the flood of attacks which followed, is told by Francis R. Fast in *The Houdini Messages.*

Some of Houdini's American colleagues made sweeping concessions. David P. **Abbot,** of the American Society for Psychical Research and E. A. Parsons investigated in 1906 the direct voice phenomena of Mrs. E. Blake. They both became convinced of its genuine nature. Abbott published his experiences in the *Omaha World Herald.* Howard Thurston, who inherited the reputation of Harry Kellar, was a convinced Spiritualist.

The current target of the skepticism of many present-day conjuring magicians is Uri **Geller.** Canadian-born magician James **Randi** ("The Amazing Randi") claims to be able to duplicate Geller's feats of telepathy and metal-bending by trickery and accuses Geller of deception. Randi is a well-known illusionist who has inherited the mantle of Houdini as the arch-enemy of psychic phenomena and psychics, and continues to issue challenges to psychics to prove themselves. Milbourne **Christopher,** another modern illusionist skeptic, is more restrained and scholarly in his books criticizing psychics and the occult.

However, an out and out dismissal of all paranormal events as fraudulent is as unreasonable as an absolute endorsement of all apparent miracles. Sincere Spiritualists themselves have often been foremost in exposing fakes, and it seems more likely that there is a reasonable proportion of genuinely paranormal phenomena as well as much ingenious trickery. (See also Milbourne **Christopher; Fraud;** Uri **Geller; Houdini**)

Recommended reading:

Christopher, Milbourne. *Houdini; The Untold Story,* Thomas Y. Crowell, 1969

Christopher, Milbourne. *ESP, Seers & Psychics,* Thomas Y. Crowell, 1970

Christopher, Milbourne. *The Illustrated History of Magic,* Thomas Y. Crowell, 1973; Robert Hale, London, 1975

Dingwall, E. J. & Harry Price (eds.). *Revelations of a Spirit Medium,* Kegan Paul, London, 1925

Dunninger, Joseph. *Inside the Medium's Cabinet,* David Kemp, New York, 1924

Ernst, Bernard M. L. & Hereward Carrington. *Houdini and Conan Doyle; The Story of a Strange Friendship,* Hutchinson, London, 1933

Fast, Francis R. *The Houdini Messages; The Facts Concerning the Messages Received Through the Mediumship of Arthur Ford,* published by the author, New York, 1929

Goldston, Will. *Secrets of Famous Illusionists,* Long, London, 1933

Houdini, Harry. *A Magician Among the Spirits,* Harper & Brothers, 1924

Proskauer, Julien J. *Spook Crooks,* A. L. Burt, New York & Chicago, 1946; Gryphon Books, Ann Arbor, 1971

Randi, James. *The Truth About Uri Geller,* revised ed., Prometheus Books, Buffalo, New York.

Randi, James. *Flim-Flam! Psychics, ESP, Unicorns & Other Delusions,* Prometheus Books, Buffalo, New York, 1982

Sexton, George. *Spirit Mediums & Conjurers,* London, 1873

Truesdell, J. W. *Bottom Facts Concerning the Science of Spiritualism,* G. W. Carleton, New York, 1883

Maginot, Adèle (c. 1848)

Early French medium, whose phenomena were carefully recorded and well attested. She was psychic from childhood and had attacks against which "magnetic" treatment was employed by Alphonse **Cahagnet.** He soon found her an excellent clairvoyant, especially for medical purposes. From this she progressed to serve as a channel for spirit communications.

From the summer of 1848, many sittings were held in which visitors were put in touch with their departed relatives. Cahagnet made them sign a statement after the sitting indicating which of the particulars was true and which false. These statements were published in the second volume of Cahagnet's book *Magnétisme Arcanes de la vie future dévoilé* (1848–60).

When Adèle was put into trance, she saw the spirits of the departed, described them and gave an intimate knowledge of their family circumstances. Baron **du Potet,** a well-known writer on **animal magnetism,** and editor of the *Journal du Magnetisme,* witnessed a striking seance in the company of Prince de Kourakine, who was secretary to the Russian Ambassador. Nevertheless, he was inclined to attribute the result to **thought-transference.**

Adèle Maginot's most extraordinary phenomena, however, did not consist in communications from the dead but in communications from the living, combined with traveling **clairvoyance.** A. M. Lucas came to inquire after his brother-in-law who had disappeared after a quarrel twelve years before. Adèle, in trance, found the man, said that he was alive in a foreign country, busy gathering seeds from small shrubs about three feet high. She asked to be awakened since she was afraid of wild beasts. M. Lucas returned a few days afterwards with the mother of the vanished man. Adèle gave a correct description of the man's appearance and of the history of his disappearance. She was asked to speak to the man.

"Get him to tell you the name of the country where you see him," says the record. "He will not answer." "Tell him that his good mother, for whom he had a great affection, is with you, and asks for news of him." "Oh, at the mention of his mother he turned around and said to me 'My mother, I shall not die without seeing her again. Comfort her, and tell her that I always think of her. I am not dead.'" "Why doesn't he write to her?" "He has written to her, but the vessel has no doubt been wrecked—at least he supposes this to be so, since he has received no answer. He tells me that he is in Mexico. He has followed the Emperor, Don Pedro; he has been imprisoned for five years; he has suffered a great deal, and will use every effort to return to France; they will see him again." "Can he name the place in which he is living?" "No, it is very far inland. These countries have no names."

A similar experience was recorded by M. Mirande, the head of the printing office in which the first volume of the *Arcanes* had been printed. His missing brother, whom he believed to be dead, was found by Adèle to be living and a plausible account of his long silence and whereabouts was given.

It must be admitted that in neither of these cases was corroboration forthcoming. But there was one instance (quoted Cahagnet's third volume) in which, a few weeks after the sitting, the mother received a confirmatory letter from her absent son.

Nevertheless, there is some force in the skeptical argument of Frank **Podmore:** "If Adèle, or any other of Cahagnet's clairvoyants really had possessed the power of conversing with the living at a distance, I cannot doubt that Cahagnet, in the course of his many years' experiments, would have been able to present us with some evidence of such power that was not purely hypothetical. Nothing would be more easy to prove. The fact that no such evidence is forthcoming affords a strong presumption that Adèle did not possess the power, and that the conversations here detailed were purely imaginary, the authentic or plausible details which they contained being filched, it may be, telepathically from the minds of those present." However, Podmore is one of the most skeptical writers on Spiritualism and the very fact that he did not question the phenomena goes a long way to indicate the extraordinary nature of Adèle Maginot's gift. Podmore stated of Cahagnet's investigations: "In the whole literature of Spiritualism I know of no records of the kind which reach a higher evidential standard, nor any in which the writers good faith or intelligence are alike so conspicuous."

Magnetic Phenomena

There appear to be connections between psychic and magnetic phenomena, giving a new slant on the old-fashioned term "animal magnetism" for mesmeric and psychic faculty.

The medium Henry **Slade** could influence the movements of a magnetic needle. Prof. **Zöllner** made convincing experiments with a glass-covered compass. Slade could also magnetize steel knitting needles and Prof. Zöllner lifted iron filings and sewing needles with their ends. Mlle. Stanislawa **Tomczvk** could exert a similar influence over the compass. The British psychical researcher and author Stanley **de Brath** also testified to a case in which a young man deflected the magnetic needle. He was searched for a concealed iron or a magnet but nothing was found.

Magnetometer

A device invented by the Abbé Fortin (c. 1864), consisting of a piece of paper cut to the shape of a compass needle. It was considered to indicate some kind of electromagnetic force. It is suspended in a glass cylinder by a silk fiber. If the cylinder is approached by a hand, the paper (over a dial of 360 degrees) will either turn towards the hand or away from it. Carried out in a more substantial form with a "metallic multiplicator," a condenser and a needle the magnetometer was used for the study of terrestrial magnetism to solve meteorological problems. Since 1904 it was used for **dowsing.** (See also **Biometer of**

Baraduc; De Tromelin Cylinder; Dowsing; Water-Divining)

Magpie

The chattering of a Magpie was formerly considered a sure omen of evil. Another folk belief was that the croaking of a single magpie round a house signified that one of the inhabitants would soon die. In parts of Britain and Ireland it was believed that evil could be averted by being respectful to a magpie—bowing or doffing one's hat. Irish folk would sometimes say "Good morning, your reverence" on seeing a magpie first thing in the morning.

The magpie figures in folklore of the American Indians and was a clan animal amongst the Hopis.

Magus

A master magician or adept. The *Magi* or magicians (plural form of *Magus*) were the "wise men" of the ancient Persian priesthood. The three Magi who brought gifts to the infant Jesus were traditionally named Kaspar, Melchior and Balthasar, and their bones are said to be in Cologne Cathedral, Germany. The term "Magus" is also used as a high degree in magical societies like the **Golden Dawn.**

"Magus"

A spirit **control** of the Rev. Stainton **Moses,** supposed to be a member of the Mystic Band which delivered occult teaching in his scripts. "Magus" did not disclose his name on earth, but he said that he lived 4,000 years ago and belonged to an ancient African wonder-working brotherhood.

In the nineteenth book of the Moses scripts, a topaz is mentioned as the material counterpart of a spiritual jewel worn by "Magus" which was to be given to Stainton Moses to help him to see visions. The stone, set in a ring, was actually dropped from the air in Stainton Moses' bedroom.

For further information on the various spirit controls of Stainton Moses, see his books *Spirit Teachings* (1883 etc.), *More Spirit Teachings* (1897), *Spirit Identity* (1902).

Maharishi Mahesh Yogi (c. 1918–)

A phenomenally successful modern **Guru** who heads a worldwide Spiritual Regeneration Movement, promoting the technique of "TM" or **Transcendental Meditation.**

Originally a physics graduate of Allahabad University, India, he worked for a time in a factory, then studied spiritual science for some years under Swami Brahmananda Saraswati Shankaracharya of Jyotir Math, a teacher of traditional Hindu transcendentalism. After the death of his teacher in 1953, the Maharishi spent some time trying to develop his own simplified non-religious version of traditional Hindu meditation.

In 1958, he conceived an ambitious plan for "the regeneration of the whole world through meditation." He unveiled his "Science of Creative Intelligence," built around the technique of "Transcendental Meditation." This involved a simple initiation ceremony in which the guru bestowed a *mantra* (sacred Sanskrit prayer) on which the pupil concentrated for a short period each day. In this easy technique, the pupil could supposedly by-pass normal intellectual activity and tap a limitless reservoir of energy and creative intelligence.

The system had limited appeal until 1967, when the Maharishi signed up the pop group The Beatles, creating waves of interest throughout the mass media world in a simple non-religious turn-on without drugs. When the Beatles defected some months later, Transcendental Meditation suffered a temporary setback, but it soon bounced back with the initiation of other showbiz personalities, many of whom made the trip East to the Maharishi's luxury ashram at Rishikesh, in the foothills of the Himalayas. The Student's International Meditation Society founded in Los Angeles, California, in 1966 became an instant success among young people tired of protest movements.

In recent years, the movement has been boosted by a well publicized scientific endorsement of the beneficial results of Transcendental Meditation, now firmly established under the initialism "TM." Organized on successful multinational corporation lines, with vice-chairmen, divisions and subdivisions, graphs and charts, computer printouts, and glossy brochures, the movement has now become a kind of ITT of meditation, embodying a host of initialisms like IMS, SIMS, CHIMS, MIU, SRM, AFSSI and today "TM" is now a registered trademark as widely recognized as TWA.

There is a World Plan to develop the full potential of the individual, to improve governmental achievements, to realize the highest ideal of education, to solve the problems of crime and all behavior that brings unhappiness to the family of man, to maximize the intelligent use of the environment, to bring fulfillment to the economic aspirations of individuals and society, and to achieve the spiritual goals of mankind in this generation."

Through all this runs the basic message that man is not born to suffer and through TM, life can be enjoyed to the full. The Maharishi himself lives simply on a vegetarian diet, but enjoys the corporation life of endless conferences, foreign junkets and chauffeured limousines. The movement's headquarters shifted from India, following income tax problems. However, the Indian medical profession has expressed interest in the benefits claimed by TM technique.

In recent years, the movement unveiled a "Siddhi" program (*siddhis* are special paranormal powers) based on the claims of the ancient Yoga Treatise *The Yoga Sutras of Patanjali*. It is claimed that students of this special course have successfully achieved the paranormal feat of **levitation.** (See **Guru; Kundalini; Meditation; Yoga**)

Mahatma Letters

Communications allegedly from the Mahatmas, Masters or Adepts of the **Theosophical Society** of Madame **Blavatsky** during the nineteenth century. These Mahatmas were said to be Eastern Teachers belonging to an occult brotherhood, living in the trans-Himalayan fastnesses of Tibet. They included Koot Humi Lal Singh (K.H.) and Morya (M.).

Notes signed with the initials of these Masters would be mysteriously precipitated out of the air, or discovered in unexpected places. Recipients of such letters included Col. H. S. **Olcott** and A. P. Sinnett (editor of the Anglo-Indian

newspaper *The Pioneer*). Sinnett was favorably impressed by such letters as well as other occult phenomena demonstrated by Madame Blavatsky, and played a prominent part in the affairs of the Theosophical Society.

However, the **Society for Psychical Research,** London, sent investigator Richard **Hodgson** to Adyar, the Madras headquarters of the Society to investigate these marvels. He reported the discovery of a shrine with a false back, used with the connivance of Madame Coulomb, an employee of the Society, as a kind of fake letter box for Mahatma letters.

In the controversy that followed, many Theosophists preferred to believe that the confession by Madame Coulomb was part of a plot to discredit Madame Blavatsky. After the death of Madame Blavatsky, further Mahatma letters were produced by Theosophist William Q. **Judge,** supporting his claim to take charge of the Society in opposition to the presidency of Annie **Besant.** Col. Olcott declared these letters to be fraudulent.

There seems little doubt that the original Mahatma letters in Madame Blavatsky's time were strongly influenced by her personality, since the handwriting and language was typical of her, although some Theosophists would claim that this resulted from the Masters using her as a medium of communication, in much the same way that a psychic delivers automatic writing.

In a paper by Charles Marshall 'The Mahatma Letters—A Syntactic Investigation Into the Possibility of "Forgery" By Helena Petrovna Blavatsky, a 19th Century Russian Occultist' (*Viewpoint Aquarius* No. 96, October 1980), the author described his attempt to prove by computer analysis that there is a strong dissimilarity between Mme. Blavatsky's language and that of the Masters.

However, the computer program, although extensive, was somewhat arbitrary, being confined to certain prepositions and conjunctions. Moreover the comparison between Mahatma Letters and Mme. Blavatsky's writings in such works as "The Secret Doctrine" ignored the extensive editorial work by others on behalf of Mme. Blavatsky's writings, and her own extensive and unacknowledged plagiarisms from other writers, thus making her claimed style unrepresentative. A less ambitious, non-computer reading of the Mahatma Letters discloses the unmistakable touch of Mme. Blavatsky herself. The whole question of the psychic powers of Madame Blavatsky remains an unsolved riddle, for it seems probable that, like many psychic mediums, she was capable of both genuine and fraudulent phenomena.

Some of the Mahatma Letters are now in the Manuscripts Department of the British Library, London.

Recommended reading:

Barker, A. T. *The Mahatma Letters to A. P. Sinnett from the Mahatmas M. and K. H.* London, 1924

Hare, H. E. & William L. *Who Wrote the Mahatma Letters?* London, 1936

Jinarajadasa, C. (ed.). *Letters from the Masters of Wisdom,* 2 vols., Theosophical Publishing House, Adyar, India, 1919–25

Jinarajadasa, C. (ed.). *The K. H. Letters to C. W. L.,* Theosophical Publishing House, Adyar, India, 1941.

Maier, Michael (c. 1568–1622)

German alchemist, born at Rensburg in Holstein. He was one of the principal figures in the Rosicrucian Controversy in Germany and the greatest adept of his time. He diligently pursued the study of medicine in his youth and settling at Rostock practiced with such success that the Emperor Rudolph appointed him as his physician, ennobling him later for his services.

Some adepts eventually succeeded in luring him from the practical work he followed so long into the complex and tortuous paths of alchemy. In order to confer with those whom he believed possessed of the transcendent mysteries he traveled all over Germany. The *Biographie Universelle* states that in pursuit of these "ruinous absurdities" he sacrificed his health, fortune and time. On a visit to England he became acquainted with Robert **Fludd,** the Kentish mystic.

In the controversy which convulsed Germany on the appearance of his Rosicrucian Manifestoes, he took a vigorous and enthusiastic share and wrote several works in defense of the mysterious society. He is alleged to have traveled in order to seek for members of the "College of Teutonic Philosophers R.C.," and, failing to find them, formed a brotherhood of his own, based on the form of the *Fama Fraternibus.* There is no adequate authority for this statement, but it is believed that he eventually, towards the end of his life, was initiated into the genuine order.

A posthumous pamphlet of Maier's called *Ulysses* was published by one of his personal friends in 1624. There was added to the same volume the substance of two pamphlets already published in German but which in view of their importance were now translated into Latin for the benefit of the European literati. The first pamphlet was entitled *Colloquium Rhodostauroticum trium personarium per Famem et Confessionem quodamodo revelatam de Fraternitate Rosæ Crucis.* The second was an *Echo Colloquii* by Hilarion on behalf of the Rosicrucian Fraternity. From these pamphlets it appears that Maier was admitted as a member of the mystical order.

He became the most profuse writer on alchemy of his time. Most of his works, many of which are adorned with curious plates, are obscure with the exception of his Rosicrucian *Apologies.* (See also **Alchemy; Rosicrucians**)

Maimonides, Rabbi Moses (1135–1204)

A great Spanish-Hebrew philosopher and theologian, author of the *Guide for the Perplexed.* His theories were Aristotelian and rational, but there remained in his viewpoint a touch of mysticism.

He was born March 30, 1135 in Cordova, southern Spain, and educated by Arabic teachers. After the Moorrish conquest of Cordova in 1148, Jews left the province, and Maimonides settled in Fez. After five years he moved to Cairo, where he became physician to Saladin and married the sister of Ibn Mali, a royal secretary.

In his famous treatise the *Guide for the Perplexed,* he sought to harmonize Rabbinical and philosophical teachings, but maintained that reason should be supplemented by revelation. His treatise has had a profound influence on his Arabic, Jewish and Christian successors. It has been suggested that Maimonides was sympathetic to the teach-

ings of Kabala in his late period. Certainly he would have been aware of mystical traditions.

He died December 13, 1204. (See also **Kabala**)

Maison des Spirites

Center founded by Jean **Meyer,** who also assisted the foundation of the **Institut Métapsychique** (concerned with psychical research).

The Maison des Spirites was located at 8 Rue Copernic, Paris and was intended to propagate knowledge of Spiritism. It became the secretariat of the Fédération Spirite Internationale (International Spiritualists' Federation), and hosted the Second International Spiritualist Congress in Paris in 1925. (See also **France**)

Maithuna

Sanskrit term for sexual intercourse in the mystic rites of **Tantric Yoga,** the left-hand path of Hindu magic.

In **Tantra,** sexual energy is supposed to be transformed into mystical energy by *coitus interruptus* with a cooperating female, in distinction to the traditional transformation of **Kundalini** energy into mystical channels by **meditation** and self-purification. It is easy to see that there are special problems arising from the use of women in sexual intercourse for claimed mystical purposes, and such practices are open to abuse. Indeed, such abuses undoubtedly occurred with such Western occultists as Aleister **Crowley** in adapting Tantric practices. (See also **Kundalini; Yoga**)

Maitland, Edward (1824–1897)

Co-founder with Anna Bonus **Kingsford** of Esoteric Christianity and the **Hermetic Society.**

Born October 27, 1824 at Ipswich, England, he graduated at Caius College, Cambridge, 1847. He had intended to become a clergyman, but had many reservations about the Church, and instead spent some years traveling in California and Australia, studying life at first hand.

Upon returning to England, he devoted himself "to developing the intuitional faculty as to find the solution of all problems having their basis in man's spiritual nature." Through his close friendship with Anna Kingsford, he became an ardent vegetarian and the interpreter of her highly individual mystical Christianity. He collaborated with her on the writing of *The Perfect Way; or, the Finding of Christ* (London, 1882 etc.), and related books. After her death in 1888, he published her biography: *Anna Kingsford; her life, letters, diary* (London, 1896).

He died in the following year on October 2, 1897.

Mak, A(rie) (1914–)

Dutch school director, who experimented in the field of parapsychology. Born November 23, 1914 at Alkmaar, Netherlands. In 1939 he married N. Jansen.

He was instructor and director at Sneek Technical School, Sneek, Netherlands, from 1939 onwards. He is a member of the Amsterdam Parapsychologische Kring, formerly research officer of the Dutch Society for Psychical Research. In 1950 he was winner of the van de Bilt gold medal for the best amateur astronomical observations, and has contributed articles to journals of astronomy.

He also studied telepathy, clairvoyance and psychokinesis and taken part in experiments (with Dr. Jan Kappers, A. H. de Jong and F. v. d. Berg) to test clairvoyance quantitatively. He also studied the question of evidence for reincarnation.

Malachite

A precious stone (a variety of topaz) of basic copper carbonate. In folklore it was believed to preserve the cradle of an infant from spells.

MALAYSIA

Malaysia now includes the mainland of West Malaysia, sharing a land border with Thailand in the north, and East Malaysia, consisting of the states of Sarawak and Sabah (formerly North Borneo). The ethnic grouping of Malaysia includes Chinese and Indian races, but the largest population is of Malays, of Moslem religion and speaking their own Malay language.

Much of the folklore and magical tradition of the Malays concerns "sympathetic magic" (see **Magic**). The traveler Hugh Clifford, writing in the nineteenth century, stated:

"The accredited intermediary between men and spirits is the *Pawang;* the *Pawang* is a functionary of great and traditional importance in a *Malay* village, though in places near towns the office is falling into abeyance. In the inland districts, however, the *Pawang* is still a power, and is regarded as part of the constituted order of Society, without whom no village community would be complete. It must be clearly understood that he had nothing whatever to do with the official Muhammadan religion of the mosque; the village has its regular staff of elders—the *Imam, Khatio,* and *Bilal*—for the mosque service. But the *Pawang* is quite outside this system and belongs to a different and much older order of ideas; he may be regarded as the legitimate representative of the primitive 'medicine-man,' or 'village-sorcerer,' and his very existence in these days is an anomaly, though it does not strike *Malays* as such. . . .

"The *Pawang* is a person of very real significance. In all agricultural operations, such as sowing, reaping, irrigation works, and the clearing of jungle for planting, in fishing at sea, in prospecting for minerals, and in cases of sickness, his assistance is invoked. He is entitled by custom to certain small fees; thus, after a good harvest he is allowed in some villages five *gantangs* of padi, one *gantang* of rice *(beras),* and two *chupaks* of *emping* (a preparation of rice and cocoa-nut made into a sort of sweetmeat) from each householder."

The *Pawang* used to regulate taboos, and employ a familiar spirit known as *hantu pusaka*—a hereditary demon. He also acted as a medium and divined through trance. To become a magician "You must meet the ghost of a murdered man. Take the midrib of a leaf of the 'ivory' cocoa-nut palm *(pelepah niyor gading),* which is to be laid on the grave, and two midribs, which are intended to represent canoe-paddles, and carry them with the help of a companion to the grave of the murdered man at the time of the full moon (the 15th day of the lunar month) when it falls upon a Tuesday. Then take a cent's worth of incense, with glowing embers in a censer, and carry them to the head-post of the grave of the deceased. Fumigate the grave, going three times round it, and call upon the murdered man by name:

' Hearken, So-and-so,
And assist me;
I am taking (this boat) to the saints of God,
And I desire to ask for a little magic.'

Here take the first midrib, fumigate it, and lay it upon the head of the grave, repeating *'Kur Allah'* ('Cluck, Cluck, God!') seven times. You and your companion must now take up a sitting posture, one at the head and the other at the foot of the grave, facing the grave post, and use the canoe-paddles which you have brought. In a little while the surrounding scenery will change and take upon itself the appearance of the sea, and finally an aged man will appear, to whom you must address the same request as before."

Malay magic may be subdivided into preparatory rites, sacrificial, lustration, divination and possession. Sacrifice took the form of a simple gift, or act of homage to the spirit or deity. Lustration was magico-religious and purificatory, principally taking place after childbirth. It might be performed by fire or water. **Divination** consisted for the most part of the reading of dreams, and was, as elsewhere, drawn from the acts of men or nature. Omens were strongly believed in.

"When a star is seen in apparent proximity to the moon, old people say there will be a wedding shortly. . . .

"The entrance into a house of an animal which does not generally seek to share the abode of man is regarded by the Malays as ominous of misfortune. If a wild bird flies into a house it must be carefully caught and smeared with oil, and must then be released in the open air, a formula being recited in which it is bidden to fly away with all the ill-luck and misfortunes *(sial jambalang)* of the occupier. An iguana, a tortoise, and a snake, are perhaps the most dreaded of these unnatural visitors. They are sprinkled with ashes, if possible to counteract their evil influence.

"A swarm of bees settling near a house is an unlucky omen, and prognosticates misfortune."

So, too, omens were taken either from the flight or cries of certain birds, such as the night-owl, the crow, some kinds of wild doves, and the bird called the "Rice's Husband" *(laki padi).*

Astrology

Divination by astrology was, however, the most common method of forecasting the future. The native practitioners possessed long tables of lucky and unlucky periods and reasons. These were mostly translations from Indian and Arabic sources.

The oldest known of these systems of propitious and unpropitious seasons was known as *Katika Lima,* or the Five Times. Under it the day was divided into five parts, and five days formed a cycle. To each division was given a name as follows: Maswara, Kala, S'ri, Brahma, Bisnu (Vishnu) names of Hindu deities, the last name in the series for the first day being the first in that of the second day, and so on until the five days are exhausted. Each of these had a color, and according to the color first seen or noticed on such and such a day would it be fortunate to ask a boon of a certain god.

Another version of this system, known as the "Five Moments" was similar in origin, but possessed a Mohammedan nomenclature.

Another scheme, *Katika Tujoh,* was based on the seven heavenly bodies, dividing each day into seven parts, each of which was distinguished by the Arabic name for the sun, moon, and principal planets.

The astrology proper of the Malays is purely Arabic in origin, but a system of Hindu invocation was in vogue by which the lunar month was divided into parts called *Rejang,* which resembles the *Nacshatras* or lunar houses of the Hindus. Each division had its symbol, usually an animal. Each day was propitious for something, and the whole system was committed to verse for mnemonic purposes.

Demonology

The demoniac form common to Malaysia was that of the Jinn, with some leaven of the older Hindu spirit. They were one hundred and ninety in number. They were sometimes subdivided into "faithful" and "infidel," and further into the Jinns of the royal musical instruments, of the state, and of the royal weapons. The *Afrit* was also known. Angels also abounded, and were purely of Arabic origin.

Besides these, the principal supernatural beings were as follows: the *Polong,* or familiar; the *Hantu Pemburu,* or specter Huntsman; the *Jadi-jadian,* or wer-tiger; the *Huntu,* or ghost of the murdered; the *Jemalang,* or earth-spirit.

Minor Sorcery

The rites of minor sorcery and **witchcraft,** as well as those of the **shaman,** were widely practiced among the Malays, and were practically identical in character with those in use among other peoples in a similar state of culture.

Recommended reading:

Clifford, Hugh. *In Court and Kampong,* Grant Richards, London, 1897

Clifford, Hugh. *Studies in Brown Humanity,* Grant Richards, London, 1898

Skeat, W. W. *Malay Magic; Being an Introduction to the Folklore & Popular Religion of the Malay Peninsula,* Macmillan, London, 1900

Swettenham, Sir Frank A. *Malay Sketches,* John Lane, London, 1895

Winstedt, R. *The Malays; A Cultural History,* Routledge, London, 1950

Mallebranche (c. 1618)

Seventeenth-century Frenchman haunted by his dead wife. M. Mallebranche was a marker of the game of tennis, living in the Rue Sainte-Geneviéve, Paris, who in 1618 was visited by an apparition of his wife, who had died five years before.

She came to advise him to repent and live a better life, and to pray for her also. Both Mallebranche and his wife (for he had married a second time) heard the voice, but the apparition did not become visible. In 1618 a booklet was published in Paris, entitled: *Histoire nouvelle et remarquable de l'esprit d'une femme qui c'est apparue au Faubourg Saint-Marcel après qu'elle a demeué cinq ans entiers ensevelie; elle a parlé a son mari, lui a commandé de faire prier pour elle, ayant commencé de parler le mardi 11 Decembre, 1618.*

Malleus Maleficarum

The most authoritative and influential sourcebook for inquisitors, judges and magistrates in the great witchcraft persecutions from the fifteenth century onwards.

The authors were Jakob **Sprenger** and Heinrich **Kramer,** leading inquisitors of the Dominican Order.

The book brought together folklore and speculation about witchcraft and magic, combining it with a fierce and relentless persecution which ensured the deaths of hundreds of unfortunate individuals accused of witchcraft. This work is in three parts. Part I fulminates against the evil of witchcraft, which is characterized as renunciation of the Catholic faith, homage to the Devil and carnal intercourse with demons. Even disbelief in witches was declared a grave heresy. Part II details the specific sorceries of witches. Part III sets forth rules for legal action and conviction of witches.

The antiquary Thomas Wright, in his book *Narratives of Sorcery and Magic* (2 vols., 1851), stated: "In this celebrated work, the doctrine of witchcraft was first reduced to a regular system, and it was the model and groundwork of all that was written on the subject long after the date which saw its first appearance. Its writers enter largely into the much-disputed question of the nature of demons; set forth the causes which lead them to seduce men in this manner; and show why women are most prone to listen to their proposals, by reasons which prove that the inquisitors had but a mean estimate of the softer sex.

"The inquisitors show the most extraordinary skill in explaining all the difficulties which seemed to beset the subject; they even prove to their entire satisfaction that persons who have become witches may easily change themselves into beasts, particularly into wolves and cats; and after the exhibition of such a mass of learning, few would venture any longer to entertain a doubt. They investigate not only the methods employed to effect various kinds of mischief, but also the counter-charms and exorcisms that may be used against them. They likewise tell, from their own experience, the dangers to which the inquisitors were exposed, and exult in the fact that they were a class of men against whom sorcery had no power.

"These writers actually tell us, that the demon had tried to frighten them by day and by night in the forms of apes, dogs, goats, etc.; and that they frequently found large pins stuck in their night-caps, which they doubted not came there by witchcraft. When we hear these inquisitors asserting that the crime of which the witches were accused, deserved a more extreme punishment than all the vilest actions of which humanity is capable, we can understand in some degree the complacency with which they relate how, by their means, forty persons had been burnt in one place, and fifty in another, and a still greater number in a third. From the time of the publication of the *Malleus Maleficarum,* the continental press during two or three generations teemed with publications on the all-absorbing subject of sorcery.

"One of the points on which opinion had differed most was, whether the sorcerers were carried bodily through the air to the place of meeting, or whether it was an imaginary journey, suggested to their minds by the agency of the evil one. The authors of the *Malleus* decide at once in favour of the bodily transmission. One of them was personally acquainted with a priest of the diocese of Frisingen, who declared that he had in his younger days been carried through the air by a demon to a place at a very great distance from the spot whence he had been taken. Another priest, his friend, declared that he had seen him carried away, and that he appeared to him to be borne up on a kind of cloud.

"At Baldshut, on the Rhine, in the diocese of Constance, a witch confessed, that offended at not having been invited to the wedding of an acquaintance, she had caused herself to be carried through the air in open daylight to the top of a neighbouring mountain, and there, having made a hole with her hands and filled it with water, she had, by stirring the water with certain incantations caused a heavy storm to burst forth on the heads of the wedding-party; and there were witnesses at the trial who swore they had seen her carried through the air.

"The inquisitors, however, confess that the witches were sometimes carried away, as they term it, in the spirit; and they give the instance of one woman who was watched by her husband; she appeared as if asleep, and was insensible, but he perceived a kind of cloudy vapour arise out of her mouth, and vanish from the room in which she lay—this after a time returned, and she then awoke, and gave an account of her adventures, as though she had been carried bodily to the assembly. . . .

"The witches of the *Malleus Maleficarum* appear to have been more injurious to horses and cattle than to mankind. A witch at Ravenspurg confessed that she had killed twenty-three horses by sorcery. We are led to wonder most at the ease with which people are brought to bear witness to things utterly beyond the limits of belief. A man of the name of Stauff in the territory of Berne, declared that when pursued by the agents of justice, he escaped by taking the form of a mouse; and persons were found to testify that they had seen him perform this transmutation.

"The latter part of the work of the two inquisitors gives minute directions for the mode in which the prisoners are to be treated, the means to be used to force them to a confession, the degree of evidence required for conviction of those who would not confess, and the whole process of the trials. These show sufficiently that the unfortunate wretch who was once brought before the inquisitors of the holy see on the suspicion of sorcery, however slight might be the grounds of the charge, had very small chance of escaping out of their claws.

"The *Malleus* contains no distinct allusion to the proceedings at the Sabbath. The witches of this period differ little from those who had fallen into the hands of the earlier inquisitors at the Council of Constance. We see plainly how, in most countries, the mysteriously indefinite crime of sorcery had first been seized on to ruin the cause of great political offenders, until the fictitious importance thus given to it brought forward into a prominent position, which they would, perhaps, never otherwise have held, the miserable class who were supposed to be more especially engaged in it. It was the judicial prosecutions and the sanguinary executions which followed, that stamped the character of reality on charges of which it required two or three centuries to convince mankind of the emptiness and vanity.

"One of the chief instruments in fixing the belief in sorcery, and in giving it that terrible hold on society which it exhibited in the following century, was the compilation of Jacob Sprenger and his fellow inquisitor. In this book sorcery was reduced to a system but it was not yet perfect; and we must look forward, some half a century before we find it clothed with all the horrors which cast so much terror into every class of society."

The work went into some thirty editions between 1486 and 1669, and was accepted as authoritative by both Protestant and Catholic witch-hunters. Its narrow-minded superstition and dogmatic legalism undoubtedly resulted in hundreds of cases of cruel tortures and judicial murders. An English translation was published London (1928; 1948; 1974) by the controversial British scholar the Rev. Montague **Summers,** who embodied in his writings a truly medieval attitude to witchcraft. With typically perverse judgment, he declared (in his learned introduction to the work) that the *Malleus Maleficarum* "is among the most important, wisest, and weightiest books of the world." (See also **Witchcraft**)

Malphas

According to demonologist Johan **Weyer,** Malphas was grand president of the infernal regions, where he appeared under the shape of a crow. When he appeared in human form he had a very raucous voice. He built impregnable citadels and towers, overthrew the ramparts of his enemies, found good workmen, gave familiar spirits, received sacrifices, and deceived the sacrificers. Forty infernal legions were under his command.

Mamaloi

An Obeah priestess (see **West Indian Islands**)

Mananan

Son of the Irish sea-god Lir, magician and owner of strange possessions. His magical boat "Ocean-sweeper" steered by the wishes of its occupant, his horse Aonban, able to travel on sea or land, and his sword **Fragarach,** a match for any mail, were brought by Lugh from "The Land of the Living" (i.e., fairyland).

As lord of the sea he was the Irish Charon, and his color-changing cloak would flap gaily as he marched with heavy tread round the camp of the hostile force invading Erin. He is comparable with the Cymric Manawiddan and resembles the Hellenic Proteus.

Mandala

A mystical diagram used in India and Tibet to attract spiritual power or for meditation purposes. The term derives from the Sanskrit word for "circle," although a mandala may embody various geometrical shapes. The Swiss psychologist C. G. **Jung** regarded the mandala as an archetypal image from the deep unconscious mind, and investigated mandalas created spontaneously by psychological patients. (See also **Yantra**)

Recommended reading:

Tucci, Giuseppe. *The Theory and Practice of the Mandala,* London, 1961

Wilhelm, Richard & C. G. Jung. *The Secret of the Golden Flower; a Chinese Book of Life* (rev. ed.), Harcourt, Brace (1962); Causeway, 1975

Mandragoras

Familiar demons who appear in the figures of little men without beards. The name is also applied to the plant popularly known as mandrake, whose roots resemble human form and were believed to be inhabited by de-mons.

The sixteenth-century **witchcraft** scholar Martin Del Rio stated that one day a *mandragora,* entering a court at the request of a sorcerer who was being tried for wizardry, was caught by the arms by the judge (who did not believe in the existence of the spirit) to convince himself of its existence, and thrown into the fire, where of course it would escape unharmed.

Mandragoras were thought to be little dolls or figures given to sorcerers by the Devil for the purpose of being consulted by them in time of need, and it would seem as if this conception sprung directly from that of the fetish, which is really a dwelling-place made by a **shaman** or medicine man for the reception of any wandering spirit who chooses to take up his abode therein.

The anonymous author of the popular magic manual *Secrets merveilleux de la magie et cabalistique de Petit Albert* (1772 etc.) stated that on one occasion, whilst travelling in Flanders and passing through the town of Lille, he was invited by one of his friends to accompany him to the house of an old woman who posed as being a great prophetess. This aged person conducted the two friends into a dark cabinet lit only by a single lamp, where they could see upon a table covered with a cloth a kind of little statue or *mandragora,* seated upon a tripod and having the left hand extended and holding a hank of silk very delicately fashioned, from which was suspended a small piece of iron highly polished.

Placing under this a crystal glass, so that the piece of iron was suspended inside the goblet, the old woman commanded the figure to strike the iron against the glass in such a manner as she wished, saying at the same time to the figure: "I command you, *Mandragora,* in the name of those to whom you are bound to give obedience, to know if the gentleman present will be happy in the journey which he is about to make. If so, strike three times with the iron upon the goblet."

The iron struck three times as demanded without the old woman having touched any of the apparatus, much to the surprise of the two spectators. The sorceress put several other questions to the *Mandragora,* who struck the glass once or thrice as seemed good to him. But the author claimed that this procedure was an artifice of the old woman, for the piece of iron suspended in the goblet was extremely light and when the old woman wished it to strike against the glass, she held in one of her hands a ring set with a large piece of magnetic stone, the virtue of which drew the iron towards the glass. This sounds very much like the folklore practice of putting a ring on a thread and holding it so that it dangles inside a glass and responds to questions put to it (see **Pendulums**).

The ancients attributed great virtues to the plant *mandragoras* or mandrake, the root of which was often uncannily like a human form, and when plucked from the earth was believed to emit a species of human cry. It was also worn to ward off various diseases. Because of the supposed danger from the resident demon when plucking the plant, an elaborate procedure was prescribed. The mandrake-gatherer was supposed to starve a dog of food for several days, then tie him with a strong cord to the lower part of the plant. The dog was then thrown pieces of meat and when he leapt forward to seize them he pulled

up the mandrake. Other folklore beliefs included the need for an elaborate prayer ritual before pulling the plant, which should only be gathered at dead of night. For a detailed study of the role of mandrakes, see *The Mystic Mandrake* by C. J. S. Thompson (1934; University Books, 1968). (See also **Alrunes; Exorcism; Ginseng**)

Mandrake

Plant whose roots often bear an uncanny resemblance to a human form (see **Mandragoras**).

Manen

The priest of the **Katean Secret Society** of the Moluccas.

Mangan, Gordon Lavelle (1924–   )

University lecturer in psychology who has made a special study of parapsychology. Born December 5, 1924 in Wellington, New Zealand, he studied at University of New Zealand (M.A. 1945), University of Melbourne, Australia (Ed.B. 1950), University of London, England (Ph.D. 1954). In 1954, he married Mary Wilshin.

After working as a high school teacher, he became a fellow of the Parapsychology Foundation, and research associate Duke University, 1954–56; assistant professor at Department of Psychology, Queen's University, Kingston, Ontario, Canada from 1956–58; lecturer in psychology at Victoria University 1958–61; senior lecturer in Psychology Department at University of Queensland, Australia from 1961 onwards.

He is a member of the American Psychological Association and British Psychological Society. In addition to his many writings on psychology, Dr. Mangan has published a monograph *A Review of the Published Research on the Personality Correlates of ESP* (Parapsychology Foundation, 1958). Other articles on parapsychology include: 'Parapsychology: A Science for Psychical Research?' (*Queen's Quarterly*, Spring 1958), 'How Legitimate Are the Claims for ESP?' (*Australian Journal of Psychology*, Sept. 1959) and contributions to the *Journal of Parapsychology*: 'A PK Experiment with Thirty Dice Released for High and Low Face Targets' (Dec. 1954), 'Evidence of Displacement in a Precognitive Test' (March 1955), 'An ESP Experiment with Dual-Aspect Targets Involving One Trial Day' (Dec. 1957).

Manning, Matthew (1955–   )

Remarkable young British psychic, whose phenomena include **poltergeist, apports, automatic writing, telepathy, precognition** and psychic art. When only a schoolboy aged eleven, Matthew was the center of extraordinary poltergeist disturbance at the family home in Shelford, Cambridge, England, involving repeated knocking and the movement of scores of small articles. After several weeks, the phenomena subsided but returned about a year later, accompanied by childish scribblings on walls and even high ceilings. Chairs and tables were disturbed and dozens of objects moved around in an extraordinary manner.

The phenomena followed Matthew to boarding school, where heavy beds were moved, and knives, nails, electric light bulbs and other objects sent flying through the air.

Showers of pebbles and pools of water manifested, and strange lights appeared on walls.

One day, whilst writing an essay in his study, Matthew found himself involved in automatic writing, which signalled cessation of the poltergeist phenomena. Since then he regularly received hundreds of communications apparently from deceased individuals, some in languages unknown to him, including Italian, German, Greek, Latin, Russian and Arabic.

Following upon the automatic writing, he produced psychic art in the manner of Thomas Bewick, Thomas Rowlandson, Aubrey Beardsley, Paul Keel, Henri Matisse, Picasso and other great names with remarkable fidelity to the styles of these artists. He also discovered an ability to bend spoons in the manner of Uri **Geller** and to record startling demonstrations of some unknown force in himself by means of **Kirlian photography.**

His strange powers were described in his book *The Link* (Colin Smythe, U.K./Holt Rinehart, 1974).

In recent times, Matthew duplicated the Uri Geller effect of starting inactive clocks and watches, as well as radios, tape recorders, music boxes and even electric lights. He had a premonition of the June 1975 plane crash near Kennedy Airport which killed 121 people, as well as the 1975 subway train disaster at Moorgate Station, England, in which 43 people died.

During a tour in Japan he appeared in a special television program, during which 1,200 callers jammed the studio switchboard with reports of bottles, glasses and other objects which exploded in their homes in the course of the transmission. Faucets turned on automatically, burglar alarms went off, auto engines switched themselves on. Lost articles reappeared, small objects materialized in homes, other objects disappeared, while watches and clocks went haywire. These and other remarkable phenomena are described in Matthew's second book: *In the Minds of Millions* (W. H. Allen, London, 1977). Matthew has also predicted that his own death will occur at an early date.

On August 7, 1977, he took part in an ESP test organized by the British newspaper *Sunday Mirror.* Matthew was stationed in London's Post Office Tower (580 ft. high). Between 6 and 6:15 p.m. he mentally transmitted three images: the color green, the number 123 and the shape of a house. Readers of the *Sunday Mirror* were asked to "tune in" to these images and send their results on a postcard. 575 of the 2,500 readers who cooperated scored the right color; one in 44 got the three-figure number right, about one in 30 identified a house-like shape. There were some 30 interesting "near-misses" in which readers reported the color green, the figure 123 and a shape of a triangle on top of a square, or the color green, the number 132 and a house. Mr. Michael Haslam, deputy honorary secretary of the Institute of Statisticians in London confirmed that the results were significantly higher than chance expectation.

Matthew was also the subject of a Canadian documentary movie "A Study of a Psychic" made by the Bruce A. Raymond Co. between 1974 and 1977. President Bruce A. Raymond was formerly Controller of Programs at the Canadian Broadcasting Corporation and one of its chief executives. The movie is an objective record of Matthew's career, including interviews with members of his family, his headmaster and school friends. Extracts were shown on British television on the Brian Inglis "Nationwide" program produced by Granada TV.

In December 1977, Matthew created something of a sensation by stating that henceforth he preferred to be described as a "mentalist" instead of a "psychic." This statement came after three years of worldwide publicity as the western world's most gifted psychic, on the same day that Matthew appeared on the Russell Harty Independent Television talk show in London, which included filmed accounts from three first-hand witnesses of the poltergeist phenomena which surrounded Matthew when a schoolboy.

During the program he demonstrated automatic drawing and attempted telepathy tests. He also stated: "I believe also that a lot of people who are doing debunking in the name of science are merely forming a religion of their own, which I call humanism. . . . They believe there is no more to life than everything they can perceive physically, there is nothing beyond the five senses and that when one dies that is the end. They turn that into a religion. Obviously, what I am doing is to them threatening. That is why they will attack me."

During his 1977 U.S. tour, Matthew had been vigorously criticized by the U.S. magician James **Randi,** a well-known hostile opponent of paranormal phenomena who formerly spent much time in a campaign of denouncing Uri Geller as a "clever magician," whose metal-bending abilities are "merely tricks accomplished by sleight of hand." Randi is a member of the **Committee for the Scientific Investigation of Claims of the Paranormal** (originally sponsored by the American journal *The Humanist*) and author of *The Magic of Uri Geller* (Ballantine Books, 1975) in which he accused Geller of "massive fraud." In September 1977, Randi attacked the British *Sunday Mirror* ESP test in the Post Office Tower, suggesting that Matthew Manning could have sent in "an important fraction of the postcards" himself. This and other implications of trickery were strongly refuted by Matthew, who stated: "The man who talks of 'falsehoods' makes statements himself which can be seen to be totally false by anyone who reads my book" *(In the Minds of Millions).* For reports on this controversy see the British newspaper *Psychic News* (September 10, 1977).

It seems possible that Matthew Manning's disclaimer of the term "psychic" in favor of "mentalist" may have been a defensive tactic in response to aggressive campaigns such as Randi's. The full statement by Matthew, delivered to Peter **Bander,** his former publisher and agent, was a front-page story in Britain's *Cambridge Evening News* (December 3, 1977), also reported in *Psychic News* (December 10, 1977). The statement reads:

"Dear Peter,—Without any disrespect to anything which may have been said or done in the past, I would prefer from now on to be known as a mentalist and not as a psychic, a description I have always resented and never liked.

"As I have no intention of giving interviews during my short stay in England, I would like you to be the first person to know. Perhaps you might also be so good as to pass this on to any pressmen or future inquirers.

"Certain events in America, for example, have made

me reconsider my position. I feel this is probably the best description to explain them.

"I reiterate that I do not wish to withdraw anything I have said or done in the past, and that I wish to be judged by what I'm doing now rather than by what I have been doing in the last four years.

"I have no intention of explaining this any further at present."

In his first book *The Link* (1974) which went into nineteen editions and was translated into many languages, Matthew had accepted the description "teenage psychic" and had described the first occasion that he "entered into direct communication with spirit entities." It may be that like other sensitive individuals in the history of psychic science and parapsychology, he felt threatened by a hostile debunking attitude going beyond criticism and speculation into the realms of psychic persecution.

Whilst no one would wish to defend uncritical acceptance of all claimed paranormal phenomena, it is equally unreasonable to denounce psychics as frauds without positive evidence, or to hound them with hostile criticism and attempt to trap them by trickery. Such bullying goes far beyond acceptable standards of public courtesy and creates a negative atmosphere which can have a damaging effect upon the personality and actions of sensitive individuals with rare and little-understood talents. In certain instances it may even result in actual frauds through the creation of a strongly suggestive atmosphere.

Mansfield, J. V. (c. 1870)

Nineteenth-century American medium, advertised as the "spirit postmaster" in the *Banner of Light.* He obtained thousands of letters in sealed envelopes addressed to spirit-friends, read them clairvoyantly and wrote out replies automatically in various languages. German, Spanish, Greek, Arabic, Sanskrit and even Chinese answers were sometimes given.

Many witnesses testified to his powers. His scripts were preserved in evidence. His mediumship is described in Dr. N. B. Wolfe's *Startling Facts in Modern Spiritualism* (1875).

However, in The Report of the **Seybert Commission,** Dr. Furness, the acting chairman, discredited Mansfield's powers on the basis of a clairvoyant sitting and a sealed letter test.

For a detailed account of Mansfield's handling of an ingeniously sealed letter, see the *Spiritual Magazine* (1868, p. 425).

Manson, Charles M. (1934–   )

Habitual criminal who achieved notoriety as charismatic leader of an infamous "Family" that indulged in sex orgies and brutal murders. Manson demonstrated that drugs, sex, occultism and crime can be an incredibly dangerous mixture.

As a young man, he was frequently arrested on such charges as car theft, parole violation, stealing checks and credit cards. He spent most of the 1960s in jail, where he learnt to play the guitar and studied hypnotism, psychological conditioning, **Scientology** and occultism, as well as reading avidly on the contemporary outside scene of the Vietnam War, peace rallies, rock and roll and the music of the Beatles. He was also greatly impressed by Robert

Heinlein's science-fiction story *Stranger in a Strange Land,* which related how an alien intelligence formed a power base of sex and religion on the earth.

In 1967, Manson was released from jail and wandered around Berkeley, California, as a guitar-toting minstrel, picking up girls and spending time in the Haight-Ashbury section, experiencing the drug scene, occult boom and communal living. In the course of time he collected a kind of tribal family, mostly young girls, and established a hippie-style commune at various locales in the Californian desert, ranging over Death Valley in stolen dune buggies in a freaked-out atmosphere of drugs and sex orgies.

In time, Manson developed paranoid fantasies of a forthcoming Doomsday situation, supposedly revealed to him by an album of rock-music songs by the Beatles, particularly "Helter-Skelter" and "Piggies." Manson and his followers shared a delusion that "Helter-Skelter" symbolized an uprising of blacks, which could be exploited by the Family.

In 1969, under the influence of Manson's fantasies, his Family accepted him as a Satanic Jesus Christ, and indulged an orgy of sadistic murders. Manson, with Patricia Krenwinkle, Susan Atkins and Leslie Van Houten were found guilty of the murders of actress Sharon Tate (pregnant at the time) and four other people at her Bel-Air home in Los Angeles—Voyteck Frykowski, Abigail Folger, Jay Sebring and Steven Parent, as well as Leno La Bianca and his wife Rosemary, also in Los Angeles. Nine weeks after the verdict, the jury voted death sentences for all the accused. The trial, which opened July 21, 1970 had taken 32 weeks. During 1976, a movie reconstructing the trial, titled *Helter-Skelter,* was shown on television programs in the U.S.

On February 18, 1972, the California State Supreme Court abolished the death penalty in the state of California, thus reducing the sentence of condemned persons to life imprisonment, which permits a prisoner to apply for parole in seven years. However, this law does not appear to allow parole in the Manson case.

For a general account of the horrifying story of Manson and his family, see *The Family* by Ed Sanders (E. P. Dutton, 1971; Avon paperback, 1972). For detailed information on the trial of Manson and associates including the aftermath of the trial, with comprehensive data on other murders, see *Helter Skelter* by prosecuting attorney Vincent Bugliosi, with Curt Gentry (Norton, 1972; Bantam paperback, 1975; Penguin Books, 1977). Susan Atkins claims to have become a born-again Christian during imprisonment and has published (with Bob Slosser) *Child of Satan, Child of God* (Logos, 1977; Hodder & Stoughton paperback, 1978). (See also **Cults;** Rev. Jim **Jones; Rosemary's Baby; Snapping**)

Mantra (or Mantram)

In Hindu mysticism, a mantra is a speech vibration which has a material effect on mind, emotions, physical body or even on physical processes in nature. The term is derived from the root *man,* "to think," and a mantra is thus an instrument of thought.

In Hindu religion, the material universe is said to be formed from divine vibration, a concept echoed in the Judeo-Christian concepts of divine utterance preceding creation—"And God said, let there be light . . ." (*Genesis*

I, 3), "In the beginning was the Word, and the Word was with God, and the Word was God" (*John,* I, 1). In Hinduism, the verses of the sacred scriptures the *Vedas* are regarded as mantras, because they have been transmitted from a divine source, rather like the Christian concept of the Bible as having power as the Word of God, but Hindus also recognize words and phrases as having special powers as expressions of the hidden forces of nature. Divine creation becomes manifest in form throughout nature, and the latent reality behind form may be affected by correctly uttering the sounds which represent the ideal reality. These mantras were discovered by ancient sages skilled in the knowledge of the *Mantra Shastra* scripture, and taught to initiates.

The universe is called *Jagat,* "that which moves," because everything exists by a combination of forces and movement, and every movement generates vibration and has a sound which is peculiar to it. These subtle sounds have correspondences in the grosser sounds of speech and music, and so everything in the universe has an exact relationship. Everything has its natural name, the sound produced by the action of the moving forces from which it is constructed, thus anyone who is able to utter the natural name of anything with creative force can bring into being the thing which has that name.

The greatest mantra is the trisyllable A-U-M which precedes and concludes reading from the *Vedas* and is chanted as an individual mantra or magical prayer. The three syllables are associated with the processes of creation, preservation and dissolution and with the three states of consciousness (dreaming, deep sleep and waking). The scripture *Mandukya Upanishad* describes how the trisyllable AUM is the basis of all the other letters in the Sanskrit language and associated with the universe and the human microcosm (analagous concepts exist in such Kabalistic works as the *Sepher Yesirah*). A mantra may also be associated with a Yantra, or mystical diagram. The whole paraphernalia of Western magic spells is clearly a decadent descent of such ancient Hindu mysticism.

Mantras are usually uttered in rhythmic repetition known as *japa,* often with the aid of a *mala,* the ancient Hindu precursor of the Christian rosary. In Japa Yoga, the power of a mantra is enhanced by the accumulation of repetitions. Although mantras have an automatic action, that action is enhanced by proper concentration and attitude of mind. The spoken mantra is also an aid to the mental mantra, which contains the inner meaning and power.

Popular spiritual mantras common in India include variants of the "Hari Rama, Hari Krishna" formula which has been introduced to the West by the Krishna Consciousness movement (see **International Society for Krishna Consciousness**) and the Gayatri Mantra, normally recited by Brahmins and which involves meditation on the sun. Special mantras are connected with the basic states of matter in connection with the *chakras* or subtle centers of the human body. These are known as *bija* mantras. (See also **Chakras; Kabala; Kundalini; Yoga**)

Recommended reading:

Easwaran, Eknath. *The Mantram Handbook*, Routledge & Kegan Paul, London, 1978

Gopalacharlu, S. E. *An Introduction to the Mantra Sastra,* Theosophical Publishing House, Adyar, India (paperback), 1934

Kalisch, Isidor (transl.). *Sepher Yezirah. A Book on Creation,* New York, 1877, reprinted A.M.O.R.C., San Jose, California 1950, etc.

Narayana, Har (transl.). *The Vedic Philosophy; or An Exposition of the Sacred and Mysterious Monosyllable AUM; The Mandukya Upanishad,* Bombay, 1895

Woodroffe, Sir John. *The Garland of Letters (Varnamala); Studies in the Mantra-Shastra,* Ganesh & Co., Madras, India, 1951 etc.

Manu

According to **Theosophy,** a grade in the theosophical hierarchy below the Planetary Logoi or Rulers of the Seven Chains. The charge given to *Manus* is that of forming the different races of humanity and guiding its evolution. Each race has its own *Manu,* who represents the racial type.

This Theosophical concept derives from Hindu mythology of *Manu* (man; thinker), a series of fourteen progenitors of the human race, each creation being destroyed in a Mahayuga (vast cycle of time) involving a deluge. The *Manu* of the present creation is *Manu Vaivasvata,* who built an ark during a cosmic deluge and afterwards renewed the human race. He is the reputed author of the *Manava Dharma Shastra* or *Laws of Manu,* an ancient Hindu treatise which prescribes human religious and social duties.

Mapes, James Jay (1806–1866)

Professor of Agricultural Chemistry, member of various learned societies, one of the early American converts to **Spiritualism.** His conversion was the result of an investigation started to save his friends from "running to imbecility." Mrs. Cora L. V. Hatch (later **Richmond**) produced for him phenomena which he could not explain. Eventually Prof. Mapes became a believer in Spiritualism.

His wife, a lady of advanced age with no talent for art, developed **automatic drawing and painting** mediumship. She executed in a marvelously rapid manner several thousand watercolor drawings which met with praise. His daughter became a writing medium.

One of the early messages that came through the latter agency purported to emanate from Prof. Mapes' father, asking him to look up an encyclopedia, stored in a packing case 27 years before, and there on page 120 he would find his father's name written which he had never seen. This was found true. With increasing interest Prof. Mapes investigated Katie Fox (See **Fox Sisters**), the **Davenport Brothers,** with whom he heard the first **direct voice** phenomena, and the manifestations of "John **King.**" He followed every new psychical discovery with keen interest.

Maple, Eric (William) (1915–   )

British authority on witchcraft, demonology, the supernatural and folklore. In addition to his books on such subjects, he has also lectured widely and was a consultant on the publication *Man, Myth & Magic* (1967–70). He has given special attention to the role of the so-called "white witch" in the history of witchcraft persecutions, and has also shown the interrelationship of witchcraft with ghost lore, **Spiritism** and the cult of the dead. His books include: *The Dark World of Witches* (1962), *The Realm of Ghosts* (1964), *The Domain of Devils* (1966), *Magic, Medicine & Quackery* (1968), *Superstition and the Superstitious* (1971), *The Magic of Perfume* (1973), *Witchcraft—the Story of Man's Quest for Psychic Power* (1973), *The Ancient Art of Occult Healing* (1974), *Deadly Magic* (1976), *Supernatural England* (1977), *Ghosts: Monsters* (1978), *The Ancient Lore of Garden Flowers* (1979).

Marabini, Enrico (1923–   )

Italian specialist in gynecology and obstetrics, also active in the field of parapsychology. Born November 12, 1923, at Casinalbo, Italy, he studied at Bologna University (M.D. cum laude 1949). In 1950 he married Sofia Cifiello. He is a member of Bologna Center of Parapsychological Studies. In 1948, he was one of the founders of the Centro Studi Parapsicologici (Center for Parapsychological Studies).

Dr. Marabini has taken special interest in clairvoyance, telepathy, psychokinesis and mediumship. He worked with mental and physical mediums for several years in controlled experiments concerned with psychosomatic aspects of paranormal behavior. However, he was unable to validate the authenticity of physical mediumship. He has since studied quantitative testing methods.

Some of his views are embodied in his article 'Una Nuova ESP?' (*Bulletin of the Italian Society for Parapsychology,* Jan.-June 1959). Other articles by Dr. Marabini include: 'La Telapatia' (Telepathy, *Metapsichica,* Nos. 1, 2, 3, 4, 1953), 'Esperienze di Telepatia collectiva eseguite nella Citta' di Bologna' (Experiments in Mass Telepathy in Bologna, *Metapsichica,* No. 1, 1954), 'Proposta di una modifica al test di Stuart per la Chiaroveggenza' (Proposal of a Modification of the Stuart Test for Clairvoyance, *Metapsichica,* No. 3, 1954); in *Parapsicologia di Minerva Medica* 'Esperienze trienneli di lettura della mano con una sensitiva Bolognese: Maria Guardini' (Three Years of Experiments in Hand-reading with the Sensitive Maria Guardini of Bologna, June 1957), 'Sogno paragnosico' (Paragnostic Dreams, June 1957), 'Il Comportamento paranormale in rapporto a stati neuro-endocrini) (Paranormal Behavior in Connection with Neuro-Endocrinological Conditions, Nov. 1957); in *Bulletin of the Italian Society for Parapsychology* 'Il Metodo scientifico in parapsicologia' (Scientific Method in Parapsychology, July-Dec. 1957), 'La Psi e' stata dimonstrata sperimentalmente?' (Has Psi Been Experimentally Demonstrated?, July-Dec. 1959); in *Proceedings* of the Third Congress of the Italian Society for Parapsychology 'Esperienze di psicometria con la sensitiva Luisa Godicini' (Experiments in Psychometry with the Sensitive Luisa Godicini, May 1956); in *Medicina psicosomatics* 'Problemi parapsicologici e psicosomatica' (*Parapsychological Problems and Psychosomatics,* No. 1, vol. 2, 1957).

Maranos

A Jewish secret fraternity which arose in Spain in the fourteenth and fifteenth centuries during the persecution of Jews in that country. Its members met in the greatest secrecy at inns, disguised, and used grips, signs and passwords (see *Freemasons' Magazine,* 1860, III, p. 416).

The term "marranos" (hogs) was used contemptuously at the time to denote Moors and Jews.

Marcellus Empiricus (c. 395 A.D.)

A Gallic-Roman writer born at Bordeaux in the fourth century. He was *magister officiorum* under Theodosius (379-395 A.D.). He wrote a work called *De medicamentis conspiricis physicis ac rationalibus,* a collection of medical recipes, for the most part absurd and worthless, and having more in common with popular superstition than with medical science.

Margaritomancy

Divination by means of pearls. A pearl was covered with a vase and placed near the fire, and the names of suspected persons pronounced. When the name of the guilty one was uttered the pearl was supposed to bound upwards and pierce the bottom of the vase.

"Margery"

Pseudonym of famous medium Mina Stinson **Crandon** (189?-1941).

Margiotta, Domenico (c. 1896)

Presumed author of *Souvenirs d'un Trente-Troisième; Adriano Lemmi chef suprême des francs-maçons* (1896) and *Le Palladisme, culte de Satan-Lucifer dans les triangles maçonniques* (1895), which violently impeached the Grand Master Lemmi of the crimes of Satanism and sorcery. These statements were amply proved to be without foundation.

It transpired that these books were part of the astonishing "Diana **Vaughan**" conspiracy of Gabriel **Jogand-Pagès** ("Leo Taxil"), designed to embarrass the Roman Catholic Church and **Freemasonry**. (See also Gabriel **Jogand-Pagès**)

Marie of Agreda (or Maria de Jesus) (1602–1665)

A Spanish nun, who founded and was abbess of the Franciscan Recollects at Agreda. She published a work entitled *La mystica ciudad de Dios (The Mystic City of God, a Miracle of the All-powerful, the Abyss of Grace: Divine History of the Life of the Most Holy Virgin Mary, Mother of God, our Queen and Mistress, manifested in these last times by the Holy Virgin to the Sister Marie of Jesus, Abbess of the Convent of the Immaculate Conception of the town of Agreda, and written by that same Sister by order of her Superiors and Confessors).*

This work, which was condemned by the Sorbonne, described many strange and miraculous happenings said to have befallen the Virgin Mary from her birth onwards, including a visit to Heaven in her early years, when she was given a guard of nine hundred angels.

These revelations appear to have been the result of genuine spiritual raptures, but of a confused kind, being full of inaccuracies. Marie herself was said to have lived a pious life.

Marion, Frederick (1892–   ?)

Stage name of Josef Kraus, famous European performer of stage telepathy and clairvoyance during the 1930s, who also claimed paranormal powers. Born in Prague, Czechoslovakia, October 15, 1892, he was the son of a business man and grew up in a practical atmosphere.

When he manifested psychometric and clairvoyant talents, his family was annoyed rather than impressed, and prescribed castor oil for an over sensitivity. At school, however, the boy became adept at games of locating hidden objects, and sometimes enlarged this talent by giving detailed descriptions and information relating to the owners of the objects. Towards the end of his schooldays, he found it expedient to present his psychic abilities in the form of so-called "tricks" at school concerts and other entertainments. He passed his final examination in mathematics, not because he understood the principles involved, but because he had the unusual talent of being able to memorize the test volume of problems and formulae from beginning to end.

After matriculation, he saw a newspaper report about a Viennese performer named Rubini who claimed special powers of finding concealed objects. Stimulated by his student friends, Marion issued a challenge that he could rival Rubini's feats. The story was taken up by a local newspaper, and a committee was appointed from amongst the Prague police and personalities of the city. Marion undertook to find, in a stipulated time, several objects hidden by the committee in different parts of Prague and described in a sealed envelope deposited at police headquarters.

Marion later stated that his spectacular success was due to the fact that he established telepathic communication with the chairman of the committee, and indeed, there seems no other way in which he could have obtained access to the sealed information.

He became an overnight celebrity, and at the age of nineteen was invited to perform at music halls throughout Europe. He was billed as "The Telepathic Phenomenon" or "The Man with Six Senses." In 1913, he appeared in Moscow on the same bill as Fred Karno's "Mumming Birds," a show which included Stan Laurel and a little clown who later became world famous as Charlie Chaplin. In England, Marion was sometimes billed as "The Human Bloodhound," since he had assisted the police in various continental countries to unravel crime mysteries through his telepathic powers.

During World War I, Marion served in the Austrian Army, and while stationed in Albania, tried his hand at water divining. He rapidly became so well known as a talented dowser that the military authorities presented him with a commission as an officer, and sent him to different areas to find water for the troops. He found traveling around the country somewhat arduous, and experimented with what has since become known as "Teleradiesthesia," holding his divining twig *over a large-scale map* instead of visiting the area (see **Radiesthesia**). He was remarkably successful, and this gave him more time to spare, which he spent in giving shows to entertain the troops. After a bullet wound and a bout of malaria, he was sent back to base at Innsbruck in the Tyrol.

After the war, he returned to his music hall demonstrations, and in 1920 met the remarkable stage clairvoyant Erik Jan **Hanussen,** who combined extraordinary talents with blatant trickery. Marion warned Hanussen that his growing preoccupation with black magic would have disastrous consequences, but the warning was not heeded. According to Marion, it was Hanussen who instructed the inner circle of the young Nazi Party in the power of signs

and words, and first proposed the **swastika** as the Party symbol. Hanussen was later murdered by Nazi thugs in 1933, after disclosures which were embarrassing to the Party.

In his later years, Marion appeared less frequently at music halls, and confined his talents chiefly to lecture demonstrations and private consultations. In 1934, he visited England and gave impressive demonstrations of his psychic talents. During a lecture at the Aeolian Hall, New Bond Street, London, he was challenged by Lady Oxford, who stated that his reconstructions of past incidents in the lives of members of his audience were too precise to be genuine, and must have involved confederates. Thereupon Marion correctly reconstructed an incident in the life of Lady Oxford's husband Lord Asquith, in August 1914, which no other person could have possibly known. Lady Oxford was tremendously impressed, and made a public apology, acknowledging that Marion's talent was genuine.

In 1934, Marion submitted to a long series of scientific experiments directed by Prof. S. G. **Soal** at the **National Laboratory of Psychical Research,** London. Soal was skeptical of Marion's ESP, but concluded that Marion had unusual **hyperaesthesia** or unusual acuity of the senses. Soal stated: "My laboratory experiments show that Marion performs his amazing feats by the aid of remarkable powers which are probably possessed by not one man in a million. There can be no question of either collusion or trickery in his public performances, judging from what I have seen him do single-handed in the laboratory. . . ." However, this hardly did justice to Marion's amazing feats outside the laboratory, including **precognition, clairvoyance,** and **telepathy,** which were less susceptible to scientific investigation.

Marion was also tested by noted psychical researcher Harry **Price,** chiefly in locating hidden objects. Price, like Soal, concluded that Marion somehow gathered imperceptible indications from the other individuals present who had seen the objects hidden. But he could not say how minute indications were possible, since Marion had no physical contact with the audience (as in the famous **"muscle reading"** technique by which some stage performers make contact with a spectator and can interpret imperceptible movements of their muscles towards or away from objects). Price even attempted to limit Marion's view to only one member of the audience, the others being screened by curtains. Then the single agent's body was further screened off progressively by a box with adjustable panels, so that at times only a fifth of his body was visible to Marion, and eventually only his feet! Even under such extraordinary conditions, Marion had a high rate of success.

After two years laboratory experiments, Dr. R. H. **Thouless** and Dr. B. P. **Wiesner** stated: "We can say definitely that we are satisfied that Marion shows paranormal capacities of an unusually high order under strictly controlled experimental conditions."

During World War II, Marion joined ENSA (the British troop entertainment service), and traveled around army camps, demonstrating his ESP talents at troop concerts. On May 23, 1946, he took part in a B.B.C. radio program investigating his psychic abilities, one of the first

British radio presentations of a subject not then deemed quite respectable.

For detailed information on the life of Frederick Marion, see his autobiography: *In My Mind's Eye* (Rider, London, n.d., c. 1949). For reports on Marion's laboratory experiments, see *Confessions of a Ghost Hunter* by Harry Price (1936, reprinted Causeway Books, 1974); *Preliminary Studies of a Vaudeville Telepathist* (London Council for Psychical Investigation, Bulletin III, 1937). See also *Proceedings* of the Society for Psychical Research, London, vol. 50, 1949, pp. 80–85.

Mark Probert Memorial Foundation

Center which preserves tape recordings of sessions with Mark Probert, a trance medium of the 1950s. The Foundation issues a catalog on request. Address: P.O. Box 11672, Palo Alto, California 94306.

Mark Twain (1835–1910)

Pseudonym of author S. L. **Clemens.** The great humorist and creator of Tom Sawyer and Huckleberry Finn wrote an article on "mental telegraphy" in 1880. This related a personal experience of **telepathy.** He also had a vivid premonitory dream of the death of his brother Henry (see *Mark Twain* by Albert Bigelow Paine, 3 vols., 1912). Twain was an early member of the **Society for Psychical Research,** London, until 1903.

After his death, various posthumous communications and writings were claimed. In 1917, a story *Jap Herron* was published in New York, purporting to come from the discarnate Mark Twain, as received by Emily Grant Hutchings and Lola V. Hays. Mrs. Hutchings, the recorder of the *Patience Worth* material of Mrs. John H. **Curran** of St. Louis, was herself an authoress who greatly admired Mark Twain. She had a keen sense of somewhat similar humor and a strong tinge of melancholy like Mark Twain's. She had strongly wished him to communicate through her. All this furnished an ideal condition for subconscious production.

Professor J. H. Hyslop resolved the problem by interesting cross-reference experiments. The two ladies received the communications through the **ouija board,** the presence of both of them being necessary to operate it. They were brought by Hyslop to Boston. He gave each lady, at separate times, five sittings with the medium "Mrs. Chenoweth" (see Mrs. M. M. **Soule).** But he did not admit them to the seance room until "Mrs. Chenoweth," who knew nothing of them, went into trance and made them sit behind her where they could not be seen.

Instead of the usual family relatives, Mark Twain purported to communicate with each of them. He used many of the same expressions that came through the ouija board, mentioned incidents in his life to prove his identity, described what he was doing through the ladies, and revealed the password which he gave to Prof. Hyslop in a St. Louis sitting for cross reference with Miss Burton (Miss Ada **Besinnet).**

"The outcome of the experiments," concluded Prof. Hyslop in the *Journal* of the American Society for Psychical Research (July 1917), "is that there is abundant evidence that Mark Twain is behind the work connected with his name, though the student of psychology would probably find abundant evidence that it was colored more

or less by the mind through which it came." The conclusion also applied to *Brent Roberts,* another posthumous Mark Twain novel which the two ladies received.

In Prof. Hyslop's *Contact with the Other World* (1919), a long chapter was devoted to other evidential spirit communications from Mark Twain.

Marryat, Florence (1837–1899)

Mrs. Ross-Church, later Mrs. Francis Lean, British authoress, daughter of novelist Frederick Capt. Marryat, acquainted with all the celebrated mediums of the seventies-eighties both in England and America, witness of the famous farewell of "Katie King" to Florence Cook at the seance held by Sir William **Crookes.**

Florence Marryat recorded remarkable experiences in two books: *There is No Death* (1891) and *The Spirit World* (1894), both of them immensely popular, and claimed mediumistic gifts herself, among them the strange power of summoning the spirits of the living.

These two books alone created a sensation and secured hundreds of converts to Spiritualism. But this versatile woman also published some ninety novels, wrote plays and acted in them, and edited a popular magazine. Many of her novels were translated into German, French, Swedish, Flemish and Russian and were also popular in America.

She died in London October 27, 1899. Her book *There Is No Death* has been frequently reprinted in Britain and was reissued by Causeway Books, New York in 1973.

Mars, Louis (1906–   )

Professor of psychiatry and former Haitian Ambassador to the U.S. who is also interested in parapsychology. Born September 5, 1906 at Grande-Rivière du Nord, Haiti, he studied at University of Haiti Medical School, Port-au-Prince (M.D. 1927) with postgraduate training in psychiatry at Faculté de Médecine, Paris, 1935, postgraduate study Columbia University, New York, N.Y., 1939–41, 1948. In 1943 he married Madeleine Targète.

He was professor of psychiatry, Medical School, University of Haiti in 1937, professor of psychiatry at Institute of Ethnology, University of Haiti 1946–49, dean of the Medical School from 1947–51, rector of University of Haiti 1957, Haitian Minister of Foreign Affairs from 1958–59, Ambassador to France 1960–61, Ambassador to the U.S. from 1962 onwards, director of Psychiatric Institute of Port-au-Prince. He is a member of New York Academy of Medicine, Academy of the Rights of Man (Berlin); Holder of Grand' Croix, Ordre National Honneur et Mérite (Haiti); Grand' Croix, Ordre du Cèdre (Lebanon); Grand' Croix, Order of the Star of Africa (Liberia). Dr. Mars is author of *La Crise de Possession dans le Voudou* (The Crisis of Possession in Voodoo, 1955), and contributed an article 'Phenomena of Possession' to *Tomorrow* (Autumn 1954).

Marsh, Maurice Clement (1922–   )

South African university lecturer in psychology who has taken special interest in parapsychology. Born March 13, 1922 at Bloemfontein, Union of South Africa, he studied at St. Andrew's School, Bloemfontein (B.A. hons. psychology), University of South Africa (U.E.D. 1948), Rhodes University, Grahamstown, South Africa (Ph.D.

psychology 1959). In 1950 he married Audrey Rittmann.

He served as a sergeant in South African Air Force, demonstrator in the Psychology Department at Rhodes University, teacher at Training School of African Student Teachers, Healdtown Missionary Institution, South Africa, lecturer in psychology at Rhodes University from 1950-61, lecturer in psychology at University of New England, N.S.W., Australia, from 1962 onwards.

He is a member of the Society for Psychical Research, London. Dr. Marsh's Ph.D. thesis dealt with experimental work in ESP and he is interested in laboratory investigation of psychical phenomena. He was a guest researcher at the Parapsychology Laboratory of Duke University, Durham, North Carolina, from November 1951 to January 1952. He has investigated ESP from the viewpoint of relationship between subjects and agents, and also the psychological aspects of conditions favorable to poltergeist, using psychological testing techniques.

Marshall, Mrs. Mary (1842-1884)

The first British professional medium, through whom Sir William **Crookes** and Dr. Alfred Russel **Wallace** obtained their introduction to the phenomena of Spiritualism.

Her manifestations consisted of **raps, movements** and **levitations** of the table, knotting handkerchiefs under the table-leaf and writing on glass. This latter appears to have been a rudimentary form of **slate-writing** with which, in the later-known form, she also confronted her sitters some time after. The first account of this demonstration was published by Thomas P. Barkas in *Outlines of Ten Years' Investigations into the Phenomena of Modern Spiritualism* (London, 1862).

On a small scale, Mrs. Marshall exhibited most of the phenomena of later mediums. From 1867 she held sittings for direct voice in which "John **King**" manifested. In her first seances she was assisted by her niece and occasionally by her young son. Her husband developed drawing mediumship.

A writer in the journal *All the Year Round* (July 28, 1860), characterized Mrs. Marshall's performance as a "dull and barefaced imposition," but Robert Bell, the celebrated dramatist, writing in the *Cornhill Magazine,* was satisfied that the phenomena were genuine spirit manifestations. (See also **Spiritualism**)

Marsi, The

According to Pliny, these people of ancient Italy were from the earliest times skilled in magical practices and sorceries. They were able to charm poisonous serpents by means of songs. St. Augustine also wrote: "One would think that these animals understood the language of the Marsi, so obedient are they to their orders; we see them come out of their caverns as soon as the Marsian has spoken." (See also **Psylli**)

Martel, Linda (1956-1961)

Remarkable child spiritual healer, who was herself born crippled. Although she only lived for five years, she became a legend through her ability to heal a wide variety of illnesses through touch or through contact with material which she had touched. One of the most extraor-

dinary aspects of her healing was that it persisted long after her death when only five years old.

Born August 21, 1956 at St. Peter Port, Guernsey, Channel Island, U.K., she suffered from hydrocephalus and spina bifida and her legs were paralyzed. After eleven days she was taken to St. Peter Port Hospital, Guernsey, to await death. Over the next few weeks, her head grew disproportionately large. During this period, her father experienced a strange phenomenon when his room was filled with a glowing light and he heard a sound like wind blowing. Linda did not die, and soon afterwards the Matron at the hospital arranged for her to have fluid drained away from her head by means of a new American treatment for hydrocephalus. The operation was successful and the size of the head reduced. However, Linda remained crippled.

At the age of three, Linda frequently spoke about "my Lady" and about Jesus. The Lady had a blue dress and gold chain and lived in heaven with Jesus and also looked after her. At the age of five, Linda foretold her own death, saying "My Jesus Christ is not coming to see me many more times, but I shall soon be going to see Him. . . ." She died October 20, 1961.

During her brief life, Linda manifested healing gifts, even as early as the age of three. Sometimes she would simply put her finger on a painful point, when a cure would take place. At other times, she healed through handkerchiefs which she had handled. After her death, a sufferer from asthma asked Linda's father whether he could have a piece of her clothing, and the father was persuaded to give him a piece of a dress. The sufferer was healed after contact with the material. After that, there were constant demands for pieces of Linda's clothing, and claimed cures through contact with them included warts, eczema, spinal injury, bone disease and throat cancer.

Because so many pieces of material associated with Linda were used up, her father presented one of her dresses to the Guernsey Museum, in the hope that it might be effective in healing through people simply looking at it, since the material itself was only the intermediary of some unknown force.

Recommended reading:

Martel, Roy. *The Mysterious Power of Linda Martel,* pamphlet. The Toucan Press, Guernsey, C.I., 1973

Martello, Leo Louis

Contemporary Manhattan witch, hypnotist and graphologist. A self-styled exhibitionist, he has appeared on radio and television programs which he enlivens with a sharp wit.

His *Witch Manifesto* demanded $500 million damages from the Catholic Church and $100 million reparation payment from Salem, Massachusetts. Calling himself "The Gay Witch," he makes no secret of his homophile predilections. He edits various witchcraft magazines, assisted by a young lady rejoicing in the name of Witch Hazel. He is director of Witches International Craft Association (WICA), leader of the Witches Liberation Movement. He has published a number of popular books on occult subjects, including: *Weird Ways of Witchcraft* (1969), *Hidden World of Hypnotism* (1969), *Understanding the Tarot* (1972), *Black Magic, Voodoo, Satanism* (1972), *How to*

Prevent Psychological Blackmail (1974), *Witchcraft: The Old Religion* (1975).

Martial Arts

A group of Asian skills, combining mental, physical and spiritual energies for self-defense in weaponless fighting, or the achievement of apparently paranormal feats of strength and control.

The martial arts derive from the Samurai or warrior caste fighting systems of ancient Japan, which were conditioned by **Zen** Buddhism, hence they have a spiritual basis. They are closely related to similar systems in ancient China, and Japanese and Chinese martial arts are widely diffused throughout Asia.

These arts have become more widely known and taught in the U.S. since World War II, when many servicemen encountered them in Asian campaigns, and there are now many schools for specific training throughout the U.S. Another influence was that of the popular Chinese actor Bruce Lee, who popularized the art of *kung-fu* in such films as *Fist of Fury* and *Enter the Dragon.* The popular television movie series *Kung Fu* starring David Carradine also did much to popularize martial arts in the U.S. during the 1970s.

The main martial arts are: *aikido* (a kind of *judo* of graceful movement in which an opponent's force is used against him), *bando* (Burmese boxing and wrestling), *judo* (wrestling with special emphasis on balance and leverage), *jiu-jitsu* (a more comprehensive and aggressive forerunner of *judo*), *karate* (kicking, striking and blocking with arms or legs), *kung-fu* (a group of various styles of fighting and defense), *shaolin* (Chinese shadow boxing), *tae kwon do* (Korean system of kick-punching), *t'ai chi chuan* (originally a self-defense art, now a system of physical exercises to harmonize body and mind).

The various forms of martial arts have, as their basis, the attainment of spiritual enlightenment and peace, from which point remarkable feats of skill and strength in self-defense or attack can be generated. In the process of training, a subtle vital energy named **ch'i** or *ki* is accumulated, amplified and directed by willpower to specific parts of the body, which develop strength and resilience. This process is sometimes preceded by a sudden exhalation of breath, often accompanied by a shout or yell. The intake of breath which follows appears to result in hyperventilation of the system, generating vitality which can be directed to hands, feet or other parts of the body. This process has been widely demonstrated by practitioners of *karate* in apparently paranormal feats such as breaking bricks, tiles and planks of wood with a bare hand. It has been suggested that these feats are related to such psychic phenomena as **Psychokinesis,** the ability to move objects at a distance by mental action.

Recommended reading:

Barclay, Glen. *Mind Over Matter: Beyond the Bounds of Nature,* Arthur Barker, London, 1973; Pan paperback, 1975

Ching-nan, Lee & R. Figueroa. *Techniques of Self-Defense,* A. S. Barnes, 1963

Feldenkrais, Moshe. *Higher Judo,* Warne, 1952

Freudenberg, Karl. *Natural Weapons: A Manual of Karate, Judo & Jujitsu Techniques,* A. S. Barnes paperback, 1962

Huard, Pierre & Ming Wong. *Oriental Methods of Mental & Physical Fitness: The Complete Book of Meditation, Kinesitherapy, & Martial Arts in China, India, & Japan,* Funk & Wagnall paperback, 1971

Masters, Robert V. *Complete Book of Karate & Self-Defense,* Sterling, 1974

Medeiros, Earl C. *The Complete History & Philosophy of Kung Fu,* Tuttle, 1975

Nakayama, M. *Dynamic Karate,* Wehman, 1966

Tohei, Koichi. *This is Aikido,* Japan Publications, 1975

Westbrook, A. & O. Ratti. *Aikido & the Dynamic Sphere,* Tuttle, 1970

Martian Language

A language purporting to be that of the inhabitants of the planet Mars, written and spoken by the medium known as Hélène **Smith** (pseudonym of Catherine Elise Muller). Hélène was studied by the celebrated investigator, Theodor **Flournoy,** professor of psychology at Geneva. In 1892 Hélène had joined a Spiritualist circle, where she developed marvelous mediumistic powers.

In 1896, after Professor Flournoy had begun his investigations, Hélène claimed to have been spirited during a trance to the planet Mars, and thereafter described to the circle the manners and customs and appearance of the Martians. She learned their language, which she wrote and spoke with ease and consistency.

Unlike most of the "unknown tongues" automatically produced, the Martian language was intelligible, its words were used consistently, and on the whole it had every appearance of a genuine language. That it was in any way connected with Mars was, of course, out of the question. The descriptions of that planet and its inhabitants were quite impossible. And the language itself bore remarkable resemblance to French, the native tongue of the medium. The grammar and construction of both languages were the same, and even the vowel sounds were identical, so that the source of the Martian language was clearly an extraordinary construction from the medium's unconsciousness. (See also Hélène **Smith;** Speaking and Writing in **Tongues; Xenoglossis**)

Martin, Dorothy R(andolph) (1912–   )

Associate professor of psychology with special interest in parapsychology. Born April 19, 1912 at Denver, Colorado, she studied at University of Colorado, Boulder, Colo. (B.A. 1934, M.A. 1936, Ph.D. 1947). She was assistant in psychology from 1934–37, instructor in psychology 1937–48, assistant professor of psychology 1948–58 University of Colorado; visiting associate professor of psychology at University of Kansas 1948–49; associate professor of psychology at University of Colorado from 1958 onwards.

She is a member of the American Psychological Association, Rocky Mountain Psychological Association, Colorado Psychological Association, American Association of University Professors and charter associate of the Parapsychological Association. She contributed various articles to the *Journal of Parapsychology,* including: 'Chance and Extra-Chance Results in Card Matching' (vol. 1, 1937), 'Studies in Extrasensory Perception' (with F. P. Stribic): 'An Analysis of 25,000 Trials' (vol. 2, 1938), 'An Analysis of a Second Series of 25,000 Trials' (vol. 2, 1938), 'A

Review of All University of Colorado Experiments' (vol. 4, 1940).

Martin, Saint (of Tours) (c. 316–400)

One of the most venerated Christian saints in Europe during the Middle Ages. Most of the luminaries of the Christian Church were credited with working miracles, and indeed the great majority of them maintained that if the people were to be won for Christ, the one sure way was to show them extraordinary marvels. Even Columba, most engaging of saints, was not averse to practicing deception with a view to making converts, and it has often been suggested, not without considerable reason, that some of these early thaumaturgists brought science to their aid. Perhaps St. Martin was among those who essayed this practice, and certainly the list of miracles credited to him is formidable, for he is traditionally credited with considerably over two hundred.

Martin was born about the year 316 at Sabaria, in Pannonia. His parents were heathen, yet he very soon came into contact with Christians and their teaching impressed him greatly. As a young man he entered the army, and it was soon after this step that, while stationed with his regiment at Amiens, he performed his famous act of charity, dividing his cloak with a beggar who was shivering with cold. The night after this generous act he was vouchsafed a vision, Christ appearing to him and giving him his blessing. Thereupon Martin espoused the Christian faith formally, was baptized and renounced soldiering once and for all.

Going to Poitiers, he then made the acquaintance of Hilary, who wished to make him a deacon, but at his own request ordained him to the humbler office of an exorcist. A little later, during a visit to his home, Martin experienced the joy of winning his mother from heathendom to the new faith. However, his open zeal in opposing the Arians raised persecution against him, and for a considerable space he found it advisable to live at the island of Gallinaria, near Genoa, in which quiet retreat he had ample leisure for scientific researches and theological studies.

By the year 365, he was back with Hilary at Poitiers, when he founded the Monasterium Locociagense. In 371, the people of Tours chose him as their bishop, and for some time subsequently he showed great activity in trying to extirpate idolatry in his diocese, and in extending the monastic system. Nevertheless, he was anything but a fierce proseletyzer, and at Trèves, in 385, he entreated that the lives of the Priscillianist heretics should be spared, while he ever afterwards refused to have anything to do with those bishops who had sanctioned their execution.

Meanwhile, being anxious for a period of quiet study, Martin established the monastery of Marmontier les Tours, on the banks of the Loire, and here much of his remaining life was spent, although it was at Candes that his death occurred about the year 400.

Martin left no writings behind him, the *Confessio* with which he is sometimes credited being undoubtedly spurious. His life was written by his ardent disciple, Sulpicius Severus, and a curious document it is, filled with accounts of the miracles and marvels worked by the quondam bishop. Martin was duly sanctified by the church, and he is commemorated on the 11th of November, but the feast of Martinmas, which occurs on that date, and which of course derives its name from him, is, nevertheless, a survival of an old pagan festival. It inherited certain usages thereof, this accounting for the fact that Martin is regarded as the patron saint of drinking, joviality, and reformed drunkards. Certain of his miracles and other incidents in his life were figured by numerous painters of note, perhaps the finest picture of him being one by the Flemish master, Hugo van der Goes, which is now in the Municipal Museum at Glasgow. It should be said that the term "martinet," signifying a severe and punctilious person, is not derived from the saint's name, but from one Jean Martinet, a French soldier who, during the reign of Louis XIV won fame by his ardor in promoting discipline in his regiment.

Martin, Stuart (died 1947)

British Spiritualist and journalist, formerly employed on the *Daily Mirror* newspaper. He was editor of the newspaper *Psychic News* from March 16, 1946 until his death on January 17, 1947.

Martinez, Louis

Prominent Mexican physical medium, supposed to have demonstrated **levitation** and **materialization** phenomena. In 1964 he was investigated by parapsychologist W. G. **Roll,** who found evidence of fraud on the part of one of the sitters.

Martiny, M(arcel) (1897–   )

Physician with special interests in parapsychology. Born November 11, 1897 at Nice, France, he studied at Faculté de Médecine, Université de Paris, France (M.D. hons. 1925). In 1921 he married Thérèse Gagey. He worked for the Rockefeller Institute Mission during World War I, at Beaujon Hospital 1925–32, Léopold Bellan Hospital, Paris 1933–40, becoming head of medical staff 1940–45, after which he became a member of the medical staff, Hospital Foch.

From 1949 onwards he was director of the Anthropotechnical Laboratory, Prophylactic Institute, Paris. Other appointments include Secretary-General, Medico-Surgical Society of the Free Hospitals of France 1932, president of National Union of Physicians, Surgeons and Specialists of the Free Hospitals of France 1948, president of Physiopsychology Society 1958, president of Institute Métapsychique 1962; member of Paris Medical Society.

Dr. Martiny was author of various medical works and co-author with Dr. Alexis **Carrel** of *Médecine Officielle at Médecine Hérétique* (Orthodox and Unorthodox Medicine). He also spent many years investigating human bio-types in relation to parapsychological phenomena, parapsychology in relation to psychoanalysis, hypnosis and Pavlov's nervous typology in relation to parapsychology, relationships between neurology, cerebral function and parapsychology, space-time concepts in parapsychology. His articles on such subjects have been published in *Revue Métapsychique.* He also contributed papers to international conferences on parapsychology (Utrecht 1953; St. Paul de Vence 1954).

"Mary Celeste"

The name of a ship found abandoned at sea December 5, 1872, one of the most famous unsolved sea mysteries. Her sails were set, she was sound and seaworthy, with plenty of food and water, but not a soul on board. Some garments were hanging out to dry on a line. In the cabin was a slate with notes for the ship's log, with November 25 as the last date. The crew had left pipes, clothing and even oilskin boots. For some unknown reason the ship had been hurriedly abandoned.

The "Mary Celeste" was brought to Gibraltar by the crew of the British brig "Dei Gratia," who claimed salvage. On March 25, 1873, the Chief Justice awarded £1,700 to the master and crew of the "Dei Gratia" (about one-fifth of the total value).

Since then, the mystery of the "Mary Celeste" (sometimes inaccurately called "Marie Celeste") has been widely discussed and many theories advanced. There have also been various literary hoaxes, notably 'The Marie Celeste, the True Story of the Mystery' (*Strand Magazine,* November 1913) and the book *The Great Mary Celeste Hoax* by Laurence J. Keating (London, 1929).

Several years before the creation of Sherlock Holmes, author Sir Arthur Conan Doyle published 'J. Habakuk Jephson's Statement' in the *Cornhill Magazine* (January 1884), a romantic fictional yarn with an air of verisimilitude. The story was republished in Doyle's volume of short stories *The Captain of the Polestar* (London, 1890).

There is a useful discussion of the mystery in *The Stargazer Talks* by Rupert T. Gould (London, 1944; reissued as *More Oddities & Enigmas* (University Books, 1973). The most complete survey is that of Harold T. Wilkins in his book *Mysteries Solved and Unsolved* (London, 1958; reissued in paperback as *Mysteries,* 1961). For the factual background of the story see *Mary Celeste: The Odyssey of an Abandoned Ship* by Charles Eden Fay (Salem, Peabody Museum, 1942).

Maryland Center for Investigation of Unconventional Phenomena

Founded by Dr. Willard F. McIntyre and Arthur F. Rosen for the purpose of gathering and disseminating information of such phenomena as UFOs, Bigfoot, monsters, etc. The center issues a publication *Believe It.* Address: 131 Clifton Road, Silver Spring, Maryland 20904. (See also **Fortean Society; Monsters**)

Marylebone Spiritualist Association, Ltd.

One of the earliest British Spiritualist organizations, founded February, 1972. It grew out of informal meetings at the Progressive Library of James **Burns** (editor of *The Medium and Daybreak* journal). In the early years, the Association hired halls for their meetings, often with some difficulty in view of prejudice against Spiritualism. In fact, the Association had to use the name "The Spiritual Evidence Society" in the beginning.

In 1879, premises were obtained in Marylebone, West London, and some famous mediums attended meetings, including Cecil **Husk,** Frank **Herne** and Charles **Williams.** In 1891, new premises were obtained in High Street, Marylebone, at an address which had formerly been a police court. The opening ceremony was performed by the famous writer Florence **Marryat.** In 1894,

the Association was addressed by Emma Hardinge **Britten.**

Over the years, there were further changes of address, but many famous names in Spiritualism became connected with the Association. Distinguished individuals who addressed meetings included such names as Dr. J. M. **Peebles,** Mrs. Cora L. V. **Richmond,** W. J. **Colville,** Sir Arthur Conan **Doyle** (at one time an honorary vice-president), the Rev. G. Vale **Owen,** and Hannen **Swaffer.**

In the course of time, the expansion of the Association's activities and scope led to its name becoming inapplicable, and by 1960 the title was the Spiritualist Association of Great Britain, now one of the largest organizations of its kind. It is located at 33 Belgrave Square, London, W.1. in spacious premises which include meeting hall, chapel, library, prayer and meditation room, and one floor devoted to spiritual healing. It is estimated that some 150,000 people visit these premises every year. (See also **Spiritualist Association of Great Britain**)

Maskelyne, John Nevil (1839–1917)

Famous British stage magician who was a strong opponent of fraudulent Spiritualism. Born at Cheltenham, Gloucestershire, December 22, 1839, he was the son of a saddlemaker. As a boy he was fascinated by an entertainer who demonstrated spinning plates and practiced this feat himself. He was apprenticed to a clockmaker and at the age of nineteen made his first piece of conjuring apparatus, a box with a secret panel. By 1865 he was giving demonstrations of amateur conjuring. After seeing the performance of the famous **Davenport Brothers,** he believed that he had observed trickery, and to prove his case he went into partnership with George Alfred Cooke to build a cabinet similar to that of the Davenports and rival their phenomena. Maskelyne and Cooke were launched on a career of stage magic and leased the Egyptian Hall in London for their entertainments. By 1905, Maskelyne was in partnership with fellow illusionist David Devant (born David Wighton) at St. George's Hall, Langham Place in West London, where they based many of their presentations of the claimed phenomena of Spiritualism.

In 1906, he was involved in a controversy with Spiritualist sympathizer Archdeacon Thomas **Colley,** who had challenged him to reproduce the phenomena of medium F. W. **Monck** (incidentally exposed in fraud). Maskelyne staged a remarkable illusion, but Colley claimed it fell short of the requirements of his challenge. After a court case, Colley's claim was upheld, perhaps surprisingly in view of opposition to Spiritualism at that time.

Maskelyne's publications included: *The Fraud of Modern "Theosophy" Exposed* (1912), *Modern Spiritualism; A Short Account of its Rise and Progress, with some exposures of so-called spirit media* (n.d.).

Notwithstanding his sweeping denunciations of Spiritualism as fraudulent, Maskelyne did not absolutely disbelieve in the supernatural. (See also **Fraud; Magicians**)

Masleh

The angel whom the Jews believed ruled the Zodiac. According to a rabbinical legend, Masleh was the medium through which the power and influence of the Messiah was transmitted to the sphere of the Zodiac.

Mass of St. Secaire

A form of **Black Mass** originating in the Basque countryside, possibly in medieval times. It was a travesty of a Christian mass and celebrated in a ruined church. The intention was not to worship the Devil, but to direct currents of malevolent spite against a victim. It may have had its origin in ancient folklore practices. For a description, see H. T. F. Rhodes, *The Satanic Mass* (London, 1954; Arrow paperback 1964).

Masse, François (1891– ?)

Commissaire général, French Navy, with interests in parapsychology. Born May 10, 1891 at Vendome, France, he entered the French Navy and served in World War I and II, retiring as commissaire général 1946. He is Commander, Legion of Honor. In 1925 he married Colette Vignal. He was a member of the Institut Métapsychique International from 1948 onwards, serving as general secretary, and secretary-treasurer. He collaborated with Rene **Warcollier** in telepathy experiments and contributed articles on parapsychological topics to *Revue Métapsychique.*

Massey, Gerald (1828–1907)

British poet, born May 29, 1828 in Hertfordshire, England. He grew up in abject poverty and had to earn a living by working in a factory at the age of eight. He learnt to read at a penny school. He became a Socialist and edited a radical journal. He also wrote poems, which were favorably noticed by established poets such as Browning and Tennyson. His first wife was Rosina Knowles, a Spiritualist medium.

He based his volume of poetry *A Tale of Eternity* on personal experience of a haunted house. He lost some of his earlier popularity when he was said to have gone over to the Spiritualists. He admitted: "For the truth's sake I ought to explain that the spiritualism to be found in my poetry is no delusive idealism, derived from hereditary belief in a resurrection of the dead. My faith in the future life is founded upon facts in nature and realities of my own personal experience. These facts have been more or less known to me personally during forty years of familiar face-to-face acquaintanceship, therefore my certitude is not premature; they have given me proof palpable that our very own human identity and intelligence do persist after the blind of darkness has been drawn down in death."

At the meeting in London in 1872 which bade farewell to Mrs. Emma Hardinge **Britten** on her departure to Australia, Gerald Massey presided. His address with some additions was later printed under the title *Concerning Spiritualism.*

Massey's genius was unrecognized during his lifetime. In his later years he published four large volumes in which he tried to trace the origin of language, symbols, myths and religions in a similar way to that other bold thinker Godfrey **Higgins** (1772–1833).

This vast compendium, in which he cited Africa as the birthplace of mankind, was ignored or ridiculed until recent times, when archaeological discoveries have validated his main theme. His books have now been reprinted, and may earn a more tolerant evaluation. *A Book of the Beginnings,* 2 vols., first published London, 1881, reissued University Books Inc. 1974; *The Natural Genesis,* 2 vols., first published London, 1883; *Ancient Egypt,* 2 vols., first published London, 1907, reissued Samuel Weiser.

Masters

Occult adepts who are supposed to have reached a superhuman stage but elected to remain on earth and guide seekers after wisdom. The founding and guidance of the **Theosophical Society** of Madame **Blavatsky** was supposed to be due to hidden Masters or Mahatmas living in remote Tibetan fastnesses.

Much of Western occultism derives from romantic concepts of adepts with magical powers, but in Hinduism, mystical awareness or God-realization is considered superior to paranormal feats, and to the Hindu pupil the Master is his guru. The term *Mahatma* is used to indicate a special guru or "great soul," and *Maharishi* or *Maharshi* denotes a great sage of transcendental wisdom. Another Sanskrit term *Paramahansa* (literally "greatest swan") is given to a very exalted mystic. (See also **Adepts; Golden Dawn; Great White Brotherhood; Guru; Mahatma; Theosophical Society**)

The five Masters claimed by Madame Blavatsky were: Koot Hoomi Lal Singh (usually signing letters "K.H."), the Master Morya (known as "Master M."), Master Ilarion or Hilarion (a Greek), Djual Khul (or "D.K."), and the Maha Chohan.

Masters, Robert E. L.

Co-founder with wife Jean **Houston** of the **Foundation for Mind Research,** Manhattan, New York, conducting experiments in the borderline between mental and physical experience. Masters has a background of poetry and sexology and was formerly director of the Visual Imagery Research Project.

Both Houston and Masters have experimented with psychedelic drugs and hypnosis, and in their Foundation they have investigated induction of mystical experience and altered states of consciousness. In collaboration with his wife, Masters is author of: *The Varieties of Psychedelic Experience* (1966), *Mind Games; the Guide to Inner Space* (1972), *Listening to the Body* (1978). (See also **Foundation for Mind Research; Witches' Cradle**)

Mastiphal

The name given to the prince of demons in an apocryphal book entitled *Little Genesis,* which was quoted by the Greek monk and historian George Cedrenus (11th century).

Material for Thought

Journal concerned with **Fourth Way** teachings deriving from the philosophy of **Gurdjieff.** Address: Box 549, San Francisco, California 94101.

Materialization

The claimed manifestation of temporary, more or less organized, substances in various degrees of solid form and possessing human physical characteristics of limbs, faces, eyes, heads or full figures, shaped for a temporary existence out of a substance named "ectoplasm," Such materializations are generally believed by Spiritualists and some psychical researchers to be due to spirit agency, although others believe that they might arise from some rare and unknown natural force independent of departed spirits, but arising from a gifted psychic.

Materialization is certainly one of the most controversial of claimed paranormal phenomena and it is unfortunate that in modern times the phenomenon is rare and therefore not easily accessible to improved laboratory techniques of investigation. It must also be admitted that many mediums of the past have been exposed in fraudulent materializations and that trade catalogs of apparatus for such frauds were well-known.

As one of the most important of the physical phenomena of Spiritualism, materialization suggests connections with the appearance of apparitions and perhaps the tenuous "astral projection" forms of out-of-the-body experience. Other possible connections may exist with the **"thoughtforms"** of **psychic photography** and the "spirit figures" of **spirit photography.** If mental images may travel across space in **telepathy,** the claim that images might assume a more solid plastic organization under certain conditions does not appear altogether absurd.

In its earlier stages, materialization was confined to the materializing of heads and hands, or vague luminous streaks of light and later figures. In common with much of the physical phenomena of Spiritualism, it had its origin in America, where it was reported at a comparatively early period in the history of the movement.

As early as 1860, seances were held with the Fox Sisters by Robert Dale Owen and others, at which veiled and luminous figures were recognized. One sitter, Mr. Livermore, claimed to see and recognize the spirit of his dead wife during seances with Kate Fox extending over some six years. However, there were no other sitters and the seances were held in the dark.

In England, the mediums Frank **Herne** and Charles **Williams** succeeded a few months later in apparently materializing shadowy forms and faces in a dark seance room.

However, it was Florence **Cook,** whose phenomena was so strongly championed by scientist Sir William **Crookes** who produced the most sensational materializations. At the commencement of her Spiritualistic career, she was a pretty young girl of sixteen or seventeen years. She was at that time a private medium, though at the outset she held some materialization seances with Herne.

From her childhood, it was said, she had been attended by a spirit-girl, who stated that her name on earth had been "Annie Morgan," but that her name in the spirit-world was "Katie **King.**" Under the latter name Miss Cook's **control** was destined to become very famous in Spiritualist circles.

Usually the medium was put in a sort of cupboard or cabinet, tied to her chair, and the cords sealed. A short interval would ensue, during which the sitters sang Spiritualist hymns, and at length there would emerge from the cabinet a form clad in flowing white draperies, and difficult to distinguish from an ordinary human being.

On one occasion, a seance was held at Mr. Cook's house, at which several distinguished Spiritualists were present. Among the invited guests was Mr. W. Volckman, who thought to test for himself the good faith of the medium and the genuineness of "Katie." After some forty minutes close observance of the materialized spirit Mr.

Volckman concluded that Miss Cook and "Katie" were one and the same, and just as the white-robed figure was about to return to the cabinet he rushed forward and seized her. His indignant fellow-sitters released the "spirit," the light was extinguished, and in the confusion that followed the spirit disappeared. Miss Cook was found a few minutes later bound as when she was placed in the cabinet, the cords unbroken, the seal intact. She wore a black dress, and there was no trace of white draperies in the cabinet.

Sir William Crookes, whose investigations into the phenomena of this medium extended over a period of some years, had better opportunity of examining Katie's claims than Mr. Volckman, and he had left it on record that the spirit form was taller than the medium, had a larger face and longer fingers, and whereas Florence Cook had black hair and a dark complexion, "Katie's" complexion was fair, and her hair a light auburn. Moreover Sir William, enjoying as he did the complete confidence of "Katie," had on more than one occasion the privilege of seeing her and Miss Cook at the same time.

But Florence Cook was not the only medium who was controlled by "Katie King," who, with her father, "John King," became in time a most popular spirit with materialization mediums. From that time onwards materialization was extensively practiced both by private and professional mediums, among the number being Mrs. **Showers** and her daughter, Miss Lottie **Fowler,** William **Eglinton** and D. D. **Home;** while in later years materializations were stated to have occurred in the presence of Eusapia **Palladino.**

Many sitters claimed to see in such draped figures and veiled faces the form and features of deceased relatives and friends, although frequently there was but the smallest ground for such a claim—parents recognized their daughter by her hair, a man recognized his mother by the sort of cap she wore, and so on.

There is no doubt that fraud entered very largely into materialization seances. Lay figures, muslin draperies, false hair, and similar properties have been found in the possession of mediums; accomplices have been smuggled into the seance-room; lights are frequently turned low or extinguished altogether. Add to this the fact that other spirits besides "Katie" have on being grasped resolved themselves into the person of the medium, and it will be seen that skepticism is not altogether unjustified. Then, as already mentioned, the rash and premature recognition of deceased friends in draped forms whose resemblance to the medium is patent to the less-interested observer, has also done much to ruin the case for genuine spirit materialization. Yet that there is a case we must believe on the assertion of some of the most distinguished of modern investigators, men fully alive to the possibilities of fraud, trained to habits of correct observation.

Psychical Researchers and Materialization

Camille **Flammarion** attributed the materializations he had witnessed in the presence of Eusapia **Palladino** to fluidic emanations from the medium's person, while judging the recognition accorded to them the result of illusion. Other researchers stated that the physical organization formed by the spirit was composed of fine particles of matter drawn from the material world.

According to Gustav **Geley** in his book *Clairvoyance and*

Materialisation (1927), this "is no longer the marvellous and quasi-miraculous affair described and commented on in early spiritualistic works."

"I shall not waste time" stated Prof. Charles **Richet** in *Thirty Years of Psychical Research* (1923) "in stating the absurdities, almost the impossibilities, from a psycho-physiological point of view, of this phenomenon. A living being, or living matter, formed under our eyes, which has its proper warmth, apparently a circulation of blood, and a physiological respiration which has also a kind of psychic personality having a will distinct from the will of the medium, in a word, a new human being! This is surely the climax of marvels! Nevertheless, it is a fact."

He suggests that "materialisation is a mechanical projection; we already know the projection of light, of heat and of electricity; it is not a very long step to think that a projection of mechanical energy may be possible. The remarkable demonstrations of Einstein show how close mechanical or luminous energy are to one another."

"I have also, like Geley, Schrenck Notzing, and Mme. Bisson, been able to see the first lineaments of materialisations as they were formed. A kind of liquid or pasty jelly emerges from the mouth or the breast of Marthe which organises itself by degrees, acquiring the shape of a face or a limb. Under very good conditions of visibility, I have seen this paste spread on my knees, and slowly take form so as to show the rudiment of the radius, the cuvitus, or metacarpal bone whose increasing pressure I could feel on my knee."

The Marthe of Prof. Richet's account was the medium Marthe Béraud, also known as "**Eva C**" Geley related his experiences with her: "I have very often seen complete representations of a face, a hand, or a finger. In the most perfect instances the materialised organ has all the appearance and the biological properties of a living organ. I have seen admirably modelled fingers with nails; I have seen complete hands with their bones and joints; I have seen a living head and felt the skull under thick hair; I have seen well-formed and living faces—human faces. In many instances these representations have grown under my own eyes from the beginning to the end of the phenomena. The forms show some degree of self-movement, and this is physiological as well as anatomical. The materialised organs are not inert, but biologically alive. A well-materialised hand has the functional capacities of a normal hand; I have at different times been touched or grasped by its fingers. Well-constituted organs, with all the appearances of life, are often replaced by incomplete formations. Relief is often wanting, and the forms are flat. I have sometimes seen a hand or a face appear flat and then take to three dimensions, either completely or partially, as I looked. When the forms are incomplete they are often smaller than natural size-miniatures."

On June 13, 1913, the ectoplasm emerged from the medium's mouth with a materialized finger at the end. M. Bourbon took hold of the finger as it came from Eva's mouth and verified the bone in it. The tulle which covered the medium's head showed no hole.

From Thought-forms to Full Grown Phantoms

Many of the photographs taken of Eva C's materializations suggest the evolution of **thought-forms**. Prof. Daumer contended that ectoplasmic forms were neither bodies nor souls. He offered the name: eidolon (shape). A number of Eva C's phantom forms were such shapes and resembled pictures she had seen, caricatures of presidents Wilson and Poincaré, and they often had folds as if a paper had been uncreased to be photographed.

Prof. Richet remarked that the supposition of fraud would presume extreme stupidity on Eva's part as she knew that photographs would be taken, moreover that there is no ground to suppose that a materialization must be analogous to a human body and must be three dimensional. "The materialisation of a plaster bust is not easier to understand than that of a lithographic drawing; and the formation of an image is not less extraordinary than that of a living human head."

Professor Daumer's speculation is strangely contrasted by Dr. Glen **Hamilton**'s report (*Psychic Science*, January 1933) on the building and photographing of a three-dimensional ectoplasmic ship in the Winnipeg circle. The entities "John King" and "Walter" claimed responsibility for the experiment. Coming through the mediums Mary M. and X, they carried on a dialogue feigning that they were aboard John King's pirate ship and amongst a crew of piratical ruffians. It was hinted that this play-acting had a psychological purpose: the recovery of past memories and the creation of the thought image of a sailing ship. Eventually the ship was built, but owing to some indecision in giving the signal to take a flash photograph, it "came into port badly damaged." Dr. Glen Hamilton remarked:

"No matter how great we may conceive the unknown powers of the human organism to be, we cannot conceive of it giving rise to an objective mass showing purposive mechanistic construction such as that disclosed in the ship teleplasm of June 4th [1930]. We are forced to conclude that the supernormal personalities in this case (by some means as yet unknown to us) so manipulated or otherwise influenced the primary materialising substance after it had left the body of the medium, or was otherwise brought into its objective state, as to cause it to represent the idea which they, the unseen directors, had in view, namely the idea of a sailing ship."

Generally the appearance of images instead of forms may have something to do with the quantity of available power. It is suggestive that Geley often observed strange, incomplete forms, imitations or simulacra of organs. "There are simulacra of fingers, having only their general shape, without warmth, without suppleness, and without joints. There are simulacra of faces like masks, or as if cut out of paper, tufts of hair sticking to them, and undefinable forms."

In explanation Geley expressly stated: "They are often the products of weak power using still weaker means of execution; it does what it can, and rarely succeeds, because its activity, diverted from its usual course, no longer has the certainty of action which normal biologic impulse gives to a physiological act." He compared them to the strange formations called dermoid cysts, in which are found hair, teeth, divers organs, viscera, and even more or less complete foetal forms. The supernormal physiology, like normal physiology, has its finished products and its abortions, monstrosities and dermoid cysts.

The essential thing is that "the formations materialised in mediumistic seances arise from the same biological process as normal birth. They are neither more nor less miraculous or supernormal; they are equally so. The same ideoplastic miracle makes the hands, the face, the viscera, the tissues, and the entire organism of the fœtus at the expense of the material body, or the hands, the face, or the entire organs of a materialisation. This singular analogy between normal and so-called supernormal physiology extends even to details; the ectoplasm is linked to the medium by a channel of nourishment, a true umbilical cord, comparable to that which joins the embryo to the maternal body. In certain cases the materialised forms appear in an ovoid of substance. . . . I have also seen, on several occasions, a hand presented wrapped in a membrane closely resembling the placental membrane. The impression produced, both as to sight and touch, was precisely that of a hand presentation in childbirth, when the amnion is unbroken. Another analogy with childbirth is that of pain. The moans and movements of the entranced medium remind one strangely of a woman in travail."

To the legitimate objection why is one biological process regular and the other exceptional, Geley returned the answer that "normal physiology is the product of organic activity such as evolution has made it. The creative and directive idea normally works in a given sense, that of the evolution of the species, and conforms to the manner of that evolution. Supernormal physiology, on the other hand, is the product of ideoplastic activity directed in a divergent manner by an abnormal effort of the directive idea."

Geley certainly showed a greater understanding of all the complexities of the phenomena than Baron **Schrenck-Notzing** when the latter categorically concluded that "a continuation of the materialisation of organic parts beyond the field of vision of the observers is non-existent." It has been suggested that the Baron's interest in anatomy was instrumental in the immature formations, just as Dr. W. J. **Crawford**'s experiments in engineering training may have contributed to the evolution of cantilever functions. Similarly, the appearances resembling internal organs in "Margery's" mediumship may have had something to do with Dr. **Crandon**'s work as a surgeon.

In a higher degree of development we find that the ectoplasmic shapes tend to conform to the bodily pattern of the medium. "I have seen, with my natural vision," stated the Rev. J. B. **Ferguson,** "the arms, bust and, on two occasions, the entire person of Ira E. Davenport duplicated at a distance of from two to five feet from where he was seated fast bound to his seat. I have seen, also, a full-formed figure of a person, which was not that of any of the company present. In certain conditions, not yet clearly understood, the hands, arms and clothing of the Brothers Davenport and Mr. Fay are duplicated alike to the sight and the touch. In other cases, hands which are visible and tangible, and which have all the characteristics of living human hands, as well as arms, and entire bodies, are presented, which are not theirs or those of anyone present."

Crookes was satisfied that "Katie King" was independent from the medium Florence Cook. Yet on certain occasions he noted a striking resemblance between phantom and medium. There is a highly curious account in the history of the medium Mme. **d'Esperance** which seems to suggest that a total exchange is within the bounds of

possibility. Under the auspices of Alexander **Aksakof** and Matthews Fidler, savants from different parts of Europe were holding a series of sittings with Mme. d'Esperance in Sweden. A crucial test was asked and the medium bravely stated to "Walter," the spirit control, that she would take the responsibility. So wrote Mme. d'Esperance:

"A very uncomfortable feeling pervaded the circle but it afterwards gave place to one of curiosity. My senses became keenly alert, the cobwebby sensation, before described, grew horribly intense, and a peculiar feeling of emptiness, which I had previously had, became so strong that my heart seemed as though swinging loosely in an empty space, and resounding like a bell with each stroke. The air seemed to be full of singing, buzzing sounds that pressed on my ears, but through it I could hear the breathing of the sitters outside the curtains. The movements made in the air seemed to sway me backwards and forwards. A fly alighting on my hand caused a pain like that of a toothache to shoot up my arm. I felt faint, almost dying.

"At last the arranged-for signal was given, that all was ready. The curtains were thrown open, and a materialised form stood fully revealed beside me. The lens of the camera was uncovered, the plate exposed, the magnesium light flashed. Then the curtains fell together. I remember the feeling of relief and thinking: Now I can give way. It is possible that I did faint. I do not know. But I was aroused by the sound of a voice saying in my ear: She is not here, she is gone. It was one of the family who spoke and the terror in the boy's voice roused me effectually. I wanted to reassure him, and asked for water, and wondered at the same time whose voice was it that made the request. It was like my own but seemed to come from the air or from another person. The water was brought and drunk, but though I felt refreshed the act seemed to be performed by that other person who had spoken. Then I was left alone . . .

"Now comes the strangest part of this strange experiment. The photographic plate was carefully developed and a print made, which revealed a most astonishing fact. The materialised form, well in focus, was clad in white, flowing garments. The hair was hanging loosely over the shoulders, which, like the arms, were without covering. The figure might have been that of a stranger, but the features were unmistakably mine. Never has a photograph shown a better likeness. On a chair beside it and a little behind, was a figure clad in my dress, the black bands on the wrist, and the tape round the waist showing themselves clearly and intact, but the face was that of a stranger, who seemed to be regarding the proceedings with great complacency and satisfaction. Needless to say, we looked at this extraordinary photograph with something like petrifaction. We were utterly at a loss to understand its meaning, and no explanation was forthcoming, except a rueful remark from "Walter," who when questioned replied that "Things did get considerably mixed up."

In *Light* (December 19, 1903), L. Gilbertson remarked: "My own theory of the strange head is that the manifesting spirit was driven out of the materialised form by Madame's sub-self, which had gained an abnormal excess of power through the weak condition of her normal organism. Finding itself ousted, the visitor took refuge with Madame's other part, and proceeded to operate on it in the way generally known as "transfiguration." Succeeding in this operation, it is not difficult to believe, as Madame says, that it "seemed to be regarding the proceedings with great complacency and satisfaction."

If the health of the medium is weak or the power, for any other reason, low, materialization usually does not progress beyond the stage of resemblance to the medium. It is a staggering phenomenon in itself and it vindicates Prof. Enrico **Morselli**'s psycho-dynamic theory (*Psycologia e Spiritismo,* 1907) according to which the ectoplasmic substance is the result of a kind of human radioactivity and the directive idea seems to have its origin in the medium's subconscious mind. But Morselli also adds that the medium's subconscious mind may establish telepathic communication with the sitter's subconscious mind and may shape the ectoplasmic forms into conformance to their thoughts and desires. Or it may be conceived that the medium transmits her psycho-dynamic forces to the spectator and he, by a sort of catalytic action, objectifies his own emotional complexes.

The second part of the hypothesis is a far-fetched assumption. The first is borne out by many observations. St. Augustine believed that the angels make themselves visible by the agency of elements taken from the air. We know better. Surely the human body plays the paramount part. The influence of the human mind, however, is noticeable up to a certain stage only. The phantom shapes do not keep for long the physiognomy, gestures and voice of the medium and disclose, after the transitory period, an apparent independence. Their body has temperature, blood circulation, exhales carbonic acid and behaves in every way as an unrelated entity.

"I took a flask of baryta water," writes Prof. Richet of his experiments with the materialized "Bien Boa" in the Villa Carmen, "to see if his breath would show carbon dioxide. The experiments succeeded. I did not lose sight of the flask from the moment when I put it into the hands of Bien Boa, who seemed to float in the air on the left of the curtain at a height greater than Marthe could have been if standing up. While he blew into the tube the bubbling could be heard."

According to the American researcher Epes **Sargent,** a spirit has been known to cut its finger with a knife, then borrow a handkerchief to wind around the wound, and at the end of the sitting, to return the handkerchief marked with blood.

The materialized form may be physically more perfect than the medium. Crookes found that the lungs of "Katie King" were sounder at a time when Miss Cook was undergoing medical treatment for bronchitis. "Katie" also proved her distinct individuality by changing the color of her face to chocolate and jet black. She did this repeatedly because she was told that she resembled the medium too much.

The will of the phantom apparently has metamorphic powers over the temporary body.

Epes Sargent wrote in *Proof Palpable of Immortality* (1875) that a feminine spirit who manifested herself at Moravia in the seances of Mrs. Mary **Andrews** was, on one occasion, known to produce in rapid succession, facsimiles of her personal appearance at six different periods of her earth-life, ranging from childhood to old age.

"I think," stated William Oxley of a materialized spirit "Lily," "that she did not appear twice in exactly the same form; but I always recognised her and never confused her with other apparitions."

The phantoms of Mrs. Etta Roberts often transformed themselves into the forms of other persons in view of the sitters.

According to the experience of E. A. Brackett (another author of books on Spiritualism), the sitter's will has an influence over the phantom shapes as well. In his seances with Mrs. H. B. **Fay,** he found that by the exercise of his will he could cause the materialized forms to recede. If this is so, it should be expected that the willpower of the medium wields a dominant influence. There is some reason to suppose that ectoplasm has a tendency to return to the medium's body and that the invisible operators have to be constantly on guard against this propensity. As long as the medium is passive the tendency is not difficult to overcome, but as soon as his will is active or a sudden emotion sweeps over him the operators become powerless and the reversal of the creative process speedily sets in.

For the exercise of the medium's willpower or a show of emotion, however, there is but little opportunity, as most of the materialization mediums pass into trance before the phenomena begin. D. D. **Home,** Mme. **d'Esperance,** Kate **Fox,** Mrs. **Hollis,** Mrs. **Andrews,** Mrs. **Mellon,** Eglinton, Mrs. **Thompson,** Miss Florence **Cook** and **Kluski,** in the first stage of their mediumship, have given most of their materialization seances in a conscious state. Their subjective experiences should be instructive.

Interdependence of Phantom and Medium

"I feel," stated Mrs. Mellon, "as though I were that form, and yet I know I am not and that I am still seated on my chair. It is a kind of double consciousness—a faraway feeling, hard to define. At one moment I am hot, and the next moment cold. I sometimes have a choking, fainting, sinking sensation when the form is out."

Describing an early materialization seance of Mrs. Thompson, F. W. Thurstan stated: "All this while Mrs. T. was in full consciousness, but she kept exclaiming that she felt "all hollow" and another thing she noticed that whenever 'Clare's' fingers touched anyone she distinctly felt a pricking sensation in her body, very similar to her experiences when she had been placed once on an insulating stool and charged with electricity and persons had touched her to make sparks come from her."

This **community of sensations** between the medium and the phantom has important bearings. The interaction between the two bodies is constant. The blending of the two organisms may be manifest in the lines of paraffin moulds (see **Plastics**). Miss Florence Cook once had a dark stain on a covered part of her body after an ink mark had been made on the face of "Katie," while the medium was shut up in the cabinet.

Mme. d'Esperance, who never touched tobacco, suffered from nicotine poisoning if her sitters smoked during the ectoplasmic process.

W. Reichel, author of *Occult Experiences* (1906), observed that the phantoms of the medium C. W. **Miller** smelled of tobacco and even of food and wine if the medium had liberally partaken of them before the seance. When the materialized child of Florence **Marryat** filled her mouth with sugar-plums, she nearly choked the medium. "Mahedi," the Egyptian phantom of medium F. W. **Monck,** discovered a dish of baked apples in the room. "I got him to eat some" wrote Archdeacon **Colley.** "Our medium was at this time six or seven feet away from the materialised form and had not chosen to take any of the fruit, averring that he could taste the apple the Egyptian was eating. Wondering how this could be, I, with my right hand, gave our abnormal friend another baked apple to eat, holding this very bit of paper in my left hand outstretched towards the medium, when from his lips fell the chewed skin and core of the apple eaten by 'The Mahedi'—and here it is before me now after all these years in this screwed up bit of paper for any scientist to analyse."

The Archdeacon repeated the same experiments many times "but never could I see the transit from the mouth of the psychic form at my right hand of what was masticated, or swallowed, of wine from a measured glass pouring in exact measure again from the mouth or dropping from the lips of the medium six or seven feet at my left into these carefully kept papers."

In a similar account about Monck in *The Spiritualist* (December 4, 1877) the story was told of a materialized spirit who drank water. What he swallowed was instantly ejected from the medium's mouth. No such reaction was observed in the case of the materialized phantom "Zion" (of medium George **Spriggs**), who drank water and ate biscuits in Melbourne.

The sensitivity of ectoplasm is well known. It must be handled with caution and protected from light. Dr. Geley observed that the shock of sudden light is proportional to the duration of the light and not to its intensity. The magnesium flash hurts the medium less than the rays of a pocket lamp. If the ectoplasm has solidified, the danger of injuring the medium is less. But it is a danger nevertheless. The medium may suffer agonies if the phantom meets with a misadventure, but the injury may not necessarily react on the corresponding part of his body. A phantom hand may be pierced through with a knife, the medium will shriek with pain, yet his hands may bear no trace of the wound. Dr. F. L. Willis had an experience of this kind in his mediumship.

However, seance room atrocities seldom go beyond the stage of spirit grabbing. It is probably that the danger attending such attempts is somewhat exaggerated and often used as an excuse for fraud. In 1876 and 1877, it was for the first time suggested that the medium and the materialized form are in an unstable equilibrium and that whether the union is effected in the hands of the spirit grabber or inside the cabinet depended on the relative proportion of energy in the two forms at the time of the seizure.

When Florence **Marryat** was conducted into the cabinet by a materialized spirit of Miss **Showers,** she was told: "You see that Rosie is half her usual size and weight. I have borrowed the other half from her, which, combined with contributions from the sitters, goes to make up the body in which I show myself to you. If you increase the action of the vital half to such a degree, that the two halves did not reunite, you would kill her. You see that I can detach certain particles from her organism for my own use, and when I dematerialise, I restore these particles to her, and she becomes once more her normal size.

You only hurry the re-union by violently detaining me, so as to injure her."

In an earlier account given to Mr. Luxmoore by "Katie King," the danger was graphically but less scientifically pictured. On the question "When you disappear, where is it to?" she answered: "Into the medium, giving her back all the vitality which I took from her. When I have got very much from her, if anyone of you were to take her suddenly round the waist and try to carry her you might kill her on the spot; she might suffocate. I can go in and out of her readily, but understand, I am not her—not her double; they talk a deal of rubbish about doubles; I am myself all the time."

The experience of Archdeacon Colley with "Mahedi" appears to conform to the above theories. This phantom was a giant. His physical strength was so enormous that he could lift the Archdeacon from his chair to the level of his shoulders apparently without effort. He reminded the Archdeacon of a mummy of gigantic proportions he once saw in some museum.

On his first visit through medium F. W. Monck, the "Mahedi" wore a kind of "metal skull cap, with an emblem in front which trembled and quivered and glistened, overhanging the brow. I was allowed to feel it, but there was little resistance to my fingers, and it seemed to melt away like a snowflake under my touch, and to grow apparently solid again the moment after. For once (February 18, 1878) by daylight, it was arranged, as a most dangerous experiment, that I should grasp the white-attired Egyptian and try to keep him from getting back to invisibility through the body of the medium. I was, by an invisible force, levitated, as it seemed instantly some eighteen or twenty feet from my drawing room door right up to where the medium stood, whom, strangely and suddenly, wearing white muslin over his black coat, I found in my arms just as I had held The Mahedi. The materialised form had gone, and the psychic clothing that he evolved with him from the left side of my friend must also have gone the same way with the speed of thought back to invisibility through the medium. But whence its substituted drapers' stuff now on the body of our friend not wearing it an instant before?"

It is difficult to find a corroboration of this experience in the literature of Spiritualism. It has happened far more often that the spirit dissolved in the grabber's hand. Mr. Volckman had this experience with "Katie King." Mostly, however, when the light was switched on, the spirit was found to be identical with the medium. Cases of transfiguration in a state of deep trance may offer an excuse, but generally it is a safe assumption that a successful grabbing of the medium in the spirit's guise, establishes a *prima facie* case for fraud. The question which usually complicates the case is of the drapery which is visible in the dark and may serve for purposes of transfiguration. This drapery has often disappeared when the light was switched on. But often it was found and turned out to be very material and enduring.

In case of full materialization, the weight of the medium's body proportionately decreases (see **Ectoplasm**). In exceptional cases, strange means appear to have been adopted to keep the phantom in sufficient solidity.

Col. H. S. **Olcott,** in his experiments with Elizabeth J. **Compton,** shut the medium up in a small cabinet, passed threads through the bored holes of her ears and fastened them to the back of her chair. When a phantom appeared from the cabinet, Olcott asked it to stand on a weighing platform. Twice it was weighed, the records being 77 and 59 lbs. Olcott then left the phantom outside and went into the cabinet. The medium was gone. Stepping out, he again weighed the apparition. The weight this time was 52 lbs. The spirit then reentered the cabinet from which other spirits emerged. Finally, Olcott went inside with a lamp and found the medium just as he had left her at the beginning of the seance with every thread unbroken and every seal undisturbed. After the return of consciousness she was weighed. Her weight was 121 lbs.

Some Early Explanations

According to the explanation of the controls, the phenomena of materialization are not produced by a single spirit. "John King," in a seance with Cecil Husk, pictured to Florence Marryat the concerted work as follows: "When the controls have collected the matter with which I work—some from everybody in the circle, mostly from the medium's brain—I mould with it a plastic mask, somewhat like warm wax in feel, but transparent as gelatine, into the rough likeness of a face. I place this plastic substance over the spirit features and mould it to them. If the spirit will have the patience to stand still I can generally make an excellent likeness of what they were in earth life, but most of them are in such haste to manifest that they render my task very difficult. That is why very often a spirit appears to his friends and they cannot recognise any likeness."

The solidity of the materialized form greatly varies. Some mediums only produce vaporous and unsubstantial phantoms. They are called "etherealizations." Apparently, the exertion of force is not dependent on solidity. An instructive instance is told in the book *Spiritualism* by Judge J. W. Edmonds & G. T. Dexter (2 vols., 1853–55): "I felt on one of my arms what seemed to be the grip of an iron hand. I felt distinctly the thumb and fingers, the palm of the hand, and the ball of the thumb, and it held me fast by a power which I struggled to escape from in vain. With my other hand I felt all round where the pressure was, and satisfied myself that it was no earthly hand that was thus holding me fast, nor indeed could it be, for I was as powerless in that grip as a fly would be in the grasp of my hand."

The word "materialization" was first used in 1873 in America in place of "spirit-forms." Hands and arms were seen in the Davenport seances in the earliest days of modern Spiritualism. According to Epes Sargent's *The Scientific Basis of Spiritualism* (1881) "as far back as 1850, a full spirit form would not infrequently appear." D. D. **Home** produced many good manifestations.

Professor J. J. **Mapes** was the first scientist who discoursed on the means by which the semblance of such temporary organisms could be produced in accordance with the kinetic theory of gases, with a minimum employment of actual material particles, provided a sufficiently intense energy of motion were imparted to them.

Complete forms were often seen with Mrs. Mary **Andrews** of Moravia about 1860. Shortly after Kate **Fox** gave proof of the same power in the Livermore seances. Dr. John F. Gray of New York testified: "Mr. Livermore's recitals of the seances in which I participated are faith-

fully and most accurately stated, leaving not a shade of doubt in my mind as to the truth and accuracy of his accounts of those at which I was not a witness. I saw with him the philosopher Franklin, in a living, tangible, physical form, several times; and, on as many different occasions, I also witnessed the production of lights, odours, and sounds; and also the formation of flowers, cloth-textures, etc., and their disintegration and dispersion."

In America, Mrs. Hardy, Mrs. Maud Lord, Mrs. Jennie Lord Webb, Bastian and Taylor; in England, Mrs. Guppy, Herne and Williams, Florence Cook and Miss Showers were the next materializing mediums. The two extremes were well represented by D. D. Home and Florence Cook. Home's phantoms were mostly transparent. "Katie King" was flesh and blood.

Phantom Eyes and Hands

The evolution from ectoplasmic vapor to full phantoms with all the attributes of life is a fascinating subject. In his book *Mondo dei Misteri,* the journalist Luigi Barzini, who observed the phenomena of Eusapia Palladino, stated:

"From the curtain of the cabinet now and then slowly advancing towards one or another of those controlling, came Things, black and unformed, which seemed nearly always to withdraw without having touched."

A record published in the *Report on Spiritualism* of the **London Dialectical Society** (1871) narrated the metamorphosis of a psychic light into an eye: "Mr. Lindsay said there was a large bright eye in the centre of the table, from whence other eyes appeared to emanate and approach and retreat." Eyes, winking humorously were frequently reported in the Boston seances of "Margery" (Mrs. **Crandon**).

F. W. Pawlowski, professor of Aeronautical Engineering at the University of Michigan, wrote on his experiences with Franek **Kluski** in the *Journal* of the American Society for Psychical Research (1925, pp. 481–504), "Bright bluish stars appear and begin to move high above the table, near the ceiling. When they approached me at a distance of about sixteen inches I recognised to my great astonishment that they were human eyes looking at me. Within a few seconds such a pair of eyes develops into a complete human head, and with a hand moving a luminous palm illuminating it clearly. The hand will move around the head as if to show itself more clearly to the onlooker, the eyes looking at one intensely and the face smiling most pleasantly. I have seen a number of such heads, sometimes two at a time, moving through the air like drifting toy balloons from one sitter to another. On several occasions the apparitions appeared just behind my back, and I was aware of them from the sound of their breathing, which I could hear distinctly before they were noticed by the sitters opposite to me. When I turned around I found their faces just about a foot from me, either smiling or looking intently at me. Some of these were breathing violently as if after a strenuous run, and in these cases I felt their breath on my face. Once I listened to the heartbeat of an apparition. They conducted themselves as callers at a party. The expression of curiosity in their eyes is most appealing. I have seen a similar look only in the eyes of children at the age of the awakening of their intelligence. On one occasion I saw two of them flying high above our heads in the high room, illuminating each other with the plaques and performing fancy evolutions. It was really a beautiful sight, something like an aerial ballet."

Sir William **Crookes** testified that the phantom hand "is not always a mere form, but sometimes appears perfectly life-like and graceful, the fingers moving and the flesh apparently as human as that of any in the room. At the wrist, or arm, it becomes hazy and fades off into a luminous cloud." To the touch the hand sometimes appeared icy cold and dead, at other times warm and life-like. Crookes had seen a luminous cloud hover over a heliotrope, break a sprig off and carry it to a lady; he had seen a finger and thumb pick the petals from a flower in Home's button-hole and lay them in front of several persons sitting near him. Phantom hands playing the keys of an accordion floating in the air were of frequent occurrence.

William **Howitt,** S. Carter **Hall** and Mrs. Hardinge **Britten** once saw in the full light of the day in the drawing room of Mr. Hall, with Home's feet and hands in full view the whole time, twenty pairs of hands form and remain visible for about an hour. They were active and unattached, but otherwise could not be distinguished from ordinary human hands.

"One evening," wrote Dr. John Ashburner of his experiences with the medium Charles **Foster,** "I witnessed the presence of nine hands floating over the dining table." (*Notes and Studies on Animal Magnetism & Spiritualism,* 1867)

Signor G. Damiani testified before the London Dialectical Committee as having seen, at a seance of the **Davenport Brothers** in London in 1868 "five pink transparent hands ranged perpendicularly behind the door. Subsequently I placed my hand in the small window of the cabinet, when I felt each of my five digits tightly grasped by a distinct hand; while my own was thus held down, five or six other hands protruded from the hole above my wrist. On withdrawing my hand from the aperture, an arm came out therefrom—an arm of such enormous proportions that had it been composed of flesh and bone, it would, I verily believe, have turned the scale (being weighed) against the whole corporeal substance of the smaller Davenport."

A silver-colored, self-luminous hand, which began at the elbow and was seen in the process of formation was described in the report of a seance with D. D. Home in the *Hartford Times,* March 18, 1853. The question was spelled out whether the sitters would like to see the hand of a colored person. "In a moment there appeared a rather dull looking, grey hand, somewhat shadowy, and not quite so clearly defined as the first, but it was unmistakably there, and its grey hue could be clearly seen."

Eusapia **Palladino** did not produce compact, full size materializations. She was famous for her "third arm" which issued from her shoulders and receded into it. This arm was often seen independently and well materialized. The "counterpartal arms" of the Rev. Stainton **Moses,** extending generally from the shoulder, straight out, and above the true arms, presented a similar phenomenon. They simply retracted into the medium, or vanished if an attempt was made to grasp them.

Describing "John King's" materialized hand, Professor Charles **Richet** stated: "I held it firmly and counted twenty-nine seconds, during all which time I had leisure to observe both of Eusapia's hands on the table, to ask Mme. Curie if she was sure of her control, to call Courtier's attention, and also to feel, press and identify a real hand through the curtain. After twenty-nine seconds I said: 'I want something more, I want uno anello (a ring) on this hand.' At once the hand made me feel a ring: I said 'adesso uno braceletto' and on the wrist I felt the two ends as of a woman's bracelet that closes by a hinge. I then asked that this hand should melt in mine, but the hand disengaged itself by a strong effort, and I felt nothing further."

Sitting with Eusapia **Palladino,** Professor Bottazzi "four times saw an enormous black fist come out from behind the left curtain, which remained motionless, and advance toward the head of Mme. B."

Dr. Eugene Crowell stated in *The Identity of Primitive Christianity with Modern Spiritualism* (1874): "At Moravia, at one time, I saw an arm projected from the aperture of the cabinet, which with the hand, was fully three and a half feet in length. It remained in view, in free motion, for a time sufficient for all to observe and remark upon it. Its enormous length and size startled all present."

Despite such startling testimonies, the inference that telekinetic effects are produced by materialized hands should not be drawn hastily. Dr. Julien **Ochorowicz** noticed an alternative character about these manifestations. A well-materialized hand when clearly visible is mechanically inactive. Mechanical effects are generally produced by invisible hands. The same holds good for chemical, luminous and acoustic effects.

Phantoms of Fame and Name

The best records of full form materializations have been furnished by "familiar" spirits: "Katie King," who attended Florence Cook for three years; "Yolande," who appeared in Mme. d'Esperance's seances for a similar period; "Estella," who manifested in the Livermore sittings for five years and "Bertha," a niece of E. A. Brackett who appeared to him through different mediums for two years.

The materialized spirits seldom come in numbers and their range of activity is limited. The marvelous stories of C. V. **Miller's** mediumship, which was powerful enough to make twelve materialized figures appear at once, rest mostly on the testimony of W. Reichel. Corroboration, by a repetition of the occurrence, is also wanting of the peripatetic ghosts of George **Spriggs** who walked about the house and in the garden, and of the open-air materializations of William **Eglinton,** in which the spirits walked away to a distance of 66 feet from the medium. "Yolande's" case is unique in a queer respect—her body was so carnally feminine that she was assaulted by a man who took her for a real woman. This resulted in a profound injury, and almost mortal illness, to the medium.

Crookes was the first modern scientist who studied materializations under laboratory conditions. "Katie King" offered him every opportunity for investigation. She even allowed Crookes to enter the cabinet where, armed with a phosphorus lamp, he saw both the medium and "Katie" at the same time. In D. D. Home's mediumship, Crookes did not see many fully materialized figures. "In the dusk of the evening," he wrote, "during a seance with Mr. Home at my house, the curtains of a window about eight feet from Mr. Home were seen to move. A dark, shadowy, semi-transparent form, like that of a man, was seen by all present standing near the window, waving the curtain with his hand. As we looked, the form faded away and the curtains ceased to move."

A phantom form, semi-transparent, through which the sitters could be seen all the time, holding an accordion in his hand and playing continuously, was described by Mrs. Crookes as seen in the presence of her husband, the Rev. Stainton Moses, and Sergeant Cox in a Home seance: "As the figure approached I felt an intense cold, and as it was giving me the accordion I could not help screaming. The figure seemed to sink into the floor, leaving only the head and shoulders visible, still playing the accordion, which was then about a foot off the floor."

Description of a more solid case was given by Lord **Adare:** "Her form gradually became apparent to us; she moved close to Home and kissed him. She stood beside him against the window intercepting the light as a solid body, and appeared fully as material as Home himself, no one could have told which was the mortal body and which was the spirit. It was too dark, however to distinguish features. I could see that she had her full face turned towards us, and that either her hair was parted in the middle, and flowed down over her shoulders or that she had on what appeared to be a veil."

The next systematic investigation attached itself to the name of Prof. Charles **Richet.** "At the Villa Carmen I saw a fully organised form rise from the floor. At first it was only a white, opaque spot like a handkerchief lying on the ground before the curtain, then this handkerchief quickly assumed the form of a human head level with the floor, and a few moments later it rose up in a straight line and became a small man enveloped in a kind of white burnous, who took two or three halting steps in front of the curtain and then sank to the floor and disappeared as if through a trap-door. But there was no trap-door."

The phantom "Bien Boa" possessed all the attributes of life: "It walks, speaks, moves and breathes like a human being. Its body is resistant, and has a certain muscular strength. It is neither a lay figure nor a doll, nor an image reflected by a mirror; it is as a living being; it is as a living man; and there are reasons for resolutely setting aside every other supposition than one or other of these two hypotheses: either that of a phantom having the attributes of life; or that of a living person playing the part of a phantom."

In another note Prof. Richet stated: "At certain moments it was obliged to lean and bend, because of the great height which it had assumed. Then suddenly, his head sank, sank right down to the ground, and disappeared. He did this three times in succession. In trying to compare this phenomenon to something, I can find nothing better than the figure in a jack-in-the-box, which comes out all of a sudden."

Hands that Melted Like Snow

The miracle of the birth of human organs or of complete bodies is twofold as it is followed by an equally mysterious dissolution of the temporary organization. This phenomenon has been observed under very dramatic circumstances. There can be no question of delusion when a spirit hand is tightly held and melts away in the sitter's grasp.

Testimonies of this occurrence are numerous: Frank L.

Burr, editor of the *Hartford Times,* in a letter to Mrs. Home, published in *D. D. Home: His Life and Mission* by Mdme D. D. Home (1888), added the following particulars to his account of March 14, 1855 of one of Home's last seances before his departure to England: "Turning this strange hand palm towards me, I pushed my right forefinger entirely through the palm, till it came out an inch or more, visibly, from the back of the hand. In other words, I pushed my finger clean through that mysterious hand. When I withdrew it, the place closed up, much as a piece of putty would close under the circumstances, leaving a visible mark or scar, where the wound was, but not a hole. While I was still looking at it the hand vanished, quick as a lightning flash."

Crookes wrote, also of Home: "I have retained one of these hands in my own, firmly resolved not to let it escape. There was no struggle or effort to get loose, but it gradually seemed to resolve itself into vapour, and faded in that manner from my grasp." He observed that the hands and fingers do not always appear to be solid and lifelike. Sometimes they present the appearance of a nebulous cloud partly condensed into the form of a hand. This is not equally visible to all present. Only when fully formed does it become visible to all present."

H. D. Jencken read in his paper before the London Dialectical Society: "I have once been enabled to submit a spirit hand to pressure. The temperature was, as far as I could judge, the same as that of the room, and the spirit hand felt soft, velvety, dissolving slowly under the greatest amount of pressure to which I could submit it."

"Katie's" wrist was once seized in anger by Mr. G. H. Tapp of Dalston whom "Katie" struck on the chest for a joke she resented. As Tapp described it, the hand "crumpled up in my grasp like a piece of paper, or thin cardboard, my fingers meeting through it."

"John King" was seen by Florence Marryat to "hold a slate so that both hands were visible, and then let one hand dematerialise till it was no larger than a doll's, whilst the other remained the normal size."

Prof. Philippe **Bottazzi** of the University of Naples wrote: "I saw and felt at one and the same time a human hand natural in colour, I felt with mine the fingers and the back of a strong, warm, rough hand. I gripped it and it vanished from my grasp, not becoming smaller, but melting, dematerialising, dissolving."

Col. **Rochas** wrote in the *Annales des Sciences Psychiques* (vol. 18, 1908, p. 280) of a seance in which M. Montorguiel seized a materialized hand and called for a light. The hand melted and "all of us thought we saw a luminous trail from his hand to F.'s body."

Dr. Hereward **Carrington,** one of the keenest fraud-hunters among psychical researchers, wrote: "I myself have observed materializations under perfect conditions of control, and have had the temporary hand melt within my own, as I held it firmly grasped. This hand was a perfectly formed, physiological structure, warm, life-like and having all the attributes of a human hand—yet both the medium's hands were securely held by two controllers, and visible in red light. Let me repeat, this hand was not pulled away, but somehow melted in my grasp as I held it."

Dramatic Exit of Spirit Visitants

The dissolution of a full phantom is one of the most dramatic of claimed phenomena. "Katie King" agreed to demonstrate it on herself. Florence Marryat gave the following account in her book *There is no Death* (1892): "She [Katie King] took up her station against the drawing room wall, with her arms extended as if she were crucified. Then three gas-burners were turned on to their full extent in a room about sixteen feet square. The effect upon Katie King was marvellous. She looked like herself for the space of a second only, then she began gradually to melt away. I can compare the dematerialisation of her form to nothing but a wax doll melting before a hot fire. First the features became blurred and indistinct; they seemed to run into each other. The eyes sunk in the sockets, the nose disappeared, the frontal bone fell in. Next the limbs appeared to give way under her, and she sank lower and lower on the carpet, like a crumbling edifice. At last there was nothing but her head left above the ground—then a heap of white drapery only, which disappeared with a whisk, as if a hand had pulled it after her—and we were left staring by the light of three gas burners at the spot on which Katie King had stood."

Sometimes the dissolution is unexpected. The power wanes and the form cannot be held together. In a seance with Mrs. H. B. **Fay,** a deceased sister appeared to Florence Marryat. Suddenly she "appeared to faint. Her eyes closed, her head fell back on my shoulder, and before I had time to realise what was going to happen, she had passed through the arm that supported her, and sunk down through the floor. The sensation of her weight was still making my arm tingle, but Emily was gone, clean gone."

"Honto," the Indian spirit squaw of the **Eddy Brothers,** smoked a pipe. The light from the burning tobacco enabled Col. Olcott to see distinctly her copper-colored cheek, the bridge of her nose and the white of her eye. She remained out too long. Darting back she collapsed into a shapeless heap before the curtains, only one hand being distinguishable. In half a minute she appeared again.

The process of dissolution varies. Robert Dale **Owen** stated that he had seen a form fade out from head downwards. William Oxley (author of *Modern Messiahs & Wonder Workers,* 1889) said that he saw "Yolande" melting away from the feet upwards until only the head appeared above the floor, and then this grew less and less until a white spot only remained, which, continuing for a moment or two, disappeared." Her materialization, as a rule, occupied ten to fifteen minutes. Her disappearance took place in two to five minutes while the disappearance of the drapery lasted from one half to two minutes.

At one of Mrs. J. B. **Mellon**'s seances in Sydney, Australia, a form, after walking about, lay down on the platform, stretched out the limbs in the presence of all and each member of the body separately dematerialized.

Most often the figures collapse and disappear through the floor. The phantoms of Virginia Roberts, however, (as Florence Marryat testified) if they were strong enough to leave the cabinet, invariably disappeared by floating upwards through the ceiling. "Their mode of doing this was most graceful. They would first clasp their hands behind their heads, and lean backwards; then their feet were lifted off the ground, and they were borne upward in a recumbent position."

The phantoms of Carlo **Mirabelli,** the South American medium, similarly raised themselves and floated in the air before full dissolution which began from the feet upwards.

When matter apparently passes through matter or when **apports** are brought into the seance room, the process of dematerialization may be identical. At least, this is strongly suggested by the following account given by Mme. d'Esperance in *Shadow Land* (1897): "A lady brought a brilliantly coloured Persian silk scarf. Yolande took a great delight in it. She could not be induced to part with it. When she had disappeared and the seance closed, the scarf also vanished. The next time she was asked what she had done with it. Yolande seemed a little nonplussed at the question, but in an instant she made a few movements with her hands in the air and over her shoulders, and the scarf was there, draped as she had arranged it on the previous evening. She never trusted this scarf out of her hands. When sometimes she herself gradually dissolved into mist under the scrutiny of twenty pairs of eyes, the shawl was left lying on the floor and we would say 'At last she has forgotten it.' But no, the shawl itself would gradually vanish in the same manner as its wearer and no search which we might afterwards make ever discovered its whereabouts. Yet Yolande assured us gleefully that we failed to see it only because we were blind, for the shawl never left the room. This seemed to amuse her and she was never tired of mystifying us by making things invisible to our eyes."

The Story of Spirit Drapery

The drapery in which materialized phantoms are enveloped may go some way towards helping us to understand how **apparitions,** observed independent of seance conditions, appear clothed. This was always considered as one of the greatest puzzles of ghost lore. The communications received through mediums did not throw too much light on the subject.

"When the soul leaves the body," states Julia's posthumous letters (see W. T. Stead, *Letters From Julia,* 1897), "it is at the first moment quite unclothed, as at birth. When the thought of nakedness crosses the spirit's mind, there comes the clothing which you need. The idea with us is creative. We think and the thing is. I do not remember putting on any garments."

Caroline D. Larsen, in *My Travels in the Spirit World* (1927) similarly stated: "From every spirit emanates a strong aura, a pseudo-phosphoric light. This aura is completely controlled by the mind. Out of this substance is moulded the vesture of the body."

"On one occasion," stated Sylvan J. **Muldoon** of a conscious projection of his **astral body,** "I noticed the clothing forming itself out of the emanation surrounding my astral body, when only a few feet out of coincidence, and the clothing was exactly like that covering my physical body. On another occasion I awakened and found myself moving along at the intermediate speed. A very dense aura surrounded me—so dense, in fact, that I could scarcely see my own body. It remained so until the phantom came to a stop, when I was dressed in the typical ghost-like garb."

The power to form spirit-clothes may not be technically understood but seems to be indicated by observations in materialization seances. There, indeed, the formation of spirit drapery is in a way preliminary to the building up of the body. It appears to serve the purpose of covering up imperfections or vacant spots in the temporary organism, besides which it protects the ectoplasmic substance from the effects of light, of human gaze and also satisfies the requirements of modesty. Once while "Yolande," (who was often seen together with Mme. d'Esperance outside the cabinet) was talking to a sitter, "the top part of her white drapery fell off and revealed her form. I noticed," writes Oxley, "that the form was imperfect, as the bust was undeveloped and the waist uncontracted which was a test that the form was not a lay figure."

The drapery is usually white in color, sometimes of a dazzling whiteness but may also be of greyish appearance; it is often luminous and so material that it is always the last to disappear when the seance concludes. The reason apparently is that the substance of the drapery, though its texture is different and much finer, is—as pointed out by Prof. Cesare **Lombroso**—withdrawn from the medium's clothes to be molded by the invisible operators in a fashion similar to ectoplasm into all kinds of patterns. The rare instances in which the medium's body entirely vanished, during the process of materialization, point to this conclusion. It appears that it is not the body alone which disappears, but the dress as well.

The medium Franek **Kluski** noticed that the curtains and carpets of his apartment where his astounding materialization phenomena were produced had been seriously worn out in an inexplicable manner. The observation was also made at the **British College of Psychic Science** that the lining of the underarms of a medium's jacket exclusively used for seance purposes and apparently subjected to no rough wear had to be renewed frequently. The wife of medium John Lewis of Wales, who had to repair the garment, said that the wear on this was much harder than on garments worn in his occupation of a coal miner. The coloring matter in the garment is apparently of no consequence as the spirit drapery remains white, even if the original dress was black.

How is this substance extracted? The following graphic descriptions furnish little explanation: In a seance with William **Eglinton** on September 9, 1877, Dr. Nichols saw the materialized form "Joey" make, in the presence of three other persons, "twenty yards of white drapery which certainly never saw a Manchester loom. The matter of which it was formed was visibly gathered from the atmosphere and later melted into invisible air. I have seen at least a hundred yards so manufactured."

Katherine Bates wrote in *Seen and Unseen* (1907): "I stood close over her [the phantom] holding out my own dress, and as she rubbed her hands to and fro a sort of white lace or net came from them, like a foam, and lay upon my gown which I was holding up towards her. I touched this material and held it in my hands. It had substance but was light as gossamer, and quite unlike any stuff I ever saw in a shop."

F. W. Thurstan stated in a record of a seance with Mrs. Thompson in 1897, that when she produced physical phenomena, "a soft, gauzy, scented white drapery was flung over my head and seen by the others on my side of the room."

The spirit niece of E. A. Brackett, in seances with Mrs.

H. B. **Fay,** made yards and yards of spirit drapery by rubbing her hands together with bare arms. Once she made a seamless robe on Mr. Brackett and dematerialized it instantaneously.

William Harrison, editor of *The Spiritualist*, stated in an account of a seance with Florence **Cook**: "She [Katie King] threw out about a yard of white fabric, but kept hold of it by the other end, saying: 'Look, this is spirit drapery.' I said 'Drop it into the passage Katie, and let us see it melt away; or let us cut a piece off.' She replied: 'I can't; but look here.' She then drew back her hand, which was above the top of the curtain, and as the spirit drapery touched the curtain, it passed right through, just as if there were no resistance whatever. I think at first there was friction between the two fabrics and they rustled against each other, but that when she said 'Look here' some quality which made the drapery common matter was withdrawn from it, and at once it passed through the common matter of the curtain, without experiencing any resistance."

"Katie King" often allowed her sitters to touch her drapery. Sometimes she cut as many as a dozen pieces from the lower part of her skirt and made presents of them to different observers. The holes were immediately made good. Crookes examined the skirt inch by inch and found no hole, no marks or seam of any kind.

These pieces of drapery mostly melted into thin air, however carefully they were guarded, but sometimes they were rendered enduring. But in the latter cases and in instances of careless operation, it happened that the medium's dress suffered. "Katie King" said in explanation that nothing material about her could be made to last without taking away some of the medium's vitality and weakening her.

A specimen of "Katie's" drapery was taken by Miss Douglas to Messrs. Howell and James's cloth and dry goods store, London, with the request to match it. They said that they could not, and that they believed it to be of Chinese manufacture.

At a seance in Christiania with Mme. d'Esperance, a sitter abstracted a piece of drapery which clothed one of the spirit forms. Later Mme. d'Esperance discovered that a large square piece of material was missing from her skirt, partly cut, partly torn. The abstracted piece was found to be of the same shape as the missing part, but several times larger, and white in color, the texture fine and thin as gossamer. In the light of this experience Mme. d'Esperance understood a similar happening in England. "Ninia," the child control, was asked for a piece of her abundant clothing. She complied but unwillingly. After the seance Mme. d'Esperance found a hole in her new dress.

"Katie Brink," the spirit of medium Mrs. E. J. **Compton,** cut a piece of her dress for Col. Richard Cross of Montreal, but on the condition that he would buy a new dress for the medium, for a corresponding hole would appear on her skirt. The cut piece was fine, gossamer like material. The medium's dress black alpaca, and much coarser. The cut piece fitted the hole in the medium's dress.

According to the recollection of Alfred Vout **Peters** (*Light*, April 7, 1931), on two or three occasions the spirit Marie gave a piece of white drapery to the sitters. The next morning Mrs. Corner found that a hole had been cut in the middle of her black skirt. Subsequently "Marie" was able to prevent making a hole in the medium's skirt when cutting off the "ectoplasm." Sometimes this material disappeared the next day, at other times it remained, and it is possible that certain pieces are still in existence.

At the Circle of Light, in Cardiff, Wales, in a sitting with medium George **Spriggs,** a piece of rich crimson silk was cut from a girdle worn by a spirit. It began to fade after a few days, but being taken back into the seance room it was manipulated by one of the spirits and restored at once to its original luster.

The Rev. Stainton **Moses** was once given a piece of spirit drapery sweetened by "spirit musk." He sent it to his friend Mrs. Stanhope Speer. The scent on the letter was fresh and pungent seventeen years afterwards.

Part of the available power seems consumed by the creation of this spirit drapery. Sometimes before its appearance, recourse is made to the portieres of the cabinet, the spirit forms wrapping in themselves before thrusting out a hand or head. In some instances, for economical reasons, the operators have accepted ready-made cloth brought in for them to wear. "John King" was photographed in such borrowed garments. There are stories that for similar reasons wearing apparel may be apported. This, however, carries speculation to uncertain grounds where fraud may easily flourish and find ready excuse. Mrs. Cook, Florence's mother, is said to have once caught "Katie King" wearing a dress of her daughter. "Katie" confessed that she borrowed it because the power was weak. She gave an undertaking that she would never do this again as the medium might be compromised. In other cases, yards of muslin and grenadine were apported expressly for draping purposes and left in the seance room. Such accounts must obviously be treated with strong reservations.

Traces of spirit cloth appear to have been found in mediumistic **plastics.** The hand, or face seems often enveloped in drapery before the putty is impressed or a paraffin cast made.

Souvenir Locks of Hair, Materialized Jewels and Flowers

Similarly to pieces of drapery, materialized phantoms often gave locks of hair for souvenirs. "Katie King" did it very often. Once in the cabinet, she cut off a lock of her own hair and a lock of the medium's and gave them both to Florence **Marryat.** One was almost black, soft and silky, the other a coarse golden red. On another occasion she asked Florence Marryat to cut her hair with a pair of scissors as fast as she could. "So I cut off curl after curl, and as fast as they fell to the ground the hair grew again upon her head." The severed hair vanished.

In some instances these souvenirs did not disappear. Crookes in a later communication spoke of a lock of "Katie" as still before him. Similarly the lock which Prof. Charles **Richet** cut from the head of an Egyptian beauty (during the mediumship of Marthe Béraud) remained. Prof. Richet stated: "I have kept this lock, it is very fine, silky and undyed. Microscopical examination shows it to be real hair; and I am informed that a wig of the same would cost a thousand francs. Marthe's hair is very dark and she wears her hair rather short."

It would appear from this that the materialized product was finer in quality than the natural one.

The materialized phantoms apparently often wear ornaments. Admiral Usborne Moore, in his seances with the medium J. B. **Jonson** of Detroit, found these ornaments yielding to the touch. In other instances they were solid.

"Abd-u-lah," the one-armed spirit of William **Eglinton,** appeared bedecked with diamonds, emeralds and rubies. The materialization of precious stones was thus described by Mrs. Nichols in the *Spiritualist* (October 26, 1877): "For some time he moved his hands as if gathering something from the atmosphere, just as when he makes muslin. After some minutes he dropped on the table a massive diamond ring. He said: 'Now you may all take the ring, and you may put it on, and hold it while you count twelve.' Miss M. took it and held it under the gaslight. It was a heavy gold ring with a diamond that appeared much like one worn by a friend of mine worth £1,000. Joey said the value of this was 900 guineas. Mr. W. examined it as we had done. He now made, as it seemed, and as he said, from the atmosphere two diamonds, very clear and beautiful, about the size of half a large pea. He gave them into our hands on a piece of paper. We examined them as we had the others. He laid the ring and the diamonds on the table before him, and there next appeared a wonderful cluster of rubies, set with a large ruby about half an inch in diameter in the centre. These we all handled as we had the others. Last there came a cross, about four inches in length, having twenty magnificent diamonds set in it; this we held in our hands, and examined as closely as we liked. He told us that the market value of the gems was £25,000. He remarked: 'I could make Willie the richest man in the world, but it would not be the best thing, and might be the worst.' He now took the jewels in front of him and seemed to dissipate them, as one might melt hailstones in heat until they entirely disappeared."

The Rev. Stainton **Moses** was told by "Magus," one of his controls, that he would deliver him a topaz, the material counterpart of his spiritual jewel which would enable him to see scenes in the spheres on looking into it. The jewel was found in his bedroom. Stainton Moses was much exercised over it. He believed it to be an **apport,** taken without the consent of the owner. He never received any definite information as to its origin. It cannot be traced how long the stone, which was set in a ring, remained in his possession.

Gems and pearls were frequently brought to the circle of Stainton Moses. His theory was that they were made by spirits because he could see them falling before they reached the table while others could not see them until they had fallen, and because an emerald had flaws in it and therefore could not have been cut or be an imitation.

Flower materializations are comparatively more frequent. There was a remarkable instance in Mme. d'Esperance's mediumship. On June 28, 1890 at a seance in St. Petersburg, in the presence of Alexander **Aksakof** and Prof. Boutlerof, a golden lily, seven feet high, appeared in the seance room. It was kept for a week, during which time it was six times photographed. After a week it dissolved and disappeared.

In the record of the Livermore seances with Kate Fox,

under date February 22, 1862 is the following statement: "Appearance of flowers. Cloudy. Atmosphere damp. Conditions unfavourable. At the expiration of half an hour a bright light rose to the surface of the table, of the usual cylindrical form, covered with gossamer. Held directly over this was a sprig of roses about six inches in length, containing two half-blown white roses, and a bud with leaves. The flowers, leaves and stem were perfect. They were placed at my nose and smelled as though freshly gathered; but the perfume in this instance was weak and delicate. We took them in our fingers and I carefully examined the stem and flowers. The request was made as before to 'be very careful.' I noticed an adhesive, viscous feeling which was explained as being the result of a damp, impure atmosphere. These flowers were held near and over the light, which seemed to feed and give them substance in the same manner as the hand. By raps we were told to 'Notice and see them dissolve.' The sprig was placed over the light, the flowers dropped, and in less than one minute, melted as though made of wax, their substance seeming to spread as they disappeared. By raps 'See them come again.' A faint light immediately shot across the cylinder, grew into a stem; and in about the same time required for its dissolution, the stem, and the roses had grown into created perfection. This was several times repeated, and was truly wonderful."

F. W. Thurstan made the significant observation with medium Mrs. R. **Thompson** (*Light*, March 15, 1901) that when a pineapple was to be materialized the smell and notion of it was all day in "her head." He believed that ideas of shapes, actions and words that are required to be brought into objectivity at a seance were made by unseen operators to be running in the medium's head often for days beforehand.

In experiments with medium T. **Lynn** at the **British College of Psychic Science,** objects were photographed in the course of materialization. They showed flecks and masses of a luminous material, possessing string-like roots. These light masses floated over a harp lying upon the table and were visible to all present. A finger-like projection extended from a mass of this luminosity, and extended itself towards the harp as if to play upon it. As the photo plates were developed, a bone ring was seen to depend from the medium's nose, and an object similar to the top of an infant's nursing bottle appeared to hang from his lips by a cord. The medium's features also seemed somewhat altered. At a second sitting, a two-pronged fish-hook, and also a small ring materialized. The photo plates of this materialization showed that some remarkable rounded object proceeded from the region of the medium's solar plexus, which had often appeared in previous photographs, and from this a root, or string, seemed to extend to the object materializing, apparently attached thereto. In this case, the root was twisted in a remarkable manner.

Similar observations were reported by Prof. Karl Blacher of Riga University, with the **apport** medium "BX." (*Zeitschrift für Parapsychologie*, June 1933). In trance, and under control, nails, screws or pieces of iron would be visibly drawn out of his chest, his armpits or arms, as could be clearly observed by means of luminous screens. On one occasion a length of wire over a yard long was drawn from the man's bared chest; at another time Prof.

Blacher himself caught hold of an end that was protruding from the same spot and drew forth a long leather strap. At another sitting the medium produced a heavy slab of metal from his chest; and from his left arm a piece of wrought steel weighing over 3 lbs.

There is a curious meeting point between apports and materialization here to which sufficient attention has not been devoted yet. The complexity of the problem is further demonstrated by the story of Lajos **Pap,** the Budapest apport medium (*Light,* July 14, 1933) that previous to his first apport of a frog, for two days he heard continual croaking. It seemed to him to come from his stomach, and he kept on asking people if they heard nothing. Similarly he heard the chirping of apported grasshoppers a long time before their arrival; and, preliminary to the apport of a large packet of needles, he felt pricking sensations over the back of his hand. It is, however, only fair to state that in 1935 Dr. Nandor Fodor detected Lajos Pap in fraud.

Marvels of Materialization

On May 25, 1921, Mme. Bisson observed the materialization on the hand of "Eva C." of a naked female eight inches high, with a beautiful body, long fair hair, brilliantly white skin. It vanished and returned several times and either her hair was differently arranged or her height grew less. The little figure performed various gymnastic exercises and finally stood on Mme. Bisson's extended hand. The materialization of small heads of the size of a walnut in a glass of water was the peculiar feature of Mme. **Ignath**'s mediumship. "Nona," the control, asserted these heads to be plastic **thought-forms.**

Describing a visit to an unnamed materialization medium, Mrs. Gladys Osborne Leonard stated in her book *My Life in Two Worlds* (1931): "My husband was sitting with his feet and knees rather wide apart. His gaze suddenly was diverted from the materialised spirit to a kind of glow near his feet. Looking down he saw a tiny man and woman, between 12 and 18 inches high, standing between his knees. They were holding hands and looking up into my husband's face, as if they were thinking 'What on earth is that?' They seemed to be interested, if not more so, in him, and the details of his appearance, as he was in theirs. He was too astonished to call anybody's attention to the tiny people, who were dressed in bright green, like the pictures of elves and fairies, and who wore little pointed caps. A slight glow surrounded them, or emanated from them, he wasn't sure which, but it was strong enough for him to see their little faces and forms clearly. After a moment or two they disappeared, apparently melting into the floor."

In a sitting with Countess Castelwitch in Lisbon, a communicator who called himself "M. Furtado" (husband of Mme. Furtado who was present), rapped out through the table that he would not allow himself to be photographed because he had forgotten what his face was like. At the next seance he said: "I have no face, but I will make one." The photographic plate revealed a tall phantom clothed in white, having a death head instead of a face.

A similar but more gruesome instance was described in the reports of the **Academia de Estudo Psychicos Cesar Lombroso** of São Paolo, on the mediumship of Carlo **Mirabelli.** "The third sitting followed immediately while the medium was still in a state of exhaustion. A skull inside the closet began to beat against the doors. They opened and the skull floated into the air. Soon the bones of a skeleton appeared one after another from neck to feet. The medium is in a delirium, beats himself and emits a bad smell like that of a cadaver. The skeleton begins to walk, stumble and walk again. It walks round the room while Dr. de Souza touches it. He feels hard, wet, bones. The others touch it. Then the skeleton disappears slowly until the skull alone remains which finally falls on a table. The medium was bound throughout the performance. It lasted 22 counted minutes in bright sunlight."

Alfred Vout **Peters** claimed to have seen, in a seance with Cecil **Husk,** the materialization of a living friend of his who was at the time asleep in his home. Horace **Leaf** reported (*Light,* January 29, 1932) on the undoubted materialization of the head, shoulders and arm of a relative of his living 400 miles away. A conversation was carried on for several minutes on matters thoroughly appropriate, then bidding him goodbye, the head vanished.

Indeed, one is tempted to speculate whether it would not be possible to build up, through a process of dematerialization and materialization, a living organism on altered lines. Perhaps some of the miraculous cures in which organic parts of the body appear to have been restored will find an explanation along such speculative lines.

Of the mysterious "Mahedi" whose characteristics were recorded by Archdeacon **Colley,** some unique feats deserve mentioning. The phantom could not speak English. By signs, the Archdeacon Colley made him understand that he wanted him to write. He looked puzzled at the lead pencil. When he was shown how to use it, he held it as he would hold a stylus and began to write quickly from the right to the left in unknown oriental characters, being "in a most peculiar way under the control of 'Samuel' "—one spirit controlling another spirit—the medium having nothing whatever to do with the matter, he being at the time his own normal fully awake natural self some seventeen feet away at the other end of the room talking to a lady. Archdeacon Colley had samples of "Samuel's" handwriting, obtained direct, moreover he knew that "Samuel" was in control, "for while the Egyptian, left to himself, could not speak any more than he could write it, yet now, with 'Samuel' in him to operate the vocal organs, he could speak real good idiomatic English—'Samuel' speaking through him. The voice was Samuel's while the lips that moved were The Mahedi's. But 'Samuel' and 'The Mahedi' were both the outcome of the medium and the connection between our normal friend, and materialised friend, and friend in control was, as the telescopic lengthening out of a multiple personality to the power of three very remarkable. It was something like what I had before seen and publicly reported relating to the evolution of a spirit form from another spirit form, which first form, as usual, extruded from the medium, so that (December 7, 1877) there stood in line our normal friend (entranced) and next to him the Egyptian thence derived, and from the Egyptian, in turn, the extruded personality of 'Lily,' all at the same time—the three in a row ranked together yet separate and distinct entities."

After all these marvels, Archdeacon Colley's description

of the reabsorption of a phantom into the medium's side in plain view appears to lose its wild improbability. Of a seance held on September 25, 1877, the notes having been made on the same evening, Archdeacon Colley stated: "As I brought my sweet companion close up to him, the gossamer filament again came into view; its attenuated and vanishing point being, as before, towards the heart. Greatly wondering, yet keen to observe, did I notice how, by means of this vapoury cord, the psychic figure was sucked back into the body of the medium. For like a waterspout at sea—funnel-shaped or sand column such as I have seen in Egypt—horizontal instead of vertical, the vital power of our medium appeared to absorb and draw in the spirit-form, but at my desire, so gradually that I was enabled quite leisurely thus closely to watch the process. For leaning against, and holding my friend with my left arm at his back and my left ear and cheek at his breast, his heart beating in an alarming way, I saw him receive back the lovely birth of the invisible spheres into his robust corporeal person. And as I gazed on the sweet face of the disintegrating spirit, within three or four inches of its features, I again marked the fair lineaments, eyes, hair and delicate complexion, and kissed the dainty hand as in process of absorption it dissolved and was drawn through the texture and substance of his black coat into our friend's bosom."

The Archdeacon once spoke to a materialized phantom before her extrusion was accomplished and he saw recognition in her eyes and heard her whisper, during the psychic parturition "so glad to see you." On one occasion, a minister friend of Dr. Monck materialized; by common consent the medium was carefully awakened. "Dazed for a moment, and then most astonished, our aroused friend looked enquiringly at the materialised spirit form, and jumping up from the sofa on which we had placed him he excitedly rushed forward to his one-time fellow-student, shouting 'Why, it is Sam' and then there was handshaking and brotherly greetings between the two. When both friends were about to speak at once there was a momentary impasse and neither seemed able to articulate; the medium's breath appearing to be needed by Samuel when he essayed to speak, while the materialised form was also checked in his utterance when the medium began to speak."

C. V. **Miller,** the San Francisco materialization medium, as a rule did not pass into trance and took the phantoms that issued from the cabinet by the hand and introduced them to his sitters. His amazing seances were duplicated by Dr. R. H. Moore, of San Diego, California. According to the account of N. Meade Layne, in *Psychic Research* (June, 1931) he was a well-known gentleman past seventy years of age, who did not go into trance and accompanied the forms which issued from behind a curtain within a few steps into the circle. The forms were never fully materialized; as a rule they were invisible below the bust, although the ectoplasmic drapery sometimes trailed nearly to the floor. "At a recent seance one of the forms, while conversing with the person at my side, advanced to within about eighteen inches of my face. Dr. Moore then, after telling us what he was about to do, struck the head of the form lightly with his open hand to show the degree of materialization. The movement and the sound were plainly perceived. He then passed his arm through the form at the solar plexus" (*Psychic Research,* July 1930).

Animal Materializations

There is one additional phenomenon to add to the record of all these miracles—the materialization of forms other than human. There are abundant accounts to show that even this seems to have occurred. We owe the strangest reports in this field to three Polish mediums: **Kluski, Guzyk** and Burgik.

Guzyk apparently materialized dogs and other strange animals, Kluski, a large bird of prey, small beasts, a lion and an apeman. The year 1919 abounded with animal materialization in the Kluski seances. "The bird was photographed, and before the exposure a whirring, like the stretching of a huge bird's wings, could be heard, accompanied by slight blasts of wind, as if a large fan were being used . . . Hirkill (an Afghan) materialised . . . Accompanying him always was a rapacious beast, the size of a very big dog, of a tawny colour, with slender neck, mouth full of large teeth, eyes which glowed in the darkness like a cat's, and which reminded the company of a maneless lion. It was occasionally wild in its behaviour, especially if persons were afraid of it, and neither the human nor the animal apparition was much welcomed by the sitters . . . The lion, as we may call him, liked to lick the sitters with a moist and prickly tongue, and gave forth the odour of a great feline, and even after the seance the sitters, and especially the medium, were impregnated with this acrid scent as if they had made a long stay in a menagerie among wild beasts" (*Psychic Science,* April, 1926).

According to Prof. Pawlowski's account (*Journal of the American Society for Psychical Research,* September 1925), the bird was a hawk or a buzzard. It "flew round, beating his wings against the walls and ceiling, and when he finally settled on the shoulder of the medium he was photographed with a magnesium flash, as the camera was accidently focussed on the medium before, and was ready."

An anthropoidal ape showed itself first in July 1919. Dr. Gustav Geley stated in his book *Clairvoyance and Materialisation* (1927): "This being which we have termed Pithecanthropus has shown itself several times at our seances. One of us, at the seance of November 20, 1920, felt its large shaggy head press hard on his right shoulder and against his cheek. The head was covered with thick, coarse hair. A smell came from it like that of a deer or a wet dog. When one of the sitters put out his hand the pithecanthrope seized it and licked it slowly three times. Its tongue was large and soft. At other times we all felt our legs touched by what seemed to be frolicsome dogs." According to Col. Norbert Ocholowicz's book on Kluski, "this ape was of such great strength that it could easily move a heavy bookcase filled with books through the room, carry a sofa over the heads of the sitters, or lift the heaviest persons with their chairs into the air to the height of a tall person. Though the ape's behaviour sometimes caused fear, and indicated a low level of intelligence, it was never malignant. Indeed it often expressed goodwill, gentleness and readiness to obey . . . After a long stay a strong animal smell was noticed. It was seen for the last time at the seance of December 26, 1922, in the same form

as in 1919 and making the same sounds of smacking and scratching."

Mrs. Hewat **McKenzie,** from whose article the above quotation is taken, also wrote of a small animal, reminding the sitters of the "weasel," so often sensed at Guzyk seances: "It used to run quickly over the table on to the sitters' shoulders, stopping every moment and smelling their hands and faces with a small, cold nose; sometimes, as if frightened, it jumped from the table and rambled through the whole room, turning over small objects, and shuffling papers lying on the table and writing desk. It appeared at six or seven seances, and was last seen in June, 1923."

Of Burgik, Prof. Charles **Richet** wrote in *Thirty Years of Psychical Research* (1923): "In the last seance that I had with him the phenomena were very marked. I had his left hand and M. de Gielski his right. He was quite motionless, and none of the experimenters moved at all. My trouser leg was strongly pulled and a strange, ill-defined form that seemed to have paws like those of a dog or small monkey climbed on my knee. I could feel its weight very light and something like the muzzle of an animal (?) touched my cheek. It was moist and made a grunting noise like a thirsty dog."

Dogs were apparently materialized by Mrs. Etta **Wriedt.** Lieut. Col. E. R. Johnson reported in *Light* (November 11, 1922) of a seance with Mrs. Wriedt: "It was quite common to meet one's departed dogs. I had one of these, a very small terrier, placed on my knees. It remained there for about a minute, and both its weight and form were all recognised. It was not taken away but seemed gradually to evaporate or melt. Two others, a large retriever and a medium-sized terrier, came very often, and all three barked with their direct voices in tones suitable to their sizes and breeds. Other sitters saw, heard and were touched by them. Those three had died in India some thirty years previously."

A dog which the medium W. **Haxby** materialized ran about the room. The appearance and pranks of an unseen but palpable pet dog in a seance with Politi on June 18, 1900 was described by General Ballatore in *Vesillo Spiritista.* It ran about the room, jumped on the knees of one of the sitters, Major Bennati, and put its paws round its mistress's neck, besides performing several other little tricks it had been taught in life.

The psychic photographer Wyllie had on record the psychic picture of a dog.

The flight of birds was often heard in seances with D. D. **Home** and later with the Marquis Scotto **Centurione.** A tame flying squirrel was materialized by "Honto," the Indian squaw, in the seances of the **Eddy Brothers.** Another Indian girl "brought in a robin perched on her finger, which hopped and chirped as naturally as life." (See H. S. Olcott, *People from the Other World,* 1875)

Two triangular areas of light, with curved angles like butterfly wings, audibly flitting and flapping were noticed in the February 24, 1924, seance of "Margery" (Mrs. **Crandon**). The flying creature, claimed to be "Susie," a tame bat of the control "Walter," performed strange antics. The wings would hover over the roses on the table, pick up one, approach a sitter and hit him over the head with it. "Susie" pulled the hair of the sitters, pecked at their faces, flapped her wings in their eyes. Another large, beetle-like area of light which scrambled about the table with a deal of flapping was called by "Walter" his "Nincompoop." Peculiar motions were also performed by a patch of light, said to be a tame bear, over a curtain pole. Clicking and whizzing it tobogganed down the pole and climbed back again. "Walter" was so fond of poking fun at the expense of the sitters that beyond his assertions that he paraded his actual livestock, nothing definite could be established about these curious animated batches of light.

"Materialisation of both beasts and birds sometimes appeared," wrote Gambier Bolton, in his book *Ghosts in Solid Form* (1919), "during our experiments, the largest and most startling being that of a seal which appeared on one occasion when Field-Marshal Lord Wolseley was present. We suddenly heard a remarkable voice calling out some absurd remarks in loud tones, finishing off with a shrill whistle. 'Why, that must be our old parrot,' said the lady of the house.

'He lived in this room for many years, and would constantly repeat those very words.' A small wild animal from India which had been dead for three years or more, and had never been seen or heard of by the Sensitive, and was known to only one sitter, suddenly ran out from the spot where the Sensitive was sitting, breathing heavily and in a state of deep trance, the little creature uttering exactly the same cry which it had always used as a sign of pleasure during its earth life. It had shown itself altogether on about ten different occasions, staying in the room for more than two minutes at a time, and then disappearing as suddenly as it had arrived upon the scene.

"But on this occasion the lady who had owned it during its life called it to her by its pet name, and then it proceeded to climb slowly up on her lap. Resting there quietly for about half a minute it then attempted to return, but in doing so caught one of its legs in the lace with which the lady's skirt was covered. It struggled violently, and at last got itself free, but not until it had torn the lace for nearly three inches. At the conclusion of the experiment a medical man reported that there were five green-coloured hairs hanging in the torn lace, which had evidently become detached from the little animal's legs during its struggles. The lady at once identified the colour and the texture of the hairs, and this was confirmed by the other sitter—himself a naturalist—who had frequently seen and handled the animal during its earth life. The five hairs were carefully collected, placed in tissue paper, and then shut up in a light-tight and damp-proof box. After a few days they commenced to dwindle in size, and finally disappeared entirely."

The story of a materialized seal was told in detail in *Light* (April 22, 1900) on the basis of Gambier Bolton's account before the **London Spiritualist Alliance** in a discussion. It reports as follows: Being well-known as a zoologist connected with the Zoological Society, he on one occasion received a note from an auctioneer asking if he would call to see a large seal which had been sent from abroad. "The poor thing is suffering; come round and see what you can do," wrote the seal's temporary owner, and being deeply interested in the welfare of animals of all kinds, Mr. Bolton at once obeyed the mandate. He saw the seal. The poor creature had been harpooned, and was lying in a languishing state in a large basket. He saw at

once that it could not live, but wishing to do what he could to prolong its life, he at once despatched it to the Zoological Gardens. Later in the day he called to see how it was faring, and found that it had been put into the seal tank. On visiting the tank the seal rose from the water and gave him a long look, which as he humorously suggested, seemed to indicate that the animal recognized him and entertained some sentiments of gratitude for its treatment.

The seal died that night, and ten days later Mr. Bolton was at a seance at which Frederick **Craddock** was the medium. A number of people of social and scientific repute were present. Suddenly someone called out from the cabinet: "Take this great brute away, it is suffocating me." It was the seal! It came slowly from the cabinet, flopping and dragging itself along after the fashion of seals, which (unlike sea-lions) cannot walk. It stayed close to Mr. Bolton for some moments, and then returned to the cabinet and disappeared. "There is no doubt in my mind," said Mr. Bolton, "that it was the identical seal."

To a question as to the *modus vivendi* of animal materializations, Gambier Bolton obtained the following answer from the spirit controls:

"Their actions are altogether independent of us. Whilst we are busily engaged in conducting our experiments with human entities who wish to materialise in your midst, the animals get into the room in some way which we do not understand, and which we cannot prevent; obtain, from somewhere, sufficient matter with which to build up temporary bodies; coming just when they choose; roaming about the room just as they please; and disappearing just when it suits them, and not before; and we have no power to prevent this so long as the affection existing between them and their late owners is so strong as it was in the instances which have come under our notice."

In contradiction to this information, Col. Norbert Ocholowicz made it a point that at the **Kluski** seances the animal apparitions were seen to be in charge of human apparitions. The only animal which seemed to be able to act independently of a keeper was the "pithecanthropus." Generally the animal and human apparitions were not active at the same moment. When the animal was fully materialized and active, the keeper was passive and kept in the background, and vice versa.

The testimony of clairvoyants also suggests that when animal apparitions are seen the necessary link is furnished by a friend of the sitter.

The question of animal materializations may have some relevance to stories of the animal **familiars** of witches. At the trial of the Chelmsford witches in 1645, Matthew Hopkins the witch-finder, John Sterne and six others, testified that on the previous night they had sat up in the room where the accused was confined to watch for the appearance of her imps which the accused promised and that they indeed saw them: five or six, entering the room in the shape of cats, dogs and other animals. John Sterne was so convinced of the truth of what he saw that he wrote a pamphlet about his experience. (See also **Witchcraft**)

Modern Views of Materialization

Since most of the accounts of the marvels of materialization belong to the past and such astonishing phenomena do not seem to be reported in modern times, there is a tendency to be highly skeptical about the reality of materialization. There have been many undoubted frauds. One of the most impudent was that of Charles **Eldred,** who always took his "highly magnetized" armchair to seances. In 1906, the chair was examined and it was found that the back was really a box with a lock and key. Inside was found a collapsible dummy, yards of cheese-cloth for "ectoplasm," reaching rods, wigs, false beards, a musical box (for "spirit music"), and even scent (for "spirit perfumes").

Other fraudulent materialization mediums were Harry **Bastian,** Frederick F. **Craddock,** Mrs. J. B. **Mellon** (Annie Fairlamb), Francis Ward **Monck** and Charles **Williams.** Although seizure of "materialized spirits" which turn out to be the medium are not conclusive evidence of fraud, since there is at least a possibility that an entranced medium may be controlled by spirits, such events are at least presumptive evidence of fraud. The vexed question is whether mediums caught out in unconscious or deliberate personation of spirits might also at times produce genuine materialization phenomena. Clearly it would be untenable to suppose that spirits influence mediums to purchase wigs, masks, cheese-cloth and other properties used fraudulently at seances, but there is some evidence which tends to show that genuine mediums do sometimes cheat, to fulfil the strong expectation of sitters for regular remarkable phenomena.

A notable example was the famous medium Eusapia **Palladino,** who produced materialization phenomena under strict conditions with a variety of skilled observers, but was known to take short cuts and cheat if the opportunity offered. The mediumistic character is often shallow and childlike, strongly influenced by the desires and expectations of sitters and perhaps even spirits, rather like a subject under hypnosis.

Another controversial medium was Mrs. Helen **Duncan,** convicted in Edinburgh, Scotland, in 1933 for fraudulent mediumship in which an undervest was used as a "materialized spirit." Many reputable observers believed she also produced genuine phenomena, although psychical researchers like Harry **Price** insisted that his photographs of "ectoplasm" clearly indicated cheese-cloth, rubber gloves and cut-out heads from magazine covers. Price did not discover how these objects evaded search, but theorized that the cheese-cloth was swallowed and regurgitated, other properties perhaps being handled by accomplices.

The great days of materialization mediums like D. D. **Home,** with his phantom hands, or Florence **Cook,** with full-length spirit forms apparently indistinguishable from living human beings, are over. No modern mediums have come forward with comparable phenomena to be tested in the more rigorous atmosphere of present times. Until they do, materialization must remain a controversial phenomenon. But it would be unreasonable to dismiss it as totally fraudulent and the claims of reputable scientists of the past as due to incompetence or collusion.

In his book *The Spiritualists: The Story of Florence Cook and William Crookes* (1962), Trevor H. Hall sought to show that not only was the mediumship of Florence Cook shamelessly fraudulent, but that William Crookes was her active accomplice through infatuation with her. Hall is a noted hostile critic of psychical phenomena and although this book is well documented the evidence remains largely speculative and anecdotal. For a refutation of Hall's charges, see the paper 'Crookes and Cook' (*Journal* of the Society for Psychical Research, vol. 42, 1963). For a general discussion of the competence and character of Crookes, see the excellent introduction by K. M. Goldney to the book *Crookes and the Spirit World* (collected) R. G. Medhurst (1972). It must also be stressed that no evidence of fraud was ever discovered on the part of D. D. Home (also tested by Crookes). (See also Florence **Cook;** Sir William **Crookes;** Helen **Duncan;** **Ectoplasm;** **Hands of Spirits;** Einer **Nielsen**)

Recommended reading:

Abbot, David P. *Behind the Scenes with Mediums,* Open Court, Chicago, 1907, 5th revised ed. 1926

Aksakof, A. *A Case of Partial Dematerialization of the Body of a Medium,* Boston, Mass., 1898

Anon. *Confessions of a Medium,* London, 1882

Anon. (ed. Harry Price & E. J. Dingwall) *Revelations of a Spirit Medium,* Kegan Paul, London, 1922

Bisson, Juliette A. *Les Phénomènes dits de Matérialisations,* Paris, 1914

Bolton, Gambier. *Ghosts in Solid Form,* London, 1919

Brackett, E. A. *Materialized Apparitions,* Boston, 1886; William Rider, London, n.d.

Carrington, Hereward. *The American Seances with Eusapia Palladino,* Barrett/Helix, New York, 1954

Carrington, Hereward. *The Physical Phenomena of Spiritualism,* Dodd, Mead, 1920; T. Werner Laurie, London, n.d.

Colley, Archdeacon. *Sermons of Spiritualism,* London, 1907

Crookes, William. *Researches in the Phenomena of Spiritualism,* J. Burns, London, 1874 etc. (frequently reprinted)

Crossley, Alan Ernest. *The Story of Helen Duncan, Materialization Medium,* Stockwell, U.K., 1975

Delanne, Gabriel. *Les Apparitions Materialisées des Vivants et des Morts,* Paris, 1911

Gray, Isa. *From Materialisation to Healing,* Regency Press, London, 1973

Hall, Trevor H. *The Spiritualists; The Story of Florence Cook and William Crookes,* Duckworth London, 1962; Garrett/Helix, New York, 1963

Henry, T. Shekleton. *Spookland; A Record of Research & Experiment in the Much Talked of Realm of Mystery,* Chicago, 1902

Geley, Gustav. *Clairvoyance and Materialisation,* George Doran, New York, 1927; Arno Press, 1975

Geley, Gustav. *From the Unconscious to the Conscious,* William Collins, London, 1920

Medhurst, R. G. (coll.). *Crookes and the Spirit World; A Collection of Writings by or Concerning the Work of Sir William Crookes, O.M., F.R.S. in the Field of Psychical Research,* Taplinger/Souvenir Press, London, 1972

"Medium, A." (A. Lunt). *Mysteries of the Seance,* Boston, 1905

Olcott, Henry S. *People From the Other World,* American Publishing Co., Hartford, Conn., 1875; Tuttle, 1972

Putnam, Allen. *Flashes of Light from the Spirit-Land,* Boston, 1872

Sargent, Epes. *Proof Palpable of Immortality,* Boston, 1876

Schrenck-Notzing, Baron von. *Phenomena of Materialisation,* Kegan Paul, London, 1920; Arno Press, 1975

Viereborne, A. *Life of James Riley,* Werner Co., Akron, Ohio, 1911

Wolfe, N. B. *Startling Facts in Modern Spiritualism,* N. B. Wolfe, Cincinnati, 1874

Mather, Increase (1639-1723) and Cotton (1662-1728)

Father and son, two eminent divines of Boston, Massachusetts, notorious for their crusade against persons suspected of witchcraft. (See **America, United States of; Witchcraft**)

Mathers, S(amuel) L(iddell) MacGregor (1854-1918)

Leading British occultist who was one of the founders of the Hermetic Order of the **Golden Dawn.** Born in Hackney, London, January 8, 1854, he lived with his mother at Bournemouth after the early death of his father. As a boy he was intensely interested in symbolism and mysticism. He claimed a romantic descent from Ian MacGregor of Glenstrae, an ardent Jacobite who was given the title of Comte de Glenstrae by Louis XIV. Mathers became a Freemason October 4, 1877 and a Master Mason January 30, 1878, soon after his twenty-fourth birthday. His mystical interests led him to become a member of the **Societas Rosicruciana in Anglia** (Rosicrucian Society of England), where he was an associate of Dr. William Wynn **Westcott,** Dr. William Robert **Woodman** and Kenneth **MacKenzie.** Together with Westcott and Woodman, Mathers became a founder of the Golden Dawn in 1888. Meanwhile he lived in some poverty after the death of his mother in 1885, and spent much time researching occultism at the British Museum Library, London. He met Anna **Kingsford,** who introduced him to Madame **Blavatsky,** who invited him to collaborate in the formation of the Theosophical Society, but he declined. In 1890 he married Mina Bergson, sister of the French philosopher Henri Bergson. Soon afterwards he removed to Paris with his wife.

Mathers and his wife received a small allowance from Annie Horniman (daughter of the founder of the Horniman Museum, London, and a member of the Golden Dawn), so that he might continue his studies on behalf of the G.D. However, disputes developed between Annie Horniman and Mathers on financial issues, and in December 1896 Mathers peremptorily expelled her from the G.D.

Mathers was deceived by the charlatans Mr. & Mrs. **Horos,** who acquired G.D. rituals from him for their own misuse. Other disagreements developed in the G.D. During a dispute between Mathers and the British officials of the G.D., occultist Aleister **Crowley** sided with Mathers and attempted to take over the London premises and documents. The poet W. B. **Yeats,** a noted G.D. member, played a prominent part in the rejection of Crowley. Eventually Mathers himself was expelled from the G.D. He died November 20, 1918. His translations of important occult texts included: *The Kabbalah Unveiled* (1907), *The Key of Solomon the King* (1889), *The Book of the Sacred Magic of Abra-Melin the Mage* (1898; reissued Causeway, 1974). For a sympathetic study of Mathers and his circle, see *The Sword of Wisdom; MacGregor Mathers and The Golden Dawn* by Ithell Colquhoun (1975).

The MacGregor Mathers Society was founded in Britain as a dining club for men only, membership by

invitation. Address: BM # Spirotos (M.M.S.), London, W.C.1., England.

Mathur, Raghuvansh B(ahadur) (1918-   )

Indian educator who has investigated parapsychological subjects. Born September 17, 1918 at Lucknow, India, he studied at University of Lucknow (B.A. 1937), London University, England (B.A. hons. 1940), Cambridge University, England (certificate in education 1942), London University (D.P.A. 1942, Ph.D. 1947).

He was Head of the Department of Education, University of Lucknow from 1953 onwards. In 1957 he was a Whitney-Fullbright visiting professor at Washington. He is a member of the Education Society, Research Society, University of Lucknow. He is interested in clairvoyance, telepathy and psychokinesis, and has investigated ESP in school children.

"Matikon"

A mystical work printed at Frankfurt in 1784, whose theories resemble the doctrines of the Brahmins. The following is an example of its teachings. Before the Fall, Adam was a pure spirit, a celestial being, surrounded by a mystic covering which rendered him incapable of being affected by any poison of nature, or by the power of the elements.

The physical body, therefore, is but a coarse husk in which, having lost his primitive invulnerability, man shelters from the elements. In his condition of perfect glory and perfect happiness Adam was a natural king, ruling all things visible and invisible, and showing forth the power of the Almighty. He also bore "a fiery, two-edged, all-piercing lance"—a living word, which united all powers within itself, and by means of which he could perform all things.

Matter Passing Through Matter

This has been claimed frequently as a seance-room phenomenon. It is involved in the marvel of **apports** and **teleportation** of the human body and its validation under test conditions would help towards the recognition of these greater phenomena. Unfortunately it has seldom occurred under laboratory conditions that would be satisfying to modern investigators. Prof. Robert **Hare**'s notes of the passing of two small balls of platinum into two hermetically sealed glass tubes have been forgotten. The human element is too strong and in most of the cases on record the body of the medium plays some as yet not clearly understood part in the performance.

It should be first mentioned that interpenetration as such is not generally admitted. D. D. **Home** stoutly denied it and his **controls** declared that fissures or cracks are necessary to permit the passage of a solid body through another. Sir William **Crookes** stated in *Researches into the Phenomena of Spiritualism* (1874 etc.): "After several phenomena had occurred, the conversation turned upon some circumstances which seemed only explicable on the assumption that matter had actually passed through a solid substance. Thereupon a message was given by means of the alphabet: 'It is impossible for matter to pass through matter, but we will show you what we can do.' We waited in silence.

"Presently a luminous appearance was seen hovering

over the bouquet of flowers, and then, in full view of all present, a piece of china-grass 15 inches long, which formed the centre ornament of the bouquet, slowly rose from the other flowers, and then descended to the table in front of the vase between it and Mr. Home. It did not stop on reaching the table, but went straight through it and we all watched it till it had entirely passed through. Immediately on the disappearance of the grass, my wife, who was sitting near Mr. Home, saw a hand come up from under the table between them, holding the piece of grass. It tapped her on the shoulder two or three times with a sound audible to all, then laid the grass on the floor and disappeared. Only two persons saw the hand, but all in the room saw the piece of grass moving about as I have described.

"During the time this was taking place Mr. Home's hands were seen by all to be quietly resting on the table in front of him. The place where the grass disappeared was 18 inches from his hands. The table was a telescope dining table, opening with a screw; there was no leaf in it, and the junction of the two sides formed a narrow crack down the middle. The grass had passed through this chink, which I measured and found to be barely one eighth of an inch wide. The stem of the piece of grass was far too thick to enable me to force it through this crack without injuring it, yet we had all seen it pass through quietly and smoothly; and on examination it did not show the slightest signs of pressure or abrasion."

There is ground to suppose, however, that the statements of D. D. Home's controls were somewhat orthodox. Otherwise it would be necessary to discredit most of the evidence. To mention some: The psychical researcher Camille **Flammarion** described the passing of a book through a curtain in a seance with Eusapia **Palladino** on November 21, 1898. A book was held up by M. Jules Bois before the curtain at about the height of a man, 24 inches from each side of the edge. It was seized by an invisible hand and Mme. Flammarion who observed the rear of the curtain, suddenly saw it coming through, upheld in the air, without hands or arms, for a space of one or two seconds. Then she saw it fall down. She cried out: "Oh, the book, it has just passed through the curtain!"

There is some similarity between this observation of Flammarion and an account of Mrs. Speer (friend of the Rev. Stainton **Moses**) dated October 17, 1874: "Before meeting Mr. Stainton Moses had taken three rings from his hands and threaded them on to his watch chain; his watch was on one end of the chain and a small pocket barometer on the other; both of these articles he placed in side pockets of his waistcoat, the rings hanging midway on his chain in full sight of the circle. We suddenly saw a pillar of light advance from a corner of the room, stand between me and Dr. S. then pass through the table to Mr. S. M. In a moment the figure flashed back again between us and threw something hard down upon the table. We passed our hands over the table, and found the rings had been removed from the medium's chain without his knowledge."

Mr. F. Fusedale, testifying to the **London Dialectical Society** in 1869, submitted an account of spirit manifestations in his own house and wrote: "The children and my wife would see the things they [the spirits] took [in particular a brooch of my wife's] appear to pass through

solid substances, such as the wall or the doors, when they were taken from them; and they would take things out of the children's hands, as if in play, and hide them, and then after a little time return them again."

In a seance with the Italian medium Francesco **Carancini,** a dinner plate, covered with soot and out of the medium's reach, was placed in a padlocked wooden box which was in the hand of one of the sitters.

In experiments with Mrs. M. B. **Thayer,** Robert Cooper found a Japanese silk handkerchief which belonged to one of the sitters and flowers which came from nowhere in the locked box which he brought to the seance and the key of which he retained (*Light,* March 15, 1902).

"During my sixteen years of experiments, investigation into the question of the existence of this psychic force," wrote Gambier Bolton (author *Psychic Force,* 1904), "the apparent penetration of matter by matter had been such a common occurrence at our experimental meetings, that unless this happens to take place in connection with some unusually large and ponderous object that is suddenly brought into our midst, or removed from the place in which we are holding our meetings, I take but very little notice of it."

One of the occasions which he found worthwhile to notice came in a seance with the medium Cecil **Husk.** A light table was placed in the middle of the circle and was securely fastened by heavy baize curtains round the four sides, pinning the bottom of the curtain to the floor boards with drawing pins. The table was first heard rocking and tapping the floor boards and in less than three minutes it had apparently passed through the curtain and was found in its old place, 21 feet distant from the curtain.

After having been accused of fraud, the American medium, Mrs. Etta **Roberts,** in a test seance on September 3, 1891, was enclosed into a wire cage out of which many phantom forms issued. Finally Mrs. Robert herself stepped out through the padlocked and sealed door without breaking the fastenings. The same feat was witnessed by Dr. Paul Gibier, Director of the Bacteriological Institute of New York with Mrs. Carrie M. Sawyer (Mrs. Salmon) in his own laboratory on three occasions. The trellis of the cage was found to be burning hot by several sitters.

Paranormal Knot-tying

Knots tied in an endless cord was the first phenomenon Professor **Zöllner** witnessed in his experiments with the medium Henry **Slade.** Zöllner made a loop of strong cord by tying the ends together. The ends projected beyond the knot and were sealed down to a piece of paper. In the seance room he hung the loop around his neck until the moment of experiment arrived. Then he took it off, placed the sealed knots on the table, placed his thumbs on each side of the knot and dropped the loop over the edge of the table on his knees. Slade kept his hands in sight and touched Zöllner's hands above the table. A few minutes later four symmetrical single knots were found on the cord.

In his further experiments, separate loops of leather were tied together and two wooden rings, one of oak the other of alder wood, were removed from a sealed loop of catgut and passed around the leg of a table. A snail shell which Prof. Zöllner placed on the table under a larger one dropped with a clatter on the slate held under the table surface. It was so hot that Zöllner nearly let it drop. A coin from a closed box on the table passed on in daylight to the slate underneath the top. Zöllner, placing two sheets of paper prepared with lamp-black between two slates in frames, closed the slates, bound them firmly together and, keeping it on his knees all the time, asked Slade to have an impression made inside the slates. He felt a strong pressure, opened the slates and found the impression of a human foot.

Prof. Zöllner's knot-tying experiment was repeated by Dr. Nichols with the medium William **Eglinton** in the presence of six observers. Dr. Nichols cut four yards of common brown twine from a fresh ball, tied the two ends together with a single knot, then passed each end through a hole in one of his visiting cards, tied another square knot and firmly sealed this knot to the card. Sitting around a small table in daylight, the sealed card upon the center of the table, the loop hanging down upon the floor, a minute later five single knots were found tied upon the string about a foot apart.

Paranormal Release and Movement of Clothing

The release of the medium from strong bonds without disturbing the knots or seals was claimed by the **Davenport Brothers,** although justifiable skepticism surrounds their stage performances. The psychic feat was also claimed by Sir William **Crookes** in his experiments with Mrs. Corner, the former Florence **Cook.**

A kindred demonstration, of which the Davenport Brothers were the greatest exponents, was the removal and donning of coats while the medium's hands were held. In a letter to the London newspaper *Daily News,* Dion Boucicault, the famous English actor and author, spoke of a seance at his house on October 11, 1864, in which, by striking a light, they actually witnessed the coat of Mr. Fay, the fellow-medium of the Davenport Brothers, flying off. "It was seen quitting him, plucked off him upwards. It flew up to the chandelier, where it hung for a moment and then fell to the ground. Mr. Fay was seen meanwhile bound hand and foot as before."

Robert Cooper wrote in his book *Spiritual Experiences* (1867): "The coat of Mr. Fay has, scores of times, been taken from his back in my presence, and Mr. Fay at the time might be seen sitting like a statue with his hands securely tied behind him and the knots sealed. I have seen coats of various descriptions, from a large overcoat to a light paletot, put on in the place of his own in a moment of time, his hands remaining securely tied and the seal unbroken. I have known the coat that has been placed on Mr. Fay so small that it could only with difficulty be got off him. I have known a coat that was first placed on Mr. Fay transferred in a moment to the back of Ira Davenport, whose hands, like Mr. Fay's, were tied behind him, and the most curious part of the proceedings was that it was put on inside out. I have also known the waistcoat of Ira Davenport taken from under his coat, all buttoned up, with his watch and guard just as he wore it."

The same feat was witnessed in 1886 in Washington by Alfred Russel **Wallace** in a seance with Pierre L. O. A. **Keeler.**

Prof. Cesar **Lombroso** recorded a similar instance with Eusapia **Palladino.** An overcoat was placed on a chair beyond the reach of the medium whose hands and feet had been continuously controlled. Several objects from an inside pocket of the overcoat had been brought and laid on a phosphorescent cardboard on the table. All at once the medium began to complain of something about her neck and binding her tight. On light being produced it was found that she had the overcoat on, her arms being slipped into it, one in each sleeve.

It is scarcely necessary to stress that accounts of release from bonds and flying clothing must be treated with caution as they are stock feats of stage conjurers.

Ring Experiments and Chair Threading

Ring experiments and chair threading were claimed on many occasions. It would seem fraud-proof if two continuous iron rings were linked. In October, 1872, the *Religio-Philosophical Journal* of Chicago claimed to have witnessed this demonstration. The editor wrote: "We had the pleasure of attending a seance at which Capt. Winslow was the medium. The manifestations were very fine. One remarkable feat is the union of two solid iron rings, leaving them thus interlinked, and yet the metal perfectly sound."

In the majority of cases, however, this plain test was always shirked for the far less convincing demonstration of placing an iron ring on the sitter's arm after the clasping of the hands or for placing the ring which was too small to pass through the hand on the medium's wrist.

The medium Cecil **Husk** wore such a ring until his death. The Society for Psychical Research, London, investigated it and claimed that the ring could be forced off if the medium were chloroformed. The statement of Dr. George Wyld, a physician of Edinburgh, that the ring was specially made to his order and secretly marked by him, and that he held the medium's hand tight while the ring was taken from him in the dark was left unconsidered.

A similar wrought-iron ring was passed on to the ankle of the medium F. F. **Craddock.** It was very tight and caused him great discomfort and actual pain until it was filed off by a friendly blacksmith. Hearing of this occurrence, Gambier Bolton procured two welded iron rings and visiting Craddock, he fastened his hands behind his back with strong tape, then led him to a chair and fastened both arms, above the elbows, to the back of the chair with strong tapes and double knots.

Bolton stated: "Placing the two rings at his feet, I turned to the gas pendant hanging over our heads and lowered it somewhat, and before I had time to turn round again I heard the well-known ring of two pieces of iron being brought into sharp contact with each other, and walking up to him I found both rings on his wrist. To make sure that my eyes were not deceiving me, I pulled them strongly, struck one with the other, and found that they really were on his wrists; and I then carefully examined the tapes and found them not only secure, but so tight that his hands were swollen as a result of the tightness with which I had tied them. I stepped backwards, keeping my eyes on him, when suddenly with a crash both rings fell at my feet. To have withdrawn his hands and arms and replaced them in that time was a physical impossibility. On attempting to untie the tapes I found that I had pulled the knots so tightly that it was only after cutting them with a finely pointed pair of scissors, that I was able to release his hands once more, his wrists being marked for some time with a deep red line as the result."

Dr. L. Th. Chazarain, in his pamphlet *Les preuves scientifique de la survivance de l'âme* (1905) wrote of his experience in meetings organized in Paris by Dr. Puel, director of the *Revue des Sciences Psychiques:* "I took the ring which had been laid on the table and passed it round her right wrist. Immediately afterwards I took hold of the corresponding hand, and waited, holding it firmly between my own. At the end of eight or ten minutes she uttered a cry, like a cry of pain or fright, and at the same instant she woke and the ring was seen on the ground." M. August Reveillac observing the same effect found the fallen ring, when picked up, almost burning hot.

Col. W. A. Danskin in *How and Why I Became a Spiritualist* (1869) described a seance in Baltimore in which a secretly marked iron ring, seven inches smaller than the circumference of the medium's head, was repeatedly placed around the medium's neck. From the *Banner of Light* (January 11, 1868) he reproduced the following testimony, signed by thirty-two names: "We, the undersigned, hereby testify that we have attended the social meetings referred to; and that a solid iron ring, seven inches less in size than the young man's head was actually and unmistakably placed around his neck. There was as the advertisement claims, no possibility of fraud or deception, because the ring was freely submitted to the examination of the audience, both before and while on the neck of the young man."

The medium was a 19-year-old boy. Danskin further wrote: "Once, when only three persons were present—the medium, a friend and myself—we sat together in the dark room. I held the left hand of the medium, my friend held his right hand, our other hands being joined; and while thus sitting, the ring, which I had thrown some distance from us on the floor, suddenly came round my arm. I had never loosened my hold upon the medium, yet that solid iron ring, by an invisible power, was made to clasp my arm."

The medium Charles **Williams** often demonstrated the ring test. A. Smedley described instances with a ring which he secretly marked (*Some Reminiscences, an Account of Startling Spiritual Manifestations,* 1890). An interesting case was the following: Col. Lean (husband of Florence **Marryat**) mentally asked the control "John King" to fetch the half-hoop diamond ring from his wife's finger and place it on his. The ring, wrote Florence Marryat "was worn between my wedding ring and a heavy gold snake ring and I was holding the hand of my neighbour all the time and yet the ring was abstracted from between the other two and transferred to Colonel Lean's finger without my being aware of the circumstance."

In experiments with Frau **Vollhardt** in Berlin, two highly skeptical members of the Medical Society for Psychic Research, holding the hands of the medium at either side, found (after one of the crises of the medium) two unbroken wooden rings about their arms.

Robert Cooper, in a seance with the **Eddy Brothers,** experienced an electric shock at his elbow and found two iron rings on his arm which were held by the medium (reported in *Light,* March 15, 1902).

Count Solovovo Petrovo took a marked ring to a seance with the Russian medium **Sambor** on November 15,

1894. The ring was placed on M. Vassilief's arm when he was holding the medium's hands. (*Rebus,* No. 47, 1894). In seances with the same medium at the Spiritist Club, St. Petersburg, Dr. Pogorelski suddenly felt a blow on his right arm (close to the shoulder) and felt a chair passed on to his right arm. He held Sambor's hands by interlacing the fingers so that "it was impossible for our hands to become separated, even for a hundredth part of a second, without my feeling it." The experiment was repeated with another sitter whose hand was tied to Sambor's by means of a nearly ten yards long linen ribbon on the ends of which seals were placed.

John S. Farmer, Eglinton's biographer, wrote in his *Twixt Two Worlds* (1886) that in June 1879, at Mrs. Gregory's house "in the presence of Mr. Eglinton and a non-professional medium, two chairs were threaded at the same moment of time upon the arms of two sitters, each of whom was then holding the hand of the medium. Mr. Serjeant Cox was holding the hand of Mr. Eglinton and the back of the chair passed through his arm, giving him the sensation of a blow against the elbow when it did so. When a light was struck the chair was seen hanging on Mr. Sergeant Cox's arm and his hand was still grasping that of Mr. Eglinton. An immediate examination of the chair showed that the back of it was in good condition, with none of the woodwork loose or broken."

In *Planchette or the Despair of Science* (1880), Epes **Sargent** quoted many testimonies of similar occurrences with Charles Read of Buffalo and other mediums. Gambier **Bolton** wrote of his experience with Cecil **Husk** as follows: "With Mrs. Cecil Husk, on half a dozen occasions, in my own room and using my own chairs, I have held both hands of another experimenter with my two hands, about fifteen inches from the top of the back of one of the chairs, when with a sudden snap the back of the chair has passed over our wrists and has been seen by twelve to sixteen other observers hanging from our arms, in gas light, my hands never for an instant releasing those of my fellow-experimenters."

Well documented experiments in the claimed demonstration of the passage of matter through matter were carried out in June and July 1932, in the "Margery" circle in Boston (see **Crandon**). The phenomena, as reported by William H. Button in *Journal* of the American Society for Psychical Research (Aug.–Sept., 1932) consisted of the removal of a variety of objects from locked or sealed boxes and the introduction of various objects into such boxes. They were undertaken to confirm some of the results of the **Zöllner** experiments were quite impressive.

The most astonishing phenomenon of the "Margery" mediumship was the interlocking rings. Sir Oliver **Lodge** had suggested the paranormal linking of two rings made of different woods might provide an irrefutable evidence of psychic force. The rings were duly provided, one of white wood and the other of red mahogany. At a seance with "Margery" in 1932, the rings were interlocked. According to Thomas R. Tietze in his book *Margery* (1973), the Irish poet W. B. **Yeats** was present at this seance. The feat of linking two rings made from different woods was apparently repeated. One set was sent to Sir Oliver Lodge for independent verification, but unfortunately arrived cracked and broken, presumably damaged in the post.

Another set of interlocked rings of different woods was shown to the British Spiritualist journalist Hannen Swaffer when he visited the Crandons in 1934. The rings were photographed and clearly show one of white wood and the other of red mahogany. They passed into the care of William Button, then president of the American Society for Psychical Research and were kept in a sealed glass-covered box. On a return visit to Boston in 1936, Hannen Swaffer asked to see the rings again, but when they were taken out of the box it was found that one of the rings was broken. It is unfortunate that permanent evidence of such paranormal linkage should be frustrated by inexplicable accidents.

In 1979, the **SORRAT** group formed by Prof. John G. **Neilhardt,** attempted to validate such paranormal linkages in an unassailable experiment. Since it could be argued that wooden rings might be cleverly separated along the grain and glued together again, parapsychologist W. E. **Cox** proposed seamless rings made from a single layer of ordinary leather. It would not be possible to cut and rejoin leather without trace of manipulation. In the event, the experiment was successful and film records show the paranormal materializing and dematerializing process. The linkages, however, were not permanent, as the leather rings separated again after a few seconds, a curious echo of the "Margery" experiments.

The high standing of the SORRAT parapsychologists, in conjunction with the film records, would seem to argue against any claims of fraud. For an account of these and related experiments, see *SORRAT: A History of the Neilhardt Psychokinesis Experiments, 1961-1981* by John Thomas Richards (Scarecrow Press, 1982). For report on the earlier experiments of Prof. Zöllner, see *Transcendental Physics; An Account of Experimental Investigations from the Scientific Treatises of Johann Carl Friedrich Zöllner* transl. Charles C. Massey (W. H. Harrison, London, 1882; Boston, 1888; reprinted Arno Press, 1976). (See also **Apports; Asports; Materialization; Movement; Psychokinesis; Teleportation**)

Maxwell, Dr. Joseph (c. 1933)

Attorney-General at the Court of Appeal at Bordeaux, prominent French psychical investigator. The chance reading of a book on Theosophy gave him the first impulse to study occult mysteries.

He found a remarkable medium in Limoge. The result, however, was unconvincing. But he realised that certain manifestations could only be studied with the assistance of nervous and mental pathology and for six years he studied at the University of Bordeaux for a medical degree.

As a trained investigator he had the rare fortune to find a medium in a friend, M. Meurice, who could produce telekinetic phenomena in good light. He obtained further good results with Mme. Agullana, of Bordeaux, two young mediums of Agen, and others. In 1895, in l'Agnelas, he attended, with Col. **Rochas,** Dariex, Sabatier, Count de Gramont and Watteville, experiments with Eusapia **Palladino.**

He made a deep study of the phenomena of **raps** and in *Les Phénomènes Psychiques,* Paris, 1903 (English translation *Metapsychical Phenomena,* 1905) he affirmed the reality of **telekinesis** in these words: "I am certain that we are in the presence of an unknown force; its manifestations do not seem to obey the same laws as those governing other forces more familiar to us; but I have no doubt they obey some law." He admitted that the force is intelligent but wondered if that intelligence did not come from the experimenters. His theory was that a kind of collective consciousness produced the intellectual results. The book, the result of ten years of research, is a valuable contribution to psychical literature.

His later books also merited interest. They were *La Divination* (1927), *La Magie* (1928), *Les Tarots* (1933).

Mayavi-rupa

According to Theosophical teachings, based on Hindu religious philosophy, this is the invisible part of the physical body. Its appearance is exactly similar to that of the physical body. (See also **Rupa; Seven Principles; Theosophy**)

Maynard, Mrs. Henrietta Sturdevant (1841-1892)

American inspirational speaker, known as Nettie Colburn before her marriage. She was born in Bolton, Connecticut, in 1841.

President Lincoln had a high opinion of her gift and was, to an appreciable extent, influenced by her trance exhortations in the issue of the anti-slavery proclamation. Mrs. Maynard described her meetings with the President in her book *Was Abraham Lincoln a Spiritualist?* (1891). The book was reissued by Psychic Book Club, London, in 1917, revised edition 1956.

Mrs. Maynard died at White Plains, New York, June 27, 1892. (See also Abraham **Lincoln**)

Mayne, Alan James (1927–   )

British researcher and consultant. Born November 29, 1927 at Cambridge, England, he studied at Oxford University, England (B.A. 1949, B.Sc. 1951, M.A. 1953). He was Scientific Officer, United Kingdom Atomic Energy Authority from 1951–56; research statistician and consultant with A. C. Nielsen Co., Oxford, from 1956–59; research fellow with Electronic Computing Laboratory, University of Leeds from 1960–61. He edited *The Scientist Speculates,* an anthology.

He is a member of the Royal Statistical Society, Operational Research Society, British Computer Society, Mathematical Association, British Association for the Advancement of Science, Society for Psychical Research, Institute of Mathematical Statistics, Brisith Society for the Philosophy of Science, Parapsychological Association.

In addition to his articles on mathematical statistics and operational research, he has studied parapsychological phenomena and published contributions in the *Journal of the British Society of Dowsers.* He acted as director of research for the Society of Metaphysicians (Archer's Court, Hastings, Sussex, England), and was president of the **Institute of Parascience** (Spryton, Lifton, Devon, U.K.) on its foundation in 1971.

Mazdaznan

An occult organization founded by Otto Hanisch (1854–1936). The name "Mazdaznan" is supposed to derive from the Persian "Mazda" and "Znan" meaning

"Master-Thought," although this might be questioned by Persian scholars.

The cult embodied deep-breathing, physical exercises, vegetarian diet, astrology, phrenology and various occult studies, and claimed descent from Zoroastrianism.

Hanisch was born in Leipzig, Germany. When only a boy, he was supposed to have been taken to a Persian monastery of Math-El-Kharman and taught every major art and science, including occultism. At the age of 25, Hanisch traveled through Russia and eventually came to Los Angeles, California, where he established his cult, using the name Rev. Dr. Otoman Zar-Adusht Ha'nish. A European headquarters was established as a colony called "Aryana" (admitting only white-skinned Aryans) at Herliberg, Lake Zurich.

For an account of this cult, see 'A Strange Adventure in Switzerland' by H. R. Ecroyd (*The Quest,* vol. xxi, No. 1, October 1939).

Mead, G(eorge) R(obert) S(tow) (1863–1933)

Theosophist, scholar and writer on Gnosticism and early Christianity. Born 1863, he was educated at King's School, Rochester, England, and St. John's College, Cambridge (M.A. 1885). In 1899 he married Laura Mary Cooper (died 1924).

In 1884 Mead joined the **Theosophical Society** on coming down from Cambridge. In 1889 he gave up his work as a teacher to be closely concerned with the Theosophical Society and its founder Madame **Blavatsky.** Mead became her private secretary for the last three years of her life, sub-edited her monthly magazine *Lucifer,* which he renamed *The Theosophical Review* on becoming editor. Mead was one of the few associates of Madame Blavatsky to have a realistic view of her complex character. He believed her to be a Bohemian and racy personality as well as a powerful medium, and not simply the charlatan alleged by her critics.

In 1890, Mead was appointed General Secretary of the Theosophical Society, a position he held for eight years. In 1908 he resigned from the Society (in company with some 700 other members) in protest against the scandals concerning C. W. **Leadbeater.** In March 1909, Mead founded The Quest Society, a group of sincere seekers after spiritual wisdom without any taint of charlatanism. He edited *The Quest* quarterly review from 1909–1930. After the death of his wife, Mead became actively interested in psychic science, and sat with several mediums. He helped to edit the second edition of Madame Blavatsky's famous work *The Secret Doctrine* in 1890, and his own important contributions to mysticism and early religion include the following books: *Simon Magus* (1892), *Orpheus* (1896), *The Upanishads* (1896), *Fragments of a Faith Forgotten* (1900), *Apollonius of Tyana* (1901), *The Gospels and the Gospel* (1902), *Did Jesus Live 100 B.C.?* (1903), *Thrice Greatest Hermes* (1906), *Echoes from the Gnosis* (1907), *The World Mystery* (1908), *Some Mystical Adventures* (1910), *Quests Old and New* (1913), *The Doctrine of the Subtle Body* [deals with early religious traditions relative to **Out-of-the-Body** experience or astral projection] (1919), *Pistis Sophia* (1921), *The Gnostic John the Baptizer* (1924), *The Sacred Dance in Christendom* (1926). Some of his most important books were reissued in modern times by University Books, Inc. Mead died September 28, 1933.

Meddelande Fran Sallskapet for Parapsykologisk Forkning

Publication in Swedish language of Sallskapet For Parapsykologisk. Address: Forsking, Box 40 243, 103-4 Stockholm, Sweden.

Medea

In Greek mythology, an enchantress, daughter of the king of Colchis, who fell in love with Jason when he came to that country. Medea enabled him to slay the sleepless dragon that guarded the golden fleece. She fled from Colchis with Jason who made her his wife, and from whom she exacted a pledge never to love another woman. They were pursued by her father, but she delayed the pursuit by the cruel expedient of cutting her brother Absyrtus to pieces and strewing the limbs in the sea.

Medea accompanied Jason to Greece, where she was looked on as a barbarian, but having conciliated King Peleus who was now a very old man, she induced him to try to regain youth by bathing in a magic cauldron of which she was to prepare the contents. So great was his faith in her powers that the old man unhesitatingly plunged into her cauldron and was boiled alive. Her reason for this frightful act of cruelty was to hasten the succession to the throne of Jason, who in due course would have succeeded Peleus, but now the Greeks would have none of either him or Medea, and he was forced to leave Iolcos.

Growing tired of the formidable enchantress to whom he had bound himself, Jason sought to contract an alliance with Glauce, a young princess. Concealing her real intentions, Medea pretended friendship with the bride-elect and sent her as a wedding present a garment, which as soon as Glauce put it on, caused her to die in the greatest agony.

Eventually Medea parted from Jason. Having murdered her two children by him, she fled from Corinth in her car drawn by dragons to Athens, where she married Argeus, by whom she had a son, Medus. But the discovery of an attempt on the life of Theseus, forced her to leave Athens. Accompanied by her son, she returned to Colchis, and restored her father to the throne, of which he had been deprived by his own brother Perses.

A great amount of literature has been written around the character of Medea. Euripides, Ennius, Aeschylus, and later, Thomas Corneille made her the theme of tragedies. The story of Medea is very movingly told by Charles Kingsley in his book *The Heroes* (1856 etc.). (See also **Greece**)

Medhurst, R. G. (died 1971)

British writer on parapsychology, a leading member of the **Society for Psychical Research,** London. Co-author with K. M. **Goldney** of the important article 'William Crookes and the Physical Phenomena of Mediumship' (*Proceedings* of the Society for Psychical Research, vol. 54, pt. 195, March 1964).

Dr. Medhurst's degree in mathematics and his outstanding work in mathematical engineering were of special value in evaluating mathematical aspects of ESP. His paper 'On the Origin of the Prepared Random Numbers Used in the Shackleton Experiments' (*Journal* of the Society for Psychical Research, vol. 46, 1971) argued that the method of constructing quasi-random series was incorrect. Other useful contributions by Dr. Medhurst including such subjects as investigation of the paragnost Croiset, Duke University's ESP cards, a project to discover ESP agents and percipients, criticism of the Psychophysical Research unit, as well as various book reviews. His posthumous publication *Crookes and the Spirit World; A Collection of Writings By or Concerning the Work of Sir William Crookes* was edited by K. M. Goldney and M. R. Barrington (Taplinger, 1972).

Medicine, Occult

"The whole power of the occult physician," according to nineteenth century magus Éliphas Lévi, "is in the conscience of his will, while his whole art consists in exciting the faith of his patient. 'If you have faith,' says the Master, 'all things are possible to him who believes.' The confidence must be dominated by expression, tone, gesture; confidence must be inspired by a fatherly manner, and cheerfulness stimulated by seasonable and sprightly conversations. Rabelais, who was a greater magician than he seemed, made pantagruelism his special panacea. He compelled his patients to laugh, and all the remedies he subsequently gave them succeeded better in consequence; he established a magnetic sympathy between himself and them, by means of which he communicated to them his own confidence and good humour; he flattered them in his prefaces, termed them his precious, most illustrious patients, and dedicated his books to them. So are we convinced that Gargantua and Pantagruel cured more black humours, more tendencies to madness, more atrabilious whims, at that epoch of religious animosities and civil wars, than the whole Faculty of medicine could boast.

"Occult medicine is essentially sympathetic. Reciprocal affection, or at least real good will, must exist between doctor and patient. Syrups and juleps have very little inherent virtue; they are what they become through the mutual opinion of operator and subject; hence hemœpathic medicine dispenses with them and no serious inconvenience follows. Oil and wine, combined with salt or camphor, are sufficient for the healing of all afflictions, and for all external frictions or soothing applications, oil and wine, are the chief medicaments of the Gospel tradition. They formed the balm of the Good Samaritan, and in the Apocalypse, when describing the last plagues, the prophet prays the avenging powers to spare these substances, that is, to leave a hope and a remedy for so many wounds. What we term extreme unction was the pure and simple practice of the Master's traditional medicine, both for the early Christians and in the mind of the apostle Saint James, who has included the precept in his epistle to the faithful of the whole world. 'Is any man sick among you,' he writes, 'let him call in the priests of the church, and let them pray over him, anointing him with oil in the name of the Lord.'

"This divine therapeutic science was lost gradually, and Extreme Unction came to be regarded as a religious formality necessary as a preparation for death. At the same time, the thaumaturgic virtue of consecrated oil could not be altogether effaced from remembrance by the traditional doctrine, and it is perpetuated in the passage of the catechism which refers to Extreme Unction. Faith

and charity were the most signal healing powers among the early Christians. The source of most diseases is in moral disorders; we must begin by healing the soul, and then the cure of the body will follow quickly."

Recommended reading:

Hartmann, Franz. *The Life and Teachings of Paracelsus,* George Redway, London, 1887 (reprinted in one volume with *The Prophecies of Paracelsus,* Rudolf Steiner Publications, Blauvelt, N.Y., 1973)

Lévi, Éliphas. *The History of Magic,* William Rider, London, 1913 etc.

Paracelsus (transl. Robert Turner). *The Archidoxes of Magic,* London, 1656; 2nd ed., Askin Publishers, New York/Samuel Weiser, 1975

Medieval Magic

In the belief of the medieval professors of the science of magic, it conferred upon the adept power over **angels,** demons (see **Demonology**), **elementary spirits** and the souls of the dead, the possession of esoteric wisdom, and actual knowledge of the discovery and use of the latent forces and undeveloped energies resident in man. This was supposed to be accomplished by a combination of will and aspiration, which by sheer force germinated an intellectual faculty of psychological perception, enabling the adept to view the wonders of a new world and communicate with its inhabitants.

To accomplish this, the ordinary faculties were almost invariably heightened by artificial means. The grandeur of the magical ritual overwhelmed the neophyte, and quickened his senses. **Ceremonial magic** was a marvellous spur to the latent faculties of man's psychic nature, just as were the rich concomitants of religious mysticism.

In the medieval mind, as in other periods of man's history, it was thought that magic could be employed both for good and evil purposes, its branches being designated "white" and "black," according to whether it was used for benevolent or wicked ends. The term "red" magic was also occasionally employed, as indicating a more exalted type of the art, but the designation is fanciful.

White magic to a great extent concerned itself with the evocation of angelic forces and of the spirits of the elements. The angelology of the Catholic Church was undoubtedly derived from the ancient faith of Israel, which in turn was indebted to Egypt and Babylon, and the Alexandrian system of successive emanations from the one and eternal substance evolved a complex hierarchy of angels, all of whom appear to have been at the bidding of the magician who was in possession of the Incommunicable Name, a concept deriving from that of the "Name of Power" so greatly made use of in Egyptian magic (see **Egypt**). The letters which composed this name were thought to possess a great measure of occult significance, and a power which in turn appears to have been reflected upon the entire Hebrew alphabet (see **Kabala**), which was thus endowed with mystical meaning, each of the letters representing a vital and creative number. Just as a language is formed from the letters of its alphabet, so from the secret powers which resided in the Hebrew alphabet, were evolved magical variations. Comparable concepts existed in esoteric Hinduism (see **AUM**).

From the letter "aleph" to that of "jod" the angelical

world was symbolized. From "caf" to "tsed" were represented the several orders of angels who inhabited the various spheres, each of which was under the direction of a particular intelligence. From "tsed" to "thau" is in secret correspondence with the elemental world; so that there were intelligences in correspondence with each of the Hebrew letters—"aleph" with the Haioth-ha-kodesch of the seraphim, the first and supreme angelical rank; "beth" the second letter with the ophanim or angels of the second order; "gimel" with the aralim or angels of the third order, and so on to the tenth letter "jod," which completes the enumeration of the angelical spheres.

The rest of the Hebrew alphabet, however, corresponds to individual principalities and powers—all of whom hold an important place in the mystical universe. Thus "caf," the eleventh letter, is in correspondence with Mettatron who belongs to the first heaven of the astronomic world. Final "caf," the next letter, corresponds to the intelligences of the secret order whose supreme chief is Raziel, and "lamed" the twelfth letter corresponds to those of the third sphere, that of Saturn, whose lord is Schebtaiel, and so on. These intelligences under their queen, with the sixteenth letter "ain" and "pe," the seventeenth of the Hebrew alphabet, refer to the first of the mystical elements—that of Fire, which is ruled over by the seraphim. Final "pe" corresponds to the air where dwell the sylphs, who are presided over by Ariel. "Tsade" refers to water where dwell the nymphs under their queen Tharsis; "koph" corresponds to earth, the sphere of the gnomes, ruled over by the cherubim. The twentieth letter "resh" applies to the animal kingdom, including man. "Shin" corresponds to the vegetable world. "Tau" the last symbol of the Hebrew alphabet refers to the world of minerals.

There are, besides these, many other species of angels and powers, as will be seen from reference to the entries on **Angels** and **Kabala.** More exalted intelligences were conjured by rites to be found in the ancient book known as the **Key of Solomon the King,** and perhaps the most satisfactory collection of formulae for the invocation of the higher angels is that included in the anonymous *Theosophia Pneumatica,* published at Frankfurt in 1686, which bears a strong family resemblance to the *Treatise on Magic* by Arbatel. The names in this work do not tally with those which have been already given, but as it is admitted by occult students that the names of all unseen beings are really unknown to humanity, this does not seem of such importance as it might at first sight.

It would seem that such spiritual knowledge as the medieval magus was capable of attaining was insufficient to raise him above the intellectual limitations of his time, so that the work in question possesses all the faults of its age and type. But that is not to say that it is possessed of no practical value, and it may be taken as well illustrating the white magic of medieval times. It classifies the names of the angels under the title of "Olympic or Celestial Spirits," who abide in the firmament and constellations: they administer inferior destinies and accomplish and teach whatever is portended by the several stars in which they are insphered. They are powerless to act without a special command from the Almighty.

The stewards of Heaven are seven in number—Arathron, Bethor, Phaleg, Och, Hagith, Ophiel, and Phul. Each of them has a numerous host at his command, and

the regions in which they dwell are 196 in all. Arathron appears on Saturday at the first hour, and answers for his territory and its inhabitants, as do the others, each at his own day and hour, and each presides for a period of 490 years. The functions of Bethor began in the fiftieth year before the birth of Christ 430. Phagle reigned till A.D. 920; Och till the year 1410; Hagith governed until A.D. 1900. The others follow in succession.

These intelligences are the stewards of all the elements, energizing the firmament and, with their armies, depending from each other in a regular hierarchy. The names of the minor Olympian spirits are interpreted in divers ways, but those alone are powerful which they themselves give, which are adapted to the end for which they have been summoned. Generically, they are called "Astra," and their power is seldom prolonged beyond one hundred and forty years. The heavens and their inhabitants come voluntarily to man and often serve against even the will of man, but how much more if we implore their ministry.

That evil and troublesome spirits also approach men is accomplished by the cunning of the devil, at times by conjuration or attraction, and frequently as a penalty for sins. Therefore he who would abide in familiarity with celestial intelligences should take pains to avoid every serious sin. He should diligently pray for the protection of God to vanquish the impediments and schemes of Diabolus, and God will ordain that the devil himself shall work to the direct profit of the worker in magic. Subject to Divine Providence, some spirits have power over pestilence and famine; some are destroyers of cities, like those of Sodom and Gomorrah; some are rulers over kingdoms, some guardians of provinces, some of a single person. The spirits are the ministers of the word of God, of the Church and its members, or they serve creatures in material things, sometimes to the salvation of soul and body, or, again, to the ruin of both. But nothing, good or bad, is done without knowledge, order, and administration.

It is unnecessary to follow the angelical host farther here, as it has been outlined elsewhere. Many preparations, however, are described by the author of the *Theosophia Pneumatica* for the successful evocation of these exalted beings. The magus must ponder during his period of initiation on the method of attaining the true knowledge of God, both by night and day. He must know the laws of the cosmos, and the practical secrets which may be gleaned from the study of the visible and invisible creatures of God. He must further know himself, and be able to distinguish between his mortal and immortal parts, and the several spheres to which they belong. Both in his mortal and immortal natures, he must strive to love God, to adore and to fear him in spirit and in truth. He must sedulously attempt to find out whether he is truly fitted for the practice of magic, and if so, to which branch he should turn his talents, experimenting in all to discover in which he is most naturally gifted. He must hold inviolate such secrets as are communicated to him by spirits, and he must accustom himself to their evocation. He must keep himself, however, from the least suspicion of diabolical magic, which has to do with Satan, and which is the perversion of the theurgic power concealed in the word of God.

When he has fulfilled these conditions, and before he proceeds to the practice of his art, he should devote a prefatory period to deep contemplation on the high business which he has voluntarily taken in hand, and must present himself before God with a pure heart, undefiled mouth and innocent hands. He must bathe frequently and wear clean garments, confess his sins and abstain from wine for the space of three days.

On the eve of operation, he must dine sparely at noon, and sup on bread and water, and on the day he has chosen for the invocation he must seek a retired and uncontaminated spot, entirely free from observation. After offering up prayer, he compels the spirit which he has chosen to appear; that is, he has passed into a condition when it is impossible that the spirit should remain invisible to him.

On the arrival of the angel, the desire of the magus is briefly communicated to him, and his answer is written down. More than three questions should not be asked, and the angel is then dismissed into his special sphere. Besides having converse with angels, the magus had also power over the spirits of the elements. These are described in the entry on **Elementary Spirits** and we are here concerned with the manner of their evocation.

To obtain power over the salamanders, for example, the *Comte de Gabalis* of the Abbé de Villars prescribed the following procedure: "If you would recover empire over the salamanders, purify and exalt the natural fire that is within you. Nothing is required for this purpose but the concentration of the Fire of the World by means of concave mirrors in a globe of glass. In that globe is formed the 'solary' powder, which being of itself purified from the mixture of other elements, and being prepared according to Art becomes in a very short time a sovereign process for the exaltation of the fire that is within you, and transmutes you into an igneous nature."

There is very little information extant to show in what manner the evocation of elementary spirits was undertaken, and no ritual has survived which will acquaint us with the method of communicating with them. In older writers, it is difficult to distinguish between angels and elementary spirits, the lower hierarchies of the elementary spirits were also frequently invoked by the black magician. It is probable that the lesser angels of the older magicians were the sylphs of **Paracelsus,** and the more modern professors of the art.

The nineteenth-century magus Éliphas **Lévi** provided a method for the interrogation and government of elementary spirits, but he did not specify its source, and it was merely fragmentary. "It is necessary," he stated, "in order to dominate these intelligences, to undergo the four trials of ancient initiation, and as these are unknown, their room must be supplied by similar tests. To approach the salamanders, therefore, one must expose himself in a burning house. To draw near the sylphs he must cross a precipice on a plank, or ascend a lofty mountain in a storm; and he who would win to the abode of the undines must plunge into a cascade or whirlpool. Thus power being acquired through courage and indomitable energy this fire, earth and water must be consecrated and exorcised."

The air is exorcised by the sufflation of the four cardinal points, the recitation of the prayer of the sylphs, and by the following formula: "The Spirit of God moved upon the water, and breathed into the nostrils of man the breath of life. Be Michael my leader, and be Sabtabiel my servant, in the name and by the virtue of light. Be the power of the word in my breath, and I will govern the spirits of this creature of Air, and by the will of my soul, I will restrain the steeds of the sun, and by the thought of my mind, and by the apple of my right eye. I exorcise thee O creature of Air, by the Petagrammaton, and in the name Tetragrammaton, wherein are steadfast will and well-directed faith. Amen. Sela. So be it."

Water is exorcised by the laying on of hands, by breathing and by speech, and by mixing sacred salt with a little of the ash which is left in an incense pan. The aspergillus is made of branches of vervain, periwinkle, sage, mint, ash, and basil, tied by a thread taken from a virgin's distaff, with a handle of hazelwood which has never borne fruit, and on which the characters of the seven spirits must be graven with the magic awl. The salt and ashes of the incense must be separately consecrated. The prayer of the undines should follow.

Fire is exorcised by casting salt, incense, white resin, camphor and sulphur therein, and by thrice pronouncing the three names of the genii of fire: Michael, Samael, and Anael, and then by reciting the prayer of the salamanders.

The Earth is exorcised by the sprinkling of water, by breathing, and by fire, and the prayer of the gnomes. Their signs are: the hieroglyphs of the Bull for the Gnomes who are commanded with the magic sword; of the Lion for the Salamanders, who are commanded with the forked rod, or *magic* trident; of the Eagle for the Sylphs, who are ruled by the holy pentacles; and, finally, of Aquarius for the Undines, who are evoked by the cup of libations. Their respective sovereigns are Gob for the Gnomes, Djin for the Salamanders, Paralda for the Sylphs, and Necksa for the Undines. These names, it will be noticed, are borrowed from folklore.

The "laying" of an elementary spirit is accomplished by its adjuration by air, water, fire, and earth, by breathing, sprinkling, the burning of perfumes, by tracing on the ground the Star of Solomon and the sacred Pentagram, which should be drawn either with ash of consecrated fire or with a reed soaked in various colors, mixed with pure loadstone. The Conjuration of the Four should then be repeated, the magus holding the pentacle of Solomon in his hand and taking up by turns the sword, rod and cup, this operation being preceded and terminated by the Kabalistic sign of the cross. In order to subjugate an elementary spirit, the magus must be himself free of their besetting sins, thus a changeful person cannot rule the sylphs, nor a fickle one the undines, an angry man the salamanders, or a covetous one the gnomes. (The formula for the evocation of spirits is given under **Necromancy**.) The white magician did not concern himself as a rule with such matters as the raising of demons, animal transformations and the like, his whole desire being the exaltation of his spiritual nature, and the questions put by him to the spirits he evoked were all directed to that end. However, the dividing line between white and black magic is extremely ambiguous and it seems likely that the entities evoked might be deceptive as to their nature. (See also **Ceremonial Magic; Elementary Spirits; Grimoire; Magic**)

Recommended reading:

De Villars, l'Abbe de Montfaucon. *Comte de Gabalis,* Paris, 1670; Old Bourne Press, London, 1913

Lévi, Éliphas. *The History of Magic,* William Rider, London, 1913 etc.

Lévi, Éliphas. *Transcendental Magic,* George Redway, London, 1896 etc.

Mathers, S. L. MacGregor. *The Greater Key of Solomon,* George Redway, London, 1888

Shah, Sayed Idries. *Oriental Magic,* Rider & Co., London, 1956

Shah, Sayed Idries. *The Secret Lore of Magic,* Frederick Muller, London, 1956

Waite, Arthur E. *The Book of Ceremonial Magic,* William Rider, London, 1911 etc.

Waite, Arthur E. *The Holy Kabbalah,* Williams & Norgate, London, 1929; University Books, 1960

Walker, D. P. *Spiritual and Demonic Magic; From Ficino to Camperella,* University of Notre Dame Press paperback, Pennsylvania, 1975

Meditation

A traditional spiritual exercise in both Eastern and Western mystical systems, usually involving asceticism, a static sitting position, a blocking of the mind from normal sensory stimuli, and a concentration upon divine thoughts and/or mystical centers in the human body.

In the Christian tradition, meditation was often enhanced by prolonged fasts and other physical mortification, in order to assert the supremacy of the soul over all physical and sensory demands. Certain well-defined stages of spiritual growth are recorded by saints and mystics, notably the awakening of the soul, contemplation, the dark night of the soul, illumination, spiritual ecstasy.

Eastern meditation traditions also record such stages, but the methods of meditation are more numerous and complex. In general, meditation was taught by a guru only to a properly qualified pupil who had already followed a pathway of *sadhana* or spiritual discipline which ensured purification at all levels. The various **Yoga** systems describe such spiritual disciplines in detail, with special emphasis on moral restraints and ethical observances. Meditation without such preliminary training was considered premature and dangerous.

The most generally known system is that of the sage Patanjali (ca. 200 B.C.) which taught that in order to experience true reality one must transcend the body and mind. In his *Yoga Sutras,* Patanjali outlined a program of physical exercises (to strengthen a meditation posture), breathing techniques (to purify the body), withdrawal of the senses, concentration, meditation, culminating in mystical experience. In this process, supernormal powers might be manifested, but were to be ignored. The ultimate goal of meditation was spiritual illumination transcending individuality and extending the consciousness beyond time, space and causality, but also interfusing it with the everyday duties and responsibilities of the individual. Thus it was not necessary for an illuminated individual to renounce the world, and there are stories in Hindu scriptures of kings and princes who did not forsake their mundane tasks after transcendental experience.

It is clear from consideration of the practices of many religions that meditation may be active or passive, depending upon the techniques employed and the degree of purification of the meditator. Fixed concentration upon one mental image, sound or center in the body is a passive mechanical technique which may bring relaxation, a sense of well-being and other mundane achievements, but is not in itself spiritual or transcendental in the traditional sense of the terms. The popular so-called "Transcendental Meditation" technique of **Maharishi Mahesh Yogi** appears to be of this order, hence criticism from traditionalists.

In active meditation systems, there has to be purification at all levels of the individual—physical, mental, emotional and spiritual, and the mind is exercised creatively before it can transcend its own activity. Those meditators who have attained stages of higher consciousness or mystical illumination testify that there is a gradual process of refinement, arising from the activity of a mysterious energy which Hindu mystics call **Kundalini,** which modifies the entire organism.

In any case, commonsense and the laws of cause and effect suggest that no mechanical habit of meditation could be expected to transform the consciousness without special efforts in other directions. However, the expectations and attitudes of the mass media consumer society have now permeated the realms of mysticism, and the inducement of high spiritual awareness by a "simple technique" or a "single gift of money" is very compelling to a generation reared on television commercials and the "instant mysticism" of drug states. Even the desire for spiritual experience often reflects mundane egoistic attitudes, and the transcending of the mundane individual ego is one of the first stages of traditional meditation systems. (See also **Drugs; Guru; Kundalini; Transcendental Meditation; Yoga**)

Recommended reading:

Augustine of Hippo (ed. Francis J. Sheed). *Confessions of St. Augustine,* Sheed, 1943 etc.

John of Ruysbroeck (transl. P. Synschenk). *Adornment of the Spiritual Marriage,* London, 1916

Krishna, Gopi. *Kundalini; the Evolutionary Energy in Man,* London, 1970; Shambala, 1970

Luk, Charles. *The Secrets of Chinese Meditation,* London, 1964; Rider paperback, 1969

Patanjali (transl. M. N. Dvidedi). *The Yoga-Sutras of Patanjali,* Theosophical Publishing House, Adyar, India, 1890, frequently reprinted

Underhill, Evelyn. *Mysticism; a Study in the Nature and Development of Man's Spiritual Consciousness,* London, 1911, frequently reprinted

Medium

Throughout the history of **Spiritualism,** a special place has been occupied by the medium, as an individual qualified in some special manner to form a link between the dead and the living. Through the medium, the spirits of the departed may communicate with their friends still on earth, either by making use of the material organism of the medium ("automatic phenomena") or by producing in the physical world certain manifestations which cannot be explained by known physical laws.

The essential qualification of a medium is an abnormal sensitiveness, which enables him or her to be readily "controlled" by disembodied spirits. Mediums are sometimes also known as "sensitives" or "psychics," although these terms are normally applicable to psychically gifted individuals who are not controlled by spirits of the dead.

There is some doubt as to whether mediumship is an inherent faculty, or whether it may be acquired, and among some Spiritualists at least, the belief is held that all individuals are mediums, although in varying degrees, and consequently that all are in communication with spirits, from whom proceeds what we call "inspiration." Those who are ordinarily designated "mediums" are but gifted with the common faculty in a higher degree than their fellows.

Mediumship, like all the central doctrines of Spiritualism, dates back to very early times. Demoniac **possession** affords an excellent instance, so also does **witchcraft,** while the *somnambule* of the Mesmerists was comparable with the modern psychic or medium. In its usual application, however, the term medium is used only of those sensitives who belong to the modern Spiritualist movement, which had its origin in America in 1848 (see **Fox Sisters**). In this sense, then, Mrs. Fox and her daughters, the heroines of the **Rochester Rappings,** were the earliest mediums. The phenomena of their seances consisted mainly of knockings, by means of which messages were conveyed from the spirits to the sitters.

Other mediums rapidly sprang up, first in America, and later in Britain and the Continent. Their mediumship was of two kinds—"physical" and "automatic." These phases were to be found either separately or combined in one person, as in the case of the Rev. Stainton **Moses.** Indeed, it was practically impossible to find a **trance** speaker who did not at one time or another practice the physical manifestations, until the time of Mrs. **Piper,** whose phenomena were purely subjective.

The early rappings speedily developed into more elaborate manifestations. For a few years an epidemic of **table-turning** caused widespread excitement, and the motions of the table became a favorite means of communicating with the spirits. The playing of musical instruments without visible agency was a form of manifestation which received the attention of mediums from an early date, as also the bringing into the seance room of "apports" of fruit, flowers, perfume, and all manner of portable property. Darkness was found to facilitate the spirit-manifestations, and as there are certain physical processes (such as those in photography) to which darkness is essential, no logical objection could be offered to the dimness of the seance room.

The members of the circle were generally seated round a table, holding each other's hands, and they were often enjoined to sing or talk pending the manifestation of a spirit. All this, although offering grounds of suspicion to the incredulous, was plausibly explained by the Spiritualists.

As time went on, and the demand for physical manifestations increased, these became more daring and more varied. The moving of objects without contact, the **levitation** of heavy furniture and of medium or sitters, the **elongation** of the human body, the **fire ordeal,** were all practiced by the medium D. D. **Home.** At the public performances of the **Davenport Brothers** musical instruments were played and moved about the room, and

objects moved without being touched, while the brothers were bound hand and foot in a small cabinet. (However, the Davenport Brothers did not claim to be mediums and may have been simply skilled stage performers.) The **slate-writing** of "Dr." Henry **Slade** and William **Eglinton** had a considerable vogue. The tying of knots in endless cords, the passage of **matter** through matter were typical physical phenomena of the mediumistic circle. The crowning achievement, however, was the **materialization** of the spirit-form. Quite early in the history of Spiritualism, hands were materialized, then faces, and finally the complete form of the spirit "control." Thereafter the materialized spirits allowed themselves to be touched, and even held conversations with the sitters. Further proof of the actuality of the spirit "control" was offered by **spirit photography.**

To those for whom Spiritualism was a religion, however, the most important part of the mediumistic performances was the trance-utterances and the like which come under the heading of "automatic," or psychological phenomena (see **Automatic Speaking** and **Automatic Writing**). These dealt largely with the conditions of life on the other side of the grave, although in style they often tended to be verbose and vague. Spirit drawings were sometimes amazingly impressive, at other times nondescript (see **Automatic Drawing and Painting**). **Clairvoyance** and **crystal vision** were included in the psychological phenomena, and so also are the pseudo-prophetic utterances of mediums, and the speaking in unknown **tongues.**

According to the Spiritualist hypothesis already referred to, that "all individuals are mediums," it would be necessary to class inspiration, not only the inspiration of genius, but all good or evil impulses as spiritual phenomena, and that in turn suggests that the everyday life of the normal individual is to some extent directed by spirit "controls." And therein lies the responsibility of mediumship, for the medium who desires to be controlled by pure spirits from the higher spheres should live a well-conducted and principled life. Misuse of the divine gift of mediumship carries with it its own punishment, for the medium becomes the sport of base human spirits and **elementals,** his or her will is sapped, and the whole being degraded. Likewise the medium must be wary of giving up individual personality to the first spirit who comes by for the low and earthbound spirits have least difficulty in communicating with the living, having still more affinity with the things of the earth than with those of the spirit.

Great Mediums of the Past

Of the physical mediums, perhaps the most successful was Daniel Dunglas **Home** (1833–1886), who claimed to be of Scottish birth. He went to America at an early age, and it was there that his mediumistic powers were first developed, although not until he came to Britain in 1855 did he rise to fame. It is worthy of note that Home was never detected in **fraud** (as were many physical mediums at one time or another) although his demonstrations were similar in kind to those of other mediums. This may be due in part to the fact that he did not act as a professional medium. Again, all who came into contact with him were impressed by his simple manners, and frank and affectionate disposition, so that he possessed the most valuable asset of a medium—the ability to inspire confidence in his sitters.

The **Davenport Brothers,** although widely popular in their time, were of a quite different nature. Their performance consisted of allowing themselves to be securely bound in a cabinet by the sitters, and while thus handicapped producing the usual mediumistic phenomena. The Davenports were claimed to be mere conjurers however, and when the stage magicians Maskelyne and Cook successfully imitated their feats, the Davenports lost credibility.

Slate-writing, which proved one of the most widely-accepted forms of psychic phenomena, had as its principal exponents Henry **Slade** and William **Eglinton.** The best argument which can be advanced against their feats is to be found in the pseudo-seances of S. J. **Davey,** given in the interests of the **Society for Psychical Research,** London. Mr. Davey's slate-writing exhibitions were so much like those of the professional mediums that some Spiritualists refused to believe that he was conjuring, and hailed him as a renegade medium!

Automatic drawing was principally represented by David **Duguid,** a Scottish medium who attained considerable success in that line.

Prominent **trance** speakers and writers were **Duguid,** J. J. **Morse,** Mrs. Hardinge **Britten,** and Mrs. Cora L. V. Tappan-**Richmond.**

One of the best-known and most respected of private mediums was the Rev. Stainton **Moses** (1839–92), a clergyman and schoolmaster, whose normal life was beyond reproach. He produced both automatic and physical manifestations, the former including the writing of a work *Spirit Teachings* (1894) dictated from time to time by his spirit controls, while the latter comprised levitations, lights and apports. His position, character, and education gave to his support of Spiritualism a stability of considerable value.

It is to later mediums, however, that we must look for proof worthy of scientific consideration, and of these the most important were Eusapia **Palladino** and Mrs. **Piper.** Eusapia Palladino, an Italian medium, was born in 1854, and for a good many years had acted as medium for scientific investigators. In 1892, seances were held at Milan, at which were present Professors Schiaparelli, **Brofferio, Lombroso, Richet,** and others. In 1894 Professor Richet conducted some experiments with Eusapia at his house in the Ile Roubaud, to which he invited Professor **Lodge,** F. W. H. **Myers,** and Dr. **Ochorowicz.** The phenomena occurring in Eusapia's presence were the ordinary manifestations of the mediumistic seance, but their interest lay in the fact that all the distinguished investigators professed themselves satisfied that the medium, with her hands, head, and feet controlled by the sitters, could not of herself produce the phenomena. Credible witnesses asserted that Eusapia possessed the ability to project psychic limbs from her person. Professor Lodge and F. W. H. Myers were disposed to look for a new force **(ectenic force)** emanating from the medium. In 1895, however, some seances with Eusapia were held at the house of F. W. H. Myers at Cambridge, England, where it became apparent that she habitually freed a hand or a foot—in short, habitually resorted to fraud if not properly controlled. Yet even these exposures were not conclusive, for in 1898, after a further series of experiments, Myers and Professors Lodge and Richet once more

declared their belief in the genuineness of this medium's phenomena.

Mrs. Leonore E. **Piper,** the Boston medium whose trance utterances and writings contain some of the best evidence forthcoming for the truth of Spiritualism, first fell into a spontaneous trance in 1884, and in the following year was observed by Professor William **James** of Harvard. Thereafter her case was carefully studied by the **Society for Psychical Research,** London. Her first important **control** was a French physician "Dr. Phinuit," who was probably a fiction, but in 1892 she was controlled by "George Pelham," a young author who had died in February of that year. So complete was her impersonation of Pelham that more than thirty of his friends claimed to recognize him, and so well did he establish his identity by the mention of many private matters known only to himself and a few of his friends, that the hypothesis of spirit-control was almost inevitable. In 1896, "George Pelham" gave place to "Imperator," "Rector," and other spirits, who had formerly controlled the Rev. Stainton **Moses.** From that time, and especially after 1900, the interest of the sittings declined, and they offered less material for the investigator.

Another automatic medium, Hélène **Smith,** came under the observation of Professor Theodor **Flournoy.** Hélène's trance utterances were spoken in the **"Martian language,"** a variant of the "unknown tongue" of the early ecstatics, and she claimed to be a reincarnation of Marie Antoinette and a Hindu princess.

Healing Mediums

The diagnosis and cure of disease have been extensively practiced by Spiritualist mediums, following in the path of the older somnambules and magnetic subjects. These latter not only used to trace the progress of diseases, but also to diagnose and to prescribe a mode of treatment. At the outset it was not prescribed for the diseases of those with whom they were in *rapport,* and likewise the medium, having established *rapport* between his control and the patient, was influenced to prescribe a mode of treatment. It was not considered proper for the healing medium to accept any remuneration for his services, but later healers usually expected a fee. It is true that healing mediums, like Christian Scientists, mesmerists, magnetists, and others, effected a considerable proportion of *bona fide* cures, but whether by spirit influence or suggestion is a point on which there is too much diversity of opinion for discussion here (see Psychic **Healing**). It is claimed for many mediums that they have cured diseases of long standing which were pronounced incurable—heart disease, consumption, cancers, paralysis, and many more. Some also have been credited with the power to heal instantaneously, as did the **Curé d'Ars** and other miraculous healers. The marvelous potency of the waters at **Lourdes** is considered to be the gift of discarnate beings, having been in the first instance revealed to a child by her spirit **guide,** in the form of a white angel (see **Healing by Faith**).

Spiritualist Views of Mediumship

Of the various theories advanced to explain the mediumistic manifestations, the most important is the Spiritualist explanation, which claims that the phenomena are produced by the spirits of the dead acting on the sensitive organism of the medium. The evidence for such a theory, although some investigators of the highest distinction have found it satisfactory, is nevertheless generally considered to be inconclusive. Although conscious **fraud** is no longer considered to cover the whole ground, yet plays a definite part in the phenomena of both "physical" and trance mediums, it has been shown that some of the latter frequently collect through private inquiry information about possible sitters, which is later retailed by the "controls." The explanation of some Spiritualists of these lapses into fraud is that they are instigated by the spirits themselves, but this is clearly untenable in the majority of cases. However, it does not seem impossible that a genuine medium might have resort to fraud during a temporary failure of psychic powers.

Automatism covers a still wider field. That automatic utterances, writing, drawing, etc., may be quite involuntary, and without the sphere of the medium's normal consciousness, is no longer to be doubted. The psychological phenomena may be met with in small children, and in private mediums whose good faith is beyond question, and the state is recognized as being allied to **hypnotism** and hysteria. Besides automatism and fraud, there are some other factors to be considered.

Some deception may be practiced by sitters as well as by the medium. It has been said that the ability to inspire confidence in sitters is essential to a successful medium, and if at the same time the sitters be predisposed to believe in the paranormal nature of the manifestations, it is easy to imagine a lessening of the attention and observation so necessary to the investigator.

The impossibility of continued observation for even a short period is a fact that can be proved by experiment. Memory defects and proneness to exaggeration are also accountable for many of the claimed marvels of the seance room, and possible **hallucination** must be considered. When the medium is in a trance, with its accompanying hyperaesthesia, unconscious suggestion on the part of the sitters might offer a rational explanation of so-called "clairvoyance."

But when all these factors are removed, the basic reality of mediumship still remains. In the case of Mrs. Piper, for example, the least that can be said for her trance utterances is that they were telepathic, that she gathered information from the minds of her sitters, or through them from other living minds. To many investigators, however, they presented definite proof of spirit communication. To meet such instances, F. W. H. Myers formulated his doctrine of transcendental faculties, crediting the medium with **clairvoyance** and **prevision.** But no really conclusive test has ever been complied with.

Psychical researchers have left sealed letters, whose contents are known only to themselves, instructing that after their deaths the letters be submitted to a medium; but the evidence of posthumous communication of such messages is not totally unassailable. Claimed instances still remain controversial. Again, in the case of Eusapia **Palladino,** F. W. H. Myers, Sir Oliver Lodge and others have inclined to the belief in a force emanating from the medium himself or herself by which the physical manifestations are produced. Here also, the evidence cannot be considered conclusive. Skilled and scientific investigators have from time to time been deceived by what has actually proved to be sleight of hand, and in fact the only

trustworthy evidence possible would be that of automatic records.

At the same time, the testimony of such distinguished scientists as Professor Charles **Richet,** Sir Oliver **Lodge** and others makes it evident that judgment must not be hastily pronounced on the medium, but rather that an earnest endeavor be made to solve the problems in that connection.

Psychical Researchers and Mediumship

Dr. Joseph **Maxwell** defined a medium as "a person in the presence of whom psychical phenomena can be observed." Dr. Gustav **Geley**'s definition was "one whose constituent elements—mental, dynamic and material—are capable of being momentarily decentralised," an intermediary for communication between the material and spirit world. In view of this definition, F. W. H. **Myers** called the word medium "a barbarous and question-begging term" as many mediumistic communications were nothing but subconscious revelation and suggested the use of the word "automatist." By others the word "psychic" was proposed, while Prof. Pierre Janet in *L'Automatisme Psychologique* (1889) termed mediums *les individus suggestibles*—persons controlled by an idea or suggestion either self-originated or coming from without, from an unseen source.

Prof. **Lombroso** maintained that there was a close relationship between the phenomena of mediumship and hysteria. Professor **Richet** voiced a warning in saying: "Unless we assign an unwarrantable extension to this morbid state it does not seem favourable to the phenomena." He believed that "mediums are more or less neuropaths, liable to headaches, insomnia and dyspepsia. The facility with which their consciousness suffers dissociation indicates a certain mental instability and their responsibility while in a state of trance is diminished."

The same opinion was expressed slightly more circumstantially, by psychical researcher Frank **Podmore** as follows: "Physiologically speaking, the medium is a person of unstable nervous equilibrium, in whom the control normally exercised by the higher brain centres is liable, on slight provocation, to be abrogated, leaving the organism, as in dream or somnambulism to the guidance of impulses which in a state of unimpaired consciousness would have been suppressed before they could have resulted in action."

Dr. Joseph **Maxwell** advised caution. He admitted that a certain impressionability—or nervous instability—was a favorable condition for the effervescence of mediumnity. But he stressed that the term "nervous instability" was not meant in an ill sense. His best experiments were made with people who were not in any way hysterical; neurasthenics generally gave no result whatever. Nor did "instability" mean want of equilibrium. Many mediums he had known had extremely well-balanced minds from the mental and nervous point of view. Their nervous system was even superior to the average. It was a state such as appears in nervous hypertension. The mediums, perhaps, were precursors, possessing faculties which are abnormal today, but which might become normal in the future.

"There are four chief types of temperament," wrote Dr. Charles **Lancelin,** "nervous, bilious, lymphatic and sanguine. Of these, the nervous temperament is the best suited for psychic experiments of all kinds; the bilious is the most receptive; the sanguine is liable to hallucinations, both subjective and objective; while the lymphatic is the least suitable of all, from every point of view. Of course, one's temperament is usually a compound of all of these, which are rarely found in their ideal state; but the predominantly nervous temperament is the one best suited for this test."

What Mediumship Is and What It Is Not

Agreement is now nearly general that mediumship is not pathological. It is not a development of certain abnormal states like hysteria. As **Myers** remarked, the confusion which is noticeable on the point is the result of the observation that supernormal phenomena use the same channels for manifestation as the abnormal phenomena. The abnormal phenomena are degenerative, the phenomena of mediumship are developmental, they show the promise of powers as yet unknown whereas the abnormal phenomena (like hysteria or epilepsy) show the degeneration of powers already acquired.

Prof. **Flournoy,** after his exhaustive study of the mediumship of Mlle. Hélène **Smith** came to the same conclusion. He stated: "It is far from being demonstrated that mediumship is a pathological phenomenon. It is abnormal, no doubt, in the sense of being rare, exceptional; but rarity is not morbidity. The few years during which these phenomena have been seriously and scientifically studied have not been enough to allow us to pronounce on their true nature. It is interesting to note that in the countries where these studies have been pushed the furthest, in England and America, the dominant view among the savants who have gone deepest into the matter is not at all unfavourable to mediumship; and that, far from regarding it as a special case of hysteria, they see in it a faculty superior, advantageous and healthy, but that hysteria is a form of degeneracy, a pathological parody, a morbid caricature."

Dr. Guiseppe Venzano, an Italian psychical researcher, was similarly emphatic: "Mediumship only represents a temporary deviation from the normal psychic state, and absolutely excludes the idea of morbidity; it is even proved that the slightest alteration of a pathological nature is sufficient to diminish or arrest the mediumistic powers."

Indeed, as Prof. **Flournoy** discovered, the conditions for the successful exercise of mediumistic powers are the same as for the voluntary exercise of any other power—a state of good health, nervous equilibrium, calm, absence of care, good humor, and sympathetic surroundings.

Outwardly there is no sign to disclose mediumistic powers. Dr. J. Maxwell stated that he observed tiny spots in the iris of the eyes of all mediums he came in contact with. They were generally black round marks, bearing a vague resemblance to a cat's head, a bird's head, cat's paws, etc. Sometimes letters appear to be traced on the iris. He knew a medium in whose left eye the letter "M" was very clearly and distinctly marked. Nevertheless he did not affirm that there was any connection between these iris spots and the mediumistic faculties. His observations, which yet await confirmation, recall medieval assertions about tell-tale spots in the eyes of sorcerers.

In many cases, mediumship can be traced as a hereditary gift. If the heredity is not direct it is to be found in ancestors or collaterals and, according to Dr. **Geley,** it is

conditioned by a tendency to decentralization of the constituent psychological factors of the medium. Mother Shipton, supposed to have been a sixteenth-century clairvoyant and prophet, was said to have been the daughter of a witch, but she may have been entirely a legendary figure. An ancestress of the **Eddy Brothers,** nineteenth-century American mediums, was sentenced to the pyre in Harlem. The **Fox Sisters** had visionary forebears. The great medium D. D. **Home** was a descendant on his mother's side of a Scotch Highland family. The medium Franek **Kluski** inherited his gifts from his father.

In the absence of heredity, physical defects or a serious illness may be the potential cause of mediumistic development. It is (as Conan Doyle put it) as if the bodily weakness causes what may be described as a dislocation of the soul, so that it is more detached and capable of independent action. Eusapia **Palladino** had a peculiar depression of her parietal bone caused by an accident in childhood. Mrs. **Piper**'s mediumship developed after two internal operations, and "Imperator," in an automatic script of the Rev. Stainton **Moses,** said: "The tempering effect of a bodily illness has been in all your life an engine of great power with us." In the case of Mary **Jobson,** Mollie **Fancher,** Lurrency Vennum (The **"Watseka Wonder"**) and Vincent **Turvey,** prolonged physical agony was the price of their psychic gifts.

With regard to the contention that everyone is a potential medium, H. Dennis **Bradley** wrote in his book *The Wisdom of the Gods* (1925): "Mediumship, even in the most advanced and powerful stage extant, is relatively a mere incoherent fluttering towards the knowledge we may gain in the future. In fifty years from now the few great mediums of to-day will be relegated to the position of the man who first risked the drop from the first parachute."

This prophecy was too enthusiastic and has not been fulfilled so far, and with the possible exceptions of **metalbending** and **psychic surgery,** there is no new mediumistic manifestation which has not been recorded in ages past in similar, or even more marvelous volume than at present. Nor is it likely that the development of the gift simply depends on willingness to experiment. According to an automatic script of Stainton **Moses:** "the mediumistic peculiarity is one of the spirit solely, and not of body. The gift is perpetuated even after the death of the earth body. Those who on earth have been mediums retain the gift and use it with us. They are the most frequent visitors to your world."

Mediumship is a delicate gift. Its voluntary development requires great care and understanding. According to Barbara McKenzie (*Light,* March 18, 1932), who had many years of unparalleled experience at the **British College of Psychic Science,** the production and ripening of physical gifts "involves a lengthy period of homely, warm, appreciative incubation . . . which is found at its best in a family or in a very intimate home circle, in which a continuity of conditions and a warm personal and even reverent interest is assured."

Even after the attainment of a *settled psychic constitution,* "the transplantation of the medium from the home circle to public work, or to a colder scientific group, is attended with risk to the gift, and by far the best way, when it is possible, is for the scientist to join the home group as Dr.

Crawford did and try to stiffen up conditions there. . . . It would seem that the imposition of so-called test conditions, of open discussion, of reports and publication of these, and the mixed mental conditions of sitters holding divers views as against the homogeneity of the home circle, awakens the mentality and egotistic nature of the medium to an excessive degree, and endangers the necessary passivity, with the result that phenomena which had been pure and regular become mixed and irregular."

As great an authority as Sir Oliver **Lodge** stated that the medium should be treated "as a delicate piece of apparatus wherewith we are making an investigation. The medium is an instrument whose ways and idiosyncrasies must be learnt, and to a certain extent humoured, just as one studies and humours the ways of some much less delicate piece of physical apparatus turned out by a skilled instrument maker."

There is a great difference between Oriental and Occidental methods of development. The **Yoga** system is the most conspicuous among the Oriental methods. It is also highly complicated. Dr. Hereward **Carrington**'s *Higher Psychical Development* (1920) presented the system in a simple and lucid way. It must be stressed, however, that the prime aim of Yoga practice is spiritual development, and psychic faculties are regarded as side effects which should be ignored as obstacles to spiritual evolution. For a discussion of matter, see the various translations of *The Yoga-Sutras of Patanjali,* a standard text of Yoga philosophy.

Age, Race, Sex and Influence on Health and Mental Powers

Inherited mediumship usually appears spontaneously and early in life, like artistic gifts. The five-month-old son of Mrs. Kate Fox-Jencken wrote automatically. **Raps** occurred on his pillow and on the iron railing of his bedstead almost every day. The seven-month-old infant of Mrs. Margaretta Cooper (see LaRoy **Sunderland**) gave communications through raps. Alexander **Aksakof,** in his book *Animisme et Spiritism* (1906), recorded many instances of infantile mediumship. The child Alward moved tables that were too heavy for her normal strength. The nephew of Seymour wrote automatically when nine days old.

In Eugène Bonnemère's *Histoire des Camisara* (1869) and in Louis Figuier's *Histoire du Merveilleux* (4 vols., 1886–89) many cases were quoted of Camisard babies of 14–15 months of age and of infants who preached in French in the purest diction. During the persecution of the Huguenots, these babes were confined to prison in numbers as they fell into ecstasy and the psychic contagion spread to Catholic children as well.

Nationality has no influence. The fact that three Polish mediums of Warsaw specialized in animal materializations simply points to a contagion of ideas, or a spirit of emulation, resulting in a special development.

Sex, however, appears to have a mysterious relationship to mediumship. The percentage of female mediums is greater than males. The mediumship of **"Eva C."** and Willie **Schneider** was accompanied by abnormal sex phenomena.

The age of puberty seems to have a peculiar significance. In old chronicles, pure children were mentioned as the best subjects for **crystal reading. Poltergeist** cases mostly occur in the presence of young girls and boys between the age of twelve to sixteen.

Dr. Hereward **Carrington** read a paper on the sexual aspect of mediumship before the First International Congress for Psychical Research in Copenhagen in 1921 and pointed out the possibility that the sexual energies which are blossoming into maturity within the body may, instead of taking their normal course, be somehow turned into another channel and externalized beyond the limits of the body, producing the manifestations in question. He conjectured: "There may be a definite connection between sex and psychical phenomena; and this seems to be borne out by three or four analogies. First, recent physiological researches as to the activities of the ductless glands and particularly the sex glands which have shown the enormous influence which these glands have upon the physical and even upon the psychic life. Second, the observation made in the cases of Kathleen Goligher and Eva C. which show that the plasma which is materialised, frequently issues from the genitals. Third, the clinical observations of Lombroso, Morselli and others upon Eusapia Palladino, which brought to light many recognised sexual stigmata. Fourth, the teachings and practices of the Yogis of India, who have written at great length upon the connection between sexual energies and the higher, ecstatic states, and of the conversion of the former into the latter, just as we find instances of 'sublimation' in modern Freudian psycho-analysis, and connection between sex and religion, here in the West."

In his book *The Story of Psychic Science* (1930) Dr. Carrington added: "These speculations have, I believe, been amply verified by certain recent investigations, wherein it has been shown that (in the case of a celebrated European medium) the production of a physical phenomenon of exceptional violence has been coincidental with a true orgasm. From many accounts it seems probable that the same was frequently true in the case of Eusapia Palladino, and was doubtless the case with other mediums also." He also pointed out that there is said to be a very close connection between the sexual energies and the mysterious **"Kundalini,"** aroused and brought into activity by **Yoga** practices.

After prolonged exercise of mediumship, intemperance often sets in. The reason seems to be a craving for stimulants following the exhaustion and depletion felt after the seance. Many mediums have been known who succumbed to the craving and died of delirium tremens.

The health of the medium otherwise remains unaffected. Recovery is usually very quick and unless too many sittings produce an excessive drain on the vitality of the medium the results, in many respects, may prove more beneficial than harmful. The spirit guides supply constant medical advice, take care of the medium's health to a greater extent than he or she could, and even prescribe treatment in case of illness. D. D. **Home** lived much longer with his weak lungs than could have been normally expected, and many mediums have attained an age of over eighty years in spite of frail health. The withdrawal of mediumship is often evidence of care for the health of the medium. Of course, the lapse may come for entirely different reasons. But recuperative rest was given as an explanation when the "Imperator" group announced on May 24, 1911 that Mrs. **Piper**'s trance mediumship would be temporarily withdrawn. The withdrawal lasted until August 8, 1915.

In the case of the Marquis **Centurione Scotto,** it was similarly announced on November 9, 1927: "He will fall ill if he continues thus. His nerves are shattered. By superior will his mediumistic faculty will be taken from him for a time." On another occasion, his mediumship was suspended to allow him to read, study and acquire more belief in the Spiritistic explanation which the Marquis did not quite accept.

Similar experiences befell the Rev. Stainton **Moses,** who revolted against his spirit guides when they tried to convince him, a Minister of the Anglican Church, that religion is eternal, whereas religious dogmas are but fleeting. His mediumship was temporarily removed. The powerful mediumship of D. D. **Home** also lapsed from time to time. As he suffered from a tubercular diathesis, this appears to have been the reason.

For the communicator, the medium is but a delicate machine. He is often referred to as such, sometimes in amusing terms. "White Hawk," the Red Indian control of the British professional clairvoyant medium Mrs. Kathleen **Barkell,** called her "my coat."

The mediums who are conscious during the production of the phenomena appear to suffer more than those in trance. The extrication of power from their organism seems a veritable trial for nerve and flesh. The phenomena in themselves are often equivalent to putting the body on the rack. This was known from ancient days. The Neoplatonist philosopher Iamblichus (died c. 330 A.D.) said on *Divination:* "Often at the moment of inspiration, or when the afflatus has subsided, a fiery appearance is seen—the entering or departing power. Those who are skilled in this wisdom, can tell by the character of this glory the rank of the divinity who has seized for the time the reins of the mystic's soul, and guides it as he will. Sometimes the body of the man is violently agitated, sometimes it is rigid and motionless. In some instances sweet music is heard, in others discordant and fearful sounds. The person of the subject has been known to dilate and tower to a superhuman height, in other cases it has been lifted into the air. Frequently not merely the ordinary exercise of reason, but sensation and animal life would appear to have been suspended; and the subject of the afflatus has not felt the application of fire, has been pierced with spits, cut with knives and has not been sensible of pain."

However, the disagreeable result of physical phenomena soon vanishes. A quarter of an hour's rest may be quite sufficient to dispel the effect. Many books have been published by those hostile to Spiritualism in the effort to show that mediumship leads to nervous derangement and insanity. Statistical investigations, however, have proved that the percentage of Spiritualists in mental asylums is very small. Dr. Eugen Crowell, author of *The Spirit World* (1879), examined the reports of 42 institutions. He found out of a total of 32,313 male patients, 215 were clergymen. The total number of male and female Spiritualists was 45. He estimated that the proportion of insane clergymen is one to every 159 inmates, while the proportion of insane Spiritualists is 1 to every 711.

Curiously enough mediumship, if suppressed, may manifest in symptoms of disease. Dr. C. D. Isenberg of Hamburg wrote of a case in *Light* (April 11, 1931) in which a patient of his suffered from sleeplessness and peculiar spasmodic attacks which generally occurred at night. The spasms seized the whole body; even the tongue was affected, blocking the throat and nearly suffocating her. When the patient mentioned that in her youth she tried table tilting, the doctor thought of the possibility that the mediumistic energy might block his patient's organism. A sitting was tried. The lady fell into trance and afterwards slept well for a few days. When the sleeplessness became worse again, the sitting was repeated and the results proved to be so beneficial that the chloral hydrate treatment previously employed was discontinued.

"She also tells us," wrote Camille **Flammarion** of Eusapia **Palladino,** "that when she has been a long time without holding a seance she is in a state of irritation, and feels the need of freeing herself of the psychic fluid which saturates her."

As regards a deleterious influence on the mind, Mrs. Osborne Leonard wrote in her book *My Life in Two Worlds* (1931): "I myself have not found that the development of psychic awareness detracts in any way from other so-called normal studies. I am a more successful gardener than I used to be, I am a much better cook; in many quite ordinary but extremely useful directions, I know I have improved; my health and nerves are under better control, therefore they are more to be relied upon than they ever were before I developed what many people think of as an abnormal or extraordinary power."

Dangers and Duration of Mediumship; Educational Benefits

Dangers, nevertheless, do exist but of another kind. According to Hereward **Carrington,** there is a true "terror of the dark" and that there are "principalities and powers" with which, in our ignorance we toy, without knowing or realising the frightful consequence which may result from this tampering with the unseen world. For that reason, he argued that a few men of well-balanced minds should be created lifelong investigators in this field; they should be looked upon as recognized authorities, "and their work accepted upon these problems just as any other physicist is accepted on a problem in physics."

The Rev. Stainton **Moses** stated: "I do not think it would be reasonable to say that it is wise and well for everyone to become acquainted with mediumship in his own proper person. It would not be honest in me to disguise the fact that he who meddles with this subject does so at his peril. I do not say that peril is anything that should always be avoided. In some cases it is not, but I do say that the development of mediumship is sometimes a very questionable benefit, as in others it is a very decided blessing."

The peril alluded to is the liability to the intrusion and control of undesirable spirits. As Stainton Moses further stated: "In developing mediumship one has to consider a question involving three serious points. Can you get into relation with a spirit who is wise enough and strong enough to protect and good enough for you to trust? If you do not, you are exposed to that recurrent danger which the old occultists used to describe as the struggle with the dweller on the threshold. It is true that everybody who crosses the threshold of this occult knowledge does unquestionably come into a new and strange land in which, if he has no guide, he is apt to lose his way."

The nervous equilibrium of the medium during the seance may be easily disturbed. "During the physical manifestations," wrote Hudson **Tuttle,** "I was in semi-trance, intensely sensitive and impressible. The least word, a jarring question, even when the intention was commendable, grated and rasped. Words convey an imperfect idea of this condition. It can only be compared with that physical state when a nerve is exposed."

Yet as regards the moral responsibility of the medium, Hudson Tuttle was emphatic in saying: "A medium cannot be controlled to do anything against his determined will, and the plea that he is compelled by spirits is no excuse for wrong-doing. The medium, like anyone else, knows right from wrong, and if the controlling spirit urges towards the wrong, yielding is as reprehensible as it would be to the promptings of passion or the appetite."

The duration of mediumship, discounting periodical lapses, is always uncertain. The mediumship of Emanuel **Swedenborg** developed at the age of fifty-five and lasted until his death. Stainton Moses maintained his powers for eleven years only. The daughter of Dr. Segard, a friend of Prof. Charles **Richet,** showed remarkable telekinetic phenomena at the age of twelve for three days. No such experience befell her for a quarter of a century afterwards.

The question of the medium's intelligence seems to have nothing to do with the psychic powers. But it may greatly influence the power of the communicators to convey clear ideas. The most stolid mediums may exhibit an extraordinary intelligence in trance. If their brain is educated the manifestation becomes still more marvelous.

The question naturally arises whether in the long run spirit influence imparts an education to rustic minds. The Rev. J. B. **Ferguson** answered the problem in the affirmative. "Supramundane influence," he recorded, "in the unfolding and education of mind has been a common and most interesting experience since my own attention was called to this subject. In the case of Mr. H. B. Champion we have a very remarkable instance. This gentleman, now distinguished for his comprehensiveness of thought on all subjects connected with mental and moral philosophy, and for unrivalled force and beauty of expression, was, to my personal knowledge, educated entirely under these influences. He was not educated even in ordinary branches, such as the orthography of his native tongue; was never at school but a few months in life. That which was at first the gift of a supramundane power is now his own; and unless his history were known he would be considered, as he often is, as a man of the highest accomplishments."

The Rev. J. B. Ferguson testified similarly regarding George W. Harrison, another medium, educated by the psychic power and concluded: "These gentlemen are today highly educated men. They speak and write our language with great precision and accuracy. They converse with men of the first attainments on all questions that engage cultivated thought. They are sought by men distinguished as professors in various departments of science; and where their history is not known, as it is to myself and to others, they are recognised at once as men of very high order of culture."

Such education undoubtedly depends on the quality of the spiritual influence which a medium attracts. The case of Andrew Jackson **Davis** and of Hudson **Tuttle** bear out the truth of the Rev. J. B. Ferguson's testimony and suggest that "men could matriculate at universities unknown to the physical senses." On the other hand, "John King," the somewhat rustic control of Eusapia **Palladino** could not impart much education to his medium in a lifetime and she was always referred to as an illiterate, uneducated woman.

The force involved in paranormal extension of awareness may not necessarily involve the spirit world. Pandit Gopi Krishna, in his book *The Biological Basis of Religion and Genius* (1972) proposes a psycho-physical mechanism traditionally aroused under the name of **Kundalini** in Yoga practice, resulting in higher consciousness.

Classification and the Source of Power

The classification of mediums is diverse. In general, they fall into two main groups: physical and mental mediums. The dividing line is not stable, as in the aspect of motor and sensory **automatism,** physical phenomena are always present. Physical mediumship as a rule means that there is no intellectual content behind the phenomena.

The distinction is useful, as the coexistence of intellectual and physical phenomena is indeed rare. These gifts either alternate or develop along lines of specification.

Mrs. **Piper** produced no physical phenomena. Mrs. **Leonard** but very few. **Kluski** was a universal medium. **Home** was mostly famous for his telekinetic manifestations. His trance phenomena were not studied at all. The skepticism of the age in which he lived impeded the chance of invaluable experiments. The Rev. Stainton **Moses** was in a somewhat reversed position. His powerful physical manifestations occurred in a small circle of friends. He was not subject to scientific experiments as regards these phenomena, but they were recorded and a still more valuable record, affording wonderful opportunity for study, was left behind in automatic scripts of his trance phenomena.

Very young mediums usually have all the potentialities of mediumship. But once the specification has taken place it has a barring effect. Miss C. E. **Wood** could never obtain **psychic photography.** Mrs. Etta **Wriedt** was unable to become a slate writer. Mrs. William Wilkinson (see **Automatic Drawing and Painting**) could draw and paint automatically, she could play the piano in trance but she could not produce automatic scripts. The organism itself may set certain limits. The controls of Stainton **Moses** produced a variety of peculiar musical sounds, but never more than a single note. They explained that the medium's organism was peculiarly unmusical.

Mediums who receive remuneration for their services are termed professional. In a way Samuel (in the *Bible*) seems to have been the first professional medium since Saul paid him the fourth part of a shekel of silver for the recovery of his father's lost asses through his seership. In the history of modern Spiritualism, professional mediums were slow to appear on the scene. In America in 1853, the *Spiritual Telegraph* hardly contained advertisements other than those of medical clairvoyants. In Britain, in the first ten years of Spiritualism, Mrs. Mary **Marshall** was alone in the professional field.

As a rule, most mediums require assistance for the production of their phenomena. The sitters of the circle are often drained of power. According to Dr. J. **Maxwell,** Eusapia **Palladino** could quickly discern people from whom she could easily draw the force she needed. "In the course of my first experiments with this medium, I found out this vampirism to my cost. One evening, at the close of a sitting at l'Agnelas, she was raised from the floor and carried on to the table with her chair. I was not seated beside her, but, without releasing her neighbours' hands she caught hold of mine while the phenomena was happening. I had cramp in the stomach—I cannot better define my sensation—and was almost overcome by exhaustion."

Dr. Justinus **Kerner** states that the Seeress of Prevorst (Frau Frederica **Hauffe**) ate little and confessed that she was nourished by the substance of her visitors, especially of those related to her by the ties of blood, their constitution being more sympathetic with her own. Visitors who passed some minutes near her often noticed upon retiring that they were weakened.

Some mediums draw more of the sitters' vitality than others. These mediums become less exhausted and consequently can sit more often. Mrs. Etta **Wriedt,** the direct voice medium, always left her sitters weak. Vice-Admiral Usborne Moore complained that he hardly could use his legs after a sitting.

In one instance in Mme. **d'Esperance**'s mediumship the draw on the sitter proved fatal. The phantom was grabbed, and an old lady (the mother of the spirit grabber), who apparently contributed most of the **ectoplasm** was so seriously injured that, after much suffering, she died from the consequences. (*Light,* November 21, 1903).

If the sitters of the circle are mediumistic themselves, the phenomena tend to increase in strength. Perhaps the strongest mediumistic circle ever recorded was the family of Jonathan **Koons,** of Ohio. From the seven-month-old infant to the eighteen-year-old Nahum, the eldest of the family, all the children were mediumistic, making, with the parents, a total of ten mediums. The same curious power was manifest in the family of John Tipple, who had a similar spirit house at a distance of two or three miles from that of Koons'. Ten children formed his "spirit battery."

In the years of 1859–60, D. D. **Home** often gave joint seances with the American medium and editor, J. R. M. **Squire.** Later he sometimes sat with Mrs. Jencken (see **Fox Sisters**) and Stainton **Moses.** Frank **Herne** and Charles **Williams** joined partnership in 1871; Miss C. E. **Wood** sat with Miss Fairlamb (Mrs. J. B. **Mellon**). The spirit photographer William **Hope** usually sat with Mrs. Buxton. Catherine **Berry** was known as a developing medium. According to a note signed by the editor of *Human Nature,* published in Catherine Berry's *Experiences in Spiritualism* (1876), "after sitting with Mrs. Berry a medium has more power to cause the phenomena at any other circle he may have to attend. Messrs. Herne and Williams have been known to visit this lady for the purpose of getting a supply of power when they had a special seance to give. Mrs. Berry is, therefore, successful in developing mediums, and has conferred the spirit voice manifestation, as well as other gifts, upon several mediums. In a public meeting, a speaker or trance medium is benefited by having Mrs. Berry sitting near him. These

facts have not been arrived at hastily, but after years of patient investigation."

Automatic writers have often joined forces. Frederick Bligh **Bond** and the automatists with whom he received the **Glastonbury scripts,** presented a case of dual mediumship. Similarly the "Oscar Wilde" scripts were produced through the mediumship of Mrs. Travers-Smith (Hester **Dowden**) and Mr. V. On the other hand, mediums may antagonize each other and nullify the power. Florence **Cook** always objected on this ground to sitting with her sister Katie.

Harm may come to the medium through the careless disregard of the conditions by the sitters, but sometimes also from the invisible operators. An evil operator may take possession of the medium's body or a well-meaning **control** may commit a mistake, just as an experimenting scientist might. Several instances of such blunders are recorded in the scripts of Stainton **Moses.** Thus, under the heading April 18, 1874, we read: "Prophet's light and two of Chom's, W.B.C. appeared again and touched my finger, the result being that the skin was broken and the joint swollen up. The pain gradually ceased, but the mark still remains after 48 hours."

Once an apport of a bronze candlestick struck a painful blow on the head of Stainton Moses. On July 26, 1874, urgent excited messages were rapped out, urging the sitters to look at the medium. A light was struck and he was discovered to have fallen down by the bookcase, doubled up in a most awkward position, and in a profound trance. So much power was drawn from his body that his legs could not support him and his hands could not hold anything when consciousness was restored.

Things often happen against the will of the medium, quite frequently against the will of the sitter. Mme. **d'Esperance** said that she always entered the seance room "with a feeling of anxiety mixed with wonder if I should ever come out again. As a rule I always felt that I was placing my life in the hands of the persons about to assist, and that they were even more ignorant of danger than myself."

Stainton Moses was very religious, but often found in his automatic scripts statements expressing atheistic and Satanic sentiments. In the seances of Eusapia **Palladino,** the spirits often broke the promises of the medium and shattered photographic plates or blocks of paraffin which bore complete imprints. Mediumship often develops from **Poltergeist** phenomena from a ferocious persecution to make the sensitive a medium against his or her will.

The mentality of the sitters appears to have an influence. "It is of no use to disguise or try to explain away the fact," wrote "Miss X" (Ada **Goodrich-Freer**) in *Essays in Psychical Research* (1899) "that, whatever may be the special mechanism which goes to make a 'sensitive,' the machinery will never work at its best under the observation of those avowedly sceptical or even critical." On the other hand, "The Davenports and Mr. Fay never fail," stated the Rev. J. B. **Ferguson,** "and their extraordinary powers seem at times even to increase with opposition; and in the degree in which timid or inconsiderate friends tremble for their success, and obstinate opponents seek their defeat, they rise to the occasion and give more powerful and triumphant evidences of truth."

Machine Mediumship

An early idea in the history of mediumship was the possibility of mechanical communication. The first confused thought of communicating with the spirit world through instruments occurred to John Murray **Spear** (see also **New Motor**). He arranged copper and zinc batteries in the form of an armor around the medium and expected phenomenal increase of mediumistic powers through the combination of mineral and vital electricity. The **Dynamistograph,** the **Vandermeulen Spirit Indicator,** the **Reflectograph** and **Communigraph** represent later developments. The most recent developments concern the **Electronic Voice Phenomenon** (see also **Raudive Voices**) and SPIRICOM.

Animal Mediumship

The unique case of a mediumistic cat was published by Aurelian Faifofer, Professor of Mathematics at Venice. It occurred in the experience of Dr. G. B. **Ermacora** of Padua, but he died without publishing it. The medium employed by him said in trance that Macacco (the cat of the medium's house) would be able to write with its paw by drawing it over a paper blackened with smoke; this would be accomplished during the night in a little room in which the animal slept. The medium advised Dr. Ermacora to make such arrangements that the genuineness of the phenomena could not afterwards be doubted.

Dr. Ermacora made a box of two compartments, one above the other, the lower storey having a zig-zag course of five passages. The cat entered through a hole in the first course and could only enter the upper compartment through another hole at the end of the fifth passage. Over this hole, a sheet of smoked paper was fixed, the whole box was fastened by two complicated English padlocks and the spirit was asked through the medium to make the imprisoned cat write the word Vittorio.

The next morning, the box was unlocked and the cat released. On the smoked paper, as if done by a cat's paw, the word "Vitt." was found. The size of the paper did not allow more writing. While the box was examined, Macacco jumped on to a chair and shook one of her forepaws, as though she wanted to write. Dr. Ermacora made about fifteen of these experiments. Before he arrived at a degree of certainty, the cat fell from the roof of a house into the street and was killed.

The **Elberfeld horses** were suspected of mediumistic powers. Capt. A. H. Trapman, in his book *The Dog; Man's Best Friend* (1929) voiced the strange conclusion that "it is easier for the spirits of the dead to communicate with the dog than with man, even when man is represented by the parents and sisters of the departed one."

Mediumistic Induction

It appears as if, similarly to electricity, mediumistic power can be generated by induction. In religious revivals a psychic contagion is noticeable. The transference of predictive power is frequent.

D. D. **Home** was the most famous medium for imparting his powers to others. Cases are on record in which he levitated others. Once he imparted the power of **elongation** to Miss Bertolacci, and he bestowed immunity to fire (see **Fire Immunity**) in a number of cases on his sitters. But there was a condition. The sitters had to have faith. "Now if you have sufficient faith let me place this coal in your hand," he said to Miss Douglas on April 3, 1869.

Miss Douglas first dreaded the test, then held out her hand. She was not the least burned and said that the red hot coal felt rather cold, like marble. Home took the coal and requested Miss Douglas to touch it; she placed her fingers near it but withdrew them immediately, saying that it burned her.

The spread of modern Spiritualism discloses the phenomenon of mediumistic induction. Those who sat with the **Fox sisters** usually discovered mediumistic abilities in themselves. Mrs. **Benedict** and Mrs. **Tamlin,** the two best early mediums, were developed through the gift of Kate Fox. A writer in the *New Haven Journal* in October, 1850, referred to knockings and other phenomena in seven different families in Bridgeport, forty different families in Rochester, in Auburn, in Syracuse, some two hundred in Ohio, in New Jersey, and places more distant, as well as in Hartford, Springfield, Charlestown, etc.

The most famous early investigators became mediums. Judge John W. **Edmonds,** Prof. Robert **Hare,** and William **Howitt,** all confessed to having received the gift. It is little known that in his last years the psychical researcher Dr. Richard **Hodgson** was in direct contact with the Imperator group. Sir Arthur Conan **Doyle** developed **automatic writing** and **direct voice** in his family. H. Dennis **Bradley** received the power of direct voice after his sittings with George **Valiantine.** The Marquis **Centurione Scotto** developed through the same instrumentality. Eusapia **Palladino** could transfer her powers by holding the sitter's hand. She made a stool follow the movements of Dr. Hereward **Carrington's** hand. Camille **Flammarion** noted: "I hold her legs with my left hand, spread out upon them; M. Sardou holds her left hand; she takes my right wrist in her right hand and says to me 'Strike in the direction of M. Sardou.' I do so three or four times. M. Sardou feels upon his body my blows tallying my gesture, with the difference of about a second between my notion and his sensation." (See also **Apports; Automatic Drawing & Painting; Automatic Speaking; Automatic Writing; Automatism; Communigraph; Control; Dynamistograph; Elberfeld Horses; Electronic Voice Phenomenon; Evidence; Fraud; Guide; Materialization; Psychic; Psychical Research; SPIRICOM; Spiritualism; Trance**)

Recommended reading:

Bayless, Raymond. *Voices From Beyond,* University Books, 1975

Bouissou, Michaël. *The Life of a Sensitive,* Sidgwick & Jackson, London, 1955

[Britten], Emma Hardinge. *Modern American Spiritualism,* London, 1870; University Books, 1970

Britten, Emma Hardinge. *Nineteenth Century Miracles,* London & Manchester, 1883

Carrington, Hereward. *Higher Psychical Development,* Dodd, Mead, 1924

Carrington, Hereward. *Your Psychic Powers and How to Develop Them,* American Universities Publishing Co., New York, 1920; Causeway, 1973

Chaney, Robert Galen. *Mediums and the Development of Mediumship,* Books for Libraries, Freeport, New York, 1972

Christopher, Milbourne. *Mediums, Mystics & the Occult,* Thomas Y. Crowell, 1975

Ellis, D. J. *The Mediumship of the Tape Recorder,* D. J. Ellis, Pulborough, U.K., 1978

Flint, Leslie. *Voices in the Dark; My Life As a Medium,* Macmillan, 1971

Garrett, Eileen J. *Adventures in the Supernormal; A Personal Memoir,* Paperback Library, New York, 1971

Garrett, Eileen J. *My Life As a Search for the Meaning of Mediumship,* Rider & Co., London, 1939; Arno Press, 1975

Gopi Krishna. *The Biological Basis of Religion and Genius,* Harper & Row, 1972

Home, D. D. *Incidents in My Life,* London, 1863; University Books, 1973

Leaf, Horace. *Psychology and the Development of Mediumship,* London, 1926

Leonard, Maurice. *Battling Bertha; The Biography of Bertha Harris,* Regency Press, London, 1975

Leonard, Maurice. *Medium; The Biography of Jessie Nason,* Regency Press, London, 1974

Leonard, Gladys Osborne. *My Life in Two Worlds,* Cassell, London, 1931

MacGregor, Helen & Margaret V. Underhill. *The Psychic Faculties & Their Unfoldment,* L.S.A. Publications, paperback, London, 1930

Manning, Matthew. *The Link; Matthew Manning's Own Story of His Extraordinary Psychic Gifts,* Corgi paperback, London, 1975; Holt, Rinehart & Winston, 1975

Northage, Ivy. *The Mechanics of Mediumship,* Spiritualist Association of Great Britain, paperback, London, 1973

Patanjali (transl. M. N. Dvivedi). *The Yoga-Sutras of Patanjali,* Theosophical Publishing House, Adyar, India, 1890 (frequently reprinted)

Piper, Alta. *The Life and Work of Mrs. Piper,* Kegan Paul, London, 1929

Podmore, Frank. *Modern Spiritualism,* 2 vols. London, 1902 (reissued under title *Mediums of the Nineteenth Century,* 2 vols., University Books, 1963)

Price, Harry & E. J. Dingwall. (ed.) *Revelations of a Spirit Medium,* Kegan Paul, London, 1922

Roberts, Estelle. *Fifty Years a Medium,* Corgi paperback, London, Avon Books, 1975

Salter, W. H. *Trance Mediumship; An Introductory Study of Mrs. Piper & Mrs. Leonard,* Society for Psychical Research, London, 1950

Smith, Susy. *Confessions of a Psychic,* Macmillan/Collier-Macmillan, London, 1971

Spraggett, Allen & Wm. V. Rauscher. *Arthur Ford, the Man Who Talked with the Dead,* New American Library, 1973

Stemman, Roy. *Medium Rare; The Psychic Life of Ena Twigg,* Spiritualist Association of Great Britain, paperback, London, 1971

Stokes, Doris (with Linda Dearsley). *Voices in My Ear; The Autobiography of a Medium,* Futura paperback, London, 1980

Tietze, Thomas R. *Margery,* Harper & Row, 1973 [deals with the controversial medium "Margery" (Mrs. Crandon)]

Tubby, Gertrude Ogden. *Psychics and Mediums,* Marshall Jones, Boston, 1935

Turvey, Vincent N. *The Beginnings of Seership,* Stead Publishing House, London, 1911; University Books, 1969

Wallis, E. W. & M. H. *A Guide to Mediumship and Spiritual Unfoldment,* 3 parts, London, 1903

Zymonidas, A. *The Problems of Mediumship,* Kegan Paul, London, 1920

Medium and Daybreak, The (Journal)

Spiritualist weekly, started in 1869 by James **Burns,** originally published under the title *The Medium,* later absorbing *The Daybreak,* a provincial paper, founded in 1867. For years it had the largest circulation of any weekly on Spiritualism. It was published until 1895, the year of the death of its founder.

Meehl, Paul E(verett) (1920–)

Professor of psychology who has written on parapsychology. Born January 3, 1920 at Minneapolis, Minnesota, he studied at University of Minnesota (B.A. summa cum laude 1941, Ph.D. 1945). In 1941 he married Alyce Roworth. From 1951 onwards he was professor of psychology at University of Minnesota, chairman of psychology department 1951–57, professor of clinical psychology, department of psychiatry at Medical School, University of Minnesota from 1951 onwards. He has also been in practice as a psychotherapist.

He was president of Midwestern Psychological Association in 1955, Winner of Distinguished Contributor Award, American Psychological Association, 1958, editor of Prentice-Hall series of publications on psychology; member of Committee on Psychology and Religion, Lutheran Church, Missouri Synod 1956–57, American Psychological Association, Minnesota Psychological Association, American Society for Psychical Research, American Psychological Association (president from 1961–62).

In addition to his various books and many articles on psychological subjects, he has also published: (with M. J. **Scriven**) 'Compatibility of Science and ESP' (*Science,* 123, 1956), (with H. R. Klann, K. H. Breimeter) *What, Then, Is Man?* (1958).

Meerloo, Joost A(braham) M(aurits) (1903–1976)

Psychiatrist, psychoanalyst and writer on parapsychology. Born March 14, 1903 at The Hague, Netherlands, he was educated at Leyden University (M.D. 1927) and Utrecht University (Ph.D. 1932). In 1948 he married Louisa Betty Duits. His appointments include: Psychiatric-neurologic consultant, Municipal Hospital, Voorburg and The Hague 1934–42, chief of Psychological Department, Netherlands Army 1943–45, High Commissioner for Welfare in the Netherlands 1945–46, Associate in psychiatry, Columbia University 1948–57, professor, political science, New School for Social Research, New York, N.Y. 1958 onwards, Associate professor of psychiatry, New York School of Psychiatry 1962 onwards.

He was a member of: Royal Society of Medicine, American Psychiatric Association, American Academy of Psychoanalysis, secretary of Schilder Society, honorary member of Tokyo Institute for Psychoanalysis, Albany Society for Psychosomatic Medicine. He was also a member of the American Society for Psychical Research, and corresponding member of the Dutch Society for Psychical Research.

He published over 300 articles on psychology, politics and literature. His writings on parapsychological subjects included: 'Telepathy as a Form of Archaic Communication' (*Psychiatric Quarterly,* vol. 23, 1949), 'Telepathy and Foreknowledge' (*Proceedings, First International Conference on Parapsychology,* Utrecht, 1953), 'The Biology of Time' (*Tomorrow,* Winter 1954), 'Man's Ecstatic Healing' (*Tijdschrift voor Parapsychologie,* vol. 27, 1959). His books included: *Patterns of Panic* (1950), *The Two Faces of Man* (1954), *The Rape of the Mind: The Psychology of Thought Control, Menticide and Brainwashing* (1956), *Dance Craze and the Sacred Dance* (1959), *Suicide and Mass Suicide* (1962), (with Edmund Bergler) *Justice and Injustice* (1963), *Hidden Communion* (1964), *Illness and Cure* (1964), *Transference and Trial Adaptation* (1965), *Unobtrusive Communication* (1965). He died November 17, 1976.

Meher Baba (1894–1969)

Eastern mystic, born Merwan S. Irani in Poona, India. His parents were Parsees, but he was strongly influenced by Sufi mysticism, although educated at a Christian high school. At the age of nineteen, he contacted Hazrat Babajan, an elderly Moslem woman saint, who kissed his forehead and induced divine consciousness and a state of ecstatic bliss. After that, he devoted his life to religious teaching, usually expressed in a rather erratic fashion, involving journeys with disciples which apparently led nowhere, or in searching out the eccentric and sometimes deranged wandering monks of India.

In 1921 he established an ashram devoted largely to philanthropic work. He had contact with the remarkable Hindu mystic **Sai Baba,** of whom the present-day **Satya Sai Baba** is claimed to be a reincarnation.

In 1925, Meher Baba entered upon a period of silence, conversing or giving lectures with an alphabet board. He often prophesied in this way that he would one day speak the One Word which would bring spiritualization and love to the world, but he died January 31, 1969 without utterance. However, his prophecy may have been symbolic, like his mysterious life itself, and devotees continue to share the intense affection of a Sufi kind which characterized his mission during his lifetime. He is regarded by many disciples as an *avatar* or descent of divine power.

Meier, C(arl) A(lfred) (1905–)

Swiss psychotherapist who has written on parapsychology. Born April 19, 1905 at Schaffhausen, Switzerland, he was educated at University of Paris Medical School, University of Venice, and University of Zurich Medical School (M.D.). In 1936 he married Johanna Fritzsche. He was assistant and director of laboratory research at the Burghölzli Psychiatric Clinic of Zurich University from 1930–36, professor of psychology at Swiss Federal Institute of Technology, Zurich, from 1949 onwards, in private practice in 1948, president of the C. G. Jung Institute, Zurich, from 1948–57, founder (in 1957) of the International Association for Analytical Psychology, general secretary of the International Society for Medical Psychotherapy from 1933–43, vice-president, Swiss Society for Practical Psychology from 1933–48, president, Psychological Club of Zurich from 1945–50.

Dr. Meier was editor of *Studien aus dem C. G. Jung Institute* (1949–57) and *Studien zu C. G. Jung's Psychologie* by Toni Wolff (1959), as well as author of *Jung and Analytical Psychology* (1959) and many articles on psychotherapy, Jungian analysis and other psychological topics. He has special interest in relationships between the unconscious and extrasensory perception.

His articles on parapsychology include: 'Jung's "Meaningful Coincidence" ' (*Tomorrow,* Spring 1954), 'C. G. Jung's Concept of Synchronicity' (*Proceedings, First International Conference of Parapsychological Studies,* 1955), 'Psychological Background of So-Called Spontaneous Phenomena' (*Proceedings, Conference on Spontaneous Phenomena,* 1957), 'Projection, Transference and Subject-Object Relation' (*Proceedings, International Symposium on Psychology and Parapsychology,* 1957).

Meisner (or Mesna), Lorentz (c. 1608)

Early alchemist, whose work is recorded in his tract *Gemma Gemmarum Alchimistarum; oder Erleuterung der Parabolischen und Philosophischen Schrifften Fratris Basilij, der zwölff Schlüssel, von dem Stein der vharalten Weisen, und desselben aufsdrücklichen und warhaften praeparation; Sampt etlichen seinen Particularen,* published Leipzig, 1608. This edition also includes a tract on the **Philosopher's Stone** by Conrad Schülern. (See also **Alchemy**)

Mellon, Mrs. J. B. (Annie Fairlamb) (c. 1930)

British **materialization** medium. Her first supernormal experience was at the age of nine, seeing her brother at sea in danger of drowning. Later physical powers manifested in a violent trembling of hand and arm. This was followed, in the family circle by **automatic writing** with lightning-like speed, by **clairvoyance** and **clairaudience.** With bandaged eyes she would fall into a trance and describe events happening at the time many miles away, events which were subsequently verified.

In 1873, as a young girl, together with Miss C. E. **Wood,** she was employed as an official medium of the Newcastle Spiritual Evidence Society. In 1875, with Miss C. E. Wood, she sat for Prof. Henry **Sidgwick** and F. W. H. **Myers** of the Society for Psychical Research at Cambridge, England. The seances, which were held under the strictest test conditions, produced excellent results but neither Prof. Sidgwick nor F. W. H. Myers chose to announce their observations in public.

In 1877 Alderman T. P. Barkas, of Newcastle, made successful experiments to obtain spirit molds (see **Plastics**). Unknown to Miss Fairlamb, he mixed magenta dye with the paraffin. The molds were found to be tinted with magenta, which proved that they were not smuggled in ready-made.

After a Continental tour, during which German investigators found her lose almost half of her bodily weight during materializations, Miss Fairlamb went to Australia. She married J. B. Mellon, of Sydney, but continued to give sittings at her own home. Dr. Charles W. MacCarthy, at whose residence Mrs. Mellon often sat, became convinced of the reality of the phenomena.

On October 12, 1894, a disastrous exposure took place in Mrs. Mellon's house. T. Shekleton Henry, another medium and pretended friend of Mrs. Mellon, grabbed "Cissie," the materialized spirit and found it to be the medium half undressed. The missing pieces of garment were found in the cabinet. Mrs. Mellon defended herself by saying that she seemed to shoot into the grabbed form and became absorbed. She was said to have suffered serious injury in consequence of the spirit grabbing, and after her recovery she resolved never to sit in the cabinet again but always before the curtain in full view of the sitters.

The story of the exposure is told by T. Shekleton Henry in *Spookland* (Sydney, 1894), to which an answer was returned by "Psyche" under the title *A Counterblast to Spookland or Glimpses of the Marvellous* (1895).

As late as 1931, Mrs. Mellon was still active as a medium. Mr. H. L. Williams, a retired magistrate from the Punjab, wrote to Harry Price (*Psychic Research,* June, 1931): "As regards her (Mrs. Mellon), Dr. Haworth, a well-known doctor of Port Darwin, has testified before me that at Melbourne, in the presence of leading and professional men, he saw many times a spot of mist on the carpet which rose into a column out of which stepped a completely embodied human being who was recognised . . ." Sir William Windeyer, Chief Judge, and Alfred Deaking, Prime Minister of Australia were, according to the letter, convinced that Mrs. Mellon was genuine.

Melton, J. Gordon

Pastor of the Emmanuel United Methodist Church in Evanston, Illinois, formerly national field representative for **Spiritual Frontiers Fellowship,** presently director of the **Institute for the Study of American Religion.** He was a graduate of Birmingham-Southern College (A.B. 1964), Garrett Theological Seminary (M. Div. 1968) and Northwestern University (Ph.D. 1975).

An authority on different religions and small religious, psychic/occult organizations, he has lectured throughout the U.S. and Canada. His publications include: *From Log Cabins to Steeples* (1972), *A Reader's Guide to the Church's Ministry of Healing* (1972), (with J. Geisendorfer) *A Directory of Religious Bodies in the United States* (1977), (with Dorothea Melton) *The Ways of Meditation: A Guide to Meditation, Contemplation & Prayer* (1978), *Encyclopedia of American Religions* (1978).

Melusina

The most famous of the fays or fairy creatures of medieval French legend. Being condemned to turn into a serpent from the waist downwards every Saturday, she made her husband, Count Raymond of Lusignan, promise never to come near her on a Saturday. This prohibition finally exciting his curiosity and suspicion, he hid himself and witnessed his wife's transformation.

Melusina was now compelled to quit her mortal husband and destined to wander about as a specter until the day of doom. She became The Banshee of Lusignan. It is said also that the count immured her in the dungeon of his castle. (See also **Fairies; Mermaids & Mermen**)

Melzer, Heinrich (1873- ?)

German **apport** medium of Dresden, successor of Frau Rothe, first seances recorded in *Die Uebersinnliche Welt* in November 1905. These were held in darkness, but the medium allowed himself to be fastened into a sack. Flowers and stones were apported in quantities. The operators were said to be Oriental entities: "Curadiasamy," a Hindu, who spoke with a foreign accent, "Lissipan," a young Indian Buddhist and "Amakai," a Chinaman. "Quirinus," who claimed to be a Roman Christian of the time of Diocletian and "Abraham Hirsch-

kron," a Jewish merchant from Mahren, were other picturesque **controls.**

By occupation Melzer was a small tobacconist. It is said that at one time he was an actor, which may account for his powers of declamation under control.

He visited the **British College of Psychic Science** in 1923 and in 1926. Owing to a significant development in his mediumship, he was able to sit in good white or red light. In 1923, he was examined before each seance and dressed in a one-piece linen suit, secured at wrist and ankles. The flowers arrived when the medium was in deep trance. He seemed to be able to observe them clairvoyantly before they appeared to the physical sight. Occasionally sitters, who knew nothing of this, spoke of seeing shadows of flowers in the air before they arrived.

Sometimes the medium seized upon the flowers and ate them voraciously, together with stalks and soil, often wounding his mouth by thorns on rose stalks. Returning to normal consciousness he blamed a particular control for the occurrence. The flowers seemed to arrive towards the medium and were not thrown out from him.

These phenomena were very satisfactory. The same could not be said of the stone apports. They were invariably very small. In the sittings of 1926, the doctor in charge slipped his hands at the back of the ears of the medium and discovered two small light colored stones affixed by flesh-colored sticking plaster. The medium's only attempt at excuse was that by that stage his power had gone and that he had been tempted by an undesirable control.

Such an exposure of fraud tends to discredit Melzer's phenomena. However, in his report in *Psychic Science,* (April, 1927) J. Hewat **McKenzie** remarked: "But there is a difference between stones of a quarter to half an inch in size, and flowers of 18 inches stalk length, with leaves and thorns. Twenty-five anemones—or a dozen roots of lilies of the valley, with soil attached, pure bells and delicate leaves—or violets appearing fresh and fragrant, after two and a half hours sitting—have all been received, when the medium's hands have been seen empty a second before, when no friends of his were in the sittings, and when no opportunity could have presented itself to conceal them that would not have resulted in broken stems and blossoms."

Men in Black

The mysterious and sinister visitors who are supposed to have silenced flying saucer investigator Albert K. **Bender,** described in the book *They Knew Too Much About Flying Saucers* by Gray Barker (1956; 1967). (See also **UFO**)

Meng-Koehler, Heinrich Otto (1887-)

Physician, professor of mental hygiene, author and writer on parapsychology. Born July 9, 1887 at Hohnhurst, Baden, Germany, he studied at University of Heidelberg (M.D. 1912), University of Leipzig, University of Würzburg. In 1929 he married Mathilde Koehler. He was director of the Institute of Psychoanalysis, Frankfurt, from 1928–33, professor of mental hygiene at University of Basel, Switzerland, 1945–55, professor emeritus from 1956 onwards, and psychoanalyst.

Dr. Meng-Koehler edited and contributed to important

works on Mental Hygiene and was author of *Psychohygiene* (Mental Hygiene, 1960). In the field of parapsychology, he took special interest in connections with psychoanalysis. He attended the International Conference on Parapsychological Studies held in Utrecht, Netherlands, in 1953 and the Conference on Unorthodox Healing at St. Paul de Vence, 1954. His articles on parapsychology included: 'Wunderheilungen' (Miracles of Healing) and 'Parapsychologie, Psychohygiene and Aerztliche Fortbildung' (Parapsychology, Mental Hygiene and Medical Training) published in *Hippokrates,* 1954.

Mental World (in Theosophy)

Formerly known as the Manas Plane. In the Theosophic scheme of things, this is the third lowest of the seven worlds. It is the world of thought into which man passes on the death of the **astral body,** and it is composed of the seven divisions of matter in common with the other worlds. It is observed that the mental world is the world of thought, but it is necessary to realize that it is the world of good thoughts only, for the base thoughts have all been purged away during the soul's stay in the **astral world.**

Depending on these thoughts is the power to perceive the mental world. The perfected individual would be free of the whole of it, but the ordinary individual in past imperfect experience, has gathered only a comparatively small amount of thought and is, therefore, unable to perceive more than a comparatively small part of surroundings. It follows from this that although the individual's bliss is inconceivably great, the sphere of action is very limited. This limitation, however, becomes less and less with the individual's abode there after each fresh incarnation.

In the Heaven world-division into which we awake after dying in the astral world, we find vast, unthought-of means of pursuing what has seemed to us good, art, science, philosophy and so forth. Here, all these come to a glorious fruition of which we can have no conception, and at last the time arrives when one casts aside the mental body and awakens in the casual body to the still greater bliss of the higher division of the mental world.

At this stage, one has done with the bodies which form mortal personality, and which form one's home in successive incarnations, and one is now truly whole, a spirit, immortal and unchangeable except for increasing development and evolution. Into this casual body is worked all that one has experienced in the physical, astral and mental bodies, and when one still finds that experience insufficient for one's needs, one descends again into grosser matter in order to learn yet more and more.

These concepts derive from the Hindu religious classification of three bodies or states of being: gross (or physical), subtle and causal (*sthula, sukshma* and *karana shariras*), surrounded by five sheaths *(koshas):* annamayakosha (food or physical sheath), *pranamayakosha* (subtle energy sheath), *manamayakosha* (mental sheath), *vijnanamayakosha* (wisdom sheath), *anandamayakosha* (bliss sheath of spiritual unity).

Mentalphysics

A spiritual development system founded in 1927 by British born Edwin John **Dingle.** It was incorporated as a religion in 1936, and embodies belief in the universality of divine manifestation. Membership covers U.S.A., Great Britain, Australia, France, Germany and India, and there is an Institute of Mentalphysics headquarters with buildings designed by architect Frank Lloyd Wright in Los Angeles.

The system of Mentalphysics is based on diet, *pranayama* (yoga breathing techniques), chanting, meditation and development of extrasensory perception. Address: Institute of Mentalphysics, P.O. Box 640, Yucca Valley, California 92284.

"Mentor"

One of the controls of the Rev. Stainton **Moses,** said to be Algazzali or Ghazali, Professor of Theology at Baghdad in the eleventh century, the greatest representative of the Arabian Philosophical School. His main duty was to manage the phenomena at the seances. He was very successful with lights and scents and brought many **apports.** In Book XVI of the spirit communications of Stainton Moses there is a story of "Mentor" carving heads on two shells in the dining room while dinner was going on; the sound of the process was heard. (See also William Stainton **Moses**)

Mephis (or Memphitis)

A fabled precious stone which, when bruised to powder and drunk in water, was said to cause insensibility to torture.

Mercury

Also popularly known as quicksilver. A metal which has been known for many centuries, and which has played an important part in the history of **alchemy.** In its refined state it forms a coherent, very mobile liquid. The early alchemists believed that nature formed all metals of mercury, and that it was a living and feminine principle. It went through many processes, and the metal evolved was pure or impure according to the locality of its production.

The mercury of the **Philosopher's Stone** needed to be a purified and revivified form of the ordinary metal. The Arabian alchemist **Geber** stated in his *Summa perfectionis:* "Mercury, taken as Nature produces it, is not our material or our physic, but it must be added to." (See also **Alchemy**)

Merlin

A legendary enchanter of Britain who dwelt at the court of King **Arthur.** His origin is obscure, but early legends concerning him agree that he was the offspring of Satan. He was probably an early Celtic god, who in process of time came to be regarded as a great sorcerer.

There appears to have been more than one Merlin, and it is necessary to discriminate between the Merlin of Arthurian romance and Merlin Caledonius, but it is probable that originally the two conceptions sprang from the one idea.

Mermaids and Mermen

Legends of supernatural sea people, human down to the waist but with a fish tail instead of legs, have been told since ancient times. In German folklore, a mermaid was known as "Meerfrau," in Danish "maremind," Irish "murduac" (or "merrow"). In Brittany, the "Morgans" were beautiful sirenlike women, dangerous to men, while in British maritime lore, seeing a mermaid might precede a storm or other disaster. A traditional ballad "The Mermaid" (Child ballad No. 289) tells how a ship's crew saw a mermaid sitting on a rock, combing her hair and holding a mirror. Soon afterwards the ship was wrecked in a raging sea. Traditionally, one can gain power over a mermaid by seizing her cap or belt.

There are many folk tales of marriages between a mermaid and a man, and in Machaire, Ireland, there are individuals who claim descent from such a union. The medieval romance of the fair **Melusine** of the house of Lusignan in France concerns the daughter of a union between a human and a fairy who cursed the daughter Melusine so that she became a serpent from the waist down every Saturday.

Hans Christian Anderson's pathetic story *The Little Mermaid* echoes folk tales in its theme of a mermaid who falls in love with a prince in a passing ship; the mermaid takes on human form in order to gain a human soul and be close to the prince, but although constantly near him cannot speak. When the prince marries a human princess, the mermaid's heart breaks. There is a similar haunting pathos in Matthew Arnold's poem "The Forsaken Merman."

In *Curious Myths of the Middle Ages* (1884; University Books, 1967), folklorist S. Baring-Gould suggested that mermaid and merman stories originated from the half-fish half-human gods and goddesses of early religions. The Chaldean Oannes and the Philistine Dagon are typical deities of this kind, and a representation of Oannes with a human body down to the waist and a fish tail has been found on sculpture at Khorsabad. Such goddesses as Derceto (Atergatis) and Semiramis have been represented in mermaid form. The classic Venus, goddess of love, was born out of the sea-foam, and was propitated by barren couples who desired children. The Mexican Coxcox or Teocipactli was a fish god, as also some Peruvian deities. North American Indians have a legend that they were led from Asia by a man-fish. In classical mythology the Tritons and Sirens are represented as half-fish half-human.

In addition to legends of mythology and folklore, however, there are many claimed accounts of actual mermaids and mermen throughout history. The twelfth-century *Speculum Regale* of Iceland describes a mermaid called the Margygr found near Greenland; "This creature appears like a woman as far down as her waist, with breast and bosom like a woman, long hands, and soft hair, the neck and head in all respects like those of a human being. From the waist downwards, this monster resembles a fish, with scales, tail, and fins. This prodigy is believed to show itself especially before heavy storms."

In 1187, a merman was fished up off the coast of Suffolk in England; it closely resembled a man but was not able to speak. The *Landnama* or Icelandic Doomsday Book tells of a merman caught off the island of Grimsey, and the annals of the country describe such creatures as appearing off the coast in 1305 and 1329.

In 1430 in Holland, there were violent storms which broke the dykes near Edam, West Friesland. Some girls from Edam had to take a boat to milk their cows, and saw a mermaid floundering in shallow muddy water. They brought her home, dressed her in female clothing and taught her to weave and spin and show reverence for a crucifix, but she could never learn to speak.

In 1560, some fishermen near the island of Mandar off the west coast of Ceylon caught no less than seven mermen and mermaids, which were witnessed by several Jesuit fathers and M. Bosquez, physician to the Viceroy of Goa. The physician made a careful examination of the mer-people, dissected them, and pronounced that their internal and external structure resembled that of human beings. There is a well authenticated case of a merman seen near a rock off the coast of Martinique. Several individuals affirmed that they saw it wipe its hands over its face and even blow its nose; their accounts were attested before a notary.

A merman captured in the Baltic in 1531 was sent as a present to Sigismund, King of Poland, and seen by all his court; the creature lived for three days. In 1608, the British navigator Henry Hudson (discoverer of Hudson Bay) reported the discovery of a mermaid: "This morning, one of our company looking overboard saw a mermaid; and calling up some of the company to see her, one more came up, and by that time she was come close to the ship's side, looking earnestly at the men. A little after, a sea came and overturned her. From the navel upward, her back and breasts were like a woman's, as they say that saw her; her body as big as one of us, her skin very white and long hair hanging down behind, of colour black. In her going down they saw her tail, which was like the tail of a porpoise, speckled like a mackerel. Their names that saw her were Thomas Hilles and Robert Rayner."

In 1755, Erik Pontoppidan, Bishop of Bergen, published his *New Natural History of Norway* (2 vols.), in which there is an account of a merman observed by three sailors on a ship off the coast of Denmark, near Landscrona; the witnesses made a deposition on oath. In another book, *Poissons, écrevisses et crabes de diverses couleurs et figures extraordinaires, que l'on trouve autour des Isles Moluques* (published in 1717 by Louis Renard, Amsterdam), there is an illustration of a mermaid with the following description: "See-wyf. A monster resembling a Siren, caught near the island of Borné, or Boeren, in the Department of Amboine. It was 59 inches long, and in proportion as an eel. It lived on land, in a vat full of water, during four days seven hours. From time to time it uttered little cries like those of a mouse. It would not eat, though it was offered small fish, shells, crabs, lobsters, &c. After its death, some excrement was discovered in the vat, like the secretion of a cat." Several individuals testified to the truth of this account.

In 1857, two Scottish fishermen made the following declaration, recorded in the *Shipping Gazette:* "We, the undersigned, do declare, that on Thursday last, the 4th June 1857, when on our way to the fishing station, Lochindale, in a boat, and when about four miles S.W. from the village of Port Charlotte, being then about 6 p.m., we distinctly saw an object about six yards distant from us in the shape of a woman, with full breast, dark complexion, comely face, and fine hair hanging in ringlets over the neck and shoulders. It was about the surface of the water to about the middle, gazing at us and shaking its head. The weather being fine, we had a full view of it and that for three or four minutes.—John Williamson, John Cameron."

In spite of these and other circumstantial accounts, the conventional explanation for sightings of mermaids and mermen is usually that they are inaccurate or romantic viewings of a marine mammal called a Dugong *(Halicore),* of the order *Sirenia,* which also includes the Manatee or sea-cow. Such creatures suckle their young at the breast and have a vaguely human appearance. They used to be hunted for their oil, used as a substitute for cod-liver oil, and are now rare.

It is possible that the dugong known as *Rhytina gigas* or "Steller sea-cow," long believed extinct, may survive in the Bering Sea, near the Aleutian Islands. Vitus Bering, after whom the Sea is named, was a Danish navigator who was shipwrecked on the desert island of Avacha (now known as Bering Island) in 1741. His party included a naturalist named George W. Steller, who made copious notes while the party were dying of starvation. Steller observed large herds of *Sirenia* a short distance from the shore. The creatures were mammals about 25 to 35 feet long and grazed off the kelp like cows on a pasture. They were unafraid of human beings, and it was easy to harpoon them, drag them ashore and eat the flesh, which sustained the party. The top half of the creature resembled a seal, and the bottom half a dolphin. It had small flippers, and the females had mammary glands like a woman, suckling their young at the breast. Even courtship habits seemed human, as well as other behavior. When one creature was harpooned, the others would gather round it and try to comfort it, and even swim across the rope and try to dislodge the hook.

In 1977, Derek Hutchinson, a British schoolteacher, started planning an expedition to the Aleutian Islands to film the Steller sea-cow from kayaks.

Meanwhile it has to be said that *Sirenia* bear only a very vague resemblance to historic accounts of mermaids, especially those which were brought ashore and kept in captivity before they died. These also have no connection with the stuffed 'mermaids' displayed in showmen's booths in the nineteenth and early twentieth centuries, which were invariably clever fakes assembled by Japanese craftsmen.

Recommended reading:

Bassett, F. S. *Legends and Traditions of the Sea and of Sailors,* Belford, Clarke & Co., Chicago & New York, 1885

Benwell, Gwen & Arthur Waugh. *Sea Enchantress; The Tale of the Mermaid and Her Kin,* Hutchinson, London, 1961

Hutchins, Jane. *Discovering Mermaids and Monsters,* Shire Publications (booklet), U.K., 1968

Rappoport, Angelo S. *Superstitions of Sailors,* Stanley Paul, London, 1928; Gryphon Books, Ann Arbor, 1971

Merrell-Wolff, Franklin (c. 1887–   )

American teacher of a system of higher consciousness deriving from Hindu **Yoga** and related philosophies. Born c. 1887, Dr. Wolff was the son of a Christian clergyman, but felt himself drawn beyond religious orthodoxy. He graduated with Phi Beta Kappa from Stanford University in 1911, majoring in mathematics, with philosophy and psychology as minors. He did graduate work at Stanford and in the Grade School in Philosophy of Harvard.

After teaching mathematics at Stanford, he withdrew from the academic life to seek metaphysical knowledge beyond sense perception and conception. After twenty-four years he attained a state of higher consciousness, described in his books *Pathways Through to Space* (1973; Warner Books, 1976) and *The Philosophy of Consciousness Without an Object* (Julian Press, 1973).

Although then in his late 80s, Dr. Wolff continued to teach students at a community in California, originally designated The Assembly of Man and now known as Friends of the Wisdom Religion, located at the Wolff residence, near Lone Pine, California, U.S. Highway 395, about half way between Reno and Los Angeles. Meetings at which Dr. Wolff's tape-recorded lectures are played take place at the home of Mrs. James A. Briggs, 4648 E. Lafayette Blvd., Phoenix, Arizona 85018. (See also **Kundalini**)

Mesmer, Franz Anton (1733–1815)

Famous Austrian doctor, originator of the technique of **Mesmerism,** forerunner of **hypnotism.** He was born at Weil, near Constance, May 23, 1733. In 1766 he took a degree in medicine at Vienna, the subject of his inaugural thesis being *De planetarum Influxu* (De l'influence des Planettes sur le corps humain). In this, he identified the influence of the planets with magnetism, and developed the idea that stroking diseased bodies with magnets would be curative. On seeing the remarkable cures of J. J. Gassner in Switzerland, he concluded that magnetic force must also reside in the human body, and thereupon dispensed with magnets.

In 1778 he went to Paris where he was very favorably received—by the public, that is, for the medical authorities there, as elsewhere, refused to countenance him. His curative technique was to seat his patients round a large circular vat or *baquet,* in which various substances were mixed. Each patient held one end of an iron rod, the other end of which was in the baquet. In due time the crisis ensued. Violent convulsions, cries, laughter, and various physical symptoms followed, these being in turn superseded by lethargy. Many claimed to have been healed by this method.

In 1784, the government appointed a commission of members of the Faculté de Médecine, the Societé Royale de Médecine, and the Academy of Sciences, the commissioners from the latter body including Benjamin **Franklin,** Bailly, and Lavoisier. The report of the Committee stated, in effect, that there was no such thing as "**animal magnetism,**" and referred the facts of the crisis to the imagination of the patient. This had the effect of quenching to a considerable extent the public interest in Mesmerism, as animal magnetism was called, for the time at least, although it was afterwards to be revived.

Mesmer died at Meersburg, Switzerland, March 5, 1815. (See also **Animal Magnetism; Hypnotism; Mesmerism**)

Mesmerism

A system of healing, founded by Franz Anton **Mesmer** (1733–1815), a German doctor who received his degree at Vienna in 1766 and expounded the main principles of his discovery of "**animal magnetism**" in *De Planetarum Influxu,* his inaugural thesis from which the following statements are extracted:

"There is a mutual influence between the celestial bodies, the earth and animated bodies.

"The means of this influence is a fluid which is universal and so continuous that it cannot suffer void, subtle beyond comparison and susceptible to receive, propagate and communicate every impression of movement.

"This reciprocal action is subject to as yet unknown mechanical laws.

"The result of this action consists in alternating effects which may be considered fluxes and refluxes . . .

"It is by this operation (the most universal in nature) that the active relations are exercised between the heavenly bodies, the earth and its constituent particles . . .

"It particularly manifests itself in the human body with properties analogous to the magnet; there are poles, diverse and opposed, which can be communicated, changed, destroyed and reinforced; the phenomenon of inclination is also observable.

"This property of the animal body which renders it susceptible to the influence of celestial bodies and to the reciprocal action of the environing ones I felt prompted to name, from its analogy to the magnet, animal magnetism. . . .

"It acts from a distance without the intermediary of other bodies.

"Similarly to light it is augmented and reflected by the mirror.

"It is communicated, propagated and augmented by the voice."

By applying magnetic plates to the patient's limbs, Mesmer effected his first cures in 1773. The arousal of public attention was due to a bitter controversy between Mesmer and a Jesuit Father Maximilian Hell, Professor of Astronomy at the University of Vienna, who claimed priority of discovery. Mesmer won.

In 1778, after a bitter public controversy over the cure of a blind girl, Mesmer went to Paris. In a short time he became famous. His first convert was Charles d'Eslon, medical adviser to the Count d'Artois. In September 1780, d'Eslon asked the Faculty of Medicine to investigate the doctrines of Mesmer. The proposal was rejected and d'Eslon was threatened that his name would be struck off the rolls at the end of the year if he did not recant.

In the meantime public enthusiasm grew to such a high pitch that in March 1871, Minister de Maurepas offered Mesmer, on behalf of the King, 20,000 livres (francs) and a further annuity of 10,000 livres if he established a school and divulged the secret of his treatment.

Mesmer refused, but two years later accepted a subscription of 340,000 livres for lectures to pupils. In 1784, the Government charged the Faculté de Médicine and the Societé Royale de Médicine to examine Animal Magnetism. A body of nine commissioners was convened under the presidency of Benjamin Franklin, including Jean Sylvain Bailly and J. K. Lavater; four more commissioners were added from the Royal Society of Medicine. The delegates restricted their activity to the search for evidence of a new physical force which was claimed as the agent of the cure. They had seen the famous *baquet* in operation.

This *baquet* was a large circular tub, filled with bottles, which dipped into the water. The *baquet* was covered. Iron rods projected from the lid through holes therein. The rods were bent and could be applied to any part of their body by the patients who sat in rows. The patients were tied together by a cord which passed round the circle, sometimes they held hands in chain. There was music. The operator, with an iron rod in his hands, walked around, touched the patients; they fell into convulsions, sweated, vomited, cried—and were cured.

The committees, in their verdict, stated that they found no evidence of a magnetic fluid and the cures might be due to vivid imagination. M. de Jussieu was the only member who dissented. He claimed to have discovered something—animal heat which radiated from the human body and could be directed and intensified by willpower. Later magnetists adopted the theory. It marked the discovery of the human element in animal magnetism.

The next important development is attached to the name of the Marquis de Puységur. He began his cures at Busancy in the same year that animal magnetism was officially turned down. He did not employ the *baquet*. He "magnetized" a tree, fastened cords around and invited the sufferers to tie themselves to it. One of his invalid patients, a young peasant of 23 years of age, Victor by name, fell asleep in the operator's arms. He began to talk. On waking he remembered nothing. This was the discovery of the somnambulic stage.

Puységur and the earlier magnetizers attributed many curious phenomena to the state of *rapport* and they insisted on the theory of a magnetic effluence. Their patients claimed they could see it radiating as a brilliant shaft of light from the operator, from trees and other substances. Some substances could conduct it, others not. Water and milk could retain it and work cures.

Tardy de Montravel discovered the **transposition of senses.** His somnambule not only walked in the town with her eyes fast closed but could see by the pit of the stomach (see also **Eyeless Sight**). J. H. Desire Pétetin, a doctor at Lyons, enlarged upon these observations. He changed the theory of Mesmer to "animal electricity" and cited many experiments to prove that the phenomena were of an electrical nature.

J. P. F. Deleuze objected, insisted on the magnetic fluid theory and pointed out its analogies with nerve-force. He explained the phenomena of the transposition of the senses by the idea that it was the magnetic fluid which conveyed the impressions from without. He offered a similar theory to the explanation of medical diagnoses which the patients gave of others and themselves. Every phenomenon was, however, attributed to physiological causes. **Thought reading** and **clairvoyance** as transcendental faculties were rejected. The phenomena of traveling clairvoyance were yet very rare. Tardy de Montravel was alone in his supposition of a sixth sense as an explanatory theory.

The new era of thought was inaugurated by a nonmedical man, Abbé Faria. In 1813, he ascribed the magnetic phenomena to the power of imagination. General Noizet and Alexandre Bertrand adopted his view. Bertrand's *Traité du Somnambulisme* was published in 1823. It definitely established a new departure. Bertrand denied the existence of the magnetic fluid and pointed out the preternormal sensitivity of the subject to the least suggestion, whether by word, look, gesture or thought. Yet he admitted the supernormal phenomena of trance.

Marvelous stories were agitating the country. Professional clairvoyants arose. They gave medical diagnosis and treatment. Billot discovered most of the phenomena of **Spiritualism.** From Germany and Russia came rumors of a wide recognition of magnetic treatment. The Royal Academy of Medicine could not long ignore the stir.

On December 13, 1825, the proposal of P. Foissac that another investigation should be ordered was, after a bitter struggle, carried. The report of the committee was not submitted until five and a half years later. It stated that the alleged phenomena were genuine and that the existence of **somnambulism** was well authenticated. They found evidence of clairvoyance and successful medical diagnosis in the state of *rapport.* They also established that the will of the operator could produce the magnetic state without the subject's knowledge, even from another room.

In the meantime, developments in Germany proceeded. Animal magnetism ceased to remain a science of healing. Under the influence of Jung-Stilling (see Johann Heinrich **Jung**) it soon developed into a spiritual science. While Gmelin, Wienholt, Fischer, Kluge, Kieser and Weserman observed all the reported properties of the magnetic fluid and insisted on its essential importance, the practice of holding intercourse with the spirits through entranced somnambules soon gained popularity and increasing trust.

In the United States the students of Mesmerism believed they had discovered a new science—**Phreno-Mesmerism.** Dr. J. Rodes **Buchanan,** Dr. R. H. Collyer and the Rev. Laroy **Sunderland** contended for the honor of the first discovery. Dr. J. Rodes Buchanan mapped out an entirely new distribution of the phrenological organs in 1843 and developed the theory of "nerve-aura" as a connecting link between will and consciousness.

The title page of Dr. Collyer's *Psychography, or the Embodiment of Thought* (Philadelphia, 1843), represented two persons looking into a bowl, illustrating, in Dr. Collyer's words, that "when the angle of incidence from my brain was equal to the angle of reflection from her brain she distinctly saw the image of my thought at the point of coincidence."

The Rev. Laroy Sunderland discovered no less than 150 new phrenologic organs by means of mesmeric experiments. Professor J. S. Grime substituted the magnetic fluid with "etherium," the Rev. J. Bovee Dods with "vital electricity."

Andrew Jackson **Davis** was started on his career of seership by Mesmeric experiments for medical purposes. He became the herald of Spiritualism and on the bridge which he built most of the exponents of Phreno-Mesmerism and Mesmerism went over to the believers of the new faith.

In England the beginnings were slow. Not until Dr. John **Elliotson** was converted by Baron **Du Potet**'s visit in 1837 did Mesmerism assume the proportions of a widespread movement. For propaganda it relied on the journal *The Zoist* and the short-lived *Phreno-Magnet.* Three main classes of phenomena were thus distinguished: the physical effluence; phreno-mesmerism; and **community of sensations,** including clairvoyance.

The controversy between official medical science and Mesmerism raged bitterly. The evolution of "Animal Magnetism" into **"Hypnotism"** was due to James **Braid.** But James **Esdaile**'s name also occupies an important

place. While Elliotson practically introduced curative magnetism into England, Esdaile proved the reality of Mesmeric trance by performing operations under Mesmeric anaesthesia.

As early as 1841, Braid read an address before the British Association in which he expounded his discovery of hypnotism. He described it as a special condition of the nervous system, characterized by an abnormal exaltation of suggestibility, which can be brought about automatically by the mere fixation of the eyes on bright objects with an inward and upward squint.

In 1843, his address was published under the title *Neurypnology.* This work was followed three years later by his *Power of the Mind Over the Body,* in which he pointed out that the Mesmerists were not on their guard against suggestion and hyperaesthesia. He produced all the characteristic results of Mesmerism without a magnet and claimed that the sensitives could not see flames at the poles of the most powerful magnets until warned to look to them. If warned, they saw flames issuing from any object.

The influence of Dr. Braid's discoveries on the Mesmerists themselves was very slight and strangely enough, official science took little notice. The main attraction of Mesmerism was its therapeutic value. It was the discovery in 1846–47 of the anaesthetic properties of ether and chloroform that deprived Mesmeric trance of its most obvious utility. The conquest by Spiritualism soon began and the leading Mesmerists were absorbed into the ranks of the Spiritualists.

No further advance was registered in England until 1883, when Edmund **Gurney** made his first experiments in hypnotism. He pointed out that in the hypnotic age the formerly numerous cases of *rapport* became extremely rare. He and F. W. H. **Myers** reverted to the earlier theory and declared that hypnotism and Mesmerism appeared to be two different states.

Official recognition was first granted to hypnotism in 1893 by a committee of the British Medical Association which reported to have found the hypnotic state genuine and of value in relieving pain and alleviating functional ailments. Mesmerism remained a controversial subject.

In France, a great revival began in 1875. A. A. Liébeault published his work on hypnotism in 1866. He sided with Bertrand. In 1875 Prof. Charles **Richet** came to the fore. In 1879, Charcot began his work in the Salpetrière. Paris, Bordeaux, Nancy and Toulon became centers of hypnotic activity. The school of Paris, of which Charcot was the chief, adopted and completed the explanation of Braid. Charcot contended that the hypnotic conditions could only be provoked with neuropaths or with hysterical subjects.

The school of Nancy accepted hypnotic sleep but considered suggestion its potent cause. In 1886, in Prof. **Bernheim**'s famous work *Suggestion and its Application to Therapeutics,* he went so far as to declare: "Suggestion is the key of all hypnotic phenomena. There is no such thing as hypnotism, there is only suggestion." The views of Liébeault and Bernheim prevailed almost everywhere over those of Charcot.

But animal magnetism was difficult to kill. Boirac was right in saying that "Animal magnetism is a new America which has been alternately lost and found every twenty or thirty years."

In 1887, Dr. Baréty published *Le Magnetisme Animal Etudié sous le nom de' Force Neurique* in which he boldly set out to prove the reality of animal magnetism. Pierre Janet, reviewing Baréty's work, admitted that certain phenomena of attraction, anaesthesia, etc., produced on subjects apart from all apparent suggestion, by contact alone or the mere presence of the operators, had often struck him as particularly suggestive of the so-called magnetic chain.

Emil Boirac supported this position. He pointed out that although hypnotism and suggestion exist, it does not follow that animal magnetism has no existence. It may be that the effects attributed to hypnotism and suggestion are caused by a third factor. Experiments with several subjects convinced him of the truth of his theory. "We are not prevented from hoping," he wrote in *Psychic Science* (1918), "that we shall one day succeed in discovering the natural unity of these three orders of phenomena [Mesmerism or animal magnetism, suggestion and Braidic hypnotism] as we begin to discover the natural unity of heat, light and electricity. They too much resemble each other's path not to betray a secret relationship. They are perhaps the effects of one and the same cause, but these effects are assuredly produced under different conditions and according to different laws."

The claim was further supported in 1921 by Dr. Sydney Alrutz, lecturer on psychology at the University of Upsala. He claimed to have proved experimentally the existence of a nervous effluence. Professor Farny, of the Zurich Polytechnicum, showed by electrical tests an emission from the fingers and called it "anthropoflux." His results verified the previous investigations of E. K. Muller, an engineer of Zurich, director of the Salus Institute.

Eventually the phenomena of animal magnetism merged with the developing Spiritualist movement, while hypnotism became established as a valid medical technique. In 1838, Phineas P. **Quimby** began to practice Mesmerism and later developed from it his own concepts of mental action culminating in the **New Thought** movement from which **Christian Science** established a separate identity. (See also **Animal Magnetism; Community of Sensation; Emanations; Hypnotism; Metals (in Animal Magnetism); Mind-Cure; New Thought; Od; Odic Force; Odyle; Phreno-Mesmerism; Somnambulism; Spiritualism Suggestion; Transposition of Senses**)

Recommended reading:

Bernheim, H. *Hypnosis & Suggestion in Psychotherapy,* London, 1888; University Books, 1964

Bertrand, A. *Traité du Somnambulisme,* Paris, 1824

Binet, Alfred & Charles Féré. *Animal Magnetism,* Kegan Paul, London, 1887

Braid, James. *Magic, Witchcraft, Animal Magnetism, Hypnotism & Electro-Biology,* John Churchill, London, 1852

Bramwell, J. Milne. *Hypnotism and Treatment by Suggestion,* Cassell, London, 1909

Deleuze, J. P. F. *Practical Instruction in Animal Magnetism,* Samuel R. Wells, New York, 1879

Franklin, Benjamin & others. *Animal Magnetism; Report of Dr. Franklin and Other Commissioners,* H. Perkins, Philadelphia, 1837

Ince, R. B. *Franz Anton Mesmer,* William Rider, pamphlet, London, 1920

Goldsmith, Margaret. *Franz Anton Mesmer; The History of an Idea,* Arthur Barker Ltd., London, 1934

Gregory, William. *Animal Magnetism; or Mesmerism and Its Phenomena,* Nichols & Co., London, 1884

Liébeault, A. A. *Du Sommeil et des Etats Analogues,* Paris, 1886

Mesmer, F. A. (intro. Gilbert Frankau). *Mesmerism by Doctor Mesmer (1779), Being the First Translation of Mesmer's Historic 'Memoire sur la découverte du Magnétism Animal' to Appear in English,* Macdonald, London, 1948

Podmore, Frank. *Mesmerism and Christian Science,* Methuen, London, 1909

Sunderland, LaRoy. *Pathetism; Man Considered in Relation to his Form, Life, Sensation. . . . An Essay Towards a Correct Theory of Mind,* Boston, 1847

Metagnomy

Term originally coined by French psychical researcher Dr. Eugen **Osty,** indicating knowledge acquired through cryptesthesia, i.e., without the use of our five senses. The term is now generally superseded by "extrasensory perception."

Metagraphology

Term indicating psychometric power on the basis of scripts. It has nothing to do with **graphology** (interpretation of personality traits indicated in handwriting) as the reading of the present, past and the future of the subject is not effected by the study of the writing. The script simply serves as an influence.

The sole justification of the term "metagraphology" is the fact that some graphologists developed their remarkably sensitive powers from the study of scripts. Raphael **Schermann** was the most notable among the metagraphologists. Recently similar powers were discovered in Otto Reimann, of Prague, a bank clerk, born in 1903, who, by simply touching a script, can give a perfect psychometric reading, and also imitate the writing. He was studied by Prof. Fischer, of Prague. (See also **Graphology; Psychometry**)

Metal Bending

One of the very few new directions in claimed psychic phenomena in modern times. It was first publicized by Uri **Geller,** the Israeli psychic from 1976 onwards, when he apparently demonstrated paranormal deformation of metal keys and spoons. When these objects were gently stroked or subjected to passes of his hand without actual contact, they tended to bend and often actually break, allegedly by some unknown force directed by the psychic's mind. The phenomenon became known as "the Geller effect," but is now generally classified by parapsychologists as "Psychokinetic Metal Bending" or "PKMB."

In spite of many demonstrations by Uri Geller and hundreds of laboratory experiments with Geller and other subjects by parapsychologists, the phenomenon remains highly controversial. However, some of the evidence is impressive. Metal samples sealed inside glass tubes have been bent. Some samples have been bent when held by someone other than the psychic, while bends have been shown in alloys which normally break rather than bend when stressed. Videotape records appear to show paranormal bending of samples not held by the psychic concerned, but it must be said that other videotapes taken secretly have revealed fraud by some metal-benders, notably children, who have become known as "mini-Gellers."

The British scientist Prof. John **Taylor** spent three years studying the phenomenon, which he endorsed in his book *Superminds* (1975) but in 1978 he retracted to complete skepticism. However, Dr. John **Hasted,** another British scientist who tested Uri Geller and other claimed metal-benders, has continued to support the reality of PKMB. For a detailed study of his experiments and conclusions, see his book *The Metal-Benders* (1981).

The stage magician James **Randi** has demonstrated various methods of apparent metal-bending, and also caused much confusion by planting fake metal-benders in parapsychology laboratory tests, to show that scientists may be deceived. One of the commonest methods of faking metal-bending in tests with spoons is for the operator to surreptitiously weaken the spoon by prior bending, which can be achieved easily with the aid of a strong belt buckle. However, such tricks do not seem to cover all the phenomena tested and observed by parapsychologists, and a careful study of the literature is advised before jumping to simplistic conclusions.

Recommended reading:

Hasted, John. *The Metal-Benders,* Routledge & Kegan Paul, London/Boston, Mass., 1981

Panati, Charles (ed.). *The Geller Papers; Scientific Observations on the Paranormal Powers of Uri Geller,* Houghton Mifflin Co., 1976

Randi, James. *The Truth About Uri Geller,* Prometheus Books, Buffalo, N.Y., 1982

Taylor, John. *Superminds; A Scientist Looks at the Paranormal,* Viking Press, N.Y./Macmillan, London, 1975

Taylor, John. *Science and the Supernatural,* Temple Smith, London, 1980

(See also **Movement; Psychic Force; Psychokinesis**)

Metals (in Animal Magnetism)

It was claimed by the magnetists that various metals exercised a characteristic influence on their patients. Physical sensations of heat and cold, numbness, drowsiness, and so on were experienced by the somnambules on contact with metals, or even when metals were secretly introduced into the room. Dr. John **Elliotson,** especially, gave much prominence to the alleged power of metal to transmit the magnetic fluid.

Gold, silver, platinum, and nickel were said to be good conductors, although the magnetism conveyed by the latter was of a highly dangerous character. Copper, tin, pewter, and zinc were bad conductors. Dr. Elliotson found that a magnetized sovereign (British gold coin) would throw into trance his **sensitives,** the **O'Key Sisters,** and that although iron would neutralize the magnetic properties of the sovereign, no other metal would do so.

When Baron Karl von **Reichenbach** propounded his theory of odic force, his sensitives claimed to see a luminous emanation proceed from metals—silver and gold shone white; lead, blue; nickel, red, and so on. Opponents of Reichenbach's theories ascribed such phenomena to

suggestion. (See also **Od; Odic Force, Odyle; O'Key Sisters;** Baron Karl von **Reichenbach**)

Recommended reading:

Elliotson, John. *Human Physiology,* London, 1840

Reichenbach, Karl von. *Letters on Od and Magnetism,* Hutchinson, London, 1926 (reissued under title *The Odic Force,* University Books, 1968)

Metaphysical Digest (Journal)

Publication of the **Society of Metaphysicians,** Inc., Archers' Court, Stonestile Lane, The Ridge, Hastings, Sussex, England.

Metapsichica

Semi-annual publication in Italian language of the Italian Metaphysical Association (Association Italiana Scientifica di Metapsichica). Address: Corso Firenze, N.8, 16136 Genova, Italy.

Metapsychics

The term proposed by Prof. Charles **Richet** in 1905 (when he was elected president of the Society for Psychical Research, London) for phenomena and experiments in psychical research. In his inaugural address he defined metapsychics as "a science dealing with mechanical or psychological phenomena due to forces which seem to be intelligent, or to unknown powers, latent in human intelligence."

He divided it into objective and subjective metapsychics, the first dealing with material, external facts, the second with psychic, internal, nonmaterial facts.

The term was not generally approved on the Continent. In Germany, the word "parapsychic" was accepted in its stead. This was originally proposed by Emil **Boirac.** Prof. Theodor **Flournoy** suggested that "parapsychics" would be better and Richet's term should be limited to those phenomena which have been definitely proved supernormal in character.

In modern times, all three terms have now been supplanted by **"parapsychology."**

MetaScience Foundation

Nonprofit organization concerned with the pursuit of scientific information in the field of parapsychology and related areas. Formerly titled the Occult Studies Foundation, the new name reflects reservations about the contemporary connotations of the word "occult."

The Foundation follows an interdisciplinary approach to paranormal phenomena, and endeavors to maintain a high standard of academic and professional responsibility in their investigations. The Foundation publishes **MetaScience Quarterly** (formerly titled Journal of Occult Studies). Address: MetaScience Foundation, Box 32, Kingston, Rhode Island 02881.

MetaScience Quarterly

A New Age journal of parapsychology formerly titled *Journal of Occult Studies.* This quarterly is the official publication of the MetaScience Foundation (formerly Occult Studies Foundation), devoted to pursuit of scientific information in the field of parapsychology and related areas, in an academic and professionally responsible manner.

The publication is concerned with a wide range of paranormal topics, including Ufology, Kundalini, the physics of consciousness, psychokinesis, telepathy and Kirlian photography. Address: MetaScience Quarterly, Box 32, Kingston, Rhode Island 02881.

Metempsychosis (or Transmigration of Souls)

The passing of the soul at death into another body than the one it has vacated. The belief in metempsychosis was very widespread in ancient times, and still survives in Hinduism and Buddhism, as well as in European folk-tales and superstitions.

The Brahmins and Buddhists believe that the soul may enter another human body, or that of one of the lower animals, or even a plant or tree, according to its deserts in previous incarnation. Thus it is doomed to successive incarnations, until by the transcending of all desires and emotions it merges in the Supreme Being. Very similar was the idea of Pythagoras and the Greeks, who believed that all material existence was a punishment for sins committed in a former incarnation. Indeed it is probable that Pythagoras (see **Greece**) derived his theory from the Brahminical doctrine.

The ancient Egyptians would also seem to have believed in metempsychosis. Among certain tribes of Africa and American Indians transmigration was also believed. Totemism (see **Fetichism**) may perhaps facilitate a belief in the passing of the soul into the body of an animal.

In Europe also in early times the belief in metempsychosis flourished, and several popular folk-tales, such as that known in Scotland as "The Milk-white Doo," of which variants are found in many lands, contain references to the souls of the dead entering into beasts, birds, or fishes. In some places it was thought that witches were at death transformed into hares, and for this reason the people of these localities refused to eat a hare. The Jewish Kabalists also believed in the doctrine of metempsychosis, and traces of the belief are to be found in the writings of Emanuel **Swedenborg**. (See also **Reincarnation**)

Methetherial

A term coined by F. W. H. **Myers,** meaning: beyond the ether, the transcendental world in which the spirits exist.

Metratton

According to Jewish rabbinical legend, Metratton, the angel, is one of the agents by whom God the Father works. He receives the pure and simple essence of the divinity and bestows the gift of life upon all. He dwells in one of the angelic hierarchies.

MEXICO AND CENTRAL AMERICA

Sorcerers and Astrologers

Occult science among the ancient Mexicans may be said to have been in that stage between the savage simplicities of medicine men and the more sophisticated magical practices of the medieval sorcerer. The sources of information are unfortunately of a most scanty description and are chiefly gleaned from the works of the early missionaries to the country, and from the legends and myths of the people themselves.

Writing upon the sorcerers of Mexico, Bernardino de Sahagun, an early Spanish priest, stated that the *naualli* or magician among the Mexicans was one who enchanted men and sucked the blood of infants during the night. This would seem as if the writer had confounded the sorcerer with the **vampire**—a mistake occasionally made by continental writers on magic. He proceeded to say that among the Mexicans, this class was ignorant of nothing which appertained to sorcery, and possessed great craft, that they hired themselves out to people to work evil upon their enemies, and to cause madness and maladies.

"The necromancer," he stated, "is a person who has made pact with a demon, and who is capable of transforming himself into various animal shapes. Such people appear to be tired of life and await death with complaisance. The astrologer practices among the people as a diviner, and has a thorough knowledge of the various signs of the calendar, from which he is able to prognosticate the fortunes of those who employ him. This he accomplishes by weighing the power of one planet against that of another, and thus discovering the resultant applies it to the case in point. These men were called into consultation at births and deaths, as well as upon public occasions, and would dispute with much nicety on their art."

The astrological system of the Mexicans was, like that of their calendar, of the most involved description possible, and no mere summary of it could convey anything but a hazy notion of the system, for which the reader is referred to Lewis **Spence**'s *The Civilisation of Ancient Mexico* (1911), Bernardino de Sahagun's *Historia de la Conquista de Mexico* (1829), and Bulletin 28 of the United States *Bureau of Ethnology.*

In connection with the astrological science of the Aztecs, however, it is worthy of note that the seventh calendric sign was that under which necromancers, sorcerers and evil-doers were usually born. Stated Bernardino de Sahagun: "These work their enchantments in obscurity for four nights running, when they choose a certain evil sign. They then betake themselves in the night to the houses where they desire to work their evil deeds and sorceries. . . . For the rest these sorcerers never know contentment, for all their days they live evilly and know no peace."

The myths of the Mexicans give a good working idea of the status of the enchanter or sorcerer in Aztec society. For example, the Toltec god Quetzalcoatl who, in early times, was regarded as a description of culture-hero, was bewitched by the god of the incoming and rival race, Tezcatlipoca, who disguised himself as a physician, prescribed for an illness of his enemy's an enchanted draught which made him long for the country of his origin—that is, the home of the rains. From this it appears that potions or philters were in vogue amongst Mexican sorcerers.

In their efforts to rid themselves of the entire Toltec race, the traditional aborigines of Mexico, Tezcatlipoca was pictured as performing upon a magical drum in such a manner as to cause frenzy amongst the Toltecs, who leaped by thousands into a deep ravine hard by their city, and similar instances of this kind were also recorded.

Wonderful stories were told of the feats of the Huaxteca, a people of Maya race, dwelling on the Gulf of Mexico. Sahagun related that they could produce from space a spring with fishes, burn and restore a hut, and dismember and resurrect themselves. The Ocuiltec of the Toluca Valley also possessed a widespread reputation as enchanters and magicians.

Divination and Augury

Although divination was practiced among the Aztecs by means of astrology, there were other and less intricate methods in use. There was in existence a College of Augurs, corresponding in purpose to the Auspices of Ancient Rome, the members of which occupied themselves with observing the flight and listening to the songs of birds, from which they drew their conclusions, and pretended to interpret the speech of all winged creatures.

The *Calmecac,* or training college of the priests, had a department where divination was taught in all its branches. A typical example of augury from birds may be found in the account of the manner in which the Mexicans fixed upon the spot for the foundation of their city.

Halting after years of wandering in the vicinity of the Lake of Tezcuco, they observed a great eagle with wings outspread perched on the stump of a cactus, and holding in its talons a live serpent. Their augurs interpreted this as a good omen as it had been previously announced by an oracle, and upon the spot where the bird had alighted, they drove the first piles upon which they afterwards built the city of Mexico—the legend of the foundation of which is still commemorated in the heraldic arms of modern Mexico.

Dreams and visions also played a great part in Mexican divination, and a special caste of augurs called *Teopixqui,* or *Teotecuhtli* (masters or guardians of divine things) were set apart for the purpose of interpreting dreams and of divining through dreams and visions, which was regarded as the chief route between man and the supernatural.

The senses were even quickened and sharpened by the use of drugs and the ecstatic condition was induced by want of sleep, and pertinacious fixing of the mind upon one subject, the swallowing or inhalation of cerebral intoxicants such as tobacco, the maguey, coca, the snake-plant or *ololiuhqui,* and similar substances.

As among some tribes of the American Indians, it was probably believed that visions came to the prophet or seer pictorially, or that acts were performed before him as in a play. It was also believed that the soul traveled through space and was able to visit those places of which it desired to have knowledge. It is also possible that the seers hypnotized themselves by gazing at certain small highly-polished pieces of sandstone, or that they employed these for the same purpose as crystal-gazers employ the globe. The goddess Tozi was the patron of those who used grains of maize or red beans in divination. (See also **Crystal Gazing; Divination**)

Charms and Amulets

The **amulet** was regarded in Mexico as a personal **fetish.** The Tepitoton, or diminutive household deities of the Mexicans were also fetishistic. It is probable that most of the Mexican amulets were modeled on the various ornaments of the gods. Thus the traveler's staff carved in the shape of a serpent like that of Quetzalcoatl was undoubtedly of this nature, and was even occasionally sacrificed to. The frog was a favorite model for an amulet. As elsewhere, the thunderbolts thrown by the gods were supposed to be flint stones, and were cherished as amulets of much virtue, and as symbols of the fecundating rains.

Vampirism

As mentioned earlier, Bernardino de Sahagun probably confused the Mexican necromancer with the vampire, and it is interesting to note that this folk belief must have originated in America independently of any European connection. But there is also another instance of what would seem something like vampirism in Mexico.

This is found in connection with the *ciupipiltin* or ghosts of women who have died in childbirth. These haunt the crossroads, crying and wailing for the little ones they have left behind them. But as in many other countries, notably in Burma, they are malevolent—their evil tendencies probably being caused by jealousy of the happiness of the living.

Lest they should enter their houses and injure their children, the Mexicans at certain times of the year stopped up every possible hole and crevice. The appearance of these ghosts (Sahagun described them as "goddesses") at crossroads is highly significant, for we know that the burial of criminals at such junctions was merely a survival of a similar disposal of the corpse of the vampire, whose head was cut off and laid at his side, and who was entombed at crossroads for the purpose of confusing him as to his whereabouts. (See also **Vampire**)

The Cult of Nagualism

Both in Mexico and Central America a religio-magical system called Nagualism existed, the purpose of which was to bring occult influence against the whites for their destruction. The rites of this strange cult usually took place in caverns and other deserted localities, and were naturally derived to a large extent from those of the suppressed native religion.

Each worshiper possessed a magical or animal spirit-guide, with which he was endowed early in life. This system certainly flourished as lately as the last quarter of the nineteenth century.

Central America

Information on magic and sorcery amongst the Maya, Kiche, and other Central American peoples is even rarer than that relating to Mexico, and there is little else than local legends as to guide research in these areas.

The great storehouse of Central American legend is the *Popol Vuh,* a study of which was published by Lewis Spence (1908). This fascinating work of mythological history states that some of the elder gods were regarded as magicians, and the hero-twins, Xblanque and Hun-ahpu, whom they sent to earth to rid it of the Titan Vukub-cakix, were undoubtedly possessed of magical powers.

As boys they were equipped with magical tools which enabled them to get through an enormous amount of work in a single day, and when they descended into Xibalba (the Kiché Hades) for the purpose of avenging their father and uncle, took full advantage of their magical propensities in combating the inhabitants of that drear abode. Xibalba itself possessed sorcerers, for within its borders were Xulu and Pacaw, who assisted the hero-gods in many of their necromantic practices.

As regards divination, the Maya possessed a caste of augurs, called *Cocomes* or the Listeners, while prophecy appears to have been periodically practiced by their priests.

In the so-called books of *Chilan Balam,* which were native compilations of events occurring in Central America previous to the Spanish Conquest, we find certain prophecies regarding, amongst other things, the coming of the Spaniards.

These appear to have been given forth by a priest who bore the title (not the name) of "Chilan Balam," whose offices were those of divination and astrology but these pronouncements seem to have been colored at a later date by Christian thought, and hardly to be of a genuine aboriginal character.

There are certain astrological formulas in the books, all of which are simply borrowed from European almanacs of the century between 1550 and 1650.

Amulets were in great vogue amongst the Maya, and they had the same fear of the last five days of the year as had the Mexicans, who regarded them as *nemontemi* or unlucky, and did no work of any description upon them. These days the Maya called *uyayayab,* and they considered that a demon entered their towns and villages at the beginning of this period. To avert evil influence they carried an image of him through the village in the hopes that he might afterwards avoid it.

The writer Lewis Spence, who published several books on Mexico and Central America, believed that there was some evidence for the influence of an Atlantean civilization, detailed in his book *Atlantis in America* (1925). (See also **Atlantis**)

Recommended reading:

Recinos, Adrián, Delia Goetz & Sylvanus G. Morley (transl. & ed.). *Popul Vuh; The Sacred Book of the Ancient Quiché Maya,* William Hodge, London, 1951

Sahagun, Bernardino de. *Historia de la Conquista de Mexico,* Mexico, 1829

Spence, Lewis. *Atlantis in America,* Ernest Benn, London, 1925; Singing Tree Press, Detroit, 1972

Spence, Lewis. *The Civilisation of Ancient Mexico,* London, 1911

Spence, Lewis. *The Gods of Mexico,* Fisher, Unwin, London, 1913

Spence, Lewis. *The Magic and Mysteries of Mexico,* Rider & Co., London, 1930

Spence, Lewis. *The Myths of Mexico & Peru,* Harrap, London, 1913

Spence, Lewis. *The Popul Vuh; The Mythic & Heroic Sagas of the Kichés of Central America,* David Nutt, London, 1908

Meyer, G. (1868–1932)

Famous German occultist and novelist, who wrote under the name Gustav **Meyrink.**

Meyer, Jean (died 1931)

French industrialist, a fervent adherent of the Spiritist doctrines of Allan **Kardec,** founder of the **Maison des**

Spirites (8, Rue Copernic, Paris) which aimed, under his personal supervision, at the diffusion of this knowledge. He was also a founder of the Institut Métapsychique International, which pursued psychical research and was recognized as of public utility by the French Government in 1919. He endowed the institution with a portion of his fortune, took a personal interest in its work and presented it, shortly before his decease, with an infra-red installation at a cost of 200,000 francs.

The following story indicates the fair-mindedness of Jean Meyer in sponsoring both Spiritualism and scientific research. After the death of Dr. Gustav **Geley,** director of the Institut Métapsychique, M. Meyer desired to appoint Dr. Eugène **Osty** as his successor. Dr. Osty pointed out that the Institut would require complete scientific liberty, and stated "what would you say, if from the laboratory of the Institut there were to issue some day studies of fact which would suggest that the teaching of the Maison des Spirites is in whole or in part illusory interpretation of facts produced exclusively by the innate powers of man as yet unknown?"

With courageous confidence in both Spiritualism and science, M. Meyer replied: "Yes, I accept the risk. I know you for a sincere researcher. That is enough for me."

Meyrink, Gustav (1868–1932)

Pseudonym of German novelist Gustav Meyer, famous for his occult fiction. He was also actively concerned with occult and Theosophical groups in Europe before and during World War I.

Born in Vienna, he was taken by his family to Prague, Czechoslovakia, where his mother's family owned a bank. As a young man, Meyrink worked in the bank, but was attracted to occult teachings. In 1891, he was a member of the Theosophical Lodge of the Blue Star, whose members practiced occult disciplines. Meyrink translated the Tantric work on Hindu mysticism *Nature's Finer Forces* by Rama Prasad.

In 1903, he published his first collection of short stories. Many of his writings have themes of fantasy or occultism, with echoes of E. T. A. Hoffmann, Edgar Allan Poe or Franz Kafka. His best known novel was *Der Golem* (1915; translated by M. Pemberton as *The Golem,* 1928). This is a brilliant and strangely disturbing book concerned with Kabalism and the occult, based on Prague legends of the **Golem,** a mysterious man-monster said to have been created from clay by Rabbi Judah Loew of Prague in the seventeenth century.

The book had added power in relating to the real-life background of Golem legends, since the Prague ghetto had changed little at that time. Indeed, Rabbi Loew's grave may still be seen in the Old Jewish cemetery at Prague. A German silent film *The Golem,* directed and scripted by Paul Wegener, was produced in 1920, adapted very loosely from Meyrink's novel.

Meyrink converted from Protestantism to Buddhism and spent many years in occult investigations, including experiments in alchemy. He was present at some of the seances of Baron **Schrenck-Notzing** in Munich with the medium **"Eva C."** Meyrink also practiced Yoga and claimed to have achieved telepathic contact with the famous South Indian holy man Sri **Ramana Maharshi,** guru of Paul **Brunton.**

Meyrink died in December 1932 in Starnberg, Germany. For biographical information see *Gustav Meyrink* by Eduard Frank (Budingen-Gottenbach, 1957). Meyrink's own book *An der Schwelle des Jenseits* (1923) presents some of his own philosophical outlook. (See also **Golem**)

Mezazoth, The

A traditional Jewish schedule which, when fastened on the doorpost, possessed talismanic qualities. It is said in the *Talmud* that whoever has the *mezazoth* fixed on his door, and is provided with certain personal charms, is protected from sin.

Mhorag (or Morag)

A Loch Ness type monster observed and photographed in Loch Morar, West Inverness, Scotland. The loch is 12 miles long, up to 2 miles wide and 1,017 feet deep. The magazine *Fortean Times* (No. 22, Summer 1977) reproduced a photograph taken by Mrs. Hazel Jackson (of Wakefield, Yorkshire), who stayed at Morar with her husband on a touring holiday. The Jacksons, who are skeptical about monsters, took two photographs of their sheepdog by the side of the loch, and both pictures showed what appeared to be the head of a monster in the loch. Two other photographs reproduced in *Fortean Times* 22 were taken by Miss M. Lindsay of Musselburgh. However, these were also somewhat ambiguous.

A Loch Morar Expedition headed by Adrian Shine has tested underwater surveillance equipment, including a spherical submersible designed by Shine. There are hopes that such equipment may identify the Mhorag monster, since the waters of the loch are crystal clear. (See also **Loch Ness Monster; Monsters**)

Michael

An archangel, the Hebrew name meaning "He who is equal to God." In *Revelation* it is said: "there was war in heaven. Michael and his angels fought against the dragon" and from this it is deduced that Michael was the leader of the celestial hierarchy—as against Lucifer, the head of the disobedient angels.

Michael is mentioned by name four other times in the Scriptures; in *Daniel* as the champion of the Jewish Church against Persia; in *Jude* as the archangel who fought with Satan for the body of Moses; by Gabriel he is called the prince of the Jewish Church; and in the prophecy of Enoch, "Michael. . . . who commands the nations."

His design, according to genealogist Randle Holme, is a banner hanging on a cross, and he is represented as victory with a dart in one hand and a cross on his forehead. Bishop Horsley and others considered Michael as only another name for the Son of God.

In one of the Jewish rabbinical legends he is the ruler of Mercury, to which sphere he "imparts benignity, motion and intelligence, with elegance and consonance of speech." (See also **Angels**)

Microcosm, The

Or the Pentagram, a little world (Greek *Micros,* small; *Kosmos,* a world)—a five-pointed star, which represents Man and the summation of the occult forces. It was believed by **Paracelsus** that this sign had a marvelous magical power over spirits, and that all magic figures and Kabalistic signs could be reduced to two—the Microcosm, and the **Macrocosm.** (See also **Magical Diagrams; Macrocosm**)

Microprosopus, The

One of the four magical elements in the **Kabala,** probably representing one of the four simple elements—air, water, earth, or fire. The word means "creator of the little world." (See also **Kabala; Microcosm**)

Mictlan

The Mexican Hades. (See also **Hell; Mexico and Central America**)

Midday Demons

Ancient peoples frequently made mention of certain demons who became visible especially towards midday to those with whom they had a pact. They appeared in the form of men or of beasts, and let themselves be enclosed in a symbolic character, a figure, a vial, or in the interior of a hollow ring. (See also **Demonology**)

Midiwiwin, The

A secret society or exclusive association of the Ojibway Indians of North America. The myth of the foundation of this society is as follows:

"Michabo, the Creator, looking down to earth saw that the forefathers of the Ojibway were very helpless. . . . Espying a black object floating on the surface of a lake he drew near to it and saw that it was an otter [now one of the sacred animals of the *Midiwiwin*]. He instructed it in the mysteries of that caste, and provided it with a sacred rattle, a sacred drum, and tobacco. He built a *Midiwigan,* or Sacred House of Midi, to which he took the otter and confided to it the mysteries of the *Midiwiwin.*"

In short, the society was one of these "medicine" or magical associations so common among the North-American Indians (see **America, U.S. of**). When a candidate was admitted to a grade and prepared to pass on to the next, he gave three feasts, and sang three prayers to the Bear Spirit in order to be permitted to enter that grade. His progress through the various grades was assisted by several snake-spirits, and at a later stage by the power of certain prayers or invocations—a larger snake appeared and raised its body, thus forming an arch under which the candidate took his way to the higher grade.

When the Indian belonged to the second grade he was supposed to receive supernatural power, to be able to see into the future, to hear what came from far off, to touch friends and foes, however far away they might be, and so on.

In higher grades he could assume the form of any animal. The third grade conferred enhanced power, and it was thought that its members could perform extraordinary exploits, and have power over the entire invisible world. The fourth was still more exalted.

When an Indian was ready to undergo initiation, he erected a wigwam in which he took steambaths for four days, one on each day. On the evening of the day before initiation he visited his teachers in order to obtain from them instructions for the following day. Next morning the priests approached with the candidate at their head, entered the *Midiwigan,* and the proceedings commenced.

The publications of the Bureau of American Ethnology contain several good accounts of the ritual of this society.

Midwest Psychic News

Monthly publication covering psychic events in Chicago and other states. Address: 2517 West 71st Street, Chicago, Illinois 60629.

Miller, Charles Victor (c. 1908)

Remarkable **materialization** medium of San Francisco, born at Nancy, France. By profession he was a dealer in old pictures and Japanese objects of art. Detailed descriptions of his phenomena were given in Willie Reichel's *Occult Experiences* (1906). Reichel claimed to have witnessed many marvels.

For example, Miller did not go into trance as a seance started. He stood outside the cabinet from which a procession of phantoms issued. Miller took them by the hand, asked their names and introduced them to the sitters. Later he went into the cabinet, where he was seen with as many as six white robed figures. They came out one by one, spoke to the sitters and usually dematerialized in front of the cabinet, sinking through the floor. Of course, in modern times the very substantiality of materialized figures suggest fraud accomplices rather than genuine Spiritualist phenomena. However, the variety of Miller's phenomena and the certainty of witnesses leaves the question unproved either way. On one occasion Reichel's nephew disappeared by floating upwards through the ceiling. Miller was normally under the **control** of the spirits "Betsy" and "Dr. Benton."

The highest number of materialized spirits Reichel claimed to have seen in a seance was twelve. The medium was conscious and kept on talking. The phantoms spoke in various languages and many were recognized by the sitters. Once, in Reichel's own house, a materialized spirit walked out into the hall, a distance of thirty-five feet from the medium.

In the journal *Psychische Studien* (February 1904) Reichel described a seance at which a deceased friend of his materialized eight times, very near to him, at a distance of over three yards from the medium. "He drew near me," wrote Reichel, "like a floating flame, which lowered itself, and in the space of about a minute and a half developed and stood before me quite formed. He held long conversations with me; then, retiring to the curtain, where I followed him, he dematerialised, speaking up to the moment when his head disappeared."

Reichel also witnessed rotating white and blue flames whence voices issued and spoke to him, giving their complete names. In one seance the medium was completely dematerialized and transported to the first floor.

Miller paid two visits to Europe. When he first came in 1906, much criticism was directed against him because he mostly sat with Spiritists (see **Spiritism**) and avoided Col. **Rochas,** with whom he had corresponded, and a circle of scientists who had arranged to test him scientifically.

However, psychical researcher Gabriel **Delanne** concluded that the apparitions were genuine. Gaston Méry, chief editor of the *Libre Parole* and director of the *Echo du*

Merveilleux (which was not a Spiritist journal) admitted that it was highly probable that the phenomena which he witnessed were genuine but "until there is fuller information we must be satisfied with not comprehending." The seance took place in Méry's house in a room which Miller did not enter before the proceedings. Moreover, he was completely undressed in the presence of three doctors and donned Méry's own garments.

Dr. Gerard Encausse ("Papus") who also attended a seance, stated in *L'Initiation* that his expectation was fully satisfied and that Miller displayed "mediumistic faculties more extraordinary than he had hitherto encountered."

From Paris, Miller went on to Germany and gave many test seances in Munich at private residences. The accounts appear to corroborate Reichel's observations. The materialized form was often seen to develop from luminous globes and clouds which first appeared near the ceiling. If several forms were materialized at the same time they were transparent. It often happened that at the end of the seance Miller was violently thrown out of the cabinet. Yet he suffered no injury.

On his way back to the United States, Miller again visited Paris and gave a few more seances. According to Prof. Charles **Richet,** he would not accept the conditions imposed. Four of his seances were reported in *Annals of Psychic Science* (vol. 4, 1906). Psychical researcher Count Cesar **de Vesme,** who attended the last seance, and objected at not having been given an adequate opportunity to form a well-founded judgment, noted: "A white ball, as of gas, about a quarter of a yard in diameter appeared in the air at the upper extremity of the curtains. Finally it came down, rested on the floor, and in less than a minute, changing into a long shape, was transformed into a draped human form, which subsequently spoke." (*Annals of Psychic Science,* No. 21, 1906) The seance, however, was not sufficient to enable de Vesme to arrive at a very definite opinion as to the genuineness of these manifestations.

In 1908, Miller paid another visit to Paris. On June 25, in the presence of forty persons, a very successful seance was held at the house of Mme. Noeggerath under test conditions. The Committee of Control consisted of Messrs. Benezech, Gaston Méry, Cesar de Vesme and Charles Blech, Secretary of the Societe Theosophique. The medium was disrobed, medically examined and put into black garments which were furnished by the committee and had neither lining nor pockets. The evolution and dissolution of numerous phantom shapes was closely observed.

Cesar de Vesme, however, remained unconvinced. In the *Annals of Psychic Science* (vol. 7, 1908), he complained that in the series of seances which he attended in almost complete darkness Miller never allowed the control of his right hand. Sitting on the left side of the cabinet he could have introduced, with his right hand, a white drapery which he could have manipulated as a small phantom in the course of materialization. He had only been searched in a single seance when forty people were present. There was no telling whether the drapery might not have been passed to him by one of the sitters.

Leon Denis, Baron de Watteville, Charles Blech, de Fremery (director of the *Het Toekomstig Leven,* The Hague), Paul Leymarie (director of the *Revue Spirite*), M. W.

Bormann, (director of *Die Uebersinnliche Welt*) and Dr. Joseph **Maxwell** shared de Vesme's opinion.

Of Miller's public seances no more was heard after this Paris series.

Miller, Ellora Fogle (Mrs. R. DeWitt Miller) (1913–)

Writer in the fields of publicity and psychical research. Born June 8, 1913 at Philadelphia, Pennsylvania, she studied at University of Southern California (M.A. 1945). In 1937 she married R. DeWitt **Miller** (died 1958). She was a staff member of the publicity department of Young & Rubicam, Hollywood, California, and national editor of *The Baton* (publication of Phi Beta Fraternity) from 1953–56, director of honors, Phi Beta Fraternity, from 1956 onwards, member of Radio and Television Women of Southern California.

With her late husband she collaborated on various books and articles concerned with psychical research. Their books included *Forgotten Mysteries* (1947) and *You Do Take It With You* (1955), and their various articles were published in *Pageant, Tomorrow, Coronet, Popular Science, Popular Mechanics*.

Miller, R(ichard) DeWitt (1910–1958)

Writer on psychical research and parapsychology. Born January 22, 1910 at Los Angeles, California, he was educated at University of Southern California, (B.A. 1933). In 1937 he married Ellora Fogle. As a freelance writer Mr. Miller contributed many articles to *Coronet, Esquire, Pageant, Popular Mechanics, Popular Science, Tomorrow* and *Life*.

Many of his writings were concerned with parapsychological topics, and he contributed regular features 'Your Other Life,' 'Forgotten Mysteries' and 'Not of Our Species' to *Coronet* magazine. He often collaborated with his wife. His books include: *The Man Who Lived Forever* (1956), *Forgotten Mysteries* (1947), *Reincarnation* (1956), *You Do Take It With You* (1957). He contributed to the anthology *Beyond the Five Senses* edited by Eileen J. Garrett (1957). He died June 3, 1958.

Millesimo Castle

Located in Italy, province of Savona, property of the Marquis Carlo **Centurione Scotto,** scene of important psychic investigations in 1927–28 and later in the phenomena of **direct voice, apports, levitation** and **materialization.** (See **Centurione Scotto**)

Mind-Body-Spirit Festival

International festival event coordinating and presenting occult, mystical, psychical, astrological, New Age, human potential and holistic organizations and individuals. Founded in April 1977 in England by new consciousness entrepreneur Graham **Wilson,** the Festival has since been presented annually in London and the U.S., associated with similar events in British provincial centers, and in São Paulo, Brazil.

The Festival provides an annual stage for contemporary alternative lifestyles in a wide spectrum of mystical, holistic and ecological areas, where traditional philosophies and activities rub shoulders with newer cults. The Festival includes lectures, demonstrations and workshops as well as exhibits and stands promoting individuals, organizations and publications concerned with psychic phenomena, healing, yoga, astrology, health, physical fitness, dance, UFOs, meditation, organic gardening, mystical arts and crafts and alternative technologies. Address: Mind-Body-Spirit Festival, 159 George Street, London, W1H 5LB, England.

Mind Cure

A system of healing, distinct from **Mesmerism** and **hypnotism,** first developed in America by Phineas Parkhurst **Quimby** (1802–66), a professional Mesmerist who discovered that his subject, in his clairvoyant diagnosis, simply reproduced the opinion which the patient or Quimby himself had formed of the disease and that his prescriptions could be traced to the same source.

Quimby conceived the idea that disease, if the expectation of the patient is enough to dispel it, is a delusion, an error of the mind. In accordance with this idea he elaborated a new method of mental treatment and began to practice it in Portland, Maine, in 1859.

Quimby did not work out his philosophical ideas into a coherent system. He described it as the "Science of Christ," "Science of Health," and occasionally as "Christian Science."

Pupils were recruited from his patients. The Rev. F. W. Evans, a Methodist minister, was one of the earliest. He published, between 1868–86 a number of books on mental healing, differing on many points from Quimby, and established in late life, a mind-cure sanatorium in Salisbury, Mass. Julius Dresser and his wife also became Quimby's disciples and their son, Horatio W. Dresser, has been acknowledged as the ablest exponent of what came to be called the **"New Thought"** movement.

The most famous patient and pupil turned out to be a woman—Mrs. Mary M. Patterson, later Mary Baker G. Eddy. In her childhood she was delicate, heard voices at the age of eight and spent the greater part of her youth and early womanhood as a confirmed invalid.

In 1862, at the age of 41, she came to Quimby. He restored her to health and this apparent miracle determined her later course of life. Filled with enthusiasm for Quimby, she gave lectures on his doctrines and for some years considered herself as his disciple, even after Quimby's death. At this period she was known as a Spiritualist medium. In trance she received communications from her deceased brother, Albert.

Her first advertisement as a healer was published in the *Banner of Light* in 1868. Soon she began to establish the method of mental healing as her own and in 1875 when she published *Science and Health* a small band of followers grew up around her. She elaborated Quimby's teachings and as a counterpart to distant healing introduced the concept of "malicious animal magnetism," not unlike the superstition of the evil eye and bewitchment of the Middle Ages.

As the years passed, Mrs. Eddy's influence grew and mental healing developed into the religious system **Christian Science** with the following fundamental propositions: 1) God is all in all; 2) God is Good. Good is Mind; 3) God, Spirit, being all, nothing is matter; 4) Life, God, omnipotent good, deny death, evil, sin, disease.

Meanwhile the New Thought movement had developed its own momentum and an international New Thought Alliance adopted a declaration of principles affirming the basis of New Thought as a religious grouping. Important names in the New Thought movement include Norman Vincent Peale (famous for his book *The Power of Positive Thinking*), Bishop Fulton J. Sheen, and Rabbi Joseph Liebman. Other independent New Thought bodies are The Unity School of Christianity of Charles and Myrtle Fillmore and The United Church of Religious Science of Ernest Holmes.

Other interesting names stemming from Mind Cure and New Thought are those of Prentice **Mulford** (author of the famous White Cross Library) and Ralph Waldo Trine (author of *The Power of Positive Thinking*). (See also **Autosuggestion; Christian Science; Mesmerism; New Thought**)

Mines, Haunted

The belief that mines are haunted is an ancient and universal one, probably arising from the many weird sounds and echoes which were heard in them, and the perpetual gloom, stimulating apparitions. Sometimes the haunting specters were gigantic creatures with frightful fiery eyes. Such was the German "Bergmönch, a terrible figure in the garb of a monk, who could, however, appear in ordinary human shape to those towards whom he was well-disposed."

Frequently weird knockings were heard in the mines. In Germany these were attributed to the Kobolds, small black beings of a malicious disposition. White hares or rabbits were also seen at times. The continual dangers attending work underground have been productive of many supernatural "warnings," which generally take the form of mysterious voices.

In the Midland Counties of England, the "Seven Whistlers" were well known and their warnings solemnly attended to. A light blue flame settling on a full coal-tub was called "Bluecap," and his work was to move the coal-tub towards the trolley-way. Bluecap did not give his services for nothing. Every fortnight his wages were left in a corner of the mine, and duly appropriated. A more mischievous elf was "Cutty Soames," who would cut the "soams" or traces yoking an assistant putter to the tub.

Basilisks, fearsome monsters whose terrible eyes would strike the miner dead were another source of dread to the worker underground. These, as well as other mysterious foes who dealt fatal blows, may be traced to the dreaded, but by no means ghostly, fire-damp or perhaps to underground lizards.

Mines of precious metals were believed to be even more jealously guarded by supernatural beings. Gnomes, the creatures of the earth element, were the special guardians of subterranean treasure, and they were anxious to defend their province. Mines containing precious stones were equally well looked after. The Indians of Peru declared that evil spirits haunted the emerald mines, while a mine in the neighborhood of Los Esmeraldos was said to be guarded by a frightful dragon. It has also been believed that the poisonous fumes and gases which often destroy the lives of miners were baleful influences radiated by evil spirits.

Other stories of haunted mines are linked to legends of secret underground temples of occultists. (See **Subterranean Crypts and Temples**)

Miñoza, Aurora (1923–)

Assistant professor of psychology who has written on parapsychology. Born January 4, 1923 at Cebu City, Philippines, she studied at University of Michigan (B.S. English 1947, M.A. psychology 1953), University of the Philippines (Ph.D. educational psychology 1957). She was an instructor in English and psychology at Cebu College from 1947–50, instructor in euthenics and psychology from 1950–55, assistant professor in education and psychology, Graduate College of Education, University of the Philippines, from 1957 onwards.

She was president of the Parapsychological Research Society, Philippines, from 1959 onwards, and is a member of the American Psychological Association, and Parapsychological Association. Her master's thesis was *A Study of Extrasensory Perception,* published in abstract by the *Educational Quarterly,* University of the Philippines (vol. 1, No. 1 September 1953).

In 1955 Dr. Miñoza received a U.S. International Cooperation Administration educational scholarship. She attended the first Parapsychology Workshop at Duke University, June 1957. She has special interests in telepathy, clairvoyance and psychokinesis, and has experimented with the effect of thought on plant growth.

Mirabelli, (Carmine) Carlos (1889–1951)

South American physical medium of Italian parentage, born in Botucatu, São Paolo. Such extraordinary accounts of his phenomena have reached England and the U.S. that if they could be proved to the satisfaction of psychical researchers, he would have to be ranked as the greatest medium of all time. Such phenomena included automatic writing in more than thirty different languages, materialization of persons and objects, levitation, impressions of spirit hands, paranormal musical performances and he normally produced phenomena in good light.

The first description of Mirabelli's amazing case was published in Germany by the *Zeitschrift für Parapsychologie* in August 1929, on the basis of a Brazilian book, *O Medium Mirabelli,* by Amador Bueno. Fearing a hoax, the German periodical made inquiries first from the Brazilian consul at Munich as to the standing and reputation of the witnesses and supporters of Mirabelli. The answer was positive and the Consul added that fourteen persons of the submitted list were his personal acquaintances to whose veracity he would testify, nor had he the right of questioning the statements of other people on the list, known to him not only as scientists but also as men of character. Thereupon the *Zeitschrift für Parapsychologie* published a summary of the remarkable case.

The summary was further supported by E. J. **Dingwall**'s examination (*Psychic Research,* July 1930) of the original Portuguese documents. It appears that the reality of the Mirabelli phenomena was first acknowledged by psychiatrists. He was committed to an asylum for the insane for observation for nineteen days. The newspapers took up the case. They wrote of telekinetic **movement,** of **apports,** of a miraculous **teleportation** of the medium from the railroad station of Da Luz to Sao Vincenti, 90 kilometers distance, in two minutes; of his **levitation** in the street two meters high for three minutes; of how he caused a skull to float towards an apothecary; of making an invisible hand turn the leaves of a book in the home of Dr. Alberto Seabra in the presence of many scientists; of making glasses and bottles at a banquet play a military march without human touch; of causing the hat of Antonio Canterello to fly off and float ten meters along a public square; of making and quelling fire by will in the home of Prof. Dr. Alves Lima; of making a cue play billiards without touching it and finally of having the picture of Christ impressed on plaster in the presence of Dr. Caluby, Director of Police.

A conjuring magician imitated some of the phenomena, but this did not lessen the reputation of Mirabelli as a wonder worker. Owing to the heated controversy which grew up around Mirabelli, an arbitration board was instituted for the investigation of the medium, among the members of which were Dr. Ganymed de Sousa, President of the Republic, Brant, of the Institute of Technology and eighteen other men of high position and learning.

After the investigation and the hearing of witnesses, the board established that the majority of the manifestations occurred in daylight, that they occurred spontaneously and in public places, that the manifold intellectual phenomena could not well be based on trickery, that the statements of personalities whose integrity is reputed could not well be doubted.

In 1919, the **Academia de Estudos Psychicos "Cesar Lombroso"** was founded. Mirabelli submitted himself for experiments in **trance** speaking, automatic writing and physical phenomena. The report was published in 1926. It reported 392 sittings in broad daylight or in a room illuminated by powerful electric light, in 349 cases in the rooms of the Academy, attended by 555 people and the summary was as follows:

"The committee carried out with the first group (medical speaking) 189 positive experiments; with the second group (automatic writing) 85 positive and 8 negative; with the third group (physical phenomena) 63 positive and 47 negative experiments. The medium spoke 26 languages including 7 dialects, wrote in 28 languages, among them 3 dead languages, namely Latin, Chaldaic and Hieroglyphics. Of the 63 physical experiments 40 were made in daylight, 23 in bright artificial light."

The automatic writing was inspired by celebrities. Johan Huss impressed Mirabelli to write a treatise of nine pages on the independence of Czechoslovakia in twenty minutes, "Camille **Flammarion**" inspired him to write about inhabited planets, fourteen pages in nineteen minutes in French. "Muri Ka Ksi" delivered five pages in twelve minutes on the Russo-Japanese war in Japanese, "Moses" wrote in Hebrew on slandering, "Harun el Raschid" made him write fifteen pages in Syrian and an untranslatable writing of three pages came in hieroglyphics in thirty-two minutes.

The phenomena of materialization were astounding. The figures were not only complete, and photographed, but medical men made minute examinations which lasted sometimes as long as for fifteen minutes and stated that the newly constituted human beings had perfect anatomical structure. After the examination was completed, one figure began to dissolve from the feet upwards, the bust and arms floating in the air. One of the doctors exclaimed

"But this is too much," rushed forward and seized the half of the body. The next moment he uttered a shrill cry and sank unconscious to the ground. On returning to consciousness he only remembered that when he had seized the phantom it had felt as if his fingers were pressing a spongy, flaccid mass of substance. Then he received a shock and lost consciousness.

For thirty-six minutes in broad daylight the materialization of the little daughter of Dr. Souza, who died of influenza, was visible to all the sitters. She appeared in her grave clothes. Her pulse was tested. Father and child were photographed. Then the phantom raised itself and floated in the air. At the third sitting, a skull inside the closet began to beat the doors, came out and slowly grew to a full skeleton (see **Materialization**).

In another sitting Mirabelli announced that he saw the body of Bishop Dr. Jose de Carmago Barros who had lost his life in a shipwreck. "A sweet smell as of roses filled the room. The medium went into trance. A fine mist was seen in the circle. The mist, glowing as if of gold, parted and the bishop materialized, with all the robes and insignia of office. He called his own name. Dr. de Souza stepped to him. He palpated the body, touched his teeth, tested the saliva, listened to the heart-beat, investigated the working of the intestines, nails and eyes, without finding anything amiss. Then the other attending persons convinced themselves of the reality of the apparition. The Bishop smilingly bent over Mirabelli and looked at him silently. Then he slowly dematerialized."

"At the sixth sitting, Mirabelli, tied and sealed, disappeared from the room, and was found in another room still in trance. All seals on doors and windows were found in order, as well as the seals on Mirabelli himself." Once among fourteen investigators his arms dematerialized. On the photograph only a slight shadow is visible.

The British psychical researcher E. J. **Dingwall** ended his review of the documents: "I must confess that, on a lengthy examination of the documents concerning Mirabelli, I find myself totally at a loss to come to any decision whatever on the case. It would be easy to condemn the man as a monstrous fraud and the sitters as equally monstrous fools. But I do not think that such a supposition will help even him who makes it." In reviewing a German translation of a Mirabelli book in 1960, Dr. Dingwall stated that the Mirabelli case "remains another of those unsolved mysteries with which the history of parapsychology abounds."

In the November 1930 issue of *Psychic Research,* Professor Hans **Driesch** threw cold water on all such marvels on the basis of a personal investigation in São Paolo in 1928. He saw no materializations, no transportation, heard only Italian and Esthonian which may have been normally known, but he admitted seeing some remarkable telekinetic phenomena which he could not explain involving the movement of a small vase and the folding of doors in daylight without any visible cause. As to the book *O Medium Mirabelli,* he was unable to find out who had written it, not even an intimate friend of Mirabelli (the overseer of the Town Library of São Paolo) knew it. He wrote: "Might not Mirabelli have written the book—himself?" Of the investigation by the Academia de Estudos Psychicos there was no mention in Prof. Driesch's article.

Mirabelli died April 30, 1951 as the result of a road accident. For a modern discussion of this remarkable medium see the chapter 'Mirabelli!!' in *The Unknown Power* (British title *The Flying Cow*) by Guy Lyon Playfair (Pocket Book paperback, 1975). Playfair met and interviewed individuals who had known Mirabelli, including living relatives.

"Mirabilis Liber"

A collection of predictions concerning the saints and the sibyls, attributed to Saint Césaire (470–542 A.D.). The work appeared in various editions. It is surprising to find in the edition of 1522 a prophecy of the French Revolution. The expulsion and abolition of the nobility, the violent death of the king and queen, the persecution of the clergy, the suppression of convents, are all mentioned, followed by a further prophecy that the eagle coming from distant lands would reestablish order in France.

Miracles

One objection urged against Spiritualist phenomena is that they represent miracles and that miracles do not happen, therefore the phenomena cannot be genuine. A lively controversy has raged around the subject since the first days when a claim was made for scientific attention to seance room occurrences. David Hume, the great Scotch philosopher, defined a miracle "as a violation of the laws of nature." Dr. Alfred Russel **Wallace,** in his book *On Miracles and Modern Spiritualism* (1881), objected that we do not know all the laws of nature, therefore we cannot rule out the possibility of an unknown law overcoming the known one. He suggested that a miracle was "any act or event necessarily implying the existence and agency of superhuman intelligences."

According to Hume, no amount of human testimony can prove a miracle. It is perhaps on this basis that in spite of the universal belief in certain supernatural happenings, the pessimistic school of scientists generally refused to investigate their nature and the evidence of their happening. This fact is very curious as the whole history of human progress demonstrates that as Prof. Charles **Richet** stated, "the improbabilities of to-day are the elementary truths of to-morrow."

Sir Isaac Newton had to fight for so long for the recognition of his theory of gravitation that he nearly resolved to publish nothing more and said: "I see that a man must either resolve to put out nothing new, or become a slave to defend it."

Galileo was persecuted and declared "ignorant of his ignorance," the evidence of his telescope was rejected without examination; Galvani was ridiculed and nicknamed "the frog's dancing master;" Harvey, the discoverer of blood circulation, Jenner, the discoverer of preventive vaccination, were "mad;" Benjamin Franklin was laughed at for the idea of the lightning conductor; Young, the proponent of the undulatory theory of light, was scorned; Sir Humphrey Davy thought the idea of lighting London with gas ludicrous; Arago was derided by the French Academy of Sciences when he wanted to discuss the subject of the electric telegraph; learned men produced evidence that Robert Stevenson's railway idea was preposterous; the action of microbes was contested for twenty years. Bouillaud attributed the telephone to ventriloquism. Lavoisier said that stones cannot fall from the sky as there are no stones in the sky, the discovery of the stethoscope, the idea of painless operation in mesmeric coma or the discovery of anaesthetics was extremely "foolish."

As late as 1893, Lord Kelvin wrote in a letter to W. T. **Stead:** "I believe that nearly everything in hypnotism and clairvoyance is imposture and the rest bad observation." Yet he appeared to admit that miracles do exist when he said: "Every action of human free will is a miracle to physical, chemical and mathematical science."

Belief in the reality of miracles has always been one of the cornerstones of religion. In former times it was sufficient to have faith that the divine power which created the universe of matter could also transcend its laws either directly or through the agency of saints.

However, the religious skepticism of the nineteenth century, together with the remarkable advances of science and technology, threw doubt on the reality of all miracles, sacred or secular. Part of the present-day opposition to claims of the paranormal is based on the brilliant achievements of applied scientific laws, reinforcing confidence in the logic of the material world. From this viewpoint, many modern agnostics and atheists deny the possibility of either religious miracles or secular paranormal happenings, claiming that both are the result of malobservation, superstition or fraud.

Meanwhile religious authorities continue to uphold the validity of Biblical miracles as indicating God's omnipotence and intervention in human affairs. Vatican Council I denied that "miracles are impossible." However, some theologians have taken the view that miracles are no longer necessary in modern times as evidence for religious faith. The Roman Catholic Church has long been aware of the necessity for great caution in evaluating apparent miracles in modern times, since it would be foolish to ignore the possibility of misunderstanding or deception. Ever since the claimed miraculous healings associated with pilgrim centers like Lourdes, the Church has been careful to insist on satisfactory scientific and medical evidence over a prolonged period of time before a miracle can be accepted.

The most controversial problem, however, remains the distinction between religious and secular miracles. Parapsychologists and Spiritualists may point to the many reported miracles in the Bible as evidence for similar paranormal events in modern times. Church authorities would accept as miraculous only those events which have a clearly established religious purpose, and reject as unproven or false all other claimed paranormal happenings. Some more orthodox churchmen have even claimed that all psychic phenomena, including that of Spiritualism, is a mere simulacrum of the miraculous and the work of devils or deceptive spirits. Not unnaturally Spiritualists resent such accusations since they too are religious people, and it is unreasonable to claim that the miracles of one religion are genuine and those of all other faiths are false. Miracles have been reported frequently in Eastern religions, even into modern times, and clearly any attempt to establish a monopoly of miracles by one faith must necessarily cast doubt upon itself as much as on the other faiths condemned as diabolical. Such an extreme position merely echoes medieval intolerance in believing that all other religions except one's own must be false and the work of the devil. Surely there are many different paths to one point.

Nowadays, it is reasonable to suppose that miracles may occasionally occur within the context of any religion and that similar paranormal events may also occur in a secular context. It seems that faith can sometimes be a powerful factor in stimulating paranormal events, particularly in faith healing, and that such faith is often enhanced by group energies. Whether the groups are sincere and enlightened individuals or an ignorant or hysterical crowd may not substantially affect the incidence of the paranormal, although it may have some effect on its quality.

Perhaps the emphasis given to miracles by religions in the past may have been somewhat misplaced, and it is reasonable for the Roman Catholic Church to be cautious about the endorsement of miracles today. It should be noted that in the **yoga** system of Eastern religion, first place is given to performance of everyday social duties and observation of ethical principles and self-purification in spiritual development. It is claimed that paranormal events may take place in such development but they should be ignored as irrelevant to true spiritual evolution. The expansion of consciousness from the narrow hopes and fears, mental and emotional limitations of individual existence, into a broader awareness, transcending mental and physical gains and losses, is claimed as the true goal of human endeavor. (See also **Autosuggestion; Bilocation; Christian Science; Fatima; Fire Ordeal;** Psychic **Healing; Healing by Faith; Healing by Touch; Levitation; Lourdes;** Therese **Neumann;** Padré **Pio; Snake-Handling; Spiritualism; Stigmata; Yoga**)

Recommended reading:

Ebon, Martin (ed.). *Miracles,* Signet paperback, New American Library, 1981

Hill, J. Arthur. *Spiritualism; Its History, Phenomena & Doctrine,* Cassell, London, 1918

Gopi Krishna. *The Secret of Yoga,* Harper & Row, 1972

LeShan, Lawrence. *The Medium, the Mystic, and the Physicist,* Viking Press, 1974

Réginald-Omez, Fr., O.P. *Psychical Phenomena,* Burns & Oates, London, 1959

Rogo, D. Scott. *Miracles; A Parascientific Inquiry Into Wondrous Phenomena,* Dial Press, New York, 1982

Stemman, Roy. *One Hundred Years of Spiritualism,* Spiritualist Association of Great Britain, London, 1972

Summers, Montague. *The Physical Phenomena of Mysticism,* Rider & Co., London, 1950

Thurston, Herbert, S. J. *The Physical Phenomena of Mysticism,* Burns & Oates, London, 1952; Henry Regnery, Chicago, 1953

West, Donald J. *Eleven Lourdes Miracles,* Duckworth, London, 1957

Mishna, The

A compilation of Jewish oral traditions embodying the religious legal decisions relating to Old Testament laws, gathered together about the end of the second century by a certain Rabbi Judah, grandson of Gamaliel II. Its doctrines are said to be of great antiquity. It forms the framework of the *Talmud.* (See also **Kabala**)

"Miss X"

Pseudonym of psychical researcher Ada **Goodrich-Freer,** used for her early writings on psychical subjects.

Mitchell, Edgar D. (1930–   )

American astronaut with an active interest in parapsychology. Born September 17, 1930 at Hereford, Texas, he was educated at Carnegie Institute of Technology. He entered the U.S. Navy in 1952 and was commissioned a year later. On completing flight training, he was assigned to Patrol Squadron 29 in Okinawa and flew aircraft on carrier duty and Heavy Attack Squadron. He studied for his doctorate in aeronautics and astronautics at Massachusetts Institute of Technology, and became Chief, Project Management Division, Navy Field Office for Manned Orbiting Laboratory, 1964; later attended Air Force Aerospace Research Pilot School. He was selected by NASA as an astronaut April 1966, and was Lunar Module Pilot of Apollo 14 which landed on the moon February 5, 1971.

His interest in parapsychology dated from 1967, soon after his arrival at the NASA Manned Spacecraft Center in Houston. He was dissatisfied with orthodox theology and began to investigate areas of psychic phenomena and mysticism. In December 1969, Mitchell became friendly with medium Arthur **Ford,** who suggested an interesting ESP test from a man in a rocket to a contact on earth.

Mitchell planned a rocket-to-earth ESP test for the Apollo 14 mission, although Ford died January 4, 1971, twenty-seven days before the mission launch (to which he had been invited as Mitchell's guest). NASA had rejected a telepathy experiment planned by the American Society for Psychical Research in 1970, so Mitchell's test was a private affair in his own rest periods. The tests involved the transmission of symbols associated with a range of chosen numbers.

Eminent parapsychologists J. B. **Rhine** of the **Foundation for Research on the Nature of Man** and K. **Osis** of the American Society for Psychical Research offered cooperation in evaluating the test. In the event, the results of the test were ambiguous, success or failure rating depending upon the evaluation technique used.

After being the sixth man to walk on the moon, Mitchell was a member of the backup crew of further lunar probes. He retired from NASA and the Navy in 1972. His second wife Anita, whom Mitchell married in 1973 after a divorce, shared his interest in parapsychology. In the same year Mitchell founded the **Institute of Noetic Sciences** for the study of human consciousness and mind/body relationships. He supported the efforts of Andrija **Puharich** to test Uri **Geller,** and supervised experiments with Geller at Stanford Research Institute.

Mitchell, T(homas) W(alker) (1869–1944)

British physician, psychologist and active worker in the field of psychical research in Britain. Born January 18, 1869 at Avock, Ross-shire, Scotland, he was educated at Fortrose Academy and University of Edinburgh (M.B., C.M. 1890, M.D. 1906). In 1931 he married Henrietta Violet Kerans. He was president of the British Psycho-Medical Society in 1911, and edited the *British Journal of Medical Psychology* from 1920–35.

He was particularly interested in psychical research in

relation to hypnosis and multiple personality. He played a prominent part in the Society for Psychical Research, London, was president in 1921, member of Council from 1909–44, secretary of the medical section from 1911–18. He was author of *The Psychology of Medicine* (1921) and contributed to *Psychology and the Sciences* edited by William **Brown** (1924).

He published a number of contributions in the SPR *Proceedings,* including 'The Appreciation of Time by Somnambules' (1908–09), 'Some Recent Developments in Psychotherapy' (1910), 'The Hypnoidal State of Sidis' (1911), 'Psychotherapy and Psychoanalysis' (1912–13), 'A Study in Hysteria and Multiple Personality' (1912–13), 'Some Types of Multiple Personality' (1912–13), 'Psychology of the Unconscious and Psychoanalysis' (1920), 'The Doris Fischer Case of Multiple Personality' (1921). His paper 'Phenomena of Mediumistic Trance' was read to the British Association for the Advancement of Science, 1927.

Modern Times, The Socialist Community of

A community founded on Long Island, in 1851, which numbered among its members a good many Spiritualists.

Moghrebi

Arab sorcerer. (See **Semites**)

Mohanes

Shamans or medicine men of the Indians of the Peruvian Andes. Joseph Skinner referred to them in his *State of Peru* (London 1805):

"These admit an evil being, the inhabitant of the centre of the earth, whom they consider as the author of their misfortunes, and at the mention of whose name they tremble. The most shrewd among them take advantage of this belief, to obtain respect; and represent themselves as his delegates. Under the denomination of *Mohanes,* or *Agoreros,* they are consulted even on the most trivial occasions. They preside over the intrigues of love, the health of the community, and the taking of the field. Whatever repeatedly occurs to defeat their prognostics, falls on themselves; and they are wont to pay their deceptions very dearly. They chew a species of vegetable called *puripiri,* and throw it into the air, accompanying this act by certain recitals and incantations, to injure some, to benefit others, to procure rain, and the inundation of the rivers, or, on the other hand, to occasion settled weather, and a plentiful store of agricultural productions. Any such result having been casually verified on a single occasion, suffices to confirm the Indians in their faith, although they may have been cheated a thousand times. Fully persuaded that they cannot resist the influence of the *puripiri,* as soon as they know that they have been solicited by its means, they fix their eyes on the impassioned object, and discover a thousand amiable traits, either real or fanciful, which indifference had before concealed from their view.

"But the principal power, efficacy, and, it may be said misfortune, of the *Mohanes,* consist in the cure of the sick. Every malady is ascribed to their enchantments, and means are instantly taken to ascertain by whom the mischief may have been wrought. For this purpose the nearest relative takes a quantity of the juice of *floripondium,*

and suddenly falls, intoxicated by the violence of the plant. He is placed in a fit posture to prevent suffocation, and on his coming to himself, at the end of three days, the *Mohan* who has the greatest resemblance to the sorcerer he saw in his visions, is to undertake the cure, or if, in the interim, the sick man has perished, it is customary to subject him to the same fate. When not any sorcerer occurs in the visions, the first *Mohan* they encounter has the misfortune to represent his image."

It seems that by practice and tradition, the *Mohanes* acquired a profound knowledge of many plants and poisons, with which they effected surprising cures on the one hand, and did some mischief on the other. They also made use of charms and superstitions.

One method of cure was to place two hammocks close to each other, either in the dwelling, or in the open air. In one of them the patient laid extended, and in the other laid the *Mohan,* or Agorero. The latter, in contact with the sick man, began by rocking himself, and then proceeded in falsetto voice to call on the birds, quadrupeds, and fishes to give health to the patient. From time to time he rose on his seat, and made extravagant gestures over the sick man, to whom he applied his powders and herbs, or sucked the wounded or diseased parts. Having been joined by many of the people, the *Agoreros* chanted a short hymn, addressed to the soul of the patient, with this refrain: "Thou must not go, thou must not go." In repeating this he was joined by the people, until at length a terrific clamour was raised, and augmented in proportion as the sick man became still fainter and fainter so that it might reach his ears.

Mompesson, John (c. 1662)

Magistrate at Tedworth, Wiltshire, England in 1661 whose home was disturbed by **poltergeist** phenomena. (See **Drummer of Tedworth**)

Monaciello, The

The *Monaciello* or "Little Monk" was a spirit who seems to have lived exclusively in Naples, Southern Italy. The precise place where he dwelt does not appear to be accurately known, but it is supposed to have been in the remains of abbeys and monasteries.

When the *Monaciello* appeared to mortals, it was always at the dead of night, and then only to those who were in sorest need, who themselves had done all that mortals could do to prevent or alleviate the distress that had befallen them, and after all human aid had failed.

Then it was that the "Monk" appeared, and mutely beckoning them to follow, led them to where treasure was concealed stipulating no conditions for its expenditure, demanding no promise of repayment, exacting no duty or service in return.

It is not clear whether it was actual treasure that he gave, or whether it merely appeared so to the external senses, to be changed into leaves or stones when the day and the occasion of its requirement had passed. And if actual treasure, how it came in the place of its concealment, and by whom it was deposited there.

In Germany, the wood-spirit "Rubezahl" performed similar acts of beneficence and kindness to poor and deserving persons and the money he gave proved to be, or passed for the current coin of the realm. In Ireland, the

O'Donoghue, who dwelt beneath the waters of an inland lake, and rode over its surface on a steed white as the foam of its waves, was said to distribute treasures that proved genuine to the good, but spurious to the undeserving.

Monad (in Theosophy)

Theosophical term which literally means a unit (Greek *Monas*). The *Monad* is frequently described as a "Divine Spark," and this impression is particularly apt, for it is a part of the Logos, the Divine Fire.

The Logos has three aspects—Will, Wisdom and Activity and, since the *Monad* is part of the Logos, it also has these three aspects. It abides continually in its appropriate world, the monadic, but in order that the divine evolutionary purposes may be carried out, its ray is borne downwards through the various spheres of matter when the outpouring of the third life wave takes place.

It first passes into the Spiritual Sphere by clothing itself with an atom of spiritual matter and thus manifests itself in an atomic body, as a spirit possessing three aspects. When it passes into the next sphere, the Intuitional, it leaves its aspect of Will behind and in the Intuitional Sphere, appears in an Intuitional body as a spirit possessing the aspects of Wisdom and Activity. On passing in turn, from this sphere to the next, the higher Mental, it leaves the aspect of Wisdom behind, and appears in a casual body as a spirit possessing the aspect of activity.

To put this somewhat abstruse doctrine in another form, the *Monad* has, at this stage, manifested itself in three spheres. In the spiritual it has transfused spirit with Will, in the Intuitional it has transfused spirit with Wisdom, and in the higher Mental it has transfused spirit with Activity or Intellect, and it is now a human ego, corresponding approximately to the common term "soul," an ego which, despite all changes, remains the same until eventually the evolutionary purpose is fulfilled and it is received back again into the Logos.

From the higher mental sphere, the *Monad* descends to the lower mental sphere and appears in a mental body as possessing mind, then betakes itself to the astral sphere and appears in the astral body as possessing emotions, and finally to the physical sphere and appears in a physical body as possessing vitality. These three lower bodies, the mental, the astral, and the physical, constitute the human personality which dies at death and is renewed when the *Monad,* in fulfilment of the process of reincarnation, again manifests itself in these bodies. (See also **Evolution of Life; Life Waves; Logos; Sphere; Spirit**)

Monck, Rev. Francis Ward (c. 1878)

British clergyman who started his career as minister of the Baptist Chapel at Earls Barton and gave up his ecclesiastical vocation for professional mediumship.

His adhesion to Spiritualism was first announced in 1873. He claimed great mediumistic powers, toured the British Isles and healed the sick in Ireland. As a result he was called "Dr." Monck by many people, although not a physician.

In London, he convinced Dr. Alfred Russel **Wallace,** the Rev. Stainton **Moses** and Hensleigh Wedgwood (brother-in-law of Darwin) of his genuine psychic gifts by giving a remarkable **materialization** seance in bright daylight. He also excelled in **slate-writing.** An account by

Dr. Alfred Russel Wallace of a puzzling slate writing demonstration was certified by Edward T. Bennett, then assistant secretary to the Society for Psychical Research, London. He convinced Judge Dailey of America that the dead returned through his body. His reputation was high.

It suffered a severe blow, however, shortly after the trial of Henry **Slade.** At a Huddersfield seance on November 3, 1876, a conjurer named H. B. Lodge suddenly demanded the search of the medium. Monck ran for safety, locked himself into his room upstairs and escaped through the window. As a further evidence of his guilt, a pair of stuffed gloves was found in his room. In the medium's luggage were found "spirit lamps," a "spirit bird," cheesecloth, and reaching rods, as well as some obscene correspondence from women. Nor was this the first case when Monck was caught in flagrant fraud. Sir William **Barrett** wrote of "a piece of white muslin on a wire frame with a black thread attached being used by the medium to simulate a partially materialised spirit."

The trial which followed the Huddersfield exposure was a great sensation. One of the witnesses was Dr. Alfred Russel Wallace. He deposed that "he had seen Dr. Monck in the trance state, when there appeared a faint white patch on the left side of his coat, which increased in density and spread till it reached his shoulder; then there was a space gradually widening to six feet between it and his body, it became very distinct and had the outline of a woman in flowing white drapery. I was absolutely certain that it could not be produced by any possible trick."

The court found Monck guilty and sentenced him to three months' imprisonment.

The blow was a stunning one. There were, however, friends who did not give up their faith in Monck. There was no greater believer in his powers than Archdeacon Colley, who had reported the most inexplicable and astounding experiences with Monck. Colley was in India when the Huddersfield incident happened. After his return, he stoutly maintained that a dreadful miscarriage of justice must have taken place. Of a seance held on September 25, 1877, on the basis of notes made the same evening, he published the following account: "Dr. Monck, under control of Samuel, was by the light of the lamp—the writer not being a yard away from him—seen by all to be the living gate for the extrusion of spirit forms from the realm of mind into this world of matter; for standing forth thus plainly before us, the psychic or spirit form was seen to grow out of his left side. First, several faces one after another, of great beauty appeared, and in amazement we saw—and as I was standing close up to the medium, even touching him, I saw most plainly—several times, a perfect face and form of exquisite womanhood partially issue from Dr. Monck, about the region of the heart. Then after several attempts a full formed figure, in a nebulous condition at first, but growing more solid as it issued from the medium, left Dr. Monck, and stood a separate individuality, two or three feet off, bound to him by a slender attachment as of gossamer, which at my request Samuel, the control, severed with the medium's left hand, and there stood embodied a spirit form of unutterable loveliness, robed in attire spirit-spun—a meshy web-work from no mortal loom, of a fleeciness inimitable, and of transfiguration whiteness truly glistening."

Colley was so sure of his own powers of observation that

he challenged stage magician J. N. **Maskelyne** and offered him a thousand pounds if he could duplicate Monck's materialization performance. Maskelyne attempted the feat and when Archdeacon Colley declared his performance to be a travesty of what had really taken place in Monck's presence, Maskelyne sued for the money. Mainly on the evidence of Dr. Alfred Russel Wallace, on behalf of Monck, judgment was entered against Maskelyne.

In his materialization seances Monck rarely used a cabinet. He stood in full view of the sitters. Sometimes he was quite conscious. He had two chief controls: "Samuel" and "Mahedi." For a year their individual character was deeply studied by Stainton Moses and Hensleigh Wedgwood who, with two other men interested in psychic research, secured Monck's services with exclusive rights for a modest salary.

Enduring evidence of Monck's phantasmal appearances was obtained by William Oxley in 1876 in Manchester in the form of excellent paraffin molds of hands and feet of the materialized forms (see **Plastics**). Oxley described his psychic experiences in *Modern Messiahs and Wonder Workers* (1889). This disposes of the hallucination theory which psychical researcher Frank **Podmore** put forward in view of Archdeacon Colley's astounding experiences. Paraffin wax cannot be hallucinated. The supposition in itself is difficult that Monck could have played the fool with an intimate friend for many years.

In his lecture before the Church Congress at Weymouth in 1903 Archdeacon Colley said: "Often when I have been sleeping in the same bedroom with him, for the near observation of casual phenomena during the night and, specially, that came through the dark I, on such occasions, would hold my hand over his mouth, and he would now and again be startled into wakefulness not unmixed with fear. For he could see the phantoms which I could not, when I had quietly put out the night-light—for he would not sleep in the dark, which made him apprehensive of phenomena, physically powerful to an extraordinary degree."

The Archdeacon's experiences present a remarkable record in the history of materialization, equalled only by the Brazilian medium Carlos **Mirabelli.** However, Mirabelli was never found to be fraudulent.

Archdeacon Colley claimed to have witnessed astonishing marvels with Monck. He said he saw the birth and dissolution of numbers of full-sized solid forms. He saw a child appear, move about, being kissed by those present and then return to the medium and gradually melt into his body. He seized a materialized form and was flung with great force towards the medium and suddenly found himself clasping him. In 1905, when he published his experiences, he wrote: "I publish these things for the first time, having meditated over them in silence for twenty-eight years, giving my word as clergyman for things which imperil my ecclesiastical position and my future advancement."

One of the most astonishing psychic feats claimed for Monck was his teleportation from Bristol to Swindon, a distance of 42 miles. This claimed miraculous feat in 1871 was described in the *Spiritualist* (1875, p. 55).

In his later years, Monck concentrated on healing. The closing period of his life was spent in New York.

Monen

A Kabalistic term covering that branch of magic which deals with the reading of the future by the computation of time and observance of the heavenly bodies. It thus includes **astrology.** (See **Kabala**)

Money (in Occult Tradition)

Money which comes from a pact with the devil is of poor quality, and such wealth, like the fairy-money, generally turns to earth, or to lead, toads, or anything else worthless or repulsive.

"A youth," stated St. Gregory of Tours, (died 594 A.D.) "received a piece of folded paper from a stranger, who told him that he could get from it as much money as he wished, so long as he did not unfold it. The youth drew many gold pieces from the papers, but at length curiosity overcame him, he unfolded it and discovered within the claws of a cat and a bear, the feet of a toad and other repulsive fragments, while at the same moment his wealth disappeared."

It took an Irishman to outsmart the devil! In his book *Irish Witchcraft & Demonology* (1913; 1973), St. John D. Seymour told the amusing story of Joseph Damer of Tipperary County, who made a bargain with the devil to sell his soul for a top-boot full of gold. On the appointed day, the devil was ushered into the living room where a top-boot stood in the center of the floor. The devil poured gold into it, but to his surprise, it remained empty. He hastened away for more gold, but the top-boot would not fill, even after repeated efforts. At length, in sheer disgust, the devil departed. It was afterwards found that the shrewd Irishman had taken the sole off the boot and fastened it over a hole in the floor. Underneath was a series of large cellars, where men waited with shovels to remove each shower of gold as it came down!

In popular superstition it is supposed that if a person hears the cuckoo for the first time with money in his pocket, he will have some all the year, while if he greets the new moon for the first time in the same fortunate condition, he will not lack money throughout the month.

Monition

Supernormal warning. In the wider sense of the definition of psychical researcher Prof. Charles **Richet,** it is the revelation of some past or present event by other than the normal senses. The *Proceedings* of the American Society for Psychical Research (1907, p. 487) published a typical instance. Mr. McCready, editor of *The Daily Telegraph,* in church on a Sunday morning, heard a voice calling "Go back to the office." He ran and found a petroleum lamp blazing in his room. It threw out such clouds of smoke that everything was covered with soot.

Monitions may range from trifling events to warnings of death. They occur accidentally and are verifiable as true. All the monitive phenomena lie within the field of non-experimental **telepathy** and **clairvoyance** and include **apparitions** of the dead and of the living, provided that they are message-bearing. It is characteristic of monitions that they deeply impress the mind of the percipients and permit an accurate remembrance even after the lapse of many years.

They may come in the waking state or in dreams, which sometimes repeat themselves. The borderland between waking and sleeping is usually the most favorable for their reception. They may be visual or auditory—seeing apparitions, or hearing voices, and they often take a symbolical form as, for instance, the idea of death being presented by a coffin, as seen by Lord Beresford in his cabin while steaming between Gibraltar and Marseilles. The coffin contained the body of his father. On arriving at Marseilles he found that his father had died six days before and was buried on the day he saw the vision (see *Proceedings* of the Society for Psychical Research, vol. 5, p. 461).

As regards perception, monitions may be collective yet non-simultaneous and non-identical, or simultaneous and collective. The former is well illustrated by Mrs. Hunter's case, cited by Ernesto **Bozzano** in the *Annals of Psychical Science.* Mrs. Hunter saw, in the waking state and in day time, a large coffin on the bed and a tall, stout woman at the foot of the bed looking at it. The governess saw that evening a phantom woman in the same dress in the sitting room where there was nothing visible and cried: "Go away, go away, naughty ugly old woman."

To quote another instance: During the winter of 1899, Prof. Charles Richet was at home while his wife and daughter were at the opera. The professor imagined that the Opera House was on fire. The conviction was so powerful that he wrote on a piece of paper "Feu! Feu!"

About midnight, on the return of his family, he immediately asked them if there had been a fire. They were surprised and said that there was no fire, only a false alarm, and they were very much afraid. At the very time Prof. Richet made his note his sister fancied that the Professor's room was on fire.

In simultaneous and collective monitions, the phantom or symbol is perceived at the same time by several people. (See also **Monitions of Approach; Premonition**)

Monitions of Approach

These are unaccountable ideas of an impending meeting with someone. A man is seen in the street, is believed to be an old friend and the next minute the mistake is perceived, yet soon afterwards the real friend comes into view in flesh and blood. This occurrence is fairly common.

Such monitions often appear in more complicated forms. They may be auditory, when suddenly a voice may be heard, announcing the arrival of someone; they may come in dreams or, in the waking state, they may take the form of actual sight of a phantom of the coming individual. The Spiritualist contention is that in the latter case, the **double** (or **astral body**) of the coming man was unconsciously projected. In many instances, this may be the right explanation, in some others it does not cover the facts. (See also **Double; Monition; Premonition; Vardøgr**)

Monsters

On the borderland between superstition, occultism and science are the many monsters, human or animal, reported from many parts of the world over the centuries.

The word "monster" is from the Latin *monstrum* and implies a warning or portent. The term includes malformed or misshapen animals or humans as well as creatures of great size. Because of the awe and horror excited by monstrous births, they were traditionally regarded as an omen or a sign of God's wrath with a wicked world. Many street ballads of the sixteenth century moralized about monstrous animals or malformed human beings. Nowadays deformed persons like giants, dwarfs and Siamese twins are studied under the scientific label of "Teratology." Deformed and limbless children are now known to be caused by rare genetic factors or by the use of such drugs as thalidomide in pregnancy.

In modern times, much of the superstitious awe surrounding legendary monsters has passed into the world of fiction, and talented novelists have created such images of doom as the monster of **Frankenstein,** the evil vampire **Dracula,** or the *alter ego* of Dr. Jekyll's Mr. Hyde. Such literary monsters have been given a powerful representation in the realistic medium of horror movies, which have also presented terrifying creatures from swamps, ocean depths and even from other worlds. Such fictional monsters undoubtedly owe their power to the eternal fascination of the clash between good and evil in human affairs and the old theological theme of damnation.

Few stories achieved this metaphysical terror so powerfully as Robert Louis Stevenson's *Dr. Jekyll and Mr. Hyde,* in which the possibilities of evil inherent in all human beings are released from the kindly Dr. Jekyll in the shape of the demonic Mr. Hyde. Stevenson also varied this theme in his short story *Markheim,* where a debauched murderer is confronted by an angelic *alter ego.*

Another aspect of monsters is the eternal attraction and fear of the unknown represented by mysterious creatures reported from isolated places, which have an existence somewhere between myth and natural history. Some may be survivors of ancient species. The main creatures in this category are as follows:

Loch Ness Monster

This is said to inhabit the large area of Loch Ness in Scotland, about 24 miles long and a mile wide, with a depth of from 433–754 feet. Since a monster was reported in ancient Gaelic legends and in a biography of St. Columba circa 565 A.D., it is supposed that there may be a colony of monsters.

Modern interest dates from the 1930s, when a number of witnesses reported sightings. The creature has been photographed repeatedly and even filmed. It appears to be about 45 ft. long, of which 10 ft. is head and neck, 20 ft. the body, and 15 ft. the tail. The head is small and sometimes lifted out of the water on the neck, high above the body. The skin is rough and dark brown in color, and in movement the creature sometimes appears to contort its body into a series of humps. It can move at speeds of around thirteen knots, and in general appearance resembles a prehistoric plesiosaurus.

On April 8, 1976, the monster made the front page of the *New York Times,* which featured records of an underwater camera using a sonar echo technique. Known in Britain affectionately as "Nessie," the creature has been given the formal name of *Nessiteras rhombopteryx* by naturalist Sir Peter Scott in an attempt to secure official protection (see 'Naming the Loch Ness Monster,' *Nature,* Dec. 11, 1975). A British Act of Parliament requires that any rare species of animal qualifying for conservation must have a scientific name.

The Loch Ness monster is not unique, since a similar creature was reported at Lough Muck in Donegal. In other parts of England and Scotland, reported creatures include **Morgawr** in the area of Falmouth, Cornwall, and **Mhorag** (or Morag) in Loch Morar, West Inverness, Scotland. There are numerous reports of sightings, and some photographs. In 1910, a plesiosaurus type creature was reported in Nahuel Huapi, Patagonia.

Interest in the Loch Ness monster was stimulated by reports of the decomposing body of a sea creature caught by the Japanese trawler "Zuiyo Maru" about 30 miles east of Christchurch, New Zealand, on April 25, 1977. The carcase was about 30 feet long, weighed two tons, and was raised from a depth of approximately 900 feet. For a time, it was suspended above the trawler deck by a crane, but the captain feared that the evil-smelling fluid dripping from the carcase would pollute his catch of whiptail fish and ordered the creature to be dumped overboard. Before this was done, Mr. Michihiko Yano, an official of the Taiyo Fishery Company aboard the vessel took four color photographs and made a sketch of the carcase, after taking measurements. He described the creature as like a snake with a turtle's body and with front and rear flippers and a tail six feet in length. This suggests a creature resembling the plesiosaurus, which flourished from 200 to 100 million years ago.

When Taiyo Fisheries executives heard about the unusual catch, they radioed their trawlers around New Zealand, ordering them to try to recover the carcase, but without success. Japanese journalists named the creature "The New Nessie" after Scotland's famous Loch Ness Monster, and a large Tokyo department store planned to market stuffed dolls of the creature. Prof. Fujior Yasuda of the faculty of fisheries at Tokyo University has examined Mr. Yano's photographs and concluded that the creature was definitely not a species of fish, and Mr. Toshio Shikama, a Yokohama University paleontologist was convinced that the creature was not a fish or a mammoth seal. For reports of this "New Nessie" see London *Daily Telegraph* (July 21, 1977), London *Times* (July 21, 1977) and *Fortean Times* (No. 22, Summer 1977).

Yeti (or Abominable Snowman)

A giant humanoid creature which has long been part of the folklore of the high Himalayan region in Asia. The popular name "Abominable Snowman" derives from the Tibetan term *Metoh-Kangmi* or "Wild Man of the Snows." Other names in the Himalayan regions of Kashmir and Nepal are *Jungli-admi* or *Sogpa*—"Wild Men of the Woods."

There are many stories told by Sherpas of the giant Yeti which carried away human children or even adults. In 1951, such stories suddenly attracted scientific interest with the photograph of a large Yeti footprint taken by mountaineer Eric Shipton on an Everest Reconnaissance Expedition.

But the Abominable Snowman had been reported as early as 1832 by B. H. Hodgson in his article 'On the Mammalia of Nepal' (*Journal of the Asiatic Society of Bengal,* vol. 1).

The first European to see Yeti footprints was Major L. A. Waddell, who found them in the snows of northeastern Sikkim at 17,000 feet in 1889, but believed them to be tracks of the great yellow snow bear *(Ursus isabellinus).* Other reports followed over the years.

In 1925, N. A. Tombazi, a Fellow of the Royal Geo-

graphical Society, saw a large humanoid creature walking upright at a distance of 300 yards in Sikkim, and afterwards examined footprints in the snow. In February 1942, Slavomir Rawicz escaped from a Siberian prisoner-of-war camp with six companions and crossed the Himalayas to India. In his book *The Long Walk* (1956), Rawicz claimed that he saw two Yeti-type creatures, eight feet tall, in an area between Bhutan and Sikkim.

In the 1950s, various expeditions to track down the Yeti failed to produce any tangible evidence of its existence, but in 1972 a Sherpa named Da Temba saw a 4′6″ creature, possibly a small Yeti, in Nepal. The cumulative effect of a large number of reports of Yeti sightings from Sherpas reinforces the possibility that there *is* a large humanoid creature in the Himalayas, but the area is a vast one and the creature could be even more elusive than the Loch Ness monster.

Bigfoot

Other creatures of a Yeti type have been reported frequently from different areas of the world, notably isolated regions of the Pacific Northwest. The popular term "Bigfoot" seems to have been a newspaper invention for the creature named "Sasquatch" by the Salish Indians of southwest British Columbia. The Huppa tribe in the Klamath mountains of Northern California use the name *Oh-mah-'ah,* sometimes shorted to *Omah,* while the name *Seeahtiks* is used in Vancouver Island.

It is interesting to note that reports of Yeti-type creatures cover a fairly consistent trail through the remote mountainous regions of Asia across to similar regions in Alaska, Canada and North America, suggesting a rare and elusive species distributed over similar isolated areas. In the Russian areas of Asia, such creatures have been named *Almast, Alma* or *Shezhnyy Chelovek.*

Bigfoot has been frequently reported in Canadian and North American territories from the early nineteenth century onwards. In modern times, construction workers in Northern California claimed to see a large ape-like creature, eight to ten feet tall in Bluff Creek in October 1958. It walked upright and left large footprints, which indicated a creature some 800 pounds weight.

Such creatures were systematically investigated by Dublin-born Peter Byrne, explorer and big-game hunter, who organized a three-year search in 1971. He traveled many thousands of miles between Nepal, Canada and the U.S., interviewing hundreds of individuals and evaluating claimed sightings of Bigfoot. Amongst such investigations is the 16mm color film taken by Roger Patterson, a rancher in Bluff Creek, California, October 7, 1967.

This film shows what appears to be an erect ape-like figure at a distance of some 30 feet. Byrne visted Patterson before his death in 1972 and found his story and the film convincing. In 1968, a prankster in Colville, Washington state, tied 16 inch foot-shaped plywood boards to his feet and made tracks in the woods. He sent a photograph to Peter Byrne, who dismissed it as an obvious fake.

Meanwhile a County ordinance in Skamania, Washington, prohibits wanton slaying of ape-creatures, with substantial penalties. For a detailed survey of Bigfoot and Yeti sightings and legends, see the book *Bigfoot* by John Napier (1972).

Recommended reading:

Costello, Peter. *In Search of Lake Monsters,* London, 1974; Panther paperback, 1975

Florescu, Radu. *In Search of Frankenstein,* New York, Graphic Society, 1975

Heuvelmans, Bernard. *On the Track of Unknown Animals,* London, 1958

McNally, Raymond T. & Radu Florescu. *In Search of Dracula; a True History of Dracula and Vampire Legends,* New York Graphic Society, 1972; Warner paperback, 1975

Sanderson, Ivan T. *Abominable Snowman: Legend Comes to Life,* Chilton Co., 1961

Thompson, C. J. S. *The Mystery and Lore of Monsters,* London, 1930; University Books, 1968; Citadel, 1970

Witchell, Nicholas. *The Loch Ness Story,* London, 1974; Penguin paperback, 1975

Móo, Queen

According to Dr. Augustus le Plongeon, Queen of Yucatan. See his book *Queen Móo and the Egyptian Sphinx* (London, 1896). (See also **Atlantis**)

Moon, Sun Myung (1918–   )

A Korean engineer born in North Pyongan, who has founded a new cult of the **Unified Church,** based on claimed revelations made personally to him by Jesus Christ. According to the Rev. Moon, these revelations took place on numerous occasions over a period of ten years. They were received coldly by the Christian churches in Korea, and the Rev. Moon thereupon moved to North Korea, where he established an underground church in Communist territory. He was arrested and imprisoned in a concentration camp for five years.

He was released in 1950 when a U.N. force liberated the camp, and upon returning to South Korea he founded his Unified Church, later developing branches in Japan, the U.S. and thirty other countries. His followers consider him a new Messiah.

His message derives from his own interpretation of the Bible, establishing a principle of the sanctity of the family. The Rev. Moon's message is also aggressively anti-Communist and centered on right-wing politics. In the 1970s he crusaded in favor of Richard Nixon, stating "You must love Richard Nixon. God has chosen Richard Nixon to be President . . ." Moon's movement derives some of its large financial resources from a South Korean armaments factory, a Titanium plant, and a tea company. He has been accused of political interference and having C.I.A. links in Korea.

His movement has been phenomenally successful with young Americans, whose zombie-like enthusiasm is oddly reminiscent of the Communist followers whom Moon condemns, and his principle of the sanctity of the family has split up many homes by attracting young converts away from their own families. His critics accuse him of brainwashing. When he is not traveling on his evangelistic campaigns, Moon lives regally in a mansion north of New York City.

Moon Sign Book

Annual astrological almanac published since 1905 by Llewellyn Publications; includes tables and guides for astrologers, with special emphasis on signs and phases of the moon. Address: Llewellyn Publications, P.O. Box 3383, St. Paul, Minnesota 55165.

Mopses, Order of the

A secret association founded in Germany in the eighteenth century, spreading through Holland, Belgium and France. It was popularly believed to be a black magic order, replacing the Satanic goat with a dog as an object of worship. However, it seems clear that it was really a somewhat whimsical crypto-Masonic order, after the papal bull of Pope Clement XII on April 24, 1738, which condemned Freemasonry.

Immediately after their establishment the Mopses became an androgynous order, admitting females to all the offices except that of Grand Master, which was for life, but there was also a Grand Mistress, elected every six months.

The ceremonies were grotesque. The candidate for admission did not knock, but had to scratch at the door, and, being purposely kept waiting, was obliged to bark like a dog. On being admitted into the lodge, he had a collar placed round his neck, to which a chain was attached. He was blindfolded and led nine times round the room, while the Mopses present made as great a din as possible with sticks, swords, chains, shovels, and dismal howlings.

The candidate was then questioned as to his intentions, and having replied that he desired to become a "Mops," was asked by the master whether he was prepared to kiss the most ignoble part of that animal. Of course this raised the candidate's anger, but in spite of his resistance, the model of a dog, made of wax, wood, or some other material, was pushed against his face. Having taken the oath, he had his eyes unbandaged, and was then taught the secret signs, which were all of a ludicrous description.

Morag (or Mhorag)

A Loch Ness type monster observed and photographed in Loch Morar, West Inverness, Scotland. (See also **Mhorag; Monsters**)

Morgan le Fay

Sister of King **Arthur** and wife of King Urien of Gore. Arthur gave into her keeping the scabbard of his sword Excalibur, but she gave it to Sir Accolon whom she loved and had a forged scabbard made. Arthur, however, recovered the real sheath, but was again deceived by her.

Morgan le Fay figured as a Queen of the Land of Faerie and as such appears in French and Italian romance. It was she who, on one occasion, threw Excalibur into a lake. She usually presented her favorites with a ring and retained them by her side as did Venus in *Tannhaüser.* Her myth is a parallel of that of Eos and Tithonus and is possibly derived from a sun and dawn myth. (See also King **Arthur**)

Morgawr

A Loch Ness type monster observed and photographed in the area of Falmouth, Cornwall, England. On November 17, 1976, Morgawr was sighted by Tony "Doc" Shiels and David Clarke (editor of *Cornish Life* magazine) in the Helford estuary near Falmouth.

A photograph taken by Mr. Clarke was reproduced in

Fortean Times (No. 22, Summer 1977). Although the camera had unfortunately jammed, resulting in a superimposition of pictures, the general impression is of the head of a creature similar to that photographed by Tony "Doc" Shiels (*Fortean Times* 19) and some Shiels' photographs of the **Loch Ness Monster** May 21, 1977 (best one reproduced in both *Cornish Life* and London *Daily Mirror* for June 9, 1977).

Some doubts have been expressed of Tony Shiels' pictures on the grounds that he is well known in conjuring circles as an exponent of magic simulations of psychic effects. However, he claims to be an avid monster-hunter, and has collected other reports of sightings of Morgawr, as well as publishing his own photographs of the Loch Ness monster. Two photographs of Morgawr taken by Gerry Bennett of Seworgan, Cornwall, from Mawnan beach on January 31, 1977 were also reproduced in *Fortean Times* 22, together with photographs and reports of **Morag**, another Scottish monster of a Loch Ness type. (See also **Loch Ness Monster; Monsters**)

Morien (or Moriensus) (12th century A.D.)

Twelfth-century alchemist. It is commonly supposed that Morien, or Morienus as he is sometimes styled, was born at Rome, and it is also reported that, like Raymond **Lully** and several other early alchemists, he combined evangelical ardor with his scientific tastes. While still a mere boy, and resident in his native city, Morien became acquainted with the writings of Adfar, the Arabian philosopher, and gradually the youth's acquaintance with these developed into tense admiration, the result being that he became filled with the desire to make the personal acquaintance of the author in question.

Accordingly he bade adieu to Rome and set out for Alexandria, this being the home of Adfar, and, on reaching his destination, did not have to wait long before gaining his desired end. The learned Arabian accorded him a hearty welcome, and a little while afterwards the two were living together on very friendly terms, the elder man daily imparting knowledge to the younger, who showed himself a remarkably apt pupil. For some years this state of affairs continued, but at length Adfar died, and thereupon Morien left Alexandria and went to Palestine, found a retreat in the vicinity of Jerusalem, and began to lead a hermit's life there.

Meanwhile the erudition of the deceased Arabian acquired a wide celebrity, and some of his manuscripts chanced to fall into the hands of Kalid, Sultan of Egypt. He was a person of active and enquiring mind, and observing that on the cover of the manuscripts it was stated that the secret of the **philosopher's stone** was written within, he naturally grew doubly inquisitive. He found, however, that he himself could not elucidate the precious documents, and therefore he summoned *illuminati* from far and near to his court at Cairo, offering a large reward to the man who should discover the mystery at issue. Many people presented themselves in consequence, but the majority of them were mere charlatans, and thus the Sultan was duped mercilessly.

Presently news of these doings reached the ears of Morien. It incensed him to think that his old preceptor's wisdom and writings were being made a laughing-stock, so he decided that he must go to Cairo himself, and not

only see justice done to Adfar's memory, but also seize what might prove a favorable opportunity of converting Kalid to Christianity.

The Sultan was inclined to be cynical when the hermit arrived, nor would he listen to attacks on the Mahommedan faith, yet he was sufficiently impressed to grant Morien a house wherein to conduct researches, and here the alchemist worked for a long time, ultimately perfecting the elixir. However, he did not make any attempt to gain the proferred reward, and instead took his leave without the Sultan's awareness, simply leaving the precious fluid in a vase on which he inscribed the suggestive words: "He who possesses all has no need of others."

But Kalid was at a loss to know how to proceed further, and for a long time he made great efforts to find Morien and bring him again to his court. Years went by, and all search for the vanished alchemist proved vain, but once, when the Sultan was hunting in the neighborhood of Jerusalem, one of his servants chanced to hear of a hermit who was able to create gold. Convinced that this must be none other than Morien, Kalid straightway sought him out. Once more the two met, and again the alchemist made strenuous efforts to win the other from Mahommedanism. Many discussions took place between the pair, both speaking on behalf of their respective religions, yet Kalid showed no inclination to desert the faith of his fathers. And as a result Morien relinquished the quest in despair, but it is said that, on parting with the Sultan, he duly instructed him in the mysteries of the transcendent science.

Nothing is known about Morien's subsequent history, and the likelihood is that the rest of his days were spent quietly at his hermitage. He was credited with sundry alchemistic writings, said to have been translated from Arabic, but the ascription rests on the slenderest evidence. One of these works was entitled *Liber de Distinctione Mercurii Aquarum*, and it is interesting to recall that a manuscript copy of this work belonged to the great chemist Robert Boyle (1627-91), one of the founders of the Royal Society in London, while another is entitled *Liber de Compositione Alchemiæ*, and this is printed in the first volume of *Bibliotheca Chemica Curiosa*.

Yet better known than either of these, and more likely to be really from Morien's pen, is a third treatise styled *De Re Metallica, Metallorum Transumtatione, et occulta summaque Antiquorum Medicine Libellus*, which was repeatedly published, the first edition appearing at Paris 1559. (See also **Alchemy**)

Mormons

A Christian religious sect better known as The Church of the Latter-day Saints. It was founded by Joseph Smith, Jr. (1805-1844) on April 6, 1830 at Fayette, New York. From six original members, the church has now grown to over three million.

While living at Palmyra, N.Y. from 1820-23, Smith had a number of visions which led him to believe that he was chosen by God to restore the true church of Christ, and that all other Christian groups were apostate. He supported his mission by producing a miraculous scripture called *The Book of Mormon*, claimed to have been revealed to him by an angel named Moroni, who assisted Smith to discover the scripture, inscribed in strange language, on golden plates. These were transcribed by Smith around 1827 by means of magical spectacles named Urim and Thummim, after which the angel took the golden tablets away.

Another work of inspired translation by Smith was the *Book of Abraham,* purchased as a manuscript from a traveling showman in Ohio in 1833. This book, supposed to be written by the Biblical Abraham himself was in hieroglyphics, some of which Smith reproduced. However, James H. Breasted, a leading American Egyptologist, declared that Smith "was absolutely ignorant of the simplest facts of Egyptian writing and civilization."

Critics of the *Book of Mormon* have stated that it was really the work of Solomon Spaulding, a Congregational minister of Monneaut, Ohio, who composed it to support his theories of early Indian origins. Spaulding is supposed to have taken the manuscript to a printer in Pittsburgh, where it was copied by Sidney Rigdon, a Campbellite preacher of Mentor, Ohio, who was an associate of Joseph Smith and an early missionary for his cause.

The Mormon view, however, is that their missionaries called on Rigdon at Mentor, showed him the *Book of Mormon* and converted him to the cause. Whatever the true facts, the work itself quotes heavily from the Authorized Version of the English Bible and is couched in similar style. It purports to tell the story of the true church of Christ on the American continent after migrating from Jerusalem.

The growth of the Mormon sect, its persecution and eventual triumph under Brigham Young, who led 30,000 of the faithful to a permanent settlement in Utah, are part of American history and folklore. The practice of polygamy or plural "spiritual marriage" revealed by Young in 1852 was officially renounced by the church in 1890 and is no longer advocated.

The modern Church of the Latter-day Saints has a very large following and a vigorous campaign of proselytization. One of its admirable but lesser known activities has been the copying of parish registers in Britain and elsewhere which were in danger of being lost through lack of official preservation.

Recommended reading:

Brodie, Fawn M. *No Man Knows My History* (The Life of Joseph Smith, the Mormon Prophet), A. A. Knopf, 1945

Davis, Inez Smith. *The Story of the Church,* Herald, 1948

Gates, Susan Young & Leah Widtroe. *The Life Story of Brigham Young,* Macmillan, 1930

Martin, Walter R. *The Maze of Mormonism,* Zondervan, 1962

Smith, Joseph etc. *The Pearl of Great Price, a selection from the revelations, translations, and narrations of Joseph Smith,* Church of Jesus Christ Latter-day Saints, 1921

Morris, Mrs. L(ouis) A(nne) Meurig
(1899– ?)

British inspirational medium through whom an entity who chose the name "Power" delivered high religious and philosophical teaching from the platform before large audiences. Some signs of Mrs. Morris' psychic gifts were noticeable at an early age but they were stifled by an orthodox education.

However, she began to develop rapidly after a first seance with a direct voice medium in Newton Abbot in 1922. Within six weeks she went under **control.** "Sunshine," the spirit of a child spoke through her, and "Sister Magdalene," the spirit of a French nun assumed charge as principal trance control. The prediction came through that Mrs. Morris would be trained for the delivery of high teaching by a spirit called "Power." This duly occurred.

Under the control of "Power," the medium's soprano voice changed to a ringing baritone, her mannerisms became masculine and priestly and the teachings disclosed an erudition and deep philosophy which was far above the intellectual capacities of the medium.

In 1929, Laurence Cowen, well known author and playwright came in contact with Mrs. Morris. "Power" convinced him of the truth of survival and filled him with missionary spirit. Hitherto an agnostic, Cowen became a convert to Spiritualism, associated himself with Mrs. Meurig Morris and arranged a long series of Sunday meetings in the Fortune Theatre in London for the general public. Wide publicity accompanied the sermons for some time in the Press. Public attention was further aroused by provincial tours which Laurence Cowen arranged at great personal sacrifice.

The rise of Mrs. Morris into the forefront of inspired orators was marked by two publicly attested supernormal occurrences.

An attempt was made by the Columbia Gramophone Company to make a phonograph record of "Power's" voice. According to the publicly rendered account of C. W. Nixon (of the Columbia Gramophone Company), at the very commencement of the experiment an incident occurred which by all the rules should have spoiled the first side of the record.

Mr. Ernest **Oaten,** president of the International Federation of Spiritualists, was in the chair, and, being unaware that the start was to be made without the appearance of the usual red light, he whispered loudly to Mrs. Morris as she stood up: "Wait for the signal." These words were picked up by the microphone and heard by the engineers in the recording room after the apparatus had been started, and it was believed they must be on the record. Later, when the second side of the record was to be made, there was confusion in starting, and towards the end, as if to make technical failure a certainty, Mrs. Morris turned and walked several paces away from the microphone.

A week before the record was ready for reproduction, Cowen rang up Nixon and told him that "Power" had asserted that notwithstanding the technical mistakes the record would be a success, that Mr. Oaten's whispered words would not be reproduced and that the timing and volume of the voice would not be spoiled by the later accidents. This statement was so extraordinary and appeared to be so preposterous in view of technical expectations, that Nixon had it taken down word by word, and sent it in a sealed envelope to Ernest Oaten in Manchester with the request that he would keep it unopened until the record was ready, and the truth or otherwise of the prediction could be tested. The record was played in the Fortune Theatre on April 25, 1931. It was found perfect. The letter was opened and read. The prediction was true in every detail.

The second strange incident occurred in the studios of the British Movietone Company where a talking film was made of "Power's" oratory. Seventy people saw the microphones high in the air, held up by new half-inch ropes. The rope suddenly snapped (it was found cut as with a sharp knife) and a terrific crash startled all present. Within half an inch of Mrs. Morris' face, the microphone swept across the space and went swaying to and fro. A foreman rushed up and dragged the rope aside to keep it out of sight of the camera. The cameraman never stopped filming. Nor did Mrs. Morris falter. In spite of the obvious danger to her life she never stirred and went on undisturbed with her trance speech.

According to expert opinion the voice registering must have been a failure. Yet it was found that the accident had not the least influence. The record was perfect. According to "Power's" later revelation, everything was planned. The ropes were supernormally severed so as to prove, by the medium's demeanor, that she was indeed in trance (which a newspaper questioned) as no human being could have consciously exhibited such self-possession as she did when the accident occurred.

Sir Oliver Lodge, in his book *Past Years* (1931), referred to Mrs. Meurig Morris in the following terms: "When the medium's own vocal organs are obviously being used—as in most cases of trance utterances—the proof of supernormality rests mainly on the substance of what is being said; but, occasionally the manner is surprising. I have spoken above of a characteristically cultured mode of expression, when a scholar is speaking, not easily imitated by an uncultured person; but, in addition to that a loud male voice may emanate from a female larynx and may occasionally attain oratorical proportions. Moreover, the orator may deal with great themes in a style which we cannot associate with the fragile little woman who has gone into trance and is now under control. This is a phenomenon which undoubtedly calls attention to the existence of something supernormal, and can be appealed to as testifying to the reality and activity of a spiritual world. It is, indeed, being used for purposes of such demonstration, and seems well calculated to attract more and more attention from serious and religious people; who would be discouraged and offended by the trivial and barely intelligible abnormalities associated with what are called physical (or physiological) phenomena and would not be encouraged by what is called clairvoyance."

In April 1932, Mrs. Meurig Morris sued the *Daily Mail* for a poster reading "Trance Medium Found Out," and also for statements made in the article to which the poster referred. The action lasted for eleven days. The summary of Justice McCardie was dramatically interrupted by a sudden entrancement of Mrs. Morris and an address of "Power" to the Judge. The jury found for the defendants on the plea of fair comment but added that no allegations of fraud or dishonesty against Mrs. Morris had been proved, and on this judgment was given for the *Daily Mail.*

Mrs. Morris' appeal, after a hearing of four days before Lord Justices Scrutton, Lawrence and Greer, was dismissed. The House of Lords, to which the case was afterwards carried, agreed with the Court of Appeal.

Morris, Robert L. (1942-   )

Parapsychologist who has published articles and edited reprint programs. Born in Canonsburg, Pennsylvania, he studied at University of Pittsburgh (B.S. 1963) and at Duke University, North Carolina (doctorate in biological psychology). After two years of postdoctoral work in Duke Medical Center, he became research coordinator for the **Psychical Research Foundation,** Durham, N.C. He is a full-time lecturer in parapsychology at the University of California, Santa Barbara, and served as president of the **Parapsychological Association** in 1974.

He edited the Arno Press reprint program 'Perspectives in Psychical Research.' His special interests concern biological aspects of psi and ANPSI. His papers include: 'The Measurement of PK (Psychokinesis) by Electric Clock' (in *Parapsychology from Duke to FRNM* by J. G. Rhine and associates, 1965), 'Some New Techniques in Animal Psi Research' (*Journal of Parapsychology,* vol. 31, Dec. 1967), 'Obtaining Non-Random Entry Points: A Complex Psi Process' (in *Parapsychology Today,* ed. J. B. Rhine & R. Brier, 1968), 'PK on a Bio-Electrical System' (in *Parapsychology Today,* 1968), 'The Psychobiology of Psi' (in *Psychic Exploration* by E. D. Mitchell *et al.* 1974), 'Biology and Psychical Research' (in *Parapsychology: Its Relation to Physics, Biology Psychology, and Psychiatry* ed. G. R. Schmeidler, 1976). Dr. Morris was also a joint editor of *Research in Parapsychology 1972* ed. W. G. Roll, R. L. Morris & J. D. Morris, 1973; *Research in Parapsychology 1973* ed. W. G. Roll, R. L. Morris & J. D. Morris, 1974; *Research in Parapsychology 1974* ed. J. D. Morris, W. G. Roll & R. L. Morris, 1975; *Research in Parapsychology 1975* ed. J. D. Morris, W. G. Roll & R. L. Morris, 1976. This series is published by Scarecrow Press Inc., Metuchen, N.J.

Morris Pratt Institute Association

The first permanent institution of learning established under the auspices of Spiritualism. It was founded in 1901 in Whitewater, Wisconsin, by Morris Pratt, an American Spiritualist who attributed the fortune which he accumulated to wise spirit guidance. He was told by his Red Indian Guide of certain mineral deposits, unknown to any white man. In a few months he had made over $200,000.

Out of gratitude he established a school to be conducted under the aegis of Spiritualism and deeded the building and land to seven well-known Spiritualists as trustees. Originally the Morris Pratt Institute, its membership now includes individuals interested in supporting and promoting the work of the National Spiritualist Association of Churches. Address: 11811 Watertown Plank Road, Milwaukee, Wisconsin 52226.

Morrow, Felix (1906-   )

American publisher who virtually created the modern occult boom in the 1960s through his publishing house University Books, Inc. and associated Mystic Arts Book Society.

Born June 3, 1906 in New York City with Hasidic Jewish roots, he grew up in a non-religious atmosphere and became drawn to Marxism and Freudian teaching. He became a graduate student in philosophy at Columbia University from 1929–31, researching the history of religions. As editor of the theoretical monthly magazine *Fourth International,* he wrote a thoughtful article on Marxism and religion.

From 1931–46, he devoted himself to the revolutionary socialist movement and was author of an important study:

Revolution & Counter-revolution in Spain (1938; 2nd. enl. ed. 1974).

In 1946, he entered the field of publishing as executive vice president of Schocken Books, New York, and became attracted to the writings of Franz Kafka, Martin Buber and Gershom Scholen, and through them to renewed interest in his Hasidic grandfather. From 1948–70, he became immersed in Freudian psychoanalytic training and publishing. At the same time, however, his association with Beacon Press and University of Notre Dame Press made him responsive to mysticism, although a socialist at heart. This dichotomy created many personal conflicts for him, although eventually broadening his humanist outlook.

As executive vice president of British Book Center Inc., he took on American rights of *Flying Saucers Have Landed* by Desmond Leslie & George Adamski (first published Britain, 1953), and this led him to research earlier literature in psychic and occult subjects.

In 1954, he incorporated University Books, Inc. in New York, publishing important out-of-print books on occultism, mysticism, psychical research and comparative religion. These included such key works as A. E. Waite's books on the Tarot and Ceremonial Magic, Lewis Spence's *Encyclopedia of Occultism,* Montague Summers' books on Witchcraft and Vampirism, William James' *Varieties of Religious Experience,* R. M. Bucke's *Cosmic Consciousness,* F. W. H. Myers' *Human Personality and its Survival of Bodily Death,* scholarly works by Charles Guignebert on the origins of Christianity, D. T. Suzuki's books on Zen Buddhism, Nandor Fodor's *Encyclopedia of Psychical Research,* G. R. S. Mead's books on Gnosticism, Alexandra David-Neel's *Magic and Mystery in Tibet,* and scores of similar books which initiated the themes of the modern occult revival and provided basic source reference.

Each book carried a new introduction, evaluating the work in a modern context and often supplying original biographical research on the author. Some of these introductions were written by Morrow under the pseudonym 'John C. Wilson,' others were written by such authorities as E. J. Dingwall, Kenneth Rexroth and Leslie Shepard.

University Books, Inc. also published original works as the occult revival threw up names like Timothy **Leary** and new causes like the psychedelic revolution. In addition to publishing, the company marketed chosen titles each month through the Mystic Arts Book Society.

After fifteen years of creative and stimulating publishing in the fields of occultism and mysticism, Morrow relinquished the business to Lyle Stuart, Inc., which continued the University Books imprint side by side with its own Citadel Press imprint, moving from New York to Secaucus, New Jersey. In 1973, Morrow began publishing an occult series for Causeway Books, an imprint of A. & W. Publishers, Inc., New York.

The significant influence of Morrow's publishing work has recently been recognized by the National Endowment for the Humanities and the Rockefeller Foundation, which have initiated an oral history recording project on the advanced literary-intellectual life of New York City between 1925 and 1975. Tape recordings have been made of Morrow and other individuals, for eventual deposit in the Oral History division of the Columbia libraries.

In recent years, Morrow extended his psychological studies from Freudianism to Maslow's Humanist Psychology and the Holistic Depth Psychology of Ira Progoff. He was in charge of publishing projects in these areas for Dialogue House Library (80 East 11 Street, New York, N.Y. 10003) prior to an active retirement.

Morse, J. J. (1848–1919)

One of the most distinguished trance speakers of the nineteenth century, named as "the Bishop of Spiritualism" by journalist W. T. **Stead.**

Morse was left an orphan at the age of ten, had very little education and served as pot-boy in a public house before his mediumship was discovered. He was described by Sergeant E. W. **Cox** in his book *What Am I?* (2 vols., 1873–74) in the following words: "I have heard an uneducated barman, when in a state of trance, maintain a dialogue with a party of philosophers on Reason and Foreknowledge, Will and Fate, and hold his own against them. I have put him the most difficult questions in psychology, and received answers always thoughtful, often full of wisdom, and invariably conveyed in choice and eloquent language. Nevertheless, in a quarter of an hour afterwards, when released from the trance, he was unable to answer the simplest query on a philosophical subject, and was at a loss for sufficient language in which to express a commonplace idea."

James **Burns,** the well-known Spiritualistic editor and publisher, took an interest in Morse and employed him as an assistant in his printing and publishing office. "Tien Sien Tie," the Chinese philosopher, who said that he lived on earth in the reign of the Emperor Kea-Tsing, gave his first addresses through J. J. Morse in Burns' offices in 1869. Of the other spirits associated with Morse's mediumship the best known was "The Strolling Player," who supplied the humor and lighter elements in the discourses, which were models of literary grace. Many proofs of spirit identity came through, some of which were years after tabulated and republished by Edward T. Bennett.

Morse's physical mediumship was a powerful one. He could demonstrate the fire test and the phenomenon of **elongation.** He visited Australia and New Zealand, edited *The Banner of Light* in Boston in 1904, and from 1906 for many years *The Two Worlds* of Manchester. *The Spiritual Review* (1901–1902) was his own foundation. His mediumship and general propaganda activity was an important factor in the spread and growth of British Spiritualism.

His daughter, Florence, who was clairvoyant from childhood, also developed the faculty of inspirational speaking. She travelled extensively, visiting America, Australia, New Zealand and South Africa. She was almost fully conscious in the course of her inspirational addresses.

Morse published an autobiographical work: *Leaves From My Life; A Narrative of Personal Experiences in the Career of a Servant of the Spirits* (1877).

Morselli, Enrico (1852–1929)

Professor of Psychiatry at Genoa University from 1889 (previously at the University of Turin), a bitter skeptic of psychic phenomena until Eusapia **Palladino** completely convinced him of their reality in thirty sittings. His book *Psicologia e Spiritismo,* published in two volumes in Turin in

1908 was described by Prof. Cesar **Lombroso** as "a model of erudition."

In 1907 in the *Annals of Psychic Science* (Vol. 5, 1907, p. 322) Morselli wrote: "The question of Spiritism has been discussed for over fifty years; and although no one can at present foresee when it will be settled, all are now agreed in assigning to it great importance among the problems left as a legacy by the nineteenth century to the twentieth. . . .

"If for many years academic science has depreciated the whole category of facts which Spiritism has, for good or ill, rightly or wrongly, absorbed and assimilated to form the elements of its doctrinal system, so much the worse for science. And worse still for the scientists who have remained deaf and blind before all the affirmation, not of credulous sectarians, but of serious and worthy observers such as Crookes, Lodge and Richet. I am not ashamed to say that I myself, as far as my modest power went, have contributed to this obstinate scepticism, up to the day on which I was enabled to break the chains in which my absolutist preconceptions had bound my judgment."

His psycho-dynamic theory of **materialization** phenomena is a compromise between psychological orthodoxy and the spirit theory. It forms an important chapter in research history.

An earlier book, concerned with paranormal phenomena was published by Morselli under the title: *Il magnetismo animaleila fascination e gli stati ipnotici* (1886). Other books included: *I fenomei telepaticie le allucinazioni veridiche* (1897), *Psicologia e "Spiritismo"* (1908)

Morya, Master

One of the mysterious **Mahatmas** or Masters of the **Theosophical Society** of Madame **Blavatsky.** Morya is often simply referred to as "M." (See also **Adepts; Great White Brotherhood; Mahatma Letters; Masters**)

Moses, Rev. William Stainton (1839–1892)

Medium and religious teacher who became one of the most prominent British Spiritualists. He was born November 5, 1839 at Donnington, Lincolnshire. His father was headmaster of the Grammar School of Donnington. In 1852, the family moved to Bedford to give young Moses the advantage of an education at Bedford College. In his schooldays he occasionally walked in his sleep, and on one occasion in this state he went down to the sitting room and wrote an essay on a subject which had worried him on the previous evening, and then returned to bed without waking. It was the best essay of the class. No other incidents of a psychic nature of his early years were recorded.

He gained a scholarship at Exeter College, Oxford. Owing to a breakdown in his health he interrupted his studies, traveled for some time and spent six months in a monastery on Mount Athos. When he recovered his health he returned to Oxford, took his degree of M.A. and was ordained as a minister of the Church of England by Bishop Wilberforce. He began his ministry at Kirk Maughold, near Ramsey, in the Isle of Man, at the age of 24.

He gained the esteem and love of his parishioners. On the occasion of an outbreak of smallpox he helped to nurse and bury a man whose malady was so violent that it was very difficult to find anybody to approach him.

His literary activity for *Punch* and the *Saturday Review* began at this time. After four years, he exchanged his curacy with that of St. George's, Douglas, Isle of Man. In 1869 he fell seriously ill. He called in for medical aid Dr. Stanhope Templeman Speer. As a convalescent he spent some time in his house. This was the beginning of a lifelong friendship.

In 1870, he took a curacy in Dorsetshire. Illness again interfered with his parish work and he was obliged to abandon it. For seven years he was the tutor of Dr. Speer's son. In 1871, he was offered a mastership in University College School, London. This office he filled until 1889, when failing health made him resign. He lived for three more years, suffered greatly from gout, influenza and nervous prostration. He died September 5, 1892.

The period of his life between 1872 and 1881 was marked by an inflow of transcendental powers and a consequent religious revolution which completely demolished his narrow orthodoxy and dogmatism. He distrusted Spiritualism and considered all its phenomena spurious. Of Lord **Adare**'s book on D. D. **Home** he said that it was the dreariest twaddle he ever came across. Robert Dale **Owen**'s *Debatable Land* (1870) made a deeper impression.

On Mrs. Speer's persuasion, he agreed to have a closer look into the matter and attended his first seance with Miss Lottie **Fowler** on April 2, 1872. After much nonsense he received a striking description of the spirit presence of a friend who had died in the North of England. Charles **Williams** was the next medium he went to see. A seance with D. D. **Home** and sittings in many private circles followed. Within about six months, Stainton Moses became convinced of the existence of discarnate spirits and of their power to communicate. Soon he showed signs of great psychic powers himself. In 1872, five months after his introduction to Spiritualism, he had his first experience of **levitation**. The physical phenomena continued with gradually lessening frequency until 1881.

They were of extremely varied nature. The power was often so enormous that it kept the room in constant vibration. Sergeant E. W. **Cox** described in his book *What am I?* (2 vols., 1873–74) the swaying and rocking in daylight of an old-fashioned, six-feet-wide and nine-feet-long mahogany table which required the strength of two strong men to be moved an inch. The presence of Stainton Moses was responsible for the table's extraordinary behaviour. When Cox and Stainton Moses held their hands over the table, it lifted first on one then on the other side.

When Stainton Moses was levitated for the third time, he was thrown on to the table, and from that position on to an adjacent sofa. In spite of the considerable distance and the magnitude of the force he was in no way hurt.

Objects left in Stainton Moses' bedroom were often found arranged in the shape of a cross.

Apports were frequent phenomena. They were usually objects from a different part of the house, invariably small, coming mysteriously through closed doors or walls and thrown upon the table from a direction mostly over Stainton Moses' head. Sometimes their origin was unknown. Ivory crosses, corals, pearls, precious stones, the latter expressly for Stainton Moses, were also brought from unknown sources.

Psychic lights of greatly varying shapes and intensity were frequently observed. They were most striking when the medium was in trance. They were not always equally seen by all the sitters, never lit up their surroundings and could pass through solid objects, for instance, rise from the floor through the table top.

Scents were produced in abundance, the most common being musk, verbena, new mown hay, and one unfamiliar odor, which was told to be spirit scent. Sometimes breezes heavy with perfumes swept around the circle.

Without any musical instruments in the room, a great variety of musical sounds contributed to the entertainment of the sitters. There were many instances of **direct writing,** demonstration of **matter passing through matter,** of **direct voice** and of **materializations** which, however, did not progress beyond luminous hands or columns of light vaguely suggesting human forms.

The habitual circle of Stainton Moses was very small. Dr. and Mrs. Stanhope Speer and frequently Mr. F. W. Percival were generally the only witnesses of the phenomena. Sergeant Cox, W. H. Harrison, Dr. Thompson, Mrs. Garratt, Miss Birkett and Sir William **Crookes** were occasional sitters. As a rule, the invisible communicators strongly resented the introduction of strangers. The physical phenomena in themselves were of secondary importance. They were produced in evidence of the supernormal power of the communicators to convince Moses and the sitters of their claims.

"That they were not produced fraudulently by Dr. Speer or other sitters," wrote F. W. H. **Myers** in *Proceedings* of the Society for Psychical Research (vol. 9, pt. 25), "I regard as proved both by moral considerations and by the fact that they were constantly reported as occurring when Mr. Moses was alone. That Mr. Moses should have himself fraudulently produced them I regard as both morally and physically incredible. That he should have prepared and produced them in a state of trance I regard both as physically incredible and also as entirely inconsistent with the tenor both of his own reports and those of his friends. I therefore regard the reported phenomena as having actually occurred in a genuinely supernormal manner."

The character and integrity of William Stainton Moses was so high that Andrew Lang was forced to warn the advocates of fraud that "the choice is between a moral and physical miracle." Frank **Podmore** was almost the only critic who preferred to believe in a moral miracle rather than in a physical one.

Podmore suggested that the psychic lights at the seances could have been produced by bottles of phosphorised oil, and quoted a report by Stainton Moses himself in *Proceedings* of the S.P.R. (vol. 11, p. 45) stating: "Suddenly there arose from below me, apparently under the table, or near the floor, right under my nose, a cloud of luminous smoke, just like phosphorous . . ." It seems most improbable that the medium would write such a report if guilty of fraud, and even Podmore himself concluded: "That Stainton Moses, being apparently of sane mind, should deliberately have entered upon a course of systematic and cunningly concerted trickery, for the mere pleasure of mystifying a small circle of friends, or in the hope of any petty personal advantage, such, for instance, as might be found in the enhanced social importance attaching to a

position midway between prestidigator and prophet—this is scarcely credible."

The famous automatic scripts of Stainton Moses are known from his books *Spirit Teachings* (1883) and *Spirit Identity* (1879) and from full seance accounts which he commenced to publish in *Light* in 1892. The scripts began in 1872 and lasted until 1883, gradually dying out from 1877. They filled twenty-four notebooks. Except the third which was lost later, they were preserved by the **London Spiritualist Alliance** where both the originals and typed copies were accessible to students. They are completed by four books of records of physical phenomena and three books of retrospect and summary. In his will Moses entrusted the manuscripts to two friends—C. C. Massey and Alaric A. Watts. They handed them to F. W. H. Myers, who published an exhaustive analysis in *Proceedings* of the S.P.R. (vols. 9 & 11).

The automatic messages were almost wholly written by Stainton Moses' own hand while he was in a normal waking state. They are interspersed with a few words of direct writing. The tone of the spirits towards him is habitually courteous and respectful. But occasionally they have some criticism which pierces to the quick. This explains why he was unwilling to allow the inspection of his books during his lifetime. Indeed, there are indications that there may have been a still more private book into which very intimate messages were entered. This book must have been destroyed.

The scripts are in the form of a dialogue. The identity of the communicators was not revealed by Moses in his lifetime. Neither did Myers disclose it. They were made public in a later book *The Controls of Stainton Moses* by A. W. Trethewy, B.A. Considering the illustrious biblical and historical names which the communicators bore, Stainton Moses' reluctance was wise. He would have met with scorn. Moreover, for a long time, he himself was skeptical, indeed, at first shocked and was often reproved for suspicion and want of faith in the scripts.

He was the charge of an organized band of forty-nine spirits. Their leader called himself "Imperator." For some time he manifested through an amanuensis only, later wrote himself, signing his name with a cross. He spoke directly for the first time on December 19, 1892, but appeared to Moses' clairvoyant vision at an early stage. He claimed to have influenced the medium's career during the whole of his lifetime and said that in turn he was directed by "Preceptor" in the background. "Preceptor" himself communed with "Jesus."

The identity of the communicators was only gradually disclosed and Stainton Moses was much exercised as to whether the personalities of the band were symbolical or real. They asserted that a missionary effort to uplift the human race was being made in the spirit realms and as Stainton Moses had the rarest mediumistic gifts and his personality furnished extraordinary opportunity he was selected as the channel of these communications. Like "Imperator" and "Preceptor" every member of the Band had an assumed name at first. The Biblical characters included the following names, as revealed later: "Malachias" (Imperator), "Elijah" (Preceptor), "Haggai" (The Prophet), "Daniel" (Vates), "Ezekiel," "St. John the Baptist" (Theologus). The ancient philosophers and sages numbered fourteen. They were: "Solon," "Plato," "Aristotle," "Seneca," "Athenodorus" (Doctor), "Hippolytus" (Rector), "Plotinus" (Prudens), "Alexander Achillini" (Philosophus), "Algazzali or Ghazali" (Mentor), "Kabbila," "Chom," "Said," "Roophal," "Magus."

It was not until Book XIV of the communications was written that Stainton Moses became satisfied of the identity of his controls. In his introduction to *Spirit Teachings* he wrote: "The name of God was always written in capitals, and slowly and, as it seemed, reverentially. The subject matter was always of a pure and elevated character, much of it being of personal application, intended for my own guidance and direction. I may say that throughout the whole of these written communications, extending in unbroken continuity to the year 1880, there is no flippant message, no attempt at jest, no vulgarity or incongruity, no false or misleading statement, so far as I know or could discover; nothing incompatible with the avowed object, again and again repeated, of instruction, enlightenment and guidance by spirits fitted for the task. Judged as I should wish to be judged myself, they were what they pretended to be. Their words were words of sincerity and of sober, serious purpose."

Later, when the phenomena lost strength he was again assailed by doubts and showed hesitation. It is obviously impossible to prove the identity of ancient spirits. "Imperator's" answer to this objection was that statements incapable of proof should be accepted as true on the ground that others which could be tested had been verified. For such evidential purposes many modern spirits were admitted for communication. In several cases satisfactory proofs of identity were obtained. "Imperator's" statement was therefore logical. It should also be noted that each of the communicators had his distinctive way of announcing his presence. If, in the case of modern spirits, the handwriting did not agree with the characters employed while on earth, in direct scripts the communication showed the same features as the one which was automatically received.

As to the contents of the communications, Stainton Moses was well aware of the possible role which his own mind might play. He wrote: "It is an interesting subject for speculation whether my own thoughts entered into the subject matter of the communications. I took extraordinary pains to prevent any such admixture. At first the writing was slow, and it was necessary for me to follow it with my eye, but even then the thoughts were not my thoughts. Very soon the messages assumed a character of which I had no doubt whatever that the thought was opposed to my own. But I cultivated the power of occupying my mind with other things during the time that the writing was going on, and was able to read an abstruse book and follow out a line of close reasoning while the message was written with unbroken regularity. Messages so written extended over many pages, and in their course there is no correction, no fault in composition and often a sustained vigour and beauty of style."

These precautions do not exclude the free working possibility of the subconscious mind. This possibility is borne out by posthumous messages claimed as emanating from Stainton Moses and fairly well establishing his identity, according to which he made mistakes in the scripts on certain points.

The life and activity of Stainton Moses left a deep impression on Spiritualism. He took a leading part in several organizations. From 1884 until his death he was president of the **London Spiritualist Alliance.** The phenomena reported in his mediumship served as a partial inducement for the foundation of the **Society for Psychical Research.** He was on its council. Owing to the treatment which the medium William **Eglinton** received, he resigned his membership and censured the Society for its unduly critical attitude. He edited *Light,* contributed many articles on Spiritualism to *Human Nature* and other periodicals and published, under the pen name of "M. A. Oxon" the following books: *Spirit Identity* (1879); *Psychography, or a Treatise on the Objective Forms of Psychic or Spiritual Phenomena* (1878, reprinted 1952 under title *Direct Spirit Writing*), *Higher Aspects of Spiritualism* (1880), *Spirit Teachings* (1883).

Moss, Thelma

Contemporary psychologist and parapsychologist, medical psychologist at the University of California, Los Angeles. Her special interests include **telepathy,** radiation, **Kirlian Photography,** energy fields, skin vision (see **Eyeless Sight**). She visited the USSR to investigate Kirlian photography and has experimented in the field with a modified high-energy photography system.

Moss-Woman, The

According to German folklore, one of the Moss or Wood Folk, who dwelt in the forests of Southern Germany. Their stature was small and their form strange and uncouth, bearing a strong resemblance to certain trees which they flourished and decayed.

They were a simple, timid, and inoffensive race, and had little intercourse with mankind; approaching only at rare intervals the lonely cabin of the woodman or forester to borrow some article of domestic use, or to beg a little of the food which the good wife was preparing for the family meal. They would also, for similar purposes, appear to laborers in the fields which lay on the outskirts of the forests. A loan or gift to the Moss-people was always repaid manifold.

But the most highly-prized and eagerly-coveted of all mortal gifts was a draught from the maternal breast to their own little ones, for this they held to be a sovereign remedy for all the ills to which their natures were subject. Yet it was only in the extremity of danger that they could so overcome their natural diffidence and timidity as to ask this boon—for they knew that mortal mothers turned from such nurslings with disgust and fear.

It would appear that the Moss or Wood folk also lived in some parts of Scandinavia. Thus it was believed that in the churchyard of Store Hedding, in Zealand, there were the remains of an oak wood which were trees by day and warriors by night.

Mott, George Edward (1935-　)

Naval officer who has also experimented in the field of parapsychology. Born December 3, 1935 at Virginia Beach, Virginia, he studied at Duke University, Durham, North Carolina (B.S. electrical engineering 1958). In 1958 he married Priscilla Weedon. He has been a Lieutenant in the U.S. Navy from 1958 onwards. He is a member of the American Institute of Electrical Engineers, and an associate member of the Parapsychological Association.

At Duke University he assisted W. C. **Stewart** and J. E. Jenkins in developing and testing devices to investigate extrasensory perception, reported in *Journal of Parapsychology* (March 1959) in the article 'Three New ESP Test Machines and Some Preliminary Results' by W. C. Stewart.

Mountain Cove Community, The

A Spiritualist community founded in Mountain Cove, Fayette Co., Virginia, in the autumn of 1851, under the leadership of the Rev. James Scott and the Rev. Thomas Lake **Harris.** Both were mediums who had settled in Auburn in the previous year, and had obtained a considerable following.

While Harris was absent in New York the command to form a community at Mountain Cove was given through the mediumship of Scott, and about a hundred persons accompanied him to Virginia. The members were obliged to deliver up all their possessions, again at the command of the spirits. Dissensions arose and pecuniary difficulties were experienced, and only the advent of T. L. Harris in the summer of 1852 saved the community from dissolution. However, the dissensions and difficulties remained, and early in 1853 the community finally broke up. (See also **Apostolic Circle;** Rev. Thomas Lake **Harris**)

Mountain Path, The (Magazine)

Quarterly magazine founded in January 1964, dealing with the life and teachings of Sri **Ramani Maharshi** (1879-1950), celebrated Hindu saint credited with many miracles. Publication address: Sri Ramanasramam, Tiruvannamalai, South India.

Movement (Paranormal)

Paranormal movement has been given various terms—with contact, which is insufficient to explain it (parakinesis), movement without obvious perceptible or normal contact (telekinesis), the most frequent seance room phenomenon. The latter, in its apparent simplicity, is one of the widest import, since behind the displacement of objects and various other mechanical effects an invisible intelligent entity is believed to manifest, performing complicated operations and exercising a directive influence over mysteriously generated and frequently tremendous forces. The generally accepted modern term for paranormal movement is "psychokinesis" or "PK." This term could also include the recently claimed phenomenon of paranormal **metal-bending.**

Shaking of the House

Molecular vibrations appear to characterize the phenomenon in its initial stage when the seance table, under the hand of the sitters, begins to tremble, shake, jerk as signs of animation. This vibratory motion is not always restricted to the table. It may spread over the whole room.

P. P. Alexander, in *Spiritualism: A Narrative with a Discussion* (1871) wrote of a seance with the medium D. D. **Home** in Edinburgh: "The first hint or foreshine we had of the phenomena came in the form of certain tremors which began to pervade the apartment. These were of a somewhat peculiar kind; and they gradually increased till they became of considerable violence. Not only did the

floor tremble, but the chair of each person, as distinct from it, was felt to rock and—as we Scots say—dirl under him."

In a similar record, Lord Adare, author of *Experiences in Spiritualism with D. D. Home* (1870; 1924), stated: "We soon felt violent vibration of the floor, chairs and table—so violent that the glass pendants of the chandelier struck together, and the windows and doors shook and rattled in their frames not only in our room but also in the next."

The *Journal* of George Fox, the Quaker preacher, disclosed this note: "At Mansfield, where was a great meeting, I was moved to pray, and the Lord's power was so great that the house seemed to be shaken. When I had done, some of the professors said, it was now as in the days of the Apostles, when the house was shaken where they were."

The **levitation** of John Lacy (*Warnings of the Eternal Spirit,* part 2, 1707) made the chamber shake. The Rev. Maurice Davies in the *Daily Telegraph* and Dr. Gully in the *Morning Star,* described the trembling of the floor during Home's levitation as an effect reminding of an earthquake. Felicia Scatcherd wrote of a seance with Mrs. Etta **Wriedt** in *Light* (August 3, 1912): "We all felt the floor, walls and windows vibrating. I have twice experienced earthquake shocks in the Ionian Islands. The sensation was similar."

The Wesley family (see **Epworth Phenomena**), during physical manifestations, heard vast rumblings and clattering of doors and shutters. In the case of Mary **Jobson,** "a rumbling noise was heard like thunder, the tenants downstairs thought that the house was coming down." An excess of power held the room in which the Rev. Stainton **Moses** sat in seance in constant vibration.

"On several occasions," wrote Gambier Bolton in *Psychic Force* (1904), "when sitting in my own room with Mr. Cecil Husk, the whole place, floor, walls, and ceiling, have commenced to tremble and vibrate strongly, table and chairs all responding, and glass, china and pictures swaying to and fro, some of the lighter articles eventually falling over; the motion being similar to that experienced when the screw of a steamer, during a gale of wind, and owing to the pitching of the vessel, comes nearly or quite to the surface of the water, and "races"; or like the tremble of the earthquake which, as I know by experience, when once felt is never forgotten again. So decided was this tremble and vibration that several of the experimenters present not only stated that it made them feel very ill, but their appearance proved to anyone used to ocean travel, that this was not an exaggeration."

Movement of Objects

However, the average telekinetic phenomenon is on a smaller scale. A seance curtain sways and bulges out, a table moves, slides or rotates, weights are lifted, small objects stir, jump into the air and drop slowly or heavily. According to reports, such objects do not follow straight lines but move in curves, as if under the influence of an intelligent mechanical force. Their speed is sometimes alarming. They may come within an inch of one's face. Then they suddenly stop. There is no fumbling, no exploration, no accidental collision. If one puts out his hand in the dark for the reception of an object it neatly drops into his palm.

The sitters may change seats or posture, yet the objects

will seek them out perfectly. The invisible manipulator which is behind the phenomena seems to have cat's eyes. A table may incline at a considerable angle, yet the objects may remain unmoved on the leaf or they may glide up the slope.

A switch may be thrown, gas or electricity turned off, the flame of a candle depressed, cords and handkerchiefs knotted, bonds untied. There is every evidence of the operation of invisible hands. Their presence is often felt in touches and quite frequently they are said to be seen in operation.

Lord **Adare** saw, in a seance with D. D. **Home,** a hand stretch over the jet of gas. At the same moment eight jets of gas went out in the house.

Psychical researcher Hereward **Carrington** wrote of the Naples seances with Eusapia **Palladino:** "In one of our seances, a white hand appeared, remained visible to all, and untied both Eusapia's hands and one of her feet.

"Once a gentleman seated to the left of Eusapia had his cigar case extracted from his pocket, placed on the table in full view of all of us, opened, a cigar extracted, and placed between his teeth."

Sir William **Crookes** in his *Researches in the Phenomena of Spiritualism* (1874) gave a good description of the average type of telekinetic phenomena: "The instances in which heavy bodies, such as tables, chairs, sofas, etc., have been moved, when the medium was not touching them are very numerous. I will briefly mention a few of the most striking. My own chair has been twisted partly around, whilst my feet were off the floor. A chair was seen by all present to move slowly up to the table from a far corner, when all were watching it; on another occasion an armchair moved to where we were sitting, and then moved slowly back again (a distance of about three feet) at my request. On three successive evenings, a small table moved slowly across the room, under conditions which I had specially pre-arranged, so as to answer any objection which might be raised to the evidence. I have had several repetitions of the experiment considered by the Committee of the Dialectical Society to be conclusive, viz., the movement of a heavy table in full light, the chairs turned with their backs to the table, about a foot off, and each person kneeling on his chair, with hands resting over the backs of the chairs, but not touching the table. On one occasion this took place when I was moving about so as to see how everyone was placed."

Dr. J. **Ochorowitz** recorded some very curious telekinetic phenomena in his experiments with Mlle. Stanislawa **Tomczyk.** In good light, before a commission composed of physicians, physiologists and engineers, the medium placed her hands at a small distance on either side of an object.

Between her extended fingers, the object would rise into the air and float without apparent support. In fact, the support appeared to be a thread-like, non-material line of force of which Dr. Ochorowitz stated: "I have felt this thread in my hand, on my face, on my hair. When the medium separates her hands the thread gets thinner and disappears; it gives the same sensation as a spider's web. If it is cut with scissors its continuity is immediately restored. It seems to be formed of points; it can be photographed and it is then seen to be much thinner than an ordinary thread. It starts from the fingers. Needless to remark that

the hands of the medium were very carefully examined before every experiment."

When these photographs were projected enlarged upon a screen, the psychic structure became visible. There were swellings and nodes along it, like the waves in a vibrating cord. A whole number of filaments surrounded, like a net, a ball which Mlle. Tomczyk lifted.

With Eusapia **Palladino,** a marked synchronism was noticed between her movements and that of the objects. She could attract and remove pieces of furniture, cause them to rise in the air or drop to the floor by a corresponding motion of her hands. However, this was an exceptional phenomenon at her seances. Usually mediums cannot account for the movement of objects, as they do not know in advance what is going to happen.

In **poltergeist** cases and in cases of **apparitions,** spontaneous telekinetic phenomena have been witnessed. Dr. J. **Maxwell** obtained good phenomena with non-professional mediums in public restaurants in daylight. Miss Cleio made pictures swing out on the wall in the rooms of the Hellenic Society for Psychical Research in full light before dozens of invited guests.

Difficult Operations

The effect of these telekinetic manifestations is often a very complicated one. Pistols were fired in the dark seances of the **Davenport Brothers** against a minute mark which was always hit with marvellous precision. The same phenomenon was witnessed earlier in the loghouse of Jonathan **Koons,** under the control of "John King."

In the presence of the Davenport Brothers, a billiard room at Milwaukee was darkened. After a few moments the balls were heard to roll and click against each other, as if propelled by expert players. The cues moved, the game appeared to be regularly played, and it was marked and counted. However, the Davenports did not claim to be Spiritualist mediums, and are now generally regarded as clever stage performers.

There are several instances on record in which typewriters were faultlessly operated in a dark seance room. In the seances of the **Bangs Sisters,** the typewriter was held in the hands of the sitters above the table and was heard operating in rapid motion. The operators also inserted the paper, addressed the envelopes and sealed them. The *Posthumous Memoirs* of Madame **Blavatsky** (ed. G. W. N. Yost, 1896) is claimed to have been produced by this technical means. The machine, according to J. M. Wade's introduction, wrote nine sheets per hour.

Of a sitting with Franek **Kluski** on November 23, 1919, the Polish Society for Psychical Research recorded: "The typewriter on the table, fully illuminated by the red light, began to write. The sitters remarked that it wrote very quickly, the keys being depressed as if by a skilful typist. There was no one near the machine. The persons holding Mr. Kluski's hands noticed that they twitched during the writing."

In Prof. Tullio Castellani's record of a sitting on July 6, 1927, in **Millesimo Castle,** there is a description of the following artistic exhibition: "After a little while we heard in perfect rhythm with the music, a dance of two drumsticks upon the floor. Then the rhythm of the drumsticks was heard in the air. On being questioned Cristo d'Angelo described it as the dance of a celebrated American negro upon the ground and in the air. The same phenomena occurred later in the presence of Bozzano, and has been described by him. I think, however, it is useful to emphasize so that the reader may form some idea of how these phenomena took place, and the effect which this dance produced on me also, habituated though I am to spiritistic phenomenology. The dance took place upon the rug but the resonance was like that of wooden drumsticks which were dancing in the void. There was observable all the weight of a normal man dancing with vigour. Thus in the dark, by only the slight spectral light of the phosphorescence from the trumpet one is reminded of a *danse macabre.*"

Many are the mediums in whose presence musical instruments were played by invisible hands (see **Music**). Other forms of artistic expression through telekinetic movements are on record in independent painting and drawing (see **Direct Drawing and Painting**). In Volume XVI of the automatic scripts of the Rev. Stainton **Moses,** there is a description of the carving of two cameo heads by "Mentor" and "Magus." "Magus" produced his own likeness. "Mentor's" artistic efforts are thus narrated under the date August 27, 1875: "A long message was rapped out by Catherine. She said they had brought a shell and were going to cut a cameo. A light was struck, then Dr. and Mrs. S. saw a shell in the middle of the table. Then Mentor came and Imperator. After he left light was called for and in the centre of the table was a cameo and a quantity of debris of shell. Noises had been heard as of picking, and I saw a hand. The shell is more clearly cut than the first, and shows a head laurel-crowned. It is polished inside and shows plain marks of the graving tool."

According to a letter from the unpublished correspondence of Stainton Moses (see *Light,* May 3rd, 1902), "Owasso," one of Henry **Slade**'s controls, extracted, without actual pain, a bad tooth of his suffering medium. A reader of *Light* related in the following issue a similar incident, in the presence of several witnesses, in the history of the medium Miss **Wood.**

The Question of Scientific Verification

Levitation of a table in the full blaze of sunshine was witnessed by Prof. Charles **Richet** in front of his Chateau de Carqueiranne with the medium Eusapia **Palladino.** Dr. J. Ochorowitz, with Mlle. **Tomczyk,** saw a garden chair raised in full light.

An ancient instance of table levitation was described in Samuel Brent's *Judischer agestreifter Schlangen Balg,* Œtlingen, (1610) and in Zalman Zebi's reply *Judischer Theriak* (Affenhauser, 1615). Zebi admitted the levitation but he argued that it was not due to magic as "beautiful hymns are sung during the production of the phenomena and no devil is able to approach us when we think of the Lord."

Count Gasparin, Baron **Guldenstubbe,** Prof. Marc **Thury,** Prof. Robert **Hare** and Prof. James J. **Mapes** were the first investigators of table turning. Prof. Hare devised special scientific instruments. Sir William **Crookes** repeated his experiments and improved upon them. Experiments with an electric bell in a locked and sealed box were successfully carried out with the mediumship of William **Eglinton** by the research committee of the **British National Association of Spiritualists** in January 1878. The bell sounded twice and the armature was depressed

with so much force that a spring was strained and an electro-magnet disarranged.

Prof. **Zöllner**'s famous knot-tying experiments on an **endless cord** were successfully repeated with Eglinton by Dr. Nichols in his own house. The fraud-proof trick table of Harry **Price** was lifted by "Margery" (Mrs. **Crandon**) in London. The telekinetoscope and the shadow apparatus of the same researcher established the genuine powers of **"Stella C."** in the **National Laboratory of Psychical Research.** "Margery" also rivalled Prof. Zöllner's experiments by demonstrating the paranormal linking of two rings made of different woods (see **Matter Passing Through Matter**).

The first demand which the **Scientific American** Committee submitted to "Walter," "Margery's" control, at the time of this well-known investigation was to produce movements inside a closed and sealed space. For this purpose, first a sealed glass jar with a brass hook projecting down into the bottle was used and "Walter" was set the task of opening the snap of the hook and hanging upon it the wooden, brass or cord rings also enclosed into the jar. Two days later the cord ring was found on the hook. A day after its examination by Prof. Comstock, the ring was found off.

Another experiment with fine scales under a celluloid cover produced very satisfactory results. With one of the pans weighted, the other empty, "Walter" held the scales in balance and sent up the weighted pan. This dynamic feat was achieved in good visibility.

Similar results were achieved with a bell box, being physically operated first by the depression of a key or throwing a switch, and later (the instrument being revised), by the depression of the contact boards. Held in the lap of Dr. **Prince,** Research Officer of the **American Society for Psychic Research,** the instrument was operated in daylight. For details of all these experiments with Mrs. Crandon, see *"Margery" the Medium* by J. Malcolm Bird (1925).

The voice-cut-out-machine of Dr. Richardson established the independence of "Walter's" voice (see *Journal* of the American Society for Psychical Research, vol. 19, No. 12, 1925). Modern psychical research laboratories may boast of a number of other instruments which detect or prevent the slightest movement in the seance room and afford opportunities for observation under strict scientific conditions.

Display of Strength

Occasionally the power which accumulates for telekinetic phenomena is so much that astounding feats of strength are exhibited.

At Warsaw, in Dr. Ochorowitz's experiments, a dynamometer marked a force three times as great as Eusapia **Palladino**'s and in excess of that of the strongest man present.

In the mediumship of Mme. **d'Esperance** it was recorded by herself as an interesting incident that in Breslau in the house of Professor Friese, the strongest man in Silesia, a veritable Hercules, vainly tried to prevent the movements of the table.

"A violent crack was suddenly heard," recorded Prof. **Zöllner,** "as in the discharging of a large battery of Leyden jars. On turning, with some alarm, in the direction of the sound, the before-mentioned screen fell apart in two pieces. The wooden screws, half an inch thick, were torn from above and below, without any visible contact of Slade with the screen. The parts broken were at least five feet removed from Slade, who had his back to the screen; but even if he had intended to tear it down by a cleverly devised sideward motion, it would have been necessary to fasten it on the opposite side.

Prof. Zöllner estimated that the strength of two horses was necessary to achieve this effect. He mentioned that one of his colleagues seriously suggested that the medium Henry **Slade** carried dynamite about him, concealed it in the furniture in a clever fashion and exploded it with a match.

In a sitting with Countess **Castelwitch** in Lisbon, which Prof. Feijao attended, a small table, strengthened with sheet-iron was rent into 200 pieces. The fragments were found piled up in a corner of the room.

It was said in the record of a seance with Eusapia Palladino under the supervision of Prof. P. Foà, Dr. A. Herdlitzka, Dr. C. Foà and Dr. A. Aggazotti: "Dr. Arullani asked that the hand behind the curtain should grasp his. The medium replied in her own voice: 'First I am going to break the table, then I will give you a grasp of the hand.' This declaration was followed by three fresh, complete levitations of the table, which fell back heavily on the floor. All those who were on the left of the medium could observe, by a very good red light, the various movements of the table. The table bent down and passed behind the curtain, followed by one of us (Dr. C. Foà) who saw it turn over and rest on one of its two short sides, whilst one of the legs came off violently as if under the action of some force pressing upon it. At this moment the table came violently out of the cabinet, and continued to break up under the eyes of everyone present. At first its different parts were torn off, then the boards themselves went to pieces. Two legs, which still remained united by a thin slip of wood, floated above us and placed themselves on the seance table."

The astronomer Porro reported from his seance with Eusapia Palladino in 1891: "Next a formidable blow, like the stroke of the fist of an athlete is struck in the middle of the table. The blows are now redoubled and are so terrific that it seems as if they would split the table. A single one of these fist blows, planted in the back, would suffice to break the vertebral column."

The Rev. Stainton **Moses** recorded in one instance sledgehammer blows and stated: "The noise was distinctly audible in the room below and gave one the idea that the table would be broken to pieces. In vain we withdrew from the table, hoping to diminish the power. The heavy blows increased in intensity, and the whole room shook with their force."

From the Livermore seance notes with Kate **Fox,** February 15, 1862: "I asked for a manifestation of power; and we at once received the following message: 'Listen, and hear it come through the air; hands off the table.' Immediately a terrific metallic shock was produced, as though a heavy chain in a bag swung by a strong man had been struck with his whole power upon the table, jarring the whole house. This was repeated three times, with decreasing force."

In slate-writing experiments with Henry Slade, the slates were often pulverized. Paul Gibier reported in *Le*

Spiritisme (Paris, 1887): "At ten different trials the slate held by Slade under the table was broken into several pieces. These slates were framed in very hard wood. We endeavoured to break them in the same way by striking them against the table, but never succeeded even in cracking them."

Writing of a visit to a Shaker village with the mediums Miss King and H. B. Champion, The Rev. J. B. **Ferguson** said of the latter: "Although a man of most delicate physical organisation, he was, to my knowledge, without food for ten days, and during that time seemed to possess the strength of three men, when under direct spiritual influence; but when not he was as feeble as an infant, and needed all the care I had promised."

Lifting of Heavy Tables and Pianos

There has been a frequent display of great force in the paranormal lifting of heavy tables or pianos.

Sir William **Crookes** saw on five separate occasions a heavy dining table rise between a few inches and one and a half feet off the floor under special circumstances which rendered trickery impossible (see R. G. Medhurst, K. M. Goldney, M. R. Barrington, *Crookes and The Spirit World,* 1972, p. 115).

D. D. **Home** testified before the committee of the **London Dialectical Society:** "I have seen a table lifted into the air with eight men standing on it, when there were only two or three other persons in the room. I have seen the window open and shut at a distance of seven or eight feet, and curtains drawn aside and, in some cases, objects carried over our heads. In the house of Mr. and Mrs. S. C. Hall a table went up so high in the air that we could not touch it."

At a supper party in the house of Henry Dunphy of the *Morning Post,* at which thirty persons, including Miss Florence **Cook,** participated, the heavy dining table, with everything upon it, rose, in full light, bodily into the air, until the feet of the table were level with the knees of those sitting round it; the dishes, plates and glasses swaying about in a perilous manner, without, however, coming to any permanent harm." (See *Psychic Force* by Gambier Bolton, 1904)

Robert Dale **Owen** claimed to have seen in Paris in broad daylight in the dining room of a French nobleman, the dinner table seating seven persons, with fruit and wine on it, rise and settle down, while all the guests stood around without touching it.

Florence **Marryat** writes in her book *There is No Death* (1892) that after her first seance with Florence Cook the whole dinner table around which perhaps thirty people were sitting, with everything upon it, rose bodily in the air, to a level with their knees, and the dishes and glasses swayed about in a perilous manner, without, however, coming to any permanent harm."

In another seance, with Katie **Cook,** a piano was carried over the heads of the sitters. One of the ladies became nervous, broke the chain of hands, whereupon the piano dropped on the floor, the two carved legs were broken off and the sounding board smashed in.

The levitation of two pianos, in the presence of an eleven-year-old child, was described as early as 1855 in Prof. Marc Thury's *Des Tables Tournantes.* The phenomenon was witnessed by President Abraham **Lincoln** in Mrs. Laurie's house.

Mr. Jencken, the husband of Kate **Fox,** said in a paper read before the **London Dialectical Society:** "As regards the lifting of heavy bodies, I can myself testify I have seen the semi-grand at my house raised horizontally eighteen inches off the ground and kept suspended in space two or three minutes."

The Master of Lindsay, before the same body, said: "I was next to him [D. D. Home]. I had one hand on his chair and the other on the piano, and while he played both his chair and the piano rose about three inches and then settled down again."

Dr. John Ashburner, author of *Notes & Studies in the Philosophy of Animal Magnetism and Spiritualism* (1867), recorded the following personal experience: "Mr. Foster, who is possessed of a fine voice, was accompanying himself while he sang. Both feet were on the pedals, when the pianoforte rose into the air and was gracefully swung in the air from side to side for at least five or six minutes. During this time the castors were about at the height of a foot from the carpet."

"As Mr. Home and myself were entering the drawing room lighted with gas," wrote Sergeant E. W. **Cox** in *What am I?* (2 vols., 1873–74), "a very heavy armchair that was standing by the fire, thirteen feet from us, was flung from its place through the whole length of the room and fell at our feet. No other person was in the room and we were crossing the threshold of the door."

Mr. Arthur Lévy wrote in a report on Eusapia **Palladino,** November 16, 1898: "Just as if she was defying some monster, she turns, with inflamed looks, toward an enormous divan, which thereupon marches up to us. She looks at it with a Satanic smile. Finally she blows upon the divan, which goes immediately back to its place." (See Camille Flammarion, *Mysterious Psychic Forces,* 1907)

Vanishing Objects

In phenomena of **apports,** human **transportation** and frequently in the phenomenon of **matter passing through matter** there is an intermediate stage in which the objects in question or the human body apparently disappears. Sometimes nothing further than disappearance and subsequent reappearance is accomplished. Whether this is done by a great increase in the vibratory rate of the objects handled or by **dematerialization** is a matter of speculation. Instances to demonstrate the claimed phenomenon are in abundance.

A small table from underneath a larger one disappeared in a seance of Prof. **Zöllner** with the medium Henry **Slade.** They searched the room without result. Five minutes later it was discovered floating in the air upside down. It dropped and struck Zöllner on the head. The vanishing and reappearance of a book was similarly observed. It struck Zöllner on the ear in its descent. (See J. C. F. Zöllner, *Transcendental Physics,* 1882)

The records of the Rev. Stainton **Moses** dated November 27, 1892 stated: "As Dr. S. and I were pacing up and down the room a whole shower of Grimauve lozenges (the remainder of the packet out of which the cross had been made on Friday last) was violently thrown on to my head, whence they spread over the floor round about where we were standing. There were thirteen or fourteen of them, and that number, together with the nine used in making the cross, would just about make up the two ounce packet which I had. I had looked in every conceivable place for

these lozenges (which were missing after the cross was made) but could find them nowhere."

"Lily," the guide of Katie **Cook,** asked Florence **Marryat** whether she could take away her fur coat which the authoress put on her shoulders. She was given permission under the stipulation that she returned it when Florence Marryat would have to go home. "Lily" asked for the gas to be turned up. The fur coat was no more in the room. During the later course of the seance, the coat was flung, apparently from the ceiling, and fell right over the owner's head. Apparently the coat had gone through an ordeal for, although it was quite new, now all the fur was coming out and an army of moths could not have damaged it more than "Lily's" trick.

Mrs. Osborne **Leonard,** in her book *My Life in Two Worlds* (1931) told of a **control** "Joey," a famous clown in earth life, who as a proof of his power made things belonging to her husband disappear in daylight in the house and reappear days later in exactly the same place. "Yolande," Mme. **d'Esperance**'s control, often performed similar feats.

In the presence of Eleonore Zügun, objects vanished for an indeterminate period. Her patron the Countess Wassilko-Serecki coined the vivid phrase "holes in the world" to describe the effect. (See 'Some Account of the Poltergeist Phenomena of Eleonore Zügun' by Harry Price, *Journal* of the American Society for Psychical Research, August 1926)

The disappearance usually involves no injury. In experiments with the medium T. **Lynn** at the **British College of Psychic Science,** watches frequently vanished from sight without showing harm or stoppage on their reappearance (see *Psychic Science,* vol. 8, No. 2, July 1929). With the Austrian medium Frau **Silbert** it was noticed that she seemed to know intuitively a few minutes beforehand what articles would appear, as if the "cloud of invisibility" which surrounded the objects had been of ectoplasmic nature.

The objects which vanish are not necessarily solids. The invisible operators seem to have the same power over liquids. Lord **Adare** recorded that brandy was invisibly withdrawn from a glass which the medium D. D. **Home** held above his head. When Lord Adare held his hands above the glass the liquor fell over and through his fingers into the glass, dropping from the air above him. Home explained that the spirit making the experiment was obliged to form a material substance to retain the fluid.

Dr. Eugene Crowell, author of *The Identity of Primitive Christianity with Modern Spiritualism* (2 vols., 1875–79) took a small vial filled with pure water to a seance with the medium Henry **Slade** to have it "magnetized." He wrote: "We were seated in a well-lighted room, the rays of the sun falling upon the floor, and no one present but us. Twice the medium said he saw a spirit hand grasping the vial, and I supposed the spirits were magnetising it and kept my eyes directing towards it, but I saw nothing, when suddenly at the same instance we both saw a flash of light apparently proceeding from the vial and the latter disappeared. I immediately arose and inspected every part of the room which from the beginning had been closed, under the table, chairs and sofa, but the vial was not found. Then resuming my seat and questions, in about fifteen minutes, while the two hands of the medium were clasping mine upon the table, I felt something fall into my lap, and looking down I observed the vial rolling off my knees on to the floor. Upon my taking it up we both remarked that the water had acquired a slightly purple tinge, but otherwise its appearance was unchanged."

Max George Albert Bruckner described in the July 1, 1931 issue of the *Zeitschrift für Metapsychische Forschung,* a sitting with Frau Maria **Silbert** in which a bottle filled with water and sealed, was transferred from the top of the table under it. On examination it was found that the water had completely disappeared. The seal and the cord remained intact. Not a drop of water was visible on the floor.

Vice-Admiral Usborne Moore noticed that the ink in his bottle disappeared in a seance with the **Bangs Sisters** (see his book *Glimpses of the Next State,* 1911).

Theories of Explanation

Since the first days of modern Spiritualism, speculation has been rife as to the mechanical agency by which movement without contact takes place. **Animal magnetism** was first thought to furnish the clue. Many theories were formulated. All of them were more or less similar to the "odylo-mesmeric" theory (deriving from the **"Od"** of Baron K. von **Reichenbach**) of E. C. Rogers (*Philosophy of Mysterious Agents, Human and Mundane,* 1853). His definition of a medium was "a person in whom the conscious and personal control of the higher brain centres was for the moment in abeyance leaving the organism open to be acted upon by the universal cosmic forces." J. Bovee Dods (*Spirit Manifestations,* 1854) possibly came very near the truth in his explanation of rapping as "an electro-magnetic discharge from the fingers and toes of the medium." As regards table-tilting he stated that "the millions of pores in the table are filled with electro-magnetism from human brains, which is inconceivably lighter than the gas that inflates the balloon."

However, the agency of human magnetism or electricity was quickly disproved when no instrument could detect the slightest trace and neither the smallest iron filing nor the tiniest pith ball was attracted by the charged table.

Confederacy, chance, **fraud, hallucination,** or a composite of these suppositions fails to meet all reported data. The other extreme that spirits were responsible for the movement explained little. It was a comparatively early claim that the contribution of the spirits was, at the most, a directive influence and that in some mysterious way the bodily organism of the medium played a dominant role.

The spirits themselves described physical mediums to Allan **Kardec** in the following words: "These persons draw from themselves the fluid necessary to the production of the phenomena and can act without the help of foreign spirits. Thus they are not mediums in the sense attached to this word; but a spirit can assist them and profit by their natural disposition."

The "fluid" of this early age has been replaced by the **"ectoplasm"** of psychical research. The claimed existence of this substance facilitates the idea of a bridge between **telekinesis** and ordinary mechanics. W. J. **Crawford**'s cantilever theory represented the most important attempt in this direction.

It essentially claimed that out of ectoplasmic emanations psychic rods, so strong as to become semi-metallic, are formed, that this extrusion acts as a cantilever, and the phenomena are produced by an intelligent manipulation on the part of unseen operators of these rods.

The contention that structures may exist which are invisible, impalpable, yet rigid is a mechanical paradox. Rigidity means the power of resisting deformation under stress. It presupposes a force opposing the effort of deformation. This force apparently is not applied from any direction with which we are acquainted.

Is it not possible, asked psychical researcher W. Whateley **Carington,** that it is applied from the fourth dimension? We do not know. Crawford was strong in facts, but his theories were few. He found that if the object to be levitated was heavy, the psychic structure beside the medium's body, found support on the floor. He made many exact measurements. He discovered that the objects were usually gripped in a manner resembling suction. He proved the presence of the psychic rods by their pressure on a spring balance and measured their reaction on the medium's body with scales. He photographed psychic structures. He noticed that if an object was lifted or glued to the floor, the medium's body showed a nearly equivalent increase or decrease in weight. The difference was distributed among the sitters. (See W. J. Crawford, *Psychic Structures in The Goligher Circle,* 1921)

Crawford's experiments were confirmed by others. Dr. Karl Grüber, Professor of Zoology in the Polytechnic School of Munich, reported experiments with the medium Willy **Schneider** in 1922: "A rigid body seemed to emanate from the right hip of the medium. At about three quarters of a yard from the floor it traversed the gauze partition, enlarging some of its interstices, and moved objects 80 to 100 centimetres distant from the medium. It seems that the medium has to make a certain effort to cause this fluidic member to traverse the screen. By using luminous bracelets we have verified that during the levitation of a small table a dark stump like that of a member could be distinguished, that it rose up under the table, raised it, and replaced it on the floor and showed itself afresh underneath it."

The advantage of the cantilever theory is its simplicity. For that very reason it only explains an initial stage of telekinetic phenomena. Movements without contact in haunted houses, in **poltergeist** cases and the **levitation** of the human body, apparently demand a different theory.

Prof. Charles **Richet** was probably right in saying that telekinetic phenomena constitute the first stage of materialization which may be called mechanization. When phantom hands or whole bodies are formed, the presence of a separate dynamic organism is suggested. It is created at the expense of the medium and the sitters. By calculation Dr. J. Ochorowitz found that the dynamometric energy which the circle loses corresponds to the average power of a man.

If the theory of a separate dynamic organism is accepted, we can fit in experiences like Lord **Adare**'s: "Home told me to go into the next room and place outside the window a certain vase of flowers. I did so, putting the vase outside the ledge and shutting the window. Home opened the window of the room in which we were sitting. The flowers were carried through the air from the window of the next room in at our open window. We could all hear the rustling and see the curtains moved by the spirit standing there, who was bringing in the flowers; Lindsay saw the spirit distinctly."

Many psychical researchers refused to go thus far. They did not like to narrow down the medium's physical participation in the occurrences. Prof. Theodor **Flournoy** put forward the following theory: "It may be conceived that, as the atom and the molecule are the centre of a more or less radiating influence of extension, so the organised individual, isolated cell, or colony of cells, is originally in possession of a sphere of action, where it concentrates at times its efforts more especially on one point, and again on another, *ad libitum*. Through repetition, habit, selection, heredity and other principles loved by biologists, certain more constant lines of force would be differentiated in this homogeneous, primordial sphere, and little by little could give birth to motor organs. For example: our four members of flesh and blood, sweeping the space around us, would be but a more economic expedient invented by nature, a machine wrought in the course of better adapted evolution, to obtain at the least expense the same useful effects as this vague, primordial, spherical power. Thus, supplanted or transformed, these powers would thereafter manifest themselves, only very exceptionally, in certain states, or with abnormal individuals, as an atavistic reappearance of a mode of acting long ago fallen into disuse, because it is really very imperfect and necessitates, without any advantage, an expenditure of vital energy far greater than the ordinary use of arms and limbs. Perhaps it is the Cosmic power itself, the amoral and stupid 'demiurge,' the Unconsciousness of M. Hartman, which comes directly into play upon contact with a deranged nervous system and realises its disordered dreams without passing through the regular channels of muscular movements."

Edmund E. Fournier d'Albe, author of several books on psychical phenomena, wondered if the living principle of the cells which die could not in some way still be attached to us. If so, we would be actually living half in this world and half in the next. Could not then telekinesis be explained by a resumed embodiment or materialized activity of the disembodied epidermal cell principles?

Prof. Cesar **Lombroso** wrote "I see nothing inadmissible in the fact that, with hysterical and hypnotic subjects the excitation of certain centres which become active in proportion as all other centres become paralysed, may cause a transposition of psychical forces, and thus also bring about a transformation into luminous force or into motor force. It is thus conceivable how the force of a medium, which I may nominate as cortical or cerebral, might, for instance, raise a table or pull someone's beard, or strike or caress him, phenomena which frequently occur under these circumstances."

Dr. J. **Maxwell** verified a correlation between the intensity of the muscular effort and the abnormal movement. The movement sometimes may be provoked by shaking the hand about at a certain distance above the table. Rubbing the feet on the floor, rubbing the hands, the back, the arms, in fact any quick or slightly violent movement appears to liberate this force. The breath appears to exercise a great influence as though, in blowing on the object, the sitters emitted a quantity of energy.

Dr. Maxwell had the impression that, within certain limits, the quantity of force liberated varied in direct proportion with the number of experimenters. His observations were thus summed up: "There is a close and positive connection between the movements effectuated by the medium and the sitters, and the displacement of articles of experimentation; there is a relation between these displacements and the muscular contractions of the experimenters; a probable relation, whose precise nature he is unable to state, exists between the will of the experimenters and paranormal movements." (See J. Maxwell, *Metapsychical Phenomena*, 1905)

Exteriorization of motricity was postulated in the case of Eusapia **Palladino** by Prof. Enrico **Morselli,** Prof. Theodor Flournoy, Dr. Gustav Geley and Dr. H. **Carrington.** Essentially the same theory was put forward in 1875 by Francis Gerry Fairfield in *Ten Years With Spiritual Mediums,* suggesting a nerve aura which surrounds every organic structure, capable of receiving sensory impressions, acting as a force and assuming any desired shape. The nerve aura, however, involves more than **ectoplasm.** It suggests the presence of a third factor, a nervous force to which both the medium and the sitters contribute.

During the levitation of a table in the "Margery" seances on June 23, 1923, the sitters felt cold, tingling sensations in their forearms. Dr. Crandon at the same time observed faint, aurora-like emanations from the region of "Margery's" fingers. It may be yet discovered that the tremendous force which occasionally operates through the ectoplasmic structures is of purely nervous origin.

F. W. H. Myers **suggested,** as a correlative to telepathic effect, a "telergic action," by which he meant the excitation of the motor and sensory centers of the medium by an external mind. He said that in case of **possession,** the external intelligence may directly act upon the body and liberate energies of which we have as yet no knowledge. This theory goes far, as the external mind appears to dwell in the spiritual world, although it is of frequent observation that the sitters' thoughts exercise a certain influence upon the phenomena. M. Barzini, journalist of *Corriere della Sera,* wrote about his seances with Eusapia Palladino (in Genoa, 1906–07): "It was obvious that our conversations were listened to, so as to yield a suggestion in the execution of the strange performance. If we spoke of levitation the table would rise up. If we began to discuss luminous phenomena instantly a light would appear upon the medium's knees."

As soon as we switch to the spiritual world in search of the ultimate agency, we have to consider what Baron L. de P. **Hellenbach** wrote in his *Birth and Death as a Change of Form of Perception* (1886): "I am convinced," he stated, "that the unseen world has first to learn how to act, so as to make themselves accessible to our senses somewhat in the same way that we have to learn how to swim in water, or communicate with the deaf and dumb."

Experimentation was plainly apparent in the "Margery" seances. "Walter" suggested, in explanation of complicated operations with scientific instruments, that he made a psychic double of all our apparatus, working directly on this, and that, automatically or otherwise the results were duplicated on the material prototype. He was always insistent that things be left undisturbed in the seance room as much as possible. He occasionally objected even to cleaning and airing, saying that he had a lot of superphysical apparatus there which gets disturbed if the room is invaded. If his wishes were respected, better phenomena were invariably produced. In view of doubts surrounding much of the "Margery" phenomena, this may seem purely fanciful.

In the weighing scale experiments of the *Scientific American* Committee with "Margery," the photograph of a curious, semi-transparent cylinder was obtained (with flashlight and a quartz lens), looking as if made of glass or celluloid. Seven of twelve exposed plates showed this cylinder. It was five or six inches long and three or a little less in diameter. It stood on its base. When it was photographed on the scale, the pan that carried it was up; when it was photographed upon the platform of the scale, the pans balanced. The deduction was that the cylinder acted as a sort of suction pump to keep the lighter pan up. "Walter" said that if the cylinders had been taken under long exposure they would have looked as though filled with cotton wool.

But even if we admit the possibility that instruments on the other side have to be devised to achieve certain effects, we have not yet come nearer to the understanding of the actual physical operation. The cantilever theory may be but one of the many possible mechanical solutions. There are observations to prove that threads, finer than a spider's, may (somewhat in the manner of cobwebs) connect the medium with the objects of the room.

Mme. **d'Esperance** often complained of a feeling of cobwebs on her face. "Margery" and many of her sitters had the same experience. Ectoplasmic threads may be the instruments of telekinetic action in **poltergeist** cases. With Mlle. **Tomczyk,** Dr. **Ochorowitz** photographed a balance which was supernormally depressed by fine hair-like threads. The method must have been similar when Eusapia **Palladino** genuinely performed the same feat. In fact the thread was seen as (in a seance at the house of Cavalier Peretti in Genoa in 1903) it made a glass of water dance. Slowly and cautiously, Cavalier Peretti drew the thick, white thread to himself. It resisted, then it snapped and disappeared with a nervous shock to the medium.

Ernesto **Bozzano** observed such threads twenty times in the same year; Mme. **Bisson** detected them with the medium **"Eva C.,"** Dr. Jorgen Bull, of Oslo, found them instrumental in an invisible state in producing direct writing on wax tablets in the presence of Mme. Lujza Linczegh **Ignath.**

In some of the excellent photographs obtained by Dr. Glen **Hamilton** with "Mary M.," of Winnipeg, slight threads can be seen reaching up to a bell fixed high above the curtain which was rung occasionally. A similar attachment of threads to apported objects was observed in the photographs taken by Major Mowbray with the medium T. **Lynn.**

The guide of Frau Ideler explicitly stated, in the experiments conducted by Prof. Blacher of the University of Riga (*Zeitschrift für Parapsychologie*, October 1931), that she spun threads to accomplish telekinetic movement. In red light and later in blue light these attachments were observable and the medium seemed to pull the threads from the inner side of her hand with her fingertips. The threads seemed to be of a doughy, elastic substance at first thick, then pulled fine, and felt soft and dry. Even while

being handled they diminished perceptibly. A piece was secured and subjected at once to microscopic examination in an adjoining room. An enlargement of the microscopic photo showed that it was composed not of one strand but of many fine but not organized threads. In its chemical composition the structure was not that of the known textile fabrics. Curiously, fire had no power over these threads. They made the flame withdraw. But they were conductors of electricity.

The thread-connection with the medium being verified, it is easy to understand that the medium subconsciously may feel, and could indicate in advance, what objects are going to be moved. Dr. Osty established this with the medium Rudi **Schneider** at the Institut Métapsychique. The experience was also well-known to sitters with Frau Maria **Silbert.**

Modern Experiments in Psychokinesis

The bulk of the past observation and theory relating to paranormal movement belongs to a period when physical mediums with unusual phenomena appeared more frequently than in modern times. Consideration of such phenomena is influenced by the fact that much of the evidence is purely anecdotal or belonging to a period of psychical research less skeptical than in modern times.

In the modern period of parapsychology, movement of objects without contact is now studied experimentally under the general term "Psychokinesis" or "PK." The first important experimental studies of this kind were inaugurated by Dr. J. B. **Rhine** in 1934 after he had encountered a gambler who claimed that he would influence the fall of dice by willpower. Rhine, who had been involved in investigation of the controversial "Margery" mediumship, was anxious to find some type of phenomena that could be studied under control conditions in a laboratory, thus avoiding the endless arguments about fraud and malobservation involved with spontaneous phenomena. Dice fall experiments could be scientifically controlled and were repeatable and also subject to statistical assessment. Rhine and his associates duly set up classic experiments at Duke University, North Carolina, where subjects attempted to influence the fall of dice by willpower.

Over the years, other parapsychologists verified the successful scores of Rhine and others. Eventually one of Rhine's associates, W. E. Cox, introduced interesting variations such as "Placement PK," in which subjects attempted to influence movement of various objects in a target direction.

Another interesting departure in scientific PK tests is the introduction of the "Minilab," a glass tank containing various small objects as targets for PK. The Minilab can be sealed and locked, and is monitored by cine camera or video camera which is activated by a switching apparatus connected to the objects, thus, object movement is automatically recorded.

The Minilab has been used by the parapsychologist J. D. Isaacs who has investigated the phenomenon of paranormal metal-bending, introduced by the Israeli psychic Uri **Geller,** whose feats in bending spoons and keys became a worldwide focus, stimulating imitators and new experiments, as well as providing accusations of fraud. (See 'Psychokinetic metal-bending' *Psi News*, Bulletin of the Parapsychological Association, vol. 4, No. 1.)

Most of Geller's phenomena were produced under casual conditions which did not preclude trickery, although he was later tested under laboratory conditions (see *The Geller Papers*, edited Charles Panati, 1976). However, critics like stage magician James **Randi** deny the possibility of paranormal metal-bending and have questioned the validity of the laboratory tests. To demonstrate the fallibility of scientific investigations, Randi introduced two fake metal-bending subjects into a test group. However, the use of the Minilab promises a more acceptable form of evidence for the verification of paranormal metal-bending and other forms of psychokinesis. (See also W. J. **Crawford; Ectoplasm; Exteriorization of Motricity; Goligher Circle;** Nina **Kulagina; Levitation; Metalbending; Psychic Force; Psychokinesis; Sorrat**)

Recommended reading:

Adare, Viscount (later Earl of Dunraven). *Experiences in Spiritualism with Mr. D. D. Home,* privately printed, 1870; Society for Psychical Research, London, 1924

Bird, J. Malcolm. *"Margery" the Medium,* Small, Maynard & Co., Boston/John Hamilton, London, 1925

Bolton, Gambier. *Psychic Force; An Experimental Investigation,* London, 1904

Carrington, Hereward. *Eusapia Palladino and Her Phenomena,* B. E. Dodge, New York/T. Werner Laurie, London, 1909

Crawford, W. J. *Experiments in Psychical Science,* John M. Watkins, London, 1919

Crawford, W. J. *Psychic Structures at the Goligher Circle,* John M. Watkins, London, 1921

Crawford, W. J. *The Reality of Psychic Phenomena,* John M. Watkins, London, 1919

Crowell, Eugene. *The Identity of Primitive Christianity and Modern Spiritualism,* New York, 1874

D'Esperance, E. *Shadow Land or Light From the Other Side,* George Redway, London, 1897

Flammarion, Camille. *Mysterious Psychic Forces,* Small, Maynard, Boston/T. Fisher Unwin, London, 1907

Forward, Haakon. *Mind, Matter, and Graviation: A Theoretical and Experimental Study,* Parapsychology Foundation, New York, 1970

Hasted, John. *The Metal-Benders,* Routledge & Kegan Paul, London & Boston, 1981

Holms, A. Campbell. *The Facts of Psychic Science and Philosophy Collated and Discussed,* Kegan Paul, London, 1925; University Books, 1969

Leonard, Gladys Osborne. *My Life in Two Worlds,* Cassell, London, 1931

(London Dialectical Society). *Report on Spiritualism of the Committee of the London Dialetical Society,* Longmans, Green, London, 1871

Marryat, Florence. *There Is No Death,* London, 1892; Causeway Books, 1973

Maxwell, J. *Metapsychical Phenomena,* Duckworth & Co., London, 1905

Medhurst, R. G. (coll.) & K. M. Goldney. *Crookes and the Spirit World; A Collection of Writings by or Concerning the Work of Sir William Crookes, O.M., F.R.S., in the Field of Psychical Research,* Taplinger, 1972

Panati, Charles (ed.). *The Geller Papers; Scientific Observations on the Paranormal Powers of Uri Geller,* Houghton Mifflin, 1976

Rhine, Louisa E. *Mind Over Matter; Psychokinesis,* Macmillan, 1970

Rogers, E. C. *Philosophy of Mysterious Agents, Human and Mundane,* Boston, 1853

Zöllner, J. C. F. *Transcendental Physics: An Account of Experimental Investigations,* W. H. Harrison, London, 1882

Moyes, Winifred (died 1957)

The medium of the spirit **guide** "Zodiac" for the spreading of whose teachings *The Greater World* paper and The **Greater World Christian Spiritualist League** were founded in 1931.

"Zodiac" first manifested at Miss Moyes's home circle in 1921. He claimed to have been a teacher at the Temple in the time of Jesus. His earth name was not disclosed but he said he was the scribe who asked Jesus which was the first commandment and to whom Jesus said: "Thou art not far from the Kingdom of God" (Mark xii, 28-34).

Miss Moyes's trance addresses were characterized by singular clarity and lofty wisdom. Although Miss Moyes died in 1957, the work of the League continues in spreading the teachings of "Zodiac."

Mr. Jacobs of Simla (*See* Jacobs, Mr.)

MUFOB (Metempirical UFO Bulletin)

Quarterly journal concerned with reports and sightings of UFOs and Fortean type mysteries. Edited by John Rimmer, 11 Beverley Road, New Malden, Surrey, England KT3 4AW.

MUFON

Initialism for Mutual UFO Network, investigating UFO phenomena and holding conferences on the subject. Founded in 1969, it became one of the most active UFO membership organizations, claiming 1,000 investigators spread over various parts of the world. MUFON holds an annual symposium and publishes *Skylook,* a monthly bulletin. The director for investigations is Raymond Fowler, author of *UFOs, Interplanetary Visitors* (Exposition, 1974). Address: 103 Oldtowne Road, Seguin, Texas 78155.

Mufon UFO Journal

Monthly bulletin concerned with UFO sightings, published by MUFON (Mutual UFO Network), 103 Oldtowne Road, Seguin, Texas 78155.

Muktanada, Swami (1908-1982)

A charismatic Hindu guru who is a unique exponent of Siddha Yoga, the pathway of spiritual development associated with psychic powers. Born May 16, 1908 at Dharmasthala, South India, he took his Master's degree from Jabalpur University in 1964, and became a lecturer in Hindi at W. M. Ruia College, India.

In February 1966, he first met Swami Nityananda of Ganeshpuri, who became his guru. Swami Nityananda had the rare power of *shaktipat,* the imparting of spiritual force through touch, arousing the **Kundalini** energy which is latent in the human organism at the base of the spine. Through initiation by his guru, Muktananda experienced the arousal of kundalini and its manifestation in various chakras or psychic centers of the body, accompanied by strange visions and enhanced consciousness.

He described his remarkable experiences in his book *Guru* (Harper & Row, 1971), which corroborates comparable experiences of Pandit **Gopi Krishna,** a Kashmir mystic who also aroused Kundalini. Muktananda became spiritual head of Shree Gurudev Ashram at Ganeshpuri, near Bombay, and attracted followers from all over India. He taught a traditional Hindu mystical doctrine of *sadhana* or spiritual discipline, enhanced by his strange ability to awaken spiritual force in others through *shaktipat.*

He first visited the U.S. in 1970, and four years later made a triumphal tour in California, where he gave an address to a convention of some 500 psychologists and psychotherapists in San Diego. Charles Garfield, clinical psychologist at the University of California, described Muktananda as "a highly developed being."

American ashrams were established in New York, Chicago, Los Angeles, Dallas and Piedmont. Muktananda also made successful visits to Britain. Known affectionately as "Baba" to his devotees, he is also given the courtesy title "Paramahansa," indicating the highest type of Hindu holy man.

Unfortunately after his death in October 1982, there have been serious allegations by former disciples claiming illicit sexual activities on the part of the guru, who had claimed to be completely celibate (see *Cult Awareness Network News,* Citizens Freedom Foundation, April-May, 1984).

Mulchuyse, S.

Dr. Mulchuyse is co-author with Prof. F. A. Heyne of the book *Vorderingen en Problemen van de Parapsychologie* (Progress and Problems in Parapsychology, 1950).

Muldoon, Sylvan J(oseph) (c. 1903–1971)

Pioneer American investigator of **Astral Projection** (**Out-of-the-Body** traveling). His first experience was at the age of twelve, stimulated by a visit with his mother to a Spiritualist Camp at Clinton, Iowa.

After going to sleep, he apparently awoke to discover himself outside his physical body, looking down at it, and connected by a kind of elastic cord or cable. He thought at first that he had died, and prowled through the house trying to awaken members of his family, but was eventually drawn back into his physical body. This was the first of hundreds of other projections.

In 1927, Mr. Muldoon read some books on occult and psychical science by the famous researcher Hereward **Carrington,** in which Carrington had stated that the book *Le Fantôme des Vivants* by Charles Lancelin covered practically all that was known on the subject of astral projection. Mr. Muldoon wrote to Carrington, challenging this statement and saying that he could write a whole book on things that Lancelin did not know.

As a result, Carrington invited Muldoon to collaborate on the book *The Projection of the Astral Body,* first published 1929, followed by *The Case for Astral Projection* (1936) and *The Phenomena of Astral Projection* (1951). These books have become classic works of their kind on this obscure subject. Two other books by Muldoon are: *Sensational Psychical Experiences* (1941) and *Famous Psychic Stories* (1942).

During much of his life, Muldoon suffered from ill health, and it is thought that this may have facilitated his frequent separation from the physical body in astral projections. In the latter part of his life, his general health improved, but his ability in astral projection correspondingly decreased and he devoted less time to the subject.

Mulford, Prentice (1834–1891)

American journalist and philosopher, a very individual blend of New Thought writer and mystic. He was born at Sag Habour, Long Island, April 5, 1834 and followed a rambling life. He served as a seaman, ship's cook and whalerman, before becoming a gold prospector. He attempted to run a mining, prospecting and teaching school, then turned to journalism.

From 1863 to 1866, he wrote for the *Democrat,* San Francisco, then *The Golden Era* (a leading literary paper) and the *Dramatic Chronicle.* In 1868 he spent a few months as editor of The Stockton Gazette, a Democratic journal.

In 1872, he persuaded a group of San Francisco business men to sponsor him for a lecture tour, promoting California in England, a project which lasted for two years. Afterwards he worked on the New York *Graphic,* conducting a news column "History of a Day" and in 1878 acted as Paris correspondent for the *San Francisco Bulletin.*

After six years, he retired to the wilderness of New Jersey, where he built a small shanty and commenced writing his famous White Cross Library series of philosophical and occult essays. These covered a wide range of occult, mystical and practical topics, involving a science of thought, and the nature and application of individual powers. The titles of some of these essays give a good idea of the range of subjects: 'God in the Trees,' 'The God in Yourself,' 'The Doctor Within,' 'Mental Medicine,' 'Faith: or, Being Led of the Spirit,' 'The Material Mind versus the Spiritual Mind,' 'Healthy and Unhealthy Spirit Communion,' 'You Travel When You Sleep,' 'Prayer in All Ages,' 'The Law of Success,' 'The Slavery of Fear,' 'Some Laws of Health and Beauty,' 'Self-Teaching; or, The Art of Learning How to Learn.' The first of these essays appeared in May 1886, published in Boston, Massachusetts. One of these White Cross Library series of special interest is 'Prentice Mulford's Story,' a vigorous autobiographical study to about 1872. The White Cross Library essays have been a great source of insight and inspiration to a large readership and still make stimulating reading.

On May 27, 1891, Mulford set out in a small boat, apparently for a vacation cruise, but died on board during his sleep, while anchored off Long Island the same evening. (See also **Mind Cure; New Thought**)

Müller, Fräulein Auguste (c. 1817)

German somnambulist of Carlsruhe, the first sensitive in the age of **animal magnetism** who claimed intercourse with spirits.

Her trance history was carefully recorded by Dr. Meier in his *Höchst Merkwürdige Geschichte der Magnetisch Hellsehenden Auguste Müller* (Stuttgart, 1818). She was controlled by the spirit of her dead mother and gave frequent exhibitions of a remarkable traveling clairvoyant faculty.

She gave correct medical diagnoses of herself and others

and claimed to discern in trance both the thoughts and the character of others. She could also project herself (see **Out-of-the-Body**) and appeared in the night in the bedroom of her friend Catherine, as she promised her.

Muller, Karl E(ugen) (1893–)

Electrical engineer who took a great interest in parapsychology. Born July 14, 1893 at New Orleans, Louisiana, he studied at the Technical University of Switzerland (B.E.E., D.Sc.Tech.). He was a measurement engineer at Swiss Electrotechnical Association in 1918, test engineer with Oerlikon Engineering Co., Zürich in 1919, laboratory director, Mexican Light & Power Co., Mexico City from 1920–25, member of engineering staff of Oerlikon, Zürich from 1925–27 and 1930–34, engineering consultant 1934–40, director of publicity at Oerlikon 1940 until retirement in 1958.

He was president of the International Spiritualist Federation from 1958 onwards, research officer of the International Spiritualist Federation from 1957 onwards; member of Swiss Electrotechnical Association, Society for Psychical Research, London, American Society for Psychical Research, Swiss Society for Parapsychology.

In addition to his many articles in technical journals Dr. Müller published contributions on parapsychology, and also experimented with infra-red photography in the investigation of physical mediumship. His publications relating to parapsychology include: 'Proofs for Reincarnation' (paper delivered before ISF Congress, London, 1960, published in *Psychic News,* (Oct.–Nov. 1960), 'Aspects of Astral Projection' (introduction to book *Excursions to the Spirit World* by F. C. Sculthorp, London, 1962), 'Spiritualist Doctrine' (*Tomorrow,* Autumn 1960). He also published articles in *Yours Fraternally, Chimes* and other magazines. Some of his articles were translated into Swedish, Danish and German.

Mullin, Albert Alkins (1933–)

Mathematician who has studied the relationship between parapsychology and cybernetics. Born August 25, 1933 at Lynn, Massachusetts, he studied at Syracuse University (B.E.E. 1955) and Massachusetts Institute of Technology (M.S. electrical engineering 1957). In 1955 he married Lorraine M. Agacinski.

He was a teaching assistant at Massachusetts Institute of Technology from 1955–57, research assistant at University of Illinois from 1957 onwards. He is a charter associate of the Parapsychological Association, member of American Institute of Electrical Engineers, Institute of Radio Engineers, American Mathematics Society, American Rocket Society. In addition to his technical papers concerned with engineering and mathematics, he contributed the article 'Some Apologies by a Cyberneticist' to the *Journal of Parapsychology* (vol. 23, No. 4, 1959).

Mullins, John (1838–1894)

One of the most famous British water diviners. He was born at Colerne, near Chippenham, Wiltshire on November 12, 1838 in a family of eleven children. His father was a stone mason and John followed the same trade. At the age of 21, while employed by Sir John Ould to build a house in Gloucestershire, a dowser (water diviner) was employed to locate a water supply. Various people pre-

sent tried their hand with the rod, including Sir John's daughter, who was frightened when the rod suddenly turned over violently. An abundant water supply was found at the spot.

Sir John was most impressed and later on asked all the workmen on his estate, about one hundred and fifty men, to try divining with a rod. When John Mullins tried in his turn, the rod moved so violently that it snapped in two. Thereafter Mullins was considered a dowser, although continuing his trade as a mason. At his first attempt to locate a water source for Sir John, he located a spring yielding 200 gallons per hour. After that, Mullins was much in demand as a water diviner.

He married in 1859 and continued his trade as a mason, but from 1882 onwards he devoted the last twelve years of his life to dowsing and well-sinking. Such was his confidence in his talent that he made no charge for the expensive work of well-sinking if a good supply of water was not found. In fact, he was immensely successful, locating over five thousand sources of water. After his death in May 1894, his business was carried on by his sons, one of whom was a dowser, although not so successful as his father. The firm of John Mullins & Sons was one of the most famous businesses of its kind, claiming royal patronage. A book by John Mullins, *The Divining Rod and Its Results in Discovery of Springs,* published in 1880, went into several editions. (See also **Divining Rod; Dowsing; Pendulum; Radiesthesia**)

Mumler, William H. (died 1884)

The first spirit photographer, living in Boston, Massachusetts. He was head engraver of the jewellery firm Bigelow, Kennard & Co., of Boston.

One day, in a friend's studio, he tried to take a photograph of himself by focusing the camera on an empty chair and springing into position on the chair after uncapping the lens. When developing the plate he discovered an extraneous figure, a young, transparent girl sitting in the chair, fading away into a dim mist in the lower parts. He recognized in this his cousin who had died twelve years before.

The experiment was repeated and he became satisfied that the extra faces appearing on his plates were of supernormal origin. The news of Mumler's discovery began to spread and he was besieged with so many requests for sittings that he gave up his position and became a professional spirit-photographer.

Among the first to investigate Mumler's powers was Andrew Jackson **Davis,** then editor of the *Herald of Progress* in New York. He first sent a professional photographer to test Mumler and on his favorable report conducted an investigation himself. He was satisfied that the new psychic manifestation was genuine.

It apparently did not matter whether Mumler worked in his own studio or in that of others, whether he used his own chemicals or not. Photographers came and went, one searching inquiry followed another. Black of Boston, inventor of the nitrate of silver bath, was anxious to establish whether a true spirit photograph was possible. He first sent Horace Weston, a fellow photographer, to Mumler, then came himself, made the most scrupulous examination, developed the plate himself and to his utter amazement found another form on it besides his own, a man leaning on his shoulder.

Mumler's reputation was established, he became in vogue and did tremendous business. His most famous picture was a photograph of the widowed Mrs. Abraham Lincoln, on which appeared a spirit portrait of her late husband.

The first scandal, however, was not long in coming. It was discovered that he obtained from time to time the spirit portraits of men who were very much alive. Apologists claimed that the pictures must be genuine since they had been recognized by relatives and that the processes of production had been properly supervised to obviate trickery. It was thought that the living individuals might be doubles of the "spirits." Mumler himself could not explain the result, but eventually even Spiritualists accused him of trickery and such a hue and cry was raised that in 1868 he transferred his headquarters to New York.

He prospered here for a while until he was arrested by the order of the Mayor of New York on an accusation of fraud raised by a newspaperman. The journalist, Mr. P. V. Hickey, of the *World,* approached Mumler for a spirit photograph, giving a false name, hoping to get a good story for his newspaper. At the trial professional photographers and independent citizens testified for Mumler and he was acquitted.

His further career was full of vicissitudes. He died in poverty. The story of his life is told in his book *Personal Experiences of William H. Mumler in Spirit Photography* (1875). Examples of his spirit photos are to be found in Aksakof's *Animisme et Spiritisme* and in James Coates's *Photographing the Invisible.* (See also **Psychic Photography;** Ted **Serios; Spirit Photography; Thoughtography**)

Mundle, Clement Williams Kennedy (1916-   )

Professor of philosophy who was actively involved in the study of parapsychology. Born August 10, 1916 in Fife, Scotland, he studied at the University of St. Andrews (M.A. 1939). From 1940–45 he was a Royal Air Force officer, Technical Branch. He took his B.A. in 1947 at Oxford University, and from 1948–50 was holder of a Shaw Philosophical fellowship at Edinburgh University. In 1946 he married Sheila MacGregor Falconer.

He was Head of Philosophy Department, University College of St. Andrews, Dundee, Scotland from 1947–55, Head of Philosophy Department, University College of North Wales, Bangor from 1955 onwards. His memberships include International Conference of Parapsychological Studies, Utrecht, Netherlands (1953), International Conference on Philosophy and Parapsychology, St. Paul de Vence, France (1954), charter member of Parapsychological Association.

Professor Mundle assisted in the ESP investigations reported by S. G. **Soal** and H. T. Bowden in their book *The Mind Readers* (1959). His own articles on parapsychology include: 'Is Psychical Research Relevant to Philosophy?' (*Proceedings, Aristotelian Society,* Supplemental vol. 24, 1950), 'Professor Rhine's Views on Psychokinesis' (*Mind,* July 1950), 'The Experimental Evidence for Precognition and Psychokinesis' (Society for Psychical Research, *Proceedings,* July 1950), 'Selectivity in Extrasensory Perception' (*SPR Journal,* March 1951), 'Some Philosophical

Perspectives for Parapsychology' (*Journal of Parapsychology,* Dec. 1952). He also contributed the chapter 'Broad's Views about Time' in the book *The Philosophy of C. D. Broad* (1959).

Prof. Mundle was president of the Society for Psychical Research, London, 1971–74.

Munnings, Frederick T(ansley) (c. 1928)

British fake medium, an ex-burglar whose claims to **direct voice** mediumship were dismissed by author and writer on psychic phenomena H. Dennis **Bradley,** who held several experimental sittings in his home. Bradley stated that the sittings were entirely valueless and, in February 1926 a public warning against Munnings was issued in the press by Sir Arthur Conan **Doyle,** Dr. Abraham Wallace, R. H. Saunders and H. D. Bradley.

For publication of the warning, Munnings brought an action for libel against the *Daily Sketch* and the *Sunday Herald* in 1928. However, he did not face the issue before the court and judgment was entered for the defendants. Thereupon Munnings sold his "Confessions" to *The People* newspaper. It appeared in installments for several weeks, written by journalist Sydney A. Moseley, branding Munnings whole psychic career as fraudulent. The understanding between Moseley and Munnings, however, was not perfect and in an interview to the *International Psychic Gazette,* Munnings entered a mild protest against his own sensational disclosures.

Psychical researcher Harry **Price** was instrumental in the exposure of Munnings, who claimed to produce the independent voices of "Julius Caesar," "Dan Leno" (famous nineteenth-century comedian), "Dr. Crippen" (a murderer), and "King Henry VIII." Price had invented a Voice Control Recorder and after testing Munnings, proved that all the voices were those of Munnings.

Murphy, Gardner (1895–1979)

Distinguished psychologist and pioneer figure in psychical research and parapsychology. Born July 8, 1895 at Chillicothe, Ohio, he studied at Yale University (B.A. 1916), Harvard University (M.A. 1917) and Columbia University (Ph.D. 1923). In 1926 he married Lois Barclay. He was a lecturer in psychology at Columbia University from 1921–25, instructor, assistant professor from 1925–29; professor, chairman of the Department of Psychology, City College of New York from 1940–52, director of research at Menninger Foundation, Topeka, Kansas from 1952 onwards. He is a member of the American Psychological Association (president in 1944), American Association for the Advancement of Science.

Dr. Murphy was a member of the Society for Psychical Research, London, as early as 1917, and his graduate work at Harvard as Richard Hodgson Fellow concerned psychical research. He served as vice-president of the American Society for Psychical Research from 1940–62, after which he was elected president. He initiated the first telepathic experiments through "wireless" (radio) in Chicago and Newark.

Dr. Murphy's many books on psychology and parapsychology include: *Historical Introduction to Modern Psychology* (first published 1925, still a standard college text in modern editions), *Personality* (1947), *In the Minds of Men* (1953), *Human Potentialities* (1958), (with Robert Ballou)

William James and Psychical Research (1960), *The Challenge of Psychical Research* (1961). Some of his important contributions to the ASPR *Journal* include: 'Concentration versus Relaxation in Relation to Telepathy' (Jan. 1943), 'Psychical Phenomena and Human Needs' (Oct. 1943), 'Removal of Impediments to the Paranormal' (Jan. 1944), 'An Outline of Survival Evidence' (Jan. 1945), 'Difficulties Confronting the Survival Hypothesis' (April 1945), 'An Approach to Precognition' (Jan. 1948), 'Needed: Instruments for Differentiating Between Telepathy and Clairvoyance' (April 1948), 'Psychical Research and Personality' (Jan. 1950), 'The Natural, the Mystical and the Paranormal' (Oct. 1952), 'Triumphs and Defeats in the Study of Mediumship' (Oct. 1957), 'Progress in Parapsychology' (Jan. 1959).

Dr. Murphy became open-minded about paranormal phenomena as a result of his personal experiences with unorthodox healing. In 1927 he suffered from near-blindness and persistent influenza. His sight was restored by Dr. Frank Marlow of Syracuse who taught him eye muscle exercises, and Dr. William H. Hay prescribed diet and exercise which overcame his semi-invalid condition.

He visualized ESP as "an extended self, an archipelago of mankind," and was quoted as saying "One of the main questions of psychic research is whether we can give up our precious folklore and intuition above vast regions of the unknown without throwing out the useful data."

Dr. Murphy died in George Washington University Hospital, Washington, D.C., March 20, 1979. He was a great psychologist and historian of psychology, as well as a distinguished parapsychologist.

He is survived by his wife Lois (Barclay) Murphy, whom he married in 1926, and who collaborated with him on some of his psychical researches.

In 1960, some of Dr. Murphy's former psychology students prepared a *Festschrift for Gardner Murphy,* ed. John G. Peatman & Eugene L. Hartley, published to honor his 65th birthday. Parapsychologist Prof. Gertrude **Schmeidler,** another former student, also published a tribute to Dr. Murphy in an article 'Some Lines About Gardner Murphy, the Psychologist's Parapsychologist' (*Parapsychology Review,* July–August, 1976). There is an obituary of Dr. Murphy in the May-June 1979 issue of *Parapsychology Review.*

Murphy-Lydy, Mrs. Mary (c. 1870– ?)

American **materialization** and **trumpet** medium, who practiced for many years in Chesterfield Camp, Indiana. Her chief controls were "Dr. Green" and "Sunflower." She was secured for a year by the Indiana Psychic Research Society at Indianapolis, toured the United States and attained prominence in 1931 in England by platform demonstration of direct voice.

Impressive accounts of her phenomena were published in the press, but British author and writer on psychic phenomena H. Dennis Bradley considered her performances highly suspicious. In his book . . . *And After* (1931) he described sittings with the medium whom he roundly condemned as "deliberately fraudulent." He also stigmatized her public appearances, stating "There was no semblance whatever of spirituality during the medium's proceedings. The effect produced was merely the boredom of a material and dreary exhibition." The main

charge was that in a private sitting the author actually heard the medium speak into the trumpet.

Murray, (George) Gilbert (Aime) (1866–1957)

Regius Professor of Greek at Oxford University, born January 2, 1866, president of the Society for Psychical Research, London, 1915-16. He is a famous figure in psychical research for his experiments in **thought-transference** which Mrs. **Sidgwick** (*Proceedings* of the Society for Psychical Research, vol. 34, 1924), which he considered "perhaps the most important ever brought to the notice of the society."

In an interview for the *Sunday Express* in the summer of 1929, he declared that he discovered his thought-reading faculty by accident. Playing guessing games with his children, one person going out of the room, the others deciding the subject he was to guess and writing it down he found, to his surprise, that in some intangible way an impression would be conveyed to him and he would actually know what the children were thinking.

On the insistence of his wife, he commenced experimenting with grown-ups and though by temperament and training he was intensely skeptical, in the interest of truth he admitted before the public that he was able to read thoughts.

He believed with psychologist William **James** that there exists the "stream of consciousness, with a vivid centre and dim edges." In moments of inattentiveness, subconscious impressions register themselves and afterwards form a sort of dim **memory.** This may account for certain phases of clairvoyance. But William James' "dim edges" idea should be further extended. Prof. Murray suspected that around our perceptions is a fringe of still more delicate sensing apparatus. The "feelers" of this apparatus are constantly registering contacts with their surroundings, but the impressions are too weak to enter the field of normal consciousness. This fringe of consciousness is the key to **telepathy.** Prof. Murray did not believe in communication with the dead.

He published a number of books concerned with Greek traditions in literature and poetry. He related his experiences in telepathy to the meaning of the original Greek term "sympathy" as "the sharing of a feeling of 'co-sensitivity.'"

He died at Oxford, England, May 20, 1957.

Murray, Margaret A(lice) (1863–1963)

British archaeologist whose writings on **Witchcraft** played a prominent part in the modern witchcraft revival. Born in Calcutta, India, July 13, 1863, she entered University College, London, 1894; Fellow of University College, London, D.Lit., F.S.A. (Scot.), F.R.A.I. She was junior lecturer on Egyptology in 1899, University Extension Lecturer at Oxford University in 1910, London University in 1911. She retired from her Assistant Professorship in Egyptology at University College in 1935, and excavated sites in Egypt from 1902-04, Malta from 1921-24, Hertfordshire, England in 1925, Minorca from 1930-31, Petra in 1937, Tell Ajjul, South Palestine in 1938.

She was a member of the Society of Visiting Scientists, and President of the Folklore Society, London, from 1953-55. She published a number of valuable works on archaeology, but is better remembered for her controversial books on witchcraft.

In *The Witch Cult in Western Europe* (1921), she explained witchcraft as a pre-Christian religion in its own right, rather than a heretical deviation from established Christianity. The book had a great influence on Gerald B. **Gardner** (1884-1964), pioneer of the modern witchcraft revival. Dr. Murray contributed an introduction to his book *Witchcraft Today* (1954). She also wrote two other books on witchcraft: *The God of the Witches* (1933) and *The Divine King in England* (1954).

She died November 13, 1963, soon after her hundredth birthday. For biographical information, see her autobiography *My First Hundred Years* (London, 1963).

Muscle Reading

According to Prof. James H. **Hyslop,** "the interpretation by the operator of unconscious muscular movements in the subject experimented on." As no paranormal perception is involved in the interpretation, psychical research is not specifically concerned in muscle reading, although the special sensitivities involved may have some relevance to the mechanisms of paranormal cognition. The subject is well treated in George Miller Beard's monograph, *The Study of Trance, Muscle Reading and Allied Nervous Phenomena* (New York, 1882). The *Proceedings* of the Society for Psychical Research, London, contain two studies on the subject: 'Note of Muscle Reading' by the Rev. E. H. Sugden (vol. 1, pt. 4, 1882-83) and 'Experiments in Muscle Reading and Thought Transference' by Max Dessoir (vol. 4, pt. 10, 1886-87).

Musès, C(harles) A(rthur) (1919-   )

Mathematician, physicist, cyberneticist, philosopher, who has worked in the field of parapsychology. Born April 28, 1919 in New Jersey, he studied at City College, New York (B.Sc.), Columbia University (A.M., Ph.D. philosophy). From 1941-43 he was a chemist at Gar-Baker Laboratories Inc.; from 1944-54 consultant; from 1954-59 editor-in-chief of Falcon's Wing Press, Colorado (concerned with philosophical and occult books); from 1960-62 research director of Barth Foundation; from 1963-69 research contributor in mathematics and morphology in Switzerland and California; edited *Journal for the Study of Consciousness*. He is a member of New York Academy of Science, Royal Astronomical Society, Canada.

He worked with the late Dr. Norbert Wiener, pioneer of Cybernetics, whose posthumously published lectures he edited. In the field of mathematics, Musès discovered root and logarithm operations for hyper-numbers following the square root of minus one. In the field of anthropology, he has studied the Maya people, the Lacadones of Chiapas, Mexico, and symbolic systems in India. He is editor of *Journal of Psychoenergetic Systems* and holds editorial positions with *Kybernetes, International Journal of Bio-Medical Computing, Impact of Science on Society* (UNESCO). He also edited *Proceedings of the First International Symposium on Biosimulation* (Locarno, 1960), *Aspects of the Theory of Artificial Intelligence* (New York, 1962). He is presently director of research for the Center for Research on Mathematics and Morphology, Santa Barbara, California.

At Falcon's Wing Press, he introduced publication of

Count Stefan Colonna Walewsky's *A System of Caucasion Yoga* (1955), a facsimile of a fascinating occult manuscript of a Gurdjieff type compiled in the 1920s. Musès own books include: *Illumination of Jacob Boehme; the work of Dionysius Andreas Freher* (1951), *An Evaluation of Relativity Theory after a Half-Century* (1953), *East-West Fire; Schopenhauer's Optimism and the Lankavatara Sutra; An Excursion toward the Common Ground between Oriental and Western Religion* (1955), (ed.) *Prismatic Voices; An International Anthology of Distinctive New Poets* (1958), (ed.) *Esoteric Teachings of the Tibetan Tantra* (1961; 1981), (ed. with A. M. Young) *Consciousness and Reality; the Human Pivot Point* (1972).

In the field of parapsychology, Musès has made important contributions to the study of the nature, alterations and potentials of consciousness, to which he gives the name **Noetics.**

His articles include: (in *Journal for the Study of Consciousness*) 'Hypernumber and Metadimension Theory; Unusual States of Consciousness' (vol. 1, 1968), 'The Limits of Consciousness' (vol. 1, 1968), 'The Noetic Relevance of Psychoactive Molecules' (vol. 2, 1969), 'Altering States of Consciousness by Mathematics' (vol. 3, 1970), 'The Emerging Image of Man and "Tain't Necessarily So"' (vol. 4, 1971). Other papers include 'Trance-inducing Techniques in Ancient Egypt' (in *Consciousness and Reality,* ed. C. Musès and A. M. Young, 'Communication of Consciousness Necessitates the Vacuum as Transducer' (*Proceedings of First International Conference on Psychotronics, Prague, 1973*), 'The Psi Dimension in Sciences' (*UNESCO's Impact of Science on Society,* 1974), 'Aspects of Some Crucial Problems in Biological and Medical Cybernetics' (in *Progress in Bio-Cybernetics,* vol. II, ed. N. Wiener & J. P. Schade, 1975), 'Psychotronic Quantum Theory; A Proposal for Understanding Mass/Space/Time/Consciousness Transductions in Terms of a Radically Extended Quantum Theory' (*Proceedings of International Association for Psychotronic Research,* 1975), 'The Politics of Psi; Acculturation & Hypnosis' (in *Extrasensory Ecology; Parapsychology and Anthropology* by Joseph K. Long, 1977).

Museum of Magic and Witchcraft

Founded in 1950 by witchcraft revivalist Gerald B. **Gardner** (1884-1964) at the Witches Mill, Castletown, Isle of Man, Great Britain. It contained witchcraft relics, as well as reconstructed scenes of occult rituals and instruments.

After Gardner's death, the Museum passed to Scottish witch Monique Wilson (witch name "Lady Olwyn"). Later the collection was sold to Ripley International, who created a Museum of Witchcraft and Magic at Fisherman's Wharf, San Francisco, California, and another at Gatlinburg, Tennessee. (See also Cecil H. **Williamson**)

Mushrooms

The narcotic and hallucinogenic properties of certain mushrooms have been known since ancient times. Certain mushrooms were even regarded as sacred and their use prohibited to ordinary people. In modern times, serious medical and scientific interest in hallucinogenic mushrooms dates from the pioneer work *Phantastica; Narcotic and Stimulating Drugs* by Louis Lewin (London, 1931). In this important book, Lewin discussed the use of fly agaric, and incidentally identified the peyotl plant (which he named *anholonium Lewinii*) and the substance mescaline obtained from it.

Over two decades later, the New York banker R. Gordon Wasson with his wife Valentina published their classic study *Mushrooms Russia and History* (Pantheon, 1957). This important work launched a new science of ethno-mycology, i.e., the study of the role played by wild mushrooms in various human cultures throughout history.

The Wassons had undertaken field trips into Mexico during 1955 to study at first hand the sacred mushroom ceremonies of the Indian people. Their record album *Mushroom Ceremony of the Mazatec Indians of Mexico* (Folkways Records, New York, 1957) was the first documented recording of its kind. The Wassons have also given special attention to fly agaric *(A. muscaria)* in history, and believe it was the source of the nectar named *soma* in the ancient Vedic literature of India. The studies of the Wassons reinforced the suggestions in Aldous Huxley's book *The Doors of Perception* (1954).

Unfortunately it was from popularization of such serious works that the psychedelic revolution and the widespread sickness of modern drug-addiction developed. It is not easy for sophisticated civilizations to recapture the cultural values and beliefs of primitive peoples who used hallucinogenic substances in religious rituals, and the over-intellectualized synthetic models of rituals mocked up by such experimenters as Timothy **Leary** and Richard **Alpert** lacked emotional and cultural integrity. On a lower level still are the reckless seekers of drug experience as an escape from social responsibility, and the sordid underworld of hard drugs and dope pushing which has grown up around them. (See also John M. **Allegro;**) **Drugs**)

Music (Paranormal)

There are various different types of paranormal music, ranging from inspired performances by mediums or compositions dictated by "spirit musicians," to music which is heard without any apparent earthly source. Perhaps this latter form of paranormal music is the most impressive. There are two distinct types of its occurrence.

During the persecution of the Huguenots in France, the hearing of music from invisible sources became a widespread phenomenon. The *Letters of Pastor Jurieu* (1689) referred to dozens of instances with names. The sound of trumpets, as if an army were going to charge, and the singing of psalms, a composition of many voices, and a number of musical instruments were heard day and night at many places.

After the church in Orthez was razed to the ground, there was hardly a house in Orthez in which people did not hear the music, ordinarily between eight and nine at night. The Parliament of Pau and the Intendant of Bearn forbade men to go and hear these psalms under a forfeiture of 2,000–5,000 crowns. The scale of the phenomenon was too vast to be attributed to **hallucination.** It was experienced throughout the Cevennes. It was largely under the effect of this supernormal phenomenon that Cavalier, Roland and Marion rose against Louis XIV.

Beriah G. Evans, in his account of the Welsh Religious Revival wrote in the *Daily News* (February 9, 1905): "From all parts of the country come reports of mysterious music descending from above, and always in districts where the Revival fire burns brightly."

In the second type of paranormal music, there are several cases cited in the *Phantasms of the Living* by E. Gurney, F. W. H. Myers & F. Podmore (1886), in which music was heard around the deathbed. After the death of Mrs. L. (p. 446), three persons in the death chamber heard for several seconds three female voices singing softly, like the sounds of an Æolian harp. Eliza W. could distinguish the words: "The strife is o'er, the battle done." Mrs. L. who was also present did not hear anything.

Before Mrs. Sewell's little girl died (vol. 2, p. 221) "sounds like the music of an Æolian harp" were heard from a cupboard in the room. "The sounds increased until the room was full of melody, when it seemed slowly to pass down the stairs and ceased. The servant in the kitchen, two storeys below, heard the sounds." The sounds were similarly heard for the next two days by several people, except the child, who was passionately fond of music. She died when the music was heard for the third time.

Following the death of her 21-year-old daughter, Mrs. Yates heard the sweetest spiritual music, "such as mortals never sang" (vol. 2, p. 223).

Music was heard around the sick bed of John Britton, a deaf-mute (*Journal* of the Society for Psychical Research, vol. 4, p. 181) who was dangerously ill with rheumatic fever. His face was lighted up and when he had recovered sufficiently to use his hands he explained that he heard "beautiful music."

In the case of an old Puritan, narrated in *John Bunyan's Works,* "when his soul departed from him the music seemed to withdraw, and to go further and further off from the house, and so it went until the sound was quite gone out of hearing."

The British *Daily Chronicle* reported on May 4, 1905, the case of a dying woman of the Salvation Army, "For three or four nights mysterious and sweet music was heard in her room at frequent intervals by relatives and friends, lasting on each occasion about a quarter of an hour. At times the music appeared to proceed from a distance, and then would gradually grow in strength while the young woman lay unconscious."

There are cases in which the experience may have been subjective. According to a story told by Count de la Resie in the *Gazette de France* of 1855, Urham's *chef d'œuvre Audition* was supernormally produced. In a narrow glade in the Bois de Boulogne, he heard a sound in the air. Urham beheld a light without form and precision and heard an air and the accompaniment with the accords of an Æolian harp. He fell into a kind of ecstasy and distinctly heard a voice which said to him: "Dear Urham, write down what I have sung." He hurried home and noted down the air with the greatest facility.

In the famous **Versailles Adventure** of C. A. E. Moberley and E. J. Jourdain, two English ladies were apparently transported to the Trianon of 1789, during which experience they heard period music, which has since been transcribed.

On a more hearsay level, folklore abounds with stories of mortals who heard the enchanting music of fairies.

Music Through Mediums Without Instruments

As a mediumistic manifestation the production of music without instruments is rare, the telekinetic playing of instruments fairly frequent. The sitters of D. D. **Home** and the Rev. Stainton **Moses** were often delighted by music from an invisible source.

D. D. Home wrote in *Incidents In My Life* (1863): "On going to Boston my power returned, and with it the most impressive manifestation of music without any earthly instrument. At night, when I was asleep my room would be filled as it were with sounds of harmony, and these gradually grew louder till persons in other parts of the house could hear them distinctly; if by any chance I was awakened, the music would instantly cease."

In the second volume of his biography, Home quoted the following well-attested experience at Easter Eve 1866, in the home of S. C. Hall: "First we had simple, sweet, soft music for some minutes; then it became intensely sad; then the tramp, tramp as of a body of men marching mingled with the music, and I exclaimed 'The March to Calvary.' Then three times the tap-tapping sound of a hammer on a nail (like two metals meeting). A crash, and a burst of wailing which seemed to fill the room, followed; then there came a burst of glorious triumphal music, more grand than any of us had ever listened to, and we exclaimed 'The Resurrection.' It thrilled all our hearts."

To Lord Adare, who published *Experiences in Spiritualism with Mr. D. D. Home* (1870; 1924), we owe many interesting records of the same phenomenon. "We had not been in bed more than three minutes," he wrote of an experience in Norwood, London, "when both Home and myself simultaneously heard the music: it sounded like a harmonium; sometimes, as if played loudly at a great distance, at other times as if very gently, close by."

On another occasion "the music became louder and louder, until I distinctly heard the words: 'Hallelujah! Praise the Lord God Almighty!' It was no imagination on my part." The music was the same as at Norwood.

The aerial musical sounds sometimes resembled drops of water. According to Home, they were produced by the same method as **raps.**

Dr. James H. Gully, in whose house at Malvern, Home was a guest, wrote: "Ears never listened to anything more sweet and solemn than these voices and instruments; we heard organ, harp and trumpet, also two voices." (*Spiritualist,* vol. 3, p. 124)

In the presence of the Rev. Stainton **Moses,** "drum, harp, fairy bells, trumpet, lyre, tambourine and flapping of wings" were heard (*Proceedings* of the Society for Psychical Research, vol. 11, p. 54). No such instruments were in the room. They were also heard in the open. Mrs. Speer stated (*Light,* January 28, 1893): "September 19, before meeting this evening we heard the fairy bells playing in different parts of the garden, where we were walking; at times they sounded far off seemingly playing at the top of some high elm trees, music and stars mingling together, then they would approach nearer to us, evidently following us into the seance room which opened on to the lawn. After we were seated the music still lingered with us, playing in the corner of the room and over the table, round which we were seated. They played scales and chords by request, with the greatest rapidity and copied notes Dr. Speer made with his voice. After

Moses was in trance the music became louder and sounded like brilliant playing on the piano! There was no instrument in the room."

There were similar observations, previous to D. D. Home and Moses, in the case of Mary **Jobson,** a psychic invasion taking place during a spell of mysterious illness; there are experiences in Dorothy Kerin's *The Living Touch* (1919), and there are modern cases on record as well.

Taps "as on a bell so pure as to bear no vibration, in the most exquisite tones, quite beyond description" were produced by "Walter" in the "Margery" seances (see **Crandon**) without any visible instrument. Notes were struck on a "psychic piano," the English Call to Arms was rendered on a "psychic bugle," sounding at a distance and in an open space, the British Reveille was played, an invisible mouth organ and the striking of a "celestial clock" were heard, the latter's character different from any clock known to be in the house or in the neighborhood. (See J. Malcolm Bird, *"Margery" the Medium,* 1925)

Music Telekinetically Produced

According to E. W. Capron in *Modern Spiritualism; Its Facts and Fanaticisms* (1885), "Mrs. Tamlin was, so far as I have been able to learn, the first medium through whom the guitar or other musical instrument was played, without visible contact, so as to give recognisable tunes. In her presence it was played with all the exactness of an experienced musician, although she is not acquainted with music, or herself able to play on any instrument. The tones varied from loud and vigorous to the most refined touches of the strings that could be imagined."

The playing of a locked piano in a seance with James Sangster was reported in the *Age of Progress* (March, 1857).

In the presence of Annie and Jennie **Lord,** of Maine, both unable to play upon any instrument, a double bass violincello, guitar, drums, accordion, tambourine, bells and various small instruments were played "with the most astonishing skill and power" wrote Emma Hardinge in *Modern American Spiritualism* (1870; 1970), "sometimes singly, at others all together, and not unfrequently the strange concert would conclude by placing the young medium, seated in her invalid chair, silently and in a single instant in the centre of the table, piling up all the instruments around her."

In D. D. Home's mediumship, musical feats of **telekinesis** were particularly well attested. Sir William **Crookes** witnessed it under fraud-proof conditions. The quality of the music was mostly fine. William **Howitt** had an experience to the contrary. He is quoted in a letter in D. D. Home's *Incidents In My Life* (1863): "A few evenings afterwards, a lady desiring that the "Last Rose of Summer" might be played by a spirit on the accordion, the wish was complied with, but in so wretched a style that the company begged that it might be discontinued. This was done, but soon after, evidently by another spirit, the accordion was carried and suspended over the lady's head, and there, without any visible support or action on the instrument, the air was played through most admirably, in the view and hearing of all."

Lord Adare noted this peculiarity: "The last few notes were drawn out so fine as to be scarcely audible—the last note dying away so gradually that I could not tell when it ceased. I do not think it possible for any human hand to produce a note in that way."

At another time: "Then there were sounds like echoes, so fine as to be scarcely audible."

Robert Bell wrote in the *Cornhill Magazine* (August, 1860), under the title *Stranger than Fiction:* "The air was wild and full of strange transitions, with a wail of the most pathetic sweetness running through it. The execution was no less remarkable, for its delicacy than its powers. When the notes swelled in some of the bold passages, the sound rolled through the room with an astounding reverberation; then gently subsiding, sank into a strain of divine tenderness."

The experience was the same when Bell held the accordion in his own hand, with full light upon it; during the loud and vehement passages it became so difficult to hold, in consequence of the extraordinary power with which it was played from below, that he was obliged to grasp the top with both hands."

In a letter to the *Morning Star* (October 1860), Dr. Gully stated: "I have heard Blagrove repeated; but it is no libel on that master of the instrument to say that he never did produce such exquisite distant and echo notes as those which delighted our ears."

Alfred Russel **Wallace** wrote in his own book *My Life* (1902) of his first seance in the company of Sir William **Crookes** with D. D. Home: "As I was the only one of the company who had not witnessed any of the remarkable phenomena that occurred in his presence, I was invited to go under the table while an accordion was playing, held in Home's hand, his other hand being on the table. The room was well lighted and I distinctly saw Home's hand holding the instrument which moved up and down and played a tune without any visible cause. He then said "Now I will take away my hand," which he did; but the instrument went on playing, and I saw a detached hand holding it while Home's two hands were seen above the table by all present."

There were other mediums who apparently performed similar feats of telekinetic music, Henry **Slade** and the Rev. F. W. **Monck** amongst them. Of Eusapia **Palladino,** Hereward **Carrington** wrote, in *The Story of Psychic Science* (1930):

"One of the most remarkable manifestations, however, was the playing of the mandolin, on at least two occasions. The instrument sounded in the cabinet first of all—distinct twangings of the strings being heard, in response to pickings of Eusapia's fingers on the hand of one of her controllers. The mandolin then floated out of the cabinet, on to the seance table, where, in full view of all, nothing touching it, it continued to play for nearly a minute—first one string and then another being played upon. Eusapia was at the time in deep trance, and was found to be cataleptic a few moments later. Her hands were gripping the hands of her controllers so tightly that each finger had to be opened in turn, by the aid of passes and suggestion."

H. Dennis **Bradley** wrote in . . . *And After* (1931) "I have had instruments of an orchestra placed in the centre of my own study, with luminous paint covering them so that every movement could be seen instantly, and these instruments have been played by unseen forces in perfect harmony. Whilst operatic selections were being played

upon the gramophone, they have been supernormally conducted with a luminous baton in a majestic manner."

Musicians Who Were Mediums

There were also musical mediums who achieved fame, although often without proper musical training or unable to play in a conscious state. Amongst these, Jesse F. G. **Shepard** was the most astonishing.

Well-known classical composers were said to play through George **Aubert,** a non-professional medium who was investigated at the Institut Général Psychologique in Paris.

At the International Psychical Congress in 1900, Professor Charles **Richet** introduced Pepito **Ariola,** a three-and-a-half-years-old Spanish child, who played classical pieces.

Blind Tom, a Negro child of South Georgia, almost an idiot, played the piano impressively with both hands, using the black and the white keys, when four years of age. When five years old, he composed his *Rainstorm* and said it was what the rain, wind and thunder had said to him. He could play two tunes on the piano at the same time, one with each hand, while he sang a song in a different air. Each tune was set to a different key as dictated by the audience.

In 1903, the famous palmist "Cheiro" (Count Louis **Hamon**) introduced to London M. de Boyon, a French musical medium to whose extraordinary gift Victorien **Sardou,** M. Massenet, M. Emile Waldteufel, M. Felicien Champsaur and actress Mme. Sarah Bernhardt testified. M. de Boyon had no memory of what he played. He employed a unique fingering and he could not play the same piece twice.

The most remarkable musical medium of recent times is Rosemary **Brown,** a British housewife who performs musical compositions on the piano, claimed to originate from such dead composers as Beethoven, Mozart, Liszt and Chopin. Miss Brown has not had proper musical training, but these psychic compositions have been endorsed by established musicians.

Paranormal Aspects of Music

Because of its powerful effects directly on emotions, music often achieves remarkable effects on the human organism and even on animals. Music therapy is now a recognized treatment for mentally handicapped children.

Ancient legends tell of the paranormal effects of music. Orpheus of ancient Greece charmed wild animals and even trees by his music, and the modal system of the Greeks was said to influence powerfully the social and emotional attitudes of listeners. Naik Gopal, a musician of ancient India, was said to have caused flames to burst forth by his performance of *Dipak Raga* (associated with heat), even when the musician stood in water.

The musical system of India has always emphasized the powerful effects of musical vibration. Different *ragas* (scale patterns) are regarded as specific for certain times of the day or season of the year, and their microtonal intervals and grace notes involve vibrations which are unknown to the well-tempered scale of Western nations. *Ragas,* properly performed, are said to evoke beautiful forms or have paranormal effects.

In Hinduism, the first manifestation of creation was said to be that of subtle sound vibration, giving rise to the forms of the material world. Each sound produced a form, and combinations of sound created complicated shapes. This is also the basis of Mantra Yoga, from which developed the system of Western magical spells. The creative power of sound is also echoed in the Judeo-Christian scripture in the formulation "In the beginning was the Word, and the Word was with God, and the Word was God."

Legendary traditions may have some basis in fact. The great Indian scientist Sir Jagadis Chunder **Bose** devised sensitive apparatus to demonstrate subtle plant reactions, many of which resembled nervous responses in animal or human life. Prof. T. C. N. Singh and Miss Stells Ponniah of Annamalai University, India, showed by their experiments that musical sounds excite growth in plants (see **Plants, Psychic Aspects**). Western scientists have demonstrated that ultrasonic sounds beyond human hearing can destroy bacteria, guide ships in the dark and weld together materials.

In recent years, the Hindu musician Swami **Nadabrahmananda Saraswati** has demonstrated an ancient **yoga** of music, involving the arousal of **Kundalini** energy through the psychic power of music vibrations. In a Western context, psychic aspects of music were claimed by the singing teacher Alfred **Wolfsohn.**

In contrast, the aggressiveness and violence of much of modern popular rock music seems to have had a negative and sinister influence on a younger generation, recalling the fears of the ancient Greeks that certain musical modes would have a harmful social effect. It will be remembered that rock music was associated with diabolical themes by Charles **Manson,** culminating in sex orgies, crime and brutal murders. Other rock music has been associated with drug addiction and violence in an overall decadence. (See also Pepito **Ariola;** Rosemary **Brown;** Charles **Manson; Mantra; Nada; Plants;** Jesse F. G. **Shepard; Vibrations**)

Recommended reading:

Brown, Rosemary. *Immortals At My Elbow,* Bachman & Turner, London, 1974 (U.S. title *Immortals By My Side,* Henry Regnery, Chicago, 1975)

Crookes, William. *Researches in the Phenomena of Spiritualism,* J. Burns, London, 1974 etc. (frequently reprinted)

Danielou, Alain. *The Ragas of Northern Indian Music,* Barrie & Rockliff, London, 1968

Gurney, Edmund. *The Power of Sound,* Smith, Elder, London, 1880; Basic Books, New York, 1966

Parrott, Ian. *The Music of 'An Adventure'* (paperback), Regency Press, London, 1966

Podolsky, Edward. *Music Therapy,* Philosophical Library, New York, 1954

Rogo, D. Scott. *Nad; A Study of Some Unusual "Other-World" Experiences,* 2 vols., University Books, 1970–72

Scott, Cyril. *Music; Its Secret Influence Throughout the Ages,* 6th enlarged edition, Rider & Co., London, 1956

Sivananda, Swami. *Music As Yoga,* Yoga-Vedanta Forest University, Sivananda Nagar, India, 1956

Musso, J(uan) Ricardo (1917–   )

Business consultant, author, editor, professor of parapsychology. Born June 9, 1917 at Buenos Aires, Argentina, he studied at the School of Economic Sciences, Buenos Aires University (Doctor of Economic Sciences 1944). In 1940 he married Elvira Germana Canales. He

was professor of parapsychology and psychostatistics at the School of Philosophy, Letters and Educational Sciences, National Littoral University, Rosario Argentina from 1959 onwards, lecturer on parapsychology at National University of the South, Bahia Blanca, Argentina in 1957 and Argentine Institute of Parapsychology, Buenos Aires from 1956–58.

He was president of the Argentine Institute of Parapsychology from 1956 onwards, and a member of the College of Economic Science Graduates, Society for Psychical Research, London, consultant to Parapsychology Foundation, director of Biblioteca de Parapsicología (Parapsychology Publications), director and editor of *Revista de Parapsicología* (Parapsychology Review).

He tested ESP by statistical methods and is author of *En los Límites de la Psicología: Desde el Espiritismo hasta la Parapsicología* (On the Frontiers of Psychology: From Spiritualism to Parapsychology, 1954) and various pamphlets on parapsychology issued by the Argentine Institute of Parapsychology.

His articles in *Revista de Parapsicología* include: 'Las Etapas del Proceso de ESP' (The Stages of the ESP Process, No. 3, 1955), 'La Posesion Espirita: Cuestión Cerrada?' (Spirit Possession: A Closed Question?, No. 4, 1955), 'Insulto pero Opertunidad: Replica a Price' (Insult but Opportunity: A Reply to Price, Nos. 1 & 2, 1956), 'Experimentos con Mediums de Trance' (Experiments with Trance Mediums, No. 3, 1956), and in the *International Review of Parapsychology:* 'Il Movimiento Parapsicologico in Argentina' (The Parapsychology Movement in Argentina, 1956), in *Revista de Educación* (Argentine Ministry of Education): 'La Percepcion Extrasensorial' (Extrasensory Perception, Jan. 1957).

In 1971, he attended the Twentieth International Conference of the Parapsychology Foundation, held at Le Piol, St. Paul de Vence, France.

Myers, A(rthur) T(homas) (1851–1894)

Brother of F. W. H. **Myers** and a founding member of the Society for Psychical Research, London, serving on the Society's Council from 1888–94. He used his medical knowledge to investigate cases of alleged paranormal healing and also made a special study of hypnotism.

He was largely responsible for forming the Edmund Gurney Library of books and pamphlets on hypnotism and related subjects. He also participated in the experiments of the French neurologist Pierre Janet in telepathic hypnotism, as well as some of the SPR sittings with the American medium Mrs. Leonore **Piper.** In addition to his contributions to medical journals and notes in the SPR *Journal,* he also published the following articles in the SPR *Proceedings:* 'Report on an Alleged Physical Phenomenon' (vol. 3, part 9, 1885), 'Mind-Cure, Faith-Cure, and the Miracles of Lourdes' (with F. W. S. Myers, vol. 9, part 24, 1893). He died in London, England, January 10, 1894.

Myers, Frederic William Henry (1843-1901)

A leading mind in psychical research, founder of a cosmic philosophy which may yet revolutionize scientific thought, a profound scholar, a poet of distinction and a brilliant psychologist.

He was born February 6, 1843, at Keswick, Cumberland, England, educated at Trinity College, Cambridge. In 1880 he married Eveleen Tennant.

For thirty years he filled the post of an inspector of schools at Cambridge. Here his resolve to pursue psychical investigation was born in 1869 after a starlight walk and talk with Prof. Henry **Sidgwick.**

His starting point was that if a spiritual world ever manifested to man, it must manifest now, and that, in consequence, a serious investigation must end by discovering some unmistakable signs of it. For "if all attempts to verify scientifically the intervention of another world should be definitely proved futile, this would be a terrible blow, a mortal blow, to all our hopes of another life, as well as of traditional religion" for "it would thenceforth be very difficult for men to be persuaded, in our age of clear thinking, that what is now found to be illusion and trickery was in the past thought to be truth and revelation."

He had in mind the same methods of deliberate, dispassionate and exact inquiry which built up our actual knowledge of the visible world. It was in this spirit that the Society for Psychical Research, London, of which he was a fellow-founder came to be established in 1882. He devoted all his energies to its work and concentrated with a deep grasp of science on the psychological side.

Of the sixteen volumes of the Society's *Proceedings* published while he lived, there is hardly one without an important contribution from his pen.

In *Phantasms of the Living,* a collaboration with Edmund **Gurney** and Frank **Podmore,** the system of classification was entirely his idea. The words "telepathy," "supernormal," "veridical" and many others less in use were coined by him. He played a large part in organizing the International Congress of Psychology and acted as secretary to the one held in London in 1892. In the Society for Psychical Research he filled the post of honorary secretary. In 1900, he was elected to the presidential chair, a post which only distinguished scientists had previously filled. To periodicals such as the *Fortnightly Review,* the *Nineteenth Century,* he contributed many articles. They were collected and published, in 1893, under the title *Science and a Future Life,* and *Other Essays.*

His chief work, *Human Personality and its Survival of Bodily Death,* was posthumously published in 1903. The University of Madras adopted it as a textbook for its courses on lectures on psychology at the faculty of philosophy and letters. It is an exposition of the potential powers of the subliminal self, which he pictured as the real ego, a vast psychic organism of which the ordinary consciousness is but an accidental fraction, the life of the soul, not bound up with the life of the body, of which the so-called supernormal faculties are the ordinary channels of perception.

It is a theory of tremendous implications. It challenged the Spiritualist position that all, or most, of the supernormal phenomena were due to the spirits of the dead. Myers contended that by far the largest proportion was due to the action of the still embodied spirit of the agent or of the percipient himself. The theory brought order into a chaotic mass of psychical phenomena. On the other hand, it greatly enhanced the probability of **survival** after death. As the powers which he claimed for the subliminal self did not degenerate during the course of evolution and served no purpose in this life they were obviously destined for a future existence. Why, for instance, should the subconscious so carefully preserve all thoughts and memories if there will be no use for them?

Professor William **James** suggested that the problems of the subliminal mind should be called "the problem of Myers." "Whatever the judgment of the future may be on Mr. Myers' speculation," he stated, "the credit will always remain to them of being the first attempt in any language to consider the phenomena of hallucination, automatism, double personality, and mediumship as connected parts of one whole subject."

"If future discoveries confirm his thesis of the intervention of the discarnate, in the web and the woof of our mental and physical world," wrote Prof. Theodor **Flournoy,** "then his name will be inscribed in the golden book of the initiated, and, joined to those of Copernicus and Darwin, he will complete the triad of geniuses who have the most profoundly revolutionised scientific thought, in the order, Cosmological, Biological and Psychological."

The same author, a profound psychologist himself, considered Myers "one of the most remarkable personalities of our time in the realm of mental science." Dr. Leaf compared him to Ruskin and considered him in some respects his peer. According to Prof. Charles **Richet** "if Myers were not a mystic, he had all the faith of a mystic and the ardour of an apostle, in conjunction with the sagacity and precision of a *savant.*"

"I never knew a man so hopeful concerning his ultimate destiny," wrote Sir Oliver Lodge in memoriam. "He once asked me whether I would barter—if it were possible—my unknown destiny, whatever it might be, for as many aeons of unmitigated and wise terrestrial happiness as might last till the secular fading of the sun, and then an end. He would not."

Myers was so convinced of survival that his friends often heard him say: "I am counting the days until the holidays."

In *Human Personality and Its Survival of Bodily Death,* physical phenomena received but little consideration. Myers believed in the occurrence of telekinetic phenomena (see **Telekinesis**), but in spite of the experiments of Sir William **Crookes** and his own, their genuine occurrence, from the viewpoint of the public, did not appear to him sufficiently believable to justify their discussion in his book. Nevertheless, in dealing with **possession** he suggested an ingenious explanation, i.e., that the possessing spirit may use the organism more skillfully than its owner and may emit some energy which can visibly move ponderable objects not actually in contact with the flesh. Of his own investigations between 1872–76 he said that they were "tiresome and distasteful enough."

On May 9, 1874, in the company of Edmund Gurney, he made the acquaintance of the Rev. Stainton **Moses.** The acquaintance led to friendship. When Stainton Moses died on September 5, 1892, his notebooks were handed to Myers for study. His articles in *Proceedings* of the Society for Psychical Research (vols. 9 & 11) contained the best accounts of this remarkable mediumship, but his conclusions were not only based on personal experiences with Moses. When he had some startling ones with Miss C. E. **Wood** and Miss Annie Fairlamb (Mrs. J. B. **Mellon**) in 1878 he kept strangely silent. Alfred Russel **Wallace** saw his notes on the seances held under the auspices of the Society for Psychical Research with the two mediums at

Cambridge in Prof. Henry **Sidgwick**'s rooms. The notes stated that the wrists of the mediums were securely tied with tapes and the ends were tacked down to the floor and sealed. Many **materialization** forms came out of the cabinet, both adults and children. The seals were found untampered. The color of the tape and the sealing wax was varied at each seance, the medium put into a hammock which was connected with pulleys to a weighing machine; nevertheless the phenomena occurred as before without the least suspicious cause.

In 1894, on the Ile Roubaud, he was the guest of Professor Richet and participated with Professor Lodge and Dr. Julien **Ochorowitz** in the experiments conducted with Eusapia **Palladino.** He could not refrain from expressing an opinion and admitted that the phenomena were genuine. The Cambridge exposure shook his belief and he then wrote: "I had no doubt that systematic trickery had been used from the first to last, and that there was no adequate ground for attributing any of the phenomena occurring at these sittings to a supernormal cause."

Later, however, he participated in another series of sittings with **Palladino** in Paris and at the solemn adjuration of Prof. Richet he declared himself convinced that both **telekinesis** and **ectoplasm** were genuine phenomena. He also sat with Mrs. Thomas **Everitt,** Mme. **d'Esperance,** and David **Duguid.** He had the strange experience of seeing objective pictures in a crystal ball (see **crystal gazing**) and he investigated the haunted Ballechin House in Perthshire, Scotland. As a result, he published two papers in *Proceedings of the* S.P.R. 'On Alleged Movements of Objects without Contact, occurring not in the Presence of a Paid Medium' (vol. 7, pts. 19, 20, 1891–92).

Still, he was not enthusiastic for physical phenomena. It was owing to his discouragement that Mrs. R. **Thompson** ceased to sit for physical demonstrations and developed chiefly as a trance medium for the S.P.R. Myers had his reward. A communication received through Mrs. Thompson finally confirmed his belief in survival. Before the International Psychological Congress in 1900 he read a paper on his experiences.

Attention to some remarkable omissions in Myers' great work was called by James Robertson in an address printed in *Light* (May 30, 1903). He objected that Andrew Jackson **Davis** was passed by only a single remark and stated that "a clear, unbiased examination of the life and writings of this extraordinary man would have given him more than all he has gathered together in these long drawn out statements as to disintegration of personality, hypnotism, trance, possession, etc."

Myers died January 17, 1901 in Rome, Italy. After his death, a flood of claimed communications from his spirit came from many mediums. The most important ones were those received through Mrs. **Piper,** Mrs. **Verrall** and Mrs. Holland (Alice K. **Fleming**). As regards the latter, Frank **Podmore** and Miss Alice **Johnson** agreed that the "Myers" **control** was a subconscious creation of the medium. The views there expressed were alien to the mentality of the living Myers. Mrs. Verrall apparently obtained the contents of a sealed letter which Myers had written in 1891 and left in the care of Sir Oliver **Lodge** for such a test. However, when the letter was opened in 1904 the contents were found to be entirely different.

In 1907, Mrs. **Sidgwick** obtained good identity proofs through Mrs. Piper. On her behalf, Mrs. Verrall asked some questions to which she did not know the answer and received correct replies as regards the contents of the last conversation that had taken place between Mrs. Sidgwick and Myers.

Many other impressive indications of his surviving self were found in **cross-correspondences,** especially during Mrs. Piper's second visit to England in 1906–07. The whole system of cross-correspondences appears to have been elaborated by him and the wealth of classical knowledge displayed in the connected fragments given by several mediums, raises a strong presumption that they emanated from Myers' mind.

The most striking evidence of this nature was obtained after Mrs. Piper's return to America by Mr. G. B. Dorr in 1908. Frank Podmore considered it "perhaps the strongest evidence yet obtained for the identity of any communicator." In *The Road to Immortality* (1932) which was automatically produced by Miss Geraldine **Cummins,** a stupendous vista was opened up by F. W. H. Myers of the soul's progression through the after-death states. As regards the authorship of the book, Sir Oliver Lodge received independent testimony through Mrs. Leonard from "Myers" of his communications through Miss Cummins. Sir Oliver Lodge saw no reason to dissent from the view that the remarkable accounts of the fourth, fifth, sixth and seventh state "are the kind of ideas which F. W. H. Myers may by this time [1932] have been able to form."

Myers, John

Prominent contemporary British medium who demonstrated psychic healing and spirit photography. Originally a London dentist, he visited a psychical research society in 1931 and was given a psychic warning about his automobile by a medium. The warning disclosed a defect.

Becoming interested in psychic phenomena, Myers visited the Stead Bureau (see **Julia's Bureau**) founded by W. T. **Stead.** He met the medium Mrs. A. E. **Deane,** who practiced **psychic photography** and tried the phenomena for himself, with successful results. He also discovered a mediumistic talent.

In his seances, he would enter into semi-trance while standing, being controlled by "Blackfoot," a Red Indian. From clairvoyant impressions, he would describe the presence of spirit forms and, quite frequently, the extra which would appear on a photographic plate.

He was challenged by the Marquess of Donegall. In the presence of the art editor of the *Sunday Dispatch,* journalist Hannen **Swaffer** and stage magician Will Goldston, Lord Donegall filled Myers' camera, which he examined, with his own marked plates, took six pictures in bright light while Myers simply stood by, and developed them himself.

Two of the plates showed extras which neither Lord Donegall nor the art editor could explain (*Sunday Dispatch,* October 9, 1932). The following week, however, as a result of a further sitting, Lord Donegall accused Myers of substitution of plates and claimed gross trickery. The accusation left part of his previous admissions unaffected.

In the 1930s, Myers was consulted by Laurence Parish, a New York businessman, who was greatly impressed by the psychic photography demonstrated by Myers. Myers was also instrumental in the psychic healing of Parish's sciatica and restoring normal eyesight after years of defective vision. After these miraculous cures, Parish invited Myers to join his company in New York. Myers accepted and eventually became vice-president of the company.

His life story is told in the book *He Walks in Two Worlds; The Story of John Myers, Psychic Photographer, Healer and Philanthropist* by Maurice Barbanell (London, 1964).

Myomancy

A method of divination by rats or mice, supposed to be alluded to in the *Bible* (*Isaiah* lxvi., 17). Their peculiar cries, or some marked devastation committed by them, was taken for a prognostic of evil. Ælian related that Fabius Maximus resigned the dictatorship in consequence of a warning from these creatures, and Cassius Flaminius (according to Varro) retired from the command of the cavalry for no greater reason.

Herodotus stated that the army of Sennacherib when he invaded Egypt was infested by mice in the night, and their quivers and bows gnawed in pieces; in the morning, therefore, being without arms, they fled in confusion, and many of them were slain.

Such a foreboding of evil could not very well be questioned, or its consequences averted, by the commander, but very different was the case when one of Cato's soldiers told him in fright that the rats had gnawed one of his shoes. Cato replied that the prodigy would have been much greater if the shoe had gnawed a rat!

Horapollo, in his curious work on the Hieroglyphics of Egypt, described the rat as a symbol of destruction, and that the Hebrew name of this animal is from a root which signifies to separate, divide, or judge. It has been remarked by one of the commentators on Horapollo that the mouse has a finely discriminating taste.

An Egyptian MS. in the Bibliothèque Royale at Paris contains the representation of a soul going to judgment, in which one of the figures is depicted with the head of a rat and the well-known wig. It is understood that the Libian rats and the mouse of Scripture are the same as the Arabian *jerboa*, which is characterized by a long tail, bushy at the end, and short fore-legs.

The mice and emerods of gold (I. *Samuel* v., 6, 7) were essentially charms having a precise symbolic meaning.

Mysteria Mystica Aeterna

A lodge of the occult society O.T.O. (Ordo Templi Orientis) licensed to Rudolf **Steiner** (1861–1925) in 1906, some years before fully developing his own interpretations of mysticism, culminating in his concept of Antroposophy ('man-wisdom'). See also **Anthroposophical Society.**

Mysteria Mystica Maxima

Name given to the British lodge of the occult society **O.T.O.** (Ordo Templi Orientis) when Theodor **Reuss,** head of the German order, proposed that Aleister **Crowley** should start a British section.

Mysteries

From the Greek word *muein,* to shut the mouth, and *mustes* an initiate: a term for what is secret or concealed in a religious context. Although certain mysteries were undoubtedly part of the initiatory ceremony of the priests of ancient Egypt, we are ignorant of their exact trend, and the term is usually used in connection with certain semi-religious ceremonies held by various cults in ancient Greece.

The mysteries were secret cults, to which only certain initiated people were admitted after a period of preliminary preparation. After this initial period of purification came the mystic communication or exhortation, then the revelation to the neophyte of certain holy things, the crowning with the garlands, and lastly the communion with the deity. But the mysteries appear to have circled round the semi-dramatic representation or mystery-play of the life of a deity.

It has often been advanced as a likely theory to account for the prevalence of these mystic cults in Greece, that they were of pre-Hellenic origin, and that the Pelasgic aboriginal people of the country strove to conceal their religions from the eyes of their conquerors. But against this has to be weighed the evidence that for the most part the higher offices of these cults were in the hands of aristocrats, who, it may be reasonably inferred, had but little to do with the inferior strata of the population which represented the Pelasgic peoples.

Again, the divinities worshiped in the mysteries possess for the most part Greek names and many of them are certainly gods evolved upon Hellenic soil at a comparatively late period. We find a number of them associated with the realm of the dead. The earth-god or goddess is in most countries often allied with the powers of darkness. It is from the underworld that grain arises, and therefore it is not surprising to find that Demeter, Ge, and Aglauros, are identified with the underworld. But there were also the mysteries of Artemis, of Hecate, and the Cherites,—some of which may be regarded as forms of the great earth-mother.

The worships of Dionysus, Trophonious, and Zagreus were also of a mysterious nature. The Eleusinian and Orphic mysteries are undoubtedly those of most importance to the occult student, and from the results of archaeology (such as vase-painting) it is possible to glean some general idea of the trend of these. That is not to say that the heart of the mystery is revealed by any such illustrations, but that these supplemented by what the Christian fathers were able to glean regarding these mystic cults, giving useful hints for further investigations.

Eleusis

The mysteries of Eleusis had for their primal adoration Demeter, Kore or Persephone (the mother and the daughter) whose myth is too well-known to require repetition here. Pluto, the third figure in the drama, is so unimportant as to be relegated to the background.

Other "nameless" divinities appear to have been associated with these, under the name of "the gods" and "the goddesses," but the theory that those are supposed to descend from an aboriginal period, when gods were nameless, seems absurd. The nameless god seems of little value and mythological science surely suggests that such nameless gods are merely those whose higher names are hidden and unspoken.

In Egypt, for example, the concept of the Concealed Name was extremely common. The "name of power" of a god, if discovered, bestowed on the discoverer sway over that deity, and we must therefore dismiss the idea of the nameless divinities of Eleusis as not in accordance with mythological fact. A more probable view is that which would make these gods later titles of the married pair Pluto and Kore, but this, in view of the facts just stated, is also unlikely.

Dionysus is also a figure of some importance in the Eleusinian mystery, and it has been thought that Orphic influence brought about his presence in the cult, but traces of Orphic doctrine have not been discovered in what is known of the mysteries.

A more baffling personality in the great ritual drama is that of Iacchus, who appears to be none other than Dionysus under another name. But Dionysus (or Iacchus) does not appear to be a primary figure of the mystery.

In early Greek legends there are allusions to the sacred character of the Eleusinian mysteries. From the fifth century, their organization was in the hands of the Athenian city, the royal ruler of which undertook the general management, along with a committee of supervision. The rites took place at the city of Eleusis, and were celebrated by a hereditary priesthood, the Eumolpedie. They alone (or rather their high priest) could penetrate into the inner-most holy of holies, but there were also priestesses and female attendants on the goddesses.

The celebration of the mysteries, so far as can be gleaned, was somewhat as follows: In the month of September, the Eleusinian Holy Things were taken from the sacred city to Athens and placed in the Eleusinion. These probably consisted to some extent of small statues of the goddesses. Three days afterwards, the catechumens assembled to hearken to the exhortation of one of the priests, in which those who were for any reason unworthy of initiation were solemnly warned to depart. All must be Greeks or Romans above a certain age, and women and even slaves were admitted, but foreigners and criminals might not partake.

The candidates were questioned as to their purification, and especially as regards the food which they had eaten during that period. After this assembly, they went to the sea-shore and bathed in the sea, being sprinkled afterwards with the blood of pigs. A sacrifice was offered up, and several days afterwards the great Eleusinian procession commenced its journey along the sacred way, its central figure being a statue of Iacchus. Many shrines were visited on the way to Eleusis, where, upon their arrival, they celebrated a midnight orgy.

It is difficult to know what occurred in the inner circle, but there appear to have been two grades in the celebration, and we know that a year elapsed before a person who had achieved one grade became fit for election to the higher. Regarding the actual ritual in the hall of mystery, a great deal of controversy has taken place, but it is certain that a dramatic representation was the central point of interest, the chief characters in which were probably Demeter and Kore, and that the myth of the lost daughter and the sorrowing mother was enacted before a highly-impressed audience. It has been stated that the birth of Iacchus was announced during the ceremony, but this has not been handed down on good authority. Of scenic display, there was probably little or none, as

excavation has proved that there was not room for it, and we find nothing regarding scenery in the accounts presented in many inscriptions; but the apparel of the actors was probably most magnificent, heightened by the Rembrandtesque effect of gloom and torchlight.

But certain sacred symbols were also displayed before the eyes of the elect. These appear to have been small idols of the goddesses, of great antiquity and sanctity. We know that the original symbols of deity are jealously guarded by many primitive priesthoods. For example, the Uapes of Brazil kept careful watch over the symbols of Jurupari, their god, and these were shown only to the initiated. Any woman who cast eyes on them was instantly poisoned.

It was also stated by Hippolytus that the ancients were shown a cut corn stalk, the symbol of Demeter and Kore. This, however, can hardly be trusted any more than the theory that the Eleusinians worshiped the actual corn as a clan totem. Corn as a totem is not unknown elsewhere, as for example in Peru, where the *cconopa* or godlings of the maize fields were probably originally totemic, and we know that amongst primitive people totemism often carried in its train the concept of the full-fledged mystery. But if the Eleusinian corn was a totem, it was certainly the only corn totem known to Greece, and corn totems are rare. The totem was usually initiated with the hunting condition of peoples. When they arrived at the agricultural stage we generally find that a fresh pantheon has slowly evolved, in which full-fledged gods took the place of the old totemic deities. The corn appears as a living thing. It is growth, and within it resides a spirit. Therefore the deity which is evolved from this concept is more likely to be of animistic than of totemistic origin.

The neophyte was then made one with the deity, by partaking of holy food or drink. It will be recalled that when Persephone reached the dark shores of Hades she partook of the food of the dead—thus rendering it impossible for her to return. Once the human soul eats or drinks in Hades, it may not return to earth. This belief is universal, and it is highly probable that it was symbolized in the Eleusinian mysteries.

There was nothing, however, particularly secret about this sacrament, as it is painted on many vases which have been brought to light. A great deal of the ritual undoubtedly partook of the character of agricultural magic, a type of sympathetic sorcery. Among barbarians the medicine-man sprinkles water over the soil to incite the rain spirit to do likewise. It is not long ago since, in the Isle of Mull, Scotland, a long carved stone in a certain churchyard was filled with water, until the depressions upon it overflowed, to symbolize a well-watered country. All sorts of imitative rites took place on similar occasions, most of which will be familiar to students of folklore.

It has been thought that the token of the growing corn may have served as an emblem of human resurrection, and the fact that most persons approached the Eleusinian mysteries for the purpose of ensuring themselves a happy immortality would go far to prove this.

M. Foucart ingeniously put forward the theory that the object of the Eleusinian mysteries was much the same as that of the Egyptian *Book of the Dead,* i.e., to provide the initiates with elaborate rules for avoiding the dangers of the underworld, and to instruct them in the necessary magical formulae. But it does not appear that any such purpose was attained in the mysteries, and we know of no magic formulae recited in connection with them. Friendship with the Holy Mother and Daughter was, to the Eleusinian votary, the chief assurance of immortality.

A great many offshoots of the Eleusinian cult were established in several parts of Greece:

Dionysiac

The most important cult next to the Eleusinian was the Orphic, which probably arose in Phrygia, and which came to be associated with the name of Dionysus, originally a god of vegetation, who was of course also a divinity of the nether world. In this case, it was also desired to enter into communion with him so that immortality might be assured. His celebrations were marked by orgies of a bacchic description, in which it was thought that the neophyte partook for the moment of the character and the power of the deity himself.

The rites of the cult of Dionysus were on a much lower grade than those of Eleusis, and partook more of the barbarian element, and the devouring of an animal victim was supposed to symbolize the incarnation, death and resurrection of the divinity. Later the Dionysiac mysteries became purified, but always retained something of their earlier hysteric character. The cult possessed a fairly wide propaganda, and does not appear to have been regarded by the sages of its time with great friendliness.

The golden tablets relating to the Orphic mystery found in tombs in Greece, Crete and Italy, contain fragments of a sacred hymn. As early as the third century B.C. it was buried with the dead as an **amulet** to protect him from the dangers of the underworld, and the fragments bear upon them incantations of a magical character.

Attis and Cybele

These mysteries arrived at a later period on Hellenic soil. Passionate and violent in the extreme, they yet gained considerable sway in a more degenerate age, and communion with the deity was usually attained by bathing in blood in the *taurobolium* or by the letting of blood.

These Phrygian mysteries were full of the conception of the rebirth of the god Attis, who was also of an agrarian character; and in brief it may be said of these mystic cults as a whole that they were primarily barbarian agricultural rites to some extent intellectualized.

Mithraic Mysteries

The Mithraic cult was of Persian origin, Mithra, a personification of Light being worshiped in that country some five hundred years before the Christian era. Carried into Asia Minor by small colonies of **magi,** it was largely influenced by the religions with which it was brought into contact.

Chaldean **astrology** contributed much of the occult traditions surrounding the creed of the Sun-god, while to a certain extent it became hellenized when the **Magi** strove to bring the more barbaric portion of their dogma and its usages into harmony with the Hellenic ideal. To the art of Greece also it owed that ideal representation of Mithra Tauroctonous which formed the central object in the temples of the cult. The wide geographical area it traversed and the immense influence thus exercised was, however, due to the Romans.

According to Plutarch, the rites originally reached Rome, through the agency of Cilician privates conquered and taken there by Pompey. Another source, doubtless, was through the large number of Asiatic slaves employed in Roman households. Again the Roman soldiery must have carried the Mithraic cult to Rome as they certainly were the means of its diffusion, as far north as the mountains of Scotland, and southwards to the borders of the Sahara Desert.

Mithraism may be said to have been the only living religion which Christianity found a need to combat. It was strong enough to exert a formative influence on certain Christian doctrines, such as those relative to the end of the world and the powers of hell.

Mithra was essentially the divinity of beneficence. He was the genius of celestial light, endowing the earth with all its benefits. As in his character of the Sun he puts darkness to flight, so by a natural transition he came to represent ethically truth and integrity, the sun of goodness which conquers the night of evil. To him was ascribed the character of Mediator betwixt God and man. His creed promised a resurrection to a future life of happiness and felicity.

Briefly the story of Mithra is as follows. He owed his life to no mortal mother. Mithra sprang to being in the gloom of a cavern from the heart of a rock, seen by none but humble shepherds. He grew in strength and courage, excelling all, and used his powers to rid the world of evil.

Of all his deeds of prowess, however, the one which became the central motive of his cult was the slaying of a bull, itself possessed of divine potentialities, by which Mithra dowered the earth with fruitfulness and miraculous crops.

From the spinal cord of the bull sprang the wheat of man's daily bread, from its blood the vine, source of the sacred drink of the Mysteries, and from its seed all the different species of useful animals. After this beneficent deed, Mithra ruled in the heavens, yet still keeping watch and ward over human beings, granting the petitions asked in his name. Those who followed him, who were initiated into his mysteries, passed under his divine protection, especially after death when he would rescue their souls from the powers of darkness which sought to seize upon the dead. And yet again Mithra would come when the earth was failing in her life-sustaining powers, and again he would slay a divine bull and give to all abundant life and happiness.

The mysteries and rites inspired the votaries with awe while giving to their hearts hope of a future life, transcending that which they had known. The temples, mithræums as they were called, were either built underground or were caves and grottoes in the depths of dark forests, symbolizing the birthplace of their god.

Among his worshipers were slaves and soldiery, high officials and dignitaries, all mingling fraternally in a religion which called them Brethren.

The rites were of magical significance. In order to bring their lives into closer communion with the divinity of Mithra, the neophytes must pass through seven degrees of initiation successively assuming the names of Raven, Occult, Soldier, Lion, Persian, Runner of the Sun and Father.

Each of these grades carried with them symbolic garments and masks, donned by the celebrants. The masks represented birds and animals and would seem to indicate the existence of belief in the doctrine of metempsychosis, or perhaps they were a remnant of totemic belief. An almost ascetic habit of life was demanded, including prolonged fasting and purification.

The oath of silence regarding the rites was taken, and before entering the higher grades a ceremony called the Sacrament was held where consecrated bread and wine were partaken of. Dramatic trials of strength, faith and endurance were gone through by all, a stoical attitude and unflinching moral courage being demanded as sign of fitness in the participant.

The drinking of the sacred wine, and the baptism of blood were supposed to bring to the initiate not only material benefit but wisdom. They gave power to combat evil, the power to attain to an immortality such as that of their god. An order of priests was connected with this cult, which faithfully carried on the occult tradition and usages, such as that of initiation, the rites of which were arduous, the tending of a perpetual fire on the altars, prayers to the Sun at dawn, noon and evening. There were sacrifices and libations, musical rites including long psalmodies and mystic chants.

The days of the week were each sacred to a planet, the day of the Sun being held especially holy. There were seasonal festivals, the birth of the Sun being solemnized on the 25th of December, and the equinoxes were days of rejoicing, while the initiations were held preferably in the spring, in March or April.

It is believed that in the earliest days of the cult, some of the rites were of a savage and barbaric character, especially the sacrificial element, but these, as indicated, were changed and ennobled as the beneficence of Mithra took precedence over his warlike prowess.

The Mithraic brotherhoods took temporal interests as well as spiritual ones under their care and were in fact highly organized communities, including trustees, councils, senates, attorneys and patrons, people of high status and wealth. The fact of belonging to such a body gave to the initiate, be he of noble birth or but a slave, a sense of brotherhood and comradeship which was doubtless a powerful reason for the ascendancy which the Mithraic cult gained over the Roman army, whose members, dispersed to the ends of the earth in lonely solitudes amid wild and barbaric races, would find in this feeling of fraternity, this sharing in the worship and ritual of the Sun-god, an infinite comfort and solace.

Recommended reading:

Angus. *The Mystery Religions and Christianity,* John Murray, London, 1928; Dover, 1975

Cumont, F. V. M. *Mysteries of Mithra,* Kegan Paul, London/Open Court, Chicago, 1910; Dover, n.d.

Harrison, Jane E. *Prolegmena to the Study of Greek Religion,* Cambridge University Press, U.K., 1922; Arno Press, 1976

Mylonas, George E. *Eleusis and the Eleusian Mysteries,* Princeton University Press (paperback), 1961

Nilsson, Martin P. *The Dionysian Mysteries of the Hellenistic and Roman Age,* C. W. K. Gleerup, Lund, Sweden, 1957; Arno Press, 1976

Ouvaroff, M. *Essay on the Mysteries of Eleusis,* Rodwell & Martin, London, 1817

Wright, Dudley. *The Eleusinian Mysteries & Rites,* Theosophical Publishing House, London/"The Square & Compass," Denver, Colorado, n.d.

Mystical Night (of the Sufis)

It was believed by the **Sufis** that to attain to the coveted state of mystical contemplation, it was necessary to close the gateway of the physical senses, so that the inner or spiritual senses might operate more freely. This injunction was sometimes taken literally, as by the Brahmin Yogis, who carefully closed eyes, ears, nose and mouth, in order to attain to visionary ecstasy. The Mystical Night was thus a shutting out of all external sense-impressions, of hope, fear, consciousness of self, and every human emotion, so that the interior light might be more clearly perceived. (See also **Meditation; Sufism; Yoga**)

Mysticism

The attempt of man to attain to the ultimate reality of things and experience communion with the Highest. Mysticism maintains the possibility of a relationship with God, not by means of revelation or the ordinary religious channels, but by introspection, and **meditation** in conjunction with a purified life, culminating in the awareness that the individual partakes of the divine nature.

Mysticism has been identified with pantheism by some authorities, but it differs from pantheism in that its motive is spiritual. But mysticism is greatly more speculative than ordinary religion and instead of commencing its flights of thought from the human side, starts from the divine nature rather than the human.

The name mysticism cannot be applied to any particular system. Whereas religion teaches submission of the will and the ethical harmonies of life, mysticism strains after the realization of a union with the divine source itself. The mystic desires to be as close to God as possible, if not indeed part of the Divine Essence itself, whereas the ordinary devotee of most religious systems merely desires to walk in God's way and obey His will.

Historical Survey

Mysticism may be said to have originated in the East, where it probably evolved from kindred philosophic concepts. The unreality of material things is taught by most Asiatic religions, especially by Hinduism and Buddhism, and the sense of the worth of human ego in these is small (see **India**). The **Sufis** of Persia may be said to be a link between the more austere Indian mystics and those of Europe.

Sufism first arose in the ninth century among the Persian Moslems, probably as a protest against the severe monotheism of their religion, but in all likelihood more ancient springs contributed to its revival. In the Persia of Hafiz and Saadi, pantheism abounded, and their magnificent poetry is read by Moslems as having a deep mystical significance, although for the most part it deals with the intoxication of love. It is certain that many of them exhibit the fervor of souls searching for communion with the highest.

The rise of Alexandrian **Neoplatonism** was the signal for the introduction of mysticism to a waiting Europe, and as this stage of mysticism has been fully reviewed in another entry on the subject, there is no necessity to follow it here. It may be mentioned, however, that Neoplatonism made a definite mark upon early Christianity, and we find it mirrored in many of the patristic writings of the sixteenth century.

It was Erigena who, in the ninth century, transmitted to Europe the so-called writings of Dionysius the Areopagite, thus giving rise to both the scholasticism and mysticism of the Middle Ages. Erigena based his own system upon that of Dionysius. This was the so-called "negative theology" which placed God above all categories and designated Him as Nothing, or The Incomprehensible Essence from which the world of primordial causes is eternally created. This creation is the Word or Son of God, in Whom all substantial things exist; but God is the beginning and end of everything. On this system Christian mysticism may be said to have been founded with little variation.

With Erigena, reason and authority were identical, and in this he agrees with all speculative mystics, whereas scholasticism is characterized by the acceptance by reason of a given matter which is presupposed even when it cannot be understood. It seemed to Erigena that in the scholastic system, religious truth was external to the mind, while the opposite view was fundamental to mysticism. That is not to say that mysticism according to Erigena is a mere subordination of reason to faith. Mysticism indeed places every confidence in human reason, and it is essential that it should have the unity of the human mind with the divine as its main tenet, but it accepts nothing from without, and it posits the higher faculty of reason over the realization of absolute truth.

Medieval mysticism may be said to have originated from a reaction of practical religion against dialectics in which the true spirit of Christianity was then enshrined. Thus St. Bernard opposed the dry scholasticism of Abelard. His mysticism was profoundly practical, and dealt chiefly with the means by which human beings may attain the knowledge of God. This is to be accomplished through contemplation and withdrawal from the world. Thus asceticism is the soul of medieval mysticism, but St. Bernard mistakenly averred regarding self-love that it is proper to love ourselves for God's sake, or because God loved us, thus merging self-love in love for God. We must, so to speak, love ourselves in God, in Whom we ultimately lose ourselves. In this, St. Bernard is almost Buddhistic, and indeed his mysticism is of the universal type.

Perhaps Hugh of St. Victor, a contemporary of St. Bernard's, did more to develop the tenets of mysticism, and his monastery of Augustinians near Paris became, under his influence, a great center of mysticism. One of his apologists, Richard of St. Victor, declared that the objects of mystic contemplation are partly above reason, and partly, as regards intuition, contrary to reason.

The protagonists of this theory, all of whom issued from the same monastery, were known as the Victorines, who put up a stout fight against the dialecticians and schoolmen. Bonaventura, who died in 1274, was a disciple of this school, and a believer in the faculty of mystic intuition.

In the twelfth and thirteenth centuries, the worldliness of the church aroused much opposition amongst laymen, and its cold formalism created a reaction towards a more spiritual regime. Many sects arose such as the **Waldenses,** the Cathari (see **Gnosticism**) and the Beguines, all of which strove to infuse into their teachings a warmer

enthusiasm than that which burned in the heart of the church of their time.

In Germany, mysticism made great strides, and Machthild of Magdeburg, and Elizabeth of Thuringia, were, if not the originators of mysticism in Germany, perhaps the earliest supporters of it. Joachim of Flores and Amalric of Bena wrote strongly in favor of the reformed church, and their writings are drenched with mystical terms, derived for the most part from Erigena. Joachim mapped out the duration of the world into three ages, that of the Father, that of the Son, and that of the Spirit—the first of which was to commence with the year 1260, and to be inaugurated by the general adoption of the life monastic and contemplative. A sect called The New Spirit, or The Free Spirit, became widespread through northern France, Switzerland and Germany; and these did much to infuse the spirit of mysticism throughout the German land.

It is with Meister Eckhart, who died in 1327, that we get the juncture of mysticism with scholastic theology. Of his doctrine it has been said: "The ground of your being lies in God. Reduce yourself to that simplicity, that root, and you are in God. There is no longer any distinction between your spirit and the divine—you have escaped personality and finite limitation. Your particular, creature self, as a something separate and dependent on God, is gone. So also, obviously, your creaturely will. Henceforth, therefore, what seems an inclination of yours is in fact the divine good pleasure. You are free from law. You are above means. The very will to do the will of God is resolved into that will itself. This is the Apathy, the Negation, the Poverty, he commends.

"With Eckhart personally this self-reduction and deification is connected with a rigorous asceticism and exemplary moral excellence. Yet it is easy to see that it may be a merely intellectual process, consisting in a man's thinking that he is thinking himself away from his personality. He declares the appearance of the Son necessary to enable us to realize our sonship; and yet his language implies that this realization is the perpetual incarnation of that Son—does, as it were, constitute him. Christians are accordingly not less the sons of God by grace than is Christ by nature. Believe yourself divine, and the Son is brought forth in you. The Saviour and the saved are dissolved together in the blank absolute substance."

With the advent of the Black Death, a great spirit of remorse swept over Europe in the fourteenth century, and a vast revival of piety took place. This resulted in the foundation in Germany of a society of Friends of God, whose chief object was to strengthen each other in intercourse with the Creator. Perhaps the most distinguished of these were Tauler, and Nicolas of Basle, and the society numbered many inmates of the cloister, as well as wealthy men of commerce and others. **Ruysbroeck,** the great Flemish mystic, was connected with them, but his mysticism is perhaps more intensely practical than that of any other visionary. It is the machinery by which the union with God is to be effected which most attracts him. In Ruysbroeck's lifetime, a mystical society arose in Holland called the Brethren of the Common Lot, who founded an establishment at which Groot dispensed the principles of mysticism to Radewyn and Thomas à Kempis.

The attitude of mysticism at the period of the Reformation is peculiar. We find a mystical propaganda pretending to be sent forth by a body of **Rosicrucians** denouncing Roman Catholicism in the fiercest terms, and we also observe the spirit of mysticism strongly within those bodies which resisted the coldness and formalism of the Roman Church. On the other hand, however, we find the principles of Luther strongly opposed by some of the most notable mystics of his time. But the Reformation past, mysticism went on its way, divided, it is true, so far as the outward theological principles of its votaries were concerned, but strongly united in its general principles.

It is with Nicolas of Kusa, who died in 1464, that mysticism triumphs over scholasticism. Nicolas was the protagonist of super-knowledge, or that higher ignorance which is the knowledge of the intellect in contra-distinction to the mere knowledge of the understanding. His doctrines colored those of Giordano Bruno and his theosophy certainly preceded that of **Paracelsus.**

The next great name in mysticism is that of **Boehme,** who once and for all systematized German philosophy.

The Roman Church produced many mystics of note in the sixteenth and seventeenth centuries, notably Francis of Sales, Mme. Guyon and Molinos,—the last two of which were the protagonists of Quietism, which set forth the theory that there should be no pleasure in the practice of mysticism, and that God did not exist for the enjoyment of man. Perhaps the greatest students of Boehme were William **Law** (1686 to 1761) and Saint **Martin** (1743 to 1803).

The Universality of Mystical Experience

It is clear from the statements of mystics that they are not limited to any given religion or theology. When Meister Eckhart stated "If I am to know God directly, I must become completely He, and He I: so that this He and this I become and are one I," he comes to the same point as the Adwaita Vedanta doctrine of Hinduism, where the *jiva* (individual soul) merges with Brahma the creator before absorption in Brahman, the non-personal divine ground.

The apparent differences between Hindu mysticism and Christian mysticism are nominal. Although Christian theology postulates the divine in the form of God as Father, Son and Holy Spirit, such distinctions vanish in the actual mystical experience. Similarly popular Hinduism postulates hundreds of different gods and goddesses, but these are merely legal fictions to the Indian mystic, melting away in the totality of higher consciousness.

Because mind and emotion are transcended in the higher reaches of mysticism, they are merely ways of reaching a reality which lies beyond them, a totality of consciousness without object, beyond the normal human limitations of individual body, ego, personality or hopes and fears.

Like Christianity, Hindu Vedanta (inquiry into ultimate reality), has different schools of theology, ranging from *Advaita* (Monism or Non-dualism, claiming that All is One and only the Divine Ultimate has actual existence, all else being illusory) to degrees of *Dvaita* or Dualism (claiming that there is One Ultimate Divine Principle of God but that the soul is a separate principle with independent existence). Such schools are not really contradictory, but rather different degrees of interpretation of one reality on the way to an actual mystical experience in which intellectual distinctions vanish.

The Way of the Mystic

In both Eastern and Western mysticism, withdrawal from the everyday life of a householder is recognized as an aid to mystical progress, thus both have monastic establishments at which one follows a life of prayer and meditation. In the initial stages, self-purification is facilitated by dedicated service to others, prior to the more secluded life of the contemplative.

Mystics have sometimes been accused of escapism, in retreating from the responsibilities of everyday life into a private world, and indeed, the descriptions of the ecstasies of spiritual awareness often sound rather like a selfish indulgence, oblivious to the problems of the outside world.

It is clear that the ideal mystic partakes fully of the duties and social responsibility of life after spiritual enlightenment, since mystical experience should give deeper meaning to the numinous reality behind the everyday mundane world. For most individuals, however, a period of retreat from everyday life is helpful in disengaging oneself from the fears, desires and egoism of mundane existence.

Hinduism places great stress on *dharma*, the duties and responsibilities of the individual, which took priority over any desire for transcendentalism. During this period one would observe the everyday religious rites and rituals related to the gods and goddesses of an individual's life. Later, however, when one had fulfilled one's responsibilities, married, begat a family and provided for them, the realization that everything connected with the material world and physical life was transient would grow steadily, culminating in a hunger for knowledge of what is eternal. At such a time, one might seek a qualified *guru* or spiritual preceptor and follow an ascetic life, discarding all material possessions, egoism and hopes and fears in the quest for a higher spiritual awareness not subject to birth and death, change or decay.

Various pathways of *yoga* facilitated that quest, involving self-purification, service to others and refinement of perception based upon physical health and its spiritual counterpart.

The modern Western preoccupation with pop *gurus* ignores the traditional emphasis given to ethical restraints and moral observance as essential preliminary to all spiritual training.

The Hindu emphasis on the duties and responsibilities of a householder taking priority over the quest for mystical enlightenment, have something in common with Judaism, which does not seek to separate mystical experience from everyday life. Judaism is essentially pragmatic in its approach to the spiritual life and requires that mystical experience be interfused with daily life and religious observance. The Jewish mystic typified in the period of eighteenth to nineteenth century Hasidism, was a pious rabbi, living a life of prayer, study and meditation within his community and sharing everyday social life and responsibility. In this respect he resembled the Eastern *guru*, around whom a group of pupils would gather for spiritual teaching and experience. The necessity for individual religious experience seems to have been ignored in the rules and regulations and formal worship of modern religions, and clearly the charismatic revival movements seeks to restore that essential experiential aspect.

The Mechanisms of Mysticism

It is clear that the concept of self-purification in mystical progress involves psycho-physical mechanisms. Fasting, asceticism, mortification and intense meditation have profound effects on the individual nervous system and other aspects of the body and mind. Very little discussion on this important area appeared in Western literature until Aldous Huxley published *The Doors of Perception* (1954) and *Heaven & Hell* (1956). These two books have had a profound effect on contemporary life.

The starting point for Huxley's speculations about the psycho-physical mechanisms of mystical experience was his own experiment in taking the psychedelic drug mescalin, and it is unfortunate that this particular stimulus has overshadowed the wider implications of his discussion.

A simplistic interpretation of Huxley's speculations led to the psychedelic revolution of the 1960s, spearheaded by Timothy **Leary** and Richard **Alpert,** based on the conviction that merely taking a chemical substance resulted in a spiritual experience comparable with that of the great mystics of history. This was a result that Huxley himself regretted in his later years.

It is now obvious that the chemical ecstasy and visions produced by psychedelic drugs are qualitatively different from transcendentalism experienced by the mystic who has devoted many years to self-purification of mind, emotions and spiritual perception, and that unless there is such a purification of the individual, any psychedelic experience lacks integrity. The search for chemical ecstasy unfortunately led to the worldwide modern problems of hard drug addiction, criminal rackets, violence and wasted lives.

The modern mass-media society, geared to consumer products, television commercials and life-styles (as distinct from living itself), is unfortunately susceptible to such simplistic instant recipes for mysticism, to be purchased with no more difficulty than the latest color television set or automobile. Most of the pop *gurus* of the West, with their thousands of adulating devotees, present a spurious mysticism which is merchandized like any detergent or aspirin. The slow patient processes of self-purification and social responsibility are ignored.

A similar over-simplification of Eastern teachings was the popularization of **Zen** Buddhism for the American campus, in which it seemed that merely reading a book of Zen *koans* (spiritual conundrums) by Dr. Suzuki or Christmas Humphreys was all that was needed to gain instant *satori* or spiritual enlightenment. In fact, as Dr. Suzuki himself did not disguise, more was required than a simple intellectual exercise. The traditional Zen student might spend months or years working hard in the mundane tasks of the Zen monastery, and it was against this background of hard work in the physical field that the intellectual gymnastics of the sound of one hand clapping or the chicken in the bottle were pondered. A student would be fully stretched to the limit on the physical and mental plane so that the resolution of a paradox would be on a higher plane of transcendental enlightenment.

It is now clear that the gradual transformation of the personality on all levels—physical, mental, emotional and spiritual—involves specific psycho-physical concomitants. Some of these may be accessible to scientific inspection. It may also be possible to evaluate various degrees of transcendental experience, ranging from emotional euphoria to progressively profound areas of higher consciousness.

The Hindu mystic Pandit **Gopi Krishna,** who experienced a dramatic development of higher consciousness following a period of intense yoga discipline and meditation, has published his experiences and the profound perceptions accompanying them in a series of books, and has attracted the attention of scientists in investigating the phenomenon. The Pandit has revived the ancient Hindu concept of **Kundalini** in a scientific context, and suggested a biological aspect of religious experience and the inspiration of geniuses. *Kundalini* is a static force located at the base of the human spine, which is activated dynamically in the processes of procreation, but which may also be aroused in mystical centers in the body (associated with the plexi of the sympathetic nervous system), resulting in activity in a higher center in the head, traditionally associated with meditation, and a consequent enlargement of consciousness beyond the individual mental and emotional limits. It is interesting to notice that symbolic representation of this schema are found in most great religions of the world which describe an Edenic garden, a tree of knowledge with the divine fruit, and the serpent which tempts to sexual activity. These can be taken as symbols of the twin currents of sex and mysticism in the human body.

Paranormal Side Effects

Most religions have reported miraculous phenomena associated with the path of mysticism, including visions, disembodied voices, levitation and gifts of healing. Christian saints have their miracles and the *yogis* have their occult powers. It would seem that with the transcendence of normal mental and emotional life, there is an area of transcendence of normal physical law.

However, the mystic is warned not to be snared by such phenomena, since it will activate egoism and pride, common faults of the beginner on the spiritual path.

It remains to be seen whether there is a *modus vivendi* for mysticism, in which the undoubted benefits of some paranormal side effects such as miraculous healing might manifest freely without hindering spiritual development. Clearly there are also theological problems involved in the eternal play of good and evil, of creation, destruction and balance, which are characteristic of the physical world and its laws. (See also **Drugs; Gnosticism; Guru; Hasidim; Kundalini; Meditation; Vedanta; Waldenses; Yoga**)

Recommended reading:

"AE" (George W. Russell). *The Candle of Vision,* Macmillan, London, 1919; University Books, 1965

Augustine, St. (transl. Edward Pusey) *Confessions,* Dent, London/Dutton, 1954

Blakney, Raymond B. *Meister Eckhart; A Modern Translation,* Harper, 1941

Brinton, Howard H. *The Mystic Will; Based on a Study of the Philosophy of Jacob Boehme,* Macmillan, 1930

Buber, Martin. *Tales of the Hasidim; The Early Masters,* Thames & Hudson, London, 1956; Schocken paperback, 1961

Bucke, Richard M. *Cosmic Consciousness; A Study in the Evolution of the Human Mind,* 1901; University Books, 1961 etc. (frequently reprinted)

Cheney, Sheldon. *Men Who Have Walked with God,* Alfred A. Knopf, 1968; Dell paperback, 1974

Gall, Edward. *Mysticism Throughout the Ages,* Rider & Co., London, 1934

Gopi Krishna. *The Biological Basis of Religion and Genius,* Harper & Row, 1972

Gopi Krishna. *Higher Consciousness; The Evolutionary Thrust of Kundalini,* Julian Press, 1974

Huxley, Aldous. *The Doors of Perception,* Chatto & Windus, London, 1954 etc.

Huxley, Aldous. *Heaven & Hell,* Chatto & Windus, London, 1956

James, William. *The Varieties of Religious Experience,* London, 1902; University Books, 1963

Lawrence, Brother. *The Practice of the Presence of God,* London, 1691; New York, 1895 etc. (frequently reprinted)

Maeterlinck, Maurice. *The Great Secret,* Methuen, London, 1922; University Books, 1969

Maeterlinck, Maurice. *Ruysbroeck and the Mystics,* London, 1908

Patanjali (transl. M. N. Dvivedi). *The Yoga-Sutras of Patanjali,* Theosophical Publishing House, Adyar, India (paperback), 1890; 1947 etc.

Puroheet Swami, Shri. (transl.) *The Geeta, The Gospel of the Lord Shri Krishna* [*Bhagavad Gita*] Faber, London, 1935 etc.

Swedenborg, Emmanuel. *Divine Love & Wisdom,* Swedenborg Foundation, n.d.

Underhill, Evelyn. *The Mystic Way; A Psychological Study in Christian Origins,* London & New York, 1913

Underhill, Evelyn. *Mysticism; A Study in the Nature & Development of Man's Spiritual Consciousness,* Methuen, London/Dutton, 1911 etc. (frequently reprinted)

Waite, Arthur E. *Lamps of Western Mysticism,* Kegan Paul, London/Alfred A. Knopf, 1923; Multimedia, Blauvelt, N.Y., 1973

Waite, Arthur E. *Studies in Mysticism,* Hodder & Stoughton, London, 1906

Zaehner, R. C. *Mysticism, Sacred & Profane,* Oxford paperback, 1957

N

Nacht, Sacha (1901–)

Physician and psychoanalyst who has been concerned with relationships between psychology and parapsychology. Born September 23, 1901 at Bacau, Rumania, he studied at the Faculté de Médecine de Paris, France, and was director of the Institut de Psychanalyse de Paris from 1952 onwards. He is author of *La Psychanalyse d'aujourdi'hui* (1956, American ed. 1959).

Nada

A Sanskrit term used in Hindu musical theory to denote subtle aspects of musical sound. There are two kinds of *Nada: Anahata* is the mystical essence of sound, *Ahata* is the conscious realization of musical sound by human beings. *Anahata* is heard by yogis in **meditation** and related to different *chakras* or psychic centers in the human body. *Nada Upasana* is the yoga of music, which brings God-realization through pure forms of music and meditation. (See also **Music; Vibrations;** Alfred **Wolfsohn**)

Recommended reading:

Rogo, D. Scott. *Nada; a study of some unusual "other-world" experiences,* 2 vols., University Books, 1970–72

Sivananda, Swami. *Music as Yoga,* Rishikesh, India, 1956

Nadabrahmananda Saraswati, Swami (1896–)

A Hindu musician who has developed a yoga of music, involving the arousal of **Kundalini** energy through the psychic power of sound vibrations. Born May 5, 1896 in Mysore, India, he studied music under Shri Sadasiva Bua, and Ustad Alladiya Khan of Dolahpur, eventually becoming a disciple of Tata Bua of Benares. He spent fifteen years in perfecting his skills.

He not only plays various instruments like Swara Mandala (Indian zither) and tabla (drums) with fantastic skill, but is also a master of the intricate graces of Thaan or vocal exercises. During his vocal performances he directs the sound vibration to any part of his body, and can send out vibrations through his ears and the top of his head when his mouth is covered.

In his performances on the tabla (Indian drums), he suspends respiration for nearly half an hour in a state of trance, playing the most intricate and complex rhythms without movement of his eyes or head. He can also use sound vibrations for psychic **healing.** He is a devotee of the late Sri Swami Sivananda, and has taught music to many students at the Sivananda Ashram (Divine Life Society), Rishikesh, Himalayas, North India. (See also **Nada**)

Naddeo, Alighiero (1930–)

Italian professor of statistics who has conducted investigations in parapsychology. Born August 18, 1930 at Rome, Italy, he studied at University of Rome (LL.B. 1952, B.S. statistics 1953). In 1960 he married Maria Teresa Patriarca.

He was lecturer in statistics from 1954–58, assistant professor econometrics and methodological statistics from 1958–61 at University of Rome, professor of statistics at University of Trieste from 1961 onwards. He is author (with M. Boldrini) of *Le statistiche empirische e la teoria dei campioni* (Empirical Statistical Studies on the Sample Theory, 1950). In his investigation of ESP ability with 500 students he concluded that the correct results were higher than random expectation.

Napellus

A plant with narcotic properties, with which J. B. Van Helmont (1577–1644) experimented. He stated that, having on one occasion roughly prepared the root, he tasted it with his tongue, and in a very short time found that the center of thought and intellect was situated in the pit of his stomach.

An unusual clarity and distinctness of thought rendered the experience a pleasant one, and he sought on future occasions to repeat it by the same means, but without success. After about two hours he felt a slight dizziness and thereupon thought in the normal fashion with his brain. But throughout the strange experience he claimed that he was conscious that his soul still remained in the brain as a governing power.

The plant with which Van Helmont experimented was *Aconitum napellus* or monkshood, a species of aconite, which is poisonous. (See also **Drugs;** Seeing with the **Stomach**)

Napper (or Napier), Richard (1559–1634)

British astrologer and doctor of medicine of Great Linford, Buckinghamshire, who, according to William **Lilly** (1602–1681), "outwent Forman in physic and holiness of life, cured the falling-sickness perfectly by constellated rings, and some diseases by amulets." Napper was a pupil of astrologer Simon Forman (1552–1611). He was probably of the stock of the Scottish Napiers although his family had been settled in England since the time of Henry VIII.

Nash, Carroll B(lue) (1914-)

Professor of biology and director of the Parapsychology laboratory at St. Joseph's College, Philadelphia, Pa. since 1956. Born January 29, 1914 at Louisville, Kentucky, he studied at George Washington University, Washington, D.C. (B.S. 1934) and University of Maryland (M.S. 1937, Ph.D. 1939). In 1941 he married Catherine Stifler. He was instructor in zoology at University of Arizona from 1939-41, associate professor of biology at Pennsylvania Military College, Chester from 1941-44, assistant professor of biology at American University, Washington, D.C. from 1944-45, chairman of biology department at Washington College, Chestertown, Maryland from 1945-48, professor of biology at St. Joseph's College from 1948 onwards, chairman of biology department at St. Joseph's College. He is a member of the American Association for the Advancement of Science.

Dr. Nash was a founding member of the *Parapsychological Society*, president in 1963. He was director of the Parapsychology Laboratory at Duke University, North Carolina in 1956 and received the William McDougall Award in 1960. His special interests include precognition, PK, and personality variables in Psi. Dr. Nash was consultant and adviser for a television production "ESP" in 1958, and has taught college-level courses in parapsychology at St. Joseph's College. His articles on parapsychology published in the *Journal of Parapsychology* include: 'Comparison of Two Distances in PK Tests' (11, 1947), 'A Comparison of Combined and Single Target Symbols' (20, 1956), 'Correlation Between ESP and Religious Value' (22, 1958), (with M. G. Durkin) 'Terminal Salience with Multiple Digit Targets' (23, 1959), 'Can Precognition Occur Diametrically?' (27, 1963), 'Note on Precognition of the Percipient's Calls as an Hypothesis to Telepathy' (39, 1975), in *Journal of the American Society for Psychical Research:* 'Psychokinesis Reconsidered' (45, 1951), 'An Exploratory Analysis for Displacement in PK' (50, 1956), (with C. S. Nash 'Checking Success and the Relationship of Personality Traits to ESP' (52, 1958), 'The Chesebrough-Pond's ESP Television Contest (53, 1959), 'Retest of High Scoring Subjects in the Chesebrough-Pond's ESP Television Contest' (57, 1963); in *Science:* 'Psi and Probability Theory' (120, 1954), in the *International Journal of Parapsychology:* 'The Unorthodox Science of Parapsychology' (1, 1959).

Nash, Catherine S(tifler) (Mrs. Carroll B. Nash) (1919-)

Assistant professor of biology, and charter associate of the Parapsychological Association. Born August 31, 1919 at Woodbrook, Maryland, she studied at Goucher College, Baltimore, Maryland (B.A. 1939) and Ohio State University (M.S. 1950). In 1941 she married Carroll B. Nash. She was a lecturer in biology at Temple University, Philadelphia, Pa. from 1942-43, instructor in biology at Pennsylvania Military College, Chester, Pa. from 1943-44, instructor in biology at American University, Washington, D.C. from 1944-45, instructor in biology at Washington College, Chestertown, Maryland from 1945-58, assistant professor of biology at St. Joseph's College, Philadelphia from 1948 onwards.

She has taken particular interest in telepathy and clairvoyance, and her published articles include: 'Checking Success and the Relationship of Personality Traits to ESP' (*Journal of the American Society for Psychical Research*, vol. 52, 1958), 'Experiments in Plant Growth' (*International Journal of Parapsychology*, Autumn 1959), 'Report on the Second Annual Convention of the Parapsychological Association' (*Newsletter, Parapsychology Foundation*, Sept.-Oct. 1959), 'A Test of Adding Extrasensorially Perceived Digits' (*Journal of Parapsychology* 23, 1959).

NASO International Astrological Directory

Directory of individuals, organizations, services and publications concerned with astrology; international coverage. Published every two years by the National Astrological Society. Address: 127 Madison Avenue, New York, N.Y. 10016.

NASO Journal (Journal of the National Astrological Society)

Available to members of the National Astrological Society, New York. The Journal acts as an information bulletin of current events in astrology, lists study programs, current research, news of conferences, and includes scholarly articles. Address: 127 Madison Avenue, New York, N.Y. 10016.

NASO Newsletter

Information bulletin of current events in astrology and related fields, listing study programs, current research, international visitors, news of members and conferences. Issued to members of National Astrological Society, 127 Madison Avenue, New York, N.Y. 10016.

Nastrond

The Scandinavian and Icelandic Hell, said to be of an icy temperature. It lies in the lowest depths of Niflheim; it is a "dark abode far from the sun;" its gates face "the cutting north;" "its walls are formed of wreathed snakes, and their venom is ever falling like rain."

It is surrounded by dark and poisonous streams, and Nidhog, the great dragon, who dwells beneath the central root of Ygdrassil, torments and gnaws the dead. Here it is that Loki is chained to a splintered rock, where the venom of the snake Skada falls on him unceasingly, and it was believed that his shuddering was the cause of earthquakes. (See also **Hell**)

Nat

An evil spirit. (See **Burma**)

National Astrological Society

Non-profit organization founded in 1969 to promote high standards of practice and instruction in astrology, to facilitate communications among astrologers through meetings and publications and to foster cooperation among persons and organizations concerned with astrology. NASO holds an annual conference in cities throughout North America, acts as an educational institution, maintains a library, and facilitates access to IBM computing for members with high level projects.

Voting membership is open to professional or qualified astrologers, non-voting membership for associates. The Society publishes **NASO Journal.** Address: 127 Madison Avenue, New York, N.Y. 10016.

National Colored Spiritualist Association of the United States of America

Established April 21, 1925 at 206 West 136 Street, New York, N.Y., president Rev. John R. White, vice-president Rev. Sarah Harrington. No longer active.

National Enquirer (Newspaper)

Popular nationally distributed newspaper which gives special attention to psychical phenomena and the paranormal, often being the first to report new aspects or developments. Although presentation is popular, reports are usually comprehensive. Reports on **UFO** sightings are often published. Published weekly from: 600 S.E. Coast Avenue, Lantana, Florida 33462.

National Investigations Committee on Aerial Phenomena (NICAP)

Founded in 1956 for persons interested in aerial phenomena, particularly unidentified flying objects (UFOs). Its panel of advisers includes scientists, engineers, aviation experts, clergymen, retired military officers, and professors.

It exists to gather, analyze, evaluate and disseminate reliable information on aerial phenomena and promotes scientific investigation, carried out in the field by technically oriented subcommittees.

It provides bibliographic and source materials to students, exchange data to scientific societies and individual scientists, and semitechnical reports to scientists, Congress and the press. It maintains a large library on aerial phenomena, aviation, astronomy, and a collection of magazine articles, newspaper clippings, letters and other documents.

It publishes *The U.F.O. Investigator* monthly and *UFO Evidence, UFO Wave of 1947, Strange Effects from UFOs.* Address: 5012 Del Ray Avenue, Washington, D.C. 20014. Current membership 4,000. (See also **UFO**)

National Investigations Committee on UFOs (NICUFO)

Non-profit organization founded in 1967 organizing conventions, lectures, seminars and various activities related to Unidentified Flying Objects, with special interest in claimed contacts with UFO occupants. Publishes *Confidential* Newsletter. Address: Suite 207, 7970 Woodman Avenue, Van Nuys, California 91402. (See also **UFO**)

National Laboratory of Psychical Research

Established by psychical researcher Harry **Price** in 1925 at 13 Roland Gardens, London, S.W.7, "to investigate in a dispassionate manner and by purely scientific means every phase of psychic or alleged psychic phenomena." The honorary president was The Lord Sands, K.C., LL.D., acting president H. G. Bois, honorary director Harry Price.

Publications included: *British Journal of Psychical Research,* bi-monthly, discontinued in 1929, *Proceedings of the National Laboratory of Psychical Research,* Vol. I., discontinued in 1929; *Bulletins of the National Laboratory of Psychical Research:* I. *Regurgitation and the Duncan Mediumship,* by Harry Price, 1932, II. *Fraudulent Mediums,* an essay by

Prof. D. S. Fraser-Harris, repr. from *Science Progress,* Jan., 1932, III. *The Identification of the "Walter" Prints,* by E. E. Dudley, 1933, IV. *An Account of Some Further Experiments with Rudi Schneider,* by Harry Price, 1933, V. *Rudi Schneider; the Vienna Experiments of Prof. Meyer and Przibram,* 1933.

One of the most valuable issues of the NLPR *Proceedings* was vol. 1, pt. 2 (April 1929), comprising *Short-Title Catalogue of Works on Psychical Research, Spiritualism, Magic, Psychology, Legerdemain and Other Methods of Deception, Charlatanism, Witchcraft and Technical Works for the Scientific Investigation of Alleged Abnormal Phenomena from circa 1450 A.D. to 1929 A.D.* compiled by Harry Price. This Catalog (supplemented by Bulletin 1 (1935) listed the splendid collection formed by Price himself. The collection is now in The Harry Price Collection, University College, London.

The Laboratory is no longer in existence.

National Psychic Science Association

A group of lecturers, healers, preachers and ministers, founded 1929, "to promote the religion of Spiritualism, psychic science and morality and demonstrate the phenomena of the continuity of life through spirit communication and psychic healing through prayer." Address: 532 Springfield Avenue, Newark, New Jersey 07103.

National Psychological Institute, Inc.

Founded for scientific research in normal and abnormal psychology and spirit **obsession** by Dr. Carl A. **Wickland,** headquarters Los Angeles, California.

National Spiritual Alliance of the United States of America

Founded in 1913 as an organization of individuals who believe that "intercommunication between the denizens of different worlds is scientifically established."

It promotes studies of Spiritualism, prescribes qualifications of ministers, method of examination and ceremony by which they are set apart, also qualifications of associated ministers, licentiates, healers, mediums, missionaries and other official workers, and issues certificates. Present membership over 3,200. Address: % Mrs. Wilma Doucette, 14 Edgewood Street, Stafford Spring, Connecticut 06076.

National Spiritualist Association of Churches

Founded in 1893; current membership over 8,000, comprising fifteen state groups. It is an association of 178 churches, 12 camps and 5 societies "to teach and proclaim the science, philosophy and religion of modern Spiritualism; to protest against every attempt to compel mankind to worship God in any particular or prescribed manner; to advocate and promote spiritual healing and to protect and encourage spiritual teachers and mediums in all laudable efforts in giving evidence or proof to mankind of a continued intercourse and relationship between the living and the so-called dead."

It maintains a library of books published for and against Spiritualism since 1948, and publishes the **National Spiritualist** monthly magazine. Address: P.O. Box 128, Cassadaga, Florida 32706.

National Spiritualist (Magazine)

Monthly magazine published by the National Spiritualist Association of Churches, P.O. 128, Cassadaga, Florida 32706.

Another magazine of the same name was published by the **Spiritualists National Union** in England.

Natsaw

Burmese wizards. (See **Burma**)

Nature Spirits or Elementals

According to **Theosophy,** nature spirits have bodies composed of the finer kinds of matter. There are countless hosts of them, divided into seven classes, which allowing for two unmanifested forms, belong to the ether, air, fire, water, and earth—the last four being called by some **Kabalists,** sylphs, salamanders, undines, and gnomes respectively. At the head of each class is a *deva* or inferior god.

Nature spirits are said to work in unsuspected ways, sometimes lending their aid to human beings in the form of certain faculties, while those in the **astral world** are engaged in the creation of form out of the matter which the outpouring of the **Logos** has quickened, hence they form minerals, flowers, and other aspects of nature. These nature spirits of the astral worlds of course have bodies of astral matter, and they frequently form mischievous or other impulses, change the appearance of these bodies. They are just beyond the limits of normal human vision, but many sensitives of more acute vision can see them, while the action of drugs is also believed to make them visible. (See also **Elementary Spirits; Fairies**)

Nayler, James (c. 1617–1660)

An English religious fanatic of the seventeenth century, born in the diocese of York. He served for a time in the army, then joined the Quakers where his discourses gained for him a reputation for sanctity. His followers hailed him as a Messiah and he entered Bristol in 1656, mounted on a horse led by a man and a woman, while others ran behind chanting "Holy, holy, holy, is the god of Sabaoth."

He was arrested, charged with blasphemy and punished by having his tongue pierced with a hot iron, and his forehead marked with the letter "B" (blasphemer). This done, he was forced to ride into Bristol in disgrace, his face turned towards the horse's tail.

After two years in prison, Nayler was released sobered and penitent. His return to Quaker preaching was sanctioned by George Fox and Nayler preached with George Whithead. After a period of ill health, Nayler died in October 1660.

Nazca "Spaceport"

A mysterious area of desert markings on the plains of Nazca, Peru, about 250 miles southeast of Lima between the towns of Nazca and Palpa. This barren plateau covering 200 square miles has over 13,000 lines, 100 spirals, trapezoids and triangles, and about 800 large animal drawings, etched in the desert through removal of surface stones with lighter colored soil underneath. Many of the lines extend for miles, radiating from centers like star shapes. It is estimated that the markings were made between 400 B.C. and 900 A.D. and their construction may have occupied several centuries.

It has been suggested that these markings were the work of ancient spacemen who landed on the plain and marked out an airfield for their spacecraft. This theory has been propagated by Erick **von Däniken,** author of the book *Chariots of the Gods* (1970) which posed the question "Was God an Astronaut?" In a later book *Gods From Outer Space* (1973), von Däniken stated: "At some time in the past, unknown intelligences landed on the uninhabited plain near the present-day town of Nazca and built an improvized airfield for their spacecraft which were to operate in the vicinity of the earth." In his article 'Von Däniken's Golden Gods' (*The Zetetic,* Vol. II, No. 1, 1977), Ronald D. Story examines this theory and points out a number of weaknesses in von Däniken's reasoning.

First of all, there should be no need for a runway several miles long for a space vehicle capable of vertical landing (only modern air liners need a long runway). Secondly, many of the lines run right into hills, ridges and the sides of mountains. Thirdly, the markings are on soft, sandy soil, unsuitable for any heavy vehicle to land on. Maria Reiche, an expert on Nazca, has commented: "I'm afraid the spacemen would have gotten stuck."

Story cited Professor Kosok of Long Island University, who first mapped and photographed the mysterious markings from the air in June 1941 and discovered apparent alignment with solstices and equinoxes. Perhaps the markings were "the largest astronomy book in the world." Similar astronomical ground markings have been interpreted in Glastonbury, England (see **Glastonbury Zodiac**).

Whilst the ideal viewing position for such markings as Nazca is from a point about 600 feet above the plain, it does not necessarily follow that they were actually designed for viewing from the air. They could be interpreted as a giant image of astronomical mysteries, in which construction and traversing of completed markings might be in the nature of a religious ritual. Most magical ceremonies involve physical traversing of geometrical forms inscribed on the ground.

An ingenious theory cited by Story is that of the International Explorers Society of Florida, who suggested that the "chariots of the gods" sailing over Nazca might have been ancient smoke balloons piloted by early Peruvians. This theory is impressively presented by IES member Jim Woodman in his book *NAZCA: Journey to the Sun* (1977). Woodman has discovered that the thousands of ancient gravesites around Nazca contain finely woven textiles (suitable for balloon fabric), braided rope and ceramic pottery. One clay pot has a picture suggesting a hot-air balloon with tie ropes.

It is not generally known that manned balloon flights were recorded in Brazil as early as 1709, when Bartolomeu de Gusmao made his first flight on August 8. Jim Woodman has actually tested his theory in collaboration with balloonist Julian Nott. They constructed a balloon using the same materials as those available to the ancient Nazcans. The envelope used cotton fabric similar to that in the gravesites; the basket for pilot and co-pilot was woven from native fibers. On November 28, 1975, Woodman and Nott actually flew their balloon (named *Condor I*) over the Nazca plains. However, this impressive demonstration hardly settles the mystery of Nazca, since it is not plausible that the Nazcans would have spent centuries constructing these markings for the benefit of occasional balloonists to view from the air. Validation of the theory would require evidence of a religious and cultural milieu in which such balloonists maintained an elitist status for hundreds of years, and it is hardly likely that such balloons would have vanished without trace. (See also **Chariots of the Gods; Erich von Däniken**)

Ndembo (or **Kita**)

A former African secret society which had widespread ramifications on the lower Congo, and especially in the districts lying to the south of that river. Initiation was made through the *ganga* or chief, who instructed the neophyte at a given signal suddenly to lie down as if dead. A shroud was spread over him, and he was carried off to an enclosure outside the village called *vela,* and pronounced to have died a *Ndembo.*

Perhaps twenty, thirty, or even fifty candidates "died" at the one time. It was then assumed that persons "dying" in this manner decayed until only a single bone remained, and this the *ganga* took charge of. The process varied from three months to as many years, and the *ganga* was supposed by art magic to bring every one of the dead back to life within that period.

On a festival day of the *Ndembo,* the members marched through the village in a grand procession amidst universal joy, carrying with them the persons who were supposed to have died. The neophytes who were supposed to have perished comported themselves as if in reality they had come from another world. They took new names, pretended that everything in the terrestrial sphere was new to them, turned a deaf ear to their parents and relatives, and even affected not to know how to eat. They further desired to have everything they set eyes on, and if it was not granted to them immediately, they might fall upon the unhappy owner and beat and even kill him without any consequence to themselves. It was assumed that they were mere children in the affairs of the terrestrial sphere, and therefore knew no better.

Those who went through this rite were called *Nganga,* or the "knowing ones," while the neophytes were designated *Vanga.* During their occupation of the *vela* they learned an esoteric language, which they constantly employed. Perhaps the best picture of their cult was given by ethnologist Adolf Bastian (1826–1905) who stated:—

"The Great Nkissi (who here replaces the fetish) lives in the interior of the woodlands where nobody can see him. When he dies the Nganga carefully collect his bones in order to bring them back to life, and nourish them that they may again put on flesh and blood. But it is not well to speak about it. In the Ambamba country everybody must have died once, and when the Nganga (replacing the fetish-priest) shakes his calabash against a village, those men and youths whose hour is come fall into a state of lifeless torpor, from which they generally rise up in three days.

"But the man whom the Nkissi loves he carries off to the bush and often buries him for a series of years. When he again awakens to life, he begins to eat and drink as before, but his mind is gone, and the Nganga must himself educate him and instruct him in every movement, like the smallest child. At first that can only be done with the rod, but the senses gradually return, so that you can speak with him, and when his education is finished the Nganga takes him back to his parents. These would seldom recognise him but for the positive assurance of the Nganga, who at the same time reminds them of earlier occurrences. Whoever has not yet undergone the experience in Ambamba is universally despised, and is not allowed to join in the dances."

This account is curiously reminiscent of the Haitian tradition of **Zombies.**

Necromancy

Divination by means of the spirits of the dead, from the Greek *nekros,* dead, and *manteia,* divination. It is through its Italian form *nigromancia* that it came to be known as the "Black Art." With the Greeks it originally signified the descent into Hades in order to consult the dead rather than summoning the dead into the mortal sphere again.

The art is of almost universal usage. Considerable difference of opinion exists among modern adepts as to the exact methods to be properly pursued in the necromantic art, and it must be borne in mind that necromancy, which in the Middle Ages was called "sorcery," shades into modern Spiritualist practice. There is no doubt, however, that necromancy has long been regarded as the touchstone of occultism, for if, after careful preparation the adept can carry through to a successful issue, the raising of the soul from the other world, he has proved the success of his art. The occult sages of the past have left full details as to how the process should be attempted.

In the case of a compact existing between the sorcerer and the devil, of course, no ceremony is necessary, as the **familiar** is ever at hand to do the bidding of his masters. This, however, is never the case with the true sorcerer, who preserves his independence and trusts to his profound knowledge of the art and his powers of command. His object therefore is to "constrain" some spirit to appear before him, and to guard himself from the danger of provoking such beings.

The magician, it must be understood, normally has an assistant, and every article and procedure must conform to rules well known in the black art. In the first place, the magician and his assistant must locate a suitable venue for their procedures, which may be either in a subterranean vault, hung round with black, and lighted by a magical torch, or else in the center of some thick wood or desert, or upon some extensive unfrequented plain, where several roads meet, or amidst the ruins of ancient castles, abbeys, and monasteries, or amongst the rocks on the sea shore, in some private detached churchyard, or any other solemn, melancholy place between the hours of twelve and one in the night, either when the moon shines very bright, or else when the elements are disturbed with storms of thunder, lightning, wind, and rain, for in these places, times, and seasons, it is contended that spirits can manifest themselves to mortal eyes with less difficulty and continue visible with the least pain in this elemental external world.

When the proper time and place is fixed on, a magic circle is to be formed, within which the master and his associate are carefully to retire. The dimensions of the circle are as follow: a piece of ground is usually chosen, nine feet square, at the full extent of which parallel lines are drawn one within the other, having sundry crosses and triangles described between them, close to which is formed the first or outer circle, then, about half-a-foot within the same, a second circle is described, and within that another square correspondent to the first, the center of which is the seat or spot where the master and associate are to be placed.

According to one authority: "The vacancies formed by the various lines and angles of the figure are filled up with the holy names of God, having crosses and triangles described between them. The reason assigned by magicians and others for the institution and use of circles, is, that so much ground being blessed and consecrated by such holy words and ceremonies as they make use of in forming it, hath a secret force to expel all evil spirits from the bounds thereof, and, being sprinkled with pure sanctified water, the ground is purified from all uncleanness; besides, the holy names of God being written over every part of it, its force becomes so powerful that no evil spirit hath ability to break through it, or to get at the magician or his companion, by reason of the antipathy in nature they bear to these sacred names. And the reason given for the triangles is, that if the spirit be not easily brought to speak the truth, they may by the exorcist be conjured to enter the same, where, by virtue of the names of the essence and divinity of God, they can speak nothing but what is true and right. The circle, therefore, according to this account of it, is the principal fort and shield of the magician, from which he is not, at the peril of his life, to depart, till he has completely dismissed the spirit, particularly if he be of a fiery or infernal nature. Instances are recorded of many who perished by this means; particularly 'Chiancungi,' the famous Egyptian fortune-teller, who was so famous in England in the 17th century. He undertook for a wager, to raise up the spirit 'Bokim,' and having described the circle, he seated his sister Napula by him as his associate. After frequently repeating the forms of exorcism, and calling upon the spirit to appear, and nothing as yet answering his demand, they grew impatient of the business, and quitted the circle, but it cost them their lives; for they were instantaneously seized and crushed to death by that infernal spirit, who happened not to be sufficiently constrained till that moment, to manifest himself to human eyes."

The magic circle is consecrated by special rituals. The proper attire or "pontificalibus" of a magician, is an ephod made of fine white linen, over that a priestly robe of black bombazine, reaching to the ground, with the two seals of the earth drawn correctly upon virgin parchment, and affixed to the breast of his outer vestment. Round his waist is tied a broad consecrated girdle, with the names "Ya, Ya,—Aie, Aaie,—Elibra,—Elchim,—Sadai,—Pah Adonai,—tuo robore,—Cinctus sum." Upon the magician's shoes must be written "Tetragrammaton," with crosses round about; upon his head a high-crowned cap of sable silk, and in his hand a Holy Bible, printed or written in pure Hebrew.

Thus attired, and standing within the charmed circle, the magician repeats the awful form of exorcism, and presently, the infernal spirits make strange and frightful noises, howlings, tremblings, flashes, and most dreadful shrieks and yells before they become visible. Their first appearance is generally in the form of fierce and terrible lions or tigers, vomiting forth fire, and roaring hideously about the circle, during which time the exorcist must not suffer any tremor of dismay, for, in that event the spirits would gain the ascendancy, and the consequences may endanger his life. On the contrary, he must summon up firm resolution and continue repeating all the forms of constriction and confinement, until the spirits are drawn nearer to the influence of the triangle, when their forms will change to appearances less ferocious and frightful, and become more submissive and tractable.

When the forms of conjuration have in this manner been sufficiently repeated, the spirits forsake their bestial shapes and enter into human form, appearing like naked men of gentle countenance and behavior, yet the magician must remain warily on his guard so that they do not deceive him by such mild gestures, for they are exceedingly fraudulent and deceitful in their dealings with those who constrain them to appear without compact, having nothing in view but to suborn his mind, or accomplish his destruction.

With great care also the spirit must be discharged after the ceremony is finished and he has answered all the demands made upon him. The magician must wait patiently until he has passed through all the terrible forms which announce his coming, and only when the last shriek has died away and every trace of fire and brimstone has disappeared, may he leave the circle and depart home in safety.

If the ghost of a deceased person is to be raised, the grave must be resorted to at midnight, and a different form of conjuration is necessary. Still another is the infernal sacrament for "any corpse that hath hanged, drowned, or otherwise made away with itself," and in this case the conjurations are performed over the body, which will at last arise, and standing upright, answer with a faint and hollow voice the questions that are put to it.

The occultist Éliphas **Lévi** stated in his book *Transcendental Magic* (1896) that "evocations should always have a motive and a becoming end, otherwise they are works of darkness and folly, dangerous for health and reason." The permissible motive of an evocation may be either love or intelligence. Evocations of love require less apparatus and are in every respect easier.

According to Lévi, the procedure is as follows: "We must, in the first place, carefully collect the memorials of him (or her) whom we desire to behold, the articles he used, and on which his impression remains; we must also prepare an apartment in which the person lived, or otherwise one of a similar kind, and place his portrait veiled in white therein, surrounded with his favourite flowers, which must be renewed daily. A fixed date must then be observed, either the birthday of the person, or that day which was most fortunate for his and our own affection, one of which we may believe that his soul, however blessed elsewhere, cannot lose the remembrance; this must be the day for the evocation, and we must provide for it during the space of fourteen days.

"Throughout this period we must refrain from extending to anyone the same proofs of affection which we have the right to expect from the dead; we must observe strict chastity, live in retreat, and take only one modest and light collation daily. Every evening at the same hour we must shut ourselves in the chamber consecrated to the memory of the lamented person, using only one small light, such as that of a funeral lamp or taper. This light should be placed behind us, the portrait should be uncovered and we should remain before it for an hour, in silence; finally, we should fumigate the apartment with a little good incense, and go out backwards.

"On the morning of the day fixed for the evocation, we should adorn ourselves as if for a festival, not salute anyone first, make but a single repast of bread, wine, and roots, or fruits; the cloth should be white, two covers should be laid, and one portion of the bread broken should be set aside; a little wine should also be placed in the glass of the person we design to invoke. The meal must be eaten alone in the chamber of evocations, and in presence of the veiled portrait; it must be all cleared away at the end, except the glass belonging to the dead person, and his portion of bread, which must be placed before the portrait. In the evening, at the hour for the regular visit, we must repair in silence to the chamber, light a clear fire of cypress-wood, and cast incense seven times thereon, pronouncing the name of the person whom we desire to behold. The lamp must then be extinguished, and the fire permitted to die out.

"On this day the portrait must not be unveiled. When the flame is extinct, put more incense on the ashes, and invoke God according to the forms of the religion to which the dead person belonged, and according to the ideas which he himself possessed of God.

"While making this prayer we must identify ourselves with the evoked person, speak as he spoke, believe in a sense as he believed; then, after a silence of fifteen minutes, we must speak to him as if he were present, with affection and with faith, praying him to manifest to us. Renew this prayer mentally, covering the face with both hands; then call him thrice with a loud voice; tarry on our knees, the eyes closed and covered, for some minutes; then call again thrice upon him in a sweet and affectionate tone, and slowly open the eyes. Should nothing result, the same experiment must be renewed in the following year, and if necessary a third time, when it is certain that the desired apparition will be obtained, and the longer it has been delayed the more realistic and striking it will be.

"Evocations of knowledge and intelligence are made with more solemn ceremonies. If concerned with a celebrated personage, we must meditate for twenty-one days upon his life and writings, form an idea of his appearance, converse with him mentally, and imagine his answers; carry his portrait, or at least his name, about us; follow a vegetable diet for twenty-one days, and a severe fast during the last seven.

"We must next construct the magical oratory. This oratory must be invariably darkened; but if we operate in the daytime, we may leave a narrow aperture on the side where the sun will shine at the hour of the evocation, and place a triangular prism before the opening, and a crystal globe, filled with water, before the prism. If the operation be arranged for the night the magic lamp must be so placed that its single ray shall upon the altar smoke. The purpose of the preparations is to furnish the magic agent with elements of corporeal appearance, and to ease as much as possible the tension of imagination, which could not be exalted without danger into the absolute illusion of dream. For the rest, it will be easily understood that a

beam of sunlight, or the ray of a lamp, coloured variously, and falling upon curling and irregular smoke, can in no way create a perfect image. The chafing-dish containing the sacred fire should be in the centre of the oratory, and the altar of perfumes close by. The operator must turn towards the east to pray, and the west to invoke; he must be either alone or assisted by two persons preserving the strictest silence; he must wear the magical vestments, which we have described in the seventh chapter, and must be crowned with vervain and gold. He should bathe before the operation, and all his under garments must be of the most intact and scrupulous cleanliness.

"The ceremony should begin with a prayer suited to the genius of the spirit about to be invoked and one which would be approved by himself if he still lived. For example, it would be impossible to evoke Voltaire by reciting prayers in the style of St. Bridget. For the great men of antiquity, we may see the hymns of Cleanthes or Orpheus, with the adjuration terminating the Golden Verses of Pythagoras. In our own evocation of Apollonius, we used the magical philosophy of Patricius for the ritual, containing the doctrines of Zoroaster and the writings of Hermes Trismegistus. We recited the Nuctemeron of Apollonius in Greek with a loud voice and added the following conjuration: 'Vouchsafe to be present, O Father of All, and thou Thrice Mighty Hermes, Conductor of the Dead. Asclepius son of Hephaistus, Patron of the Healing Art; and thou Osiris, Lord of strength and vigour, do thou thyself be present too. Arnebascenis, Patron of Philosophy, and yet again Asclepius, son of Imuthe, who presidest over poetry. Apollonius, Apollonius, Apollonius, Thou teachest the Magic of Zoroaster, son of Oromasdes; and this is the worship of the Gods.'

"For the evocation of spirits belonging to religions issued from Judaism, the following Kabalistic invocation of Solomon should be used, either in Hebrew, or in any other tongue with which the spirit in question is known to have been familiar: 'Powers of the Kingdom, be ye under my left foot and in my right hand! Glory and Eternity, take me by the two shoulders, and direct me in the paths of victory! Mercy and Justice, be ye the equilibrium and splendour of my life! Intelligence and Wisdom, crown me! Spirits of *Malchuth*, lead me betwixt the two pillars upon which rests the whole edifice of the temple! Angels of *Netsah* and *Hod*, strengthen me upon the cubic stone of *Jesod!* O *Gedulael!* O *Geburael!* O *Tiphereth!* *Binael*, be thou my love! *Ruach Hochmael*, be thou my light! Be that which thou art and thou shalt be, O *Ketheriel!* Tschim, assist me in the name of *Saddai!* Cherubim, be my strength in the name of *Adonai!* Beni-Elohim, be my brethren in the name of the Son, and by the power of *Zebaoth!* Eloim, do battle for me in the name of *Tetragrammation!* Malachim, protect me in the name of *Jod He Vau He!* Seraphim, cleanse my love in the name of *Elvoh!* Hasmalim, enlighten me with the splendours of *Eloi* and Shechinah! Aralim, act! Ophanim, revolve and shine! Hajoth a Kadosh, cry, speak, roar, bellow! Kadosh, Kadosh, Kadosh, *Saddai, Adonai, Jotchavah, Eieazereie:* Hallelu-Jah, Hallelu-jah, Hallelu-jah. Amen.'

"It should be remembered above all, in conjurations, that the names of Satan, Beelzebub, Adramelek, and others do not designate spiritual unities, but legions of impure spirits. 'Our name is legion, for we are many,' says the spirit of darkness in the Gospel. Number constitutes the law, and progress takes place inversely in hell—that is to say, the most advanced in Satanic development, and consequently the most degraded, are the least intelligent and feeblest.

"Thus, a fatal law drives the demons downward when they wish and believe themselves to be ascending. So also those who term themselves chiefs are the most impotent and despised of all. As to the horde of perverse spirits, they tremble before an unknown, invisible, incomprehensible, capricious, implacable chief, who never explains his law, whose arm is ever stretched out to strike those who fail to understand him. They give this phantom the names of Baal, Jupiter, and even others more venerable, which cannot, without profanation, be pronounced in hell. But this Phantom is only a shadow and remnant of God, disfigured by their wilful perversity, and persisting in their imagination like a vengeance of justice and a remorse of truth.

"When the evoked spirit of light manifests with dejected or irritated countenance, we must offer him a moral sacrifice, that is, be inwardly disposed to renounce whatever offends him; and before leaving the oratory, we must dismiss him, saying: 'May peace be with thee! I have not wished to trouble thee; do thou torment me not. I shall labour to improve myself as to anything that vexes thee. I pray, and will still pray, with thee and for thee. Pray thou also both with and for me, and return to thy great slumber, expecting that day when we shall wake together. Silence and adieu!'"

Paul Christian, in his *Historie de le magie* (Paris, 1871) stated: "The place chosen for the evocation is not an unimportant point. The most auspicious is undoubtedly that room which contains the last traces of the lamented person. If it be impossible to fulfil this condition, we must go in search of some isolated rural retreat which corresponds in orientation and aspect, as well as measurement, with the mortuary chamber.

"The window must be blocked with boards of olive wood, hermetically joined, so that no exterior light may penetrate. The ceiling, the four interior walls, and the floor must be draped with tapestry of emerald green silk, which the operator must himself secure with copper nails, invoking no assistance from strange hands, because, from this moment, he alone may enter into this spot set apart from all, the arcane Oratory of the Magus. The furniture which belonged to the deceased, his favourite possessions and trinkets, the things on which his final glance may be supposed to have rested—all these must be assiduously collected and arranged in the order which they occupied at the time of his death. If none of these souvenirs can be obtained, a faithful likeness of the departed being must at least be procured, it must be full length, and must be depicted in the dress and colours which he wore during the last period of his life. This portrait must be set up on the eastern wall by means of copper fasteners, must be covered with a veil of white silk, and must be surmounted with a crown of those flowers which were most loved by the deceased.

"Before this portrait there must be erected an altar of white marble, supported by four columns which must terminate in bull's feet. A five-pointed star must be emblazoned on the slab of the altar, and must be com-

posed of pure copper plates. The place in the centre of the star, between the plates, must be large enough to receive the pedestal of a cup-shaped copper chafing-dish, containing dessicated fragments of laurel wood and alder. By the side of the chafing-dish must be placed a censer full of incense. The skin of a white and spotless ram must be stretched beneath the altar, and on it must be emblazoned another pentagram drawn with parallel lines of azure blue, golden yellow, emerald green, and purple red.

"A copper tripod must be erected in the middle of the Oratory; it must be perfectly triangular in form, it must be surmounted by another and similar chafing-dish, which must likewise contain a quantity of dried olive wood.

"A high candelabrum of copper must be placed by the wall on the southern side, and must contain a single taper of purest white wax, which must alone illuminate the mystery of the evocation.

"The white colour of the altar, of the ram's skin, and of the veil, is consecrated to Gabriel, the planetary archangel of the moon, and the Genius of mysteries; the green of the copper and the tapestries is dedicated to the Genius of Venus.

"The altar and tripod must both be encompassed by a magnetized iron chain, and by three garlands composed of the foliage and blossoms of the myrtle, the olive, and the rose.

"Finally, facing the portrait, and on the eastern side, there must be a canopy, also draped with emerald silk, and supported by two triangular columns of olive wood, plated with purest copper. On the North and South sides, between each of these columns and the wall, the tapestry must fall in long folds to the ground, forming a kind of tabernacle, which must be open on the eastern side. At the foot of each column there must be a sphinx of white marble, with a cavity in the top of the head to receive spices for burning. It is beneath this canopy that the apparitions will manifest, and it should be remembered that the Magus must turn to the east for prayer, and to the west for evocation.

"Before entering this little sanctuary, devoted to the religion of remembrance, the operator must be clothed in a vestment of azure, fastened by clasps of copper, enriched with a single emerald. He must wear upon his head a tiara surrounded by a floriated circle of twelve emeralds, and a crown of violets. On his breast must be the talisman of Venus depending from a ribbon of azure silk. On the annular finger of his left hand must be a copper ring containing a turquoise. His feet must be covered with shoes of azure silk, and he must be provided with a fan of swan's feathers to dissipate, if needful, the smoke of the perfumes.

"The Oratory and all its objects must be consecrated on a Friday, during the hours which are set apart to the Genius of Venus. This consecration is performed by burning violets and roses in a fire of olive wood. A shaft must be provided in the Oratory for the passage of the smoke, but care must be taken to prevent the admission of light through this channel.

"When these preparations are finished, the operator must impose on himself a retreat of one-and-twenty days, beginning on the anniversary of the death of the beloved being. During this period he must refrain from conferring on any one the least of those marks of affection which he was accustomed to bestow on the departed; he must be absolutely chaste, alike in deed and thought; he must take daily but one repast, consisting of bread, wine, roots, and fruits. These three conditions are indispensable to success in evocation, and their accomplishment requires complete isolation.

"Every day, shortly before mid-night, the Magus must assume his consecrated dress. On the stroke of the mystic hour, he must enter the Oratory, bearing a lighted candle in his right hand, and in the other an hour-glass. The candle must be fixed in the candelabra, and the hour-glass on the altar to register the flight of time. The operator must then proceed to replenish the garland and the floral crown. Then he shall unveil the portrait, and erect it immovable in front of the altar, being thus with his face to the East, he shall softly go over in his mind the cherished recollections he possesses of the beloved and departed being.

"When the upper reservoir of the hour-glass is empty the time of contemplation will be over. By the flame of the taper the operator must then kindle the laurel wood and alder in the chafing-dish which stands on the altar; then, taking a pinch of incense from the censer, let him cast it thrice upon the fire, repeating the following words:— 'Glory be to the Father of life universal in the splendour of the infinite altitude, and peace in the twilight of the immeasurable depths of all Spirits of good will!'

"Then he shall cover the portrait, and taking up his candle in his hand, shall depart from the Oratory, walking backward at a slow pace as far as the threshold. The same ceremony must be fulfilled at the same hour during every day of the retreat, and at each visit the crown which is above the portrait, and the garlands of the altar and tripod must be carefully renewed. The withered leaves and flowers must be burnt each evening in a room adjoining the Oratory.

"When the twenty-first day has arrived, the Magus must do his best to have no communication with any one, but if this be impossible, he must not be the first to speak, and he must postpone all business till the morrow. On the stroke of noon, he must arrange a small circular table in the Oratory, and cover it with a new napkin of unblemished whiteness. It must be garnished with two copper chalices, an entire loaf, and a crystal flagon of the purest wine. The bread must be broken and not cut, and the wine emptied in equal portions into the two cups. Half of this mystic communion, which must be his sole nourishment on this supreme day, shall be offered by the operator to the dead, and by the light of the one taper he must eat his own share, standing before the veiled portrait. Then he shall retire as before, walking backward as far as the threshold, and leaving the ghost's share of the bread and wine upon the table.

"When the solemn hour of the evening has at length arrived the Magus shall carry into the Oratory some well-dried cypress wood, which he shall set alight on the altar and the tripod. Three pinches of incense shall be cast on the altar flame in honour of the Supreme Potency which manifests itself by Ever Active Intelligence and by Absolute Wisdom. When the wood of the two chafing-dishes has been reduced to embers, he must renew the triple offering of incense on the altar, and must cast some seven

times on the fire in the tripod; at each evaporation of the consecrated perfume he must repeat the previous doxology, and then turning to the East, he must call upon God by the prayer of that religion which was professed by the person whom he desires to evoke.

"When the prayers are over he must reverse his position and with his face to the West, must enkindle the chafing-dishes on the head of each sphinx, and when the cypress is fully ablaze he must heap over it well-dried violets and roses. Then let him extinguish the candle which illuminates the Oratory, and falling on his knees before the canopy, between the two columns, let him mentally address the beloved person with a plenitude of faith and affection. Let him solemnly entreat it to appear and renew this interior adjuration seven times, under the auspices of the seven providential Genii, endeavouring during the whole of the time to exalt his soul above the natural weakness of humanity.

"Finally, the operator, with closed eyes, and with hands covering his face, must call the invoked person in a loud but gentle voice, pronouncing three times all the names which he bore.

"Some moments after the third appeal, he must extend his arms in the form of a cross, and lifting up his eyes, he will behold the beloved being, in a recognisable manner, in front of him. That is to say, he will perceive that ethereal substance separated from the perishable terrestrial body, the fluidic envelope of the soul, which Kabalistic initiates have termed the *Perispirit.* This substance preserves the human form but is emancipated from human infirmities, and is energised by the special characteristics whereby the imperishable individuality of our essence is manifested. Evoked and Evoker can then intercommunicate intelligibly by a mutual and mysterious thought-transmission.

"The departed soul will give counsel to the operator; it will occasionally reveal secrets which may be beneficial to those whom it loved on earth, but it will answer no question which has reference to the desires of the flesh; it will discover no buried treasures, nor will it unveil the secrets of a third person; it is silent on the mysteries of the superior existence to which it has now attained. In certain cases, it will, however, declare itself either happy or in punishment. If it be the latter, it will ask for the prayer of the Magus, or for some religious observance, which we must unfailingly fulfil. Lastly, it will indicate the time when the evocation may be renewed.

"When it has disappeared, the operator must turn to the East, rekindle the fire on the altar, and make a final offering of incense. Then he must detach the crown and the garlands, take up his candle, and retire with his face to the West till he is out of the Oratory. His last duty is to burn the final remains of the flowers and leaves. Their ashes, united to those which have been collected during the time of retreat, must be mixed with myrtle seed, and secretly buried in a field at a depth which will secure it from disturbance of the ploughshare."

The last two examples are, of course, those of "white" necromancy. The evocation procedure followed by primitive tribes is totally different. Among certain Australian tribes the necromants were called "Birraark." It is said that a Birraark was supposed to be initiated by the "mrarts" (ghosts) when they met him wandering in the bush. It was from the ghosts that he obtained replies to questions concerning events passing at a distance, or yet to happen, which might be of interest or moment to his tribe.

An account of a spiritual seance in the bush is given in a discussion of the Kamilaroi and Kurnai peoples: "The fires were let down; the Birraark uttered the cry 'Coo-ee' at intervals. At length a distant reply was heard, and shortly afterwards the sound as of persons jumping on the ground in succession. A voice was then heard in the gloom asking in a strange intonation 'What is wanted?' At the termination of the seance, the spirit voice said, 'We are going.' Finally, the Birraark was found in the top of an almost inaccessible tree, apparently asleep." (See also **New Zealand**)

In Japan, ghosts were traditionally raised in various ways. One mode was to "put into an andon [a paper lantern in a frame] a hundred rushlights, and repeat an incantation of a hundred lines. One of these rushlights is taken out at the end of each line, and the would-be ghost-seer then goes out in the dark with one light still burning, and blows it out, when the ghost ought to appear. Girls who have lost their lovers by death often try that sorcery."

The mode of procedure as practiced in Scotland was thus. The haunted room was made ready. He, "who was to do the daring deed, about nightfall entered the room, bearing with him a table, a chair, a candle, a compass, a crucifix if one could be got, and a Bible. With the compass he cast a circle on the middle of the floor, large enough to hold the chair and the table. He placed within the circle the chair and the table, and on the table he laid the Bible and the crucifix beside the lighted candle. If he had not a crucifix, then he drew the figure of a cross on the floor within the circle. When all this was done, he rested himself on the chair, opened the Bible, and waited for the coming of the spirit. Exactly at midnight the spirit came. Sometimes the door opened slowly, and there glided in noiselessly a lady sheeted in white, with a face of woe and told her story to the man on his asking her in the name of God what she wanted. What she wanted was done in the morning, and the spirit rested ever after. Sometimes the spirit rose from the floor, and sometimes came forth from the wall. One there was who burst into the room with a strong bound, danced wildly round the circle, and flourished a long whip round the man's head, but never dared to step within the circle. During a pause in his frantic dance he was asked, in God's name, what he wanted. He ceased his dance and told his wishes. His wishes were carried out, and the spirit was in peace."

In Sir N. W. Wraxall's *Memoirs of the Courts of Berlin, Dresden, Warsaw, and Vienna* (2 vols., 1799), there is an amusing account of the raising of the ghost of the Chevalier de Saxe. Reports had been circulated that at his palace at Dresden there was secreted a large sum of money, and it was urged that if his spirit could be compelled to appear, interesting secrets might be extorted from him. Curiosity, combined with avarice, accordingly prompted his principal heir, Prince Charles, to try the experiment, and, on the appointed night, Schrepfer was the operator in raising the apparition. He commenced his proceedings by retiring into the corner of the gallery, where, kneeling down with many mysterious ceremonies, he invoked the spirit to appear. At length a loud clatter

was heard at all the windows on the outside, resembling more the effect produced by a number of wet fingers drawn over the edge of glasses than anything else to which it could well be compared. This sound announced the arrival of the good spirits, and was shortly followed by a yell of a frightful and unusual nature, which indicated the presence of malignant spirits. Schrepfer continued his invocations, when "the door suddenly opened with violence, and something that resembled a black ball or globe rolled into the room. It was enveloped in smoke or cloud, in the midst of which appeared a human face, like the countenance of the Chevalier de Saxe, from which issued a loud and angry voice, exclaiming in German, 'Carl, was wollte du mit mich?' " (Charles, what would thou do with me?). By reiterated exorcisms Schrepfer finally dismissed the apparition, and the terrified spectators dispersed fully convinced of his magical powers.

Since the rituals of magical evocation date back to the ancient East, it is not surprising to find that European rituals have parallels in Arabia, Persia, India, China, Tibet and Japan. In the modern occult revival, such rituals have been revived and popularized, side by side with European traditions and revivals and various hybrid forms have evolved. (See also **Ceremonial Magic; Magic; Magical Diagrams; Magical Instruments and Accessories**)

Recommended reading:

Christian, Paul. *The History and Practice of Magic,* Forge Press, London, 2 vols., 1952

Lévi, Éliphas. *The History of Magic,* William Rider & Co., London, 1913 etc.

Lévi, Éliphas. *Transcendental Magic; Its Doctrine and Ritual,* George Redway, London, 1896 etc.

Shah, Sayed Idries Shah. *Oriental Magic,* Rider & Co., London, 1956

Shah, Sayed Idries Shah. *The Secret Lore of Magic; Books of the Sorcerers,* Frederick Muller, London, 1957

Smedley, Edward, W. C. Taylor, Henry Thompson & Elihu Rich. *The Occult Sciences,* Richard Griffin, London & Glasgow, 1855

Waite, Arthur E. *The Book of Ceremonial Magic,* William Rider & Son, London, 1911; University Books, New York, 1961; (under title *The Book of Black Magic and Ceremonial Magic*) Causeway Books, 1973

Necronomicon, The

A fabled **grimoire** or textbook of black magic for evoking demons, supposedly compiled by the "mad Arab Abdul Alhazred"—in fact, an invention of H. P. **Lovecraft,** writer of supernatural and fantasy fiction. The name "Abdul Alhazred" was adopted playfully by Lovecraft around the age of five, after reading an edition of *The Arabian Nights,* and was used in later life in Lovecraft's fiction. It may also contain a reference to the name "Hazard," an old Rhode Island family.

In 1936, Lovecraft wrote a pseudo-scholarly essay titled *A History of the Necronomicon,* which claimed that its original title was *Al Azif,* deriving from the word used by Arabs to designate the nocturnal sound of insects resembling the howling of demons. There followed an account of various editions of the *Necronomicon* from A.D. 730 onwards. Lovecraft had claimed that there was a copy of the work in the library of Miskatonic University, in Arkham (a city invented by him in his fiction). Lovecraft's essay was published in leaflet form by Wilson H. Shepherd, Alabama, 1938, and has since been reprinted. The *Necronomicon* was cited in various stories by Lovecraft, and gradually acquired a spurious life of its own. Someone inserted an index card for the book in the files of Yale Library. A New York bookseller could not resist inserting an entry for a Latin edition in one of his sale catalogs.

Eventually a group of writers and researchers headed by occult scholar Colin **Wilson** solemnly presented *The Necronomicon: The Book of Dead Names* as a newly discovered lost masterpiece of occult literature. In an introduction to this publication, Wilson suggested that Lovecraft's invention may have had some substance in fact, perhaps revealed through Lovecraft's subconscious mind. Wilson told a story as fabulous as that of the origin of the **Golden Dawn** cipher manuscript, concerning a Dr. Stanislaus Hinterstoisser, president of the Salzburg Institute for the Study of Magic and Occult Phenomena, who claimed that Lovecraft's father was an Egyptian Freemason, that he had seen a copy of *The Necronomicon* in Boston, U.S. (where Lovecraft senior had worked), which was a section of a book by Alkindi (died A.D. 850) known as *The Book of the Essence of the Soul.*

Science-fiction writer L. Sprague de Camp (who published an excellent biography of Lovecraft in 1975) is said to have acquired an Arabic manuscript from Baghdad titled *Al Azif.* The British occultist Robert Turner, after researching in the British Museum Library, claimed that the Alkindi work was known to the famous magician John **Dee** (1527-1608) who had a copy in cipher manuscript. This book, known as *Liber Logaeth,* was recently examined by computer analysis, and so *The Necronomicon: The Book of Dead Names* has now been published, edited by George Hay, introduced by Colin Wilson, researched by Robert Turner and David Langford (Neville Spearman, U.K., 1978; Corgi paperback, 1980).

No doubt other recensions of *The Necronomicon* will be discovered in the course of time. Meanwhile, librarians need no longer be embarrassed by requests for this elusive work.

Neihardt, John G(neisenau) (1881-1973)

Eminent American poet and author, who also founded a remarkable organization for parapsychological research known as SORRAT (Society for Research on Rapport and Telekinesis).

Neilhardt was born January 8, 1881 near Sharpsburg, Illinois, son of a farmer. He was educated at Nebraska Normal College (now Nebraska State Teachers College at Wayne), obtaining a diploma in science 1897. From 1901-07 he lived among Omaha Indians, later among the Sioux. From 1911-20 he was literary editor of the *Minneapolis Journal.* In 1923, he was appointed professor of poetry at University of Nebraska, Lincoln. From 1926-38 he was literary editor of the *St. Louis Post-Dispatch.* From 1943-46 he worked for the U.S. Department of Interior, Bureau of Indian Affairs, Washington, D.C.; director of information at Chicago office from 1943-46, field representative, 1946-48. From 1949-65, he was lecturer in English and poet-in-residence at University of Missouri-Columbia; Honnold Lecturer, Knox College, 1939, also lecturer at other colleges and universities.

His many books included: *The Divine Enchantment* (1900), *The Lonesome Trail* (1907), *The River and I* (1910, 1927), *The Quest* (1916), *The Song of Three Friends* (1919), *The Splendid Wayfaring* (1920), *The Song of the Indian Wars* (1925, 1928), *Poetic Values—Their Reality and Our Need of Them* (1925), *Collected Poems* (1926), *Indian Tales and Others* (1926), *Black Elk Speaks* (1932), *The Song of the Messiah* (1935), *All Is But a Beginning* (autobiography, 1972).

He was honored by the Poetry Society of America Prize for best volume of verse in 1919, named poet laureate of Nebraska by an act of the legislature 1921. He was awarded the Gold Scroll Medal of Honor of National Poetry Center in 1936, Writers Foundation award for poetry, 1964, LL.D., Creighton University 1928, Litt.D., University of Nebraska 1917, University of Missouri 1947, Midland Lutheran College 1972. He was elected to Nebraska State Hall of Fame in 1974. A bronze bust of Neilhardt was placed in the rotunda of the Nebraska capital by an act of the state legislature in 1961 and there is another monument in the city park, Wayne, Nebraska. The Garden Club of Bancroft, Nebraska acquired the cottage in which he lived and wrote as a museum of Neihardt memorabilia, and there is a special Neihardt Memorial Collection at the University of Missouri.

Neihardt was friendly with Dr. Joseph B. Rhine, famous parapsychologist and director of the Foundation for Research on the Nature of Man. Neihardt's experience with Omaha and Sioux Indians probably influenced his philosophical views expressed in what has been called "Pragmatic Mysticism," involving the heightened awareness of prayer and meditation being applied to everyday life. In 1908, he married Mona Martensen who had earlier spent some time as companion to a Spiritualist and who was convinced that psychic experience could not be dismissed. Apparently she had considerable mediumistic talents herself.

From the 1920s onwards, Neihardt spent some time investigating psychic phenomena at first hand. He was also well aware of paranormal experiences amongst the Sioux Indians. In 1926, he met Caspar Yost, a journalist who had investigated the famous phenomena of Mrs. Pearl **Curren,** through whom the **"Patience Worth"** scripts were produced. Neihardt himself made an in-depth study of the phenomena. In 1960, with Dr. John T. Richards and other associates, Neihardt formed the Society for Research on Rapport and Telekinesis (see **SORRAT**) in order to develop investigation of psi faculties under conditions which would be favorable. Some remarkable effects of psychokinesis were obtained. The story of the group has been recorded in *SORRAT: A History of the Neihardt Psychokinesis Experiments,* 1961-1981 by John Thomas Richards, published Scarecrow Press, 1982. Neihardt died November 3, 1973. (See also **Movement; Psychokinesis; SORRAT**)

Neil-Smith, the Rev. Christopher

Vicar of a London, England church, and the leading British exorcist. He was ordained in 1944 and became aware of a healing power, which he has since used for dealing with possessed individuals.

He performed his first exorcism in 1949, and has since performed more than 500 exorcisms a year. By 1974, he had performed some 2,200 exorcisms, one of which was filmed for television.

He has appeared on radio and television programs in the U.S., Canada, Italy, Belgium, Switzerland, Germany and Africa, as well as Britain. He described his experiences and beliefs in his book *The Exorcist and the Possessed; the Truth about Exorcism* (Cornwall, U.K., 1974)

Nengraphy

Japanese term for the psychic photography (or "Thoughtography") of the young Japanese psychic Masuaki **Kiyota.** The Japan Nengraphy Association, headed by Tsutomu Miyauchi, investigates such phenomena. Address, Awiji-cho 2–25, Kannda, Chioda, Tokyo. (See also T. **Fukurai; Japan; Psychic Photography;** Ted **Serios; Thoughtforms; Thoughtography**)

Neoplatonism

A mystical philosophical system initiated by Plotinus of Alexandria, 233 A.D., which combined the philosophy of ancient Greece with later spiritual cravings. Although to some extent founded on the teaching of Plato, it was undoubtedly sophisticated by a deep mysticism, which in all probability emanated from the traditions of the land in which it originated. To a great extent it colored the thought of medieval mysticism and magic.

Plotinus, its founder, commenced the study of philosophy in Alexandria at the age of twenty-eight. He early experienced an earnest desire to reach the truth concerning existence, and to that end made a deep study of the dialogues of Plato and the metaphysics of Aristotle. He practiced the most severe austerities, and attempted to live what he called the "angelic" life, or the life of the disembodied in the body.

He was greatly drawn to **Apollonius of Tyana** by reading his *Life* by Philostratus, and gave credence to many of the marvels recorded therein. The union of philosopher and priest in the character of Apollonius fired the imagination of Plotinus, and in his Pythagorean teachings the young student discovered the elements of both Orientalism and Platonism, for both Pythagoras and Plato strove to escape the sensuous, and to realize in contemplative abstraction that tranquility superior to desire and passion which made men approach the gods, although in the hands of the later Pythagoreans and Platonists, the principles of the Hellenic masters degenerated into a species of theurgic freemasonry. Many of the Pythagoreans had joined the various Orphic associations, and indeed became little more than itinerant vendors of charms.

It is probable that at Alexandria Plotinus heard from Orientals the principles of eastern theosophy, which he did not find in Plato. But everywhere he found a growing indifference to religion as known to the more ancient Greeks and Egyptians. By this time, the pantheons of Greece, Rome and Egypt, had become fused in the worship of Serapis, and this fusion had been forwarded by the works of Plutarch, Apuleius, and Lucian.

The position of philosophy at this time was by no means a strong one. In fact, speculation had given place to ethical teaching, and philosophy was regarded more as a branch of literature, or an elegant recreation. Plotinus persuaded himself that philosophy and religion should be

one, that speculation should be a search after God. It was at this time that he first heard of Ammonius Saccas, who shortly before had been a porter in the streets of Alexandria, and who lectured upon the possibilities of reconciling Plato and Aristotle.

"Skepticism," stated Ammonius, "was death." He recommended men to travel back across the past, and out of the whole bygone world of thought to construct a system greater than any of its parts. This teaching formed an epoch in the life of Plotinus, who was convinced that Platonism, exalted into a species of illuminism and drawing to itself like a magnet all the scattered truth of the bygone ages, could alone preserve mankind from skepticism. He occupied himself only with the most abstract questions concerning knowledge and being.

"Truth," according to Plotinus, "is not the agreement of our comprehension of an external object with the object itself, but rather the agreement of the mind with itself. For the philosopher the objects we contemplate, and that which contemplates are identical; both are thought." All truth is then easy. Reduce the soul to its most perfect simplicity, and we find it is capable of exploration into the infinite; indeed it becomes one with the infinite. This is the condition of ecstasy, and to accomplish it, a stoical austerity and asceticism was necessary.

The Neoplatonists were thus ascetics and enthusiasts. Plato was neither. According to Plotinus, the mystic contemplates the divine perfection in himself; all worldly things and logical distinctions vanish during the period of ecstasy. This, of course, is Oriental rather than Platonic, and is reminiscent of the stages of **Yoga** meditation. Plotinus regarded the individual existence as phenomenal and transitory, and subordinated reason to ecstasy where the Absolute is in question. It is only at the end of his chain of reasoning that he introduced the supernatural. He is first a rationalist, afterwards a mystic, and only a mystic when he finds that he cannot employ the machinery of reason. The following letter of Plotinus, written about 260 A.D., well embodies his ideas on these heads:

"Plotinus to Flaccus.—I applaud your devotion to philosophy; I rejoice to hear that your soul has set sail, like the returning Ulysses, for its native land—that glorious, that only real country—the world of unseen truth. To follow philosophy, the senator Rogatianus, one of the noblest of my disciples, gave up the other day all but the whole of his patrimony, set free his slaves, and surrendered all the honours of his station.

"Tidings have reached us that Valerian has been defeated and is now in the hands of Sapor. The threats of Franks and Allemanni, of Goths and Persians, are alike terrible by turns to our degenerate Rome. In days like these, crowded with incessant calamities, the inducements to a life of contemplation are more than ever strong. Even my quiet existence seems now to grow somewhat sensible of the advance of years. Age alone I am unable to debar from my retirement. I am weary already of this prison-house, the body, and calmly await the day when the divine nature within me shall be set free from matter.

"The Egyptian priests used to tell me that a single touch with the wing of their holy bird could charm the crocodile into torpor; it is not thus speedily, my dear friend, that the pinions of your soul will have power to still the untamed body. The creature will yield only to watchful, strenuous constancy of habit. Purify your soul from all undue hope and fear about earthly things, mortify the body, deny self,—affections as well as appetites, and the inner eye will begin to exercise its clear and solemn vision.

"You ask me to tell you how we know, and what is our criterion of certainty. To write is always irksome to me. But for the continual solicitations of Porphyry, I should not have left a line to survive me. For your own sake, and for your father's, my reluctance shall be overcome.

"External objects present us only with appearances. Concerning them, therefore, we may be said to possess opinion rather than knowledge. The distinctions in the actual world of appearance are of import only to ordinary and practical men. Our question lies within the ideal reality which exists behind appearance. How does the mind perceive these ideas? Are they without us, and is the reason, like sensation, occupied with objects external to itself? What certainty could we then have, what assurance that our perception was infallible? The object perceived would be a something different from the mind perceiving it. We should have then an image instead of reality. It would be monstrous to believe for a moment that the mind was unable to perceive ideal truth exactly as it is, and that we had not certainty and real knowledge concerning the world of intelligence. It follows, therefore, that this region of truth is not to be investigated as a thing external to us, and so only imperfectly known. It is *within* us. Here the objects we contemplate and that which contemplates are identical,—both are thought. The subject cannot surely *know* an object different from itself. The world of ideas lies within our intelligence. Truth, therefore, is not the agreement of our apprehension of an external object with the object itself. It is the agreement of the mind with itself. Consciousness, therefore, is the sole basis of certainty. The mind is its own witness. Reason sees in itself that which is above itself as its source; and again, that which is below itself as still itself once more.

"Knowledge has three degrees—Opinion, Science, Illumination. The means or instrument of the first is sense; of the second, dialectic; of the third intuition. To the last I subordinate reason. It is absolute knowledge founded on the identity of the mind knowing with the object known.

"There is a raying out of all orders of existence, an external emanation from the ineffable One [*prudos*]. There is again a returning impulse, drawing all upwards and inwards towards the centre from whence all came [epistrophe]. Love, as Plato in the *Banquet* beautifully says, is the child of Poverty and Plenty. In the amorous quest of the soul after the Good, lies the painful sense of fall and deprivation. But that Love is blessing, is salvation, is our guardian genius; without it the centrifugal law would overpower us, and sweep our souls out far from their source toward the cold extremities of the Material and the Manifold. The wise man recognises the idea of the Good within him. This he develops by withdrawal into the Holy Place of his own soul. He who does not understand how the soul contains the Beautiful within itself, seeks to realize beauty without, by laborious production. His aim should rather be to concentrate and simplify, and so to expand his being; instead of going out into the Manifold, to forsake it for the One, and so to float upwards towards the divine fount of being whose stream flows within him.

"You ask, how can we know the Infinite? I answer, not by reason. It is the office of reason to distinguish and define. The Infinite, therefore, cannot be ranked among its objects. You can only apprehend the Infinite by a faculty superior to reason, by entering into a state in which you are your finite self no longer, in which the Divine Essence is communicated to you. This is Ecstasy. It is the liberation of your mind from its finite consciousness. Like only can apprehend like; when you thus cease to be finite, you become one with the Infinite. In the reduction of your soul to its simplest self (aplosis), its divine essence, you realize this Union, this Identity [enosin].

"But this sublime condition is not of permanent duration. It is only now and then that we can enjoy this elevation (mercifully made possible for us) above the limits of the body and the world. I myself have realized it but three times as yet, and Porphyry hitherto not once. All that tends to purify and elevate the mind will assist you in this attainment, and facilitate the approach and the recurrence of these happy intervals. There are, then, different roads by which this end may be reached. The love of beauty which exalts the poet; that devotion to the One and that ascent of science which makes the ambition of the philosopher; and that love and those prayers by which some devout and ardent soul tends in its moral purity towards perfection. These are the great highways conducting to that height above the actual and the particular where we stand in the immediate presence of the Infinite, who shines out as from the deeps of the soul."

Plotinus appears to have been greatly indebted to Numenius for some of the ideas peculiar to his system. Numenius attempted to harmonize Pythagoras and Plato, to elucidate and confirm the opinions of both by the religious dogmas of the Egyptians, the **Magi** and the Brahmans, and he believed that Plato was indebted to the Hebrew as well as to the Egyptian theology for much of his wisdom. Like Plotinus he was puzzled that the immutable One could find it possible to create the Manifold without self-degradation, and he therefore posited a Being whom he calls the Demi-urge, or Artificer, who merely carried out the will of God in constructing the universe.

Expressed in summary, the mysticism of Plotinus is as follows: One cannot know God in any partial or finite manner. To know Him truly we must escape from the finite, from all that is earthly, from the very gifts of God to God Himself, and know Him in the infinite way by receiving, or being received into Him directly. To accomplish this, and to attain this identity, we must withdraw into our inmost selves, into our own essence, which alone is susceptible of blending with the Divine Essence. Hence the inmost is the highest, and as with all systems of mysticism introversion is ascension, and God is found within.

Porphyry entered the school of Plotinus when it had become an institution of some standing. At first he strongly opposed the teachings of his master, but soon became his most devoted scholar. He directed a fierce assault on Christianity, and at the same time launched strictures at Paganism, but both forces were too strong for him. The attempt of the school to combine religion and philosophy robbed the first of its only power, and the last of its only principle. Religion in the hands of the Neoplatonists lost all sanctity and authoritativeness, and philosophy all scientific precision, and the attempt to philosophize superstition ended in mere absurdity. But they succeeded in one thing, and that was in making philosophy superstitious—no very difficult task.

Porphyry modified the doctrine of Plotinus regarding ecstasy, by stating that in that condition the mind does not lose its consciousness of personality. He called it a dream in which the soul, dead to the world, rises to a species of divine activity, to an elevation above reason, action and liberty. He believed in a certain order of evil genii, who took pleasure in hunting wild beasts, and others of whom hunted souls that had escaped from the fetters of the body, so that to escape them, the soul must once more take refuge in the flesh. Porphyry's theosophical conceptions, based on those of Plotinus, were strongly and ably traversed by the theurgic mysteries of Iamblichus, to whom the priest was a prophet full of deity. Criticizing Porphyry, Iamblichus stated:

"Often, at the moment of inspiration, or when the afflatus has subsided, a fiery Appearance is seen—the entering or departing Power. Those who are skilled in this wisdom can tell by the character of this glory the rank of divinity who has seized for the time the reins of the mystic's soul, and guides it as he will. Sometimes the body of the man subject to this influence is violently agitated, sometimes it is rigid and motionless. In some instances sweet music is heard, in others, discordant and fearful sounds. The person of the subject has been known to dilate and tower to a superhuman height; in other cases, it has been lifted up into the air. Frequently, not merely the ordinary exercise of reason, but sensation and animal life would appear to have been suspended, and the subject of the afflatus has not felt the application of fire, has been pierced with spits, cut with knives, and been sensible of no pain. Yea, often, the more the body and the mind have been alike enfeebled by vigil and by fasts, the more ignorant or mentally imbecile a youth may be who is brought under this influence, the more freely and unmixedly will the divine power be made manifest. So clearly are these wonders the work, not of human skill or wisdom, but of supernatural agency! Characteristics such as these I have mentioned, are the marks of the true inspiration.

"Now, there are, O Agathocles, four great orders of spiritual existence,—Gods, Dæmons, Heroes or Demigods, and Souls. You will naturally be desirous to learn how the apparition of a God or a Dæmon is distinguished from those of Angels, Principalities, or Souls. Know, then, that their appearance to man corresponds to their nature, and that they always manifest themselves to those who invoke them in a manner consonant with their rank in the hierarchy of spiritual natures. The appearances of Gods are uniform, those of Dæmons various. The Gods shine with a benign aspect. When a God manifests himself, he frequently appears to hide sun or moon, and seems as he descends too vast for earth to contain. Archangels are at once awful and mild; Angels yet more gracious; Dæmons terrible. Below the four leading classes I have mentioned are placed the malignant Dæmons, the Anti-gods.

"Each spiritual order has gifts of its own to bestow on the initiated who evoke them. The Gods confer health of body, power and purity of mind, and, in short, elevate and restore our natures to their proper principles. Angels and Archangels have at their command only subordinate

bestowments. Dæmons, however, are hostile to the aspirant, afflict both body and mind, and hinder our escape from the sensuous. Principalities, who govern the sublunary elements, confer temporal advantages. Those of a lower rank, who preside over matter, often display their bounty in material gifts. Souls that are pure are, like Angels, salutary in their influence. Their appearance encourages the soul in its upward efforts. Heroes stimulate to great actions. All these powers depend, in a descending chain, each species on that immediately above it. Good Dæmons are seen surrounded by the emblems of blessing, Dæmons who execute judgment appear with the instruments of punishment.

"There is nothing unworthy of belief in what you have been told concerning the sacred sleep, and divination by dreams. I explain it thus:

"The soul has a twofold life, a lower and a higher. In sleep that soul is freed from the constraint of the body, and enters, as one emancipated, on its divine life of intelligence. Then, as the noble faculty which beholds the objects that truly are—the objects in the world of intelligence—stirs within, and awakens to its power, who can be surprised that the mind, which contains in itself the principles of all that happens, should, in this its state of liberation, discern the future in those antecedent principles which will make that future what it is to be? The nobler part of the soul is thus united by abstraction to higher natures, and becomes a participant in the wisdom and foreknowledge of the Gods.

"Recorded examples of this are numerous and well-authenticated; instances occur, too, every day. Numbers of sick, by sleeping in the temple of Æsculapius, have had their cure revealed to them in dreams vouchsafed by the god. Would not Alexander's army have perished but for a dream in which Dionysius pointed out the means of safety? Was not the siege of Aphutis raised through a dream sent by Jupiter Ammon to Lysander? The nighttime of the body is the day-time of the soul."

We thus see how in the process of time the principles on which the system of Plotinus rested were surrendered little by little, while **divination** and evocation were practiced with increasing frequency. Plotinus had declared the possibility of the absolute identification of the divine with human nature—the broadest possible basis for mysticism. Porphyry took up narrower ground and contended that in the union which takes place in ecstasy, we still retain consciousness of personality. Iamblichus diminished the real principle of mysticism still farther in theory, and denied that man has a faculty, eternally active and inaccessible, to passion: so that the intellectual ambition so lofty in Plotinus subsided among the followers of Iamblichus into magical practice.

Proclus was the last of the Greek Neoplatonists. He elaborated the Trinity of Plotinus into a succession of impalpable triads, and surpassed Iamblichus in his devotion to the practice of theurgy. With him, theurgy was the art which gave human beings the magical passwords that carry them through barrier after barrier, dividing species from species of the upper existences, till at the summit of the hierarchy he arrives at the highest.

Above all being is God, the Non-Being, who is apprehended only by negation. When we are raised out of our weakness and on a level with God, it seems as though reason were silenced for then we are above reason. In short we become intoxicated with God.

Proclus was an adept in the ritual of invocations among every people in the world, and a great magical figure. With the advance of Byzantinism, he represented the old world of Greek thought, and even those who wrote against him as a heathen show the influence he exercised on their doctrines. Thus Dionysius attempted to accommodate the philosophy of Proclus to Christianity, and greatly admired his asceticism.

The theology of the Neoplatonists was always in the first instance a mere matter of logic. They associated Universals with Causes. The highest became with them merely the most comprehensive.

As has been said, Neoplatonism exercised great power among the scholiasts and magicians of the Middle Ages. In fact all that medievalism knew of Plato was through the medium of the Neoplatonists. In Germany in the fourteenth century it became a vivifying principle, for although its doctrine of emanation was abandoned, its allegorical explanation, its exaltation of the spirit above the letter was retained, and Platonism and mysticism together created a party in the church—the sworn foes of scholasticism and mere lifeless orthodoxy. (See also **Divination; Greece; Meditation; Yoga**)

Recommended reading:

Brehier, Emile. *The Philosophy of Plotinus,* University of Chicago Press, 1958

Mead, G. R. S. *Essay Written as a Preface to a New Edition of T. Taylor's "Select Works of Plotinus,"* Theosophical Publishing Society, London, 1895

Rist, J. M. *Plotinus; the Road to Reality,* Cambridge University Press, U.K., 1967

Turnbull, Grace (ed.). *The Essence of Plotinus,* Greenwood Press, 1934

"Nessie"

Popular affectionate name for the Monster of Loch Ness, Scotland. In an article in *Nature* titled 'Naming the Loch Ness Monster,' naturalist Sir Peter Scott and Robert Rines bestowed the scientific name *Nessiteras rhombopteryx.*

They felt obliged to do this following the recent photographic evidence for the reality of the Monster, because a British Act of Parliament (1975) requires a scientific name for any rare species of animal qualifying for conservation. Unfortunately some newspapers gleefully pointed out that this scientific name may be converted to the anagram "Monster Hoax by Sir Peter." (For fuller information on "Nessie" see **Monsters; Loch Ness Monster**).

Nessletter (Newsletter)

Newsletter concerned with reports and news of monsters, especially the Loch Ness Monster. Published by Ness Information Service, Huntshieldford, St. Johns Chapel, Bishop Aukland, Co. Durham DL13 1RQ, England.

Nester, Marian L(ow) (1910–)

Researcher in parapsychology. Born June 8, 1910 at Jamaica Plain, Massachusetts, she studied at Smith College (B.A. 1932) and Boston University (M.Ed. 1940). In 1951 she married J. E. Nester. She was a teacher from 1933–44, staff member of United Service Organization, Travelers Aid Society from 1944–46, worked in publishing from 1946–51, free-lance editor, secretary and researcher from 1951 on, research assistant at Parapsychology Foundation 1958–62. She is an associate member of the Parapsychological Association.

Mrs. Nester worked on experiments at the Parapsychology Foundation connected with survival and mediumship, and assisted in a survey of death-bed hallucinations. Her articles include: 'New Methods of Parapsychology' (*Tomorrow,* vol. 9, No.4, 1961) and a review of Rene Sudre's book *Parapsychology* (*International Journal of Parapsychology,* vol.3, No.1 1961).

Neuburg, Victor (Benjamin) (1883–1940)

Poet, editor and associate of occultist Aleister **Crowley.** Born May 6, 1883 in Islington, London, England, he was educated at the City of London School, southwest London, and at Trinity College, Cambridge. An early Freethinker, his first poems were published in the *Agnostic Journal* and *Freethinker.* In 1892 he married Kathleen Rose Goddard.

Around 1906 at Cambridge, Neuburg came in contact with Crowley, also a poet, who had read some of Neuburg's pieces in the *Agnostic Journal.* Crowley initiated Neuburg into his secret society the **A.∴.A.∴.** giving him the name "Frater Omnia Vincam." He also initiated Neuburg into homosexuality, to enhance their joint occult powers through sex-magic.

In 1909, Crowley took Neuburg to Algiers, and they set off into the North African desert, where they performed occult rituals. Afterwards, with characteristic callousness, Crowley appears to have abandoned Neuburg in the desert. Neuburg fortunately survived.

In 1913, Crowley and Neuburg again joined forces in a homosexual ritual magic operation known as "The Paris Working." Neuburg appears to have broken with Crowley some time in 1914, before Crowley left for the U.S. on a magickal tour. Neuburg was ritually cursed by Crowley and suffered a nervous breakdown.

From 1916–19 he served in the Army in World War I. Thereafter he avoided Crowley and spent most of his time at Vine Cottage, Steyning, Sussex, where he operated a hand-printing press. Many of his poems were issued under the imprint "Vine Press." In addition to works published under his own name, he used a number of pseudonyms: Alfricobas, Benjie, M. Broyle, Richard Byrde, Christopher Crayne, Lawrence Edwardes, Arthur French, Paul Pentreath, Nicholas Pyne, Harold Stevens, Shirley Tarn, Rold White. His books included: *The Green Garland* (1908), *The Triumph of Pan* (1910), *Lillygay, an Anthology of Anonymous Poems* (1920), *Swift Wings, Songs in Sussex* (1921), *Songs of the Groves* (1921), *Larkspur, a Lyric Garland* (1922).

In 1933, Neuburg edited a section called the Poet's Corner in the British newspaper the *Sunday Referee.* This encouraged new talent by awarding weekly prizes. A group of talented young writers and poets grew up around Neuburg. He showed his excellent taste and judgment by an award to a then unknown poet named Dylan Thomas. As a result of Neuburg's enthusiasm, the publisher of the *Sunday Referee* sponsored the first book of poems by Dylan Thomas, titled *18 Poems.* The first publication is now a much prized collector's item.

Neuburg died May 31, 1940. Although a minor poet,

his work has a magical lyric quality. Known affectionately as "Vickybird," he was a generous and warmhearted friend of other writers, but his natural mystical inclinations were ruthlessly exploited by Aleister Crowley. There is an account of Neuburg in Arthur Calder-Marshall's *The Magic of My Youth* (1951), and a sympathetic biography *The Magical Dilemma of Victor Neuburg* was published by Jean Overton **Fuller** (1965).

Neumann, Thérèse (1898–1962)

Bavarian peasant girl of Konnersreuth, whose **stigmata,** vision of the Passion of Christ and other supernormal phenomena aroused world-wide attention. Born April 8, 1898, she was educated to a religious mentality and aspired to become a missionary sister. Constitutionally she appeared robust.

In March, 1918, while she aided in putting out a fire which broke out in a neighboring house by passing buckets of water up the roof, she was stricken by a violent pain in the lumbar regions and collapsed. In the hospital of Waldsassen she was seized with terrible cramp, became blind, from time to time deaf, and paralyzed, first in both legs, then in the right and left cheek. She spent miserable years at the home of her parents in constant suffering and religious meditation.

On April 29, 1923, the beatification day of St. Thérèse, she suddenly recovered her sight. On May 3, 1923 an ulcer between the toes of her left foot which might have necessitated amputation, was unaccountably healed, after she put three rose leaves from the tomb of St. Thérèse in the bandage.

On May 17, 1925, the canonization day of St. Thérèse de Lisieux, she saw a light and heard a voice which comforted and assured her that she would be able to sit up and walk. She sat up immediately and afterwards could walk about the room with the help of a stick and a supporting arm. On September 30 she dispensed with this support and went to the church alone.

In December she was seized with violent intestinal pains. An urgent operation for appendicitis was recommended. She had a vision of St. Thérèse and heard a voice which told her to go to Church and thank God. During the night the pus found a natural outlet and she was cured.

The stigmata appeared during Lent in 1926. An abscess developed in her ear, causing violent headaches. She saw in a vision Jesus in the Garden of Olives and felt a sudden stinging pain in the left side. A wound formed which bled abundantly. It was followed by stigmatic wounds in the hands and legs. There was no pus, no inflammation, but there was a fresh flow of blood every Friday. She also shed tears of blood and became, by Friday, almost blind.

With an awe-inspiring dramatic vividness she lived through the whole tragedy of the crucifixion and in ancient Aramaic (which famous linguists established as such and found more perfect than they knew it from present-day research), she reproduced the words of Christ and the vile swearing of the crowd as she clairaudiently heard them. There was no scholar who could emulate her command of this archaic language, for some of the phrases, like the words spoken by the Apostles when Jesus was betrayed do not exist in print. Her pronunciation was always phonetic and it is difficult to escape the conclusion that she was in communication with someone who was a spectator of the Passion.

At Christmas in 1922, an abscess developed in Thérèse Neumann's throat and neck. From this date until Christmas 1926, she abstained from solid food. She took a little liquid, three or four spoonfuls of coffee, tea or fruit juice. After Christmas 1926, she only took a drop of water every morning to swallow the sacred host. From September 1927 until November 1928, she abstained even from this drop of water. Nevertheless she retained her normal weight. But four Roman Catholic sisters declared on oath that during the Friday ecstasies Thérèse lost four pounds of weight which she regained by the following Thursday without taking nourishment in any form.

On August 15, 1927, Thérèse had a vision of the death, burial and ascension of Mary. She visualized Mary's tomb as at Jerusalem, and not at Ephesus as usually assumed.

In the Socialist and Communist press of Germany, Russia and Austria many libellous statements and quasi-exposures were published about Thérèse Neumann. Whenever they were followed by suits for libel the editors were found guilty and sentenced to imprisonment and fine.

Thérèse Neumann was something of an embarrassment to the Nazis during World War II, and the authorities made difficulties for visitors to Konnersreuth. After the war, hundreds of thousands of American and other servicemen queued to visit Neumann. She often gave accurate information on distant events through **out-of-the-body** travel, and appears to have traveled astrally to the death chamber of Pope Pius XII.

Although pilgrims presented many gifts to her, she would not use these for her own comfort, and before her death September 18, 1962, she had contributed to the Church a training seminary for priests, as well as a convent. During her lifetime over 133 books or papers were written about her including: R. W. Hynek, *Konnersreuth: A Medical and Psychological Study of the Case of Teresa Neumann* (1932); Frederick von Lama, *Thérèse Neumann, une stigmatisée de nos jours* (1928); K. Fahsel, *Konnersreuth: le mystère des stigmatisés* (1933); J. Danemarie, *The Mystery of Stigmata from Catherine Emmerich to Theresa Neumann* (1934). Recommended English works include: Hilda Graef, *The Case of Thérèse Neumann* (Mercier, Irish Republic, 1952); Paul Siwek, *The Riddle of Konnersreuth* (Browne & Nolan, Irish Republic, 1954), Johannes Steiner, *Thérèse Neumann; a portrait based on authentic accounts, journals, and documents* (Alba, 1967). (See also Padre **Pio; Stigmata**)

Neurypnology

James **Braid**'s first term for **hypnotism.**

New Age

A general term for the modern culture complex of organic farming, macrobiotics, environmentalism, alternative energy, unorthodox healing, meditation, spiritual development, higher consciousness, experimental communes. A related term is "holistic," implying wholeness, embracing "New Age" subjects, whole grain foods and an ambience of youth opposition to the modern consumer society and materialism.

However, there is nothing essentially new about most

New Age factors. Sensible vegetarian foods, organic gardening, whole grain bread, yoga, meditation, etc., were all pioneered by older people decades back, but their modern revival owes much to the trendiness of the mass media society and the commercial exploitation of the generation gap. Discriminating older people who were aware of the value of such things long ago will be glad to see them revived but will regret any tendency to cultishness.

The term "New Age" is now generally synonymous with **Aquarian Age,** but there are hopeful signs that its holistic aspects may become part of a general positive movement in modern society and culture rather than an eccentric counterculture. The New Age has familiarized a generation with topics and words formerly of esoteric significance, as well as a whole set of new attitudes and terms. A useful guide to this largely semantic revolution is *The New Age Dictionary* edited by Alex Jack, Kanthaka Press, Brookline, Mass., 1976. Publications of special significance in the field of New Age teachings include *East West Journal* (P.O. Box 305, Dover, New Jersey 07801) and *New Age* Journal (32 Station Street, Brookline Village, Mass. 02146). (See also **Findhorn; Lindisfarne;** William Irwin **Thompson**)

New Atlantean Journal

Quarterly publication of New Atlantean Research Society, dealing with research and discussion on Atlantis, UFO sightings and earth changes. Address: 4280 68th Avenue North, Pinellas Park, Florida 33565.

New Church, The

Religious organization devoted to the teachings of Swedish mystic Emanuel **Swedenborg** (1688–1772). The New Church embodies the writings of Swedenborg which were originally known as the Church of the New Jerusalem.

Followers of Swedenborg believe that the Second Coming of Christ took place in 1757 in the form of the revelation of Swedenborg's esoteric interpretation of the scriptures, as a fulfilment of John's vision of the New Jerusalem coming down out of heaven from God, with the declaration "Behold, I make all things new."

Salvation is regarded as deliverance from sinning itself, and hell a free choice on the part of those who prefer an evil life. Jesus is worshiped directly as Creator, Redeemer, the Word and the Revelation. Swedenborg's teachings had some influence in America through Jonathan Chapman, known as "Johnny Appleseed," a Swedenborgian who wandered through nineteenth-century settlements planting apple trees and leaving Swedenborg literature at log cabins. Some of Swedenborg's concepts passed into early American spiritual and occult cults. Andrew Jackson **Davis** (1826–1910), an American Spiritualist, claimed that Swedenborg was one of three spirits who revealed the secrets of the universe to him in 1844.

The New Church has more than forty churches in Britain, administered by a General Conference. For further information, consult The New Church Enquiry Centre, 20 Bloomsbury Way, London, WC1A 2TH. (See also **Swedenborg Society**)

New Dimensions (England)

Quarterly publication dealing with Qabalah and magical teachings in the tradition of the Golden Dawn and Dion Fortune. Address: 8 Acron Avenue, Braintree, Essex, England.

New Dimensions (Florida)

Occasional newsletter of the Florida Society for Psychical Research, Inc., dealing with Society activities and psychic topics. Address: Florida Society for Psychical Research, Inc., 2837 First Avenue North, St. Petersburg, Florida 33713.

New England Journal of Parapsychology

Quarterly journal which publishes papers from undergraduates of a college course in parapsychology. Address: Franklin Pierce College, Rindge, New Hampshire 03461.

New Existence of Man upon the Earth (Journal)

British journal founded in 1854 by socialist reformer Robert **Owen** (1771–1858), the only journal of the period concerned with **Spiritualism.** The issues included an early report on automatic writing by a child of four years, who wrote in Latin. The journal ceased publication after the death of Owen.

New Horizons (Journal)

Semi-annual journal of New Horizons Research Foundation, Canada. Contains articles on researches of the Toronto Psychical Society and other parapsychological work. Edited by Dr. A. R. G. Owen, a mathematician at the University of Toronto, who was one of the group of experimenters who created the experimental ghost **"Philip."** Address: New Horizons Research Foundation, P.O. Box 427, Station F, Toronto, Ontario, Canada M4Y 2L8.

New Horizons Newsletter

Monthly publication devoted to spiritual movements, alternate energies and related New Age subjects. Address: 1 Palomar Arcade, #124, Santa Cruz, California 95060.

New Isis Lodge

A sister-lodge of the secret occult organization **O.T.O.** (Ordo Templi Orientalis), which grew out of the Brotherhood of Light at the end of the nineteenth century. The O.T.O. was organized with ten degrees of initiation by Dr. Karl Kellner, an Austrian occultist in 1895. Its most precious secret was that of sex-magic, the techniques of utilizing the energies of sex for occult purposes.

After the death of Kellner in 1905, the head of the O.T.O. was Theodore Reuss, who was also a member of the German Secret Service, and had spied upon the Socialist League in England. Reuss concluded from reading publications of occultist Aleister **Crowley** that Crowley had discovered the secret of sex-magic, and in 1912 he invited Crowley to head a British branch of the O.T.O.

When Crowley died in 1947, Karl Germer became head of the O.T.O. and about 1951 granted a charter to Kenneth **Grant,** a Crowley enthusiast in Britain. In 1955, Grant set up the New Isis Lodge of the O.T.O. with eleven rituals. The "New" was a pun on "Nu" (or

"Nuit"), a term borrowed from Egyptian mythology, symbolizing absolute consciousness, associated with the Crowley concept of the Scarlet Woman, whose formula was "love under will." "New-Isis" or "Nu-Isis" therefore symbolized the heavenly and earthly goddess. (See also Aleister **Crowley; Golden Dawn;** Kenneth **Grant**)

New Motor, The

A strange machine constructed in 1854 by Spiritualist medium John Murray **Spear** in association with another medium Charles Hammond, at the instigation of the "Association of Electricizers," one of the bands of spirits by whom he was controlled.

The Motor was to derive its motive power from the magnetic store of nature, and was therefore to be as independent of artificial sources of energy as was the human body. The machine was hailed as the "Physical Saviour of the race," the "New Messiah," and Mrs. Alonzo Newton, wife of one of Spear's collaborators, in obedience to a vision, went to High Rock, Lynn, Massachusetts, where the New Motor was located and for two hours suffered "birth-pangs," whereby she judged that the essence of her spiritual being was imparted to the machine. At the end of that time it was claimed that pulsations were apparent in the Motor. Mrs. Newton continued to act as nurse to the contraption for several weeks, but the only observed movements seemed to be a slight oscillation of some of the metal balls which adorned it. One disappointed Spiritualist complained that the New Motor could not even turn a coffee mill.

Andrew Jackson Davis visited the New Motor at High Rock and expressed the belief that the design was the work of spirits of a mechanical turn of mind, but was of no practical value. The New Motor was finally smashed by a mob at Randolph, New York, where it had been taken. In all it cost its builder some two thousand dollars. In common fairness to the Spiritualists it must be said that Spear was widely recognized as a kind and honest man who had championed many liberal reforms. His earlier experience of spirit messages was remarkable, resulting in a healing ministry. It seems that he was deceived by misleading communications from the Association of Electricizers (which claimed to include the spirit of Benjamin Franklin).

It is possible that the New Motor fiasco may have suggested a line of research to John Worrell Keely (1837–1898), who claimed the discovery of a new motive force in his invention of the Keely Motor. This force was said to be "vibratory etheric force" or cosmic energy. After the death of Keely, evidence of fraud was revealed.

From time to time, Spiritualists have constructed various apparatus to facilitate communication with the spirit world, sometimes basing their constructions on spirit messages. Amongst modern inventors who were more successful than Spear were those comprising the group known as the Ashkir-Jobson Trianion, c. 1930, who built various apparatus which seemed to work. The psychotherapist Wilhelm Reich also claimed the discovery of a cosmic motor force in "Orgone energy." (See also **Communication; Communigraph;** John E. W. **Keeley; Orgone;** Wilhelm **Reich;** J. M. **Spear**)

New Realities Magazine

A continuation under new title of *Psychic* Magazine. Vol. 1, No. 1, of *New Realities* appeared in 1977, dedicated to a broader scope of "developments in the emergent areas of human possibilities that affect our everyday lives."

In addition to psychic phenomena and parapsychology, *New Realities* deals with "holistic health" (total approach to human well-being on physical, mental, emotional and spiritual levels), changing consciousness, different life styles in the modern world and mysticism of both East and West.

The Editor and Publisher is James G. Bolen. Address: New Realities, P.O. Box 26289, San Francisco, California 94126.

New Thought

A relatively modern religious movement which, in some of its tenets resembles faith-healing. Unlike the separate development of **Christian Science,** however, it does not affect entirely to dispense with all material medical aids such as drugs, the setting of broken bones, and so on. Nor does it give the whole credit for cures to the imagination of the patient, as in **hypnotism.** But striking a point midway between the two, it gives considerable prominence to the mind in the healing process, while not altogether despising the doctor.

Mind is considered as highly refined matter and therefore the "mind" cure is, in a measure, a material cure. It is clear that the part of the New Thought which deals with bodily healing had its roots in the **Animal Magnetism** and **Mesmerism** of bygone times. So much have they in common that it is needless to trace mental-healing as such further back than Dr. Phineas Parkhurst **Quimby** (1802–1866), the first to make use of the terms "mental-healing" and "Christian Science."

Dr. Quimby was the son of a New Hampshire blacksmith, and was himself apprenticed to a clockmaker, having had but little education. At the age of thirty-six he attended a lecture on Mesmerism, and thereafter practiced for himself. With the aid of a clairvoyant youth he cured diseases, and so successful was his treatment that he soon adopted magnetic healing as a profession.

At length, however, he got a glimpse of the true reason for his success—the expectation of the patient. The diagnoses of his clairvoyant he attributed to the latter's telepathic reading of the patient's own thoughts, and he judged that the treatment prescribed depended for its efficacy on the confidence it inspired rather than on its intrinsic merits. From this point he gradually evolved his doctrine that disease was a mere delusion, a traditional error that had fixed itself in men's minds, which it behoved them to be rid of as soon as might be. The way to cure disease, therefore, was to destroy the error on which it rested.

Besides Christian Science, Quimby called his doctrine the Science of Health, or the Science of Health and Happiness. He had many disciples, among whom were Mrs. Mary Baker G. **Eddy,** the founder of the Christian Science Church. Others whose influence was felt more in the direction of the New Thought movement were the Rev. W. F. Evans and Mr. and Mrs. Julius Dresser, whose son, Horatio W. Dresser, remained one of the ablest exponents of the New Thought.

As has been said, the method of healing practiced by this school is not considered to be entirely immaterial. It is no longer believed that a fluid emanates from the fingertips of the operator, or that he radiates a luminous odic force (see **Od**), but Mr. Dresser himself stated that the communication was of a vibratory character, made up of ethereal undulations directed and concentrated by the thought of the healer. The power was equally efficacious at a distance and could be used without the patient's knowledge or even against his will.

This belief in action at a distance became a problem for the New Thinker, who feared the ascendancy of an evil influence much as the superstitious of the Middle Ages feared bewitchment. But there is a spiritual aspect of the New Thought as well as a physical one. The health of the soul is as fully considered as the health of the body. Spiritual sanity, then, is to be procured by lifting oneself to a higher plane of existence, by shutting out the things of the earth and living "in tune with the infinite." We must realize our own identity with the Infinite Spirit and open our lives to the Divine inflow. Ralph Waldo Trine, himself a New Thinker, stated in an expressive metaphor, "To recognize our own divinity and our intimate relation to the Universal, is to attach the belt of our machinery to the power-house of the Universe." In short, we must have sufficient self-confidence to cast our fears aside and rise unfettered into the Infinite.

Other influential individuals in the New Thought movement include Emmet Fox (who developed his own interpretation of Christianity), Charles and Myrtle Fillmore, Ernest Holmes, Prentice Mulford, Thomas Troward (famous for his *Edinburgh Lectures on Mental Science*), Frederick Bailes (director of the Science of Mind Church), the Rev. David Thompson, Norman Vincent Peale (author of *The Power of Positive Thinking*), Bishop Fulton J. Sheen, Rabbi Joseph Liebman, Lewis Dunnington and Gleen Clark.

In modern times, New Thought exists both as a religious movement of organized and independent churches, and as a secular principle expounded by independent authors. The organized church groupings are: United Churches of Religious Science, Unity Churches, Divine Science Churches, International Churches of Religious Science, Independent New Thought Churches.

An international New Thought Alliance has affirmed a declaration of New Thought principles as follows:

We affirm the inseparable oneness of God and man, the realization of which comes through spiritual intuition, the implications of which are that man can reproduce the Divine perfection in his body, emotions, and in all his external affairs.

We affirm the freedom of each person in matters of belief.

We affirm the Good to be supreme, universal, and eternal.

We affirm that the Kingdom of Heaven is within us, that we are one with the Father, that we should love one another, and return good for evil.

We affirm that we should heal the sick through prayer, and that we should endeavor to manifest perfection "even as our Father in Heaven is perfect."

We affirm our belief in God as the Universal Wisdom, Love, Life, Truth, Power, Peace, Beauty, and Joy, "in whom we live, move, and have our being."

We affirm that man's mental states are carried forward into manifestation and become his experience through the Creative Law of Cause and Effect.

We affirm that the Divine Nature expressing Itself through man manifests Itself as health, supply, wisdom, love, life, truth, power, peace, beauty and joy.

We affirm that man is an invisible spiritual dweller within a human body, continuing and unfolding as a spiritual being beyond the change called physical death.

We affirm that the universe is the body of God, spiritual in essence, governed by God through laws which are spiritual in reality even when material in appearance. (See also **Christian Science; Mary M. B. Eddy;** Psychic **Healing; Healing by Faith; Mind Cure;** Prentice **Mulford;** Phineas P. **Quimby**)

Recommended reading:

Beebe, Tom. *Who's Who in New Thought,* CSA Press, Lakemount, Georgia, 1977

Braden, Charles S. *Spirits in Rebellion,* Southern Methodist University Press, Dallas, 1963

Collier, Robert. *The Secret of the Ages,* Collier Publications, Tarrytown, N.Y., 1954 etc.

Dresser, Horatio W. (ed.). *The Quimby Manuscripts,* Julian Press, 1961

Dresser, Horatio W. *The Spirit of New Thought,* Thomas Y. Crowell, 1917

Fillmore, Charles & Cora Fillmore. *Twelve Powers of Man,* Unity School of Christianity, Missouri, 1943

Fillmore, Myrtle. *How to Let God Help You,* Unity School of Christianity, Missouri, 1956

Fox, Emmet. *Power Through Constructive Thinking,* Harper & Bros., 1946; Harper & Row, 1940 etc.

Goldsmith, Joel S. *The Art of Spiritual Healing,* Harper & Bros., 1959

Holmes, Ernest S. *Complete Course of Lessons in the Science of Mind and Spirit,* Dodd, Mead, 1926 etc.

Judah, J. Stillson. *The History and Philosophy of the Metaphysical Movements in America,* Westminster Press, Philadelphia, 1967

Larson, Christian D. *The Creative Power of Mind,* privately printed, Los Angeles, 1930

Meyer, Donald. *The Positive Thinkers,* Doubleday, 1965

Mulford, Prentice. *Your Forces and How to Use Them,* White Cross Library, F. J. Needham, New York, 1888–92.

Murphy, Joseph. *The Miracles of Your Mind,* Willing Publishing Co., San Gabriel, California, 1953 etc.

Peale, Norman Vincent. *The Power of Positive Thinking,* Prentice-Hall, 1952 etc.; Fawcett paperback, 1976

Podmore, Frank. *Mesmerism and Christian Science,* Metheun, London, 1909

Trine, Ralph Waldo. *In Tune With the Infinite,* Thomas Y. Crowell, 1897 etc.; Dodd, Mead, 1921; Bobbs Merrill paperback, 1970

Troward, Thomas. *The Edinburgh Lectures on Mental Science,* London, 1904; Dodd, Mead, 1904

Troward, Thomas. *The Hidden Power and Other Papers on Mental Science,* Dodd, Mead, 1917, 1958

Wilbur, Sybil. *The Life of Mary Baker Eddy,* The Christian Science Publishing Co., 1907

New Thought Magazine

Quarterly journal concerned with New Thought and religion; includes directory of affiliated organizations. Address: New Thought Alliance, 6922 Hollywood Boulevard, Los Angeles, California 90028.

New Ways of Consciousness Foundation

Founded by Alan Vaughan, a former editor of *Psychic* magazine, to develop consciousness technology and encourage consciousness research. The Foundation was opened in June 1979 and contains a library on consciousness research. Address: 3188 Washington Street, San Francisco, California 94115.

New York Circle

The first experimental Spiritualist organization in America. It was an exclusive body in the initial stages, later broadening its membership.

The principal medium was Edward P. **Fowler,** who had sat with Kate and Margaretta **Fox.** Mr. Fowler provided premises for the use of the group. Early members included John W. Edmonds, Dr. J. B. Gray, Charles Partridge, Dr. & Mrs. Warner, Dr. and Mrs. R. T. Hallock, Robert T. Shannon, W. J. Baner, Dr. Hull, Miss Fowler, Professor Bush, Rev. S. B. Britain and Almon Roff. At one sitting of the circle, the medium Henry Gordon demonstrated the feat of floating in the air, in the presence of many unimpeachable witnesses.

At the initiative of the Circle, the New York Conference was established in November 1851, providing a focal point for the growing Spiritualist movement. (See also **Spiritualism**)

NEW ZEALAND

Maori Superstitions

"Spirits of the dead" played a very prominent part in Maori tradition. The priests or "Tohungas" were unmistakably mediums in the modern sense of the term. Sometimes they were born with their gift, sometimes they were devoted to the priestly office by their parents and acquired their power after the fashion of Eastern ecstatics, by prayer, fasting and contemplation. That good prophets existed amongst the Maoris has been abundantly proved. During the time when Great Britain busied herself in colonizing New Zealand, her officials frequently wrote home that the Maori would never be conquered wholly. Information of the parties sent out to attack them, the very color of the boats and the hour when they would arrive, the number of the enemy, and all particulars essential to their safety were invariably communicated to the tribes beforehand by their Tohungas, or prophets.

The best natural prophets and seers amongst the Maoris were of the female sex, and although the missionaries tried to account for the marvelous powers they exhibited above all for the sound of the spirit voice, which is a common phase in their communion with the dead—on the hypothesis that the women who practiced "the arts of sorcery," were ventriloquists, this attempted explanation rarely covered the ground of the intelligence received.

In his book *Old New Zealand* (1863), F. E. Maning cited an interesting case of Tohungaism. A certain young chief had been appointed Registrar of births and deaths, when he suddenly came to a violent end. The book of registries was lost, and much inconvenience ensued. The man's relatives notified their intention of invoking his spirit, and invited General Cummings to be present at the ceremony, an invitation which he accepted.

"The appointed time came. Fires were lit. The Tohunga repaired to the darkest corner of the room. All was silent, save the sobbing of the sisters of the deceased warrior-chief. There were thirty of us, sitting on the rush-strewn floor, the door shut and the fire now burning down to embers. Suddenly there came a voice out from the partial darkness, 'Salutation, salutation to my family, to my tribe, to you, pakeha, my friend!' Our feelings were taken by storm. The oldest sister screamed, and rushed with extended arms in the direction from whence the voice came. Her brother, seizing, restrained her by main force. Others exclaimed, 'Is it you? Is it you? Truly it is you! aue! aue!' and fell quite insensible upon the floor. The older women and some of the aged men were not moved in the slightest degree, though believing it to be the spirit of the chief.

"Whilst reflecting upon the novelty of the scene, the 'darkness visible' and the deep interest manifest, the spirit spoke again, 'Speak to me my family; speak to me, my tribe: speak to me, the pakeha!' At last the silence gave way, and the brother spoke: 'How is it with you? Is it well with you in that country?' The answer came, though not in the voice of the Tohunga-medium, but in strange sepulchral sounds: 'It is well with me; my place is a good place. I have seen our friends; they are all with me!' A woman from another part of the room now anxiously cried out, 'Have you seen my sister?' 'Yes, I have seen her; she is happy in our beautiful country.' 'Tell her my love so great for her will never cease.' 'Yes, I will bear the message.' Here the native woman burst into tears, and my own bosom swelled in sympathy.

"The spirit speaking again, giving directions about property and keepsakes, I thought I would more thoroughly test the genuineness of all this: and I said, 'We cannot find your book with the registered names; where have you concealed it?' The answer came instantly, 'I concealed it between the tahuhu of my house, and the thatch; straight over you, as you go in at the door.' The brother rushed out to see. All was silence. In five minutes he came hurriedly back, with the book in his hand! It astonished me.

"It was now late, and the spirit suddenly said, 'Farewell my family, farewell, my tribe; I go.' Those present breathed an impressive farewell, when the spirit cried out again, from high in the air, 'Farewell!'

"This, though seemingly tragical, is in every respect literally true. But what is that? ventriloquism, the devil, or what! . . ."

Mrs. Emma Hardinge Britten stated in her book *Nineteenth Century Miracles* (1883): "The author has herself had several proofs of the Mediumistic power possessed by these 'savages' but as her experiences may be deemed of too personal a character, we shall select our examples from other sources. One of these is furnished by a Mr. Marsden, a person who was well-known in the early days of New Zealand's colonial history, as a miner, who grew rich 'through spiritual communications.' Mr. Marsden was a gentleman who had spent much time amongst the Maoris, and who still keeps a residence in 'the King country,' that is—the district of which they hold control.

"Mr. Marsden informed the author, that his success as a gold miner, was entirely due to a communication he had received through a native woman who claimed to have the power of bringing down spirits—the Maoris, be it remembered, always insisting that the spirits descend through the air to earth to visit mortals.

"Mr. Marsden had long been prospecting unsuccessfully in the gold regions. He had a friend in partnership with him, to whom he was much attached, but who had been accidentally killed by a fall from a cliff.

"The Spirit of this man came unsolicited, on an occasion when Mr. Marsden was consulting a native seeress, for the purpose of endeavouring to trace out what had become of a valuable watch which he had lost.

"The voice of the Spirit was first heard in the air, apparently above the roof of the hut in which they sat, calling Mr. Marsden by his familiar name of 'Mars.' Greatly startled by these sounds, several times repeated, at the Medium's command, he remained perfectly still until the voice of his friend speaking in his well-remembered Scotch accent sounded close to his ear, whilst a column of grey misty substance reared itself by his side. This apparition was plainly visible in the subdued light of the hut, to which there was only one open entrance, but no window. Though he was much startled by what he saw and heard, Mr. Marsden had presence of mind enough to gently *put his hand through the misty column* which remained intact, as if its substance offered no resistence to the touch. Being admonished by an earnest whisper from the Maori woman, who had fallen on her knees before the apparition, to keep still, he obeyed, when a voice—seemingly from an immense distance off—yet speaking unmistakably in his friend's Scotch accents, advised him to let the watch alone—for it was irreparably gone—but to go to the stream on the banks of which they had last had a meal together trace it up for six miles and a half, and then, by following its course amidst the forest, he would come to a *pile* which would make him rich, if he chose to remain so.

"Whilst he was waiting and listening breathlessly to hear more, Mr. Marsden was startled by a slight detonation at his side. Turning his head he observed that the column of mist was gone, and in its place, a quick flash, like the reflection of a candle, was all that he beheld. Here the seance ended, and the astonished miner left the hut, convinced that he had heard the Spirit of his friend talking to him. He added, that he followed the directions given implicitly, and came to a mass of surface gold lying on the stones at the bottom of the brook in the depth of the forest. This he gathered up, and though he prospected for several days in and about that spot, he never found another particle of this precious metal. That which he had secured he added, with a deep sigh, was indeed enough to have made him independent for life, had it not soon been squandered in fruitless speculations."

"Many degrees of superstition exist among the Maoris," stated a writer in the *Pall Mall Gazette*, "In the recesses of the Urewera country for example, diablerie has lost little of its early potency; the *tohunga* there remains a power in the land. Among the more enlightened natives a precautionary policy is generally followed; it is always wiser and safer, they say, to avoid conflict with the two mysterious powers *tapu* and *makuta*. Tapu is the less dangerous of the two; a house, an individual, or an article may be rendered tapu, or sacred, and if the tapu be disregarded harm will befall someone. But makuta is a powerful evil spell cast for the deliberate purpose of accomplishing harm, generally to bring about death. The *tohunga* is understood to be in alliance with the spirits of the dead. The Maori dreads death, and he fears the dead. Places of burial are seldom approached during the day, never at night. The spirits of the dead are believed to linger sometimes near places of burial. Without going to experts in Maori lore, who have many and varied theories to set forth, a preferable course is to discover what the average Maori of to-day thinks and believes respecting the strange powers and influences he deems are at work in the world around him.

"A Maori of this type—who can read and write, is under forty years of age, and fairly intelligent—was drawn into a lengthy conversation with the writer. He believed, magistrates notwithstanding, that *tohungas*, somehow, had far more power than ordinary men. He did not think they got that power from the 'tiapo' (the devil?); they just were able to make themselves masters of men and of many things in the world. There are many degrees of Tohungaism. An ordinary man or woman was powerless against a *tohunga*, but one *tohunga* could overcome another. The speaker knew of an instance of one *tohunga* driving the tohunga power entirely out of a weaker rival. It was a fairly recent east coast occurrence. Three Maoris had accidentally permitted their pigs to trespass into the *tohunga's* potato paddock, and much damage and loss was the result. The *tohunga* was one of the dangerous type, and being very wroth, he *makutued* the three men, all of whom promptly died. Nobody was brave enough to charge the *tohunga* with causing the death of the men; they were all afraid of this terrible *makuta*. At length another *tohunga* was heard of, one of very great power. This oracle was consulted, and he agreed to deal effectively with *tohunga* number one, and punish him for killing the owner of the pigs. So, following his instructions, the first-mentioned individual was seized, and much against his will, was conveyed to the home of the greater magician. Many Maoris, it should be known, stand in awe of hot water, they will not handle it, even for purposes connected with cooking or cleaning. Into a large tub of hot water the minor *tohunga* struggling frantically, was placed, then he was given a page torn from a Bible, which he was ordered to chew and swallow. The hot water treatment, combined with the small portion of the white man's sacred volume, did the expected work; the man was no longer a *tohunga*, and fretting over his lost powers, he soon afterwards died."

Spiritualism in New Zealand

Amongst the earliest investigators in Dunedin was Mr. John Logan. Before he had become publicly identified with the cause of Spiritualism, an association had been formed, the members of which steadily pursued their investigations in private circles and semi-public gatherings.

One of the most marked events in connection with the early development of Spiritualism in Dunedin, however, was the arraignment and church trial of Mr. Logan, the circumstances of which may be briefly summed up as follows. This gentleman, although holding a high position in the first Presbyterian church of the city, had attended circles and witnessed Spiritualistic phenomena and it was currently reported that one of his own near relatives was a very remarkable medium. On March 19, 1873, Mr. Logan was summoned to appear before a Church Convocation, to be held for the purpose of trying his case, and if necessary, dealing with his "delinquency." Mr. Logan was in the event deprived of his church membership.

In many of the principal towns besides Dunedin, circles held at first in mere idle curiosity, produced their usual fruit of mediumistic power, and this again was extended into associative action, and organization into local societies. For over a year, the Spiritualists and Liberalists of Dunedin secured the services of Charles Bright as their lecturer. This gentleman had once been attached to the editorial staff of the *Melbourne Argus,* and had obtained a good reputation as a capable writer, and liberal thinker.

Mr. Bright's lectures in Dunedin were highly appreciated, and by their scholarly style and attractive manner, served to band together the liberal element in the city.

In Auckland, the principal town of the North Island, the same good service was rendered to the cause of religious thought by the addresses of the Rev. Mr. Edgar, a clergyman whose Spiritualist doctrines had tended to sever him from sectarian organizations, and draw around him, the Spiritualists of the town.

Besides the good work effected by these gentlemen, the occasional visits of well-known personalities like the Rev. J. M. Peebles, and J. Tyerman, and the effect of the many private circles held in every portion of the islands, tended to promote a general, although quiet, diffusion of Spiritual thought and doctrine, throughout New Zealand.

In 1879, a lecture tour by Mrs. Emma Hardinge Britten gave a powerful impetus to public interest and discussion concerning Spiritualism and its doctrines.

By 1930, the Spiritualist Church of New Zealand in Wellington had branches throughout New Zealand. One of the most prominent mediums was Miss Pearl **Judd,** who demonstrated direct voice phenomena in full light.

Psychical Research

One prominent New Zealand personality in the field of psychical research was the entomologist R. J. Tillyard, who in 1926 became vice-president of the National Laboratory of Psychical Research in England.

At the present time, there is an Auckland Psychical Research Society (P.O. Box 5894, Wellesley Street) and a Churches' Fellowship for Psychical and Spiritual Studies, as well as a Federation of Spiritual Healers. There is also a UFO Research Group at Auckland University.

Newbold, William Romaine (1865–1926)

Educator, psychologist and investigator in the field of psychic science. Born November 20, 1865 at Wilmington, Delaware, he studied at University of Pennsylvania (B.A. 1887, Ph.D. 1891), graduate study at University of Berlin 1891–92, and University of Pennsylvania (Hon. LL.D. 1921). In 1896 he married Ethel Kent Sprague Packard. He was a member of the faculty of the University of Pennsylvania for thirty-seven years, and was Adam Seybert Professor of Intellectual and Moral Philosophy from 1907–26.

He was an authority on European politics, archaeology, genealogy, Oriental languages and Greek philosophy. He became famous for his achievement in deciphering a medieval manuscript which he showed to be the work of Roger Bacon, and for his translation of Semitic scrawls on the walls of the Roman catacombs.

He was a member of the American Philosophical Association, the American Philosophical Society, the American Psychological Association, the Society for Psychical Research, London, and the American Society for Psychical Research. He was deeply interested in psychical research and contributed a number of important articles on the subject to the *Journal* and *Proceedings* of the ASPR and the SPR.

He died September 26, 1926 at Philadelphia, Pennsylvania.

Newbrough, Dr. John Ballou (1828–1891)

New York dentist, clairvoyant and clairaudient from childhood, automatic writer and painter. He could paint in total darkness with both hands at once. It was claimed that closing his eyes he could read printed pages of any book in any library, that he could bring back recollections of astral travels (see **astral projection**) and that under control he could lift enormous weights, even a ton, without apparent effort.

He is chiefly remembered in Spiritualism for **OAHSPE,** *A Kosmon Bible in the Words of Jehovah and his Angel Ambassadors,* first published in 1882 in New York. It is a new Bible purporting to come from the higher heavens, and "to have been directed and looked over by God, the creator's chief representative in the heavens of this earth." In a letter dated January 21, 1883, Dr. Newbrough wrote to the editor of the *Banner of Light:*

"I was crying for the light of Heaven. I did not desire communication from friends or relatives or information about earthly things; I wished to learn something about the spirit world; what the angels did, how they travelled, and the general plan of the universe. . . . I was directed to get a typewriter which writes by keys, like a piano. This I did and I applied myself industriously to learn it, but with only indifferent success. For two years more the angels propounded to me questions relative to heaven and earth, which no mortal could answer very intelligently. . . .

"One morning the light struck both my hands on the back, and they went for the typewriter for some fifteen minutes very vigorously. I was told not to read what was printed, and I have worked myself into such a religious fear of losing this new power that I obeyed reverently. The next morning, also before sunrise, the same power came and wrote (or printed rather) again. Again I laid the matter away very religiously, saying little about it to anybody. One morning I accidentally (seemed accidental to me) looked out of the window and beheld the line of light that rested on my hands extending heavenward like a telegraph wire towards the sky. Over my head were three pairs of hands, fully materialised; behind me stood another angel with her hands on my shoulders. My looking did not disturb the scene, my hands kept right on printing . . . printing. For fifty weeks this continued, every morning, half an hour or so before sunrise, and then it ceased, and I was told to read and publish the book *Oahspe.* The peculiar drawings in Oahspe were made with pencil in the same way."

Newcomb, Simon (1835–1909)

Astronomer, mathematician, first president (1885–86) of the American Society for Psychical Research. Born March 12, 1835 at Wallace, Nova Scotia, he studied at Lawrence Scientific School, Harvard University (B.S. 1858). In 1863 he married Mary Caroline Hassler.

He was professor of mathematics, U.S. Navy in 1861, assigned to the U.S. Naval Observatory 1897; Director of the American Nautical Almanac 1877–97, professor of mathematics and astronomy at Johns Hopkins University from 1884–94.

A world famous astronomer and mathematician, Dr. Newcomb's researches made possible the construction of accurate lunar tables. In spite of his interest in psychical research, he remained something of a skeptic. His viewpoint is explained in his *Reminiscences of an Astronomer* (1903). He died July 11, 1909.

News, The

A British journal devoted to "Fortean data," i.e., strange phenomena, curiosities, prodigies, portents, coincidences and mysteries in the spirit of the late Charles **Fort,** who first correlated and studied such things. Vol. 1, No. 1, of *The News* was published November 1973. From No. 16 (June 1976) onwards, the title was changed to *Fortean Times.* Published by Robert J. M. Rickard, Fortean Times, 96 Mansfield Road, London NW3 2HX, England. (See also **INFO**)

Newsletter of the Parapsychology Foundation

Former publication of the **Parapsychology Foundation** (29 West 57 Street, New York, N.Y. 10019) which appeared as a bimonthly, giving news in the field of parapsychology and psychical research with world coverage, from vol. 1 (1956) through vol. 16 (1969), when it was subsumed in **Parapsychology Review.** Back issues of the Newsletter available from the Parapsychology Foundation.

Newspaper Tests

Ingenious experiments devised by seance-room communicators to exclude **telepathy** as an explanation. The Rev. C. Drayton **Thomas** in *Some Recent Evidence for Survival* (1922) published many remarkable instances as recorded in sittings with the medium Mrs. Osborne **Leonard.**

The method of the communicators was to give in the afternoon names and dates that were to be published in certain columns of next day's *The Times* newspaper, or, if so requested, in coming issues of magazines. The information so obtained was immediately posted to the **Society for Psychical Research,** London. The results when verified were so much more striking since neither the editor nor the compositor in the offices of *The Times* could tell at the hour when the communication was made what text would occupy the column mentioned in the next edition.

The following tests were given on February 13, 1920:

The first page of the paper, in column two and near the top the name of a minister with whom your father was friendly at Leek. (Perks was found, a name which was verified from an old diary.)

Lower in this column, say one quarter down, appears his name, your own, your mother's and that of an aunt; all four within the space of two inches. (John and Charles were correctly found, then came the name Emile Souret which presumably suggested Emily and Sarah, his aunt and mother.)

Near these the word "Grange." (It was not found.)

In column one, not quite half-way down, is a name which is your mother's maiden name or one very like it. (The maiden name was *Dore,* the name found *Dorothea.*)

Somewhat above that is named a place where your mother passed some years of her girlhood. (Hants. Correct. Shirley, where she spent her girlhood, being in Hampshire.)

Close to the foregoing is a name, which suggests an action one might make with the body in jumping. (Cummock, a bad pun: come knock.)

Towards the bottom of the column one is named a place where you went to school. (Lincolnshire. Correct.)

There is a word close by which looks to your father like Cheadle. (Not found.)

Higher in column one, say two-thirds down, is a name suggesting ammunition. (Found the ecclesiastical title Canon.)

Between that and the teacher's name is a place-name, French, looking like three words hyphened into one. (Braine-le-Chateau.)

About the middle of this page, the middle both down and across, is a mistake in print; it cannot be right. Some wrong letters inserted or something left out, some kind of mistake just there. (The word "page" printed imperfectly: "Paae.")

Out of the items in this test, two entirely failed, the others forecast at 3 p.m. the day previous to the publication of the paper were correct. At 6 p.m. a copy of this test was posted to the Society for Psychical Research. Inquiries at *The Times* revealed the fact that in some cases the particular notices referred to might have already been set up in type at the time of the sitting, in other cases they were probably not set up and in any case their ultimate position on the page could not be normally known until late in the afternoon.

By the spirit of his father the following explanation was furnished to the Rev. C. Drayton Thomas: "These tests have been devised by others in a more advanced sphere than mine, and I have caught their ideas. I am not yet aware exactly how one obtains these tests, and have wondered whether the higher guides exert some influence whereby a suitable advertisement comes into position on the convenient date. I am able to sense what appear to me to be sheets and slips of paper with names and various information upon them. I notice suitable items and, afterwards, visualise a duplicate of the page with these items falling into their places. At first I was unable to do this. It seems to me that it is an ability which throws some light upon foretelling, a visualising of what is to be, but based upon that which already is. Sometimes I see further detail upon visualising which I had not sensed from the letters. I think there is an etheric foreshadowing of things about to be done. It would probably be impossible to get anything very far ahead, but only within a certain number of hours, and I cannot say how many. I scarcely think it would be possible to get a test for the day after the morrow, or, even if possible, that it could result in more than a jumble of the morrow's with a few of the day following. I think they should impress people more than book tests. It becomes clear that telepathy cannot explain; you find in the paper that for which you seek, but given in a form which you did not expect and about which you could, in the nature of the case, have known nothing. Two sets of memory are combined to produce them, my memories of long ago, and my memory of what I found this morning about preparations for the Press." (See also **Book Tests; Prediction; Prevision**)

Newton, Dr. J. R. (1810–1883)

American healing medium. He began his healing career in 1855 and is said to have cured thousands of sufferers from a variety of ailments. However, he cured only a few of the many who came to him.

He claimed to be aided by Christ and other spirits. He usually healed in large halls or other areas with space to move about in and used to handle patients, often giving a sufferer a push and telling him he was cured, which he usually was. He gave most of his healing free. Many of his cures were reliably recorded both in the United States and in England, which he visited the first time in 1870.

Nganga

Members of the **Ndembo** secret society of the Lower Congo. *Nganga*—literally "the knowing ones"—is a term applied to those who have passed certain curious rites to distinguish them from the *Vanga* or uninitiated. (See also **Ndembo**)

NICAP

Initialism for **National Investigations Committee on Aerial Phenomena,** founded in the U.S. in 1956 to investigate unidentified flying objects (see also **UFO**).

Nichusch

Cabalistic term for prophetic indication, in accordance with the view that all events and natural happenings have a secret connection, and interact upon one another. It was believed that practically everything could become an object of soothsaying—the flight of birds, movement of clouds, cries of animals, events happening to man, and so on. Man himself might become *Nichusch* by saying that if such and such a thing took place it would be a good or a bad omen. (See also **Divination; Kabala**)

"Nick" or "Old Nick"

A well-known British nickname for the Devil, comparable with the American "Mr. Splitfoot" or "Old Scratch." It seems probable that this name is derived from the Dutch *Nikken,* the devil, which again comes from the Anglo-Saxon *næc-an,* to slay, deriving from the theological view that the devil was "a murderer from the beginning."

In northern countries there is a river spirit named "Neck," "Nikke," or "Nokke," of the same nature as the water Kelpie and the Merman or Triton. (See also **"Old Scratch"; "Splitfoot"**)

Nicol, Betty (Elizabeth) Humphrey (Mrs. J. Fraser Nicol) (1917–)

Psychologist and parapsychologist. Born June 7, 1917 at Indianapolis, Indiana, she studied at Earlham College, Richmond, Indiana (B.A. philosophy 1940), and Duke University, Durham, North Carolina (Ph.D. psychology 1946). She was visiting research fellow (psychology) at Radcliffe College, Cambridge, Massachusetts from 1957–58. In 1955 she married parapsychologist J. Fraser **Nicol.**

Mrs. Nicol collaborated in parapsychology experiments with her husband, with J. B. **Rhine,** J. G. **Pratt,** E. A. **McMahan.** She also undertook a detailed analysis of published precognition cases in order to ascertain optimal psychological and physical conditions for spontaneous precognition. This project was sponsored by a grant from the Parapsychology Foundation. She has contributed articles to the *Journal of Parapsychology* and is author of the publication *Handbook of Tests in Parapsychology* (1948).

Nicol, J(ohn) Fraser

Contemporary parapsychologist. Born in Edinburgh, Scotland, he was educated at Heriot's School, Edinburgh and Heriot-Watt College, Edinburgh University. In 1955 he married Betty M. Humphrey.

He was a researcher member of the Society for Psychical Research, London from 1934–51, research associate at Parapsychology Laboratory, Duke University, Durham, North Carolina from 1951–52, research grantee, Parapsychology Foundation from 1954 onwards, research associate of American Society for Psychical Research from 1960–63. Member of American Statistical Association, corresponding member of the Society for Psychical Research, London (council member from 1948–57).

Mr. Nicol's researches and experiments have included telepathy, psychokinesis, precognition with falling dice, paranormal cognition in relation to personality factors, spontaneous psychical phenomena, paranormal communication. He has also collaborated with his wife on various experiments and reports. His articles in the *Proceedings* of the Society for Psychical Research include: 'Some Experiments in Willed Dice-Throwing' (with W. W. **Carington**) and 'In Memoriam: Whately Carington' (vol. 48, 1947), in the SPR *Journal:* 'The Fox Sisters and the Development of Spiritualism' (vol. 34, 1948), 'Randomness: The Background and Some New Investigations' (vol. 38, 1955), in the ASPR *Journal:* 'The Exploration of ESP and Human Personality' (with Betty Humphrey, vol. 47, 1953), 'The Feeling of Success in ESP' (with Betty Nicol, vol. 52, 1968), in *International Journal of Parapsychology:* 'The Statistical Controversy in Quantitative Research' (vol. 1, 1959), 'Apparent Spontaneous Precognition' (vol. 3, 1961), in *Tomorrow:* 'Buried Alive—Saved by Telepathy' (with Betty Nicol, vol. 5, 1957), 'Keeping Up with the Joneses' (vol. 8, 1960). He contributed a paper on 'Some Difficulties in the Way of Scientific Recognition of Extrasensory Perception' to the book *Ciba Symposium on Extrasensory Perception* (1956) and collaborated with Betty Nicol on the report 'Experimental Uses of Chemical Compounds' published in *Proceedings of Two Conferences on Parapsychology and Pharmacology* (1961).

Nicolai, Christoph Friedrich (1733–1811)

German critic, novelist and bookseller of Berlin, who was of special interest from the occult point of view because of his peculiar experiences which he described in his account read before the Royal Society of Berlin. The case is one of the most celebrated in the annals of psychology. His own account is as follows:

"In the first two months of the year 1791," he stated, "I was much affected in my mind by several incidents of a very disagreeable nature; and on the 24th of February a circumstance occurred which irritated me extremely. At ten o'clock in the forenoon my wife and another person came to console me; I was in a violent perturbation of mind, owing to a series of incidents which had altogether wounded my moral feelings, and from which I saw no possibility of relief, when suddenly I observed at the distance of ten paces from me a figure—the figure of a deceased person. I pointed at it, and asked my wife whether she did not see it. She saw nothing, but being much alarmed, endeavoured to compose me, and sent for the physician. The figure remained some seven or eight minutes, and at length I became a little more calm, and as I was extremely exhausted, I soon afterwards fell into a troubled kind of slumber, which lasted for half an hour. The vision was ascribed to the great agitation of mind in which I had been, and it was supposed I should have nothing more to apprehend from that cause, but the violent affection had put my nerves into some unnatural state. From this arose further consequences, which require a more detailed description.

"In the afternoon, a little after four o'clock, the figure which I had seen in the morning again appeared. I was alone when this happened, a circumstance which, as may be easily conceived, could not be very agreeable. I went therefore to the apartment of my wife, to whom I related it. But thither also the figure pursued me. Sometimes it was present, sometimes it vanished, but it was always the same standing figure. A little after six o'clock several stalking figures also appeared, but they had no connection with the standing figure. I can assign no other cause for this apparition than that, though much more composed in my mind, I had not been able so soon entirely to forget the cause of such deep and distressing vexation, and had reflected on the consequences of it, in order, if possible, to avoid them; and that this happened three hours after dinner, at the time when digestion just begins.

"At length I became more composed with respect to the disagreeable incident which had given rise to the first apparition, but though I had used very excellent medicines and found myself in other respects perfectly well, yet the apparitions did not diminish, but on the contrary rather increased in number, and were transformed in the most extraordinary manner.

"The figure of the deceased person never appeared to me after the first dreadful day, but several other figures showed themselves afterwards very distinctly, sometimes such as I knew, mostly, however, of persons I did not know, and amongst those known to me, were the semblance of both living and deceased persons, but mostly the former, and I made the observation, that acquaintance with whom I daily conversed never appeared to me as phantasms; it was always such as were at a distance.

"It is also to be noted, that these figures appeared to me at all times, and under the most different circumstances, equally distinct and clear. Whether I was alone, or in company, by broad daylight equally as in the night-time, in my own as well as in my neighbour's house; yet when I was at another person's house, they were less frequent, and when I walked the public street they very seldom appeared. When I shut my eyes, sometimes the figures disappeared, sometimes they remained even after I had closed them. If they vanished in the former case, on opening my eyes again, nearly the same figures appeared which I had seen before.

"I sometimes conversed with my physician and my wife concerning the phantasms which at the time hovered around me; for in general the forms appeared oftener in motion than at rest. They did not always continue present—they frequently left me altogether, and again appeared for a short or longer space of time, singly or more at once; but, in general, several appeared together. For the most part I saw human figures of both sexes. They commonly passed to and fro as if they had no connection with each other, like people at a fair where all is bustle. Sometimes they appeared to have business with one another. Once or twice I saw amongst them persons on horseback, and dogs and birds; these figures all appeared to me in their natural size, as distinctly as if they had existed in real life, with the several tints on the uncovered parts of the body, and with all the different kinds and colours of clothes. But I think, however, that the colours were somewhat *paler* than they are in nature.

"None of the figures had any distinguishing characteristic, they were neither terrible, ludicrous, nor repulsive; most of them were ordinary in their appearance—some were even agreeable.

"On the whole, the longer I continued in this state, the more did the number of the phantasms increase, and the apparitions became more frequent. About four weeks afterwards I began to hear them speak. Sometimes the phantasms spoke with one another, but for the most part they addressed themselves to me, these speeches were in general short, and never contained anything disagreeable.

Intelligent and respected friends often appeared to me, who endeavoured to console me in my grief, which still left deep traces on my mind. This speaking I heard most frequently when I was alone; though I sometimes heard it in company, intermixed with the conversation of real persons; frequently in single phrases only, but sometimes even in connected discourse.

"Though at this time I enjoyed rather a good state of health both in body and mind, and had become so very familiar with these phantasms, that at last they did not excite the least disagreeable emotion, but on the contrary afforded me frequent subjects for amusement and mirth, yet as the disorder sensibly increased, and the figures appeared to me for whole days together, and even during the night, if I happened to awake, I had recourse to several medicines."

Nicolai then recounted how the apparitions vanished upon blood being let.

"This was performed on the 20th of April, at eleven o'clock in the forenoon. I was alone with the surgeon, but during the operation the room swarmed with human forms of every description, which crowded fast one on another. This continued till half-past four o'clock, exactly the time when the digestion commences. I then observed that the figures began to move more slowly; soon afterwards the colours became gradually paler; every seven minutes they lost more and more of their intensity, without any alteration in the distinct figure of the apparitions. At about half-past six o'clock, all the figures were entirely white, and moved very little, yet the forms appeared perfectly distinct. By degrees they became visibly less plain, without decreasing in number, as had often formerly been the case. The figures did not move off, neither did they vanish, which also had usually happened on other occasions. In this instance they dissolved immediately into air; of some even whole pieces remained for a length of time, which also by degrees were lost to the eye. At about eight o'clock there did not remain a vestige of any of them, and I have never since experienced any appearance of the same kind. Twice or thrice since that time I have felt a propensity, if I may be allowed to express myself, or a sensation as if I saw something which in a moment again was gone. I was even surprised by this sensation whilst writing the present account, having, in order to render it more accurate, perused the papers of 1791, and recalled to my memory all the circumstances of that time. So little are we sometimes, even in the greatest composure of mind, masters of our imagination."

Nicolai was a greatly respected writer who became the organizer and leader of the Enlightenment, together with G. E. Lessing and Moses Mendelssohn. He died January 1, 1811.

His true story 'An Account of the Apparition of Several Phantoms' was published in *The German Museum* (London, 1800).

Nicoll, (Henry) Maurice (Dunlop)
(1884–1953)

Prominent British physician and psychologist who became a leading exponent of the teachings of G. I. **Gurdjieff** and P. D. **Ouspensky.** Born 1884, he was educated at Aldenham School and Caius College, Cambridge University, going on to study medicine at St. Bartholomew's Hospital, London, and in Vienna, Berlin, Paris and Zurich (B.A., M.B., B.C. Cambridge, M.R.C.S. London). He was Medical Officer to Empire Hospital for Injuries to the Nervous System; lecturer in medical psychology at Birmingham University, England; member of the British Psycho Medical Society. He became a member of the editorial staff of *Journal of Neurology and Psychopathy.* In World War I he served in Gallipoli in 1915, Mesopotamia in 1916.

His publications included: *Dream Psychology* (1917; 1920), *The New Man; an Interpretation of Some Parables and Miracles of Christ* (1950; 1951); *Living Time* (1952), *Psychological Commentaries on the Teaching of G. I. Gurdjieff & P. D. Ouspensky* (5 vols., 1954–1966); *The Mark (On the Symbolism of Various Passages from the Bible)* (1954).

He died August 30, 1953.

Nictalopes

Name given to human beings who can see in the dark. They are extremely rare. Dr. Tentin of Paris reported in 1874 the case of Marie Verdun, a girl of eighteen: "Although her eyes do not present any special morbid character she is forced to keep her eyelids closed during the day, and to cover her head with a thick veil. On the other hand, when the shutters of the room are hermetically fastened, she reads and writes perfectly in the deepest darkness."

Auguste Müller, the Stuttgart somnambulist, saw perfectly well and recognized all persons and objects in the greatest darkness.

In view of the remarkable precision with which objects move in the darkness of the seance room, it was suggested that some mediums might be nictalopes. As, however, the same precision has been observed when the medium goes into trance, the theory as a normal explanation seems untenable. (See also **Eyeless Sight**)

Nielsen, Einer (died 1965)

Remarkable Danish materialization medium, experiments with whom were recorded by Baron **Schrenck-Notzing** in his book *Physikalische Phaenomene des Mediumismus* (1920).

In 1922 in Christiania, Oslo, Nielsen was pronounced a fraud but he had completely reinstated himself in 1924 in Reykjavik, in sittings for the Psychical Research Society of Iceland. The report of the novelist Einar H. Kvaran, endorsed by scientists and other people of high standing, is a remarkable record of the materialization of forms, sometimes two appearing simultaneously near the medium while he himself was within view. Levitations and other telekinetic phenomena were seen in abundance (see **Levitation; Movement**).

However, several years later in Copenhagen, he could not regain the lost confidence of serious researchers. He was again accused of fraud by Johs. Carstensen, the leader of his circle, and a convinced Spiritualist. After his exposure in a pamphlet the medium went to court, but lost his case in April, 1932.

He died February 26, 1965.

Nielsen, Winnifred Moon (1917–)

Assistant professor of psychology who experimented in the field of parapsychology. Born August 16, 1917 at Key West, Florida, she studied at University of Florida (B.A. 1958, Ph.D. 1962). In 1937 she married Major Kenneth Cooper Smith (died 1943); her second marriage was in 1944 to William Andrew Nielsen (died 1953).

She was a research fellow at the Parapsychology Laboratory, Duke University, Durham, North Carolina from 1954–56, thereafter assistant professor of psychology at Mary Washington College, University of Virginia. She is a charter associate of the Parapsychological Association. Mrs. Nielsen has investigated relationships between Psi and personality. She published reports on her researches in the *Journal of Parapsychology;* these include 'An Exploratory Study in Precognition' (March 1956), 'Mental States Associated with Precognition' (June 1956).

Nielsson, Harald (died 1928)

Professor of Theology in the University of Iceland, who became convinced by experiences with the medium Indride **Indridason,** that modern Spiritualism was identical with primitive Christianity. Three lectures in which he affirmed this faith were published in a small book: *Mes Expériences en Spiritualisme Experimentale.* Professor Nielsson died in 1928.

Nif

An Egyptian symbol in the form of a ship's sail widely spread, symbolizing breath. (See also **Egypt**)

Nightmare

Possibly deriving from the Old English *night* and *mara,* a specter, indicating a terrifying dream. It is said to be caused by a disorder of the digestive functions during sleep, inducing the temporary belief that some animal or demon is sitting on the chest. Among primitive people it was thought that the affection proceeded from the attentions of an evil spirit.

Johann Georg Keysler, in his very curious work *Antiquitates selectae Septentrionales et Celticae* (1720), collected many interesting particulars concerning the nightmare. *Nachtmar,* he stated, is from *Mair,* an old woman, because the specter which appears to press upon the breast and impede the action of the lungs is generally in that form. The English and Dutch words coincide with the German. The French *cochemar* is *Mulier incumbens* or *Incuba.* The Swedes use *Mara* alone, according to the *Historia de omnibus Gothorum Sueonumque Regibus* of J. Magnus (1554), where he stated that Valender, the son of Suercher, succeeded to the throne of his father, who was suffocated by a demon in his sleep, of that kind which by the scribes is called *Mara.*

Others, "we suppose Germans," continued Keysler, "call it *Hanon Tramp.*" The French peasantry called it *Dianus* which is a corruption either of Diana or of *Dæmonium Meridianum* for it seems there is a belief which Keysler thought might not improbably be derived from a false interpretation of an expression in the 91st Psalm ("the destruction that wasteth at noon-day") that persons are most exposed to such attacks at that time and therefore women in childbed are then never left alone.

But though the *Dæmonium Meridianum* is often used for the Ephialtes, nevertheless it is more correctly any sudden and violent attack which deprives the patient of his senses.

In some parts of Germany, the name given to this disorder is *den alp,* or *das Alp-dructen,* either from the "mass" which appears to press on the sufferer or from *Alp* or *Alf* (elf). In Franconia it is *die Drud* or *das Druddructen,* from the Druid or Weird Women, and there is a belief that it may not only be chased away, but be made to appear on the morrow in a human shape, and lend something required of it by the following charm:

> "Druid to-morrow
> So will I borrow."

These Druids, it seems, were not only in the habit of riding men, but also horses, and in order to keep them out of the stables, the salutary *pentalpha* (which bears the name of *Druden-fuss,* Druid's foot) should be written on the stable doors, in consecrated chalk, on the night of St. Walburgh. It should also be mentioned that the English familiar appellation "Trot" is traced to "Druid," "a decrepit old woman such as the Sagas might be," and the same might perhaps be said of a Scottish Saint, Triduana or Tredwin.

In the *Glossarium Suiogothicum* of Johann Ihre (1769), a somewhat different account of the *Mara* is given. Here again, we find the "witch-riding" of horses, against which a stone **amulet** was suggested by the antiquarian John Aubrey, similar to one described below.

Among the incantations by which the *nightmare* may be chased away, Reginald Scot recorded the following in his *Discovery of Witchcraft* (1584 etc.)

> "St. George, St. George, our lady's knight,
> He walked by day so did he by night:
> Until such times as he her found,
> He her beat and he her bound,
> Until her troth to him plight,
> He would not come to her that night."

"Item," continued this author, "hang a stone over the afflicted person's bed, which stone hath naturally such a hole in it, as wherein a string may be put through it. and so be hanged over the diseased or bewitched party, be it man, woman, or horse."

Readers of the above lines may be reminded of the similar charm which Shakespeare put into the mouth of Edgar as Mad Tom in *King Lear:*

> "Saint Withold footed thrice the Wold;
> He met the night-mare and her ninefold
> Bid her alight,
> And her troth plight
> And aroint thee, witch, aroint thee."

Another charm of earlier date occurs in Chaucer's *Miller's Tale.* When the simple Carpenter discovers the crafty Nicholas in his feigned abstraction, he thinks he may perhaps be hag-ridden, and addresses him thus:

> "I crouch the fro Elves and fro wikid wightes
> And therewith the night-spell he seide arightes,
> On four halvis of the house about,
> And on the dreshfold of the dore without,
> 'Jesu Christ, and Seint Benedight,
> Blesse this house from evrey wikid wight,

Fro the night's mare, the wite paternoster,
Where wennist thou Seint Peter's sister."

A later author has pointed to some other formularies, and has noticed that Asmodeus was the fiend of most evil repute on these occasions. In the *Otia Imperiala* of Gervase of Tilbury, some other protecting charms are said to exist.

To turn to the medical history of the **Incubus, Pliny** recommended two remedies for this complaint, one of which was the herbal remedy wild peony seed. Another, which it would not be easy to discover in any modern pharmacopœia, was a decoction in wine and oil of the tongue, eyes, liver, and bowels of a dragon, wherewith, after it has been left to cool all night in the open air, the patient should be anointed every morning and evening.

Dr. Bond, a physician, who stated that he himself was much afflicted with the nightmare, published an *Essay on the Incubus* in 1753. At the time at which he wrote, medical attention appears to have been very little called to the disease, and some of the opinions hazarded were sufficiently wild and inconclusive. Thus, a certain Dr. Willis said it was owing to some incongruous matter which is mixed with the nervous fluid in the cerebellum *(de Anima Brutorum)*, while Bellini thought it imaginary and to be attributed to the idea of some demon which existed in the mind the day before.

Both of these writers might have known better if they would have turned to Fuchsius (with whom Dr. Bond appeared to be equally acquainted), who in his work *de Curandi Ratione*, published as early as 1548, had an excellent chapter (I, 31) on the causes, symptoms, and cure of nightmare, in which he attributed it to repletion and indigestion, and recommends the customary discipline.

Much of Gothic literature has been ascribed to dreams and nightmares. Horace Walpole's famous story *The Castle of Otranto* (1764) derived from a dream in which Walpole saw upon the uppermost banister of a great staircase a vision of a gigantic hand in armor. In 1816, Mary Shelley had a gruesome and vivid nightmare which was the basis for her story *Frankenstein.* Nearly seventy years later, novelist Robert Louis Stevenson had a nightmare that inspired his famous story *The Strange Case of Dr. Jekyll and Mr. Hyde*, which he completed in only three days. Bram **Stoker**'s immortal creation of *Dracula* (1897) was claimed to be the result of a nightmare after a supper of dressed crab, although clearly many of the elements in the story had been germinating in the author's mind much earlier. Many horror stories have also inspired nightmares. (See also **Fiction,** Occult English; **Incubus; Succubus**)

Noetics

Term used by scientific writer Charles A. **Musés** and others to denote the science of consciousness and its alterations. In his paper 'The Politics of Psi: Acculturation and Hypnosis' (included in *Extrasensory Ecology* edited Joseph K. Long, Scarecrow Press, 1977), Musés stated 'Noetics is concerned with the nature, alterations and potentials of consciousness, and especially human consciousness.' However, this parapsychological use of "Noetic" is distinct from its existing use as a synonym for "Noachian," meaning pertaining to Noah and his period.

An early use of the word "Noetic" in relation to states of consciousness was the article 'Psychic and Noetic Action' by occultist Madame H. P. **Blavatsky** (1831–1891), originally published in the journal *Lucifer* during the last years of her life. In this article, Madame Blavatsky equated "noetic" with *manasic* (deriving from *manas*, a Sanskrit term for mind) and compares materialistic psychological views of her time with ancient Hindu religious teachings and occultism. She concluded that there is a higher noetic character of the Mind-Principle than individual ego, a "Spiritual-Dynamical" force relating to divine consciousness, as distinct from mechanistic psychological dogmas or passive psychicism. This interesting article was reprinted in *Studies in Occultism* by Helena Petrovna Blavatsky (Dennis Wheatley Library of the Occult, London, 1974). (See also **Institute of Noetic Sciences;** Edgar D. **Mitchell**)

North Door

A possible remnant of pagan beliefs in some old Christian churches in Europe is a bricked-up doorway on the north side. There is a tradition that witches used to enter on the north, which is connected with superstitions of the Devil.

Norton, Thomas (died c. 1477)

The exact date of this alchemist's birth is wrapped in mystery, while comparatively little is recorded about his life in general. But at least it is known that he was born in Bristol, England, towards the end of the fourteenth century, and that, in the year 1436 he was elected to represent that town in Parliament. This suggests that he was an upright and highly-esteemed person, and the conjecture is strengthened by the fact that Edward IV made him a member of his privy council and employed him repeatedly as an ambassador.

At an early age Norton showed curiosity concerning **alchemy,** demonstrating his predilection by attempting to make the personal acquaintance of George **Ripley,** sometime Canon of Bridlington, who was reputedly a man of extraordinary learning, author of numerous alchemical works.

For many months Norton sought this person in vain, but at length the Canon, yielding to the other's importunity, wrote to him in the following manner: "I shall not longer delay; the time is come; you shall receive this grace. Your honest desire and approved virtue, your love of truth, wisdom, and long perseverance, shall accomplish your sorrowful desires. It is necessary that, as soon as convenient, we speak together face to face, lest I should by writing betray my trust. I will make you my heir and brother in this art, as I am setting out to travel in foreign countries. Give thanks to God, Who next to His spiritual servants, honours the sons of this sacred science."

After receiving this very friendly and encouraging letter, Norton hurried straightway to Ripley's presence, and thereafter for upwards of a month the two were constantly together, the elder man taught the novice many things, while he even promised that, if he showed himself an apt and worthy pupil, he would impart to him the secret of the **philosopher's stone.** And in due course this promise was fulfilled, yet it is reported that Norton's own alchemical researches met with various disappointments. On one occasion, for instance, when he had almost perfected a certain tincture, his servant absconded with the crucible containing the precious fluid; while at a later time, when the alchemist was at work on the same experiment and thought he was just about to reach the goal, his entire paraphernalia was stolen by a Mayoress of Bristol. And this defeat must have been doubly galling to the unfortunate philosopher, for soon afterwards the Mayoress became very wealthy, presumably as a result of her theft.

Norton himself does not appear to have reaped pecuniary benefit at any time from his erudition, but to have been a comparatively poor man throughout the whole of his life. This is a little surprising, for his *Ordinall of Alchimy* was a popular work in the Middle Ages, and was repeatedly published. The original edition was anonymous, but the writer's identity has been determined because the initial syllables in the first six lines of the seventh chapter compose the following couplet:

"Tomas Norton of Briseto
A parfet master ye maie him trowe."

Norton died circa 1477, and his predilections descended to one of his grandsons. This was Samuel Norton, who was born in 1548, studied science at St. John's College, Cambridge, and afterwards became a Justice of the Peace and Sheriff of Somersetshire. He died about 1604, and in 1630 a collection of his alchemistic tracts was published at Frankfort. (See also **Alchemy**; George **Ripley**)

Nostradamian, The

Monthly journal which analyzes the predictions of **Nostradamus** (1503–1566), discussing prophecies fulfilled and interpreting those which have not yet come to pass. Address: Nostradamus Research, P.O. Box 6463, Lincoln, Nebraska 68506.

Nostradamus (Michael de Nostradame)
(1503–1566)

French physician, counselor and astrologer to the kings Henry II and Charles IX, renowned for his predictions both of events of his day and of the distant future.

In 1555, and in later years, he published ten "centuries," each containing 100 quatrains (with the exception of the 7th, containing 42 only). The prediction of the fatal death of Henri II was fulfilled in his own lifetime. "En champ bellique par singulier duelle" (In a field of combat in single fight) is a fitting description of his accidental death in 1559 at the hands of Montgomery.

Nostradamus foresaw the decline of the Church as a result of the advance in astronomy and gave the date as 1607 (Lippershey invented his telescope in 1608); he prophesied the prosecution of the astronomers, the seizure of their books and the coming of rationalism for "there would be not an end to the eye." The "commun advenement," the reign of the people is another event in which he foresaw disaster for the Church and named correctly the year of 1792. The details of the French revolution and of the Napoleonic period are almost overwhelming.

But the decipherment of all this requires scholarly erudition. The knowledge of the future was dangerous, so Nostradamus veiled his meaning in a medley of languages, using French, Spanish, Portuguese, Italian, Latin,

Greek and Hebrew words, making anagrams and syllable permutations.

He succeeded so well that the Church did not put his book on the Index until 1781. Nostradamus was a Roman Catholic and no enemy to the Church. In fact he predicted the coming of a purified faith in the faraway future when "le corps sans âme plus n'estre en sacrifice" (the death of the body will no more be considered a sacrifice) and "Jour de la mort mis en nativité" (the day of death will become another birthday). This might even apply to Spiritualism.

Other forecasts apply closely to the Great War (see **Prediction**), some others to years to come. Their meaning, however, can only be grasped in the light of fulfilment. Hundreds of quatrains still await convincing explanation. The following (IX.20) illustrates the difficulties of interpretation:

"De nuict viendra par la forest de Reines
Deux pars, vaultorte, Herne la pierre blanche
Le moyne noir en gris dedans Varennes:
Esleu Cap. cause tempeste, feu, sang, tranche."

"Forest" stands for the Latin "fores," door, "pars" for "part" (in old French, husband or wife), "vaultorte" is a composite of "vaulx" (valley) and "de torte" (tortuous), "Herne" is an anagram for "reine" (Queen), "moyne" is Greek for "seul," "noir" another anagram for "roi(n)," "esleu" means "elu" (elected), "Cap." Capet, "tranche" knife.

The meaning is: Two married people, the King alone, dressed in grey, and the Queen, the white precious stone, will leave one night through the "door" of the Queen, take a tortuous road, enter into Varennes. The election of Capet will cause storm, fire, bloodshed, decapitation.

The historical facts are: Louis XVI wore a grey suit, the Queen was dressed in white, on her return her hair had become white (Prudhomme: *Revolutions de Paris*, VIIIe. Semèstre, No. 102, p. 544) their escape was furtive through the "door" of the Queen (*Op. Cit.* VII, p. 57), the road was altered by Louis XVI, to lead from Verdun into Varennes. The absolute monarchy had been changed in 1791 into an elective one.

In modern times, some commentators have claimed that there are quatrains that foretold World War II, the part played by Mussolini and Hitler and even the name "Hister," which can be taken either as an equivalent of the long "s" instead of "t," or a typical Nostradamian pun on "the upstart from the Danube." Ironically, Hitler himself became interested in Nostradamus and faked prophecies were circulated predicting the victory of Hitler, as part of psychological warfare. The allies also employed fake predictions.

Nostradamus appeared to predict the end of the world around the year 2,000, but in this he may have been echoeing millenial speculations of his time rather than relying on visions.

Skeptics maintain that the quatrains of Nostradamus are so involved and symbolical that they may be twisted to prove anything after the event. Moreover, since they do not follow a consistent time sequence, the sudden jumps between quatrains are misleading.

In spite of these criticisms, some of the prophecies are so remarkably clear that they seem beyond coincidence or wishful thinking. Bearing in mind the necessity for Nostradamus to protect himself by using deliberately involved symbolism and hidden meanings, it is difficult to avoid the conclusion that he did in fact have a rare gift of prophetic vision.

Nostradamus died in the night on July 1, 1566. He had accurately foreseen his death in minute details:

> "De retour d'ambassade, don de Roy Mis au lieu,
> Plus n'en fera, sera allé à Dieu,
> Parens plus proches, amis, freres du sang,
> Trouve tout mort près du lict et du banc." (Présage CXLI)

> ("On return from the embassy, the King's gift safely put away, he will do no more, for he will have gone to God. By his near relations, friends and brothers he will be found dead near the bed and the bench")

He had, in fact, gone to Arles as representative of the town of Salon and had been given a gift of money by the King. The bench was one which he used to help hoist his body into bed, and he was found by the bench in the morning.

The only comparable prophet, capable of a broad sweep over a vast area of the future, with its events and individuals, seems to have been the Hindu sage Bhrigu, who is said to have had a vision of the births of all souls in every country, and compiled a vast astrological treatise, in which every name and destiny is said to be recorded (see **Bhrigu-Samhita**). (See also **Prediction; Second Sight**)

Recommended reading:

Cheetham, Erika. *The Prophecies of Nostradamus,* Putnam, 1972; Neville Spearman, London, 1973; Corgi paperback, 1975

Du Vignois, Elisée. *Notre histoire racontée à l'avance par Nostradamus,* Paris, 1910

Howe, Ellic. *Urania's Children; The Strange World of the Astrologers,* William Kimber, London, 1967 (revised and condensed edition: *Astrology and Psychological Warfare During World War II,* London, 1972; U.S. title *Astrology; A Recent History Including the Untold Story of Its Role in World War II,* Walker & Co., New York, 1968)

Laver, James. *Nostradamus, or the Future Foretold,* Collins, London, 1942; Penguin Books, U.K., 1952; George Mann, London, 1973

Le Pelletier, Anatole. *Les Oracles de Michel de Nostredame,* 2 vols., Paris, 1867

Prieditis, Arthur A. *Fate of the Nations,* Neville Spearman, London/Llewellyn Publications, St. Paul, Minnesota, 1973

Torné-Chiavigny, H. *L'Histoire prédite et jugée par Nostradamus,* 3 vols., Bordeaux, 1860-62

Voldben, A. *After Nostradamus,* Neville Spearman, London, 1973; Citadel, 1974, Mayflower paperback, 1975

Ward, Charles A. *Oracles of Nostradamus,* London, 1891; Modern Library, New York, 1942

(For a bibliography of the twenty-five oldest editions of Nostradamus until 1689, compiled by Carl Graf von Klinckowstroem, see *Zeitschrift für Bücherfreude,* March, 1913)

Noualli

Aztec magicians (see **Mexico and Central America**).

Nous Letter (Journal)

Semi-annual journal of **Noetics,** science of states of consciousness. (This publication also incorporates *Astrologica,* formerly a separate journal.) Address: 1817 De La Vina Street, Santa Barbara, California 93101.

Nuan

In ancient Irish romance, the last of the sorceress-daughters of Conaran. Having put **Finn Mac Cummal** under taboo to send his men in single combat against her as long as she wished, she was slain by Goll Mac Morna, her sister's slayer.

Numerology

A popular interpretative and prediction system deriving from the mystic values ascribed to numbers. In Jewish mysticism, **Gematria** was the association of numbers with Hebrew letters, discovering hidden meanings in words by systematically converting them into numbers.

Modern numerology was popularized by the palmist and fortune-teller **"Cheiro"** (Count Louis Hamon), who developed a system of what he called "fadic" numbers. These were arrived at by adding together all the digits in the subject's birth date, giving a number of destiny to which special planetary and other significance was attached.

In general, numerology systems assign numerical values to letters of one's name or birthplace. These are added together to ascertain a basic number, which has a special symbolic interpretation, much as astrological types are traditionally assigned particular characteristics of helpful and harmful influences. Sometimes lucky or unlucky numbers are related to the twenty-two symbols of the Major Arcana of the Tarot pack.

Recommended reading:

Bosman, Leonard. *The Meaning and Philosophy of Numbers,* Rider, London, 1974 (originally published 1932)

Cheiro (Count Louis Hamon). *The Book of Numbers,* London, n.d. (1926)

Coates, Austin. *Numerology,* Muller, London, 1974

Kozminsky, Isidore. *Numbers, Their Meaning and Magic,* London, 1912

Moore, Gerun. *Numbers Will Tell,* Barker, London/Grosset & Dunlap, 1973

Sepharial (W. G. Old). *The Kabala of Numbers,* 2 vols., London, 1913

Westcott, W. W. *Numbers: Their Occult Power and Mystic Virtue,* London, 1890 etc.

O

Oahspe

A "New Bible" revealed to Dr. John Ballou **Newbrough** (1828–1891), a New York medium, manifested through automatic writing on the newly invented typewriter in 1881.

Newbrough spent ten years in self-purification so that he could become inspired by a higher power each day just before dawn. The result was *Oahspe, the Kosmon Bible in the words of Jehovah and his angel ambassador.* It took fifty weeks to complete, working half an hour each morning. The Kosmon Church was founded to practice the teachings of *Oahspe,* but this has since become known as the Confraternity of Faithists.

Oak Apples

In folklore, oak apples could be used in **divination.** To discover whether a child be bewitched, three oak apples were dropped into a basin of water under the child's cradle, at the same time preserving the strictest silence. If the oak apples floated, the child was not fascinated, but if they sank, the child was believed to be bewitched.

Oak Tree

Much folklore belief surrounds the oak tree. From time immemorial it has held a high place as a sacred tree. The Druids worshiped the oak and performed many of their rites under the shadow of its branches.

When St. Augustine preached Christianity to the ancient Britons, he stood under an oak tree. The ancient Hebrews evidently held the oak as a sacred tree. There is a tradition that Abraham received his heavenly visitors under an oak. Rebekah's nurse was buried under an oak, called afterwards the oak of weeping. Jacob buried the idols of Shechem under an oak. It was under the oak of Ophra that Gideon saw the angel sitting, who gave him instructions as to what he was to do to free Israel.

When Joshua and Israel made a covenant to serve God, a great stone was set up in evidence under an oak that was by the sanctuary of the Lord. The prophet sent to prophesy against Jeroboam was found at Bethel sitting under an oak. Saul and his sons were buried under an oak, and, according to Isaiah, idols were made of oak wood. Abimelech was made king by the oak that was in Shechem.

During the eighteenth century the oak was believed to have influence in curing diseases. The toothache could be cured by boring with a nail the tooth or gum until blood came, and then driving the nail into an oak tree. A child with rupture could be cured by splitting an oak branch, and passing the child through the opening backwards three times; if the splits grew together afterwards, the child would be cured.

Oaten, Ernest W(alter) (c. 1937)

Prominent British Spiritualist, former president of the International Federation of Spiritualists, and president of **Spiritualists National Union** from 1915 onwards.

He edited the journal *Two Worlds* from 1919–36. He was also an excellent medium and believed that his leading articles were inspired by the spirit of Mrs. Emma Hardinge **Britten.**

Oaten studied every phase of psychical phenomena and was a clear forceful lecturer. He did valuable work as chairman of the Parliamentary Committee of the Spiritualists National Union in pressing for reform of the archaic British law relating to mediumship (see **Fortune Telling Act**).

OBE (or OOBE or OOB)

Initialism for **Out-of-the-Body** experience, also known as **Astral Projection,** Etheric Projection or Ecsomatic Experience.

Obercit, Jacques Hermann (1725–1798)

Swiss mystic and alchemist. Born December 2, 1725 in Arbon, Switzerland, Jacques Obercit was the son of a scientist keenly interested in Hermetic philosophy, and no doubt the boy's own taste developed the more speedily on account of the parental predilection.

Very soon Jacques became determined to discover the **philosopher's stone,** hoping thereby to resuscitate the fortunes of his family, which were at a low ebb, presumably because the elder Obercit had expended large sums on his alchemistic pursuits. The young man worked strenuously to gain his ends, maintaining all along that whoever would triumph in this endeavor must not depend on scientific skill alone but rather on constant communion with God.

Notwithstanding this pious theory, he soon found himself under the ban of the civic authorities, who came to his laboratory, and forced him to forego further experiments, declaring that these constituted a danger to public health and safety. At least they gave this as their reason, but the likelihood is that, in their ignorance, they were unsympathetic to all scientific researches.

Obercit was bitterly incensed and appears to have left his native place and to have lived for some time thereafter with a certain Lavater, a brother of the noted physiognomist of that name. At a later date, Obercit renounced the civilized world altogether and took up his abode in the lofty fastnesses of the Alps.

However, he did not live the solitary life of a hermit, since according to his own account, he took as bride an angel shepherdess named Theantis, with whom he dwelt peacefully during a number of subsequent years. Whether children were born of this union between the terrestrial and the ethereal is not recorded, and the alchemist's account of the affair reads like a romance, as also did two books which he published: *Les Promenades de Gamaliel, juif Philosophe,* and *La Connexion Originaire des Esprits et des Corps, d'après les Principes de Newton* (Augsburg, 1776). His other writings included *Disquisitio de Universali Methodo Medendi* (1767). *Défense du Mysticisme et de la Vie Solitaire* (1775). Obercit was undoubtedly a picturesque character, and it is matter for regret that so little is known about his life. He died at Weimar February 2, 1798. (See also **Alchemy; Philosopher's Stone**)

Oberion

One of three spirits (the others were "Andrea Malchus" and "Inchubus") said to have been raised up by the parson of Lesingham and Sir John of Leiston in Norfolk, England, c. 1528. (See **England**)

Object Reading

Modern term for **Psychometry,** in which the operator may form impressions of events relating to an object associated with those events, usually by holding the object in the hand.

Objective Phenomena

Term used by psychical researchers, together with "subjective phenomena" as an alternative classification to "physical" and "mental" phenomena. (See also **Psychical Research; Spiritualism**)

Obsession and Possession

Obsession, from Latin *obsessionem—obsidere,* to besiege, is a form of insanity caused, according to traditional belief, by the persistent attack of an evil spirit from outside the individual, this being the opposite of possession, control by an evil spirit from within. Both meanings, however, involve the usurpation of the individuality and control of the body by a foreign and discarnate entity.

Historical Background

This belief may be found in the earliest records of human history, and in the magical rites and formulæ of ancient religions, used as charms against and **exorcism** of these invading influences. Ancient Indian, Greek and Roman literature teem with instances. The Bible also furnishes many, from the case of Saul ("troubled with an evil spirit" only to be dispossessed by the music of David's harping) to the miracles of Jesus Christ who cast out legions of possessing spirits.

Plato in his *Republic* not only spoke of demons of various grades, but mentioned a method of treating and providing for those obsessed by them. Sophocles and Euripides described the possessed, and mention of the subject is also to be found in Herodotus, Plutarch, Horace, and many others of the classics.

Terrible and appalling episodes in the Middle Ages are to be traced to the unquestioned belief in the possibility of possession and obsession by the Devil and his legions. All madness was caused by this and was, indeed, the visible manifestation of the Evil One, only to be exorcised by charms, averted by the observance of sacred rites, or later, to be burned and destroyed bodily for the good of the tortured soul within. The rites of Black Magic, in all ages and places, deliberately evoked this possession by the Devil and his demons for the communication and benefit of the infallible knowledge it was believed they conferred and its consequent power and control of man and his destinies.

Modern science with its patient and laborious researches into human psychology, has shown the human mind to be an incomparably delicate instrument, peculiarly at the mercy of the perceptions of the senses and their multitudinous impressions on the brain, its balance so easily shaken by a shock, a drug, a momentary excitement, oftener by prolonged and intense concentration upon single groups of ideas. It is to be noted that in the hallucinatory epidemics of all ages and countries there is to be found this unvarying characteristic: they are connected with some dominant cause, train of thought or religious sentiment prevalent at the time.

In the Middle Ages, when there flourished an intense belief in the positive apparitions of angels, saints and devils, the people's imagination was dominated and rendered intensely dramatic thereby.

The transmigration of the human soul into animals was another popular belief and to this again can be traced the terrible superstition of **Lycanthropy** which possessed large numbers of people in France and Germany in the fourteenth and sixteenth centuries. The mania of **Flagellation** took its rise at Perouse in the thirteenth century, caused by the panic attendant upon an outbreak of plague. These people maintained that there was no remission of sins without flagellation. This they preached with fanatical fervor and bands of them, gathering adherents everywhere, roamed through city and country, clad in scanty clothing on which were depicted skeletons and with frenzied movements publicly lashed themselves. It was to these exhibitions, the name of the "Dance of Death" was first applied.

The Dancing mania, accompanied by aberration of mind and maniacal distortions of the body was very prevalent in Germany in the fourteenth century, and in the sixteenth century in Italy where it was termed "Tarantism" and as a variant in source, was ascribed to the bite of the Tarantula spider. The music and songs employed for the cure are still preserved.

Edmund Parish in his book *Hallucinations and Illusions* (1897) made the following observations on this subject: "If not reckoned as true chorea, the epidemic of dancing which raged in Germany and the Netherlands in the Middle Ages comes under this head. Appearing in Aix it spread in a few months to Liège, Utrecht and the neighbouring towns, visited Metz, Cologne and Strasburg (1418) and after lingering into the sixteenth century gradually died out. This malady consisted in convulsions, contortions accompanying the dancing, hallucinations and so forth. The attack could be checked by bandaging the abdomen as well as by kicks and blows on that part of the body. Music had a great influence on the dancers, and for this reason it was played in the streets in order that the attacks might by this means reach a crisis and disappear the sooner. Quite trifling circumstances could bring on these seizures, the sight of pointed shoes for instance, and of the colour red which the dancers held in horror. In order to prevent such outbreaks the wearing of pointed shoes was forbidden by the authorities. During their dance many of the afflicted thought they waded in blood, or saw heavenly visions."

The same author remarked on other instances: "To this category also belongs the history of demoniacal possession. The belief of being possessed by spirits, frequently met with in isolated cases, appeared at certain periods in epidemic form. Such an epidemic broke out in Brandenburg, and in Holland and Italy in the sixteenth century, especially in the convents. In 1350-60 it attacked the convent of St. Brigitta, in Xanthen, a convent near Cologne, and others. The nuns declared that they were visited by the Devil, and had carnal conversation with him. These and other 'possessed' wretches were sometimes thrown into dungeons, sometimes burnt. The convent of the Ursulines at Aix was the scene of such a drama (1609-11) where two possessed nuns, tormented by all kinds of apparitions, accused a priest of witchcraft on which charge he was burnt to death [see Urbain **Grandier**]. The famous case of the nuns of Loudun (1632-39) led to a like tragic conclusion, as well as the Louvier case (1642) in which the two chief victims found their end in life-long imprisonment and the stake."

Religious Possession

The widespread belief in and fear of magic and **witchcraft** operating on superstitious minds produced the most extraordinary hallucinations. Certain levels of religious ecstasy partake of the same character, the difference being that they involve possession by and contact with so-called good spirits. The sacred books of all nations teem with instances of this and profane history can also furnish examples. The many familiar cases of ecstatic visions and revelations in the Old Testament may be cited, as well as those found in the legends of saints and martyrs, where they either appear as revelations from heaven or temptations of the Devil.

In the latter case, the eminent sexologist R. Von Krafft-Ebing, pointed out the close connection of religious ecstasy with sexual disturbances. That this ecstatic condition was sought and induced, the following passage amply indicates: "Among Eastern and primitive peoples such as Hindoos, American Indians, natives of Greenland, Kamtschatka and Yucatan, fetish-worshipping Negroes, and Polynesians, the ecstatic state accompanied with hallucinations is frequently observed, sometimes arising spontaneously, but more often artificially induced. It was known also among the nations of antiquity. The means most often employed to induce this state are beating of magic drums and blowing of trumpets, howlings and hour-long prayers, dancing, flagellation, convulsive movements and contortions, asceticism, fasting and sexual abstinence. Recourse is also had to narcotics to bring about the desired result. Thus the flyagaric is used in Western Siberia, in San Domingo the herb coca, tobacco by some tribes of American Indians, and in the East opium and hashish. The ancient Egyptians had their intoxicating drinks, and receipts for witch's salves and philtres have come down to us from medieval times."

In many countries this condition of possession was induced for religious and prophetic purposes, also for mere fortune-telling. The extent to which this belief in obsession and possession persisted in recent times was testified by Edward Tylor in *Primitive Culture* (2 vols., 1871): "It is not too much to assert that the doctrine of demoniacal possession is kept up, substantially the same theory to account for substantially the same facts, by half the human race, who thus stand as consistent representatives of their forefathers back in primitive antiquity."

Such beliefs persisted in the development of Spiritualism. The obsessional theory was also used to account for forms of insanity and crime. The following passage taken from the publication *Diakka and their Victims* by the seer Andrew Jackson **Davis** (1873) indicates this recent belief: "The country of the diakka is where the morally deficient and the affectionately unclean enter upon a strange probation . . . . They are continually victimizing sensitive persons still in the flesh making sport of them and having a jolly laugh at the expense of really honest and sincere people. They [these demon-like spirits] teach that they would be elevated and made happy if only they could partake of whiskey and tobacco, or gratify their burning free-love propensities . . . . Being unprincipled intellectualities their play is nothing but pastime amusement at the expense of those beneath their influence." These creatures were also said to be of a malignant and bloodthirsty nature, inciting the beings they possessed to murder, often of a terrible character.

Signs of Demoniac Possession

Philipp Melanchthon (1497-1560) in one of his letters, stated that though there may occasionally be some natural causes for a frenzy or mania, it is also quite certain that devils enter certain persons and there cause torment and fury with or without natural causes, just as one sees at times maladies cured with remedies which are not natural. Moreover, such spectacles were in the nature of wonders and forecasts of things to come. Twelve years before a woman of Saxony who could neither read nor write, being controlled by a devil, spoke after the torment was over, words in Greek and Latin to the effect that there would be great distress among the people.

The following have been cited in the past as possible signs of possession:

Imagining oneself possessed; leading an evil life; living alone; chronic ailments, unusual symptoms, a deep sleep, the vomiting of strange things; blaspheming and frequent reference to the Devil; making a compact with the Devil; being controlled by spirits; having a face that inspires horror and fear; being tired of living and the giving up of hope; being enraged and violent in action; making the cries and noises of a beast.

A much more detailed review of objective and subjective indications is found in the authoritative work *Possession Demoniacal & Other* by T. K. Oesterreich (1930; 1966).

In an account of the possession of the nuns of **Loudon** in the seventeenth century, we find the questions put to the University of Montpellier by Santerre, priest and founder of the bishopric and diocese of Nimes touching on the signs and the judicial answers of this University.

Q.—Whether the bending and moving of the body, the head at times, touching the soles of the feet, with other contortions and strange positions are good signs of possession?

A.—Mimics and acrobats make such strange movements, bending and twisting themselves in so many ways that one must conclude that there is no sort of position which men and women cannot take up, after long practice and application, even being able, with the ease of experience, to extend and spread out abnormally the legs and other parts of the body, by the extension of the nerves, muscles and tendon—such performances are not without the bounds of nature.

Q.—Whether the rapidity of the movement of the head backwards and forwards, touching the chest and the back, is an infallible sign of possession?

A.—This movement is so natural that nothing need be added to what has been said about the movements of the other parts of the body.

Q.—Whether the sudden swelling of the tongue, the throat and the face, and the sudden changing of color, are sure signs of possession?

A.—The swelling and disturbance of the chest through interruption are the efforts of breathing or inspiration—the normal actions in respiration—and possession cannot be inferred from them. The swelling of the throat may proceed from the retention of the breath and that of the other parts from the melancholic vapors which are often observed wandering through all parts of the body. Hence it follows that this sign of possession is inadmissible.

Q.—Whether a feeling, stupidly heedless, or the lack of feeling, to the point of being pricked or pinched without complaining or moving and not even changing color are certain signs of possession?

A.—The young Lacedemonian who allowed himself to be bitten by a fox which he had stolen without seeming to feel it, and those who flog themselves, even to death, before the altar of Diana, without turning a hair, they all show that, with resolution, pin-pricks can be endured without complaining. Moreover, it is certain that in the human body, small areas of skin are met with in some persons, which are insensitive, although the neighboring parts may be quite sensitive, a condition which occurs the more frequently after some previous illness. Such a condition has, therefore, no bearing on possession.

Q.—Whether the total lack of bodily movement which, at the command of the exorciser, occurs in those supposedly possessed during, and in the middle of, their most violent actions, is an undeniable sign of a true diabolic possession?

A.—The movements of the parts of the body being voluntary it is natural for well-disposed persons to move themselves or not at will, so that such a cessation of movement, if there is not entire lack of feeling, is not sufficient ground from which to infer a diabolic possession.

Q.—Whether the yelping or noise like that of a dog, which comes from the chest rather than from the throat, is a mark of possession?

A.—Human skill adapts itself so easily to the counterfeiting of all kinds of expressions, that persons are met with every day who can give perfectly the expressions, cries and songs of all sorts of animals, and that with a practically imperceptible movement of the lips. Again, many are to be found who form their words in the stomach and they would seem to come from some other

object rather than from the one who forms them. Such persons are called ventriloquists. However, such a condition is natural, as Pasquier shows, in Chap. 38 of his *Researches,* with one Constantin, a jester, as an example.

Q.—Whether keeping the gaze fixed on some object without moving the eye, is a good sign of possession?

A.—The movement of the eye is voluntary, like that of the other parts of the body, and it is natural to move it or keep it still—there is therefore, nothing of note in this.

Q.—Whether the answers, given in French, to questions put in Latin, to those supposedly possessed, are a mark of possession?

A.—We assert that to understand and speak languages which one has not learnt is certainly supernatural, and would lead to the supposition that it occurred through the ministrations of the Devil or from some other cause beyond; but merely to answer some questions suggests nothing more than long practice, or that one of the number is in league with them and able to contribute to such answers making it appear a fallacy to say that the devils hear the questions put to them in Latin and answer in French and in the tongue natural to the one who is to pass for the demoniac. It follows from this that such a result does not infer the occupation by a demon, more especially if the questions are of few words and not involved.

Q.—Whether the vomiting of such things as one has swallowed is a sign of possession?

A.—Delrio, Bodin, and other authors say that by witchcraft, sorcerers sometimes manage to vomit nails, pins, and other strange things, by the work of the devil, who is able to do the same for the truly possessed. But to vomit things one has swallowed is natural, there being people with weak stomachs who keep down for several hours what they have swallowed and then return it as they have taken it; also the lientery returns food through the bowel as it has been taken by the mouth.

Q.—Whether pricks with a lancet, in different parts of the body, without the drawing of blood, are a good sign of possession?

A.—This is related to the composition of the melancholic temperament, in which the blood is so thick that it cannot issue from such small wounds and it is because of this that many when pricked by the surgeon's lancet, even in their very veins, do not bleed a drop, as is shown by experience. There is thus nothing extraordinary here.

Recorded Instances of Possession

The sixteenth-century writer Jean Boulaese told how twenty-six devils came out of the body of the possessed Nicoli of Laon: "At two o'clock in the afternoon, the said Nicoli, being possessed of the Devil, was brought to the said church, where the said de Motta proceeded as before with the exorcism. In spite of all entreaty the said Beelzebub told them in a loud voice that he would not come out. Returning to their entreaties after dinner, the said de Motta asked him how many had come out, and he answered, 'twenty-six.' 'You and your followers,' then said de Motta, 'must now come out like the others.' 'No,' he replied, 'I will not come out here, but if you like to take me to Saint Restitute, we will come out there. It is sufficient for you that twenty-six are out.' Then the said de Motta asked for a convincing sign of how they had come out. For witness he told them to look in the garden of the treasury over the front gate, for they had taken and carried away three tufts (i.e., branches) from a green may-pole (a small fir) and three slates from above the church of Liesse, made into a cross, as others in France commonly, all of which was found true as shown by the Abbot of Saint-Vincent, M. de Velles, Master Robert de May, canon of the Church Notre-Dame of Laon, and others.''

The same author gave an account of the contortions of the demoniac of Laon: "As often as the reverend father swung the sacred host before her eyes, saying, 'Begone, enemy of God,' so did she toss from side to side, twisting her face towards her feet, and making horrible noises. Her feet were reversed, with the toes in the position of the heel, and despite the restraining power of eight of the men, she stiffened herself and threw herself into the air a height of six feet, the stature of a man, so that the attendants, sometimes even carried with her into the air, perspired at their work. And although they bore down with all their might, still could they not restrain her, and torn away from the restraining hands, she freed herself without any appearance of being at all ruffled.

"The people, seeing and hearing such a horrible sight, one so monstrous, hideous and terrifying cried out, 'Jesus, have mercy on us!' Some hid themselves, not daring to look; others, recognising the wild cruelty of such excessive and incredible torment, wept bitterly, reiterating piteously, 'Jesus, have mercy on us!' The reverend father then gave permission to those who wished to touch and handle the patient, disfigured, bent, and deformed, and with the rigidity of death. Chief among these were the would-be reformers, such men as Francois Santerre, Christofle, Pasquot, Gratian de la Roche, Masquette, Jean du Glas, and others well-known for their tendencies towards reform, all vigorous men. They all endeavoured, but in vain, to straighten her limbs, and bring them to a normal position, and to open her eyes and mouth—it was futile. Further, so stiff and rigid was she, that the limbs would have broken rather than give, as also the nose and ears. And then, as she said afterwards, she was possessed, declaring that she was enduring incredible pain. That is, by the soul torment, the devil makes the body become stone or marble."

Jean Le Breton (in *Recveil de pièces sur les possessions des religieoses de Louviers,* Rouen, 1879) stated the following concerning those possessed in Louviers:

"The fourth fact is that many times a day they show transports of rage and fury, during which they call themselves demons, without, however, offending anyone or even hurting the fingers of the priests, which were put into their mouths at the height of their fury.

"The fifth is that during these furies they show strange convulsions and contortions, bending themselves back, among other things, in the form of a circle, without the use of the hands, and in such a way that their bodies are supported as much on the forehead as on the feet. The rest of the body is unsupported and remains so for a long time—the position being repeated seven or eight times. After such feats as this and many others, kept up sometimes for four hours, chiefly during the exorcism and during the warmest parts of the dog days, they are found on coming to, to be as normal, as fresh and with a pulse as even as if nothing had happened to them.

"The sixth is that some of them faint away at will during the exorcism and this condition occurs at a time when the face is the most suffused with blood and the pulse is the strongest. They come to of themselves and the recovery is more remarkable than the swooning—it begins as a movement of the toe, then of the foot and in their order, of the leg, thigh, abdomen, chest and throat, the movement of the last three being one of wide dilation. The face, meanwhile is apparently devoid of expression, which finally returns with grimaces and shoutings, the spiritual element returning at the same time with its former disturbing contortions."

Doctor Ese gave the following particulars of the case of Sister Mary, of the Convent at Louviers:

"The last was Sister Mary of St. Esprit, supposedly possessed by Dagon, a large woman, slender-waisted, and of good complexion, with no evidence of illness. She came into the refectory . . . . head erect and eyes wandering from side to side, singing, dancing and skipping. Still moving about and touching lightly those around her, she spoke with an elegance of language expressive of the good feeling and good nature which were his (using the person of the devil). All this was done with movements and carriage alike haughty, following it up with a violence of blasphemy, then a reference to his dear little friend Magdalen, his darling and his favourite mistress. And then, without springing or using effort of any kind, she projected herself into a pane of glass and hanging on to a central bar of iron passed bodily through it, but on making an exit from the other side the command was given in Latin, 'est in nomine Jesu rediret non per aliam sed per eadem viam.' After some discussion and a definite refusal to return she, however, returned by the same route, whereupon the doctors examined her pulse and tongue, all of which she endured while laughing and discussing other things. They found no disturbance such as they had expected, nor any sign of the violence of her actions and words, her coming to being accompanied with some trivial remarks. The company then retired."

Another writer on those possessed in Louviers gave the following astonishing statement:

"Placed in the middle of the nave of this chapel was a vase of some kind of marble, some two feet in diameter and a little under a foot deep, with sides about three fingers' breadth in thickness. So heavy was it that three of the most robust persons would have had difficulty in raising it while on the ground, yet this girl, to all appearances of very low vitality, came into the chapel and grasping the vase merely by the ends of her fingers, raised it from the pedestal on which it was placed, turned it upside down and threw it on to the ground with as much ease as if it had been a piece of cardboard or paper. Such great strength in one so weak astonished all those present. Moreover, the girl, appearing wild and possessed, ran hither and thither with movements so abrupt and violent that it was difficult to stop her. One of the clerics present, having caught her by the arm, was surprised to find that it did not prevent the rest of her body from turning over and over as if the arm were fixed to the shoulder merely by a spring. This wholly unnatural performance was carried out some seven or eight times and that with an ease and speed difficult to imagine."

The *Relation des Ursulines possedées d'Auxonne* (c. 1660) contains the following:

"M. de Chalons was no sooner at the altar (at midnight) than from the garden of the monastery and around the house was heard a confused noise, accompanied by unknown voices and some whistling; at times loud cries with strange and indistinct sounds as from a crowd, all of which was rather terrifying among the shadows of the night. At the same time stones were thrown from different places against the windows of the choir where they were celebrating holy mass and this despite the fact that these windows were a good distance from the walls which enclosed the monastery which made it improbable that they came from without. The glass was broken in one place but the stone did not fall into the choir. This noise was heard by several persons, inside and out. The sentinel in the citadel on that side of the town took alarm at it as he said the next day, and at the altar the bishop of Chalons could not but feel a suspicion that something extraordinary was going on in the house and that demons or sorcerers were making some attempts at that moment which he repelled from where he was by secret imprecations and inward exorcisms."

"The Franciscan nuns of the same town heard the noise and were terrified by it. They thought that the monastery shook beneath them and in this confusion and fear they were compelled to have recourse to prayer."

"At the same time voices were heard in the garden, weak and moaning and as if asking for help. It was nearly an hour after midnight and very dark and stormy. Two clerics were sent out to see what was the matter and found Marguerite Constance and Denise Lamy in the monastery garden, the former up a tree and the latter seated at the foot of the stairway into the choir. They were at liberty and in the full possession of their senses, yet appeared distracted, especially the latter, and very weak and pale, though with blood on her face; she was terrified and had difficulty in composing herself. The other had blood on her face also though she was not wounded. The doors of the house were tightly closed and the walls of the garden were some ten or twelve feet high."

"In the afternoon of the same day the bishop of Chalons, with the intention of exorcising Denise Lamy, sent for her and when she was not found, he inwardly commanded her to come to him in the chapel of St. Anne where he was. It was striking to see the prompt obedience of the demon to this command, formulated merely in the mind, for in about a quarter of an hour a violent knocking was heard at the door of the chapel, as if by one hard pressed. On opening the door this girl entered the chapel abruptly, leaping and bounding, her face changed greatly and with high colour and sparkling eyes. So bold and violent was she that it was difficult to restrain her, nor would she allow the putting on of the stole which she seized and threw violently into the air despite the efforts of four or five clerics who did their best to stop her, so that finally it was proposed to bind her, but this was deemed too difficult in the condition in which she was."

"On another occasion, at the height of her frenzy . . . . the demon was ordered to stop the pulse in one of her arms, and it was immediately done, with less resistance and pain than before. Immediate response was also made to the further order to make it return. The command being given to make the girl insensible to pain, she avowed that she was so, boldly offering her arm to be pierced and burnt as wished. The exorcist, fortified by his earlier experience, took a sufficiently long needle and drove it, full length, into the nail and flesh, at which she laughed aloud, saying that she felt nothing at all. Accordingly as he was ordered, blood was allowed to flow or not, and she herself took the needle and stuck it into different parts of her arm and hand. Further, one of the company took a pin and, having drawn out the skin a little above the wrist, passed it through and through so that the two ends were only visible, the rest of the pin being buried in the arm. Unless the order was given for some no blood issued, nor was there the least sign of feeling or pain."

The same account gave, as proofs of the possession of the Auxonne nuns, the following:

"Violent agitation of the body only conceivable to those who have seen it. Beating of the head with all their might against the pavement or walls, done so often and so hard that it causes one to shudder on seeing it and yet they show no sign of pain, nor is there any blood, wound or contusion.

"The condition of the body in a position of extreme violence, where they support themselves on their knees with the head turned round and inclined towards the ground for a foot or so, which makes it appear as if broken. Their power of bearing, for hours together without moving, the head being lowered behind below the level of the waist; their power of breathing in this condition; the unruffled expression of the face which never alters during these disturbances; the evenness of the pulse; their coolness during these movements; the tranquil state they are in when they suddenly return and the lack of any quickening in the respirations; the turning back of the head, even to the ground, with marvellous rapidity. Sometimes the movement to and fro is done thirty or forty times running, the girl on her knees and with her arms crossed in front; at other times, in the same position with the head turned about, the body is wound around into a sort of semicircle, with results apparently incompatible with nature."

"Fearful convulsions, affecting all the limbs and accompanied with shouts and cries. Sometimes fear at the sight of certain phantoms and spectres by which they say they are menaced, causes such a change in their facial expression that those present are terrified; at other times there is a flood of tears beyond control and accompanied by groans and piercing cries. Again, the widely-opened mouth, eyes wild and showing nothing but the white, the pupil being turned up under cover of the lids—the whole returning to the normal at the mere command of the exorcist in conjunction with the sign of the cross.

"They have often been seen creeping and crawling on the ground without any help from the hands or feet; the back of the head or the forehead may be touching the soles of the feet. Some lie on the ground, touching it with the pit of the stomach only, the rest of the body, head, feet and arms, being in the air for some length of time. Sometimes, bent back so that the top of the head and the soles of the feet touch the ground, the rest of the body being supported in the air like a table, they walk in this position without help from the hands. It is quite common for them, while on their knees to kiss the ground, with the face twisted to the back so that the top of the head touches the soles of the feet. In this position and with the arms crossed on the chest they make the sign of the cross on the pavement with their tongues.

"A marked difference is to be noticed between their condition when free and uncontrolled and that which they show when controlled and in the heat of their frenzy. By reason of their sex and delicate constitutions as much as from illness they may be weak, but when the demon enters them and the authority of the church compels them to appear they may become at times so violent that all the power of four or five men may be unable to stop them. Even their faces become so distorted and changed that they are no longer recognisable. What is more astonishing is that after these violent transports, lasting sometimes three or four hours; after efforts which would make the strongest feel like resting for several days; after continuous shrieking and heart-breaking cries; when they become normal again—a momentary proceeding—they are un-wearied and quiet, and the mind is as tranquil, the face as composed, the breathing as easy and the pulse as little changed as if they had not stirred out of a chair.

"It may be said, however, that among all the signs of possession which these girls have shown, one of the most surprising, and at the same time the most common, is the understanding of the thought and inward commands which are used every day by exorcists and priests, without there being any outward manifestation either by word or other sign. To be appreciated by them it is merely necessary to address them inwardly or mentally, a fact which has been verified by so many of the experiences during the stay of the bishop of Chalons and by any of the clergy, who wished to investigate, that one cannot reason-ably doubt such particulars and many others, the details of which cannot be given here."

A number of archbishops or bishops and doctors in the Sorbonne made the following notification with regard to the condition at Auxonne.

"That among these differently-placed girls there are seculars, novices, postulants and professed nuns; some are young, others old; some from the town, others not; some of high estate, others of lesser parentage; some rich, others poor and of low degree. That it is ten years or more since the trouble began in this monastery; that it is remarkable that a reign of deceit was able for so long to preserve the secret among girls in such numbers and of conditions and interests so varied. That after research and a stricter enquiry, the said Bishop of Chalons has found nobody, either in the monastery or in the town, who could speak other than well of the innocence and integrity, alike of the girls and of the clergy who worked with him in the exorcisms, and, for himself, he finds them with the bearing of persons of uprightness and worth—evidence which he gives in the interest of truth and justice.

"Added to the above is the certificate of Morel, doctor and present at everything, who asserts that all these things exceed the bounds of nature and can only occur as the work of a demon; in short, we consider that all the extraordinary findings with these girls are beyond the powers of human nature and can only be instigated by a demon possessing and controlling their bodies."

Simon Goulart in *Histoires admirables et mémorables de nostre temps* (2 vols., 1610) culled many stories of demoni-acs from Johan **Weyer,** including the following:

"Antoine Benivenius in the eighth chapter of the *Livre des causes cachées des maladies* tells of having seen a girl of sixteen years whose hands contracted curiously whenever she was taken with a pain in the abdomen. With a cry of terror her abdomen would swell up so much that she had the appearance of being eight months pregnant—later the swelling went down and, not being able to lie still, she tossed about all over the bed, sometimes putting her feet above her head as if trying a somersault. This she kept up throughout the throes of her illness and until it had gone down by degrees. When asked what had happened to her, she denied any remembrance of it. But on seeking the causes of this affection we were of opinion that it arose from a choking of the womb and from the rising of malignant vapours affecting adversely the heart and brain. We were at length forced to relieve her with drugs but these were of no avail and becoming more violent and congested she at last began to throw up long iron nails all bent, brass needles stuck into wax, and bound up with hair and a part of her breakfast—a mass so large that a man would have had difficulty in swallowing it all. I was afraid, after seeing several of these vomitings, that she was possessed by an evil spirit, who deluded those present while he removed these things and afterwards we heard predictions and other things given which were entirely beyond human comprehension.

"Meiner Clath, a nobleman living in the castle of Boutenbrouch in the duchy of Juliers, had a valet named William who for fourteen years had had the torments of a possession by the devil, and when, at the instigation of the devil, he began to get ill, he asked for the curé of St. Gerard as confessor . . . . who came to carry out his little part . . . . but failed entirely. Seeing him with a swollen throat and discoloured face and with the fear of his suffocating, Judith, wife of Clath and an upright woman, with all in the house, began to pray to God. Immediately there issued from William's mouth, among other odds and ends, the whole of the front part of the trousers of a shepherd, stones, some whole and other broken, small bundles of thread, a peruke such as women are accus-tomed to use, needles, a piece of the serge jacket of a little boy, and a peacock's feather which William had pulled from the bird's tail eight days before he became ill. Being asked the cause of his trouble he said that he had met a woman near Camphuse who had blown in his face and that his illness was the result of that and nothing else. Some time after he had recovered he contradicted what he had said and confessed that he had been instructed by the devil to say what he had. He added that all those curious things had not been in his stomach but had been put into his throat by the devil despite the fact that he was seen to vomit them. Satan deceives by illusions. The thought comes at times to kill oneself or to run away. One day, having got into a hog-shed and protected more carefully than usual he remained with his eyes so firmly closed that it was impossible to open them. At last Gertrude, the eldest daughter of Clath, eleven years old, came along and advised him to pray to God for the return of his sight, but he asked her to pray and the fact of her praying, to the great surprise of both, opened his eyes. The devil exhorted him often not to listen to his mistress or anyone else who bowed the head at the name of God, who could not help him as he had died once, a fact which was openly preached.

"He had once attempted rudely to touch a kitchen-maid and she had reproved him by name, when he answered in a voice of rage that his name was not William but Beelzebub, at which the mistress asked—'Do you think we fear you? He Whom we serve is infinitely more powerful than you are.' Clath then read the eleventh chapter of St. Luke where mention is made of the casting out of the dumb devil by the power of the Saviour and also of Beelzebub, prince of devils. Finally William began to rest and slept till morning like a man in a swoon, then taking some broth and feeling much relieved he was sent home to his parents, after having thanked his master and mistress and asked God to reward them for the trouble they had been caused by his affliction. He married afterwards and had children, but was never again tormented by the devil.

"On the 18th March, 1566, there occurred a memorable case in Amsterdam, Holland, on which the Chancellor of Gueldres, M. Adrian Nicolas, made a public speech, from which is the following: "Two months or so ago thirty children of this town began to be strangely disturbed, as if frenzied or mad. At intervals they threw themselves on the ground and for half an hour or an hour at the most this torment lasted. Recovering, they remembered nothing, but thought they had had a sleep and the doctors, sorcerers, and exorcists were all equally unable to do any good. During the exorcism the children vomited a number of pins and needles, finger-stalls for sewing, bits of cloth, and of broken jugs and glass, hair and other things. The children didn't always recover from this but had recurrent attacks of it—the unusualness of such a condition causing great astonishment."

Jean Languis, a learned doctor, gave the following examples in the first book of his *Epitres,* as having happened in 1539 in Fugenstall, a village in the bishopric of Eysteten and sworn to by a large number of witnesses:

"Ulric Neusesser, a ploughman in this village, was greatly troubled by a pain in the side. On an incision being made into the skin by a surgeon an iron nail was removed, but this did not relieve the pain, rather did it increase so that, becoming desperate, the poor man finally committed suicide. Before burying him two surgeons opened his stomach, in front of a number of persons, and in it found some long round pieces of wood, four steel knives, some sharp and pointed, others notched like a saw, two iron rods each nine inches long and a large tuft of hair. One wondered how and by what means this mass of old iron could be collected together into the space of his stomach. There is no doubt that it was the work of the devil who is capable of anything which will maintain a dread of him.

"Antoine Lucquet, knight of the order of the Fleece, of high repute throughout Flanders, and privy counsellor of Brabant, had married in Bruges, and his wife, soon after the nuptials, began to show the torments of an evil spirit, so much so that at times, even in company, she was suddenly taken up and dragged through rooms and thrown from one corner to another, despite the efforts of those around to restrain and hold her. She was little conscious of her bodily welfare while in this frenzy and it was the general opinion that her condition had been induced by a former lover of her young and light-hearted husband. Meanwhile she became pregnant without a

cessation in the evil torment and the time of her delivery being at hand the only woman present was sent for the midwife but instead, she came in and herself acted as midwife which disturbed the invalid so much that she fainted. She found, on recovering, that she had been delivered, yet to the astonishment of both there was no sign of a child. The next day on wakening up she found a child in swaddling clothes in the bed and she nursed it a couple of times. Falling asleep shortly afterwards the child was taken from her side and was never seen again. It was reported that notes with the hall-mark of magic had been found inside the door."

Simon Goulart gave an account from Johan Weyer, of the multitude of terrible convulsions suffered by the nuns of the convent of Kentorp near Hammone: "Just before and during the attack their breath was fœtid and sometimes continued so for hours. While affected they did not lose their power of sound judgment nor of hearing and recognising those around them, despite the fact that owing to the spasm of the tongue and respiratory organs they could not speak during the attack. All were not equally affected but as soon as one was affected the others, though in different rooms, were immediately affected also. A soothsayer, who was sent for, said they had been poisoned by the cook, Else Kamense, and the devil taking advantage of the occasion increased their torment, making them bite and strike each other and throw each other down. After Else and her mother had been burnt some of the inhabitants of Hammone began to be tormented by an evil spirit. The minister of the Church took five of them home to warn them and strengthen them against the machinations of the enemy. They laughed at him and mentioned certain women of the place whom they would like to visit on their goats, which were to carry them there. Immediately one straddled a stool calling out that he was off, while another, squatting down, doubled himself up and rolled towards the door of the room which opened suddenly and through which he went falling to the bottom of the steps without hurting himself."

"The nuns of the Convent of Nazareth at Cologne [according to the same writer] were affected much the same as those of Kentorp. After being troubled for a long time and in various ways by the devil they were more terribly affected in 1564 when they would lie out on the ground, with clothing disordered, as if for the companionship of man. During this their eyes would be closed and they would open them later with shame and feeling that they had endured some deep injury. A young girl of fourteen named Gertrude who had been shut up in this convent was subject to this misfortune. She had often been troubled by wild apparitions in bed as witness her mocking laughter, although she tried in vain to overcome it. A companion slept near her specially to protect her from the apparition but the poor girl was terrified at the noise from Gertrude's bed, the devil finally controlling the latter and putting her through a variety of contortions. . . . The beginning of all this trouble was in the acquaintance picked up with one or two of the nuns on a neighbouring tennis court by some dissolute young man who kept up their amours over the walls."

"The torments suffered by the nuns in Wertet in the county of Horne are also wonderful. The beginning is traced to a poor woman who borrowed from the nuns during Lent some three pounds of salt and returned double the amount before Easter. From that they began to find in their dormitory small white balls like sugar-plums, and salt to the taste, which they did not eat, nor did they know whence they came. Shortly after they heard a moaning as of a sick man, then warnings to rise and go to the help of a sick sister, which they would do but would find nothing. Sometimes in endeavouring to use a chamber it would be pulled away suddenly with a consequent soiling of the bed. At times they were pulled out by the feet, dragged some length, and tickled so much on the soles of the feet that they nearly died with laughter. Pieces of flesh were pulled out of some, while others had their legs, arms and heads twisted about. Thus tormented some would throw up a large quantity of black fluid, although for six weeks previously they had taken nothing but the juice of horseradish without bread. This fluid was so bitter and so sharp that is blistered their mouths and one could evolve nothing which would give them an appetite for anything else. Some were raised into the air to the height of a man and as suddenly thrown to the ground again. When some thirty of their females visited this convent to congratulate those who seemed relieved and practically cured, some of them immediately fell backwards from the table they were at, losing the power of speech and of recognising anyone, while others were stretched out as if dead with arms and legs turned around. One of them was raised into the air against the restraining efforts of those present and then brought again to the ground so forcibly that she seemed dead. She rose, however, as if from a deep sleep and left the convent uninjured. Some moved about on the fronts of their legs as if lacking feet and as if dragged in a loose sack from behind. Others even climbed trees like cats and came down as easily. The Abbess told Margaret, Countess of Bure, that she cried aloud when pinched in the leg; it was as severe as if a piece had been pulled out, and that she was carried to bed at once and the place became black and blue, but she finally recovered. This derangement of the nuns was an open secret for three years but has been kept dark since.

"What we have just said applies equally to the early case of the Bridget nuns in their convent near Xanthus. Now, they gambol or bleat like sheep or make horrible noises. Sometimes they were pushed from their seats in church where their veils would be fastened above their heads. At other times their throats would be so stopped up that they could swallow no food, and this affliction lasted for ten years in some of them. It was said that the cause of all this was a young nun whose parents had refused to allow her to marry the young man she loved. Further that the devil in the form of this young man had come to her at the height of her passion and had advised her to return to the convent which she did at once and when there she became frenzied and her actions were strange and terrible. The trouble spread like the plague through the other nuns, and the first one abandoned herself to her warder and had two children. Thus does Satan both within and without the convent, carry out his hateful schemes.

"Cardan relates that a ploughman . . . . often threw up glass, nails and hair and, on recovering, felt within a large quantity of broken glass which made a noise like that from a sackful of broken glass. This noise he said troubled

him greatly and for some eighteen nights towards seven o'clock, although he had not observed the time and although he had felt cured for some eighteen years, he had felt blows in his heart to the number of hours which were to strike. All this he bore not without great agony."

"I have often seen," stated Goulart, "a demoniac named George, who for thirty years on and off was tormented by an evil spirit and often I have seen her swell up, and become so heavy that eight strong men could not raise her from the ground. Then, exhorted and encouraged in the name of God and the hand of some good man extended to her, she would rise to her feet and return home, bent and groaning. She did harm to no one whether by day or night while in this condition, and she lived with a relative who had a number of children so used to her ways that when they saw her twisting her arms, striking her hands and her body swelling up in this strange way, they would gather in some part of the house and commend her to God and their prayers were never in vain. Finding her one day in another house of the village in which she lived I exhorted her to patience. . . . She began to roar in a strange way and with a marvellous quickness shot out her left hand at me and enclosed in it my two hands, holding me as firmly as if I had been bound with stout cords. I tried, but in vain, to free myself, although I am of average strength. She interfered with me in no other way nor did she touch me with her right hand. I was held as long as it has taken to tell the incident and then she let me go suddenly, begging my pardon, and I commended her to God, and led her quietly home. . . . Some days before her death being much tormented she went to bed with a low fever. The fury of the evil one was then so much curtailed that the patient, wonderfully strengthened inwardly, continued to praise God who had been so merciful to her in her affliction and comforting all who visited her. . . . I may add that Satan was overcome, and that she died peacefully, calling on her Saviour."

According to Goulart, "there was, in the village of Leuensteet and duchy of Brunswick, a young girl of twenty years, Margaret Achels, who lived with her sister. Wishing to clean some shoes one day in June she took a knife some six inches long and sat down in a corner of the room for she was still weak from a fever of long standing, whereupon an old woman entered and inquired how she was and whether she still had the fever and then left without further words. After the shoes were cleaned she let the knife fall in her lap but subsequently could not find it despite a diligent search. The girl was frightened and still more so when she found a black dog under the table. She drove it out, hoping to find the knife, but the dog got angry, showed its teeth and growlingly made its way into the street and fled.

"The girl at once seemed to feel something indefinable which passed down her back like a chill and fainting suddenly she remained so for three days when she began to breathe better and to take a little food. When carefully questioned as to the cause of her illness she said that the knife which had fallen into her lap had entered her left side and that there she felt pain. Although her parents contradicted her, attributing her condition to a melancholic disposition, her long abstinence and other things, she did not cease to complain, to cry and to keep a continuous watch, so much so that her mind became deranged and sometimes for two days at a time she would take nothing even when kindly entreated to do so, so that sometimes force had to be used. Her attacks were more severe at times than others and her rest was broken by the continuous pains which beset her, being forced as she was to hold herself doubled over a stick.

"What increased her pain and lessened the chance of relief was her firm belief that the knife was buried in her body and the stubborn contradiction of the others who said it was impossible and thought it nothing but a phantom of the mind, since they saw nothing which would give them ground for believing her unless it were her continual complaints and tears. These were kept up for some months and until there appeared on her left side between the two false ribs a tumour as large as an egg which fluctuated in size with the changes in her own girth. Then the girl said to them: 'Up to the present you haven't wanted to believe that the knife was in my side, but you will soon see now that it is.'

"On the 30th June, that is after almost thirteen months of the trouble, the ulcer which developed on her side poured out so much material that the swelling began to go down and the point of the knife showed and the girl wanted to pull it out but her parents prevented her and sent for the surgeon of Duke Henry who was at the Castle of Walfbutel. This surgeon arrived on the 4th July and begged the curate to comfort, instruct and encourage the girl, and to take particular note of her answers since she was regarded as a demoniac. She agreed to be attended by the surgeon, not without the idea that a quick death would follow. The latter, seeing the point of the knife projecting, grasped it with his instruments and found that it was just like the other in the sheath and very much worn about the middle of the blade. The ulcer was finally cured."

Goulart, quoting Melanchthon, stated that "there was a girl in the marquisate of Brandebourg who pulled some hairs off the clothing of some person and that these hairs were at once changed into coins of the realm which the girl chewed with a horrible cracking of the teeth. Some of these coins are kept still by persons who snatched them away from the girl and found them real. From time to time this girl was much tormented but after some months got quite well and has remained so since. Prayers, but nothing more, are often offered up for her."

The same author also stated: "I have heard that there was in Italy a demented woman who when controlled by a devil and asked by Lazare Bonami for the best verse of Virgil, answered at once:

'Discite Justitiam Moniti et non temnere divos.' 'That,' she added, 'is the best and most-deserving verse that Virgil ever wrote; begone and don't come back here again to try me.'

Louise Maillat, a young demoniac who lived in 1598, lost the use of her limbs and was found to be possessed by five demons who called themselves, "wolf," "cat," "dog," "beauty" and "a griffin." At first, two of these demons came out from her mouth in the form of balls the size of the fist, the first fire-red, the second, which was the cat, quite black; the others left her with less violence. On leaving her they all made a few turns round the hearth and disappeared. Frances Secretain was known to have made this girl swallow these devils in a crust of bread the colour of manure."

Modern Views of Obsession in Psychical Research

Obsession in psychiatry means that the mind of the patient is dominated by fixed ideas to which an abnormal mental condition corresponds. In traditional belief, obsession is an invasion of the living by a discarnate entity, tending to a complete displacement of normal personality for purposes of selfish gratification which is more or less permanent. The difference between mediumship and obsession is not in principle but in purpose, in duration and in effect.

Mediumship, or to be more precise, trance possession, does not interfere with the ordinary course of life, does not bring about a demoralizing dissociation or disintegration; it shows consideration for the medium and its length is limited. After a certain time it ceases automatically and the medium's normal self, held in voluntary abeyance for the time being, resumes its sway.

Obsession is always abnormal, it is an accompaniment of a shock, organic lesion, or, in cases of psychics, of low morale and weakening will power, induced by an unstable character and debility of health. Once the existence of spirits is admitted, the possibility of obsession cannot be disregarded. Perhaps, a lesser assumption is just as sufficient to point out the possibility.

"If we believe in telepathy," wrote Dr. James H. **Hyslop** in *Contact with the Other World* (1919), "we believe in a process which makes possible the invasion of a personality by someone at a distance." "It is not at all likely," he stated, "that sane and intelligent spirits are the only ones to exert influence from a transcendental world. If they can act on the living there is no reason why others cannot do so as well. The process in either case would be the same; we should have to possess adequate proof that nature puts more restrictions upon ignorance and evil in the next life than in this in order to establish the certainty that mischievous personalities do not or cannot perform nefarious deeds. The objection that such a doctrine makes the world seem evil applies equally to the situation in the present life."

How are we to distinguish obsession from multiple **personality?** It was explained to Hyslop by the "**Imperator**" group of controls of the Rev. Stainton **Moses** that even for the spirits it is sometimes difficult to state how far the subconscious self of the patient is acting under influence and suggestion from spirits or as a secondary personality. Nevertheless Hyslop found a highly satisfactory method to find out the truth in **cross reference.** He wrote: "I take the patient to a psychic under conditions that exclude from the psychic all normal knowledge of the situation and see what happens. If the same phenomena that occur in the patient are repeated through the medium; if I am able to establish the identity of the personalities affecting the patient; or if I can obtain indubitably supernormal information connecting the patient with the statements made through the psychic, I have reason to regard the mental phenomena observed in the patient as of external origin. In a number of cases, persons whose condition would ordinarily be described as due to hysteria, dual, or multiple personality dementia precox, paranoia, or some other form of mental disturbance, showed unmistakable indications of invasion by foreign and discarnate agencies."

This method was a revolutionary innovation. To reach the conviction of the reality of obsession which preceded it, a long time was necessary. "Before accepting such a doctrine," stated Hyslop in *Life After Death* (1918), "I fought against it for ten years after I was convinced that survival after death was proved. But several cases forced upon me the consideration of the question. The chief interest in such cases is their revolutionary effect in the field of medicine. . . . It is high time for the medical world to wake up and learn something."

Prof. William **James,** shortly before his death, surrendered to the same belief. He wrote: "The refusal of modern enlightenment to treat obsession as a hypothesis to be spoken of as even possible, in spite of the massive human tradition based on concrete experience in its favor, has always seemed to me a curious example of the power of fashion in things "scientific." That the demon theory (not necessarily a devil theory) will have its innings again is to my mind absolutely certain. One has to be 'scientific' indeed to be blind and ignorant enough not to suspect any such possibility."

It was the report of the Thompson-Gifford case in *Proceedings* of the American Society for Psychical Research (vol. 3, part 8, 1909) which overcame his resistance to the idea of obsession. The short history of this famous case is as follows: Mr. F. L. Thompson, a Brooklyn goldsmith, was seized in 1905 with an irresistible impulse to sketch and paint. The style was plainly that of Robert Swain Gifford. This well-known American artist had died six months previously but this fact was unknown to Thompson who hardly knew him and, except for a slight taste for sketching in his early years, never showed artistic talents.

He had visions of scenes of the neighborhood of Gifford's country house and often had the hallucination that he was Gifford himself. He saw a notice of an exhibition of Gifford's paintings. He went in and heard a voice whisper: "You see what I have done. Can you take up and finish my work?" The desire to paint became stronger. Soon it was so overpowering that he was unable to follow his former occupation.

He grew afraid that he was losing his sanity. Two physicians diagnosed the case as paranoia. One of them, without offering to cure it, expressed a desire to watch the progress of the malady. Thompson came to Prof. Hyslop for advice, who took him to three different mediums. They all sensed the influence of Gifford, described his character and life and confirmed the vague possibility which Dr. Hyslop wished to investigate that the case was not the result of mental disorder. As soon as the case was proved as spirit obsession, treatment was comparatively simple. Gifford was reasoned with and persuaded to desist.

Spirit Obsession and Personality Displacement

The importance of such treatment on the assumption of spirit obsession is apparent. An obsessing spirit, if driven out by strengthened willpower of the victim or by psychotherapeutic means, will seek and find another subject, but if it is convinced of the error of its ways the danger is eliminated.

A systematic practice of curing obsession through such means was taken up by Dr. and Mrs. Carl **Wickland** in

their Psychopathic Institute of Chicago. The patient was brought to Mrs. Wickland. She went into trance. Her controls influenced the obsessing spirit to step into Mrs. Wickland's body. If the obsessor was unwilling it was forced to do so by means known to the controls. Dr. Wickland then began to parley with the spirit, explained the position and usually ended in convincing the invader that it did a great wrong to its spiritual evolution by strengthening ties to the earth. The invader usually promised to depart and the patient became normal.

Later Dr. Wickland moved to California and founded the National Psychological Institute for the treatment of obsession. His experiences were narrated in his book *Thirty Years Among the Dead* (1924).

Similar work was done in *The Temple of Light* in Kansas City in 1910. Dr. Hyslop was so much impressed with the importance of this cure that he established a foundation in his will for the work. The headquarters of the James J. Hyslop Foundation for the Treatment of Obsession were in New York; Dr. Titus **Bull** was its director.

The obsessors are mostly earthbound spirits. They do not necessarily mean harm. All they wish is to enjoy earthly existence once again. But some of them may commit acts of revenge or do other harm, owing to their ignorance. And if an evil personality gets into control, the obsessed individual may be driven to criminal, insane acts.

Just as the trance control will become perfect by practice, the obsessor will feel more at home in the victim's organism after repeated possession and will settle as permanently as possible. Certain historic records suggest that obsession may attain an epidemic character. The case of the Ursuline Nuns of Loudon in 1632–34 has already been cited. Several of the nuns of the convent, including the Mother Superior, were seized with violent convulsions, symptoms of catalepsy and demoniac possession. Blasphemies and obscenities were pouring forth from their mouths, confessed to come from the devil. The curé, Urbain **Grandier,** was accused of grave immoralities, preceding the outbreak. The devils indicated him as the author of their troubles. He was burnt alive in April, 1634.

Obsessions by evil spirits were of frequent occurrence in the congregation of the Rev. Edward **Irving** in 1831. The bystanders rebuked the evil spirits and bade them to come forth. In one such case, recorded by Robert Baxter in his pamphlet *A Narrative of Facts* . . . (1833), the possessed man when released by the "tongue" fell upon the ground crying for mercy, and lay there foaming and struggling like a bound demoniac.

In February 1874, Franklin B. Evans was executed in Concord, New Hampshire, for the murder of a twelve-year-old child. In his confession made just before his execution he said that "for some days before the murder I seemed to be attended continually by one who seemed to bear a human form, urging me on to the deed. At length it became fixed in my mind to take her life."

Hudson Tuttle, in his book *The Arcana of Spiritualism* (1876) described a suicidal obsession as follows: "While sitting in a circle at the home of the venerable Dr. Underhill, I was for the time in an almost unconscious state, and recognised the presence of several Indian spirits. The roar of the Cayahoga River over the rapids could be heard in the still evening air, and to my sensitive ear was very distinct. Suddenly I was seized with a desire to rush away to the rapids, and throw myself into the river. As I started up someone caught hold of me, and aroused me out of the impressible state I was in, so that I gained control of myself. Had the state been more profound, and had I once started, the end might have been different. The desire remained all the evening."

Sometimes the obsession serves beneficial ends. An excellent instance is the "**Watseka Wonder,**" the case of Lurancy Vennum. Her malicious obsessors were forced out by the spirit of Mary Roff who departed from earth life eighteen years previously in the same city. Mary Roff lived in Lurancy Vennum's body, but in the house of her own parents for sixteen weeks and satisfied everybody of her identity. Her long inhabitation somehow made the body safe from malicious invasions and when she finally yielded its control to the returning ego of Lurancy Vennum, the girl's health was mentally and physically reestablished.

In the famous Beauchamp case (see **Personality**), "Sally," one of the four chief personalities, marked as B.III showed evidence of obsession. The case was never treated as such. "Sally," however, claimed to be a spirit, wrote automatically, had a will of her own by which she could hypnotize the other personalities, was always conscious and had no perception of time. She was the connecting link between the memories of the other personalities and was a mischievous entity.

She would go out in the country in the last car and leave the first self to walk home. She would put into a box spiders, toads or other animals to frighten the first self when she opened it, and she waged formal war on the fourth personality. An electric shock, like in the Wickland cases, had the effect of bringing about her eclipse but this fact was not sufficiently noted by Dr. Morton **Prince.**

In the Doris Fischer case investigated by Dr. Walter F. **Prince** (see **Personality**), "Margaret," one of her five personalities, appeared to be a similarly mischievous entity. She would steal so that Doris would be blamed for the theft. She would hide her books at school so that she could not study her lessons. She would scratch the body of the real Doris until it bled, then go out and leave the normal personality to suffer the pain. She would eat the candy that Doris bought for herself. She would jump into a dirty river with clothes on that Doris should suffer from the filth which stuck to her.

But she did not claim to be a spirit; she did not write automatically and showed no ignorance of time. It was with difficulty that her history was traced. Dr. Walter F. Prince succeeded in treating Doris Fischer sufficiently by suggestion to bring her from California to Boston. Dr. Hyslop took her to Mrs. Chenoweth (Minnie M. **Soule**). Dr. Hodgson came through when Mrs. Chenoweth went into trance and compared the case to that of Sally Beauchamp, remarking that it was "as important as any that Morton Prince ever had." He knew the Beauchamp case from personal experience. He also communicated that a little Indian was connected with the case.

Soon afterwards, Doris developed **automatic writing** through the **planchette.** A little Indian personality manifested and gave her name as "Minnehaha" or Laughing Water. Later Mrs. Chenoweth's control, "Starlight,"

found Minnehaha and in trying to give her name said: "I see, like a waterfall, just like water falling over and whether it is Water Fall or—something like that." Then she remarked: "She laughs after she shows me the water." Still later "Minnehaha" herself communicated and confessed a number of pranks that she played upon the girl.

As a result of his twenty years' study of obsession at the head of the James Hyslop Institute, Dr. Titus Bull published in 1932 some startling conclusions. He stated:

"An obsessing personality is not composed of the soul, mind and will of one disembodied being, but is, in reality, a composite personality made up of many beings. The pivot obsessor, or the one who first impinges upon the sensorium of the mortal, is generally one with little resistance to the suggestions of others. He or she, therefore, becomes an easy prey to those who desire to approach a mortal in this way.

". . . Some people, moreover, may be born with tendencies which make it easier for them to become victims of mental alterations later in life. . . . There is an influence which can be exerted upon the minds of mortals by ideas embodied in thoughts from their departed ancestors. In other words, some departed ancestors, whenever possible, attempt to mould the lives of those incarnated who are akin. . . . There is a type of mortal whose mind is easily influenced by the stronger minds of the family group. . . . The more clannish the family group, the more likely is this to be true on both sides of the veil. It is, however, not to be considered as spirit obsession in the true sense. . . . The intervention of shock, however, or anything that could upset the nerve balance of a member of such family group, would place him in actual danger of becoming a victim of true spirit obsession. . . . The primary obsessor, in this case, would likely be one who claimed the right by ties of blood, who had no desire to do anything but to keep the mortal in line with family ideals."

According to Dr. Bull, obsessors "have three major points of impingement; namely, the base of the brain, the region of the solar plexus and at the center governing the reproductive organs. As there are three major points of impingement, it may be assumed that there can be three composite groups, each starting with a pivot entity. What satisfaction is to be gained this way includes the whole gamut of human emotions."

The pivot entities "upon which the mound of entity obsession is built" act as automatic channels for the others. Many of them were victims of obsession before their passing. Others may become obsessors "through the machinations or wiles of others." Not understanding what has happened to them they may be readily influenced to turn to obsession.

Another important point is "the possibility of obsessions passing on to the body of mortal pangs which were part of their own physical life." They retained in their memory the possibility of producing pain and as often they are unable to inhibit the production of it in the obsessed body, it must be beyond their control. "Therefore," stated Dr. Bull, "it is a fair assumption to say that often the migratory pains of the living are caused by the memory pangs of the dead." The prime reason of why the production of pain should be beyond control is "the domination of another and more crafty entity who is using the pain-producer for his own purpose. . . ."

Objections to the Concept of Spirit Obsession

Much of the evidence for spirit obsession is subjective, based on the observations and feelings of investigators, many of whom have been reputable individuals. However, so far no really conclusive evidence has been found which will resolve this question definitively.

It should not be overlooked that the subconscious mind has the ability to weave convincing fantasies of personality, while novelists have created imaginary characters who now seem to have a reality of their own. Some cases of apparent secondary or multiple personality seem to be a dramatization of the subject's unconscious emotional desires and fears. Children often pretend to be different personalities, while even the effect of a powerful movie portrayal often awakens both conscious and unconscious imitation of personality traits amongst impressionable viewers.

For a time, it was thought that the technique of hypnotic regression, in which a subject's memory is progressively explored into the past and then into apparent former lives, might offer reliable evidence of the continuity of personality from one life to another. However, although there are some impressive case histories, the evidence so far is not conclusive.

It may well be discovered that there is no one simple explanation for or against the concept of spirit obsessions, that certain cases may be genuinely spirit obsession, others subconscious personation.

The concept of spirit possession is still very much alive in various African and West Indian areas, especially amongst Voodoo cults.

Exorcism

The pagan and Christian belief in demonic obsession and possession brought about complex rituals of exorcism, designed to drive out the diabolical entities. Although such rituals had virtually fallen into disuse in Christian countries during the more pragmatic materialist philosophy of the twentieth century, they were revived on a startling scale with the occult boom of the 1960s, which generated a widespread public obsession with claimed demonic possession, factual and fictional. The theme permeated popular books and movies, and led to a revival of forgotten rituals of exorcism. It should be noted that the belief in demonic possession seems to generate hundreds of apparent cases. (See also Arnall **Bloxham;** Titus **Bull; Exorcism; Personality; Personation, Reincarnation; Rescue Circles; Voodoo; Watseka Wonder;** Carl August **Wickland**)

Recommended reading:

Ebon, Martin (ed.). *Exorcism; Fact Not Fiction,* Signet paperback, 1974

Holzer, Hans. *Possessed!,* Fawcett paperback, 1973

Huxley, Aldous. *The Devils of Loudon,* Chatto & Windus, London, 1952; Harper & Row paperback, 1971

Nicola, John T. *Diabolical Possession and Exorcism,* Tan Books, Rockford, Illinois, 1974

Oesterreich, T. K. *Possession, Demoniacal & Other,* Kegan Paul, London/R. R. Smith, New York, 1930; University Books, 1966 (variant title *Possession and Exorcism,* Causeway Books, 1974)

Pettiward, Cynthia. *The Case for Possession,* Colin Smythe, U.K., 1975

Sargant, William. *The Mind Possessed; A Physiology of Possession, Mysticism & Faith Healing,* Heinemann, London, 1973; J. B. Lippincott, 1974

Shepard, Leslie. *How to Protect Yourself Against Black Magic & Witchcraft,* Citadel, 1978

Walker, Sheila S. *Ceremonial Spirit Possession in Africa and Afro-Americana,* E. J. Brill, Leiden, Netherlands/Humanities Press, New York, 1972

Occult

General term (derived from Latin *occultus, occulere,* to hide) to denote that which is hidden, mysterious, known only to the initiated, imperceptible by normal senses, thus embracing all the pseudo-sciences of **magic** belief and practice, such as **alchemy, astrology, demonology, ghosts, miracles, poltergeists, prediction** of the future, psychic powers, spells, **Spiritism,** sympathetic magic, etc. The term is also used to include abnormal or rare phenomena such as reported monsters unknown to contemporary science or paranormal events, all of which might some day become part of normally accepted knowledge, much as so many natural phenomena thought by primitive peoples to be magical. There is also a specialized scientific use of the term "occult" in astronomy, denoting the hiding or obscuring from view of one heavenly body (as the moon or a planet) by another.

"Occult" is properly used as an adjective, roughly synonymous with "magic," but in common usage it is also employed as a noun, thus "the occult" implies the body of occult belief or practice.

In ancient times, it was believed that apparent deviations from natural law involved mysterious and miraculous "supernatural" or occult laws, deriving from gods, invisible entities or the souls of the dead. The rituals of magic were designed to evoke entities and spirits to ward off misfortune or perform actions in defiance of natural law, such as obtaining knowledge of distant or future events, causing injury or death of one's enemies, or securing sudden wealth (usually in the form of gold). Most primitive peoples had witch-doctors or shamans who claimed such specialized ability to work magic.

Modern **Spiritualism** is basically a revival of ancient belief in the claimed evidence for the continued existence of personality after death and the evolution of the individual soul to perfection. The Spiritism inaugurated by Allan **Kardec** is a form of Spiritualism with emphasis on reincarnation. Both Spiritualism and Spiritism are essentially religious movements, endorsing the miracles cited in the Bible and citing continuing paranormal phenomena as evidence of survival.

Much of primitive occultism was an aspect of religion, deriving from the mystery, wonder and fearfulness of the world in which human beings found themselves. At other times in history, the occult was clearly a degenerate form of earlier belief and practice of the higher religions. Thus, the magic spells and rituals of the Middle Ages are a decadent descent from the more refined religious beliefs and practices of Eastern religions, which were in turn a higher form of primitive beliefs.

Much of the aims and objects of ritual magic and **witchcraft** rituals appear tawdry, egocentric, selfish, immature and power-seeking, lacking in more civilized ethics of self-purification, service to the community, and desire for truth and knowledge. The occult often promises short cuts to wealth, success and power in this life, but has nothing inspiring to contribute on the hereafter.

Opinion of the validity of the occult and the meaning of claimed paranormal phenomena must depend upon one's philosophical or religious viewpoint. From the early nineteenth century onwards, the successes of science and technology in achieving apparent miracles developed a materialistic view of life and its laws, encouraging agnosticism and atheism. It became fashionable (with much justification) to ridicule simplistic literal belief in Biblical teachings, such as the probably allegorical story of creation in *Genesis* and point to the abuse of power by religious authorities in the establishment of the Christian church and the suppression of heresies, and the bloodthirsty power games of religious wars (which are still unfortunately present). At the same time, it is impossible to deny the validity of the ethical teachings of Christianity, which are shared by all great religions and even the ethical teachings of rationalists.

In modern times, Christianity has tended to play down the question of miraculous phenomena, although there is persuasive evidence that it still occasionally occurs. The Creator of the world and the universe must surely be assumed to have power to suspend created laws. However, certain theological problems are involved in the concept of such intervention, notably the side effects of causation, and their apparently indiscriminate action. Clearly suspension of natural law in one area will tend to create side effects in adjacent areas, while favoring one individual, however devout or worthy, might involve problems for another individual. Again, although the empirical evidence for miraculous healing is quite impressive, it is by no means clear why some sufferers should be healed and others never have access to healers. Why are certain noble individuals doomed to suffer disease and pain while immoral and vicious individuals die comfortably in their beds? It would seem that religious explanations for miracles are at present simplistic and inadequate, indicating the need for more complex investigation.

Belief has always appeared to be a powerful creative factor in occult practice, and it is not impossible that even initial fraud could sometimes be a stimulating factor in producing paranormal phenomena by "priming the pump," so to speak. Ancient religions sometimes used mechanical contrivances to simulate divine power, rather like religious conjuring tricks. The power of prayer may be more closely connected with a creative power of mind rather than validating the actual nature of the gods. Prayers to Eastern and Western deities appear to produce results, while spirit entities also appear to perform magical feats. The mental state of the petitioner may be the dominant factor. Allied with belief is the willpower of the operator in magical practice, which again has some relevance to the mystical concept of concentration and meditation being preliminaries to the manifestations of paranormal phenomena.

At a secular level, psychical researchers and parapsychologists have attempted to bring scientific method into the investigation of claims of the paranormal, removing the subject from a religious context. This is in many ways

a welcome development for scientific knowledge, but sometimes tends to bypass the possible religious dimension and ignore the broader aspects of the meaning and purpose of life and the interpretation of natural phenomena. The clinical atmosphere of a parapsychology laboratory, with its scientific controls, specialized jargon and mathematical evaluation removes the paranormal from a natural setting.

By comparison, the sincere Spiritualist views paranormal phenomena in a context of personal knowledge and meaning, and if the evidence of survival of loved ones and hopes of spiritual evolution are not scientifically verifiable, the evidence nevertheless carries its own verisimilitude in a way which is not accessible to objective scrutiny. The experience of happiness or being in love, or recognizing the individual personality of a friend or relative are all areas which science may comment upon but cannot share. Of course, simple-minded people are often imposed upon by cheats, but that is surely a case for more general education and clear thinking rather than delegation to "experts." Clearly a fully developed emotional, intellectual and spiritual framework for all phenomena, whether normal or paranormal, is the ultimate desirable context for evaluation.

The senses and the mind are mirrors of reality, but the experience of waking consciousness in the brief span of one's life limits the totality of contact with ultimate reality. Bishop George Berkley (1685–1753) questioned the actual existence of matter outside the idealism of the human mind, explaining the more or less uniformity of shared sensory and mental experience as due to a divine idea which regulated human impressions. In this he echoed ancient Eastern religions, which also stressed that the reality picture of minds is not the ultimate criterion. Time, space and causation are only limiting adjuncts of human experience, and the minimum data for any valid philosophical scheme are surely the contents of all minds, past, present and future, and all interrelationships in the cosmos. In the absence of this, any individual human mind or sensory impression is a defective instrument, often additionally flawed by immature development or emotional problems.

Eastern religions have proposed a "cosmic consciousness" to which a purified human consciousness may have access and share, and this experience has also been claimed by Western mystics. It would seem that there are various levels of higher consciousness, and that the experience of extended consciousness is sometimes accompanied by paranormal phenomena. Does the experience involve an occasional release of energy that momentarily deforms the mental picture of empirical reality? On a more mundane level, various advocates of New Thought techniques have claimed that intense mental concentration brings about paranormal effects such as healing or obtaining desired aims.

It may be that the empirical reality of waking consciousness is no more substantial than a dream. A dream seems real so long as one is dreaming, but upon awakening, time, space and causation have a different and more extended quality. But even waking life is conditioned by perceptual limitations imposed by the experience of matter and natural law, and it may well be that consciousness itself ultimately has infinite dimensions that transcend the matter and natural law in which it occurs.

Clearly, psychical researchers, parapsychologists, occultists, witches, and gurus of both Eastern and Western religions will act within their own terms of reference, and it may well be that their discoveries and teachings will eventually form part of a more complex and inspiring view of life than the mere question of whether or not occult phenomena are a valid part of life. Like so many other aspects of life, the results of investigation are conditioned by the attitudes of the investigators. (See also **Ceremonial Magic; Consciousness; Evidence; Fraud; Magic; Meditation; Miracles; Mysticism; Parapsychology; Psychical Research; Spiritualism; Witchcraft; Yoga**)

Recommended reading:

Bucke, Richard M. *Cosmic Consciousness; A Study in the Evolution of the Human Mind,* Innes & Sons, Philadelphia, 1901; E. P. Dutton, 1946 etc.; University Books, 1961

Crow, W. B. *A History of Magic, Witchcraft & Occultism,* Aquarian Press, U.K., 1968; Abacus paperback, 1972

Freedland, Nat. *The Occult Explosion,* Putnam/Michael Joseph, London, 1972

Godwin, John. *Occult America,* Doubleday, 1972

Gopi Krishna. *The Biological Basis of Religion and Genius,* Harper & Row, 1972

Grattan-Guinness, Ivor. *Psychical Research; A Guide to Its History, Principles & Practices,* Aquarian Press, U.K. (paperback), 1982

Grant, Kenneth. *The Magical Revival,* Frederick Muller, London, 1972

James, William. *The Varieties of Religious Experience,* London, 1902; University Books, 1963

Rhine, J. B. & associates. *Parapsychology From Duke to FRNM,* Parapsychological Press, Durham, N.C. (paperback), 1965

Thomas, Keith. *Religion and the Decline of Magic,* Charles Scribner's Sons, 1971

Underhill, Evelyn. *Mysticism; A Study in the Nature and Development of Man's Spiritual Consciousness,* Metheun & Co., London, 1911 etc.

Waite, Arthur E. *The Book of Ceremonial Magic,* William Rider & Son, London, 1911; University Books, 1961; Causeway Books, 1973

Wilson, Colin. *The Occult,* Hodder & Stoughton, London/Random House, 1971; Vintage Books, New York, 1973; Mayflower paperback, U.K., 1973

Occult Americana (Magazine)

Bi-monthly magazine with articles, interviews and other material relating to occultism and psi phenomena. Address: P.O. Box 667, Painesville, Ohio 44077.

Occult Observer (Magazine)

British journal first published May 1949 by Michael **Houghton,** London. Houghton was a well-known occultist, proprietor of the **Atlantis Book Shop.** The journal contained much useful information, but ceased publication after completion of one volume.

Occult Review, The

British monthly journal founded in 1877, devoted to the investigation and discussion of paranormal phenomena.

In September 1933 its title was changed briefly to *The London Forum.*

From January 1936 to Christmas 1948, it resumed the title *Occult Review,* but in 1949 it changed again to *Rider's Review,* after which it ceased publication.

It was undoubtedly one of the finest British journals of the occult ever published, and contained many notable contributions from authorities in the field.

The high standard of this periodical was due to the intelligent and broadminded approach of the original editor, the Hon. Ralph **Shirley.** He ceased editing when the publication changed hands with the sale of William Rider publications to Hutchinson, but his high standards and good judgment were continued for a time by Harry J. Scrutton.

Occult Studies Foundation

Former name of **MetaScience Foundation,** Rhode Island.

Occultism

The doctrine, theories, principles or practices of the pseudo-sciences of **magic,** including **alchemy, demonology, ghosts, miracles, poltergeists, prediction,** psychic powers, **spells, Spiritism,** sympathetic magic, etc. The term "the occult" is often used synonymously with "occultism." (See **Occult**)

Ochorowicz, Julien (1850–1917)

Lecturer in psychology at the University of Lemberg, co-director from 1907 of the Institut Général Psychologique of Paris, distinguished psychical researcher. He was born in Radzyn, Poland, February 23, 1850 and educated at the University of Warsaw.

The famous medium Eusapia **Palladino** was his guest from November 1893 until January 1894 in Warsaw. His conclusions did not favor the spirit hypothesis and he expressed his conviction that the phenomena were due to a "fluidic action" and were performed at the expense of the medium's own powers and those of the persons present. The hypothesis that for the greater part of the phenomena a "fluidic double" can, under certain conditions, detach itself and act independently of the body of the medium, appeared to him to be necessary.

After the exposure of the medium's cheating in seances in Cambridge, England, he came to the defense of Eusapia and offered very plausible reasons for her constant attempt to free her hand. He condemned the method employed at Cambridge as a blundering one.

The mediumship of Mlle. **Tomczyk** was discovered by Dr. Ochorowitz. His experiments with her were very important. He achieved conspicuous success in **psychic photography,** having photographed an etheric hand on a film rolled together and enclosed in a bottle, and objects suspended in the air without contact. For this, in 1911 the Comité d'Etude de Photographie Transcendental awarded him a prize of 1,000 francs. A similar prize was awarded to him by the Academie des Sciences de Paris.

He was an honorary member of the Society for Psychical Research, London, the American Society for Psychical Research, and other societies in Hungary and Germany. He was author of over a hundred books, papers and articles on psychology, philosophy and psychical research.

His books included: *Mediumistic Phenomena* (1913), *Psychology and Medicine* (1916), *Psychology, Pedagogics and Ethics* (1917). His articles in the journal *Annales des Science Psychiques* include: 'La question de la fraude dans les expériences médiumniques' (The Question of Fraud in Mediumistic Experiments, 1896), 'Un nouveau phénomène médiumnique' (A New Mediumistic Phenomenon, 1909).

He died in Warsaw, Poland, May 1, 1917.

Od (Odic Force, Odyle)

The term first used by Baron Karl von **Reichenbach** to denote the subtle effluence which he claimed emanated from every substance in the universe, particularly from the stars and planets, and from crystals, magnets and the human body.

The term "Od" was derived from *Odin,* the Norse deity, indicating a power that permeated the whole of nature. The name "Od" was retained by Dr. John Ashburner (1816–1878) in his translation of Reichenbach's writings, but another translator, Prof. William Gregory (1803–1858) substituted "Odyle," probably hoping it would sound more scientific than "Od."

Od or Odyle was perceptible to sensitives, in whom it produced vague feelings of heat or cold, according to the substance from which it radiated. A sufficiently sensitive person might perceive the odic light, a clear flame of definite color, issuing from the human fingertips, the poles of the magnet, various metals, crystals and chemicals, and hovering like a luminous cloud over new-made graves.

The colors varied with each substance; thus silver and gold had a white flame; cobalt, a blue; copper and iron, a red.

The English Mesmerists speedily applied Reichenbach's methods to their own sensitives, with results that surpassed their expectations. These observations were confirmed by experiments with persons in perfect health. Prof. D. Endlicher of Vienna saw on the poles of an electromagnet flames forty inches high, unsteady, exhibiting a rich play of colors, and ending in a luminous smoke, which rose to the ceiling and illuminated it. The experiments were controlled by Dr. William Gregory, who was Professor of Chemistry in the University of Edinburgh and Dr. Ashburner in England.

According to the sources from which the energy proceeded, Reichenbach employed the following nomenclature: Crystallod, electrod, photod, thermod, etc. He claimed that this peculiar force also existed in the rays of the sun and the moon, in animal and human bodies, that it could be conducted to distances yet unascertained by all solid and liquid bodies, that bodies may be charged with od, or od may be transferred from one body to another. This transference was apparently affected by contact. But mere proximity, without contact, was sufficient to produce the charge, although in a feebler degree. The mouth, the hands, the forehead and the occiput were the main parts of the body in which the od force manifested.

Reichenbach claimed that the odic tension varied during the day; it diminished with hunger, increased after a meal and also diminished at sunset. He insisted that the odic flame was a material something, that it could be affected by breath or a current of air and that it exhibited a suggestive likeness to the aurora borealis.

The thoroughness of Reichenbach's experiments, and the apparent soundness of his scientific methods, made a deep impression on the public mind. The objections of James Braid, who at this time advanced his theory of suggestion, were ignored by the protagonists of od. In after years, when Spiritualism had established itself in America, there remained a group of "rational" defenders of the movement, who attributed the phenomena of Spiritualism as well as those of **poltergeist** to the action of odylic force. **Table-turning** and rapping were also referred to this emanation by many who laughed to scorn Faraday's theory of unconscious muscular action.

Others again, such as Mr. Guppy, regarded the so-called "spirit" intelligences producing the manifestations as being compounded of odic vapors emanating from the medium, and probably connected with an all-pervading thought-atmosphere—an idea sufficiently like the "cosmic fluid" of the early magnetists.

Reichenbach's Odic Force clearly had possible relevance to psychical research, and in 1883 the Society for Psychical Research, London, formed a committee to report on "Reichenbach Phenomena." The committee's first report was published in the Society's *Proceedings* (vol. 1, part 3, 1883) and contributions on the subject also appeared from time to time in the S.P.R. *Proceedings* and *Journal.*

Reichenbach's experiments with Od make interesting comparison with the phenomenon of the human **Aura** reported by Dr. Walter J. **Kilner,** Oscar Bagnall and others, and also with the researches of Dr. Wilhelm **Reich** and his concept of "Orgone energy." (See also **Aura; Emanations; Orgone;** Baron von **Reichenbach**)

Recommended reading:

Bagnall, Oscar. *The Origin and Properties of the Human Aura,* University Books, 1970

Kilner, Walter J. *The Human Aura,* University Books, 1965

Reich, Wilhelm. *The Discovery of the Orgone* (2 vols.), New York, 1942, 1948

Reichenbach, Karl von (transl. John Ashburner). *Physico-Physiological Researches on the Dynamics of Magnetism, Heat, Light, Crystallization, and Chemism, in their relations to Vital Force,* London, 1851 (an alternative translation by William Gregory was issued under the title *Researches on Magnetism, Electricity, Heat, Light, Crystallization and Chemical Attraction, in their relations to the Vital Force,* London, 1850; University Books, 1974)

Reichenbach, Karl von (transl. F. D. O'Byrne). *Letters on Od and Magnetism,* London, 1926 (reissued as *The Odic Force; Letters on Od and Magnetism,* University Book, 1968)

O'Donnell, Elliott (1872–1965)

Author of popular books on occult subjects. Born in England, he claimed descent from Irish chieftains of ancient times, including Niall of the Nine Hostages (the King Arthur of Irish folklore) and Red Hugh, who fought the English in the sixteenth century. O'Donnell was educated at Clifton College, Bristol, England, and Queen's Service Academy, Dublin, Ireland.

He had a psychic experience at the age of five, in a house where he saw a nude elemental figure covered with spots. As a young man, he was half strangled by a mysterious phantom in Dublin. In later life he became a ghost hunter, but first he traveled in America, working on a range in Oregon and becoming a policeman in the Chicago Railway Strike of 1894. Returning to England, he worked as a schoolmaster and trained for the theater. He served in the British army in World War I, later acted on the stage and in movies.

His first book, written in his spare time, was a psychic thriller titled *For Satan's Sake* (1905). From this point onwards, he became a writer. He wrote several popular novels but specialized in what were claimed as true stories of ghosts and hauntings. These were immensely popular, but his flamboyant style and amazing stories suggest that he embroidered fact with a romantic flair for fiction.

As an authority on the supernatural, he achieved fame as a ghost hunter. He lectured and broadcast on the subject in Britain and the U.S. and also appeared on television. In addition to his books he wrote scores of articles and stories for national newspapers and magazines. He claimed "I have investigated, sometimes alone, and sometimes with other people and the press, many cases of reputed hauntings. I believe in ghosts but am not a spiritualist."

The O'Donnells were reputed to have a **Banshee**—the wailing ghost that heralds a death, and O'Donnell wrote the only book devoted entirely to the subject. It is not known whether his own passing evoked this eerie phantom, but he lived to the ripe old age of ninety-three years. He died May 6, 1965.

He achieved the distinction of an entry in the prestigious British publication *Who's Who,* in which he listed his hobbies "investigating queer cases, inventing queer games, and frightening crooks with the Law." The latter pastime seems a piece of whimsical romanticism, since there are no reports of any criminals being scared by him.

He published over fifty books, including the following typical titles: *For Satan's Sake* (1905), *Unknown Depths* (1906), *Some Haunted Houses* (1908), *Haunted Houses of London* (1909), *Reminiscences of Mrs. E. M. Ward* (1910), *The Meaning of Dreams* (1911), *Byways of Ghostland* (1911), *Scottish Ghost Stories* (1912), *Werewolves* (1912), *The Sorcery Club* (1912), *Animal Ghosts* (1913), *Ghostly Phenomena* (1913), *Haunted Highways and Byways* (1914), *The Irish Abroad* (1915), *Twenty Years' Experience as a Ghost Hunter* (1916), *The Haunted Man* (1917), *Spiritualism Explained* (1917), *Fortunes* (1918), *Haunted Places in England* (1919), *Menace of Spiritualism* (1920), *More Haunted Houses of London* (1920), *The Banshee* (1926), *Ghosts, Helpful and Harmful* (1926), *Strange Disappearances* (1927; reprinted University Books, 1972), *Strange Sea Mysteries* (1927), *Confessions of a Ghost Hunter* (1928), *Fatal Kisses* 1929), *Famous Curses* (1929), *Great Thames Mysteries* 1929), *Rooms of Mystery* (1931), *Ghosts of London* (1932), *The Devil in the Pulpit* (1932), *Family Ghosts* (1934), *Strange Cults & Secret Societies of Modern London* (1934), *Spookerisms; Twenty-five Weird Happenings* (1936), *Haunted Churches* (1939), *Dead Riders* (1953), *Phantoms of the Night* (1956), *Haunted Waters* (1957), *Trees of Ghostly Dread* (1958).

Odor of Sanctity

Perfume said to be exhaled by Christian saints, even after death. The idea that sin has a disagreeable odor and holiness a sweet perfume occurs in Romance literature and reflects folk beliefs of medieval times.

In Malory's *Morte d'Arthur* (c. 1469, translated as *History of Prince Arthur*), the death of the wicked Sir Corsabrin is described as follows: "Then they smote off the head of sir Corsabrin, and therewithal came a stench out of the body, when the soul departed." And in contrast, the death of the noble Sir Launcelot is described thus: "When sir Bors and his fellows came to sir Launcelot's bed, they found him stark dead, and the sweetest savour about him that ever they did smell."

St. Benedicta (c. 1643) claimed that angels had perfumes as various as those of flowers; Benedicta herself was supposed to exhale the sweet perfume of the love of God. The body of St. Clare (A.D. 660), abbot of Ferriol, exhaled a sweet odor after death, which pervaded St. Blandina's church. When St. Hubert of Britanny (A.D. 714) died, the whole province was said to be filled with sweet perfume. St. Casimir, Patron of Poland, died in 1483, and when his body was exhumed one hundred and twenty years later, it exhaled a sweet smell. (See also **Perfumes**)

Oesterreich, Traugott Konstantin (1880-1949)

German professor of philosophy, an authority on religious philosophy and one of the first modern scientists in Germany to declare publicly his belief in psychic phenomena.

He taught philosophy at Tübingen University in 1910 and was appointed Professor in 1922. He somehow survived in Nazi Germany, in spite of his Jewish wife and his anti-militarist views, although he was dismissed from his post in 1933, reinstated in 1945 and again forced into retirement on reduced pension soon afterwards. He died in 1949.

He was originally skeptical of psychic phenomena, and in the fourth volume of Friedrich Ueberweg's *Geschichte der Philosophie* (Berlin, 1916) he referred to Baron **Schrenck-Notzing,** pioneer of investigations into **materialization** phenomena, as the dupe of tricksters. In private correspondence with Oesterreich, Schrenck-Notzing protested at this sweeping charge, and submitted his entire literary and photographic material on **Eva C.,** the famous medium. Oesterreich became interested, investigated the mediumship of Frau Maria **Silbert** and Willi **Schneider** and became convinced of the reality of such phenomena.

In 1921, he published two books: *Grundbegriffe de Parapsychologie* and *Der Okkultismus im modernen Weltbild;* the latter book testified to materializations and **telekinesis** as facts. He also revised his earlier views in a new edition of Ueberweg's *Geschichte der Philosophie* published in 1923. His book *Weltbilder der Gegenwart* contained further important contributions to psychic science. As an active and thorough psychical researcher, Professor Oesterreich also published a number of scientific papers and monographs supporting psychic science.

His classic work, however, was undoubtedly his careful study of psychic possession (see **Obsession and Possession**), translated into English by D. Ibberson from the German publication of 1921 as *Possession: Demoniacal and other among primitive races, in antiquity, the Middle Ages, and modern times.* This is an immensely detailed study of possession and multiple **personality** from earliest times onwards and must be regarded as the standard work on the subject. For many years it failed to secure other than a highly specialized readership, but following the 1966 reprint by University Books, New York, it attracted the attention of William Peter Blatty, who derived much of the background material for his sensational book *The Exorcist* (1971) from it. After the equally sensational movie of the book, there was a new wave of interest in demonic possession and exorcism, and Oesterreich's book was again reprinted by various publishers, sometimes under variant titles *Possession and Exorcism* and *Possession and Obsession.*

For biographical information on Oesterreich, see the book *Traugott Konstantin Oesterreich—Lebenswerk und Lebensschicksal* (1954) published by his widow Dr. Maria Oesterreich.

Recommended reading:

Oesterreich, T. K. *Occultism at the Present Day,* London, 1922

Oesterreich, T. K. *Occultism and Modern Science,* McBride, 1923

Oesterreich, T. K. *Possession: Demoniacal and Other . . .* (transl. from German *Die Bessessenheit*), University Books, 1966

Official UFO

Magazine published nine times per year, giving articles, photographs, charts and other information relating to extraterrestrial phenomena. Address: Countrywide Publications, 257 Park Avenue South, New York, N.Y. 10010.

Ohio Sky Watcher

Quarterly publication of Ohio UFO Investigators League, Inc. Includes news and discussion of UFO sightings and other mysteries such as monsters, Bermuda Triangle. Address: 5852 East River Road, Fairfield, Ohio 45014.

Ointment, Witches'

It was believed in medieval times that the wonders performed by witches such as changing themselves into animals, or being transported through the air, were wrought by anointing themselves with a potent salve.

As ointments have been used in Oriental countries as a means of inducing visions, it is possible that something of the kind may account for the hallucinations which the witches seem to have experienced.

Francis Bacon (1561–1626) stated: "The *ointment,* that witches use, is reported to be made of the *fat* of *children,* digged out of their *graves;* of the *juices* of *smallage, wolfebane,* and *cinque foil,* mingled with the *meal* of fine *wheat:* but I suppose that the soporiferous medicines are likest to do it, which are *hen-bane, hemlock, mandrake, moonshade, tobacco, opium, saffron, poplar leaves,* etc."

Other recipes which have been handed down as flying ointments for witches include the following:

1) Parsley, water of aconite, poplar leaves and soot
2) Water parsnip, sweet flag, cinquefoil, bat's blood, deadly nightshade and oil
3) Baby's fat, juice of water parsnip, aconite, cinquefoil, deadly nightshade and soot.

It should be noted that such poisonous drugs as aconite, hemlock and belladonna, absorbed through the skin, would probably cause mental confusion, dizziness, irregular heart action and shortness of breath. These effects might give the sensation of flying through the air, although witchcraft authorities during the great witch hunts have claimed that witches did actually travel in the air. (See also **Drugs; Transvection; Witchcraft**)

O'Key Sisters, Jane & Elizabeth (c. 1838)

Two somnambules or hypnotized subjects of Dr. John **Elliotson,** early British experimenter in **Animal Magnetism.**

The two girls were put into trance by passes on the part of Dr. Elliotson and two different states induced: a condition of coma with insensibility and lack of consciousness, and ecstatic delirium in which they spoke, sometimes making clairvoyant predictions and were also subject to the operator's suggestions. In the ecstatic condition, sometimes lasting for days, one of the girls claimed to be able to see with the back of her hand.

After many successful demonstrations, Dr. Elliotson one day met with a complete failure, which excited his opponents to accusations of imposture on the part of the girls, Dr. Elliotson being stigmatized as a weak and credulous man. Eventually he was obliged to resign his position as physician at University College Hospital, London. However, Dr. Elliotson persisted with his experiments and published his conclusions in an appendix to his *Human Physiology* (London, 1840), in which he detailed his further experiments with the O'Key sisters.

Olcott, Henry Steel (1832–1907)

Joint founder with Madame **Blavatsky** of the **Theosophical Society.**

Olcott was born August 1, 1832 at Orange, New Jersey, where his father had a farm. At the age of twenty-six, Olcott was associate agricultural editor of the New York *Tribune* and traveled abroad to study European farming methods. In 1860, he married Mary E. Morgan and they had three sons. They later divorced. Olcott served in the Civil War and afterwards became a special commissioner with the rank of Colonel. In 1866, he was admitted to the New York bar. In 1878 he was commissioned by the president to report on trade relations between the U.S. and India.

His first contact with psychical phenomena was established in 1874. The *New York Daily Graphic* had assigned him to investigate the phenomena of the **Eddy Brothers** in Vermont. He spent ten weeks at the Chittenden farm and came away convinced of the genuineness of the phenomena which he witnessed. The fifteen articles in which he summarized his experiences started him on the career of a psychical investigator.

His next opportunity was afforded by the Holmes scandal, when the **materialization** mediums Mr. and Mrs. Nelson **Holmes** were accused of fraud. Olcott sifted all the records, collected new affidavits and came to the conclusion that as the evidence of fraudulent mediumship is very conflicting, the mediums should be tested regardless of the past. After making his tests, he affirmed his belief in their genuine powers.

His book *People from the Other World* (1875) into which the Eddy articles were incorporated, contained an account of his experiences with the medium Mrs. Elizabeth **Compton,** whose history presents a strange case of entire dematerialization. The book was made the subject of scathing criticism in D. D. **Home's** *Lights and Shadows of Spiritualism* (1877). It was denounced as "the most worthless and dishonest" book. The bias of D. D. Home against the author, however, was strongly apparent.

As a result of the Eddy and Holmes investigation, Col. Olcott was soon acknowledged as a competent psychical researcher. When the professors of the Imperial University of St. Petersburg decided, by the wish of the Grand Duke Constantine of Russia, to make a scientific investigation of Spiritualism, Olcott and Mme. Blavatsky were asked to select the best American medium they could recommend. Their choice fell on Henry **Slade.**

The association between Col. Olcott and Mme. Blavatsky sprang out of their meeting at the Chittenden farm. Mme. Blavatsky had strong leanings towards Spiritualism and went to the Vermont farm to satisfy her curiosity. For some time she wrote articles on psychic subjects, but she broke with the Spiritualist movement soon after her larger conception, the Theosophical Society, came into being.

It was founded in December 1875. Col. Olcott was elected as chairman and he threw himself with unbounded energy and zeal into the task of founding and organizing the society all over the world. It is a great credit to his organizing genius that the society became firmly established in New York and that it withstood later the emotional earthquake of the Blavatsky exposure by the Society for Psychical Research (see Mme. H. P. **Blavatsky**).

Nobody witnessed more apparent Theosophic marvels accomplished through the agency of Mme. Blavatsky than Olcott. In those early days, Mme. Blavatsky professed to have been controlled by the spirit "John King." She first specialized in precipitated writing, independent drawing and supernormal duplication of letters and other things (among them a $1,000 banknote in the presence of Olcott and the Hon. J. L. Sullivan). To Olcott's great regret, the duplicate had mysteriously dissolved in the drawer. In justice, it should be remarked that Col. Olcott was convinced that Mme. Blavatsky could produce such illusions by hypnotic suggestion. Apparently the Colonel was a good subject, for Mme. Blavatsky once disappeared from his presence in a closed room and appeared again a short time afterwards from nowhere. The admission of this miracle vitiates Col. Olcott's observations and records, and makes it at once intelligible that he could have testified in good faith to the appearance of **Mahatmas** and to the souvenirs they left behind.

In 1878, Col. Olcott sailed with Mme. Blavatsky for Bombay. On the way, they stopped in London for a short period. A. P. **Sinnett** in his book *The Early Days of Theosophy in Europe* (1922) suggested that the manners of Mme. Blavatsky and Col. Olcott were liable to cause offense in polite society and that the beginning of the unfriendly attitude of the Society for Psychical Research was to be traced to a meeting of that body at which Col. Olcott made a speech in his worst style.

The great Blavatsky exposure in 1895 left Col. Olcott's honor unimpugned. According to Dr. Richard Hodgson, who compiled the famous S.P.R. Report, Olcott's statements were unreliable either owing to peculiar lapses of memory or to extreme deficiency in the faculty of observation. Hodgson could not place the slightest value upon Olcott's evidence. But he stated definitely also: "Some readers may be inclined to think that Col. Olcott must himself have taken an active and deliberate part in the fraud, and been a partner with Mme. Blavatsky in the conspiracy. Such, I must emphatically state, is not my own opinion." On the other hand V. Solovyoff in *A Modern Priestess of Isis* (1895) called Olcott a "liar and a knave in spite of his stupidity."

The accusation is unjust, although it must be admitted that there are many Theosophic marvels in the Indian history of Theosophy which, on the basis of Dr. Hodgson's findings, make the hypothesis of collusion on the part of the Colonel very plausible. One of the most problematic of such instances is the story of the William **Eglinton** letter which, from the boat "Vega," was claimed to be "astrally" conveyed first to Bombay, then with superimposed script of Mme. Blavatsky carried to Calcutta, where it was precipitated from the ceiling in Mrs. Gordon's home whilst Col. Olcott pointed to the apparition of two Brothers outside the window. According to Mrs. Gordon's testimony, Col. Olcott told her that the night before he had an intimation from his Chohan (teacher) that K.H. (a Mahatma) had been to the "Vega" and had seen Eglinton. If then the delivery of this letter was fraudulent (and it has been convincingly claimed by experts that the K.H. letters were written by Mme. Blavatsky), the only excuse for Col. Olcott lies in the supposition that Mme. Blavatsky made him dream, by her powers of suggestion, what she wanted—a supposition which, in view of Mme. Blavatsky's record, is not entirely preposterous. It should be remembered that Hodgson stated "writing about him [Olcott] from America to a Hindu in Bombay, she characterised him as a 'psychologised baby', saying that the Yankees thought themselves very smart and that Colonel Olcott thought he was particularly smart, even for a Yankee, but that he would have to get up much earlier in the morning to be as smart as she was." The revelation of this cruel flippancy by a woman he had loyally supported caused the Colonel to contemplate suicide momentarily.

One of Olcott's greatest achievements was undoubtedly his public espousal of Buddhism, which popularized this religion in Western countries. His *Buddhist Catechism* stemmed from his conversion to Buddhism, publicly affirmed in Ceylon in 1880. First issued in 1881, the book was widely used as a textbook by Western Buddhists, and editions have remained in print every since.

Olcott died February 17, 1907 at Adyar, India. For biographical information on Olcott, together with valuable sidelights on the early history of the Theosophical movement, see Olcott's *Old Diary Leaves*, 4 vols. first published Theosophical Publishing House, 1895–1910, frequently reprinted. His book *People From the Other World* (1875) was reissued by Charles E. Tuttle, 1971. (See also Mme. H. P. **Blavatsky;** Richard **Hodgson; Mahatma Letters; Theosophical Society**)

Old, Walter G(orn) (1864–1929)

British author of works on astrology. Originally named Walter Richard Old, he wrote under the name Walter Gorn Old and the pseudonym "Sepharial." He was born March 20, 1864 at Harndsworth, Birmingham, England and educated at King Edward's School, Birmingham.

At an early age he studied books on **Kabala** and **astrology.** He became friendly with astrologer Alan **Leo**

(1860–1917). Old studied a variety of subjects, including medical dispensing, Orientalism and ancient languages, but without a successful career until he eventually found his feet in professional astrology and authorship. He moved to London in 1889 and joined the Theosophical Society, where he became a member of the Inner Group around Madame **Blavatsky.** He also introduced Alan Leo to Theosophy.

Old had special psychic talent in **astral projection (out-of-the-body** traveling). He left the Society after the death of Madame Blavatsky.

He developed a system of astrological prediction for the stock market, and predicted futures in basic commodities. His most profitable income was from astrological horse-racing systems. He died December 23, 1929, a year before the popularity of newspaper astrology columns, at which he would doubtless have been highly successful. He contributed a number of articles to the *Occult Review.* His books include: *Book of the Crystal and the Seer* (1897), *Prognostic Astronomy* (1901), *Second Sight* (1911), *The Kabala of Numbers* (2 vols., 1913), *The Book of Charms and Talismans* (n.d., c. 1923).

Old Hat Used for Raising the Devil

A popular mode of raising the devil in former times was to make a circle, place an old hat in the center, and repeat the Lord's Prayer backwards. This was really a caricature of magical incantation.

"Old Moore"

Pseudonym assumed by a succession of British astrologers for more than three centuries. The original Dr. Francis Moore, physician, was born in 1657 and published his *Vox Stellarum* almanac in 1701.

The title was still being used in the nineteenth century. A later "Old Moore" was Henry Andrews, whose editions of *Vox Stellarum* reached half a million circulation. *Vox Stellarum* had become *Old Moore's Almanack* by the twentieth century, and in the 1960s "Old Moore" was Edward W. Whitman, secretary of the Federation of British Astrologers. There is a "Genuine Old Moore" ("Beware of Spurious Editions") credited to John Arigho which at one time featured a portrait of one Theophilus Moore, said to have lived c. 1764. The Irish Old Moores contain an interesting regular feature of word games, conducted by "Lady Di."

Until recently, there were four rival Old Moores in Britain, issued by Roberts, Blakemore, Walker and Foulsham, all claiming "Original Editions." Today Foulsham states that their own original Old Moore ("Beware of Imitations") dates back to a copyright of 1697. Their predictions are now calculated by a team of four astrologers.

A comparable American publication is the *Old Farmer's Almanac,* whose Robert B. Thomas rivals Old Moore in claiming centuries of continuous publication. It maintains the tradition of quaint wit established by Benjamin Franklin's *Poor Richard's Almanac,* which started in 1732. (See also **Astrology; "Zadkiel"**)

Recommended reading:

Capp, Bernard. *Astrology & the Popular Press; English Almanacs 1500–1800,* Faber & Faber, London & Boston, 1979

Howe, Ellic. *Urania's Children; The Strange World of the Astrologers,* William Kimber, London, 1967; (revised *Astrology and Psychological Warfare During World War II,* & condensed ed. Rider, 1972) (Part I deals with the historical background of British astrology)

Old Religion, The

Folklore term for witchcraft as paganism displaced by Christianity. (See also **Witchcraft**)

"Old Scratch"

One of the appellations given to the Devil. It is supposed to have been derived from *Skrati,* an old Teutonic faun or Satyr, half-man and half-goat, and possessed of horns. (See also **"Nick"; "Splitfoot"**)

Om (or AUM)

A Sanskrit word of special sanctity in the Hindu religion. It is pronounced at the beginning and end of every lesson in the *Vedas* (ancient scriptures), and is also the introductory word of the *Puranas* (religious works embodying legends and mythology). It is stated in the *Katha-Upanishad:* "Whoever knows this syllable obtains whatever he wishes."

Various accounts are given of its origin; one that it is the term of assent used by the gods, and probably an old contracted form of the Sanskrit word *evam* meaning "thus." The *Manu-Sangita* (Laws of Manu), a religious work of social laws, states that the word was formed by Brahma himself, who extracted the letters *a-u-m* from the *Vedas,* one from each, and they thus explain its mysterious power and sanctity. *Om* is also the name given by the Hindus to the spiritual sun, as opposed to *Surya,* the natural sun. (See also **AUM**)

Omarr, Sydney

One of the most successful modern astrologers in the U.S. Born in Philadelphia, he served with the Air Force in the Pacific during World War II. After predicting the death of President Roosevelt, the Armed Forces Radio assigned him to a horoscope show; he thus became the first official astrologer in U.S. Army history.

After the war, he wrote many articles on astrology and appeared in radio shows. He was also a CBS radio news editor in Los Angeles. His astrology columns appeared in some 225 newspapers, and at the height of his success he moved to Hollywood. His many books on astrology include: *Astrology; Its Role in Your Life* (1963), *My World of Astrology* (1965), *Sydney Omarr's Astrological Guide to Sex and Love* (1971), *Dream-Scope* (1973), *The Thought Dial Way to a Healthy & Successful Life* (1973), *Sydney Omarr's Astrological Guide* (1974).

Omega Magazine and Directory

Monthly publication giving news of psychic matters in the Southwest area; includes articles, interviews and information on regional groups. Address: P.O. Box 2145, Scottsdale, Arizona 85252.

Omez, Réginald, O. P. (Order of Dominicans) (1895–   )

Dominican priest who has studied parapsychological subjects. Born October 12, 1895 at Tourcoing (Nord),

France, he studied at Le Saulchoir, Université Francaise des Dominicains (D. Theol. 1922) and Dominican University, Rome, Italy (Ph.D. 1924). He was professor of the International Dominican University, Rome, from 1922–40, French and international chaplain of Catholic Writers and Journalists from 1942 onwards, member of French Association for Metapsychical Studies, Society of Friends of the Institut Métapsychique International, Academy of Social Education and Mutual Aid.

In addition to his many articles and books on religious subjects, he has published: *Le Subconscient* (The Subconscious Mind), vol.1 *Sciences Psychiques et Morale Catholique* (Psychic Sciences and Catholic Morality, 1949), vol.2 *Metapsychique et Merveilleux religieux* (Metapsychics and the Religious Supernatural, 1950), vol.3 *Le Subconscient destructeur ou serviteur du Moi?* (The Subconscious: Destroyer or Servant of the Ego?, 1951), vol.4 *Présence de nos morts* (Our Dead Are With Us, 1952), vol.5 *Subconscient et Liberté* (The Subconscious and Freedom, 1953), *Etudes sur le subconscient* (Studies of the Subconscious, 1954), *Peut-on communiquer avec les morts?* (Can We Communicate with the Dead? 1955, also translated into German and Portuguese), *Supranormal ou surnaturel?* (Supernormal or Supernatural? 1956, Spanish ed. 1958 English translation titled *Psychical Phenomena* 1959), *Religione E. Scienze Metapsichiche* (Religion and the Metaphysical Sciences, 1957), *Psychical Phenomena* (U.S. ed. 1958), *Médecine et Merveilleux* (Medicine and the Supernatural, 1956), *Le Gouvernement Divin: Coopération des hommes et des esprits* (God's Rule: Cooperation of Men and Spirits, 1959), *Le monde des ressuscités* (The World After Resurrection, 1961), *Jeunesse eternelle* (Everlasting Youth, 1962), *L'Occultisme devant la science* (Occultism and Science, 1963). He has published articles in a number of journals, including: *Revue Métapsychique, Schweizer Rundschau, Présences, La Tour Saint Jacques, Tomorrow, International Journal of Parapsychology.*

Onimancy (or Onycomancy)

An elaborate ritual of **divination** said to be based on the observation of the angel Uriel. Upon the nails of the right hand or the palm of the hand of an unpolluted boy or a young virgin is put some oil of olives, or what is better, oil of walnuts mingled with tallow or blacking. If money or things hidden in the earth be sought, the face of the child must be turned towards the east. If crime be inquired into, or the knowledge of a person out of affection, towards the south; for robbery towards the west, and for murder towards the south.

Then the child must repeat the seventy-two verses of the Psalms, which the Hebrew Kabalists (see **Kabala**) collected for the Urim and Thummim. These are found in the third book of Johann Rechlin on the Kabalistical art (De arte cabalistica, 1517) and in a treatise *De verbo mirifico* (c. 1480). In each of these verses occurs the venerable name of four letters, and the three lettered name of the seventy-two angels, which are referred to the sacred name **Shemhamphorash,** which was hidden in the folds of the lining of the tippet of the high priest. When the curious student has done all this, he is assured that he will "see wonders."

Other authorities give the name Onycomancy to the interpretation of the spots on the human nails. (See also **Divination; Onychomancy**)

Onion

The onion was regarded as a symbol of the universe by the ancient Egyptians, and many curious beliefs were associated with it. It was believed that it attracted and absorbed infectious matters, and was thus usually hung up in rooms to prevent maladies. This belief in the absorptive virtue of the onion is prevalent even in modern times.

"When a youth," stated British folklorist James Napier, "I remember the following story being told, and implicitly believed by all. There was once a certain king or nobleman who was in want of a physician, and two celebrated doctors applied. As both could not obtain the situation, they agreed among themselves that the one was to try to poison the other, and he who succeeded in overcoming the poison would thus be left free to fill the situation. They drew lots as to who should first take the poison. The first dose given was a stewed toad, but the party who took it immediately applied a poultice of peeled onions over his stomach, and thus abstracted all the poison of the toad. Two days after, the other doctor was given the onions to eat. He ate them, and died. It was generally believed that the poultice of peeled onions laid on the stomach, or underneath the armpits, would cure anyone who had taken poison."

Onomancy (or Onomamancy)

Divination by names, satirically said to be nearer to divination by a donkey, and more properly termed Onomamancy or Onomatomancy. The notion that an analogy existed between men's names and their fortunes is supposed to have originated with the Pythagoreans; it provided some speculations to Plato and was the source of some witticism by Ausonius, which may amuse the classical scholar to collate from his epigrams.

Two leading rules in the science of Onomancy were first, that an even number of vowels in a man's name signifies something amiss in his left side; an uneven number a similar affection on the right. Between the two, perfect sanity was little to be expected. Secondly, of two competitors, that one would prove successful when the numeral letters in whose name when summed up exceeded the amount of those in the name of his rival; and this was one of the reasons which enabled Achilles to triumph over Hector.

The Gothic King Theodotus was said, on the authority of Cælius Rhodiginus to have practiced a peculiar species of Onomancy on the recommendation of a Jew. The diviner advised the prince, when on the eve of a war with Rome, to shut up thirty hogs in three different sties, having previously given some of them Roman and others Gothic names. On an appointed day, when the sties were opened, all the Romans were found alive, but with half their bristles fallen off; all the Goths, on the other hand, were dead. From this the onomantist predicted that the Gothic army would be utterly destroyed by the Romans, who, at the same time, would lose half their own force.

The system recalls the rationale of Jewish **gematria,** which assigns numerical values to the letters of names. (See also **Divination**)

Onychomancy

Divination by the fingernails. It was practiced by watching the reflection of the sun in the nails of a boy, and judging the future by the shape of the figures which showed themselves on their surface. (See also **Divination; Onimancy**)

Onyx

A precious stone whose properties were believed to resemble those of Jasper, besides increasing saliva in boys, and bringing terrible shapes to the dreamer. If applied to the eye it was said to act as if it were alive, by creeping about and removing anything noxious.

The onyx was further believed to create strife, to cause melancholy and to cure epilepsy.

According to the authorized text of the Bible, an onyx was the eleventh stone in the breastplate of the High Priest, but it is more probable that this stone was a **beryl.**

Oom the Omnipotent

Title given to Pierre **Bernard,** pioneer of Hatha Yoga study in the U.S. and founder of the New York Sanskrit College in 1909.

Ooscopy and Oomantia

Two methods of divination by eggs. An example under the former name was related by the Roman historian Suetonius (c. 98–138 A.D.), who stated that Livia, when she was anxious to know whether she should be the mother of a boy or girl, kept an egg in her bosom at the proper temperature, until a chick with a beautiful cockscomb came forth.

The name Oomantia denoted a method of divining the signs or characters appearing in eggs. The custom of pasche or paste eggs, which are stained with various colors and given away at Easter is well known, and was described at considerable length by John Brand in *Observations on Popular Antiquities* (2 vols., London, 1813 etc.). The custom was most religiously observed in Russia, where it is derived from the Greek Church. Gilded or colored eggs were mutually exchanged both by men and women, who kissed one another, and if any coolness existed previously became good friends again on these occasions.

The egg is one of the most ancient and beautiful symbols of new birth, and has been applied to natural philosophy as well as the spiritual creation of man.

Opal

Beautiful gemstone of quartz or silica, highly praised by **Pliny** (c. 23–79 A.D.), who wrote: "For in them you shall see the living fire of the ruby, the glorious purple of the amethyst, the green sea of the emerald, all glittering together in an incredible mixture of light." In ancient times many legends grew up around its claimed virtues. It was believed to recreate the heart, preserve from contagion in the air, and dispel sadness. It was also good for weak eyes. The name *poederos,* applied to the opal, is understood to indicate the beautiful complexion of youth.

The superstition that opals were unlucky seems to have been popularized by Sir Walter Scott's novel *Anne of Geirstein* (1829), in which the opal worn by Baroness Hermione of Arnheim has a drop of holy water fall upon it, whereupon a brilliant spark shot out of the gem and it lost its luster.

Open Letter

Bi-monthly publication of the **Findhorn Community,** Scotland, a famous **"New Age"** spiritual center. Address: Findhorn Publications, The Park, Findhorn Bay, Forres, Moray, Scotland.

"Ophiel"

Pseudonym of Edward C. Peach, modern popular writer on occultism. In 1961, after receiving a claims settlement of $1,000 for an accident, he spent the money publishing his own manuscript *The Art and Practice of Astral Projection,* using a Hong Kong printer. The book hit the market at the peak of the occult revival and sold so well that Llewellyn Publications were happy to take it over for their Gnostic Institute imprint.

Since then, "Ophiel" has published five successful occult books for them. Now in his sixties, he lives in an apartment in Hollywood, California, which he claims to have obtained by the method detailed in his book *The Art of Getting Material Things by Creative Visualization* (1966). His other books include: *Art and Practice of the Occult* (1968), *Art and Practice of Clairvoyance* (1969), *Oracle of Fortuna* (1972), *Art and Practice of Talismanic Magic* (1973), *Art and Practice of Cabala Magic* (1976), *Art and Practice of the Occult* (n.d.).

Ophites

This Gnostic sect seems to have dated from the second century. A full system of initiation was in vogue among the members, and they possessed symbols to represent purity, life, spirit and fire. The whole appears to have been a compound of the mysteries of the Egyptian goddess Isis, concepts of Oriental mythology, and Christian doctrine.

According to the theologian Origen (c. 185–c. 254 A.D.), they were founded by a man named Euphrates, but it seems more likely that this was a symbolic reference to the water of life in *John* (iv, 10). The sect was believed to have given special prominence to serpents in their rituals. (See also **Gnostics**)

Oracles

Shrines where a god was believed to speak to human beings through the mouths of priests or priestesses. The concept of the god becoming vocal in this manner was by no means confined to ancient Greece or Egypt.

Probably most primitive gods of the fetish class (see **Fetishism**) were consulted as oracles, and from **animism** this was transmitted later to gods of the most advanced type. In early times, the great question was whether man would have food on the next day and perhaps the first oracle was the spirit which directed the hungry primitive in hunting and fishing expeditions. The Esquimaux used to consult spirits for this purpose, and their wizards were as familiar with the art of giving ambiguous replies to their anxious clients as were the well-informed keepers of the oracles of Greece. As advancement proceeded, the direction of the gods was obtained in all the affairs of private and public life.

The Oracle of Delphi at Greece

When Jupiter was once desirous to ascertain the central point of the earth, he dispatched two eagles, or two crows, as they were named by Strabo. The messengers took flight in opposite courses, from sunrise and sunset, and they met at Delphi, which place was thenceforward dignified with the title "The navel of the earth" an "umbilicus" being represented in white marble within its celebrated temple.

Delphi thus became a place of great distinction, but it was not yet oracular until the fumes which issued from a neighboring cave were first discovered by a shepherd named Coretas. His attention was forcibly attracted to a spot around which whenever his goats were browsing they gambolled and bleated more than usual.

Whether these fumes arose in consequence of an earthquake, or whether they were generated by demoniacal art is not recorded; but the latter hypothesis was suggested by one commentator. Anyway, the story goes that Coretas, on approaching the spot, was seized with ecstacy and uttered words which were deemed inspired. It was not long before the danger arising in consequence of the excitement of curiosity among the neighbors, the deadly stupefaction often produced among those who inhaled the fumes without proper caution, and the inclination which it aroused in some to plunge themselves into the depths of the cavern below, occasioned the fissure to be covered by a sort of table, having a hole in the center and called a tripod, so that those who wished to try the experiment could resort there in safety.

Eventually a young girl of unsophisticated manners became the chosen medium of the responses, now deemed oracular and called "Pythian," as proceeding from Apollo, the slayer of Python, to whom Delphi was consecrated. A sylvan bower of laurel branches was erected over the spot, and at length the marble temple and the priesthood of Delphi arose where the Pythoness, seated on her throne, could be charged with the divine "afflatus," and was thus rendered the vehicle of Apollo's dictation.

As the oracle became more celebrated, its prophetic machinery was constructed of more costly materials. The tripod was then formed of gold but the lid, which was placed in its hollow rim in order to afford the Pythoness a more secure seat, continued to be made of brass. She prepared herself by drinking out of a sacred fountain (Castalia) adjoining the crypt, the waters of which were reserved for her only (and in which she bathed her hair) and by chewing a laurel leaf and circling her brows with a laurel crown.

The person who made inquiry from the oracle, first offered a victim, and then having written his question in a notebook, handed it to the Pythoness before she ascended the tripod, and he also, as well as the priestess, wore a laurel crown. In early times the oracle spoke only in one month of the year named "Byssus," in which it originated, and at first only on the seventh day of that month, which was esteemed the birthday of Apollo and was called "Polypthonus."

Virginity was at first an indispensable requisite in the Pythoness, on account (as Diodorus relates) of the purity of that state and its relation to Diana; moreover, because virgins were thought better adapted than others of their sex to keep oracular mysteries secret and inviolate. But after an untoward accident had occurred to one of these consecrated damsels, the guardians of the temple (in order, as they imagined, to prevent its repetition for the future) permitted no one to fulfil the duties of the office until she had attained the mature age of fifty. They still indulged her, however, with the use of a maiden's habit. The response was always delivered in Greek.

The Oracle of Dodona

Another celebrated oracle, that of Jupiter, was at Dodona in Epirus (from which Jupiter derived the name of Dodonus). It was situated at the foot of Mount Tomarus, in a wood of oaks, and there the answers were given by an old woman under the name of Pelias.

"Pelias" means dove in the Attic dialect, from which the fable arose that the doves prophesied in the groves of Dodona.

According to the historian Herodotus (c. 484–425 B.C.), this legend contains the following incident, which gave rise to the oracle.

Two priestesses of Egyptian Thebes were carried away by Phœnician merchants; one of them was conveyed to Libya, where she founded the oracle of Jupiter Ammon, the other to Greece. The latter one remained in the Dodonian wood, which was much frequented on account of the acorns. There she had a temple built at the foot of an oak in honor of Jupiter, whose priestess she had been in Thebes, and here afterwards a regular oracle was founded. Herodotus added that this priestess was called a dove, because her language could not be understood.

The Dodonic and African oracles were certainly connected, and Herodotus distinctly stated that the manner of prophecy in Dodona was the same as that in Egyptian Thebes. Diana was worshiped in Dodona in conjunction with Zeus, and a female figure was associated with Amun in the Libyan Ammonium. Besides this, the dove was the bird of Aphrodite, the Diana of Zeus, or the Mosaic divine love which saved mankind from complete destruction. According to other authors, there was a wondrous intoxicating spring at Dodona, and in later times more material means were employed to produce the prophetic spirit.

Several copper bowls and bells were placed upon a column with the statue of a boy beside them. When the wind moved a rod or scourge having three bones attached to chains, this struck upon the metallic bowls and bells, the sound of which was heard by the applicants. These Dodonian tones gave rise to a proverb: *æs Dodonæum*—an unceasing babbler.

The oracle at Dodona was dedicated to the Pelasgian Zeus, who was worshiped here at the same time as the almighty ruler of the world, and as the friendly associate of mankind. In the course of the theogonic process, Diana was associated with him as his wife, mother of Aphrodite. The servants of Zeus were Selles, the priests of Diana, the so-called Peliades. According to Homer, the Selles inhabited the sanctum at Dodona, sleeping upon the earth, and with naked unwashed feet. They served the Pelasgian Zeus. It is probable that they slept upon the earth on the hides of newly-sacrificed animals, to receive prophetic dreams, as was customary at other places, Calchos and Oropus amongst many others.

As regards the oracular divination of Dodona, it was partly natural, from the excitement of the mind, partly artificial. Of the latter we may mention three modes—the ancient oak of Zeus, with its prophetic doves, the miraculous spring, and the celebrated Dodonian bowls of brass.

The far-spreading speaking tree, the "incredible wonder," as Æschylus calls it, was an oak, a lofty beautiful tree, with evergreen leaves and sweet edible acorns, which according to the belief of the Greeks and Romans, were the first sustenance of mankind. The Pelasgi regarded this tree as the tree of life. In this tree the god was supposed to reside, and the rustling of its leaves and the voices of birds showed his presence. When the questioners entered, the oak rustled and the Peliades said, "Thus speaks Zeus." Incense was burned beneath it, which may be compared to the altar of Abraham under the oak Ogyges, which had stood there since the world's creation. According to the legend, sacred doves continually inhabited the tree, like the Marsoor oracle at Tiora Mattiene, where a sacred hawk foretells futurity from the top of a wooden pillar.

At the foot of the oak, a cold spring gushed as it were from its roots, and from its murmur the inspired priestesses prophesied.

Of this miraculous fountain, it is related that when lighted torches were thrust into it they were extinguished, and that extinguished torches were re-lit; it also rose and fell at various seasons. Ernst von Lasaulx in *Das pelasgische Orakel d. Zeus zu Dodona* (1841) stated: "That extinction and rekindling has, perhaps, the mystical signification that the usual sober life of the senses must be extinguished, that the prophetic spirit dormant in the soul may be aroused. The torch of human existence must expire, that a divine one may be lighted; the human must die that the divine may be born; the destruction of individuality is the awakening of God in the soul, or, as the mystics say, the setting of sense is the rising of truth."

The extinguishing of a burning light shows that the spring contained carbonic acid gas, which possesses stupifying and deadly properties, like all exhalations arising especially from minerals. The regular rising and sinking of the water is a frequent phenomenon, and has been observed from the earliest ages.

It appears that predictions were drawn from the tones of the Dodonian brass bowls, as well as from the rustling of the sacred oak and the murmuring of the sacred well.

The Dodonian columns, with that which stood upon them, appears to express the following: The medium-sized brazen bowl was a hemisphere, and symbolized heaven; the boy-like male statue was a figure of the Demiurgos, or constructor of the universe; the bell-like notes were a symbol of the harmony of the universe and music of the spheres. That the Demiurgos was represented as a boy is quite in the spirit of Egypto-Pelasgian theology as it reigned in Samothrace. The miraculous bell told all who came to Dodona to question the god that they were on holy ground, must inquire with pure hearts, and be silent when the god replied. It is easily imagined that these tones, independent and uninfluenced by human will, must have made a deep impression upon the minds of pilgrims. Those who questioned the god were also obliged to take a purificatory bath in the temple, similar to that by which the Delphian Pythia prepared herself for prophecy.

Besides this artificial soothsaying from signs, natural divination by the prophetic movements of the mind was practiced. Where there are prophesying priestesses, there must also be ecstatic ones, similar to those in the magnetic state. Sophocles called the Dodonean priestesses divinely inspired. Plato (Phædrus) stated, more decidedly, that the prophetess at Delphi and the priestesses at Dodona had done much good in sacred madness, in private and public affairs, to their country, but in their senses little or nothing.

We may infer from this that the Delphian Pythia as well as the Dodonian priestesses did not give their oracles in the state of common waking consciousness but in real ecstasy, to which the frequent incense (and drink) offerings would assist. Aristides stated still more clearly than the others, that the priestesses at Dodona neither knew (before being seized upon by the spirit) what would be said, nor remembered afterwards when their natural consciousness returned, what they had uttered, so that all others, rather than they, knew it.

The Oracle of Jupiter Trophonius

Trophonius, according to Pausanias (c. 470 B.C.), was the most skillful architect of his day. Concerning the origin of his oracle there are many opinions. Some say he was swallowed up by an earthquake in the cave, which afterwards became prophetic; others, that after having completed the Adytum of Apollo at Delphi (a very marvelous specimen of his workmanship, he declined asking any specific pay, but modestly requested the god to grant him whatever was the greatest benefit a man could receive—and in three days afterwards he was found dead.

This oracle was discovered after two years of scarcity in its neighborhood, when the Pythoness ordered the starving population who applied to her, to consult Trophonius in Lebadæa. The deputation sent for that purpose could not discover any trace of such an oracle until Saon, the oldest among them, obtained the desired information by following the flight of a swarm of bees.

The responses were given by the genius of Trophonius to the inquirer, who was compelled to descend into a cave, of the nature of which Pausanias left a very lively representation. The votary resided for a certain number of days in a sanctuary of good fortune, in which he underwent customary lustrations, abstained from hot baths, but dipped in the river Hercyna, and was plentifully supplied with meat from the victims which he sacrificed.

Many, indeed, were the sacred personages whom he was bound to propitiate with blood; among them were Trophonius himself and his sons, Apollo, Saturn, Jupiter, Vasileus, Juno Henioche, and Ceres Europa, who is affirmed to have been the nurse of Trophonius. From an inspection of the entrails, a soothsayer pronounced whether Trophonius was in fit humor for consultation. None of the "exta," however favorable they might have been, were of the slightest avail unless a ram, immolated to Agamedes at the mouth of the cave on the very night of the descent, proved auspicious. When that propitious signal had been given, the priests led the inquirer to the river Hercyna, where he was anointed and washed by two Lebadæan youths, thirteen years of age, named "Hermai."

He was then carried farther to the two spring-heads of the stream, and there he drank first of Lethe, in order that he might forget all past events and present his mind to the oracle as a "tabula rasa" (cleaned tablet); and secondly of Mnemosyne, that he might firmly retain remembrance of every occurrence which was about to happen within the cave. An image, reputed to be the workmanship of

Dædalus, was then exhibited to him, and so great was its sanctity, that no other eyes but those of a person about to undertake the adventure of the cave were ever permitted to behold it.

Next he was clad in a linen robe, girt with ribbons, and shod with sandals peculiar to the country. The entrance to the oracle was a very narrow aperture in a grove on the summit of a mountain, protected by a marble parapet about two cubits in height, and by brazen spikes above it. The upper part of the cave was artificial, like an oven, but no steps were cut in the rock, and the descent was made by a ladder brought to the spot on each occasion.

On approaching the mouth of the adytum itself, the adventurer lay flat, and holding in each hand some honeyed cakes, first inserted his feet into the aperture, then drew his knees and the remainder of his body after them, till he was caught by some hidden force and carried downward as if by a whirlpool.

The responses were given sometimes by a vision, sometimes by words, and a forcible exit was then made through the original entrance, and in like manner feet foremost. There was only a single instance on record of any person who had descended failing to return and that one deserved his fate, for his object was to discover treasure, not to consult the oracle.

Immediately on issuing from the cavern, the inquirer was placed on a seat called that of Mnemosyne, not far from the entrance, and there the priests demanded a relation of everything which he had seen and heard; he was then carried once again to the sanctuary of good fortune, where he remained for some time overpowered by terror and lost in forgetfulness. By degrees, his former powers of intellect returned, and, in contradiction to the received opinion, he recovered the power of smiling.

The antiquary Dr. Edward D. Clarke (1769–1822) during his visit to Lebadæa found everything belonging to the hieron of Trophonius in its original state, excepting that the narrow entrance to the adytum was choked with rubbish. The Turkish governor was afraid of a popular commotion if he gave permission for cleansing this aperture. Mr. J. M. Cripps (who accompanied Dr. Clarke) however, introduced the whole length of his body into the cavity, and by thrusting a long pole before him found it utterly stopped. In modern times, the waters of Lethe and Mnemosyne supplied the washer-women of Lebadæa.

The Oracles of Delos and Branchus

The oracle of "Delos," notwithstanding its high reputation, had few peculiarities. Its virtue was derived from the nativity of Apollo and Diana in that island. At Dindyma, or Didyma, near Miletus, Apollo presided over the oracle of the "Branchidæ," so called from either one of his sons or of his favorites Branchus of Thessaly, whom he instructed in soothsaying while alive and canonized after death.

The responses were given by a priestess who bathed and fasted for three days before consultation, and then sat upon an axle or bar, with a charming-rod in her hand, and inhaling the steam from a hot spring.

Offerings and ceremonies were necessary to render the inspiration effectual, including baths, fasting, and solitude, and Iamblichus (c. 330 A.D.) censured those who despised them.

The Oracle of the Clarian Apollo at Colophon

Of the oracle of Apollo at Colophon, Iamblichus related that it prophesied by drinking of water: "It is known that a subterranean spring exists there, from which the prophet drinks; after he has done so, and has performed many consecrations and sacred customs on certain nights, he predicts the future; but he is invisible to all who are present. That this water can induce prophecy is clear, but how it happens, no one knows, says the proverb.

It might appear that the divine spirit pervades this water, but it is not so. God is in all things, and is reflected in this spring, thereby giving it the prophetic power. This inspiration of the water is not of an entirely divine nature, for it only prepares us and purifies the light of the soul, so that we are fit to receive the divine spirit. There the divine presence is of such a nature that it punishes every one who is capable of receiving the god. The soothsayer uses this spirit like a work-tool over which he has no control. After the moment of prediction he does not always remember that which has passed; often he can scarcely collect his faculties. Long before the water-drinking, the soothsayer must abstain day and night from food, and observe religious customs, which are impossible to ordinary people, by which means he is made capable of receiving the god. It is only in this manner that he is able to hold the mirror of his soul to the radiance of free inspiration."

The Oracle of Amphiaraus

Another very celebrated oracle was that of Amphiaraus, who distinguished himself so much in the Theban war.

He was venerated at Oropus, in Bœotia, as a seer. This oracle was consulted more in sickness than on any other occasion. The applicants had here, also, to lie upon the skin of a sacrificed ram, and during sleep had the remedies of their diseases revealed to them.

Not only were sacrifices and lustrations performed here, but the priests also prescribed other preparations by which the minds of the sleepers were to be enlightened. They had to fast one day, and refrain from wine for three.

Amphilochus, as son of Amphiaraus, had a similar oracle at Mallos, in Cilicia, which Pausanias called the most trustworthy and credible of the age. Plutarch spoke of the oracles of Amphilochus and Mopsus as being in a very flourishing state, and Lucian mentioned that all those who wished to question the oracle had to lay down two oboles (small silver coins).

Egyptian Oracles

The oracles of ancient Egypt were as numerous as those of Greece. It must have been due to foreign influence that the oracle, that played so important a part in the Greek world at this time, was also thoroughly established on the banks of the Nile.

Herodotus knew of no fewer than seven gods in Egypt who spoke by oracles. Of these, the most reliable were considered to give an intimation of their intentions by means of remarkable events. These were carefully observed by the Egyptians, who wrote down what followed upon these prodigies.

They also considered that the fate of a person was fixed by the day of his birth, for every day belonged to a special god. The oracle of Jupiter Ammon at the oasis of that name and the same deity at Thebes existed from the twentieth to the twenty-second Dynasty. He was consulted not only concerning the fate of empires but upon such trifling matters as the identification of a thief. In all serious matters, however, it was sought to ascertain his views. Those about to make their wills sought his oracle, and judgments were ratified by his word.

According to the inscriptions, intercourse between king and god was arranged as follows: "The King presented himself before the god and preferred a direct question, so framed as to admit of an answer by simple yes or no; in reply the god nodded an affirmative, or shook his head in negation. This has suggested the idea that the oracles were worked by manipulating statues of divinities mechanically set in motion by the priests. But as yet no such statues have been found in the Valley of the Nile, and contrivances of this kind could have had no other object than to deceive the people, a supposition apparently excluded in this case by the fact that it was customary for the king to visit the god alone and in secret. Probably the king presented himself on such occasions before the sacred animal in which the god was incarnate, believing that the divine will would be manifested by its movements."

The Apis bull also possessed oracles. Bes, too, god of pleasure or of the senses, had an oracle at Abydos.

American Oracles

Among the American races, the oracle was frequently encountered. All the principal gods of aboriginal America universally acted as oracles. With the ancient inhabitants of Peru, the *huillcas* partook of the nature of oracles. Many of these were serpents, trees, and rivers, the noises made by which appeared to the primitive Peruvians (as, indeed, primitive folk all over the world) to be of the quality of articulate speech. Both the Huillcamayu and the Apurimac rivers at Cuzco were *huillca oracles* of this kind, as their names, "Huillcariver" and "Great Speaker," denote. These oracles often set the mandate of the Inca himself at defiance, occasionally supporting popular opinion against his policy.

The Peruvian Indians of the Andes mountain range within recent generations continued to adhere to the superstitions they had inherited from their fathers. A rare and interesting account of these says that they "admit an evil being, the inhabitant of the centre of the earth, whom they consider as the author of their misfortunes, and at the mention of whose name they tremble. The most shrewd among them take advantage of this belief to obtain respect, and represent themselves as his delegates. Under the denomination of *mohanes*, or *agoreros*, they are consulted even on the most trivial occasions. They preside over the intrigues of love, the health of the community, and the taking of the field. Whatever repeatedly occurs to defeat their prognostics, falls on themselves; and they are wont to pay for their deceptions very dearly. They chew a species of vegetable called *piripiri*, and throw it into the air, accompanying this act by certain recitals and incantations, to injure some, to benefit others, to procure rain and the inundation of rivers, or, on the other hand, to occasion settled weather, and a plentiful store of agricultural productions. Any such result, having been casually verified on a single occasion, suffices to confirm the Indians in their faith, although they may have been cheated a thousand times."

There is an instance on record of how the *huillca* could refuse on occasion to recognize even royalty itself. Manco,

the Inca who had been given the kingly power by Pizarro, offered a sacrifice to one of these oracular shrines. The oracle refused to recognize him, through the medium of its guardian priest, stating that Manco was not the rightful Inca. Manco therefore caused the oracle, which was in the shape of a rock, to be thrown down, whereupon its guardian spirit emerged in the form of a parrot and flew away. It is possible that the bird thus liberated had been taught by the priests to answer to the questions of those who came to consult the shrine. But upon Manco commanding that the parrot should be pursued, it sought another rock, which opened to receive it, and the spirit of the *huillca* was transferred to this new abode.

Like the greater idols of Mexico, most of the principal *huacas* of Peru seem to have been also oracles. The guardians of the great speaking *huacas* appear to have exercised in virtue of their office an independent influence which was sometimes sufficiently powerful to resist the Apu-Ccapac-Inca himself. It was perhaps natural that they should be the exponents of the popular feeling which supported them, rather than of the policy of the sovereign chiefs, whose interest it was to suppress them. There was even a tradition that the Huillac-umu, a venerable *huillac* whom the rest acknowledged as their head, had in old times possessed jurisdiction over the supreme war chiefs.

Many Indian tribes employed fetishes (See **Fetichism**) as oracles, and among the ancient Mexicans practically all the great gods were oracular. (See also **Greece**)

Recommended reading:

Bouché-Leclercq, A. *Histoire de la divination dans l'antiquité*, Paris, 1879

Dempsey, T. *The Delphic Oracles*, Oxford, U.K., 1918

Halliday, W. R. *Greek Divination*, Macmillan, London, 1913

Parke, Herbert W. *Greek Oracles*, Hutchinson, London, 1967

Parke, Herbert W. *Oracles of Zeus*, Blackwell, Oxford, U.K., 1967

Parke, H. W. & D. E. W. Wormell. *The Delphic Oracles*, Blackwell, Oxford, U.K., 1956

Oram, Arthur T(albot) (1916–)

British accountant and statistician who conducted research on card guessing. Born June 27, 1916 at Devizes, Wiltshire, England. In 1947 he married Reith Eleanor Bettine Williams. He served in the Civil Service and industry, and has been a council member of the Society for Psychical Research, London. His work on the 'displacement effect' in card guessing was reported in *Nature* (vol. 157, 1946). He also published 'An Experiment with Random Numbers' (*Journal of the Society for Psychical Research*, vol. 37, 1954; vol. 38, 1955).

Orbas

The name given by the French to a species of metallic electrum. According to **Pliny**, a vessel of this substance has a certain magical property; when it is filled with liquor it discovers poison by showing semicircles like rainbows, while the fluid sparkles and hisses as if on the fire. The occult qualities of electrum are of a tell-tale nature.

Orchis, Root of

In ancient times, Root of the *Satyrios Orchis* of the orchid family was believed to be a sure remedy against enchantment.

Order of Bards, Ovates & Druids

A British Druid Order which claims to continue the traditions of the ancient Bardic and Druid Order. The outer grade is concerned with the arts and also studies in history and archaelogy, with outdoor ceremonies. The initiatory order undertakes mystical studies.

Public ceremonies are arranged at ancient sites at times based on the solstices of summer and winter, and the equinoxes of March and September. Address: The Secretary, 42 Gledstanes Road, London, W14 9HU, England.

Order of Elect Cohens

An occult Masonic group founded by Martinès de Pasqually (1710–74) in Bordeaux, France. The French title "des Élus Cohens" with the French plural is corrupt Hebrew, and the order was also known as the Rite of Elect Priests.

It appears to have had a Sovereign Tribunal at Paris in 1767 with Pasqually at its head. After the death of Pasqually in Port-au-Prince September 20, 1774, the Order continued to exist, probably until the advent of the French Revolution.

Other individuals connected with the Order were Louis Claude de **Saint-Martin** ("The Unknown Philosopher") and "Papus" (Gérard **Encausse**).

Order of New Templars

German occult sect organized between 1894 and 1907 by Austrian occultist Jörg **Lanz von Liebenfels** (1874–1954) at Burg Werfenstein near the river Danube. Temples were also founded at Marienkamp, near Ulm and at Rügen.

The Order used the swastika symbol and claimed divine support for Hitler style race theories. White-robed members held mysterious "Grail" ceremonies. In his journal *Ostara,* von Liebenfels published racist propaganda.

The Order of New Templars went underground after the German invasion of Austria in 1938, but there is little doubt that its fascist ideas directly or indirectly influenced Adolf Hitler and the Nazi party.

Order of the Cubic Stone

A secret order in the **Golden Dawn** tradition, founded in Britain in the 1930s by Theodore Howard and two young technicians, David Edwards and Robert Turner.

The Order teaches a system of "Enochian Magic" and claims to 'train the student in our approach to Ceremonial Magic in order that he may use this medium to obtain knowledge and to reach his goal.' The Order publishes a magazine *The Monolith.* Address: The Wardens, Order of the Cubic Stone, P.O. Box 40, Wolverhampton, West Midlands, WV2 3PH, England.

Order of the Silver Star

The A∴A∴ (Argenteum Astrum), a secret order founded by occultist Aleister **Crowley.**

Ordo Rosae Rubeae et Aureae Crucis (Order of Rose of Ruby and Cross of Gold)

The Second Order of the Hermetic Order of the **Golden Dawn,** usually known by the initials R. R. et A. C. It was formed in 1892 by S. L. M. Macgregor **Mathers,** with W. W. **Westcott** as Chief Adept.

It was kept secret from ordinary members of the G.D. and accessible only to those who qualified as 5°=6° Adeptus Minor grade. The R. R. et A. C. gave instructions in ritual magic. The poet W. B. **Yeats** was initiated into the 5°=6° grade January 20–21, 1893. During later controversies in the G.D. in 1901, Yeats privately published a pamphlet titled *Is the R. R. et A. C. to Remain a Magical Order?*

Ordre Kabbalistique de la Rosecroix

A French Rosicrucian order founded by Joséphin Péladan (1858–1918) and the Marquis Stanislas de Guaita (1860–98). The occultist Gérard **Encausse** (known as "Papus") was a member on the Supreme Council.

Orenda

A magical force. (See **America, United States of**)

Orgone

Primordial cosmic energy, claimed to be discovered by Wilhelm Reich between 1936 and 1940. It is supposed to be universally present and demonstrable visually (a blueness in the atmosphere), thermically, electroscopically and by means of a Geiger-Müller counter; manifest in living organisms as biological energy.

Reich invented an "orgone energy accumulator," a device which was claimed to concentrate orgone energy in a kind of box constructed from metallic material covered by organic material. Reich found a significant temperature difference between the inside and outside of the accumulator, and believed that the accumulated energy had a therapeutic effect on individuals.

He made a number of experiments using the accumulator on cancer patients, and reported substantial improvement in the health of patients. He authorized widespread use of the accumulator for therapeutic purposes provided that it was used in conjunction with reputable medical advice. As a result, he was the subject of court action instituted by the F.D.A. in the States, equating the accumulator with worthless crank cures.

As Reich was a reputable physician and psychotherapist and had never sought to make money out of the accumulator, he rejected these charges and denied the right of federal inspectors to arbitrate in matters of natural science. Eventually he was imprisoned for contempt of court, his apparatus destroyed and his books burned. He died in prison (see Wilhelm **Reich**).

Nowadays the notion of a static device accumulating some form of energy does not seem extravagant, and all over the world people have experimented with pyramid forms which are claimed to have this effect and even to sharpen old razor blades (see *The Secret Power of Pyramids* by Bill Schul & Ed Pettit, Fawcett, 1975).

Reich's discovery of a motor force in orgone energy may be compared with other mysterious motors (see entries under John Ernest Worrell **Keely,** and John Murray **Spear**). Another related motor is described in the august columns of the British medical journal *The Lancet* (July 30, 1921): 'An Instrument Which is Set in Motion by Vision or by Proximity of the Human Body' by Charles Russ.

Orgone energy concepts also resemble earlier ideas of **"Od,"** investigated by Baron von **Reichenbach** in the nineteenth century, as well as occult concepts of vital force. The biological manifestation of orgone energy in the human organism as described by Reich is strongly reminiscent of the **Kundalini** energy of Hindu **yoga** science.

For an account of the construction of an orgone accumulator, see: *The Cancer Biopathy* (vol. 2 of *The Discovery of the Orgone*) by Wilhelm Reich, Orgone Institute Press, or the booklet *The Orgone Energy Accumulator* published by Orgone Institute Press. Some valuable observations on Orgone energy were published in the mimeographed journal *Orgonomic Functionalism* edited by Paul & Jean Ritter, published between 1954 and 1963 from Nottingham, England, and in *Energy and Character; the Journal of Bioenergetic Research* published from 1970 onwards by David Boadella (an associate of Paul Ritter) from: Abbotsbury, Dorset, England. The official American Association for Medical Orgonomy has published *Orgonomic Medicine* from June 1955 onwards (Orgonomic Publications Inc., 515 East 88 Street, New York, N.Y. 10028). (See also **Kundalini; Od; Psychic Force;** Wilhelm **Reich; Reichenbach**)

Ornithomancy

The ancient Greek term for augury, the method of **divination** by the flight or the song of birds, which, with the Romans, became a part of their national religion, and had a distinct priesthood. (See also **Almoganeses; Birds**)

Orton

A mysterious spirit alluded to by the historian Jean Froissart (1338–c. 1410) as the **familiar** of the Lord of Corasse, near Orthes. A clerk whom his lordship had wronged set this spirit the task of tormenting his superior, but by fair words the Lord of Corasse won him over to himself so that Orton became his familiar. Nightly Orton would shake his pillow and waken him to tell him the news of the world. Froissart wrote of their connection:

"So Orton continued to serve the Lord of Corasse for a long time. I do not know whether he had more than one master, but, every week, at night, twice or thrice, he visited his master, and related to him the events which had happened in the different countries he had traversed, and the lord of Corasse wrote of them to the Count of Foix, who took a great pleasure in them, for he was the man in all the world who most willingly heard news of strange countries.

"Now it happened that the Lord of Corasse, as on other nights, was lying in his bed in his chamber by the side of his wife, who had become accustomed to listen to Orton without any alarm. Orton came, and drew away the lord's pillow, for he was fast asleep, and his lord awoke, and cried, 'Who is this?' He answered, 'It is I, Orton.' 'And whence comest thou?' 'I come from Prague, in Bohemia.' 'And how far from hence is this Prague, in Bohemia?' 'Why,' said he, 'about sixty days' journey.' 'And thou hast come so quickly?' 'Faith, I go as quickly as the wind, or even swifter.' 'And thou hast wings?' 'Faith,

none.' 'How then canst thou fly so quickly?' Orton replied—'It does not concern thee to know.' 'Nay,' said he, 'I shall be very glad to know what fashion and form thou art of,' Orton answered, 'It does not concern thee to know; it is sufficient that I come hither, and bring thee sure and certain news.' 'By G—, Orton,' exclaimed the lord of Corasse, 'I should love thee better if I had seen thee.' 'Since you have so keen a desire to see me,' said Orton 'the first thing thou shalt see and encounter to-morrow morning, when you rise from your bed, shall be—I.' 'That is enough,' said the Lord of Corasse. 'Go, therefore; I give thee leave for this night.'

"When the morrow came, the Lord of Corasse began to rise, but the lady was so affrighted that she fell sick and could not get up that morning, and she said to her lord, who did not wish her to keep her bed, 'See if thou seest Orton. By my faith, I neither wish, if it please God, to see nor encounter him.' 'But I do,' said the Lord of Corasse. He leapt all nimbly from his bed, and seated himself upon the edge, and waited there to see Orton, but saw nothing. Then he went to the windows and threw them upon that he might see more clearly about the room, but he saw nothing, so that he could say, 'This is Orton.' The day passed, the night returned.

"When the Lord of Corasse was in his bed asleep, Orton came, and began speaking in his wonted manner. 'Go, go,' said his master, 'thou art a fibber: thou didst promise to show me to-day who thou wert, and thou hast not done so.' 'Nay,' said he, 'but I did.' 'Thou didst not.' 'And didst thou not see anything,' inquired Orton, 'when thou didst leap out of bed?' The Lord of Corasse thought a little while, and said—'Yes, while sitting on my bed, and thinking of thee, I saw two long straws upon the pavement, which turned towards each other and played about.' 'And that was I,' cried Orton, 'I had assumed that form.' Said the Lord of Corasse: 'It does not content me: I pray thee change thyself into some other form, so that I may see and know thee.' Orton replied: 'You will act so that you will lose me.' 'Not so,' said the Lord of Corasse: 'When I have once seen you, I shall not want to see you ever again.' 'Then,' said Orton, 'you shall see me to-morrow; and remember that the first thing you shall see upon leaving your chamber, will be I.' 'Be it so,' replied the Lord of Corasse. 'Begone with you, therefore, now. I give thee leave, for I wish to sleep.'

"Orton departed. When the morrow came, and at the third hour, the Lord of Corasse was up and attired in his usual fashion, he went forth from his chamber into a gallery that looked upon the castle-court. He cast therein his glances, and the first thing he saw was the largest sow he had ever seen; but she was so thin she seemed nothing but skin and bones, and she had great and long teats, pendant and quite attenuated, and a long and inflamed snout.

"The Sire de Corasse marvelled very much at this sow, and looked at her in anger, and exclaimed to his people, 'Go quickly, bring the dogs hither, and see that this Sow be well hunted.' The varlets ran nimbly, threw open the place where the dogs lay, and set them at the sow. The sow heaved a loud cry, and looked up at the Lord of Corasse, who supported himself upon a pillar buttress in front of his chamber. She was seen no more afterwards, for she vanished, nor did any one note what became of her.

The Sire de Corasse returned into his chamber pensively, and bethought himself of Orton, and said, 'I think that I have seen my familiar; I repent me that I set my dogs upon him, for I doubt if I shall ever behold him again, since he has several times told me that as soon as I should provoke him I should lose him, and he would return no more.' He spoke truly; never again did Orton return to the Lord of Corasse, and the knight died in the following year."

Osborn, Edward Collet (1909–1957)

British publicist and parapsychologist. Born November 4, 1909 at Irvingdean, Sussex, England, he studied at Giggleswick School, Yorkshire. In 1938 he married Pauline Rhoda Whishaw. He was a council member of the Society for Psychical Research, London from 1947–57 and edited the SPR *Journal* from 1947–57 and the *Proceedings* from 1951–57. For some years he worked with the publishing company of Benn, and from 1932 onwards with the Royal Institute of International Affairs.

He played an important part in research and organization at the Society for Psychical Research and contributed articles to the *Journal,* including 'The Woman in Brown, an Investigation of an Apparition' (1939), 'An Experiment in the Electro-Encephalography of Mediumistic Trance' (with C. C. Evans, 1952).

Oscilloclast

An apparatus invented by unconventional healer Dr. Albert **Abrams** (1863–1924), pioneer of **Radionics.** For a detailed description of the apparatus see *The Abrams Treatment in Practice; an Investigation* by G. Laughton Scott (London, n.d., c. 1925). (See also **Black Box**)

Osis, Karlis (1917–   )

Distinguished modern parapsychologist who has investigated extrasensory perception, spontaneous psi phenomena and mediumship. Born December 26, 1917 at Riga, Latvia, he studied at University of Munich (Ph.D. psychology 1950). In 1951 he married Klara Zale. He became a U.S. citizen in 1959. He was research associate at the Parapsychology Laboratory, Duke University, Durham, North Carolina from 1951–57, director of research at Parapsychology Foundation, New York, N.Y. from 1957–62, director of research at American Society for Psychical Research 1962, council member of the Parapsychological Association (president 1961–62), member of the American Psychological Association.

Dr. Osis's doctorate from the psychology department of University of Munich was for a thesis that reviewed all previous work on the theoretical basis of ESP. Since then he devoted a lifetime to research and study of parapsychology.

In his period at Duke University from 1951–57 he worked with J. B. **Rhine,** and explored the relationship between ESP and psychokinesis, precognition, and psi between men and animals. He investigated the well-publicized poltergeist phenomena at Seaford, Long Island, N.Y. in 1958, although he concluded that the facts did not support a paranormal explanation. His report was published in the *Newsletter* of the Parapsychology Foundation (March–April 1958).

One of his important studies concerned the effect of distance on ESP. He recently conducted an extensive study on the relationship between meditation and ESP. His contributions to the *Journal of Parapsychology* include: 'A Test of the Occurrence of Psi Effect Between Man and Cat' (vol.16, No.4, 1952), 'A Test of ESP in Cats' (with Esther Bond **Foster,** vol.17, No. 3, 1953), 'A Test of the Relationship Between ESP and PK' (vol.17, No.4, 1953), 'Precognition Over Time Intervals of One to Thirty Days' (vol.19, No.2, 1955), 'ESP Tests at Long and Short Distances' (vol.20, No.2, 1956), 'ESP Over a Distance of 7,500 Miles' (with D. C. **Pienaar,** vol.20, No.4, 1956). Dr. Osis is also author of *Deathbed Observations by Physicians and Nurses* (published Parapsychology Foundation, 1961), (with Erlendur Haraldsson) *At the Hour of Death* (1977), *Man Among His Peers* (1977).

Osmond, Humphrey (Fortescue) (1917–   )

Psychiatrist who has made special contributions to the study of psychedelics and parapsychology. Born July 1, 1917 at Milford, Surrey, England, he studied at the Royal College of Physicians and Surgeons, Canada (certificate in psychiatry 1952), Guy's Hospital, London, England (M.R.C.S., L.R.C.P. 1942) and St. George's Hospital, London from 1949–51 (diploma in psychological medicine 1949). In 1947 he married Amy Edith Roffey.

He was a surgeon lieutenant in the Royal Navy from 1942–47, specialist in neuropsychiatry, command psychiatrist at Military Hospital, Malta from 1945–57. In 1948 he was in the Neurology Department, Guy's Hospital, London, was first assistant in Department of Psychological Medicine at St. George's Hospital, London, from 1949–51; clinical director (1951–53), physician superintendent and director of research (1953–61) at Saskatchewan Hospital, Weyburn, Canada; director of the Bureau of Research in Neurology and Psychiatry for the State of New Jersey thereafter.

His memberships include British Medical Association, Canadian Medical Association, Royal Medico-Psychological Association, Canadian Psychiatric Association (editorial staff of Canadian Psychiatric Association *Journal*), Group for Advancement of Psychiatry, Collegium International, Neuro-Psychopharmacology, Saskatchewan Psychiatric Association (president in 1958).

Dr. Osmond has taken special interest in psychedelics, the study of mental activities and states of consciousness in relation to drugs or pharmacological substances. He contributed a paper on 'Analogues of Mediumship and their Bearing on Parapsychology' at the Conference on Parapsychology and Psychedelics held in New York in 1958. He was also co-chairman with Dr. Emilio **Servadio** at the Conference on Parapsychology and Pharmacology held in 1959 at St. Paul de Vence, France. His articles on parapsychology include 'A Call for Imaginative Theory' (*International Journal of Parapsychology,* Autumn 1959) and (with Dr. Robert **Sommer**) 'Studies in Precognition' (International Journal of Parapsychology' (Summer, 1960). He has given special attention to imagery in relation to mediumship and telepathy. With Dr. Abram **Hoffer** he was co-author of *The Chemical Basis of Clinical Psychiatry* (1960), *How to Live With Schizophrenia* (1966, 1974); *The Hallucinogens* (1967); *New Help for Alcoholics* (1968). He was editor (with Bernard Aaronson) of *Psychedelics: The Uses and Implications of Hallucinogenic Drugs*

(1970). His other publications include: (with H. Yaker & F. Cheek) *The Future of Time; Man's Temporal Environment* (1971), (with Miriam Sieyler) *Models of Madness, Models of Medicine* (1974), *Predicting the Past* (1981).

Osmont, Anne (1872–1953)

Clairvoyant, author and lecturer. Born August 2, 1872 at Toulouse, France. Miss Osmont published articles on psychic subjects in *Initiation et Science* and *Psychic* magazine (a French journal).

Her books included: *Le Mouvement Symboliste* (The Symbolist Movement), *L'Art d'etre Heureuse* (The Art of Being Happy), *Le Rythme Créateur de forces et de formes* (The Creative Rhythm of Forces and Forms), *Les Plantes médicinales et magiques* (Medical and Magic Plants), *Clartés sur l'occultisme* (Light on Occultism). Her book *Envoutements et exorcismes à travers le ages* (Sorcery and Exorcism Through the Ages) was published posthumously in 1954. She died in Paris May 13, 1953.

Ossowiecki, Stephan (1877–1944)

Polish engineer, one of the most remarkable and scientifically tested clairvoyants.

He inherited his psychic gifts from his mother's side, and could read thoughts from early childhood. In the Engineering Institute at Petrograd, where he studied, he astounded his professors by answering questions enclosed in an envelope without opening it. He could see colored **auras** of surrounding people, heard raps and could move objects telekinetically. When he practiced **telekinesis** his clairvoyant powers diminished. At the age of thirty-five he lost his telekinetic powers and his gift of reading sealed papers developed remarkably.

With human subjects he showed even more penetration. Most of the persons he met had no secrets from him. He knew their most intimate thoughts, and read their past, present and future as in an open book. On several occasions, mostly involuntarily, but once by an effort of will, he has externalized. His friends to whom he manifested himself received the impression that he was near in flesh and blood.

His powers were nearer to **psychometry** than **clairvoyance.** He never read the sealed letters word by word. He perceived the ideas. Typewritten or printed texts failed to bring his powers into play. They had to be written by a living person. Nevertheless if the writing was in a strange language which he did not know, he could not disclose the contents but could tell all the circumstances connected with the writer and the writing.

He gave remarkable evidence of clairvoyance to Professor Charles **Richet,** Dr. Gustave **Geley** and many other scientists in reading sealed letters, the contents of which in many cases were unknown to the experimenters. To Geley, he read the contents of a letter as follows: "I am in a zoological garden; a fight is going on, a large animal, an elephant. Is he not in the water? I see his trunk as he swims. I see blood."

Geley said: "Good, but that is not all."

Ossowiecki: "Wait, is he not wounded in his trunk?"

Geley: "Very good. There was a fight."

Ossowiecki: "Yes, with a crocodile."

The sentence which Geley wrote was "An elephant bathing in the Ganges was attacked by a crocodile who bit off his trunk."

At the time of the International Psychical Research Congress in Warsaw in 1923, Ossowiecki was asked to read the contents of a note sent by the **Society for Psychical Research** and carefully sealed by Dr. E. J. **Dingwall** in an envelope after having been wrapped in several folds of paper of various colors. The note contained the sketch of a flag, a bottle and, in a corner, the date of August 22, 1923. Ossowiecki reproduced correctly the flag and the bottle, and wrote the numerals of the date, although not in correct order. The seal being broken, Ossowiecki was warmly acclaimed by the Congress. The psychical researcher Baron **Schrenck-Notzing** cried: "Thank you, thank you, in the name of science." For an account of this remarkable experiment see 'Une sensationelle expérience de M. Stephan Ossowiecki au Congrès de Varsovie' by Gustave Geley (*Revue Métapsychique,* Paris, September–October 1923). Additional reference to Ossowiecki's powers will be found in Geley's book *Materialisation and Clairvoyance* (London, 1927). See also *Collected Papers on the Paranormal* by Theodore Besterman (New York, 1968).

Osty, Dr. Eugèn (1874–1938)

French physician, director of the **Institut Métapsychique Internationale.** He was born May 16, 1874. He trained for a medical career and was physician at Jouet sur l'Aubor's from 1901–24. In 1910 he set out to investigate psychical phenomena and summed up his researches three years later in *Lucidity and Intuition* (1913).

He admitted that the acquisition of knowledge through paranormal means was possible. His subsequent researches were embodied in *Supernormal Faculties in Man* (1923). He neither affirmed nor denied survival, inclining to find the source of after-death communication in a "crypto-psychism" which lingers after bodily death.

As the successor of Dr. Gustave **Geley** at the head of the Institut Métapsychique he had unequalled opportunities for investigation and by painstaking care and strictly scientific methods considerably advanced the cause of psychical research. Geley considered him "the first living authority on lucidity as applied to a human being, both under its practical and its theoretical aspect. His book, *Supernormal Faculties in Man* (La Connaissance Supranormale) [1923] is truly epochal in the study of subjective metapsychics."

In 1931 and 1932, with the collaboration of his son, Marcel Osty, he employed, for the first time in mediumistic research, infra-red and ultra-violet rays in the study of physical and physiological phenomena of Rudi **Schneider,** the results of which were published in *Les Pouvoirs inconnus de l'esprit sur la matiere* (1932) and formed another important contribution to psychical research. Dr. Osty died August 20, 1938.

Otani, Soji (1924–   )

Japanese psychologist who has conducted research in parapsychology. Born December 8, 1924 in Chiba Prefecture, Honshu, Japan, he studied at University of Tokyo (B.A. 1949). In 1958 he married Yoko Okamoto. He was a research fellow at the National Institute of Education, Tokyo from 1951–52, instructor at Chiba University,

Chiba-shi from 1952–56; lecturer in psychology from 1956–60, assistant professor from 1960 onwards at Defense Academy Yokosuka-shi. He is a charter associate of the Parapsychological Association, and councilor at Japan Psychic Science Association, Tokyo.

Prof. Otani investigated relationships between mental and physiological conditions and ESP scoring. His articles in the *Journal of Psychical Research and Spiritualism* include: 'A Survey of Public Opinion on Psychical Phenomena' (1951), 'The Method of ESP Card Testing' (1951), 'The Aim of Parapsychology' (1955), and in *Journal of Parapsychology:* 'Relations of Mental Set and Change of Skin Resistance to ESP Scores' (vol.19, 1955), and in *Journal of the Department of Liberal Arts* (Defense Academy): 'Studies on the Influence of Mental and Physiological Conditions Upon ESP Function' (1959).

In 1979, a group headed by Prof. Otani studied the remarkable phenomena of the Japanese psychic Masuaki Kiyota in **metal-bending** and Nengraphy (psychic photography).

O.T.O.

Initialism of the *Ordo Templi Orientis* or Order of Templars of the East, an occult society founded in Germany at the beginning of the twentieth century. One of the leaders was Karl Kellner from Vienna, who had toured in the East and met various yogis and fakirs. He learned about the sexual magic of **Tantric Yoga** and together with other associates (including Heinrich Klein and Franz **Hartmann**) launched the O.T.O., combining Eastern sex-magic with Masonic rituals.

The title of the order was a romantic reference to the sex practices which were the downfall of the original Templars in the fourteenth century, and also intended to suggest that the order had descended from the Knights Templars. Glorification of the Templar idol **Baphomet** was a feature of the O.T.O. ceremonies.

Kellner died in 1905, and his place was taken by Theodor Reuss, once a Socialist and associate of Eleonor Marx, but expelled from the British Socialist League because he was a spy for the German Secret Service.

British occultist Aleister **Crowley** had independently discovered the secret of sex magic and made guarded references to it in his writings. Reuss noticed these and visited Crowley in London, suggesting that he join the O.T.O. and be head of a British order. Accordingly Crowley visited Berlin and was initiated, returning as "Supreme and Holy King of Ireland, Iona, and all the Britains there are in the Sanctuary of the Gnosis." He also decided to call himself "Baphomet," in addition to his many other self-bestowed titles (which included "Beast 666").

For a time, Rudolf **Steiner** was also a member of the O.T.O., but he left to found his own society of **Anthroposophy,** with broader and more humanitarian aims than the occultism of the O.T.O.

The O.T.O. seems to have been inactive in Germany during the Nazi regime, but was kept alive elsewhere by Crowley and his associates. After the death of Crowley in 1947, Karl Germer claimed to be head of the order. In 1955, Kenneth **Grant** set up the **New Isis Lodge** of the O.T.O. in Britain and is now the present head.

Ouija Board

Apparatus for psychic **communication.** The name derives from the French *oui* and the German *ja:* yes and the apparatus consists of a wooden tripod on rollers which, under the hand of the medium, moves over a polished board and spells out messages by pointing out letters with its apex.

As an invention it is very ancient. It was in use in the days of Pythagoras, about 540 B.C. According to a French historical account of the philosopher's life, his sect held frequent seances or circles at which "a mystic table, moving on wheels, moved towards signs, which the philosopher and his pupil, Philolaus, interpreted to the audience as being revelations supposedly from the unseen world."

An improvement of the original ouija board is the finger-like pointer at the narrow end, and a simplification is the replacement of the wooden board by a piece of alphabetical cardboard. If the pointer and the roll at the apex is replaced by a pencil thrust through a bored hole so as to form the third leg, the ouija board is transformed into a **planchette.**

Mrs. Hester **Dowden,** one of the best English automatists, found the ouija board very efficient. "The words come through so quickly that it is almost impossible to read them, and it requires an experienced shorthand writer to take them down when the traveller moves at its maximum speed." She also believed that the cooperation of two automatists leads to the best results. Three seemed to create confusion. She and her fellow-sitter mostly worked blindfolded. The communications were recorded in silence by a friend. She found these blindfold sittings very exhausting. But they had the great advantage of barring any subconscious guidance of the indicator.

As a rule the ouija board as a method of communication is slow and laborious. But it frequently works with those who fail to get automatic writing with a pencil. (See also **Automatic Writing; Communication; Planchette**)

Oupnekhat, The

According to Lewis **Spence** in *An Encyclopaedia of Occultism* (1920), the *Oupnekhat* or *Oupnekhata* (Book of the Secret) is a work written in Persian which gives the following instructions for the production of visions. "To produce the wise Maschqgui (vision), we must sit on a four-cornered base, namely the heels, and then close the gates of the body. The ears by the thumbs; the eyes by the forefingers; the nose by the middle; the lips by the four other fingers. The lamp within the body will then be preserved from wind and movement, and the whole body will be full of light. Like the tortoise, man must withdraw every sense within himself; the heart must be guarded, and then Brahma will enter into him, like fire and lightning. In the great fire in the cavity of the heart a small flame will be lit up, and in its center is Atma (the soul); and he who destroys all worldly desires and wisdom will be like a hawk which has broken through the meshes of the net, and will have become one with the great being." Thus will he become Brahma-Atma (divine spirit), and will perceive by a light that far exceeds that of the sun. "Who, therefore, enters this path be Brahma must deny the world and its pleasures; must only cover his nakedness, and staff in hand collect enough, but no more, alms to maintain life. The lesser ones only do this; the greater throw aside pitcher and staff, and do not even read the *Oupnekhata*."

This book is clearly from a somewhat garbled recension of one of the Hindu *Upanishads*. This is probably from a nineteenth century German translation titled *Das Oupnekhat; die aus den Veden zusammengefasste Lebre von dem Brahm* (Dresden, 1882) in turn deriving from an earlier Latin edition of 1801.

There is no single *Upanishad* "Book of Secrets." All the *Upanishads* contain the esoteric wisdom of Hindu metaphysics (deriving from the *Vedas*) and comparable forms of meditation to that prescribed above are also found in various Hindu *Yoga* treatises and also in the *Bhagavad-Gita*, a popular Hindu scripture derived from the *Mahabharata* religious epic. (See also **Meditation; Vedanta; Yoga**)

Oursler, Will (William Charles) (1913–)

Author who is concerned with certain areas of parapsychology. Born July 12, 1913 at Baltimore, Maryland, he studied at Harvard College (B.A. cum laude 1937). In 1939 he married Adelaide Burr. He was formerly a police reporter, magazine editor, and war correspondent accredited to U.S. Army and U.S. Navy in World War II. Memberships include: Overseas Press Club, Dutch Treat Club, The Players, P.E.N., Harvard Club of New York, Baker Street Irregulars. His books include: (with the late Fulton Oursler) *Father Flanagan of Boys Town* (1949), (with Lawrence Dwight Smith) *Narcotics; America's Peril* (1952), *The Boy Scout Story* (1955), *The Healing Power of Faith* (1957), *The Road to Faith* (1960), *Marijuana; The Facts and the Truth* (1968), *Religion; Out or Way Out?* (1968). He has published a number of articles dealing with human problems and religious faith in such magazines as *Collier's, Reader's Digest, True, American Weekly, Photoplay*.

Ousby, W(illiam) J(oseph) (1904–)

British authority on hypnosis, who has also studied yoga and African witchcraft at first hand. Born in Liverpool, England, he became a journalist. He later set up as an industrial psychological consultant and studied hypnosis.

He lectured and taught self-hypnosis in Britain, Australia and New Zealand. He spent several years in Africa, where he studied the methods of witch doctors. In India he trained in hatha yoga and investigated fire walking and trance conditions. He now practices as a specialist in hypnosis and self-hypnosis in Harley Street, London. His writings include: *A Complete Course of Auto-Hypnosis—Self Hypnotism and Auto-Suggestion* (London & Durban, 1950), *Methods of Inducing and Using Hypnosis* (London, 1951), *The Theory and Practice of Hypnotism* (London, 1967).

Ouspensky, P(eter) D(emianovitch) (1878–1947)

A prominent follower of mystic and occultist G. I. **Gurdjieff** (1877?–1949) and an interpreter of his system. Born in Russia, he was the son of an army officer whose wife was a painter, and the artistic and military characteristics of both parents played a large part in the personality of Ouspensky. He became a student of mathematics at Moscow University, then went on to become a successful journalist.

In 1907 he became aware of Theosophical literature and became interested in the possibility of a synthesis of religion, mysticism and science. In 1909 he published *The Fourth Dimension*, dealing with abstract mathematical concepts. He went on to publish a book on Yoga, then followed his major philosophical work *Tertium Organum; the third canon of thought; a key to the enigmas of the world* (English translation London, 1923). It was a remarkable synthesis of concepts of time, space, relativity, Theosophy, cosmic consciousness, and Eastern and Western philosophy. The Latin title of the book implied a complete reorganization of thought under a Third Canon.

From 1913 onwards, Ouspensky traveled in the East, searching for the miraculous, and upon his return gave a series of lectures on his experiences. In 1915 he met Sophia Grigorievna Maximenko (who later became his wife) and the mystic G. I. Gurdjieff (who became his guru).

Although Gurdjieff had already discovered many of the occult truths for which Ouspensky had searched, his approach was in sharp contrast to Ouspensky's more formal mathematical mind. Ouspensky became an enthusiastic disciple and interpreter of Gurdjieff's system until 1924, when he decided to follow his own pathway, although still impressed by his teacher. He lectured and conducted study groups in England and the U.S. on the work of Gurdjieff until his death in 1947.

His later works, published posthumously include: *A New Model of the Universe* (London, 1948), *In Search of the Miraculous* (London, 1950), *The Strange Life of Ivan Osokin* (English translation of *Kinemadrama*, London, 1948).

For an eyewitness account of Ouspensky's lectures, see Chapter VIII of *God Is My Adventure* by Rom Landau (London, 1935); the book also includes reminiscences of meetings with Gurdjieff.

Out-of-the-Body Travel

The belief that individuals can leave their physical bodies during sleep or trance and travel to distant places in an etheric or astral counterpart is a very ancient one. It was an important part of early religious teaching that men and women are essentially spiritual beings, incarnated for divine purpose and shedding the body at death, surviving in an after-life or a new incarnation.

Hindu teachings recognize three bodies—physical, subtle and causal. The causal body builds up the characteristics of one's next reincarnation by the desires and fears in present life, but the subtle body may sometimes leave the physical body during lifetime and reenter it after traveling in the physical world. The ancient Hindus were well aware of the phenomenon of out-of-the-body traveling, which features in such scriptures as the *Yoga-Vashishta-Maharamayana* of Valmiki. Ancient Egyptian teachings also represented the soul as having the ability to hover outside the physical body in the *Ka* or subtle body.

But it was not until comparatively modern times that any detailed study of experiments in out-of-the-body traveling was published. This was the series of articles in the British journal *The Occult Review* from 1920 onwards by "Oliver Fox" (pseudonym of Hugh G. **Callaway**), later author of the pioneer book *Astral Projection* (1939). Meanwhile an American experimenter Sylvan J. **Muldoon** in collaboration with Hereward **Carrington** published *The Projection of the Astral Body* (1929).

Both Callaway and Muldoon gave detailed firsthand accounts of consciously controlled and involuntary journeys outside the body. Sometimes these involved appearances to other individuals or the obtaining of information which could not have been ascertained by other means. Such accounts were thus highly evidential.

Certain techniques were described by both Callaway and Muldoon for facilitating the release of the astral or etheric body from the physical body. These included visualizing such mental images as flying, or being in an elevator traveling upwards, just before going to sleep. Some involuntary releases occurred as a result of regaining waking consciousness while still in a dream condition. This was often stimulated by some apparent incongruity in the dream, such as dreaming of one's own room but noticing that the wallpaper had the wrong pattern, so that one thought "I must be dreaming!" but continuing in the dream state. Such awareness sometimes resulted in normal consciousness *outside* the physical body, and being able to look down at it.

Those who have experienced astral projection describe themselves as joined to the physical body by an infinitely extensible connection, rather like a psychic umbilical cord. This would snatch the astral body back to the physical body if disturbed by fear.

Some cases of astral projection have been reported as a result of anesthetics or even a sudden shock.

In spite of the great importance of out-of-the-body experiences, both as a parapsychological phenomenon and for its relevance to the question of survival after death, it did not receive the attention it deserved until recently, when the British scientist Dr. Robert **Crookall** published a number of books in which he cataloged and analyzed hundreds of cases of astral projection from individuals in all walks of life. It seems that the phenomenon is much more widespread than generally supposed, but some people are sensitive about discussing such experiences. Moreover the majority of cases are of involuntary projection and consciously controlled projection under laboratory conditions is rare.

Dr. Crookall distinguishes between the physical body of everyday life, a "vehicle of vitality" and a "Soul Body," connected by an extensible cord. Movement from one body to another is often accompanied by strange sounds and sensations—a "click" in the head, a "blackout" or a "journey down a long tunnel." The projector often sees his own physical body lying on the bed and sometimes the semi-physical vehicle of vitality is observed by other people. Dr. Crookall also cites instances of the strange condition of consciousness in which one sees a "double" of oneself (see also **Double** and **Vardøgr**). Sometimes the transition from the physical body appears to be assisted by "deliverers" or spirit helpers, or even obstructed by "hinderers." Again, whilst much astral travel is in the world of everyday life, one sometimes moves in regions of other-worldly beauty or depression, characterized by Dr. Crookall as "Paradise condition" (the finer aura of earth) or "Hades condition" (a kind of purgatorial area). Here one sometimes encounters friends and relatives who died, or even angelic or demonic beings. Return to the physical body is often accompanied by violent loud "repercussion" effects.

Projection may be preceded by a cataleptic condition of the body in which there are **Hypnogogic** illusions. Because of the close association of dreaming and hallucinatory images, many people have dismissed claimed out-of-the-body experiences as illusory or merely dreams, but considerable evidence for the reality of astral projection has been collated by Dr. Crookall and other investigators.

One of the most remarkable controlled experiments in astral projection was that undertaken in 1934 by the talented medium Eileen J. **Garrett,** when a test was set up between observers Dr. Mühl in New York and Dr. D. Svenson in Reykjavik, Iceland. Mrs. Garrett projected her astral double from New York to Iceland and acquired test information afterwards verified as correct. The case is described in her book *My Life as a Search for the Meaning of Mediumship* (1939), although at the time the experimenters were not named, in order to protect their anonymity, and "Newfoundland" was substituted for Reykjavik.

Modern parapsychologists have now given special attention to the phenomenon of out-of-the-body experience, now termed "OBE" or "OOBE." A number of special terms were devised by Celia Green, director of the Institute of Psychophysical Research, Oxford, England, in a scientific study of approximately 400 individuals claiming out-of-the-body experiences. The general term "ecsomatic" was applied where objects of perception appeared organized in such a way that the observer seemed to observe from a point of view not coincident with the physical body. "Parasomatic" was defined as an ecsomatic experience in which the percipient was associated with a seemingly spatial entity with which he felt himself to be in the same kind of relationship as, in the normal state, with his physical body. "Asomatic" denoted an ecsomatic state in which the subject was temporarily unaware of being associated with any body or spatial entity at all. The project was discussed fully in Celia Green's book *Out-of-the-Body Experiences* (Oxford, U.K., 1968).

An American investigator who has given special attention to OBE is Dr. Charles T. **Tart** of the University of California at Davis. In 1969 he conducted a number of experiments under control conditions in which the subject was required to read a five-digit number placed on a shelf about five feet above the head. Electrodes were attached to the subject's head and EEG records made, to ensure that the subject did not move physically from the bed. In one of four tests, the subject correctly read the number. Other experiments have been conducted at the American Society for Psychical Research in New York and the Psychical Research Foundation, Durham, North Carolina. At the ASPR Dr. Karlis **Osis** used a special target box designed to eliminate ordinary ESP. Subjects were invited to "fly-in" astrally and read the target. Over a hundred volunteers participated in the test. Although Dr. Osis reported that the overall results were not significant, some of the subjects were tested further under laboratory conditions. For a progress report on the experiments see ASPR *Newsletter* (Summer 1974). At the Psychical Research Foundation, brain wave recordings were taken from OBE subjects, with special attention given to detection of the subject at the target location. There is a suggestion that some subjects may have been able to manifest PK effects while projecting. PK effects had been reported earlier in the experiments of Sylvan J. Muldoon in the book *The Projection of the Astral Body* (1929).

In 1956, Dr. Hornell **Hart** made a survey of reported apparitions of the dead, which he compared with apparitions of living persons when having OOB experiences. He concluded that "the projected personality carries full memories and purposes."

As with other laboratory experiments in parapsychology, OBE tests lack the incentive or intrinsic interest of involuntary experiences, and acceptable evidence is correspondingly reduced. Many laboratory experimenters regard OOB experiences as a form of traveling clairvoyance. It remains to be seen whether scientists can devise techniques which can validate objectively the important phenomenon of OOB experience.

Meanwhile in the many cases of involuntary projection, the experience itself often has a profound effect on the outlook of the subject, since it seems to give firsthand subjective evidence for the existence of a soul that survives the death of the physical body. Those who attempt to explain away the phenomenon as "hallucination" or "dreaming" are clearly expressing an opinion without evidence, since they would need to have had such an experience themselves in order to evaluate it. (See also **Astral World; Double; Etheric Double; Ka**)

Recommended reading:

Battersby, H. F. Prevost. *Man Outside Himself,* London, 1942; University Books, 1969

Black, David. *Ekstasy; Out-of-the-body Experiences,* Bobbs-Merrill, 1975

Crookall, Robert. *The Study and Practice of Astral Projection,* London, 1960; University Books, 1966

Crookall, Robert. *Out-of-the-Body Experiences,* University Books, 1970

Crookall, Robert. *Case-Book of Astral Projection, 545–746,* University Books, 1972

Crookall, Robert. *Ecstasy; The Release of the Soul from the Body,* Darshand International, Moradabad, India, 1975

Fox, Oliver. *Astral Projection,* London, 1939; University Books, 1963

Green, Celia E. *Out-of-the-Body Experiences,* Oxford, U.K., 1968

Greenhouse, Herbert B. *Astral Journey; Evidence for Out-of-the-Body Experiences from Socrates to the ESP Laboratory,* Doubleday, 1975

King, Francis. *Astral Projection, Ritual Magic and Alchemy; Being Hitherto Unpublished Golden Dawn Material,* Neville Spearman, London, 1971

Mead, G. R. S. *The Doctrine of the Subtle Body in Western Tradition,* London, 1919

Monroe, Robert A. *Journeys Out of the Body* (introduction by Charles T. Tart), Doubleday, 1971; London, 1972; Corgi, 1974

Muldoon, Sylvan J. & Hereward Carrington. *The Projection of the Astral Body,* London, 1929

Muldoon, Sylvan J. & Hereward Carrington. *The Phenomena of Astral Projection,* London, 1951

Shirley, Ralph. *The Mystery of the Human Double,* London, (1938); University Books (1965)

Smith, Susy. *The Enigma of Out-of-body-Travel,* Garrett/Helix, 1968; Signet, 1968

Turvey, Vincent N. *The Beginnings of Seership,* London, 1911; University Books, 1969

Wilkins, Hubert & Harold Sherman. *Thoughts Through Space,* Frederick Muller, London, 1971 (U.S. edition gives authors as Sherman, Harold & Hubert Wilkins, published Fawcett paperback, 1973)

Yram [pseudonym of Marcel L. Forham]. *Practical Astral Projection* (translated from the French 'Le Medecin de l'Ame'), London (1935); Weiser (c. 1966)

Owen, Alan Robert George (1919–　　　)

British university lecturer who has investigated parapsychology. Born July 4, 1919 at Bristol, England, he studied at Cambridge University (B.A. 1940, M.A. 1945, Ph.D. 1948). In 1952 he married Iris May Pepper. He was a research fellow at Trinity College, Cambridge from 1948–52, university lecturer in genetics at Cambridge from 1950 onwards, fellow and lecturer in mathematics, Trinity College, Cambridge from 1962 onwards. He is a member of the Genetical Society, the Society for Psychical Research and the Biometric Society.

He is the author of a number of scientific papers, and has also taken an interest in **telepathy** and **poltergeist** phenomena. He has contributed a number of papers to the *Journal* and *Proceedings* of the Society for Psychical Research. He studied poltergeist cases in collaboration with Trevor H. **Hall,** and conducted a comprehensive card-guessing test with forty subjects.

Owen, Rev. George Vale (1869–1931)

An outstanding British religious teacher of Spiritualism. He was born in Birmingham, England, and was educated at the Midland Institute and Queen's College there. After curacies at Seaforth, Fairfield and Liverpool, he became vicar of Orford, near Warrington. Here he created a new church and worked for twenty years.

After some psychic experiences he developed **automatic writing,** and received, from high spirits, an account of life after death and philosophical teachings. Lord Northcliffe published them in his newspaper the *Weekly Dispatch.* The result was persecution from the Church superiors of the Rev. Vale Owen, whereupon he resigned. After a lecturing tour in America and in England he became pastor of a Spiritualist congregation in London.

His most notable book is *Life Beyond the Veil* which comprises five volumes. Other works included: *Facts and the Future Life* (1922), *On Tour in U.S.A.* (1924), *Paul and Albert* (1925), *The Kingdom of God* (1925), *Problems Which Perplex* (1928), *Body, Soul and Spirit* (1928), *Jesus the Christ* (1929), *How Spirits Communicate* (n.d.), *What happens After Death* (n.d.), *The Priesthood of the Laity* (n.d.), and, in collaboration with H. A. Dallas, *The Nurseries of Heaven* (1920). His key books were frequently reprinted.

A Voice from Heaven (1932) received automatically by clairvoyant Frederick H. **Haines,** contains messages which purported to emanate from the surviving ego of Vale Owen.

Owen, Robert (1771–1858)

Famous British socialist and humanitarian. He was born May 14, 1771 at Newtown, Montgomeryshire. He had some success in the cotton mill industry and in 1800 established a new kind of society based on his cotton mills at New Lanark. Many years after his socialist experiments and writings, he embraced Spiritualism in his 83rd year after several sittings with Mrs. Hayden, the first American medium who visited England.

In his journal, the *Regional Quarterly Review,* Owen published a formal profession of his new faith and of the grounds on which it rested. In the same year he issued as a separate pamphlet a manifesto, *The Future of the Human Race; or great, glorious and peaceful Revolution, to be effected through the agency of departed spirits of good and superior men and women.*

The periodical instalments of his *New Existence of Man Upon Earth* were, for some time, the only English publications dealing with Spiritualism.

Owen established a community at New Lanark, news of which induced the settlers of the Harmony Society in Indiana to sell land to Owen, who purchased Harmony with its mills, factories, houses and land when the Harmonists moved to Pennsylvania. Owen came to the U.S. in December 1824 and established the community of New Harmony, based on socialist principles.

The experiment seems to have been ahead of its time and through mismanagement did not succeed, although Owen's ideals were commendable. For an account of New Harmony see *Strange Cults & Utopius of 19th Century America* by J. H. Noyes (Dover, 1966; former title *History of American Socialisms,* 1870). On May 14, 1856 at The First Meeting of the Congress of the Reformers of the World, detailed plans, based on spiritually-inspired architectural conceptions, were submitted through Owen's agency for building Homes of Harmony.

Nevertheless, he cannot be ranked as a typical Spiritualist. Communication with the Beyond for him was but another means for the advancement of mankind for which he labored. But it is curious to note that Andrew Jackson Davis, who saw him when lecturing in America in 1846, should have written in November 1847, some months before the advent of the Rochester knockings that according to a message which he received from the spiritual spheres, Robert Owen was destined to hold "open intercourse" with the higher world. Some of the communications which apparently fulfil this prophecy were printed in Owen's autobiography *The Life of Robert Owen* (2 pts., London, 1857–58). Another biography of the same title was published by F. A. Packard (Philadelphia, 1866). Owen died at Newtown November 17, 1858.

Owen, Robert Dale (1801–1875)

Son of the British socialist Robert Owen. He was born November 9, 1801 in Glasgow, Scotland and educated in Switzerland. He eventually emigrated to America, where he hoped to find more scope for his reforming zeal. He lived for several years in his father's socialistic community New Harmony in Indiana, and served in the Indiana legislature and in Congress.

He introduced the bill organizing the Smithsonian Institution and in 1846 became one of its regents and chairman of its Building Committee. He was a member of the Constitutional Convention in Indiana in 1850. W. Hepworth Dixon calls him, in one of his volumes, "the Privy Councillor of America."

In 1853 Owen was appointed Chargé d'Affaires at Naples and Minister in 1855. He remained there until 1858.

Of his father's attachment to Spiritualism, he heard with pain and regret. But experiences with the famous medium D. D. **Home** during his stay in Naples started him on a career of psychic investigation. He vowed not to rest until he proved **survival** a certainty or delusion.

In the event, he found overwhelming evidence in favor of survival. His book *Footfalls on the Boundaries of Another World* was published in 1860, *The Debatable Land Between this World and the Next* in 1870. Both books attracted wide attention and popularity and were influential in the Spiritualist movement. To Robert Dale Owen Spiritualism became the most profound of all revelations. Until the end of his life he continued to write and speak boldly on the subject.

He had his trials and disappointments in its championship, for example, the scandal surrounding the controversial accusation of cheating on the part of the mediums Mr. and Mrs. Nelson **Holmes** in 1874 almost broke his spirit, but he never went back on the proclamation of its truth.

He died June 17, 1875.

Owens, Ted

Individual who claims contact with Space Intelligences from flying saucers. Unlike most other contactees, he does not claim to have taken a ride on a saucer, but merely uses his brain as a kind of radio set for telepathic messages, which he passes on to anyone interested. He lives with his wife Martha in Virginia Beach, Virginia. The ultimate purpose of the Space Intelligences is that Owens will act as a kind of ambassador for them to world governments. (See also **Space Intelligence; UFO**)

Ozanne, Charles E(ugene) (1865–1961)

History and philosophy teacher, who devoted many years to research in parapsychology after retirement from teaching. Born April 14, 1865 in Cleveland, Ohio, he studied at Western Reserve University, Cleveland (B.A. 1889), Yale University (B.S.T. 1892), Harvard University (M.A. 1895). He was a history instructor at Harvard and Radcliffe colleges from 1896–97, history and civics teacher at Central High School, Cleveland between 1869 and 1935, instructor in philosophy at Fenn College, Cleveland from 1935–36. Mr. Ozanne provided financial support for research in parapsychology at Duke University, Durham, North Carolina, and after 1951 moved to Durham so that he could be more closely connected with research at the Parapsychology Laboratory. In 1961 he took a leading part in setting up the **Psychical Research Foundation, Inc.** at Durham, N.C., an independent research organization concerned with mental, spiritual or personality characteristics and survival after death. The director of the Foundation is W. G. **Roll.** Mr. Ozanne's own writings include 'Significance of "Non-Evidential" Material in Psychical Research' (*Hibbert Journal,* Oct. 1913), 'A Layman Looks at Psychical Research' (*Journal of the American Society for Psychical Research,* April 1942).

DATE DUE

PRINTED IN U.S.A.